THE BLUE G

MW00439437

Church of Sta María, Tonantzintla

BLUE GUIDE

Mexico

John Collis and David M. Jones

Atlas, maps, and plans by John Flower

Archaeological site plans by David M. Jones

A&C Black
London

WW Norton
New York

First edition

Published by A & C Black (Publishers) Ltd
35 Bedford Row, London WC1R 4JH

A CIP catalogue is available from the British Library.

ISBN 0-7136-2776-X

Published in the United States of America by
W. W. Norton & Company
500 Fifth Avenue
New York, NY 10110

ISBN 0-393-30072-2

Photographs by the authors, Creenagh Lodge and Anne Jones, and courtesy of INAH.

John Collis, who has traveled all over Mexico, is a specialist in, and enthusiast for, the Art and Architecture of Viceregal Mexico (1521-1810).

David M. Jones is a writer and archaeologist, with wide experience of Mesoamerica, its archaeology and prehistory, and the ethnography of its ancient peoples.

1 2 3 4 5 6 7 8 9 10

Printed in the United States of America

CONTENTS

Mexico City and its Environs 127

Sierra Madre Occidental 333

Maps and Plans

PREFACE

Blue Guide Mexico has, necessarily, been long in its compilation. The size of the task and the difficulties facing anyone who attempts to include the amount of detail expected of the series are great. It is a study not only of breadth, but also of extraordinary depth. Mexico is truly kaleidoscopic, with century after century of artistic wealth. We have given equal prominence to the remains of its ancient civilizations, to the monuments and art of the period between the Conquest and Independence, and to the 20C. The consistency and quality of Mexico's art and heritage are amazing. Even so, this Guide can only be of the nature of an interim report. Much has had to be left out to achieve a manageable book. Much remains to be discovered, as specialists in Mexico acknowledge.

The ancient civilizations of Mesoamerica and the art and architecture of the period between the Conquest and the early 20C are not nearly as well known outside Mexico as they deserve to be. Although the Mexicans have been keen to emphasize their prehispanic past, one cannot escape the feeling that they have not been as keen on emphasizing the later period. Even so, Europeans appear to have only a vague idea of the gambit of Mexico's prehispanic and Spanish past, unlike their general knowledge of the sequence of civilization in Europe. Most people have some idea of who the ancient Aztecs were, but the wealth of other ancient Mesoamerican civilizations is too little known. All of Mexico's art and architecture are a part of its people's heritage, as recent, and excellent, works by Mexican, US, and Spanish specialists have abundantly shown. We have been firm in our resolve to provide a guide to the whole of Mexico, for indeed there is much continuity through the two somewhat arbitrarily defined periods of prehispanic and post-Conquest Mexico. No culture with such diverse roots could be otherwise, its modern art and architecture including inspiration from both its native and European heritages.

Work on the Guide has proceeded during a period of great difficulty for Mexico. Yet during our travels throughout the country we have never ceased to be impressed by, and grateful for, the great kindness and often heartwarming welcomes that we have received. An editorial on the earthquake of 1985 in 'The Times' of London justly paid tribute to Mexico as 'a proud and stoical country'. It might have added that Mexico is a grand country, in every sense of the word. Mexicans, rather like the English, are apt to go through periods of self-doubt and self-criticism. But they have so much to be proud of. Many Mexicans, whose names we never learned, helped us in our travels around Mexico, from hotel clerks to ticket collectors to tourist information personnel. We wish to thank them for their valuable help and for striving to make our visits pleasant as well as productive.

Our specific debts are many. Among the friends who have been indispensable are **Warwick Bray**, who has advised and made valuable suggestions on Mexico's prehispanic past; and **Nicola Coleby**, who has written the Introduction to modern Mexican art and architecture, and has generously given us the benefit of her expert knowledge of Mexican mural painting. Both have unfailingly provided the answers to all sorts of awkward and persistent questions. **Elizabeth Baquedano Pope** and **Ligia Baquedano** most kindly drew on all their considerable experience to write the section on Mexican food and drink. The enthusiasm and wide interests of **Martine Chomel** have been infectious, and she has supplied material on many aspects and accompanied us on visits to important places. **Clara Bargellini**, an authority on the cathedrals and churches of N Mexico, has cheerfully given us her time to discuss various problems, and furnished us with much invaluable material. **Jaime Abundis** provided a vital reading list and helped with the topography of the historic centre of the city of Mexico. **Creenagh Lodge** has come with us on many journeys and taken many photographs, which have been vital for study purposes; likewise, **Anne Jones** has been a photographer in Mexico and a source of continual encouragement. To **Christopher** and **Madeleine Humphrys,** who gave us our first welcome in Mexico, we are grateful for much kindness and hospitality. **Lorenzo Lazo-Margain,** former cultural attaché at the Mexican embassy in London, and **Elena Uribe,** also at the embassy, gave us our first introductions to experts in Mexico and to essential works of reference.

We are grateful to the following who have helped in a variety of ways: *Vicente Medel Martínez, Marco Díaz, Enrique Bautista Villegas, José Luis Martínez H., Guillermo Turner Rodríguez, David Brading, Peter Ward, Geraldine Scanlon, Valerie Fraser, Fr Charles Dilke, Padre Luis Avila Blancas, David Fox, Alison Frater, Francisca Denegri, Marco Arturo González Rodríguez, María Dolores Páez Cruz, Rebeca Romero Pérez, Annie Galliano, Susannah Edmunds, Henry Coelho, Alan Cameron,* the late *Harold Blakemore, Barry Brown,* and *Peter Calvert,* and to *Patricia Rodríguez Lozano* of Ciudad Victoria, *Roberto de Jesús Luna Martínez* of Zacatecas, *José Guadalupe Treviño Castillo* of Monterrey, *Mario Guzmán* of Puebla, and *Antonio Ortiz Peralta* of Aguascalientes. We are also grateful to *Muriel Kilvert* for her hospitality and kindness when we visited her to talk about Mexico.

Needless to say, none of these kind people are responsible for any mistakes, for which the authors alone are accountable. And our interpretations are our own.

Some quotations have deliberately been left in the original Castilian. No translation could convey the flavour. It will take only a little effort for non-Spanish speakers to get their meaning. For essential words in the Mexican fine arts repertory, like estípite or estofado, for which there is no translation, the reader is referred to the glossary.

Abbreviations

The population figures given in this Guide can only be regarded as very approximate. They are nearly always those of an urban area and its wider municipio.

abp archbishop
attr. attributed to
Av. Avenida = Avenue
b. born
Banamex Banco Nacional de México
Bl. Blessed
bp bishop
c circa
C century
C. Calle = Street
Calz. Calzada = Highway
Cap. Capilla = Chapel
Carr. Carretera = Motorway
Cda Calle Cerrada (blind alley)
Cjón Callejón = Alley
Col. Colonia
d. died
H hotel
ha. hectares

IMSS Instituto Mexicano de Seguro Social
INAH Instituto Nacional de Antropología e Historia
incl. including
l. left
m metre
M motel
MW Megawatts
P petrol
Pal. Palacio
Pl. Plaza
PRI Partido Revolucionario Institucional
r. right
R restaurant
Sta Santa
Sto Santo
UNAM Universidad Nacional Autónoma de México

BACKGROUND INFORMATION

Mexico's Prehistory

'...Columbus was the last, rather than the first, to discover America.' R. A. Diehl

Introduction

To summarize in a few pages the whole of Mexico's history before the permanent arrival of Europeans is virtually impossible. The most obvious problem is that of modern political geography, for to confine the cultural sequence of ancient Mesoamerica within modern political boundaries is an inappropriate concept: prehistoric cultural regions did not anticipate later political boundaries, nor were the limits of prehistoric and modern regions drawn up for the same political or social motives.

Physical Geography

Mexico comprises many geographical zones. The basic division is between drier *Highlands* and more humid *Lowlands*, defined by mountain chains and blocks, and by more and less humid tropical jungles, grasslands, and marshes.

There are three major highland regions, each subdivided, constituting land above 1000m and rising to peaks of over 5000m. The *Mesa Central*, or Central Highlands, is one of, if not the, most prominent regions in Mesoamerica's prehistory: general unifying forces originated from Central Highland centres. It is formed by the converging Sierra Madre Occidental and Sierra Madre Oriental ranges from the N, ending in a massive clump of mountains and valley systems in S-central Mexico. It is drained by four great rivers: to the NW—the Lerma/Santiago; to the NE—the Pánuco; to the SW—the Balsas; and to the SE—the Papaloapan. The Mesa Central has been likened to one of the great pyramids typical in its prehistory, with 'precincts' and 'terraces' to the N, S, E, and W. Its central 'platform' is the Basin of Mexico, with its snow-crested volcanic rim. More familiarly known as the Valle de México, it was in fact once a true valley, draining S into the Balsas and Papaloapan rivers. It became a basin, partly filled with five shallow lakes mostly drained in viceregal times, when cut off by the Pliocene eruption of a 'transverse volcanic axis', running E–W across the natural drainage course.

N of the Basin of Mexico a subregion of increasing aridity, ultimately a desert, stretches into the Southwest USA. Within it are 'oases', where irregularities of terrain form shielded, specialized climatic and vegetational pockets. These were variously isolated or influenced by cultures both to the N and S, and often acted as points of transmission for Mesoamerican culture traits to the N.

W of the Basin is the Valle de Toluca, roughly equal in height, but separated by the Basin's W rim; to the E is the Valle de Puebla, with similar characteristics. Mountain passes link the Basin to these valleys, and ultimately to the Pacific and Gulf coasts. To the S lie three corresponding lower 'terraces': the valles de Tenancingo (S of Toluca), Morelos (S of the Basin), and Atlixco (S of Puebla). To the E and W are the coastal strips—the Lowlands (described below).

The Southern Highlands lie S of the Balsas and Papaloapan rivers, centred on the three arms of the Oaxaca Valley system (Etla, Tlacolula, and Zaachila), and drained by the Río Atoyac. They comprise a high, flat plateau, bordered on the W and S by the Sierra del Sur along the Pacific coast.

The SE Highlands form SE Mexico and Guatemala, separated from the Southern Highlands and central Mexico by the Isthmus of Tehuantepec, a narrow break between the 1000m contour lines. The SE Highlands comprise two younger, steeper-sided volcanic chains, Alta Verapaz and Sierra de Sta Cruz, stretching across Chiapas in Mexico and central and S Guatemala, then down the spine of Central America.

The Lowlands form the peripheries of the highland zones, and also comprise several distinct regions. The W coastal strip is narrow, barely more than 19km at its widest. It is mostly hot and dry, but is more humid to the S where the hilly piedmont provides a land corridor across Tehuantepec and Soconusco. The E Lowlands form more than just a coastal strip, being nearly 73km at their widest. Generally very hot and humid, their tropical vegetation is broken in two places by more arid bush and grasslands: in central Veracruz, and in the NW Yucatán Peninsula. Between these zones are the central Gulf Coast tropical lowlands, separating central Mexico from Yucatán. Drained by winding, sluggish rivers—the Coatzacoalcos, Tonalá, Grijalva, Usumacinta, and Candelaria—they penetrate southwards to the Chiapas and Guatemalan uplands, linking the SE and Southern Highlands across the Isthmus of Tehuantepec in upland forests interspersed with marshes and grasslands.

Thus ancient Mesoamerica comprised many units within and across modern borders. A second system of division is based on rainfall and vegetation, bisecting Mesoamerica on either side of the E escarpment: the windward, or Caribbean-Atlantic, side has heavy, tropical soils and is warm and moist; while the leeward, or inland, side, is more seasonal with summer rains and lighter, intermittent, cultivable soils. Finally, a third system of division is based on altitude and micro-vegetational zoning. Certain products were grown or available in the valleys and basins, others on the piedmont slopes, and still others in the higher slopes, a diversity affecting the development of many of Mesoamerica's culture traits.

Mesoamerica as a Culture Concept

The idea of a geographical area called Mesoamerica that shared a general cultural cohesion was proposed by Walter Lehmann in the 1920s, then defined by Paul Kirchhoff in 1943 using a trait list of common cultural 'items', both physical and conceptual. Kirchhoff's list was based on historical and ethnographical evidence, and primarily on the situation revealed by these sources at the time of the Spanish conquest.

As archaeological evidence accumulated from excavations and field surveys, the question arose of how far back into prehistory the concept could be applied. Gordon Willey, René Millon, and Gordon Ekholm reviewed the evidence in 1964 and further defined the concept in archaeological terms, adding more evidence of artefacts, and ideas on technology, subsistence, social organization, and settlement patterns. They defined Mesoamerica as a 'diffusion sphere' in which important events in one region eventually affected the whole area. It was recognized that Mesoamerica's geographical diversity encouraged both cultural diversity and a general unity—by stimulating the development of ideas to overcome the physical obstacles within and between regions, by redistributing the products of the regions, and by making use of the natural communication routes between regions. The geographical features of Mesoamerica were realized to have less well-defined limits than the cultural traits.

A long list of culture traits is now recognized to have been confined en bloc to central and S Mexico, the Yucatán Peninsula, Guatemala, Belize, and El Salvador, and parts of Honduras, Nicaragua, and Costa Rica. The N limit followed the Sinaloa, Lerma, and Pánuco rivers, although the NW portion of the boundary fluctuated in time. N of this line the populations were mobile hunter-gatherers (as far N as the agriculturalists of Southwest USA and adjacent N Mexico); S of it the populations were agriculturalists. The S limit, less definite, ran from the mouth of the Motogua river in Guatemala, SE via Lake Nicaragua to the Gulf of Nicoya in Costa Rica. (Conversely, this is the N limit of penetration of primarily S American cultural influences.) Individual traits were present N and S of these limits, but not the entire set. The most famous example is perhaps adaptations of the ball game, originally Mesoamerican, in the South-western cultures of the USA and in the Antilles, especially Puerto Rico.

Mesoamerican civilization thus comprised: the Central Highlands, Western Mexico, the NW Frontier, the Huasteca (NE Frontier), the PueblaOaxaca Highlands, the Valle de Oaxaca and adjacent Pacific coast, the Gulf Coast of Veracruz and the adjacent Isthmus of Tehuantepec and Pacific Coastal Plain (Soconusco), the Maya Lowlands of Yucatán, and the Maya Highlands of Chiapas and Guatemala.

The first recognizable Mesoamerican traits appeared c 2500 BC and continued, with additions, to the Spanish conquest in AD 1519, some still lingering today. From c 1500 BC widespread trade connections, themselves a Mesoamerican culture trait, and later, military conquest, contributed to unity. Thus the N and S limits were both economic and political, sometimes simultaneously. The S boundary fluctuated with developments in the Maya regions; the N boundary fluctuated with changes in rainfall, affecting the practice of agriculture.

The cultural traits listed below were related within a complex religious and ceremonial context, and through constant interaction between regions in long-distance trade in goods, raw materials, and ideas:

ball courts with rings and ceremonial ball game
volador ceremony in which several men 'fly' (their ankles tied to ropes) from the top of a tall pole down to the earth
human and auto sacrifice

stepped pyramid temple platforms and other platforms, arranged around cere-monial plazas
architecture in stone, plaster and mortar, incl. stucco floors

society organized around agricultural villages; agricultural economy based on maize

cacao (chocolate)
chia cultivation (a plant used as food, to make a drink, and as oil)
chinampa agriculture (artificial islands around lake shores or marshes, created by dredging up soil into a constructed frame and planting on it)
use of coa (digging stick)
grinding of corn mixed with ash or lime

long-distance trade and periodic, centralized local markets

hieroglyphic writing on stone and in books made of amate paper or deer-skin parchment (codices)
positional numerals and use of 13 as a ritual number
solar and ritual calendars, incl. a year of 18 months of 20 days each plus five extra days at the end, and a 52-year cycle
cosmic concept of four cardinal points or directions from a centre, each with a special colour and deity
ritual uses of rubber and paper
complex pantheon of deities with specific traits and functions

sandals with heels
woven rabbit-hair garments
feathered garments
turbans
one-piece outfits for warriors
labrets, lip ornaments, body-painting/tattooing

polished obsidian artefacts (esp. knives)
pyrite mirrors
wooden clubs with obsidian or flint blades set into them
clay pellets for the blow tubes

Development of Archaeology in Mexico

Mexican archaeology developed through two principal periods of activity, subdivided into phases of similar functional and intellectual focus. The first period was from the Spanish conquest into the 19C, and overlaps with the second, of the 19C and 20C.

Characteristic of the first period were simple collection and recording of data about the natives of Mesoamerica. It was heavily biased in subject and function: the Aztecs and Maya were over-represented, and there was usually some polemic stance or specific purpose involved. There was no systematic collection of antiquities, rather a concentration on recording ethnographic and historical data. Some artefacts (many of materials not normally preserved in archaeological contexts) were shipped back to Europe as curiosities and survive in modern museum collections, incl.: wooden shields; masks inset with turquoise, lignite, and shell mosaic-work; headdresses and shields decorated with feathers of several colours; carved and gilded wooden atlatls (spear throwers); three Maya hieroglyphic codices, and several 'Mixtec' codices (see *Writing, Counting, and Calendrics* below); and a 16C copy of Moctezuma's tribute list for the provinces of the Aztec empire.

The second period saw the beginnings of scientific interest in archaeological data—ruins and artefacts. It began with data-gathering explorations and gradually developed into the modern practice of archaeology, incl. more recently an interest in the history of Mexican archaeology itself.

In the first period viceregal officials and missionaries were the principal collectors, but the earliest sources for much first-hand information on the Aztec and Maya states are chronicles and semi-official reports written by the conquistadores themselves. Cortés wrote five long letters to Charles V (Charles I of Spain), reporting his discovery, exploration, and conquest of central Mesoamerican civilization. Other officers wrote similar reports, on a more official basis, in the 1520s and 1530s as other regions of Mesoamerica were conquered—eg, Francisco de Montejo for Yucatán. In addition to Cortés' there were four other more or less contemporary eyewitness accounts: Bernal Díaz del Castillo, López de Gómora, Andrés de Tapia, and the 'Anonymous Conqueror'. Of these, the first is the most famous—Díaz del Castillo's 'Historia verdadera de la conquista de la Nueva España'. One factor in his decision to write was a claim to correct the inaccuracies of the others, especially the chaplain Francisco López de Gómora, who had also taken down Cortés' dictation for the first of the five letters. Ethnographic information in all of these accounts was therefore mostly incidental.

Conscious efforts to gather and record information on the native inhabitants began soon after colonial status was established. Andrés de Olmos, one of the earliest clergy to arrive, began collecting native books, 'translating' them into Spanish, and adding supplements based on interviews with natives. Unfortunately, his books are lost, but in his footsteps followed a handful of fellow clergy and a few native nobles educated by the Spaniards. Of these, two are especially important: Diego de Landa ('Relación de las cosas de Yucatán') and Bernardino de Sahagún ('Historia general de las cosas de Nueva España').

Landa, a Franciscan in Yucatán and later bp of Mérida, recorded aspects of Maya life in the 16C. Sahagún, also a Franciscan, in central Mexico, learned Náhuatl and systematically collected, recorded, and collated Aztec ethnography of a surprisingly professional and modern standard. Curiously, these two still-indispensable sources were written from opposite sides of the socio-political coin: Landa recorded his information while systematically destroying original Maya hieroglyphic books along with stone idols and temples; Sahagún, although equally eager to convert the natives to Christianity, collected and wrote with genuine concern for and interest in the native culture, and to argue against its indiscriminate destruction and exploitation of the Indians.

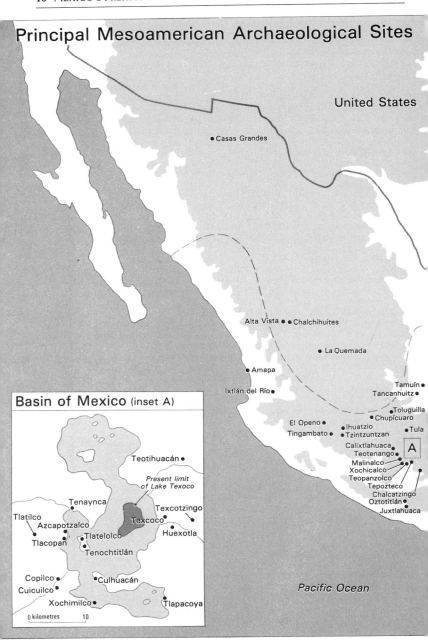

Principal Mesoamerican Archaeological Sites

United States

• Casas Grandes

Alta Vista • • Chalchihuites

• La Quemada

• Amapa

Ixtlán del Río •

Tamuín •
Tancanhuitz •

• Toluguilla
• Chupícuaro

El Openo •
Tingambato •

• Ihuatzio
• Tzintzuntzan

• Tula

Calixtlahuaca •
Teotenango •
Malinalco •
Xochicalco •
Teopanzolco •
Tepozteco •
Chalcatzingo •
Oztotitlán •
Juxtlahuaca •

[A]

Pacific Ocean

Basin of Mexico (inset A)

Teotihuacán •

Present limit of Lake Texoco

Tenaynca

Texcotzingo

Tlatilco •
Azcapotzalco •

Texcoco •

Tlacopan •
Tlatelolco •

Huexotla •

Tenochtitlán •

Copilco •
Cuicuilco •

• Culhuacán

Xochimilco •

• Tlapacoya

0 kilometres 10

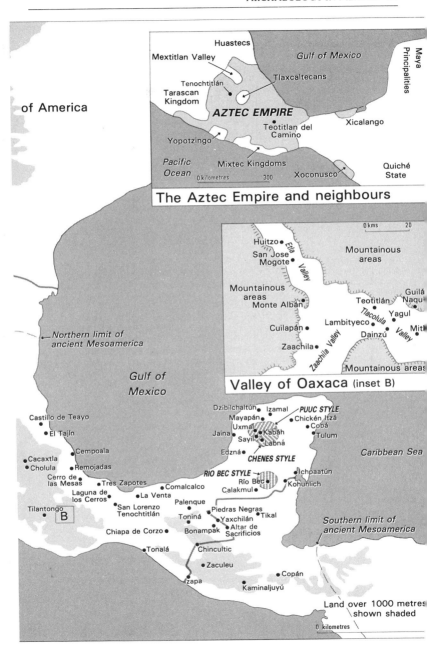

The Aztec Empire and neighbours

of America

Huastecs

Gulf of Mexico

Mextitlan Valley

Maya Principalities

Tlaxcaltecans

Tenochtitlán

Tarascan Kingdom

AZTEC EMPIRE

Teotitlan del Camino

Xicalango

Yopotzingo

Pacific Ocean

0 kilometres   300

Mixtec Kingdoms

Xoconusco

Quiché State

Valley of Oaxaca (inset B)

0 kms   20

Huitzo

San Jose Mogote

Etla Valley

Mountainous areas

Mountainous areas

Monte Albán

Teotitlán

Guilá Naquí

Tlacolula Valley

Yagul

Lambityeco

Mitl

Cuilapán

Dainzú

Zaachila Valley

Zaachila

Mountainous areas

Northern limit of ancient Mesoamerica

Gulf of Mexico

Castillo de Teayo

El Tajín

Cempoala

Cacaxtla

Cholula

Remojadas

Cerro de las Mesas

Tres Zapotes

Laguna de los Cerros

Comalcalco

La Venta

Dzibilchaltún   Izamal   *PUUC STYLE*

Mayapán   Chichén Itzá

Uxmal   Kabáh   Cobá

Jaina   Sayil   Labná   Tulum

Edzná   *CHENES STYLE*

RIO BEC STYLE →   Río Bec   Ichpaatún

Calakmul   Kohunlich

Caribbean Sea

Tilantongo   B

San Lorenzo Tenochtitlán

Palenque

Piedras Negras   Tikal

Toniná   Yaxchilán

Chiapa de Corzo   Bonampak   Altar de Sacrificios

Southern limit of ancient Mesoamerica

Tonalá   Chincultic

Zaculeu

Copán

Izapa   Kaminaljuyú

Land over 1000 metres shown shaded

0 kilometres

On the secular side, Antonio de Mendoza, the first viceroy, had the 'Codex Mendoza' compiled as a guide for his officials. Its primary concern was to discover Aztec tribute amounts and sources in order to know what could be expected by the Spanish collectors.

Once viceregal administration and the initial distributions of lands and native tributaries had been accomplished, there began a longer phase of documentation, lasting from c 1570 to 1800. A few works of the type summarized above were collected, especially as Spanish conquests advanced into the N provinces; but most material was in the form of official documents, collected on royal orders and for special purposes. These began with the 'Relaciones geográficas', ordered by Philip II, and collected mostly in 1578–80. Their format was a questionnaire requesting details of the size and distribution of native (and Spanish) populations, their towns, products, and the natural history of each minor Spanish political jurisdiction, plus a pintura (map). A second set of such comprehensive 'Relaciones' was ordered and completed between 1740 and 1792 (one set, referred to by historians as the 'Padrones', was compiled in 1790–92). There were several other, less complete, compilations in the 17C.

Not until the very end of the viceregal period was any systematic interest taken in the ruins of Mesoamerica. Explorations began to locate and carefully record these ruins, beginning with that of Capt. Antonio del Río at Palenque in 1787. In the late 18C wave of historical and scientific inquiry in Europe and America, Spain began to take a renewed interest in the antiquities of its colonial possessions, and to encourage its officials to collect artefacts and information. Del Río actually cleared parts of Palenque and made the first maps of the site. His report, however, remained unpublished until 1822; it included 17 engravings by Frédéric Waldeck, who later explored sites in his own expeditions and wrote a book on Palenque in 1864.

The German mining engineer Alexander von Humboldt spent five years (1799–1804) travelling throughout the Spanish colonies of N and S America and produced 30 volumes on their geography, geology, meteorology, botany, zoology, and ethnography. His work included the first study of prehispanic architecture: he measured and drew the monuments, related them to his ethnographic data, and even distinguished between different styles. Independently, the retired Mexican cavalry officer Capt. Guillaume Dupaix was commissioned by Charles IV to survey the antiquities of central and S Mexico. His reports and drawings include the rediscovery of such important highland sites as Xochicalco in Morelos, Zapotec cities in Oaxaca, and Palenque and other Maya sites.

These pioneers aroused the interest mainly of fellow scholars; popular awareness of the ancient antiquities of Mexico was to be stimulated by others—adventurer-collectors. Among these was William Bullock, who built a private exhibition gallery in London in 1812. In 1823 he spent six months in Mexico where he saw Dupaix's unpublished drawings and visited known ruins; he collected antiquities and took casts of architectural sculptures, all of which he transported back to London for a grand exhibition. Another 19C collector was Henry Christy, who collected through the middle decades and who gave his 1805-piece collection (602 of which were Mexican) to the British Museum in 1865. A travelling companion of Christy's was Sir Edward Tylor, who in 1861 wrote a popular account of Mexico and its ancient history and antiquities entitled 'Anahuac', before settling in Cambridge to found the first formal Anthropological studies in England.

Dupaix's and del Río's books on the Maya stimulated much new scholarly interest. Chief among the new explorers was the single-minded Lord Kingsborough, who published (1830–48) a multi-volume, hand-coloured set on Maya ruins (incl. the first publication of Dupaix's material), impoverishing himself in the process. Also in the 1830s Juan Galindo studied and published reports on Palenque, Copán, and many Guatemalan sites. The general popularity of Maya ruins was greatly enhanced by the Anglo-American team of John Lloyd Stephens and Frederick Catherwood. Stephens, an American lawyer, managed to get himself appointed US 'Special Confidential Agent' in Central America in 1839; and with the experienced British architect and artist Catherwood, explored the Maya ruins of Central America and Yucatán for the next three years. They visited all the known ruins and discovered more than 40 new sites. Their immense popularity lay in the entertaining accounts of their 'adventures' published in two two-volume sets: 'Incidents of Travel in Central America, Chiapas, and Yucatán' (1841) and 'Incidents of Travel in Yucatán' (1843).

In the latter half of the 19C interest focused on making complete records of known ruins and ancient cultures, and the first problem-oriented excavations, although crude by today's standards, were undertaken. Four figures, among many, who did extensive work were: Désiré Charnay, Alfred P. Maudslay, Teobart Maler, and Leopoldo Batres.

Charnay worked in Mexico between 1858 and 1882, travelling throughout Mayaland and central Mexico as director of a special programme sponsored by the French Ministry of Public Instruction. He was a pioneer in many ways, conducting some none-too-careful excavations at Tula and at Teotihuacán (sometimes using dynamite!), using a huge, primitive camera to take some of the first photographs of ancient Mexican sites, and experimenting with the use of papier mâché to take mouldings of architectural sculptures and hieroglyphs. In his book, 'The Ancient Cities of the New World', he questioned the lack of respect for and interest in the ancient civilizations of the New World simply because they were believed so recent in comparison to ancient cities in the Old World. Maudslay, an Englishman, worked during 1881–94, making several trips to the Maya region to explore, photograph, and make plans of Copán, Quirigua, Tikal, Yaxchilán, and many other major Maya sites in Central America. His report was part of a huge English work on the Natural History of Central America. Maler, a German-American, worked for the Peabody Museum of Harvard University in the late 19C. Concentrating on Guatemala and Yucatán, he recorded texts, drew plans, and took photographs of Maya ruins and published a well-illustrated scientific set of volumes. Leopoldo Batres, a Mexican, was official director of antiquities under Porfirio Díaz. Working in the late 19C and early 20C, he carried out excavations at Teotihuacán in preparation for Mexico's centennial Independence celebrations. The work of these men, and others, established two trends in Mexican archaeology which continue up to the present: international participation and the beginnings of Mexican pride in its past.

Alongside site exploration there was a scholastic movement in document collection and historiography by the newly independent Mexican intellectuals. Among these were José Fernando Ramírez, Joaquín García Icazbalceta, Alfredo Chavero, Francisco Paso y Troncoso, and Manuel Orozco y Berra, all of whom made invaluable collections and collations of documents and ethnographic sources 'buried' in haphazard viceregal archives. One example of the hundreds of discoveries was Diego de Landa's manuscript, in 1863. Orozco y Berra made one of the first attempts to synthesize these materials into a monumental history of Mexico's prehispanic cultures in his 'Historia antigua y de la conquista de México' (1880). From 1887, his German counterpart, Edouard B. Seler of the Berlin Ethnographical Museum, began systematically to compare chronicles, native documents, linguistics, and archaeological evidence in trying to understand the native Mesoamerican mind and culture. In the mid-century the Aztecs were made extremely popular to a wide reading public by an American historian with a skill for synthesis and a flair for dramatic writing—William H. Prescott, who wrote his seminal 'The Conquest of Mexico' in 1843.

These 19C explorations and excavations took place against the backdrop of several important scientific developments in Europe which were crucial to the growth of modern archaeology. In geology, Charles Lyell's careful explanation and proof of the idea of stratigraphy gave 'antiquarians' a method for making sense of the layers in their excavations and for relating to each other the artefacts within the layers. The growing realization of the antiquity of man in the Old World, and of his association with extinct animals and primitive tools, led some to begin looking for evidence of early man in the New World as well. Equally important, the implied associations of tools, animals, and ancient men were proved by Lyell's stratigraphic principles; and Charles Darwin's proposal of the theory of biological evolution gave a theoretical framework for the evidence and implied a long time-span to these ancient men. The idea of cultural (or at least technological) evolution implied by the Three Age System of stone, bronze, and iron tools in Europe had less effect in the New World except to provide another theoretical framework for cultural evolution and for the systematic organization of artefacts.

Another new development in the 19C study of Mexico's past, perhaps also inspired by earlier work in Europe, was interest in its ancient languages. By the final decades of the century many copies of Maya hieroglyphs had been published, and in these decades and the first years of the 20C three men had been working independently on decipherment: Ernst Förstemann, Joseph Goodman, and Charles Bowditch. By 1887 Förstemann had recognized the Maya use of and symbol for zero, and began working out Maya arithmetic and calendrical systems; by 1905 Goodman had put forward a formula for converting Maya dates into their Christian equivalents.

In the 20C the growth of Archaeology as a recognized field of study took place within the wider field of Anthropology in the New World and in broad terms the development of archaeology in Mexico has followed the N American model. It has not, however, ever abandoned European connections, and permanent or long-term German and other 'Scientific Projects' have played a major part in the excavation of Mexican sites.

A convenient date for the beginning of modern Mexican archaeology is 1908, when the anthropologists Edouard Seler, Franz Boas (of Columbia University), and Alfred Tozzer (of Harvard) founded the School of American Studies in Mexico City. With the already well-known Mexican anthropologist and historian Manuel Gamio, projects were begun to explore Mexico's past on a more controlled, problem-oriented basis. Armed with the intellectual developments outlined above, the anthropological orientations of Boas and Tozzer, scientific excavation techniques worked out by Alfred Kidder in the Southwest USA, and the historical tradition of the 19C Mexican school (which he learned under Nicolás León, Director of the Museo Nacional), Gamio began his famous Teotihuacán Valley project in 1917. The time-scope of the project was from the prehistoric beginnings of settlement in the valley to the study of the modern population. Similarly Sylvanus G. Morley and Alfred Kidder began a long-term project in 1914, in the Maya region, under the auspices of the Carnegie Institution of Washington, DC.

Thereafter the nature of archaeological work in Mexico has been on a monumental scale, by both national and foreign teams. Alfonso Caso began work in the Valle de Oaxaca, at Monte Albán, in 1927; George Vaillant worked in the Maya region and in the Basin of Mexico through the 1930s and 1940s, and was a pioneer in focusing on the chronological details of Mexico's past. He was equally influential in synthesizing the mounds of new data in both scholarly and popular publications.

Archaeological work in Mexico since the second world war has advanced at an ever-increasing pace and volume. A major trend has been the continuation of a strong international, as well as national, aspect, and in this respect Mexico's Instituto Nacional de Antropología e Historia (INAH), created in 1939 out of several earlier institutes, has been generous in allowing and in working alongside foreign expeditions. Projects have frequently been large-scale and a particular emphasis since the war has been the long-term, large-area project, involving survey and test excavation over huge areas (eg, Teotihuacán Valley, Oaxaca Valley, Basin of Mexico, Tehuacán Valley, Olmec, and Tula projects). Projects have been problem-oriented both in terms of specific goals or questions about past cultures, and in terms of more general questions of cultural development. In the last four decades virtually every region of Mexico has had some exploration; huge amounts of information have been discovered, including the recognition of unsuspected civilizations such as that of the Olmecs of the Gulf Coast region. In all this work the use of scientific techniques and applications has played an increasing role: everything from the now familiar radiocarbon (C14) dating to powerful statistical techniques on computers. Palaeoenvironmental analyses are now an integral part of every project alongside the excavation of monumental structures.

A final, but by no means less important, aspect of archaeology in Mexico has been oriented towards the public. The Mexican government has given equal importance to the restoration of monuments after excavations and a considerable part of the national budget goes towards restorations, museums, and tourism.

Outlines of Mesoamerican Prehistory

Earliest Occupation

The New World was peopled from the Old World from NE Asia; groups of nomadic hunters, presumably following herds of game, migrated across the Bering Strait into what is now Alaska. There were several periods in the Pleistocene Era when such a migration on land could have occurred, but there is no evidence for man's presence in the New World before c 50,000 years ago. In each of these periods the sea level was many metres lower than today's level and there was consequently a vast area of dry land around the Bering Strait—referred to as Beringia. Optimum conditions for land migration existed c 20,000 years ago, during the final phases of the Wisconsin Glaciation of N America; however, the bulk of uncontroversial dates for man's presence in the New World falls between 12,000 and 6000 BC. There are a few much older dates but arguments to support or question them are extremely technical.

Various theories propose a single migration, several migrations, migration by sea, and combinations of routes. There is good evidence for man's presence in highland Peru by c 13,000 BC, if not earlier, and abundant evidence for his presence in Mesoamerica by 10,000 BC, with more isolated earlier evidence, theoretically necessitated by the Peruvian materials. Another source of disagreement between scholars is the route of migration southwards once the Bering Strait had been crossed. Substantial evidence supports the ice-free 'corridor' E of the Rocky Mountains, but other evidence suggests a coastal route as well.

Between c 20,000 and 10,000 years ago there was gradual change in the technology of the migrants' tool-kits. Tools became more specialized and several regional styles developed; in general, large lanceolate and fluted projectile points became hallmarks of different regional traditions, especially in N America, where the evidence is more abundant. A second major change, the extinction of the big-game animals hunted by man (camel, horse, a primitive bison, woolly mammoth, mastodon), occurred during the warmer climatic phases following the end of the Pleistocene Period, c 9000 BC.

Evidence of early man in Mesoamerica is scattered. In NW Sonora surface finds of crude chopping and scraping tools are claimed to be dated c 17,000 BC; later in date, in Sonora, Coahuila, Durango, and Jalisco, more specialized fluted projectile points, similar to 'Clovis' points from adjacent regions of the USA, have been found, again, mostly as surface finds. At Tlapacoya, SE of Mexico City, hearths have been found with bones of extinct game and stone tools; a date of c 20,000 BC has been obtained (some scholars believe it should be a few thousand years earlier), but the problem is with the associations between layers dated and the artefacts and bones. (Interestingly, although most of the tools are made of the local andesite, others are of imported obsidian, quartz, and basalt— the earliest evidence of the transportation of these materials in Mesoamerica.) The Tlapacoya finds strengthen evidence from near Tequixquiac, N of Mexico City, where bones of extinct animals and some 20 claimed stone and bone implements have been found in the late Pleistocene gravel and sand beds, incl. scrapers, lanceolate-like blades, and awls. From Tequixquiac also came the earliest carved bone 'art' in Mesoamerica—a camelid sacrum (18cm wide) carved to look like a dog's or coyote's head. To the SE in Puebla, around the Valsequillo reservoir, have come more tools, similar to those from the Basin, and also in Pleistocene gravels rich in fossil bones. A buried charcoal sample has been dated c 36,000 BC, but its association with the artefacts is uncertain. Finally, in San Luis Potosí stone tools and bones have been found at El Cedral, suggesting man's presence before 30,000 BC.

After c 8000 BC the evidence is both more abundant and less controversial. At Sta Isabel Iztapán in the NE Basin of Mexico a 'kill-site' had two imperial mammoths (*Mammuthus imperator*) around and among the ribs of which were various stone tools: obsidian scrapers and prismatic knives, flint blades, part of a bifacially-flaked knife, and three projectile points (all resembling types found further N in Mexico and the USA). Radiocarbon dates from the associated sediments, and from nearby similar finds at San Bartolo Atepehuacán, range between 7800 and 7300 BC. Of similar date are two human fossil finds, the most substantial from Tepexpan, less than 3.5km NE of Sta Isabel: 'Tepexpan Man', the more or less complete skeleton of a woman, c 1.6m tall, interred face-down on the former NE shore of Lago de Texcoco. The second find, the jaw of an infant, came from Xico, S of Mexico City.

Outside the Basin of Mexico the most complete and continuous evidence of early man, from c 8000 BC, comes from SE Tamaulipas and from Tehuacán. From cave sites in these two regions come oval and leaf-shaped projectile points, end scrapers, flake scrapers, and, from Tamaulipas, some crude-looking chopper tools. In both cases, however, the hunters were not primarily big-game hunters but subsisted as much by foraging and by hunting the 'new', modern fauna, incl. deer, fox, coyote, rabbit, skunk, ground squirrel, lizards, and turtles.

Although the different sites are widely scattered, it seems a plausible hypothesis that they represent home and away activities, possibly the roving, hunting bands creating immediate purpose kill-sites, while the cave sites were permanent home bases.

Incipient Agriculture and the First Villages

Early domestication and the rise of village farming have been especially intensely studied since about 1950. There are two aspects: the comparatively straightforward evidence for where and when it occurred, and the more tentative theorizing about why it took place. Theories abound, but it is generally agreed that the process took place gradually and at different paces in different regions. Some regions only knew of agriculture by diffusion, not by independent development, and some regions never practised agriculture in the prehistoric period. The archaeological evidence suggests that agriculture developed through several phases of increasing reliance on plant foods, and several readjustments in the proportions of reliance on various species. No society in Mesoamerica ever became totally reliant on grown plant foods—some hunting, fishing, and collecting played a part even in the most urbanized agricultural states of central Mexico.

Proportional readjustments in food sources not only took place over a long period of time but also fluctuated seasonally or over short spans of years. Numerous factors were relevant to both long-term and short-term fluctuations: climate, rainfall, population increases and decreases, population movements, natural selection, human selection; so complex is the entire ecological realm involved that arguments in general stem from the selection of one or a few factors as primary. A safer position is that the interplay of factors was constant and intricate, and that no single cause can be named. Nevertheless different regions developed different kinds of agriculture and some factors were more important in some regions than in others. In general, environmental changes were at the heart of the earliest developments, but man's reactions to them varied within the limits of his ingenuity and of his environment's resources at any particular time—a desert can be irrigated for agriculture, if the technology and economic machinery are available to do so. Mesoamerican agriculture was once generally thought to have been extensive in lowland zones and intensive in highland zones, but a growing body of evidence has shown this to be too simplified. Both zones varied according to population density through time, and we now know that the Lowland Maya also had many intensively cultivated drained field plots as they refined their agricultural techniques.

Animal domestication played only an insignificant role. Dogs, the earliest domesticates, are known in Idaho by c 9000 BC and in Peru by c 6000 BC; they may have accompanied man across the Bering Strait. They were an important food source in Veracruz by c 1500 BC (nearly half the total meat supply). The only other animal domesticates were the turkey, the muscovy duck, and the stingless bee. Otherwise early Mesoamericans focused their attention on plants. Long before the Spanish conquest about 100 different plants were cultivated (see below). By then Mesoamerican farming systems were consciously designed to provide a recognized balanced and varied diet, plus other items for daily use: containers, fishing net floats, fibres, dyes, ornaments, medicines, ritual objects, and hallucinogens.

Recognition of the earliest occurrence of domesticated plants is not straightforward. The earliest phases are obscure because morphological changes (greater size; differences in shape and colour) do not occur until long after actual domestication, defined as deliberate planting and harvesting with an expected result and planned use of the product, has taken place. Evidence of early tended crops is indistinguishable from wild progenitors or counterparts. The best evidence of plant domestication comes from cave sites where long-term, intensive projects have been done: Tamaulipas (NE Mexico), Tehuacán (Puebla), and the Valle de Oaxaca. In Tehuacán and Oaxaca there were no major climatic changes during the transition from Pleistocene to Holocene (modern) times, and although cooler and drier, their climates were not significantly different from today's. The horse and camel became extinct but deer and small mammals remained or were replaced by their modern equivalents.

In the cave sites of the Valle de Tehuacán, from c 7500 BC, the preponderance of the meat supply was small game. In an annual cycle of movements and collecting, seed pods of mesquite (a leguminous tree) and other wild plants were harvested. In the succeeding millennium the antelope left the valley and an increasing variety of plant foods was collected: setaria grass, amaranth, prickly pear, avocado, and chupandilla fruit. In Oaxaca the process was similar. The principal evidence comes from Guilá Naquitz cave, dated c 8800–6800 BC, occupied by people who hunted deer, rabbit, and mud turtles, and collected mesquite pods, acorns, piñon and susi nuts, maguey, prickly pear, tree fruits and berries, pumpkins and squashes, beans, and a weedy 'grass' that was either an early form of maize, or teosinte, its nearest wild relative.

In both regions populations shifted in accordance with a cyclical pattern governed by the seasonal availability of food. During most of the year, in the dry season, the population scattered in small groups to hunt deer and small mammals and to collect cactus leaves and edible roots; during the rainy season, especially in abundant years, larger groups could congregate to collect, intensively and quickly, seasonal cactus fruits, wild cereals, and mesquite pods before they rotted or were eaten by birds and animals. Eventually some of these plants were cultivated—deliberately sown and harvested—but as such only contributed a minor part of the diet. The proportion grew as efforts increased and crops, by trial and error, could be seen to be more productive in terms of time and effort (eg, selection and care). Preserved human faeces, a major source of dietary information in cave sites, clearly show, however, that virtually anything was eaten—faeces contain bits of charred snail shell, mouse, lizard, snake and bird bones, feathers, eggshell, grubs, and insects.

Artefacts from the caves illustrate the inhabitants' way of life: stone-tipped darts, thrown with atlatls, for hunting deer and peccary; roasting pits for cooking meat with heated stones; shattered long bones from which the marrow was eaten; wooden clubs, spring traps, and fibre snares and nets, for trapping; net bags and baskets of plant fibre for collecting; grinding stones for processing plant foods; miscellaneous flint tools for making wooden, bone, and shell ornaments, cleaning hides, and striking fire; and fibre mats for repose. Not until c 5700 BC can morphological changes be recognized in cultivated plants. The proportions of wild and cultivated foods changed slowly, although in the regions destined to become 'fully' agricultural the pace accelerated.

Simultaneously, settlement patterns changed. In the earliest phases settlements were seasonal: in the dry season, two- or three-hearth campsites were the norm, with no permanent dwellings; in the wet season, larger camps and cave sites. As population increased and eventually exceeded the numbers supportable by seasonal hunting and gathering, selection of certain more productive plants (especially maize) changed at some point from an unconscious (or semi-conscious) to a conscious, deliberate activity. It became recognized that actually clearing areas and fostering the growth of, or even planting, selected crops were worthwhile. Groups were thus able to remain in one place, in larger numbers, and to build more permanent structures. Trial, error, and intelligent observation led to improvements in techniques and selection of sites for cultivation.

By the fifth millennium BC the most important plant of those cultivated was maize. However, as late as 3800 BC cobs remained small and of little more calorific value than wild mesquite pods; but with selection and experimentation, by c 2000 BC it had reached a yield of c 200 kilos a hectare—much more productive than any wild plant. At about the same time the first small sedentary villages and pottery-making appeared in highland Mexico.

The pace of change from hunting and gathering to sedentary village agriculture varied throughout Mesoamerica. Sedentary villages were possible in drier regions only after irrigation systems had been invented. Some regions, such as the desert N of Mexico, never had permanent settlements in most of their areas. In other environments, where wild food sources were sufficiently abundant, settled life occurred even before agricultural development or diffusion. On the sea coasts, for example, shellfish were available year-round and large shell-mounds may indicate permanent or semi-permanent residence. Very few coastal sites date before c 4000 BC, however. In the Basin of Mexico, Zohapilco has the oldest evidence that could be used to argue sedentary life as early as 6000 BC. Peat-like deposits near the former shores of the Basin's freshwater lakes show that abundant plant and animal foods were available in or near the water: three species of fish, waterfowl, deer, rabbit, snakes, turtles, axolotls (small, eel-flavoured amphibians), teosinte amaranth, physals, and squash. Stone grinding tools, too heavy for easy and frequent transport, feature in the tool-kit. But until many other such sites are known, the main evidence of continuous, permanent settlements remains the early agricultural villages. Generally speaking, settlement patterns reflect the agricultural techniques: dispersed in extensively cultivated lowlands and nucleated in intensively cultivated highlands.

Some of the principal domesticated plants of ancient Mesoamerica, with dates and locations of earliest domestication in Mesoamerica, were:

amaranth	Tehuacán c 4900–4400 BC
avocado	Tehuacán c 1800 BC
beans:	
common	Tamaulipas and Tehuacán c 5000 BC
jack	Dzibilchaltún c 430 BC
runner	Tamaulipas (wild?) c 7500 BC; Tehuacán (cultivated) c 1800 BC
sieva	Tamaulipas, Tehuacán, Yucatán c AD 100–850
tepary	Tehuacán c 4300–3000 BC
chili pepper	Tehuacán (wild?) c 7000–5700 BC; (cultivated) c 1170–400 BC
cotton	Tehuacán c 4300 BC
gourd (bottle)	Tamaulipas and Oaxaca c 7500 BC; Tehuacán c 5700 BC

maize	Guilá Naquitz (maize or teosinte pollen?) c 8800–7500 BC;
(cultivated maize cobs)	Tamaulipas c 3700 BC; Tehuacán c 5700 BC
manioc	Lake Gatún (Panama; pollen?) c AD 150; ceramic manioc griddles in S America by c 1300 BC; later in Mesoamerica
pumpkin	Guilá Naquitz (wild?) c 8800–8100 BC;
(cultivated)	Tamaulipas c 7500 BC; Tehuacán c 1800 BC
quinoa	grown when Spaniards arrived; earlier in S America
setaria	Tamaulipas c 4400 BC; Tehuacán c 1800 BC
squash	Tamaulipas c 1900–1700 BC; Tehuacán c 6000 BC
sunflower	Tamaulipas 400 BC

The Preclassic Period (c 2500 BC–AD 1/300): The Birth of Civilized Societies

The Preclassic, also called the Formative, was a period of major new developments, during which all the classic features of Mesoamerican civilization were established: planned ceremonial centres, monumental architecture, long-distance trade, hieroglyphic writing, calendrics, the ball game, and socioeconomic specialization. It can be subdivided into four phases, each with distinctive features: Early Preclassic c 2500–1250 BC, Middle Preclassic c 1250–400 BC, Late Preclassic c 400 BC–AD 1, and Protoclassic c AD 1–300.

In the Early Preclassic, agriculture spread throughout highland and lowland Mesoamerica. We have seen the highland evidence; in the lowlands it is more difficult to find, because of the dense tropical vegetation, and because it is thought that the earliest domesticates were root crops, which leave little trace in the archaeological record. Sedentary villages were established beside rivers and lakes where high rainfall, a high water table, and well-drained lands were preferred. As population increased, less favourable marginal lands were also settled, and by c 2000 BC experiments were being made to control, collect, and store water: diversion of slope wash and eventually canals to direct water from slope to field, dams, and pot irrigation (the sinking of small wells at intervals in fields where the water table is high). These methods were particularly advanced in central Mexico and Oaxaca.

In the lowlands of Yucatán and the Gulf Coast soils were especially fertile and well-watered; annual flooding on river levees and delta flood-plains made it possible to raise two crops a year. On the loamy soils, where milpa agriculture (slash-and-burn clearance) was practised, periodic fallowing was necessary, but two annual crops were still possible. As population increased, more sophisticated techniques were developed to drain swamps and create raised fields. Everywhere, maize became the staple crop, followed closely by beans and squash, plus various regionally cultivated plants.

The outstanding technological development of the phase was pottery. Whether it was independently discovered in Mesoamerica or diffused from S America is debated. That there was contact is certain, however, as maize was transmitted S while root-crops were transmitted N, each along with other items. The oldest known pottery in Mesoamerica (c 2450 BC) comes from coastal Guerrero (Puerto Marqués, known as Pox Ware), the Central Highlands (Purrón Ware in Tehuacán), the Oaxaca region (Purrón-like wares), and Cuello in Belize. Pox Ware and Purrón Ware show many similarities. The earliest named regional traditions were in S Mexico and W Guatemala (Ocós Complex) and in Yucatán (Swasey Complex).

The mano (grinder) and matate (grinding surface) for processing maize, and prismatic obsidian blades for a multitude of purposes, became two other essential tools of civilization. Use of obsidian was particularly important as it necessitated the development of permanent long-distance trading from about ten highland sources in Mexico and Guatemala (there may be other, undiscovered, sources).

In the Middle Preclassic regional centres and hierarchies of sites developed simultaneously in the Gulf Coast region (Olmec), the Basin of Mexico, the Valle de Oaxaca, and the extreme S of Mexico. Centralized ceremonial sites were established to serve the surrounding small farming villages.

Gulf Coast Olmec centres were not residential, except perhaps for a few élites who served in them, but they focused the communities' ideas in planned centres of monumental architecture, around a cosmology based on certain art forms (especially the were-jaguar) and on astronomical observations. There was insufficient population density, political complexity, and control of centralized forced-labour for true statehood, but the creation of the centres and the development of ceremonial art mobilized manpower for their construction and maintenance, and nurtured specialized crafts and long-distance trade to fetch exotic materials such as jade, obsidian, mica, serpentine, and basalt.

At least three principal Olmec centres were built, succeeding one another, but overlapping in their dates of occupation. The earliest was San Lorenzo Tenochtitlán, where a huge platform was raised, with an open ceremonial court, surrounding mounds, and a system of dams and lagoons. More than 60 stone monuments were set up, incl. at least 10 colossal stone heads (possibly ruler-'portraits'), massive altars, and other freestanding sculptures. An eleventh colossal head was found in the Tuxtla mountains E of Tres Zapotes. When it was abandoned, c 900 BC, the monuments, for uncertain reasons, were deliberately defaced, toppled into trenches dug for the purpose, and buried. Contemporary with San Lorenzo Tenochtitlán were three other centres, each with similar features on a smaller scale: Río Chiquito, Potrero Nuevo, and Laguna de los Cerros.

The second Olmec centre was La Venta. Its main features included a man-made, fluted, conical mound and several raised earthen platforms, the whole precinct oriented on an axis 8° W of N. Within the ceremonial complex were several buried mosaic jade pavements (in the form of stylized jaguar faces) and a basalt tomb. Four colossal stone heads and other freestanding sculptures were also set up. La Venta was abandoned c 600 BC in similar manner to San Lorenzo Tenochtitlán.

Succeeding it was a centre at Tres Zapotes, whose occupation extended into the Late Preclassic. Here there were about 50 mounds in groups around four plazas. At least two colossal stone heads were erected, although one of them is, more accurately, from *Cerro Nestepe*. There were large, flat stone altars, and a stele stone with the Long Count date of 31 BC (see *Writing, Counting, and Calendrics* below). One of its rectangular pyramid-mounds was faced with cut stone but no lime mortar was used to secure it.

Two important features of Olmec culture were long-distance trade and a distinctive art style. Trade was essential to obtain raw materials, especially stone, for cult objects. The Olmec art style was manifested in naturalistic, chubby-faced 'portraiture' (colossal heads), in distinctive infantile (or 'baby-face') sculptures in small objects, and in feline (jaguar) features, often highly stylized. We can only surmise the nature of Olmec religion, although we can identify many of their gods (see *Mesoamerican Religion* below); the artistic elements it fostered formed the beginnings of the religious iconography of the Classic Maya and central Mexican Highlands.

Olmec and Olmecoid influence was widespread. Whether the evidence shows Olmec influence, control, or mere presence as traders is debated. It spread southwards into lowland Mexico and mingled with the earlier Ocós Complex sites in S Chiapas, Guatemala, and Costa Rica. Some evidence of Olmec art is found as far S as El Salvador and Honduras. To the W and NW actual Olmec presence seems certain throughout highland Guerrero, Morelos, and Oaxaca, where there are cave paintings (Oxtotitlán and Juxtlahuaca in Guerrero), numerous portable objects and stelae, and rock reliefs (Chalcatzingo in Morelos). In the Basin of Mexico, Olmec figurines and pottery were included in burials at Zohapilco and Tlatilco, alongside local art objects and pottery.

Contemporary Middle Preclassic developments elsewhere in Mesoamerica included less of monumental scale at first. In the Basin of Mexico, at Tlatilco and several other agricultural villages around the lake shores, there were hundreds of burials whose grave-goods included a distinctive figurine style mixed with Olmecoid features and imports. From c 900 BC there was a rapid population increase and several new settlements: Zacatenco, Copilco, Cuicuilco, El Arbolillo, Teotihuacán, Texcoco, and Cuautitlán. Olmec influences declined and disappeared at these sites as the Basin style waxed, best represented in the solid clay figurines from Tlatilco graves. These represent young girls in short skirts, with coiffeured hair, mother-and-child groups, dancers, acrobats, ball players, hunchbacks, dogs, and peculiar two-headed figures and monster-faces of half flesh–half skeleton. Towards the end of the Middle Preclassic the first ceremonial mounds were erected in the S Basin, at Cuicuilco. Here, grave-goods included new ceramics, especially white-paste wares with incised double-line-back decoration on their rims and sun-bursts on their interiors (see *Mesoamerican Pottery* below).

In the Valle de Oaxaca there was a similar tradition of farming villages. In the Middle Preclassic Tierras Largas, San José Mogote, and Huitzo grew more rapidly than the rest, but no monumental ceremonial architecture was constructed until after c 850 BC, and then not on the scale of the contemporary Olmec sites. Between c 850 and 550 BC San José Mogote grew to 15 times the size of any other town in the region and incorporated a natural hill, on which masonry buildings were erected, oriented to the cardinal points. At the threshold between two main buildings was a carved stone slab depicting a Classic 'captive' figure and the oldest known Mesoamerican hieroglyphic symbol, c 600 BC—'One Earthquake'. Thus, at the threshold of the Late Preclassic, the development of hieroglyphic writing was well under way. Other new settlements were established in the valley, most notably Monte Albán, on the hilltops overlooking the three arms of the Valle de Oaxaca; its establishment seems to have been a deliberate and co-operative effort by the valley towns.

In the Late Preclassic, from c 400 BC, the tradition of ceremonial centres was well established in the Gulf Coast zone and became more common elsewhere. In the Basin of Mexico many towns constructed platforms, temples, and pyramids. At Tlapacoya a temple and pyramid were built; at Cuicuilco a large and a smaller stepped pyramid, both round, were built, plus 11 other mounds. The Cuicuilco pyramid was the earliest stone-faced structure in Mesoamerica. At Teotihuacán rapid growth was encouraged by control of the local obsidian sources just N of the site, and irrigation works (if later, more substantial, evidence can be pushed back into this period) indicate the beginnings of centralized political control. By c 200 BC Cuicuilco was some 400ha with a population of perhaps 20,000. It dominated the S Basin and its only serious rival was Teotihuacán, equally dominant in the N Basin. The contest was soon ended, however, by the eruption of Xitle in c 50 BC (and again c 1 BC–AD 1), burying Cuicuilco in a layer of lava several metres thick.

In Oaxaca, Monte Albán was used as the ceremonial and political centre by the valley towns and rapidly dominated the region. The construction of a large, carefully planned ceremonial plaza included intensive agriculture on the surrounding, terraced hillsides, differential burial in specially constructed tombs, the establishment of fixed calendrical cycles (especially of a 260-day cycle; see *Writing, Counting and Calendrics* below), the Zapotec hieroglyphic system, and the military domination of the region. Several other smaller centres also developed in the valleys, at Mitla, Tlacolula, and Monte Negro.

In S Chiapas, near the Guatemalan border, another major centre was Izapa. Here a distinctive art style specialized in relief-carving in an easy, curvilinear style and a more violent, elaborate narrative style on altars and stelae. Glyphs appear to be ancestral to Maya writing and include some of the earliest recorded dates, between 35 BC and AD 36. Izapa was influenced by the Olmecs and in turn influenced early Maya styles.

In the Maya Lowlands the first small villages began to grow and to manifest glimmerings of what would become the Classic Maya civilization. As more people moved into the region ceremonial structures were erected at Uaxactún, El Mirador, and Tikal (Guatemala). In the N Lowlands there is evidence for sites at least as early as c 700 BC. During the final centuries of the Preclassic we know that settlements existed at Becán, Chichén Itzá, Yaxuná, Maní, Chacchab, Aké, and Dzibilchaltún. (As excavations continue at sites in Yucatán it may turn out that the sequence of occupation here is as early as elsewhere in S Mesoamerica.) In the Highlands of S Guatemala the principal centre was Kaminaljuyú, where a ceremonial plaza was built with temple-pyramids, burial mounds, stelae, and colossal stone sculptures.

Independently and somewhat isolated from all these developments, the W Mexican region of Michoacán, Jalisco, Colima, Nayarit, Sinaloa, and Guanajuato developed its own distinctive culture. A unique tradition of shaft- and chamber-tomb construction was established in part of the region (eg, El Opeño, Etzatlán, Colima), some being as early as 1500 BC. Both this and the local ceramic styles suggest contact by sea with S America, although the evidence is disputed. A tradition of glossy, red, burnished hollow figurines, and of solid figurines depicting everyday life, for which W Mexico is justly famous, began. At Chupícuaro in Guanajuato, about 400 graves were dug and stone alignments made; another distinctive ceramic style emerged, incl. figurines with long, thin eyes and polychrome vessels with geometric designs in black and cream on red. By the Classic Period activity at the site had ceased.

The major achievements of the Preclassic, up to c AD 1, are impressive: the plaza-plan for ceremonial centres, the appearance of stepped pyramids and the corbel arch in the Maya region; differentiation in housing and burial—ie, the beginnings of class structures and occupational specialization (farmers, builders, craftsmen, merchants, rulers, and slaves); writing, development of the 260-day calendar, and date-recording using the Long Count system; permanent, well-established, and organized long-distance trade routes, distinctive art styles, regional pottery and figurine traditions; the beginning of the ball game, originating in the Veracruz area of the Gulf Coast region; and the beginning of organized warfare and the fortification of important sites.

The Protoclassic of c AD 1–300 is a useful concept as a phase during which a few regions advanced rapidly towards the highly urbanized civilization of the Classic Period. A few sites began to dominate—socially, economically, and sometimes politico-militarily—large Mesoamerican regions, and grew into huge cities with elaborate socio-political structures: Teotihuacán, Monte Albán, and Tikal. Each region—Central Highlands, Southern Highlands, and Maya Lowlands—while firmly remaining part of greater Mesoamerican civilization, developed artistic, religious, and socially distinctive characters.

The Classic Period (AD 1/300–900): Urbanization and the Growth of Trading Empires

The principal themes of the Classic Period were the development of true urbanism and diversification. A few large cities became dominant, Mesoamerican culture expanded in both geographical range and scope, and there were many intellectual, artistic, socio-political, and agricultural innovations.

Technologically the Classic Period differed little from the Late Preclassic. Stone tools, especially the adaptable obsidian blade, the digging stick, and the mano and matate remained the principal implements. A more efficient hoe, in general use by c AD 500, and the bow and arrow were invented. Likewise, dietary patterns changed little, but several inventions and improvements in agriculture enabled more land to be cultivated and produced greater crop returns, in particular, higher-yielding varieties of maize. In the Central Highlands, dams, irrigation canals, and terracing came into widespread use and greater sophistication gave more refined control of water. In the Maya Lowlands ridged terraces and raised plots in bajos (broad, swampy areas) were used to increase the amount of land under cultivation; short-cycle slash-and-burn agriculture was introduced into more and more regions. Water supply, always crucial, was ensured by building reservoirs and wells, and by taking advantage of natural pots, wells, and underground pools (chultunes and cenotes; but note that the chultún, a small subterranean chamber dug into solid material, could be used for water or food storage, or burial).

Mesoamerica's geographical limits expanded northwards when climatic shifts increased rainfall along the E flanks of the Sierra Madre Occidental. Cultivation spread into a narrow strip almost up to the present-day borders of Chihuahua; E of this 'tongue', the great central desert region remained inhabited by nomadic Chichimec tribes, who played an important periodic role in developments to the S in central Mexico. Although cultivation had long since been part of the cultures of W Mexico, it was not until late in the Classic, c AD 600, that other Mesoamerican features became established in the region. Shaft-tombs were no longer constructed, and westerners began to build plazas with ball courts, stepped pyramids, and temples (eg, Amapa in Nayarit), and to participate more actively in the long-distance trade networks controlled from central Mexico.

Increased agricultural production and dramatic population increases were reciprocal. Large, dense populations became possible for the first time. At their respective peaks Teotihuacán, Monte Albán, and Tikal reached c 200,000 (maximum estimate), c 30,000, and c 70,000. Many other urban ceremonial centres reached populations of 10–15,000. The constituents of these settlements emphasize a change from purely ceremonial centres, inhabited by priests and ruling élites serving a large scattered population, to urban centres, inhabited by ruling and priestly élites surrounded by a variety of craftsmen, traders, and farmers in humbler dwellings.

Climate, tradition, social structure, terrain, agricultural methods, and artistic inclination all contributed to a variety of morphological features, but scholars identify at least four general settlement patterns (each further subdivided): (1) a nucleated grid, compact, densely populated, and rigidly planned—Teotihuacán is the archetypal example; (2) a more dispersed pattern, typical of the Maya Lowlands and Gulf Coast cities, with compact, well-planned central zones, and decreasing population density outwards from the centre, the dwellings carefully planned as individual units or small groups of units, but not regularly sited on a grid system—eg, Tikal, Chichén Itzá, Palenque, and El Tajín; (3) a less nucleated pattern, typical of SE Mesoamerica (especially in what is now Belize), with ceremonial centres strung out along river-frontages, serving dispersed populations—eg, Labaantún (Belize); and (4) the unique co-operative settlement at Monte Albán, a centre established specifically as a large, terraced, élite city to serve the numerous agricultural towns of the valley bottoms and slopes. Around the urban sites villages, hamlets, and coastal settlements remained numerous, and, where limiting factors operated, some regions never rose above village level.

The Early Classic (AD 1–300), sometimes called the Protoclassic, was a developmental phase during which Teotihuacán, Monte Albán, and Tikal began to dominate their respective regions. Scores of other urban or urban-like sites dominated smaller regions and were ever ready to take advantage of any chance to increase their own political or commercial influence.

Teotihuacán quickly dominated the Basin of Mexico once Cuicuilco had collapsed. Several factors contributed to its growth: improved agriculture, the construction of a sophisticated irrigation system, careful civic planning and control by a hierarchical élite over the increasing labour force, and control of the nearby obsidian mines of the Pachuca–Tulancingo–Tepeapulco area, whose exploitation began in earnest for an increasingly demanding market. The population was densely packed in the city in contiguous housing units, with only small outlying villages to exploit the lakeshores of the Basin, and industrial settlements for exploiting obsidian (eg, Tepeapulco) or salt. Long-distance trade became increasingly controlled and extended in direct routes as far S as Guatemala and Belize. Diplomatic relations with other cities were cultivated and maintained, and prospecting, eventually colonizing, groups of Teotihuacanos searched the N and W regions of Mesoamerica and beyond for rare mineral resources. Teotihuacán's city plan was early established, especially the ceremonial core. By c AD 100 Calle de los Muertos and its E–W-running counterpart were established as axes of the city, and the Pirámide del Sol completed; around these characteristic Teotihuacán apartment-complex dwelling units were built in uniform blocks along the grid of streets and alleys.

Simultaneously, Monte Albán strengthened its position in S Mexico. Its huge central ceremonial plaza was constructed, and trade and political links were formed with Teotihuacán and other Central Highland cities, and with cities in the Maya region. Although warfare had become more organized towards the end of the Preclassic, the relationship between Monte Albán and Teotihuacán was peaceful, and contributed to the prosperity of both.

In W Mexico, commercial contacts with Teotihuacán were also important. However, relative isolation during the Preclassic had allowed the development of distinctive regional artistic styles, social structure, and burial practices, which were only slowly replaced by central Mexican and other Mesoamerican features. Nevertheless, the area remained distinctive in the tradition of large, hollow, red pottery figurines and for its shaft- and chamber-tombs, the latter until the Middle Classic.

The Early Classic was also an embryonic phase E of the Isthmus of Tehuantepec. Characteristic features of Maya civilization spread rapidly throughout the lowlands: distinctive pottery called Chicanel, the corbel arch, and a strong 'cult' of erecting monolithic monuments (stelae) with Long Count dates. The Petén region of present-day N Guatemala and S Yucatán was a hive of activity, where several regional, chronologically overlapping, architectural styles developed. One outstanding site was Tikal, whose growth from c 200 BC coincided roughly with that of Teotihuacán. At the top of a settlement-pattern hierarchy, it and a few other regional capitals dominated the Maya Lowlands and collected tribute from groups of smaller cities, who in turn collected from towns and villages. In highland Guatemala, Kaminaljuyú and San Antonio Frontal were rivals for power and influence. The former developed a special relationship with Teotihuacán, which apparently maintained a resident group there, while Frontal clove more to its Maya origins and traded to the E and S. At Tikal (by the 4C AD) and Kaminaljuyú the beginnings of dynasties, which later led to intricate power alliances, are recorded in stelae sculptures.

Throughout Mayaland the landscape was infilled by increasing population and land reclamation: at first along selected riverine systems; then on more loamy soils and swampy regions as populations exceeded the agricultural capacities of earlier settlements. Competition for land and friction over tribute control undoubtedly fostered political alliances and warfare.

In the Middle Classic (AD 300–700) Teotihuacán, Monte Albán, Tikal, and Kaminaljuyú reached the heights of their powers. From c AD 300 to c 650 Teotihuacán had no rival in the Central Highlands and its products were distributed all over Mesoamerica. Nevertheless, its 'empire' seems more commercial than political. Its influence was supreme in the Central Highlands and it may have maintained a certain measure of control over Kaminaljuyú's rulers; it also jealously guarded its virtual monopoly on land access to W Mexico and northern prospecting. Its relationships with other powerful cities, however, remained peaceful coexistence. Teotihuacano products appear alongside, not in exclusion of, the products of Monte Albán, El Tajín (by then of rising importance in the N Gulf Coast), and the Maya centres.

By c AD 600 Teotihuacán had achieved its maximum size of more than 20 sq km. Its population, estimated between 100,000 and 200,000, was between 80 and 90 per cent of the total population of the Basin of Mexico. A regular grid of compact courtyard-housing spread in a continuous mass in the four quarters formed by main avenues running N–S and E–W. There were four zones: the ceremonial core, with the Pirámides del Sol and de la Luna, and over 100 smaller temples and shrines; élite palace-compounds in the adjacent streets; huge market areas, each surrounded by merchants' and craftsmen's quarters; and the mass of apartments, arranged in complexes around patios, of the agricultural bulk of the population. Social divisions are evident in differences in scale and luxury of the houses, incl. the quality of materials, size of rooms, and extent of carved and painted decorations. In élite compounds the plastered walls were covered with frescoes and stone columns around the courtyards carved and inset with obsidian and other stones for the eyes of the carved figures. It is estimated that c 25 per cent of the population were full-time craftsmen and merchants rather than farmers. More than 500 workshops have been identified. At least one large residence-workshop barrio of the city was a foreign enclave, a sort of Oaxaqueño quarter of craftsmen, merchants, and their families from Monte Albán; it is probable that Kaminaljuyú and other Maya cities also maintained such enclaves. Reciprocally, Teotihuacán must have maintained merchants of its own in Monte Albán, Kaminaljuyú, and Tikal, and perhaps in El Tajín and in W Mexican cities. From the site of Chalchihuites in Zacatecas, Teotihuacano prospectors penetrated N as far as modern New Mexico, in search of turquoise and other rare stones; from colonies in Jalisco turquoise and other minerals were mined; and from N Querétaro came cinnabar.

Kaminaljuyú continued to have a special relationship with Teotihuacán and was the regional advocate of Teotihuacano culture. Some scholars even suggest that it was actually ruled by Teotihuacán. Tláloc, a Central Highland deity, was prominent there, and the huge ceremonial complex was built in pure Teotihuacano style. The ruling élite maintained strong political and economic ties with Teotihuacán, and with most of the major Maya cities.

The Valle de Oaxaca remained dominated by Monte Albán throughout the Classic Period. Around the ridge-top ceremonial centre the hillsides were terraced for residential suburbs. Many other Zapotec towns were scattered on the slopes and floors of the three valleys overlooked by the capital. Commercially and politically Monte Albán maintained its independence and status as an important economic power, especially in its relationship with Teotihuacán. Its rulers were buried in tombs of a distinctive artistic style, constructed in the hills around the ceremonial plaza. Later, as Teotihuacán waned, Monte Albán remained vigorous.

The Maya Lowlands were equally prosperous in the Classic Period. Tikal's ruling dynasty dominated the city and region, arranged strategic marriages and political alliances with other Maya cities, conquered territories and exacted tribute, and buried their dead in sumptuous tombs recording their histories on altars, stelae, and door lintels. More than 1800 hieroglyphic dates commemorate special events and cycles. At least two of Tikal's rulers probably came from Kaminaljuyú, bringing with them a taste for things Teotihuacano.

Artistic expression reached a feverish pitch and extensive building programmes were continuous in every city. Regional styles, chronologically overlapping, borrowed from each other, spread in area, and went out of style—Petén, Río Bec, Chenes, Puuc, Palenque, and N Yucatán styles. Common to all were the extensive use of the corbel arch, massive masonry temples, pyramids, courtyard palaces, and the erection of commemorative stelae.

Tikal reached its maximum size and prosperity, with a population estimated between 50,000 and 70,000, dispersed over c 120 sq km. It thus contrasted with the dense settlement patterns of Central Highland cities, and had no grid plan. Nevertheless, it comprised a similar set of zones: a ceremonial core, linked by causeways (sacbéob) to the surrounding city; élite palaces immediately around the core, but secluded and not open to common access; and thousands of small house-clusters, more and more dispersed the farther they were from the central core. Each cluster comprised 2–5 houses around an open patio with croplands between the clusters. Tikal was a regional capital, at the top of the hierarchy, with its own hieroglyphic emblem. Its rulers presided over the flourishing trade necessitated by élite demands for luxury items only available from outside the Petén region, and by the general need of utilitarian raw materials such as obsidian, hard stone for grinding tools, salt, jade, seashells, and manufactured objects, such as Teotihuacán pottery. In return the Maya exported their own distinctive polychrome wares, exotic bird feathers, skins, and other tropical products.

As other Maya centres grew and ruling alliances and marriages became more complex, Tikal found itself sharing power with three other regional capitals, each also with its own emblem: Palenque, Calakmul, and Copán (Honduras). Tension and military rivalry prevailed among them and their tributaries, but building projects continued unabated and trade remained brisk. Many of the larger cities were fortified.

Between c AD 600 and 700 the extensive Teotihuacán trade 'empire' collapsed. The reasons are uncertain. The N end of the city suffered drastically from a fire which devastated the structures and presumably dispersed the population. Although its trading activities were generally peaceful, there is some evidence in murals and sculpture, from c AD 500, to suggest increasing militarism. One theory, although there is no specific evidence for it, is that outsiders sacked the city, or at least took advantage of the catastrophe. Another theory is that the sheer strain of maintaining such extensive commercial and political connections became too great, and caused internal strife.

The city was not abandoned but its population was at least halved. Several cities, which had prospered within the shadow of Teotihuacán's commercial world, began to assert themselves as regional powers: El Tajín in the Gulf Coast Lowlands, Xochicalco and Cholula in the Central Highlands S of Teotihuacán. Each developed its own eclectic art style drawing from Teotihuacano tradition and from local styles. At Xochicalco, a special event seems to have occurred c AD 650, recorded on its Serpent Pyramid, whose style includes central Mexican, Maya, and Oaxaqueño elements, and Zapotec and Mixtec date glyphs. One interpretation is that Mesoamericans convened at Xochicalco to synchronize their calendars, and it seems fitting and prescient that the meeting was held, or at least recorded, at one of the newly assertive cities and not at one of the old power capitals such as Teotihuacán or Monte Albán.

The Late Classic (c AD 700–900) was thus a time of change. Teotihuacán continued to decline but remained the largest centre of about half a dozen in the Basin of Mexico. It lost control over the black obsidian mines of Tepeapulco and began to exploit a new source of grey obsidian from nearby Otumba. In Mayaland, rivalry continued as Palenque, Calakmul, Copán, and Tikal vied for territory, and new centres such as El Tajín and Chichén Itzá developed new trade routes. Kaminaljuyú and its rivals declined as a new power at Cotzumalhuapa grew. The inland trade routes on which Classic Maya cities relied so heavily were rivalled by sea routes, skirting around the Yucatán coast and bringing port-cities into greater prominence. In all these newly assertive cities, as well as the old, the ball game cult became extremely important; solid, massive masonry ball courts, with temples and highly ornate carved narrative panels, were constructed in several cities.

In the Petén a final spurt of building activity only heralded the end. During the 9C Maya society slowly broke down and by c AD 900 major building activity had ceased. One by one the Maya cities had erected their last hieroglyphic inscriptions, and full lunar observations were no longer recorded when Short Count dates began to replace the Long Count system (see *Writing, Counting and Calendrics* below); public buildings ceased to be maintained and a rapid decline in population caused some ceremonial centres to cease to function, others to be abandoned entirely. Territorial borders were contracted, and there are signs of foreign intruders from the N and W in the appearance of new pottery types and stone sculptures of Mexican character. Trade had begun to decline as early as the 7C when the established long-distance routes between Teotihuacán, Monte Albán, and Mayaland were disrupted. Maya products, especially ceramics, deteriorated in quality. There is also evidence of environmental over-exploitation—as early as AD 300 the city of El Mirador (Guatemala) apparently collapsed chiefly for this reason.

These factors define the Maya collapse, but to explain it is not so easy. Rival theories will no doubt exercise scholars for generations to come. Many reasons have been proposed, and, as in most such cases, all must have contributed. The collapse seems sudden because most of the major centres recorded their last Long Count date in the early 9C; but there were early-warning signs: the environment was increasingly strained by rapid population growth in the Middle Classic centuries, until further expansion was no longer possible and overpopulation began to tell; moreover, ecological studies have discovered evidence of 9C climatic shifts that caused moisture decrease and a consequent inability to produce sufficient crops; a larger and larger proportion of the population was no longer engaged in farming and a top-heavy, dependent group of élites, traders, and craftsmen taxed the resources; internal stress and strain were notable from the Middle Classic as cities fought over tributary territories; foreign intrusions included new groups of Maya-speakers from the W (Tabasco)—the Putún-Itzá—some of whom occupied and revitalized Chichén Itzá and others continued S to capture Seibal in AD 830, and to attack Becán and cities along the Usumacinta river and its tributaries. Whether sudden or gradual, the result was the same: a dramatically altered Maya world. While the trigger of the collapse was one or a few factors, the result involved many major and minor factors over a longer period.

In the N half of the Yucatán Peninsula there was no corresponding decline. Maya cities here profited by encroaching on earlier trade networks and by developing sea trade. During the 9C the Puuc architectural style flourished in revitalized N centres. Highland Mexican influences from the Basin of Mexico, Oaxaca, and Veracruz spread into Yucatán via the S Gulf Coast. Every new centre, or revitalized old one, had at least one ball court. Long-established, heretofore peripheral, centres came into their own: Dzibilchaltún, Chichén Itzá, Cobá, Tulum, Uxmal, Kabah, Labná, and Sayil. New Maya influences were carried N and W to Teotihuacán and to Xochicalco, El Tajín, and Cacaxtla.

In Oaxaca, Monte Albán was abandoned shortly after AD 700 and its place was taken by several prominent valley cities (eg, Mitla).

In the N of the Central Highlands a new power began to emerge just after AD 900. The rivalry and disunity following Teotihuacán's decline began to coalesce as migrant peoples from the N and W were effectively led by semi-mythical, later deified, chiefs. The first of these Tolteca-Chichimeca leaders was one Ce Tecpatl Mixcóatl (Cloud Serpent). His son and heir, Ce Acatl Topiltzin, established the Toltec capital of Tula c AD 968 or 980. It is at this time that historical legends begin to provide another source of information in addition to archaeology and the brief narrative scripts on stelae and stone masonry.

What can we list as the most prominent features of Classic civilization? Foremost is the advent of urbanism; and with it, great artistic and architectural innovations, and intellectual achievements. Improvements in agricultural techniques and outputs, and population increases were both the mechanisms of these developments and the results. Classic Period ceremonial centres no longer served as places of pilgrimage from a wide hinterland, but formed the cores of vast residential cities, either compact or loosely settled.

It was perhaps this proximity of the religious and the secular that fostered a greater sharing of power between these two social elements. The vast trade, craft, and agricultural populations, and the careful planning of civic centres required an increasingly secular bureaucracy which increased its control over everyday life at the expense of the influence of religious élites. Secularization increased as class structure became more complex; specialization demanded a categorization of society into rulers, nobles, priests, bureaucrats and administrators, merchants and traders, craftsmen, farmers, and slaves. Secularization of power was also manifested in a keenness to record family histories and to emphasize one's ancestry and legitimacy. Such records were publicly displayed on panels, stelae, altars, and lintel stones. Intellectual discoveries included the zero and the invention of vigesimal mathematics. The Maya scrutinized the skies and invented calculations for predicting eclipses of the sun and moon, and for plotting the movements of planets, stars, and comets. Astronomical cycles became intimately linked with the agricultural seasons and with various ceremonies for appeasing increasingly defined and specialized gods. If the interpretation of the Serpent Pyramid at Xochicalco is correct, the 'convention' held there was a crowning achievement to these intellectual discoveries.

The extensive public building programmes were manifestations of political, economic, and artistic might. Long-distance trade brought a wealth of materials, 'capital', and ideas for secular and religious leaders to use in glorifying their cities. Several artistic media were employed throughout Mesoamerica. At Teotihuacán mural-painting and polychrome ceramics were especially important; the Maya also painted murals, specialized in stone and stucco sculpture, and developed their own distinctive polychrome ceramics. Most Teotihuacano scenes depicted formal religious and iconographic themes, with abundant allegory and symbolism. Later, there was an increase in pictures of warriors, weapons, ball game contests, and violence, but only in terms of individual combats, not in massed armies. Other paintings at Cholula, Cacaxtla, Chichén Itzá, Mul-Chic, and Bonampak depict similar, valuable historico-mythological and ethnographic information. Warfare was also depicted in stone relief; and fortifications, or defensible features, were present from the Early Classic at several sites.

Regional styles were also expressed in smaller artefacts, especially in pottery. Decorative techniques included carving, incising, and detailed polychrome painting. As with architectural decoration these depict narrative scenes, dates and texts, and religious scenes, all of which provide more historical and ethnographic information. Equally important is the distribution of ceramics and other small artefacts, whether exquisitely decorated luxury vessels or common utilitarian items. Extensive trade networks distributed both raw materials and finished products all over Mesoamerica, mingling the artistic styles of every region, and another 'invention' of Classic Mesoamerica was the standardization and mass-production of goods—eg, figurines made in moulds and the ubiquitous cylindrical tripod vessel. Certain wares were widely distributed: Usulután pottery from El Salvador throughout S Mesoamerica; Thin Orange Ware from central Mexico; and Fine Orange Ware from Mayaland, both throughout Mesoamerica.

Finally, some measure of standardization was also evident in architectural decoration, in the use of pre-cut masonry blocks, especially in Puuc façades, and in the use of stencils in mural-painting.

The Early Postclassic (AD 900–c 1150/1250): Early Military States

The Early Postclassic was a time of sweeping change in the political geography of Mesoamerica. Settlement patterns; art and architectural styles; economic relationships, controls, and routes; military practices; and religious emphases all changed significantly. As the power of great Classic cities waned, other cities, some newly founded, asserted themselves to establish regional states. Two sites stand out from the rest: Tula and Chichén Itzá and for both of these cities, and for their respective spheres of rule, we have the first truly historical sources.

However, because these histories were passed down for half a dozen centuries before they reached Spanish chroniclers and converted native historians, we can only guess at how compressed, how legendary or accurate, or how much reinterpreted to suit later needs, they were.

It was a time of mass movements of people. In S Mesoamerica the Petén was virtually abandoned according to one interpretation; but there was no noticeable influx of Petén traits into N Yucatán, so the movements of peoples are not completely understood. Other groups may have moved S, to establish hilltop settlements in highland Guatemala. In Oaxaca, Mixtec principalities were established in the vacuum of Monte Albán's abandonment.

In N Mesoamerica the Chichimecas, comprising numerous tribes, migrated S into the Central Highlands. Of these, the Toltecs were a coalition of the remaining incumbent peoples of central Mesoamerica, and of the Tolteca-Chichimecas from N and W Mexico. A second group, the Nonoalca, were described in Toltec histories, as wisemen, priests, merchants, and craftsmen, and as speaking several languages—Náhuatl, Popoloca, Mixtec, Mazatec, and Maya. Their origin is uncertain but their language abilities suggest a sort of international Mesoamerican scholarly élite.

Tula—ancient Tollán—was established in the later days of Teotihuacán's heyday, c AD 650, although there is also evidence of Late Preclassic-Early Classic settlement at the site (see Rte 19). Between c AD 900 and 1150 Tula became the largest and most important urban centre of central Mexico. In an area of c 12 sq km, later 16.5 sq km, lived an estimated 30,000 urban dwellers, with an equal number of farmers around them. Social stratification followed familiar Mesoamerican patterns—élites, craftsmen, merchants, and farmers—but at Tula secular power was supreme. In addition to the two large pyramid-temples there was a luxurious, capacious colonnaded palace and two huge ball courts, attesting to the continued, perhaps increased, importance of the game.

Judging by their art and colossal sculpture the Toltecs were the first to introduce full-scale, organized warfare into Mesoamerica, on a pattern that prevailed until the Spanish conquest. Warrior élites formed a new social class; and there was increased emphasis on human sacrifice—manifested in the tzompantli (skull rack) in the main plaza—and on cannibalism, both practices favoured later by the Aztecs as ritual acts and in emulation of the Toltecs.

Through military conquest, migration, and commerce the Toltecs rapidly expanded their power. They controlled the obsidian industry at Tepeapulco, formerly under Teotihuacán's control, and practised several craft specialities in cotton textiles and ixtle-plant fibres, and in ceramics, incl. distinctive wares—Coyotlatelco and Mazapán (both red-on-buff wares) and Blanco levantado (Tula water-coloured)—and ceramic drain tubes. They also initiated the practice of confiscating and storing food surpluses, anticipating the formalized Aztec system of tribute collection.

Toltec trade extended to the far N of Mexico and as far S as lower Central America, but there were gaps. Contact with the Gulf Coast was restricted by the rival cities of El Tajín and Cempoala, although a trade route did reach the Gulf Coast Maya. The Puebla-Tlaxcala region also has little sign of Toltec presence, and Cacaxtla and Cholula seem to have been effective competitors. Similarly, the Mixtec principalities of Oaxaca were uninterested in formal contact with the Toltecs. In W Morelos the site of Xochicalco had been all but abandoned by c AD 1000. Contact to the S thus followed a narrow corridor weaving between these regions, most probably through the Valle de Toluca via the city of Teotenango, which had been founded about the same time as Tula, then through N Guerrero to the Pacific coast. Thence trade routes went by sea to Guatemala, where Plumbate Ware was made, and E across the Isthmus of Tehuantepec for trade with S Veracruz and Tabasco—for Silho Fine Orange pottery—and with Yucatán—for Maya polychromes.

With much of their access to the S hindered, the Toltecs had a previously unequalled interest in the N. Trade goods reached as far N as the site of Casas

Grandes in Chihuahua, which prospered from c AD 1050 for c 200 years as a major trading post town with earthen ball courts, plaza groups, and workshops for trade goods. Derivatives of Toltec-Mesoamerican features are recognizable even farther N in the Chaco Canyon sites of present-day New Mexico. Nearer Tula, the fortified citadels of La Quemada and several others in Zacatecas formed a bulwark against the Chichimec frontier. La Quemada sat on the main N–S trade route through the agriculturally rich Malpaso valley; and a little farther N the sites of Chalchihuites, Alta Vista, and others marked the NW route into Sinaloa. All show signs of Toltec presence and influence in trade goods and architecture.

In Sonora, small chieftainships or 'statelets' developed as a result of population increase and burgeoning participation in local and longer distance trade, incl. trade and later influence from Casas Grandes. To the NE, in Veracruz, S Tamaulipas, and E San Luis Potosí, the Toltecs developed contact with the Huastec 'state' from c AD 900. From only a few Toltec items, traded along with items from W Mexico, a brisk E–W trade gradually developed across N Mesoamerica. The circular Corral temple at Tula may reflect Huastec religious influence (see *Mesoamerican Architecture* below). The Huastecs remained politically independent, however, and undertook similar trade with central Mexico and Gulf Coast cities to the S. Although an integral part of Mesoamerican civilization, Huastec culture had several distinctive features: the use of asphalt for floors and for surfacing mounds, the predominance of round temple-platforms (eg, Las Flores, Pavón, Tancol, Buenavista Huaxcama), distinctive stone-carving (especially on yugos, hachas, and palmas used in the ball game), and their own pottery styles.

Despite their military reputation, the Toltec 'empire', if it was like later Aztec, Tarascan, or Mixtec states, must have had borders that varied frequently and have been based mainly on the collection of tribute payments. Power and influence SE to Tulancingo and Tepeapulco were strong. To the W, large amounts of Mazapán pottery and Toltec figurines indicate healthy trade, and many Toltec tools were of obsidian from the Zinapécuaro (Michoacán) mines; but the extent of their political control in Michoacán, Jalisco, and Nayarit is uncertain. To the S they controlled only the N half of the Basin of Mexico, and seem to have had a healthy respect for Cholula and S Basin cities, causing them to skirt around the Basin altogether, via the Valle de Toluca.

Cholula reasserted itself in the Early Postclassic after a period of weakness coinciding with the demise of Teotihuacán. Another Chichimeca group and new rulers established themselves in the city and revitalized trade with the S Basin city of Chalco, with the Gulf Coast, and with the Mixtec principalities of Oaxaca. The city's huge pyramid was enlarged four times, reaching its largest c 1100. It became a centre for the production and trade of Mixteca-Puebla Ware, a distinctive polychrome style reflecting the city's close association with Oaxaca. Although its production began in the Early Postclassic, the style reached its peak in beauty and distribution in the Late Postclassic.

Oaxaca, the main obstacle to Toltec expansion into S Mexico, comprised a loose confederation of Mixtec city-states. Since the abandonment of Monte Albán Mixtec peoples had pushed S into the formerly Zapotec Valle de Oaxaca, where the two cultures remained uneasy rivals. Their relationship vacillated within a mixture of military rivalry, diplomacy and noble intermarriage, and occasional alliance. New sites were settled and some older sites remodelled. There were valley cities, such as Mitla or Tilantongo, and hilltop fortress towns, such as Yagul. The hallmark of Mixtec cities, however, was their stone slab mosaic style, featuring a variety of stepped-fret and lattice facings. 'Mixtec' codices from the Postclassic give us valuable insights into Mixtec society and legendary histories of their ruling houses.

With such resistance in central Mexico and Oaxaca, it seems unlikely that Toltec influence should have been strong in the far SE, yet beyond Oaxaca evidence of Toltec presence becomes stronger. Although settled in the Preclassic, Chichén Itzá was revived as the legendary Toltec founding of Kukulkán, traditionally in AD 987 and thus only shortly after the founding of Tula. The old city was expanded, incl. a new section architecturally and sculpturally almost identical to Tula.

The remarkable similarity of the two cities and ambiguities about their foundation dates as Toltec cities have even led one group of scholars to suggest that their relationship was reversed—that Tula was the N outpost of Toltec Chichén Itzá. The historical sources are unclear on whether the Itzás arrived in Yucatán before, after, or with the legendary leader Kukulkán, and the nature of Kukulkán's relationship with the Toltec ruling factions at Tula is uncertain. More generally, there is always difficulty in correlating archaeological materials with specific movements of peoples. There may have been more than one group of Itzás, arriving at different times; and there may be confusion within the historico-legendary sources between the earlier Putún Maya migrants into N Yucatán and the Itzás. The Maya Postclassic use of the Short Count based on a 260-day cycle, makes it more difficult to calculate the year (ie, which 260-day period is referred to in the Short Count date in question). And because there is little archaeological material along the potential migration routes, the direction and progress of movement cannot be determined with certainty.

Examination of the details of Tula and Chichén Itzá architecture, sculpture, and other objects shows many features that could be claimed to be of Classic Maya derivation; equally, however, the planning, much of the architectural construction, and sculptural and ceramic traditions of Tula are definitely of central Mexican derivation. To confuse the issue still further, Tohil Plumbate Ware, a typical item associated with Toltec sites—found at both Tula and Chichén Itzá—was of Guatemalan (S Highlands) origin, and Silho Fine Orange Ware was of S Lowlands origin.

Finally, the historical record seems to make it necessary (depending on date calculations and the legendary version used) for a large faction of Toltecs to have left Tula only shortly after its foundation as the Toltec capital, in order to have moved S to found Chichén Itzá; there is no inherent reason for or against such a development, but some scholars think such a move unlikely. But what is certain, from careful comparison of textual and modern place-names, is that Tula was ancient Tollán, the Toltec capital by their own admission. The special relationship between Tula and Chichén Itzá was manifested in many shared features, the most important of which included: long, colonnaded palaces, or courts—a new architectural form, and virtually identical at both sites; architectural embellishments incl. processions of similarly-dressed and armed warriors, and relief sculpture featuring jaguars, eagles, skull-and-bones, and human hearts; small atlante figures with raised arms to support altar-slabs (but the colossal atlante warrior roof-columns occur only at Tula); chacmool stone figures, of unknown origin (seven from Tula and 14 from Chichén Itzá); roof support columns carved as feathered-serpents (Quetzalcóatls), their heads resting on the ground (ie, the pyramid-platform surface), bodies upright and tails supporting the roof—they were incomplete at Tula but well preserved at Chichén Itzá.

From the mid-10C AD Chichén Itzá rapidly established its rule over N Yucatán. In a Triple Alliance with Mayapán (founded c AD 1000) and Izamal (or Uxmal according to some scholars) it controlled trade and exacted tribute from smaller cities. Most of the Puuc Maya cities to the S were controlled by Chichén Itzá, but these declined rapidly in the Early Postclassic and most were severely depopulated. Rule was not without tension and many more sites were fortified, and the key to power was control of maritime trade around the coasts of Yucatán. Major products included salt, slaves, honey, blue dye, Silho Fine Orange and Tohil Plumbate pottery, ixtle-plant fibres, and other, perishable, items. Chichén Itzá's power prevailed until c AD 1250, when a conspiracy led by Mayapán sacked the city.

One other Early Postclassic innovation remains to be mentioned—metallurgy. All documented finds of metal artefacts in Mesoamerica are of Postclassic date except a few trade items of the Late Classic brought to Maya cities from Central America. Some evidence suggests that Maya metalworking may have begun at this time. But the sudden appearance between c AD 800 and 900 of large quantities of copper, and a few gold, objects in Western Mexican graves (eg, Amapa in Nayarit) suggests the introduction of metallurgy from outside; there is no evidence of local smelting until much later. A second place of introduction was Guatemala. The majority of items were of copper—awls, needles, tweezers, knives, rings, beads, bracelets, and bells—but gold, silver, and alloys were also worked. When Mesoamericans themselves began to smelt, the skill was virtually full-blown, supporting the conclusion that the technology was diffused rather than independently discovered. During the Postclassic, W Mexico, and especially the Tarascans, and Mixteca Oaxaca became famous for their skills as smiths.

The date of the fall of Tula is as enigmatic as are its origins. The historical sources give no clear date, but range between AD 1168 and 1179. Tula's colonnaded palace was burnt and we suspect that the city was sacked and much of its population dispersed; excavators found the adobe bricks baked and charred, and fragments of burnt wood, ash, and carbon throughout the rooms and patios, but the evidence is not conclusive on the actual cause. The ceramic sequence shows that the site remained occupied by a small population down to Aztec times. Those who left migrated into the Basin of Mexico, in particular to the city of Culhuacán; and to Puebla and Veracruz.

The destruction coincided roughly with a reversal of the climatic shift which had extended the N limits of Mesoamerican agriculture at the beginning of the Classic Period. The change was so severe that large parts of N and central Mexico were desiccated, leaving their populations facing drought and starvation. Large-scale migrations of Chichimec tribes began again, creating irresistible pressures on Tula and its neighbours. Historical sources recount acute crises in the rulership, ideological struggles between rival factions, and civil war. Tula lost control of the obsidian trade at Tepeapulco, a loss which had previously proved detrimental to Teotihuacán.

After its destruction Tula's cultural heritage continued for another 70–80 years at Chichén Itzá until that city's sacking. Tula itself became a legendary city; central Mexican kingdoms and empires of the Late Postclassic looked back to the Toltecs and their times as a golden age of glory, prosperity, and purity. Toltec accomplishments were preserved, embellished, and emulated, especially by the Mexica Aztecs.

The Late Postclassic or Protohistoric (AD 1150/1250–1519): The Aztec Empire and Other States

After the sack of Tula central Mexican peoples were on the move again, but the Mixtec-Zapotec states of Oaxaca remained stable and in Mayaland the change was one of rulers and trading arrangements.

Mayapán and the Postclassic Maya. Mayapán was the last centralized capital of the Yucatán Peninsula. Unlike the more dispersed cities of earlier periods, it was bounded by massive stone walls pierced by six gateways. Its 12,000 inhabitants were prosperous, and powerful enough to exact tribute from a large part of Yucatán, but there was little public building, no town-planning, and little of the outward manifestations of grandeur exhibited by the Classic Maya cities. Most of its monuments were less skilful imitations of earlier examples. International trade was as strong as ever, and now almost wholly by canoe around the coasts of Yucatán, wherever land transport could be avoided. Several new or rejuvenated port-cities became international emporia: Tulum, Xelha, Tancah, Cozumel, Ichpaatún, and Sta Rita (Belize), all fortified, along the E coast, and Coatzacoalcos, Comalcalco, Cerillos (or Xicalango), and Isla Carmen on the Gulf Coast.

Resentment of tribute demands eventually erupted in civil war and Mayapán was overthrown c 1450 by a coalition of Uxmal and allied cities. Political authority was thereafter fragmented into 17 city-states or principalities, most controlling a stretch of coast and extending inland: Acalán, Ah Canul, Ah Kin Chel, Canpech, Cehpech, Chakan, Champotón, Chetumal, Chikenchel, Cochuah, Cupul, Ecab, Hocabá, Maní, Sotuta, Tazes, and Uaymil. Spanish invasions of Yucatán after 1520 met stiff resistance, especially from the E coast cities, and several campaigns were necessary to subdue Yucatán, by 1550.

In highland Guatemala new unification also took place. The Quiché State formed a confederation of cities, each with a certain autonomy and all claiming Toltec ancestry: Utatlán, Iximché, and Zacuelu. Their architecture, religious rites, and calendrical practices were heavily influenced by the Postclassic traditions of central Mexico.

In Oaxaca the Mixtec states prospered on Pacific coastal trade from Soconusco port-cities. Mixtec craftsmen were highly skilled in metallurgy, jewellery-making, featherwork, ceramics, and manuscript illumination. Some scholars suggest that the Aztecs imported Mixtec craftsmen to Tenochtitlán, but the evidence in the chronicles is unclear. Most of the Mixtec states were eventually subjugated and made to pay tribute by the Aztecs, but remained semi-autonomous in local affairs and allowed to retain their princely lineages and social organization. The principal cities included Tilantongo, Coixtlahuaca, Tlaxiaco, Yanhuitlán, Tututepec, Chachoapan, and Nochixtlán.

The Mexica and the founding of Tenochtitlán. In earlier migrations Tolteca-Chichimeca tribes had settled in the Basin of Mexico and the surrounding valleys, establishing city-states either as new settlements or by mingling with indigenous populations. In the central and S Basin there were a few dominant city-states, incl. Azcapotzalco and Tenayuca on the W shores of Lago de Texcoco, Huexotla/Texcoco and Coatlinchan on the E shores, and Culhuacán, Xochimilco, Cuitlahuac, Mixquic, Chalco, Xico, and Amecameca around Lagos Xochimilco and Chalco in the S. As Basin populations increased, the first experiments with chinampa agriculture began in earnest—cultivated plots of land, created by dredging soil from the lake bottoms into large wooden frames.

Into this arena moved yet another Chichimec group, known to the indigenous peoples as tamime—'semi-civilized'.

The tamime used the 52-year cycle, played the ball game, used irrigation agriculture, built in stone, dressed in maguey-fibre clothes, and organized themselves into calpulli (clans) with hereditary headmen—all trappings of a civilized life-style. On the other hand, they repeatedly raided other groups, stealing their women and crops, and sacrificed prisoners of war in a belief that it was necessary to feed the sun with human blood to avoid disaster—all unconducive to a quiet life in a crowded Basin. Although such practices had long histories in Mesoamerica, the tamime were exceptional in their singleminded ferocity and in the scale with which they pursued them.

The name Aztec comes from the legendary homeland—Aztlán (place of the seven legendary caves). The legends come from several sources. Aztlán was a land in NW Mexico within which lay Chicomoztoc, the 'seven caves', from which came the seven Aztec tribes: the Alcolhua (or Texcoca), Chalca, Mexica, Tepaneca, Tlahuica, Tlaxcalteca, and Xochimilca. Assuming correct identification of tribes with archaeological materials, they migrated S at different times.

The Alcolhua, Chalca, Tepaneca, and Xochimilca settled in the Basin in the Early Postclassic, founding the city-states of Texcoco, Chalco, Azcapotzalco, and Xochimilco, respectively; they were thus well established in the Basin before the arrival of the Mexica. The Tlahuica settled farther S, in the Valle de

Morelos, and the Tlaxcalteca settled in Tlaxcala, E of the Basin. The Mexica were also known as the Tenochca, after their early leader Ténoch, and whence the name of their city, Tenochtitlán ('land of the Tenochca'); and as the Culhua-Mexica, after their early alliance with Culhuacán, the old Toltec city.

The Mexica therefore entered a crowded Basin of well-established city-states. For about 50–60 years they were driven from one site to another in semi-nomadic existence by their more powerful neighbours. Between c 1250 and 1298 they served Azcapotzalco as mercenaries; in the early 14C they moved S and became allies of Culhuacán in a war against Xochimilco and from a judicious marriage alliance with Culhuacán's ruling house they later claimed Toltec ancestry, a lineage of which they were very proud.

Several dates are traditionally given for the foundation of Tenochtitlán, ranging between AD 1325 and 1370. The more important fact is that the Mexica had by this time succeeded in alienating themselves, alliances notwithstanding, from virtually all their Basin neighbours, and in the mid-14C were forced to occupy a muddy, none-too-fertile island off the W shore of Lago de Texcoco. Here, their first dynastic ruler was Acamapichtli (1372–91). A few years after the foundation of Tenochtitlán another group settled on an island just to the N and founded Tlatelolco (traditional dates range between 1358 and 1370). The two new cities coexisted, not without jealousy, until Tlatelolco was forcibly incorporated into greater Tenochtitlán in 1473.

From Tenochtitlán the Mexica continued to fight for status in the Basin, to ally and alienate themselves by turns. Under Huitzilihuitl (1391–1415) and Chimalpopoca (1415–26; son and grandson, respectively, of Acamapichtli), as vassals of Azcapotzalco, they served in wars of expansion against Chalco, Xaltocán, and Texcoco. Tension rose, however, as the Mexica chaffed under Tepanec rule; in various accounts Chimalpopoca was poisoned, strangled, starved to death in a cage, or committed suicide. In any case the Tepaneca were held responsible and the alliance broken. Under Itzcóatl (1426–40) alliance was made with Texcoco (which was threatened by Azcapotzalco when the Tepanec ruler slew its king, Ixtlilxóchitl I [1409–18]) and Tlacopán (modern Tacuba; an equally disgruntled Tepanec vassal-city)—the Triple Alliance—and Azcapotzalco was defeated and razed.

Aztec expansion and Empire. During the reigns of Itzcóatl and Moctezuma I Ilhuicamina (1440–68) Tenochtitlán and Texcoco, under Ixtlilxóchitl's son Nezahualcóyotl (c 1431–72), remained firm allies until near the end of Moctezuma I's reign, and systematically subdued other city-states of the Basin. Together they built aqueducts and causeways, began the expansion of chinampa agriculture out into the lakes, and constructed huge ceremonial precincts with temples, palaces, ball courts, and coatepantli (serpent walls). At the death of Nezahualcóyotl, Tenochtitlán became pre-eminent in the Basin. Under Axayácatl (1468–81) Tlatelolco was seized and campaigns were extended outside the Basin.

A successful campaign subdued the Matlazinca of the Valle de Toluca by 1480. Attempts to conquer territories farther W met stiff resistance, however, from the Tarascan state in Michoacán. Revolt against Tizoc (1481–86) made a second campaign against the Matlazinca necessary under Ahuítzotl (1486–1502), who was chiefly responsible for the creation of the coast-to-coast dimensions of the Empire.

After resubjugating Toluca, the Huasteca region of NE Mexico was invaded and defeated, and tribute exacted. Campaigns to the SW carried Aztec rule and tribute to the coast of Guerrero and N Oaxaca; a trading port was conquered in the Isthmus of Tehuantepec, giving the Aztecs direct control of Pacific coastal trade with Central America. In 1502 Moctezuma II Xocoyotzin ascended the throne and began new campaigns to the E. The territory of the Tlaxcalteca, whom he never succeeded in defeating, was skirted and the campaign carried to the Gulf Coast against the Totonacs of Veracruz. Further campaigns captured the Tabascan port-city of Xicalango, and subjugated the Oaxaqueño Mixteca Baja. A brief Mixtec-Zapotec alliance had defeated the Aztecs at the hilltop fortress of Guiengola in 1497, but the rich market-cities of Coixtlahuaca and Tlaxiaco fell in the early 16C.

Thus, by 1519 the Empire extended from coast to coast and reinforced its power and wealth by exacting tribute in goods, raw materials, and sacrificial victims. Territorial borders were not always neatly defined, but lines of garrisoned forts were established between the Aztec and Tarascan states, and revolts were endemic and periodically successful. The 'empire' comprised a loose confederation, often based on forced allegiance and tribute. Especially troublesome districts were garrisoned but no attempts were made to reorganize or move local populations.

Tenochtitlán was a huge metropolis for specialized crafts, commerce, and bureaucratic, religious, and military offices. It was a carefully planned city, the largest ever known in Mesoamerica, with gridded regularity around the prestigious and intimidating central Templo Mayor (or Teocalli). It was a reflection of the equally well-defined, tightly stratified Aztec social structure. All aspects of society were regulated by a combination of religious ceremony, special law codes, and the demands of the economy. Agriculture stretched S and E around the capital in a grid of chinampa plots divided by canals on Lagos Xochimilco, Chalco, and Texcoco, covering some 10,000ha. The specially regulated pochteca system of professional traders controlled the economy and maintained its spy network on Aztec tributaries and beyond.

Aztec economy, based on productive chinampas, water control, and long-distance trade and tribute, supported a much greater population in the Basin than ever before. For the most part, however, the Aztecs were imitators rather than innovators. Their religious and social structures were based on long-evolved central Mexican precedents. They imitated Toltec architecture and probably modelled the Templo Mayor on the examples of Tenayuca, Tlatelolco, and other earlier ceremonial precincts in the Basin. In their claims of Toltec descent, they deliberately altered their history books to coincide with a warlike, empire-building image of themselves, emulating their image of the Toltecs. They were perhaps the first people in Mesoamerica to keep a majority of the male population trained for war. Although not strictly speaking a standing army, garrisons were kept in many tributary cities, ports, and border forts. Toltec methods of human sacrifice were copied and taken to extremes; rough estimates from the historical sources suggest that in the late 15C–early 16C 10–15,000 victims were sacrificed each year to feed the insatiable gods Huitzilopochtli and Tezcatlipoca.

The collapse of the Empire. Aztec bloodthirstiness, however, is often exaggerated or at least overemphasized. There is no denying its immensity and repulsiveness, nor its integral function in Aztec cultural psyche, but it should not be allowed to obscure the positive aspects of the Aztec state. To the average Aztec life had never been so good. Trade and craftsmanship flourished; agriculture and tribute together ensured a stable standard of living; law and justice, if sometimes rough, could be counted on; the calpulli social structure provided predictable social position and stability; and the architectural magnificence of Tenochtitlán instilled a sense of civic pride. And there was always the glory of the warrior and the chance to die in battle (or give your son or husband to the glory of the state). To borrow the words of one author, they may have 'worshipped deities who required human blood and sacrificial victims, fought wars with gusto, and even practised cannibalism. Yet they also planted crops, made love, raised children, argued about the petty affairs of daily life, composed poetry, appreciated the beauty of flowers, tried to understand man's place in the universe, and worried about the future just as we do'.

But all was not well when Cortés arrived on the shores of Veracruz in 1519. Constant warfare and conquest had become a necessity. Despite the rich chinampas the Empire needed tribute to help feed its ever-growing urban populations. The newly conquered territories, some of them only just subdued, lacked the socio-political cohesion of the core area in the Basin of Mexico. In time the Empire may have been consolidated and a more stable administration established; as it was in 1519, the Spanish arrival caught it just at the raw stage when the conquerors were still expanding and merely exploiting their victims. Several weaknesses were still inherent: the humiliation and strain of tribute on conquered peoples, themselves having reached a high standard of civilization, and requirement of sacrificial victims made revolt ever-imminent; local rulers were usually kept in place rather than taken hostage, and colonial groups were not shifted about within the Empire to confuse loyalties—thus the local nobility retained local loyalty while chaffing under the daily chagrin of defeat; before Aztec justice and social organization could be imposed, the sole enforcement for good behaviour was the threat of violence, Tarascan and Tlaxcalan resistance demonstrated that Aztec armies were not invincible, and the inevitably frequent revolts were often put down by reliance on allies and tributaries, themselves under the same threat.

All of these psychological and economic pressures contributed to rapid collapse. The real 'conquest' by Spain came after the escapade of Cortés and his 500 soldiers. Glory must go to Cortés for his courage and audacity, but the conquest of Tenochtitlán was as much a civil war, the unstable conditions of which were skilfully, if brutally exploited by him. Had Cortés not had the help of thousands of Tlaxcalan and other native troops he could never have overcome the Aztec army with his small band of adventurers, guns and horses notwithstanding.

Aztec social structure. Aztec society comprised several rigidly defined social classes, generally divided between nobility and commoners. Membership in most positions was controlled to a great extent by birth, but opportunities for advancement were possible by a combination of ascription and achievement. The nobility controlled this to some extent by tending to marry endogamously, thus assuring themselves of most of the higher civil and religious positions. The major groups within the class structure are as follows:

(1) The *tlatoque* (sing. *tlatoani*) were the highest rulers—the sovereign of the Empire, king of a city-state or other empire. The *tetecutin* (sing. *tecutli*) included both the Aztec *tlatoani* and numerous high military and administrative-governmental positions: the four high counsellors, the palace administrator, the *calpullec* (imperial administrative officers), military and district chiefs, and town chiefs. A soldier could obtain *tecutli*-status by capturing four or more prisoners of war, and simultaneously the title of *tequihua* (tribute-holder). On an equal footing with the highest governmental officials were the *tlenamacac* (high priests to Huitzilopochtli and Tláloc).

(2) The general reservoir of nobility were the *pipiltin* (sing. *pilli*—'son of someone'), the children and descendants through subsequent generations of the *tlatoque* and *tetecutin*. *Pipiltin* occupied most of the lower-ranking governmental, military, and religious positions, and had the privilege of being educated in the *calmecac*, colleges run by priests specifically to prepare pupils to take up state and religious offices. The *calmecac* was strictly male, women aspiring to priestesshood being trained in the temples themselves.

(3) The intermediate social ranks comprised the *pochteca* (sing. *pochtecatl*) and the *tolteca* (sing. *toltecatl*), the merchants and artisan-craftsmen, respectively. The *pochteca* were organized into guilds to trade over long-distance routes throughout the Empire. They could also be used as agents or spies to watch and investigate new territories for the Empire; if killed in these activities they became, as did warriors killed in battle, a star to nourish the sun. As an exclusive class the *pochteca* arranged marriages between their own sons and daughters; had special, well-defined living quarters in the city; their own special gods and ceremonies; the privilege of sacrificing slaves; exemption from the military levy; and were judged for crimes in their own special courts. They paid tax in the form of goods, but were forbidden by law to flaunt their wealth in public. Their class was further kept exclusive by only allowing sons to inherit their business territories. While normally educated in the 'state' schools called *telpochcalli*, places, if available, were open to them in the *calmecac* as well.

The *tolteca* were those who worked in gold, feathers, and other exotic materials, making jewellery and ornament. They were highly esteemed and could obtain high prestige, but were generally less privileged than the *pochteca*. Some artisans were organized into guilds while others were employed directly by the state.

(4) The general mass of the population were the *macehualtin* (sing. *macehualli*), organized into unstratified social groups called *calpulli*, with councils of elders and elected members (although leadership tended to be hereditary in practice). Originally based on kinship, the *calpulli* were later just as often organized around craft and agricultural specialization. They were makers of utilitarian goods, farmers, fishers and hunters, salt makers, charcoal makers, and other rural specialists of Aztec society. Educated in the *telpochcalli*, a student who showed special promise could, through the influence and sponsorship of a friendly *tetecutin*, gain admittance to the *calmecac*. Their obligations were heavy: state labour (ie, in monument-building, chinampa-construction, causeway, aqueduct and canal maintenance), taxes, and military service. On the other hand, they owned land and could, by their skill, rise in rank. The living standards of the *macehualtin* varied throughout the Empire and in general those of Tenochtitlán were in the best position.

(5) Below the *macehualtin* were the *mayeque* (sing. is same) or *tlalmaitec* (sing. *tlalmaitl*), agricultural workers who served on the private lands of nobility. They had few privileges but were exempt from taxation and statute labour. Their condition was hereditary and they were subject to the military levy, leaving this their only avenue for bettering themselves. Both *mayeque* and *macehualtin* were under the ultimate jurisdiction of the *tlatoque*, to whom they could appeal.

(6) At the very bottom of Aztec society were the *tlacotin* (sing. *tlacotli*), the slaves. They provided part of the urban labour force for the nobility, and their condition varied according to their individual merit and their masters. Slave status was imposed for several reasons, such as gambling, economic need, or crime (especially theft). War prisoners could also be sold into slavery, although most eventually ended up on the sacrificial block. Azcapotzalco was famous, before its razing, as a slave market and the Tlatelolco market also sold slaves. Freedom could be bought, or, at the owner's discretion, earned.

Assessment of Late Postclassic Civilization

The most notable feature of the Late Postclassic is its continuity with Early Postclassic and Classic patterns. There was little innovation except in empire-building and this was itself regarded by the Aztecs as following the Toltec lead. Emphasis was on adapting and restructuring older themes, some of which reached unprecedented proportions—human sacrifice, the religious overtones of almost all actions, emphasis on organized warfare and new forms of fortifications, tribute demands, and the extent of chinampa agriculture. On the other hand, the old themes of central ceremonial precincts, city-planning, long-distance trade, traditional gods, calendrics, and hieroglyphic writing continued.

The architecture of ceremonial centres was composed of familiar constructions. In Yucatán workmanship declined and artistic zeal dampened, but the forms were imitative. Similarly the Aztecs copied the idea of twin temple-pyramids, ball courts, and circuit walls; the ominous dominance of the Aztec Teocalli as a focus for human sacrifice was in emulation of the Toltecs. Perhaps the only architectural innovations in the Postclassic were the Huastec emphasis on round structures and the yácata temples of the Tarascans (see *Mesoamerican Architecture* below).

In form, Aztec stone sculpture was distinctive. It emphasized three-dimensional works and detail within an imposing bulk; sculptors' skills in blending horror, tension, and grace were remarkable.

Another new theme was fortification, in both Mayaland and central Mexico outside the Aztec homeland. There was a long history of warfare and fortification in these regions, but massive walls, and in some cases towers, were part of nearly every city-state in Postclassic Yucatán and Oaxaca. Late Postclassic warfare was innovative in scale, its unrelenting nature, and in the increasing size of armies and practice of garrisoning cities. Although possibly modelled on Toltec precedent, the pochteca spy-system was more sophisticated than any previous practice.

The normal arrangement in the Late Postclassic, apart from the short-lived Aztec Empire, was the city-state. Urbanism had reached its apogee and the island-city of Tenochtitlán, skilfully planned, protected, and serviced, was unprecedented in scale. The Basin of Mexico in the 16C comprised some 50–60 semi-autonomous city-states, each with its own princely lineage and 8–10,000 subjects within 1–2 sq km. The two cities of Tenochtitlán and Texcoco stood above the rest, Texcoco having c 20–30,000 in 4 sq km and Tenochtitlán c 150–200,000 in 12 sq km. Altogether about 500 such city-states throughout central Mexico were exploited by the Aztecs.

Finally, Aztec engineering skill deserves mention. The depth of learning, so quickly acquired, for building aqueducts, ditches, sluice gates, and causeways in vast systems to service their city was as remarkable as was the idea of an island city. The pressures of population growth and the need to produce more food brought under state control the construction and use of floodwater-irrigated terracing and chinampas, enabling them to be built and managed on a huge scale.

Religion, commerce, and warfare were intricately related and inseparable in Aztec society; on these rested the growth, prosperity, and ultimate collapse of Aztec civilization.

Mesoamerican Writing, Counting, and Calendrics

Writing

Several hieroglyphic writing systems were used in Mesoamerica, evolving from pictographs (picture glyphs representing the subjects), to ideographs (glyphs representing ideas or things, often abstractly or symbolically), to phonetic. Single glyphs, groups of glyphs—like 'captions'—and longer texts were carved in stone on altars, building façades, stairways, ramps, lintels, tomb and temple walls, ball court walls, and on upright stelae, worked in stucco and painted on murals and pottery. Less frequently they were carved on special objects of bone, shell, or jade and other semi-precious stones. Lastly, there are the codices, all extant examples dating from the Late Postclassic and post-Conquest Periods.

The most sophisticated system was that of the Maya, with some 750 symbols incl. consonant-vowel combinations. Different, but related through the early development of writing in Oaxaca and the S Gulf Coast regions, were the Teotihuacán, Xochicalco, Ñuiñe (upper Río Balsas region of S Puebla), and Zapotec systems. Later systems, most to a certain extent related, include: the Mixtec or Borgia codices; Aztec in the Basin of Mexico; Toltec, related to the Xochicalco script; El Tajín, possibly related to the Mixtec and Borgia groups; and scripts used in Guatemala at Cotzumalhuapa and Kaminaljuyú (where a unique group of symbols appears on Stele 10). None of these systems was fully phonetic, but the Maya used some phonetic glyphs and the Aztecs were on the verge of becoming phonetic at the time of the Spanish conquest.

No Mesoamerican writing system has been totally deciphered, but the Maya code has been 'broken' and up to 85 per cent of Maya texts can be read. Maya inscriptions usually follow a pattern: first comes a date glyph, followed by an event glyph, then the name and title of the ruler or élite person concerned, incl. details of position, dynasty, and lineage; then follows a 'distance number' of days passed between events, before the day and month of another event and glyphs for that event. Scenes illustrating the events are equally important as keys to understanding the 'embedded text', for example the verb may be provided by the image.

Earlier interpretations of the 'Mixtec' codices, based on central Mexican concepts and languages, are being restudied, relating them to S Mexican languages. Similarly, the texts, formats, dress of the figures depicted, and many other details of other codices are being used to argue for origins within a wide area, incl. Náhuatl, Popoloca, Chocho, Mazatec, Cuicatec, and Otomí.

The subject of most inscriptions and codices was concerned mainly with calendrical cycles, religious rites, and the recording of specific events—a conquest, marriage, birth, death, or accession. Only a few codices are narrative history, detailed genealogies, or more scholastic works of literature, philosophy, medicine, law, or science (other than astronomical observation).

Codices survive in several forms. The tira is a painted manuscript on long strips of animal skin or paper, glued together. It could be written up or down the strips, and from r. to l. or l. to r. A 'screen-fold' is a tira folded in pleats, each pleat being a page and the 'text' continuing onto the opposite side at the end. Most pre-conquest codices are of this form, the central Mexican ones on skins and the Maya ones on bark paper. Tiras were also rolled. A lienzo refers to a codex painted on cotton or maguey-fibre cloth, sewn together; while a mapa is a general term used to denote any post-conquest, single-panel paper manuscript. Lastly, the Huehuetlatolli were Náhuatl texts setting out in a formal way the ideals, traditions, and philosophy of Aztec life; they were not written, but memorized and orally transmitted by the elders. One example has been preserved in the 'Florentine Codex'. There are 14 (or 15, the authenticity of one is disputed) pre-conquest codices and a few hundred early post-conquest and later codices. The authenticity, reliability, and amount of European influence in examples from the latter group varies widely. A complete census of both the pre-and post-conquest codices is given in the *Handbook of Middle American Indians*, volume 14 (Austin, Texas, 1975).

Counting

Mesoamerican arithmetic was a vigesimal system (base-20). The Maya (or their neighbours) independently invented the concepts of zero and of place value.

Maya numbers were expressed in several sets of symbols but the most commonly used set was the dot (for one) and bar (for five). With the use of place values based on multiples of 20, the higher numbers could be expressed economically because the first place group=units, the next=20s, the next=400s (ie, 20 x 20), and so on. In Maya numbers the places proceeded from bottom to top (rather than the Western r. to l.) in columns. To express the number 20, or 400, the 'empty' places had to be occupied in order to indicate the value of the vigesimal symbol; therefore the concept of, and a symbol for, zero was essential. (The concept of zero, so far as we know, has only been invented thrice: by the Babylonians, by the Hindus, whence it passed to the West via the Arabs, and by the Maya, or their neighbours.) The Maya used a set of glyphs or the dots and bars set upright, for carving numbers on stone; and the dots and bars set horizontally, for painting them in codices. The dot and bar system was also used by the Zapotecs and Mixtecs, and the bar appears at Teotihuacán, Xochicalco, and Teotenango. The Aztecs also used a vigesimal system, but they did not use the zero and thus had no place values. The numbers 1 to 19 were expressed as the corresponding number of dots; larger numbers of vigesimal multiples were simply represented by established, originally arbitrarily chosen, symbols (eg, a banner for 20, a feather for 400, and so on).

	Maya	*Aztec*		*Maya*	*Aztec*
1	hun	ce	8	uaxac	chicueyi
2	ca	ome	9	bolon	chicnahui
3	ox	yeyi	10	lahun	mahtlactli
4	can	nahui	15	ho lahun	mahtlactli ihuan macuilli
5	ho	macuilli	19	bolon lahun	mahtlactli ihuan chicnahui
6	uac	chicuacen			
7	uuc	chicome			

Calendrics

Two principal calendrical cycles dominated Mesoamerican lives: a 260-day ritual calendar and a 365-day solar calendar, together called the Calendar Round. The Aztec Calendar Round, inherited from the Classic Period, represents the culmination of its evolution.

The invention of these calendars is an unsolved problem. There are no known Olmec calendrical inscriptions, but four Olmec astronomical symbols were inherited by the Maya and used in Maya calendars: sun, moon, Venus, and 'celestial bands'. The earliest known evidence of the 260-day cycle is the carved stone threshold at San José Mogote (Oaxaca), dated c 600 BC, where the glyph 'One Earthquake' was carved between the legs of a figure. The earliest known date-glyph is on Stele 2 at Chiapa de Corzo, which converts to 36 BC (see below). Present evidence, therefore, indicates that the calendar was invented outside the Maya region, perhaps in the Southern Highlands—S Gulf Coast area.

The Aztecs used three chronological systems: *Xihuitl* (or *Xiuhpohualli*), the 365-day solar year; *Tonalpohualli*, the 260-day cycle based on numbers and day-names; and a Venusian system. The first two were combined to form the *Xiuhmolpilli*, the 52-year cycle. In Aztec mythology the calendar was invented by Cipactonal and his wife, Oxomoco, the 'first man and woman', sorcerer and sorceress of astrology.

The *Xihuitl* comprised 18 months (*Cempohualli*) of 20 days each, plus five extra days of ill-omen (*Nemontemi*) at the end of the year. Thus: 18 x 20 = 360 + 5 = 365. Each month was named and had special rites celebrated at its end. Each day was also named with a glyph depicting a plant, animal, element, or abstract symbol. The day was divided into 13 'hours' of day-time and 9 'hours' of night-time, respectively ruled by 13 Lords of Day and 9 Lords of Night, and of the 13 Aztec heavens and 9 underworlds. (But no other Mesoamerican group divided the day thus; and the Aztec division bears no relation to our hours.) In theory the year was named after the day on which it began, but because the sequence of days in the month was fixed, the system shifted by five days each year; in practice, therefore, year-names were restricted to four (ie, dividing the extra five days of *Nemontemi* into the 20 day-names shows that only four will constantly turn up to begin a year or month): *Acatl* = reed, *Tecpatl* = flint knife, *Calli* = house, and *Tochtli* = rabbit.

(The equivalent Maya solar calendar was called *Haab*, and the five end-days *Uayeb*; the four year-days were originally *Ik*, *Manik*, *Eb*, and *Caban*, but later shifted, presumably in a calendrical adjustment, to *Ben*, *Eznab*, *Akbal*, and *Lamat*; and at the Spanish Conquest, to *Muluc*, *Ix*, *Cauac*, and *Kan*.)

The *Tonalpohualli* ('counting of the days') was a combination of the numbers 1 to 13 and the 20 day-names counted in sequence, one number against each day-name (see lists below). Thus, *1 Cipactli, 2 Ehecatl, 3 Calli... 13 Acatl*; then continuing the day-names, but beginning the numbers again, to get *1 Océlotl, 2 Cuahtli*, etc. to *13 Miquiztli*. Because 13 and 20 have no common denominator the same day-name and number occurs only every 260 days. (The equivalent Maya calendar was called *Tzolkin*; the Zapotecs called it *Piye* or *Yza*, with four quarters of 65 days each [4 x 65 = 260], and each quarter divided into five parts of 13 days each.)

The *Xiuhmolpilli* was a sort of Aztec (or Mesoamerican) 'century', occurring every 52 years as a result of the frequency of certain combinations of the above two systems. The same combination of numbered day and month positions of the two systems occurred only every 18,980 days, as 52 sets of 365 days each (52 x 365 = 18,980) and as 73 sets of 260 days each (73 x 260 = 18,980). Thus the two systems fit together, as the early Mayanist Sylvanus Morley so aptly demonstrated, like the teeth of two cog-wheels, one smaller than the other.

The drawing to completion of a 52-year cycle was the cause of much fear and trepidation as it was uncertain, in the Mesoamerican world-view, whether the sun would rise again to begin a new cycle or the world would end. At such a coalition of cycles the Aztecs performed a special rite known as the *Toxiuhmolpilia* ('tying of the years') or New Fire Ceremony on top of the Cerro de la Estrella to sustain the sun. The end of a cycle was symbolized by a reed bundle, whence 'the tying or binding of the years'.

The Venusian system, borrowed by the Aztecs from the Mixtecs, possibly originated in the Oaxaca–S Gulf Coast region. It was based on the 584 days taken by Venus to complete the apogees of its orbit, and was divided into four periods of 236, 90, 250, and 8 days (=584): that is, Venus, visible for 236 days as the morning star, unseen for 90 days (during its superior conjunction), visible again as the evening star for 250 days, and then invisible again for 8 days (during its inferior conjunction). Thus eight *Xiuhuitl* equalled five Venusian cycles (8 x 365 = 2920 and 5 x 584 = 2920). (The Maya also used the Venusian calendar; and observation points for Venus were located in Tehuacán and at Teotitlán del Camino.)

The *Huehuetiliztli* was the concurrence of all four systems (365-day cycle, 260-day cycle, 584-day cycle and 2 x 52-year cycles), to begin anew on the same day, a cause for superlative celebrations, omens, prophecy, fear, etc., and no doubt many resolutions, every 104 years.

The 260-day and 365-day calendars, and the 52-year cycle were widely used in Mesoamerica; the Calendar Round was celebrated by the Huastecs, Matlazincas, Mixtecs, Otomís, Tarascans, Totonacs, and several other groups.

The Maya Long Count and Short Count

Only the Maya went beyond the 52-year and 104-year cycles, and used yet another cycle which related each 52-year cycle to the 'beginning of time' as they knew it. Known as the Long Count or Initial Series, it enabled them to calculate the exact number of days since they began the calendrical count—ie, the same as we do when we start at AD 1. To do this they used a number of cumulative positions—like place values in counting: 1 *kin* = 1 day, 1 *uinal* = 20 days (20 *kins*), 1 *tun* = 360 days (18 *uinals*), 1 *katun* = 7200 days (20 *tuns*), 1 *baktun* = 144,000 days (20 *katuns*), and 1 *piktun* = 2,880,000 days (20 *baktuns*).

The system obviously bears a close relation to the vigesimal counting system except that the *tun* was only 18 *uinals*, not 20, because as 360 days it was closer to the 365-day solar year. The Maya 'zero' date was *13.0.0.0.0. 4 Ahau, 8 Cumkú*—that is, *13 baktuns* on the day *4 Ahau* and the month *8 Cumkú*, the day-month being the starting day and month of the next *baktun*.

There is more than one system for converting Maya dates into Christian dates, but the most accepted system, referred to as the Goodman-Martínez-Thompson Correlation (GMT; used throughout this book), converts the starting date to 13 Aug. 3114 BC. (The oldest Long Count dates are on monuments outside Mayaland: Stele 2 at Chiapa de Corzo = 36 BC and Stele C at Tres Zapotes = 31 BC; at El Baúl [Guatemala] Stele 1 = AD 36; and in the Tuxtla region around Tres Zapotes the La Mojarra stele = AD 143 and 156, while the San Andrés Tuxtla statuette = AD 162. The oldest date on a Maya site is on Stele 29 at Tikal [Guatemala] = AD 292, and the youngest = AD 909 from inscriptions at La Muñeca [Campeche] and at Dzibanché [Quintana Roo].)

Long before the Spaniards arrived the Maya had abandoned the use of the Long Count and had begun to use a briefer system, referred to as the Short Count. Instead of counting from a zero date of *13 baktuns*, the Short Count began at the end of *katun 13 Ahau* and used only *tuns*, which were numbered consecutively, and *katuns*, which were named. The *katun* cycles thus established always finished on a day in *Ahau* in the following sequence: *katun 13 Ahau, katun 11 Ahau, katun 9 Ahau*, then *7, 5, 3, 1, 12, 10, 8, 6, 2 Ahau*; and after 256.43 years, back to *katun 13 Ahau*. The cyclical nature was again important, and certain events were expected to be repeated.

Finally, the Maya and others also used a lunar count (called *Meztlipohualli* by the Aztecs), with up to eight glyphs. In it there were 29-and-a-fraction days between new moons.

The Aztec, Maya, and Zapotec day- and month-names were:

Day-names

day	Aztec	Maya	Zapotec
1	Cipactli (crocodile)	Imix (earth-monster)	Chilla (crocodíle)
2	Ehecatl (wind)	Ik (breath; wind)	Quij (or Laa) (wind)
3	Calli (house)	Akbal (darkness)	Guela (night)
4	Cuetzpolin (lizard)	Kan (ripe maize)	Ache (lizard)
5	Cóatl (serpent)	Chicchan (serpent)	Zee (or Zij) (serpent)
6	Miquiztli (death)	Cimi (death)	Lana (blackness)
7	Mazatl (deer)	Manik (hand)	China (deer)
8	Tochtli (rabbit)	Lamat (Venus)	Lapa (rabbit)
9	Atl (water)	Muluk (water)	Niza (or Queza) (water)
10	Itzcuintli (dog)	Oc (dog)	Tella (dog)
11	Ozomatli (monkey)	Chuen (monkey; craftsman)	Loo (or Goloo) (dog)
12	Malinalli (grass)	Eb (bad or poor rain)	Pija (draught)
13	Acatl (reed)	Ben (?growing maize)	Quij (or Ij; or Laa) (reed)
14	Océlotl (ocelot)	Ix (jaguar)	Geche (jaguar)
15	Cuauhtli (eagle)	Men (moon; wise one; eagle)	Naa (eagle)
16	Cozacuauhtli (vulture)	Cib (wax)	Loo (or Guiloo) (crow)
17	Ollin (earthquake)	Caban (earth)	Xoo (earthquake)
18	Técpatl (flint knife)	Etz'nab (cutting edge)	Opa (cold)
19	Quiáhuitl (rain)	Cauac (rain; storm)	Ape (cloudy)
20	Xóchitl (flower)	Ahau (lord)	Lao (flower)

Month-names

month	Aztec	Maya
1	Izcalli (resurrection)	Pop
2	Atlcahualo (they leave the water)(also Cuauhuitlehua and Xilomanaliztli)	Uo
3	Tlacaxipehualiztli (flaying of men)	Zip
4	Tozoztontli (short watch) (or Xochimanaalo—offering of flowers)	Zotz
5	Hueytozoztli (great watch)	Tzec
6	Tóxcatl (dry thing) (also Tepopochtli)	Xul
7	Etzalcualiztli (meal of maize and beans)	Yaxkin
8	Tecuilhuitontli (small feast of the lords)	Mol
9	Hueytecuilhuitl (great feast of the lords)	Chen
10	Miccailhuitontli (small feast of the dead) (also Tlaxochimaco)	Yax
11	Hueymiccailhuitl (great feast of the dead) (also Xocotlhuetzi)	Zac
12	Ochpanitztli (road sweeping) (also Tenahuatiliztli)	Ceh
13	Pachtontli (a bit of hay) (also Ecoztli and Teotleco)	Mac
14	Hueypachtli (much hay) (also Pillahuana and Tepeílhuitl)	Kankin
15	Quecholli (valuable feather) (also Tlacoquechotli and Tlamiquecholli)	Muan
16	Panquetzaliztli (raising of banners)	Pax
17	Atemoztli (the water falls)	Kayab
18	Títitl (shrunken; wrinkled)	Cumku
year-end	Nemontemi (five unhappy days)	Uayeb

Aztec Lords of Day and Night:

Day (Tonalteuctin)
1. Xiuhtecuhtli (fire-god)
2. Tlaltechutli (earth-god)
3. Chalchiúhtlicue (water-goddess)
4. Tonatiuh (sun-god)
5. Tlazoltéotl (goddess of love)
6. Teoyaomiqui (god of fallen warriors)
7. Xochipilli-Centétl (god of pleasure/ maize-god)
8. Tláloc (rain-god)

Night (Yohualteuctin)
1. Xiuhtecuhtli (fire-god)
2. Itztli-Técpatl (obsidian-god)
3. Piltzintecuhtli (young sun-god)
4. Centéotl (maize-god)
5. Mictlantecuhtli (god of death)
6. Chalchiúhtlicue (water-goddess)
7. Tlazoltétl (goddess of love)
8. Tepeyolohtli (heart of the mountain)

9	Quetzalcóatl (wind-god)	9	Tláloc (rain-god)
10	Tezcatlipoca (god of sustenance)		
11	Mictlantecuhtli (god of death)		
12	Tlahuizcalpantecuhtli (god of dawn)		
13	Ilamatecuhtli (sky-goddess)		

Corresponding Maya Lords of Day and Night, unknown individually, were called *Oxlahun ti Ku* and *Bolon ti Ku*, respectively.

Mesoamerican Religion

Mesoamerican art and architecture were manifestly religious in symbolism, execution, and function. Knowledge of Mesoamerican religion is biased towards information on Aztec gods and practices, due chiefly to the work of Bernardino de Sahagún, who collected so much ethnography in the Basin of Mexico. For the Mixtecs and Maya much can be gleaned from codices, but for the Huastecs, Totonacs, Tarascans, and others there is much less information.

Religious themes were important to Mesoamericans from very early times, but their physical manifestations appear most clearly with the construction of ceremonial centres in the Gulf Coast region. Details of the ceremonies in these early centres will never be known, but many of the early gods can be identified. Many attributes remained constant throughout Mesoamerican prehistory, although various combinations and recombinations were attributed to different gods or goddesses over time. The Maya and Aztec pantheons are well known and were frequently depicted in sculpture, in murals, on pottery, on architectural façades, and in the codices.

There were several Pan-Mesoamerican themes. The first was duality. In central Mexico the concept of the 'creator pair', a male and a female deity, was widespread. Most of the gods, in fact, had a consort. And more generally, opposing concepts were a frequent feature throughout Mesoamerican religions: fertility v. barrenness, life v. death, good v. evil, night v. day. Many myths illustrate such oppositions, such as the daily battle between sun and moon each dawn.

A second theme was death and the underworld. Both Maya and Aztec religion had ruler-gods of the underworld, and their consorts, supplemented by gods for caves and for the 'night sun'. From very early times caves were important as shrines, such as the partly natural-partly artificial cave under the Pirámide del Sol at Teotihuacán, the seven caves of Chicomoztoc of the Aztec tribes in Aztlán, the cave origin of the Mixtecs, underground water caverns of the Maya, and perhaps the cave-like tombs built in several regions of Mesoamerica.

A third theme was the specialized functions of individual gods. In Aztec daily life nearly every act, craft, day, month, or city had its special deity. Tribes often had patron deities, such as the Mexica's Huitzilopochtli, or the Xochimilca's Xochipilli and his consort Xochiquetzal. The structure of the Mesoamerican pantheon became extremely complex, and gods and goddesses frequently took on multiple aspects and functions for different occasions, being described as god X in the guise of god Y. For most functions there was a male and a female deity.

The gods were also personified in relation to the four cardinal directions and to special colours. The colour-directional combinations varied from one region to another; for the Maya and the Aztecs they were:

Maya	*name*	*colour*	*year-bearer*
N	Xamen	zac (white)	Muluk
S	Nohol	kan (yellow)	Canac
E	Likin	chac (red)	Kan
W	Chikin	ek (black)	Ix

Aztec	*name*	*colour*	*sky-bearer*
N	Mictlampa	black (red; white)	a fire-god
S	Huitzlampa	blue (red; white)	Mictlantecuhtli
E	Tlapcopa	red (yellow; blue green)	Tlahuizcalpantecuhtli
W	Cihuatlampa	white (yellow; blue green)	Ehecatl-Quetzalcóatl

In each case the fifth (or fifth and sixth), or central, direction was in the centre and went up, to the heavens or sky layers, and down, to the earth and under-world. The Maya centre was represented by a *ceibe* tree whose roots penetrated the earth and branches spread into the sky; the Aztec centre was ruled by the god and goddess Ometecuhtli and Omecíhuatl.

A fifth theme was sacrifice, both of time to participate in special ceremonies and of flowers, animals, humans, and auto-sacrifice. Human sacrifice seems to have begun in the Preclassic (eg, the Late Preclassic mutilated 'dancers' at Monte Albán), but its institutionalization was a Toltec-Aztec, Postclassic speciality. Some difference is notable in Maya and Aztec views on sacrifice: to the Maya the victim's blood was needed to replenish and ensure the smooth progress of cyclical events, but also demonstrated Man's obeisance to the gods and his willingness to obey them; to the Aztecs the sacrifice of humans was necessary on a huge scale to hold the universe together and to strengthen the sun for its night-journey and battle against the forces of darkness. In practice, Aztec human sacrifice also became a means of political coercion and social control.

A final theme was cyclical time ruling both men and gods from everyday life to world view to social evolution. Calendrical cycles have been described; other cycles were also cosmological. Perhaps the most famous was the Aztec creation myth of the five suns: the first was ruled by Tezcatlipoca and was destroyed when Quetzalcóatl caused the earth-giants (quinametzin) to be eaten by jaguars; the second was ruled by Quetzalcóatl and was destroyed by winds; the third was ruled by Tláloc and was destroyed by a rain of fire; the fourth was ruled by Chalchiútlicue and was destroyed by floods; and the fifth is the present, ruled by Tonatiuh, and will end in destruction by earthquake, when mankind will be eaten by descending tzitzimime—'demons of darkness'. The Maya creation myth had three parts with two destructions, both by floods: from a world of darkness and water, the gods created the earth and the animals; man was created from mud but was destroyed because he lacked speech and could not worship his makers; man was then made from wood—he could speak and procreate but had no mind, and was again destroyed because he could not worship the gods; survivors of this flood became monkeys; a third man-type was made, this time from yellow and white maize dough—he could speak, procreate, and on the first dawn of his existence worshipped the creator-gods. Such cyclical beliefs were intimately connected with Aztec collapse: in Moctezuma II Xocoyotzin's reign Quetzalcóatl would return to reclaim his rightful place as ruler, a belief that helps to explain the complex and varied reactions to the Spaniards.

Mesoamerican worship focused on public display and on a certain amount of public participation, although the performance of most rites was the preserve of specially trained priests. Public display was the function of the ceremonial centres, into which the surrounding countryside or city populations could gather. Private, or small-group worship was also practised, and many residential blocks in cities had small shrines with private altars. There were also many sacred cave sites with shrines and special temples for the worship and rites of secret societies (eg, the Eagle and Jaguar warriors of the Toltecs and Aztecs; see Rte 11). Certain sites were revered for their sacredness during and long after their principal occupation, such as the cave beneath the Pirámide del Sol at Teotihuacán, a sacred site before the pyramid was built and honoured for several hundred years by the construction of the pyramid and its additions; or the Sacred Cenote at Chichén Itzá, heavily used for rites, offerings, and sacrifices during the city's occupation, and a site of pilgrimage even after the Spanish conquest. Teotihuacán itself was reoccupied by a small Aztec colony and Moctezuma II Xocoyotzin revered it as an ancient shrine where he regularly performed special rites. And shrines on the islands of Cozumel, Isla de Sacrificios, and Jaina around the Yucatán coast were places of pilgrimage (and on Jaina, burial) for the Maya.

To understand many aspects of Aztec behaviour a knowledge of their religion is essential. Their pantheon was all-embracing and they maintained an open capacity for taking in the gods and ceremonies of their predecessors and contemporaries. There were some 1600 gods with considerable overlap in functions and characteristic features. In general, Aztec religion was pervaded by a sense of dread and impending doom. The cyclical nature of their universe, even to the minutiae of Huitzilopochtli's daily battle to rise, called for continuous preparations, rites, sacrifices, and appeasements.

The more spectacular of these rites were the various forms of human sacrifice that have captured modern interest. To nourish Huitzilopochtli, victims were forced down onto their backs over a convex sacrificial stone at the entrance to the temple; while four priests held the victim's limbs (and sometimes a fifth held his neck with a rope or U-shaped tool) a fifth (sixth) priest slit the chest cavity with an obsidian knife and literally ripped out the beating heart, which was then burnt. Such was the enthusiasm of some victims, that they apparently 'danced' up the steps of the pyramid to show the honour they felt in the life-giving role they were paying to the nation; but the overwhelming majority must have been unwilling victims. To honour Xipe Totec, god of springtime, victims were flayed alive and their skins donned by the performing priests to signify renewal. Two forms of special sacrifice, often performed on captured warriors, were the 'gladiatorial combat' (tlahuahuanaliztli) and the arrow-sacrifice (tlacacaliliztli). In the first, the victim was tied to a heavy stone to restrict his movements, and given a wooden club, often set with feathers, with which to defend himself against several Aztec warriors, fighting with obsidian-bladed clubs. In the second, the prisoner was tied to a wooden frame, set upright, and used for 'target practice'. Flaying in honour of Xipe Totec and the arrow-sacrifice are thought to have been introduced into central Mexico by the Toltecs, who had copied them from the Huastecs of NE Mexico.

Other Aztec rites, inherited from thousands of years of evolution, included tlachtli (the ball game), the voladores ceremony, and patolli (a board game). The ball game was a religious exercise and its outcome was believed to be determined in the heavens, sometimes with dire results for the losers, who in some contests were sacrificed for their pains; ball courts were often dedicated to specific gods. The voladores ceremony of the Huastec and Totonac people was more than a dance or display, as it is usually referred to today; it involved men dressing in elaborate costumes, in imitation of gods, and flinging themselves off the platform of a tall pole, having fixed ropes, which were carefully wound around the pole, to their waists or ankles. As the ropes unwound they 'flew' slowly down to the ground as centrifugal force kept them out away from the pole. Just before touching the ground, by inches, and revealing themselves to be mere men, they pulled themselves up to land on their feet, a no less remarkable feat considering the thrust of the centrifugal force. A fifth volador stood on a small platform playing a flute and beating a small drum. Patolli, a game resembling pachisi and known at least as early as Teotihuacán, also had religious overtones; it was played under the auspices of a special god of games and the outcome, notwithstanding invocations to the gods, was presumed to be predetermined. Patolli boards have been found at Benque Viejo (Belize), Chichén Itzá, Cuahtetelco, Dzibilchaltún, Palenque, Seibal (Guatemala), Stann Creek (Belize), Teotihuacán, Tula, and Uxmal.

Glossaries of gods

Olmec gods

God I: a monster creature with flaming eyebrows, large nose, L-shaped or trough eyes, and composite features incl. crocodile, eagle, human, jaguar, and serpent; associated with earth, sun, water, and fertility; possibly ancestral to Maya Itzamná and Aztec Xiuhtecuhtli.

God II: the Maize god, depicted as a toothless infant were-jaguar with almond-shaped eyes, flat nose, and plump flaring lips; a maize symbol sprouts from a cleft in his head.

God III: a bird-monster with composite features of birds and reptiles, incl. flaming eyebrows, L-shaped or trough eyes, paw-wings with talons, a raptor's beak, and sometimes a single, cleft fang; sometimes also, a harpy eagle crest on his head; generally associated with celestial matters and with agricultural fertility.

God IV: a rain god, depicted as an infant were-jaguar incl. almond eyes, flat nose, flaring lips, and toothless mouth turned down at the corners; he usually wears a distinctive, sectioned headband, crenellated ear ornaments, and pectoral with crossed bands; a fertility god ancestral to Maya Chac and Aztec Tláloc.

Designation *V* is no longer used.

God VI: a mysterious god possibly representing spring and renewal; portrayed with a disembodied, cleft head and distinctive band across its almond-shaped, open eye, and a grinning, toothless mouth with prominent gums; possibly ancestral to Aztec and Huastec Xipe Totec.

God VII: possibly an early version of the 'feathered serpent', with attributes similar to *Gods I* and *III*.

God VIII: a fish-monster with crocodile and shark-like features, crescent eyes, human nose, and fish body, often with cross-bands; associated with the ocean and with standing water (not rivers) in general.

Designation *IX* is no longer used.

God X: another were-jaguar creature with many attributes similar to *God VI*, but without eye-bands and with figure-of-eight motifs in the nostrils.

Maya gods

The Maya universe was conceived in two ways. In the first, the earth rested on the back of a caimán (crocodile), with 13 celestial sections above and 9 under-world sections below. The celestial stations were six steps up from the E horizon to the seventh station, then six steps down to the W horizon; the underworld stations descended four steps from the W to the fifth level, then four steps up to the E. There were therefore only seven and five levels, respectively (comp. Aztec levels, below). In the second conception the world was tzamná ('iguana house'), in which iguanas formed the roof, walls, and floor to represent the sky and earth.

The gods are listed alphabetically; the letter-list is a designation of 1904 by P. Schellhaus, still sometimes seen in texts.

A	=	*Ah Puch, Cizin, Hun Ahau,* and *Yum Cimil.*
B	=	*Chac.*
C	=	*Monkey-faced god* and *Xamen Ek.*
D	=	*Itzamná.*
E	=	*Ah Mun* and *Yum Kaax.*
F	=	*War god.*
G	=	*Kinich Ahau.*
H	=	*Chicchan god.*
I	=	*Ix Chel.*
J	=	not used.
K	=	*Bolon Dz'acab.*
L	=	*Old Black god.*
M	=	*Ek Chuah.*
N	=	*Bacabs, Pauahtun,* and *Uayeb god.*
O	=	*Ix Chebel Yax.*
P	=	not used.
Q	=	*Etz'nab* and *Evil god.*
R	=	*Buluc Ch'Abtan* and *Earth god.*

Ah Mun: Maize god; portrayed as youth, often with a maize plant sprouting from his head; ruler of day *Kan*; symbolized by number 8; also called *Yum Kaax.*

Ah Puch: Death god; portrayed with a skull and long spine; ruler of Underworld and of day *Cimi*; symbolized by number 10 and motif \5; associated with Moan bird, owl, and dog.

Bacabs: sons of Itzamná and sky supports at the four corners of the earth; see *Uayeb god.*

Bolon Dz'acab: 'the nine generations'—god of lineage and descent; portrayed with an extended upper-lip (sometimes confused as a long nose), sometimes with serpent-feet on a manikin sceptre of power; ruler of day *Muluc*; associated with the E and with years beginning with day *Kan.*

Buluc Ch'Abtan: see *Earth god.*

Chac: Rain god; portrayed with long nose (often up-curled) and lolling tongue; ruler of day *Ik*; symbolized by number 6; associated with the cardinal points and with four assistants—*Zac Xib Chac* (N, white), *Kan Xib Chac* (S, yellow), *Chac Xib Chac* (E, red), and *Ek Xib Chac* (W, black); equivalent of Aztec *Tláloc.*

Chaneques: dwarf-like poltergeists who resemble *Chac*, dwell in the forests, and cause mischief; probably of Olmec origin.

Chicchan god: a rain god; ruler of day *Chicchan*; symbolized by number 9.

Cizin: see *Ah Puch.*

Earth god: the Earth god was probably an anthropomorphic, primitive earth-monster, portrayed as a youth; possibly *Buluc Ch'Abtan.*

Ek Chuah: god of merchants (benevolent aspect) and god of war (malevolent aspect); portrayed as a merchant with staff and backpack, or as old man with one or no teeth; also god of cacao; equivalent to Aztec *Yacatecuhtli.*

Etz'nab: see *Evil god.*

Evil god: god of evil and probably of human sacrifice, possibly called *Etz'nab*; symbolized by number 2.

Hunab Ku: supreme, single Maya creator god, but invisible; possibly an abstraction preached by Early Postclassic priests; thought of as the father of *Itzamná.*

Hun Ahau: see *Ah Puch.*

Hunahpú: see *Xibalba.*

Hun Hunahpú: see *Xibalba.*

Itzamná ('iguana house'): Maya superdeity, second only to *Hunab Ku* and—with goddess *Ix Chebel Yax*—father of the gods, of the sky and earth, and of science and the arts; portrayed with a Roman nose and a single tooth; ruler of day *Muluc* and month *Zip*; associated with the sun glyph *Kin.* The *Bacabs* were his sons.

Ix Chebel Yax: the 'old red goddess', spouse of *Itzamná* and mother of the gods; goddess of painting, weaving, and brocading.

Ix Chel: Moon goddess and goddess of childbirth, procreation, medicine, and water; wife of *Kinich Ahau*; portrayed as a female warrior with spear and shield; ruler of day *Caban.* On Cozumel there was a special shrine dedicated to her.

Ixtah: goddess of suicide; portrayed suspended in a rope noose; possibly an aspect of *Ix Chel.*

Jaguar god: god of day *Akbal* and of number 7.

Kinich Ahau: the Sun god; portrayed with a Roman nose and square eyes; symbolized by number 4; associated with *Itzamná.*

Kukulkán: the Maya translation of central Mexican *Quetzalcóatl*, introduced by the Putún Maya in the 10C AD. He was also the legendary Feathered Serpent leader who brought Mexican (Toltec) civilization to Yucatán.

Monkey-faced god: probably ruler of day *Chuen* and possibly called *Xamen Ek*, the North Star god.

Old Black god: a lord of the Maya Underworld, associated with *Ah Puch*; portrayed smoking a cigar and wearing a Moan bird headdress; ruler of day *Akbal.*

Pauahtun: winds of the cardinal points; see *Uayeb god.*

Uayeb god: god of the five ill-omened days of the solar calendar; portrayed as an old man, identified with the *Bacabs* and *Pauahtun*; also portrayed as an altar atlante; symbolized by number 5, by a snail or turtle shell worn on his back; also a ruler of the Underworld.

Vucub Hunahpú: see *Xibalba.*

War god: god for war and human sacrifice (see also *Evil god* and *Ek Chuah*); resembled Aztec *Xipe Totec*; related to *Ah Puch*; ruler of day *Manik.*

Xamen Ek: North Star god, possibly the *Monkey-faced god.*

Xbalanqué: see *Xibalba.*

Xibalba: Highland Quiché Maya Underworld and, by association, the gods thereof; in the 'Popul Vuh' text they defeated *Hun Hunahpú* and *Vucub Hunahpú,* the sons of *Xmucané;* when *Hun Hunahpú's* head was hung up in a calabash tree as a trophy, a daughter of a *Xibalba* lord fell in love with it, was impregnated by its spittle, and gave birth to the hero twins *Hunahpú* and *Xbalanqué;* they returned to *Xibalba,* defeated its lords, and ascended into the sky as sun and moon.

Xmucané: Highland Quiché Maya 'grandmother' creator goddess and wife of *Xpiyacoc;* mother of *Hun Hunahpú* and *Vucub Hunahpú,* grandmother of *Hunahpú* and *Xbalanqué;* equivalent to Aztec *Oxomoco.*

Xmulzencab: bee gods who take part in the creation-myth, each as a cardinal direction and world colour, in the 'Chilam Balam'.

Xpiyacoc: Highland Quiché Maya 'grandfather' creator god and husband of *Xmucané;* father of *Hun Hunahpú* and *Vucub Hunahpú,* grandfather of *Hunahpú* and *Xbalanqué;* equivalent to Aztec *Cipactonal.*

Yum Cimil: see *Ah Puch.*

Yum Kaax: see *Ah Mun.*

Aztec gods

The Aztec universe comprised 13 celestial and 9 underworld layers. The first level in both sets was the earth, pictured as a huge crocodile lying in the water. The levels can be imagined thus:

level	name	character
13	*Omeyocán,*	duality
12	*Teotl Tlatlauhcán,*	place of red god
11	*Teotl Cozauhcán,*	place of yellow god
10	*Teotl Iztacán,*	place of white god
9	*Itztapal Nauatzcayán,*	place of crashing stone slabs
8	*Ilhuicatl Xoxouhcán,*	blue heaven
7	*Ilhuicatl Yayauhcán,*	black heaven
6	*Ilhuicatl Mamalhuazocán,*	fire drill heaven
5	*Ilhuicatl Huixtotlán, Huixtocíhuatl,*	heaven of salt-goddess
4	*Ilhuicatl Tonatiuh,*	sun heaven
3	*Ilhuicatl Citlalícue,*	heaven of star-skirted goddess
2	*Ilhuicatl Tlalocán Ipan Meztli,*	heaven of *Tláloc* and the moon
1	*Tlaltícpac,*	earth
2	*Apanohuayán,*	water passage
3	*Tepetl Imonamiquiyán,*	place of clashing hills
4	*Itztepetl,*	hill of obsidian knife
5	*Itzehecayán,*	place of obsidian-bladed wind
6	*Pancuecuetlayán,*	place of flourishing banners
7	*Temiminaloyán,*	place of arrow-sacrifice
8	*Teyollocualoyán,*	place where the heart is eaten
9	*Iz Mictlán Opochcalocan,*	place of the dead,'where streets are on the left'

The gods are listed first in groups after their general spheres of influence, then alphabetically:

1 Principal deities: *Huitzilopochtli, Quetzalcóatl, Tezcatlipoca.*

2 Creator deities: *Cipactonal, Omecíhuatl, Ometecuhtli, Ometeotl, Oxomoco, Tloque Nahuaque, Tonacacíhuatl, Tonacatecuhtli.*

3 Fertility deities: *Ahuiatéotl, Ahuiatl, Centéotl, Chalchiuhcíhuatl, Chicomecóatl, Cihuacóatl, Coatlícue, Ilamatecuhtli, Ixcuinan, Macuilxóchitl, Quilaztli, Teteoinnan, Tlazoltéotl, Toci, Tonantzin, Xilmen, Xipe Totec, Xochipilli, Xochiquetzal.*

4 Fire deities: *Ahuiateteo, Chantico, Cuaxólotl, Huehuetéotl, Xiutecuhtli.*

5 Pulque deities: *Centzóntotochtin, Mayáhuel, Ometochtli, Patécatl, Tepoztécatl, Tezcatzontécatl.*

6 Sky or heavenly deities: *Camaxtli, Centzonhuitznahuac, Centzonmimizcoa, Citlalicue, Citlalinicue, Citlatona, Coyolxauhqui, Itzpapálotl, Meztli, Mixcóatl, Nanahuatzin, Omeyocán, Piltzintécuhtli, Tecciztécatl, Tlahuizcalpantecuhtli, Tonatiuh, Tzitzimime.*

7 Underworld deities: *Chalchiuhtecólotl, Chalmecatecuhtli, Huahuatli, Mictecacíhuatl, Mictlantecuhtli, Teoyaomiqui, Tepeyolohtli, Tlaltecuhtli, Yohualtecuhtli.*

8 Weather deities (rain, wind, storm): *Chalchiúhtlicue, Ehecatl, Huixtocíhuatl, Naapatecuhtli, Tepictoan, Tláloc.*

9 Miscellaneous deities: *Atlatonan, Chalchiuhtotolin, Chimalmqm, Cihuateteo, Huehuecóyotl, Itztlacoliuhqui, Itztli, Ixtlilton, Matlalcueitl, Matlalcueyo, Omácatl, Opochtli, Paynal, Tlalchitonatiuh, Tlaltícpac, Xólotl, Yacatecuhtli, Yáotl.*

Ahuiatétl: god of voluptuousness; a manifestation of *Xochipilli;* see also *Macuixóchitl.*

Ahuiateteo: five 'jin' of the S, companions to *Ahuiatéotl.*

Ahuiatl: see *Macuilxóchitl.*

Atlatonami: goddess, impersonated by virgins who gave themselves to the young warrior, impersonating *Tezcatlipoca,* in the year prior to his sacrifice at the *Tóxcatl* rites (see *Tezcatlipoca).*

Camaxtli: Tlaxcalan god of the hunt and war; same as *Mixcóatl.*

Centéotl: central Mexican god of the maize plant; son of *Tlazoltéotl;* possibly descended from Olmec *God II.*

Centzonhuitznahuac: stars of the S constellation; brothers of *Huitzilopochtli.*

Centzonmimizcoa: stars of the N constellation and 'cloud serpent' (Milky Way); brothers of *Huitzilopochtli.*

Centzóntotochtin: '400 rabbits', a collective term for the pulque gods.

Chalchiuhcíhuatl: a harvest goddess.

Chalchiutecólotl: 'precious owl', god of night as an aspect of black *Tezcatlipoca.*

Chalchiúhtlicue: female counterpart of *Tláloc;* goddess of rivers, oceans, and floods; ruler of day *Cóatl,* Third Lord of Day, Sixth Lord of Night.

Chalchiuhtotolin: 'precious turkey', an aspect of *Tezcatlipoca;* patron of night and mystery; ruler of day *Técpatl.*

Chalmecatecuhtli: god of sacrifice and of the Underworld; sometimes substituted for *Mictlantecuhtli* as Eleventh Lord of Day.

Chantico: goddess of the hearth and of smiths, especially goldsmiths; related to *Mictlantecuhtli* and principal deity of Xochimilco.

Chicomecóatl: 'seven serpents', goddess of maize and vegetation; usually portrayed with red face and body, wearing a paper mitre with rosettes, or, in sculpture, holding maize ears; also called *Chicomolotzin* and related to *Centéotl, Chalchiútlicue,* and *Xilonen.*

Chicomolotzin: see *Chicomecóatl.*

Chimalman: feminine personification of divinity and female *teomama*—bearer of a cult object in the Aztec migrations; manifested as legendary mother of Ce Acatl Topiltzin Quetzalcóatl of Tula, and in one myth the mother of *Huitzilopochtli* (rather than *Coatlícue).*

Cihuacóatl: 'serpent woman'; Earth goddess and patroness of the *Cihuateteo;* other forms include *Coatlícue* and *Tonantzin;* transferred into Mexican folklore as 'La Llorona' ('weeping woman').

Cihuateteo: spirits of women who died in childbirth; they lived in the W paradise *Cincalco* and helped convey fallen warriors to the world of the dead.

Cipactonal: mythologically the 'first man', spouse of *Oxomoco;* sorcerer and inventor of astrology and the calendar.

Citlalícue: 'star-skirted goddess' of the heavens (see sky-level 3); female counterpart to *Citlatona*, and feminine aspect of *Ometeotl*; see also *Omecíhuatl*.

Citlatinicue: same as *Citlalícue*.

Citlatona: masculine aspect of *Ometeotl*—duality; see *Ometecuhtli*.

Coatlícue: Earth goddess, mother of *Centzonhuitznahuac, Coyolxauhqui,* and *Huitzilopochtli;* ruler of the rainy season and concerned with agriculture in general; also called *Teteoinnan, Toci,* and *Tonantzin.*

Coyolxauhqui: Moon goddess, daughter of *Coatlícue;* conspired with the *Centzonhuitznahuac* for the death of her mother, for which she was decapitated by her brother *Huitzilopochtli.*

Cuaxólotl: another name for *Chantico;* portrayed with two heads to symbolize the good and evil potentials of fire.

Ehecatl: the Wind god and a manifestation of *Quetzalcóatl;* portrayed wearing a bird-beak mask; ruler of day 2 (*Ehecatl*) and corresponding Maya day *Ik,* Zapotec day *Quij;* also the Fourth Aztec Sun (see creation myth, above).

Huahuantli: see *Teoyaomiqui.*

Huehuecóyotl: the 'coyote-god', patron of amantecos—feather-workers; possibly of Otomí origin.

Huehuetéotl: the Old Fire God, descended from Olmec *God I;* usually portrayed as a wrinkled, toothless old man holding a brazier on his head; also called *Xiuhtecuhtli.*

Huitzilopochtli: the special, and exclusively Aztec, god of the sun and war; patron deity of Tenochtitlán and the tribal god of the Mexica; he led them from Aztlán into the Basin of Mexico, where he gave them the sign of the eagle (his representative) alighting on a cactus to show them where to settle and build their city. In one legend he is son of the creator couple *Omecíhuatl* and *Ometecuhtli;* in another he is son of *Coatlícue,* whom he saved by decapitating his sister *Coyolxauhqui,* who conspired to kill her mother; this brother-sun/sister-moon struggle symbolized the day and night, respectively, and the rising of the sun after battling against darkness. In his daily journey he is accompanied by the souls of fallen warriors to the centre of the sky (noon) and then by the *Cihuateteo* until his descent in the W as a falling eagle. As his 'chosen people' the Mexica worshipped him in repeated, necessary, human sacrifices for his blood-nourishment.

Huixtocíhuatl: sister-goddess of *Tláloc* and inventor of salt; one of the four women who gave themselves to the warrior-youth during his year before the *Tóxcatl* rites (see *Tezcatlipoca*); related to *Tlazoltéotl.*

Ilamatecuhtli: an ancient Moon goddess, and goddess of old, dried-up maize ears; see also *Centéotl.*

Itzpapálotl: 'obsidian butterfly', she was an ancient Chichimec Earth-goddess and wife of *Mixcóatl;* also one of the *Tzitzimime.*

Itztlacoliuhqui: a form of *Tezcatlipoca,* representing ice, cold, sin, misery, black.

Itztli: 'obsidian knife', the sacrificial knife—deputy of *Tezcatlipoca.*

Ixcuinami: one aspect of *Tlazoltéotl,* probably of Huastec origin.

Ixtlilton: god of health and medicine; brother of *Macuilxóchitl* and *Xochipilli.*

Macuilxóchitl: god of pleasure, of tlachtli (the ball game), and of patolli; related to *Xochipilli,* but given more to excess.

Matlalcueitl: 'lady of the green skirts'; second wife of *Tláloc.*

Matlalcueye: another name for *Matlalcueitl* and the ancient name for a volcano between Puebla and Tlaxcala, now called La Malinche.

Mayáhuel: goddess of maguey-plants and of pulque distilled from them; consort of *Patécatl;* portrayed with '400 breasts' (ie, 'without number') to feed the '400 gods'; goddess of drunkenness—centzóntotochtin; ruler of day *Tochtli;* symbolized by *Ce Tochtli* ('one rabbit'); see also *Ometochtli.*

Meztli: Náhuatl for moon and used for the nocturnal aspect of *Tezcatlipoca.* In legend the moon was born at a cremation self-sacrifice which took place at an assembly of gods at Teotihuacán. Poor and syphilitic *Nanahuatzin* leapt into the fire first and came out as the brilliant sun; rich and cowardly *Tecciztécatl* was next and came out as the moon, equally brilliant until a god obscured his light by throwing a rabbit into his face.

Mictecacíhuatl: wife of *Mictlantecuhtli.*

Mictlantecuhtli: god of the Underworld; portrayed covered with human bones and wearing a skull mask with human bone earplugs, black-haired, curly, and with starlike eyes so he can see in the dark; ruler of day *Itzcuintli,* Sixth or Eleventh Lord of Day, and Fifth Lord of Night; associated animals include bats, owls, and spiders.

Mixcóatl: legendary Toltec-Chichimec leader, father—with *Chimalman*—of Ce Acatl Topiltzin Quetzalcóatl; deified as god of the hunt after his murder; Náhuatl meaning is 'cloud serpent', probably the Milky Way; see also *Camaxtli.*

Naapatecuhtli: 'four times lord'—one of the *Tlálocs.*

Nanahuatzin: syphilitic god, an aspect of *Xólotl;* became the sun in the legend of the gods' assembly at Teotihuacán—see *Meztli.*

Omácatl: an aspect of *Tezcatlipoca,* as god of banquets.

Omecíhuatl: female counterpart of *Ometecuhtli.*

Ometecuhtli: masculine aspect of *Ometeotl* (duality), the creative energy from which all other gods descended; he and his consort *Omecíhuatl* lived in the thirteenth level of heaven, the *Omeyocán* ('place of two'); their four sons were the world directions and colours, viz. N—Black *Tezcatlipoca,* S—Blue *Tezcatlipoca,* E—Red *Tezcatlipoca,* and W—White *Tezcatlipoca.*

Ometeotl: primitive bisexual divinity, duality, literally 'twice god'; an abstraction used by Aztec priests, but too subtle for active cult worship. Cf. *Tloque Nahuaque.*

Ometochtli: 'two rabbits', a generic name for the *Centzóntotochtin;* see also *Mayáhuel* and *Patécatl.*

Omeyocán: supreme, thirteenth heaven, literally 'place of two'; home of *Omecíhuatl* and *Ometecuhtli,* symbols of masculine-feminine, light-dark, and all dualities.

Opochtli: one of the *Tlálocs;* god of those who lived on or near water; inventor of the fish net, bird net, harpoon, spear-thrower, and boatman's pole.

Oxomoco: mythologically the 'first woman', wife of *Cipactonal;* sorceress and inventor of astrology and the calendar.

Patécatl: god of pulque, husband of *Mayáhuel;* he made the maguey juice 'change' into pulque; also associated with herbs, medicine, and narcotic plants; ruler of day *Malinalli.*

Paynal: messenger of *Huitzilopochtli.*

Piltzintécuhtli: a youthful aspect of *Tonatiuh* and *Xochipilli;* Third Lord of Night.

Quetzalcóatl: a major god all over Mesoamerica, especially in the Postclassic (eg, *Kukulkán* to the Maya, *Gucumatz* to the Quiché Maya of highland Guatemala, *Ehecatl* to the Huastecs of NE Mexico). Literally 'feathered serpent', he was important at Teotihuacán, possibly descended from Olmec *God VII.* He was a father and creator god, father of the priesthood, learning, science, the arts, and agriculture. In different manifestations he was god of wind (*Ehecatl*), the morning star (*Tlahuizcalpantecuhtli*), the evening star (*Xólotl*), the legendary Toltec leader Ce Acatl Topiltzin Quetzalcóatl, and the Maya-Toltec leader Kukulkán. His brothers were *Huitzilopochtli, Tezcatlipoca,* and *Xipe Totec.* He ruled the second sun of the creation myth and was Ninth Lord of Day. He was portrayed with many attributes in many combinations: a conical hat (copilli) painted half dark, half light; a hat-band with tools for autosacrifice; a flower to symbolize blood; a fan at his neck, of black crow and red macaw feathers; a bird-beak mask and beard; black front and yellow back; jade disc and spiral-shell ear ornaments; a breastplate cut from a conch shell; and a spear-thrower, symbol of the Fire god.

Quilaztli: an aspect of *Cihuacóatl,* goddess of pregnancy, childbirth, and the sweat bath.

Tecciztécatl: god of the Moon; with both masculine and feminine aspects; became the moon in the legend of the assembly at Teotihuacán—see *Meztli;* also, god of fertility and ruler of day *Miquiztli.*

Teoyaomiqui: god of warriors who died in the 'Flower Wars'—wars to obtain prisoners for sacrifice; sometimes replaced *Mictlantecuhtli* as Sixth Lord of Day.

Tepictoton: little *Tlálocs,* gods of mountain rains; portrayed as dwarfs.

Tepopochtli: see *Tóxcatl.*

Tepoztécatl: a pulque god and patron deity of Tepoztlán; see also *Patécatl.*

Teteoinnan: 'mother of the gods', an earth-mother concept; more primitive but related to *Cihuacóatl, Coatlícue, Tlazoltéotl,* and *Toci.*

Tezcatlipoca: 'smoking mirror', a creator god with many forms and aspects; god of night, evil, death, destruction, and mystery; patron of robbers and sorcerers. He intervened directly in human affairs. His left foot, replaced by the smoking mirror, had been ripped off by the Earth Monster and he was the perpetual rival of his brother *Quetzalcóatl*. He was also special to Texcoco, and probably important to the Mexica for that reason. Tenth Lord of Day. Associated with the cardinal points, directional colours, and many aspects: N, black, 'smoking mirror', god of Texcoco and of day *Acatl*; S, blue, 'hummingbird sorcerer', *Huitzilopochtli*—Sun and War god, god of Tenochtitlán; E, red, 'the flayed one', *Xipe Totec, Camaxtli,* and *Mixcóatl,* god of Tlaxcala, god of day *Cuauhtli*; W, white, 'plumed serpent', *Quetzalcóatl,* god of Cholula, god of education and the priesthood. Ruler of the First Sun and abductor of *Xochiquetzal,* *Tláloc*'s first wife. *Tezcatlipoca* was honoured in a special ceremony in the month *Tóxcatl*: a young warrior impersonated him for a year, during which he lived a life of pleasure, incl. the enjoyment of four virgins impersonating goddesses; at the end of the year, however, he was led to sacrifice watched by the Aztec nobility and crowds. The 'massacre of *Tóxcatl*' took place when Cortés's lieutenant Pedro de Alvarado impetuously used the ceremony as an excuse to attack, killing more than 8500 unarmed Aztecs.

Tezcatzontécatl: a god of pulque, possibly identifiable as the chacmool sculptures.

Tlahuizcalpantecuhtli: a Venus deity both as evening star, *Xólotl,* and morning star *Quetzalcóatl*; Twelfth Lord of Day.

Tlalchitonatiuh: an early god originally worshipped at Teotihuacán and introduced from there into highland Guatemala and later to Yucatán; referred to as the Jaguar Sun or Falling Sun, and the special god of the Jaguar and Eagle warrior cults.

Tláloc: an early god, possibly descended from Olmec *God IV*; the Rain god, associated with all forms of precipitation—rain, hail, ice, snow, flood, drought, thunder, and lightning; also with mountains and frequently with serpents (eg, paired with *Quetzalcóatl* at Teotihuacán); portrayed with rings or 'spectacles' around his eyes, fangs, and a volute across his mouth; his sister was *Chalchiútlicue,* and two wives were *Xochiquetzal* (abducted by *Tezcatlipoca*) and *Matlalcueitl*; ruler of the day *Mázatl,* Eighth Lord of Day, Ninth Lord of Night; conceived as fourfold, representing the four world colours and cardinal points; directly equivalent to Maya *Chac,* Mixtec *Dzahui,* Totonac *Tajín,* and Zapotec *Cocijo.*

Tlaltecuhtli: the Earth Monster; portrayed as a huge, fat toad with fangs and claws, and of dual gender; he ate the hearts of sacrificial victims and was frequently carved on the underside of cuauhxicalli (stone boxes for the heart and blood of victims); he ate the sun every evening and regurgitated it every morning; Second Lord of Day.

Tlaltícpac: 'earth'—ie, the here and now.

Tlazoltéotl: 'goddess of filth', an Earth goddess related to *Cihuacóatl* and *Coatlícue*; patroness of carnality and fertility; ruler of day *Océlotl,* Fifth Lord of Day, and Seventh Lord of Night; portrayed with raw cotton and spindles or bobbins in her headdress, and sometimes wearing a flayed skin; originally from the Huastec pantheon.

Tloque Nahuaque: 'lord of everywhere', an abstract concept, invisible spirit, proposed by the Texcocan king Nezahualcóyotl; worshipped in temples but not represented by idols; not generally popular after the proponent's death in 1472. Cf. *Ometeotl.*

Toci: 'our grandmother', another name for *Tlazoltéotl,* the Huastec, later Aztec, Earth goddess.

Tonacacíhuatl: see *Omecíhuatl.*

Tonacatecuhtli: see *Ometecuhtli.*

Tonacatépetl: 'sustenance mountain', where *Quetzalcóatl* was led by Azcatl, the red ant, who changed into a black ant and showed *Quetzalcóatl* maize grains for mankind; sometimes identified with Iztaccíhuatl volcano.

Tonantzin: 'little mother', the benevolent aspect of the Earth goddess; the shrine of the Virgin of Guadalupe at Tepeyac was the location of the temple of Tonantzin.

Tonatiuh: Sun god, related to *Huitzilopochtli,* the young warrior; as the sun itself—*cuauhtlehuánitl* ('ascending eagle') was the rising sun and *cuauhtémoc* ('descending eagle') the setting sun; ruler of day *Quiáhuitl* and Fourth Lord of Day; see also *Yohualtecuhtli.*

Tóxcatl: see *Tezcatlipoca.*

Tzitzimime: 'demons of darkness'—stars visible only during a solar eclipse, who in the creation myth would one day come down to earth and devour mankind at the end of the Fifth (present) Sun.

Xilonen: goddess of young maize; closely related to *Chicomecóatl* and *Centéotl.*

Xipe Totec: god of Spring, seeds and planting; his special ceremony was a human sacrifice and flaying, after which the priests dressed in the victims' skins to signify renewal, taking place in the month *Tlacaxipehualiztli;* ruler of the day *Cuauhtli* and represented as the E, *Red Tezcatlipoca;* ultimately of Zapotec origin, possibly even from Olmec *God VI;* especially honoured in Tlaxcala; patron of metal and stone craftsmen. Also worshipped by Tarascans and Zapotecs.

Xiuhtecuhtli: Fire god, an ancient deity ultimately descended from Olmec *God I* (see *Huehuetéotl*); ruler of the day *Atl,* First Lord of Day and First Lord of Night; represented by number 3, symbolizing the three hearthstones of the traditional Aztec household.

Xochipilli: 'flower prince', a manifestation of the young Sun god, god of pleasure, male lust, joy, and poetry; closely related to *Ahuiatl* and *Macuilxóchitl;* especially popular with the Xochimilca tribe, along with his female counterpart, Xochiquetzal.

Xochiquetzal: 'feathered flower' or 'rich-plumed flower'; portrayed with two large quetzal feathers; female counterpart of *Xochipilli,* and personification of love and beauty; patroness of domesticity, flowers, the *anianime* or *maqui* (lady companions of unwed Aztec warriors), and courtesans; ruler of day *Xóchitl.* According to legend, she was the first wife of *Tláloc* but was abducted by *Tezcatlipoca.*

Xólotl: god of Venus, evening aspect of *Tlahuizcalpantecuhtli* and twin of *Quetzalcóatl* as the morning star; portrayed with a dog's head, probably as guide to the Underworld; ruler of day *Ollin;* see also *Nanahuitzin.*

Yacatecuhtli: special god of the pochteca merchants; symbolized by a bamboo staff and a fan; worshipped especially at Cholula and Tlatelolco; equivalent of Maya *Ek Chuah.*

Yáotl: general Náhuatl word for enemy; synonym for *Huitzilopochtli* and *Tezcatlipoca* in their malevolent aspects.

Yohualtecuhtli: 'lord of the night'; as the night-sun he was counterpart to *Tonatiuh*—day-sun; representative of both the sun and Venus as they joined in the Underworld ending each cosmic cycle, he was identified with the star appearing in centre-sky at midnight at the completion of a 52-year cycle; generally associated with darkness, midnight, and cyclic completion.

Yohualtonatiuh: see *Tonatiuh* and *Yohualtecuhtli.*

Yope or *Yopi:* a linguistic group in Guerrero, possibly the origin of *Xipe Totec* and thus a synonym for him.

Various other gods

Acpaxaco: Otomí Water goddess; equivalent to *Chalchiútlicue.*

Beydo: 'wind' or 'seeds'; Zapotec name for deity objects or natural forces.

Chupithiripeme: Tarascan Rain god.

Cocijo: 'lightning'; Zapotec Rain god; portrayed with composite human-jaguar-serpent face and forked tongue symbolizing lightning; equivalent to *Tláloc,* but see also *Mdi.*

Coqui-Bezelao: Zapotec god of death and the Underworld.

Cozaana: Zapotec creator god; spouse of *Nohuichano.*

Cuerauáperi or *Cueraváperi:* Tarascan goddess of creation, birth, and sewing; consort of *Curicaueri.*

Curicaueri or *Curicaveri:* Tarascan Sun god and fire god, and masculine creation element; husband of *Cuerauáperi.*

Dubdo: Zapotec Corn god and a Lord of Night; related to Aztec *Centéotl.*

Dzahui: Mixtec god of rain and lightning; equivalent to *Tláloc.*

Huehuecóyotl: Otomí 'coyote god'.

Kedo: Zapotec god of justice and a Lord of Night; equivalent to *Mictlantecuhtli.*

Mbaz: Zapotec Earth god/goddess and Lord of Night; equivalent to *Tepeyolohtli* and *Tlazoltéotl;* see also *Mse.*

Mdi: Zapotec Rain god and Lord of Night; similar to *Tláloc,* but see also *Cocijo.*

Mse: Zapotec Earth goddess and Lord of Night; similar to *Tlazoltéotl;* see also *Mbaz.*

Ndan: Zapotec god/goddess of oceans and a Lord of Night.

Ndo'yet: Zapotec god of death and of natural forces.

Ndozin: Zapotec god of death and justice, messenger of *Ndan* and a Lord of Night.

Nohuichano: Zapotec creator goddess; consort of *Cozaana.*

Otontecuhtli: a fire god and special deity of the Otomí, Mazahua, and Tepaneca tribes.

Pijetao: Zapotec supreme creator god.

Pitao Cozobi: Zapotec god of maize, agriculture, and fertility; benevolent influence; portrayed as a bat.

Quiepelagayo: 'fire flower'; Zapotec god of flowers, music, and pleasure; cf. Aztec *Xochipilli.*

Serpent mask god: Zapotec god of learning, wealth, and the wind.

Tajín: Totonac Rain god; equivalent to *Tláloc.*

Tariácuri: Tarascan giver of life, god of the wind, learning, and wealth.

Tihuime: Tarascan god of death and the Underworld.

Tzahui: see *Dzahui.*

Xarátanga: Tarascan Moon goddess and goddess of germination, fertility, growth, and sustenance; daughter of *C_erauápe_ri* and Curicaueri.

Xócatl: see *Otontecuhtli.*

Xonaxi-Quecuya: Zapotec god of death and the Underworld.

Young Fire god: Zapotec Fire god.

Mesoamerican Pottery

The oldest known pottery in Mesoamerica, dated c 2450 BC, comes from coastal Guerrero (Puerto Marqués), from sites in the Central Highlands, from Oaxaca, and from Cuello in Belize. Whether or not pottery was independently discovered or diffused to Mesoamerica from S America is uncertain. Pottery, like plant domestication, is likely to have been 'discovered' more or less simultaneously in several regions. Early ceramics were crude and shared certain basic characteristics. Early ceramics in S America, dated c 3600 BC, come from Ecuador (Valdivia), Colombia (Puerto Hormiga), and from shell mounds at the mouth of the Amazon, although new evidence from these regions has recently produced dates as early as the 6th millennium BC. Contact between Mesoamerica and N South America was nearly as early, as claimed in arguments for the diffusion of certain domesticated plants. By c 2000 BC pottery-making was well established in Mesoamerica and the first distinct 'traditions' or styles recognizable.

The potter's wheel was unknown in prehistoric Mesoamerica. Four methods were employed: modelling from a solid lump of clay; building up the vessel with long coils of clay; building it up by sections of modelled clay; and casting the piece in horizontal or upright moulds. The colour-range of clay fabrics from fired pieces shows that Mesoamerican kilns rarely exceeded temperatures of c 950°C. To reach this temperature an enclosed kiln is needed, and although orange-fabric pottery from excavations indicates that such kilns existed, few examples have been found. Most kilns were of two types: an open fire on the ground (in the coals of which pots were buried for firing); and pits with fires. A few kilns have been found at Las Peñitas (Nayarit) and in Oaxaca, and the native temescal might have doubled in use as a kiln. Excavations at Tula recovered a pit in a house group that showed remains of a duct system and of a top-covering of large potsherds and stones to retain the heat.

During the course of Mesoamerican prehistory many decorative techniques were used: applied before firing, in the naturally-dried ('leather-hard') stage, after firing, or in combinations of the two. Important techniques included:

> *appliqué*: embellishment added to the completed pot- form as lumps and strips of clay.
> *blanco levantado*: known also as 'Tula Watercoloured'—painted decoration of white, transparent streaked lines.
> *burnishing*: rubbing with a stick or bone before firing, to create a smooth surface.

champ-levé: design background cut away, leaving the design standing in relief; especially popular in *Teotihuacán III*.

cloisonné, or *paint cloisonné*: surface colour is cut out, the hollow filled with a new colour, then smoothed down level with the original surface; extensively used in Teotihuacán, Mixteca-Puebla, and W Mexico regions.

cord-marking: impressing a length of cord into the partially-dried surface of the vessel to create patterns, usually bands.

double-line-break: a rim decoration of two parallel, *incised* lines, one or both of which turns up and continues over the lip; wide distribution, especially in the Preclassic.

excising: cutting out of grooves, strips, or shapes from the surface, often painting inside the excised surface.

incising: using a sharp tool to score thin lines on a vessel's surface (but not cutting out a piece of clay); done after firing either before or after applying a *slip* of liquid clay or paint.

iridescent painting: painting the vessel, either entirely or in strips, with an iridescent colour to give the surface a metallic sheen.

painting: monochrome—original clay colour or single-colour *slip*; bichrome—two colours; polychrome—more than two colours; all were extensively used in Mesoamerica, ranging from geometric designs to narrative scenes.

resist painting (sometimes called 'negative painting'): design is created by covering parts of the vessel with paint-resistant material (eg, wax or clay bits) before painting, creating a positive-negative design pattern after the resistant material has been removed.

rocker-stamping: 'walking' the edge of a sharp-edged tool (eg, a shell) along the surface of the vessel to cut a zigzag pattern.

slips: a mixture of very fine clay, water, and pigment, applied to a vessel either before or after firing.

There were numerous regional styles, using: geometric, naturalistic, symbolic, and narrative decoration, and style distinctiveness lies in its combination of techniques, vessel forms, and the artistic execution of animal, plant, and human figures.

Preclassic Central Highlands. The earliest pottery is from the Valle de Tehuacán, c 2300 BC: crude, basic vessels presumably imitating stone or basketry containers. Monochrome grey, black, or white, flat-bottomed bowl and bottle shapes, often with rocker-stamping, predominated in the Early Preclassic. Masculine figurines depicted chubby, 'baby-face' expressions, jaguar claws, fangs, and jaguar-markings. Slightly later, in the Basin of Mexico, the Zacatenco style included highly-polished red-brown vessels, adding jar forms. Zacatenco figurines were nearly all of women, naked at this early stage except for fancy hats and hairdos.

In the Late Preclassic new traditions developed at Chupícuaro and spread S. Chupícuaro potters introduced the comal (a large, gently convex griddle), the molcajete (a bowl with deep, criss-crossed grooves inside for grinding chillies and other soft, dried vegetables), and bi- and polychrome geometric designs in red, cream, black, and brown. Appliqué embellishments on arms, legs, torso, and face were used on figurines. Towards the end of the Preclassic, larger bowls and a wide-lipped, tall-necked bottle called a florero were introduced. Details of clothing were added to figurines, and Tláloc effigies were frequently applied to the sides of vases and jars. Vessels and figurines were also imported from the Gulf Coast and Oaxaca.

Preclassic Mexico. The earliest ceramics come from Puerto Marqués and sites in Colima. Alongside the use of shaft-tombs a distinctive tradition of large, hollow glossy red figurines and highly polished vessels developed, mostly in isolation, although there is some early evidence of influence from central Mexico, the Olmecs, and possibly from NW South America.

Preclassic Oaxaca. Distinctive grey-black wares predominated, with some Olmec influence. Red and white anthropomorphic and zoomorphic effigy vessels were made, and Monte Albán funerary urns featured stylized jaguar mouths and serpentine symbolism.

Preclassic Gulf Coast. In the Olmec heartland the ceramic tradition favoured white-rimmed, black excised wares with an 'x' motif and stylized jaguar paws. Hollow 'baby-face' figurines were produced for home use and exported to the Central Highlands. In the central Gulf (eg, at Remojadas) polished black bowls and effigy vessels were popular, and incised, slant-eyed figurines were decorated with black resin and tar. Farther N, in the Huasteca, flat-bottomed bowls and tecomates (gourd-shaped vessels) were traditional.

Preclassic Mayaland. Two traditions developed, based at Chiapa de Corzo and Izapa. Olmec influence was strong. Early vessels imitated gourd and squash shapes and flat-bottomed stone vessels. The Ocós tradition of Izapa in S Chiapas and SW Guatemala used rocker-stamping, shell-impressed decoration, cord-marking, and iridescent painting down to c 1350 BC. Olmec influence introduced effigy vessels and bi- and polychrome painting.

The Chiapa de Corzo tradition featured unslipped bichromes and, later, 'waxy' slips and polished red and black wares. Olmec figurine types were made but gradually decreased. Trade wares came in from Central America.

In the Late Preclassic, Chicanel, a development of the Izapan tradition, featured wide, flanged, and everted rims, 'waxy' slips and Usulutan Ware imports from El Salvador, but almost no figurines.

Classic Central Highlands. Dominated by urbanism, Teotihuacán introduced pottery specialists, bulk manufacture, and the use of moulds. Distinctive types and qualities were made for everyday use and for ceremonial and funereal use. The variety in forms, colours, and decorative techniques increased. Colours ranged from brown to dark purple (almost black); forms included Tláloc effigy jars, whistle jars, cups, bowls with base supports, vases or jars, incense burners, miniatures, and a thin-walled, orange-paste ware called Thin Orange Ware. The exact origin of Thin Orange Ware is unknown but its distribution stemmed from Teotihuacán and was ubiquitous. Champ-levé and cloisonné decoration were much favoured.

Ritual vessels became increasingly elaborate: cylindrical tripod vessels, often with an effigy on the side wall, and decorated with religious ceremonial, celestial, and underworld scenes; elaborately sculpted incense burners made from several prefabricated sections; and 'candeleros', candlestick-like vessels possibly used as incense burners or to hold ritual, blood-splashed paper in ceremonies.

Teotihuacano figurines wore distinctive costumes: men wore loincloths and other clothing according to their social rank; women wore the triangular quechquemitl blouse, full-length skirts, wide hats, and elaborate hairstyles. New types included articulated dolls and figurines with unembellished stick-like limbs and bald heads—presumably dressed in clothing of perishable materials.

All Teotihuacano wares were widely distributed throughout Mesoamerica.

Classic Western Mexico. Colima and Guerrero had much contact with central Mexico, and Guerrero with the Maya region. Everyday pottery was heavily influenced by Teotihuacano products, and much Thin Orange Ware was imported. The tradition of large, polished red anthropomorphic and zoomorphic figures, especially of dogs, reached its peak. Solid clay figurines, equally numerous, depicted virtually every aspect of everyday life—work, play, and ceremony.

N Jalisco, Nayarit, and S Sinaloa had less contact with central Mexico. Sinaloa Chametla Ware was an independently-developed polychrome style with elaborate designs, possibly influenced by Central American wares via coastal trade. There were also engraved spindlewhorls and painted figurines.

Classic Oaxaca. Grey wares continued to compete with Teotihuacano imports. The most distinctive Oaxaqueño types were painted funerary urns (subdivided into over 40 types)—red, or yellow, or polychrome—and effigy vessels of gods and serpents. Figurines included a long-headed type with tall or low head-dresses, forms resembling miniature funerary urns, and Teotihuacano types. The increasingly abundant Thin Orange Ware imports reflected the Oaxaqueño-Teotihuacano economic relationship.

Classic Gulf Coast. The most prominent site was El Tajín, where Teotihuacano influence was strong, but Olmecoid features lingered, and there was an indigenous white, resist-painted ware. 'Smiling face' figurines with raised arms and hollow-bodied figurines with infantile faces were characteristic of Remojadas and the surrounding S Gulf region. Innovations included the use of a metallic-like slip, wheeled toys, and a multitude of ceramic flutes and whistles. Late Classic 'smiling face' figurines were mould-made and one sub-group had Maya-like features. Another figurine tradition developed at Nopiloa, featuring miniature portraits of social 'types' and of individuals. Champ-levé decorated bowls, put together from two moulded sections, were also characteristic, and a fine-grained, untempered Orange Ware was developed at Gulf Coast Plain sites and distributed within and outside the region.

Classic Mayaland. The Petén zone around Tikal, Uaxactún (both in Guatemala), and Yaxchilán (Chiapas) had a highly developed tradition of polychrome painting depicting narrative scenes in red, cream, grey, and black. Linear and curvilinear motifs, and geometric designs were used independently and in combination with narrative scenes. Cylindrical tripod jars with effigy knobs in the shapes of birds, snakes, and humans were characteristic. Monochrome wares increased in the Late Classic, and Fine Orange Ware imports from the Gulf Coast and Red Wares from N Yucatán increased.

Around the old centres of Chiapa de Corzo and Izapa, and at Kaminaljuyú, Teotihuacano influence was particularly strong, incl. Thin Orange Ware and Teotihuacano figurine types. Imports from the Petén and from Jaina island were also important. Another special ware, from the highlands around Cozumalhuapa (Guatemala), was San Juan Plumbate, vessels made from clay with a high percentage of iron compound, giving it a hard, vitrified, lustrous finish after firing at c 950°C.

Across N and central Yucatán, at Palenque and Comalcalco on the SW, Jaina island on the W, Dzibilchaltún in the centre, and Cobá and Tulum on the E, Jaina figurines were especially widespread, depicting members of all social classes, delicately modelled and painted wearing everyday dress or ceremonial regalia; later, they were mould-made, often as whistles. At Palenque a special tube-shaped form depicted heads in a vertical column. A unique blue dye, of unknown source, was used at Palenque and Jaina. More utilitarian wares were monochrome grey, orange, or red.

Classic N Mexico. Outside the Mesoamerican zone, ceramics in the Desert and Oasis cultures resembled contemporary US Southwest wares: Hohokam styles in N Sonora (eg, at Trincheras) and Mogollon styles in Chihuahua (eg, at Casas Grandes).

Postclassic Central Mexico. Teotihuacano styles waned with the collapse of the city, and migrating Chichimec tribes brought new traditions from the N. In the Early Postclassic there was confusion of styles as techniques, designs, and forms were integrated. New shapes of bowls, pipes, molcajetes, and incense burners were introduced. Out of these Toltec Coyotlatelco Ware and Mazapán Ware were developed, to which Fine Orange Ware from the Gulf Coast and Tohil Plumbate Ware from the Tajamulco area of highland Guatemala were added to form the Toltec ceramic complex. Fine Orange Ware is conspicuously absent at Tula itself although abundant at Chichén Itzá. Another tradition was 'Tula

Watercolored' or blanco levantado. Figurines were much simplified and cast in moulds, or imported from the Gulf Coast. Coyotlatelco (c AD 800–1000) was a red-on-buff ware; Mazapán (c 1000–1200), also red-on-buff, featured wavy red lines on the buff body.

In the Basin of Mexico a separate tradition, the Aztec Ceramic Sequence, developed out of the myriad N and indigenous wares. In the Early Postclassic Aztec I and II were distinctive Black-on-Orange matt wares, divided by minor changes in designs and forms (Aztec II from c AD 1200), and Plain Orange. Forms were carried over from the Classic, but base supports were slabs or spikes. In the Late Postclassic Aztec III and IV included polished Black-on-Red ware and polychrome Black-and-White-on-Red. New forms included a biconical pulque goblet and a wider variety of plates, jars, jugs, and malcates (spindlewhorls). Figurines were mould-made en masse. Aztec III and IV Orange Wares continued in use into the post-Conquest period, especially in rural areas, into the early 18C, before being replaced by European glazed wares.

In the S, especially in Puebla, in and around Cholula, polychrome Mixteca-Puebla Ware featured five- and six-colour vessels incl. black, blue, cream, orange, pale purple, and red, combining features from most preceding classic styles. At Teopanzolco (Morelos), contemporary Tlahuica Ware featured lacquered decoration in polychrome, and a related style was developed at Teotenango in the Valle de Toluca.

Postclassic W Mexico. The W received strong ceramic influences from the Mixteca-Puebla tradition and later from the Aztec Sequence. At Amapa (Nayarit) at least four sources were borrowed from the US Southwest (Pueblo styles), Mixteca-Puebla (especially in animal and deity motifs), Toltec Mazapán and Aztec sequences (especially in figurines), and Central America via coastal trade. The Colima tradition of figurines continued, incl. new double-jar forms, plates on stands, and Mixteca-Puebla decorative influences. Tarascan Michoacán had its own polychrome style, but farther S in Guerrero, Mixteca-Puebla and Aztec influences joined with elements from Costa Rica and Nicaragua and with the local flat, angularly geometric Mezcala style.

Postclassic Oaxaca. Oaxaqueño potters shared the Mixteca-Puebla style, helping to distribute it into W Mexico and possibly across the Gulf into Yucatán. Toltec Mazapán Ware and later Aztec II figurines were imported. Nevertheless, the long-established tradition of polished grey and black wares continued.

Postclassic Gulf Coast. In central Veracruz, Totonac (eg, Cempoala) fine-paste orange wares continued from the Classic. Tohil Plumbate Ware was imported through Toltec trade routes; and a new form of bottomless, cylindrical effigy censer, highly ornamented, called xantiles spread throughout the Gulf, into Puebla and Oaxaca, via Cholula into the Basin of Mexico, and into Maya N Yucatán. At El Tajín, Toltec wares frequently replaced local ones. In the Late Postclassic Mixteca-Puebla and Aztec Orange wares were imported.

In the Huastec N Gulf local styles prevailed: fine-paste Grey-on-White and pale Purple-on-Brown wares, and painting with tar (eg, on malacates). Toltec wares were imported but in the Late Postclassic new indigenous Huastec variants continued to follow earlier traditions: fine-paste, Black-on-White wares with geometric patterns, squash- and gourd-shaped vessels, and effigy vessels with Totonac scroll designs (which became popular as far inland as San Luis Potosí, to Lago de Chapala and into N Hidalgo; a few trade pieces even reached Texas and Oklahoma).

Postclassic Mayaland. Ceramic traditions of the Petén and of the S Maya zone waned as the focus of Maya civilization shifted into N Yucatán. In both regions monochrome wares increasingly replaced polychromes: red and orange in the Petén and white-slipped wares in Chiapa de Corzo. Imports included champ-levé decorated vessels and slate Grey Ware from Yucatán and the Gulf, Aztec Black-on-Red pots, and Mixteca-Puebla polychromes.

In N Yucatán a tradition of polychrome vessels in cream, grey, and orange developed in Tabasco and S Campeche. Slate Grey Ware and Plumbate Ware were traded in; and new forms included effigy vessel incense burners and 'frying pan' incense burners (a small plate and long handle form). Toltec conquest introduced Mazapán wares and Toltec figurines. Silho Fine Orange Wares were manufactured in continuance of the fine orange ware tradition of the Maya Lowlands.

Postclassic N Mexico. During the Toltec centuries Coyotlatelco and Mazapán wares were traded N into Zacatecas (eg, Chalchihuites) and Durango. Farther N Hohokam styles from Arizona filtered down into Sonora and Pueblo-Anasazi styles into Chihuahua. From c AD 1000 Casas Grandes grew into a major trade-centre between Mesoamerican and US Southwest cultures.

Mesoamerican Metallurgy

Contrary to popular belief, metallurgy in the New World was widespread and had reached a high degree of craftsmanship by the time Europeans arrived. It was independent of Old World connections. Knowledge of gold-, silver-, and copper-working was well established in Andean and NW S America by AD 1, but was not taken up in Mesoamerica until a half millennium later, when it was introduced from the N central Andes and Central America. The first known items were copper and gold trade pieces which began reaching Maya sites such as Altun Há (Belize) and Tazumal (El Salvador) in the Late Classic. Metalsmiths were working in Panama at Coclé by the 5C AD, and trade pieces found at Petén sites probably came from the site of Nicoya in Costa Rica, where similar pieces have been found, dated c AD 650. With these exceptions, all well-documented finds of metal artefacts in Mesoamerica are of Postclassic date.

Several arguments support the introduction of metallurgy from the S: abundant evidence, beginning in the Incipient Agriculture Period, of contact between NW S America, Central America, and Mexico—coastal trade along the Pacific began in the Preclassic; the sudden appearance and quantity of metal artefacts on the W coast; the lack of evidence showing early attempts at smelting—objects appear well-made and as an established craft; and similarities between many early Mesoamerican pieces and pieces from Central America. There is also a certain patterning to the introduction and spread of metalworking knowledge, proceeding from three centres: the S Maya region, spreading into Yucatán and S Mexico; and Nayarit and Guerrero on the W coast, spreading into central Mexico. Oaxaca later also became a centre of manufacture, but its craftsmen had less influence on styles of other smiths than did the Maya and W Mexican centres.

Some of the earliest finds of copper-work come from Amapa (Nayarit), dated c AD 8–900. Copper artefacts were placed in quantity in tombs and resemble pieces from Central America and Ecuador. By AD 900 copper and gold artefacts were being made in Oaxaca, knowledge having spread from Central America via Guatemala. In the Maya region, metallurgy was well established at Chichén Itzá in the Toltec phase, but fewer objects are known from Tula itself. A few of the most important Late Classic-Early Postclassic sites in W Mexico include centres at Zihuatanejo and the Barnard Site, both in Guerrero, and Apatzingán in Michoacán. Tarascan craftsmanship in copper- and gold-work became famous in Aztec times and continues to the present day. Despite a few early examples most Mesoamerican gold metallurgy is of Late Postclassic date. Most large Late Postclassic cities had metalsmiths.

The lack of iron in Mesoamerica limited the practical use of metals for tools. The base metals used were copper (most extensively), gold, silver, and tin. All were worked on their own, but alloys were also deliberately produced: bronze from copper and tin; and tumbaga from copper and gold, copper and silver, and sometimes as a naturally-occurring impurity. Several techniques were employed and developed to high standards of craftsmanship: cold-hammering was used to shape and stretch metal, even down to paper-thinness; annealing—heating the metal to restore its flexibility and workability in hammering and shaping; repoussé—pushing the sheet metal out from the back to produce the desired design in relief on the front (especially in Oaxaca, Central America, and Mayaland); casting in open moulds and with the lost wax technique—in which a wax model was made, then a clay mould around it, and fired to drain the melted wax from one or more ducts left in the clay for that purpose, molten metal poured into the clay mould, allowed to solidify, and released by breaking the mould; incising and inlaying with other metals or with precious stones; and alloying.

The metal artefacts of Mesoamerica had several functions. By far the most important was for ornament. Because nothing harder than bronze could be made, there was not a large variety of metal tools and weapons, although axes were numerous. It has also been suggested that the success of Tarascan resistance to Aztec invasions was due in part to their more extensive use of bronze. Ornaments in abundance included ear and lip spools, rings, bracelets, necklaces, beads, pins, bells, and plaques. There were also cast figurines in smaller numbers. From the Sacred Cenote at Chichén Itzá, and from other Maya sites and Central America, come large repoussé and incised dishes, plaques, and breast plates. Tools included copper awls, needles, pins, tweezers, fish hooks, small knives, and axeheads, many of the last as miniatures. In Western Mexico, particularly at the Barnard Site, bronze items were found amongst the general household refuse, indicating its widespread use for common objects rather than for luxury items only. Lastly, in certain regions metals were used as 'exchange media' (ie, money): small copper axeheads were used extensively in Western Mexico and in the Postclassic Mixtec kingdoms in the Pacific coastal trade; and amongst the items on tribute lists were quotas of copper and gold-dust in quills.

Mesoamerican Architecture

Introduction (principles, elements and construction techniques)

As in Mesoamerican ceramics and religious practices, there were several universal features alongside regional variation. From at least the Middle Preclassic, communities were laid out observing formal principles. Ceremonial centres included pyramids, temples, and other buildings, oriented to the cardinal points, and surrounded by the dwellings of élite and commoners. The first principle was therefore planning. Availability of water, defensive position, and economic advantages (for agriculture, trade, and raw materials) were important in choices of sites. Generally, sites were more compact, and domestic architecture more dense and apartment-like in the Highlands, more scattered in small groups of several dwellings each in Mayaland. The patio format was universal. Ceremonial centres were correspondingly the cores of dense metropolises or at the centre of looser communities decreasing in density away from the centre. Highland centres tended to be more quadrangular, with formal layouts of streets and blocks; Maya cities used causeways to connect scattered elements around less well-defined ceremonial plazas, palaces, and lesser buildings.

A second principle was monumentality. Ceremonial centres were special precincts, designed to transcend basic needs and to serve the ideological or spiritual needs of the community. Their monumentality was a deliberate statement of contrast with the more fundamental dwellings.

A third principle was space. To serve the community's spiritual needs, Mesoamerican planners became expert in the rhythmic ordering of open spaces. Each ceremonial plaza was the result of deliberate initial planning and adherence to that plan in subsequent rebuildings and additions.

The elements comprising ceremonial centres included platforms, terraces, and ramps, organized around plazas and esplanades; parts were connected or divided by avenues, streets, alleys, and causeways. Buildings included the stepped pyramid, temple, ball court, ceremonial precinct and coatepantli wall, market, 'palace' (élite dwelling), tzompantli, tomb, and circuit or defensive wall; functional elements included roads, canals, drains, cisterns, and aqueducts.

Different construction techniques and artistic embellishments developed into regional styles and changed through time. Techniques included talud-tablero facing, the use of cut and uncut facing slabs (veneers) over rubble cores, projecting tenons to secure facings, niches, the corbel arch, cornicing, and decorative embellishments in stucco, plaster, mosaics, and paint. Sculpture, modelling, and painting were integral parts. The Maya were famous for elaborately sculpted façades and the central Mexicans for garishly painted stone sculptured facings. Inside, murals on plastered walls were equally important. Apart from masonry, adobe bricks, thatch, and wood were used extensively in domestic architecture. Fired bricks were rarely used—they occur mostly in the Late Postclassic Maya region, but earlier examples are known at Comalcalco, Corozal (Belize), and Zacualpa (Guatemala); it is uncertain whether the bricks at Tula were deliberately fired or the result of conflagration. At Late Postclassic Tizatlán bricks were used for walls, stairs, altar tables, and benches.

Preclassic Architecture

The idea of a ceremonial centre orientated to the cardinal points may have been an Olmec invention. Simultaneously, stepped pyramids as temple platforms, staircases, and ramps were developed in the Basin of Mexico. The earliest Olmec platforms and terraces were of earth; the first stone-faced pyramid was at Cuicuilco in the Basin, although its round plan was atypical of later Mesoamerican development. The idea of the temple platform was in keeping with a longer tradition of building houses on platforms. As the houses of gods, temples were in time naturally distinguished in elevation from common dwellings. Temple buildings changed little in size and remained relatively simple in their interiors throughout Mesoamerican prehistory, while the size of platforms increased. In some cases pyramids were also used for burials, but their primary purpose was an elevated stage on and in front of which ceremonies were performed for spectators below.

Classic Central Mexico

The first architectural tradition to influence other regions as a set of elements and style, was Teotihuacán's. The entire concept of Teotihuacano architecture was one of monumentality: the ceremonial centre served as a geometric position from which to observe relations between the Sun and Earth. Its first structure was the Pirámide del Sol, oriented to coincide with the annual zenith setting of 21 June, and all subsequent planning of the city was governed by this axis. Teotihuacano style began a central Mexican tradition of opposing massive solid forms to corresponding open spaces: plazas were built in front of each pyramid, delimited by subsidiary pyramids and buildings. Around the centre, élite courtyard palaces were arranged using the same juxtaposition of mass and space on a smaller scale. Around these was the grid-plan of streets and apartments around patios.

Teotihuacán's pyramids were stepped, artificial mounds of earth and rubble, faced with stone, and periodically enlarged, encasing the earlier inside the later. The major functional component developed at Teotihuacán, and subsequently spread throughout Mesoamerica (although its origins are as yet uncertain), was the facing technique known as talud-tablero. It comprised, originally, two parts: a sloping base (talud) cantilevered by a vertical face (tablero) formed by a rectangular panel framed in mouldings. Frequently, the recessed portion of the tablero was painted or sculpted or both. Throughout central Mexico locally abundant tezontle was used.

The Pirámide del Sol at Teotihuacán was too massive, and begun before the invention of talud-tablero assemblage, to make use of them without necessitating hundreds of steps to achieve the height. Instead, it comprised huge stages with sloping sides, a style retained into the Postclassic for achieving height, reserving talud-tablero facing for smaller pyramids, platforms, and terraces.

Several regional variations of talud-tablero construction were developed in the later Classic: at Cholula tableros were given an extra moulding inside the main frame and taluds were slightly concave; at Xochicalco taluds became the main component, tableros reduced, and a 'flying' or projecting cornice added above it—all three parts completely and intricately carved. The 'flying' cornice, an inverted counterpart to the talud, originated at El Tajín. Other El Tajín developments were the use of chiaroscuro (using the effects of light and shade to create the impression of a third dimension) and niches, made up of rectangular frames of slabs each set inside the previous one and recessed (the Pirámide de los Nichos, with 365 niches, is the best known example). Teotihuacán talud-tablero use spread S and was faithfully copied at Kaminaljuyú (Guatemala), where a Teotihuacán-like centre was built.

Temple remains in central Mexico, especially before the Postclassic, are rare. Basically, all temples were rectangular, flat-roofed, one- or two-roomed buildings. They had front doorways but no windows, and were primarily backdrops for ceremonies performed in front of them. In some cases secret cult temples or altars were in caves or in circular, conical-roofed temples.

Courtyard palaces were another major element at Teotihuacán. Each side was an independent façade, most commonly with a two-columned porch. Subsidiary units filled in the corners of the rectangle, but were set back, making the courtyard appear to be open. The whole group was set atop a low talud-tablero-faced platform and many wall bases were themselves sloped, and the two resulting planes often used to divide murals on them into fields.

Finally, there is no obvious fortification at Teotihuacán. The Classic Period in central Mexico was relatively peaceful although elements of increased violence are recognizable in later murals and sculptures. The formidable compounds of the Ciudadela and the Market could, no doubt, have been used for defence and it has been suggested that the pyramid was a last resort in fighting. (Late codices depict fighting on pyramids, and the Mesoamerican symbol of defeat or capture of a town was a dominated or fallen temple–pyramid.)

Classic S Mexico

S Highland Zapotec and Mixtec styles developed contemporaneously with Teotihuacano style, using huge roughly shaped quartzite blocks. Monte Albán was on a hilltop, artificially altered to form a huge sunken plaza surrounded by platforms, some contiguous, and numerous smaller sunken plazas.

Distinctive Zapotec features include the sunken plaza, enclosed groupings, the use of monolithic lintels and jambs with masonry columns, exceptionally wide staircases, and tombs beneath courtyards and patios. Unlike Teotihuacán, an I-shaped ball court was an integral part of the site. Early practice at Monte Albán was to cover earthen mounds with flat slabs incised with figures (Danzantes) in low relief; later, from the Early Classic, these were replaced by panelled friezes on pyramids, platforms, and terraces. Zapotec talud-tablero variations included two overlapping tablero planes. As at Teotihuacán, dwellings were on the patio-plan.

Western Mexico

Development during the Late Preclassic and Classic was independent of central Mexico. The most striking architectural specialization was the shaft- or chamber-tomb, an L-shaped structure comprising a subterranean, vertical shaft, cut into the tezontle, usually 4–6m deep, with one or more projecting, horizontal burial chambers. From c AD 600 W Mexicans began to build planned, rectangular ceremonial plazas, the earliest examples using Teotihuacano talud-tablero construction and I-shaped ball courts (eg, Amapa and Tingambato).

Postclassic Central Mexico

The Toltecs inherited remnants of Teotihuacano architectural principles, incl. the lack of obvious fortifications at Tula, but contributed no major innovations in structural technique; in general their execution is said to be poorer, lacking the niceties of Teotihuacano lattice-work and cantilevered tableros. They did, however, initiate several bold styles in design, which continued into the Late Postclassic, and monumental power of structures at Tula and Chichén Itzá is impressive.

The Toltecs added 'aprons' flanking the staircases of the principal pyramid at Tula, acting as a planar-transition from the steep slope of the step faces of the pyramid and the slope of the staircase itself. Another innovation was the use of tenons, projecting from the face of the Pirámide de Quetzalcóatl and into the core, to hold the heavy facing slabs in place. The inbuilt cylindrical drainage ducts of this pyramid, also innovative, still function today.

Toltec taluds-tableros were yet another variation, the tableros being a double-square panel crowned with a frieze. The tablero and frieze were marked out with three wide, flattish, raised mouldings, and both were carved, coated in plaster, and painted. There are hints of Teotihuacano style in the jaguars and pumas, and hints of Monte Albán and Mitla styles (below) in the multi-faceted composition of the tableros, but the overall combination is decidedly Toltec. Toltec builders also adapted the courtyard palace plan. The Palacio Quemado at Tula, paralleled by the Templo de los Guerreros at Chichén Itzá, comprised three contiguous patio-units; and the whole plan included a long colonnaded hall, breaking with all previous courtyard-palace tradition. Such design was brought from the Toltecs' N homeland and was in keeping with their use of columned porticoes on palaces and temples. The use of columns allowed for larger rooms and central, skylight openings. Toltec temples differed little from their Classic predecessors: they were rectangular, one- or two-roomed, and flat-roofed. Added to these were the columned porch and stone column roof supports, in the forms of serpents and atlante warriors, respectively. These were made up of carved drum sections, fitted with mortice and tenon joints; the serpent columns supported the roof on their tails with the serpent's head resting on the platform surface, each at right-angles to the shaft of the column.

A final Toltec addition to the ceremonial centre was the idea of enclosing the sacred precinct within a wall, called a coatepantli after its serpent (cóatl) decoration. (At Tula only one section survives, and it is not certain that it entirely enclosed the precinct as it did at Aztec Tenochtitlán.) It was carved on both faces, formed by double taluds, plastered over.

Toltec houses are less well known. They were of stone foundations with adobe walls and flat roofs, apartment-like, but perhaps less contiguous than the housing at Teotihuacán. In the few that have been excavated there were hints of socio-economic differentiation, and most had a curious L-plan entrance into the courtyard or patio, thus ensuring the privacy of the unit and the intimacy of the component apartments, and possibly a defensive measure as well.

Postclassic Gulf Coast

El Tajín's talud-tablero variation has been described. The plan of the city comprised two distinct zones, earlier and later, each with a different orientation. The earlier El Tajín, of the Pirámide de los Nichos and ball court with carved narrative panels, was oriented to the cardinal points and developed the use of 'flying' cornices and niches. The later site, Tajín Chico, had structures of greater complexity, grouped on long terraces and platforms on a natural outcrop. Here there were courtyard groups reminiscent of Mitla and platforms with 'flying' cornices like those at Xochicalco. Maya influence can be seen in the use of massive roof slabs and of pumice and lime 'concrete', poured on roofs and over arches to form a solid mass when dry; arches were also sometimes formed when projecting cornice wings met at the tips of adjacent corner buildings; and Maya-like doorways were used in the buildings around courtyards. Several similar sites are scattered around central Veracruz.

In the Huasteca (N Veracruz–S Tamaulipas) there developed a style which borrowed from several sources to the S, but whose outstanding feature, by way of contrast, was a proliferation of round structures. In no other place in Mesoamerica was the round temple–platform the norm: in the Huasteca, all principal sites used wide, low, round platforms in their plazas. And a modified form passed into the Late Postclassic Aztec repertoire of temples dedicated to Ehecatl–Quetzalcóatl.

Postclassic N Mexico

For Early Postclassic N Mesoamerica, two plan-groups predominate. The first is exemplified by Las Ranas and Toluquilla on the plateau of N Querétaro. Each was a string of aligned and grouped terraces, buildings, and ball courts along narrow ridges. Except for their linear plan, their architectural features were borrowed from El Tajín, Xochicalco, and through these, from Maya traditions.

The second group is a series of hilltop forts, of which La Quemada is the best example, but including the Chalchihuites sites as well. These were acropolis towns, presumably built for defence, along the N frontiers of Toltec influence, but their precise relation to Tula is uncertain. The site of Alta Vista in Zacatecas appears to have the prototypes for the colonnaded halls and skull racks of Tula and the Late Postclassic.

The Late Postclassic

Architecture became more homogeneous in the Late Postclassic, perhaps due to Aztec expansion and influence. Regional styles were Aztec in central Mexico, Tarascan in Michoacán, and Mixtec in Oaxaca.

The Aztecs inherited much from the Toltecs, but they finally abandoned the use of talud-tablero construction. Aztec pyramid–platforms were simply steps of sloping faces. Mouldings on the faces, however, visually preserved a talud-tablero effect, indicating the endurance of the form.

The Aztec period, more than any previous period, was one of metropolitan concentrations, especially in the Basin of Mexico and the adjacent valleys of Toluca, Morelos, and Puebla–Tlaxcala; Tenochtitlán, Tlatelolco, and Xaltocán were rare as island cities. Aztec innovation engulfed the ceremonial core within the metropolis more than ever, decreasing its prominence but not necessarily its dominance. Detailed mapping of Tula, Monte Albán, and Teotihuacán has somewhat diminished this Classic–Postclassic difference, but Aztec Tenochtitlán included at least two major ceremonial precincts, many smaller ones, and precincts in each nearby city. This must have decreased the predominance of any one centre for the local populace and perhaps increased the use of precinct enclosure walls. The pyramids at Tenayuca and Tlatelolco, and of Teopanzolco in Cuernavaca, give the best idea of what the Teocalli precinct at Tenochtitlán looked like, a stereotyped form with pyramid–platform, double-staircase and twin temples on top, ball court, tzompantli, subsidiary pyramid–platforms and temples, and palaces. This 'formula' was the culmination of Toltec and earlier elements, compacted and enclosed within the metropolis. Aztec innovations included the use of twin temples and staircases, a plain pyramid profile, and a steepened section at the top of the staircases as a sort of 'crown'. From the Toltecs they copied the building of porches on temple fronts and aprons on either side of staircases.

The Aztecs also built isolated temples in places of difficult access (eg, Tepozteco near Tepoztlán, and Malinalco). Malinalco, a group of temples for the exclusive Eagle and Jaguar warrior cults, passes from architecture to truly monumental sculpture, as most of the 'buildings' were literally carved out of the cliff face, incl. figures sitting on the temple steps and porch. At other sites they adopted local traditions. For example at Calixtlahuaca, a conquered Matlazinca town in the Valle de Toluca, the monumental buildings were scattered along the hillside, on top, and at the base. Contrasting with Tenochtitlán, the hilltop cities of Teotenango and Tlaxcala were amassed groups of deep plazas surrounded by pyramids and platform–terraces up the hill-slopes.

Aztec palaces are described in 16C chronicles, and the best excavated example is Nezahualcóyotl's palace at Texcoco (Rte 20). Many were royal retreats, but Axayácatl and Moctezuma II also had palaces adjacent to the Templo Mayor in downtown Tenochtitlán. According to the descriptions these comprised courtyards with sets of surrounding buildings, some in open groups, some individual, and some long and continuous. Smaller, excavated house groups show similar patio-plans. Other Aztec buildings were the state and priestly colleges (telpochcalli and calmecac). These were also courtyards surrounded by a mass of intercommunicating buildings and perhaps a small platform and shrine.

Lastly, there are the Aztec aqueducts, causeways, and dikes. None was new, as Mesoamericans had long used dams, canals, irrigated terraces, underfloor and tube drains, and massive ramps to link hillsides; the Aztec innovation was one of scale and sheer audacity, coupled with the fact that they were building over water. The causeways connecting Tenochtitlán with the mainland were at once civilian and military—they facilitated trade but were also fitted with removable sections at intervals. The aqueducts bringing spring-water from Chapultepec and Coyoacán and the dike to hold back the brackish waters of Lago de Texcoco were large enterprises necessitated by the density of the city's population and the need to feed it. The Aztecs learned to use foundation piling and to lighten the load of a structure by facing it with tezontle to counteract the problem of subsidence.

Mesoamerican architectural traditions continued in Postclassic W Mexico, but one new form developed by the Tarascans was the yácata. This was a circular temple platform, supporting a thatched, circular temple and connected by a short rectangular platform of the same height to a wider rectangular platform, forming a 'T'. Alignments of yácatas were built on top of long rectangular platforms, with wide staircases on the side of the circular components, and with most of the top left open in front of the T-component, presumably as ceremonial space. Excavation has revealed that burials were placed in the angles of the T and circular components and sometimes periodically re-used.

A third Postclassic tradition developed in Mixtec Oaxaca. Pyramid–platforms were less important while tombs and palatial complexes became the focuses of distinctive decorations. Mixtec valley-cities developed a variation of the court-yard palace using large, square courtyard assemblages, somewhat isolated and self-sufficient—almost suburban villas. This was a departure from the centralized precinct. The classic example is Mitla, where the decorative variations in the quadrangles may represent chronological differences. In some cases the four buildings of the quadrangle have corner gaps, leaving the court-yard open; in other cases the corners are joined. The buildings are on long platforms with wide staircases up to colonnaded porches, each with a unique, independent façade. Smooth-grained, easy to work beige or pink trachyte slabs were used instead of the quartzites of Monte Albán. The Mixtecs also used poured concrete roofs, presumably learned from the Maya. On walls and in tombs beneath the courtyards decoration was of two kinds: carved in relief on the block masonry faces and framed mosaics made up of hundreds of small slabs. At Mitla alone there are some 150 surviving fretwork carvings and mosaics, composed of variations of stepped-fret, spiral, and geometric patterns and frames in repeated, mirrored, and lattice-like detail.

Another Mixtec tradition was to build hilltop fortress towns. Yagul in Oaxaca is the most accessible example but others are Tepexi el Viejo in Puebla and Zapotec Guiengola in S Oaxaca. These were isolated sites, reflecting the endemic warfare between Mixtec and Zapotec, and later Aztec. Decorative mosaics similar to those at Mitla can be seen on several structures at Yagul.

In the Late Postclassic Gulf Coast Huasteca round platforms predominated. At the neighbouring Totonac capital of Cempoala there was a mixture of styles: pyramids were squat and bulky as at Cholula, stairs included the Aztec change of pitch at the top, palaces resembled the multi-chambered buildings of the Maya, and a circuit wall may also reflect Maya influence.

Maya Architecture

Maya traditions were quite different from Mexican ones, although most of the same elements were used. Maya architects used similar combinations of mass and space but to them interiors were less important. Ceremonial centres were of two types: well-planned central cores surrounded by clustered dwelling groups; and linear patterns of ceremonial buildings along river frontages.

Maya pyramids and temples were more diverse than their Mexican counterparts, chiefly because of regional styles of embellishment. Pyramids served the same function of supporting a temple, but in many cases the temples were false ones—that is, not intended to be entered. Maya pyramids were also more complex, with more facets to their ground plans; they usually had staircases on all four sides; the sides were made up of many more, low steps, rising at much steeper angles; and they were generally smaller, their steepness making the ratio of height to plan-space much greater. They ranged, however, from the squat, many-faceted Early Classic pyramids at Tikal and Uaxactún, to the steep, tall, rectangular ones of the Late Classic.

Temples often occupied the entire top of the pyramid, the steeply-angled plane of the sides giving way only to the vertical temple walls. The massive masonry blocks used made temple interiors cramped. Roofs were flat but ceilings were formed by corbel vaults whose capstones ran the entire length of the vault. The whole was stabilized by the massive weight of rubble infill above the arch and a poured concrete roof. Elaborate crests, or 'combs', above doorways added to the height. A common grouping was of three vaulted rooms with tower-like pyramids supporting false temples with crests, individual or adjoined on a single platform.

The walls of Maya buildings were intricately and elaborately decorated. They usually comprised three or more zones: a plain lower section, a dividing cornice with decorative frieze, and the comb. The diversity of decorative styles included repetitive geometric patterns, masks of gods and monsters, and sets of colonnettes and framing cornices, executed in sculpted plaster, carving, or mosaics of small slabs.

Thus three elements of Maya architecture are distinctive: roof-combs, corbel arches, and the Maya talud-tablero, in which both parts were slopes (often nearly the same as the slope of the pyramid itself). The corbel arch was a Protoclassic invention, first used in tombs, later in temples, palaces, and staircases.

Maya palaces were also distinctive. Unlike Aztec palaces (residential) or Mixtec ones (religious and funereal), the purpose of Maya palaces is less certain. Several plans were used, but always on platforms and with multi-chambered, corbel-vaulted sets of buildings. Examples include single, long platforms, quadrangles, three-sided courts, and connected lengths at various angles. Façades were often differentially decorated and of different dates; some were a single chamber deep, others two or three chambers deep and intercommunicating.

The accumulated monuments of Maya plazas show less coherence than many central Mexican sites. Differently dated sets of buildings, coherent amongst themselves, often had several orientations, suggesting less control through time. This seeming lack of central planning may be due in part to the less rigid plans of Maya cities in general, and to difficulties in surveying alignments in jungle undergrowth. Parts of Maya cities were connected by short causeways (sacbéob, sing. sacbé) and longer ones connected cities between ceremonial plazas. Sacbéob were constructed of large stone blocks, covered with levelled gravel and plastered over. Sometimes a monumental archway was erected at the end of a sacbé, at the entrance to the plaza. The longest sacbé, c 100km, runs between Cobá and Yaxuná in Yucatán.

A long tradition in Maya city-planning was concern for defence. There are many examples of circuit walls of both Classic and Postclassic date: Aké, Becán, Chacchab, Champotón, Cuca, Ichpaatún, Mayapán, Palenque, Tulum, and Xelha. Competition between cities was well recorded on stone and plaster in the Classic, and in the codices in the Postclassic.

There were several distinct regional styles.

Classic Petén Maya Style. Elements of Classic Maya styles began to emerge in the Late Preclassic when Petén sites such as Tikal and Uaxactún laid out their ceremonial plazas with pyramids, corbelled temples, and tombs, and carved façades with masks, snakes, and repetitive geometric motifs. Three variants quickly developed.

Río Bec Style, in the N Petén during the 7C AD, was characterized by tripartite platform groups: lavishly decorated central building, flanking towers, and sometimes a central tower. Each tower was a stylized pyramid whose false stairs, at only 20° from vertical, led to a false temple, surmounted by a sculpted roof-comb. Typical sites include Río Bec, Becán, Xpuhil, and Chicanná.

Chenes Style of NW Campeche was a slightly later variant of Río Bec. It featured temples whose doorways were gaping, stylized earth-monster or serpent mouths, with fangs hanging down from the lintel, and elaborate coils and sculptured masks. Archetypal is Hochob, from which the style spread widely—eg, the Pirámide del Adivino at Uxmal and the Nunnery Annexe at Chichén Itzá.

Puuc Style was a Late Classic style developed directly from Classic Petén in central Yucatán and continuing to c AD 900. It borrowed elements from Río Bec and Chenes styles, and featured freestanding palace complexes around large quadrangles, monumental archways, and multi-storeyed interior-chambered pyramids. Buildings were multi-chambered and corbel-arched, with rectangular doorways divided by sets of columns. Façades were covered with limestone veneers divided by cornices into an undecorated lower section and upper friezes of carved stucco lattice-work, stepped-frets, serpents, and masks with protruding noses (Chac masks). Decorative bands of cornice mouldings encircled the buildings alternating with sets of attached colonnettes (half-columns) and framed friezes. Typical sites include Kabah, Labná, Sayil, Uxmal, and numerous smaller sites.

Palenque Style exemplifies the W Maya region, using Classic Petén elements but featuring less ponderous buildings of double-ranged galleries of corbelled rooms with open, colonnaded fronts, a multi-storeyed tower, latticed roof-combs, and a pyramid used as a tomb. Comalcalco and Piedras Negras (Guatemala) are similar, but only 45km away, across the Río Usumacinta, Yaxchilán is of heavy, Classic Petén style, demonstrating the overlapping ranges of styles.

In *N Yucatán* several Late Classic styles co-existed: Puuc with veneer-masonry, pyramids and palaces, carved stucco and stone façades of masks, roof-combs, and 'flying' façades. Variations included block-masonry, carving in stucco only, or the absence of flying cornices on roof-combs (eg, Cobá and Oxkintok). At Chichén Itzá block-masonry was used, but little façade decoration. Veneer-masonry gradually replaced block-masonry in the Late Classic. At Dzibilchaltún the Templo de las Muñecas is a rare example with functional windows.

Highland Maya Style. Here two distinct styles developed from typical, Early Classic Maya features. Kaminaljuyú adopted the Teotihuacán style, mixing the two liberally; talud–tablero construction was copied faithfully. Rival cities at San Antonio Frutal and Copán (Honduras) ascribed faithfully to Classic Petén Maya concepts from the N and Pacific coastal elements to the S.

Toltec-Maya Style. There was little monumental construction in the Early Postclassic S Maya Lowlands. In the N Lowlands, Classic Petén and Puuc styles were mixed with Mexican elements brought in by the Toltecs in the 10C and 11C: porches on temples, serpent columns, and long, colonnaded palaces.

Ball Courts and the Ball Game

Ball courts, built throughout Mesoamerica, were an integral part of the ceremonial complex. Versions of the game spread as far N as the Southwest USA and E to the Caribbean Antilles. The game was of Preclassic origin and by the Middle Classic had become a state cult in which human sacrifice played an important part. The earliest known ball court was at Olmec San Lorenzo, and the game is thought to have been invented in Veracruz, the home of the rubber tree. It spread quickly, perhaps with the cacao trade, and is known from figurines of ball-players with pads on their arms, knees, and hands at Tlatilco, Tlapacoya, and Cuicuilco to have been played in Preclassic central Mexico as well.

Early evidence of the game as a cult comes from relief carvings at Dainzú (Oaxaca), and there are scenes of ball-player sacrifice at Chichén Itzá, El Tajín, and Cotzumalhuapa (Guatemala). After AD 900 the game ceased to be a cult and underwent major rule changes, but remained a ritual activity. The cult game may have been a ritual re-enactment of a myth in which the Sun-god died and was reborn as the Maize god; pulque-drinking is also thought to have been connected with it. Three objects associated with ball-playing have been found in abundance, and in miniature on figurines: yugos, hachas, and palmas. Yugos are U-shaped stones (a few closed-ended examples are also known), weighing c 15–30kg, and usually elaborately carved. They appear to have been ceremonial imitations of the protective belts (probably of wood and leather) worn by players, as seen on figurines. Hachas are thin stone heads or wedges, usually carved and sometimes with a deep notch or tenon on the back. They may have been mounted ball court markers. Palmas, later in date and mostly from Veracruz, are stone, usually fan-shaped with a notch in the upper end, and concave based, possibly for mounting on a convex edging on the ball court; they were also elaborately carved. All three items were part of ball game ritual but their exact connections to the game and to each other are uncertain, although some codices depict palmas resting on yugos. Rules of play varied in time and by region: the Maya game was called pok-ta-pok, the Mexican game, tlachtli. The earliest figurines are heavily padded and Spanish chroniclers described the game as very rough. The solid rubber ball could be as large as 30cm in diameter and up to 2.25 kg. With 2 to 11 players per team, the ball had to be kept in motion using only the hips, knees, and elbows (although Dainzú carvings depict players holding the ball in their hands, and in the Tepantitla murals at Teotihuacán and in some Western Mexican figurines players are depicted with bats). Goals were scored when the ball passed through the rings or hit the hachas used as markers; in one version the game ended when one goal was scored. The consequences of losing also varied, and could result in sacrificial death, or in a free-for-all in which the winning team had rights to anything worn by the losing team's supporters—if they could be caught.

The classic ball court shape was an uppercase I, but sides varied through time. In the Classic they were usually wide viewing platforms with lower walls sloping into the court's field; in the Postclassic they were usually vertical and taller than in the Classic, with the goals set high up in the wall face. Goals were markers or stone rings set permanently in the masonry, dividing the field of play into two or three zones. The first known ring-markers were at Cobá, whence they spread to central Mexican courts (eg, Xochicalco, Tula, Teotenango, and Aztec sites).

This basic picture varied regionally. At Teotihuacán the game was played in an open field rather than in a stone court, and used end-goals. In Western Mexico the centre-marker, usually a tenoned head, was more common; at Amapa, however, the centre-marker was a cup set atop a stump. Stone courts varied from completely enclosed, with sets of steps down into the playing field (eg, Monte Albán and Yagul); to shallower enclosed courts, with wide, gently sloping sides up to a vertical wall and ring-goals (eg, Xochicalco and Tula); to large, elaborate affairs with high spectator platforms and temples at the ends (eg, Chichén Itzá); to smaller courts with separate side and end sections (eg, Copán or Amapa); to courts of earthen parts (eg, Casas Grandes).

Aztec and Texcocan rulers

Rulers of Tenochtitlán
Acamapichtli 1372–91
Huitzilíhuitl 1391–1415
Chimalpopoca 1415–26
Itzcóatl 1426–40
Moctezuma I Ilhuicamina 1440–68
Axayácatl 1468–81
Tizoc 1481–86
Ahuítzotl 1486–1502
Moctezuma II Xocoyotzin 1502–20
Cuitláhuac 1520
Cuauhtémoc 1520–25
Tlacotzin Cihuacóatl 1525–26
Don Diego Huanitzin 1539–42

Rulers of Texcoco
Quinatzin c 1300–1357
Techotlala c 1357–1409
Ixtlilxóchitl 1409–18
Tezozómoc (of Azcapotzalco) 1418–26
Maxtla (of Azcapotzalco) 1426–28
Nezahualcóyotl 1418–72 (1418–31 in exile)
Nezahualpilli 1472–1515
Cacamatzin 1515–20
Coanacochtzin 1520–21
Don Fernando Ixtlilxóchitl 1521–31

A History of Mexico

The Conquest

Spaniards from Cuba had been shipwrecked on the coast of Yucatán in 1511. In 1517 and 1518 two expeditions followed, under Francisco Hernández de Córdoba and Juan de Grijalva, the second sailing up the coast of Veracruz. In 1519, without proper sanction, Hernán Cortés, coming from Cuba with some 600 men and 16 horses in ten ships, made landfall first on the Tabasco coast and then on the coast of Veracruz. Here he founded Villa Rica de la Veracruz and struck inland, making an alliance with the Tlaxcaltecans, who joined him to march on Tenochtitlán, which he entered on 3 Nov. 1519. Moctezuma II received and lodged the Spaniards hospitably enough. Leaving a garrison in Tenochtitlán, Cortés returned to the coast to defeat the expedition of Pánfilo de Narváez, sent from Cuba to arrest him, and came back to find that the garrison, under Pedro de Alvarado, had stirred the enmity of the Aztecs. Persuaded, it is said, by Cortés to appeal to his people for calm, Moctezuma was stoned by them and died from a head wound (30 June 1520). The Spaniards' retreat that night (Noche Triste) from Tenochtitlán, with their Tlaxcaltecan allies, turned into a rout.

Cortés retired to Tlaxcala where he built brigantines to aid a fresh attempt on Tenochtitlán, at first beaten off by the Aztecs under Cuauhtémoc. After a siege of 75 days, Aztec power was destroyed, and the subject peoples of the Aztec empire submitted to the conquerors. Cortés's personal rule (1522–24) established Spanish power over what he called New Spain (a name variously interpreted; gradually to expand until the 18C, to include what is now the S USA and most of modern Mexico). He governed with moderation despite the pressure on him to grant encomiendas and lands, of which there were not enough to share among his followers and other adventurers arriving from Spain. His absence (1524–26) on a disastrous expedition to Honduras led to anarchic and corrupt government in Mexico, and the machinations of his enemies in Spain determined him to return home to defend himself. He took care to take with him many Mexican delights to please Charles V. The story of the first audiencia appointed by the Crown to rule New Spain (1527–30) is a catalogue of horrors. While extending the Conquest into Michoacán and founding the kingdom of Nueva Galicia, its president, Nuño de Guzmán, was responsible for genocide on a grand scale. When the second audiencia arrived late in 1530, to right the wrongs done by the first and at the urgent pleading of Cortés and Bp de Zumárraga, Guzmán was at large in the W and any Indian confidence in Spanish rule had all but collapsed. The second audiencia (1530–35) established law and order, and its most famous oidor, the compassionate Vasco de Quiroga, worked all out to try to make up for Guzmán's atrocities among the Tarascans in Michoacán. After a second period in New Spain (1539–40), out of government, but maintaining the state due to him as marqués del Valle de Oaxaca (a vast landholding), Cortés returned disillusioned to Spain, to die there in 1547. His arch-rival Guzmán had been sent back to face trial in 1537. In 1566 a conspiracy under the titular headship of Cortés's legitimate son Martín (2nd marqués del Valle de Oaxaca) to overthrow the government of New Spain and install himself as king was discovered. Retribution on real and supposed conspirators was so savage that Philip II disowned the judge he himself had sent.

The conquest of the SE was undertaken between 1522 and 1549: Soconusco, Tabasco, and Chiapas by Cortés's men in 1522–28; the Yucatán, after a struggle, by Francisco de Montejo and his son and nephew (both also Francisco). The discovery of silver (at Culiacán, Compostela, Bolaños, Zacatecas) helped push the frontier northwards to Nueva Vizcaya, Nuevo León, and Nuevo México, in face of constant harassment (c 1550–90) by fierce desert tribes, generically called chichimecs, who were threatened with displacement. Cortés himself tried to colonize the pearl coast of Baja California (1535–36).

The Conversion

The role of the Church in furthering and consolidating the Conquest is indisputable. Its secular organization began with the titular bishopric of Yucatán in 1519 and the see of Tlaxcala (later moved to Puebla) in 1526. Appointment to livings, supervision of the clergy, and control of church revenues were matters for the Crown. A bull of Pope Leo X, issued in 1521, gave the regulars extraordinary powers and forbade any secular priest from interfering in their sphere.

Three Flemish Franciscans arrived in 1523, the first of those Mendicant friars whose labours in New Spain were to have so staggering an effect. In 1524 arrived 12 more Franciscans, the Apostolic Twelve, who walked barefoot from Veracruz to Mexico and were received with great reverence by Cortés and his followers, to the astonishment of Cuauhtémoc and the Indian chiefs. A few more arrived each year. There were never enough of them, but they began to plant their convents—c 160 by 1590, perhaps c 600 friars—in the centre of New Spain, to the W and NW, and in Yucatán. Friars could impose a peace far more effectively than an encomendero or a garrison. The first few Dominicans arrived in 1526—it was a Dominican, Bartolomé de las Casas, who was the fieriest advocate of Indian rights against the encomenderos; the first Augustinians in 1533. The former founded some convents in the central region and then progressed SE to Oaxaca and Chiapas—75 convents by the end of the century and c 400 friars. The latter spread N and W of the Valley of Mexico, to present-day Hidalgo and to Michoacán, with roughly the same number of establishments and friars as the Dominicans. Of the Mendicants the Franciscans enjoyed the greatest popularity among the Indians for their humility, their dedication to unremitting hard work—in building, teaching and imparting skills, administering the sacraments—their quickly acquired fluency in native tongues, and the staunch protection they afforded against the cruelty and demands of Spanish civilians. Unlike any other great conversion in Christian history this one was accomplished with remarkable speed, relatively gently, and bloodlessly. The reasons deduced for such success are the strong support of the king-emperor, backed by the papacy and the viceregal government; the extraordinary character of the friars themselves; resemblances between the old and new religions (a love for images, for prayers like incantations, for holy water, for stiff physical penance); the docility of the Indians; and weariness with the barbarities and demands of paganism. The Indians took, among other things, with alacrity to baptism (coming back whenever they could to be baptized again) and to confession (often plunging into the Lago de Texcoco and swimming after the friars in their boats to confess while treading water). By the end of the 16C, the friars faced the Mexican hierarchy's determination to end their state within a state and to extend its jurisdiction over them. Secular priests were introduced into their parishes. The Crown eventually came down on the side of the seculars. Disputes with the hierarchy, seculars, civilians, and government damaged not only the friars' prestige but also their will to succeed. Fewer Indians, more mestizos, more Spaniards meant less souls to win. The decline in their power was irreversible, but they left an imprint on Mexican society which endures today, in the basic strength of Catholicism in an anticlerical State.

The Development of New Spain

Antonio de Mendoza (1535–50) and Luis de Velasco (1550–64) were the first of a long series of generally competent viceroys, subject to the laws and regulations issued by the Council of the Indies in Spain. Their powers were checked by those of the audiencia, which could hear appeals against their decisions or make complaints against their administrations, and by the account taken of their term of office on retirement. Mendoza held the restive conquistadores in check and put down an Indian uprising, known as the Mixtón war (1541), in Nueva Galicia. He succeeded in averting the full force of the New Laws of the Indies for the Good Treatment and Preservation of the Indians, promulgated by the Council of the Indies in 1542 and promoted by the Dominicans, which abolished the encomiendas and Indian slavery, and thus prevented a full-scale encomendero rebellion. Velasco applied the New Laws in modified form and the encomenderos' powers were curbed. As the 16C progressed, the population of New Spain came to consist of an upper class of Spanish settlers (peninsulares; less politely gachupines; c 7000 by mid-century); a small middle class of creoles and mestizos; and c 9 or 10 million Indians, whose treatment in mines and on haciendas was still often appalling. They were also victims of famine and plague (which the Europeans had introduced), of which seven major visitations occurred between the Conquest and 1600, when their numbers had been reduced by some four-fifths. Even then, they could be subject to the repartimiento—forced labour, often for completely inadequate wages—which pointed up the dwindling supply of workers. Debt peonage, by which the Indian became tied through debt to his employer, remained a fact of life until the Revolution. In 1598–1605 a push by the Crown to concentrate Indians in towns, the better to turn them into taxpayers, was accomplished as humanely as possible, but the cause of much suffering. The structure of the Indian village established then remains much the same today.

Silver from the mines of New Spain (two-thirds of world supply came to be shipped from Veracruz) was a mixed blessing, which brought fortunes and coveted titles to mining families, but upset the equilibrium of the Spanish (and indeed the European) economy, and made American coasts a magnet for the freebooters of Europe. The 'king's fifth' (quinto) could not assuage the chronic indebtedness of the Spanish Habsburgs. A slump in silver production was one of the factors which caused economic depression in 17C New Spain. Economic problems went hand in hand with social and political problems, exemplified in the conflict between Spanish-staffed bureaucracy and creole colonists. The creoles envied the peninsulares' preferment in high office in the State and to a lesser extent in the Church; the peninsulares despised the creoles for unreliability, supposed impurity of blood, and unsuitability for responsible positions, and suspected a restlessness at control from Madrid. Conflict was also endemic with and in the Church itself—the viceroys' support of religious orders in the countryside and desire to prevent secular priests from taking possession of Indian parishes brought them into conflict with the hierarchy, who could control seculars and who had the support of the Crown. A full-scale revolt in Mexico City in 1624 was the climax of a terrible quarrel over their respective jurisdictions between viceroy marqués de Gelves and Abp Juan Pérez de la Serna, champion of the creoles. Bp Palafox's ascendancy in the 1640s marked a further struggle between colonists and hierarchy on the one hand, whom he upheld, and bureaucracy and religious orders on the other, in this case most noticeably bitterly between Palafox and the Jesuits.

Local government appointments came to be sold or traded, or handed down from father to son. Later 17C viceroys could do little against this nascent caciquismo and the weakness of the Crown under the last Habsburgs, especially under Charles II (1665–1700), meant that no control could be exercised from Madrid.

Some among the religious orders still had a pioneering zeal, facing danger and death on the N frontier of New Spain. Franciscans pushed N into Nueva Vizcaya (Durango, most of Chihuahua and Coahuila) and Nuevo León, and as far N as Nuevo México, and, in the 18C, into Nuevo Santander and Texas. The Jesuits, the first of whom had arrived in 1572, became active in Nayarit, Sinaloa, Sonora, and Baja California, to be followed in the latter by the Dominicans. In these areas the surviving orders successfully resisted secularization until the late 18C.

The Spanish Bourbons (from 1701) had their hands full with reforms in Spain itself. Charles III (1759–88), however, determined to maximize crown revenue. By making trade with the Spanish empire free (and not just the monopoly of the port of Cadiz), he enormously increased traffic between Spain and her empire, and crown revenue. He sent José de Gálvez as visitor-general (1765–72) to reform the government of New Spain, in co-operation with viceroy marqués de Croix. In 1767 this able pair expelled the Jesuits. The reaction among Jesuit sympathizers, in Michoacán, Guanajuato, and San Luis Potosí, was fiercely and riotously resentful. Gálvez's countermeasures were even more fierce. The loss of the Jesuits, whose achievements in education, missionizing, agriculture, and other spheres were second to none, was disastrous and led to ignorance, inefficiency, and chronic disaffection in the regions where they had had most influence.

Gálvez's reforms prompted (from 1777) the creation of the Comandancia General de las Provincias Internas, to strengthen the government of the N regions, from Baja California to Nuevo Santander. The system was complicated by modifications and the viceroy's insistence on having a say. Furthermore, in 1786–90 all Spanish America was divided into intendancies, under salaried officers appointed from Madrid, in charge of all branches of government, yet subordinate to viceroy and audiencia. The new system was superimposed on the old, with consequent administrative confusion. Yet Bourbon reforms brought an effectiveness and prosperity hitherto unknown: new government monopolies produced much-needed revenue and trade was far better organized, which meant lower prices for most of the population. Viceroy conde de Revillagigedo II (1789–94) worked hard to make Gálvez's reforms effective, purged local government of corrupt officials, and so improved the civil service that crown revenues reached an unprecedented level. His successors were nothing like as efficient, and New Spain followed the old Spain of the incompetent Charles IV (1788–1808) into disaster.

The Move to Independence

The European Enlightenment had already spread scientific knowledge in New Spain, applied especially to mining and agriculture, while the French and American revolutions did not pass unnoticed. When in 1808 Napoleon forced the abdication of Charles IV, installed his brother Joseph Bonaparte as king of Spain, and provoked a Spanish convulsion, the government of New Spain was thrown into confusion. Viceroy Iturrigaray, siding with the creoles, who wanted an independent provisional government, was toppled by a revolt of peninsulares, who imposed their own nominee. The government's weakness provided the background for more or less secret creole societies throughout central New Spain which indulged their dislike of Spaniards and plotted more actively for Independence. Discovering that the authorities in Mexico City had got wind of a revolt planned for Dec. 1810 by the Literary and Social Club of Querétaro, one of its leaders, the priest Miguel Hidalgo, decided to bring the date forward and proclaimed it (the Grito de Dolores) on 16 Sept. 1810 on the steps of his parish church at Dolores in Guanajuato. He could have had no clear idea of the murderous fury that he would unleash in the Bajío, in Michoacán, and as far W as Guadalajara. His untrained army of mestizos and Indians was beyond his experience and ability to control, and the dreadful massacre it perpetrated at the Alhóndiga in Guanajuato on 28 Sept., followed by further killings of Spaniards at Guadalajara in Nov.–Dec., caused revulsion among creoles. Despite the efforts of his efficient and disapproving second-in-command, Ignacio Allende, to acquire arms and to instil some discipline into the insurgent host, it was too late. The army, 600 strong, recruited by the Spaniard Félix Calleja finally smashed the insurgents at Puente de Calderón on 17 Jan. 1811. Hidalgo, racked by remorse, was executed in Chihuahua on 31 July 1811.

It was left to the parish priest of Carácuaro in remote S Michoacán, José María Morelos, to continue the fight for Independence. Morelos, however, was in every way better fitted to be a military leader: loyal, modest, humane, a good organizer who enlisted other able men and worked through family clans in the S. At Apatzingán in 1814, when his star was on the wane after defeat at Valladolid, his peripatetic Congress of Chilpancingo wrote the first Mexican constitution, proclaiming Independence from Spain. After Morelos had been captured and executed in 1815, his remaining followers were reduced to isolated insurgent bands.

The liberal coup in Spain in 1820 determined conservative creoles, peninsulares, the church hierarchy, and the audiencia, horrified at the thought of liberalism coming from Madrid, to make a dash for Independence. The movement's military thrust was led by Agustín de Iturbide, who persuaded the insurgent guerrilla leader Vicente Guerrero to join him and to subscribe to the Plan of Iguala (made public on 24 Feb. 1821), which proclaimed the three guarantees: Independence from Spain under a monarchy; equal treatment for Spaniards and creoles; the supremacy of the Roman Catholic Church. The new, and last, viceroy could only accept the plan and thus the end of Spanish rule. On 27 Sept. 1821 Iturbide's army entered Mexico City. This sanguinary creole, whose activities on the royalist side against the insurgents had brought him notoriety, had stolen the prize which they had struggled so hard and in vain to obtain.

Independent Mexico

Iturbide cut through the objections of a constitutional congress assembled in Feb. 1822, whose members advocated a republic or a monarchy headed by a Bourbon prince, and in May had himself proclaimed emperor. He took care to conciliate neither his former comrades nor his opponents and resorted to forced loans. In March 1823 he was scuttled by the Plan of Casa Mata, proclaimed by Antonio López de Santa-Anna, commandant of Veracruz, abdicated, and went into exile in Europe. On his premature return in 1824 he was promptly executed. With monarchy discredited, conservative elements among republicans preferred the idea of a centralist regime, liberals a federal system, the former associated with freemasonry of the 'Scottish Rite', the latter with lodges of the 'York Rite'. The constitution decided upon by a reassembled congress in Oct. 1824 was a federal one, a wrongheaded rejection of the tried viceregal system, in a huge sprawling country racked by instability, whose main source of government revenue, its customs' receipts, was pledged well in advance. The mining industry was in decline and, with the forced departure of many Spaniards, the numbers of trained administrators or holders of capital were reduced. Two loans negotiated in 1823–24 with London banks on disastrous terms were used to defray government expenses. Spending to develop an economic and social infrastructure was all but impossible. Mexico's first president, the likeable Guadalupe Victoria, whose reputation had been made as a hardy lone-wolf insurgent, and his military colleagues, unaccustomed to the rigours of running a government, relied at first on Lucas Alamán, an anglophile creole guanajuatense, as minister for foreign and internal affairs. Alamán insisted on strong central control, the upholding of the Church as a guarantee of property rights and privileges, and the admission of foreign skills and foreign capital. Guadalupe Victoria's successor, Vicente Guerrero, and his finance minister, Lorenzo de Zavala, tried to establish a decent financial basis by selling nationalized church property and introducing graduated taxation (which would have helped the poor), but a conservative coup overthrew Guerrero. Honest and respected, and representing an insurgent past, he was hunted down and killed, while Alamán, having returned to his old post, was at work on laying the foundations of an industrial revival.

Political stability, however, was to be denied with a vengeance. Most well-to-do creoles were untouched by any thought of public spirit or service, and stayed aloof from the convulsions into which Mexico was to be plunged. In 1833, Santa-Anna, who had defeated a weak Spanish invasion in Tamaulipas in 1829, was elected president. For 22 years he exercised his disastrous influence on the destinies of Mexico: a man to whom the pursuit of power was far more exciting than the possession; with an excess of misdirected energy; but who could always take advantage of a surge of discontent. He held the presidency 11 times and on four occasions (1833–34) handed it over to his vice president, Valentín Gómez Farías, the pioneer of Mexican anticlerical liberalism, whose first liberal measures Santa-Anna returned to undo.

In 1835, Texas, now well populated with US settlers, rebelled. Without cash to pay them or rations to sustain them, Santa-Anna, at San Luis Potosí, organized some 7000 men for a horrendous march N to do battle with the settlers and beat them at the Alamo (March 1836). But he frittered away his advantage and in April was in turn humiliatingly beaten and captured by Sam Houston's Texans at San Jacinto. Texas won its independence at a stroke. In 1838 Santa-Anna made a comeback in a skirmish with a French force which blockaded Veracruz to enforce claims by French citizens against the government (the so-called Pastry war) and lost a leg. He staged another comeback in 1846, unsuccessfully to combat the invading armies of the USA, which had annexed Texas in 1845 and provoked a Mexican declaration of war. Despite a heroic action by starving Mexican troops at Buenavista in Feb. 1847, Santa-Anna could not prevent the fall of Mexico City in Sept. By the Treaty of Guadalupe Hidalgo, signed in Feb. 1848, Mexico officially lost Texas, New Mexico, and Upper California and was indemnified for $15 million. During this final period of power, backed by the conservatives, he sold the Mesilla Valley (100,000 sq km) in Arizona to the USA for 10 million pesos. In March 1854 the veteran insurgent Gen. Juan Alvarez issued the liberal Plan of Ayutla in Guerrero. The ensuing revolt brought an end to Santa-Anna's rule.

The Reform

Alvarez's cabinet contained the cream of liberal politicians—Miguel Lerdo de Tejada, Benito Juárez, Melchor Ocampo, Guillermo Prieto, the moderate Ignacio Comonfort—determined to carry out liberal policies. The first new law, the 'Ley Juárez', restricted church courts to trying ecclesiastical cases only. Under Alvarez's successor, Comonfort, the far more radical 'Ley Lerdo' forbade corporations (church and civil institutions) from holding real estate. It aimed to destroy the Church's economic power by forcing it to sell church lands and to provide the government with funds from a transfer tax on such sales. Only rich Mexicans and foreign speculators could afford to take advantage of the measure; the Indians remained unprovided for. A liberal constitution in 1857 incorporated both laws; established secular education; allowed friars and nuns to renounce their vows; and further reduced the Church's power and influence. After trying to conciliate the conservatives, Comonfort abandoned the liberal fight and the presidency, which was assumed by Gen. Félix Zuloaga, upheld by clericals and conservatives, who cancelled the liberal legislation. The three-year war of the Reform began: the conservatives under Zuloaga and then under the young Pres. Miguel Miramón holding Mexico City; the liberal government under Juárez finally establishing itself in Veracruz, where it controlled the customs revenue and issued a series of harsh anticlerical laws, confiscating all church property without compensation, annulling all un-civil marriages, abolishing all clerical fees, and decreeing the formal separation of Church and State. There were initial conservative successes under able young generals, but the liberal armies struck a winning streak from Aug. 1860. González Ortega's defeat of Miramón at Calpulalpan in Dec. 1860 opened the liberal way to Mexico City in Jan. 1861.

Intervention

With a country ravaged by war, and uncaught conservative caciques pursuing their own private vendettas, an unpaid army, a ruined economy, and monumental government debts, Juárez suspended for two years all payments on the foreign debt of 80 million pesos and faced the threat of a combined invasion from France, Spain, and Britain to win compensation for what their nationals had lost and claim what Mexico owed. Spain and Britain withdrew from the adventure, but Napoleon III continued, ambitious to extend French influence to the Americas. Despite a check at Puebla on 5 May 1862 (the Cinco de Mayo) the French consolidated their hold in central Mexico and in May 1863 Juárez and his government fled N. After a rigged plebiscite, which pretended to show that the Mexicans wanted him, Napoleon's nominee for the Mexican imperial throne, Maximilian of Habsburg, after much hesitation, and his ambitious wife, Charlotte of Belgium, at last arrived at Veracruz in May 1864—an unhappy marriage, but a working partnership. There had always been Mexican advocates of monarchy among those who despaired of a republic ever bringing stability, and Maximilian won the support of some moderate liberals. He held the diehard conservatives at arm's length. But comparatively few Mexicans were willing to put themselves out for him. He and Carlota soon clashed with the Church, which expected full restoration of its ancient privileges and was disappointed, and his overtures to Juárez, backed by the USA, were rebuffed. Although in 1865 he decreed laws substantially to better the lot of the Indians (laws the liberals had never even considered), they came too late. Juarista guerrillas operated with impunity, and Maximilian signed his own death warrant when in 1864–65 he decreed, on French urging, that all republicans should be classed as bandits—all captured guerrillas to be court-martialled and shot within 24 hours. In 1866 Napoleon, under pressure from the USA, and despite Carlota's frantic appeals, decided to withdraw his troops, and most of Maximilian's Mexican supporters drifted away. He stayed, loyal to those who were loyal to him, to be shot, after a final battle at Querétaro, on 19 June 1867.

The Republic Restored

It needed all the stamina and determination of the victorious Juárez to start a pacification campaign and put life into a defunct economy. He was fortunate in his collaborators. Sóstenes Rocha, controlling an army which Juárez had cut down to size, was to lean hard on banditry and disaffected caciques. The finance minister Matías Romero, faced with an internal debt of 300 million pesos, succeeded in reducing US claims and repudiated all loans contracted in Europe by the empire, postponed payments on the earlier debt to Britain, began to reform the tax system, and encouraged industry. Gabino Barreda advised on a sustained programme of educational reform. In 1867 and 1871 Juárez was re-elected, over the rebellious objections of Porfirio Díaz. Mexicans could be convinced that Juárez's re-election in no way lessened his commitment to democracy and the rule of law. He died in July 1872. His most famous utterance sums up his career: 'Respect for the rights of others is peace itself'.

His successor, Sebastián Lerdo de Tejada, was determined to show impeccable liberal credentials. Juárez had not been heavy-handed in applying the

Reform laws; Lerdo incorporated them into the constitution. In 1876 Díaz intervened to prevent Lerdo seeking another term and initiated the porfiriato.

The Porfiriato

Gen. Díaz had been the military hero of the republican fight against Maximilian. Juárez, that determined civilian, had not rewarded him as he thought fit. His rule was to be a period of unprecedented peace and economic progress, and his skill and unmatched shrewdness worked to convince many diverse groups that it was in their interest to support the regime. His alliance with the creole upper class was cemented in 1881 by his marriage, a very happy one, to the cultivated Carmen Romero Rubio, 34 years his junior. His dictatorship was served by a group of positivist ministers, advisers, and apologists—the científicos, whose pragmatic approach meant that all must be subordinated to material progress and the survival of the fittest: true democracy would come one day, but not yet. Among them were the finance minister, José-Yves Limantour, who in 1893 managed to balance the budget, and Justo Sierra, from 1905 secretary for education, the most enlightened Mexican of his day. Mexico re-established credit abroad; banking enterprise flourished; foreign investment poured in, particularly to benefit mining and the petroleum industry, and, to some extent, agriculture; railways, indispensable for economic progress as well as to ensure Díaz's continuing control over his country, were built (640 km in 1876; 24,000 km by 1910); the Church was reconciled and even encouraged. However prosperous the creoles and growing middle class of miners and rancheros were to become under Díaz, foreign capitalists fared even better, especially in the N States, where Mexicans and foreigners accumulated huge landholdings. Yet economic development was uneven. Prosperous industry required more than the limited domestic market. Only henequen (for a time) and tobacco proved reliable in export markets. The new railways were far from constituting an effective national grid and the foreign entrepreneurs who built lines which joined the capital and the mining towns of the N to US markets and business were given huge subsidies by the government. Rural workers were mercilessly exploited and trapped by getting into debt at tiendas de raya (company stores) from which they were compelled to buy. Industrial workers, though better off than their rural counterparts, could arrive at their factories at dawn, to remain locked in till 8 at night, or later; management deducted church dues from wages, fined and sacked at will; and held workers responsible for damaged machinery.

Díaz's popularity waned as the years passed and the porfiriato became trapped in its own rigidity. Privilege and access to the spoils of power remained the preserve of the few, who perpetuated themselves in office and grew old with their leader. The Senate, in the words of one acid científico, 'housed a collection of servile mummies in a state of lingering stupor'. Nor was the regime buttressed by a strong army, which was, on the contrary, a hotbed of graft and incompetence, with phantom regiments not unknown. Díaz's famous rurales (by 1910 only some 3000 in number—their bruited savagery now faded) had also grown old and complacent—and so fat that 'some of their legendary captains could only mount their horses with herculean efforts'.

The economic crisis, originating in the USA, which hit Mexico in 1907 was probably the turning point. Mineral exports had already plummeted; their decline increased after 1907. Foreign and Mexican investors lost fortunes. Banking failures shook the country's financial structure. The sharp decline in the value of henequen hit the wealthy exporters of Yucatán. Agriculture was on the whole too incompetently run to come to the rescue. Yet radical opposition to the regime, exemplified by Ricardo Flores Magón and his Partido Liberal Mexicano, had drawn few followers. The industrial labour force, which had seen some small gain by 1900 wiped out by the economic collapse, began to organize and to strike. It resented higher wages being paid to foreign workers and wanted to increase its wealth and bargaining power rather than upset the political status quo.

The Revolution

The revolt against Díaz was headed by Francisco I. Madero, a hacendado from Coahuila, who in 1908 had begun to campaign for a free choice in presidential elections, which had hitherto been rigged to ensure Díaz's return. His Plan of San Luis Potosí (Oct. 1910) denounced Díaz's latest re-election. An uprising in Chihuahua led by Pascual Orozco and Francisco Villa exposed the collapsibility of the regime. Díaz resigned in May 1911.

The period of civil war and economic chaos ushered in by the departure of Díaz and known as the Mexican Revolution had in fact little of the revolution about it. It was rather a rebellion led by a middle class which was increasingly frustrated at being kept out of office; had seen its upward mobility blocked; and gave vent to vocal nationalism which blamed Mexico's economic crisis on the USA. Emiliano Zapata took up arms on behalf of the rural poor in Morelos, robbed of their land by hacendados. But his uprising and consistency of principle were a thing apart. Few among the other rebel leaders championed the dispossessed by advocating land reform. Indeed, many (incl. Francisco Villa) displayed the soundest bourgeois instincts. Discontent did not result in socialist solutions or a dismantling of the capitalist structure. Private property was regarded as sacred and not to be interfered with. If land must be taken from hacendados to distribute among the peasants, let due compensation be paid. But to destroy the hacienda system meant harming a class on whom the welfare of millions depended, and putting paid to any hopes of increased agricultural efficiency.

The connivance of the US ambassador in Madero's murder had been particularly blatant and shocking. Interference from the USA, implacably opposed to full-blooded reform in Mexico, was always to be feared and was always a brake on radicalism. Despite their nationalism, Mexico's new leaders knew that US recognition of their rule was vital, and they could dangle the prospect of intervention to hide their own reluctance to reform.

In his 13 months' presidency Madero did little to satisfy reformers, and alienated Zapata. His betrayal and murder at the hands of his general Victoriano Huerta, who then assumed the presidency, sparked a revolt in Chihuahua and Sonora, led by Francisco Villa and Alvaro Obregón, which spurred the defiance of Venustiano Carranza, governor of Coahuila. Carranza, a conservative, a moralist, a strong nationalist, with no real interest in social issues, let alone land reform, in March 1913 was proclaimed first chief of the constitutionalist army. With the help of Obregón and Villa, and a timely, but deeply resented, US invasion of Veracruz in Apr. 1914, he forced Huerta into exile.

The Convention of Aguascalientes (Oct.–Nov. 1914), an unsuccessful effort to resolve the differences between the rival factions, led to the split between Carranza and Villa, successful and exuberant, whom he hated, and a period of civil war, ending with Villa's defeat by Obregón, Carranza's rapidly learning and successful general, at Celaya in Apr. 1915. In Oct. the USA recognized Carranza. In March 1916 the vengeful Villa raided Columbus in New Mexico, in the hope of embroiling the USA and the constitutionalists in war. This prompted Pres. Wilson to send the Pershing expedition into Mexican territory in an unsuccessful attempt to flush Villa out, which put the future of Carranza's regime at great risk. The constitutional convention at Querétaro (1916–17), respectably middle class, published articles on land reform, education, and labour. The first gave Mexico ownership of its own subsoil (thus disturbing foreigners about their Mexican investments) and allowed the subdivision (but not the total disappearance) of large estates to create a prosperous small farmer class. The second tried unsatisfactorily to provide a national system of primary education. The third sought to establish a balance between the bargaining power of labour and capital, and made the State the protector of the worker. None was fully approved by Carranza, nor did he hurry to give the articles the force of law. His election to the presidency in May 1917 confirmed the position of a man who had no stomach for reform. In 1919 his bitter war against Zapata ended with the latter's murder, which Carranza condoned. Zapata's movement allied with Obregón to unseat and murder Carranza in May 1920.

Consolidating the Revolution

The self-made Obregón strongly advocated capitalism. Only when capitalists had security for their investments would working-class problems be solved. He was lukewarm towards land reform and his ventures in this area were limited. The hacendados kept their estates virtually intact. He gained US recognition only with the Bucareli agreements of 1923, by which the US oil companies' subsoil rights acquired before and after 1917 were to be respected, and Obregón pledged to pay Mexico's foreign debt—bitterly criticized in Mexico as a sell-out to the USA and an end to all thought of land and other social reform. The regime's association with the Confederación Regional Obrera Mexicana (CROM), an all-embracing labour union, whose leaders became a byword for thuggery and corruption, meant that Obregón passed on a tested system for the manipulation of labour to his successor, Plutarco Elías Calles, during whose presidency the number of strikes dropped dramatically.

Calles, who during his governorship of Sonora had equated the harm caused by alcohol with that caused by the clergy, and had outlawed both, professed an even stronger anticlericalism than other revolutionary leaders. Unlike his predecessors, he enforced the anticlerical provisions of the Constitution of 1917, thus unleashing the Cristero war, which raged ferociously until 1929, particularly in the W and NW. Mexico was placed under an interdict, and no public religious services were held. Bishops and foreign priests and nuns were deported. Ruthless and efficient, more and more conservative as time passed, Calles presided over a measure of progress: over 3 million hectares of land distributed to peasants; roads built; railways repaired; educational advance, begun under Obregón, maintained. His continued exercise of power, as Jefe Máximo de la Revolución, was assured when Obregón, who was to be allowed to succeed him (for a six-year term) in Nov. 1928, was assassinated in July. During 1928–34 Calles ruled through interim presidents: Emilio Portes Gil, who distributed over a million hectares in a year and curbed the power of the CROM; Pascual Ortiz Rubio, 'a conservative with the backbone of a jellyfish'; and Abelardo Rodríguez. Calles's imposition of the Partido Nacional Revolucionario (PNR) in 1928 to absorb the various factions involved in the Revolution, incl. peasants who had been given land, gave him the instrument for manipulating government. This manipulation, however, ended with the election of Lázaro Cárdenas, former governor of Michoacán, who expelled Calles, together with the former leader of the CROM, Luis Morones, in 1936. Cárdenas, thoroughly sympathetic and a consistent reformer, stepped up land distribution (18.6 million hectares expropriated and redistributed during his term), mitigated anti-Catholic rigour, and reorganized the PNR as Partido de la Revolución Mexicana (PRM). He nationalized the railways and—his most daring move—in 1938 nationalized the US and British oil companies. The slump which followed, as the oil companies' boycott forced Mexico to sell oil elsewhere, only increased his popularity on a tide of patriotic fervour.

His successor, Manuel Avila Camacho, chosen by Cárdenas and backed by the PRN machine, in retaliation against German attacks on Mexican shipping, declared war on the Axis in 1942, an act which marked the end of international isolation. Land reform was halted in the interests of efficient food production and a domestic manufacturing industry was able to develop and profit from a home market lacking imported consumer goods. The USA was eager to buy minerals, oil, and food. Under an agreement with the USA thousands of Mexicans (braceros) obtained jobs across the frontier. The Mexican economy was flooded with new money and inflation rose. In 1944 new-found solvency enabled the government to pay off 248.5 million pesos of public debt.

Industrial and infrastructure development was pushed ahead after the war by the first of a series of civilian presidents, Miguel Alemán, whose dynamism encouraged a headlong boom. Fortunes were made, especially from public works contracts, and corruption was rife. Alemán reconstituted the PRM as the Partido Revolucionario Institucional (PRI), 'institutionalizing' the Revolution, celebrating its maturity and readiness for a disciplined unradical future. The party machine introduced presidents, each chosen by his predecessor, for a six-year term, but the PRI was to become arrogant and complacent in its monopoly of power, resorting to fraud in national and local elections. Nor has the six-year presidential term, with no re-election, been conducive to continuity and consistency of policy. Under the hard-working and charismatic Adolfo López Mateos, however, redistribution of land again came to the fore, along with a widening of the social security system. López Mateos also pushed Mexico into taking far more prominent a part on the international stage, and it was his urging that led to the holding of the XIX Olympiad in Mexico in 1968—an occasion catastrophically marred by student unrest and a massacre of demonstrators at Tlatelolco. On the basis of enormous new oil finds in the 1970s public spending raced ahead of oil revenue, and foreign banks eagerly supplied loans. In 1982, at the end of the term of José López Portillo, came the crash. A prolonged economic recession began. The international debt crisis had been born. Pres. Miguel de la Madrid came into a cursed inheritance. Falls in world oil prices during the 1980s could only aggravate Mexico's severe economic problems. Clashes within the PRI, between technocrats in power and displaced politicians of the older populist school, have gone hand in hand with a weakening of the PRI's grip. The bitterly disputed presidential election of 1988 was won by the PRI candidate, Carlos Salinas de Gortari, the young former planning minister who had drastically reduced the budget deficit and curbed rocketing inflation. The seemingly unstoppable challenge of Cuauhtémoc Cárdenas, son of Lázaro, and his Partido de la Revolución Democrática was somehow fended off. The Salinas government boldly embarked on a programme of reform: opening up what was once one of the world's most protected economies and starting to modernize it through deregulation, privatisation, and tax reform. Mexico's accession to the North American Free Trade Association on 1 Jan. 1994 was immediately followed by an uprising in Chiapas. The murder of the PRI presidential candidate, Luis Donaldo Colosio, in March obscured recent achievements. In August the PRI candidate, Ernesto Zedillo, was elected to succeed Salinas in the presidency; in September the PRI secretary-general, José Francisco Ruiz Massieu, was murdered. Mexico again faced a flight of capital and economic recession.

Mexican Heads of State

(omitting the less important interim presidencies)

Agustín de Iturbide (emperor) 1822–23
Guadalupe Victoria 1824–29
Vicente Guerrero 1829
Anastasio Bustamante 1830–32, 1837–39, 1839–41
Melchor Múzquiz 1832
Manuel Gómez Pedraza 1832–33
Antonio López de Santa-Anna 1833 (3 times), 1834–35, 1839, 1841–42, 1843, 1844, 1847 (twice), 1853–55
Valentín Gómez Farías 1833–34, 1846–47
Nicolás Bravo 1842–43
Valentín Canalizo 1843–44
José Joaquín de Herrera 1844–45, 1848–51
Mariano Paredes y Arrillaga 1846
Pedro María Anaya 1847–48

Manuel de la Peña y Peña 1847, 1848
Mariano Arista 1851–53
Juan Alvarez 1855
Ignacio Comonfort 1855–58
Félix Zuloaga 1858–59   conservatives in Mexico City
Miguel Miramón 1859–60
Benito Juárez 1858–67 (liberal government outside Mexico City, in Mexico City,
    and in exile), 1867–72
Regency 1863–64   2nd empire
Maximilian 1864–67
Sebastián Lerdo de Tejada 1872–76
Porfirio Díaz 1877–80, 1884–1911
Manuel González 1880–84
Francisco León de la Barra 1911
Francisco I. Madero 1911–13
Victoriano Huerta 1913–14
Venustiano Carranza 1914–17, 1917–20
Adolfo de la Huerta 1920
Alvaro Obregón 1920–24
Plutarco Elías Calles 1924–28
Emilio Portes Gil 1928–30
Pascual Ortiz Rubio 1930–32
Abelardo Rodríguez 1932–34
Lázaro Cárdenas 1934–40
Manuel Avila Camacho 1940–46
Miguel Alemán 1946–52
Adolfo Ruiz Cortines 1952–58
Adolfo López Mateos 1958–64
Gustavo Díaz Ordaz 1964–70
Luis Echeverría 1970–76
José López Portillo 1976–82
Miguel de la Madrid 1982–88
Carlos Salinas de Gortari 1988–94
Ernesto Zedillo 1994–

Mexican Architecture and Art of the Viceroyalty, 1521–1810

The Renaissance in New Spain

After the Conquest, Mexican architecture, sculpture, and painting developed in a way quite their own. Initial stylistic confusion reflected changes in Spain, where Mudéjar and Isabeline Gothic had given way to the Renaissance. Moreover, the friars, in building their first convents, were not professional enough architects accurately to memorize the buildings which had accompanied their earlier lives. They employed indigenous labour which added its own special stamp as it gained in confidence. (Later in the 16C professional architects also came to New Spain. The most famous was *Claudio de Arciniega* [c 1526–1592 or '93], some of whose work survives.) What is termed the Renaissance (16C– early 17C) in New Spain, however, can be said to embrace three co-existing modes: eclectic (a mixture of Isabeline Gothic, Mudéjar, and other influences, which sometimes introduce archaizing elements); plateresque, the form in which Spain took in the Italian Renaissance; and Mannerist. Eclecticism is made more exotic by the infusion of tequitqui—an indigenous, anachronistic, interpretation of the European. Sometimes we can look at a mixture of two of, or all, three.

The convents which stand as monuments to the great conversion incorporate standard features. A vaulted church, remarkable for solidity and strength, its thick walls supported by pier buttresses and lifted beyond the springing of the vaults to a parapet topped by merlons. It stands next to the convent proper, which includes the cloister, generally of two storeys, the walks and arches often showing much of interest, originality, and beauty in design and vaulting. Convent and church face a squarish (sometimes L-shaped) atrio, bounded by a wall, a space often of ample dimensions to accommodate a large Indian congregation. For it, Mass would be celebrated in an open chapel, sometimes raised alongside the church. Where there is no separate open chapel, Mass would be offered under the main arch of the portería, the main entrance to the convent. At or near the corners of the atrio posa chapels sometimes survive—resting places for the Host during processions of the Blessed Sacrament. The majority of convent churches consist of a single, long, high nave, generally barrel-vaulted, sometimes square domical and ribbed, ending in a triumphal arch dividing it from a polygonal, rectangular, or (rarely) curved apse, itself sometimes independently and elaborately, ribbed.

The Franciscans built many fine churches, and sometimes ornate façades. The Augustinian love of show (or perhaps more a pedantic interest in architectural detail), especially in façades, was to get them into trouble. Dominican buildings in the S, a zone of frequent earthquakes, tend to be really solid, with thickest possible walls. The area covered by carved decoration, unrelated to the bare flat mass of the rest of the building, is small, and concentrated on doorways and choir windows. Decoration can also be lavished on the exteriors of posa chapels, of open chapels, of porterías, and of atrial crosses.

A main Mudéjar legacy is the magnificent timber ceilings (alfarjes, artesonados; interlocking beams or deeply coffered), once common, but mostly destroyed, except in San Francisco at Tlaxcala. Parts survive, for example, in San Diego at Huejotzingo; in the Cap. de la Tercera Orden at Tulancingo; in the sotocoros at Yanhuitlán and Epazoyucan; and, delightfully, at Huatlatlauca. Another Mudéjar legacy is the alfíz, the rectangular space, marked out by a moulding, often the Franciscan cord, which envelops and emphasizes the doorway arch of so many churches. The tightly patterned sacristy doorway at Huejotzingo; the fountain at Chiapa de Corzo; and the Rollo at Tepeaca are also Mudéjar reminders.

Isabeline Gothic (of Mudéjar, Flemish, and Burgundian ancestry) is seen in ogee and other elaborately shaped arches and canopies, and panels of dense naturalistic, heraldic, and geometric relief. The main doorways of the convent churches at Huejotzingo, Tecamachalco, and Tepeaca, and the civic buildings of Tlaxcala carry Isabeline-influenced arches. There is priceless Isabeline façade relief at Acámbaro and Chimalhuacán-Chalco.

Eclecticism is evident at Molango and Otumba. At Molango the W portal has an alfíz made of plateresque baluster columns upholding an almost classical cornice, framing a Romanesque arch—all beneath a Gothic rose window. Arch, jambs, and columns show Isabeline and Mudéjar-inspired relief—all carved by an Indian hand. At Otumba alfices frame doorway arch and choir window. Slender colonnettes and arch mouldings divide Isabeline and plateresque relief. Eclecticism of a far more exotic, opulent kind marks the breathtaking façade at Angahuan—three alfices piled on top of one another, they and the jambs and arch all dense with Mudéjar and Isabeline relief, and heavily Indianized. Eclecticism of a majestic kind marks the open chapel at Tlalmanalco. Isabeline and Manueline Gothic seem to be the influences behind the enchanting open chapel at Tlahuelilpa, where the medallion-lozenge voussoirs form a fantastic multifoil arch.

Plateresque concentrates sculpted ornament around doorways and windows. The bare wall background is an admirable foil. An immediately recognizable support is the baluster column, the capital ionic, corinthian, or composite. Ornamental relief consists of grotesques (derived from ancient Rome)—anthropomorphic, zoomorphic, and vegetal—and shells. The purest example is at Acolman, reflected at Metztitlán and Ixmiquilpan. Yuriria follows the general scheme, but introduces extraneous, complex decoration. At Cuitzeo we find an indigenous version of academic plateresque, something distinct and in three storeys. The church façade at Tzintzuntzan is very original, the canopy a huge shell, while at Erongarícuaro the shell motifs vie with the attractive solidity of the doorway panel. At Yecapixtla, a superbly sculpted Gothic rose is placed above a lovely plateresque doorway—all incorporating delightful relief. The façade of the Casa de Montejo in Mérida is a rare survival of secular plateresque, liberally influenced by Isabeline Gothic. At Actopan the proud church façade is doubly transitional, from Romanesque to plateresque to Mannerist, with its contrast of light and shade.

The first phase of Mannerism (from c 1570) in New Spain applies classical canons, emphasizes order, proportion, obedience to Italian precepts. It is also called Renaissance purism, or Herreran, after the severe classicism of Juan de Herrera who finished the Escorial near Madrid—an expression of Counter-Reformation strength. In New Spain the façades at Tecali, Zacatlán de las Manzanas, Cuilapan, and Tlalmanalco, and the sacristy and sala capitular doorways in Mexico Cathedral, fall within this definition. The cathedral portals at Mérida and Guadalajara are further examples.

Two good examples of the second Mannerist phase (16C and into the 17C) are the W portals at Xochimilco and Tlatelolco. In them classical outlines are the basis for decorative flights, to become more marked as the 17C progresses. The façades of the 17C convent churches of San José de Gracia, La Concepción, San Bernardo, and Sta Teresa la Antigua in Mexico City are also Mannerist, with controlled employment of relief, as are those of Mexico and Puebla cathedrals, despite any use of solomonic columns. A similar use in the Altar de los Reyes of Puebla Cathedral is also within a Mannerist scheme. The façade of Sto Domingo in Oaxaca is an expertly proportioned specimen of this phase. The polychrome stucco interiors in the latter church, in the Cap. Doméstica at Tepotzotlán, and at Tlacolula, notwithstanding their baroque-seeming abundance, are Mannerist. This phase may be regarded as a transition between Mannerism and baroque. *Pedro de Arrieta* (d. 1738), an architect whose career spans the late 17C and early 18C, typifies it. His work is grounded in Mannerism, with tritóstilo columns and classical overall design, but more spacious, with more copious relief and a use of curves—as in the façade of La Profesa in Mexico City.

Indian carving skills are also notable in atrial crosses—eg, at Cuautitlán, with its portrait heads; at Huichapan, with complex Passion symbol relief; at Acolman, with the head of Christ at the crossing. Zinacantepec has a global font covered in relief; Huaquechula, a pulpit with adorable levitating angels—ingenuousness equalling, as in so many places in Mexico, a wholly endearing charm. The sumptuous relief of the posas and in the N doorway at Huejotzingo is reminiscent of Manueline Gothic. That of the posas at Calpan; on the N portal at Huaquechula; on the W portal at Tepoztlán; on the doorway of the Casa del que mató el animal in Puebla, flatter, more tequitqui.

Of the Renaissance main altarpieces, among the glories of Mexican art, results of so much care on the part of both contractors and skilled artists and workmen, precious few remain reasonably intact. Care was as nothing in face of changes in fashion and the wanton destruction of later ages. The great triptych now at Cuauhtinchán is small in proportion to its setting and has slim baluster columns. The two outstanding are at Huejotzingo and Xochimilco, gilded, proud examples of the second stage of Mannerism, full of judiciously placed relief, their sculpture unrivalled for composure and the use of estofado—that technique for displaying flow, folds, and set of a garment which specialists worked out on a gold and silver base.

Mexican Baroque

This is a style of movement, of curves, of an abundance of adornment, of spaciousness, of radiance. The structural is invaded by the ornamental. Structural features—columns, cornices, pediments—become absorbed in the ornamental. Ornament triumphs over structure. Baroque contributed much to the splendour of the city of Mexico ('la grandeza mexicana') and, thanks to the expertise and sophistication of Mexican craftsmen, made an enthusiastic progress through New Spain, taking on different characteristics in different regions. It reflects a period when the Church, presided over by gifted archbishops and higher clergy, benefited from huge endowments (especially from mining wealth). The style originally in Mexico City influenced developments northwards and westwards—façades like altarpieces, polygonal arches, a more conservative approach. From Puebla southwards to Oaxaca and Chiapas, especially after 1650, façades are more plastic, with reticulated decoration, polychrome surfaces, and multiple-curve arches.

Its earliest, transitional, phase (first half of 17C, even beyond; see above) sees the co-existence of Mannerism with incipient baroque. The spiral solomonic column in altarpieces and façades, on cupolas and church towers, emerges as a prominent feature of the second (and first full) phase (last third of 17C; first third of 18C). Sometimes the unadorned column shaft appears as a spiral. More often, heavy mouldings of various slanting types are twisted around the shaft, as on the church of San Agustín in Querétaro, Aguascalientes Cathedral, the façades of Saltillo Cathedral, or in the upper storey of the W façade of Durango Cathedral. Sometimes the spiral moulding forms a third of a tritóstilo column, as on the church of Guadalupe near Zacatecas or Chihuahua Cathedral. In San Miguel de Allende, columns on the façade of the Oratory are carved with a band of flat leaves instead of moulding. Elaboration of the solomonic column is seen at its lushest in the doorways of Sta Mónica at Guadalajara, where vegetal and fruit forms, and birds and bunches of grapes, are swathed round, and mask, the shaft. The solomonic is particularly well defined at San Francisco in the same city. Leafy and fruit relief render luxurious the columns of the façades of El Carmen and the Cathedral in San Luis Potosí. At San Cristóbal de las Casas the façade of Sto Domingo offers layer upon layer of solomonic, either invaded by or companion to, the copious relief which covers the whole façade. The heady peak of solomonic decoration is reached on the façade of Zacatecas Cathedral, a work of tremendous (almost barbarous) bravura.

In Mexico City, *Miguel Custodio Durán* (? 1700–44) developed a special baroque variation: sinuous pilasters and torchlike finials, seen in the puerta abocinada of San Juan de Dios, and on the façade of La Regina and the entrance to the Medina Picazo chapel in the church. Other baroque elaborations of the column may be seen, as around the cupola drum of the side chapel of the church of Guadalupe in Puebla: tritóstilo, with thick geometric and vegetal relief.

Baroque in Puebla is enhanced by azulejos. The façades of San Francisco Acatepec and Sta María Tonantzintla are glorious in their azulejo display. In Atlixco the mortar relief of La Merced still shows traces of the polychrome covering which must once have made it bewitching. The Cap. del Rosario in Sto Domingo (Puebla) is a paradise of the poblano stuccoist's art. If one wants a vibrant synthesis of baroque and earlier modes, the grand exterior of La Compañía in Puebla will provide it.

Solomonic altarpieces, even more magnificent and almost always gilded, and with polychrome statues and relief, abound. Their column mouldings and intervening parts of the shaft are sometimes completely disguised by lush relief decoration. Sturdy and straightforward at Oxkutzcab; in tecali alabaster at San José de Chiapa; forming part of the majestic main altarpiece of Sto Domingo at Puebla; in the Franciscan convent churches at Tlaxcala and Xochimilco; and all gilded beauty and completeness at Metztitlán and Ozumba. Those of the church of La Soledad in Puebla are among the grandest. Those of the Cap. de los Santos Angeles in Mexico Cathedral are unsurpassed for craftsmanship amid gilded and polychrome masses.

We may admire the splendid didactic reliefs which form façade centrepieces, often enclosed by a characteristic eared frame: St Augustine protecting his friars (Mexico and Oaxaca); the Assumption on Oaxaca Cathedral; the attributes of Our Lady, accompanied by merry cherubs, on La Soledad at

Puebla; Doubting Thomas at Ixtlán de Juárez; and, among the best, sleeping St Augustine in Zacatecas and Our Lady of Solitude in Oaxaca, part of a work which shows the spacious virtuosity of oaxaqueño baroque.

Mexican Churrigueresque

This flamboyant, entirely decorative, development of baroque (third stage; c 1720–80), with Mannerist features, is perversely named (after the most tenuous of connections with the Spanish Churriguera family of architects and retable-makers). Although today Mexican art historians prefer the description 'barroco estípite', we retain 'churrigueresque' in this book. As Manuel Toussaint has said, the onomatopoeia suits the fantastic style. The first craftsman-architect to adapt the inverted pyramid called the estípite (a time-honoured device, but to become the churrigueresque's conspicuous feature) is the Spaniard *Jerónimo de Balbás* (c 1670–1748), who designed the Altar de los Reyes in Mexico Cathedral. The style fades when the estípite is either much reduced in significance, or dissolves.

On the estípite are often superimposed foliage, medallions, garlands, festoons. Polychrome saints, angels, cherubs, stand, or perch, or climb, forward of them. A soaring effect is marked when the estípites stand well apart to let interestípites, full of relief, develop, as in the altarpiece of the Holy Cross in Belem de los Mercedarios in Mexico City. Estípites can be combined with ornamental niche pilasters—pointer to the later anastyle mode—as at Apan and Tepeyanco, and in Sto Domingo at Zacatecas and in San Cosme in Mexico City. No interior shows the style to greater effect than San Francisco Javier at Tepotzotlán, apogee of churrigueresque splendour, with its seven altarpieces. So prodigious and spectacular are the gilding and polychrome that estípites, cornices, and interestípites are almost lost in the total blaze.

The style was quickly adopted for façades. In Mexico City the Sagrario Metropolitano is the masterwork of the Spaniard *Lorenzo Rodríguez* (1704–74). Two portals of Las Vizcaínas and the badly abused Casa del conde de San Bartolomé de Xala are also by him, and his influence in the design of Santísima Trinidad is palpable. San Felipe Neri, all delicacy and elegance, is by *Ildefonso de Iniesta Bejarano y Durán*. La Compañía in Guanajuato is by *Felipe de Ureña*, an early exponent of the churrigueresque in altarpieces. Other outstanding examples are the façades of the churches at Tepotzotlán, creamy in the sunlight; at La Valenciana, Cata, and Rayas (results of mining wealth) in Guanajuato; at Dolores Hidalgo; Guadalupe in Aguascalientes; and Saltillo Cathedral. The puerta abocinada of Nuestra Señora de la Salud at San Miguel de Allende shows a modest churrigueresque, charming in its unskilled reticence. A pure serenity is to be found in the façade of El Encino in Aguascalientes. Rustic churrigueresque comes in the delectable façades at Huexotla and Jolalpan (in the latter as part of a provincial eclectic plum-pudding, the estípites barely tapering), to cite only two examples. A stiffer, more academic, kind is provided by the façade of San Francisco in Puebla. Nothing comes more luscious than the ivory-like mortar façade at Panotla or more exuberant than the dazzling white stucco of the Santuario de Ocotlán near Tlaxcala. Churrigueresque also appears in the brave virtuoso façades of the churches in the wild Sierra Gorda, far away in dangerous mission country. Even there they took care to be abreast of fashion.

Anastyle Baroque

The fourth phase of baroque (from c 1750) goes beyond churrigueresque and applies almost always to altarpieces. Supports, if any, are subsumed by decorative wealth. The ornamental niche pilaster is a main feature. Estípites, in a secondary role, sometimes appear, but the pervading motifs are often rococo. An overwhelming example is the Portada de los Angeles in El Carmen at San Luis Potosí, made in mortar. Here estípites are reduced by pronounced niche pilasters, amid a vertiginous swirl of stepped lines and spiralling curves. The high altar in La Enseñanza in Mexico City shows layer upon layer of curved and straight mouldings, emphatic background for the niche pilasters. Of the altarpieces in Sta Prisca at Tasco, the work of *Isidoro Vicente de Balbás*, some are churrigueresque, others profusely, exquisitely, anastyle, created at the moment when churrigueresque dissolves. The high altar, based on four detached estípites, huge and complex, and imaginative interestípites, achieves an incredible, lustrous disorder. From Querétaro a special kind of anastyle (queretano), strongly rococo-influenced, spreads through the Bajío. In Querétaro itself the interiors of Sta Clara and Sta Rosa are dazzling tours de force of this rich gilded baroque, generously heightened with polychrome. Altarpiece supports are either suppressed or take on the aspect of bulbous, opulent estípites; backgrounds are masses of petatillo and rococo effects; elaborate canopies, crowns, and softly curving frames do honour to statues and paintings. San Agustín in Salamanca has gorgeous examples, incl. two by *Pedro Joseph de Rojas*. The altarpieces at Chamacuero are among the last of their kind, fittingly opulent.

Neostyle Baroque

Also after 1750 reaction begins to set in (fifth phase). Baroque, though still with lively relief and lambrequins much in evidence, is reined in and develops within the confines of fluted, tritóstilo, or soberly solomonic columns, curved pediments, straight cornices—sometimes standing out from, and in contrast to, the plainness of a wall behind. The best-known examples are Sta Prisca in Tasco (perfectly preserved and of greatest beauty), San Felipe Neri in Querétaro, Nuestra Señora del Buen Suceso at Tianguistenco, Tlaxcala Cathedral, and San Lorenzo and the wonderfully compact La Enseñanza in Mexico City, the last possibly the work of *Francisco Guerrero y Torres* (1727–92). He is an admirable synthesizing architect, creator of the finest casas señoriales in Mexico City (San Mateo de Valparaíso, Jaral de Berrio, Santiago de Calimaya, probably Mayorazgo de Guerrero) in which he reflected the taste of the creole elite. His masterpiece, the Cap. del Pocito at Villa de Guadalupe, is the synthesis of Mexican baroque.

Neoclassical

From 1785 the Academia de San Carlos took up the cause of neoclassical architecture in New Spain. It was eagerly adopted—a delayed response to what had started in Europe many years before. The contrast between it and churrigueresque and anastyle could not be more complete (an academician described the public buildings of Mexico City as 'deformed'), yet its closeness to Mannerism, which had still influenced early 18C architects, cannot be denied.

José Damián Ortiz de Castro (1750–93) completed the towers and filled out the façade of Mexico Cathedral. *Ignacio Castera*, successful and rich (a target for his irascible, but able, Spanish contemporary *Miguel Costansó* [b. 1741]), designed the church of Loreto in Mexico City. *José del Mazo y Avilés* (d. 1819) is responsible for the Alhóndiga at Guanajuato and modernized chapels in Mexico Cathedral. *José Gutiérrez* left fine work in Guadalajara, incl. the Sagrario and the chapel of the university. *José Manzo y Jaramillo* (1789–1860) put his mark on Puebla Cathedral. The hard-working *José Antonio González Velázquez* (d. 1810) designed San Pablo el Nuevo in Mexico City, the Ciudadela, and the Cap. del Señor de Sta Teresa, and transformed the altarpieces of Jesús María.

The finest and most influential neoclassical architect and sculptor is *Manuel Tolsá* (1757–1816), a dynamic Valencian who arrived in 1791. Among his great monuments are the cupola, the top of the façade, and the tower figures of the Cathedral; the Pal. de Minería; the Pal. Buenavista; and the Pal. del Marqués del Apartado—all in Mexico City. He designed the Hospicio Cabañas in Guadalajara—the 'Escorial of America'. His El Caballito is one of the world's finest equestrian statues. His high altarpieces in La Profesa and Sto Domingo in Mexico and in Puebla Cathedral achieve a beauty and symmetry that successors strove for in vain. *Francisco Eduardo Tresguerras* (1759–1833), wayward and gifted, adept at graceful effects, beautified his native Celaya. The church of El Carmen is a masterwork. Some exterior detail seems to strain towards baroque.

After its best essays in the final 40 years of the viceroyalty, neoclassicism became all-pervading—considered 'de muy buen gusto'. So many churches were so wantonly reordered in the 19C that it degenerated into a routine. Parish priests and bishops, who might have known better, tore out beauties of the baroque and churrigueresque, and substituted their dull successors, which do so little for us today.

Mexican Painting of the Viceroyalty

The international fame of 20C Mexican muralists might lead outsiders to suppose that the art of painting begins in Mexico after the Revolution. Nothing could be further from the truth. The years following the Conquest see a sustained development. Works by native, and European, artists from the 16C onwards adorn cathedrals and churches, museums and galleries. Mexican painters are obviously influenced by copies or woodcuts of works by contemporaries in Spain, Italy, and the Netherlands. But their output is not a pallid, provincial reflection of European models. They have a stamp, style, and vigour of their own, despite the fact that they are subject to the captious inefficiency of the Inquisition.

The Indian tradition of wall painting continues and the friars favour mural decoration for their churches and convents. Friezes of grotesques and arabesques, Passion scenes, figures of saints, done by indigenous hands, still exist in cloister walks, in staircase wells, and in churches. A rigid, medieval, style in black or brown on white, with sometimes a reddish addition, may be seen, for example, at Cholula (Mass of St Gregory, Scenes from the Life of St Francis) and at Huejotzingo (Apostolic Twelve). Some murals can be frighteningly didactic—as in the amazing scenes of evil and its consequences at Ixmiquilpan or those showing condign punishment for sin at Sta María Xoxoteco. In a class of their own are the paintings by the Indian cacique Juan Gersón at Tecamachalco. More Renaissance in style are the superb murals at Actopan, denoting the Augustinians' pride in their own saints. Augustinian themes also predominate at Charo. Outstanding are the coloured Passion scenes in the cloister at Epazoyucan, where earlier Flemish, Italian, and Spanish influence can be traced, showing grief, nobility, and urgency.

Mannerism

The first European painter of note to work in New Spain is the Fleming *Simón Pereyns* (d. c1590), who arrives in 1566. Among his few extant works are the paintings of the Huejotzingo high altarpiece and a St Christopher in the Cap. de la Purísima Concepción in Mexico Cathedral. *Andrés de la Concha* (d. 1611) arrives in 1567. Influenced by Italian Mannerism, he has a good sense of colour, and knows how to distribute figures and how to give character to a face. Certainly by him are the paintings in the high altarpieces at Yanhuitlán and Coixtlahuaca. Possibly by him are a Holy Family and a St Cecilia (Pinacoteca Virreinal = PV). The cultivated Basque nobleman **Baltasar de Echave Orio** (c 1548–c 1620) arrives c 1580. His ease with anatomical detail recalls Italian Mannerism. His Visitation and Annunciation (PV) show great serenity; his Martyrdom of St Apronianus (PV) and Martyrdom of St Pontian (Museo Nacional de Arte = MNA), also with a fine sense of colour, show a pure religious spirit. His Mexican-born son *Baltasar de Echave Ibía* (c 1585–1645), known as 'de los azules' for the blue tints which mark his work, a lesser talent, is nevertheless an elegant painter who integrates landscapes into his compositions. His St John the Baptist (PV) captures an expression of sweetness and calm that is most moving. Echave Ibía's close contemporary **Luis Juárez** (c 1585–before 1639), probably Mexican-born, conveys mysticism (St Teresa of Avila [Museo Regional, Guadalajara]; Agony in the Garden [PV]), a smooth serenity (Annunciation [PV]), a childlike tenderness (Martyrdom of St Ursula; Mystic Marriage of St Catherine [MNA]). His tousled angels are to be adopted as a type and refined by later masters. Crisp treatment of drapes add to his interest, though he lacks expertise in anatomy. **Alonso López de Herrera** ('el Divino'; 1579–c 1643), b. in Valladolid in Spain, excels in paintings of the Divine Countenance and in portraiture. A portrait of Fray García Guerra, abp of Mexico, his earliest known work, is at Tepotzotlán. His Assumption (PV) shows grandness, vigour, and vivid colouring, the Virgin realistic and matronly.

Baroque

The influence of Zurbarán is evident in the work of **Sebastián López de Arteaga** (1610–53; stabbed in a fight), who comes to Mexico in 1640 as an official of the Inquisition. His use of chiaroscuro is assured, his figures and drapery realistic. Three superb canvases (PV) sum up his work. In Incredulity of St Thomas, a masterpiece, all is stillness, mystery, and wonder; the figure of Christ virile and noble. His Crucifixion, the greatest painting of the subject in Mexico, shows an agitated Christ bathed in light against a sombre background of sky and buildings. His Marriage of Our Lady, a seminal work, is supremely elegant, different in style to the former two. In his Stigmatization of St Francis (Museo de Guadalupe) the vigorous central figure is placed in a rocky landscape and under a dramatic sky. **José Juárez** (c 1615–1662 or 63), the greatest Mexican-born painter of the baroque—it would be heretical today to call him the greatest of all Mexican painters—is also influenced by Zurbarán, and by Rubens. Three gloriously coloured works (PV), Martyrdom of the Child Saints Justus and Pastor, Epiphany, and Apparition of Our Lady to St Francis, are testimony to his genius. Contrast the Virgins of the second and third paintings, the one humanized and detached, the other ethereally beautiful yet tender and gracious. Note too the panache with which he details the clothing of the kings.

Baltasar de Echave y Rioja (1632–82), son of Echave Ibía, puts chiaroscuro to dramatic use in a night scene, Burial of Christ (PV), the drama heightened by the facial expressions. **Pedro Ramírez** (d. 1678) is also influenced by Rubens. His Liberation of St Peter (Tepotzotlán) has great assurance, while the central figures of his Adoration of the Shepherds (PV) have an earthy character. *Antonio Rodríguez* (fl. 1650–86), son-in-law of José Juárez, is a careful painter of dignified saintly figures (St Augustine, St Thomas of Villanueva [MNA]).

Of lesser, but nonetheless interesting, painters of the second half of the 17C we may single out *Hipólito de Rioja*, whose martyrdoms (PV), full of crowding movement and chiaroscuro, also denote an ability to handle much lively detail. Works by the productive *Juan Sánchez Salmerón* (d. 1697) are immediately recognizable for their slightly elongated faces and looks of devotion. His SS Joachim and Gabriel and SS Joachim and Anne (Tepotzotlán) are good examples.

Late Baroque

The virtuoso of full baroque is **Cristóbal de Villalpando** (c 1645–1714), a painter for the grand occasion. In him we see the influence not only of Murillo and Rubens, but also of that febrile genius Juan de Valdés Leal. His is perhaps the most adventurous artistic spirit Mexico has ever known. He revels in exuberant effulgence, as may be seen in the divine, apocalyptic, and archangelic swirls in the Sacristy of Mexico Cathedral and in Puebla Cathedral. He excels in depicting expanses of negligent drapery, blown by a heavenly wind. Calmer, but no less magnificent and mystic, are Vision of St Teresa and other works in La Profesa in Mexico City, and Flight into Egypt (Tepotzotlán), all sumptuously coloured. He has also left us one of Mexico's most important, detailed, and absorbing historical documents—a painting of Pl. Mayor in Mexico City (1695; private ownership, England).

His friend the mulatto **Juan Correa** (c 1640–1716) may be called the sheet anchor of late Mexican baroque, even though his work is, unsurprisingly, not of consistently high quality. His paintings may be found all over Mexico, and in Guatemala (and further afield). In Mexico Cathedral we have some of his finest: Assumption and Entry of Christ into Jerusalem, in the Sacristy; and Old and New Testament scenes in the Cap. de los Santos Angeles. Utterly enchanting, and endearing (a word redolent of Mexican art throughout the viceregal period), is his Infant Christ with Musical Angels, one a mulatto (PV). Resplendent for its majestic archangel and beautiful landscape is Expulsion of Adam and Eve from Paradise (Tepotzotlán). He can also assume an extremely theatrical style: Repentant Magdalen (MNA).

The sons of Antonio Rodríguez and Antonia Juárez (see above), **Nicolás Rodríguez Juárez** (1667–1734) and **Juan Rodríguez Juárez** (1675–1728), are major talents. By Nicolás we single out the tender Child Jesus (Museo Franz Mayer), Triumph of the Church (El Carmen, Celaya), and excellent works in La Profesa. Juan's paintings in the Altar de los Reyes (Mexico Cathedral) are fully worthy to be there. His Flight into Egypt (Museo de Arte, Querétaro) rivals even Villalpando in its beauty and tenderness. His Education of the Virgin (Museo Regional, Guadalajara) has an unsurpassed serenity. He is also, like his brother, an able portraitist. His self-portrait (PV) has a startling intensity, as does his likeness of Fr Juan Rodríguez de la Parra (Sala Jesuita, La Profesa). That of viceroy duque de Linares (PV) is a superb representation of dignity, conveying a hint of sardonic humour in the heavy underlip. One of the very few works by *Nicolás de Correa* (fl. 1690s) to survive, and enough to mark him as a master of some taste, is a St Rose with Our Lady and the Infant Christ (PV), light shades predominating, as refreshing as a glass of champagne.

Of painters resident in Puebla, canvases by *José Rodríguez de Carnero* (d. 1725) line the church of La Concordia and the Cap. del Rosario in Sto Domingo. *Rodrigo de la Piedra* (d. 1682?), whose Crucifixion and Descent from the Cross are in the Cap. de la Soledad in the Cathedral, shows exceptional verve. *Juan Tinoco* (fl. 1680s) is equally vigorous, as in the Biblical Battle (PV) and the Apostolate (12 paintings; Pinacoteca Universitaria). Scenes from the Life of Our Lady by *Juan de Villalobos* (d. 1724) are included in the high altarpiece of the Medina Picazo chapel in La Regina in Mexico City. His best-known works are on the same theme in the Camarín of the Santuario de Ocotlán near Tlaxcala and in the Sacristy of La Compañía in Puebla. *Pascual Pérez* (late 17C–early 18C) has left paintings especially in Puebla and Cholula, incl. an ambitious and accomplished Patronage of Our Lady of Mount Carmel (El Carmen, Puebla). Respectable paintings by *Antonio de Santander* (fl. 1680s) are to be found in Cholula and works by *José Rubí de Marimón* (fl. 1670s–1729) in Puebla, Cholula, and Tlaxcala.

The Eighteenth Century

Although criticized for decadence, Mexican 18C painters produce much good work—for a wealthy upper class and a powerful clergy who favour elegance and suavity. Portrait-painting comes into its own, with unusual, exclusively Mexican, features.

The most famous of 18C painters are **José de Ibarra** (1688–1756) and **Miguel Cabrera** (1695–1768), both prolific, both heading overdriven studios and no doubt sometimes putting their signatures to paintings they may begin, but which are finished by their pupils. Ibarra's work may be seen in Mexico City, incl. his self-portrait (PV), and in the Museo Regional of his native Guadalajara. His Christ and the Woman taken in adultery (PV) reveals him at his most expressive and graceful. Cabrera's easy charm, sweetness, and theatricality, which so much reflect contemporary taste, may be enjoyed in the four huge canvases (Mexico Cathedral) glorifying Our Lady. As a portraitist, he is even more interesting. His *Sor Juana Inés de la Cruz* (Museo Nacional de Historia = MNH) is an accomplished posthumous portrait (from an original likeness), showing the learned, beautiful, and stately sitter in a study full of books. His *Sor María Josepha Augustina Dolores* (Tepotzotlán) is all stillness, piety, and simplicity.

Other 18C painters of note include *Antonio de Torres* (fl. 1708–28), whose works are especially evident in San Luis Potosí; *Francisco Martínez* (fl. 1718–54); *Juan Patricio Morlete Ruiz* (1715–71); *Nicolás Enríquez* (fl. 1730–87); *Diego de Cuentas* (d. 1744); *Francisco Antonio Vallejo* (fl. 1756–83); and **José de Alzíbar** (c 1725–1803), whose Adoration of the Kings (San Marcos, Aguascalientes) is very fine. His portrait of a nun in her finery on the day of her profession, *Sor María Ignacia de la Sangre de Cristo* (MNH), captures pensiveness and timidity. *Ignacio María Barreda* (fl. late 18C) is a portraitist of a popular, down-to-earth type, as his *Doña Juana María Romero* (MNH) witnesses. Works by *Andrés de Islas* (fl. 1760s) and *José de Páez* (1720–90) are not without interest.

18C painters from Puebla include *Luis Berrueco* (fl. 1727–33), *José Joaquín Magón* (fl. mid-18C), and various members of the Talavera family. The two huge canvases by *Pablo Joseph de Talavera* (fl. 1728–48) in La Soledad are most instructive for contemporary detail.

Among the best of late 18C masters is **Andrés López** (c 1740–1812). His Assumption and Our Lady of the Apocalypse (La Enseñanza, Mexico City) admirably complement that church's anastyle splendour; his Stations of the Cross (El Encino, Aguascalientes) are a considerable tour de force. He is also an expert portraitist. He skilfully catches the personality of the Belgian nun Anne-Thérèse Bonstet (private collection), who must be one of the great characters of 18C Mexico, despite his being able to concentrate only on the shrewd, humorous face—the part not enveloped by her habit.

Andrés López is but one of the 18–19C painters (many of them anon.) who do portraits of young girls on the day of their profession as nuns, dressed in much finery over their habits—a memory for the family they are rarely, if ever, to see again. Nuns are also painted, in similar finery, in death. Fascinating examples of this genre are to be found at Tepotzotlán, in the MNA, and in private collections.

The Valencian *Rafael Jimeno y Planes* (1759–1825), director of painting at the Academy, has left excellent portraits of Jerónimo Antonio Gil and Manuel Tolsá (PV). A portrait by his pupil *José María Vásquez* (fl. 1780s–1826), María Luisa Gonzaga Foncerrada y Labarrieta (PV), focuses on a personality—as though a Mexican guest has graced a Jane Austen novel.

Mexican Architecture and Art, 1821 to the Present Day

By Nicola Coleby

Early 20C developments are responsible above all for the worldwide reputation of modern Mexican art and architecture. The Mexican mural 'renaissance' of the 1920s led to the consolidation of an extraordinarily strong sense of national identity in the visual arts, which lasted until well into the 1950s, and had a powerful influence in the USA during the 1930s and 1940s. Artists such as Rufino Tamayo (1899–1991) and José Luis Cuevas (b. 1933) have achieved international reputations by working with a more universal, less nationalistic language; yet much of the imagery of earlier 20C art continues to pervade their work. Mexican architecture of the 20C owes its fame mainly to the way in which architects created buildings that draw on historical traditions, as in the

Ciudad Universitaria in Mexico City with its massive external decorations, or adapted them to their surroundings, such as the private residences built by Luis Barragán. Although much 19C artistic production is less flamboyant, it nevertheless provided strong foundations for the 20C flourishing.

Architecture

After 1821, the Academia de San Carlos was closed until 1824. It reopened with the appointment of *Pedro Patiño Ixtolinque* (1774–1835) as director, who had trained under Manuel Tolsá. It continued, however, to reflect the general turbulence of the country until 1843, when Santa-Anna decreed that it should be reorganized, with the directors of each discipline to be chosen from among European artists. Neoclassicism continued to predominate in Mexican architecture, although baroque ornamentation is present in Ixtolinque's best-known work, the high altarpiece in the Sagrario Metropolitano (completed 1827). French and Spanish influences were maintained by *Lorenzo de la Hidalga* (1810–72), who had trained in Madrid and Paris and arrived in Mexico in 1838, to serve both Santa-Anna and Maximilian. Many of his buildings no longer exist, but the structural simplicity he imposed on his neoclassical works can be seen in the elegant cupola with peristyle he erected for the church of Sta Teresa la Antigua in Mexico City (1845–58).

From 1856 to 1864 *Javier Cavallari*, formerly director of the Academy of Milan, ran the first architecture classes at the Academia de San Carlos, combining architecture with engineering. Almost his only work in Mexico is the two-storey façade of the Academia, with its elegant portico, niches with sculptures, and medallions. During this period, several churches and convents in Mexico City, such as San Francisco and Sto Domingo, were partially destroyed by the liberals in their fight to limit the power of the clerical conservatives. Simultaneously, wide new roads began to be constructed in Mexico City by the new generation of architect-engineers, with Independencia, begun in 1856, being one of the first. The road linking the Palacio Nacional to Chapultepec was begun a few years later under Maximilian. However, thanks to political turmoil, architecture did not begin to flourish in the 19C until after Juárez's death.

With the revival of architectural construction during the porfiriato, the popularity of neoclassical styles diminished as new, predominantly European, currents were introduced. French styles were emulated above all, but a general eclecticism came to characterize this period. French Mansard style was popular, as in La Esmeralda on Av. Madero in Mexico City; *Emilio Dondé* (1849–1905), who had trained in Paris, was prodigiously active, adopting various styles, in the capital. Semiclassical eclecticism was practised by *Antonio Rivas Mercado*, one of the greatest architects of the porfiriato, and can be seen in his completion of the Teatro Juárez in Guanajuato (1891–1903), with its neoclassical exterior and Moorish interior. Italianate influence can be seen both in the Secretaría de Comunicaciones y Obras Públicas begun in 1904 by the Italian architect *Silvio Contri*, and built in the style of an Italian Renaissance palace. Neo-gothic styles also appeared in Mexico, as in the ornamental details of the Correos building in Mexico City built by the Italian architect *Adamo Boari* and the engineer *Gonzalo Garita*. Neo-Islamic, neo-byzantine, neo-romanesque, and neo-baroque styles all appeared in cities throughout Mexico; even 'indigenismo' was absorbed into the eclectic range of styles practised during the porfiriato—one of the best examples being the monument to 'Cuauhtémoc' on Paseo de la Reforma in Mexico City, by *Francisco M. Jiménez* and *Miguel Noreña*. During the latter part of the porfiriato, Art Nouveau styles also became popular, of which examples can be seen in residential buildings in the Colonias Juárez and Roma. Many of the upper classes of Mexico City in these and other new colonias (Condesa, Tlalpan, Mixcoac) indulged in 'campestre romántica' flights of fancy, building their houses to resemble elegant suburban European models, such as Swiss chalets, French villas, Tudor houses.

The effects of the Revolution on architecture were an initial move towards the self-conscious definition of a Mexican style, with a final break with neo-classicism and a move away from the European eclecticism of the porfiriato. The elaborate use of prehispanic structures and motifs in designs for the Mexican pavilions in world fairs during the final years of the porfiriato had already testified to the interest stimulated by archaeological excavations. In the early 1900s, interest in the historical heritage had also begun to manifest itself, with *Jesús Acevedo* writing a number of texts urging architects to seek answers to contemporary architectural problems in historical structures. *Samuel Chávez* and *Manuel Torres Torija* were among the earliest architects to bring this into practice when in 1902–10 they built the Anfiteatro Bolívar in the Colegio de San Ildefonso, Mexico City: the reinforced concrete structure was clad with an 18C-style exterior, in keeping with the main body of the Colegio.

Enthusiasm for historical styles and traditional materials was rapidly super-seded by a more modern approach. *Carlos Obregón Santacilia* designed numerous public buildings in Mexico City, working initially in a neo-academic and then Art Nouveau style before embracing modernism. Works by him include the completion of the Monumento a la Revolución (1933), the Hotel del Prado, and the Instituto de Seguro Social, all in Mexico City. The influence of N American architecture also began to be felt in the capital, with the construc-tion of the first multi-storey building, 'La Nacional', in 1932 by *Manuel Ortiz Monasterio, Fernando Calderón* and *Luis Avila*, followed by others such as *José Cuevas'* Lotería Nacional building, completed in 1946. One of the first architects to embrace modernist practice, and influenced by such doctrines as functional-ism and the practice of Le Corbusier, was *José Villagrán García* (b. 1901), professor of architecture at the Academia from 1924. He designed numerous public buildings, incl. schools, hospitals, and markets, and was influential on the generation of students he taught. *Juan O'Gorman* (b. 1905) embraced the use of modern materials, seeking to create an economical 'machine for living', as in the studio he constructed in 1930 for Diego Rivera (now Museo Diego Rivera, San Angel). By 1950, however, he had abandoned functionalism, turn-ing instead to a high degree of ornamentation, using native materials and prehispanic motifs, as in his own house in the Pedregal de San Angel.

During the 1940s and 1950s, 'multifamiliares' were constructed by teams of architects in response to the ever-increasing expansion of Mexico City. The Miguel Alemán Multifamiliar (1947–50) was the work of *Mario Pani, Salvador Ortega, J. Gómez Gutiérrez* and *Jenaro de Rosenzweig*, with decorations by *Clara Porset*. *Mario Pani* collaborated with the artist José Clemente Orozco and sculptor Ortiz Monasterio, combining a mural and sculpture into the design of the Escuela Nacional de Maestros in Mexico City. One of the most strident collaborative architectural projects is the Ciudad Universitaria (1950–52), designed by 150 teachers and students from the Escuela Nacional de Arquitec-tura under the direction of *Carlos Lazo* (1914–55). Numerous buildings are spread over the large campus, many combining mural decorations with the architectural structure, as in the Biblioteca Central, with its mosaic mural by Juan O'Gorman; the Estadio Olímpico, by *Augusto Pérez Palacios, Jorge Bravo*, and *Raúl Salinas*, with stone and mosaic murals by Diego Rivera; and the Rectoría, by *Mario Pani* and *Enrique del Moral*, with a glass mosaic mural by David Alfaro Siqueiros.

Market complexes, churches, and public buildings throughout Mexico have continued in recent years to provide Mexican architects with opportunities for experimentation with modern materials. *Luis Barragán* has gained an interna-tional reputation for his use of monolithic walls, often with bright, traditional Mexican colours, internal patios, and incorporation of water as an architectural element in constructions built as private residences. Increasing ecological awareness has also occasioned a return to the use of traditional 'adobe', often combined with tezontle, and solar energy in private houses.

Painting and Sculpture

During the 19C, until the porfiriato, romantic and historical themes were developed by different groups of artists. Romanticism was introduced to Mexico by European traveller-artists, in parallel to the historical themes that predominated at the Academy.

The traveller-artists were among the first to depict Mexican landscapes and customs. The Englishman *Daniel Thomas Egerton* (c 1800–1842), the Frenchman *Jean-Baptiste Louis Gros* (1793–1870), and the German *Johann Moritz Rugendas* (1802–58) travelled through Mexico in the 1830s, painting panoramic landscapes and views of towns. Lithography was introduced to Mexico by the Italian *Claudio Linati* (1790–1832), and also used by the Englishman *Frederick Catherwood* (1799–1854) and the German *Carlos Nebel* (1805–55). Linati and Nebel detailed local customs and costumes, with Nebel recording contemporary townscapes as well as prehispanic buildings. Catherwood travelled throughout the Yucatán and produced some of the earliest records of prehispanic sites, adding contemporary Indian figures to them, emphasizing the splendours of the ancient buildings among the thick overgrowth. The images produced by these artists introduced new iconography, based on local landscapes and scenes, coupled with a sense of the sublime, into Mexican art.

Also outside the Academy, in the provinces, costumbrismo contributed to the development of a Mexican iconography. The Jaliscan artist *José María Estrada* (fl. 1830–60) received private commissions to commemorate traditional local events. Paintings such as 'Don Francisco Torres' (The Dead Poet [MNA]; 1846) are typical in their lack of perspective space, surface decoration, and use of script. *Agustín Arrieta* (1802–74) studied at Puebla Academy and produced more sophisticated work, but delighted in portraying local figures and still-lifes with regional foods and fruits. The self-taught guanajuatense artist *Hermenegildo Bustos* (1832–1907) made intense use of realism in portraits such as 'Doña Leocadia López de González' (1854), and in his bodegones, where depictions of Mexican fruit and vegetables are arranged geometrically over the surface of the canvas. The intense vitality of costumbrista work was later recouped by many artists in the 20C.

Developments in academic painting and sculpture were slow during the first half of the 19C until the reorganization of the Academy in 1843. Neoclassicism gained a tenuous hold, evident in many of the numerous portraits commemorating Iturbide. The sculptor *José María Labastida*, who studied in Paris and Rome (1825–35), produced neoclassical figures in marble, breaking with the earlier preference for carved wood. Painting was revitalised by the arrival at the Academy in 1846 of the Catalan **Pelegrín Clavé** (1810–80), whose Nazarene aesthetics had developed during his training in Barcelona and Rome. His preference for Biblical themes was consistent with the conservative government of the Academy, and one of his major works is 'The Seven Sacraments' painted on the cupola of the church of La Profesa in Mexico City (1861–67). His students included *José Salomé Pina* (1830–1909) and *Santiago Rebull* (1829–1902), who painted both Biblical and, later, historical compositions. Clavé's chief opponent was **Juan Cordero** (1824–84), who studied in Rome from 1844 to 1853, and painted accomplished neoclassical portraits such as 'Doña Dolores Tosta de Santa-Anna' (MNA, 1855), with fine attention to details such as the texture of materials. Both he and Clavé painted historical images of the founding of New Spain, and like Clavé, Cordero also painted church murals, the best of which is in the cupola of the Cap. del Señor de Sta Teresa (1857).

Manuel Vilar (1812–69), also Catalan, was appointed head of sculpture at the Academy in 1846, and executed a number of works in plaster commemorating national figures, incl. prehispanic ones, in neoclassical style. Landscape was introduced into the Academy for the first time in 1855 with the arrival of the Italian *Eugenio Landesio* (1810–79), who painted classical landscape compositions with small figures and attention to vegetation. His most talented students, *Luis Coto* (1830–91) and **José María Velasco** (1840–1912), developed landscape into one of the most striking genres of 19C Mexican painting. Velasco painted Mexico City from further and further afield, capturing the quality of light and the peculiarity of the landscape. Prehispanic ruins began to feature in his landscapes during the 1870s, and by the 1890s he had introduced symbols of industrial progress into his paintings, such as the steam engine in 'El Citlatépetl'.

By the 1870s, Biblical themes in academic painting and sculpture were replaced by historical themes, as the ideology of liberalism replaced the former conservatism. Prehispanic themes such as *Rodrigo Gutiérrez's* 'La Deliberación del Senado de Tlaxcala' (MNA, 1875) were used by both painters and sculptors. Notable historical works were also painted by *Félix Parra* (1845–1919), *Leandro Izaguirre* (1876–1941), and *José Jara* (1866–1939). Miguel Noreña's statue of *Cuauhtémoc* (Paseo de la Reforma, 1887) is one of the most grandiose bronze public sculptures, and is combined with the bronze statues of historical public figures that line that avenue. As in architecture, eclecticism predominated in the fine arts during the porfiriato: *Jesús F. Contreras* (1866–1902), for example, produced bronze sculptures, many of them of allegorical female figures, for public commissions throughout Mexico City, greatly influenced by French symbolism.

But perhaps the beginning of 20C modernism in Mexican art can be traced back to the late 19C movement known as *Modernismo*. A reaction against the positivist philosophy that pervaded cultural spheres during the porfiriato—with its emphasis on rationality, science, and progress—*Modernismo* was initially a literary movement that developed in Mexico during the 1890s, with artists providing illustrative work; like many other artistic manifestations, it was an eclectic movement, but this time drawing on elements of the irrational and the subconscious that were found in Symbolism, in Orientalism, in the 'decadent' art of Aubrey Beardsley, in Impressionism, and in other sources. The 'Revista Moderna' drew artists such as *Julio Ruelas* (1870–1911), who provided menacing etchings, as well as painting allegorical portraits in a naturalist style and in less overtly sinister tones. *Roberto Montenegro* (1886–1968) drew symbolist illustrations, stylistically close to Beardsley. *Alberto Fuster* (1879–1922) reveals different traits in his paintings; pale colours and classical compositions and figures, with allusions to classical Greek mythology, show yet another side of *Modernismo*. *Germán Gedovius* (1867–1937), a tutor at the Academy, influenced his students at the turn of the century with dark, allegorical oil paintings.

A different form of art, but one which was to be important during the early 20C, was political caricature, developed during the second half of the 19C. Artists such as *Gabriel Vicente Gahona* (1828–99), known as Picheta, and, above all, **José Guadalupe Posada** (1852–1913) engraved caricatures for newspapers commenting on current political events. Posada's enormous influence on later generations of artists was due, however, to his engravings on popular broadsheets for the publisher Vanegas Arroyo during the latter half of his career. Following in the tradition of an earlier engraver for Arroyo, *Manuel Manilla* (1830–90), Posada developed a range of images in which the fantastic and the supernatural describe everyday events in an expressionistic style, frequently using the calavera or skeleton figure in corrido scenes (popular songs). The predominance of the irrational in his images and their visual strength were influential on artists at the beginning of the 20C seeking a new visual iconography.

Just before the outbreak of the Revolution, a new cultural group was formed in Mexico which inherited many of the ideas of the modernistas; known as the *Ateneo de la Juventud*, the group was formed by writers and philosophers, incl. José Vasconcelos, who would become the influential Minister of Education after the Revolution, with artists affiliated on the perimeter. Concerned with developing Mexican culture, as well as with the education of the masses, and drawing on Latin American concepts, the Ateneo looked to Spanish culture and pre-

Independence cultural manifestations in Mexico, as well as some of the symbolism of the prehispanic world. The symbolist paintings of *Saturnino Herrán* (1887–1918), depicting both the Spanish and the prehispanic heritage of Mexican culture, are particularly close to the Ateneo philosophy.

Cut off from contact with Europe during the Revolution, many artists who remained in Mexico turned increasingly towards their own culture. *Dr Atl* (Gerardo Murillo; 1875–1964), who had travelled in Europe, called himself by a Náhuatl name and sought new imagery in Mexican landscape, as well as new techniques incl. an early attempt at mural decoration during the 1910s. **José Clemente Orozco** (1883–1949) painted small scenes of deprivation and poverty in Mexico City, while *Francisco Goitia* (1882–1960) depicted many of the events that occurred in the countryside during the Revolution. In 1913 Alfredo Ramos Martínez inaugurated an open-air painting school in the south of Mexico City, where students, who had rebelled against the confines of the Academy, learnt to paint out of doors alongside students with no previous formal art training, with a brightening of palettes and an interest in local scenes and subjects.

Other artists spent all or some of the years of the Revolution in Europe: Roberto Montenegro, **Diego Rivera** (1886–1957), and **David Alfaro Siqueiros** (1896–1974) absorbed both contemporary art in Paris and Barcelona, and earlier work in Italy. Both the artists who had remained in Mexico during the Revolution, and those who had been in Europe, became involved, after the Revolution, in the enormous educational programme of José Vasconcelos, who facilitated the initial development of Mexican mural painting through his plan for the decoration of public buildings in Mexico City. Early murals, incl. the decoration of the Colegio de San Pedro y San Pablo by Roberto Montenegro (1922), and the Anfiteatro Bolívar in the Escuela Nacional Preparatoria (1922) by Diego Rivera, were modernista in style, drawing on European traditions into which references to Mexican culture were inserted. Rivera, however, gradually transformed Vasconcelos' decorative intentions in the Secretaría de Educación Pública (1923–29), moving away from universal symbolism to depictions of popular Mexican customs, the struggle during the Mexican Revolution, and, as he became increasingly politicized, scenes alluding to world revolution. Similarly, in the Escuela Nacional Preparatoria (1923–26), Orozco, Siqueiros, and other artists depicted the political struggle of the Revolution. In 1923 the mural artists formed the Sindicato de Obreros, Trabajadores, Pintores y Escultores, which had close links with the Mexican Communist Party. Although short-lived as an organization, it had a lasting influence on mural painting in the degree to which murals were didactic and critical. The three main figures of the mural movement, Rivera, Orozco, and Siqueiros, had developed the characteristic styles and concerns found throughout their mural paintings by the end of the 1920s. Rivera's narrative style, use of popular types and overlapping imagery, and his depiction of Mexican history can be clearly seen in the Palacio de Cortés, Cuernavaca (1930–31), the Agricultural School of Chapingo (1923–36) and the Palacio Nacional in Mexico City (1929–51). Orozco's expressionistic style, his scepticism, and concern with universalism rather than political didacticism are well exemplified in his most ambitious project, the Hospicio Cabañas in Guadalajara (1938–39). Siqueiros remained politically uncompromising in his murals, suffering exile and imprisonment throughout his career for his beliefs; he was also the most interested in technical innovations, using new techniques and continuing to experiment in his mature works, as at the Poliforum Cultural Siqueiros in Mexico City (1965–71).

From the 1920s to the 1950s painting and sculpture in Mexico were dominated by the 'Escuela Mexicana', with the emphasis on large public commissions and nationalistic themes. The popular imagery found in the work of these artists, however, was also found in the work of others who chose to dissociate themselves from the nationalistic and frequently political themes of the 'Escuela Mexicana'. Artists such as *Miguel Covarrubias* (1904–57) and *Antonio Ruiz* (1897–1964) often painted small canvases depicting scenes of everyday life, frequently in a humorous vein. Other artists, like *Julio Castellanos* (1905–47), used forms and styles developed from the study of prehispanic motifs to depict similar scenes. *María Izquierdo* (1902–55) painted numerous still-lifes, using Mexican pottery, fruits and food, with a juxtapositioning of imagery that has sometimes led to her being called surrealist. *Frida Kahlo* (1907–54), the wife of Diego Rivera, produced a large body of self-portraits using Mexican costumes and imagery, as well as still-lifes and narrative paintings. The vibrancy and intensity of her work and its concern with the subconscious drew her to the attention of André Breton in 1938. The English *Leonora Carrington* (b. 1917) and the Spanish *Remedios Varo* (1908–63) also produced surrealist images, but with greater attention to detail and in more subdued tones. *Rufino Tamayo* (1899–1991) also rejected the political concerns of the Mexican muralists, producing bright, vibrant images in Mexican colours, often with a single central motif.

A strong photographic tradition has existed in Mexico since the Revolution. The American photographer *Edward Weston* (1886–1958) lived in Mexico from 1923 to 1926, producing portraits and photographs of local crafts, buildings, and vegetation that are distinguished for their angled and restricted viewpoint, the striking use of light, and the high degree of formalism. The Italian *Tina Modotti* (1896–1942), living and working with Weston, took formalistic and often highly symbolic photographs of people and objects. Concern with Mexican imagery is found in the work of one of Mexico's most distinguished photographers, *Manuel Alvarez Bravo* (b. 1902), who has delighted in capturing bizarre, ephemeral qualities of Mexican life and customs, as well as political imagery in his striking black and white photographs. Photography, especially in black and white, continues to thrive in Mexico, with a high proportion of excellent women photographers.

The graphic arts have also enjoyed wide practice in Mexico since the Revolution. In the 1920s and 1930s magazines and other publications were produced by different groups of artists, with striking images, often made from woodcuts. During the 1930s, graphic imagery became increasingly used for political purposes, beginning with the founding of the Liga de Escritores y Artistas Revolucionarios (LEAR) in 1933, and then the Taller de Gráfica Popular, founded in 1937 by *Leopoldo Méndez* (1902–69), *Luis Arenal*, and *Pablo O'Higgins* (1904–83). The Workshop was used by artists to produce political posters—often anti-fascist ones—but also lithographs, woodcuts, and lino-prints that were edited in portfolios, frequently depicting peasant life in Mexico.

The post-Revolutionary change in subject-matter in painting and the graphic arts also occurred in sculpture. Beginning with José Vasconcelos' commissioning in 1922 of sculptures for the Ministry of Education building in Mexico City from sculptors such as *Ignacio Asúnsolo* (1890–1965), naturalism began to predominate in sculpture with massive figures soon being used allegorically to represent the homeland, the soldier, the peasant in numerous public monuments. The female figure, both as mother earth and as an allegorical representation of the homeland, has also appeared frequently. On a smaller scale, *Germán Cueto* (1893–1975) has produced individual sculptures using different types of materials—incl. metal and glass—breaking with this naturalism. *Luis Ortiz Monasterio* (b. 1906) also moved away from nationalistic themes, using forms drawn from ancient Greek, Egyptian, or prehispanic sculpture to create symbolic sculptures. *Matías Goeritz* (b. 1915, Germany) arrived in Mexico in 1949, and introduced new ideas into Mexican sculptures with his El Eco Experimental Museum in Mexico City in 1953, using geometrical sculpture and the idea of installation work. The clean, geometrical shape of his monumental concrete sculpture, the Five Towers (1957–58; Ciudad Satélite, Mexico City), heralded abstract developments that occurred in the 1950s and 1960s in Mexico in both painting and sculpture, as artists looked outside their own country and towards international currents. A concern with more abstract forms and with the surface texture of the canvas is evident in the work of painters such as *Vicente*

Rojo (b. 1932), *Manuel Felguérez* (b. 1928), *Fernando García Ponce* (b. 1936), and *Arnaldo Coen* (b. 1940). Whilst the work of the painters *Alberto Gironella* (b. 1929) and *Francisca Corzas* (b. 1936) has remained figurative, the imagery is no longer based on Mexican themes and where references are made to history, it is frequently to European history. Gironella in particular has taken up themes related to Spanish art history, and has used montage techniques giving a sculptural quality to his work. Much of José Luis Cuevas' production is in graphic work, with strangely distorted and grotesque figures appearing in disturbing settings; his themes are often universal, sometimes dealing with Spanish historical and religious issues.

Whilst the visual arts continue to thrive in Mexico with increasing contact with Europe and the USA, international recognition of present-day Mexican art has often focussed on work that is recognizably Mexican in content. *Francisco Toledo* (b. 1940) produces paintings and works on paper that draw on Mexican mythology and nature, often with anthropomorphic figures. The delicate imagery and the unnatural use he makes of Mexican fauna, together with references to old traditions, have drawn much attention. The vitality of the Mexican visual arts, with much of their vibrancy due to the incorporation of popular art forms into 'high' art that has occurred throughout the 20C, continues today with active museum and gallery programmes.

Bibliography

There are several recently published general books on Mesoamerican prehistory. These have bibliographies of their own, which will lead the reader from the general to the specific. First and foremost is Muriel Porter Weaver's *The Aztecs, Maya, and their Predecessors: Archaeology of Mesoamerica* (3rd edn, San Diego, 1993). Its bibliography will lead the reader to almost every corner of prehistoric Mesoamerican research. Two books that together comprise a similar survey of ancient Mesoamerica are Michael Coe's *Mexico* (4th edn, London and New York, 1994) and *The Maya* (5th edn, London and New York, 1993). These are available in paperback, but their bibliographies are not so extensive as Weaver's. Sylvanus G. Morley's original book, *The Ancient Maya*, of 1946 has been updated several times. The 5th edn, by Robert J. Sharer (and now as much his authorship as Morley's) was published in 1994 (Stanford). Other surveys, somewhat older, include Michael Coe, Dean Snow, and Elizabeth Benson, *Atlas of Ancient America* (Oxford and New York, 1986); and Nigel Davies, *The Ancient Kingdoms of Mexico* (London, 1982).

Increasingly out of date, but still useful, are the volumes of the *Handbook of Middle American Indians*, a series of 16 volumes under the general editorship of Robert Wauchope (Austin, Texas, 1964–76). Since 1981 there have been several supplementary *HMAI* volumes summarizing more recent research.

Surveys of ancient Mesoamerican art and architecture include George Kubler's classic *Art and Architecture of Ancient America* (3rd edn, London, 1984) and Mary Miller's *The Art of Mesoamerica from Olmec to Aztec* (London and New York, 1986). Two large-format volumes with abundant and excellent colour photographs are Henry Stielin's *Art of the Maya from the Olmecs to the Toltec-Maya* (New York, 1981) and *Art of the Aztecs and its Origin* (New York, 1982). A definitive study of Aztec art is Esther Pasztory's *Aztec Art* (New York, 1983).

Studies of the Aztecs, with much that is relevant to earlier periods, include Nigel Davies's classic *The Aztecs: a History* (Norman, Oklahoma, 1973); the same author's more recent *The Aztec Empire: the Toltec Resurgence* (Norman, Oklahoma, 1987); Frances Berdan's *The Aztecs of Central Mexico: an Imperial Society* (New York, 1982); Rudolph van Zantwijk's *The Aztec Arrangement: the Social History of Pre-Spanish Mexico* (Norman, Oklahoma, 1985); Inga Clendinnen's *Aztecs: an Interpretation* (Cambridge, 1991); and Richard S. Townsend's *The Aztecs* (London and New York, 1992). Studies of specific aspects of Aztec society include Ross Hassig's *Trade, Tribute, and Transportation: the Sixteenth-century Political Economy of the Valley of Mexico* (Norman, Oklahoma, 1985) and the same author's *Aztec Warfare: Imperial Expansion and Political Control* (Norman, Oklahoma, 1988). The definitive study of Mesoamerican clothing, an aspect often otherwise neglected, is Patricia Rieff Anawalt's *Indian Clothing before Cortés: Mesoamerican Costumes from the Codices* (Norman, Oklahoma, 1981).

For the more ambitious, several academic periodicals that regularly have articles on ancient Mesoamerica include *American Antiquity, The Journal of Field Archaeology, The Journal of New World Archaeology*, and one devoted entirely to Mesoamerica—*Ancient Mesoamerica* (from Cambridge University Press, 1990–).

Books in English on Mexican historical art and architecture are few. The best are fundamental works by US specialists. George Kubler, *Mexican Architecture of the Sixteenth Century* (New Haven, 1948) is exhaustive. John McAndrew, *The Open-Air Churches of Sixteenth-Century Mexico: atrios, posas, open chapels, and other studies* (Cambridge, Mass, 1965) is a brilliant, witty, and elegant study of the achievements and styles of the friar builders. Elizabeth Wilder Weissman, *Mexico in Sculpture, 1521–1821* (Cambridge, Mass, 1950) is full of acute, sympathetic insights. Joseph Armstrong Baird, *The Churches of Mexico, 1530–1810* (Berkeley and Los Angeles, 1962) is a stimulating study. Pál Kelemen, *Baroque and Rococo in Latin America* (2nd edn, New York, 1967) has good coverage of Mexico. Of the many works by Manuel Toussaint (1890–1955), great Mexican pioneer of studies into the subject, his *Arte Colonial en México* has been lovingly and expertly edited and translated (with a valuable added bibliography) by Elizabeth Wilder Weissman as *Colonial Art in Mexico* (Austin, Texas, 1967). Other, more specialist, studies are Sidney David Markman, *Architecture and Urbanization in Colonial Chiapas* (Philadelphia, 1984) and Robert James Mullen, *Dominican Architecture in Sixteenth-century Oaxaca* (Phoenix, 1975).

Three indispensable works on the historical geography of New Spain by Peter Gerhard: *A Guide to the Historical Geography of New Spain* (Cambridge, 1972); *The Southeast Frontier of New Spain* (Princeton, 1979); *The North Frontier of New Spain* (Princeton, 1982). Three books on Mexican history and Mexico today: Lesley Byrd Simpson, *Many Mexicos* (4th edn, Berkeley and Los Angeles, 1966), shrewd and entertaining; Alan Riding, *Mexico: Inside the Volcano* (paperback edn, London, 1989), an essential, absorbing overview of Mexican history, politics, and the economy; Ramón Eduardo Ruiz, *The Great Rebellion: Mexico 1905–1924* (New York, 1980), a masterly reinterpretation of the Revolution. Fanny Calderón de la Barca (Frances Erskine Inglis), *Life in Mexico* (Boston, Mass, 1843, and many reprints) is a delightful, classic, account by the Scottish wife (resident in the USA) of the first Spanish minister to Mexico in 1839–42.

The text of this guide is also interspersed with quotations from other travellers. Among the English are Thomas Gage (1625–26), William Bullock (1823), George Francis Lyon (1826), Henry George Ward (1827), and Thomas Brocklehurst (1881); among Americans Joel Poinsett (1822) and John F. Finerty (1879); and among French, Mathieu de Fossey (mid-19C).

Works in Spanish abound. Though it would be invidious to mention only a few, we shall risk it. Diego Angulo Iñiguez, Enrique Marco Dorta, and Mario Buschiazzo, *Historia del arte hispanoamericano* (3 vols, Barcelona, 1945–56) is a magisterial survey, incl. much on Mexico. Manuel Toussaint, *Paseos coloniales* (2nd edn, Mexico, 1983), a collection of essays on historical monuments; *La catedral y las iglesias de Puebla* (Mexico, 1954); *Pintura colonial en México* (2nd edn, Mexico, 1982). Francisco de la Maza, *El pintor Cristóbal de Villalpando* (Mexico, 1964); *El arte colonial en San Luis Potosí* (2nd edn, Mexico, 1985). Guillermo Tovar de Teresa, *México barroco* (Mexico, 1981), beautifully illustrated. Elisa Vargas Lugo, *La iglesia de Santa Prisca de Tasco* (Mexico, 1971). Elisa Vargas Lugo, José Guadalupe Victoria, and Gustavo Curiel, *Juan Correa: su vida y su obra* (Mexico, 1985, 1991)—Tomo II (in 2 parts), Catalogue of Works, and Tomo III, Documentation, published so far. Rogelio Ruiz Gomar, *El pintor Luis Juárez* (Mexico, 1987). Clara Bargellini, *La catedral de Chihuahua* (Mexico, 1984); *La arquitectura de la plata; iglesias monumentales del centro-norte de México, 1640–1750* (Mexico and Madrid, 1991). A topographical classic: Hugo Leicht, *Las calles de Puebla* (4th edn, Puebla, 1986).

For 19C and 20C art and architecture we recommend the following. Dawn Ades, *Art in Latin America. The Modern Era, 1820–1980.* Exhibition catalogue, The Hayward Gallery (London, 1989). Oriana Baddeley and Valerie Fraser, *Drawing the Line. Art and Cultural Identity in Contemporary Latin America* (London, 1989). Anita Brenner, *Idolos tras los Altares* (Mexico; rev. edn, 1983). Jean Charlot, *The Mexican Mural Renaissance 1920–25* (Austin, Texas, 1963). Olivier Debroise, *Figuras en el Trópico, Plástica Mexicana 1920–40* (Barcelona, 1984). Emily Edwards, *Painted Walls of Mexico* (Austin & London, 1977). Justino Fernández, *El Arte del siglo XIX en México* (Mexico, 1952; rev. edn, 1983). Elisa García Barragán, *El pintor Juan Cordero* (Mexico, 1984). Shifra M. Goldman, *Contemporary Mexican Painting in a Time of Change* (Austin & London, 1977). Edward Lucie-Smith, *Latin American Art of the 20th Century* (London, 1993). *Mexico: Splendors of Thirty Centuries.* Exhibition catalogue, The Metropolitan Museum of Art (New York, 1990). Raquel Tibol, *Historia General del Arte Mexicano. Epoca Moderna y Contemporánea*, 2 vols. (Barcelona, 1975).

Glossary

ABANICO. Lit., fan. Latticed screen filling in arch of vault and shaped like a fan, above grille of coro alto in nuns' churches.

ACOMPAÑANTE. Anthropomorphic urn representing priest or devotee, found in Zapotec tombs accompanying larger deity urn.

ACRYLIC. Acrylic paint, made from acrylic resin, particularly suitable for indoor and outdoor murals.

ADOBE. Sun-dried (unfired) mud brick.

AFRANCESADO. In the French style, favoured in architecture of porfiriato.

AGUADA. Seasonal waterhole in lowland Yucatán limestone region, natural or man-made.

AHUEHUETE. Kind of giant cypress.

AJARACA. Stucco bow and ribbon relief.

AJIMEZ. Round-headed windows divided by thin colonnette.

ALCALDE. Mayor.

ALCALDIA MAYOR. Administrative division subordinate to a political unit of New Spain.

ALFARJE. Timber ceiling, planks carved and interlocking.

ALFIZ. Rectangle described above arch, helping to frame church portal.

ALGUACIL. Constable.

ALHONDIGA. Store for wheat and other grains, especially for buying and selling in times of scarcity.

ALMEHEN. Maya male noble.

ALMOHADILLA. Projecting wall stone.

ALMOHADILLADO. Pattern of square and projecting stones on a façade.

ALTEPETL. Aztec city-state.

AMATE. (i) Tree of mulberry family. (ii) Náhuatl *amatl*: paper made from inner bark of wild fig tree used for codices (sing. codex).

ANASTYLE. Extreme development of baroque (sometimes called ultrabaroque; after 1750) in church façades and altarpieces, marked by ornamental niche pilasters or seeming absence of any support amid wealth of decoration.

ANTESACRISTY. Room between sacristy and presbytery of church.

ARCHITRAVE. Lowest of three main parts of entablature, below frieze and cornice, forming horizontal beam.

ARCHIVOLT. Moulding of face of arch.

ART DECO. Eclectic architectural style, emphasizing individuality, of 1920s and 1930s.

ART NOUVEAU. Stylized adaptation of floral and plant forms giving graceful linear patterns, a decorative style much favoured in late 19C and early 20C Mexico.

ARTESONADO. Coffered (square or polygonal) or panelled ceiling, typical of Mudéjar style, covered with repeated relief (sometimes gilded) ornament of wooden ribs either intersecting or forming rows of polygonal coffers.

ARZOBISPADO. Archbishop's palace.

ASHLAR. Masonry of dressed rectangular stones laid in regular horizontal courses, usually with a regular pattern of joints.

ASTRAGAL. Narrow moulding, semicircular in section, at top or bottom of column.

ATADURA. Upper and lower moulding defining decorative frieze on upper façade of Classic Period Maya structures, esp. in Puuc style.

ATECOCOLLI. Ancient Mesoamerican conch shell trumpet; Maya *hub*.

ATLANTE. Male figure as decorative column supporting roof of structure.

ATLATL. Spear-thrower (Náhuatl), comprising short grooved stick with notch or hook at one end (to hold spear butt) and finger loops at other end (to propel missile); Maya HULCHE.

ATRIO. (i) Large quadrangular open-air space limited by wall, in front of convent, where Indians could hear Mass offered in open chapel. (ii) Courtyard in front of church.

AUDIENCIA. Supreme court.

AUTO DE FE. Execution in public by civil tribunal of sentence pronounced by Inquisition.

AYUNTAMIENTO. (i) Seat of town government. (ii) The government itself.

AZULEJO. Glazed, coloured tile.

BAJOS. Broad, swampy depressions in the Maya Petén, cultivated with chinampa-like fields.

BALAM. Maya for jaguar.

BALCHE. Maya ritual alcoholic drink of honey and balché tree bark.

BALDACHIN. Decorative canopy covering altar.

BALUSTER. Column shaped like baluster—hallmark of plateresque.

BARGUEÑO. Desk of a type originating from Burgos (prov. of Toledo).

BAROQUE. In Mexican architecture the style may be taken as developing from a more subjective and imaginative approach than the Mannerist, leading to a dramatic focus of design elements and manifesting various phases: (i) transitional (from mid-17C); (ii) solomonic baroque, marked by use of solomonic column (late 17C–early 18C); (iii) churrigueresque (c 1720–80);

(iv) anastyle baroque; (v) neostyle baroque (both after 1750).

BARRIO. District of city or town.

BEVELLED. Square edge cut to more obtuse angle.

BLANCO LEVANTADO. Unburnished, painted decoration on pottery of white, transparent, streaky lines.

CABILDO. (i) Town council. (ii) Cathedral chapter.

CACAO. Chocolate bean tree; in Mesoamerica, a major trade item, used to make a drink for the Aztec privileged class, also as 'coinage' in market places.

CACIQUE. (i) Native term (West Indian origin) for chief. (ii) Local political boss.

CACIQUISMO. Rule by political boss.

CAJA-ESPIGA. Peg and socket elements in securing columnar sections from lateral movement (eg, ATLANTE figures).

CALENDAR ROUND. Ancient Mesoamerican 52-year cycle of the permutation of the 260-day and 365-day calendrical systems.

CALMECAC. Aztec school or college for the sons of kings and nobility.

CALPULLI. In Aztec society, a corporate kin group of patrilineages that owned land and largely regulated its own affairs; there were 20 calpulli in Tenochtitlán.

CAMARIN. Small chamber.

CAMPESINO. Agricultural worker.

CAÑA DE MAIZ. Corn pith.

CANDELERO. Small pottery incense burner in candlestick-like shape; esp. common at Teotihuacán.

CANEPHORA. Sculptured female figure carrying basket on her head.

CAÑITAS. Small Preclassic Period solid figurine type, Cuicuilco area, Basin of Mexico—simple, nude females, with large holes for eyes, surrounded by circle or punctations.

CANTERA VERDE. Greenish soft stone characteristic of Oaxaca.

CARCEL. Prison.

CASA SEÑORIAL. Nobleman's mansion.

CELOTEX. Artificial paint substance.

CENOTE. In Yucatán, a natural well formed when limestone crust collapses, exposing underlying ground water.

CHACMOOL. Life-sized, reclining stone figure, with legs flexed and head turned to one side; figure often holds a stone box on the abdomen to receive offering; associated with temples.

CHALCHIHUITL. Náhuatl for jade or other prized green stones, incl. jadeite, green obsidian, green rock crystal; represented in sculpture as disc with central hole.

CHAMP-LEVE. Decoration technique on pottery in which part of design is heavily carved.

CHANCEL. Space in church, immediately in front of apse, reserved for clergy.

CHEMIN-DE-RONDE. Exterior walkway round upper part of building, usually shielded by parapet protected by battlements.

CHIA. Lime-leafed sage, used in ancient Mesoamerica to make a soft drink.

CHIAROSCURO. Distribution of light and shade, apart from colour, in a painting.

CHICHIMEC. Generic term for nomadic peoples N of Mesoamerica proper, who frequently caused problems for urbanized Mesoamericans by invasions/migrations.

CHINAMPA. Artificial rectangular fields separated by canals extending from lakeshore; created and kept fertile by dredging lakebed mud and spreading it over the surface within a wooden and reed framework; anchored to the lakebed by trees, not 'floating' gardens.

CHINESCO. Hollow ceramic figurine type with generalized oriental facial features.

CHOIR. In Mexico, usually balcony at back end of nave, to accommodate singers.

CHULTUN. Bottle-shaped underground water storage cistern in N Yucatán; in S Yucatán, with lateral chambers, for food storage.

CHURRIGUERESQUE. In Mexico, extremely ornamental architectural style (c 1720–80) marked by use of estípite.

COA. Mesoamerican digging stick used in planting.

COATEPANTLI. Wall formed by stone serpents around Postclassic Period Central Highland sacred precincts.

CODEX (pl. codices). Painted book of AMATE paper or deer skin, folded concertina-like or rolled; both prehispanic and post-conquest.

COFFER. Square or polygonal sinkage in ceiling, or in soffit or archivolt of arch or in beam.

COLONNETTE. Small decorative column.

COMAL (Náhuatl *comalli*). Slightly convex round pottery griddle for cooking tortillas.

CONGREGACION. Indian settlement in New Spain, to facilitate religious instruction and use of labour.

CONVENT (CONVENTO). (i) In New Spain community of friars and missionizing centre. (ii) Community of nuns in town.

COPAL. Incense from resins of various tropical trees; used in ancient Mesoamerican rituals.

COPILLI. Huastec conical headdress, typical of the god Quetzalcóatl.

CORBEL. Block of stone projected outwards beyond faces of stones below in order to support something above.

CORD MARKING. Pottery decoration made by pressing fine cord, wrapped around a wooden paddle, into unfired vessel.

CORNICE. Projecting group of mouldings usually used to crown building or important part of building.

CORO ALTO, CORO BAJO. Higher and lower choirs in nuns' churches.

CORREGIDOR. Under viceroyalty, executive officer appointed by crown and enjoying political and judicial authority in his district.

COSTUMBRISTA. Showing local customs and manners.

CRATICULA. Opening by grille of a coro bajo, through which nuns received communion.

CREOLE. Someone of Spanish or other European blood born in New Spain.

CUAUHXICALLI. 'Eagle cup'; stone box-like receptacle for receiving and burning the hearts of sacrificial victims.

CUPOLA. Dome, on semicircular or polygonal base.

DADO. Finishing of wood or tiles running along lower part of wall.

DANZANTE. Life-sized or near life-sized low relief carved figures of prisoners or sacrificial victims on stone slabs; esp. at Monte Albán.

DELEGACION. One of 16 large divisions of Federal District.

DENTIL. Tooth-like block used as moulding in classical cornices.

DOCTRINA. Indian congregation or parish.

DOMICAL. Pertaining to vault shaped like dome.

DRUM. Hollow cylinder of wall carrying cupola.

EARED FRAME. Feature of 17–18C church façades where corners of frame of relief are developed in rectangular shapes.

EJIDO. (i) Small plot of land rented out by government. (ii) Land held in common by villagers.

ENCARNACION. In New Spain, tinted finish to wooden sculpture to represent flesh.

ENCOMIENDA. Royal grant of native labour to Spanish settler.

ENTABLATURE. That part of classical order above column—architrave, frieze, cornice.

ENTRECALLE. Space between columns or estípites.

ENTRESUELO. Mezzanine.

ERMITA. Small independent chapel, often out of town.

ESPADAÑA. Wall pierced with arches in which bells are hung.

ESTIPITE. Inverted obelisk base with various ornamental blocks above, covered with decorative capital.

ESTOFADO. In New Spain, technique in sculpture of representing flow of garment, worked out in colour on gold or silver base.

EXTRADOS. Outer curved face of arch.

FINIAL. Ornament placed as final touch on gable or roof.

FLORERO. Ceramic jar with tall, restricted neck and flared rim; esp. at Teotihuacán.

FRAY. Title given to friar, and even to secular priest.

FRESCO. Mural painted on wet plaster. On the wall beneath is made the sketch in red earth pigment and the full-size preparatory drawing is transferred on to the fresh plaster before the fresco is begun either by pricking the outline with small holes over which a powder is dusted, or by means of a stylus which leaves an incised line on the wet plaster.

GADROON. One of series of convex curves joined at extremities to form pattern.

GARITA. Sentry-box.

GESSO. Prepared plaster surface as ground for painting.

GRISAILLE. Painting in grey monotone to represent relief.

GROIN. Square vault formed like intersection of two barrel vaults at right angles.

HAAB. Maya 365-day calendar; Aztec XIHUITL.

HACHA. Associated with the Mesoamerican ball game: thin, stone slabs resembling hatchet blades in general shape, decoratively carved.

HACIENDA. (i) Landed estate. (ii) Treasury.

HALACH UINIC. Hereditary Maya civic ruler in Yucatán, with some priestly functions as well.

HUEHUETL. Vertical, skin-headed drum, played with fingers and palms.

HUIPIL. Traditional Mesoamerican 'native' cotton blouse, formed by two woven rectangles; frequently brocaded or embroidered.

HULCHE. Maya spear-thrower (ATLATL).

HUMILLADERO. Wayside shrine containing Crucifix.

IMPOST. Part of pier or wall on which rests lowest part of arch.

INCENSARIO. Ceramic vessel for coal and incense used in ancient Mesoamerican ceremonies.

INTENDANCY (INTENDENCIA). Administrative division of late 18C New Spain.

INTERESTIPITE. Space (often highly ornamented) between estípites.

INTRADOS. Inner curve or underside of arch.

ISABELINE GOTHIC. Late 15C Spanish architectural manner in which Mudéjar, Flemish, Burgundian, and other exotic motifs are used to elaborate Gothic elements.

IXTLE. Náhuatl for maguey.

JAMB. Side post of doorway.

JUEGO DE PELOTA. Mesoamerican ball court.

KEYSTONE. Central stone of arch.

LABRET. Ornament inserted in lower lip, usually cylindrical.

LAMBREQUIN. Hanging cut-paper ornament, feature of Mexican churrigueresque and of anastyle and neostyle baroque.

LAPIDA. Carved stone slab, smaller than usual stele, characteristic of Zaachila and Late Zapotec culture.

LONJA. Covered gallery.

LUNETTE. Semicircular space in vault or ceiling, or above door or window, often decorated with a painting or relief.

MACEHUAL. Aztec commoner.

MACUAUHUITL. Aztec 'broad sword' of hardwood set on opposing edges with obsidian blades.

MAESTRO DE OBRAS, MAESTRO MAYOR. Chief architect.

MALACATE. Spindle whorl, usually ceramic—perforated disc used as weight in drop-spinning.

MANDORLA. Almond-shaped frame to enclose figure of Christ or Our Lady.

MANNERIST. In late 16C and 17C New Spain, the final phase of the Renaissance style. In its first stage, purist and classicizing, the strict application of Renaissance ideals in architecture and art; in its second, involving a play with accepted rules, a sort of pre-baroque, where coldness gives way to lively decoration.

MANO. Cylindrical rubbing stone for grinding maize on a METATE.

MANUELINE GOTHIC. Late Gothic style of Portugal, which flourished during the reign of Manuel I (1469–1521), tinged with exotic influences from Mudéjar, African, and perhaps Indian art.

MARIACHIS. Strolling singers and players, of loud trumpet-infected music, in distinctive, heavily-decorated costumes.

MASONITE. Cement or plastic based substance used as support for murals by Orozco and Siqueiros.

MAXTLATL. Central Mesoamerican breechcloth.

MAYEQUE. Aztec bondsman or 'slave'.

MAYORAZGO. Entailed estate.

MERLON. Single battlement.

MESTIZO. Person with mixture of Spanish and Indian blood.

METATE. Mesoamerican flat or dished quern stone for maize grinding with a MANO.

METOPE. Square space between two triglyphs in classical frieze.

MEXICA. One of the traditional seven Aztec tribes; more commonly called Aztec.

MILPA. Náhuatl for cornfield, in which 'slash and burn' agriculture was practised.

MIXTILINEAR. Of an arch partly of straight and partly of curved lines.

MODILLION. Small bracket supporting cornice.

MOLCAJETE. Bowl with interior surface scored or roughened for grinding vegetables and fruit; usually ceramic and tripod.

MONSTRANCE. Display vessel for Host on altar or for processions of the Blessed Sacrament.

MUDEJAR. Art in Muslim or Muslim-influenced style made for Spanish Christians.

MUNICIPIO. An urban area and surrounding country in its jurisdiction.

NAHUATL. Language of the Aztecs; became lingua franca of the Aztec Empire.

NEMONTEMI. Five unlucky days at end of Aztec year (cf. UAYEB).

NEOCLASSICAL. Influential revival of classical architectural and sculptural style, in Mexico from the late 18C.

NEOSTYLE. Soberer baroque, with classical elements, of late 18C.

NICHE PILASTER. Elaborate, disguised, support holding richly decorated niche—hallmark of anastyle baroque. Sometimes also forming interestípite.

OBSIDIAN. Natural, volcanic glass (grey, black, dark green, red, streaked).

OCTLI. Náhuatl for fermented drink, usually for PULQUE.

OGEE. Pointed arch with S-curved sides—concave below and convex above.

OIDOR. Judge who is member of audiencia.

OLLAMA. Náhuatl for ball game.

OMICHICAHUAZTLI. Notched bone (usually human or deer) rasp played with a stick.

OPEN CHAPEL. Open-air chapel, alongside main church, wherein Mass was celebrated for Indians assembled in atrio of convent.

PAINT CLOISONNE. Cutting out of the surface colour, filling the hollow with a different colour paste, and smoothing down to the original surface level.

PALACIO DE GOBIERNO. Headquarters of State government in State capital.

PALACIO FEDERAL. Contains representation of federal government in State capital.

PALACIO MUNICIPAL. Town hall.

PALMA. Associated with the Mesoamerican ball game: narrow, spade-shaped stone artefacts, decoratively carved.

PARROQUIA. Parish church.

PATOLLI. Mesoamerican game, similar to pachisi, played on a divided, cross-shaped board; esp. by Aztecs, Toltecs, Teotihuacanos and Maya.

PEDIMENT. Triangular or curved gable outlined by cornices.

PENATE. Small stone Mixtec amulet(?) figure.

PENDENTIVE. Concave spandrel beneath dome.

PEON. Rural labourer, farmhand.

PETATE (Náhuatl *petatl*). Woven straw mat; ancient Mesoamerican symbol of authority.

PETATILLO. Relief in mat-like, or basket-weave, pattern.

PILLI. Aztec privileged class.

PLATERESQUE. Adaptation in 16C New Spain of type of Renaissance architectural decoration which flourished in Spain in first half of 16C. Relief is concentrated around portals and windows, in contrast with smooth emptiness of rest of façade. Plateresque can contain elements of Isabeline Gothic, a style it supersedes—flattish dense patterns (heraldic, vegetal, geometric) of Mudéjar type, elaborating Spanish Gothic features.

PLAZUELA. Small plaza.

POCHTECA. Aztec professional trader class, who also served as spies; often used generically for ancient Mesoamerican long-distance traders.

POK-TA-POK. Maya for ball game.

POLYCHROME. Painted in several colours.

POLYSTYRENE. Special paint, suitable for use on cement, eg, by Rivera in the Cárcamo del Río Lerma murals, largely destroyed by chlorinated water.

PORFIRIATO, PORFIRIAN. Reign of Porfirio Díaz (1876–1911); adjective pertaining to it.

PORTADA. Frontispiece, façade.

PORTALES. Arcades surrounding plaza.

PORTERIA. Porch at main entrance to convent.

POSA. Small chapel with open entrances at each corner of atrio, used as stopping place in processions of the Blessed Sacrament.

PREDELLA. Long, narrow section forming base of altarpiece.

PRESBYTERY. Far part of chancel where altar stands.

PRESIDIO. Garrison.

PRONUNCIAMIENTO. Military rising.

PUEBLO. People; village.

PUERTA ABOCINADA. Concave façade.

PUERTA CHATA. 'Flat doorway'—flattening of corner of building to accommodate a doorway.

PULQUE. Mesoamerican alcoholic drink made from maguey or agave.

PYROXYLIN. Cellulose nitrate. Paint used on metals, wood, masonite, cloth; applied with air pistol, brush, or spatula.

QUECHQUEMITL (QUEXQUEMITL). Sleeveless blouse of two rectangular parts joined so as to hang in a point front and back.

QUETZAL. Tropical bird of mountainous Chiapas, Guatemala, and Honduras, whose green tail feathers were used in Mesoamerica for decoration, costume, and symbol; Maya *kuk*.

REAL DE MINAS. Mining settlement.

REFORM. Crucial phase (1855–61) in Mexican history marked by implementation of the Reform laws to abolish power of Roman Catholic Church and to deprive it of its wealth, so that this could be put to uses of the State; culminating in three years' war (1858–61) between liberals and conservatives, in which former emerged victorious.

REGIDOR. Municipal councillor.

RENAISSANCE. 15–16C architectural style. In New Spain: eclectic, plateresque, Mannerist.

RESIST PAINTING (NEGATIVE PAINTING). Pottery decoration technique in which design is covered, before firing, with wax or other substance, and paint applied; when wax is removed, design remains in base colour. Alternatively, design on fired vessel is covered with clay slip, a vegetable substance rubbed on and low heat applied; after cooling, vegetable substance is removed.

RETABLE. Set of decorated panels of sculpture or painting rising above back of altar.

ROCAILLE. Rococo decoration, with shell and coral forms, and C and S curves.

ROCKER-STAMPING. Pottery decoration made by 'walking' a sharp, curved edge (eg, a shell) along vessel surface to create an incised zigzag line.

ROCOCO. Development of late baroque, stressing asymmetry. ·

ROLLO. Tower in plaza, from whose base justice was dispensed.

ROOF-COMB. Tall stone superstructure on Lowland Maya temples; often covered in stucco, then elaborately carved and painted.

RURALES. Repressive rural police under Pres. Díaz.

SACBE (pl. SACBEOB). Maya causeway of huge stone blocks with gravel and plaster paving; both within and between sites.

SAGRARIO. Parish church.

SALA DE PROFUNDIS. Chapter hall in convent.

SALON DE ACTOS. Hall of university reserved for academic ceremonies.

SANCTUARY. Apse and space in front of altar.

SECRETARIA. Department of State.

SERPENT-COLUMN. Toltec support column in form of serpent: upright sections form the serpent's body, the open-mouthed head (at right angles to body) forms the base, and the tail (also at right angles) forms the top.

SGRAFFITO. Technique of decorating wall by scraping through thin surface layer of plaster to lower coat, usually of different colour.

SHAFT-TOMB. Tomb form in W Mexico comprising a vertical shaft down to one or more horizontal galleries for burials.

SOFFIT. Exposed underside of arch.

SOLOMONIC. Of twisted column, so-called for its supposed use in Solomon's temple, and a hallmark of Mexican baroque.

SOTOCORO. Space in church beneath choir.

SPANDREL. Triangular space between outer edge of arch and vertical member beside it—or triangle between two adjacent arches.

STEPPED FRET. Painted and stone architectural abstract decorative form comprising diagonally rising steps ending in a curved hook; possibly inspired by serpents or waves.

STRAPWORK. Relief decoration similar to fretwork or cut leather.

TABLERO. Elongated rectangular concave or convex panel in façade.

TALUD-TABLERO. Ancient Mesoamerican architectural form comprising a sloping face (*talud*) surmounted and cantilevered by a rectangular, vertical panel (*tablero*); esp. Classic Period Teotihuacán, but many regional variations; often decoratively carved, plastered, and painted.

TAMIMES. Semicivilized Chichimecs in the Late Postclassic Period; eg, Mexica Aztecs before founding Tenochtitlán.

TECALI. Mexican onyx: banded calcite, travertine, or translucent alabaster.

TECHCATL. Sacrificial stone, shaped so as to arch the victim's back and thrust the chest forward for cutting open the chest and extracting the heart.

TECOMATE. Early Mesoamerican spherical ceramic vessel form with restricted mouth and no collar.

TECUHTLI. Privileged class in Tenochtitlán; also Aztec honorary title.

TELPOCHCALLI. Aztec school for MACEHUALS; incl. training in warfare.

TEMALACATL. Circular stone platform on which special sacrificial victims were allowed to defend themselves, armed with a feather-edged MACUAUHUITL, against Aztec warriors armed with obsidian-edged ones.

TEMESCAL. Mesoamerican sweat bath, for both cleansing and ritual.

TEMPERA. Method of painting in distemper.

TEOXIHUITL. Náhuatl for turquoise.

TEPETATE. Yellow-beige, compact, fine-grained volcanic-derived natural subsoil.

TEPONAZTLI. Horizontal cylindrical wooden drum with tongue-like slots, played with rubber-tipped sticks to produce different tones.

TEQUITQUI. Post-Conquest art using European motifs with Indian sense of pattern.

TEZONTLE. Porous reddish-brown, grey, or black volcanic rock; esp. in Basin of Mexico.

TINDALO. Philippine cedar.

TLACHTLI. Náhuatl for ritual ball court.

TLATOANI. Aztec hereditary ruler.

TONALPOHUALLI. Aztec 260-day cycle of 13 'months' of 20 days each; Maya TZOLKIN.

TRACHYTE. Volcanic rock with gritty surface.

TRIGLYPHS. Blocks separating metopes in classical frieze.

TRIPLAY. Three layers of wood compressed together, used as support for paintings or murals.

TRITOSTILO. Describing column of which one-third is decorated in a distinctive way; or divided into three distinct parts.

TUMP-LINE. Traditional porter's strap in ancient Mesoamerica, for carrying heavy loads on back, passing over chest or forehead.

TYMPANUM. Triangular space enclosed by mouldings of pediment.

TZOLKIN. Maya 260-day cycle; see TONALPOHUALLI.

TZOMPANTLI. Skull rack, either to hold actual skulls of human sacrificial victims skewered on poles, or of carved stone; usually associated with temple.

UAYEB. Five unlucky days at end of Maya year (cf. NEMONTEMI).

VILLA. Settlement in New Spain with privileges granted by crown.

VISITA. Dependency of convent where friars did not live, but visited to say Mass and administer sacraments.

VOLADOR. 'Flyer'; Mesoamerican ceremony in which men, dressed as gods or birds, descend to the ground from a rotating platform atop a pole, on ropes secured to their waists and wrapped around the pole; sometimes a musician stands on the platform playing a flute and small drum.

VOLCANIC DIVIDE. 'Sierra Volcánica Transversal', extending from San Blas on Pacific coast to State of Veracruz near Gulf coast.

VOLUTE. Double-spiral scroll.

VOUSSOIR. One of wedge-shaped blocks which constitute arch.

XIHUITL. Aztec 365-day calendar; Maya HAAB.

YACATA. Tarascan stepped platform-mound of keyhole plan with elongated T at the shaft end.

YUGO. Associated with the Mesoamerican ball game: richly-carved U-shaped stone artefact to fit around the hips of a ball player; stone yugos are thought to have been used only in ritual, whereas similar gear made of wood and leather, as padding, was worn in actual play.

PRACTICAL INFORMATION

TRAVEL TO MEXICO

Numerous **Air Services** operate direct from major US cities. Examples are given below.

PanAm run daily flights to Mexico City from New York, Washington DC, Houston, Los Angeles, and Miami.

Delta. Daily to Mexico City and to Acapulco from Dallas/Fort Worth. Daily to Mexico City from Atlanta. Daily to Acapulco, to Guadalajara, to Ixtapa/Zihuatanejo, to Mazatlán, to Mexico City, and to Puerto Vallarta from Los Angeles. Daily to Puerto Vallarta and to Mazatlán from Phoenix.

American Airlines. Daily to Acapulco, to El Paso/Ciudad Juárez, to Mexico City, and to Puerto Vallarta from Chicago. Daily to Mexico City, to Acapulco, to Guadalajara, to Puerto Vallarta, and to Monterrey from Dallas/Fort Worth. Weekly to Cancún from New York, to Mexico City from Miami, and Mexico City from Cincinnati.

Mexicana de Aviación. Daily to Cancún, to Guadalajara, to Mazatlán, to Mexico City, and to Puerto Vallarta, and 4 times weekly to Zacatecas, from Los Angeles. Daily to Cancún and to Puerto Vallarta from Dallas/Fort Worth. 4 times weekly to Guadalajara and to Cozumel, and 3 times weekly to Monterrey, from Dallas/Fort Worth. Daily to Cancún and to Cozumel from Miami. Daily to Mexico City from New York. Daily to Guadalajara, to Mazatlán, and to Puerto Vallarta, and 3 times weekly to Los Cabos and to Manzanillo, from San Francisco. Daily to Cancún from Baltimore. Daily to Mazatlán and 4 times weekly to Puerto Vallarta from Seattle. 4 times weekly to Puerto Vallarta and 3 times weekly to Monterrey from San Antonio.

Travellers from Canada may take one of the numerous *Air Canada* flights to Miami and continue thence by another airline. *Delta* run a service from Calgary to Los Angeles and Mexico City.

From Europe, *Aeroméxico* fly 3 times weekly to Mexico City from Paris via Madrid and Miami. *British Airways* 3 times weekly to Mexico City from London (Heathrow). *Air France* 4 times weekly to Mexico City from Paris via Houston. *KLM* daily to Mexico City from Amsterdam via Houston. *Iberia* 3 times weekly to Mexico City from Madrid.

Bus. Greyhound buses from the USA serve El Paso, Laredo, and Brownsville (Texas), across the frontier from Ciudad Juárez (Chihuahua), Nuevo Laredo, and Matamoros (Tamaulipas); and Calexico and San Diego (California) across the frontier from Mexicali and Tijuana (Baja California). Other lines serve Eagle Pass (Texas), across the frontier from Piedras Negras (Coahuila), and Nogales (Arizona), across the frontier from Nogales (Sonora). Greyhound and Trailways buses cross the frontier at the larger towns and deposit passengers at the Mexican bus station for onward journeys.

Railway. Amtrak from the USA to El Paso, with connection across the frontier at Ciudad Juárez with Ferrocarriles Nacionales de México (FF.CC) for Chihuahua and further S; and to San Diego (connecting road service to Tijuana). There is no direct link between the US and Mexican rail networks.

By Car. Some 16 frontier entry towns (see itineraries in the main text) are spread over California, Arizona, New Mexico, and Texas. Drivers intending to take their cars into Mexico must obtain a vehicle permit, issued at the frontier, though this is not needed for Baja California and Mexican frontier cities. To get such a permit, the vehicle registration certificate must be shown. Proof of ownership or the authorization of the owner will also be needed. Mexican car insurance is essential, and may be obtained from offices of the American Automobile Association (AAA) or from various agencies on both sides of the frontier. Long-term parking lots in major US frontier towns offer reasonable rates to those who do not wish to take their cars into Mexico. US, Canadian, British, and other European driving licences are valid in Mexico, but British and other European drivers will do well to arm themselves as well with an international driving licence (obtainable, for example, from the Automobile Association in London), as their national licences may not be easily recognizable to the Mexican authorities.

Passports are necessary for all foreigners entering Mexico. It is essential to keep a record of the passport number in case of loss, accompanied, if possible, by an expired passport or a copy of a birth certificate and passport photographs, which will facilitate the issuing of a fresh passport or travelling papers by the nearest consulate, to whom, and to local police, a loss should be reported.

A **Tourist Card** is needed by all visitors to Mexico. This is obtainable, on production of a valid passport, from Mexican embassies, consulates, or tourist offices abroad, or at the frontier or airport on arrival. The top copy is surrendered to the customs on arrival, the carbon copy on departure. A tourist card is generally valid for 90 days or for 180 days if the traveller can satisfy the authorities that he or she has sufficient funds for a stay of this length of time. The document must be carefully kept and carried at all times. Its loss can involve much bureaucratic inconvenience and long delays. A replacement can only be issued at the Secretaría de Gobernación (Department of the Interior) in Mexico City.

Customs. Customs officers at Mexican international airports are reasonable and quick. Each visitor may bring in a maximum of 200 cigarettes or 50 cigars or 250 grammes of tobacco; 500 grammes (600 cc) of scent; one litre of spirits and one litre of wine. He may also bring in one camera and one 8mm movie camera, with 12 rolls of film for each; and a reasonable amount of personal possessions, except drugs, weapons, and pornography. US visitors are advised to register valuable personal possessions, such as jewellery, cameras, binoculars, etc, at the US port of exit. It is prohibited to take archaeological remains and 16–19C works of art out of Mexico.

Customs officers are generally stricter at the US land frontier. Immigration checkpoints some 30 km into Mexico check documents. If all is not in order, travellers will be sent back.

TRAVEL IN MEXICO

Air travel is the quickest way for those whose time is limited. Flights between the main cities are frequent. If there are no direct flights, one can easily be routed via Mexico City.

Aeroméxico and Mexicana de Aviación maintain flights throughout the republic; Aero California operates within Baja California, Sonora, Sinaloa, and Jalisco; Inter and Aviacsa in Yucatán and the SE; Litoral along the Gulf Coast from Veracruz and Ciudad del Carmen; etc. Taxi and colectivo bus services connect airports with city centres at fixed tariffs. Tickets for taxis are bought at a special booking office before one joins the queue.

Railway travel (Ferrocarriles Nacionales de México; FF.CC) is cheap, but slow and only for railway enthusiasts, who may enjoy the pullman carriages dating from the 1930s. The journey from Mexico City to Mérida, for example, can take 42 hrs. The cheapest, second-class (segunda clase) carriages are generally crowded and hot, and none too clean; having to stand can be an extreme trial. First-class (primera general) should mean getting a seat, but is no guarantee of comfort. Primera clase especial (or reservada) assures a seat and comfort. Sleepers are available at extra cost. These may take the form of a high or low bunk (cama alta or cama baja), a small private room (camarín), or a larger room with washing facilities (alcoba)—all priced accordingly.

Buses are the best method of travel. The Mexican bus system deserves all praise, with frequent services connecting population centres round the clock. Tickets are obtainable at, and buses leave from, the main bus station (central camionera) in or near each town and city. Sometimes there is more than one station, each company having its own headquarters. Fares range from amazingly cheap to thoroughly reasonable. First-class buses are comfortable and smooth, and sometimes have a washroom and air-conditioning. Seats are bookable in advance. Second-class buses are not so comfortable. Sometimes one has to stand, although the booking clerks will recommend waiting for the next bus for a seat. Smaller buses (colectivos) or combis (even smaller) connect main towns with country destinations in the locality.

Passengers are recommended to visit the bus station well before their intended departure to check the times of services, displayed on boards at the booking offices of the various companies, and to book their tickets then if they can. There is generally no problem getting a seat at the starting-point of a route. If starting a journey at a stopping-point along a route (long-distance buses make several stops of between 10 and 30 minutes to set down and take on passengers, and to allow crews and passengers to refresh themselves), in theory only as many tickets are sold as there are seats available. In practice a passenger may find himself having to stand, either because there are no seats or because a seat allotted is already occupied. The less chivalrous will enlist the crew's help in ejecting the occupier.

Most bus stations have a left-luggage office (equipaje) where travellers can leave luggage during a break in a journey, enabling them to spend a few hours in a place worth visiting. Charges are reasonable.

Seats for travel by any means during public holiday seasons are booked well in advance. It is best to avoid travel at such times. The only alternative is to try one's luck in the queues for non-bookable seats at bus stations or railway stations—a daunting prospect.

Travel by car in Mexico will give the serious traveller independence and enable him to get to more places than he otherwise would. But he should be aware of the inconveniences. Those who wish to bring their own cars into Mexico from the USA and have the necessary document (see above) should be warned that heat, bumpy roads, floods and landslides after rain, can make driving hazardous and take their toll of all but the toughest vehicles. Spare parts are available only for those automobiles—Volkswagen, Datsun, Ford, Dodge—manufactured in Mexico. It is essential to bring spare fan belts, spark plugs, air and fuel filters, oil, and at least one spare tyre.

A cheerful point is that the Mexicans are probably the world's greatest improvisers and Mexican mechanics (at talleres de reparación) can be relied on to do their best in a case of mechanical trouble. Another is the fleet, of green emergency service vans, funded by the federal Department of Tourism and staffed by English-speaking mechanics, called Angeles Verdes, which patrols main highways and is well known for courtesy and efficiency. The service is free, but payment must be made for petrol and parts.

Maximum speed on highways is 100 km an hour. At approaches to and exits from population centres, one must keep a look-out for, and take great care in negotiating, speed bumps (topes). Petrol available on main highways includes Nova Plus (leaded) and Magna Sin (unleaded). Tyre pumps at petrol stations are calibrated in kg (1 kg = 2.2 lb). Petrol stations cannot be relied on to accept credit cards. One is generally advised not to drive at night, especially in out of the way places. At the approach to a narrow bridge (puente angosto or solo carril), the first driver to flash headlights has right of way. Away from cities, care should always be taken for cattle straying on to the road. Mexican drivers can be erratic and careless, forgetting to signal a lane change or a stop, so one should allow plenty of room. At an approach to roadworks, drivers should slow down and make sure they understand the often confusing signs given by construction workers before gingerly moving on.

Toll (cobra) is payable on well-maintained and faster stretches of main highways (toll road—cuota). Rates are displayed well in advance of the booth (caseta de cobre).

Authorized parking zones (Estacionamiento—E) should always be used and fees are payable. Parking on the street may well be illegal and those who do this, or join other double-parked cars in dire emergency, may find themselves confronting a policeman demanding an on the spot fine. In some cases, a car illegally parked may be towed away. The owner should go without delay to reclaim it at the nearest police station, and his wait there may be frustratingly long. If stopped by the police for a real or imaginary offence, an on the spot fine will also be demanded and a foreign visitor will only be let off if the police officer relents in the face of quietly injured innocence, bewildered ignorance, or an obvious inability to understand and speak Spanish. If the officer persists, however, it is better to pay up, though bargaining is possible. It is often possible to pay a bystander to look after a car while it is left for a short period.

Especially in small towns and villages, one will often be approached by children offering to clean the car or look after it while one is absent. It is inadvisable to refuse such offers, though only the obvious leader should be paid.

Possession of a car will be entered on a tourist card and it is forbidden to leave the country without it (which means that one cannot sell one's car in Mexico). If a car breaks down, or is damaged and needs extensive repairs, special permission must be got to leave without it (through local offices of the Secretaría de Hacienda—Treasury). The owner has 45 days after expiry of the vehicle permit to return to reclaim the car.

Hiring a car obviates many difficulties. Agencies compete for custom, though local ones are cheaper than the well-known names. Rates are reasonable. It is advisable to enquire about unlimited mileage offers, which may turn out a better bargain than hire for the day. A valid driving licence is required and there may be an age limit. It is essential to check that the car is in good working order before accepting it. Insurance, arranged by the hire company, should be regarded as mandatory. All new cars produced by the home auto industry must be fitted with catalytic converters.

Taxis are available everywhere and fares are reasonable. An exception can be the saloon cars which wait outside hotels. If hiring one of these (and there are occasions when it is unavoidable), the customer should enquire about the tariff before he gets in. If the price is too high, and the driver will not come down, he should be told that a report will be made to the local tourist office. In cities, taxi drivers cannot be relied on to be conversant with out of the way areas.

Tourist Offices exist in cities and sizeable towns. In State capitals they are run by the State government and are sometimes commodious and well-equipped with maps, town plans, hotel lists, ideas for excursions, etc. English-speaking staff, except in Mexico City, Guadalajara, Puebla, and the large beach resorts, are few.

Tourist offices, however, are not very knowledgeable about art history, archaeology, or topographical detail. The serious traveller who wants detailed information on local monuments will often find what he needs at the local INAH headquarters (if there is one—a glance through the local telephone directory will tell).

Maps and town plans. Pemex (Petroleos Mexicanos) publish an excellent 'Atlas de Carreteras y Ciudades Turísticas', with introductory text in Spanish and English, obtainable both in Mexico and in specialist book and map shops abroad. It is revised at intervals to take account of new roadbuilding. Detenal, the official map printer, publishes a variety of specialized and detailed maps. Its Carta Turística, covering the republic in seven parts, is still an excellent buy, though in need of revision. A helpful series of Traveller's Reference Maps to Mexico (scale 1:1,000,000) comes from International Travel Map Productions (Vancouver).

Guía Roji of Mexico City publishes a series of maps of the States and detailed city plans, with helpful notes. It is a pity that the detail takes account of only a very few important buildings.

Town plans obtained from tourist offices are sometimes very sketchy. In places with no tourist office, stationers' shops often stock plans, some helpful.

ACCOMMODATION

Hotels. Mexican hotels range from the luxurious (Mexico City, Monterrey, Guadalajara, Manzanillo, Acapulco, Cancún) to the appalling, in the seediest districts. Better-class hotels in popular resorts are apt to be booked up months in advance. Except in such places, a traveller arriving late at night will quite easily find somewhere to stay. Taxi drivers will invariably oblige by taking him to the sort of hotel he specifies. If a business or other convention is being held, however, accommodation can be impossible to find and he may have to rough it in an unsalubrious neighbourhood or stay some distance from the town centre.

Prices are controlled by the Department of Tourism and in theory should be permanently displayed. With high inflation (and after recent substantial tariff rises) this is sometimes not done, and one should establish the tariff, incl. IVA tax, before one registers. Even so, those in search of comfort and services, and backed by hard currency, will still find that prices are very fair, and, except perhaps in Mexico City and the prime coastal resorts, cheaper than in the USA and Europe.

Old-fashioned hotels (sometimes called posadas) in some provincial towns, with rooms around the upper floors of flower- and plant-filled patios, can be as delightful as the welcoming staff, with plenty of comfort, a private bathroom, and at reasonable rates. Generally speaking, the cheapest hotels are in the centre of town, but here the noise from the street, or the main plaza, will keep all but the soundest sleepers awake, unless a quieter back room is available. One should always inspect the rooms, lavatories, and washing facilities (if there are no private bathrooms) before making a decision; and also find out whether the tariff includes breakfast or any other meal. Valuables should not be left in hotel rooms and one should enquire at the reception of higher-class establishments if a caja de seguridad (of which one keeps the key) is available. All but the plainer establishments will accept credit cards.

In more remote areas, a supply of lavatory paper, soap, and a towel will be necessary. Electric current is 110 v 60 cycles AC. Electric appliances will therefore need adaptors for the two-pin plugs in use.

Food and Drink

By Elizabeth Baquedano Pope and Ligia Baquedano

RESTAURANTS

Mexican food is usually good and inexpensive. The least pretentious restaurant often provides the best value. The service charge is not included in the bill. A 10 per cent tip is acceptable. The menu posted outside the restaurant shows the charges the customer can expect. Many simpler establishments do not offer a menu. Here the choice is limited, but the standard good. Lunch is normally at about 1400 and is the main meal of the day. Dinner is at about 2000.

Tacos (popular and cheap) and other *tortilla*-based dishes (*antojitos mexicanos*) are served in a *taquería*, *tortería*, or *fonda*. Antojitos are numerous, but *sopes* and *quesadillas* should also be sampled if real familiarity with Mexican food is to be gained. They are utterly unlike famous 'Mexican' dishes known in the USA and Europe, such as enchiritos, or TexMex. A *Cantina* often sells beer and wine, and simple food, at very reasonable prices. *Bares* (Bars; open midday till late at night) serve varieties of refreshments and cocktails. Even in taquerías the customer pays at the end of the meal, generally at the till, having left a 10 per cent tip on the table. Black coffee (*café americano* or *express*) can be ordered with milk (*café con leche*) or with cream (*crema*), which often comes in plastic containers. Many restaurants serve *café de olla*—black coffee with molasses and cinnamon.

FOOD AND WINE

In Mexico food varies with region, climate, and prehispanic heritage. Maize, which has been cultivated since c 5700 BC, was and still is a staple food, together with beans, tomatoes, squashes, and chillies. The earliest corn (6000–5000 BC) was found at Tehuacán. By 100 BC the cob had increased from c 1.9 to 10 cm in length. Maize is made into dough (*masa*), then pancakes (*tortillas*) are formed, which are cooked on a griddle. Numerous prehispanic sculptures are dedicated to tortilla-making. The 'Codex Mendoza' in the Bodleian shows a mother instructing her daughter in the art.

Dishes from all over the country are included in the menu below.

Entremeses (hors d'oeuvre)
Aguacate con camarones, Avocado with prawns
Aguacate con atún, Avocado with tuna
Coctel de camarones, Shrimp cocktail
Ceviche, Marinated fish with lemon, tomatoes, avocado, onion, chilli
Ceviche de ostión, Oyster ceviche

Sopas
Sopa de tortilla or *Sopa azteca*, Tortilla soup, usually served with chicken broth, tomatoes and avocados, cream, and grated cheese
Sopa de fideo, Pasta soup (the pasta fried and then cooked in chicken broth and tomatoes)
Sopa de frijol, Bean soup
Sopa de verduras, Vegetable soup
Sopa de lentejas, Lentil soup
Sopa de flor de calabaza, Courgette flower soup
Arroz, Rice as part of the menu (especially in a *comida corrida*—fixed menu)
Sopa de elote, Cream soup with maize and bacon
Caldo de pollo, Chicken broth
Caldo de pescado, Fish broth
Caldo de mariscos, Seafood broth
Crema de aguacate, Avocado soup
Crema de jitomate, Tomato soup
Caldo xóchitl, Shredded chicken in its broth cooked with vegetables and herbs

Pescados
Filete sol, Fillet of sole
Huachinango a la veracruzana, Red snapper, Veracruz style
Pescado al mojo de ajo, Fillet fried with garlic
Camarones al mojo de ajo, Shrimps cooked in garlic
Pescado empanizado, Fish fried in breadcrumbs
Robalo, Bass
Pulpos en su tinta, Octopus cooked in its own ink
Jaibas al chipotle, Crab cooked with a red chilli
Mojarra frita, Fried fish (a kind of tuna)
Bacalao, Salted cod
Almejas, Mussels
Trucha, Trout
Tomates rellenos de atún, Tomatoes stuffed with tuna
Calamares, Squid

Carnes (Entrées)
Bistec, Beef rib steak (usually fried)
Pollo, Chicken
Pechuga, Chicken breast
Pollo rostizado, Roast chicken
Mole poblano, Chicken cooked with spices and chocolate
Mole verde, Chicken cooked in a chilli and green tomato sauce
Lomo de puerco, Pork loin
Tinga, Pork loin and chorizo cooked with tomatoes, potatoes, chillies, and onions
Chicharrón en salsa verde, Pork skin cooked in a green chilli sauce
Milanesa empanizada, Veal cutlet, fried in breadcrumbs
Barbacoa, Lamb
Carnitas, Fried pork
Cochinita, Pork cooked in achiote (a seed with a red tint giving a flavour similar to saffron)
Albóndigas, Meat balls

Ternera, Veal
Carne tampiqueña, Fried or grilled steak Diane
Costilla, Pork cutlet
Hígado, Liver
Conejo, Rabbit
Sesos, Brains
Riñones, Kidneys
Lengua, Tongue
Tocino, Bacon
Carne mexicana, Beefsteak cooked in a tomato sauce
Chorizo, Spanish-type paprika sausage
Picadillo, Minced meat cooked with tomatoes, onions, and raisins
Brocheta de filete, Fillet steak cooked on a skewer
Guajolote or *Pavo*, Turkey
Venado, Venison
Pato, Duckling
Cabrito, Goat

Verduras
Ensalada verde, Green salad
Espárragos, Asparagus
Ensalada mixta, Mixed salad
Calabazas, Courgettes
Jitomates, Tomatoes
Huitlacoches, Fungi from maize
Calabacitas rellenas, Courgettes cooked with cheese and fried with egg batter in a tomato sauce
Espinacas, Spinach
Chícharos, Peas
Chiles rellenos, Green chillies stuffed with cheese and covered with batter cooked in a tomato and oregano sauce
Pipián, A dough made with pumpkin seeds
Frijoles, Beans
Frijoles refritos, Beans fried in oil, or refried
Papas, Potatoes
Alcachofas, Artichokes
Zanahorias, Carrots
Acelgas, Chard
Hongos, Mushrooms
Elote, Corn
Nopales, Cactus leaves
Guacamole, Avocado dip made with tomatoes, onions, garlic, and green chillies
Jícama, white tuber similar to radish

Postres
Crepas con cajeta, Crepes with a kind of buttermilk
Higos en almíbar, Figs with syrup
Duraznos, Peaches
Plátano, Banana
Guayaba, Guava
Flan, Flan
Piña, Pineapple
Almendrados, Almond pudding
Arroz con leche, Rice pudding
Calabaza en tacha, pumpkin in molasses
Torrejas, Bread pudding
Dulce de nuez, Nut pudding
Fresas con crema, Strawberries and cream
Ensalada de fruta, Fruit salad
Naranjas, Oranges
Cocada, Coconut sweet
Papaya en dulce, Pawpaw in syrup
Manzanas, Apples
Manzanas en horno, Baked apples
Manzanas en almíbar, Apples in syrup
Gelatina, Jelly
Chongos zamoranos, Curdled milk cooked with cinnamon and syrup

Mangos, Mangoes
Natilla, Milk pudding
Merengues, Meringues
Sandía, Watermelon

Antojitos are mostly from Mexico City. Although strictly speaking these are not entremeses, people eat them before meals.

Quesadillas, among the simplest and tastiest, are small fried or grilled tortillas with cheese and *epazote* (a herb); they can be seasoned with *salsa* (a chilli sauce). *Tacos de pollo* (tortillas filled with chicken), covered with cream, cheese, lettuce, fresh onions, and an optional layer of chilli sauce, are a favourite entremese. *Ceviche* is always excellent. *Ensalada de nopalitos* is common in fondas: cactus leaves are cooked and then seasoned with olive oil, coriander, oregano, green chillies; a basket of tortillas comes too, so that they can be eaten as a taco (rolled tortilla). Some fruits, such as *jícama,* are often served as salad, or as a starter.

Besides sopa de tortilla and caldo xóchitl, *sopa de hongos* is delicious, particularly common during the rains. Several kinds of mushroom combine to make it rich. *Caldo tlalpeño* is a chicken broth seasoned with tomatoes, onions, chicken breast, and red hot peppers. Cactus fruits are added—a distinctive taste. *Sopa de aguacate* is popular and combines soured cream with avocados. *Sopa de poblano,* mild yet exotic, consists of green peppers, onions, cream, and fried sliced tortillas. *Arroz a la mexicana* accompanies many dishes, but is served also in its own right. The basic recipe is with onions, tomatoes, garlic, and chicken broth. There are other varieties, such as *Arroz poblano,*which combines green peppers, cheeses, onions, and cream.

Of the main courses *Mole poblano* is similar to a prehispanic recipe based on a thick, rich sauce. Most moles are served with chicken, but the dish was originally with turkey. The sauce is made with a variety of chillies, pepper, many spices, and chocolate. Although chocolate with chicken may seem off-putting, it is in fact a delicious combination, especially for those who enjoy rich food. *Mole negro de Oaxaca* is made with a sauce of overcooked chillies and spices. *Carne tampiqueña* is a thin, long piece of fillet steak, fried in a little oil, freshly ground pepper, and salt. It is served with many typically Mexican side dishes: *Rajas* (sliced hot green chillies fried and mixed with onions, melted cheese, and cream); *arroz a la mexicana*; *guacamole*; *enchiladas* (tortillas simmered in mole sauce and filled with chicken); and refried beans. This is as Mexican as one can get—excellent even in modest restaurants. *Sabana* (a long, thin piece of beefsteak) is popular in Mexico City; although thin, the size is usually generous. Sometimes it is served with refried beans or with lemon juice on top.

Barbacoa is another prehispanic recipe. A leg of lamb is wrapped in cactus leaves with salt. (In prehispanic times, venison was used.) An underground oven is lit and the meat is left to cook overnight. The flavour is unique and the meat very tender. Several sauces may accompany it. The famous *Salsa borracha* (drunkard's sauce) is made with dried red chillies and mixed with pulque. *Tacos de barbacoa* are another variety on the same theme, but the meat is a lot nicer by itself.

Both barbacoa and *carnitas* (small pieces of pork loin fried and served like barbacoa with at least three different salsas to moisten the meat) are usually sold in what are called restaurantes mexicanos in Mexico City.

Carne a la mexicana (rump steak cooked in tomato sauce with onions, garlic, and a touch of green peppers) is another very Mexican dish: pieces of fillet cooked in a hot chilli sauce with tomatoes, garlic, and spices. It is not recommended for fragile stomachs. Another version is called *Puntas de filete al albañil.* Mexican albañiles (stonemasons) are supposed to be able to handle chillies of any heat; so the meat is extremely hot, served with green fried chillies and onions. *Albóndigas al chipotle* is a well-known, and cheap, dish: meat balls made of minced beef and minced pork, cooked over a low heat with *chipotles* (red chillies), and tomatoes, onions, and garlic.

Milanesas are more often than not beefsteaks fried in breadcrumbs. In Italian restaurants they tend to be veal steaks cooked in the same way—mild and served with a green salad and chips. *Huachinango a la veracruzana*, a renowned dish, cooked in a tomato sauce with olives, olive oil, garlic, and onions, and a layer of long, green peppers, is not hot. A good appetite is essential because a whole red snapper is generally served. *Filete sol* is simple and tasty, prepared with a touch of garlic and fried. In *Enchiladas suizas*, not heard of in Switzerland, the basic ingredients are chicken, a tomato sauce, and a mixture of cheese and cream. *Pollo almendrado* (almond chicken), cooked with a tomato sauce, is well known in Oaxaca. *Cochinita pibil* (red colour), from Yucatán, is a delicious pork stew, flavoured with achiote and served with radish, fresh coriander, red onion, and a sauce made from chile habanero (from Havana). It is a time-honoured Maya dish and was formerly based on peccary or turkey. *Cabrito al pastor* is grilled kid, a speciality of Monterrey. *Pozole*, from Guadalajara, is a kind of broth which includes pork, chicken, and boiled maize, and is seasoned with oregano, onions, lemon, radishes, lettuce, and dried red chillies.

Desserts

Chongos zamoranos is a traditional Mexican dessert based on clotted milk mixed with lemons and cinnamon. *Crepas con cajeta* is another popular sweet: crepes filled with cajeta. *Cocada*, made with grated coconut, coconut milk, eggs, milk, and cinnamon, is also served in traditional Mexican restaurants. *Ate con queso* is a combination of guava made into a paste and served with a mild cheese. *Mousse de mango* made with fresh mangoes is not to be missed. *Calabaza en tacha* is a pumpkin pulp cooked in syrup. *Pastel de chocolate* is a cake with a real chocolate taste. Fruit is so plentiful in Mexico that a *coctel de frutas* is always a good choice.

Mexican Wine

Although vines were brought to New Spain in the 16C, only recently has the potential of the Mexican wine industry been fully realized. The reason for this resurgence was the ban on wine imports in the 1980s. Large houses, such as Martel and Pedro Domecq, therefore invested in vineyard development in Baja California, where a unique microclimate (by Mexican standards) allows the grapes to develop fully. The secret of enjoying Mexican wine is to look for the combination of well-known grape varieties (Chardonnay, Riesling, Cabernet, Sauvignon) with recognized producers (Domecq, Martell, La Cetto, Santo Tomás, and Don Angel). Wines from Querétaro and Aguascalientes have a deserved reputation.

Mexican beer is also excellent and there is a lot to choose from. *Dos Equis* and *Corona* are popular. *Noche Buena* is a type of lager produced especially at Christmas. *Bohemia, Lager, Carta Blanca, Brisa* (low alcohol) are all lagers.

Mexican cocktails should not be ignored, but their strength should be respected. *Tequila* is an alcoholic drink made from the fermented and distilled sap taken from the *agave* (maguey). Cocktails based on it are popular, such as *cocktel margarita*, served with lime and salt around the rim of the glass. (Some fine tequilas, such as *Centenario* or *Conmemorativo*, are put in oak barrels and take on a brandy colour and flavour, with an equally strong alcoholic content.) *Piña colada* and other rum-based cocktails are common in Mexico, as is Bloody Mary. *Mezcal* is an agave liquor made into a kind of spirit and sometimes served in restaurants with *botanas* (snacks), such as fried ants and maguey worm—supposed to be a delicacy. Pulque, another fermented agave drink, can be mixed with fruits: *pulque de fresa, pulque de guayaba*, etc.

Aguas Frescas

There is an endless variety of fresh fruit drinks, such as *agua de guanabana* (a tropical fruit with a wonderful flavour), *agua de tamarindo, agua de guayaba*, *agua de limón*, *agua de sandía*, *agua de plátano*. They are safe to drink in restaurants, but are not recommended from street vendors as the water is often contaminated.

Refrescos

Another kind of fruit drink, but bottled. *Horchata* is made with almonds, *chufas* (tubers), and a dash of cinnamon. *Tepache* is generally pineapple, left to ferment for a few days. It is served sieved with sugar. *Refresco de tuna* is cactus fruit mixed with water and sugar.

Language

In Mexico the official language is Castilian, but more noticeably flexibly used than in Spain, the sound softer, far more attractive and musical (particularly when spoken by educated women) to the ear of an English-speaker. Various words derived from Indian tongues enrich it: in the central States, words from the Otomí, Tlaxcaltecan, and Náhuatl tongues; in Oaxaca, words from the Zapotec and Mixtec; in the Yucatán, words from the extraordinarily expressive language of the Maya. Vowel sounds are often shortened and consonants more strongly pronounced (possibly an Aztec legacy). The less cultured often hasten over word endings. Although a Spaniard may speak Spanish-style in Mexico without a native Mexican batting an eyelid, the same speech from foreigners from other countries will be received with surprise, and some displeasure.

The following few, approximate, pronunciation hints may be useful:

a somewhere between r*a*ther and Sp*a*nish
e as in p*e*nny when ending a word
                 as in f*a*te when accented
                 as in b*e*t when followed by a consonant
i as in fl*ee*ce when accented
                 as in l*i*neage when not
o as in h*o*tel when accented
                 as in h*o*t when not
u always as in l*oo*t

Consonants are pronounced as in English, except:
b hardly sounded, the lips barely touching
c like k before a, o, u, but like ss before e and i
cc as in ta*cks*
ch as in *ch*oke
g as in *g*o before a or o, or before u followed by a consonant; like h before e and i; *gu* before a vowel is like *w*; and *gü* like *woo*
h not sounded
j very lightly aspirated, softer than the English h
ll as y (*y*acht), except in Indian words, where it is like a single l
ñ as ny (ca*ñ*ón—ca*ny*on)
qu like k (*qu*e)
rr rolled
s like ss, never like z
v as a soft b (*v*ino)
x like x in words derived from Latin (má*x*imo), and in some Mexican names, eg, Ne*c*axa. In Indian words, originally like sh (I*x*miquilpan), now often modified to *s* (Mi*x*teca), especially at the beginning of a word (*X*ochimilco) and sometimes eroded to an h (Oa*x*aca).
y before a vowel like y; otherwise like ee in m*ee*k
z always ss

The rules of Castilian place stress on a syllable marked with an orthographic accent ('). If there's no accent, the stress falls on the last syllable in all words, except those ending in a vowel or the letters n or s, in which case it falls on the penultimate syllable. There are no exceptions. The accent is not always used in Indian words, but its use can aid pronunciation. A tendency of Mexican speech, however, is to transfer stress to the last syllable, sometimes lengthened for emphasis, when it should fall on the penultimate.

Except in the cities of the northern frontier region, a knowledge of English is not as widespread in Mexico as one would suppose. In the capital and the prime tourist resorts the staff at the main hotels, shopkeepers, and various others generally speak some English. A knowledge of Spanish is therefore desirable for visitors to Mexico, and a lack of it can be an uncomfortable disadvantage. Those intending to venture further afield than Mexico City and the popular resorts are advised to learn some basic Spanish, both in self-defence and to make their stay more enjoyable. Mexicans of all stations will listen patiently and will be only too willing to encourage the faltering speaker.

Manners and Customs

To a visitor from Europe, Mexico resembles more a continent than a country. It takes little effort to realize that one should not generalize about the Mexicans, who are not a homogeneous people (certainly not a nation), but a collection of different peoples and types, formed by traditions and a turbulent history, during which they have suffered much.

Yet in a small space some generalization, to satisfy the intending traveller, will have to be attempted. In general, then, Mexicans are not xenophobic, are extremely courteous—indeed, their reputation for courtesy and kindness is a historical fact and thoroughly deserved, often putting people from more developed countries to shame—friendly and helpful towards a foreigner. Mexicans are sensitive and anxious that the visitor to their country should enjoy it and show appreciation. In Mexico, formalities and symbolism are just as important as concrete reality. The foreigner should always remember to show respect and an awareness of his host's sensitivities; should make a request, however urgent, in a quiet and pleasant way, with a smile; should never be brusque or raise his voice in the supposed interests of efficiency or be quick to criticize. If he returns courtesy for courtesy, he will find it easy to get along. If he does not, he will not get results. Mexicans are fatalistic and a sense of urgency does not count much with them.

The essential rituals of politeness in everyday behaviour include such phrases as 'para servirle' (to serve you), 'a sus órdenes' (at your service), 'su servidor'. Such assurances that a Mexican host's house is 'su casa' (your home) and that anything in it one may admire is 'yours' must not be taken at face value. Timekeeping is lax. An appointment made in seeming good faith will, in all probability, not be kept. One should never arrive on time at the host's house for a dinner or lunch engagement.

In a society still conservative and male-dominated, a woman can expect to be treated with a courtesy which to her may seem exaggerated and patronizing. Even though she may feel that her independence is not being recognized, she should still respond with quiet humour, and a smile, not with a glare.

The tendency, away from coastal resorts, of some holidaymakers from abroad to dress as though they were about to step on to the beach is deplored. In cities and larger towns, it is considered to be in extremely bad taste, however hot the climate. In more remote areas it can invite revulsion, or worse trouble. Shorts should not be worn in such areas, nor in churches, where women should cover their heads and arms.

Obligatory greetings are 'buenos días' in the morning; 'buenas tardes' in the afternoon and early evening; 'buenas noches' in the late evening and at night. Never forget to say thank you ('gracias'; 'muchas gracias').

The abrazo (bear hug) between Mexican male relatives or friends should not be imitated by the foreigner; if he is to be the object of one, he should wait until a Mexican takes the initiative. A special Mexican handshake (very firm, with thumbs entwined, and forearms often held vertically against each other) is a sign of great favour.

To the Mexican, 'México' really means Mexico City. The country which the foreigner calls Mexico is more often referred to as 'La república' or 'La república mexicana' or 'nuestro país'.

General Information

Climate. There is no tourist season. It is possible to find warmth and sun at all times of year, even though Mexican weather is not as universally sunny as some would have it and its most unpredictable extremes can be treacherous.

In the desert and semi-desert regions N of the Tropic of Cancer the climate is sunny and dry, especially towards the W. Winters can be fairly cold and summers very hot indeed (well over 40°C), for instance in Mexicali and Monterrey. Rain falls in the higher areas and winter snows are not unknown. In Baja California it hardly ever rains and the summer months are intensely hot. The central high plateau, at altitudes over 2000m (tierra fría), enjoys a pleasantly temperate all year round climate (average 17–18°C), with afternoon rains during June–Sept. April, May, and June are the hottest months. But evenings and early mornings can be chilly. At altitudes of between 900 and 2000m (tierra templada) rainfall is the same as in the higher regions and temperatures higher (22–24°C), but still with a pleasing lack of humidity. Along the Gulf, Pacific, and Caribbean costs (tierra caliente) the climate is tropical, with extremes of summer heat and humidity, especially in the Yucatán (42°C at Mérida); at Acapulco (39°C) and Veracruz (36°C). Sea breezes, however, can often mitigate the heat. In the SE States of Tabasco and Chiapas temperatures are constant throughout the year and in parts of Tabasco there is an excess of rain. In winter the coasts of the Gulf of Mexico are battered by violent winds. Hurricanes and cyclones have wreaked havoc.

Insurance and Health. It is essential to take out travel (in case of loss of possessions) and medical insurance before leaving for Mexico. A timely visit to a doctor before leaving is also advisable. Vaccination certificates are not needed, but a physician may recommend inoculation against typhoid, paratyphoid, polio, tetanus and hepatitis, and the commencement (and completion) of a course of tablets against malaria, especially if visiting the low-lying area of SE Mexico—the Yucatán, Chiapas, and Tabasco. Travellers should also arm themselves with a mosquito repellent for these and other tropical areas.

Those with a tendency to heart and lung complaints should check carefully about the advisability of going to Mexico. Thin high-altitude air causes initial breathlessness for all new arrivals, however healthy. Stomach upsets (the most savage vulgarly known as Moctezuma's revenge, accompanied by vomiting, cramps, fever, chill, and diarrhoea) are common, caused by dietary change and bacteria in food and water. Preventative medicines are of limited efficacy. New arrivals should not indulge straight away in food (especially spicy food) which they are not used to and in alcohol. They should drink only bottled water and soft drinks, and avoid aguas frescas (which may be made with unpurified water) and ice. Most better-class hotels have purified water (agua purificada) on hand, and this should be used to brush teeth. Open-air foodstalls and roadside restaurants and cafés should be avoided. Unpeeled fruit; fruit (and vegetable) salads suspected of being washed in unpurified water; unwashed vegetables; and greasy food should also be avoided. Papayas are recommended as good stomach settlers. If stomach upsets do strike, plenty of rest should be taken; pure water and fruit juices drunk to guard against dehydration; and dry toast and plain rice eaten. Local doctors and pharmacists are well acquainted with the problem and will treat sympathetically.

The sun, particularly at high altitudes, is very strong—deceptively, for in a dry climate, the heat does not seem so severe. The fair-skinned should not hesitate to wear a protective cream on face, arms, and neck, and a hat (sombrero), to avoid painful and dangerous sunburn.

Currency exchange. Banks (for exchange of money and traveller's cheques—Banamex, Bancomer, and Banco del Atlántico are recommended) are open Mon.–Fri. 9–1.30. Exchange bureaux in the larger cities keep more flexible hours. Most large hotels will change money (preferably dollars), but at something less than the official rate. At international airports exchange bureaux often stay open until late, convenient for arrivals who should change enough money into pesos for a taxi into town and other immediate expenses. Payment by credit card can be to the advantage of visitors backed by hard currencies. When entering a bank a customer should immediately find out at which counter foreign currency is changed, and thus save a long wait. Credit cards are not accepted in remote areas.

Taxes. A 15 per cent tax (IVA) is payable on hotel bills, airline tickets, and restaurant bills.

Money. The Mexican currency unit is the peso (nuevo peso—N$—from January 1993, when 1000 old pesos became 1 N$), divided into 100 centavos (¢). Notes of N$10, 20, 50, and 100 (or 10,000, 20,000, 50,000, and 100,000 old pesos) and of 2000 and 5000 old pesos—equal to N$2 and N$5—are in circulation. There are coins of 5¢, 10¢, 20¢, 50¢, N$1, N$2, N$5, and N$10. Coins of 50, 100, 200, 500, 1000, and 5000 old pesos (equal to 5¢, 10¢, 20¢, 50¢, N$1, and N$5) are also in circulation.

Begging is an inevitable accompaniment to travel in Mexico. Although beggars (adults and children) are not usually aggressive, the visitor should remember that they are driven by extreme poverty and not refuse to give them some change.

Working hours are variable in Mexico, depending on climate and local custom. Offices usually open at 9 or 10, close at 1 or 2, and reopen at 2 or 3, or even 4, often staying open until 7.30. Shop hours are more generous, sometimes extending until late at night without a break for lunch. Sat. and Sun. opening is common.

Postal, telegram, and telephone services. Stamps (timbres) are obtainable from post offices (correos), which, except in large cities, can be tucked away in side streets, as if to defy discovery. The Mexican postal services are cheap, but unbelievably slow. Airmail is no guarantee of quick delivery. Street postboxes, which may not be emptied for days at a time, should not be used and all letters and postcards sent from the main post office in large cities or from international airports.

Most larger towns have separate telegram offices (telégrafos). Telegrams may also be sent from the better-class hotels.

Telephone booths are ubiquitous and charges for local calls cheap. Long-distance calls (larga distancia) are best made from a public telephone office (teléfonos), where one pays the operator on duty after one has finished the call, or from a hotel, where a surcharge will be made. International calls are subject to swingeing taxes.

Theft in urban areas is, alas, quite common, and generally accomplished discreetly and quietly, unaccompanied by violence to the person. Guests at the better-class hotels can use a strongbox (caja de seguridad) for valuables, cash, and traveller's cheques that will not immediately be needed. Money, passports, wallets, and tourist cards should on no account be carried in hip pockets or in the side pockets of jackets.

Police. The Mexican police have gained a poor reputation, partly, it is said, because their salaries are so low they have to supplement them through unofficial levies (mordidas) on the public, incl. foreign travellers. Serious crime by the police has also been reported. If accused of an infringement of the law, the traveller should politely say that he is a tourist unversed in the ways of the country, in which case he will probably be let off. If accused of a motoring offence, he can either demand to go to the nearest police station and plead his case there, or pay an on-the-spot fine, which will go into the officer's pocket.

There is a more cheerful side. In provincial towns, and smaller localities, the police will nearly always take pains to help a traveller in difficulty or in search of a missing museum curator or church custodian. Even in Mexico City there are friendly policemen who will give directions or warn a visitor that a neighbourhood may not be safe.

Drugs are the most serious cause of trouble both with and within the police. In certain areas government action against corrupt local forces has been sudden and firm. Frequent police and army crackdowns can result in such measures as the stopping of buses on the highway and the ordering-off of all male passengers to be searched. The innocent traveller should bear it all with gentle patience. Anger and impatience will be counterproductive. Suspicious approaches by strangers should be firmly rejected. Never agree to carry items for a fellow, but otherwise unknown, traveller.

Churches are often closed during the middle of the day. In out of the way places they may be kept closed outside occasional services. In this case it is necessary to seek out the custodian or parish priest who has the key. Local people, even the police, are nearly always only too happy to aid in the search. A tip for such help is welcome. Permission should be sought from the sacristan of those churches easier of access to enter the sacristy, often containing the church's finest treasures.

Museums are generally closed on Mon. and there may be departures from advertised times. Enquiries of locals or at the police station can often turn up the curator. Times given in the itineraries of this guide are the latest known to the authors, but are constantly subject to change. Except for the largest and most famous museums in the capital and large cities, fees, when charged, are nominal. To complicate the compilation of the Blue Guide, dispositions within museums are also subject to sudden change. Visitors may have to make their own adaptations. Similar comments apply to archaeological sites. On the largest and most famous there is often a long-term programme of restoration work.

Photography. There are few restrictions in Mexico, but permission should be sought to photograph interiors (churches, museums). It is possible to apply to INAH (43, 45–47 C. Córdoba, Col. Roma, México DF) for written permission to take photographs at archaeological sites, museums, and historic monuments if the traveller can provide evidence that he is a serious student of Mexican archaeology or architecture and needs a photographic record for study purposes. It need hardly be said that attempts to take photographs in a church while a service is in progress will cause grave offence.

Public holidays. Mexican national holidays, when banks, offices, and some shops close, are as follows: 1 Jan. (New Year); 6 Jan. (Epiphany); 5 Feb. (Constitution of Querétaro—1917); 21 March (Birthday of Benito Juárez); 1 May

(Labour Day); 5 May (Cinco de Mayo—Battle of Puebla, 1862); 1 Sept. (President's State of the Union address to reassembled Congress); 15–16 Sept. (Independence Day); 12 Oct. (Columbus Day—Día de la Raza); 1–2 Nov. (Día de todos los santos, Día de Muertos); 20 Nov. (Revolution of 1910); 12 Dec. (Our Lady of Guadalupe); 25 Dec. (Christmas Day).

Other celebrations, although not official holidays, may still entail the closure of local banks and offices if on a weekday. 18 Jan. (Sta Prisca—Tasco); Pre-Lenten carnival week (most famous at San Juan Chamula, Huejotzingo, Mazatlán, and Veracruz); Palm Sunday (throughout the republic); Holy Week (Tasco—enacting of the Passion); Good Friday (processions in Mexico City—Col. Roma; San Luis Potosí); 25 April (San Marcos—Aguascalientes); 2nd and 3rd Mondays of June (Guelaguetza—Oaxaca); 16–24 Dec. (Posadas in Querétaro and Tasco).

Time. Mexico is on central time (6 hrs behind Greenwich Mean Time) throughout the year, except for Baja California Sur, Sonora, Sinaloa, and Nayarit, which are on mountain time (7 hrs behind GMT). Baja California (Norte) is on Pacific Time (8 hrs behind GMT).

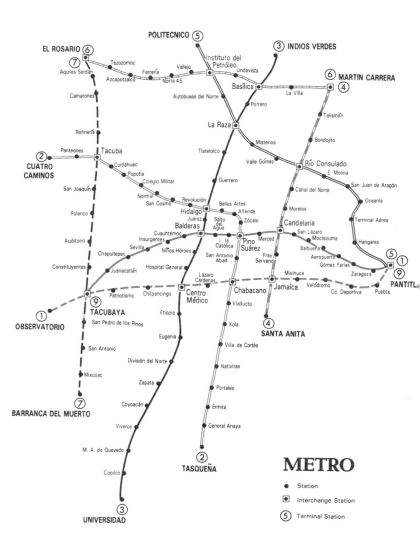

MEXICO CITY AND ITS ENVIRONS

MEXICO CITY (to the Mexican, simply **MEXICO**), capital of the federal republic of Mexico (the United Mexican States—Estados Unidos Mexicanos), is the largest and most densely populated city in the world, dominating all aspects of Mexican life. It has been allowed haphazardly to develop in the Valley of Mexico, surrounded by mountains and volcanoes, on a subsoil too soft to support it, and in an earthquake zone, far removed from fresh water and energy sources—in short, just where a city of any size should not be. The fumes and toxic substances sent up by traffic and by heavy industry on its outskirts into high-altitude air, lacking in oxygen, point up the harm caused by unchecked environmental pollution and massive immigration. No urban area enjoys a worse press (national and international). Yet the extraordinary resilience of its people (capitalinos; colloquially, chilangos) has meant that it has not lost its soul. And, thanks to its strong cultural and intellectual traditions, the architectural beauties and interest of its historic centre, its archaeological remains, its cathedral and churches, its splendid museums and art galleries and mural paintings, its parks and old plazas, as well as the more modern grandeur of its famous Paseo de la Reforma, and the old-world charm of its once outlying villages, it is still, in its strange and paradoxical way, and for all its faults, a magnificent city. It is never dull.

Its population (1990) is probably c 20 million, c one-quarter of the republic's total. The altitude of the Federal District (Mexico DF; see below) averages c 2400m. There is no winter, properly speaking, and the climate is cool to warm, and dry. The rainy season lasts from May to Sept. (afternoon rain) and the average annual temperature is 64°F (18°C). July and Aug. are warmer, with an average temperature of 70°F (21°C). The strain of day-to-day living tells on its inhabitants and affects the visitor, who should take things very easily at first. Those on short stays should not try to do too much, and stick to an unhurried plan of visits to a few of what seem the most desirable places.

Exploration of the historic centre is best done on foot, even though this is a tiring business. Except on Sun., the streets teem with people and traffic, and the pavements and pedestrian precincts are often clogged by street vendors and their stalls, which can make walking hazardous as well. At times the polluted air descends in an unpleasant smog which can cause sore throats and smarting eyes. This is hemmed in by the mountain ring and frequent temperature inversions. At other times, a pleasant breeze blows, clearing away the pollution. Then one can appreciate what Mexico has to offer, even today: a wonderful light and clear views of the surrounding mountains, seeming close at the end of straight thoroughfares.

Airport. Benito Juárez International Airport, 6.5km E of the centre. Flights to all parts. Taxi services, for which one buys tickets at official rates at the ticket booth, to other parts of the city. Metro 'Aeropuerto' on the Observatorio-Pantitlán line.

Railway station. Estación Buenavista. At the corner of Av. Insurgentes Norte and C. Mosqueta. Trains, stopping at intermediate stations, to *Ciudad Juárez* (36 hrs); to *Monterrey* (15 hrs); to *Guadalajara* (14 hrs); to *Veracruz* (12 hrs); to *Puebla* (9 hrs); to *Oaxaca* (15 hrs); to *Mérida* (36 hrs); to *Nuevo Laredo* (Aguila Azteca; 25 hrs); etc.

Bus stations (Centrales Camioneras; Centrales de Autobuses.) *Central del Norte* (Metro, Autobuses del Norte on Politécnico-Pantitlán line). Av. Lázaro Cárdenas, beyond junction with Av. Insurgentes Norte. For all destinations N of the city: Pachuca, Tampico, Matamoros, Querétaro, Guanajuato, Guadalajara, Morelia, Puerto Vallarta, Aguascalientes, San Luis Potosí, Durango, the frontier cities, etc.

Central de Oriente (Metro, San Lázaro on Observatorio-Pantitlán line), on Calz. Ignacio Zaragoza. For all destinations E of the city: Puebla, Tlaxcala, Veracruz, Orizaba, Jalapa, Villahermosa, Mérida, Campeche, Oaxaca, San Cristóbal de las Casas, etc.

Central de Poniente (Metro, Observatorio). At the corner of C. Sur 122 and Av. del Río (Tacubaya). For the service to Toluca.

Central del Sur (Metro, Tasqueña), Calz. Tasqueña. For destinations S of the city: Tasco, Cuernavaca, Acapulco, Ixtapa, Zihuatanejo, etc.

Tickets for taxis are obtainable from booths inside the stations.

Secretaría de Turismo. 172 Av. Presidente Masarik (Col. ChapultepecPolanco). For comprehensive information and complaints. There is also a 24-hour telephone service (English spoken) for emergencies and complaints. There is a federal tourist office at 54 C. Amberes (Col. Juárez).

Embassies. *British*, 71 Río Lerma (Col. Cuauhtémoc); *US*, 305 Paseo de la Reforma; *Canadian*, 529 C. Schiller (Col. Polanco); *Australian*, 11 C. Jaime Balmes, Pl. Polanco (Torre B, 10th Floor; Col. Los Morales; *New Zealand*, 229 Av. Homero (Col. Polanco); *German*, 707 C. Byron (Col. Rincón del Bosque); *French*, 15 C. Havre (Col. Juárez); *Spanish*, 2105 Parque Via Reforma (corner with Paseo de las Palmas; Col. Lomas de Chapultepec); *Guatemalan*, 1025 Av. Explanada (Col. Lomas de Chapultepec).

Anglo-Mexican Cultural Institute (*British Council*). 127 C. Maestro Antonio Caso (Col. San Rafael).

Benjamin Franklin Library. 16 C. Londres (Col. Juárez). Mon.–Fri., 9–8.

Post Office. E side of Alameda; Mon.–Sat., 8–midnight; Sun., 8–4.

Bookshops. *British*, Río Ganges (Col. Cuauhtémoc). *American*, 25 Av. Madero (Col. Centro)—both with large second-hand sections. *Porrúa* (one of Mexico's great institutions; superb selection of academic books), at the corner of Cs Justo Sierra and Argentina (Col. Centro)—no browsing; an assistant will bring books to the counter for the customer to inspect. *Misrachi*, SE side of Alameda. The second-hand bookshops in C. Donceles near the corner with C. Brasil (Col. Centro) offer a wide selection.

Newspapers. 'La Jornada', radical; 'El Norte de Monterrey'; 'El Excelsior'; 'El Universal'—all influential. 'El Financiero' and 'El Economista'—also influential, important for business and financial communities. 'El Heraldo' and 'El Novedades'—more superficial, but read for social and high society news. 'El Nacional'—formerly belonging to the government, put up for sale in 1993. 'La Prensa'—tabloid, relished for sensational reporting. 'Mexico City News'—English language. 'El Proceso' and 'Siempre' are influential weekly magazines, the former with a popular appeal, the latter more for intellectuals. Another magazine, 'Tiempo Libre', appeals to the artistic community. An outstanding journal (4 times a year) is 'Artes de México', recently reconstituted, with articles on all aspects of Mexican art, architecture, and culture, and plentiful illustrations.

Hotels. Finding accommodation is never difficult, and prices are still reasonable. The most expensive hotels are on, and just off, Paseo de la Reforma, in the Zona Rosa (Col. Juárez), and on the N side of Chapultepec. There are first-class hotels in the historic centre (Col. Centro), but a room facing the street lets in much noise. Those who are willing to sacrifice quiet to convenience will have no problem. There are cheaper, and very cheap, establishments in the same colonia, in the area S of the Alameda, for example, and between Pl. de la República and Estación Buenavista (Col. Buenavista).

Restaurants. Everywhere at all prices, and all types of cuisine, to cater for Mexicans, who eat out whenever they can, and foreign visitors. Expensive and elegant in the Zona Rosa; N and W of Chapultepec (Colonias Polanco and Lomas de Chapultepec); and along and N of Paseo de la Reforma (Col.

Cuauhtémoc); and in San Angel and Coyoacán. Reasonable or cheap, and characterful, in Col. Centro, near the Zócalo and the Alameda, and near Pl. San Fernando (Col. Buenavista).

Buses. Usually green, displaying route they cover on windscreen. Cheap flat fares. The extreme E corner of Chapultepec, between the W end of Av. Chapultepec and Paseo de la Reforma, is a convenient terminus. 'Villa' indicates Guadalupe.

Taxis are plentiful and cruise for hire, but can be difficult to find during rush hours. Cheapest are the small yellow and white, or green cabs. For the larger, saloon-type cabs it is as well to agree a fare in advance.

Metro. Efficient and clean, but very crowded, and therefore tiring, especially in the early morning and evening. Travellers are advised to arm themselves with a plan (sometimes obtainable at booking offices of more important stations). Cheap flat fares, with tickets obtainable in blocks—essential if one is to avoid queues. Tickets are surrendered at automatic machines which lift the entrance barriers. Stations connecting with another line are called correspondencias. The sign 'Andenes' signifies platforms; 'Salidas' means way out. The walk within a correspondencia to the platforms of another line can be a long one. Heavy luggage is forbidden.

At *Pino Suárez* station a small semicircular *Adoratorio*, dedicated to Ehecatl, was discovered and preserved during the metro excavations and construction. It was one of what must have been hundreds of such small centres for worship in Greater Tenochtitlán. Artefacts recovered in its excavation are also on display.

At *Bellas Artes* station the walls have cast, full-sized, reproductions of famous Mexican prehistoric stone sculptures and stelae from all over the country.

Hospitals. British-American Cowdray Hospital (private), C. Sur 136 (Col. Las Américas), off Av. Observatorio, W of Tacubaya. Centro Médico, Av. Cuauhtémoc (Col. Doctores), for specialist help in emergencies.

Founding of the city. The Mexica Aztecs entered the Basin of Mexico in the mid-13C, but, as newcomers to an already populous region, found difficulty in finding a place to settle. After basing themselves in several locations, incl. Chapultepec and Culhuacán, they were allowed to settle on the island in Lago de Texcoco which became Tenochtitlán.

Having been twice expelled from the rock of Chapultepec by the Tepaneca of Azcapotzalco, the Mexica established an alliance with the Culhua, who allowed them to live in the rocky wastes of Tizapán, E of Culhuacán. From the Culhua they accepted their first princely ruler, Acamapichtli (1372–91). They served both the Culhua and others as mercenaries, but Culhua favour was lost when the Mexica requested of them a 'marriage' alliance, by which they meant a spiritual alliance, through their principal deity, Huitzilopochtli. The Aztec aim, it seems, was to secure a claim of descent from the Tolteca, through Culhuacán, which was originally a Toltec foundation. The unsuspecting Culhua duly proffered a daughter and prepared for the wedding feast, only to arrive and find a frenzied Aztec priest dancing in the skin of their sacrificed and flayed princess, a sacrifice to prepare her for a symbolic marriage to Huitzilopochtli! Attacked by the infuriated Culhua the Aztecs fled and took refuge in the marshlands along the shores of Lago de Texcoco, and it was here, on a nondescript island off the W shore, that Aztec priests and leaders received the famous 'message' from their god—to settle where they witnessed an eagle perched on a prickly pear cactus devouring a snake (the scene now commemorated on the Mexican national flag). Here they built the city of Tenochtitlán and the great ceremonial precinct, the Teocalli, with its pyramids, skull rack, and twin temples dedicated to Huitzilopochtli and Tláloc, and where they sacrificed so many victims to nourish the life-giving sun with blood.

The exact date of the founding of Tenochtitlán is uncertain. Older sources give the year as 1325, but more recent research favours either 1345 or 1369–70. Simultaneously, another group established a twin city, Tlatelolco, on an island just N of Tenochtitlán, traditionally in 1358, or, according to more recent sources, in 1370. After more than 100 years of uneasy coexistence, however, Tlatelolco was annexed to Tenochtitlán in 1473 by Axayácatl (1468–81).

Development of the city and domination of the Basin of Mexico. For the remainder of the 14C and early 15C Tenochtitlán was only one of the 50–60 rival city-states in the Basin of

0 metres 500

MEXICO HISTORIC CENTRE

Key to Numbers
1 Puerta de Veracruz
2 Fábricas Univerales
3 Casa May.de Avila
4 Casa Mayorazgo López Peralta
5 Casa Torre Cossio
6 Casa Humboldt

Mexico, where the limited resources were a continuous cause for competition and conflict. Two of the more powerful cities were Azcapotzalco, which had succeeded in dominating much of the W side of Lago de Texcoco, and Texcoco, which dominated the E side. As their power and confidence grew, strengthened by alliance to Texcoco, the Mexica settled old scores with the Tepaneca of Azcapotzalco by declaring war on, and eventually razing, the city in 1428. With the help of Texcoco's new ruler, Nezahualcóyotl (1418–72), they began to expand Tenochtitlán and many joint building projects were undertaken. By the time Cortés had arrived in 1519, virtually all the cities of the Basin had been made tributary to either Tenochtitlán or Texcoco, and Aztec expansion had been extended beyond the Basin to the Pacific and Gulf coasts. Many regions, however, had only recently been conquered and the process of consolidation was incomplete.

Defence, Water, and Food. Tenochtitlán was at first supplied with fresh water from a spring within the precincts of the Teocalli, the sacred ceremonial core of the city; but the growing population soon rendered this supply inadequate. Dikes and causeways, to section off the surrounding lake, and to give dry access to the city, were designed and begun by Itzcóatl (1426–40) and Nezahualcóyotl after the defeat of Azcapotzalco. Each causeway was broken by several drawbridges or removable sections; Moctezuma I Ilhuicamina (1440–68), Itzcóatl's successor, began to supplement the city's water supply by using the W causeway to support an aqueduct carrying water from a spring at the old Mexica settlement at Chapultepec; and in the reign of Ahuítzotl (1486–1502), a second aqueduct was built alongside the causeway from the S, from Coyoacán (whose flow proved too difficult to control, and to prevent flooding was eventually blocked up when Ahuítzotl himself was drowned in a flood).

There were eventually several causeways joining the city to the mainland, but their number and exact routes are uncertain. The descriptions of Spanish chroniclers conflict and access to archaeological evidence is limited by the modern city. One main causeway entered the S gate of the Teocalli. It forked before reaching the shore, one part going to Ixtapalapa via Mexicalzingo—the branch used by Cortés—and the other part to Coyoacán via Huitzilopochca.

At least four other main causeways joined the mainland from the N and W gates, via Tlatelolco. One went W to Tlacopan (modern Tacuba), with a branch causeway to Azcapotzalco. Another, carrying the aqueduct, went to Chapultepec. Two others went N, one by the shortest route, to the peninsula of Tepeyac (where the shrine of the Virgen de Guadalupe now stands), and another by a slightly longer route, to Tenayuca.

By 1519 the estimated population of Tenochtitlán–Tlatelolco was some 200–300,000, living in a vast grid-plan of compact housing around the central Teocalli. Feeding this multitude presented considerable difficulties, but was managed by the ingenious extension of cultivable land in chinampas, the misnamed 'floating gardens'. They varied in size, but were laid out in a planned grid with interconnecting canals between them. By 1519 the construction of chinampas had reached an estimated 10,000ha, and stretched from Tenochtitlán, S to Xochimilco (where a few still survive), and E into Lago de Chalco. There were also smaller chinampa systems in Lago de Texcoco on its E shore, and in Lago de Xaltocán to the N.

Post-conquest Mexico. During the bloody siege of May–Aug. 1521 Cortés and the conquistadores began the destruction of Tenochtitlán, whose beauty had so enchanted them. After some indecision he resolved to build the capital of New Spain on the same site. He had the remaining Aztec edifices razed, but the soft watery subsoil would prove unsuitable for buildings of the scale and mass that the Spaniards were to introduce, and would present continuous problems of subsidence and drainage. Not until the 20C was it realized that the Valley of Mexico owed its existence to the invisible fault line that lay directly under the site of the proposed city, which was to be shaken through the centuries by earthquakes; against them the soft ground was, ironically, to afford some protection. The traza (plan) for the Spanish city of Mexico envisaged a centre, on as rectangular a grid as the site permitted, divided among the conquerors. The Indians were confined to four barrios on the outskirts. Where possible, the streets and canals which traversed the city followed the plan of Tenochtitlán. A firm stone causeway was constructed to allow the Spaniards an escape route to Tacuba.

Created in 1530, the bishopric of Mexico, to which the formidable Juan de Zumárraga was consecrated in 1533, was raised to an archbishopric in 1546 and became the primatial see of a province stretching from Nicaragua to Alta California. Its significance matched that of Mexico as the most important capital in the Americas. The personal rule of Cortés gave way in 1527 to that of the audiencia, whose rule in turn gave way, from 1535, to that of audiencia and viceroy. Public buildings, the university, hospitals, convents of friars and, from 1570 (with one exception), of nuns helped to increase the city's prestige and grandeur. In the 17C building and rebuilding continued. It gradually lost the aspect of a fortress and began to take on the style of the Renaissance. The water supply came to be provided by two aqueducts: one from Sta Fe along Calz. de Tacuba; the other from Chapultepec to Pl. San Juan.

During the early 17C the streets were a network of canals, with pavements on each side, supplemented by drainage channels. Their inadequacy was pointed up by floods, especially during the first half of the century. Those of 1629–34 did much damage and caused loss of life. Floods would still be a feature into the 19C, and many bridges were needed. A permanent drainage system, to take off surplus water and sewage (aguas negras), would not be complete until 1900. Mexico was already elegant in the 17C; the 18C was its golden age. Noble buildings reflected the pride and wealth of a creole and Spanish minority sustained by legions of mixed-race and Indian servants and slaves. A construction feat of exceptional skill (1711–79) was the arches of the aqueduct of Belem, to carry the 'agua gorda' of Chapultepec into the city. Under viceroy conde de Revillagigedo II (1789–94) improvements were made to enhance a civilized urban life: street lighting (by vegetable oil lamps) under the care of nightwatchmen; street name plaques in azulejos; a police force recruited; garbage collections; clean and paved streets; noisome drainage channels closed in; a piped sewage system; taps attached to water pipes to ease collection of fresh water; sidewalks built; new plazas and tree-lined avenues opened up. The census of 1790 probably understates the number of inhab. at 112,000, and the city's splendour, wealth, and confidence ensured that it had no equal in the New, or even the old, World.

In 1836 the English traveller Charles Joseph Latrobe could praise it as a 'luxurious City of Palaces'. In the Independence struggle and civil and military disturbances (under a new aristocracy of generals) and invasions that followed, urban renewal, and intellectual and artistic life, suffered. The Reform closed convents and sequestered their properties. Churches were put to other uses. When Juárez returned in 1867, the capital wore a ramshackle aspect. Maximilian's projected Calz. del Emperador, however, gave a push to new development from the 1860s, and the colonias of Sta María la Ribera, San Rafael, and Guerrero, on the NE, were a pointer of growth to come. Gas lighting arrived in 1869; electricity in 1880; electric trams in 1896.

Expansion began in earnest under the porfiriato. Outside the historic core, developments went ahead in conspicuously eclectic styles. By 1900 the population was c 350,000. Indians were discouraged from entering the city, unless they wore European-style dress. In 1910, for the Independence centenary celebrations, beggars were collected by the cartload and dumped beyond the outskirts so as not to scandalize foreign visitors by their presence.

During the Revolution the city became a prize to be won by the various factions, and numbers were swollen by refugees from the countryside. The much-feared zapatistas, who arrived in 1915, came diffidently and almost apologetically. Little harm was done to its fabric, but thousands died of typhoid and typhus, and in the influenza epidemic of 1919. In 1920–50 much building was unplanned and opportunistic. Unrestrained private initiative spawned apartment blocks, and factories and warehouses spread far out along the arterial roads. In 1930 the population reached 1 million; in 1940, 1.5 million. Utter transformation followed. Mexico City became a magnet for peasants seeking work in new industries and relief from rural misery. By 1970 the population had grown to over 8 million; by 1980 to 14 million.

Firm planning policies to accommodate an environment overwhelmed by too many people and the growth of slums, such as Nezahualcóyotl on the E side of the city (most unsuitably plumped on the desiccated bed of the Lago de Texcoco); squatter invasions; the demands of a transport system unable to cope; the pollution caused by cars, buses, and factories (of which only a small percentage comply with anti-pollution laws), and dust storms (tolvaneras), caused by deforestation and the drying-up of the bed of the Lago de Texcoco, are hampered by the waiving or ignoring of regulations when political or economic imperatives are in the way.

The earthquake of 1957 caused damage, but had less effect in a less crowded city. That of 1985 was much more serious: officially 8000 dead (probably more); 200,000 homeless; and damage put at $4000 million. It struck haphazardly. Old buildings, some without foundations, withstood the shocks; newer, speculative, poorly built edifices in the centre collapsed. The spontaneous and heartwarming response of the capitalinos and the community spirit they showed in often heroic works of rescue caught the admiration of the world and contrasted with the hesitant efforts of the seemingly (perhaps understandably) bewildered national and local authorities. Rebuilding and repair, often egged on by determined local associations, have on the whole been quicker than at first seemed possible.

Mexico City is officially capital of the **Distrito Federal** (DF; 1483 sq km), created in 1824 to centralize, and preserve the dignity of, the government of a federal republic. It is governed by a regent appointed by the president, and is divided into 16 large areas called delegaciones. Each delegación is itself divided into colonias. The situation has now been reached where the delegaciones of Milpa Alta (extreme S), Cuajimalpa (extreme W), and Tláhuac (extreme E) are mainly composed of rural communities engaged in agriculture, while parts of Tlalpan, Xochimilco, Alvaro Obregón, and Magdalena Contreras preserve rural areas. The main urban area, however, has spilled N, W, and E into the State of México.

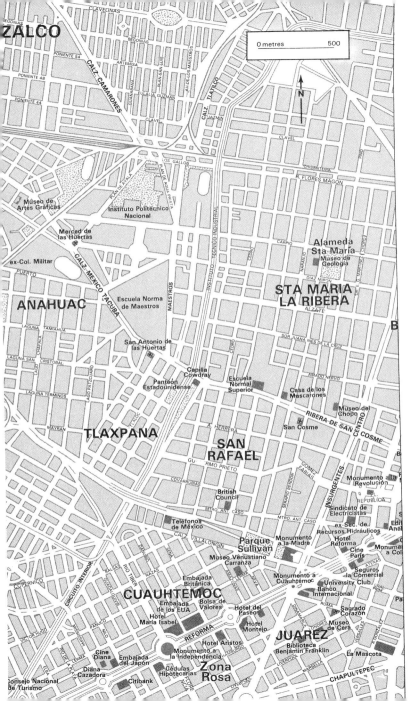

Hospital de la Raza

Monumento a la Raza

E. VILLANUE

RIO CONSULADO

CAJONAL

GERANIO

INSURGENTES NORTE

GUERRERO

LERDO

CALZ. SAN SIMON

M. GONZALEZ

CLAVEL

CRISANTEMA

R. FLORES MAGON

M. GONZALEZ

NONOALCO-TLATELOLCO

LAZARO CARDENAS

CARPIO

NARANJO

PINO

MARTINEZ

DIAZ MIRON

Alameda Sta María

Museo de Geología

R. FLORES MAGON

SATURNO

ESTRELLA

ROSAS

Sta María de los Angeles

STA MARIA LA RIBERA

ALZATE

SOR JUANA INES DE LA CRUZ

Estación Buenavista

ALTAMIRA

ZARAGOZA

CAMELIA

Inmaculado Corazón de María

BUENAVISTA

GONZALEZ

GUERRERO

TORRE MOSQUETA

AMADO NERVO

MAGNOLIA

Casa de los Mascarones

VIOLETA

ZARO

PL. ASCENCIO

PERU

Museo del Chopo

RIBERA DE SAN COSME

CENTRO

BELISARIO

San Cosme

Pal. Buenavista

ALVARADO

TIZIANO

GOMEZ FARIAS

INSURGENTES

Monumento a la Revolución

Frontón México

Lotería Nacional

HIDALGO

SERAPIO RENDON

REPUBLICA

Lotería Nacional

Alameda

MTRO. ANT. CASO

Sindicato de Electricistas

Sanborns

JUAREZ

5 DE MAYO

ex-Sec. de Recursos Hidráulicos

Edificio Anáhuac

MADERO

Monumento a la Madre

Hotel Reforma

Café Colón

See Historic Mexico

ue van

Cine París

Monumento a Colón

INDEPENDEN.

16 DE SEPTIEMBRE

BUCARELI

LAZARO CARDENAS

URUGUAY

Monumento a Cuauhtémoc

Seguros la Comercial

MORELOS

BALDERAS

VICTORIA

REP. SALVADOR

University Club

GRAN PRIX

AYUNTAMIENTO

Banco Internacional

ROMA

Sagrado Corazón

Pal. Cobián

Edificio Gaona

E. PUGIBET

ISABEL

JUAREZ

Museo de Cera

Edificio Vizcaya

Talleres Gráficas

CUAUHTEMOC

ejo

Biblioteca Benjamín Franklin

TOLSA

LIVERPOOL

MARSELLA

La Mascota

CHAPULTEPEC

Arena México

DR. RIO DE LA LOZA

ARCOS DE BELEN

San Salvador el Seco

N

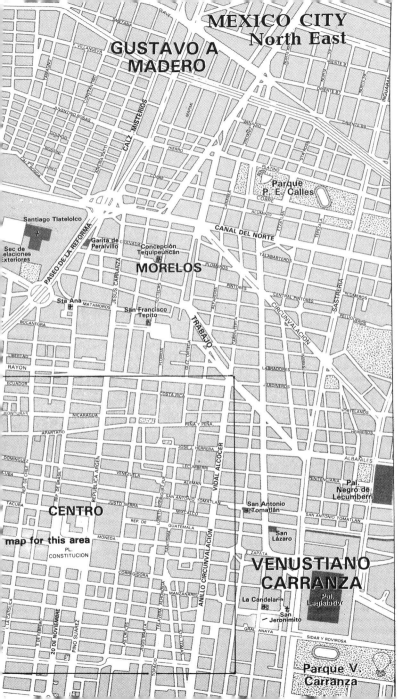

RIBERA DE SAN COSME

Museo del Chopo

San Cosme

CENTRO

0 metres 500

Pal. Buenavista

ALVARADO

Monumento a la Revolución

Frontón México

Lotería Nacional

REFORMA

HIDALGO

Alameda

GOMEZ FARIAS

INSURGENTES

N

REPUBLICA

MTRO. ANT. CASO

SERAPIO RENDON

Sindicato de Electricistas

ex-Sec. de Recursos Hidráulicos

Hotel Reforma

Cine París

Sanborns

Edificio Anáhuac

Monumento a Colón

Café Colón

BUCARELI

Lotería Nacional

JUAREZ

5 DE MAYO

See Historic Mexico

INDEPENDENCIA

MADERO

Monumento a la Madre

Monumento a Cuauhtémoc

Seguros la Comercial

University Club

Banco Internacional

ROMA

Sagrado Corazón

Museo de Cera

JUAREZ

Biblioteca Benjamin Franklin

La Mascota

LIVERPOOL

MARSELLA

DINAMARCA

ATENAS

PASEO PRIM

VERSALLES

DONCELES

BERLIN

Edificio Gaona

Pal. Cobián

Edificio Vizcaya

Talleres Gráficos

TOLSA

MORELOS

VICTORIA

AYUNTAMIENTO

E. PUGIBET

BALDERAS

18 DE SEPTIEMBRE

URUGUAY

REP. SALVADOR

LAZARO CARDENAS

BOLIVAR

CUAUHTEMOC

ARCOS DE BELEN

DR. RIO DE LA LOZA

CHAPULTEPEC

Arena México

Romita

CORDOBA

JALAPA

DURANGO

MERIDA

FRONTERA

Sagrada Familia

PL. RIO DE JANEIRO

COLIMA

ROMA

ALVARO OBREGON

ORIZABA

PL. E. CABRERA

GUANAJUATO

Nuestra Señora del Rosario

QUERETARO

SAN LUIS POTOSI

DR. LAVISTA

Tesorería del DF

Campo Florido

Pal. de Justicia

CLAUDIO BERNARD

DR. I. VELASCO

DR. LUCIO

DR. JOSE TERRES

HEROES

NIÑOS

DR. MA. VERTIZ

San Salvador el Seco

DIAZ 20 NOV

BOLIVAR

JOSE T. CUELLAR

DOCTORES

DR. PASTEUR

DR. JOSE TERRES

DR. BARRAGAN

DR. ANDRADE

Hospital General

Instituto de Cardiología

CUAUHTEMOC

Multifamiliar Juárez

Hospital Infantil

DR. NORMA

DR. DURAN

DR. MARQUEZ

J. M. ROA BARCENAS

Centro Médico

DR. M. UGARTE

MANUEL CABALLERO

CENTRAL

LAZARO CARDENAS

HERNANDEZ DAVALOS

Panteón Francés

BAJIO

VIADUCTO

MIGUEL ALEMAN

DR. BOLAÑOS

DR. ANDRADE

DR. DEVOX

BENITO JUAREZ

Nuestra Señora de la Piedad

CALZ. CASA OBRERO MUNDIAL

ESPERANZA

MA. VERTIZ

BOLIVAR

CORUÑA

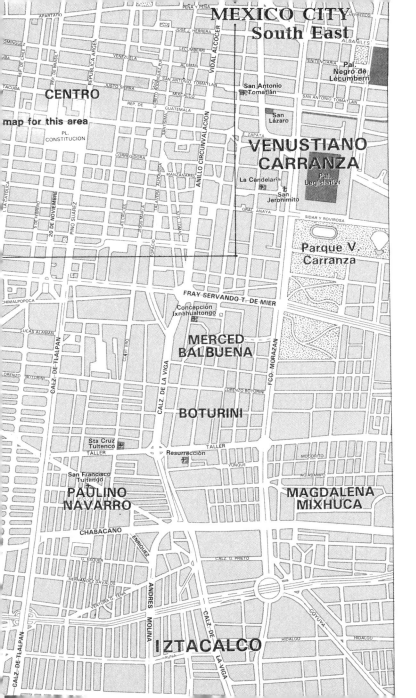

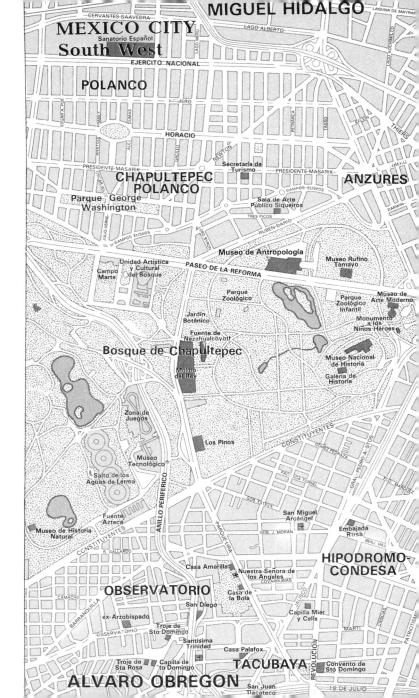

The chronic water shortage has meant that hydraulic engineers, however resourceful and brilliant, have had to go even further afield in their search for sources to tap, leaving a trail of environmental and ecological disasters in their wake. At the same time, unbelievably, with the disappearance of the waters of the Valley of Mexico, the city sinks lower and lower, and has to be drained to prevent flooding after heavy rain. A drainage canal (Gran Canal) on the E side, running to Tequixquiac (c 60 km N) and connected by tunnel with the Río Tula, was opened in 1900. Continued subsidence has reversed the direction of its flow and giant pumping stations have had to be built to pump flood water and sewage away from the centre. Three interceptor canals at depths of up to 220 m were built in the 1970s to catch water coming down from the heights during the rains. In 1993 British and French water companies won contracts to rebuild the water system, incl. a water census, accurate metering to eliminate waste, and the repair of 12,000km of pipes.

1 The Zócalo

The **ZOCALO**, officially *Pl. de la Constitución* (once known as Pl. Real, Pl. de Armas, or Pl. Mayor), second only in size (approx. 57,600sq m) to Red Square in Moscow, is one of the world's most imposing city centres, heir to a triumphal pivot of viceregal town-planning, teeming with life and full of architectural and historical interest.

The original Pl. Mayor, taking shape in the 1520s to the plan of Alonso García Bravo, was considerably smaller than today's plaza. To its N the Pl. Chica (or Plazuela del Marqués) faced on the W the Casas Viejas of Axayácatl, where Cortés built his own mansion. S of this, on the W, was built the Portal de Mercaderes, later to incorporate three houses: of Rodrigo de Albornoz; of Rodrigo de Castañeda; and of the conde de Santiago. On the SW side rose the Casa del Cabildo, separated from the Portal de las Flores (SE) by a narrow street. On the E the Casas Nuevas of Moctezuma, also acquired by Cortés, became the Pal. de los Virreyes. At its first auto de fe, on 28 Feb. 1574, 'in the middest of the market place ... right over against the head church' the newly formalized Inquisition sentenced survivors of John Hawkins's worsted fleet (see Rte 72) in the presence of the viceroy and 300 dignitaries of Church and state: one, George Rively, to be burned; c 25 to the lash and the galleys; c 8 (among them Miles Philips and Paul Hawkins) to wear the sanbenito and to serve in convents. After an auto in 1575 John Martin from Cork, another Hawkins man, was sentenced, garrotted, and burned. In 1610 space was made for two days of bullfights—50 bulls were killed—to celebrate the canonization of St Ignatius.
    In 1695–1703 the Parián, a permanent masonry structure divided into two blocks by a narrow passage, probably intended as a cavalry barracks, was fitted into the SW part, but was soon taken over by stallholders. Those who could not fit into it soon spilled over into the plaza, which the diarist and bookseller Francisco Sedano described in the late 18C as 'an ugly and disagreeable sight', complete with gallows and pillory facing the viceregal palace. From 1789, on the orders of Viceroy Revillagigedo II, the plaza was cleared. In 1796 the SE part was redesigned by José Antonio González Velázquez as a setting for the statue of Charles IV (see Rte 8). In 1812 the assembled citizens swore allegiance to the Constitution of Cadiz and in May 1813 Viceroy Calleja renamed it Pl. de la Constitución. In Dec. 1818 an enthusiastic mob shouting 'Death to the Spaniards' fired the Parián and badly damaged it. In 1843 Santa-Anna ordered its demolition and launched a competition for a monument to Independence to grace the centre, won by Lorenzo de la Hidalga, who put down the base (zócalo); but the project remained unfulfilled, and 'zócalo' was adopted as a name for the whole plaza.
    During the second empire, parterres, fountains, and iron benches were laid out; gas lighting was introduced; and by 1878 a bandstand had been installed on top of the zócalo: 'every afternoon and evening Beethoven, Wagner, and Suppé'. Early this century, zócalo and bandstand were removed. After 1914 garden and park areas gradually disappeared. Since the 1960s only the national flagpole remains.

On the N side of the Zócalo stands the **Catedral Metropolitana de Nuestra Señora de la Asunción**, largest of Mexican cathedrals, centre of the archdiocese of Mexico, and noblest ecclesiastical edifice in the Americas. It is built of grey stone and basalt, which introduces a vibrant pinkish ochre. Its combination of different styles, from Renaissance to neoclassical, is a reflection of the 250 years it took to complete.

The incomplete cathedral of Mexico City (mid-18C)

The first cathedral (iglesia mayor), begun by Cortés and finished by Bp Juan de Zumárraga (c 1524–32), was orientated E–W, just SW of the present building. Considered small and insignificant, nevertheless some of New Spain's finest artists and craftsmen embellished its interior, and its treasure was considerable. In 1626 it was demolished and its magnificent gilded retables destroyed. Some of its column bases, brought to light during excavations in 1881, may still be seen facing Av. 5 de Mayo.

A new cathedral was ordained in 1536 and again in 1552. Actual building, to a modified plan by Claudio de Arciniega, did not begin until 1573. Early in the 17C Juan Miguel de Agüero introduced further modifications; still another plan, by Juan Gómez de Mora, sent by Philip III, was rejected. By 1615 the walls were half projected height and the N doorways completed, followed in 1623 by the vaults of the sacristy, where in 1626 Mass was being said. Soon after, the first two side chapels on the E side were finished. In 1635–40 work resumed on the Cap. de los Reyes. In 1656 the imperfect cathedral was dedicated. A few days before the ceremony viceroy duque de Alburquerque, his wife, and little daughter swept the chancel clean, 'shaking themselves free of dust, *que fué mucho*'—an act of humility, we are told, which edified all who saw it. On 13 July 1659 Oliver Cromwell's death was celebrated with Te Deum, High Mass, and litanies of Our Lady. In 1664–67 interior and cupola were brought to fruition, an occasion for a second dedication, when viceroy marqués de Mancera, on the eve of the great day, detailed relations, friends, and servants to see to the final touches and to do the cleaning up. In 1672–89, S, E, and W portals were finished. José Damián Ortiz de Castro, having won the competition to finish the work, designed and raised the higher storeys of the towers (1787–91) and filled out the façade. He also devised a carriage, with many wheels, to bring the largest bell from its foundry at Tacubaya and a machine to haul it up into the W tower. It was left to Manuel Tolsá to raise the façade by a semicircular pediment surmounted by a clock; add the balustrades; modify and reinforce cupola and lantern; and supervise the adornment of the towers, work completed in June 1813.

On 21 July 1822 Agustín de Iturbide and Ana María Huarte were crowned emperor and empress of Mexico in a splendid ceremony. The crown was too small for Iturbide's head: 'Your majesty must not let the crown fall', whispered Rafael Mangino, president of Congress, who

CATHEDRAL AND SAGRARIO, MEXICO

0 metres   25

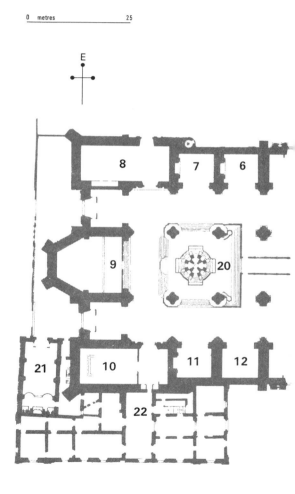

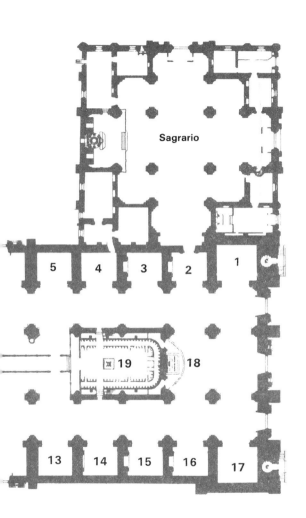

crowned him; 'it shall not fall', Iturbide hissed back. (On 27 Oct. 1838 his remains were brought here in solemn procession, so long that its head had arrived at the main portal before its tail had left the starting point at San Francisco.) In 1847 Santa-Anna confiscated treasure to fund the war against the USA. In 1836–50 the original retables and gilded wooden grilles of some side chapels were destroyed; in 1868 the chapter started to destroy more, but Juárez himself ordered them to desist. In 1888 Abp Labastida wanted to tear out the Altar de los Reyes, but, to his everlasting credit, Ignacio de la Hidalga refused the commission to build a new.

EXTERIOR. The main (S) façade is of three Mannerist portals recessed between solid buttresses. Their lower storeys (1667–72) have two pairs each of fluted columns ending in doric capitals; the friezes are of triglyphs and metopes. The upper storeys were finished in 1687: those of the side portals have solomonic columns, the earliest exterior use in Mexico City, with Corinthian capitals. All three contain beguilingly detailed stone reliefs in eared frames: on l., St Peter receiving the keys of the kingdom; in centre, Assumption; on r., ship of the Church. The statues of SS Peter and Paul (lower storey) and SS Matthew and Andrew (upper storey) are by Miguel and Nicolás Ximénez (1687). The upper central part is by Tolsá: curved pediment enclosing a post-Independence medallion of the eagle and serpent and supporting the clock tower (clock by José Francisco Dimas Rangel), topped by masterly statues of Faith, Hope, and Charity. The festoons, candelabra, urns, cherubs, and garlands above the portal panels are the work of Ortiz de Castro's collaborators, José Santos Castillo, Mariano Paz, and Nicolás Xirón.

The tower bases date from the 17C, as does the first storey of the E tower; that of the W was in place by the 1760s. The inner octagons of the second storeys (1787–91) are enclosed by clustered corner pilasters; the capping stone bells are an original and striking consummation. Both towers house 39 bells, the oldest, Doña María, dated 1578; the largest, Sta María de Guadalupe, dated 1791. The eight statues of saints on the W tower and two on the E, all designed by Tolsá, were sculpted by José Zacarías Cora; the remaining six on the E are by Santiago Cristóbal and Ignacio de Sandoval. The cupola, 'the most spiritual in Mexico', owes much to Tolsá's elegant brand of neoclassicism. Above each window of the high drum is a curved pediment (an archiepiscopal shield perched on each). The lantern, surrounded by a balustrade, is a marvel of slenderness and lightness.

The N doorways, facing C. Guatemala, are in austere Renaissance style. The E and W portals (finished in 1688 and 1689) show Renaissance influence in their lowest storeys. Baroque ornamentation in their first and second storeys was eliminated in 1804. There remain the beautifully patterned window frames and two inner solomonic columns in the second storey.

The illusion of great height in the INTERIOR is achieved by central intersecting barrel vaults, divided by lunettes, and clerestory resting on heavy pilasters and fluted columns, which in two rows divide the nave (c 130m long and 57m wide), with its more medieval-style vaults, from the groin-vaulted side aisles and chapels.

The CHOIR (19) occupies, Spanish-style, the S end of the nave. On either side, along the aisles, its walls are topped by an elaborately ornamented gallery in carved and gilded wood (1734), which curves outwards at the corners to form a kind of pulpit borne up by young male figures: the work of José Eduardo de Herrera and Domingo Arrieta. Above the walls are the two great organs, their cases magnificently carved: the one on the W (1736) by José de Nazarre, who also updated the other, by Jorge de Sesma, ordered in 1688 and brought from Aragón by the brothers Tiburcio and Félix Sanz. On the S the choir is closed by the restored Altar del Perdón (18; finished 1732; dedicated 1737; ravaged by fire 1967), graced by four slender estípites, with a fan-like top, by Jerónimo de Balbás; backing it is a late 16C painting of the Holy Family. The N side is a superb screen of two oriental precious-metal alloys, tumbaga and calaín: the first a good bronze containing gold; the second similar, but lighter in colour. It was made in Macao to the design of Nicolás Rodríguez Juárez and modified and put in place by Jerónimo de Balbás in 1730. The choirstalls (c 1696–1709; extensively restored) are by Juan de Rojas; adorned with twisted columns and panels of saints in high relief. The ebony and tíndalo lectern (by José Núñez,

1762; arrived 1770), decorated with ivory statuettes, was the gift of Manuel Rojo del Río, abp of Manila.

The choir is joined to the high altar (20) by a low balustrade-type passage of bronze (1734–45), made in Mexico by José de Lemus; the anthropomorphic torchholders at intervals along the top are fashioned in tumbaga.

The first high altar (1673) was replaced in the 18C by a splendid one by Jerónimo de Balbás. This in turn was destroyed and replaced in the mid-19C. During restoration in 1943 the present alabaster altar, which does not obstruct the view of the Cap. de los Reyes, was put here. Two small pulpits, that for the epistle carrying apostle figures, that for the gospel the four evangelists, are probably by the same artist who fashioned the larger one attached to the column on the E in front of the choir, decorated with floral designs, cherubs, and a central panel carved with an image of Our Lady. All three are of alabaster; the third was put in place in 1683.

In the apse is the matchless ALTAR DE LOS REYES (9; 1718–37; main construction finished 1725), a forerunner of Mexican churrigueresque and the masterwork of Jerónimo de Balbás. Estípites of varying sizes soar into the vault. Polychrome statues of sainted kings and queens, attended by fluttering cherubs, stand at the bases of the main estípites and in canopied side niches, emphasizing the beauty of the central paintings, Adoration of the Kings and Assumption (1718–28), by Juan Rodríguez Juárez. The gilding (1736–43) is by Francisco Martínez.

This sculptural wonder, like a magic golden cave, named for the royal personages seen here honouring, with the three kings, the Christ child, takes on a different aspect according to the light. Two large compound lateral pilasters supporting the archivolt and two more at the back divide the piece into three main vertical parts, the central one appearing slim, but forming a high retable in itself. Each section gathers in its own major and minor estípites and all three are capped by a 'quarter-orange' vault. The semicircular shape disguises the pentagonal apse. The four main estípites are easily seen, but the side sections immured between them are not, even though they are slanted. These are framed by smaller estípites, between which, in rectangular frames, are statues of Louis IX of France and Ferdinand III of Castile (r.); above the elaborate cornices, on the volutes of the broken pediments sit angels holding fruits. In the centre the lower painting is similarly framed, the cornice and top especially plastic; the higher painting rises above the large estípites and breaks into the topmost decoration, which in turn invades the vault.

At the lowest level stand royal female saints: from l., Margaret of Scotland, Empress Helena, Elizabeth of Hungary, Isabel of Portugal, Empress Cunegund, Edith of England. Above them, stiffer than the more graceful ladies, are SS Hermenegild, Emeric of Hungary, Edward the Confessor, Casimir of Poland. The four angels above the monumental estípites carry attributes of Our Lady; the archivolt, with its central medallion of God the Father, has a Romanesque look.—To l. and r. are groups of paintings, Scenes from the Life of Our Lady, by the same master, framed to resemble retables, rococo in inspiration.

The SACRISTY (8), entered by a Renaissance portal from the NE aisle, has Gothic vaulting and the original chests for storing vestments. Six sumptuous paintings, on the grandest scale, by Juan Correa and Cristóbal de Villalpando (1684–86) line the walls. The colours and the swirl of angels, heroic figures, horses, are breathtaking. Alas, there is neither light nor space enough fully to admire them.

The four by the latter begin with (above and round the entrance) the Apotheosis of St Michael, the archangel dominating the top half. The lower part, divided by the door, shows (l.) a bull drinking from a rocky pool in a lush landscape, a wounded man behind it—perhaps symbolizing St Michael's victory over idolatry. On the r., at the lowest level, Abp Aguiar y Seijas is attended by five canons and the painter himself; to the r., a priestly group kneels, facing away from the New Jerusalem. On the same wall is the Woman of the Apocalypse, a painting in two parts: in the lower, St John and St Michael; in the upper, Our Lady and God receiving the Child. On the N wall is the Church Militant and the Church Triumphant, in three parts. The Church Militant is a young woman in pontifical robes; Charity, a lovely figure, nurses the infant Christ below. The Church Triumphant sits in a chariot attended by a heavenly orchestra. On the E wall is the Triumph of the Eucharist, the Host carried to church in a chariot, drawn by two effulgent women representing Prudence. On the S and E walls

Correa's Assumption (1689) and Entry of Christ into Jerusalem (1691) reveal fascinating human, divine, and landscape detail.

Corresponding with the Sacristy in the W aisle is the *Sala Capitular* (10; Chapter Hall), with an identical doorway, containing portraits of the abps of Mexico; the Last Supper and Triumph of the Faith, by José de Alzíbar; Descent of the Holy Ghost, by José de Ibarra; and 16–17C furniture.

SIDE CHAPELS, R. (E) AISLE. *Cap. de las Angustias de Granada* (1). The main altarpiece (c 1750) shows fading churrigueresque and outer low-relief niche pilasters, its central painting a Pietà by Francisco Antonio Vallejo. The small retable (r.) frames a painting of St Raphael and Tobias by the late 16C Flemish master Marten de Vos. On l., the tabernacle is a relic of the old high altar (1850), by Lorenzo de la Hidalga. *Cap. de San Isidro Labrador* (2), with original vaulting (1626), communicates with the Sagrario by an ornate early 18C doorway. On l., a 17C black Christ, originally in the church of Porta Coeli; on r., a churrigueresque altarpiece. *Cap. de la Purísima Concepción* (3) contains an anastyle altarpiece (after 1755). The centre paintings are St Christopher by Simón Pereyns and Flagellation of Christ by Baltasar de Echave Orio. The outer paintings are by José de Ibarra. *Cap. de Nuestra Señora de Guadalupe* (4; 1808–11). Neoclassical, by José Antonio González Velázquez and José del Mazo y Avilés. *Cap. de Nuestra Señora de la Antigua* (5), once chapel of the musicians' guild. Coolly neoclassical. The paintings inserted into the main altarpiece (Birth of Our Lady; Presentation in the Temple) are by Nicolás Rodríguez Juárez. The crystal-covered niche in the centre holds a small early 17C statue, Sto Niño Cautivo. After the crossing, *Cap. de San Pedro* (6), with three retables.

The central one (c 1672–73), transitional between Mannerism and baroque, assembled by Tomás Juárez and gilded by Alonso de Jerez, is in three storeys on a base. In the centre of this is a small shrine (sagrario), an 18C addition flanked by estípites and with a tiny marble relief of the Crucifixion on top of its frame, possibly from the Philippines. In the niche is a late 16C statue, Niño Llorón (weeping infant Christ). Above it, in the lowest storey, in a glass-covered niche flanked by slender solomonic columns, is a statue of St Peter, a fine late 16C survival, but repainted; the niche pediment broken by an 18C statue of St John Nepomuk, under a canopy held by two angels. In the centre of the middle storey is the Crucifixion of St Peter, an early 17C painting, attr. Baltasar de Echave Orio. The lower storey columns are encrusted with relief giving an effect known as entorchadas. The estípites framing the window are later additions. The other, anon., paintings show scenes from the life of St Peter.

On l., the retable of St Teresa, in delicate churrigueresque, incorporates a statue of the saint showing estofado and four paintings of scenes from the Life of Our Lady on copper plates framed in ebony. The flanking paintings on the St Teresa theme are by Baltasar de Echave y Rioja (c 1670). The r. altarpiece, similar to the main, includes a painting, Holy Family in St Joseph's Workshop (1720), by Juan de Aguilera. *Cap. de las Reliquias* or *del Cristo de los Conquistadores* (7). The gate screen is a faithful mid-20C replica of the 17C original. In the intrados of the arch, four paintings (c 1723)—Moses, Solomon, David, Zachary—by Bentura Miranda. The main altarpiece, a mass of graceful gilding, is mid-17C (central niche) and early 18C (base and wings) and preserves its original statues of saints and angels and, in the centre, a Crucifixion (Cristo de los Conquistadores), probably a survival from an earlier retable and a gift from Charles V. Beneath it is an affecting painting of the Descent from the Cross, either 15C Flemish or an excellent copy. The paintings of saints (1698) on the wooden panels of the predella enclosing reliquaries are by Juan Herrera: originally 12, one lost and replaced by an 18C substitute (Juan Diego before Bp Zumárraga). Note the elaborate scroll supports, complete with heads, of the upper storeys. The flanking retables date from c 1770. The central medallion (painted by Ibarra) of the retable of the Patrocinio de Nuestra Señora de Guadalupe (l.), small and rococo (in a Renaissance frame), figured in a ceremony in Apr. 1737 when the city was dedicated to her protection. Behind, a vigorous Crucifixion by José de Villegas (late 17C), set in a Renaissance niche, once frame for an archiepiscopal tomb. The curious retable of the Virgen de Confianza (r.), in one section, hints at a mixture of styles, with its anachronistic solomonic columns. In the upper niche, St Joseph and the infant Christ; on either side of the anon. painting of the Virgin and Child, SS Anne and Joachim—three fine late 17C statues; in the niche below the painting, 17C ivory St Joseph and Child, from the Philippines. In the background, anon. 18C paintings of the Passion.

Closing the N end of the E aisle is an altarpiece (mid-18C), now dedicated to Nuestra Señora de Zapopan, with a copy of her miraculous image, probably from San Pedro y San Pablo. On the wall (l.), Circumcision, attr. Andrés de la Concha.

L. (W) AISLE (from N end). The churrigueresque retable which closes the aisle was originally moved in 1770 to the Sagrario from San Pedro y San Pablo. It was placed here in 1958. On the wall (l.), Annunciation by Juan Sánchez Salmerón; higher up, SS Teresa and John of the Cross with the Virgin and Child, by Luis Juárez.

SIDE CHAPELS. *Cap. de San Felipe de Jesús* (11). The main retable (1770–80), anastyle, and reaching up in thin vertical lines, frames a 17C statue of Mexico's own saint. The contemporary paintings of scenes from his life show a delicate blue tint. At the entrance has been preserved (since 1648) the font in which he is said to have been baptized. On r., an urn contains the remains of Agustín de Iturbide. *Cap. de los Dolores* (or *Sta Cena*; 1808–11; 12). By González Velázquez and José del Mazo. Sculpture by Clemente Terrazas; painting by J.M. Vásquez. *Cap. de San Eligio* (13), once chapel of the silversmiths' guild. Its neoclassical retable shelters the revered statue of the Señor del Buen Despacho (16C), made in Andalucía, traditionally a gift from Charles V. *Cap. de Nuestra Señora de la Soledad* (14). The main retable is a fine late 17C work with substantial solomonic columns. Its central panel is a painting of Our Lady of Solitude, copy of an original in Madrid. The surrounding paintings of Scenes from the Passion (c 1670–80) are by Pedro Ramírez. The beautiful painting (r. wall) of the Holy Family with SS Anne and Joachim (Los Cinco Señores) is a late 16C work, attr. Andrés de la Concha, probably from the old cathedral. *Cap. de San José* (15), with an elongated churrigueresque altarpiece brought here from Monserrate. On r., the Señor del Cacao, a crude 16C work, once at the entrance to the old cathedral where the faithful left alms of cacao seeds, then used as currency. *Cap. de los Santos Cosme y Damián* (16), with two notable retables. The main in a dignified Mannerist-accented style (mid-17C) with splendid gilding. The paintings of scenes from the saints' lives, with background detail, are later 17C works by Sebastián López Dávalos. In the centre niche is the image of Sto Cristo de la Salud. The side retable (l.) is later 17C baroque, incorporating an Adoration of the Shepherds, once part of a late 16C retable from Zinacantepec—a lovely work, possibly by Concha, but gone over by a later hand. Above it, an Annunciation; the four saints of the outside panels are by Nicolás Rodríguez Juárez. In the arches above the altarpieces, three paintings (c 1684) by Cristóbal de Villalpando: Marriage of Our Lady (l.); Beheading of John the Baptist (r.); and Christ in Glory with Angels, part of a fuller mural, the rest lost.

On the choir wall opposite the chapel, two paintings (1704; retouched) of Souls in Purgatory by Juan Correa.

Cap. de los Santos Angeles (17). Perhaps the finest of all, dating from 1713 and financed by Juan Caballero y Ocío of Querétaro. The three retables are stunning in their gilding and in the beauty of the polychrome and gilded figures. The lateral paintings by Juan Correa are among his best. On l., retable of St Raphael, with paintings of the Agony in the Garden (centre), Liberation of St Peter (below l.), Conversion of St Paul (below r.), and five of the nine orders of angels. On r., Retable of St Gabriel, with paintings of the Annunciation (centre), Jacob's Ladder (above), Tobias and St Raphael (below l.), Jacob wrestling with an angel (below r.), and the remaining four of the nine orders.

In the crossing by the side entrances are four huge oval paintings (mid-18C) by Miguel Cabrera, for the Cap. de la Purísima in the church of San Francisco. On l. (W) side, Our Lady Queen of Martyrs, incl. (l.) San Felipe de Jesús in blue habit carrying his own cross; Our Lady Queen of Patriarchs, incl. patriarchs and founders of religious orders. On r. (E) side, Our Lady Queen of Angels, receiving the homage of the nine orders of the celestial hierarchy; Our Lady Queen of Apostles, with the apostles, the three Marys, and SS Luke and Mark.

The crypt, entered down stairs by the W door, contains the tombs of Juan de Zumárraga, first bp and abp of Mexico, and his successors.

Flanking the NW side of the Cathedral is the *Mitra* (22), dating from 1659, but handsomely rebuilt in the 18C, now offices of the archdiocese. Between it and the NW side, facing C. Guatemala, is the former *Cap. de las Animas* (early 18C), once used as an extension to the crypt.

Adjoining the Cathedral to the E is the **Sagrario Metropolitano**, the main parish church of the city and a monument to the genius of Lorenzo Rodríguez, who here gave an irresistible impulse to the switch of the churrigueresque style from the retable to the church façade.

Rodríguez's design was first discussed in 1740. Building began in 1749; the façades were finished in 1759; and the church was dedicated in 1768. The foundations, however, were unsound, and earthquakes in 1858 and 1895 did great damage. A rescue operation in the 1930s averted collapse.—Miguel Domínguez and Josefa Ortiz (see Rte 37) were secretly married in this church in Jan. 1793.

The three EXTERIOR walls are of red tezontle ('a rock bathed in blood'); the two façades on S and E superimposed in stone. These are of two storeys: four rotund estípites in the lower; six, more slender, in the upper. The interestípites add more delicate touches to the overall luxuriance. The lower-storey cornice forms an arch in the centre, repeated in the upper storey of the S façade; while on the E the upper cornice curves slightly downward. On either side of the S façade stand richly decorated lateral doorways and the stone wall frame undulates downward to embrace a pair of windows framed in dressed stone.

The statues and reliefs of the S portal represent New Testament figures. The wooden door reliefs, SS Peter and Paul. Framed in the arch above the door, St Joseph and the infant Christ; beneath them, St Ildefonsus. In the medallions on each face of the lower-storey estípite cubes, the 12 apostles; in the niches of the interestípites, SS Ignatius and Francis Xavier with medallions of SS Michael and Raphael above them. In the medallion which unites the lower and upper storeys, St Lawrence. Christ the Redeemer occupies the central niche of the upper storey, flanked by four doctors of the Church: SS Ambrose, Gregory, Augustine, and Jerome. Below the ornate crest, the Apocalyptic Lamb; above the Lamb, the monstrance surrounded by 14 stars representing the corporal and spiritual works of mercy. Alternating with the topmost pinnacles (Arms of León and Mexico), Faith, Hope, Charity, and Temperance.

The E portal door reliefs are the Immaculate Conception and St Joseph and the infant Christ. In the arch above the door, St John the Baptist; beneath him, St Louis IX. In the lowest-storey estípite cube medallions, 12 prophets and patriarchs, and, in the interestípite niches, SS Peter and Paul with St Gabriel and the infant Christ's guardian angel. The Immaculate Conception occupies the central upper-storey niche, with St John Nepomuk in the medallion beneath. The flanking niches contain the Four Evangelists. At the top on either side, statues of SS Gabriel and Raphael.

The INTERIOR, neoclassically cold, is on a Greek cross plan, the splendid cupola above the crossing. Communication with the Cathedral is through a doorway of the same pattern as the façade side portals. The main altarpiece (1829) is by Pedro Patiño Ixtolinque. Several of the eight side altars (c 1869) are by Luis G. Anzorena. Inside the E entrance, the giant ornamental niche pilaster is a survival from the original interior (nearly gutted by fire in 1796), as is the windbreak, also decorated with rocaille motifs (both c 1770).

On the W side of the Cathedral, facing Av. 5 de Mayo, is the **Monumento Hipsográfico** (1878–81), a bronze statue on a marble plinth representing the city of Mexico, in honour of Enrico Martínez.

Martínez (Heinrich Martin; d. 1632), a native of Hamburg, devised the Cut of Nochistongo to drain the Valley of Mexico (1607–) and to put an end to the yearly flooding of the city from the Lake of Texcoco. The monument was designed by Francisco M. Jiménez; the statue cast in Paris by Miguel Noreña. Further N is a fountain monument (1976) to Fray Pedro de Gante, a gift from the city of Ghent.

At the SE corner of Av. Madero and the Zócalo the *Hotel Majestic*, built in 1925 as the Hotel Plaza in neo-historical style by Rafael Goyeneche, occupies the site of the house of Rodrigo de Castañeda (1539) on the N side of the **Portal de Mercaderes** (1529; rebuilt 1754–70; restored since). On the Portal's S side (NE corner of Av. 16 de Septiembre), the **Gran Hotel Ciudad de México** is on the site of the house of Rodrigo de Albornoz (1529), finally demolished in 1895. In 1898 a sumptuous Art Nouveau emporium, the *Centro Mercantil*, was raised here by Daniel Garza, with lavish use of wrought-iron, cage lifts, and stained-glass lobby ceiling (1908) by Jacques Gruber of Nancy. Its conversion into the hotel in the 1930s enhanced its elegant reputation.

On the SW side of the Zócalo rises the **Ayuntamiento**. It owes its present appearance to transformations (1906–10) begun by Manuel Gorozpe.

The rioters of 1692 all but destroyed the first building. Of the two-storey structure of 1720–24, to which Ignacio Castera gave a new façade in 1789, only the arcade is left. On it Gorozpe raised two storeys, an unembarrassedly grand essay in nationalistic style. In 1921–34 what is now the second storey (note the estípites) was fitted in between the first and the arcaded top, and the grand staircase put in place. City archives and library are housed here, with other offices of the Federal District. The *Sala de Cabildos* (decoration of 1888–92 respected in rebuilding) is full of portraits and busts of past mayors.

On the SE side, separated from the Ayuntamiento by Av. 20 de Noviembre, is its seeming twin, the **Pal. del Departamento del Distrito Federal** (1935–48) by Federico Mariscal.

Here once stood the *Portal de las Flores*, demolished in 1935 to open up Av. 20 de Noviembre. The offices of the regent of the Federal District and other local government departments are found here. On its E side, facing the Supreme Court, is a monument to the city's foundation (1970) by Francisco Olaguíbel.

The E side of the Zócalo is taken up by the vast **Pal. Nacional**, seat of the Treasury (*Hacienda*) and of the Federal government, in its day an edifice of immense dignity, and still imposing despite the changes it has suffered. Its façade reaches 205m.

In Jan. 1562 the crown bought the house (*Casas nuevas de Moctezuma*) which Cortés had built on the site where Moctezuma II had had his palace and gardens as a palace for the viceroys, and as seat of the audiencia. It was the focal point of a great uprising in Jan. 1624 when viceroy marqués de Gelves, excommunicated by Abp Pérez de la Serna, was besieged by a mob running amuck in Pl. Mayor and only just managed to escape being torn to pieces. In June 1692, during even worse riots, the mob pelted the palace with stones and set fire to it. Rebuilding, under Diego Valverde and Felipe de Roa, began in 1693. The new palace, incomplete, was blessed in 1697. In 1711 the first Mexican opera, 'La Parténope' by Manuel Zumaya, was performed in it. The palace's reputation continued tarnished. Taverns were set up in the principal patio and the public got easy access, a practice Revillagigedo stopped after 1789. In July 1840, during Gómez Farías's abortive coup, a 12-day siege left it 'with its innumerable smashed windows and battered walls, as if it had become stone blind in consequence of having the smallpox'. In Sept. 1847 Gen. Winfield Scott had the US flag hoisted over it, while US marines chased out a band of convicts who had taken up residence. In 1864 Maximilian briefly occupied it. He spent his first night in Mexico City sleeping on a billiard table, to keep clear of the vermin scuttling about the floor. Pres. Juárez died here in 1872. Changes were made to the N wing in 1892–1902 to provide more space for the Hacienda. The home of all viceroys and presidents until 1884 (when Pres. González, notoriously venal, made off with the best furniture and fittings), it has always been used by succeeding presidents, with the exception of Pres. Alemán, as administrative headquarters.

The palace was drastically changed in 1926–27 by Augusto Petriccioli, who added the third storey, restored façade ornamentation lost in the 19C, repositioned and elaborated the three gables above the portals, and refaced the walls with tezontle, and window frames, cornices, and gables with stone. The miniature battlements signify authority. The *Puerta de Honor* (S) is reserved for the president, visiting heads of State, and ambassadors. The central *Puerta Principal* incorporates an elegantly framed balcony. Here, at 2300 hours every 15 Sept., the president rings the Campana de Dolores and repeats the Grito de Dolores, echoed by the patriotic throng filling the Zócalo: 'Viva México, viva la independencia'. The Campana, cast in 1768, was brought from Dolores Hidalgo in 1896 and fixed in a specially made niche above the balcony.

The N portal, *Puerta Mariana*, was added for Pres. Mariano Arista (1851–53) by Vicente E. Manero. The square, tower-like NW and SW corners are successors to the bastions reinstated after 1693 as a defensive measure.

INTERIOR. The public may enter (guided visits Mon.–Fri., 9–6) through the Puerta Principal, which gives on to the Patio Principal. The fountain and patio floor were added during stabilization after the building of the nearby Metro in the late 1960s. The grand staircase (l. of the gateway), in white marble, dates from 1926–27. On the staircase walls and the N and E corridors of the first floor of the principal patio are the famous murals of Diego Rivera, a vast panorama of Mexican history up to the Revolution and a vision of the world to come (and a fascinating exercise in spotting his heroes and villains). On the E side of the first floor the semicircular former Chamber of Deputies (by José Agustín Paz; 1821–30), ruined by fire in 1872, was reinaugurated as a historic precinct in 1972. On the S side was the Senate chamber.

The theme of the staircase murals (1929–35) is the history of Mexico from the prehispanic epoch to the future. On N wall, an idealized representation of prehistory, emphasizing creative work. Quetzalcóatl presides, appearing to instruct a group of priests. Behind, two pyramids; and Quetzalcóatl flying away on a serpent with forked fang. On l., a volcano erupts Quetzalcóatl as the feathered serpent in tongues of flame; above all, the sun upside down—sunset symbolizing the end of prehispanic tradition. The central (W) wall is covered by a mass of figures and may be read both vertically and horizontally. In the truncated pyramidal base, the Conquest (a bloody confrontation between two cultures) and subjugation of the indigenous, presided over by an eagle perched on a prickly pear, the Aztec symbol of war in its beak. To r., Cuitláhuac grasps a flint-tipped lance; below, Cortés on a white horse. Forced Indian labour; tortures and executions of the Inquisition; destruction of Indian culture (Bp Zumárraga burning codices) are all depicted. On r. of the eagle, Bernardino de Sahagún, Vasco de Quiroga, Bartolomé de las Casas, Pedro de Gante—friends of the Indians. Further l., Cortés, La Malinche with a child, symbol of the mingling of the races. Above, modern Mexican history unfolds on the wall marked off by five arches. Those at either end enclose the 19C invasions: on the N, the US invasion of 1847; on the S, the defeat of the French invasion in 1867, with the death of Maximilian. Juárez looks on with Escobedo, Negrete, and Zaragoza. In the central arch are heroes of Independence, the central figures Hidalgo and Morelos (Rivera's favourite and with his features). On Hidalgo's l., Allende, Josefa Ortiz, Guerrero, Iturbide, and, below him, Quintana Roo and Leona Vicario. Behind Morelos appears Guadalupe Victoria. In the upper part, Revolutionary figures. On r., Zapata, Carrillo Puerto, and the communist leader José Guadalupe Rodríguez, behind a zapatista banner 'Tierra y Libertad'. Opposite on l., Obregón and Calles. The arch to the r. contains history between Independence and Reform. At bottom l. appears a fat friar, symbolizing the Church; on his r., Santa-Anna, and at his side Abp Labastida. Above r., Juan Alvarez, who finally defeated Santa-Anna; on his r., Santos Degollado. Below, Miramón surrounded by clergy. On l., above Santa-Anna, Juárez holding a parchment: 'Constitución y Leyes de Reforma'. On his r., Ignacio Ramírez; on his l., Ignacio Altamirano and Melchor Ocampo. Below them, Comonfort; at his side, Leandro Valle; and below, Gómez Farías, instigator of Reform. The arch to the l. shows the Revolution of 1911. At bottom l., liberal intellectuals who made the base on which was built the porfiriato: Guillermo Prieto, Gabino Barreda, and Justo Sierra Méndez among them. Above preside Díaz, his wife, José Yves Limantour, and Huerta, and, arranged behind, symbols of the groups which kept them in power. Facing them are the diverse groups which took part in the Revolution, here presented as unified, centred on Madero; with him, Pino Suárez; above, Aquiles Serdán. Next to Zapata appears a bandaged Otilio Montaño, author of the Plan of Ayala; below, a smiling Francisco Villa; and, further below, Carranza. Beneath Madero, Vasconcelos, José Guadalupe Posada, and Ricardo Flores Magón. Their banner 'Tierra, libertad y pan para todos' is held up by Carrillo Puerto and Juan Sarabia. Below them, the constitutionalist Lucio Blanco and Eulalio Gutiérrez, elected president by the convention of Aguascalientes.

The S wall shows 'Mexico today and tomorrow' (1935; done after Rivera's stay in the USA), an industrialized city in which the worker is paramount, promoting change, while the campesino takes second place. At bottom l., one of a worker group holds 'Das Kapital'. Higher up, a classroom at the university, with the legend 'Socialismo Nacional Mexicano', the students of different races. Below, in centre, an altar of Our Lady of Guadalupe, a kneeling man, his arms outstretched, before it; the faithful place their alms in a collection box below it, but the money is diverted by tubes to other purposes above. Meanwhile children and teachers read from Karl Marx; one teacher resembles Frida Kahlo, Rivera's wife. On r., campesinos work; others are threatened with pistols. Below, a knight of Columbus, one of an association of militant Catholics, wearing an enormous sombrero. In middle, strikers are attacked by fascist soldiers; the cruel fate of some strikers illustrated on r. On l., a series of tableaux of bourgeois society, framed by tubing and machinery: one of a semi-nude woman embracing a priest, with high society carousing. Above, a group of US capitalists awaits developments on Wall Street: Nelson A. Rockefeller, Harry Sinclair, William Durant, J.P. Morgan, Cornelius Vanderbilt, Andrew Mellon. To r. sits Calles, flanked by a general and a bishop. Below, a representation of the Press. Above r., a worker incites others to riot; in the distance a city enveloped in flames and smoke signifies revolt. To l., the prosperous, industrialized world of the future. In centre, Karl Marx shows this future to a worker, a campesino, and a soldier.

The N and E walls of the first-floor corridors are covered by murals of prehispanic Mexico (1941–51), in colour and in grisaille, the former accompanied beneath by rectangular grisaille panels, simulating reliefs, amplifying the scenes above. Flanking a doorway at the W end of the N corridor are two long grisaille panels detailing the natural riches of Mexico. Next comes the first coloured mural: View of Tenochtitlán from the market of Tlatelolco, marvellous in its detail; in background, Popocatépetl and Iztaccíhuatl, and the two temples of the city centre, one of them flowing with sacrificial blood. In background two figures stand out: the market inspector in a litter and a beautiful courtesan, with a feathered head-dress, exposing her r. leg.

The following panels describe the Tarascan civilization of Michoacán; the Zapotec civilization of Oaxaca, the landscape dominated by the Río Balsas; the Totonac civilization of Veracruz, with the pyramid of El Tajín. The next mural shows the extraction of rubber. Next comes the Huastec civilization of Veracruz, San Luis Potosí, Hidalgo, and Tamaulipas, celebrating the production and harvesting of maize. Next, harvesting of cacao and production of chocolate. Last, the use of maguey, incl. the production of pulque.

On the E wall is the Arrival of the Spaniards: a friar and Cortés (shown, mistakenly, as deformed) on either side of the Cross, presented with a gift from Moctezuma. In background, Cuauhtémoc hangs from a tree. Indians are hanged, whipped, or work as slaves. A burning village symbolizes Spanish pillage. In foreground, a redheaded Spaniard (Pedro de Alvarado ?) points to an Indian woman, another reference to slavery. In centre, Cortés appears again, collecting the king's fifth from a colonist.

In the Patio de Honor (entered from the Patio Principal) are column bases from the 16C edifice. The upper part of this wing was once the viceroy's apartments. The marble staircase was designed by Lorenzo de la Hidalga for Maximilian.

The *Puerta Mariana* gives access to the former apartments of Pres. Juárez on the ground floor of the N wing (extreme N side), arranged as the *Museo Recinto Homenaje a Benito Juárez* (Tues.–Fri., 10–6; Sat., Sun., 10–3). At its entrance, a statue of Juárez, cast from captured conservative cannon and from shot fired by the French at Puebla in 1863. Four rooms display mementoes of the president, contemporary furniture, a library, and portraits of those associated with the Reform.

E of the Sagrario, Pl. del Seminario was where from 1881 the Circo-Teatro Orrin gave famous performances. Two English clowns were great favourites with the Mexican public: Richard Bell excelled as Napoleon the Great in the pantomime 'La Cenicienta' and, wrote Thomas Brocklehurst, 'never was a better clown than Mr Henry Cook, and his effort in making a comic speech in Spanish every evening was received with deafening applause'.

2 The Templo Mayor

The area immediately around the huge Templo Mayor pyramid, which supported the twin temples of Tláloc and Huitzilopochtli, has been excavated, restored, and made into an open-air museum. Tues.–Sun., 9–5; free.

The Teocalli (Sacred Precinct): Excavations and Present Remains. Descriptions by Spanish chroniclers and excavation make it possible to reconstruct and describe the ancient capital, especially its ceremonial centre, with considerable accuracy.

Tenochtitlán was razed by Cortés to make way for the building of the new capital, and much of the material of the ancient monuments was re-used for that purpose. However, since the late 18C ancient foundations and architectural sculptures have been discovered. In 1790 the two great sculptures of Coatlícue and the Piedra del Sol were discovered on 13 Aug. and 17 Dec. respectively, and in 1791 the Piedra de Tizoc was found across the road (now Pl. de Armas). In 1900 sewerage excavations along present-day C. Guatemala encountered and destroyed part of the Templo Mayor, to a depth of c 2m. In the same year Leopoldo Batres found part of the staircase of the VIth Stage of the Templo Mayor along C. Guatemala behind the Cathedral. In 1901, at the corner of Cs Donceles and Argentina, P. Díaz discovered steps to a small pyramid and a huge sculpture of a jaguar (ocelotl-cuauxicalli), now in the Museo Nacional de Antropología. In 1913–14 Manuel Gamio conducted excavations at the corner of Cs Seminario and Guatemala, and located the SW corner of the Templo Mayor, incl. one of the heads of the great decorative serpent sculptures of the staircase to the Templo de Huitzilopochtli. In 1933, near the NE corner of the Cathedral, Emilio Cuevas exposed the staircase of a small pyramid now known to be part of the VIth Stage of the Templo Mayor. In 1948 excavations by Hugo Moedano and Elma Estrada Balmori expanded Gamio's excavation, and located the base of the great platform, lined with sculptures of small serpent heads, also finding a larger serpent head and a huge brasero (brazier). In 1964 Eduardo Matos Moctezuma excavated a small adoratorio decorated with masks of Tláloc (god of rain), to the N of C. Justo Sierra and forming the NE corner of the Teocalli. On 21 Feb. 1978, workers of the Power and Electricity Company discovered the huge stone sculpture of Coyolxauhqui (goddess of the Moon and daughter of Coatlícue) at the corner of Cs Argentina and Guatemala. INAH was called in and from 1978 to 1981 excavations, restoration, stabilization, and reconstruction were directed by Eduardo Matos Moctezuma, under the Director of INAH, Gastón García Cantú.

A spacious catwalk and explanatory panels guide the visitor around the site. In C. Seminario, a stone and brass scale model of the ancient city has been constructed in a fountain-pond on a raised platform, simulating the lakes of the Basin. It is extremely useful for visualizing the position of the Templo Mayor within the Teocalli, and the latter within Tenochtitlán; the relative positions of Tenochtitlán and Tlatelolco; and of these within the Basin. On the walls of buildings to the NE, quotations describe the ancient city: 'El Informe al Rey' (from the second 'Carta de Relación' of Cortés; 1522), 'El Asombro del Conquistador' (from the 'Historia verdadera de la conquista de la Nueva España' of

Bernal Díaz del Castillo; 1568), and 'El Testimonio del Fraile' (from the 'Memoriales' of Toribio de Benavente [Motolinía]; 1549).

The Sacred Teocalli

The sacred precinct of Tenochtitlán formed a huge plaza c 300m each side, now bounded, approximately, by Cs González Obregón and San Ildefonso on the N, Moneda and the Cathedral precinct on the S, Carmen and Correo Mayor on the E, and Monte de Piedad and Brasil on the W. The precinct was constructed around the spring, called Tozpalatl, which had been blocked up in the early 16C and was later reopened by Cortés in 1528.

The precinct was defined by a coatepantli (serpent wall), within which were c 40 structures, incl. major pyramids supporting temples at the corners, the Templo Mayor in the centre of the E side, and numerous smaller pyramids and other structures. (Bernardino de Sahagún described Tenochtitlán as having some 78 major buildings, incl. 25 pyramids; these must have included Moctezuma II Xocoyotzin's palace, numerous subsidiary precincts such as the one in Tlatelolco and the temple-platform in the Pino Suárez metro station, and Moctezuma II's second palace on the Ixtapalapa road.)

S of the Teocalli were a palace of Moctezuma II (where the Pal. Nacional now stands) and the palace of Axayácatl where Cortés was entertained.

Templo Mayor

The Great Pyramid of the Teocalli is that now exposed in the open-air museum. It supported the twin temples of Tláloc (on the N) and Huitzilopochtli (on the S), and in legend was built on the exact spot where the eagle was seen devouring the serpent. Its massive double staircase rose up the W side and faced the precinct, with the sculpture of Coyolxauhqui at the foot of the S staircase. Huitzilopochtli's name is derived from the two words, huitzil—hummingbird, and opochtli—left or south; thus 'hummingbird on the left'. To the Aztecs the hummingbird represented or symbolized warriors who gave their blood to ensure the sun's survival. So important were these temples, and their function in sustaining the life-giving sun with sacrificial blood, that Aztec chronicles record the slaying of 80,000 victims in front of them during the reign of the eighth emperor, Ahuítzotl (1486–1502), alone.

Excavation of the Templo Mayor has enabled archaeologists to interpret the several stages in its construction. It underwent at least four complete rebuildings with several additional renovations to add new façades, probably following the long-established Mesoamerican tradition of renovating structures in accordance with calendrical cycles and historical events. These may be summarized under the Aztec emperors concerned. Acamapichtli (1372–91)—began Stage II. Huitzilíhuitl (1391–1415)—continued Stage II. Chimalpopoca (1415–26)—completed Stage II. Itzcóatl (1426–40)—Stage III. Moctezuma I (1440–68)—Stage IVa. Axayácatl (1468–81)—Stage IVb. Tizoc (1481–86)—Stage V. Ahuítzotl (1486–1502)—Stage VI. Moctezuma II (1502–20)—Stage VII.

Beneath the floors of many constructions offerings were found in stone-lined cists. Cist 1, for example, was c 1m sq, and lined with red and black tezontle. In it were more than 800 artefacts in several layers, incl. copper bells; stone, shell, and turquoise beads; seated figurines; lidded stone Tláloc vases; 17 flint sacrificial knives with inlaid shell decorations; six human undamaged skulls, and others with enlarged earholes for the insertion of the tzompantli (skull rack) pole; a polished obsidian mace head; turquoise mosaics; shells, vegetable fibres, and other plant remains. The whole rested on a floor of fine sand, on which lay fish scales, delicate bird bones, and larger bones. The faunal remains throughout the layers included crocodile, a complete fish, eagle, jaguar, corals, and marine shells from the Gulf Coast, the Caribbean, and the Pacific. Leaning against the pyramid were found a greenstone figure (possibly representing Coyolxauhqui) and eight other stone figures.

TEOCALLI—TEMPLO MAYOR, Tenochtitlán

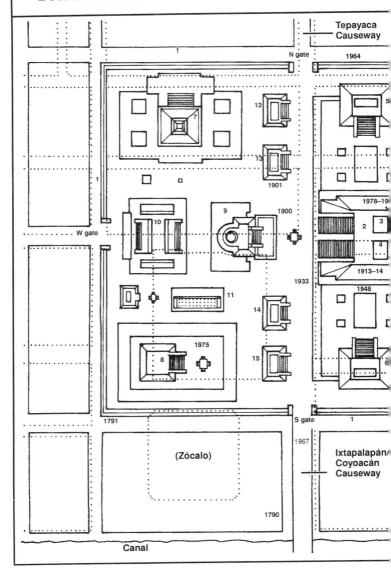

— ancient monument (reconstructed)
··· modern streets
1933 location/year of excavation

1 coatepantli (serpent wall)
2 Templo Mayor (Great Pyramid)
3 Templo de Tláloc
4 Templo de Huitzilopochtli
5 unidentified temple
6 Templo de Tezcatlipoca
7 Templo del Sol
8 Templo de Xipe Totec
9 Templo de Quetzalcóatl–Éhecatl
10 Juego de Pelota
11 Tzompantli
12 temple to conquered gods
13 Templo de Cihuaccóatl
14 Templo de Chicomecóatl
15 Templo de Xochiquetzal
16 Museo del Templo Mayor

0   50   100m

N

The remains of the earliest temple, not often found on sites with so many reconstructions, included the base for the statue of Huitzilopochtli and the sacrificial stone in situ (of tezontle, c 5cm high). Over this the victim would have been stretched and his heart torn out of his just sliced-open chest cavity. Next to this, in the Templo de Tláloc, was a chacmool sculpture. The doorway of the Templo de Tláloc was flanked by stone pillars, which still retain their painted stripes and human figures; along the interior wall was a bench to support the Tláloc idol. Most of the stone sculptures in the Templo Mayor are in the Mezcala style from Guerrero (see Rte 82).

Around the Templo Mayor the other structures of the Teocalli were arranged semi-symmetrically. On the E were priests' quarters and the Calmecac (a training college for priests). N and S were smaller temple-pyramids facing it across open areas. The temple to the N is unidentified, but that to the S is known to have been dedicated to Tezcatlipoca (the Creator god), and is reported to have been c 20m high with 80 steps. Corresponding temple-pyramids stood in the NW corner (the Templo del Sol) of the precinct, and the SW corner (the Templo de Xipe Totec, god of springtime). On this last platform the 'gladiatorial' sacrifices of special captives would have been held.

W of the Templo Mayor, ie, in front of it, stood the *Templo de Quetzalcóatl*, in the guise of Ehecatl, god of wind. It may have resembled the Templo de Quetzalcóatl at Calixtlahuaca, whose final construction phase took place about the same time.

According to the reconstruction of Ignacio Bernal, an I-shaped *Juego de Pelota* (ball court) stood in the middle of the W side of the precinct (cf. the model of the Teocalli in the Museo Nacional).

SE of the Juego de Pelota, Ignacio Marquina has placed the *Tzompantli*. This was a long wall on which the skulls of sacrificial victims were aligned on poles. When the Pl. de las Tres Culturas was cleared for the construction and preservation of the Tlatelolco ceremonial precinct (Rte 8), the earliest excavators found a large pile of skulls with enlarged holes, obviously once stacked on a tzompantli; and Cortés and his men, when they were Moctezuma II's guests, counted more than 136,000 skulls in Tenochtitlán, on the Tzompantli and stacked in storage. Carved stone skull racks were also made.

The **Museo del Templo Mayor** is on the E side of the site. Its eight rooms contain extraordinary finds from the excavations and chart the rise and fall of Tenochtitlán, Aztec religion, government, and commerce. On the uppr floor is the circular votive-stone of Coyolxauhqui (8 tonnes).

3 East of the Zócalo

To the N of the Pal. Nacional, CALLE DE LA MONEDA, still a beguiling evocation of old Mexico, leads E. The house on the corner with C. Seminario (late 18C, its corner niche a reminder of its historic associations) is on the site of that of Catalina de Montejo, first home of the University after its foundation in 1553 (see Rte 15). Next door is the former **Arzobispado**, originally c 1546, but completely rebuilt in 1730–47 and enlarged in the later 18C. Quietly imposing, with its balconies and the inverted arches and merlons of its skyline, its main doorway includes engaged estípites.

On the landing of the staircase leading to the first floor is a mural, 'Canto a los Héroes' (1952), by José Gordillo. It is brilliantly coloured, in polystyrene, and is partly an attack on the exploitation of Mexican workers by industry and US companies. In the palace was held prisoner and died Francisco Primo de Verdad (1768–1808), precursor of Mexican Independence.

Opposite, at the corner of Cs Lic. Verdad and Moneda, is a simple early 19C edifice, where once was the house of Juan Pablos (Giovanni Paoli of Brescia; fl. 1539–60), who established the first printing press in the Americas with a treatise on Christian doctrine 'in the Mexican and Castilian tongues' (1539).

C. Lic. Verdad leads to the church of **Sta Teresa la Antigua** (1678–84; restored 1983–; secularized) by Cristóbal de Medina Vargas, its beautiful doorways and windows a good example of Mannerism, despite solomonic columns (an early architectural use) and copious relief.

It belonged to a convent of discalced Carmelite nuns, founded (as San José) in 1616 after persistent efforts by two Conceptionists, Sor Inés de la Cruz (Inés de Castillet; c 1567–1633) and Sor Mariana de la Encarnación. Their long wait for premises in which to follow a stricter rule was rewarded when Abp Pérez de la Serna said Mass in a house on the site (which the nuns had been bequeathed, but could not get possession of), then turned out the tenants as living in a sacred building. Such was Sor Inés's reputation for sanctity that vicereine marquesa de Cerralvo served as her nurse, 'in the most difficult offices', during her last painful illness.

EXTERIOR. The slim, beautifully proportioned dome of the *Cap. del Señor de Sta Teresa* (1845–48) is by Lorenzo de la Hidalga.

INTERIOR. The neoclassical chapel (1798–1813), by José Antonio González Velázquez, was built to house a venerated Crucifixion from Ixmiquilpan. It lost its first dome in an earthquake in 1845. The second has a scattered pattern interior and good stained glass. The tempera paintings (c 1857) are by Juan Cordero and created a sensation in their time. In the apse vault, Divine Providence; in the lunettes, the Evangelists. (The Matthew, by Rafael Jimeno y Planes, is a relic of the previous decoration.) In the panels at the sides of the central windows, Astronomy, History, Poetry, Music. In the dome, God the Father surrounded by Virtues. Between the pilasters, four apostles; on walls and in choir vault, six allegories of the Passion. Above entry to sacristy, Purification; opposite, Birth of Our Lady. For the side altars Cordero copied Raphael's Transfiguration and Titian's Assumption.

Opposite in C. de la Moneda, the former **Casa de Moneda** (Mint) is the NE part of the Pal. Nacional complex. Built in 1731–34 by Luis Díez Navarro, perhaps using the plans of a Spanish architect, Juan Peinado, its portal, with engaged columns, rich cornice, and upper-level decoration, is a judicious baroque flowering.

The Casa de Moneda, one of three in Spanish America, stood here from 1569, the 18C rebuilding becoming necessary as its responsibilities increased. It was enlarged in 1772–80 by Miguel Costansó, the E façade on Correo Mayor most likely his work. In 1847 the Mint acquired new premises and in 1865 the national historical, natural history, and archaeological collections were brought together here; the façade was then adapted by Lorenzo de la Hidalga.

Today the building houses the **Museo Nacional de las Culturas** (Mon.–Sat., 9.30–6), inaugurated in 1965, illustrating the archaeology and ethnography of five continents. Reproductions (incl. 19C plaster casts of Greek and Roman pieces) illustrate the fine arts of various countries. On the W wall of the entrance corridor, a mural, 'Revolución' (1938), by Rufino Tamayo.

Further along C. de la Moneda, on either side of Correo Mayor (l.), are the similar, but not identical, houses **Mayorazgo de Guerrero**. Note the larger portal, with beautifully framed upper window and gable, the corner towers, the asymmetry of the ground-floor windows, and the strong tezontle and stone façades.

Both buildings were reconstructed, probably by Francisco Antonio Guerrero y Torres, in the late 1770s. From the 1890s the lesser house (Nos. 18–22) contained the studio of José Guadalupe Posada. In 1912–46 the greater (Casa Mayor; Nos. 14–16) was the *Conservatorio Nacional de Música*. On the staircase walls, a mural, 'La Música' (1933), by Rufino Tamayo.

Next door the church of **Sta Inés**, with neoclassical twin portals, was dedicated in 1790. The carved wooden doors show reliefs of the martyrdom of St Agnes and the figures of the founders.

The convent, for Conceptionist nuns, was founded in 1596 by Diego Caballero and Inés de Velasco. The first church (burial place of the painters Cabrera and Ibarra) was built by 1600. The convent has been restored. It is now the *Museo José Luis Cuevas*, for art exhibitions.

INTERIOR. The coros alto and bajo remain, but without grilles. Above the latter is a relief of St Augustine, perhaps a relic of the old church. On either side, the cratícula and doorway were converted in 1877 into tombs for the Anda family. In the finials and below the friezes are reliefs of saints and of the Lamb of God.

C. Academia (typical 18C and 19C houses) runs N of the church to meet C. Guatemala. Near the junction, at Nos 88–92, are the former premises of the Hospicio de San Nicolás, where from 1792 the *Real Tribunal de Minería* (see Rte 8) taught its first Mexican pupils.

At the SE corner of Cs de la Moneda and Academia is the former **Academia de San Carlos**, which did most to promote the fine arts in Mexico. Its exterior (1863–64) is by Javier Cavallari, who also transformed the painting galleries and salón de actos. The medallion reliefs (Raphael, Michelangelo, Charles III, Charles IV, Mangino, and Gil; 1855) are by Felipe Sojo.

The building was once the *Hospital del Amor de Dios*, founded in 1539 by Bp Zumárraga primarily for the treatment of syphilitics. In 1541 he assigned it his former residence. Its chaplain from 1682 was the renowned polymath Carlos de Sigüenza y Góngora. In 1788 the patients were removed to San Andrés (see Rte 8).
  In 1784 Jerónimo Antonio Gil, master engraver, sent from Spain to improve the coinage and to establish an engraving academy, with the blessing of the superintendent of the Casa de Moneda, Fernando José Mangino, founded the Academia de las Nobles Artes de San Carlos de la Nueva España. In 1791 it moved into the former hospital. José Antonio González Velázquez was director of architecture; Manuel Tolsá became director of sculpture, and Rafael Jimeno y Planes director of painting. In the early 19C it decayed and was closed. In 1843 Santa-Anna ordered its re-establishment and a national lottery to cover the costs. Pupils were sent to Europe to study and new instructors attracted thence by large salaries. In 1847 it reopened, the new director of engraving being the Londoner John Baggally (called Juan Santiago in Mexico; 'die sinker and engraver' of the Old Kent Road). From 1856 the Palermitan Cavallari reorganized it. The building now houses the Escuela de Artes Plásticas. The late 18C patio was covered to the design of Antonio Rivas Mercado in the early 1900s.

Beyond the Academia, C. de la Moneda crosses C. Jesús María. To the r., at the corner of C. Soledad, is the church of **Jesús María** (c 1596–1626) by Pedro Briseño.

The Conceptionist convent was founded in 1578 by Pedro Tomás Denia for descendants of conquistadores on land owned by Juan Jaramillo, husband of Doña Marina, Cortés's former interpreter and mistress. In 1583 it came under royal patronage, to provide an asylum (it is said) for the mad illegitimate daughter of Philip II and the sister of the abp of Mexico, Pedro Moya y Contreras. In the later 17C it earned the praise of Sigüenza y Góngora—as 'el Paraíso Occidental'. The convent was secularized in 1867 and adapted to other uses.

EXTERIOR. Tower and portals, with clean, classical lines, curved pediments, urns, and garlands, date from an early 19C remodelling, possibly by Tolsá. The INTERIOR was neoclassically redecorated under González Velázquez (1799–), though the grille of the coro alto remains. The semicircular mural above the high altar, Christ disputing with the Doctors (c 1855), is by Juan Cordero. The paintings by Jimeno y Planes which decorated the side altars of El Señor de Sta Teresa were removed here in the 1850s. The convent building (1692), with ornate parapet and corner niche, may be seen to the S of the church.
  The S of the convent faces CALLE CORREGIDORA, lined with mainly late 18C and early 19C buildings (note Nos. 62 [N side] and 73 [S side]). Here once ran a stretch of the *Acequia Real*, widest and largest of the canals which crossed the city (mostly W to E) carrying passengers and goods. It was channelled into a conduit and built over after 1753. Recent restoration works, however, have uncovered its course. At the NE corner with Correo Mayor is the former *Colegio de Sta María de Todos Santos*, founded in 1573 for postgraduates, sold off in 1843, remodelled in 1981. No. 76 preserves a rondel relief of Our Lady and St

Anne. This street leads E to meet (l.) Pl. Alhóndiga, named after the **Alhóndiga**, the public grain store which sold to the poor at low prices and released grain in times of scarcity.

The first alhóndiga was established in 1573, rebuilt in the 18C, and demolished at its end. Only the portal remains, at 10 C. Alhóndiga, on the plaza's E side.

C. Roldán, which goes SSE, marks the course of a branch of the CANAL DE LA VIGA, the waterway which joined the city to the Lago de Chalco, so-called because it ran from the r. side of the Acequia Real to the Garita de la Viga (a distance of 1848 m), at the SE border of the city's jurisdiction. Along it were brought cereals, wood, vegetables, flowers, etc. to the daily market of La Merced here, next to the landing stage at Puente de Roldán. Its banks were bordered by *Paseo de la Viga*, a favourite promenade lined by double rows of willows, already vanishing in the 19C.

One block N, at the corner of Cs Santísima and Emiliano Zapata (continuation of Moneda), is the church of **Santísima Trinidad** (1755–77; dedicated 1783), its façades, in tezontle and chiluca, two of the best examples of churrigueresque.

Doubtfully attr. Lorenzo Rodríguez, the church almost at once started to subside and had to be shored up (by José del Mazo) in 1805. More drastic repairs were made in 1855–58. In 1861 the church and its neighbouring hospital, closed by the Reform, became property of the English Compañía Lancasteriana, which propagated the educational system founded by the English Quaker Joseph Lancaster (1778–1838) throughout Mexico. In 1864, thoroughly dilapidated, they were reported in the middle of a lake caused by floods. The church was restored to Catholic worship at the end of the 19C. Its chronic but unequal sinking tilts it towards the S. Excavations during major works in 1924 revealed the pedestals of the lower estípites measuring 2.85m below the pavement. A band of carved masonry wedged between the N buttress and the façade is an attempt to remedy the subsidence.

EXTERIOR. The main (W) façade is divided horizontally into three rectangular storeys, the highest somewhat top-heavy. The lowest-storey estípites stand free of the wall and are encrusted with vegetable, lambrequin, angel, and cherub relief, and the Maltese cross. The upper estípites are smaller and simpler. The cornices break in the centre to make way for the intricacies and reliefs of the central panel above the doorway arch: the smaller, covered by a flourish of volutes meeting at a cherub head, is the papal tiara and the keys of St Peter; the larger, Holy Trinity, shows acute pathos, a strong correction amid liveliness, which includes two children sitting on its frame and holding horns of plenty. Apostle heads appear on the lower estípites, while in upper and lower entre-calles, full of delightful relief, framed by pronounced mouldings, and on elegant bases, are ten formalized statues: four popes, five bishops, one presbyter. Estípites also surround the beautiful tower, crowned by a truncated papal tiara. The tile-decorated dome, its panels adorned with pontifical coats-of-arms, is topped by a lantern whose niches hold statues of the Evangelists.

The S portal, between buttresses, is more refined, obviously influenced by Rodríguez, and its verticality is assured by the closeness of its supports. The lower estípites are partly sunk; the upper storey combines slim estípites, pinnacles, and niche pilasters, held up by decorative corbels, sprouting medallions and scrolls. The sculptured saints are Paul (centre); below him, Antony Abbot holding a piglet; John the Baptist (r.); an anon. saint (l.); and, above the arch, Ildefonsus receiving the chasuble (a dove perched on it) from a crowned Virgin and angel. Further E along the S wall is a niche, flanked by estípites, containing a relief: under a canopy, a monstrance containing the Host rests on the heads of two cherubs; on either side, kneeling on clouds, two adoring angels. Above it, a Latin cross rests on a pedestal ornamented with a relief of John the Baptist.

The INTERIOR lost its churrigueresque splendour in the early 19C, although the high altar is all that survives from early 19C 'improvement'. Its present aspect owes much to the restoration of 1966. In the main entrance, a good carved windbreak. Along the nave walls, 12 paintings of martyrdoms and the Crucifixion (late 18C) by Michael Rudesindo Contreras. To the N and E are what remains of hospital and seminary, finished in 1789 (attr. Ildefonso de

Iniesta Bejarano y Durán). The handsome two-storey cloister (gained at 8 C. de la Santísima) has been restored.

C. de la Santísima leads N to reach C. Mixcalco, where we turn l. for PL. DE LORETO, in its centre a fountain by Manuel Tolsá which once stood in Paseo Bucareli, removed here in 1929. On the N side is the church of **Loreto** (1809–16), by Ignacio Castera and José Agustín Paz, known for the purity and proportion of its façades and its mighty dome.

In 1680 a chapel was inaugurated in what had been the baptistery of the Jesuit church of San Gregorio, probably on this site, to house the replica of the statue of Our Lady of Loreto brought from Italy by Fr Giambattista Zappa. The present edifice was paid for by Antonio de Bassoco (1738–1814), onetime alcalde. But the architects had used heavy stone for the W side and tezontle for the E; in 1832 the church began to sink on the E and had to be closed. It held together so well, however, that it did not crack, and reopened in 1850. Restoration has been undertaken since 1982.

The superb INTERIOR, lit from the windows of the cupola drum and clerestory, is marked by a vigorous cornice and entablature which envelop small nave and spacious transept—two semicircular chapels on each side. The painting of Fr Zappa on his deathbed (sacristy) is by Cabrera.

On the W side of the plaza the two corner houses (Nos 2, 4, and 14; 1739–42), by José Eduardo de Herrera, boast elaborate corner niches and the cross of Caravaca motif (symbol of episcopal authority), echoed above the portals of the church opposite. A companion house survives on the E side. On the S side, No. 83 C. Justo Sierra, once a synagogue, has been heavily altered.

Facing the E side of Loreto, at the corner of Cs San Antonio Tomatlán and Rodríguez Puebla, is the former *Colegio de Nuestra Señora de Guadalupe (Las Inditas)*, founded in 1753 for the education of Indian girls. In 1811, it was enlarged as the convent of *Nuestra Señora de Guadalupe de Indias*, also called *Enseñanza Nueva*. In 1827 subsidence forced evacuation. Conversion into shops has rendered what remains almost unrecognizable.

On the E side of the plaza is the church of **Sta Teresa la Nueva** (1715), by Pedro de Arrieta, almost Mannerist in style, with two W portals. The interior, much gone over, still has the original coro bajo, framed in stone, its grille studded with stout spikes.—The convent building (entrance in C. Mixcalco), rebuilt in the late 19C, is now the *Escuela Nacional para Ciegos* (for the Blind).

The convent was founded in 1700–01 by Sor Teresa de Jesús, prioress of Sta Teresa la Antigua. In their vows the nuns promised not to drink chocolate.

C. San Antonio Tomatlán leads E, across the busy Anillo Circunvalación, to the little church of **San Antonio Tomatlán** (1740), in its small plaza at the intersection with C. Bravo. Its façade, with a good relief of its patron and attractively highlighted round windows, exhibits a rustic baroque. The interior contains three churrigueresque retables. Behind it, to the SE, at the corner of Cs Alarcón and FFCC de Cintura, the former hospital church of **San Lázaro** (1728), by Miguel Custodio Durán, has a striking baroque portal with excellent relief. Badly mangled by misuse (by the late 19C it was already a warehouse), the church has deserved a better fate. The former *Garita de San Lázaro* stands at the corner of Av. Morazán and C. Zapata, SE of the church. 1km E, reached by following C. Nacozari, which runs parallel with C. San Antonio Tomatlán one block N, is the **Pal. Negro de Lecumberri**, until 1976 the Federal District penitentiary (5.5 hectares), built in 1885–1900 by Antonio Torres Torija. The remodelled interior holds the **Archivo General de la Nación**, dating back to the 1530s.

C. Rodríguez Puebla leads N from Pl. Loreto. On the corner (l.) with C. Venezuela is the MERCADO ABELARDO RODRIGUEZ (1933–35), built, by Antonio Muñoz, on the site of the Colegio de San Pedro y San Pablo, and incorporating part of its structure. The interior murals (1933–35) are by artists of the Liga de Escritores y Artistas Revolucionarios, on food production and distribution.

In SW corner, on ceiling and l. wall inside first lobby along C. Venezuela, 'Los alimentos y los problemas del obrero', by Antonio Pujol, showing mining dangers and diseases, bad food, and interaction between city labourers and peasants. Through gate at back of lobby, on ceilings and walls of cloister arcade, 'La lucha de los obreros contra los rentistas', by Pablo O'Higgins. Past the main entrance portal, farther up C. Venezuela, a second entrance hall, with a large stairway (r.). On ceiling above stairs, 'Influencia de las vitaminas', by Angel Bracho—three panels showing effects of vitamin deficiency. Higher up same street another entrance vestibule contains murals 'La vida del pueblo' by Pablo Rendón. Almost at the corner of the street an entrance with stairs leading up to a second level. Here (with permission) may be seen murals now in a back room. R. wall, 'Historia de México' by Isamu Noguchi. On l. side of stair walls opposite, 'La industrialización del campo' by Marion Greenwood, showing food marketing on the Canal de la Viga; on r., the fight of the unemployed against fascism. In between, a mural by Grace Greenwood showing the mining, minting, and distribution of gold and oppression of workers. On ground floor at SE corner, 'Las labores del campo', showing food production on haciendas before the Revolution, by Ramón Alva Guadarrama. A short way down N side, on Cjón de Girón, is 'Los mercados', a Maya market scene in light tones facing a darker exploitation scene, by Raúl Gamboa. On staircase, 'Los mercados', by Miguel Tzab.

Further N, C. Rodríguez Puebla leads into PL. TORRES QUINTERO, the former Pl. San Sebastián, a typical part of old Mexico, preserving 18C houses. To the r. is the church of **San Sebastián** (with an adjoining chapel, known as *La Soledad*), founded in the 16C as a Franciscan chapel in the barrio of Atzacoalco and in 1607 assigned to the Augustinians. Though altered in the 18C and restored in the 1930s, it preserves a 16C look, with single nave and flat beamed ceiling (1558–61). The pulpit is 18C work. Viceroy duque de Linares was buried here (1716). Off the N side of the plaza opens a smaller plaza, with 18C houses on two sides.

From Pl. Loreto, C. San Ildefonso leads W past, on its N side, the former premises of the **Nuevo Colegio de San Gregorio** and the **Colegio de San Pedro y San Pablo**, two time-honoured and related Jesuit foundations.

The Colegio Máximo de San Pedro y San Pablo, for creole boys, was established by 1576. The Society opened three more colleges (San Gregorio, San Bernardo, and San Miguel, amalgamated as San Ildefonso in 1588) and acquired the land bounded by today's Cs del Carmen and San Ildefonso and Mercado Abelardo Rodríguez. In 1612, yet another college, Nuevo Colegio de San Gregorio, was founded, to instruct Indian boys in catechism and basic letters. San Pedro y San Pablo was amalgamated with San Ildefonso in 1618 (comp. below). San Gregorio and San Pedro y San Pablo occupied neighbouring premises on the same site. The regimen of the former included 'music on all kinds of instruments … and dancing … rosary and litany on Sat. afternoons, and little talks on Sundays'. It acquired its own rector and the communicating door with San Pedro y San Pablo was permanently closed. Rebuilding of both colleges started in the 1720s. After the expulsion of the Jesuits in 1767, from 1775 the Nacional Monte de Piedad had its first home in the San Pedro y San Pablo premises. From 1922 the buildings were reconstructed under the auspices of José Vasconcelos and in 1933 much of the part formerly occupied by San Pedro y San Pablo was demolished. Since 1936 what remains, fronting C. San Ildefonso, has been the *Universidad Obrera* (Working Men's University), founded by Pres. Cárdenas.

EXTERIOR. The plain façade on C. San Ildefonso is that of the former San Gregorio. In the early 1930s the 18C portal of the salón de actos of the old University was reassembled here in modified form (with upper mosaic pattern by Montenegro).

INTERIOR. The W patio is mainly later 18C. The E patio is possibly earlier. In the NW corner of the latter the staircase walls are decorated with murals (1923–33) by Montenegro. On the E (r.), 'La fiesta de la Sta Cruz' (3 May), when buildings in construction are decorated with paper banners and festoons. On the N wall the mural called 'Reconstrucción' celebrates the building of a new country. Included in the decoration of the S wall are portraits of the artist's assistant Hermilio Jiménez and the Russian film director Sergei Eisenstein who came to Mexico in 1930 and whom Montenegro accompanied on his travels through the country.

Of the former church of **San Pedro y San Pablo**, at the corner of Cs San Ildefonso and del Carmen, little of the fabric of 1576–1603 remains. Its neoclassical portal belongs to the early 19C.

In 1822–29 it housed the legislative assembly before which Iturbide took the oath on his election as emperor. Thoroughly run down after a variety of uses in the 19C and early 20C, incl. ballroom, madhouse, and stables, it was saved from ruin by Vasconcelos, Secretary of Public Instruction under Pres. Obregón (1921–24), who organized its redecoration as a conference hall. During 1944–80 it was the *Hemeroteca Nacional* (Newspaper and Periodical Library).

The skirting of decorative tiles was designed by Gabriel Fernández Ledesma and Roberto Montenegro; the tempera decoration of arches and vaults painted by Xavier Guerrero and Hermilio Jiménez; the stained glass of the transepts ('Jarabe tapatío' on W; 'Parakeet-seller' on E) designed by Montenegro and that of the façade by Jorge Enciso. On the N wall is the mysterious mural 'El árbol de la vida' (1922) by Montenegro, open to various interpretations. In 1944 it was heavily overpainted in oil (on the original tempera) by Miguel Querol and Gerardo Esquivel, much to Montenegro's indignation. The dome of the chapel on the r. (E) is painted with a Zodiac (1921) by Guerrero.

C. San Ildefonso continues across C. del Carmen (17–18C houses). On its S side is the former **Colegio de San Ildefonso**, still known as the **Escuela Nacional Preparatoria**, large and imposing, faced with tezontle, finished in 1749 to the design of the Jesuit Cristóbal de Escobar y Llamas.

Although in theory merged with San Pedro y San Pablo in 1618, in fact San Ildefonso continued to function separately and grew in importance as what amounted to a boarding school for sons of the governing class. One of its most famous rectors was the Irish Jesuit Michael Wadding (Godínez; 1586–1644). In 1767 there were 300 pupils. In 1868 the Escuela Nacional Preparatoria began its classes here in accordance with the Law on Public Instruction decreed in 1857. In 1910 the School formed part of the National University and since 1929 has been a part of UNAM.

EXTERIOR. The façade is lined with square windows curving outwards on each of their sides. Subdued estípites flank two noble portals in their lower storeys; the upper storeys are baroque. Both use lambrequins. That on the W (entrance to Colegio Grande) displays a relief of the Investing of St Ildefonsus; that on the E (entrance to Colegio Chico) is richer, a statue of Our Lady of the Rosary on a half-moon, and, above, a relief of St Joseph holding the Child and protecting Jesuits under his cloak.

INTERIOR. The college buildings are disposed from the E around three patios aligned with C. San Ildefonso. The small square *Patio del Colegio Chico* (1712–18) has three storeys of five arches on either side. In the centre of the building is the *Patio de Pasantes* (once for assistant masters); beyond (W side), the great square *Patio del Colegio Grande* has a lordly air, three storeys of varied arches resting on strong pilasters. On its W side is the great hall (altered 1868–96). From the N side we gain the *Salón de Actos* (or *Generalito*). The five arris vaults are an 'improvement' of the 1890s. Its chief treasure is a large part of the former choirstalls (1701–02) from the church of San Agustín, carved in the workshop of Salvador de Ocampo, perhaps helped by his father Tomás Juárez. Delightfully ingenuous touches heighten the effect.

Of the original 254 biblical panels, 153 were set up here in 1890–94 and restored by Nicolás Fuentes. Note, for instance, the caryatids and the leafy and fruity motifs separating the panels; God creating sun, moon, birds, and fishes; Adam and Eve expelled from the Garden of Eden; Sacrifice of Abraham, watched by parrots in the tree; Building Noah's Ark, with busy detail; Rebecca and Jacob, with animals, birds, and household effects; Joseph and Potiphar's wife—indignation and seductiveness; and the seven archangels.

On the E side of the Patio Grande is the great staircase, also serving the Patio de Pasantes. The first flight starts after a notable portal. On the N side of the Patio de Pasantes is the former chapel, now the library, entered through a matching portal. The sacristy contains a Pentecost and a Holy Family, two fine works by Francisco Antonio Vallejo.

MURALS. On the l. wall of the entrance to the Patio Grande is 'La llegada de la Cruz a la Nueva España' (1922–23), the first post-Revolutionary mural using the fresco technique, by Ramón Alva de la Canal. Opposite, 'Alegoría de la Virgen de Guadalupe' (1923) by Fermín Revueltas, a homely image in a Mexican environment. To the r. on entering the patio, a series of murals by José Clemente Orozco (1923–24). Immediately r., 'Maternidad', the only remaining of a first series, followed by four more on a Revolutionary theme: 'Destrucción del viejo orden', 'La trinchera' (Trench), 'La huelga' (Strike), and 'La trinidad' (Revolutionary Trinity). The head above the door in 'La huelga' is all that remains of an earlier mural, 'Cristo destruyendo su cruz'. The last mural here, 'La banquete de los ricos', a caricature, is retaliation on public criticism of his earlier murals. Criticism of Mexican society continues in the *First Floor* murals. R. to l., 'Los ricos' (Reactionary Forces; Money Box), 'La basura' (Political Junk-heap), 'Las acechanzas' (False Leaders), 'La libertad', 'Jehová entre los pobres y los ricos' (Last Judgment), 'La ley y la justicia'. After dismissal in 1924, Orozco returned in 1926 to paint the *Second Floor* murals. R. to l., 'Revolucionarios' (Return to the Battlefields), 'La familia', 'La despedida' (Mother's Farewell), 'Los trabajadores' (Return from Work), 'La bendición' (Mother's Blessing), 'El sepulturero' (Gravedigger), 'Mujeres'. *Staircase.* On either side of entrance, 'Hombres sedientos' (Thirst) and 'Los ingenieros' (Engineers). Between ground and first floors, 'Cortés y la Malinche', 'Razas aborígenes' (Ancient Warring Races), 'Franciscano auxiliando a los enfermos' (Aiding the Sick). Between first and second floors, 'La conquista de Tenochtitlán' (1922–23) by Jean Charlot and 'Fiesta de Chalma' (1922–23) by Fernando Leal.

The staircase at the E end of the Patio Chico is decorated with the first murals (1923–25) of David Alfaro Siqueiros. On ceiling over first flight, 'Los Elementos', a winged woman with Mexican features incorporated into an essentially classi-cal composition. L. wall, first landing, 'Hombre cargando al niño'; opposite, Mexican peasant woman. Above, the face of an angel is reminiscent of popular Mexican imagery. Below the abstract ceiling motifs over the third and fourth flights are the most interesting, and unfinished, murals. L. wall, 'El llamado de la libertad' (Call of Liberty); central wall, 'Los Mitos' (Myths), a strange group-ing: lower l., the Monarchy; lower r., the Clergy. R. wall, 'El entierro del obrero sacrificiado', prefiguring Siqueiros' dynamic mature work, alluding to the death of Felipe Carrillo Puerto (see Rte 95). On back wall, symbols of the Mexican communist party.

The S wing, on C. Justo Sierra (entrance at Nos 14 and 16), was started in an attempt at matching style by Samuel Chávez in 1902, continued until 1911 by Manuel Torres Torija, and finished in 1928–31 by Pablo Flores, to house the **Anfiteatro Bolívar** and the offices of the vice chancellor. Enquire for permission to enter at reception.

In the lobby of the amphitheatre are a series of nine frescoes (1931–33) by Fernando Leal, 'Libertadores de América', showing the liberators who freed Spanish America and Haiti from European rule and incl. in the last panel, above the death of Bolívar, an allusion to the dominance of other foreign powers in Latin America. Above the podium is an encaustic mural, 'La Creación' (1921–22), by Diego Rivera, who uses Christian and pagan iconography: the central hand pointing to Man emerging from the tree of life, around which are symbols of the four evangelists. On r., female figures portray Fable, Knowledge, Erotic Poetry, Tradition, Tragedy; four standing figures represent the four Cardinal Virtues; on l., Dance, Music, Song, Comedy, and the three Theological Virtues. In centre, Wisdom unites the composition into a central focus.

No. 19 C. Justo Sierra opposite belongs to the *Sociedad Mexicana de Geografía y Estadís-tica*, a learned society, founded in 1833. It has a famous library and map room.

4 North of the Zócalo

On the W side of the Cathedral (N corner of Av. 5 de Mayo and C. Monte de Piedad) is the **Nacional Monte de Piedad** (National Pawn Shop), once part of the *Casas Viejas de Moctezuma*, on the site of the palace of Axayácatl (1468–81), which Cortés adapted and built on for his own residence in 1522–29. The present huge tezontle-faced edifice, with stone-framed doorways and windows, dates in part from a rebuilding in 1758.

Cortés's heirs retained ownership of the site, rebuilt from 1611. In 1836 Lucas Alamán, their trustee, sold the building to the Monte de Piedad for 134,000 pesos. In 1878 it was modernized by Ricardo Orozco and in 1881 the façade on Av. 5 de Mayo was adapted by the architect Juan Manuel Bustillo. The fourth storey, which helped regularize façades of unequal height, is a later addition (1948). The Sacro y Real Monte de Piedad de Animas was founded in 1774, thanks to the efforts (and a donation of 300,000 pesos) of Pedro Romero de Terreros, conde de Regla, mainly as a resource for poorer citizens. The modernized interior, with a few traces of former times, contains innumerable objects (mainly jewellery, furniture, and antiques), pawned and never reclaimed. Special sales advertised in the press (Mon.–Fri., 10–2, 5–7; Sat., 10–2).

AV. 5 DE MAYO, a broad thoroughfare, essentially a 19C development, with its hotels (which have seen better days) and shops, leads W to the Alameda. Among its more notable buildings are the former *Hotel Washington* (c 1890), in functional style, at the NW corner with C. Palma; No. 40, the former *Hotel Comonfort* (c 1870), now the characterful *Café La Blanca*; the bar *La Opera* and the *Café París*, two famous meeting-places, recalling fin-de-siècle splendour; and, most seductive of all, the *Dulcería de Celaya* (No. 39), established in 1874, the city's most famous sweetshop.

Past the E façade of the Monte de Piedad, C. Monte de Piedad leads N to meet C. Guatemala (r.). No. 18, behind the Cathedral apse, is the 18C **Casa Vallarta**.

It occupies the site of the house of Juan Engel, from Hamburg, who came to New Spain from Seville in 1536 to establish the proper founding and exploitation of silver. Ignacio Luis Vallarta (1830–93), foreign minister (1876–78) and president of the Supreme Court, lived here.

The so-called **Casa de las Ajaracas**, at the corner of Cs Guatemala and Argentina, is an enchanting early 17C survival, with irregularly placed windows and faced in lacy stucco which culminates in a corner niche sustained by eloquent angels. The Mudéjar influence is palpable. The third floor is an early 20C addition.

C. Brasil goes N from C. Monte de Piedad, crossing Cs Tacuba and Donceles. The corner house, 87–89 C. Donceles, was residence of Gabriel de Yermo, who headed the conspiracy which dethroned Viceroy Iturrigaray in 1808. C. Brasil leads into PL. STO DOMINGO, redolent of historic Mexico; in its centre are a fountain and a monument (1900) to Josefa Ortiz, heroine of Mexican Independence, by Jesús Contreras; the statue by Enrique Alciati. On the N side rises the church of **Sto Domingo**, finished and dedicated in 1736, to the initial design of Pedro de Arrieta.

EXTERIOR. The wide (solemn baroque) façade, largely projected by 1685, is admirably set off by a tasteful tower; the first and second storeys display small estípite pilasters and lambrequins. The central relief, in an eared frame, showing the descent of the Holy Ghost on St Dominic, flanked by SS Peter and Paul, is academic and somewhat lifeless. The upper relief shows an Assumption. Tritóstilo columns with Corinthian capitals flanking the doorway have finely carved lower thirds and are wavily fluted; and the statues in niches—St Augustine (l.) holding a church and St Dominic—add to the more effective lowest storey, possibly the work of Miguel Custodio Durán. On C. Brasil, the E doorway relief shows SS Francis and Dominic upholding the House of God.

The cruciform INTERIOR is lit (not always adequately) through the stained glass of the cupola. The side chapels of nave and transept contain superb 18C

Plaza de Sto Domingo (mid-19C)

altarpieces. The first to r. and l. are churrigueresque; the third and fourth l., baroque with solomonic columns. The painting on the l. wall of the fourth chapel r. is an Investing of St Ildefonsus, probably by Alonso López de Herrera, notable for the portrait of the donor (lowest r.), a likeness of extraordinary strength. In the transept are two churrigueresque altarpieces: Virgen del Camino (r.), enriched by sculpture and paintings from the church's earlier retables, incl. a St Dominic (lower storey; r.) by López de Herrera; Virgen de Covadonga (l.), with varied estípites and lovely frames for paintings. The neo-classical high altarpiece, an unsuitable contrast, but undeniably fine, is by Manuel Tolsá. The statues are by Pedro Patiño Ixtolinque.

In the choir are excellent 18C cedarwood stalls, the 32 seat-backs showing saintly figures in high relief. Most of the convent, with two sumptuous 18C chapels, was destroyed during the Reform—bulldozed to make way for a meaningless street, C. Leandro Valle. To its SW, the *Cap. de la Expiración* is a relic of the second 16C foundation on the site, though modernized after 1716 for the district's poor and again in the later 19C. Before it, in July 1867, Santiago Vidaurri was shot on Díaz's orders.

On the W side of the plaza *Portal de Sto Domingo* (1685; modified), which belonged to the convent, has served as workplace for evangelistas, public scribes who deciphered official letters and composed replies for the illiterate. Today their successors use typewriters and printing presses.

On the S side of the plaza, Nos. 95–97 C. Cuba are an 18C house built on the site of that of Juan Jaramillo, husband of La Malinche. No. 9, *Casa del Mayorazgo de Pacheco y Bocanegra*, is another 18C residence.

Facing the Portal de Sto Domingo, on the E, is the former **Real Aduana** (Royal Customs), large and handsome with its windows, portals, and gables framed in chiluca stone, and its parapet lined with merlons.

From 1676 the customs occupied the house (NW part of the present site) of Francisca María Bellvis, marquesa de Benavides y Villamayor. In 1729 she was forced to sell it. On the S part of the site new customs headquarters were built (1729–34). In 1777–78 this was expanded to its present dimensions. Here goods entering the city were liable to inspection and tax. The large portals were built to accommodate waggons and carriages. The section on C. Venezuela may be an adaptation of the marquesa's house. Since 1958 the whole has been offices of the Ministry of Public Instruction.

Walls and ceiling of the grand stairway are covered by a mural of David Alfaro Siqueiros, 'Patricios y Patricidas', begun in 1945 with the application of pyroxylin to a celotex surface moulded over the stone. It gives the artist's Marxist view of history: punishment due to villains and exaltation of the oppressed. The E wall, painted first, shows the Descent of the Old Order. An Ascent of the New Order was originally planned for the W wall and ceiling, but work was interrupted. The more geometric W side (1966–71) centres on the portrait of a woman, a likeness of the artist's wife. The different compositions on E and W sides are formally united in the arch ceiling.

Next, across C. Venezuela, is the former **Pal. de la Inquisición**, once the *Escuela Nacional de Medicina*, now an arm of the faculty of medicine at UNAM, built in 1732–36 to the design of Pedro de Arrieta.

The Inquisition existed in New Spain from 1522, although it was not formally established until 1571. Its main purpose was to maintain the purity of the Catholic faith and to combat heresy and outrages against public morals. Indians remained outside its jurisdiction. Although its reputation for cruelty and terror has become heightened in the telling, those killed at its hands (generally by garotting before the corpse was burned) numbered c 43–50 between the 1520s and 1815. The majority of victims were sentenced to other punishment after consignment to the secular arm, or given absolution after abjuring their fault. The ceremony of condemnation (auto de fe) was held, at frequent intervals, and sometimes with great pomp, most often in Pl. Mayor, and burnings carried out in Pl. del Quemadero, on the W side of the Alameda. Procedures were slow and inefficient, with fiercest concentration directed against judaizers, especially during 1600–50, climaxed during the visitor-generalcy of Bp Palafox in 1642–49. A caller at the building in 1813 wrote that the miserable prisoners were wont to distract themselves by scribbling on walls and doors imprecations against their judges and 'horrorosas exclamaciones llenas de rabia y desesperación'. One of its last victims was José María Morelos, disgracefully treated and publicly degraded before execution in 1815. In 1822, two years after abolition, Joel Poinsett viewed the building: 'It was shut up. God grant it may remain so'. It houses the *Museo de la Historia de la Medicina en México* (Mon.–Sat., 8–3), which illustrates medical practice in Mexico from the 13C.

EXTERIOR. The wide, bevelled portal, 'puerta chata', has two storeys with a gable holding the cross emblem of the Inquisition, supported by angels. Singularity and grandity within the baroque tradition are also manifested by semi-octagonal arches in the centre and, on either side, plain columns and repeated pilasters, all with Corinthian capitals, the outer pilasters at an angle to the rest.

INTERIOR. The corner ground-floor arches of the imposing main patio are without column support. Behind, on the E, the grand staircase is reached through contrasting arches springing from sturdy pilasters—a dignified effect. At the rear, also E, is the smaller *Patio de los Naranjos*, its upper storey a 19C addition. On the NE side, where the auditorium now is, was the *Cárcel Perpetua*, for long-term prisoners.

To the N, at the corner of Cs Brasil and Colombia, is the **Casa de Leona Vicario** (18C), residence of a heroine of Mexican Independence.

A woman of intellect and character (b. 1789), she informed the insurgents of events in Mexico City and was locked up. She escaped to Oaxaca and accompanied the Congress of Chilpancingo, alongside Andrés Quintana Roo, whom she married. She returned to Mexico after a viceregal pardon in 1820, and died in this house, part of her reward from a grateful people, in 1842.

C. Brasil continues N to Pl. Sta Catarina, facing which (l.) is the church of **Sta Catarina Mártir** (1740). The niche containing a statue of the saint is framed by slim estípites.

It was spared by the Reform laws, thus giving it an unbroken tradition of parish life. Among its parish priests was Thomas Twaites (1869–1959), a native of Birmingham in England, poet, canon lawyer, and mexicanist, later archdeacon of the Cathedral.

From the plaza C. Honduras leads W, across C. Chile, to Cjón Vaquita, which goes N to the nucleus of MERCADO LAGUNILLA, whose reputation for raffishness has faded somewhat since permanent buildings have been set up to contain some of it. On Sun. (best day for visiting) it spills over into the streets to the N and into C. Allende, with stalls selling antiques (some doubtful), arts and crafts, and second-hand books.

C. Brasil (N) crosses C. Ecuador, which leads (r.) to Cjón Ecuador (l.), No. 10 in which is an 18C house, known as *Casa de las Ajaracas*, still preserving rustication, lacy stucco fringing, and elaborate gables. About 400m N in C. Brasil are Pl. Sta Ana and the church of *Sta Ana* (1754), another to escape closure during the Reform. The priest and future insurgent Mariano Matamoros (1770–1814) sang his first Mass in this church. At No. 124 C. Peralvillo, continuation of C. Brasil, is the 18C *Garita de Peralvillo* which marked the N entry into, and functioned as a customs check for pulque supplies for, the city. From C. Peralvillo, C. Constancia goes E to Pl. Concepción and the little church of *Concepción Tequipeuhcan*, 18C successor to a 16C ermita. Beyond this plaza C. Toltecas goes S to PL. SAN BARTOLOME DE LAS CASAS. Here is the church of *San Francisco Tepito*, another 16C foundation, rebuilt in the 18C. Its façade is simple yet effective, with a niche above the doorway holding a statue of St Francis.

TEPITO, a poor, crowded area, but extremely characterful, has developed a culture, behaviour patterns, even a language, of its own. Its vecindades (overpopulated, one-storey tenements round a single courtyard) have become a magnet for sociologists. Four markets (designed by Pedro Ramírez Vázquez) dispose of second-hand goods. Tepito has a reputation as a forcing ground for Mexican boxing champions.

Off the W side of the plaza C. Aztecas goes S. The fourth turning l., C. Nicaragua, brings us to **Nuestra Señora del Carmen**.

The first Carmelite friars to arrive in Mexico (1585) moved to their new convent in 1607. An ambitious rebuilding scheme (1790s and early 1800s) to the designs of José del Mazo, amended by Ignacio Castera, was left unfinished, except for the Cap. de la Tercera Orden, on which the present church was elaborated. Modernization by Manuel G. Calderón in 1900–03 accounts for its present appearance. Parts of the convent remain at Nos. 4, 6, and 16 C. Aztecas. On the S side of the neighbouring Pl. del Estudiante is the former *Casa del Estudiante* (1905) by Genaro Alcorta.

At Nos. 13–23 C. Apartado, the next street S from C. Nicaragua, is the **Apartado** (c 1770), the mint from 1850, after its removal from the old Casa de Moneda, until 1970. During the viceroyalty the building was headquarters of the apartador, responsible for purchases of minerals and for extracting (apartando) gold and silver for coining from the ore.

C. Argentina leads back towards the Zócalo, passing (l.), after the junction with C. Venezuela, the former church of **Sta Catalina de Sena** (1619–23), by Juan Márquez Orozco, the twin portals showing classicism in their lower storeys, delicate baroque touches in the upper (18C additions).

Founded in 1593 for Dominican nuns, the convent came to possess wealth and property. For three years it was prison for Josefa Ortiz (see Rte 37) and she was buried in the church after her death in 1829. The nuns were finally expelled after the fall of Maximilian. The church is now the Presbyterian temple of *El Divino Salvador*. The INTERIOR has lost its once famous baroque altarpieces, but parts of the coros bajo and alto remain, incl. the latter's wrought-iron screen.

Opposite is the **Secretaría de Educación Pública** (1922–37), a vast and solid adaptation of the neoclassical by Federico Méndez Rivas, displacing the convent of **La Encarnación**, but incorporating much of its inner structure, incl. the late 18C cloisters, rusticated in their lower storeys and not very conventual in style. It is chiefly notable for the murals (1923–28) by Diego Rivera. Above the main entrance is a sculptural group (Apollo, Minerva, Dionysus) by Ignacio Asúnsolo.

The Conceptionist convent was founded in 1594. Rebuilding started in 1639. Modernizing began in 1779, under Miguel Costansó. 'I heard the nuns sing very well', wrote the Italian Francesco Gemelli Carreri in 1697, 'there are about a hundred of them, and they have about 300 servants'. The convent was expropriated during the Reform.

Rivera's fresco murals show the gradual maturing of his style. E patio (Patio de Trabajo), ground floor: labour and industrial scenes from Mexican regions and revolutionary ideals. 1st floor: the Sciences (in grisaille). 2nd floor: the Arts (also in grisaille), and rigid portraits of revolutionary martyrs on N wall. On the S side of the patio the stairway walls are painted with regional scenes, from sea-level to highland areas.

Originally planned as a collaborative programme, which Rivera stopped in 1923, the murals in the larger W PATIO still show intact on the N wall 'Lavanderas' (Washerwomen) and 'Cargadores' (Carriers) by Jean Charlot; 'Baile de los Santiagos' and 'Toritos' (Dance of the Bullocks) by Amado de la Cueva. The rest of the ground floor shows mainly folklore scenes (1925–27) by Rivera. On W wall in centre, 'La asamblea', with his portrait among the workers on the l. At l., a politician, a priest, and a general (Judases) are burned. On S wall in centre, redistribution of land. 1st floor: frescoes by Emilio Amero, Charlot, De la Cueva, and Guerrero, showing coats-of-arms of the Mexican states. 2nd floor: Rivera murals showing two corridos (popular ballads; written across the upper parts). On N and W walls, a Revolutionary corrido, showing peasants and the capitalists (incl. Rockefeller—N wall) they will overcome. In 'Los sabios' (Experts; N wall) Rivera attacks Vasconcelos, sitting on a white elephant and using a spitoon as an inkwell. On S wall (1927–28), scenes of the international proletarian revolution, incl. portraits of contemporary Mexican intellectuals. In 'El que quiera comer, que trabaje' (Whoever wants to eat, let him work), he criticizes the elitist group of artists and intellectuals called contemporáneos. In the last mural, 'El arsenal', Frida Kahlo and Tina Modotti (Rivera's friend) hand out arms to the workers.

In C. González Obregón, the former church of **La Encarnación** (1639–48) has good bas-reliefs in the doorway panels (Annunciation, Martyrdom of St Lawrence), among the earliest in the city, and a tower decorated with azulejos. It is now the **Biblioteca Iberoamericana** (Mon.–Sat., 9–8).

INTERIOR. The recess of the coro alto, with three stone frames for reliefs above it, may still be seen. The tempera mural on the back wall, commissioned by Vasconcelos, was painted in 1923–24 by Roberto Montenegro. In the upper half, the Renaissance-style map includes politicians and revolutionaries who participated in the Independence movements. In the lower frieze, a central female figure symbolizing Latin American spirituality. To the r., discoverers and conquistadores; to the l., liberators. On the r. wall, another Montenegro mural portrays Fray Servando Teresa de Mier.

One block S, in C. Donceles, is the church of **La Enseñanza** (1772–78), possibly by Francisco Guerrero y Torres, uniquely and excitingly arranged.

The convent of Nuestra Señora del Pilar, founded in 1754, belonged to the Company of Mary, dedicated to improving education for girls. Its initiator was the nun María Ignacia de Azlor y Echeverz (1715–67), daughter of José de Azlor y Virto de Vera, marqués de San Miguel de Aguayo, governor of Coahuila and Texas. The church was built under her successor, Anne-Thérèse Bonstet, a native of Brussels, who organized lotteries and raffles to raise the cash. The nuns were expelled in 1863. In 1906 the church came within an ace of being demolished.

EXTERIOR. The neostyle baroque façade, for all its limited space, is a marvel of exuberance and precision. Intricate relief covers much of the upper surfaces and the lowest thirds of the columns. Those of the lowest storey have doric capitals and vertical fluting; between them are niches sheltering images of SS John Nepomuk (l.) and Michael (r.); those of the middle storey have ionic capitals and wavy fluting; between them, niches for SS Ignatius (l.) and Benedict (r.). Above the mixtilinear arch of the doorway is a gently humorous St Joseph, patron of New Spain, holding the infant Christ. In front of the lovely choir window, framed by layers of curved and angular moulding, is a statue of the Virgen del Pilar. The gable holds a relief of the Trinity.

INTERIOR. The sotocoro, at the S end, covered by a low groin vault, gives on to the nave through a three-lobed arch, with a triglyph and metope frieze. The coro alto is closed in by a wrought-iron grille reinforced by a wooden lattice. On either side, its galleries, closed by a similarly styled lattice, encroach along both sides of the nave, shaped, unusually, as an octagon, lit by the lantern above the cupola. Above the coro alto is a gilded low abanico containing the shield of the Company of Mary, adorned with strapwork and edged in a Greek pattern. The chancel is preceded and emphasized by a great arch framing the high altar and two coros bajos, behind whose grilles the nuns assisted at Mass. The cratícula, on the r. of the apse, is carved with a relief of the Trinity and a well flanked by two sirens. The apse vault holds an anon. fresco of the Virgen del Pilar; the blind skylights are octagonal paintings: Vision of Jacob (l.) and King David (r.).

Apse, nave, and sotocoro are ablaze with nine late 18C anastyle altarpieces (some possibly by Joaquín de Sállagos), gilded, adorned with polychrome statues and paintings. Their beautiful disorder, contained within the order imposed by, sometimes undulating, vertical lines and symmetrically placed figures, is most marked in the high altar (1778). Here the manipulation of surface planes shows astonishing finesse and dexterity.

The vertical lines resemble layers of ornate engaged pilasters renewing themselves beyond capitals and cornices, soaring upwards until they curve inwards in the topmost part to form a mighty multilayered archivolt. The convexity of the central section is emphasized by tabernacle, glass shrine of the Virgen del Pilar, canopied niches, and fluttering cherubs. On either side, four rows of shallow niche pilasters, from which statues stand forward, form entrecalles. The statues are saints concerned with education and youth: Andrew Avellino, Cajetan, John of God, Philip Neri, and Jesuit saints, incl. Francis Xavier, Francis Borgia, Ignatius. On either side are huge, effective paintings (1779) by Andrés López: Assumption and Our Lady of the Apocalypse.

The four other nave altarpieces, contained within arches, show various themes. To l., Catholic Reform, with statues and busts of SS Augustine, Thomas Aquinas, Vincent Ferrer, Ignatius, etc; Lineage of Our Lady, with figures of SS Anne, Joachim, John at the foot of the Cross, the archangel Gabriel; the backing paintings of scenes from the lives of Our Lady and St Joseph (1778) are by José de Alzíbar, to whom have also been attr. these two retables. To r., Christian Martyrs, the only altarpiece to preserve its original glass case, beneath which is a painting of the scourging of Christ by Francisco Antonio Vallejo; and, after the pulpit, an altarpiece with more figures of saints, incl. Cajetan, Stanislaus Kostka, John Nepomuk. The four retables in the sotocoro lack most of their original statues. Two good paintings, SS John Evangelist and Mary Magdalen, by Vallejo, enhance the one on r. nearer the nave.

The former convent buildings were adapted for other uses in the later 19C. Nos. 104–6 C. Donceles (r. of the church) were modified in 1899–1900 as the *Pal. de Justicia*. Its N side (corner of Cs González Obregón and Argentina) is now the *Colegio Nacional*, founded in 1943 to represent the finest in Mexican scholarship and the arts.

The *Pinacoteca de la Enseñanza* (Mon.–Fri., 7.30–7; on application at 104 C. Donceles) contains religious paintings and photographs illustrating restoration processes and techniques. No. 98 C. Donceles was the house of Joaquín Dongo, a merchant whose murder in Oct. 1789, with ten members of his household, was a cause célèbre of viceregal Mexico. Through the vigorous action of Viceroy Revillagigedo the three assassins were brought to justice and garotted within 15 days.

Opposite the church, at 99 C. Donceles, are the former premises of the **Colegio de Cristo** (mid-18C), with a beautiful portal, the lower part showing a more sober yet rich baroque influence; the upper incorporating churrigueresque motifs and relief of great finesse. The patio is a peaceful refuge from the noisy street.

The college was founded in 1612 with 12 poor scholars (huérfanos de padre) and a rector. In 1774 it was amalgamated with San Ildefonso.

Next door, fronting C. Argentina, is the **Casa del Marqués del Apartado** (1790s), by Manuel Tolsá—with hallmarks of neoclassical nobility.

It was destined for the 2nd marqués, José Fagoaga de Leisaur, partisan of Independence. In 1900–01 it was modernized. Today it houses a library and a museum of the building's history.—Beneath the patio are preserved remains of one of the temples of the Teocalli (Rte 2).

Diagonally opposite, on the corner of Cs Argentina and Justo Sierra, is an 18C house occupied since 1910 by the **Librería Porrúa Hermanos**, leading booksellers and publishers.

On the site was the house of Luis de Castilla, regidor of Mexico City in 1534. The Porrúa business was started in 1900 by Francisco, Indalecio, and José Porrúa Estrada, brothers from Asturias. The books, with an educational and academic slant, are companions of generations of students and bibliophiles.

5 South of the Zócalo

At the SE corner of the Zócalo and facing the S side of the Pal. Nacional, the block bounded by Avs Pino Suárez (W) and Venustiano Carranza (S), and by Cs Corregidora (N) and Castellanos Quinto (E), is taken up by the **Suprema Corte de Justicia** (1935–41), Mexico's highest judicial tribunal, in massive, simple style, by Antonio Muñoz García.

The INTERIOR (Mon.–Fri., 9–1) contains two sets of murals, by José Clemente Orozco (1941) and the US artist George Biddle (1945).

Orozco's murals, on the lobby walls (recinto de los pasos perdidos) at the top of the main staircase, depict a pessimistic vision of corruption and betrayal in the legal system, without explicit references to Mexico. Chaos and disorder are shown (N and S walls) in compositions based on jarring diagonals, where black tones predominate. Justice herself, a far from graceful figure, sleeps on her pedestal. Democracy, clad with the attributes of the Statue of Liberty, flees, her scales unbalanced. On the W wall the phantasmal figure of Juárez appears— vague and almost forgotten. On the E wall an allegory, 'La patria', is full of symbols (eg, oil pouring from a macabre and bloody head) of Mexico suffering through betrayal and death. Biddle's triptych mural is on the library entrance wall, reached by turning l. on the first landing of the main staircase. It alludes to the destruction caused by the second world war.

The Supreme Court occupies what was the PL. DEL VOLADOR, a precinct bought by Cortés and owned by his heirs until 1937. In Apr. 1649 the Inquisition liquidated the élite of Mexican Jewry here at an extraordinary auto de fe. A later market was demolished in 1930. The block immediately E was the site of the *Universidad de México* from 1589 to 1910, when it was finally demolished (see Rte 15).

On the S side of the Supreme Court, in Av. Venustiano Carranza, is the church of **Porta Coeli**, dedicated in 1711. Its classical façade was restored, and the pilasters smoothed to characterlessness, by Luis. G. Anzorena in 1891, who also designed the high altar. The neo-byzantine frescoes (1951–71) are by Manuel Pérez Paredes.

It is all that remains of a Dominican college founded in 1603 to train missionaries for the Philippines. One of its pupils was Fray Servando Teresa de Mier (1765–1827), indefatigable apologist of Independence, who in 1794 preached a notorious sermon casting doubts on the miracle of Guadalupe, for which he was hounded by the authorities and which began his colourful career as one of the foremost prison-breakers of the day. The church is now owned by Uniate Catholics of the Melkite rite.

Beyond it C. Tabaqueros leads S to join Av. Uruguay, lined with interesting old buildings: No. 117 is a two-storey late 18C casa señorial. Beyond C. Yucatán is the former Conceptionist convent church (now Maronite) of **Nuestra Señora de Valvanera** (less correctly, but more popularly, *Balvanera*; 1667–71), with typical twin S doorways, classicizing and baroque motifs contending—all probably restyled in the early 19C. The blue and yellow azulejos of the 18C tower offer a delightful contrast. In the sacristy are paintings by Carlos Clemente López (1750).

Opposite, at the NE corner of Av. Uruguay and CORREO MAYOR (another historic street, lined with 18–19C houses, named after the royal official in charge of the mails, who had his residence here) survives the portal of the **Colegio de San Ramón** (1654–1840; for the training of secular priests of pure Castilian descent), showing the coat-of-arms of its founder, Alonso Enríquez de Toledo (d. 1628), bp of Michoacán. Part of the interior remains.

By going N up Correo Mayor we join Av. Venustiano Carranza and turn r. No. 135 (18C; good doorway) was the house of Joaquín García Icazbalceta (1825–94), historian, philanthropist, and tireless promoter of Mexican culture. We pass C. Las Cruces, which runs S, and has 17–18C domestic architecture, especially No. 20 (17C). No. 148 Av. Venustiano Carranza was birthplace of the insurgent Mariano Matamoros (1770–1814). No. 153 was the house of another, Andrés Quintana Roo (1787–1851).

We then come to PL. GARCIA BRAVO, with a monument to Alonso García Bravo (d. c 1560), who laid out the post-Conquest city. On its S side is the stunning baroque cloister of the former convent of **La Merced**.

Dedicated to collect alms for the release of captives, the Mercedarian order was established on the site by the late 16C. Its sumptuous adjoining church (1630–54) was pulled down in 1862—for the lead tiles between the roof and alfarje vaults. Thomas Gage reported the scandalous election of a new provincial in 1625–26: 'such was their [the priors'] various and fractious differences that upon the sudden all the convent was in an uproar, their canonical election was turned to mutiny and strife, knives were drawn, and many wounded'. Such was the scandal that viceroy marqués de Cerralvo had to sit in until the proper election was made.

The lower arcade (mid-17C) is rich enough, with the arch voussoirs alternating plain blocks and squares of relief; the keystones jutting framed carvings of saints of the Order; and the spandrels resting on doric capitals. The upper arcade (c 1700) is Mudéjar-inspired: double arches in relation to each lower-arcade arch; columns, arches, capitals, and surfaces encrusted with relief, the diamond-point arch profiles especially noticeable. The railings may have been rescued from the old University (see above).

From the plaza we may diverge E along the narrow C. Manzanares to the **Cap. de Manzanares**, a late 18C barrio chapel containing churrigueresque altarpieces.

From here, across Anillo de Circunvalación, lined with traders' stalls, C. Manzanares continues E to C. Sta Escuela, which goes N to the church of **La Soledad de Sta Cruz** (1750–92), its wide, balanced, strangely handsome façade showing the continuous influence of classicism and maximum effect in simplicity. Beneath the curved pediment, the mandorla containing the central statue of Our Lady is a delightful touch. The high altar, bearing a venerated image of Our Lady, is a later neoclassical work.

From behind the church C. Rosario runs S to meet C. Candelaria, which goes E. Reached along it are two barrio chapels: *La Candelaria de los Patos* (early 17C; corner with C. San

Convent of La Merced (mid-19C)

Ciprián; serving an area once known for duck-breeding and selling), unhappily rebuilt in 1924; and *San Jeronimito* (16C; corner with C. de la Granja). Beyond, across Av. Morazán, looms the *Pal. Legislativo*, home since 1982 of the Chamber of Deputies (murals by José Chávez Morado).

Anillo de Circunvalación runs S to pass the former Augustinian church of **Sto Tomás de la Palma** (18C; l.; between Cs G. Pedraza and Palma), facing an atrio, its stone portal, with a relief of the Crucifixion, set against rusticated masonry. It has been recently remodelled.

Behind it, bounded on the N by C. General Anaya, on the E by C. Rosario, on the S by C. Gurrión, and on the W by C. Cabaña, is the MERCADO DE LA MERCED (1957), damaged by the earthquake of 1985. Its giant concrete shell covers four blocks.

Av. Uruguay leads W from La Merced back to Correo Mayor, which goes S two blocks to reach C. Mesones. On the r. is the church of **San José de Gracia** (1659–61), whose twin portals display emphatic broken pediments, repeated above the windows, and relief—all Mannerist. The drum of the cupola was the city's first.

The adjoining convent (Sta María de Gracia; now demolished) was founded in 1610 for Conceptionists from La Valvanera, next to a retreat house for pious widows and married women. Sometime before 1621 the nuns (led by the aggressive Sor Bárbara de Jesús) bored a hole through the wall, turned the laywomen out, and took over their premises. In 1871 the church was sold to the Episcopalians, whose services Pres. Juárez used to attend.

C. Mesones runs W to join Av. Pino Suárez (the former Cs Real and Estampa de Jesús). In this stretch during the 16–17C noble residences were aligned with that of the viceroy to the W. Opposite as we turn r. are the hospital and church of **Jesús Nazareno**, the first hospital in the Americas, founded c 1524–28 by Cortés at the place where he first met Moctezuma on his entry into Tenochtitlán in 1519. Much rebuilt and mutilated, it still has parts of the 16C structure.

They are hemmed in behind the five-storey hospital (by José Villagrán García; 1943) on Av. Pino Suárez; by a modern building on C. Mesones; and by a shopping arcade (through which is another entrance) on the W side, which fronts Av. 20 de Noviembre.

The Hospital de la Purísima Concepción (a name it retained until 1663) was inspired by the great Spanish foundations: Compostela, Granada, Seville, Toledo. It occupied c 8320 sq m; and was originally in the shape of a T, with a double chapel on two floors where the two corridors met (facing Av. Pino Suárez). In the S r.-angle (facing C. Mesones) were two patios, still in place. The E front was finished in 1535. On their arrival, exhausted, in the city late in 1568 Miles Philips and his companions (see Rtes 7, 62) were kindly treated by the Spaniards, even though 'many of the company ... dyed within the space of fourteene dayes'. The survivors stayed at 'Our Ladies hospitall' until cured, their Spanish visitors bringing them 'marmilads' and other gifts. From 1577 the works were under Claudio de Arciniega and completed by the end of the century. In the 1950s, with the widening of Av. Pino Suárez, the decayed E façade was tragically demolished.

The entrance in Av. Pino Suárez (No. 35) leads into the modern hospital, from which may be gained access to the patios of the old. The pilasters supporting the lower arcade are replacements (1800–09) by González Velázquez. Reminders of Arciniega's work can still be seen in the upper storeys, the sturdiness of the arches on Tuscan columns continued in the splendid beams of the ceiling. On the upper floors are 16C survivals: friezes of grotesques and, above them, between the beam ends, human portraits.

On the N side stands the rusticated church of **Jesús**, mostly finished in 1608, although the nave remained uncovered until 1684. The tower (1704) is topped by a St Michael.

EXTERIOR. The side door, facing Av. El Salvador, with its upper-storey reliefs of Faith and Hope on either side of the Virgen de las Maravillas, was finished in the late 18C. The main (W) door preserves Arciniega's work in the lower storey: fluted pilasters with Tuscan capitals. The upper storey (17C) niche holds a statue of Jesus the Nazarene.

Adjoining it, facing N, is the entrance to the *Cap. de la Sta Escuela*, a brotherhood associated with the hospital since the late 17C.

INTERIOR. On the N side of the sanctuary the bones of Hernán Cortés at last found a resting place. From Castilleja de la Cuesta in Andalucía where he died in 1547, they were brought to Texcoco in 1566 and in 1629 to San Francisco in Mexico City. In 1794 they were placed in this church. In 1823, fearing profanation, Lucas Alamán hid them. They were discovered and reinterred here, behind a simple slab and inscription, in 1947. Alamán (1792–1853) also rests here, in the N transept.

Orozco's mural 'Apocalipsis' (1942–44), in the vault and on the walls covering the first two sections at the choir end, is the first part of an uncompleted project. It interprets conflict and destruction. In the centre of the vault, a rectangular prism crowned by a T and emitting rays of light is the only regular, geometrical form in the mural, and through this abstract notion of order, divinity is symbolized amidst chaos. To the S of the prism, an angel ties the Devil upside down to a post; in the r.-angle of the wall below, two human figures are powerless to intervene; on the opposite wall, he is freed to sow war and destruction. This is shown in the first section of the ceiling vaults. The Babylonian whore sits on the apocalyptic beast—here the Mexican jaguar.

The sacristy has a beautiful (restored) artesonado ceiling. Among its and the adjoining room's paintings is an anon. work (1781) of a procession to the hospital in 1663, giving a contemporary view of the vanished E front.

The plaza opposite the church has a monument to Francisco Primo de Verdad y Ramos. On the other side of Av. Pino Suárez rises the **Casa de los Condes de Santiago de Calimaya**, well preserved, in its present state (1779) by Francisco Guerrero y Torres.

The condado was created by Philip III in 1616 for Fernando de Altamirano y Velasco (1597–1657); in 1651–52 corregidor of Mexico City; in 1655–57 governor of Guatemala.

The great portal's main influence is baroque—columns with ionic capitals resting on claw feet flanking an intricately curved arch in the lower storey; fluted columns with Corinthian capitals on either side of the ornately framed window in the upper. Above, the gable holds the coats-of-arms of Altamirano, Velasco, Castilla, and Mendoza, supported by atlantes perched on tightly rolled scrolls. Around the parapet are gargoyles resembling cannon. At the SW corner is a prehispanic snake head, relic of the original house (c 1536). The interior has more upper-storey gargoyles resting against the arch spandrels and an ornate shell fountain, with a siren musician.

It houses the **Museo de la Ciudad de México** (Tues.–Sun., 9.30–5.30), a didactic collection of scale models, relief maps, plaster casts, paintings, drawings, furniture, porcelain, sculpture, etc., to chart the history, geography, and customs of Mexico City from earliest times to the present day.

GROUND FLOOR. 1. Geography of the Valley of Mexico. 2. Man in the Valley of Mexico: prehispanic cultures. 3. Classic Teotihuacán: first ethnic groups. 4. Peregrination of Náhuatl-speaking tribes. 5. Foundation of Tenochtitlán. 6. Splendour of Tenochtitlán. 7. Conquest and destruction of Tenochtitlán. 8. Mexico in the 16–17C, incl. floods. UPPER FLOOR. 9. Mexico City, fount of American culture. 10. Splendour of New Spain. 11. Independent Mexico. 12. Lithography in Mexico. 13. Reform and empire. 14. Restoration of the republic. 15. Revolution.

On the r. of the staircase, the Sacristy contains a St Viridiana by Baltasar de Echave Ibía and a Death of St Joseph by Ibarra. The chapel (its façade 19C) contains an Assumption attr. Simón Pereyns and Our Lady of Sorrows by Cristóbal de Villalpando.

In the NE part of the upper floor is the former studio of the painter Joaquín Clausell (1866–1935; kept locked). The walls are covered with symbolist-impressionist sketches and paintings, done straight on to the surfaces.

The next turning along Av. Pino Suárez, Av. Uruguay, runs W to meet Av. 20 de Noviembre. To the r. across the road is the former Conceptionist convent church of **San Bernardo** (1685–90), by Juan de Cepeda (in collaboration with Pedro de Arrieta ?). Its elaborate portals span Mannerist and baroque, and are remarkable for their relief, a combination of wavy and fluted patterns in the upper parts of the columns and lace-like in the lower; the latter tendency transferred to the outer supports (with exotic capitals) of the upper storeys and the delicately ornate niche frames. The niches contain statues in yellowish tecali alabaster: Our Lady of Guadalupe, with a relief of God the Father and angels above (E portal); St Bernard (N), with the Holy Ghost and angels.

The convent was demolished after 1861. The church has twice been truncated on the E for road-widening. In 1935 the easternmost of the twin N doors was realigned to face Av. 20 de Noviembre. The semicircular high altar is neoclassical.

S of the church, at the corner of Avs 20 de Noviembre and Uruguay, is the late 18C **Casa del Conde de la Cortina**, still impressive, with imposing portal and windows in rusticated stone, despite the mauling it suffered through road-widening. Next door, 90 Av. Uruguay is the **Casa del Conde de la Torre de Cosío** (1781), whose modified façade retains some dignity. Note the turret covered with azulejos.

Further W, on the NE corner of Av. Uruguay and C. 5 de Febrero, Nos. 86 and 20 are what remains of the *Casa del Mayorazgo de los López Peralta* (17C), modernized in 1938, its original Mudéjar stucco remade in cement. Next door, at 18 C. 5 de Febrero, is the **Casa del Mayorazgo de Avila**.

It is named after the 16C house of Hernando de Avila on the site. The present is a rebuilding (1762–66; since altered) for Nicolás Cobián y Valdés. The relief and lovely window frame of the portal panel remain. In the roof garden is the finest azulejo work in the city.

Further N on the same side, at the corner of C. 5 de Febrero and Av. Venustiano Carranza (No. 79), is the department store built for *Fábricas Universales* (1909) by Miguel Angel de Quevedo. On the opposite side of Av. Venustiano Carranza (No. 84), and backing on to the Ayuntamiento, is the *Pal. de Hierro* (1920) by Paul Dubois, a replacement for the earliest department store in the city, burned down in 1914. Another store, *El Puerto de Veracruz* (1904; restored), by Rafael Goyeneche, faces Fábricas Universales at the SW corner of C. 5 de Febrero and Av. Venustiano Carranza. On the same side (15 C. 5 de Febrero) is an 18C house with ajaraca facing (third floor a later addition). Around the corner, at 80 Av. Uruguay, is the 18C house occupied by Alexander von Humboldt in 1803.

The SE corner of C. 5 de Febrero and Av. Uruguay is occupied by the *Hotel Ontario* (1923), a throwback to casa señorial and Mudéjar influences, with corner niche and curvetting cornice, by Luis Robles Gil. Opposite, at 23 C. 5 de Febrero, is a late 18C house attr. Manuel Tolsá. Other 18C houses are at Nos. 26, 28, and 30 opposite.

6 The Alameda

The **ALAMEDA**, named after the álamos (poplars) with which it was first planted, is the main park of central Mexico City: a large rectangle containing four smaller, each divided by broad pathways in the shape of a St Andrew's cross. In addition to its recreational attractions, it is a focus of city festivities, especially between Christmas and Epiphany. Its ancient ash are prominent. Its fountains date from early and mid-century. (An undulating parapet is all that survives of a once famous 18C central fountain.) The statuary dispersed about it is mainly by 19C Mexican academic sculptors: Jesús Contreras, 'Malgré-tout' (c 1897–1902); José María Labastida, 'Gladiators' (1825–35); Agustín Ocampo, 'Desespoir' (1898); Tomás Pérez, 'Venus' (1854); James-Jacques Pradier, 'Bacante recostada' (1823). At the E end, facing the Pal. de Bellas Artes, the monument to Beethoven (1927) was a gift from the German community. Facing S towards Av. Juárez is the *Hemiciclo a Benito Juárez* (1910), by Guillermo Heredia.

The Alameda was laid out, on marshy terrain, in 1592–94. In the early 17C the neighbourhood was hardly upper-class: 'Spanish vagabonds, mestizos and mulattos, villains, and other persons', who cut down the trees, tore up the soil, and let their cattle break in. Yet in 1625, recorded Thomas Gage, it was 'somewhat like unto our Moorfields, where do meet as constantly as the merchants upon our exchange about two thousand coaches, full of gallants, ladies, and citizens, to see and to be seen, to court and to be courted'. In 1770–79 it was gradually extended to E and W, achieving its present dimensions. On 8 May 1810 Francisco Javier Lizana y Beaumont, abp of Mexico since 1803, having just resigned as viceroy (since 1809), stepped into his coach and ordered the coachman to take him to the Alameda, which he had never yet seen. On 12 Nov. 1855 the French and English residents held a party here to celebrate the victory of Sebastopol: 'telle que Mexico n'en avait jamais vu', wrote Mathieu de Fossey. Lawns and a rose garden were laid out in the 1860s at Carlota's order.

After 1868 the railings were removed, lighting introduced, and bordering streams closed up. On the W side, facing San Diego, was Pl. del Quemadero, where from 1574 those judged by the Inquisition to have deserved the extreme penalty were burned. This infamous spot was erased by order of Viceroy Revillagigedo in 1791.

On the N side of the Alameda two churches face one another across a sunken plaza. That on the E is **La Santa Veracruz** (1730–). Its W façade (1776) is routinely churrigueresque; its S more compact and much livelier. Note the jolly cherubs carrying horns of plenty perched above the volutes. The towers (1776) display tableros and the dome gold leaf decoration.

In 1568 the Archicofradía de la Cruz, dedicated to giving paupers a decent funeral, built a church here, later promoted as the third parish church of the city. The niche above the S doorway holds a statue of St Blaise, bp of Sebastea, patron of the archbrotherhood. Manuel Tolsá was buried in the church.

Opposite, facing E, is **San Juan de Dios**, dedicated in 1729, by Miguel Custodio Durán.

EXTERIOR. The puerta abocinada is a reminder of the open chapel. The wavy pilasters, running between the beautifully framed niches, are continued above the jagged cornice in the form of flame-like obelisks. Wavy movement goes on into the rays of the canopy above. Walls and tower base are covered in hexagonal ajaracas, continued in the former hospital building, facing N next door.

The INTERIOR was reconditioned in the 19C and contains paintings by Germán Gedovius: SS Benedict and Sebastian, Holy Trinity, Our Lady of Mount Carmel, Our Lady of Guadalupe.
The hospital of *Nuestra Señora de los Desamparados* (distressed), founded in the 16C by the physician Pedro López (1527–97), was taken over in 1604 by the Brothers of St John of God, who ran it until c 1820. Later it became the hospital for women, famous for obstetrics, until 1965–67, when larger premises became imperative.

It has been restored and rearranged to house the **Museo Franz Mayer** (Tues.–Sun., 10–5; fee), with pieces from the most extensive private collection of fine and applied art in Mexico.

Franz Mayer (1882–1975), b. in Mannheim, emigrated first to London, then to New York. He finally settled in Mexico City in 1905, where he became a stockbroker and financier. He also became an enthusiastic collector, and succeeded in repatriating works of art. He left his collection (c 9000 objects, and 20,000 azulejos) to a trust on the understanding that it should be kept intact in a museum. The museum's scope is of the widest, particularly the Mexican ceramics and silver sections. It offers an ideal introduction to Mexican historical art. Only part can be displayed at any one time. An area on the ground floor is reserved for concerts and lectures. Several original baroque doorways and traces of murals have been left in place.

VESTIBULE. 17C Mexican Santiago, in carved and gilded wood, one of various examples in the collection. Silver gilt early 17C Spanish processional cross. S. CLOISTER WALK. 16–18C Flemish, Nuremberg, and Brussels tapestries. 18–19C English, Spanish, and German glass. Late 18C Sheffield tea and coffee pots. 18C Dutch porcelain. 18–19C German pewter. 17–18C Spanish barguenos, with bone and mother-of-pearl inlay. 17–18C Asian furniture. Among Mexican work: 18–19C lacquerware from Pátzcuaro (a miniature commode, clawfeet [patitas de garra] in upper part) and Olinalá; 18–19C soup tureens; an 18C San Diego is an excellent example of glazed Talavera pottery. There follow first-rate 17–18C Mexican sculpture and relief, polychrome and gilded, some from altarpieces. Among European works: 16C Entry of Christ into Jerusalem.

SCULPTURE ROOM (E side of cloister). Christ (caña de maíz) in arms of God the Father; God the Father blessing—two stark 17C Mexican polychrome works. 18C examples of Tecali alabaster. Outstanding polychrome wooden sculpture (17–18C) from Guatemala. St Anne enthroned (the throne with clawfeet, modish in 18C Mexico). 17–18C Mexican popular sculpture. Among European works: Descent from the Cross, an expertly crowded late 15C Flemish work; 18C Spanish St Raphael; St Catherine, in polychrome stone (15C Flemish or French); Adoration of the Kings (17C Spanish polychrome wood in high relief), fluent and natural despite lack of perspective and errors in proportion and anatomy. Among other 16–17C wooden relief sculpture is an intense Death of Our Lady, probably early 17C Spanish.

PORCELAIN ROOM (N side of cloister). Pieces produced for export under the Ch'ing dynasty (late 18C). 18C E India Co porcelain brought to New Spain in the Manila galleon. Lustrous 16C Spanish porcelain from Manises (Valencia); 17–18C pieces from Aragón and Catalonia. 17–18C ware from Talavera de la Reina (Toledo).

The SILVER ROOM (E side of cloister behind stairs to upper floor) contains a wealth of 16–19C Mexican silver and silver plate, often chased and embossed, mostly for use in church.

UPPER FLOOR. On the staircase wall, 18C English tapestry inspired by a harvest festival scene by David Teniers the Younger. At top of stairs, 17C Mexican folding screen, both sides with oil paintings of the Conquest of New Spain (repaying detailed study). We turn right into the E side of the upper cloister walk. SPANISH AND ITALIAN PAINTING. Anon. 15C Aragonese, St Christopher. Lluis Borrassá (c 1360–1426; Gerona/Barcelona), St Hippolytus blessing his family (oil and tempera on wood). Disciple of Alonso Sánchez Coello (c 1531–88), Infanta Isabel Clara Eugenia, daughter of Philip II and governor of the Netherlands. Juan de Castillo (1584–1640), Nativity. José de Ribera (Lo Spagnoletto; 1589–1652), 'El sentido de la vista'. Zurbarán, Bernardo del Carpio and one of the seven Infantes de Lara (figures from medieval Spanish legend); Miraculous discovery of the statue of Our Lady of Puig. School of Velázquez, Lady in black. Juan Miranda (18C), Immaculate Conception. Vicente Salvador y Gómez de Valencia (1637–80), Liberation of St Peter. Paintings by Joaquín Sorolla y Bastida (1863–1923), incl. portrait of Adelina Patti, and Ignacio Zuloaga y Zabaleta (1870–1945). *Italian*. Aniello Falcone (1607–56), Battle Scene. Alessandro Allori (Bronzino; 1535–1607), Eleonora di Toledo. Lorenzo Lotto (1480–1556), Antiquarian. Attr. Paolo Domenico Finoglia (1590–1645), Nativity. Luca Giordano (1634–1704), Lucretia.

NETHERLANDS AND GERMAN PAINTING (N side of upper cloister walk). Attr. Joseph Heintz the Younger (1600–78; German), Building works. School of Jacob Grimmer (1526–c 1590; Dutch), Landscape with castles. Master of the Legend of St Mary Magdalen (late 15C; Dutch), SS Louis of Toulouse and Elizabeth of Hungary with donors. Master of the Altar of Seydfriedberg (16C; German), Adoration of the Kings. Anon. 16C Augsburg, Presentation in the Temple. Master of the Embroidered Leaves (early 16C; Dutch), St Christopher. Bartholomeus Bruyn the Elder (1493–1555; Dutch, resident in Cologne), Nativity (with donor on l.). Lanceloot Volders (1657–1703; Flemish), Ladies and Servants. School of Frans Pourbus the Elder (c 1570–80; Flemish), Love Feast. Ferdinand van Kessel (1648–96; Flemish), Allegory of Brazil. Justus Sustermans (1597–1681; Flemish), Matteo de Medici. School of Paul de Vos (c 1596–1678; Flemish), Wild boar confronting hunting dogs. Joos de Momper and Jan Jordaens III (1564–1635; d. 1643; Flemish), Laban searching for the statues of his household gods in Rachel's tent. Frans Francken the Younger (1581–1642; Flemish), Lazarus and Dives. Studio of Willem van Herp (1614–77; Flemish), Allegory of the Five Senses. Abraham Hondius (c 1625–after 1695; Dutch), Hunt after wild boar. Gerrit van Honthorst (1590–1656; Dutch), Violinist with glass of wine. Attr. Frans van Mieris the Elder (1635–81; Dutch), Doctor's visit. Philips Wouwerman (1619–68; Dutch), Boar hunt.

We retrace our steps to the room beyond the E side of the upper cloister walk, devoted to CERAMICS FROM PUEBLA, pre-eminently a sumptuous collection of the tin-glazed earthenware, or majolica, known in Mexico as Talavera poblana. Its production in Puebla, inspired by the styles created in Talavera de la Reina (Toledo), began in the 16C and reached its apogee in the 17–18C. Three main types may be distinguished: in blue and white, influenced by Chinese styles; in polychrome (blue, black, yellow, orange, and green); and fashioned like mosaic. Religious statuary, though rare because of the great skill needed to model it, was also part of the genre. The collection of glazed tiles (azulejos), coloured and patterned in the same way as Talavera poblana, is also of the finest and in many styles, from rare 17C examples to those of the 18C, when their manufacture reached its peak.

The N cloister walk continues with an excellent collection of MEXICAN PAINTING. Manuel Arellano, St Luis Gonzaga expounding virtue to Roman children (1691), sweet-natured and typically Mexican. Juan Correa, St Michael; Christ with the woman taken in adultery; Our Lady of Valvanera (in a lush landscape); St Ignatius Loyola; St Francis Borgia. Pedro Ramírez, Birth of Our Lady. Nicolás Rodríguez Juárez, the Child Jesus, sweet and appealing. Juan Rodríguez Juárez, St Francis Xavier baptizing Indians. Antonio Sánchez Salmerón, Annunciation to SS Anne and Joachim. Francisco Martínez, St Louis

IX with Our Lady. Miguel Jerónimo Zendejas, Christ of the Fountain. Anon. 18C, María Josepha Tobío y Estrada; Juan Francisco de Güemes y Horcasitas, conde de Revillagigedo I, viceroy 1746–55. Miguel de Herrera, Portrait of a lady. 19C works by Fernando Best, Félix Parra, and José María Velasco.

A recess has been furnished as a typical 18C SACRISTY, containing contemporary furniture, sculpture, and vestments.

On the W side of the upper cloister begins a series of rooms devoted to the decorative arts from the 16C. *16C*. Flemish tapestry; Spanish walnut chairs with velvet seats and examples of Spanish embroidery with silken and gold thread; patents of nobility; Catalan wooden chest, gilded and polychrome. From the *17C* come a bronze German clock, a Spanish walnut table, mother-of-pearl Our Lady of Guadalupe, Mexican shell paintings (shell fragments under a painted surface), Mexican feather paintings, and a lantern clock (1680) made by Daniel M. Quare of London. Note also a 15C Spanish chest covered in velvet. Silver is represented by Spanish processional crosses and an Italian chased and embossed casket (for ecclesiastical use), topped by a statue of St Michael; ivory, by figures of Our Lady and St Joseph, from the Philippines. Mexican writing desk with bone inlay. Small cabinet (bufetillo) from Oaxaca, profusely encrusted with lacy rosettes, foliage, and volutes. Italian oak cabinet of small drawers. Collection of similar cabinets (cajoneras) with mother-of-pearl and shell inlay. Mexican travelling case—its framework of reed fibre woven by the technique known as petate (basket-weave), covered in leather embroidered with yarn made from the maguey plant; wrought-iron locks and handles. 17–18C Mexican chests. Lacquered wooden cabinet from Pátzcuaro. Collection of 17–18C Mexican wooden boxes, covered in gilding and polychrome, with silver embellishments. Mexican kitchen furniture. A section is furnished as an early 18C (?) chemist's shop.

There follows one of the most interesting and beautiful pieces: six surviving panels from a late 17C folding bedroom screen painted with scenes of the four elements and the liberal arts by Juan Correa, the only 17C Mexican painting on a humanist theme so far known to have survived. It was perhaps done for Abp Payo Enríquez de Rivera (viceroy 1673–80; d 1683) and taken by him back to Spain where it remained until recently in the possession of his collateral descendants.

Obverse. Earth is represented by Ceres and Cybele in a chariot drawn by a white ox and a black bull; Air by Flora, Chloris, and Zephyr, in a chariot drawn by two powerful birds. *Reverse*. Five liberal arts—Grammar, Astronomy, Rhetoric, Geometry, Arithmetic—are symbolized by dignified female figures with appropriate attributes. In the sixth panel are four more figures seated on the shore of a lake, either part of the next (cut-off) art scene or representing Music.

18C. Mexican relief of the Death of St Augustine, ministered to by angels. Polychrome Mexican sculpture. Mexican furniture, some in Queen Anne style, and silver frames. Dutch grandfather clock by Jan Volker. Mexican and European miniature sculpture in alabaster and marble. English clock by Robert and Peter Higgs. Two views of Zacatecas (1833) by Daniel Thomas Egerton (see Rte 16). English clock by Johannes Fromanteel—the face a painted landscape; a circle moving through the sky through 180 degrees pointing to the hour—designed to be visible at night. Urbano López, two (NW and SW) of a series of four panoramic views of 19C Mexico City. 18–19C Mexican, English, and Spanish glass. English globe (1812).

At 39 Av. Hidalgo is the *Museo Nacional de la Estampa* (Tues.–Sun., 10–6), a collection of prints, engravings, lithographs, aquatints, etc., showing the development of the genres in Mexico. Works by Manuel Manilla, José Guadalupe Posada, Orozco, José Chávez Morado, Rufino Tamayo are included.

Av. Hidalgo runs W to meet Paseo de la Reforma. At the NE corner is the **Hotel Cortés** (1780), finished in tezontle. The baroque doorway encloses a statue of St Thomas of Villanueva, patron of the destitute, a reminder that this was once a hospice for discalced Augustinians.

On the W side of the Alameda, C. Dr Mora leads past the former church of **San Diego**, once part of a convent (1594–1621) of discalced Franciscans (dieguinos). The church's neoclassical aspect dates from an early 19C rebuilding. It has been altered since (most recently after earthquake damage in 1985). The convent was closed and sold off from 1860; the church finally closed for worship in 1926.

It and part of the cloister have been adapted for the **Pinacoteca Virreinal** (Tues.–Sun., 10–5), installed in 1964, a collection of the highest importance. Even the most hurried visitor to Mexico City should try to spend a little time here. Some works are of the first rank; even the minor canvases have a naive charm.

In the mid-19C José Bernardo Couto (1803–62) set about building a display of paintings from the viceregal period: he added to the collection of the Academia de San Carlos by taking the best from the deposits of confiscated convents and getting donations from religious and lay orders. Further additions have been made since.

The disposition may be changed from time to time, and one or two rooms shut. The staff will generally grant access on request.

ROOM 1 (below choir). Anon. 16C, Holy Family with St John; St Cecilia—both wrongly attr. Simón Pereyns, more likely by Andrés de la Concha; the former retinted in the 19C by José Salomé Pina. Anon. early 17C, Virgin and Child with St Augustine, from the convent of Tlayacapan (Morelos), perhaps by an Indian hand using a Flemish source. Attr. Luis Juárez, Visitation. Antonio Rodríguez, St Thomas Aquinas. Juan Tinoco, Battle of Hebrews and Amalechites—an exceptionally vigorous baroque work.

R 2 (nave). Baltasar de Echave Orio, Martyrdom of St Apronianus (1612); Annunciation and Visitation (1609), dignified and serene, the main figures in dark green backgrounds—from the Tlatelolco altarpiece; Adoration of the Kings (c 1595); Presentation in the Temple (doubtful, heavily retouched). Alonso López de Herrera, Assumption—Italianate below, Flemish above. Attr. Luis Juárez, Investing of St Ildefonsus. Sebastián López de Arteaga, Incredulity of St Thomas (the painter's own likeness upper l.); Marriage of Our Lady; Crucifixion (1643); The Apostles. José Juárez, Martyrdom of the child saints Justus and Pastor; Apparition of Our Lady to St Francis; Adoration of the Kings—magnificent, gloriously coloured works.

R 3 (Cap. de Nuestra Señora de los Dolores) contains 18C works. Miguel Cabrera, Our Lady of the Apocalypse. José de Ibarra, Woman taken in adultery; Our Lord healing the woman with an issue of blood; St Mary Magdalen washing Christ's feet—note the catching of His expression; Christ and the Samaritan woman; 12 small paintings of the apostles. Francisco Juan de Aguilera, Immaculate Conception (1720).

In the tympanum above the entrance is a mural, 'Los ángeles músicos', by Federico Cantú. In the presbytery is another by him, 'Los informantes de Sahagún', in which the conversion of New Spain, initiated by the friars, is seen as a process of interchange, in which the Indians also participated. Both were finished in 1954.

R 4 (sacristy). Baltasar de Echave Ibía ('de los azules'), Our Lady of the Apocalypse, full of symbolism above a strange landscape, infused with the blue shades for which the painter is famous. Luis Juárez, Guardian Angel, the devil and a woman representing worldly temptation lower l.; St Michael vanquishing Satan; Agony in the Garden—note the treatment of Christ's robe; Annunciation. Attr. Luis Juárez, Our Lady and St Anne; St Thomas Aquinas. Pedro Ramírez, Adoration of the Shepherds, showing character and realism. Baltasar de Echave y Rioja, Burial of Christ (1665), fascinating and full of chiaroscuro effects, the apostle holding the torch (l.) to light the scene and the blonde woman (r.) imposing urgency on to general grief; St Catherine disputes with the philosophers (1678). José Mora, Christ of Chalma (1719). Anon. mid-18C, Allegory of St Joseph as Protector of the Faith. Diego Sanabria, St John of the Cross.

R 5 (lower cloister) is dominated by Francisco Antonio Vallejo's huge canvas of the Immaculate Conception (1774).

The higher level shows Our Lady in glory surrounded by angels and saints: top l., SS John Nepomuk, Thomas Aquinas, Anselm, Peter Canisius, and Paul (doctors of the Church and patrons of education); top r., SS Catherine, Bernard, Ildefonsus, and Luis Gonzaga (patrons of the University). In the lower level are (l.) Pope Clement XIV, Abp Francisco Antonio de Lorenzana y Buitrón (a good portrait of an intellectually brilliant and beneficent man), behind him, St Bonaventure; and (r.) King Charles III and Viceroy Bucareli. The work was commissioned by the Real y Pontificia Universidad, for a fee of 600 pesos, to commemorate the papal granting of the royal wish to have the invocation Mater Immaculata added to the Litany of Our Lady.

Baltasar de Echave Orio, Agony in the Garden. Attr. Echave Orio, St Diego of Alcalá. Alonso López de Herrera, Resurrection. José Juárez, Martyrdom of St Lawrence, the authorship disputed by some. Luis Lagarto, Annunciation; Adoration of the Shepherds; Assumption (1611), delicate watercolours on vellum. Cristóbal de Villalpando, St Francis; Marriage of Our Lady; Annunciation. Juan Correa, Musical Angels and the infant Christ, an enchanting piece. Nicolás Correa, St Rose with Our Lady and the infant Christ (1691), delightful in its freshness. Nicolás Rodríguez Juárez, St Christopher. Juan Rodríguez Juárez, St Stanislaus Kostka; St John of God; Our Lady of Mount Carmel (1708). José Mora, Last Supper. José de Ibarra, Our Lady of Mount Carmel of Guatemala. Miguel Cabrera, Our Lady of Mercy; St Bernard; St Anselm (1759). Anon. 18C, St Philip Neri. Miguel de Mendoza, Visitation (1739). José de Alzíbar, Holy Family at table.

R 6 (upper cloister). Anon. early 19C, Still Life, with a jug in the background inscribed NELSON and a profile which could represent the admiral. Antonio Pérez de Aguilar, Cupboard (1769). Hipólito de Rioja, Martyrdoms of St Lawrence, Catherine, and Ursula, three crowded canvases (1668). Baltasar de Echave Ibía, SS Paul and Antony in the wilderness; St Luke; St Mary Magdalen—grief reinforced by the rocky landscape and dramatic sky; Baptism of Christ; St John the Baptist, most expressive; St Matthew. Attr. Sebastián López de Arteaga, Madonna and Child. Juan Rodríguez Juárez, Adoration of the Kings; Assumption—copies (or drafts) of the paintings in the Altar de los Reyes—the artist himself lower l. in the first. José de Ibarra, Adoration of the Shepherds; St Catherine. Juan Patricio Morlete Ruiz, St Luis Gonzaga; Immaculate Conception; Christ scourged, consoled by angels; Heart of Mary; Heart of Jesus. Nicolás Enríquez, Intercession of Saints (1738). Rafael Jimeno y Planes, Crucifixion. Padre Manuel Jesuita, Immaculate Conception. José del Castillo, Virgen de Belén (1686).

R 7 (choir) contains some of Mexico's most famous portraits. Portraits of nuns: anon. 18C, Sor María Tomasa de San Gabriel; Sor María Clara Josefa (María Rosa Chamorro from Zacatecas), a Capuchiness; Sor Manuela de la Sangre de Cristo. Baltasar de Echave Ibía, Portrait of a lady praying (a vicereine ?). José de Alzíbar, Fr Manuel Bolea Sánchez de Tagle (1738–1813), Oratorian official of the Inquisition, renowned too for his charity. José Joaquín de la Vega, the painter Manuel Carcáneo (1783). Nicolás Rodríguez Juárez, Joaquín Fernández de Sta Cruz (1695), at the age of four. Juan Rodríguez Juárez, Self-portrait; Fernando de Alencastre Noroña y Silva, duque de Linares (1717), 36th viceroy. (His advice to his successor: 'treat everyone well, expect nothing from anyone, trust very few'.) José de Ibarra, Self-portrait. Rafael Jimeno y Planes, Jerónimo Antonio Gil; Manuel Tolsá—handsome, assured, richly dressed, the mirror of success. José María Vásquez, María Luisa Gonzaga Foncerrada y Labarrieta (1806), full of understated charm.

C. Dr Mora runs S to join Av. Juárez. To the r. is the **Museo Mural Diego Rivera** (Tues.–Sun, 10–6), containing his mural 'Sueño de una tarde dominical en la Alameda Central' (A Sunday afternoon's dream in the Alameda), an idiosyncratic vision of Mexican history.

It was painted for the lobby of the Hotel del Prado in 1947–48, but remained hidden from public view until 1956—for two causes of offence. First, one of the figures combined the features of Calles, Avila Camacho, and Miguel Alemán. Secondly, another figure, Ignacio Ramírez, held a paper with the words 'Dios no existe', a phrase eventually changed.

Among the figures on the l. are Cortés, his hand bloody, with executioners and victims of the Inquisition; Abp Juan de Zumárraga; and Viceroy Luis de Velasco II. To his r., Sor Juana Inés de la Cruz; to her r., Agustín de Iturbide, and, below him, Santa-Anna facing Winfield Scott and handing over keys representing Mexican territory. Above, on the r., Juárez holds the Constitution of 1857. Below appear Maximilian, Miramón, and Escobedo. Below Cortés is a group of porfirian personages, incl. José Yves Limantour. Towards the centre, on either side of belles of porfirian society, the Mexican poet Manuel Gutiérrez Najera (El duque Job) and the Cuban poet José Martí raise their hats. Next to Martí, Diego Rivera himself, aged ten; Frida Kahlo; the Calavera Catrina, an allegory of death figure; and its creator, Posada. Behind rises the balloon in which Joaquín de la Cantolla flew from Mexico to Puebla in 1903. In front, in yellow dress, the prostitute La Lupe contrasts with a veteran weighed down by medals. Above him, Porfirio Díaz. Below, on r., a policeman strikes an Indian who cannot afford the 25 centavos entry to the park. Middle r., revolutionary figures. Further r., the artist's second wife, Guadalupe Marín, with her two daughters; higher up, Huerta; above, a composite president with a New York banker and Luis María Martínez, abp of Mexico. Madero encourages the revolutionaries.

Almost opposite, at the corner with C. Revillagigedo, is the site of the *Hotel del Prado*, victim of the earthquake in 1985. On the opposite corner, the *Cine Variedades* (c 1885) was designed as a private house by Ignacio and Eusebio de la Hidalga.

Along C. Revillagigedo, the neoclassical portal, with fluted columns, and windows at No. 31 are a survival of the house (begun c 1785) of the architect Ignacio Castera. Its grounds occupied c 18,000 sq m. No. 44 is the former *Inspección de Policia* (1906–09), a neo-Gothic fantasy, with hints of an English castle, by Federico Mariscal.

Further W in Av. Juárez, the former church of **Corpus Christi** (1724), by Pedro de Arrieta, preserves a finely balanced façade of greatest charm, with a central relief of the Blessed Sacrament. This is flanked by barely perceptible estípite-like motifs. The triangular pediments are a Mannerist legacy.

The convent (demolished), for Poor Clares of the strict rule, to which the church belonged was founded by viceroy marqués de Valero (who bequeathed his heart to it) for noble Indian ladies. A descendant of Moctezuma, María Teresa de los Reyes Valeriano y Moctezuma, was professed in 1773. In 1867 they were turned out and the building became a school for deaf mutes. In 1925, during the fierce anti-Catholic persecution, the church was consigned to the short-lived and schismatic Iglesia Nacional Mexicana.

It has (since 1960) been adapted as the *Museo Nacional de Artes e Industrias Populares* (Mon.–Sat., 9–5), with, (upstairs) a display of Mexican handicrafts and a shop where they may be bought. Facing the entrance is a mural map of Mexican popular art by Miguel Covarrubias (1951).

On the E side of the Alameda stands the **Pal. de Bellas Artes**, an unfailingly eyecatching pile, originally destined to be the symbol of early 20C culture and wealth, and a National Theatre. But its building history and consequent mixture of styles have left it rather extemporaneous, removed from the overall Art Nouveau often claimed for it; indeed with more than a hint of classical balance.

The plans were drawn up by Adamo Boari, a native of Ferrara, and the builders, Milliken Brothers of Chicago, began construction in 1905 (on foundations by W.H. Birkmire of New York): a huge iron frame covered, front and sides, in cement and Carrara marble. Soon after the 40,000 ton grillage had been laid, however, foundations and building began to sink under their enormous weight—which caused great scandal. In 1916 work was suspended when Boari returned to Italy. It was resumed in 1919–23 under Antonio Muñoz who modified the plan, to enlarge the auditorium and dome. Not until 1932–34, under Federico Mariscal, was completion achieved.

EXTERIOR. The upper parts of the façades, influenced by the prevailing Paris Exhibition mood, with large layered central tympana, resemble a Byzantine church, the lower have a classical emphasis. A kind of Mexican art nouveau can be seen in the details; for instance, the heads of tigers, coyotes, and serpents (echoing a prehispanic tradition) in the arches of the ground-floor windows, and in the masks and festoons of the portico parapet. The sculpture on top of the dome and the mosaic of the principal arch are by Geza Marotti; Leonardo Bistolfi sculpted the figure and relief within it; the garlands, masks, and other motifs are by Gianetti Fiorenzo; the lateral façade sculptures by another Italian, Boni; the great dome (which Boari had wanted covered in glass) by Roberto Alvarez Espinosa. The corners of the plaza display the four Pegasi designed by Agustín Querol, cast by Boari in Italy, first placed at the corners of the Zócalo.

Performances by the famous Ballet Folklórico are the chief present-day attraction (advance booking advisable). The former museum collection has been largely dispersed to other museums.

The INTERIOR decoration shows Mariscal's specifically Mexican adaptation of art deco: geometrical patterns and landscape themes against dark Mexican marble; and outstanding work in metal and rare woods. The theatre's fireproof glass curtain, made by the Tiffany Studios of New York during the first building period, is enriched by a myriad opalescent crystals designed by Dr Atl as the Valley of Mexico and its two volcanoes.

The upper-floor rooms are given over to temporary art exhibitions, but permanently in place on first and second floors are murals, strongly revolutionary in theme, by Diego Rivera, José Clemente Orozco, and David Alfaro Siqueiros.

SECOND FLOOR. Diego Rivera's 'El hombre en el cruce de los caminos' (Man at the Crossroads; 1934), on the l. wall, is a replica of the work he had done for the RCA building at the Rockefeller Center in New York and which was erased because of its communist sympathy. Man the technician at the centre, aided by all refinements of science, controls the world, flanked by confronting communism and capitalism; beneath, the natural world. On the r. side of the N wall are three panels of a four-part mural (1936) for the banqueting hall of Alberto Pani's Hotel Reforma. Pani toned down Rivera's satire on contemporary political figures and caused a court case, after which he was ordered to make restitution. In 'La dictadura' the colossal head is a synthesis of Hitler, Mussolini, Roosevelt, and Hirohito. An officer with the head of a pig dances with a woman (Mexico) and steals fruit from her basket. 'La danza de los Huichilobos' shows Rivera's view of the sequel of armed intervention and its effect on Mexican culture. 'México folklórico y turístico' ridicules the pretentious foreigner who meddles in, without understanding, traditional celebrations (here at Yautepec). On r. (E) wall, 'Kátharsis' (1934) by Orozco is an explosion of trauma and violence which ensues when irreconcilable forces clash.

Siqueiros's murals are done in pyroxylin. On l. side of N wall, 'La nueva democracia' (1945; on celotex), a huge female bursting with superhuman force from a volcano. Diagonally opposite, backing on to the staircase, 'Monumento a Cuauhtémoc' (1951) has two parts: 'El tormento' shows Cuauhtémoc and the lord of Tlacopan undergoing the torments of fire, the former stoically, the latter begging for relief; 'La apoteosis de Cuauhtémoc' shows a resurrected hero killing the centaur, symbol of the Conquest.

Other paintings on this floor are 'La humanidad liberándose' (1963) by Jorge González Camarena; 'La piedad en el desierto' (1942) by Manuel Rodríguez Lozano; and 'Alegría', a fragment by Roberto Montenegro.

FIRST FLOOR. Two works by Rufino Tamayo: 'Nacimiento de la nacionalidad' (1952), in dark but soft colours and cubist-influenced; 'México de hoy' (1953), column and talud framing the flames which represent fusion.

7 South-East of the Alameda

Av. Juárez runs parallel with the S side of the Alameda as far as the crossing with Av. Lázaro Cárdenas (the former Av. San Juan de Letrán), the main façade of the Pal. de Bellas Artes on the l. On the SW corner of the crossing is the *Edificio La Nacional* (1930) by Manuel Ortiz Monasterio, Bernardo Calderón, and Luis Avila; functional and solid, its ten storeys were considered a daring departure. Stability was assured by the first use in Mexico of pilotes de control, piles driven through a deep concrete foundation. Opposite soars the **Torre Latinoamericana** (10am–11pm; fee), highest building in the city, its 44 storeys a triumph for the architects Manuel de la Colina and Augusto H. Alvarez, and the engineers Leonardo and Adolfo Zeevaert.

So carefully planned was the construction in 1950, using floating foundations, that the earthquakes of 1957 and 1985 left it undamaged. A lift takes visitors to the 44th floor, with a spectacular view (atmosphere permitting) of the city and valley of Mexico.

The continuation of Av. Juárez, AVENIDA MADERO, was formerly C. San Francisco. Opposite the Torre Latinoamericana is the *Edificio Guardiola* (1938), now offices of the Banco de México, by Carlos Obregón Santacilia, on the site of the late 17C house of the 2nd marqués de Sta Fe de Guardiola. Separated from it by C. Condesa is the incomparable **Casa del Conde del Valle de Orizaba** (more popularly known as **Casa de los Azulejos**), built probably c 1730 and entirely faced with glazed tiles.

It was a rebuilding of the seat of the Vivero family, condes since 1657, according to the wishes of the 5th condesa, who died in 1737. In 1881 it became headquarters of the Jockey Club; after 1914 of the Casa del Obrero Mundial, a revolutionary workers' group. Here in Dec. 1914 Francisco Villa and Emiliano Zapata celebrated their entry into the capital. In 1918 the building was acquired by Frank Sanborn (1870–1956), from Piqua (Ohio), who with his brother and sons established a restaurant, soda fountain, and general store here—quickly and lastingly in vogue.

The tiles, in shades of blue, yellow, and cream, cover the facings divided by ornate pilasters, door and window frames, cornices, and mouldings, all of soft grey stone. The tiled parapet, decorated with inverted mixtilinear arches and pinnacles, is broken by two niches, one at the corner, the other above the main doorway, both highlighted by elaborate scrolls.

Soon after 1900 the house was enlarged and given a S façade on Av. 5 de Mayo by Guillermo Heredia. He installed estípites, but lost the house's proper proportions.
The adapted interior preserves the patio whose octagonal pillars support a prolonged lintel. Tiles continue along the dado of the monumental stairway and round the upper gallery, with richly carved doorways. The bronze railings are original, probably from Asia. The stairway is setting for Orozco's privately commissioned mural 'Omnisciencia' (1925). In the centre, an indigenous female figure looking towards the light of inspiration represents Art; at her sides Strength and Intelligence, male and female figures, are held in check by two arms. The spiritual experience is beyond them both.

Opposite, on the S side of Av. Madero, is the entrance to the church of **San Francisco**, once part of the great convent set up where once had been the private zoo of Moctezuma II.
A small atrio faces the chapel of **La Valvanera** (dedicated in 1766 and built by the lay congregation of Our Lady of Valvanera) which forms the antechapel on the N side of the church. Its façade combines churrigueresque and anastyle. Ubiquitous lush decoration heightens the crowded and exotic effect. The statues and further decoration were removed c 1864. The interior preserves a contemporary main altarpiece.

Recent restoration uncovered in its S wall remains of the portal of one of the chapels (second station) of the Way of the Cross which began in the church next door and continued, after two

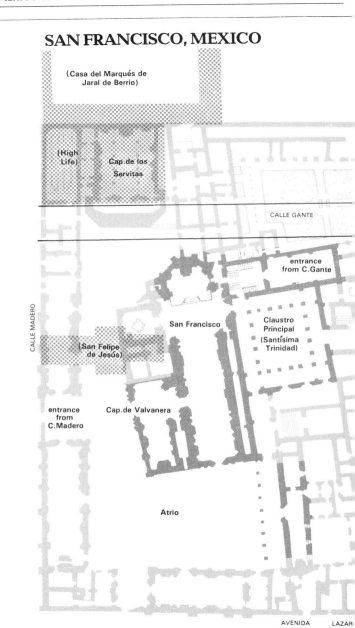

SAN FRANCISCO, MEXICO

(Casa del Marqués de Jaral de Berrio)

(High Life)

Cap. de los Servitas

CALLE GANTE

entrance from C. Gante

CALLE MADERO

San Francisco

Claustro Principal (Santísima Trinidad)

(San Felipe de Jesús)

entrance from C. Madero

Cap. de Valvanera

Atrio

AVENIDA   LAZAR

Buildings in, or next to, convent area.

Surviving buildings.

Area of former convent.

C. INDEPENDENCIA
(C. 16 DE SEPTIEMBRE)

0 ————————— 30 metres

←N—

C. VENUSTIANO CARRANZA

area of former
garden, converted
into Hotel del Jardín

Cap.
de
San Antonio

CARDENAS

more in the atrio, to end at the convent of San Diego. This chapel was partially destroyed to make way for the Valvanera chapel; the others completely in 1825–61.

A baroque portal leads into the single-nave church (1710–16; architect Diego de los Santos, succeeded after 1712 by Feliciano Cabello), much interfered with. The high altarpiece (early 20C) is overladen and curves with the apse.

The first permanent church on the American mainland, with four resident friars, was built in 1525 and finally demolished in 1590. A grander one was built in the 1590s; in turn demolished.

In the atrio was set up **San José de los Naturales**, the first open chapel, most original of the historical buildings of New Spain, project of the influential Fray Pedro de Gante (c 1480–1572; Peeter van der Moere), a Flemish lay brother of imperial blood (either uncle or great-uncle to Charles V). In its earliest form it was built and maintained by the Indians (naturales) and much loved by them. By c 1562 it was described as 'majestic [solemne]': seven naves with seven altars, laid out like a mosque; c 46m wide, 25m deep, 6m high. From the 17C it was allowed to fall into ruin. Its site is now occupied by High Life (see below). Also off the atrio Fray Pedro founded what was to become the best-known convent school in New Spain, for a thousand Indian boys.

By the 18C convent and dependencies covered a huge area, bordered by today's Avs Madero, Lázaro Cárdenas, Venustiano Carranza (N, W, and S), and a line drawn between Cs Gante and Bolívar (E).

In Jan. 1624 viceroy marqués de Gelves, hounded by a murderous mob, found sanctuary in San Francisco. On 27 Oct. 1821 the first solemn Te Deum to celebrate Mexican Independence was sung in the church; exactly 17 years later Iturbide's funeral was held in it. 'I was absolutely lost amidst its multiplicity of passages and labyrinths, nor could I find my way to return until conducted by one of the courteous Padres who had observed my dilemma', wrote William Bullock in 1823. In 1856 the convent was suppressed and its dismemberment began, despite protests by various liberals. In 1868 the church was sold to one Henry C. Riley (Catholic Church of Our Lord Jesus Christ) for a revival of the Mozarabic liturgy. In 1940 the Franciscans returned and started renovation. At the corner of Avs Lázaro Cárdenas and Venustiano Carranza, a modern building incorporates the former 17C chapel of *San Antonio*, its dome visible from the street.

Flanking San Francisco on the E is the church of **San Felipe de Jesús** (1886–97), a neo-Romanesque creation by Emilio Dondé. The interior (paintings by Bartolomé Galloti) is neo-byzantine.

It occupies the site of two chapels from the convent of San Francisco: Tercera Orden and Nuestra Señora de Aranzazu. It commemorates Mexico's first native martyr, beatified in 1627 and canonized in 1862, Felipe de las Casas (b. 1572). On his way back from Manila to Mexico to be ordained as a discalced Franciscan a storm drove his ship on to the Japanese coast. With a company of Jesuits, other religious, and Japanese catechists he was crucified at Nagasaki on 5 Feb. 1597. After his proclamation as patron of Mexico in 1629, his mother was said to have been so overcome by the attention paid her by the viceroy and the honour done to her son that she died of joy.

Beyond San Felipe we turn r. into C. Gante. At No. 5 is the Methodist church of *Santísima Trinidad*, in fact part of the former cloister of San Francisco, in grey chiluca stone, now covered by metal and glass roofing.

The lower cloister dates mainly from a rebuilding in 1649; the upper, by Juan Antonio de la Cruz and his son Antonio de Rojas, from c 1701–02.

The wealth of arch, column, and frieze decoration is exceptional. In the lower storey, slightly swelling, smooth Tuscan columns; in the upper, slimmer columns, enveloped in their lower part by delicate vegetal motifs, and topped by complex composite capitals. The lower arches show almohadilla carving, with jutting keystones in tightly curled relief. The elaborate spandrels include exotically carved corbels. The frieze carries triglyphs and metopes. Five layers of contrasting moulding compose the upper arches, with even richer spandrels: in their centres, busts of cherubim whose wings disintegrate in an eddy of leafy and vegetal relief. A flowery frieze undulates above.

In 1868 Giuseppe Chiarini opened a circus here, 'Gran Salón de Chiarini', succeeded by the Teatro Variedades. In 1873 the cloister was sold to the Episcopal Methodist church of New York.

On the opposite corner of Av. Madero and C. Gante the *High Life* building (1922), by Silvio Contri, occupies the site of San José de los Naturales. Next door is the **Casa del Marqués de Jaral de Berrio (Hotel de Iturbide;** 1779–c 1785), most sumptuous of casas señoriales, by Francisco Guerrero y Torres; finished by Agustín Durán, his brother-in-law.

It was commissioned by Miguel de Berrio y Saldívar, marqués de Jaral de Berrio, husband of Ana María de la Campa y Cos, condesa de San Mateo de Valparaíso, and progressed amid a bitter family dispute. The house was destined for their only child, married to a Palermitan, Pedro de Moncada, marqués de Villafont, better known as the marqués de Moncada. The Moncadas, whose public rows kept contemporary society agog, were also notorious spend-thrifts. The widowed condesa tried in vain to keep her husband's estate intact and to exclude her son-in-law. In 1821 Juan de Moncada, 2nd marqués de Jaral de Berrio, put the house at Iturbide's disposal, who lived here until his abdication in 1823. On 21 July 1822, after their coronation, the emperor and empress tossed specially minted coins from the balcony to the delighted crowd below. In 1855 a new owner, Germán Landa, reopened it as a luxury hotel. By 1872 it boasted the finest restaurant in Mexico, run by Carlos Recamier, where one dined amid artificial waterfalls, flowers, and caged songbirds 'in an ecstasy of champagne'. In 1898 Emilio Dondé modernized it, added a fourth gallery to the main patio, and raised another storey. The hotel closed in 1928 and in 1969 the building was bought by Banamex, which has restored it to the original design. Temporary exhibitions, from Banamex's own art collections, are held here.

It has three storeys, a mezzanine separating the ground floor and the high first floor, the top storey composed of two wide tower-like structures, unusually crenellated, at the E and W corners, joined by a five-arched gallery. The portal, reaching through the frieze to the jutting cornice and first-floor balcony, is framed by exuberantly carved pilasters which seem to set off similar supports beneath the towers and inspire the opulent window frames. Above the doorway two atlantes stand on exaggerated scrolls either side of a beautifully detailed valence-type relief, repeated beneath the mezzanine windows. Throughout the façade run variations of a meander pattern, done with such mastery that it never becomes monotonous. The very richness of the relief contrasts with the smooth tezontle panels studded with large medallions on the E and W sides, and small delicately carved vegetal and figural badge motifs towards the centre.

The patio shows a Sicilian influence, the lower arches, on slender columns with sturdy square bases, daringly high. The meander pattern is repeated in jambs and window frames, and the spandrel medallions and gargoyles have a Renaissance air. The chapel, with a fine portal and interior dome, is reached from the upper gallery.

Nos. 27–33 Av. Madero, at the corner with C. Bolívar, are the **Casa Borda**, finished probably in 1775, town house of José de la Borda (1699–1778). Only the exterior remains, though the principal portal has disappeared.

Two more storeys in 18C style were added facing Av. Madero in the early 20C, which spoil the effect. From Aug. 1906 it housed the *Salón Rojo*, Mexico's first cinema.

Opposite, at No. 32, is the *Banco Serfín*, which contains a mural, 'Alegoría de la Producción' (1933), by Fermín Revueltas. No. 30, next door, is the **Hotel Ritz** (1927), by Francisco Martínez Gallardo.

The extension, at 20 C. Bolívar, dates from 1936.—In the bar is a colourful mural (1937) by Miguel Covarrubias, showing Mexicans and US visitors enjoying a tranquil Sun. afternoon at Xochimilco.

Soon after, Av. Madero is crossed by C. Motolinía. No. 39 is the **Casa del Marqués del Prado Alegre**, another 18C casa señorial, former residence of Francisco Fernández de Tejada y Arteaga, marqués del Prado Alegre from 1771 and alcalde of the city. Its ornate portal and crenellations are arresting preservations. The handsome building opposite, *La Perla* (c 1900–02), at the NE corner of Av. Madero and C. Motolinía, with elevated ground floor and huge windows, was designed as a jewellery store by Hugo Dorner and Luis Bacmeister.

Av. Madero next reaches C. Isabel la Católica. On the NW corner is the church of **La Profesa** (1720), a masterwork of classically based baroque. It is a monument of great importance, full of art treasures, especially paintings by Mexican masters of the 17–19C. Permission to view those not in the church itself should be sought in advance.

This, the main Jesuit church in the city, was first built in 1597–1610. Pedro de Arrieta's rebuilding, though keeping original interior elements, was done at a cost of 150,000 pesos, paid for by Gertrudis de la Peña, marquesa de las Torres de Rada. In 1771 the Oratorians were put in possession, with a rededication to San José el Real, a name which never stuck. In 1820, in an adjoining house for retreats, took place the juntas de la Profesa—meetings of conservatives, headed by Matías Monteagudo, provost of the Congregation—to distance Mexico from the liberal coup in Spain and to agitate for Iturbide as army chief, a situation from which he took maximum advantage. The church avoided suppression in 1861, but the house was largely demolished after 1862 to make way for Av. 5 de Mayo.

Powerful buttresses punctuate the EXTERIOR, covered in tezontle. The towers enclose the E façade and blend well with it. The lowest storey carries statues of SS Barbara and Gertrude between fluted columns with Corinthian capitals; the doorway arch has a hint of the ogee and is topped by clustering relief. The middle-storey columns, enclosing statues of SS John the Baptist and Louis IX, are richer, their lower thirds encrusted with succulent foliage and enclosing reliefs of a horseman jumping a bridge, a motto above: 'Por pasar la puente me puse a la muerte' (to cross the bridge I put myself to death)—a reference to a benefactor, José de la Puente y Peña, marqués de Villapuente. In the middle of the broad band containing rectangular bases, loaded with more relief, for the columns appears the Oratorian badge. The central relief (17C) shows a vision of Christ carrying the Cross to St Ignatius, witnessed by God the Father and angel musicians. The statues of SS Joseph and Paul are late 18C additions. In its lower storey the S doorway bears signs of the church's earlier, classical, period. In the keystone of the arch, the infant Christ holds the world in his hands. The broken pediment of the harmonious upper storey incorporates an Oratorian shield. The niche shelters St Ignatius; the keystone, Our Lady of Sorrows, her expression dramatic.

The INTERIOR preserves its original basilical plan: nave, wide aisles, high crossing, sustained by clustered columns, Gothic in detail. The magnificently proportioned high altar (c 1800) is by Tolsá, its round tabernacle with a bell-like top and the upper storey fastidiously ornamented with statuary, garlands, and urns. The lower-storey statues, inferior pieces, are by Pedro Patiño Ixtolinque. By the E door are two paintings: Our Lady of the Rosary (l.), rich in brocades and a profusion of pearls, with flower arrangements in the bottom corners, by Cristóbal de Villalpando; Baltasar de Echave Orio, Pentecost, with fine detail.

R. (N) AISLE. *Altar del Carmen*. Señor de la Columna (17C Mexican), in wood. *Altar de la Purísima Concepción*. Statue by Tolsá, exquisite, combining classical purity and baroque drapery. *Altar de Guadalupe*. Painting by Andrés López (1805); the four paintings of Scenes from the Life of Christ (Rescuing Peter, Storm on the Lake, Transfiguration, Ascension—the latter two dated 1720) are by Juan Rodríguez Juárez. *Altar de San José*. Four paintings (1696) of apostles by Nicolás Rodríguez Juárez, part of a series on copperplate, the rest in the sacristy; José Juárez, Crucifixion, Christ and the two thieves dramatic against the dark background. At W end, *Altar de Nuestra Señora de los Dolores*, attr. Tolsá. 17C Crucifixion in wood; Tolsá, Our Lady of Sorrows—reputed a likeness of María Ignacia Rodríguez de Velasco y Osorio Barba (La Güera Rodríguez; 1778–1850), considered the greatest beauty of her day and called by Mathieu de Fossey 'la Ninon de Lenclos de son epoque'; 18C statues of SS Mary Magdalen and John.

L. (S) AISLE. Cristo del Consuelo, an expressive 17C Crucifixion in wood. At W end, *Altar de Nuestra Señora de las Nieves* (Snows). 18C statues of Our Lady and of St Ignatius and Stanislaus; Juan Correa, St Luke painting Our Lady (incorporating a late 16C Italian painting of the Virgin, a reproduction of the Evangelist's supposed likeness of her in S. Maria Maggiore in Rome, copies of which were distributed by St Francis Borgia to Jesuit colleges abroad).

The Stations of the Cross are later 18C paintings, with skilled foreshortening and vigorous figures.
To the r. of the Altar of Our Lady of Sorrows a door leads into the dependencies of the church and the remaining part of the Oratorian house, which contain the bulk of the art collection.

The antesacristy leads into the SACRISTY, preserving a 17C wooden partition and containing 17–18C furniture, incl. cabinets inlaid with ivory and tortoise-shell. The polychrome busts of Our Lady of Sorrows and Christ crowned with thorns are by the 18C Spanish sculptor Juan de Mena. Miguel Cabrera, Annunciation; Marriage of Our Lady. Nicolás Rodríguez Juárez, Heads of apostles (see above). CAP. DE GUADALUPE. Nicolás Rodríguez Juárez, Scenes from the Life of St Joseph (especially the Dream and the Marriage). Francisco Martínez, Annunciation; Visitation. Anon. 18C, Scenes from the Life of SS Anne and Joachim. On first floor: ROOM 1 (Sala Jesuita). Alonso López de Herrera, St Francis Borgia. Anon. late 17C, Death of St Francis Xavier in China (note the weeping disciple). Francisco Martínez, Our Lady's Patronage of the Jesuits. Juan Rodríguez Juárez, Fr Juan Rodríguez de la Parra, SJ. Cabrera, SS Ignatius and Francis Xavier before Our Lady; Bl. Alonso Rodríguez. Andrés López, Death of St Joseph (1803). Anon. 18C, Martyrdom of Jesuits in Japan. Nicolás Enríquez, St Ignatius in retirement at Manresa (1762). R. 2 (Sala Newman). Portraits of founders and provosts of the Oratory. Antonio de Torres, Scenes from the Life of St Philip Neri. José de Alzíbar, St Joseph's Patronage of the Oratorians, incl. portraits of Viceroy Bucareli and Abp Núñez de Haro y Peralta (c 1775). R. 3 (Library). Nicolás Rodríguez Juárez, Abp Aguiar y Seijas (1682–98), dramatic and enigmatic, in pontificals and black chasuble. José de Alzíbar, portraits of Charles III; Viceroy Bucareli; Juan José de Eguiara y Eguren (1696–1763), bibliographer, theologian, canon of the Cathedral.
R. 4 (Sala Tres Siglos) contains 17–19C paintings. Cristóbal de Villalpando, Vision of St Teresa (in which Our Lady and St Joseph cover her in a white veil and give her also a collar of gold and precious stones), intensely baroque; St Teresa writing; St Jerome; four Scenes from the Life of Joseph (Joseph and his Brethren, Dying Jacob blesses Joseph's sons, Joseph in Pharoah's Chariot, Marriage of Joseph), the last sumptuous, in golden brown, showing the artist's facility in representing jewels and rich fabrics; Christ, St Peter, and the Eucharist (note the expressive hands); Ecce Homo (c 1680–90), large and commanding; Abp Aguiar y Seijas, the artist's only known portrait. Juan Correa, St Francis; St Dominic. Nicolás Rodríguez Juárez, Isaiah (1690). Antonio Rodríguez, Elijah. Juan Rodríguez Juárez, St Teresa transfixed (1692); St Raphael and Tobias. Cabrera, Agony in the Garden; Crucifixion (both 1761). Andrés de Islas, Scourging of Christ; Christ carrying the Cross (1762), with a haunting quality; Way of the Cross. José Miranda, St Emigdius (1768). Nicolás Enríquez, Christ mocked (1762). Andrés López, Our Lady of the Dawn. Diego de Cuentas, the Four Evangelists (1720).

Among anon. 18C works are two (suitably gruesome where necessary) for Indian consumption—Pains of Hell and Good and Bad Confession.

At 17 C. Isabel la Católica, the *Hotel Gillow* (1869; by Ramón Rodríguez Arangoity, altered since, with art deco touches) once formed part of the vast inheritance of Eulogio Gregorio Gillow (1841–1922), abp of Oaxaca, son of the Lancastrian Catholic Thomas Gillow and María Zavalza y Gutiérrez, marquesa de Selva Nevada. Opposite the E door of La Profesa, on the NE corner of Av. Madero and C. Isabel la Católica, the portentously grand *La Mexicana* building

(1906) by Genaro Alcorta occupies the site of the *Café la Concordia*, favourite resort of 19C high society.

Here in 1881 Thomas Brocklehurst would step across the street from his rooms in the Hotel Gillow to order 'a little private dinner' in the evening and consume 'a cup of chocolate and a large spongy bun' before his early morning ride.

At the SE corner of the crossing is the former **Joyería la Esmeralda** (1890; now the *Banca Cremi*), by J. Francisco Serrano and Eleuterio Méndez, one of the first iron-built edifices (iron and reinforced concrete) in Mexico. A grand jewellery establishment, with its sumptuous mirror-like dormers abounding with relief completing the changes in window styles, venturesome cornice cum balcony, and Mansard roof, it created a delighted stir among contemporaries. One block further E, where C. Palma and Av. Madero cross, on the NW corner is another late 19C example of a multi-storey metal-structure building in eclectic style (with neoclassical garlands), by Manuel Francisco Alvarez; opposite (SE corner) is the *Ciudad de Londres* (1900) by Dorner and Bacmeister.

No. 35 in C. Palma (N), though with a later third floor added, is a good example of an 18C house, preserving a palm motif on its façade. Beyond Av. 5 de Mayo the street was once the C. Alcaicería, named after the old silk market, between it and C. Isabel la Católica. Nos. 6, 12, and 14 in the latter and 21 in the former incorporate remains of the market buildings. The final stretch of Av. Madero beyond La Profesa was the old C. Plateros (silversmiths).

We turn r. into C. Isabel la Católica. On the r., No. 31 is the **Casino Español** (1903) by the Spanish architect Emilio González del Campo. Built in the grand manner, the exterior with a sumptuously relieved portal panel, its interior a lavish mixture of classicizing and neo-baroque.

Further down on the l. No. 30 is the **Casa de los Condes de Miravalle** (now the *Edificio Jardín*), perhaps the oldest surviving noble house in the city, with doorways and windows of rusticated stone, but altered in the 19C and since. The patio still has charm, despite its filled-in arches.

It dates from the late 17C, probably a combining of several houses for Alonso Dávalos y Bracamonte, created conde de Miravalle in 1690. In 1846 it housed the Ateneo Mexicano, founded by Angel Calderón de la Barca, first Spanish minister to the Mexican republic and husband of Fanny. From the late 1840s until 1930 it was the Hotel del Bazar, launched by Estanislao Lanit, who advertised, among other refinements, 'a superb table service of glass and porcelain; breakfasts will be served until noon; waiters will wear uniforms for better cleanliness'. Here, on 17 June 1854, the great German soprano Henriette Sontag died of cholera at the age of 49. Since 1930 the lower storey has been altered to accommodate shop windows. Here lived Francisco Sergio Iturbe, patron of arts and letters, who in 1942 commissioned the mural, on the staircase wall at the E end of the principal patio, by Manuel Rodríguez Lozano. Integrated into the composition is the window, on whose sill rests a wooden sculpture by Mardonio Magaña, 'Los dos comrades', contemporary with the mural. This, entitled 'Holocausto', shows the body of a man in the form of an arch curving round the window, attended by sorrowing women.

To the r., at the NW corner of the crossing with Av. 16 de Septiembre (Nos 56–60), is the former *Casa Boker* (1898–1900), designed by the US partnership Lemos and Cordes and built, using iron and reinforced concrete, by Gonzalo Garita as a hardware store for the German Robert Boker.

At the corner of Av. 16 de Septiembre and C. Palma (to the E) is the **Bella Unión**, handsome and unfussy, built by José Besozzi in 1840, often wrongly called the first brick building in Mexico. The first floor is enhanced by balconies and medallion reliefs of the heroes of Independence; the top floor is a later addition.

Following C. Isabel la Católica further S we come to No. 44 (l.), on the corner with Av. Venustiano Carranza, the **Casa de los Condes de San Mateo de Valparaíso** (1769–72), of unsurpassed and imaginative dignity, by Guerrero y Torres.

It was commissioned by the condesa de San Mateo de Valparaíso and her husband (see above). In 1882 the last private owner sold the house to the Banco Nacional Mexicano, later Banco Nacional de México, whose headquarters it has remained to this day. Adaptations were made in the late 19C by Ignacio de la Hidalga.

The EXTERIOR chiluca stonework, contrasting with the tezontle panels, is a marvel of vigour and luxuriant relief. The pilasters, framed by wavy carving, enclose sunken elongated rectangles. The main portal panel is most delicately done. Above the unusually flat arch two cherubic atlantes perched on frail volutes hold the shield (for the family coat-of-arms), enclosed by lovely vegetal relief. The lower-storey cornice is bold enough; that of the upper storey runs above a beautiful frieze punctuated by angelic corbels supporting the gargoyles. Above, ornate finials are placed at intervals along the parapet and at the angles of the tower—its niche a quintessence of decorative detail.

The INTERIOR (adm. not always allowed) decoration is just as sumptuous. The wide, low-slung spanning and crossing arches of the lower storey of the main patio create an unconfined and daring effect. A massive, exceptionally carved, portal gives on to the unique, double-ramp staircase, once used by servants on the one hand and owners and guests on the other, without the two having to meet. A lovely cupola crowns it, as does another, smaller, the former chapel next door, now adapted for the elevator. Rustic paintings (late 18C) decorate window embrasures.

Opposite, beyond the junction with C. Palma, at No. 73 is the **Casa de los Condes de San Bartolomé de Xala** (1763–64), by Lorenzo Rodríguez, a two-storey house in tezontle, with stone embellishments. It has been put to quite inappropriate uses.

It was built for Manuel Rodríguez Sáenz de Pedroso, created conde in 1749, who wanted no expense spared. His son Antonio, 2nd conde, became a priest after widowhood in 1784. The marriage of Antonio's daughter María Josefa (3rd condesa) to Pedro Ramón Romero de Terreros, 2nd conde de Regla (son of the mining magnate), took place here in 1780, amid much ostentation.

The mauled EXTERIOR repays examination for the beauty of its relief, especially the main doorway and the former cochera (carriage entrance; l.), framed by solid pilasters which reach to the elaborate cornice above the mezzanine. Note the lambrequin motifs at their tops, the strapwork above the ornate lintels, and the delicate undulations framing the mezzanine windows: all hallmarks of the period. These contrast with the startling canopied frames of the upper-floor windows and the vigorous almohadilla frieze. The parapet is probably of later date.

The badly neglected INTERIOR still preserves blue and white azulejos on what was once the staircase of honour and on the smaller staircase. In the former second patio a charming, original fountain survives. No. 67, next door, is another 18C house.

At the SW corner of the junction of C. Isabel la Católica and Av. Venustiano Carranza is the main building of the **Nacional Financiera** (1966), Mexico's development bank, by Ramón Marcos Noriega. The wrought-iron work facing C. Isabel la Católica is by Herbert Hoffmann; the interior stained glass by Kitzia Hoffmann. Further W in Av. Venustiano Carranza, No. 57 is a two-storey 18C house (*Casa del Conde de la Cadena*), now the *Banco Mercantil*. On the first floor is the central section (all that remains) of a mural triptych, 'La industria, la banca, y el comercio' (1945), by Jorge González Camarena. No. 49 is a much-altered late 18C residence, *Casa del Marqués de Selva Nevada*. It retains its old stone window frames and doorways.

We continue W to the junction with C. Bolívar, with a Lebanese-style clock (*Reloj turco*; 1910), by G.M. Oropeza, donated by the Turkish community, in front of the *Bancomer* building (1964), on the site of the house where the 15-year-old Simón Bolívar stayed in Feb.–March 1799 and the house of Porfirio

Díaz. Facing it, and running the whole block between Avs 16 de Septiembre and Venustiano Carranza, is the former **Colegio de Niñas**.

The *Colegio de Nuestra Señora de la Caridad* was founded in the 1540s to provide a basic education and refuge for poor mestizas. Spaniards gradually excluded mestizas. The tone became more aristocratic, with a regimen like that of a nunnery. In 1682, Isabel Ribero, a seasoned pupil, asked permission to attend the profession of her niece as a nun in the convent of La Concepción: 'she was given the said permission, taking into consideration that for more than forty years she has never left the College; but on the strict understanding that she must be back before five in the afternoon'. In 1862 it was closed. In 1909 the reconditioned building reopened as the *Teatro Colón*, with a performance of Bizet's 'Carmen'. From the 1920s it served as a cinema and in 1950 returned to use as theatre, until its ruinous state forced closure a few years later.—In the late 19C the church was assigned to the French community and renamed *Nuestra Señora de Lourdes*.

The church dates from a rebuilding by José Eduardo de Herrera, finished in 1744, and from further changes in 1846–47 by Lorenzo de la Hidalga. The façade was discreetly restored c 1930–40.

EXTERIOR. The façade, facing E, has two similarly designed portals. On both sides are pairs of estípites, truncated during De la Hidalga's reform. Above the estípites of the l. portal are reliefs of SS Joachim and Anne with the child Mary; above those of the r. portal, reliefs of SS Peter and Paul. The large reliefs above show Visitation (l.) and Baptism of Christ (r.). The single-nave INTERIOR, producing a suave effect even though early 20C stained-glass deprives it of light, is given a unity by the high altarpiece and six side altarpieces, all by De la Hidalga. Their marble, colour, and gilding, as well as the Italian-style grotesques, make a baroque-inspired ensemble. The high-altar relief of the Visitation is a 17C survival.

The college itself, as built by Claudio de Arciniega after 1570 and partly rebuilt by Ildefonso de Iniesta Bejarano y Durán in 1768, but following the old style, was altered out of all proportion at the turn of the century: its clean historic lines, simple windows high up, and arcade, tortured into a hybrid, Franco-Italian style.

To the W, at the SE corner of Av. 16 de Septiembre and C. Gante, is the imposing *Banco Mexicano Somex* (early 1900s) by José Luis Cuevas. No. 10 Av. 16 de Septiembre, opposite, is the *Restaurante Prendes*, a traditional meeting place of politicians and intellectuals.

Diagonally opposite the former college is the erstwhile building of the *Banco de Londres y de México* (1910–12) by Miguel Angel de Quevedo, now the *Banco Serfín*, though still carrying the BLM monogram.

No. 31 Av. Venustiano Carranza, beyond the C. Bolívar turning, is a remodelled 18C house. Further along, at No. 25, is the *Nacional Financiera* building (1944–45) by Manuel Ortiz Monasterio and Luis Avila. On the first floor is a mural, 'Jugando con luces' (1949), by Leopoldo Méndez, to celebrate Mexican industrial development. C. Bolívar runs S to Av. Uruguay. On the SW corner, at 31 Av. Uruguay, is the *Casa de los Marqueses de Uluapa*, another 18C casa señorial, though modified by time. Further E, at 45 Av. Uruguay, is the building designed for the *Bancos Agrícola e Hipotecario y Mutualista* (1904) by Nicolás and Federico Mariscal.

Following C. Bolívar S and turning l. into Av. El Salvador we reach the former headquarters of the Oratorians and their two churches.

In 1751 Ildefonso de Iniesta Bejarano y Durán was commissioned to design a new church 'so exquisite in structure and execution that it will inspire the envy of art, the despair of generosity, and the admiration of Solomon's temple', provided with 'all permissible ornaments and refinements where with dignity and decorum the retables will be installed ... accompanied by those daring profusions which are a feature of the [Mexican churrigueresque] style'. This to replace an existing church (1687; largely destroyed by earthquake in 1768). In 1771 the Oratorians moved to La Profesa. The unfinished church was left forlorn. In 1875 it was enveloped in the *Teatro Arbeu*, the incomplete nave forming part of the auditorium. The theatre was closed in 1954 and a garage succeeded it. In 1969 the Secretaría de Hacienda began rescue operations to tear away the accretions and restore the beauty of the original.

No. 47 is the entrance to the former Oratorian house, with a two-storey cloister (early 18C). No. 49 is the doorway to **San Felipe el Viejo** (1687), recessed within an arch; its lower storey an echo of classicism; the upper charmingly and delicately baroque, the relief of St Philip Neri, inspired by the Holy Ghost and attended by cherubs, protecting members of the Congregation in an unusually elaborate frame. Nos. 51–55 include the façade of **San Felipe el Nuevo**, a major work of the churrigueresque. It is framed by plain pilasters on either side and a curvetting cornice above. Flanking the doorway, pairs of estípites are continued by smaller tentative versions above the cornice. In the entrecalles are ornamental niche pilasters, the medallions containing images of SS Peter and Paul. Above the doorway is a beautiful relief of the Baptism of Christ flanked by typically Mexican angel atlantes. Above the jagged pediment is a framed relief of the Holy Ghost. Everywhere relief detail, achieved with utmost delicacy, is staggering: note especially the bands of floral and vegetal motifs descending on either side of the large upper niche.

Since 1970 the church has housed the reading room of the *Biblioteca Miguel Lerdo de Tejada* of the Secretaría de Hacienda, concentrating on economics. The walls are covered with bright murals: that on the S wall, by the Russian-Mexican artist Vlady, depicts the Freudian revolution.

No. 59 Av. El Salvador, still with a fine exterior, the **Casa del Conde de Regla**, was once home of the richest man in New Spain, Pedro Romero de Terreros (1710–81), created conde de Regla in 1769 (see Rte 62). The house was unostentatious in his lifetime and the interior later suffered from being converted into a tenement and rebuilt in 1928. It was then bought for restoration by the Comisión Nacional Bancaria y de Seguros y Fianzas.

Beyond this house C. Isabel la Católica soon crosses Av. El Salvador. Bounded by the latter on the S, C. Isabel la Católica on the W, and Av. Uruguay on the N is the former church and convent of **San Agustín** (1677–97), the work of Fray Diego de Valverde.

The Augustinians' first church and convent were sumptuously built, mostly during 1541–87. Charles V made 102,000 pesos available; doña Isabel de Moctezuma, daughter of Moctezuma II, gave 'con tanta largueza'. After the auto de fe of 1574 Miles Philips and William Lowe, survivors from Hawkins's fleet, were sentenced to serve as overseers of the Indian workmen. (The friars treated them well and commiserated with them on their sufferings. Philips liked and admired his Indian charges and learned Náhuatl.) A fire in Dec. 1676 gutted the old church, the hero of the hour being Juan de Chavarría, who rescued the Blessed Sacrament from the flames. In 1859 the convent was closed and the church dismantled. The former fell into utter neglect. The atrio became 'a cesspool which fouled the centre of the city'. During 1868–82 the church was converted into the *Biblioteca Nacional* by Vicente Heredia and Eleuterio Méndez, who did their best to hide the building's ecclesiastical origins. Today the church is used as reading rooms and can be adapted as a concert hall.

The N façade, rebuilt by Heredia, faces on to Av. Uruguay. The magnificently and stylishly framed central relief shows St Augustine, his left hand sustaining the Church, sheltering members of his Order under his cloak, held up by angels. Underfoot are discomfited Eastern heretics. It is probably all that survives of 16C work by Claudio de Arciniega.

Heredia added the third storey, with two caryatids (one on either side of the octagonal choir window), two enormous volutes, and curved pediment to sustain a flagpole. The vast N and W windows are also his impositions, as are the urns around the parapet—the whole acquiring a bulky look, not helped by the removal of the E and W towers. Busts of distinguished Mexicans (late 19C embellishments) rest on the columns of the atrio wall. The statue of Humboldt was a gift from Germany in 1910.

The adjoining *Cap. de la Tercera Orden* escaped alteration, but the lower part of its original façade was covered after 1903, when it became headquarters of the night watch. At 74–76 Av. El Salvador is the entrance to the *Cap. de San Agustín*, reopened for worship in 1957, and the cloisters.

The INTERIOR, once full of altarpieces and paintings, was oppressively altered in the 1870s: transepts and choir closed up; semicircular window in the sanctuary (to provide badly needed light); artificial vaulting; statues, busts (St Paul, Dante, Descartes, Voltaire, Humboldt, etc.), and medallions to promote a scholarly atmosphere.

No. 81, with a medallion enclosing an image of Our Lady of Guadalupe above the door, is the former Augustinian novitiate, once connected with the convent by a bridge across the street, demolished in 1828.

No. 68 Av. Uruguay, opposite San Agustín, is the former *Bolsa de Valores* (Stock Exchange), built in 1955 to the designs of Enrique de la Mora and Fernando López Carmona. The doubly curved vault of the main hall (second floor) is by Félix Candela. No. 69, E of the front of San Agustín, is the *Hotel Monte Carlo*, where D.H. Lawrence stayed in 1923–24. 'a little Italian place— we pay only 4 pesos a day each ... I like it very much'.

Continuing S on C. Isabel la Católica, the second turning r., C. Regina, leads to a plaza facing the church of **Regina Coeli** (more popularly *La Regina*), largely rebuilt by Miguel Custodio Durán.

The Conceptionist convent, founded in 1573, was rebuilt in 1656; the new church opened in 1731. In 1867 the nuns were finally expelled. The convent was saved from ruination by the will of María Concepción Béistegui (d. 1873) who left funds for the adapted premises to be used as a hospital, opened in 1886.

EXTERIOR. The main (N) portal, more Mannerist than baroque, is flanked by fluted and engaged pilasters; spandrels and frieze showing delicate vegetal relief. The upper storey encloses a delightful relief, in an eared frame, of the Birth of Our Lady, with angels holding a canopy over SS Anne and Joachim. The wavy pilasters and flame-like outer finials are a hallmark of Custodio Durán. More relief in the frieze and in the grooved broken pediment completes the harmonious whole. The smaller portal is a fainter version. Discreet buttresses and two cupolas (one above the crossing, the other above the side chapel) reinforce an aspect of solidity.

INTERIOR. Until the Reform, the walls, vaulting, and cupola were covered in gilded ornamentation. The carved wooden furniture formed a magnificent set. Today only the windbreaks and one or two confessionals remain. Off the S aisle is the CAP. DE LA PURISIMA CONCEPCION, bequeathed by Buenaventura de Medina Picazo (d. 1729) and finished by Custodio Durán in 1733. The undulating pilasters of the portal seem to inspire the rippling broken pediment. Note the polychrome statue of the benefactor. The early churrigueresque main altarpiece holds five paintings of scenes from the life of Our Lady (possibly the property of don Buenaventura, specially adapted) in the first two storeys by Juan de Villalobos. In the top storey is an anon. 18C Assumption. To the l. of the altar is a cratícula. Of the two baroque side altarpieces, that on the l., with paintings by Nicolás Rodríguez Juárez, is dedicated to Our Lady's patronage over the Dominicans; that on the r. to Our Lady of Sorrows. The choir, at the back of the chapel, connects with the tribune and main choir in the nave of the church. Its fan-like gilded wooden screen shows, between estípites, monograms of Jesus, Mary, and Joseph, and, to each side, of SS Anne and Joachim.

The sumptuous late 18C high altarpiece has heavily encrusted ornamental niche pilasters and holds a profusion of polychrome saints and cherubs, and scrolls, volutes, fruits, and foliage. In the l. aisle beneath the tribune the small 17C altarpiece of Guadalupe stands next to that, churrigueresque, of the Virgen de la Fuente. Further up the aisle, the 18C altarpiece of San Francisco, with bulbous solomonic columns on baluster bases. Beyond the side chapel entrance is that of St John Nepomuk, smaller, but with columns of the same type, and ingenuous anon. paintings of scenes from his life. At the back of the church are the coros alto and bajo, now without grilles.

The keystone of the entrance doorway arch to the convent is in the form of a niche holding a polychrome stone statue of St Christopher. Against the back wall of the coro bajo are eight paintings of the Passion by Francisco Antonio Vallejo (the third from the r. partly destroyed and unsuitably covered).

The anastyle altarpiece of the Coronation of Our Lady (c 1770s) in the r. aisle is based on four huge ornamental niche pilasters and loaded with statues, busts, and relief.

Nos. 7 and 9 C. Regina give access to the heavily restored cloister, now part of the *Hospital Béistegui*, with an original tiled fountain. Both Cs Bolívar and San Jerónimo bound the convent buildings. No. 20 in the latter (17C doorway) is the entrance to the *Celda de la Marquesa de Selva Nevada*, a suite of rooms by Tolsá for Antonia Rodríguez de Pedroso y Soria, who became a nun in 1797.

From Pl. Regina, C. Echeveste (18–19C houses; restored) leads W to the **Colegio de las Vizcaínas** (1734–53), a vast feat of a building (more than 12,000 sq m). The initial design was by Pedro Bueno Basorí; continued by Miguel de Mora Quiera, with interventions by Lorenzo Rodríguez.

The **Colegio de San Ignacio de Loyola** was founded in 1732 by three Basque philanthropists, Ambrosio Meave, Manuel de Aldaco, and Francisco Echeveste, for girls (some aimless and vagrant) of Spanish (preferably Basque) descent. It was opened in 1767 under crown patronage and run by the lay confraternity of Nuestra Señora de Aranzazu. Earthquake necessitated repairs by Lorenzo de la Hidalga in 1845, and parts of the building were taken for other uses. The college escaped the Reform, but the arrival of disorientated females from suppressed convents upset its equilibrium. It flourished under the porfiriato with a new programme of studies, and ancient nuns were allowed to stay on undisturbed. Part is still a school.

EXTERIOR. Facing C. de las Vizcaínas, the N façade is marked by three portals and two window storeys. Tezontle panels are separated by pilasters topped by pyramidal finials, which add to a fantastic air. The octagonal upper windows, in eared frames, catch the eye. Access to the college and to the former chaplains' house is gained by the NE and NW doorways, notable for their staggered eared frames, the upper storeys aligned with the lower by two great volutes. In the niches of the former are statues of St Ignatius and Our Lady of Aranzazu; of the latter, St Francis Xavier and Our Lady of Begoña, the figures in pink stone contrasting with the grey of the framing stone. In the centre is the portal, effortlessly graceful, to the chapel, by Lorenzo Rodríguez, the niches elegantly canopied: St Ignatius in the middle, SS Luis Gonzaga and Stanislaus Kostka on either side.

INTERIOR. The finely proportioned principal patio keeps its old tiled floor, its wrought-iron railings, and its central fountain. Two staircases lead to the upper floor—one monumental, occupying the central part of the S side, covered by a cupola, illuminated by four round windows. The single-nave CHAPEL has kept intact its coro alto, where the inmates worshipped. (The coro bajo has been removed.) The five magnificent altarpieces (c 1745–81) are by Joaquín de Sállagos. In the central upper part of the churrigueresque high altarpiece the Christ crucified (probably 17C, one of the college's earliest donations) is flanked by statues of SS Francis and Dominic. The anastyle side altarpieces, of Our Lady of Sorrows and Our Lady of Aranzazu, and, towards the back, of Our Lady of Guadalupe and Our Lady of Loreto (paintings by Andrés de Islas), have beautifully canopied saints and bold, forward decoration.

The houses of two famous Mexicans are nearby. At 11 C. Aldaco (to the N), that of Angela Peralta (1845–83), the great soprano, 'Angelica di voce e di nome', in the words of her Italian maestro; at 10 C. Mesones (to the E), that of Guillermo Prieto (1818–97), poet, dramatist, journalist, and liberal politician.

Parallel with C. Regina, to the S, C. San Jerónimo leads to the church and former convent of **San Jerónimo**, facing an elongated plaza.

A foundation of c 1585 by Conceptionist nuns who changed to the Jeronymite order, the convent has achieved lasting fame through its most illustrious inmate, the beautiful poet, playwright, and polemicist Sor Juana Inés de la Cruz (Juana Asbaje y Ramírez; 1651–95), 'the Tenth Muse'. She finally took the veil in 1669, but not before viceroy marqués de Mancera had submitted her to a rigorous intellectual contest against 40 of Mexico's leading academics and described her as like a royal galleon defending herself against a few little boats. In June–July 1810, with Spain fighting for her life under Napoleonic occupation, the image of the Virgen de los Remedios did the rounds of the convents (with great pomp and 88 sermons) to implore her help for Spain, the king, and the pope. The nuns of San Jerónimo gave her a baton (as 'capitana-generala of the Army of America') and the child a sabre—even in those heady days regarded by the citizens as a lapse of good taste. The convent was closed in 1863 and ransacked in succeeding years. In the 1940s the cloister housed a cabaret.

The convent (Mon.–Fri., 9–5), rebuilt in the 18C and early 19C, contains the *Museo del Claustro de Sor Juana Inés de la Cruz*, showing Mexican, European, and oriental ceramic pieces and other objects (17–19C), many thrown up during excavations in the 1960s. The Centro Universitario de Ciencias Humanas (UNAM) is also housed here.

The church (1623), its Mannerist portal facing N, was restored in 1964–65, after chronic neglect and even use as barracks. The coro alto (with beamed ceiling) and coro bajo have regained their old dignity; part of the cratícula and the confessionals have also survived. Sor Juana's bones lie in the ossuary beneath the coro bajo.

S of San Jerónimo, on the opposite side of Av. José María Izazaga, is the restored Benedictine priory of **Nuestra Señora de Monserrate**. The church façade is of the 18C.

Benedictine monks took over a small church on the site in 1614—the only Benedictine monastery in New Spain. Although respected for educational, charitable, scholarly, and farming activities (they introduced plum cultivation), they never achieved influence and were suppressed in 1821.

The church now contains the *Museo de la Charrería* (Mon.–Fri., 10–6), illustrating the art of Mexican horsemanship. The convent, modernized in the 18C and in the 1970s, is headquarters of the Federación Nacional de Charros (Horse Society).

From here we may turn W along Av. Izazaga eventually to regain the Alameda, see below. However, a side excursion may be made to places S and SE, an unattractive quarter, but not unrewarding for the energetic.

Three blocks S of Monserrate, at the corner of Avs Pino Suárez and Izazaga, is **San Miguel** (1690–92; by Pedro de Arrieta), its huge cupola a landmark in this part, facing E.

Erected as a parish church free of control by the Orders, it was left untouched during the Reform. The bulky EXTERIOR (altered in the 18–19C) has an excellent façade relief in burnished marble. The azulejos on the tops of the towers and in the lantern above the cupola add a dash of colour.

The INTERIOR was neoclassically modernized in 1850 and the walls are lined with azulejos. The columns, frieze, and pediment of the retable in the l. aisle (opposite the r. aisle side chapel) cover the remains of a mid-16C funerary monument to Alonso de Villaseca (once in San Pedro y San Pablo), still showing plateresque detail. Under the arch, a superb relief of Charity. In the l. transept is a painting by Pedro Ramírez, Christ waited upon by angels (1656). To the r. of the high altar, the parish office contains a painting of St John Nepomuk hearing confession (c 1735) by Nicolás Enríquez. The sacristy has a fine panelled ceiling and more (anon.) 18C paintings.

Opposite San Miguel, the continuation of C. San Jerónimo E contains (Nos. 108–110, 112–114, 128, 134–138) houses built by the Camillan fathers (Order of Clerics Regular, Servants of the Sick), whose ministry in Mexico, from 1756, was to nurse the dying. (Their church, called *Sagrado Corazón de Jesús*, was at 111 C. Regina.)

C. San Jerónimo ends at the junction with Correo Mayor. Opposite, facing Pl. de San Pablo, is the former church of **San Pablo el Viejo**, a 16C foundation, but dating in its present form from 1793–99.

After 1847 the attached Augustinian convent and college were converted into a hospital for the wounded in the US-Mexican war. In 1877 it became the *Hospital Juárez*, which, with its newer buildings, was a casualty of the earthquake of 1985. The church is used as a lecture hall and is not open to the public. It contains, however, an anastyle side altarpiece in stone (c 1770).

Further E, along Av. San Pablo, is the huge and heavy church of *San Pablo el Nuevo* (1789–1803) by José Antonio González Velázquez.

From San Pablo, C. San Miguel leads S to the former chapel of *La Magdalena*, set up in 1808 by the Inquisition as a haven for penitent prostitutes. Further along is the church of *San Lucas*, a late 17C barrio chapel. From Pl. San Lucas we may gain Calz. San Antonio Abad, continuation of Av. Pino Suárez. On its W side, a little S, is *La Concepción Tlaxcoaque*, another former barrio chapel (early 18C; no adm.), with a pretty doorway, the supporting pilasters topped by angels.

The busy Calz. San Antonio Abad runs S. At No. 18, near the corner with the callejón of the same name, is the former church of **San Antonio Abad** (1687), now in decay. The façade bears signs of an earlier style, which has caused an attribution to Claudio de Arciniega.

It was once attached to a hospital of canons regular of the order of St Antony Abbot, who (from 1628 in Mexico) specialized in the treatment of erysipelas (St Antony's fire).

Further S, in its own plaza, is *Sta Cruz Acatlán* (1693–94), which, though repaired and altered, still keeps a baroque façade.

Going W along Av. Izazaga we come to the junction with C. Bolívar. Two blocks S, across C. Nezahualcóyotl, is the little 18C chapel of *San Salvador el Seco*, in its own plaza with humble houses of the same period. The next junction is that with Av. Lázaro Cárdenas. On an island on the E side is the church of **Purísima Concepción** (1750–61; also known as *Nuestra Señora del Salto del Agua*), in grey chiluca stone and tezontle, noted for the beauty of its baroque façade. It was restored after road-widening in the 1940s. It faces the replica of the *Salto del Agua* fountain, with its mermaids, dolphins, and chubby twisted columns.

The original (1779) marked the end of one of the aqueducts (largely destroyed in 1859–97) which brought water from the spring of Chapultepec into the city.

Further W, along Av. Arcos de Belén and facing its pleasant garden, is the church of **Belem de los Mercedarios** (also known as *Nuestra Señora de Merceditas*), in its present form a rebuilding of 1730–35, the exterior remodelled in 1973.

It was formerly attached to the Mercedarian seminary of San Pedro Pascual de Belem, opened in 1678, but closed and sold off in 1861.

The façade, facing E, is a charming classical reminder. The S doorway was rebuilt in 1906. The INTERIOR preserves two superb gilded altarpieces: in the r. transept, dedicated to the Birth of Our Lord (del Nacimiento), representing the full glory of churrigueresque (mid-18C). Especially fine are the statues of SS Anne and Joachim, l. and r. in the lower storey. Nearly as good is the altarpiece of the Holy Cross (de la Sta Cruz; l. transept), with emphatic, richly decorated estípites. On the high altar, disguised by crowns and other appendages, is a venerable, priceless, polychrome and estofado statue of Our Lady of Ransom (c 1525–50), a Guatemalan work of rare beauty. She is carved standing, holding the Child, who seems about to fly from her arms, and shielding under her mantle two captives and two friars.

Two blocks S, at 42 C. Dr Lavista, is the chapel of *Campo Florido* (1822). It served a cemetery, in a swamp, in 1846–78, filled after a cholera epidemic in 1853.

Av. Arcos de Belén leads further W. At the corner with Av. Niños Héroes is the **Centro Escolar Revolución** (1933), designed by a group of architects, headed by Antonio Muñoz, as a symbol of the post-Revolutionary regime and destined for an enlightened socialist education programme. Panels at the entrance are painted with murals (1936) by Raúl Anguiano, Aurora Reyes, Everardo Ramírez, Gonzalo de la Paz Pérez, Antonio Gutiérrez, and Ignacio Gómez Jaramillo on the theme of socialist education. In the buildings at either side of the school, originally libraries, are four large stained-glass windows (1934), designed by Fermín Revueltas.

It occupies the site of *San Miguel de Belem*, a refuge and religious retreat for pious and indigent women, founded in 1683–84, suppressed in 1861, and taken over as a prison in 1862. At 9 C. Tolsá, which runs straight W from this junction, is the building which once housed the *Talleres Gráficos de la Nación*, founded in 1936 to promote painting and the graphic arts.

Between Belem de los Mercedarios and the Salto del Agua, C. Buen Tono runs N to PL. SAN JUAN, on the E side of which is the *Mercado San Juan*, good for handicrafts. On the W side is the church of *Nuestra Señora de Guadalupe*, more popularly known as **Buen Tono** (1912), by Miguel Angel de Quevedo.

Formerly on this site was the church and convent of *San Juan de la Penitencia*, belonging since 1591 to urbanist Poor Clares and demolished in 1908. The new church (probably the only one in the world owing its name to a cigarette) was raised at the expense of Ernest Pugibet, a French tobacco magnate whose adjoining *Buen Tono* factory, designed by the same architect in 1896–1904, and other business interests made him one of the richest men in pre-Revolutionary Mexico. The church has good stained glass and the interior is notable for its use of marble.

On the N side of the plaza, somewhat hidden by intrusive newer buildings, but with a noticeable cupola and classical portal, is the tezontle-covered parish church of **San José** (c 1790), the work of José del Mazo y Avilés. It was rebuilt in 1858 after earthquake damage and fell heir to some of the fittings from San Francisco.

8 North-East of the Alameda

On the E side of the Pal. de Bellas Artes, at the W end of Av. 5 de Mayo, is the building known as **La Mutua**, raised in 1903–05 by the US architects De Lemos and Cordes, with the engineer Gonzalo Garita, for the Mutual Life Insurance Co. in Italian Renaissance style and enlarged and modernized by Carlos Obregón Santacilia in 1926–27 for the Banco de México, the country's central bank. Backing on to it and fronting Av. Lázaro Cárdenas to the W and C. Tacuba to the N is the colossal **Correos** (Central Post Office; 1902–07), a major work by Adamo Boari (with Gonzalo Garita) in which he harmoniously combined various features of Romanesque, Gothic, Spanish Renaissance, and even touches of Mexican baroque.

One of the main inspirations seems to have been façades of 16C buildings in Salamanca. The rich neo-plateresque decoration is concentrated around doors and windows: baluster and candelabra motifs reaching vertically, medallions, and finely judged canopies falling gracefully over the arches. The greatest decorative emphasis is above and below the gallery, which separates the layered frieze punctuated by the slender engaged column finials and the tightly ornate balustrade. The wrought ironwork came from the Pignone foundry of Florence, the steel frame from Milliken Brothers of New York. On the first floor is the *Museo Postal* (Mon.–Sat., 9–2), which illustrates every aspect of Mexican postal history. At 2 C. Marconi, first turning l. along C. Tacuba, on the first floor of the Banco de México building, is the *Museo Numismático* (Mon.–Fri., 10–5; adm. in small groups preferred), containing Mexican medals, coins, paper money, and other objects of exchange from the 1530s to the present day.

CALLE TACUBA, an historic thoroughfare, widens into an imposing plaza, in its centre the bronze **El Caballito**, a majestic monument to unworthy majesty, by Manuel Tolsá.

In 1795 viceroy marqués de Branciforte secured from his brother-in-law Godoy, Charles IV's chief minister, permission to erect a statue of the king, destined for Pl. Mayor. Tolsá was commissioned and the plaza rearranged by González Velázquez to receive it. At its inauguration in Dec. 1796, a wooden facsimile had to do because Tolsá took his time. The statue was cast in Aug. 1803 by Salvador de la Vega and made its debut in Dec. It found no favour with patriotic Mexicans and in 1822 was consigned to the patio of the old University. In 1852 it was placed at the N end of Paseo Bucareli, at the spot where it would meet Paseo de la Reforma, where it remained until finding its present position in 1979.

Although said to have been inspired by a statue (now lost) of Louis XIV by Girardon and to have followed the model closely, Tolsá's genius informs the whole with extraordinary vigour and command. The spring of the horse, the balance of animal and rider, the flow of the king's robe, the grand attitudes of head and arm, and the marvellous attention to detail give it a place second only to the statue of Marcus Aurelius in Rome.

It faces Tolsá's crowning achievement as architect, the renowned neoclassical **Pal. de Minería**, attesting the boom of 1775–1810, and the importance and respectability of the silver-mining community.

A royal decree of 1 July 1776 set up the Real Tribunal General de Minería: to govern the mining guild, to manage a bank, and to establish the Royal Mining College. The definitive plan was by Tolsá, who began work in 1797. In 1811 the students moved in; in 1813 the building was finished—at a cost of 1.5 million pesos. Its weight, however, was too much for the subsoil. There began a slump, corrected only in 1830–34 by a French architect, Antoine Villard. The School of Mines was in occupation until 1867. Today the building is part of UNAM. It remains in constant danger, so much so that its dismantling and re-erection on a safer site have been advocated. In the 19C it played host to glittering social occasions, among them a ball given on 24 May 1840 by the British minister, Richard Pakenham, to celebrate the marriage of Queen Victoria. 'Nothing could be more splendid', wrote Fanny Calderón de la Barca, 'than the general effect of this noble building, brilliantly illuminated … the president of the corps diplomatique in full uniform, and the display of diamonds was extraordinary … there were assembled what is called *all* Mexico'. Pres. Bustamante, guest of honour, proposed the queen's health, which was drunk by all the company.

EXTERIOR. The façades (90m long on N and E; 81m on W), with two main floors and a mezzanine, have well-proportioned windows; cornices above ground and mezzanine floors, entablature above the upper; balustrades punctuated by urn finials; and, on the main N façade, a central panel crowned by a pediment. (The cube above is a rebuilding by Villard.) In the noble central piece, fluted columns (doric capitals below, ionic above) uphold friezes of triglyphs and metopes, with roses nestling in the latter. The upper windows are beautifully framed; above, in semicircular niches, corbels with bead motifs sustain miniature pediments resting on jutting slabs, curved in the centre; the bead motif is repeated in the keystones of the arches and in the tympana. The side doors, with their broken pediments, are models of balance and perfectly judged ornamentation. The four meteorites were installed in the porch in 1893.

INTERIOR. Tolsá combined monumentality with the utilitarian and functional. Much is composed of small rooms and offices. But main emphasis is on the patio. On the ground floor the five semicircular arches on each side, in dressed stone, are flanked by engaged columns. The upper floor is much more striking: low-slung arches supported by elegant double columns with ionic capitals (three-column groups in the corners). The staircase is wide and handsome, the columns and capitals of corridors and patio combining as we climb in an effect of awe-inspiring grandeur.

The chief rooms are on the upper floor. Above the central portico, the Salón de Cosmografía and Observatory on two floors. The *Gran Salón de Actos*, on the E side, was also the scene of balls and receptions. S of the staircase is the *Chapel*, another fine work, in Tolsá's best tradition of 'buen gusto'. The ceiling is decorated with two murals in tempera by Rafael Jimeno y Planes, Assumption and Miracle of the Well of Guadalupe.

Opposite, on the N side of C. Tacuba, is the former **Pal. de Comunicaciones y Obras Públicas** (1904–11), eclectically designed, with more than a nod to the Italian Renaissance, by Silvio Contri in collaboration with the engineer Manuel Marroqui: another celebration of porfirian confidence.

The iron and stone ornaments and interior decorative painting were entrusted to the Florentine house of Coppedé (Mariano Coppedé and his sons Gino, Adolfo, and Carlo); the ironwork came from the Pignone foundry in Florence; and the iron frame and other materials from Milliken Brothers of New York. The site was once occupied (1779–1903) by the Hospital of *San Andrés*. In 1867 the corpse of Maximilian was re-embalmed there and Juárez is said (incorrectly) to have paid a secret midnight visit to view the body of his arch-foe.

The **Museo Nacional de Arte** (Tues.–Sun., 10–5; fee) housed here shows Mexican painting and sculpture. Its arrangement is subject to frequent change.

Art of New Spain. Mannerism. Baltasar de Echave Orio, La Porciúncula (1609), from the Tlatelolco retable; Martyrdom of St Pontian (1605). Attr. Echave Orio, St Anne. Alonso López de Herrera, Divine Countenance (oil on copper plate). Baltasar de Echave Ibía, Virgin of the Apocalypse, infused with blue tints; Our Lady with St Anne. Luis Juárez, St Augustine; Mystic Marriage of St Catherine; Investing of St Ildefonsus, both luminous and mystic; Choir of Virgins (from a Martyrdom of St Ursula); St Simon Stock receives the scapular. *Baroque.* José Juárez, St Salvator of Horta receives the viaticum. Antonio Rodríguez, St Thomas of Villanueva; St Augustine (both 1668). Baltasar de Echave y Rioja, Martyrdom of St Sebastian; Martyrdom of St Peter Arbues (1666), the painter ignoring the Inquisition's instructions for a second version after the first had been rejected. Cristóbal de Villalpando, Adoration of the Shepherds. Juan Correa, St Catherine; Repentant Magdalen—two contrasting works, the first serene, the second histrionic. Miguel de Mendoza, Visitation, with good landscape.

Among the 18C works are Nicolás Enríquez, Christ scourged, stark for its time; José de Ibarra, Eight scenes from the life of Our Lady; José de Alzíbar, Ministry of St Joseph, Ecce Homo; Cabrera, Conversion of St Ignatius; José María Vásquez, Crucifixion.

Sculpture, engravings, drawings, and paintings (late 18C and 19C) by tutors and students of the Academia de San Carlos, incl. sculpture by Miguel Noreña (1834–94) and oil paintings, Madness of Isabel of Portugal by Pelegrín Clavé (1811–80) and Bacchanal by Antonio Fabrés (1854–1938), both directors. Works by foreign artists who portrayed the regions, architecture, and customs of Mexico after Independence. Pietro Gualdi, Lithographs and Interior of the Cathedral; Paseo de la Independencia (1841). Edouard Pingret, Iztaccíhuatl and Popocatépetl from the aqueduct of Tlaxpana. Costumbrista oil sketches by Johann Moritz Rugendas (1802–58), showing provincial life.

19C Religious Painting, showing the influence of the Roman Nazarene school on those artists who went to Rome on scholarships. Neoclassical simplicity and pre-Raphaelite influences are reflected in works by Luis Monroy (1845–1918), Prodigal Son; Roman Charity. Santiago Rebull (1829–1902), Sacrifice of Isaac; Crucifixion; Death of Abel. Joaquín Ramírez (1830–86), Noah's Ark; Moses in Rafidin. Rafael Flores (1832–86), Holy Family; Christ waited upon by angels; Good Shepherd. Ramón Sagredo (1834–72), Jesus at Emaus. José Salomé Pina (1830–1909), Samson and Delilah; Agar leaves for the desert (1852); Abraham and Isaac. Felipe Gutiérrez (1824–1904), St Bartholomew. José María Ibarrarán y Ponce (1854–1910), Early Christian Charity.

19C History Painting, incl. outstanding nationalistic works. Leandro Izaguirre, Torture of Cuauhtémoc (1892). Rodrigo Gutiérrez, Senate of Tlaxcala. Félix Parra, Fray Bartolomé de las Casas (1876); Massacre of Cholula; Galileo. José María Obregón, Discovery of Pulque; Young Columbus. Juan Urruchi, Sor Juana Inés de la Cruz takes the habit. Juan Cordero, Columbus before the Catholic Kings. Alberto Fuster, Apotheosis of Peace, allegory of the 'peace and progress' of the porfiriato. Felipe Gutiérrez, Amazon of the Andes (revealing another aspect of Latin American nationalism). Manuel Vilar's plaster statue of Tlahuicole (1851) shows nationalism in sculpture.

19C designs for a series of children's board games by José Guadalupe Posada (1852–1913). In the room, zinc engravings by him, used for penny fly-sheets and in anti-Díaz newspapers; coloured book-cover engravings. Wood prints by the popular illustrator Manuel Manilla

(1830–90). Engravings by the Englishman George Austin Periam, contracted by the Academy in 1853 to revive techniques.

Academic Sculpture. Neoclassical sculpture and bas-reliefs by artists working in the tradition of Tolsá; an Immaculate Conception by him is included. Works by Academy artists trained by Manuel Vilar (director of sculpture 1846–60), showing his Romantic predilection for religious and historic themes. Work by Martín Soriano, the first to sculpt marble in Mexico, and Miguel Noreña. *19C Academic Portraiture and Provincial Painting*. Juan Cordero. The sculptors Pérez and Valero (1847), done in Rome, in which he combined indigenous facial traits with classical treatment of colour; self-portrait (1848) and portraits of his mother, the daughters of Manuel Cordero, and his wife María de los Angeles Osio (1860); superlative portrait of doña Dolores Tosta (1855), a mixture of daintiness and deliberate imperiousness. Portraits by Pelegrín Clavé, director of the Academy and Cordero's rival: José Bernardo Couto and Andrés Quintana Roo.

Works, generally rigidly naive, but influential in post-Revolutionary years, by non-Academic provincial painters. Among them, Agustín Arrieta from Puebla, Hermenegildo Bustos from Guanajuato, and José María Estrada from Guadalajara.

19C Landscape Painting. Works by the Italian Eugenio Landesio (1810–79), who came to Mexico in 1855 and initiated the Academic tradition of Romantic landscapes. Works by his pupils Luis Coto (1830–91) and Salvador Murillo (1840–?); and an excellent collection by José María Velasco (1840–1912). Carlos Ribera (1856–?), 'La Barranca de Metlac' (1886) shows Velasco's enormous influence on contemporary and later artists. Impressionist paintings by the Modernist Joaquín Clausell.

19C Sentimental and Literary Painting. Rodrigo Gutiérrez (1848–1903), 'Ariadna Abandonada', and Manuel Ocaranza (1841–82), Tricks of Love, both turned to Greek history and mythology to convey moral messages. Luis Monroy, Death of Atala. Gonzalo Pineda, Othello and Desdemona (1879). Rafael Flores, Dante and Vergil. Felipe Gutiérrez, Death of Lucretia.
   Symbolist Painting and Sculpture, favoured during the porfiriato. Sculpture was often worked in marble imported from Italy. Early plaster works by Enrique Guerra (1871–1943), 'Fleur Fanée' and 'El Beso', and others by Gabriel Guerra, Jesús Contreras, and Arnulfo Domínguez Bello. Paintings of the Modernista and Ateneista generations: the triptych 'El Adios' by Alberto Fuster and 'Ex-voto a San Sebastián' by Angel Zarraga show the influence of French symbolism; 'Nuestros Dioses' by Saturnino Herrán (1887–1918), a sketch (1917) for a state-commissioned mural for the National Theatre, never executed. Ink drawings from the early 1900s, showing Aubrey Beardsley's influence, by Roberto Montenegro. 'Velorio' (Vigil) by José Jara (1866–1939) is one of the first paintings to take contemporary Indians as its theme. Julio Ruelas's famous etching 'La crítica' is also a self-portrait. Paintings by Dr Atl (Gerardo Murillo).
   Escuelas al Aire Libre. Sculpture and naive paintings by mainly popular artists who attended post-Revolutionary open air schools. Clay handicrafts from the Roberto Montenegro collection.
   Mexican Painting School (Escuela Mexicana), realistic style, first and second post-Revolutionary generations of artists, most of whom participated in state-sponsored mural commissions. Among works by José Clemente Orozco: early watercolours from the 'Casa del Llanto' series (1912–13), several mural projects, and late works, using new materials, such as 'La Vela' (Wake; 1948; pyroxylin and masonite). Diego Rivera, Cubist works from the 1910s; later works in social realism style. Adolfo Best Maugard, 'Autorretrato' (1923), displaying 'petatillo' technique. David Alfaro Siqueiros, 'Madre Proletaria' and 'El Coronelazo' (self-portrait; 1943; pyroxylin on celotex).
   20C Prints. Lithographs by Orozco, Siqueiros, Montenegro, and Alfredo Zalce. Woodprint 'Tierra y Libertad' by Xavier Guerrero, used as headpiece of 'El Machete', initially put out by the muralists' union and later converted into the organ of the Mexican communist party. Socialist-oriented prints and posters by members of the Taller de la Gráfica Popular, founded in 1937, offspring of the anti-fascist Liga de Escritores y Artistas Revolucionarios.

Further E, on the corner of Cs Tacuba and Filomeno Mata, is the former church of **Nuestra Señora de Belem**, once attached to the hospital of the Bethlemites, a nursing order founded in 1656 in Guatemala.

Church, convent, and hospital were established in 1681–87, the latter for convalescents. (It has been wittily said that the sick emerged so ill from hospital treatment that other institutions were needed for them to recover in.) In 1820 the Order was suppressed. Since 1964 the church, keeping signs of an austere façade, has housed the *Museo de la Asociación del Heroico Colegio Militar* (Mon.–Sat., 10–2), which commemorates the war against the USA (1847–48) with a muster of documents, maps, flags, etc. Survivals of the convent and hospital (the main part by Lorenzo Rodríguez; 1758–68) are found at 17–19 C. Tacuba and 1–13 C. Bolívar, with remains of a fine cloister and monumental staircase. At 14 C. Bolívar (then 9 C. Vergara), during the night of 20–21 June 1876, at the age of 82, died Antonio López de Santa-Anna.

On the opposite corner is the former church of **Sta Clara** (1661), by Pedro Ramírez, with twin Mannerist portals.

It was part of a convent for urbanist Poor Clares, founded in 1570 and opened in 1579. In the main street of old Mexico, it was patronized by viceregal society and disposed of much wealth and property. In the 18C, we are told, the nuns were addicted to bellringing, which caused friction with their neighbours. The convent was suppressed in 1861 and later destroyed. The church served as a livery stable. Since 1936 it has housed the **Biblioteca del Congreso de la Unión** (Library of Congress). By law two copies of every book published in the republic must be deposited here.

No. 48 C. Tacuba was the house of the poet Francisco González Bocanegra (1824–61), who wrote the verses of the Mexican national anthem ('Mexicanos, al grito de guerra'; 1853–54). At this point C. Tacuba meets C. Isabel la Católica (r.), No. 7 in which preserves the façade of an early 17C house, with a lacy stucco pattern. C. Chile, continuation of C. Isabel la Católica, leads N to the crossing with C. Donceles. Spanning 6–8 C. Chile and 51 C. Donceles is the **Casa de los Condes de Heras Soto** (c 1760). Its stone decoration is perhaps the finest in the city. The outstandingly beautiful portal, with notable cornices, is alive with delicate carving. At the corner, a chubby little boy, a basket of fruit

Convent of Sta Clara in Calle Sta Clara (19C)—now Calle Tacuba

on his head, stands on a lion and is surrounded by a panel of rococo relief, daringly intricate.

Further E, at 66 C. Donceles, an 18C house, is the headquarters of the *Academia Mexicana de la Lengua*, founded in 1875. It contains the *Museo del Recuerdo* (Mon.–Fri., 10–2; adm. on previous application), with a collection of manuscripts by famous Mexican writers. Following C. Donceles W we pass Nos. 43–49, 18–19C houses once property of the condes de Heras Soto, and come, at No. 39, to the former **Hospital Real del Divino Salvador**, with an 18C doorway, now a clinic of the Ministry of Public Health.

The hospital originated in viceregal Mexico's most remarkable manifestation of charity, when, c 1680, the carpenter and retable-maker José Sáyago, moved by the plight of madwomen destitute in the city streets and subjected to much cruelty, began to take them into his own house and to care for them. He soon received the enthusiastic support of Abp Aguiar y Seijas, a notorious misogynist (giving thanks that his myopia prevented him from seeing women too well), who provided the money for more adequate premises. In 1700 the hospital was settled on the present site in the care of the Congregation of the Divine Saviour. It was closed in 1910. The building's present aspect dates from modernization and enlargement by José Joaquín García de Torres in 1802–09. The second floor was added between 1809 and 1864.

Opposite, at 36–38 C. Donceles, is the handsome **Teatro de la Ciudad** (1917), neoclassically based, with exotic additions, by Federico Mariscal, restored in 1976–84. Parallel in C. Cuba, to the N, is another famous theatre, *Teatro Lírico* (by Manuel Torres Torija; 1905–07).

It adjoins the former (until 1982) *Cámara de Diputados* (1909–10), at the corner of Cs Donceles and Allende, an appropriately classical design by Mauricio Campos.

On the S side of C. Donceles, No. 27, further W, is the **Cámara de Senadores**, a reconditioned late 18C house, once part of the Colegio de San Andrés.

The INTERIOR contains murals by Jorge González Camarena. On the E side of the courtyard two (1974) commemorate the restoration of the Senate under Juárez and Lerdo de Tejada, and the creators of the Republic and the Senate. On the staircase walls and its ceiling is Fight against Tyranny (1958), in honour of Belisario Domínguez (1863–1913), senator from Chiapas and implacable and courageous opponent of Pres. Huerta, killed on the president's orders. High-coloured works of extraordinary strength, they culminate in a ceiling allegory of Mexico, the eagle, killing the still struggling monster. The centre wall is a heroic representation of Domínguez.

C. Allende leads N to meet C. Belisario Domínguez. To the r., at Nos. 44–50, is the former *Beaterio de Niñas* (*Nuestra Señora de Covadonga*; 1775), another, much altered, house of retreat for girls of Spanish descent, preserving a plain doorway (No. 46) with a touch of elegance. Opposite are three more modified 18C houses: No. 37, *Casa Villanueva*; No. 39; and No. 43, a casa señorial, with an added top storey, but with traces of original external decoration. Still further E, at the junction with C. Chile, No. 58 is a 17–18C house, the top floor added in the late 19C. Nos. 61 and 62 C. Belisario Domínguez and 27–33 and 35–37 C. Chile are two 18C houses, *Casas de los Marqueses de San Miguel de Aguayo*, once fine tezontle and stone structures. Nos 76–80 are three connected 18C houses.

On the l. of the junction of Cs Allende and Belisario Domínguez is **San Lorenzo** (1785), in tezontle, and buttressed, with high windows.

It belonged to a convent of Augustinian nuns, who were said to make the best alfeñiques (sugar paste flavoured with almonds) and toffees in Mexico, until final suppression after the fall of Maximilian. Fire damaged the church in 1939; restoration was finished in 1953.—The convent, adapted in 1878 by Manuel Francisco Alvarez for secular use, partly survives (38 C. Allende).

EXTERIOR. Above the doorway of the neostyle portal the cornice rises into an arched niche enclosing a statue of St Lawrence holding his grille flanked by two saints of the Order. Above perch cherubs holding horns of plenty. The pattern is repeated, more grandly, in the upper storey: the elaborate niche, its frame studded with shell and rose motifs and a crowning medallion, a setting for a statue of St Augustine holding a church.

INTERIOR. The S end preserves its two choirs. The *coro bajo*, now without its grille, has a low domical vault, reinforced and ornamented by an undulating moulding; its keystone an eight-pointed star in white stucco, from which fly cherubim. The *coro alto* has part of its original screen. On the wall between the two is a relief of the Annunciation in white stone, once polychrome and gilded, laden with enchanting detail: a gracious and reassuring St Gabriel; a sweetly expressive Virgin. The apse mural, part of the restoration, is by Matías Goeritz.

Further W along C. Belisario Domínguez is the church of **La Concepción** (c 1655).

It was part of a Conceptionist convent, founded by Bp Zumárraga in 1540. The community was to become the biggest and richest in Mexico. By 1612 there were 130 nuns, accompanied by 500 servants and slaves. In the 18C the sisters engaged in a shrill and unseemly quarrel with the church authorities about the number of servants they should be allowed to have. In 1775 the servants were sent packing by royal command. After suppression in 1867 (when 21 nuns were left) the present Cjón del 57 was driven through the convent. A considerable section survives, at 5 C. Belisario Domínguez, at 6–16, 24, and 30–34 Cjón del 57, and further along C. Belisario Domínguez (No. 33), almost opposite San Lorenzo.

EXTERIOR. The twin N portals show elaborate Mannerism. Corinthian columns flank the double-arched (polygonal within semicircular) doorways and support sumptuous friezes. Above the cornice, fancifully framed shields stand either side of the windows flanked by similar columns, with ornate friezes and broken pediments above, on which rest 18C gables enclosing the arms of the Order. The cupola (1645) was the first in the city.

In the mid-19C, all the 17–18C altarpieces were torn out to make way for an updated version of neoclassical in white and gold. The grille of the old *coro bajo* (a children's theatre in anticlerical days) survives.
  Opposite the church is the exquisite round chapel of *La Concepción Cuepopan* (mid-17C). Abandoned in the late 18C, it was later (till 1893) repository for the corpses of bankrupts. It is now a library.

Further N, across C. Perú, is PL. GARIBALDI, haunt of Mariachi bands, especially on Fri. and Sat. evenings. It adjoins the N continuation of Av. Lázaro Cárdenas (still known as Av. Sta María la Redonda). On the other side of the avenida, facing a small plaza off C. Riva Palacio, is the church of **Sta María la Redonda** (1677–1734), with a simple façade.

In the apse its small, single-nave interior is a hexagonal rotunda, its airiness emphasized by high arches upheld by pilasters.—The neighbouring burial ground, established in 1784 for the destitute, was acquired and enlarged by the authorities in 1836–42 as *Panteón de Sta Paula*. In Sept. 1842, with great ceremony, Santa-Anna's left leg, blown off by French cannon at Veracruz in 1838, was reinterred here. The president wore a new cork leg for the occasion. The cemetery (now disappeared) was closed in 1871.

From here may be reached points of interest N of the centre. Av. Lázaro Cárdenas crosses the extension of Paseo de la Reforma and reaches (c 1km; l.) C. Luna, which leads to PL. DE LOS ANGELES. On its W side is the church of *Nuestra Señora de los Angeles*, finished in 1808.
  Beyond, Av. Lázaro Cárdenas runs through UNIDAD NONOALCO-TLATELOLCO, a development of the 1950s and 1960s to provide low-cost housing, the work of a team of town-planners under the direction of Mario Pani. High-rise apartment blocks create a chilly, impersonal atmosphere, not improved after earthquake damage in 1985. Its focal point is PL. DE LAS TRES CULTURAS, inaugurated in 1964 after clearance since 1960. Today it embodies prehispanic, historical, and modern Mexico.

The ancient city of **Tlatelolco** was established c 1358 (1370 in some sources) by one of the many migrant tribes in the Basin of Mexico, on an island N of Tenochtitlán island in the Lago de Texcoco. At first it was a ceremonial and commercial city in its own right, and was powerful enough by the early 15C to undertake campaigns into Puebla, where it conquered Quauhtlin-chán in 1438 and established marriage alliances with Tepexi el Viejo and other S Puebla towns. In 1473, however, it was captured by the Mexica Aztecs under Axayácatl, who caused its ruler, Moquihuixtli, to be thrown to his death from the top of its great pyramid.

Tlatelolco nevertheless retained a special status in the Aztec city for its huge market, visited daily by tens of thousands. The great market was formed sometime in the 15C, when an association of merchants known as the pochteca from 18 towns of the Basin banded together and established themselves in Tlatelolco. Causeways were built connecting its ceremonial centre S to Tenochtitlán, W to Tlacopan (Tacuba) and the mainland, and N to Tenayuca. In the market officials inspected the quality of merchandise and checked prices, both of which were government regulated. The pochteca dealt specifically with long-distance trade, but combined their travels with spying out lands for future Aztec conquest. Established trade routes went from Tlatelolco SE out of the Basin, via Chalco, Amecameca, and Cuautla, to Izúcar de Matamoros. There they split and followed routes to the market cities of the S and E: to Coixtlahuaca, Cuilapa, and Tlaxiaco in N and central Oaxaca; and to Teotitlán del Camino and Tuxtepec in N and E Oaxaca, where they split again. Routes went SE to Coatzacoalcos, Cimatan, Potonchán, and Xicalango, where canoe trade plied the Gulf Coast to the Maya principalities of Yucatán. Other routes went SW, to Tehuantepec, to tap the Pacific coastal trade from Central America. Trade items included gold ornaments, precious stones, garments, slaves, obsidian knives and mirrors, copper bells, needles, combs and other jewellery, feathers, ceramics, honey, and salt; media of exchange varied, and could include cacao (chocolate beans), cotton cloaks, quills of gold dust, or small copper axes. In the market itself both local and imported goods were sold; Bernal Díaz lists foods of all sorts, cacao, honey, cotton and fibre cloth, thread, rope, feathers, manufactured garments and sandals, animal skins, various live animals (incl. snakes, dogs, turtles, turkeys, ducks, and other birds), slaves, pottery, wood, paper, stone tools, precious stones, and jewellery of all sorts, made of metal, shell, bone, and stone.

During the siege of Tenochtitlán, Tlatelolco witnessed some of the fiercest fighting. Several conquistadores, in an attempt to capture the market place, were themselves taken, and later sacrificed on the great pyramid, from which their screams could be heard by their comrades below.

Early excavations at the site of the ceremonial centre were conducted in 1948 by Francisco González Rul for INAH. Further work was done in 1962–66 by César A. Sáenz, Víctor Segovia, and Eduardo Contreras to uncover the monuments of the sacred teocalli for restoration.

The main structure comprises the foundations of the several successive building phases of the main temple-pyramid, one behind the other. Remains of each include a wide double staircase divided and flanked by ramps, which would have led to twin temples at the top. When excavated, two almost complete sets of the 20 Aztec calendrical day-signs were found carved on stone slabs set upright around three sides of the platform. Various other foundations are scattered around the great pyramid, incl. smaller rectangular pyramids with steps; circular platforms, which perhaps supported temples dedicated to Ehecatl, the Wind god; long walls of terraces mounted by multiple sets of steps at regular intervals; and the remains of two walls on the N side of the plaza, which mark the route of one of the ancient causeways. A rectangular platform E of the great pyramid once supported a tzompantli (skull rack), and the exca-vators found nearly 200 skulls in alignments around the base, as if once put on shelves or poles. Inhumation and cremation burials of both individuals and groups were also found in the excavations.

The plaza was scene of a massacre on 2 Oct. 1968 (ten days after the opening of the XIX Olympiad) when several thousand students and others met to protest against the govern-ment's occupation of the UNAM campus and its methods in suppressing dissent. Troops and police opened fire on the crowd and flares were dropped from helicopters. Between 300 and 400 are said to have been killed.

In 1536 the Franciscans inaugurated the **Colegio Imperial de Sta Cruz de Tlatelolco**, for the training of Indian novices—'one hundred boys, sons of caciques, between ten and 12'. Among the founding masters who added to its reputation were Andrés de Olmos, Bernardino de Sahagún, and Juan de Gaona. It had ceased to exist by 1612.

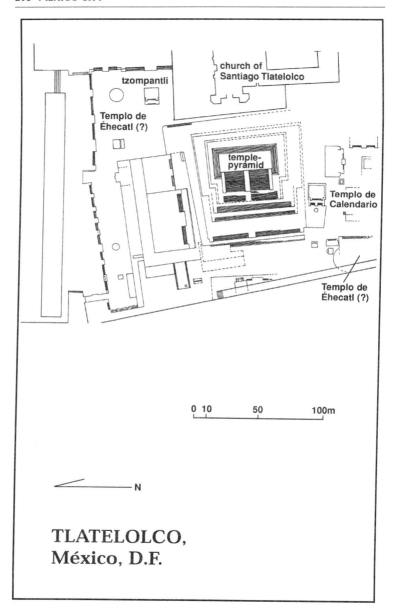

church of
Santiago Tlatelolco

tzompantli

Templo de
Éhecatl (?)

temple-
pyramid

Templo de
Calendario

Templo de
Éhecatl (?)

0 10   50   100m

N

TLATELOLCO,
México, D.F.

The church of **Santiago Tlatelolco**, on the E side of the plaza, dates from 1603–10. On its S side is the former *Colegio de San Buenaventura*, founded in 1660.

The church accompanied the Franciscan convent, founded in 1543. The college was for friars dedicated to higher studies; it functioned until the 1820s, after which the building, together with the church, was abused by a variety of profane uses. The church was reconstructed from 1944–48. In 1973–75 the college was restored.

EXTERIOR. The main W doorway displays a development of Renaissance modes, the upper two storeys elegant variations of Mannerism. The N doorway continues the latter influence, its upper storey with a relief of the imperial eagle and five flowers representing the stigmata of St Francis.

The INTERIOR was refashioned in 1960–64 by Ricardo de Robina, but still has old traces: the great St Christopher mural (17C) above the side door and, in the apse, a bas-relief of Santiago Mataindios, a hardly apt reminder of the vast early 17C altarpiece, destroyed in the later 19C.

The college cloister is still a good example of 17C work. In the patio are remains of the second Franciscan church (c 1540). Superimposed on the E side is the façade (1771–79) of the *Tecpan*, until c 1850 the seat of Indian local government. On the S side of the plaza is the tall building (20 floors) of the *Secretaría de Relaciones Exteriores* (1963).

At the W end of Nonoalco-Tlatelolco, at the corner of Avs Insurgentes Norte and Flores Magón, is the *Torre Banobras* (127m high) with 24 floors of offices, its tip a tower containing a 47-bell carillon cast in Belgium. Av. Insurgentes Norte runs NE; c 1km further, at a major junction, looms the pyramidal *Monumento a la Raza*, projected in 1940 by Luis Lelo de Larrea, to celebrate Mexico's fusion of races.

On the NW of the junction (main entrance in Calz. de Vallejo) is the **Hospital de la Raza** (1936–40, 1946–52; by Enrique Yáñez), which contains murals by Siqueiros and Rivera (behind locked glass doors; permission to view essential).

Just inside the entrance gates on the l. is an auditorium where Siqueiros painted a parabolic mural, 'Por una seguridad social completa y para todos los Mexicanos' (1952–54), using pyroxylin and celotex, to cover all the walls and ceiling of the lobby. Inside the hall at the end of the entrance way is Rivera's last mural, 'El Pueblo en demanda de Salud' (1935–55), showing the history of medicine in Mexico. In the centre of the fresco is the Aztec goddess of medicine, Tlazolteotl, her skirt bearing a design taken from the Codex Badiano (1542), a treatise on medicinal herbs and the first book on medicine to be written in the New World. To the r., Aztec medicinal practice is shown underneath the sun, presided over by Quetzalcóatl's priest, whose paper headdress signifies potent magic. At the l., under a new moon, modern medicine—the demand for it in peacetime and its technology.

9 West of the Alameda

Beyond the NW corner of the Alameda, Paseo de la Reforma runs diagonally NE to divide Av. Hidalgo and Puente de Alvarado. At the corner of the latter and C. Zarco is the church of **San Hipólito**, finished in 1739.

It marks the action of the Noche Triste (30 June–1 July 1520) when Cortés withdrew the Spanish and Tlaxcaltecan forces from Tenochtitlán after the Aztecs had risen against the Spanish garrison and Moctezuma had been killed. The line of retreat was along today's C. Tacuba, Av. Hidalgo, and Puente de Alvarado, W to Tacuba. Loaded with their treasure and heaving a portable wooden bridge to negotiate gaps in the causeway, the Spaniards successfully got over the first channel. Then an old woman sounded the alarm, taken up on conch shells by the sentries. Soon the Mexicans were flanking the causeway in canoes, shooting at the retreating mass. The Spanish formations broke and their bridge collapsed. Panic and confusion reigned. Cortés and his companions raced for the mainland and swam the remaining breaks in the causeway, though he later spurred back to the mêlée. Pedro de Alvarado, commanding the lead column, leapt the last channel on a lance vault. Cortés had lost c 450 men, more than 4000 Tlaxcaltecans, 46 horses, all his guns. Few escaped to the mainland unwounded. The treasure of Moctezuma disappeared in the rout. Cortés led the tattered remnant of his forces back to Tlaxcala.

A chapel to St Hippolytus was built where once stood the fortification guarding the causeway. From the 1530s it became the custom for the viceroy to head a procession every 13 Aug. to San Hipólito, to the sound of trumpets, the banner of the saint held high—a celebration of Spanish arms. In 1566 the site was ceded to Bernardino Alvarez (1514?–1584), a merchant who had decided to devote himself to the care of the sick. Here he built a hospital for aged priests and schoolteachers, whose numbers were swollen by poverty stricken conquistadores and the insane, to be cared for by his new Order, Hermanos de la Caridad (Brothers of Charity). The new church, started in 1602, took 138 years to complete. The hospital was rebuilt in 1776–79. The Order was suppressed in 1821. Today the former hospital is the *Hostería del Bohemio.*

EXTERIOR. The façade, both Mannerist and baroque influenced, has pilasters, and unexpected flourishes. The simple lowest storey is overshadowed by the upper two, with emphatic statuary, and the soaring gable. Unusually placed, the tower bases are covered with ajaraca relief; their upper storeys show estípites. At the corner of the atrio is a singular monument (late 1780s ?), enclosing a relief commemorating Moctezuma's dream portending defeat—done free of charge by José Damián Ortiz de Castro, to promote his candidature for the post of chief architect of the city. The INTERIOR was gone over, with more than a nod to the byzantine, by Manuel Francisco Alvarez in 1893.

Puente de Alvarado runs S of PL. SAN FERNANDO, in the centre of which is a statue (1868–70) of Vicente Guerrero by Ramón Rodríguez Arangoity and Miguel Noreña. At its N end is the church of **San Fernando** (1735–55).

Franciscan missionaries founded the church and accompanying *Colegio Apostólico de Propaganda Fide* (their third; 1733; see Rte 37). They were expelled in 1860, while restoration of the church was in progress; destruction of the college began in 1862.

EXTERIOR. The façade, its original proportions altered by sinkage, is baroque in conception, but with exceptional features which may owe something to Jerónimo de Balbás. The doorway, with unusual variations of tableros grafted on to the extrados and soffit of the arch and its thick supports, is flanked by pairs of Tuscan half-columns rippling with wavy fluting and backed by sturdy pilasters. The canted niches between them, topped by shell canopies, are rare and effective. The first-storey relief of Santiago Matamoros stands between pairs of discreet estípites—all on bases incised with tableros. An octagonal rose, framed by delicate relief which overflows around the medallions on either side, dominates the second storey. Above, doubly curved moulding joins the pinnacles of the broken pediment.

The INTERIOR was once famous for its churrigueresque retables, torn out in 1860. An attempt has been made to revive the high altar in its old style. The beautifully carved pulpit dates from 1778.

E of the church is the **Panteón de San Fernando** (*Panteón de Hombres Ilustres*), declared public in 1835. Among famous Mexicans buried here are Pres. Benito Juárez (monument by Juan and Manuel Islas; 1874–80) and other presidents, incl. Vicente Guerrero, José Joaquín de Herrera, and Ignacio Comonfort; Miguel Lerdo de Tejada (1812–61), Ignacio Zaragoza (1829–62), Leandro Valle (1833–61); and Tomás Mejía (1820–67).

On the E side of the Panteón, C. Héroes runs N. At the corner with C. Esmeralda is the *Biblioteca Miguel de Cervantes Saavedra*, founded in 1924 (murals by Ramón Alva de la Canal). No. 46 (l.) is the house (late 19C) specially designed for himself by Antonio Rivas Mercado (see Rte 12). Six blocks N from the Panteón is Pl. Martínez de la Torre in COL. GUERRERO (once the estate of Rafael Martínez de la Torre [1828–76], politician, orator, and Maximilian's defending lawyer), developed as the city's fourth colonia from the 1870s. Here is the ambitious neo-Gothic church of *El Inmaculado Corazón de María* (1887–1902), by Ismael Rego.

Further W, at 50 Puente de Alvarado, is the neoclassical **Pal. Buenavista**, by Tolsá.

It is not without baroque hints and has a concave façade, remodelled in 1914 when the art deco window grilles were added. It was begun c 1795 for María Josefa Rodríguez de Pinillos y Gómez, marquesa de Selva Nevada, and destined for her son, the conde de Buenavista, who died before it was completed in 1803. The family sold it soon after. Subsequent owners included Santa-Anna, who used it as a summer residence. In 1865 Maximilian granted it to Marshal Bazaine, commander of the French forces, on his marriage to Josefa Peña y Azcárate.

Since 1968 it has been home to the **Museo de San Carlos** (Tues.–Sun., 10–7; fee), Mexico's finest collection of paintings (16–19C) by European masters. The majority were formerly in the Academia de San Carlos; the kernel of the collection is the legacy of the Academy from the 1780s.

The entrance gives on to the beautiful oval patio. The ground-floor rooms are devoted to temporary exhibitions.

FIRST FLOOR. Rooms VI–VIII contain 14–16C Spanish, Catalan, Netherlandish, and German paintings. R. VI. Lluis Borrassá (Gerona/Barcelona; c 1360–1426), Road to Damascus, a predella; Noli me tangere, a triptych (Resurrection; Christ appears to St Mary Magdalen; SS Catherine, Agatha, and Lucy), both works in Catalan Gothic style. Pere Espallargues (1425–95), Altarpiece of the Incarnation, a rare work showing Italian and Flemish tendencies. R. VII. Anon. late 14C Catalan, Scenes from the Life of Lazarus, with byzantine touches and marvellous detail. Anon. late 15C Catalan, Beheading of Santiago. Anon. 15C Valencian, Holy Trinity with SS Andrew and Basil; Pietà with supporting angels—both showing Italian and Flemish influences. Attr. Juan de Levi (Aragón; fl. 1378–1407), SS Luke and Matthew. Maestro de Palanquinos (15C León; a precursor of the Spanish Renaissance), SS Peter, Andrew, and Matthew. Anon. 15C German, St Jerome, full of superb detail. School of Jan Provoost (1462–1529; Bruges), Virgin and Child with St Anne and donors. Juan de Flandes (d. 1519), Descent from the Cross. Master of Osma (early 16C), SS Catherine and Mary Magdalen. Pedro Berruguete (c 1450–1504), Adoration of the Kings, by an artist trained in Naples and Urbino. Sch. of Giovanni Bellini, Virgin and Child. Sch. of Botticelli, Virgin and Child. R. VIII. Master of the Tiburtine Sibyl (15C Netherlandish), Raising of Lazarus—a little masterpiece, meticulously painted, wonderfully observed. Pieter de Kempener (1503–80; Brussels), The Seven Virtues. Jan Gossaert (c 1478–c 1536; Antwerp), Adoration of the Kings (a copy). Gillis I. Mostaert (c 1534–98), Christ in Limbo. Sch. of Gerard David (early 16C), Madonna and Child. Anon. 16C German, Creation of Eve, Original Sin, Expulsion from Eden—a triptych. Lucas Cranach the Elder (1472–1553), Frederick of Saxony; Adam and Eve. Luis de Morales (el Divino; c 1509–86), Madonna and Child writing in a book, a beautiful example of Mannerism and the influence of Raphael.

R. IX. Mannerism. Tintoretto, Man in a fur coat—an early work; Judith and Holofernes; Portrait of an old man. Pontormo, Madonna and Child, a typically startling work by a singular genius. Giovanni Biliverti (Jan Bilivert; 1576–1664), Marriage of Sarah and Tobias, by a Dutch painter settled in Florence. R. X. 17C Masters. Copy of José de Ribera, Jacob looking after Laban's flock. Mateo Cerezo (c 1626–66), Still Life with fish. Pedro de Orriente (1588–1644), Making cheese. Zurbarán, St Augustine; Supper at Emaus—mysterious in its tenebrism; St John of God. School of Velázquez, Portrait of a man. Rubens, Diana hunting; Portrait of a Spanish nobleman; Portrait of a man.

Three important works; the portraits emphasizing heads, features, and huge ruffles against dark backgrounds; the hunting scene full of movement—a type which was to influence Cristóbal de Villalpando.

Attr. Hyacinthe Rigaud, The future James III of England (1699). Pierre Mignard, Portrait of a man—a sympathetic work. Joris van Son (c 1623–67), Still Life—a closely observed Flemish work. Ferdinand van Kessel (1648–c 1696; Antwerp), Feasting monkeys. Joos van Craesbeeck (c 1606–61; Flemish), Cardplayers— homely and realistic. Adriaen van de Venne (1589–1662; Dutch), Quarrel over trousers. Jan Dirksz. Both (c 1618–52; Dutch), Landscape with figures and cattle. Attr. Albert Jansen Klomp (c 1618–88; Amsterdam), Bull tied to a tree, an exercise in stillness. Meindert Hobbema (1638–1709; Amsterdam), Landscape, with a beautiful sky. Van Dyck, Head of a bearded man. Frans Hals, Portrait of a man (c 1630). Luca Giordano, Ancient astronomer. Andrea Vaccaro (c 1598– 1670; Naples), St Agatha—dramatic and ecstatic, laterally illuminated for major emphasis. Rutilio di Lorenzo Manetti (1571–1639; Siena), Samson and Delilah, with notable chiaroscuro. Ciro Ferri, St Mary Magdalen and angels—a gorgeous baroque work, richly coloured and textured.

R. XI. 18–19C Works. Goya, Water-carrier; Marquesa de San Andrés—the minute detail of the clothing, frills, and jewels most unusual for Goya. Thomas Lawrence, Nicholas Vansittart, Lord Bexley, chancellor of the exchequer 1812–23; Man going shooting. Reynolds, Sir William Stanhope. John Opie, Portrait of a lady. Fragonard, Coquette and admirer. Sch. of Greuze, Head of a girl. Attr. J.-L. David, Portrait of a lady. Honoré Daumier, The Old Concièrge—a marvellous caricature. A.C.H. Vernet, Games in honour of Patroclus. Johann Friedrich Overbeck (1789–1869; German), Annunciation and Visitation—watercolour on parchment by an inspirer of the Nazarenes (see Rte 8). Ingres, St John the Baptist as a child. Francesco Coghetti (1804–75), Scene from the Flood—an Italian academic work (Coghetti was president of the Accademia di San Luca in Rome), commissioned direct by the Academia de San Carlos. Henri Decaisne (1779–1852; Belgian), Odalisque. Antoine Carte (1886–1954; Belgian), Miners. Joaquín Sorolla y Bastida (1863–1923; Spanish), Weaving nets. Ladislas de Czachorski (1850–1911; Polish), Confidants. Victor-Emile Cartier (1811–66; French), Bull frightened by serpent. Rosa Bonheur (1822–99; French), Calves. Pierre Puvis de Chavannes, Allegory of sadness. Pelegrín Clavé, Portraits of Ana Philips and Rosario Almanza de Echeverría—the latter his first work in Mexico (1846). Gustave Mascart (late 19C; French), Outskirts of Paris. Eugenio Landesio, Valley of Mexico; Vallefrenda—painted in Rome before he came to Mexico; Self-portrait.

Puente de Alvarado runs W. Beyond the busy intersection with Av. Insurgentes, Av. Ribera de San Cosme continues the traffic-laden road towards Tacuba. No. 10 in the first turning r. beyond the intersection, C. Dr Enrique González Martínez, is the *Museo Universitario del Chopo* (Wed.–Sun., 10–2, 4–7), for temporary exhibitions, concerts, plays, and other cultural activities. The build- ing, of iron, glass, and brick, was prefabricated in France, and put together by the engineers Luis Bacmeister and Aurelio Ruelas for a Japanese exhibition of 1910.

Further along Av. Ribera de San Cosme, at the corner with C. Serapio Rendón, is the much-restored church of **San Cosme**.

In 1667–75 Franciscan observants built the present church with a convent for retreats attached. In 1861 the church was closed and the convent sold to the heirs of Santos Degollado. It was broken up into lots, but part survives to the S of the church. During the final US assault on the city in Sept. 1847, Lt Ulysses S. Grant mounted a howitzer on the tower and shelled the neighbourhood. In the convent building in 1871 died doña Margarita Maza, the staunch and selfless wife of Pres. Juárez. Fr Augustine Fischer (1825–87), reputed eminence grise of Maximilian, ended his days as curate of the parish.

The façade, facing E, preserves a relief of the Holy Family watched over by God the Father and the Holy Ghost. On either side, statues of SS Cosmas and Damian, in medallion frames. The INTERIOR's chief beauty is the high altar- piece (mid-18C), once in San Joaquín (Tacuba), rearranged here in 1937. It beautifully combines churrigueresque and anastyle. The elegant, slender estípites on the inside are flanked by outer pairs of niche pilasters, almost obscured by the statuary, cherubs, and busts bursting through oval frames.

Across Av. Ribera de San Cosme, C. Sta María la Ribera runs N in the colonia of the same name (the third in the city, begun by c 1870) past (r.) the church of *Sagrada Familia de los*

Josefinos (1901–06), a neo-byzantine pile by Carlos Herrera. It reaches ALAMEDA STA MARIA LA RIBERA, whose centre is graced by the Moorish pavilion designed in 1884–85 by José Ramón Ibarrola for the international exhibition in New Orleans, and moved here in 1900. On the W side is the neo-Renaissance former building of the *Instituto Geológico Nacional* (1900–06), by Carlos Herrera. It now houses the *Museo de Geología de UNAM* (Mon.–Fri., 9–5). Besides the geological and natural history collections, it contains paintings by José María Velasco on geological and botanical themes. Three blocks E, in the colonia of BUENAVISTA, is the city's main railway station, **Gran Estación Central de Buenavista**, completed, by Jorge L. Medellín, in 1959.

From the station C. Buenavista runs S to join Puente de Alvarado, through Pl. de Buenavista. Here is a bronze monument to Columbus, modelled (1856–58) by Manuel Vilar and cast in 1892.

At 71 Av. Ribera de San Cosme (corner with C. Naranjo) is the **Casa de los Condes del Valle de Orizaba** (called *Casa de los Mascarones*), a one-storey country house built in 1766–71 for José Vivero Huertado de Mendoza, then holder of the title, and left unfinished at his death. It is remarkable in the adaptation of churrigueresque to the secular.

Exceptional estípites mark the stone façade, only substantial remaining part of the original building. On them stand male caryatids supporting the rich frieze. These alternate with wonderfully framed windows, still enclosed by original grilles.

Av. Ribera de San Cosme ends at the junction with Calz. Melchor Ocampo, former *Calz. Verónica*, which marked the line of the aqueduct of *Tlaxpana* (built in 1603–20; demolished in 1852–79), bringing water from the springs of Sta Fe and Chapultepec, running along the line of Av. Ribera de San Cosme, Puente de Alvarado, and Av. Hidalgo to end at the Caja Mariscala, behind where the Pal. de Bellas Artes now is.

On an island stands the small, circular *Cap. Cowdray* (Cap. Británica; 1908–09) by Charles J.S. Hall. It was the chapel of the *Panteón Inglés*, established in 1824, for British subjects. Burials ceased in 1926 after the opening of the new cemetery (see below). After road widening, its remaining area was converted into a small park. Behind, at 31 Calz. Melchor Ocampo, is the *Panteón Estadounidense* (US Cemetery), founded after 1847 for US war dead. Over 400 were buried here. Along Calz. Verónica on 13 Sept. 1847, Gen. Worth's division marched relentlessly on to turn along the San Cosme road and enter the city from the NE on the 14th.

From here Calz. México-Tacuba runs NW through a crowded inner suburb to (3km) *Tacuba*.

The quickest way to reach the places described is by taxi, bus, or metro—the Normal station is two blocks beyond the junction.

The road passes (No. 70; l.) the church of *San Antonio de las Huertas* (1952–57), designed by Enrique de la Mora and built by Félix Candela—one of their ingenious shell-concrete structures. We pass (r.) Mexico's main teacher-training college, the *Escuela Normal* (more strictly *Nacional*) *de Maestros* (1945–47), designed by Mario Pani.

Its long open-air theatre has six tiers of balcony corridors on either side. The stage, backed by a curved concrete wall, is covered by a mural, a national allegory (1947–48) by José Clemente Orozco, painted in ethyl silicate. In the centre, the Serpent held fast by the Eagle; on the l., Man, head in the clouds, ascends up a giant staircase from the material to the spiritual; on the r., an Indian hand puts a block of stone into place above symbols of a prehispanic past. The mural surrounds a reconstituted 18C portal from the old university building, integrated into the composition as the Spanish element in Mexico. The lobby contains more murals by Orozco: a commentary on education bringing hope for a brighter future.

C 500m N of the college is the *Instituto Politécnico Nacional* (1937–)which boasts an outdoor mural by David Alfaro Siqueiros illustrating man's mastery of technology. A long concave rectangle, and a remarkable exercise in perspective, it is painted in pyroxilin on aluminium.

Beyond the Escuela Normal we pass (l.) the former headquarters of the *Colegio Militar* (see Rtes 10, 15), erected, for a teacher training college, in 1908–10. At 305 Calz. México-Tacuba is the 18C church of *Nuestra Señora de la Merced de las Huertas* which contains, on the r. of the nave, an altarpiece with the slenderest of estípites incorporating paintings (1751) on the Guadalupe theme by Cabrera. At 8 C. Mar Arafura, NE from Popotla metro station, is the **Museo de Artes Gráficas** (Mon.–Fri., 9–6; adm by appointment), illustrating the history of typesetting and printing in Mexico from prehispanic times. The first printing press, brought by Juan Pablos in 1539, and a mid-16C psalter (reputed the largest of its type in the world) are shown.

Calz. México-Tacuba continues to the *Arbol de la Noche Triste*, under which Cortés is supposed to have sat and wept after the disasters of 30 June 1520. A venerable, gnarled, shored-up ahuehuete tree, set off by a modern fountain, it suffered from arson in 1872. Opposite stands the simple 18C church of *San Esteban Popotla*.

C 1km further, Calz. México-Tacuba is crossed by Calz. Marina Nacional, running SE to meet Calz. Melchor Ocampo and N to Azcapotzalco and the NW suburbs. Opposite Tacuba metro station is the church of **San Gabriel**, part of a Franciscan convent built in the 1560s under the auspices of Antonio Cortés Chimalpopoca, grandson of Moctezuma.

The church is substantially of the early 18C. In the upper storey of the Mannerist main portal, the relief of the Annunciation (1733) is unusual in including the infant Christ bodily present below God the Father and the Holy Ghost. The side portal shows undulating lines and flame-like motifs, a baroque tendency. The INTERIOR has kept its 18C pulpit. Part of the choir arch dates back to the 16C, as does a column in the Cap. del Señor del Claustro. Restoration in the late 1960s rescued part of the small 16C cloister and the two original entry arches into the convent.

Tacuba was an area of rural settlement in the Classic Period, and part of the hinterland of Teotihuacán. In the Postclassic, sometime during the 12C, it became a Tepanec city, known as *Tlacopan*, when the Tepaneca ('those on the rocks') Aztecs migrated into the Basin of Mexico; another ancient name for the district was *Atlacuihayán*.

During fighting between Azcapotzalco (capital of the Tepanec state) and the Mexica Aztec–Texcoco alliance, Tlacopan, no doubt chafing under the harsh rule of the Tepanec king Tezozómoc (1343–1426), contrived to remain neutral. Under these conditions it became accepted as the third, but weakest, member of a Triple Alliance formed in 1428. It received only one-fifth of the tributes from the subject towns of the Alliance, while Tenochtitlán and Texcoco each received two-fifths.

It was eventually swallowed up in Aztec-Tenochtitlán empire-building, although there were princes of Tlacopan right up to the reign of Moctezuma II Xocoyotzin (1502–20), and it remained an important provincial city. Causeways joined the ceremonial centres of Tacuba-Tlacopan and Tenochtitlán–Tlatelolco across W Lago de Texcoco. The Aztec king Axayácatl (1468–81) had a palace built in Tlacopan.

Av. Azcapotzalco runs N to **AZCAPOTZALCO**, an industrial area still maintaining its prehispanic tradition as a metal-working centre, and conspicuous for its *18 de Marzo* oil refinery (closed).

The site, *Amantla*, was founded in the 9C AD by Otomí and Teotihuacano immigrants, who carried on Teotihuacano traditions there into the 9C and 10C.

In the 12C the Tepaneca, one of the seven Aztec tribes, migrated into the Basin of Mexico and under their ruler, Tezozómoc (1343–1426), founded a city-state ruled from Azcapotzalco. During their conquests they drove the Mexica Aztecs from Chapultepec and subdued several other city-states in the W Basin, incl. Culhuacán in 1367 and Tenayuca in 1371. The Mexica, under Acamapichtli (1372–91), were tributaries to Tezozómoc; and Huitzilhuitl (1391–1415), Acamapichtli's successor, married one of his daughters. In c 1417 Tezozómoc ordered the assassination of Chimalpopoca (1415–26), the third Mexica ruler, and himself slew Ixtlilxóchitl (1409–18), king of Texcoco. Ixtlilxóchitl's son, Nezahualcóyotl (b. 1402; king 1428–72), later allied with the Mexica under Itzcóatl (1426–40) and his nephew Tlacaelel, and with the city of Huexotzingo, to destroy Azcapotzalco and make the Tepaneca tributaries to the Triple Alliance of Texcoco, Tenochtitlán, and Tlacopan in 1428. Under the Mexica Aztecs the city was an important provincial centre with a noted slave market and a causeway joined to the causeway between Tlatelolco and Tacuba.

At the junction of the avenida with C. Juárez, on the E side of Pl. Hidalgo, is the former Dominican convent of **San Felipe y Santiago**, its tree-planted atrio, surrounded by a high wall, a peaceful haven.

The convent was built during the 1560s and 1570s at the instance of the learned friar Lorenzo de la Asunción (1523–1607; b. and d. on the feast of the Assumption). The present church dates mainly from the late 17C; the adjoining Cap. del Rosario was mainly finished by c 1720. The Indian population of Azcapotzalco, estimated at 17,000 at the Conquest, was especially hit during the later 16C cocoliztli epidemics and many of the friars, tending the sick, themselves caught the pestilence. During the early 17C the convent was reduced to a doctrina dependent on the mother house in Mexico City. After a resurgence of fortune in the late 17C and 18C, by 1843 the community was reduced to two friars. By 1860 the buildings were in full decay. In Aug. 1821 a final action of the war of Independence was fought in the atrio.

ATRIO. The surrounding wall shows prehispanic masonry. In the NW corner a small 18C chapel is an elaboration of an original posa. At the SW angle, embedded in the wall of the Pal. Municipal, is the façade, undeniable 16C work, of another posa.

EXTERIOR. The church walls retain much from the 16C structure, but were raised higher at N and S in the late 17C to allow for vaulting. The W façade (1785–90) has neostyle baroque and churrigueresque tendencies, the lambrequin motif dominant. The tower dates from c 1750. The adjoining Cap. del Rosario has its own small atrio. Above its baroque doorway is a statue of Our Lady of the Rosary, a 16C survival.

INTERIOR. On the r. of the nave is a baroque altarpiece (1681), notable for its varied solomonic columns and ornate upper pilasters, incorporating 16 paintings of the Life of St Rose, early works by Cristóbal de Villalpando.

Opposite opens the CAP. DEL ROSARIO; above its entrance a relief of Our Lady with SS Francis and Dominic. The interior contains more, excellent, altarpieces. In the nave the retable of Our Lady of Guadalupe (l.) is a simple late 18C work; that of St Joseph (r.; 1738) is churrigueresque, with firm estípites. In the r. transept a baroque altarpiece, dedicated to St Anne, contains upper panels painted with Scenes from the Life of Our Lady and, in the predella, SS Jerome, Gregory the Great, Augustine, Thomas Aquinas, St Anne and Our Lady, and St Roch (the latter two smaller, in the centre), by Juan Correa (1681). The late 17C central statue of St Anne is superb. On the lower part of the N wall of the transept are two paintings (1670s), detached from a retable, by Pedro Ramírez: Immaculate Conception with SS Michael and Teresa (l.); Assumption with SS Gabriel and Rose (r.). The anastyle high altarpiece (1779) is a soaring glorification of Our Lady, composed of a central and outer pairs of ornamental niche pilasters.

The latter are obscured by medallions, mouldings, and figures; and those of the lower storey are joined to those of the upper by spiralling broken pediments. At the sides of the central Virgin and Child stand SS Anne and Joachim, and, a little below, SS Elizabeth and Zachary. Above are Our Lord and St Joseph, and, higher up on either side, SS Peter and Paul and SS John the Baptist and John the Evangelist. Higher still, St Michael holds the banner of Guadalupe and annihilates Lucifer. In the charming polychrome medallions, the Mysteries of the Rosary. Attached to the pillars on either side are two small corner retables, almost unique survivals, of the same period. The niches contain statues of SS John Nepomuk and Gertrude. The chapel arch keystones hold small niches for saintly images.

In the three-arched portería, on the S side of the church, are remains of late 16C murals. The beautiful two-storey CLOISTER (finished c 1565), with low arches, retains its wooden-beam ceilings, especially elaborate at the corners, at which are niches framed by stone coffering. Some of the original painted friezes remain. Also on the S side of the church, joining presbytery and antesacristy, is the *Cap. de San Francisco*, retaining 16C work, but changed in the 17–18C, probably an adaptation of the first church on the site. C 1.5km N, on Av. Manuel Acuña, between Avs Azcapotzalco and Reforma, the *Cap. de la Concepción* is a charming 16C survival.

Beyond the road junction, Calz. México-Tacuba runs SW through the NW part of the delegación MIGUEL HIDALGO, NW edge of the Federal District. At the corner of the calzada and C. Lago Saima begins the series of panteones (cemeteries) allotted to foreign residents of Mexico. First the *Panteón Alemán*; then, at 1129 Calz. México-Tacuba, the *Panteón Inglés* (see above). On its W side, the *Panteón Moderno* adjoins the *Panteón Español*, inaugurated in 1886, with its neo-Romanesque chapel by Ignacio and Eusebio de la Hidalga and fine metalwork gateway (1891–92).

At Panteones metro station the road forks. Calz. México-Tacuba now goes SW, after c 1km skirting the *Panteón Sanctorum*, on land once occupied by the Carmelite convent of *San Joaquín*, founded in 1696, whose church was restored with the laying-out of the cemetery. In the chapel to the r. of the r. transept is a Transfixing of St Teresa by Juan Correa. Off C. Arista is the restored early 17C church of *Sanctorum*, with intricately carved main portal and interior triumphal arch. Further SE is the *Panteón Francés*, opened in 1942. Calz. México-Tacuba ends at the junction with the Anillo Periférico, just N of the *El Toreo* bullring (see Rte 19).

10 Chapultepec

The **Bosque de Chapultepec**, the great park W of the centre, is the unrivalled recreational area of Mexico City. It covers approx. 12 sq km and counts seven museums, the National Auditorium, theatres, a zoo, four lakes, botanical gardens, a marine park, and other attractions, as well as the residence of the president. The easternmost part, Bosque Antiguo, is divided from the two W parts by the Anillo Periférico; the continuation of Paseo de la Reforma cuts through to the N; Av. Constituyentes is the boundary on the S. Planted with ahuehuete trees, which give ample shade, and intersected by walks and drives, its welcome spaciousness is apt to be invaded by crowds on public holidays and the litter they leave behind—a phenomenon by no means peculiar to Mexico.

According to legend, in AD 1256 the Mexica migrated into the Basin of Mexico and settled on the rocky hill, *Cerro de la Sauterelle*, in the E part of the park. They were twice expelled by the Tepaneca of Azcapotzalco and retreated to Culhuacán on the N shore of Lago de Xochimilco, only to be evicted by its ruler, Tizapán, to a volcanic wasteland E of the city. Here the Mexica thrived, however, serving the Culhua as mercenaries and establishing the descent from the Toltecs that they sought by receiving prince Acamapichtli (1372–91) from Culhuacán as their first king. (The Aztec king, Itzcóatl [1426–40] later took the title 'Lord of Culhuacán' in order to exclude others from claims to Toltec succession.)

The Mexica were eventually bold enough to ask the Culhuacán ruler for political alliance through marriage between his daughter and their chief. Not realizing what this meant, he agreed and arrived at the wedding ceremony only to find that his daughter had been sacrificed to the Mexica's god, Huitzilopochtli (some sources say Xipe Totec), and flayed. The infuriated Culhua drove the Mexica into the marshes of Texcoco. The Mexica were 'told' by their patron god that their final resting place must be where they saw an eagle perched on a prickly pear cactus (nopal), in some sources with a snake in its mouth, which they duly witnessed on the island later named Tenochtitlán in W Lago de Texcoco.

In the 15C Chapultepec (Náhuatl 'grasshopper hill') became a recreational area for Aztec rulers after Moctezuma I Ilhuicamina (1440–68) converted an existing fortress and temple into a summer palace. The earliest park may have been laid out by, or at least encouraged by, Nezahualcóyotl (1418–72), ruler of Texcoco and ally of Moctezuma I. Together they also built an aqueduct to carry water from Chapultepec's springs to Tenochtitlán.

In 1456–57 Moctezuma I allegedly caused a memorial relief to be carved in the cliff-side. Barely visible today, it depicts him standing in the guise of Topiltzin Quetzalcóatl (see *Tula*) wearing a flamingo-feather shirt, a quetzal-feather loincloth, and a feather headdress. Other carvings—depicting Tlacaélel, his chief counsellor, and Moctezuma II Xocoyotzin (1502–20)—are said to have been destroyed in 1539 by order of Juan de Zumárraga.

From springs on Chapultepec potable water was carried to Tenochtitlán by aqueducts designed and built by Moctezuma I and Nezahualcóyotl. These went N and joined the causeway between Tenochtitlán and Tacuba.

By the early 17C a viceregal residence had been built here, to be used on arrival before formal reception in the city centre. In 1702 viceroy duque de Alburquerque held his first receptions amid much festivity, incl. bullfights. Such jollity, however, could give rise to intemperate behaviour and in 1739 it was ordered that in future viceroys should proceed straight to the viceregal palace. Another cause of royal worry was the state of the road into the city: 'pitted with ruts on all sides, into which men, waggons, and horses fall by the hour'. In 1784 a gunpowder factory nearby blew up, and took the decayed house with it. In 1785 Viceroy Bernardo de Gálvez began building a summer palace, but this was stopped by the crown in 1787. The suspended building became something of a white elephant. In 1843, after repairs, it was turned into the Colegio Militar. In Sept. 1847, poorly prepared, far from artillery-proof, and defended by an inadequate force under Gen. Nicolás Bravo, it was the final obstacle to the US forces' progress into the city. At dawn on 13 Sept. troops from Gen. Gideon Pillow's division began the assault. At 9.30 Bravo surrendered and the stars and stripes were raised. 'If we planted our batteries in hell', exclaimed Santa-Anna, 'the damned Yankees would take them from us'. 'God is a Yankee', muttered one of his aides. Some of the youngest cadets had refused to leave the building. Seven of them, who heroically gave their lives, have achieved immortality as the Niños Héroes.

We enter Chapultepec at its E end. A broad entrance pavement leads to the *Monumento a los Niños Héroes* (1952), by Enrique Aragón Echegaray and Ernesto Tamariz. It incorporates a crystal urn containing their remains. To the r. is the **Museo de Arte Moderno** (entrance at the corner of Paseo de la Reforma and Calz. Gandhi; Tues.–Fri., 10–6), with a permanent collection of Mexican art; temporary exhibitions are also held here.

The permanent collection is in Rooms II and III in the first building reached from the entrance. R. II. Mexican Painting 1920s–1970s. Starting in the outer circle, moving r., the first section shows work by the 'Contemporáneos' (1924–34), artists concerned with formal experimentation related to Paris vanguardisms. Early works by Rufino Tamayo; small oils from the 'Muerte de Sta Ana' series (1932) by Manuel Rodríguez Lozano; 'La mesera' (1923) by Abraham Angel. Next, work by the 'Escuela Mexicana' (1940–50), mostly muralists who also did easel paintings. Portraits by Diego Rivera show the thematic divorce between his murals and easel work; unity is maintained in the work of Orozco and Siqueiros. Frida Kahlo, 'Los dos Fridas' (1939); Olga Costa, 'Vendedora de Frutas' (1951). Early black and white photographs by Manuel Alvarez Bravo, still an influence in present-day Mexican photography.

Mexican Surrealism (1940–50): Leonora Carrington, Remedios Varo, Kati Horna (all foreign artists). A fourth section shows the antecedents of geometricism in Mexico in the 1950s, among them the Russian Vlady and the German Matías Goeritz. Gunther Gerszo and Carlos Mérida developed their respective geometric and landscape figures from an interest in Maya architecture and folk art respectively. Photographs relating to the experimental museum 'El Eco' (1951–52), directed by Goeritz, based on the unity of art and architecture, with participation, among others, from the US Merce Cunningham dance group.

The new 'Escuela Mexicana' (1950s): largely abstract, reflecting US abstract expressionism: works by Roger van Gunten, Antonio Rodríguez Luna, Lilia Carrillo, Alberto Gironella, Francisco Corzas. 'Neofiguration' (1960s), strongly influenced by Orozco. Large silk-screen print, 'El gigante', by José Luis Cuevas. 'Nueva Presencia' group (1960s): works by Javier Arevalo and Arnold Belkin.

The next section includes abstract geometric paintings by Vicente Rojo, Fernando García, Federico Silva, and Manuel Felguérez.

In the centre circle, mainly figurative paintings, of the new 'Escuela Mexicana': Ricardo Martínez, 'Dos figuras' (1958), evoking the massiveness of prehispanic sculpture; Juan Soriano, 'Apolo y las Musas' (1954), influenced by the bright colours of Mexican folk art. Rufino Tamayo, paintings (1950s) in bright colours. Francisco Toledo, paintings reflecting an oaxaqueño environment.

Among the sculpture are pieces by Luis Ortiz Monasterio, using prehispanic themes; Francisco Zúñiga, 'Los dos esperanzas' (bronze; 1959); Germán Cueto, recent abstract work. Tapestry by Marta Palau.

FIRST FLOOR. R. III. Mexican art of the 1970s and 1980s. Art groups within local communities in Mexico City: 'Proceso Pentágono' (discontinued); 'Tepito Arte Acá'—murals and artistic endeavours among the people; 'Suma' (1976–81), organized by students from the Academia, specializing in political street art.

Victor Hugo Núñez, 'Espacio Tiempo de Odio' (1984); paintings by the four Castro Lonero brothers, Arnold Belkin, and Alberto Gironella, etc (predominantly figurative representations of politics in everyday life); photographs by José Luis Neyra, Nacho López, Graciela Iturbide, and others.

Past the Monumento a los Niños Héroes a road winds up to the Cerro de Chapultepec towards the castle. Just before the castle gates, to the r., is the **Galería de Historia—la Lucha del Pueblo Mexicano por su Libertad** (Tues.– Sat., 10–5; Sun. and holidays, 9–2), a helicoid building (1960; designed by Pedro Ramírez Vázquez), in which scale models, dioramas and cycloramas, photographs, etc., illustrate scenes in Mexican history from the 18C to the Constitution of 1917. To the l. in the entrance lobby is a bronze panel by José Chávez Morado representing the fusion of Mexican and Spanish cultures.

The **Castillo de Chapultepec** crowns the hill at the E end of the park. It combines the late 18C base with the refashioning of 1864–65 by Ramón Rodríguez Arangoity (helped by Eleuterio Méndez) to the orders of Maximilian and substantial changes made by later regimes. The conspicuous round tower (*Caballero Alto*) was amplified in 1878 by the architect and astronomer Angel Anguiano as first home of the *Observatorio Nacional*.

Maximilian conceived Chapultepec as a second Miramar, his beloved palace near Trieste. Rodríguez Arangoity began to modernize the W wing and made improvements to the E wing, known as the Alcázar. The interior (Pompeian) decoration was entrusted to Santiago Rebull. Here Maximilian and Carlota held their brilliant, fated court and transacted state business. In 1872 the castle was nominated a presidential residence. In 1883 a two-floor complex on the W side was ordered, to rehouse the Colegio Militar. From 1884 Pres. Díaz began the conversion of the Alcázar, in the prevailing afrancesado style, as his summer residence. From here on 9 Feb. 1913 Pres. Madero, escorted by members of the college, started his fateful journey to the Pal. Nacional and his death. In 1916 began the demolition of part of the former college and adaptation of the rest as presidential offices. Later presidents occupied the castle, and made modifications. In 1939 Pres. Cárdenas transferred it to INAH: the W wing for a museum; the Alcázar for preservation as a historic monument.

The **Museo Nacional de Historia** (daily, 10–6; fee) is the foremost museum dedicated to Mexico from the Conquest to the Revolution. Its exhibits are unsurpassed in their variety and interest, and a tour is enlivened by masterworks by leading 20C muralists.

The museum's collections (of paintings in particular) are so extensive that much has to be kept in storage. Dispositions are changed from time to time, to allow hitherto unknown objects to be brought forward.

The entrance is by the S doorway of the W wing. MAIN ENTRANCE HALL STAIRCASE. On the ceiling, a mural (1970) by Gustavo Flores celebrating the Niños Héroes. On the l. wall, a fresco allegory of the Revolution (1933) by Eduardo Solares Gutiérrez, showing Madero in the centre. Opposite, J. Cusachs, Capture of Puebla in Apr. 1867 by Porfirio Díaz (1902). We enter the W patio and turn sharp r. to ROOM I. New Spain. Jorge González Camarena, 'La fusión de dos culturas' (1963)—the struggle between eagle warrior and conquistador. 16C cannon from Veracruz. 16C armour; suit of chain mail. Biombo de la Conquista, late 17C folding screen painted with 12 scenes from the capture of Tenochtitlán (once property of the duques de Moctezuma). Portraits of four viceroys: Antonio de Mendoza (1535–50); Luis de Velasco (1550–64); attr. Simón Pereyns, Martín Enríquez de Almanza (1568–80); Luis Enríquez de Guzmán, conde de Alva de Liste (1650–53). Codice Mendocino (Mendoza Codex; c 1548): a history of Mexico City, tax register, and report on ancient Mexican customs. Marquetry bargueño (late 16C). Portrait of Gaspar de la Cerda Sandoval Silva y Mendoza, conde de Galve (viceroy 1688–96). Attr. Diego Correa, 17C painting of Mexico City. European religious objects in enamel (16–17C). Attr. Nicolás Rodríguez Juárez, Baptism of Maxixcatzin, one of the four lords of Tlaxcala. Four more viceroys: attr. Simón Pereyns, Pedro Moya y Contreras (1584–85); Juan Palafox y Mendoza (1642); Payo Enríquez de Rivera (1673–80); Juan de Ortega y Montañés (1701). Two 17C Mexican gilded polychrome reliefs: St Joseph and the Child Jesus; Heavenly Patronage over the Church. Collection of 16–17C Mexican silver.

R. II. Viceroyalty. 16–17C coins. 17C ivories. 16C Flemish astrolabe. Coins of Charles III, Charles IV, and Ferdinand VII. 18C ivories, silver, and porcelain. Miguel Cabrera, St Joseph and the Infant Christ; Sor Juana Inés de la Cruz (1750), a superlative portrait. R. III. Later Viceroyalty. José de Alzíbar, Sor María Ignacia de la Sangre de Cristo, a 22-year-old in finery on the day of her profession in the convent of Sta Clara. 18C anon. painting of St Roch, surrounded by silver filigree. Bronze copy of Tolsá, Bust of Cortés (for his tomb, destroyed before 1844; see Rte 5). Rafael Jimeno y Planes, Francisco Javier Lizana y Beaumont, abp of Mexico and unworldly viceroy (1809–10). José Luis Rodríguez Alconedo, silver relief portrait of Charles IV (late 18C), which won him the rank of académico de mérito.

R. IV. Later Viceroyalty and Independence. Anon., Pl. Mayor in Mexico City (c 1770).

The viceroy in his carriage, with full escort, approaches the cathedral, accompanied by oidores. The plaza is crowded with stallholders and customers. Looming on its W is the Parián. The detail is enough to give hours of study.

Portraits of the Jesuit philosopher and historian Francisco Javier Clavijero (1731–87); Viceroy Martín de Mayorga (1779–83); Charles III by Ramón Torres; and Viceroy Bernardo de Gálvez (1785–86) on horseback, a calligraphic portrait by Fray Jerónimo and Fray Pablo de Jesús. 18C pictorial explanation of Mexican castes. Pedro Gualdi, Pal. de Minería (mid-19C). Juan Nepomuceno Illescas, Portrait of Josefa Ortiz and purse belonging to her. Portraits of insurgents and opposing viceroys. Painting of the entry into Mexico City of the Army of the Three Guarantees (1821). Table on which were signed the Treaties of Córdoba (1821). Chair used by Miguel Hidalgo, and his baptismal font (from Cuitzeo). Standard of Our Lady of Guadalupe hoisted by Hidalgo in Sept. 1810 in the church of Atotonilco. Standard of José María Morelos and sword he carried at Cuautla. Drum played during the celebratory procession for the Plan of Iguala (Feb. 1821). Insurgent banner (1812). Banner of the Army of the Three Guarantees.

R. V. Juan O'Gorman, 'Retablo de la Independencia' (1960–61), painted after Diego Rivera's death, on a concave wall surface he had originally designed for Rivera.

The l. section shows Mexican society at the end of the viceroyalty, with the Inquisition and precursors of Independence. The central part shows principal locations and characters of the war of Independence, and the different ideological currents. At r., Hidalgo bears the banner of Our Lady of Guadalupe. Further r., Congress of Chilpancingo (1813–14). Morelos is shown twice, once as general at the Congress; once, in civilian dress, during his pre-1814 campaigns. At far r., Vicente Guerrero. The l. side of the mural is done under the moon and a dark sky; at r., the dawning of independent Mexico occurs under the light of the new day and by the open sea, alluding to physical and political separation from Spain.

R. VI. Nation and Independence. Among the possessions of Agustín de Iturbide are his sword, the crucifix he carried at his execution, a crystal set made in Bohemia. Chocolate cup belonging to Guadalupe Victoria. Pascual Alamán's portrait of Lucas Alamán, politician and historian. Material relating to the governments of Guerrero, Bustamante, and Santa-Anna. Carlos Nebel, Lithographs of scenes of the US invasion in 1847. Coat, knife, and sword belonging to Guerrero. Uniforms, prints, medals, and guns associated with Santa-Anna's dictatorship (1853–55). Material relating to the revolution of Ayutla (1854) and the Constitution of 1857. Juan Cordero, Portrait of the children José and Julia Iglesias Calderón (1865).

Between RR. VI and VII (archway between two inner patios). On r. wall, acrylic mural (1960) by Angel Bolívar showing the battle of Zacatecas (1914). Opposite, acrylic mural (1959) by José Reyes Meza showing distribution of prehispanic cultures in Mesoamerica and the arrival of the Spaniards by boat from the E.

R. VII. Along back wall, fresco by José Clemente Orozco, 'La reforma y la caída del Imperio' (1948).

In centre, the head of Juárez symbolizes the triumph of the republic. Below, the mummified corpse of Maximilian is borne by his supporters, who include Napoleon III (r.). Upper l., the republican flag, below which soldiers ward off reactionary clergy. Upper r., another soldier attacks a caricature bishop.

RR. VIII and IX. Victory of the Republic 1857–76. Portraits of Juárez, Ignacio Zaragoza, Sebastián Lerdo de Tejada, and Díaz (by José Obregón; 1883). Costumes of the period. Felipe Sojo, Bust of Maximilian. The sword he surrendered to Escobedo is displayed, as are guns used at his execution, and his imperial ring. English spyglass (mid-19C) belonging to Zaragoza.

R. X. Dictatorship 1876–1911. Clothing, uniforms, books, pamphlets, china, fans, letters, and documents help to give the atmosphere of the period, as does an early Mexican telephone. Presidential chair, used by Francisco Villa on his visit to Chapultepec in Dec. 1914. Jesús Contreras, Bust of doña Carmen Romero Rubio.

On end wall of R. XI the fresco 'Retrato de Francisco I. Madero: la Revolución 1910–1914' (1968) by Juan O'Gorman shows in the foreground Madero setting out from Chapultepec in Feb. 1913. At l., Gen Huerta and Henry Lane Wilson, US ambassador, in a doorway allude to Madero's betrayal and murder. In the centre, political factions supporting Madero; in the lower part of this section, José Guadalupe Posada holding a print of Madero. At r., 'El Santañón', a woman revolutionary general. At far r., Madero's wife and one of his brothers, and Pino Suárez are shown underneath a doorway.

On opposite wall O'Gorman's mural 'Feudalismo porfirista' (1973) shows (l.) the dictatorship: Díaz enthroned surrounded by científicos, incl. Justo Sierra and José Yves Limantour. In background, allusions to the regime's extravagance. In centre, barracks of the rurales, towards which moves a group of peasants intending to set it alight. On r., repression: caciques and a hacienda foreman torture a peasant family, while behind, an old man motions them to remain silent. Further back, behind the élite's mansions, peasant housing, with a tienda de raya guarded by rurales. On r. wall, a fresco panel shows Francisco Villa and Felipe Angeles, leaders of the División del Norte, with a script below referring to their influence on the course of the Revolution. The remaining walls were still unfinished when O'Gorman died in 1982.

R. XII. Revolution 1910–17. Jorge González Camarena's mural 'Constitución de 1917' (1966): Carranza in the centre, flanked by his colleagues, an enveloping eagle backing them, and the constitutionalist army. R. XIII. From Porfiriato to Revolution. The monumental mural 'Del Porfiriato a la Revolución' by David Alfaro Siqueiros was begun in 1957; work was interrupted in 1960–64 when Siqueiros was jailed on political grounds, and finally completed in 1966. The materials are acrylic and fibre glass mounted on celotex and triplay.

On l. wall, four texts by Francisco I. Madero and Ricardo Flores Magón refer to their political ideologies. The mural opposite the entrance commemorates martyrs of the Revolution, based on a photograph taken in Nochistlán (Zacatecas) in 1913. In foreground, the corpse of the artist's father-in-law, Lt-Col Leopoldo Arenal Bannet. The mural at right-angles to this wall celebrates the Horse, fundamental to the revolutionary struggle. On l. wall behind, the Nation up in arms, villistas and zapatistas representing the popular forces, carrancistas the constitutionalists, each faction differentiated by its own type of sombrero. Behind are principal figures from the period, and female members of the liberal party. The l. part of the back wall panel shows the ideological precursors of the Mexican liberal party: Marx, Lenin, and Prud'hon among the intellectuals. Journalists and caricaturists opposed to the Díaz regime are also here, incl. José Guadalupe Posada. In centre of back panel, Strike at Cananea (1907), antecedent of the Revolution, with workers seeking protection from oppression. In foreground, Fernando Palomares, a liberal, fights for the Mexican flag with the US owner of the mining company, William Greene. To r., Vice President Ramón Corral and ministers are protected by rurales. Red and white strike banners drape the panel's upper part.

On r. wall, Díaz, his foot on the 1857 Constitution. To his r., Victoriano Huerta; to his l., Limantour. In front of Díaz, dancing aristocratic women. The final panel by the entrance shows Díaz petrified in a wasteland—the barrenness of the porfiriato.

UPPER FLOOR. RR. XIV, XV, and XVI. Fine Arts 1760–1917. From religious painting of the viceroyalty to costumbrista themes, landscape and historical painting by Mexican and foreign artists (eg, Edouard Pingret, J.M. Rugendas, Pedro Gualdi), lithographs, and 19C and early 20C caricatures. A selection of the museum's large store of portraits (incl. works by Ignacio María Barreda and Juan Cordero, and wax reliefs) is also on display. Sculpture, woodcarving, silverwork, furniture, ceramics, objects in tortoiseshell, etc. (17–19C). The ponderous malachite pieces, carved in Italy and bought in France, were destined for the Pal. Nacional during the porfiriato, but were never installed.

In RR. XVII and XVIII photographs illustrate aspects of two Articles in the Constitution of 1917: Article 27, which enunciated principles on the ownership of land and land reform; Article 123 (labour laws), on the rights to strike, to social security, to an eight-hour working day and a weekly rest day, and incl. provisions on the prohibition of child labour. RR. XIX, XX, and XXI. Economic Organization and Social Structure 1760–1917. Paintings, lithographs, photographs, handicrafts, agricultural implements, etc. illustrate economic and social conditions and developments, and the 19C contrast between owners of the means of production and labouring classes.

The museum also possesses a large, movable acrylic painting (1979) by Arnold Belkin: arrival of Villa and Zapata at the National Palace on 6 Dec. 1914, in which he uses photography, a technique learnt from Siqueiros.

To the r. of S entrance (W end of Alcázar) is the CARRIAGE ROOM. This contains the carriage for the everyday use of Maximilian and Carlota. Their state carriage, built in Milan by Cesare Sola, is in stark contrast to the two simple carriages of Juárez, used by him during his continuous journeys in N Mexico in the mid-1860s. On l. wall, acrylic mural (1972) by Antonio González Orozco—Juárez as symbol of the Revolution against French intervention: in upper l., the battle of Puebla (5 May 1862); to r., the Castillo de Chapultepec appears as it was before Maximilian's alterations; lower l., French troops, with republican guerrillas at r. On r. wall, another acrylic mural (1967) by the same artist showing Juárez's triumphant return to the National Palace in 1867.

ALCAZAR. On the S side opens the Flag Room, containing standards and colours belonging to Mexican regiments (19C). Facing E on the ground floor are the restored Imperial Apartments (no entry; well viewed through large windows). Salón de Música: portraits of Maximilian and Carlota (1865) by Albert Graeffe, of Maximilian's parents Franz Karl of Habsburg and Sophia of Wittelsbach (1865) by Rudolf Müller, of Napoleon III (c 1860) attr. Pelegrín Clavé; furniture, chairs and sofas covered in Aubusson tapestry, a gift from Napoleon III. Empress's Recámara: decorated in Boulle style. Cuarto de Baño: onyx bath, thought to belong to Carlota. At the SE corner are the salón de espera (waiting room) for secretaries of state under Díaz and the reception room used by his wife; at the NE corner, Díaz's dining room (restored).

Recently restored on the upper floor are (SE corner) their bedrooms; the sumptuous central Salón de Embajadores flanked by the Galería de Emplomados, notable for its late 19C stained glass made in Paris by Champigneulles fils; the Salones Azules on the N side, used as guest rooms.

From the Museo de Arte Moderno the continuation of Paseo de la Reforma through the park reaches (r.) the **Museo Rufino Tamayo** (Tues.–Sun., 11–7; fee), the building designed by Abraham Zabludovsky and Teodoro González de León, and inaugurated in 1981, a magnificent collection of 20C painting, sculpture, and engravings donated to the Mexican republic by the artist Rufino Tamayo and his wife, Olga Flores Rivas.

The museum is so singularly designed for ease of viewing, with rooms of different sizes and variations of light both artificial and natural, that one loses all sense of the level one is on.

The central patio is devoted to the sculpture collection. Three rooms are reserved for temporary exhibitions and there is an auditorium with capacity for 250. The 300 or so works by some 150 Mexican and foreign artists include some of Tamayo's finest, and others by Dalí, Picasso, Miró, Carlos Mérida, Manuel Felguérez, Francis Bacon, José Luis Cuevas, Vassarely, and others. Notable among the paintings are Fernand Léger, 'Los clavadistas circulares' (1942). Picasso, 'Nude on Divan' (1961). Mark Tobey, 'Restricted Space' (1950). Jacques Lipchitz, 'Allegory of Orpheus' (c 1941). Max Ernst, 'Tired People' (1943), a disconcerting surrealist piece. Joan Miró, 'Pintura' (1927). André Masson, 'Vampires' (1961). René Magritte, 'Treasure Island' (1942). Jean Dubuffet, 'Man shivering' (1959). Willem de Kooning, 'Figure' (1964). Mark Rothko, 'Untitled work' (1947). Victor Pasmore, 'Blue Development' (1967). Roberto Matta, 'Homo Tumultum' (1974). Robert Motherwell, 'Collage' (1974). Pierre Soulages, '15.1.55' (1955). Antoni Tápies, 'Figures' (1960). Pierre Alechinsky, 'Old tapestry' (1974). Rufino Tamayo, 'La gran galaxia' (1976); 'Mujer en blanco' (1976); 'Retrato de Olga' (1964); 'Dos mujeres' (1981); 'Sandías' (1968).

On the other side of Paseo de la Reforma, a little further W, is a small children's zoo. Next, on the r., is the road leading to the entrance to the *Museo Nacional de Antropología* (see Rte 11). Opposite its S side, across Paseo de la Reforma, is the *Lago de Chapultepec*. On its N shore is the *Casa del Lago* (late 19C), now a cultural centre belonging to UNAM. The Gran Avenida, to the S, separates the lake from a smaller boating lake. Beyond the Lago de Chapultepec, on the l., is the **Jardín Zoológico** (Tues.–Sun., 8–6), the city's principal zoo.

Paseo de la Reforma continues W to the **Unidad Artística y Cultural del Bosque de Chapultepec**, centred on the *Auditorio Nacional*, inaugurated in 1953 for the second Panamerican Games. From the mid-1950s a series of theatres has been built next to it: the small *Teatro Villaurrutia* and the *Teatro del Granero* (both 1956); the *Teatro del Bosque* and the *Teatro Orientación* (both 1957), the latter for children; the *Teatro de la Danza* (1969); and the *Teatro el Galeón*, an experimental theatre, and the *Teatro Titiriglobo*, another children's theatre (both dating from the 1970s). The headquarters of various cultural and educational organizations also form part of the complex. Immediately to the W is the *Campo de Marte*, a military parade ground.

Calz. Chivatito leads S beyond a Korean pagoda to (l.) the **Jardín Botánico** (daily, 9–5), incl. plant and tree varieties from Mexico and abroad, and a lake filled with exotic fish; and the **Molino del Rey** (l.; beyond the roundabout), scene of a famous battle on 8 Sept. 1847 when US troops under Gens. Winfield Scott and William J. Worth, approaching from Tacubaya, defeated a depleted Mexican force in the penultimate action of the war before the fall of Mexico City on 14 Sept.

The Molino del Rey, a range of stone buildings at the W end of Chapultepec, contained a mill, a gunpowder factory, and a cannon foundry; c 450m NW, another building, the Casamata, contained a gunpowder store. All were covered by the artillery at the castle. Devastating Mexican fire and a counter-attack from the E repulsed initial US attacks. Eventually a US barrage forced the Casamata defenders to flee and the US 11th Infantry breached the Molino, which was captured and ordered destroyed. The Casamata blew up; 2000 Mexicans were killed or wounded; US losses were 116 killed, 665 wounded, 18 missing. A monument, erected in 1856, commemorates the Mexican dead in an engagement described by Gen. Ulysses S. Grant as one of the unnecessary battles of an unholy and unjust war.

To the E, in Calz. de la Milla, is the **Monumento a Nezahualcóyotl** (1956) by Luis Ortiz Monasterio. The 4m-high statue of the lord of Texcoco is flanked by the shields of Texcoco, Tenochtitlán, and Tlacopan against a wall of tezontle; the fountain, at right-angles to it, is backed by a tezontle wall studded with reliefs in prehispanic style.

From Molino del Rey, Calz. Chivatito runs S to join Calz. Molino del Rey, which continues to the S boundary of the park, Av. Constituyentes. On the l. is **Los Pinos**, official residence of the President of the Republic.

It was once part of the ranch of La Hormiga, bought in 1858 by José Pablo Martínez del Río, distinguished obstetrician and imperialist, whose property was later confiscated. Although in 1923 the estate was bought by the government for conversion into a presidential residence, it did not begin to serve as such until 1934, after Pres. Cárdenas adapted the house. Since then it has been rebuilt and modernized, with adjoining administrative offices and barracks.

To the W of the Anillo Periférico lies the **Nuevo Bosque**, opened up in 1964. On the SE side is the **Museo Tecnológico** (Tues.–Sat., 9–5; Sun., 9–2), run by the Comisión Federal de Electricidad. It illustrates the development of technology and its application in industry, transport, and communications in general. Included are a Planetarium and a room devoted to the petroleum industry. Adjoining it on the N is the *Parque de Diversiones* (amusement park; Wed., Sat., Sun.; fee), with its huge roller-coasters.

To the W is the **Cárcamo del Agua del Río Lerma**, the complex which receives water from the Río Lerma, processing it for distribution to the city.

Diego Rivera, using natural-coloured stones to give a polychromatic effect, designed a fountain here in the form of Tláloc, lying on his back in a shallow pool. In the small building immediately behind, he painted murals (1951) on the walls of the basin into which the water first flows, using polystyrene and liquid rubber, materials unresistant to water. The parts above it are all that remain of a work which represents water in the evolution of species. On the walls of the tunnel where the water enters the basin are paintings of two large hands, as if spilling it into the pool. On the walls round the tunnel mouth are paintings of miners carving it through the rock face; at either side, the fecundity brought by water, and the contrary effects of drought; in centre, a negro man and mongolian woman symbolize the first races in human evolution. On back wall, portraits of Fernando Casas Alemán, responsible for the Lerma processing system, and other engineers.

N and W of the Cárcamo are two boating lakes, large and small. Beyond the latter, at the SW extremity of the second (middle) section of Chapultepec, is the *Museo de Historia Natural* (Tues.–Sat., 10–5; Sun. and holidays, 10–7; fee), contained in ten large halls covered by conspicuous hemispherical shells, designed by Leónidas Guadarrama and opened in 1964.

The park's third section stretches to the SW and includes the huge **Panteón Civil** (*Panteón de los Dolores*). It includes the *Rotonda de los Hombres Ilustres*, resting-place of renowned Mexicans.

Among artists: Dr Atl (Gerardo Murillo); José Clemente Orozco; Carlos Pellicer; Silvestre Revueltas; Diego Rivera; David Alfaro Siqueiros. Among poets and writers: Ignacio Manuel Altamirano; Salvador Díaz Mirón; Francisco González Bocanegra; Ramón López Velarde; Amado Nervo; Guillermo Prieto; Luis G. Urbina. Among military men: Mariano Escobedo; Jesús González Ortega; Donato Guerra; Sóstenes Rocha. Among statesmen: Juan Alvarez; Mariano Arista; Santos Degollado; Sebastián Lerdo de Tejada; Melchor Ocampo; Andrés Quintana Roo and Leona Vicario; Ignacio Ramírez; Vicente Riva Palacio; Justo Sierra O'Reilly. Archaeology is represented by Alfonso Caso; music by Angela Peralta; philosophy by Antonio Caso; the Church by Francisco Javier Clavijero, SJ (remains moved in 1970 from Bologna).

The marine park *Atlantis* (Tues.–Sun., 10–5; daily in summer; fee) lies SW of the Panteón, reached along Av. Constituyentes.

At the junction of Paseo de la Reforma and Anillo Periférico (NW extremity of the park) rises the *Monumento a la Industria Petrolera* (1952), by Vicente Mendiola, with bronze statuary by Juan Olaguíbel. The central obelisk is of chiluca stone.

The W extension of Paseo de la Reforma climbs into the LOMAS DE CHAPULTEPEC, an area to which viceroy marqués de Cerralvo suggested transferring the capital after the floods of 1629–34. It began as a suburb early in the 20C, promoted, as Chapultepec Heights, by the US Mexican International Trust Co. Its main development (plan by José Luis Cuevas) took place from 1922, with the building of desirable residences, in conspicuously ornate neo-baroque, for the richer classes. Today it bears all the hallmarks of a well-to-do residential district.

Directly N of Chapultepec is the POLANCO district, another well-to-do area, with some distinctive, profusely decorated, domestic architecture, 'Californian baroque', in vogue during the 1920s and 1930s. Not far N of the Museo Nacional de Antropología and next door to the *Hotel el Presidente Chapultepec*, at the corner of Campos Elíseos and C. George Eliot, is the *Centro Cultural de Arte Contemporáneo*, a striking building designed by Juan Sordo Madaleno for Televisa (state television service), and housing the World Cup soccer championship of 1986. To the E, at 29 C. Tres Picos, is the **Sala de Arte Público Siqueiros** (Tues.–Fri., 10–2, 5–8; Sat., 10–2), the studio and house of David Alfaro Siqueiros (1896–1974), donated to the Mexican people a year before his death. It contains sketches and studies for his murals; ten lithographs inspired by the Canto General of Pablo Neruda; his 'Cristo Mexicano', painted in prison; a library; and many documents on his life. Temporary exhibitions are also held here.

At 8 Av. Presidente Masarik, to the NE, the *Seguros Monterrey* building (1960) by Enrique de la Mora, Leonardo Zeevaert, and Alberto González Pozo represents an architectural departure. The foundations, based on earth replacement, are on the seventh floor.

At Polanco's N extremity (corner of Av. Ejercito Nacional and C. Lago Victoria) is the *Sanatorio Español* complex, founded in 1842 as the Sociedad de Beneficencia Española, with contributions from resident Spaniards. It has functioned at its present site since 1932. The chapel (1955) is by Juan Sordo Madaleno.

11 Museo Nacional de Antropología

The Museo Nacional de Antropología is one of the world's great museums. Its inauguration by Pres. Adolfo López Mateos took place on 17 Sept. 1964. Some 15,000 ethnographic items and 12,000 prehistoric artefacts are exhibited from all over Mexico. A whole day to see the museum at a moderate pace, or more than one visit, is highly recommended.

The building was designed by Pedro Ramírez Vázquez, in collaboration with 42 engineers and 52 other architects, planners, and designers, incl. his chief assistants, Rafael Mijares and Jorge Campuzano. The basic construction is steel-reinforced concrete, and the various facings include marble from Sto Tomás (Puebla), light brown Tepeaca marble, white marble from Carrara, and travertine from Apaxco and Puebla. It comprises three storeys, one of which is underground. The central patio of the museum supports a single huge pillar, 11m high, supporting an anodized aluminium roof, 53m by 82m, and weighing 1600 tonnes. The pillar is faced in bronze sheeting with relief sculpture, and water cascades from its capital to the patio below. Beyond it is an artificial pond, planted with papyrus, with a huge conch shell at one end. The whole scene is enlivened by the booming of a tape recording of a conch shell horn.

The museum includes archaeology and prehistory, and public facilities on the ground floor; ethnography and the National Library and School of Anthropology (open to the public; free) on the floor above; and a restaurant, Educational Service (incl. a special children's section), and research facilities (not open to the public) in the basement.

Before the main entry on Paseo de la Reforma stands an immense monolithic sculpture, identified as either Tláloc, god of rain, or Chalchiúhtlicue, goddess of water, which has come to symbolize the museum. It was cut from rock quarried in the Sierra de Ajusco, and originally erected in the foothills above the E shore of Lago de Texcoco, near Coatlinchán. It is of Late Preclassic Period date, c 100 BC (see Rte 20), and weighs 167 tonnes. It stands 7m high and has a span of 4m at the base.

The museum's single entrance is approached up broad, shallow marble steps, to an esplanade over the approach road to the car-park. The centre of this plaza is filled with a fountain shooting water up from a pool below, and is flanked by bench-walls. Above the glass doors of the entrance is the national crest of the eagle, nopal, and serpent, to remind us of Mexico's ancient heritage, and the legend of the Aztec peregrination and the founding of Tenochtitlán.

Inside the museum there are 12 ground-floor rooms of archaeology and pre-history, and 11 first-floor rooms of ethnography. Upon entering, to the l. are a bookshop and cloakroom; straight ahead is a raised area with a sculpture at its summit, and a small orientation cinema below; and to the r. is a hall for temporary exhibitions. Just ahead and to the r. are the ticket counter and multilingual guides in red jackets, who will conduct individuals and parties around the museum. (Descriptions below generally proceed anticlockwise in each room.)

The arrangement of the archaeological collections is designed to move from the general to the specific, to show the development of Mesoamerican and other prehistoric cultures of Mexico from the earliest times up to the Spanish Conquest. The visitor is given an introduction to anthropology, then has his attention focused on the Mesoamerican geographical region and chronology, and then, in succeeding rooms, proceeds chronologically and regionally through Mexico's past, from the first hunter-gatherer traditions to the urban states of the Aztec, Maya, and their neighbours. References below to other items are to items in that same room, unless otherwise stated.

We begin the tour of the museum at the first doorway on the r. of the central patio, past the ticket desk. The first three rooms contain an introduction to anthropology, its subfields and their interrelationships; the definitions of the Mesoamerican cultural and geographical region; and the beginning of New World prehistory with the arrival of man migrating across the Bering Strait.

ROOM 1: Introducción a la Antropología, providing the theoretical framework for all subsequent exhibits. We begin on the r., proceeding anticlockwise. **1**. The evolution of man and the primates. **2**. Fossil evidence for human evolution. **3**. Modern physical anthropology, incl. racial types throughout the world. **4**. Skeletal materials illustrating physical types, stature, variation. **5**. Man's physiology, and the development of the brain and nervous system. **6**. Genetic interrelationships and world blood group patterns. **7**. Model illustrating the concept of stratigraphy in archaeological excavation. **8**. The development of archaeology and a large comparative chronological chart. **9**. Diorama—Vida en el Paleolítico Inferior. **10**. Palaeolithic tools and their evolution from the earliest crude stone 'choppers' to the more refined techniques of the Late or Upper Palaeolithic. **11**. Diorama—Vida en el Paleolítico Superior. **12**. Life and technology in the Post-Pleistocene (Post-Ice Age)—the Mesolithic ('Middle' Stone Age); and the beginnings of agriculture and sedentary village life in the Neolithic. **13**. Cases of artefacts from four of the world's 'primary' regions for early developments in agriculture, sedentary village life, and the earliest independent urban developments in both the Old World and the New World— India (Indus river valley); Mesopotamia (Tigris and Euphrates river valleys); Mesoamerica, and Andean and coastal Peru; and Egypt (Nile river valley). **14**. A Neolithic burial. **15**. Circular display unit illustrating linguistics: evolution of language, language groups and families, the study of languages today. **16**. The discipline of ethnology, its history and modern practice, incl. comparative ethnographic collections from all over the world.

ROOM 2: Mesoamerica: the Mesoamerican region and its fringes, physical setting, comparative chronology, and thematic concepts for subsequent archaeology rooms. We look l. first, then r. and proceed anticlockwise. **1**. Huge colour wall-map (l. of entrance) showing Mexico with the principal prehistoric cultural regions and sites. **2**. (opposite entrance and to r.). Stone atlante sculpture from a *Toltec Phase* altar at Chichén Itzá, a site displayed more fully in the Maya Room; also a large comparative chart of the cultural regions shown in No. 3 below. **3**. Turning r. (on low central display island), engraved map on a white Carrara marble slab: Mesoamerica and its neighbouring regions, with the principal cultural regions outlined. **4**. The evolution of agriculture in Mesoamerica, incl. the paramount food staples of maize corn, tomatoes, squashes, and gourds. **5**. Hunting and gathering subsistence: a complement to agriculture and the main subsistence where agriculture was not practicable. **6**. Figurines of animals hunted in Mesoamerica for food, skins, feathers, bones, etc., incl. jaguar, deer, rabbit, peccary, armadillo, iguana, and others; and various birds, incl. wild turkey, duck, eagle, macaw, and quetzal. **7**. Photographs illustrating Mesoamerican physical types. Two carved stone slabs with jaguars from Aztec Tenochtitlán.

8. In a central display island, a series of displays illustrates comparative aspects of prehistoric Mesoamerican lifeways. First, the practice of mutilation, incl. cranial deformation, dental filing, blackening the teeth with tar, encouragement of a squint and cross-eyed look, deformation of legs; also body painting and tattooing, and shaving of body hair. Such mutilation in ancient Mesoamerican cultures was used to delineate rank, social status, and individual prowess. **9**. Comparative pottery display. **10**. Diorama of daily life in early village farming communities. **11**. Comparative burial customs in various regions and through time, incl. individual and multiple burials, urn burials, flexed and unflexed burials. **12**. Ancient festivals: copies of codices, musical instruments, and figurines engaged in festive activities (eg, drummers, dancers, ball game players). **13**. Mesoamerican science, incl. copies of codex pages showing different writing systems; astronomical, mathematical, and calendrical systems; table showing Aztec numbers; pages showing medicinal knowledge; literature; and architectural methods. **14**. Metal, bone, and shell ornament; and figurines illustrating tattooing and body painting. **15**. Ancient Mesoamerican warfare and the imposition and payment of tribute. **16**. (opposite 15, on the central island). Stone working, incl. yugos and palmas used in the ball game cult, axe-heads, knives, and other stone tools. **17**. Scale-models comparing Mesoamerican pyramid architecture: hut model meant to represent the earliest form of sacred structure (reconstructed from archaeological features in the lowest levels of Preclassic sites), circular pyramid (Cuicuilco), Tikal (Guatemala), Palenque (Classic Period temple), Chichén Itzá (Pirámide de Kukulkán, of the *Maya-Toltec* phase), Tenochtitlán (twin-pyramid temple), and Teotihuacán (Pirámide del Sol). **18** (opposite 17). Cases, photographs, and panels showing painting on pottery, architectural friezes, and murals (examples from Teotihuacán). **19**. Scale-model of the Valle de Teotihuacán (fully illustrated in Room 5). **20** (l. of exit to central patio). Stele from Izapa (Chiapas), c 1C AD, depicting god with snake feet and serpent masks, with a jaguar mask, representing the heavens, above his head. The style and iconography indicate some Olmec influence.

ROOM 3: Los Origenes. The cultural development of the earliest inhabitants of Mexico, incl. their routes of arrival and way of life. **1**. Overhead is a panoramic painting 'Los Origenes', showing Palaeolithic hunters following game herds across the Bering Strait from Asia into America. Such migration could have taken place during several periods when glacial freezing lowered the sea level to create a partly frozen and partly land bridge across the gap, c 24,000 and c 10,000 years ago. (There were earlier land bridge periods also, but there is no confirmed, unequivocal evidence for migrations then.) **2–3**. Examples of the earliest stone tools used by these migrants. **4**. Mural illustrating Mexican fauna of the migratory period, and examples of fossils of that date. **5**. (In pit in middle of room). Fossilized skeleton of the Imperial Mammoth (*Mammuthus imperator*), as discovered and excavated at Sta Isabel Iztapan in the NE Basin of Mexico (c 7700–7300 BC). In single display case opposite, carved camelid sacrum from Tequixquiac, deliberately carved to resemble a dog or coyote (c 14–17,000 BC); Mexico's earliest art. **6** (opposite side of the panel). Early Man in Mexico; and opposite it, another panel showing the migratory routes of the peopling of N America. **7**. Fossil human skulls from locations in Mexico. **8**. Diorama depicting trapping and slaying of a Mammoth in the marshlands edging the ancient lakes in the Basin of Mexico, c 10,000 years ago. **9**. Large-scale model of Basin of Mexico, with overlay of Aztec Tenochtitlán. **10–12**. Early evolution of culture in Basin of Mexico: earliest stone tool traditions and later ground and polished pieces; early grinding tools and stone vessels; earliest pottery and weaving. **13**. Earliest types of domesticated plants and their evolution from wild species to their control by man. **14**. Wall painting of 'La Primera Aldea' (The First Village)—an artist's rendering based on archaeological evidence. **15**. Early ceramics from the early agricultural period. For Room 4 return to the central patio and turn r., then r. again into the next doorway.

ROOM 4: Preclásico displays artefacts of the Preclassic Period (c 2500 BC–AD 300), the final phase of which is often referred to as Protoclassic (c AD 1–300). Displays and descriptive materials illustrate prehistoric techniques of stoneworking and early pottery-making, and highlight various cultural achievements and early civic developments. These include early calendrical systems, the Maya counting system, ceramic painting and moulding techniques, carved vessels, distinctive identities for special deities (eg, Tláloc, god of rain, and Huehuetéotl, god of fire), and the development of the first ceremonial centres. In particular, the Olmec culture of the central and S Gulf Coast is illustrated by various Olmec and Olmec-influenced figurines (woman-and-child groups, acrobat, priest in tiger skin, dancers, musicians, magicians; and cf. No. 19 in Room 9); and vessels with incised jaguar designs, with labial mouldings, and in the shapes of animals.

1. On the r., double-sided panel illustrating the Preclassic with a mural of the Altiplano and, on the reverse, a map of the principal Preclassic sites. **2**. Early Preclassic artefacts, incl. pottery and figurines. **3**. Six more cases containing figurines and incised pots. In particular, note the Acrobats Vase from Tlatilco, Tumba 154. This piece was an offering in the tomb, dated Middle Preclassic. It illustrates the early excellence of Mesoamerican art while at the same time giving practical information—one of the chief values of figurines—by indicating something of the nature of early agricultural offerings and celebrations, and Preclassic dress. **4**. Continuous case going around the corner, containing Middle Preclassic pottery and more figurines. **5**. More figurines, and Middle Preclassic adornments. The Tlatilco figurines seen in these and the previous cases include numerous mujer bonita examples—young women with brilliantly painted bodies (yellow, black, white, and violet, plus red hands, feet, and hair), and with elegant jewellery and coiffered hair.

These are believed to be anthropomorphic representation of maize corn ears (ie, multicoloured corn cobs), or women participating in a harvest ceremony. From Fray Bernardino de Sahagún, writing almost 3000 years later, we have descriptions of the Aztec corn ceremony seemingly descended from the Preclassic one: a young woman, chosen to represent the Maize goddess Xilonen, painted her face and dressed in rich clothing and jewellery, red sandals, and a headdress of quetzal feathers; in the ceremony she was decapitated by a priest. In contrast, there are relatively few male figurines at early Tlatilco, and these are usually deformed specimens (eg, hunchbacks).

6. Middle Preclassic technology, incl. grinding tools, obsidian projectile points, bone awls, and other stone tools. **7**. Reproduction of a sculpture from Chalcatzingo. **8**. Another stone sculpture from Chalcatzingo. **9**. Late Preclassic artefacts. **10**. Reconstruction of the Tlatilco excavations, showing a complete burial, and its grave offerings. **11**. From the windows, a reconstruction of the earliest Preclassic ceremonial structure at Cuicuilco (see Rte 15), which predated the later, circular pyramid there. **12**. Late Preclassic artefacts from important sites, incl.: Cuicuilco, Tlapacoya, Ticoman, and Zacatenco.

ROOM 5: **Teotihuacán** is devoted to the site and its influence in the Proto-classic and Classic Periods (c AD 1–900). On a patio just outside the room is a large-scale composite model of the site. Inside are diagrams, photomurals (eg, of the Pirámide del Sol and the Pirámide de la Luna), and drawings of ground plans showing the phases of development, expansion, and contraction of the ancient city through its 900-year history. Around the room exhibits include pottery and other artefacts, facsimiles and reconstructions of wall paintings, and of the talud-tablero architectural style of wall-facing, corresponding to the chronological subdivisions of the site's occupation (for developmental phases see Rte 18).

1. Stone ring composed of four parts which fit together; thought to be a ball game goal; from La Ventilla. **2**. Scale model of the Valle de Teotihuacán and ceremonial complex; and following it, case of materials illustrating the ancient population of the valley. **3**. **Teotihuacano pottery**, and pottery from contemporary sites in the Basin of Mexico.

Proto-Teotihuacán (c 200 BC–AD 1)—chiefly monochrome wares. Decorations included impressing various designs with sticks, grooving, burnishing and polishing, and occasionally 'negative' painting in pink with geometric patterns. The later *Proto-Teotihuacán* (or *Patlachique*) phase also included slip decoration, plus 'negative' painting, incised designs, appliqué decoration, and decorative differential burnishing.

Tzacualli or *Teotihuacán I* (c AD 1–150)—decoration included pastel-work, incised designs, incl. stick impressing, serration, and differential burnishing and rubbing, of various geometric patterns. Bichrome vessels became more prominent and polychromes also appeared. The ceramic assemblage also included imported pieces, generally grey and orange wares from Oaxaca and from the Gulf Coast. In *Late Tzacualli* moulded vessels became popular, depicting stylized Tláloc features. Finally, *Anaranjada Fina* (Thin Orange Ware—not to be confused with the Fine Orange Wares of W Maya Lowlands origin) made its appearance and was subsequently exported far and wide beyond the Basin of Mexico. Although definitely distributed by Teotihuacán, there is no evidence to prove that it was actually manufactured there.

Miccaótli or *Teotihuacán II* (c AD 150–250)—Anaranjada Fina was prominent; moulded Tláloc vases became increasingly common; decorations included painting, engraving, burnishing and polishing, and added wavy-lined patterns to the usual geometric repertoire.

Tlamimilolpa or *Teotihuacán IIa–III* (c AD 250–450)—forms and decorations were carried over from the previous phase, but some new forms and techniques were added. Appliqué work, excision, denticulation, and incrusting all became popular, as did one-hole 'candlesticks' and miniature pieces (especially dishes). Most decoration was still geometric, but symbols for the year-names, snakes, feathers, and anthropomorphic representation were all increasingly used. Vessel variety increased in the later part of the phase (c AD 375–450), when braseros (braziers) with appliqué figures, double braseros, and cylindrical vessels all appeared, together with new types of base supports. Moulded vessels increased in proportion and decoration in general became more elaborate and varied: painted stucco (a secco), anthropomorphic serpents, feathers, stars, glyphs, concentric circles, eyes, shells, and the usual geometric patterns were all used. More Teotihuacano ware was exported, and correspondingly more foreign wares were imported, particularly from the Gulf Coast, but also from Oaxaca as the result of increased trading contacts.

Xolalpan or *Teotihuacán III* (c AD 450–650)—all of the older forms of the previous phase continued. Again there was an increase in form variety, especially in the addition of miniatures, and of ceramic funerary masks. Many more motifs were added: other gods (eg, Xipe Totec, god of springtime), deformed figures, birds, houses, and glyphs. Snakes also remained popular. In the later part of the phase braseros and burial urns with conical lids were highly decorated with numerous figures (Tlálocs and other masks, monkeys, feathers, stars, butterflies, and flowers). All the previously mentioned decorative techniques were employed. A final addition was ceramic toys on clay wheels, probably introduced from the Gulf Coast (see Rte 71).

Metepec or *Teotihuacán IV* (c 650–750)—generally represents continuity, but the city began its economic decline during this phase. Notable new imports included Maya ceramics (Fine Orange Wares and polychromes).

Oxtoticpac and *Coyotlatelco* (or *Xometla* c 750–950)—Teotihuacano wares continued to be produced, but the city's economic power was all but gone. An addition was a long-handled spoon- or 'frying pan'-shaped instrument of uncertain purpose (possibly for burning incense). During these phases polychrome pottery from Cholula and from the Huasteca region began to be imported, as did Toltec wares and forms in the 9–10C.

4. *Teotihuacán III* pottery vessels, especially funerary urn with carved mask with nose ring, within a temple façade. **5**. Wall map with Teotihuacán and contemporary sites, and large display of daily life at Teotihuacán, incl. discussions of architectural techniques, painting, jewellery-making, and other crafts. Artefacts to illustrate these include ground and polished stone axeheads, quarry hammers, various sculpting tools (chisels, wedges, scrapers, abrasives), stone sculptures (note in particular one head which had inset eyes and cheek ornaments), painted vessels, clay figurine art, and bone and shell ornaments.

Wall painting is illustrated, incl. both fresco (application of the colours while the plaster is still wet, then tracing the figures and designs in a pigmented plaster) and a secco (dry surface painting). One case includes samples of the pigments used at Teotihuacán, and the tools used to prepare and apply them. **6**. *Teotihuacán IIa–III* ceramics. **7**. More *Teotihuacán III* and *IV* ceramics; and in centre of room, another display shows domestic vessels of everyday use.

Sub-section decorated with reproduced murals from the Tepantitla compound at Teotihuacán: the scenes show 'Tlalocán' (Paradise of Tláloc), depicting a sort of Teotihuacano Garden of Eden in which figures (in Teotihuacano mythology, the victims of drowning or of certain diseases) frolic in an ideal landscape; and 'Tonatiuh Ichan' (paradise for warriors killed in battle). On either side of this section is a case displaying incense pots decorated with Teotihuacano gods: Tláloc, a fat Gulf Coast imported god, Huehuetéotl (ancient Fire god), Xipe Totec (god of springtime), Chalchiútlicue (goddess of water), Quetzalpapálotl (the Plumed Butterfly), and Yacatecuhtli (god of merchants).

Above the next main section of displays is suspended a large mural of the Basin of Mexico in the Classic Period. **9**. Brasero, depicting (?)Quetzalpapálotl. The principal figure is a highly stylized butterfly, with a nose ring; around it are moulded quetzal birds, other butterflies, flowers, chalchihuites (discs symbolizing jade, jadeite, greenstone, and other green-coloured stones), and glyphs. **10**. **Statue of Xipe Totec**, associated with the East. He wears the skin of a flayed sacrificial victim as a symbol of renewal and new growth.

His cult seems to have originated in the Oaxaca-Guerrero region and was maintained throughout the Classic and Postclassic Periods in Mesoamerica. He was patron of the Aztec day Cuauhtli and honoured during Tlacaxipehualiztli, second month of the Aztec year, by priests performing their ceremonial rituals dressed in the flayed skins of sacrificial victims. During wartime, Aztec kings dressed in the guise of Xipe Totec, his cult being especially favoured by Axayácatl (1468–81).

This example was excavated in the Tlamimilolpa residential compound, and comprises three joined parts. **11**. Ritual objects excavated at Teotihuacán, incl.: greenstone yugo depicting a (?)frog; inscribed shell used as a musical instrument in ceremonies; tripod vessel with appliqué heads and a tripod brasero; two stone sculptures of Huehuetéotl (cf. No. 29, below); alabaster mask from Azcapotzalco. **12**. Three almenos—crenellated stone blocks carved with year glyphs. **13**. Large stone block or plaque, an architectural decoration from a ball court or temple; its carved motif probably represents the concept of time. **14**. Stone relief **carving of Tláloc**. **15**. Full-scale reproduction of a corner of the Templo de Quetzalcóatl at Teotihuacán. It shows the alternating Tláloc and Quetzalcóatl heads in the full glory of their red, green, white, and black paint (traces of which can still be seen on the originals, see Rte 18). **16**. Reproductions of the murals in the Subestructura de los Caracoles Emplumados beneath the Pal. de Quetzalpapálotl (Rte 18). **17**. Reproductions of frescoes of various plants from the now disintegrated originals in the Templo de la Agricultura (see also No. 21, below). **18**. Reproductions of the frescoes in the Atetelco residential compound, depicting two priests (see Rte 18).

19. **Large sculpture of Chalchiúhtlicue** excavated by Jorge Acosta in the Plaza de la Luna. She was goddess of water and female counterpart of Tláloc, patroness of the fifth Aztec day (*Cóatl*), and third of the 13 Lords of Day, sixth of the Nine Lords of Night. The Gulf of Mexico was known as Chalchiuhcueyecatl ('water of the goddess Chalchiúhtlicue'). In this example she wears a huipil and quechquémitl (cotton blouse of woven rectangles, often embroidered, and triangular shaped overblouse), sandals, headdress, earplugs, and three-stranded necklace and bracelets. **20**. **Double sculpture**, depicting a back-to-back skull, probably Mictlantecuhtli, Lord of the Underworld, and of *Itzcuintli*, tenth Náhuatl day; Mictlantecuhtli was sixth or sometimes eleventh Lord of Day, fifth Lord of Night. This example comes from the Pl. del Pirámide del Sol. Originally painted bright red with jade or obsidian insets in the eye slots and nose.

Outside the windows at this point may be seen another scale model of the ceremonial centre of Teotihuacán, laid out on a small patio. **21**. Reproduction painting from the Templo de la Agricultura (see also No. 17, above). **22**. Photomural of the Pirámide de la Luna and its plaza; below it, reproduction of a fresco from the Tetitla residential compound. **23** (near corner). **Stylized jaguar sculpture** from the side-ramp of a staircase of one of the many pyramid-platforms at Teotihuacán. **24**. Photomural of the Pirámide del Sol and its plaza; below it, reproduction of a Teotihuacán fresco depicting a procession of gods, or priests dressed as gods. **25**. **Sculpture of Huehuetéotl** in characteristic pose, holding a brasero on his head (see also No. 29, below). **26** (near corner). Relief carving excavated in the Edificios Superpuestos (Rte 18). The most familiar features are the mouth used on Tláloc masks, and the serpent's forked tongue. **27**. Photomural of the Ciudadela and Templo de Quetzalcóatl; below it, architectural frieze with four eagles. **28**. Column carved with chalchihuites, green discs symbolizing water, or, when combined with other water symbols, human blood. **29. Sculpture of Huehuetéotl**, oldest of Mesoamerica's functionally identifiable gods, probably originating as the Olmec God I. Also called Xiuhtecuhtli, he was the first Lord of Day and first Lord of Night. **30. Stone stele** from the Pal. de Quetzalpapálotl, depicting a priestly figure.

31. Polychrome pottery from Cholula, a contemporary site. Much Cholula polychrome was imported into Teotihuacán during the Coyotetelco Phase (see after No. 3, above). **32.** Scale model of the Cholula pyramid, largest in the New World, contemporary with the Pirámide del Sol. This model shows the Cholula Estructura B, which utilized the talud-tablero architectural technique. **33.** Stone almena (crenellated slab), carved with a knot representing the conclusion of a calendrical cycle; from the façade of the Pirámide del Sol. **34. Burial masks** carved on basalt, jade, andesite, and other stones, and clay; made with inset mother-of-pearl and obsidian eyes and other decorations. One, from (?) Guerrero, has an inset mother-of-pearl, turquoise, and coral mosaic. Superb alabaster jaguar, carved with a butterfly on his forehead and a year glyph on his tail. Greenstone vase carved with Tláloc holding a (?)thunderbolt and possibly a pouch for copal incense; recognizable by his 'spectacle' eyes and long fangs. **35.** As we leave Room 5 to proceed along a corridor to Room 6, there is a large, polished stone sculpture of Mictantecuhtli, double-faced Lord of the Underworld (cf. No. 20, above).

Connecting Rooms 5 and 6 is a short corridor, at the end of which is a small display of artefacts from and models of the site of Xochicalco, with an emphasis on the cultural and artistic links between Teotihuacán and the Toltecs of the Early Postclassic.

1. Photomural display of **Xochicalco**. **2.** Stone stele with two Nahua glyphs above and two Zapotec glyphs below, illustrating the internationalism of both the site and the calendrical system. **3.** Stone stele from a ball court, depicting a ball player with the head of a macaw. **4.** The three famous **stelae from the Templo de las Estelas: Stele 1** depicts, from bottom to top, the 584-day cycle of the planet Venus; the creation of the Venus 'star' is represented by the glyph 'seven eye of reptile' or 'seven wind'. In the realm of Tlahuizcalpantecuhtli, the planet is represented in different aspects as the morning star (jaguar head) emerging from the Underworld, and as the evening star (reed mat) returning to the Underworld. The central theme of Stele 1 is Quetzalcóatl, representing the morning star, while his twin, Xólotl, represents the evening star on Stele 3 (below). **Stele 2** has as its central theme a large mask of Tláloc. **Stele 3** depicts Xólotl, as a dog and guide into the Underworld, and thus god of Venus as the evening star. He was patron of the Aztec day *Ollin*. Both Stelae 1 and 3 are also associated with the Central Mesoamerican Creation Myth of the Five Suns (for details on which, see No. 43 in Room 7). **5.** Pottery and other artefacts from Xochicalco.

ROOM 6 is devoted to the Toltecs and the ancient site of Tula (Tollán), of the Early to Middle Postclassic Period in the Central Highlands. It includes materials from the height of Tula's power and influence, domestic and imported ceramics, and a large number of Toltec stone sculptures. After the main room, which concentrates on Tula itself, subsections follow with displays of later Toltec material, plus items from contemporary Texcoco and Tenayuca.

6. Basalt head of Quetzalcóatl, as the Toltec priest-king and founder (see Rte 19). **7.** Two stone atlantes, used as altar supports; one still has traces of its original paint. **8–9. Two stone chacmools** from Tlaxcala and from the Pal. Quemado at Tula.

Chacmools were first found at Chichén Itzá, and misnamed 'red jaguar' (in Maya—chac mool), but their origin has been traced to Tula and the Toltecs. One suggestion is that they represent the 'divine messenger' who received and carried the hearts of sacrificial victims in the small receptacle on their stomach—but this is speculation, and there is no direct evidence to support it. Other scholars have suggested a connection with the cult of Tláloc. Jorge Acosta has suggested that they functioned as altars, a reasonable suggestion prompted by their unquestionable association with temples at both Chichén Itzá and Aztec Tenochtitlán. Six of the seven chacmools at Tula had been deliberately decapitated at the time of the site's abandonment, or sometime afterwards, leaving only this one complete.

10. Row of **Toltec bas-relief sculptures**. These demonstrate the artistic links between Teotihuacán and the Aztecs, who used Toltec pieces as models. **11–12**. Two **Toltec standard-bearers** represented as a jaguar and as a man, both from Tula. These would have held standards in front of one of the temples. **13** (above No. 9). A painting by Alfredo Zalce shows a reconstruction of the Pl. Central and its pyramids and temples. **14**. Reconstruction of a **bench from the Pal. Quemado**, covered with sculpted plaster and painted. It depicts a ceremonial 'banquet' scene (cf. No. 25 in Room 7). **15** (above). Mural by Zalce showing construction of the Templo de Tlahuizcalpantecuhtli on Pirámide B at Tula. Stonemasons are shown cutting and hauling the huge Atlante statue columns up to the top of the pyramidal platform, under the direction of a figure in a green, quetzal-feather cloak. Other stonemasons are cutting crests for the top of the Coatepantli (Serpent Wall). **16**. On a platform in the centre of this section are **four small Toltec warrior sculptures**—small atlantes used to support the large slabs of altars in temples. **17**. **Reproduction** of one of the huge **Atlante** columns from the **Templo de Tlahuizcalpantecuhtli**. These were roof supports inside the temple atop Pirámide B. **18**. In the centre, on a low platform, four fragments of sculptures from Tula temples (perhaps deliberately smashed at the time of the abandonment of the city): (a) a small atlante altar-slab support; (b) a column support; (c) another small atlante; and (d) a column drum carved with quetzalcóatls (feathered serpents). **19**. Original wall or roof crenellation in the shape of a spiral, or stylized snail. **20**. Stele carved with a ball player wearing feathered headdress and nose ornament common in the Huasteca region. **21**. Toltec ceramic vessels, in front of which is another stone sculpture—depicting Tláloc. **22**. Stone brasero depicting priest in Tláloc mask. **23–25**. Cases of Toltec pottery, figurines, and stone sculpture. **26**. Copies of three square temple columns from the Templo de Tlahuizcalpantecuhtli. These stood behind the large Atlante columns. **27**. Stone sculpture of Tláloc. **28**. Toltec pottery with a distinctive metallic sheen, from the Highland Maya region of present-day Chiapas and Guatemala, known as Tohil Plumbate Ware. **29**. Sculpture of a woman in a quechquémitl from Tula.

30. **Mexica Aztec ceramics from 15C Tula**, when the site was reoccupied by the Aztecs after its 12C destruction and abandonment. The Aztecs' primary purpose in establishing a colony at Tula seems to have been to loot the site for Toltec sacred sculptures, which they re-erected in Tenochtitlán, and copied. **31**. Sculpture of a wild beast covered in mother-of-pearl mosaic, holding a human mask or head between its jaws. **32**. Unfinished travertine vessel, illustrating Toltec skill at stone carving with copper tools. **33**. Stele depicting a large jaguar. **34**. Stele depicting a warrior; the bird on his chest represents his transformation into a brilliantly plumed bird after following the Sun to its zenith—the fate of warriors killed in battle. **35**. Sculpture of a double-headed serpent. **36**. Sculpted head wearing a triangular headpiece. The facial features are typical of the central Mexican Plateau and presumably of 'José Tolteca'. **37**. More Tohil Plumbate Ware and other ceramics. **38** (on wall). Mural of the Toltec market. **39**. Damaged sculpture with the glyph for 'flower' in its headdress—presumably Xipe Totec. **40**. **Skin codex**, showing the descent of the Texcoca kings from Tzoltzin, founder of Texcoco and nephew of the legendary Chichimec leader, Xólotl. **41**. Aztec II Ware—from Tenayuca (see Rte 18). **42**. Scale model of the Tenayuca pyramid, showing the various stages of construction.

ROOM 7: The Mexica Aztecs. A short ramp leads from the central patio into the Mexica Room. The Mexica were one of the seven Aztec tribes, usually referred to now simply as the Aztecs. They were, however, relative latecomers to the Basin of Mexico (see *La Quemada*). The Hall is divided into display areas by partial walls, forming a central area and four further subdivided side sections. The Hall contains over 100 sculptures and display units, and at first seems somewhat chaotic. Nevertheless, it does describe all aspects of Aztec daily life in a logical sequence if one takes the time to move around the sections systematically.

Panels along the walls describe the Basin, and the Mexica Aztec migration into it in the late 13C and their early history there. Murals and information panels describe the rise of the Mexica to power and the building of Tenochtitlán. The far wall illustrates Aztec daily life, warfare, religion and ceremonies, science, arts, and commerce and economy. Sculptures and cases are arranged to illustrate the themes of these panels and diagrams.

1. Immediately ahead is a large **Ocelotlcuauhxicalli** (Náhuatl *ocelotl* = jaguar; *cuauhcalli* = eagle house, or vessel). It has a hollow receptacle for the hearts of sacrificial victims, and inside the hollow, the symbol for life-giving blood adorned with eagle feathers and precious stones. The interior wall is carved with two gods: Huitzilopochtli (god of war) and Tezcatlipoca (god of the smoking mirror and Creator god; see also No. 50, below), each engaged in auto-sacrifice by drawing blood from his ear. To the l. of the vessel is the head of an 'Eagle Knight', wearing an eagle-shaped helmet; and (opposite side of screen) a sacrificed jaguar. The jaguar shape of the vessel represents the First Sun, Sun of the night (see No. 43, below). **2**. The **pyramidal block** to the r. of the Ocelotlcuauhxicalli is known as the Teocalli de la Guerra Sagrada, signifying the sacred war waged by the Aztecs to take prisoners as victims for the sacrifices. It was thought to be a call from the gods to men to take part in the sacred war, to ensure that the Sun continued to receive sustenance, ie, blood. Relief carvings on the r. side of the pyramid represent Tláloc and Tlahuizcalpantecuhtli (cf. No. 4 between Rooms 5 and 6, above); on the l. side, Xiuhtecuhtli (god of fire) and Xochipilli (the Flower Prince). In front of each figure's mouth is the glyph sign for 'war'—streams of water and fire—and thus the name of the monument, given to it by the archaeologist Alfonso Caso.

The stairway of the pyramid is flanked by side ramps carved at the bases with the year glyphs *Ce Tochtli* ('one rabbit') and *Ome Acatl* ('two reed')—referring to the coming of the Fifth Sun (see No. 43, below), and with sacrificial vessels. At the top of the platform is a sun disc, or calendar stone, flanked by two priestly figures engaged in ceremonial rites. On the back of the block is the emblem signifying the legendary founding of Tenochtitlán and of the Aztec nation—emerging from the mouth of the Earth Monster is the eagle, perched on a nopal cactus, eating a serpent.

From these two entrance pieces, there is a good view of the huge Sun Disc or Calendario Azteca (No. 63, below). **3**. Several Aztec sculptures, notably an atlante, emphasizing the actual link between the Toltecs and the Aztecs, as well as the desired link which the Aztecs cultivated (see Introduction: The Late Postclassic). **4**. **Documents** relating to the migration of the Mexica tribe into the Basin of Mexico, and their eventual settlement of the Isla Tenochtitlán. This 22-page codex is known as the *Tira de la Peregrinación* (Band of Wanderings), and was compiled in Náhuatl using Latin script shortly after the Spanish conquest. Footprints show the route of Aztec wanderings, guided by Huitzilopochtli through their priests, until the sight of the eagle, serpent, and nopal cactus indicated the final resting place. **5**. Sculptures illustrating Mexica social structure in their own eyes, incl. a macehualli (man of the people—ie, commoner), priest, woman, old man, hunchback, and other natural and sacredly inflicted deformities. **6** (on wall). Painting of the Basin of Mexico and map of the Náhuatl-speaking region of central Mexico. **7**. **Sculpture of Teteoinnan**, mother of the gods. She represents the mother-goddess cult of the Late Postclassic in central Mexico and on the Gulf Coast. Associated with fertility, she enjoyed a highly developed cult practice in the chinampa agricultural areas of the Basin of Mexico. She was often represented by Toci, Coatlícue, Tlazoltéotl, or Citluacóatl—all various aspects of the mother-goddess, of different origins in Mesoamerica. She was honoured at the Ochpanitztli, twelfth monthly feast of the Aztec year. Temescalli (steam baths) were often dedicated to her, as pregnant women believed these made the childbirth easier. In this example, note the fine inset mother-of-pearl eyes and the glyph sign for *Yeyi Ozomatli* ('three monkey') on her clothes. **8. Ceremonial carved stone vessel**, depicting warriors approaching a zacatapoyolli from either side. Such vessels were used to store cactus thorns in autosacrificial rites, in which blood was let by piercing one's ears, tongue, and lips. This example was excavated in Tenochtitlán itself.

9. Along the wall, opposite, display panels illustrate aspects of Aztec life. They begin with reproductions of codices showing the arrival of the Mexica in the Basin and their settlement of Tenochtitlán island; then continue with scenes of their rise to empire, and the genealogy of their rulers. **10. Bas-relief sculpture** known as **'great dog of the water'**, depicting the glyph sign of Ahuítzotl, eighth Aztec ruler (1486–1502). (He succeeded his older brother, Tizoc (1481–86), and was father of Cuauhtémoc (1520–25).) It was he who used especially extensively the pochteca class of merchants as spies and agents to help expand the empire far beyond the Basin of Mexico and the adjacent valleys. **11. Stone sculpture** from the **Acuecuexatl spring** at Coyoacán, commemorating Ahuítzotl's building of an aqueduct along the S causeway from Coyoacán to the Teocalli (Sacred Precinct) of Tenochtitlán. The waterflow, however, proved to be difficult to control, and often caused flooding. It was eventually blocked up after Ahuítzotl himself was drowned in a flood. Ahuítzotl is depicted on the stone, piercing the lobes of his ears, the Aztec equivalent of a ribbon-cutting ceremony to dedicate the works in the year *Chicome Acatl* ('seven reed' = 1499), shown on the inscribed glyph. The feathered serpent carved on the stone represents water.

12. Sculpture of a warrior, one of the '**Eagle Knights**' of the sacred wars, symbolized by his feathered shirt.

The Eagle Knights (Sun) and the Jaguar Knights (Earth) were two Aztec military orders or cults originated, or at least more formally organized, by the Toltecs, whose military prowess was legendary and highly revered by the Aztecs. Members of the orders were picked, high-ranking members of Aztec society. Eagle Knights were dedicated to the Sun as the Solar Star, and Jaguar Knights to the Setting Sun (tlachitonatiuh). Each dressed in an appropriate costume of feathered helmet and/or shirt, or a jaguar skin. The rites of their mystical order involved special knowledge and initiation procedures in which the aspirant, according to the 16C chronicler Diego Muñoz Camargo, was confined in the temple for 30–40 days to practise fasting and autosacrifice. One of their privileges was to take part in the 'gladiatorial' sacrifice of princely captives. The victim was secured to a stone weight to restrict his movements, and given a wooden club set with feathers in imitation of clubs set with razor-sharp obsidian blades, which, needless to say, were given to the brave knights. The outcome was virtually inevitable, but in theory the victim could be freed if his prowess proved impressive (ie, if he succeeded in defeating a string of successive knights).

13. Case of artefacts. **14. Piedra de Tizoc**, a **colossal stone cylinder** erected at the foot of the great staircase of the Templo Mayor at the temple's dedication ceremonies. It is 0.93m high and 2.65m in diameter. In the Codex Telleriano-Remensis (reputedly derived from the lost Codex Huitzilopochtli, and covering the period AD 1198–1562) Tizoc began the new temple in the year *Nahui Acatl* ('four reed' = 1483), but it was not completed until 1487 by his younger brother and successor Ahuítzotl. Reputedly 80,000 sacrificial victims were slain in celebration of the completion. The stone is carved in bas-relief depicting Tizoc and Ahuítzotl practising autosacrificial rites, with the year glyph *Chicueyi Acatl* ('eight reed' = 1496). The figures around them are in 15 pairs, each pair incl. Tizoc in the guise of Huitzilopochtli (with Tizoc's name glyph), and a figure representing one of the conquered provinces of the empire (each with a location and ethnic identification glyph). Huitzilopochtli was worshipped in one of the twin temples of the Templo Mayor at Tenochtitlán. Below each pair is the hide of a cayman (crocodile) symbolizing the earth, while the upper part of the stone symbolized the Sun. The hollowed-out cavity and the channel cut into the stone are of later date and of unknown purpose.

Three sculptures along the wall behind the Piedra de Tizoc. **15**. Bas-relief to commemorate the Templo Mayor by Ahuítzotl in 1496. **16**. Warrior, a Jaguar Knight of the sacred wars (see No. 12, above). **17**. Eagle, cuauhtli, representing Nagual, the Solar Star—ie, the Sun, the Eagle Knights, and prisoners sacrificed to sustain the Sun with their blood. **18**. **Sculpture of the 'Indio Triste'**—in fact, a standard-bearer from the Templo Mayor (cf. Nos. 11 and 12 in Room 6). Found in an excavation near Cs Seminario and Guatemala in 1913–14, this example represents a seated man with hands folded at the knees with a hole to take the shaft of the standard. Such figures were placed on the staircase side ramps of pyramids, and in front of the temples on the tops.

19. **Copy of the plan of ancient Tenochtitlán** known as the Plan of Cortés, reputedly drawn just after the Conquest, before the razing of the city was begun. It was first published in Nuremberg in 1524, along with the letters of Cortés to Charles V, the plan being part of the second letter. It shows the Teocalli and the various city districts, incl. Tlatelolco on its own island to the N, but 'connected' by chinampas. Other plans illustrate the development of the city, and compare it to modern Mexico. **20**. Long case containing a reconstructed feathered headdress. This is an example of the sort of work done by a toteccatl (artisan). It is made up of various feathers, incl. most conspicuously, the large, brilliant green feathers of the quetzal, still extant in the mountainous areas of Chiapas and Guatemala. Such headdresses figure prominently in sculptures depicting ceremonies and in codices, where they are worn by high-ranking individuals and priests. **21**. Architectural fragment from Tenochtitlán, and smaller fragments from a wall or roof crenellation—possibly a coatepantli (serpent wall), judging by their stylized double-headed serpent shapes. **22**. Fragments of sculpted architectural embellishments, incl. serpent heads, a monkey between serpent heads, and shell-encrusted crenellations. **23** (on other side of dividing screen). **Sculpture of Xiuhcóatl** (2.5m), the Turquoise Serpent— alter ego symbolizing Xiuhtecuhtli, god of fire. This particular example is thought to have embellished one of the corners of the main platform of the Templo Mayor.

Repeated in a continuous series, they crested the coatepantli of the Teocalli at Tenochtitlán, and two of them encircle the edge of the great Calendario Azteca (No. 63, below). In Aztec mythology, Xiuhcóatl carries the Sun across the sky from daybreak to zenith. Personified as Xiuhtecuhtli, he contrasts with the benevolent Quetzalcóatl, and symbolizes aridity and drought. He was first of the 13 Lords of Day, first of the Nine Lords of Night, and often shown as an accoutrement of Huitzilopochtli or of Tezcatlipoca. As a very ancient god, with origins in the Preclassic Olmec pantheon, he was known as Huehuetéotl. In this example, his crown of stars symbolizes his role as Huitzilopochtli's helper in the battle against the Moon and Stars before dawn. In other examples his entire body is divided into 13 parts to symbolize the 13 Mexican constellations.

24. Fragment of a standard-bearer (cf. No. 18, above). This example depicts a figure seated on a throne decorated with skulls, with a hole at its base for the shaft of the standard. Note also the rattlesnake-shaped ears and tail. **25**. Fragment of a bench, probably taken by the Aztecs from Tula for re-use at Tenochtitlán (cf. No. 14 in Room 6). It depicts a ceremonial banquet or procession, with figures of warriors approaching a zacataypolli vessel, holding maguey thorns for ritual autosacrifice. Beneath the cornice is a row of feathered serpents. **26**. Fragment of architectural embellishment, a serpent head, possibly from a coatepantli; it bears the glyph sign *Chicueyi Acatl* ('eight reed' = 1496). **27**. Large serpent head from the base of a pyramidal staircase, found in one of the early excavations of the Templo Mayor.

28. **Large scale model of the sacred Teocalli of Tenochtitlán**. It is based on the various descriptions of the ancient city given by the conquistador chroniclers (eg, Bernal Díaz del Castillo) and on archaeological evidence from the various excavations. Recent discoveries have added fresh evidence and detail, but have not significantly altered the basic layout (see Rte 2). **29**. On the main wall above the model is a panoramic painting of ancient Tenochtitlán, amidst the lakes of the Basin of Mexico. Below it is a wooden, hollowed out canoe of the type used for traffic and commerce on the lakes, and along the canals between chinampas. **30**. Huge **serpent head** from the base of a pyramidal staircase; this example has a crown of eagle feathers symbolizing the Sun. **31**. Rodent sculpture. **32**. Fragment of architectural decoration, a rattlesnake tail, with ears of maize corn between the rattles and spikes. **33**. Vessel, decorated with maize corn ears, reputedly used in 'first harvest' ceremonies. **34**. **Sculpture of a turtle**; used extensively by the Aztecs as food, and the shell for jewellery and drum bases for religious ceremonies and dancing.

35. Information panels and diagrams illustrating Aztec economy, subsistence, and commerce. Various foods from the lakes and lakeshores supplemented the chinampa agriculture, incl. a variety of fish and freshwater fowl—taken in nets; water-fly eggs (called axayácatl), water larvae (called aneneztli), algae (called tecuitlatl), tadpoles (called atepocatl), and freshwater shrimps (called acociltin).

36. Serpent sculpture from the Templo Mayor. **37**. Artefacts illustrating Aztec commerce.

Generally speaking, the Aztecs imported raw materials and exported manufactured items, although many manufactured items were included in the tributes lists. Long-distance trade was the exclusive business of the intermediate-ranking class called the pochteca (for routes, see No. 38 below). As there were no draught animals all materials were carried on the backs of men organized in vast caravans. Overland and coastal trade extended to both the Pacific and Gulf Coasts; trade items incl. fabrics, garments, jewellery, gold items and ingots, copper tools, obsidian tools, herbs, dyes, perfumes, cocoa, salt, vanilla, feathers, jade, jadeite, turquoise and other precious stones, sea shells, turtle shells, skins, copal incense, cotton, slaves, and foodstuffs.

The Aztecs also prospected for rare minerals into the far N (as far as present-day New Mexico), and maintained several garrisoned cities on both coasts and outposts in the N. The former acted as international 'free-trade' zones between the Aztec Empire and the various Maya and Central American provincial principalities (cf. *Coatzacoalcos*, Cimatán [Rte 83], Potonchán, and Xicalango [Rte 91A]).

38. **Diorama of the Tlatelolco Market**. Tlatelolco was an independent city-state on an island N of Tenochtitlán, conquered and annexed by the Mexica under Axayácatl in 1473. The two islands were connected by a causeway and the intervening waters were eventually 'filled in' by chinampa plots.

All long-distance trade routes commenced here, and the pochteca families had a special residential section around the market plaza. The market had a special police force whose duty was to inspect the quality of goods and to enforce the market regulations and prices. (In the diorama, r. background, three officials are seated in judgement of a person accused of shoplifting.) Eyewitness accounts of the market remark on its size and the variety of goods available. As many as 60,000 people a day are reputed to have visited it.

39. More wall panels and diagrams illustrating Aztec daily life. A diagram shows, as the Aztecs saw it, the 'stages' of a man's life in Aztec society, from birth to death. **40**. Two sculptures, complementing the information panels, represent a macehualli (commoner) and a tecutli (nobleman), wearing large ear ornaments.

41. Collection of figures—**agricultural deities**: Xilonen, goddess of young, unripe maize; Centéotl, god of ripened maize; Chicomecóatl, goddess of maize and cultivated vegetation in general (also called Chicomolotzin). They clutch maize ears in their hands and have them embroidered on their triangular quechquémitl garments; and are embellished with various headdresses and accoutrements such as staves with bells (called chicahuaztli) used in rituals to encourage the growth of crops. These gods and goddesses were almost household deities judging from the large numbers of them found on every site throughout the Basin from the Preclassic Period onwards (cf. No. 5 in Room 4, above).

The Aztec harvest ceremonies were held in September, and the principal act was for a priest, dressed in the flayed skin of a freshly sacrificed woman, to represent Tlazoltéotl, the Earth goddess (or, more accurately, one of her many manifestations). In the ritual he imitated the actions of a woman giving birth, as Tlazoltéotl giving birth to the Maize god; a second priest, dressed as the young Maize god, then acted out the battle against threats to the harvest. In another ceremony a young woman was dressed as Xilonen in rich clothing and jewellery, red sandals, and a green quetzal feather headdress, and was beheaded by a priest.

42. Sculpture of a man with a statue of the Maize goddess. **43. Carved monolith** illustrating the central Mesoamerican **Creation Myth of the Four Suns**, incl. glyph dates for each Sun's destruction: creation proceeded through five suns, each destroyed by an element, the Fifth Sun being the present one.

First Sun, Sun of Night, was ruled by Tezcatlipoca (Creator god, represented by the glyph *Nahui Océolt*—'four jaguar'); he defeated Quetzalcóatl and destroyed the giants of the earth by letting them be eaten by jaguars (representing Earth). Second Sun, Sun of Air, was ruled by Quetzalcóatl (represented by the glyph *Nahui Ehecatl*—'four wind'); it was destroyed by winds and the survivors turned into monkeys. Third Sun, Sun of the Rain of Fire, was ruled by Tláloc (represented by the glyph *Nahui Quiáhuitl*—'four rain'); it was destroyed by a rain of fire and the survivors became birds. Fourth Sun, Sun of Water, was ruled by Chalchiúhtlicue (Tláloc's sister and represented by the glyph *Nahui Atl*—'four water'); it was destroyed in floods and the survivors became fish. Fifth Sun, Sun of Union and Stability, was ruled by Tonatiuh (Sun god, and represented by the glyph *Nahui Ollin*—'four movement'); in its age the four basic elements (earth, air, fire, and water) have been brought together in harmony and stability; the prediction is that it will be destroyed by earthquakes.

44. Composite goddess sculpture with symbols for both earth and fire. As Cihuateteo she would represent a woman who had died in childbirth; her duty was to meet at midday warriors killed in battle, as they were carried by the Sun, and lead them to the world of the dead in the West. As Cihuacóatl she would represent the 'serpent woman' Earth goddess, patron of the Cihuateteo. The sculpture is richly dressed and bears a multitude of symbols: in her l. hand she grasps a bell, symbolizing thunder and rain; in her r., a snake, for lightning and rain. The xicalcolhiuqui (stepped-fret or 'key' pattern on her skirt), and the Chalchiúhtlicue figure (female counterpart of Tláloc), and plumed-serpents embroidered on the back of her cape also symbolize running water and rain. Along the back of the cape also runs the skeleton of a snake, with feathers issuing from it and various figures of (?)butterflies and serpent heads. On the bottom of the support column, eagle claws perhaps symbolize the function of the Cihuateteo in leading fallen warriors and women who died in childbirth.

45. Sculpture of Xólotl. Normally represented as a dog or coyote, he was twin brother of Quetzalcóatl and god of the evening star (Venus). He was patron of *Ollin*, seventeenth Aztec day, and associated with the creation of man by taking bones from the Underworld, pulverizing them, and mixing them with the blood of the gods. It was a central Mexican custom to bury a dog, slain by an arrow in the neck, with the body so that it could lead the dead person to the Under-world. **46**. Stone discs, perhaps weights used in the gladiatorial slayings of Eagle and Jaguar Knights—see No. 12, above. **47. Sculpture of Tlahuizcalpan-tecuhtli**, god of the planet Venus as the morning and evening stars. He appears as both Quetzalcóatl, the morning star, and Xólotl, the evening star, and is therefore often depicted in the codices as simultaneously a living human and a skull. He was twelfth of the 13 Lords of Day.

In the 'Anales de Cuauhtitlán' (also known as Codex Chimalpopoca), Quetzalcóatl, as ruler of Tollan (Tula), is defeated by his political rival Tezcatlipoca and driven into exile. After a long journey he is transformed into the morning star, as Tlahuizcalpantecuhtli in his Quetzal-cóatl guise. As the dual human-skull representation, he was also considered the god of evil omens and of sickness.

48. Tlecuil (or ritual stone brasero). Copal incense was burned in such braziers in ceremonies dedicated to Xiuhtecuhtli (god of fire); and the sacred fire of the New Fire ceremony at the end of a 52-year calendrical cycle was transferred to them after being kindled in the chest cavity of the sacrificial victim (see *Cerro de la Estrella*). **49**. Three stone solar discs; associated with human sacrificial rites. **50**. **Sculpture** (fragmentary) **of Tezcatlipoca**. This example depicts him ascending, with his l. foot being devoured by the Earth Monster, and the glyph sign *Ome Acatl* ('two reed') in his headdress.

Tezcatlipoca was a complex Creator god, represented in numerous aspects. His Náhuatl name means smoking mirror, a symbol often used to replace his devoured l. foot. He was greatly feared because he frequently interfered directly with people's lives, and was associated with many other deities of evil, destruction, and death. As such he was the patron god of sorcerers and thieves, but was also regarded as 'inescapable justice'. In other aspects he was associated with the directional colours: red for East, in the guise of Xipe Totec and Camaxtli (patron god of Tlaxcala); black for North, the Smoking Mirror (a god special to Texcoco) and the 'Warrior of the North'; White for West, the god of Cholula, and, in the guise of Quetzalcóatl, god of learning and of the priesthood; and blue for South, as Huitzilopochtli (god of war and of the Sun), and the 'hummingbird sorcerer' and principal god of Tenochtitlán.

He was reputedly transformed into the Great Bear constellation, and as Black Tezcatlipoca he was patron god of the day *Acatl* (thirteenth of the 20 Aztec days). Alternatively, as Chalchiuhtotolin ('precious turkey'), he represented the Night and Mystery, and was patron of the day *Técpatl* (eighteenth day). In the Creation Myth he ruled the First Sun; and in another myth he abducted Tláloc's first wife, Xochiquetzal. He was also a War god, associated with Huitzilopochtli, and patron of the telpochcalli ('house of war', ie, the war colleges). He was also prominent in Toltec mythology, particularly as an opponent of Quetzalcóatl (see No. 47, above) and appears on Toltec columns at Chichén Itzá. He was titulary god of Texcoco, which perhaps explains his importance to the Aztecs, who were early influenced by both Tula and Texcoco. In Aztec Tenochtitlán he was the tenth of the 13 Lords of Day.

51. **Fractured bas-relief of Tonatiuh**, Sun god. As the rising sun he was called Cuauhtlehuánitl ('ascending eagle') and as the setting sun, Cuauhtémoc ('descending eagle'). He was fourth of the 13 Lords of Day and patron of Quiáhuitl, nineteenth Aztec day. In this example he is shown kneeling, with the solar disc carved on the back buckle of his belt.

52. Case of artefacts associated with sacrificial rites, incl.: two obsidian knives embellished with mother-of-pearl handles (reconstituted), numerous other knife blades, etc., and illustrations of the sacrificial rites. **53**. **Carved zacatapayolli**, a receptacle for maguey thorns used in autosacrifice. On the sides are the zacate (hay ball) in which the thorns were 'planted', and several priestly figures. The glyph names for Chicomóztoc and Culhuacán refer respectively to the location of the seven caves, from which the seven Aztec tribes emerged (see *La Quemada*), and to a city-state in the S Basin of Mexico which was settled by the Culhua leader Mixcóatl, founder of the Toltec dynasty. From the Culhua the Mexica Aztecs took their first ruler, Acamapichtli (1372–91), thus establishing a Toltec dynastic link.

54. In the centre of the room, collection of ceremonial items: two examples of carved cuauhxicalli ('eagle boxes'), possibly used to hold the hearts of sacrificial victims before they were burnt (one with plumed serpents on the sides and the other with skulls, interlaced patterns, and the zacate with maguey thorns 'planted' in it for autosacrifices); xicalcoliuhqui, or stepped-fret decorated vessel; tlachtimalácatl, stone cylinder used to restrict the movement of the sacrificial victim in the 'gladiatorial' fights of the Eagle and Jaguar Knights (see No. 12, above). **55**. **Sculpture of Xiuhcóatl** (see No. 23, above). **56**. **Sculpture of Quetzalcóatl**, the Plumed Serpent, with a sacrificial stone knife on his tongue.

Quetzalcóatl was a clear favourite among the Mexican pantheon, and, like Tezcatlipoca, complex in his many manifestations. He was a creator god and sometimes assumed the attributes of other gods. His origins are at least as early as Teotihuacán, where he was venerated alongside Tláloc, and may be connected to the Olmec God VIII. He was revered as the great civilizer, having brought man into being, taught him how to feed himself (through the gift of multicoloured maize), clothe himself, and make tools. He taught man moral judgement, and was father of the priesthood, learning, art, and science. In mythology he was brother and equal of Tezcatlipoca (see No. 50, above), Xipe Totec, and Huitzilopochtli. In Aztec cosmography he was both Tlahuizcalpantecuhtli (the morning star—see No. 47, above) and Xólotl (twin, and evening star); in the Creation Myth he ruled the Second Sun (see No. 43, above). He was patron deity of Ehecatl (second of the 20 Aztec days), and was often manifested as the Wind god Ehecatl; and he was ninth of the 13 Lords of Day.

In legend he is identified as a real person, leader of the people, founder of cities, and bringer of civilization. As Ce Acatl Topiltzin he led the Toltecs, founded Tula, and was defeated by rivals and forced into exile. In some versions he ended his life by setting fire to himself and was transformed into the morning star; in other versions he was the Maya leader known as Kukulkán and founded Chichén Itzá and other cities in Yucatán. The prophecy of his eventual return from the East, in the year Ce Acatl ('one reed'; 1519), was exploited psychologically by Cortés when he learned of it.

Quetzalcóatl's obvious importance at Teotihuacán helps to explain his widespread popularity throughout central Mesoamerica in the Classic Period, when Teotihuacano influence itself was so widespread. It seems possible that his legendary status in Toltec history stems from the Late Classic Chichimec-Toltec conquest of Teotihuacán and the Basin of Mexico. The earliest Toltec settlement, in their own histories, was Culhuacán, founded by Ce Tecpatl Mixcóatl, father of Ce Acatl Topiltzin and founder of the Toltec dynasty. The moral, generally benevolent character of Quetzalcóatl seems betrayed by Toltec and Aztec bloodthirstiness.

57. Sculpture of a coiled plumed serpent—another personification of Quetzalcóatl, and two other plumed serpents. On the front of the coiled serpent the sign of xochiyaóyotl ('flower war' for obtaining sacrificial captives) is carved in the form of intertwined streams of water and fire. **58.** Sculptures of atlantes, used as altar-slab supports. Here, Quetzalcóatl is seen in the guise of Ehecatl, wearing the bird-beak mask. **59.** Plumed Serpent. **60. Sculpture of (?)Yolotlicue**, an Earth goddess. Her head and arms are missing but were apparently composed of serpents; her feet are eagle talons; and her skirt is composed of human hearts!

Proceed now into the central section, through the partition walls. **61.** Flanking the gap are two large terracotta braseros. **62.** Sculpture of a god with attributes of both Coatlícue (see No. 77, below) and Huitzilopochtli. She/He sits crosslegged, with eagle talons for hands, and wears a skirt and belt of human skulls and bones, a pectoral of human hands and hearts, and several bracelets. Found during the construction of the Metro system.

63. Calendario Azteca—the Aztec Calendar Stone or Piedra del Sol. Mounted on a special display block of white Carrara marble, this huge monument is carved on a basalt block weighing 24 tonnes, and has a diameter of 3.6m.

It was found lying in a horizontal position on a platform in front of the Templo del Sol in Tenochtitlán. It was supported on a low dais and eight postholes around it indicated that it was covered by a canopy. It was apparently broken in two at some point in its transfer from the quarry, or in setting it up, and some scholars conclude that it was never actually used because the Aztec priests would not have tolerated such an imperfection. Its date is also disputed, but is thought to be very late Postclassic, perhaps in the reign of Moctezuma II Xocoyotzin (1502–20). It was found in 1790, by accident, during excavations for repairs to the Cathedral. The entire face is carved with the rich symbolism of the Aztec cosmography, telling how the world began, how it would continue, and how it would end. Because it includes the calendrical glyphs for the 20 day-names, it has been misleadingly called the Calendar Stone, but it is much more than a mere clock. Like the rest of ancient Tenochtitlán, the details of relief would have been painted in brilliant reds, greens, blues, yellows, oranges, and white.

The centre is the Sun, carved as a stylized human face, variously interpreted as Tonatiuh or Yohualtonatiuh (Tonatiuh's nocturnal manifestation). From his mouth protrudes a sacrificial knife, and two rounded arms (in the first ring, r. and l. of the face) contain claws clutching human hearts, leading some scholars to conclude that the stone, and others like it, was used horizontally as a sacrificial table. Around this face are concentric rings of hieroglyphic signs.

In the first ring, framing the face, is the predicted date of the end of the Fifth Sun, *Nahui Ollin* ('four movement'; the pointed symbol directly above the face of the god—not the pointed symbol higher up). The dates of the preceding four Suns—Night, Air, Rain of Fire, and Water—are carved in the four rectangular arms to the r. and l. (see No. 43, above).

The next ring contains the glyphs for the 20 day-names. Starting with day 1, just above and to the l. of the *Ollin* symbol, counterclockwise, these are:

crocodile, wind, house, lizard, serpent, death, deer, rabbit, water, dog, monkey, grass, reed, jaguar, eagle, vulture, movement, flint knife, rain, and flower. Next, there is a narrow ring of repetitive design, then a broad ring containing various repeated symbols representing turquoise and jade, the colours of the heavens and symbolic of the equinoxes and solstices. Around the outer border, two circling Xiuhcóatl (Turquoise Serpents or Fire Snakes) signify cyclic and cosmic order, and the present. Their heads, wearing appropriately elaborate head-dress, meet at the bottom of the stone, and their pointed tails, at the top, end on either side of a glyph for the ritual date 'Thirteen Reed' = AD 1011, the beginning of the Fifth Sun.

64. Sculpture of a huge stone drum, carved with feathers. **65**. **Sculpture of Mictecacíhuatl**, with the bulging eyes and protruding ribs of an emaciated face and body; goddess of the dead, consort or female counterpart of Mictlantecuhtli, god of the dead and of the Underworld. **66**. **Large ritual vessel** carved with the Chichimec goddess Itzapapálotl (obsidian butterfly), principal deity of Cuauhtitlán. She was goddess of war and of the Earth, venerated by a cult of the 'first generation'. This example has the symbols of the 'flower war' and of human sacrifice—streams of water and fire intermingled—carved on its sides. The wings of Itzapapálotl have stone knives on them, symbolizing the souls of women who have died in childbirth. **67**. **Sculpture of Tlaltecuhtli**, the Earth Monster, or Lord of the Earth, depicted here with its head back-to-front. It is frequently shown in the form of a grotesque toad with tusks and claws on its feet. In Aztec mythology, the Earth Monster swallowed the Sun every evening and spat it out every dawn. It was often depicted on the bottoms of cuauhxicalli, the stone boxes used to hold the hearts and blood of sacrificial victims, and on other sacrificial stone containers, and was believed to eat and drink the contents after the sacrifice. As an Earth god, it was second of the 13 Lords of Day. **68**. Stone sculpture of a skull—death's head. **69**. Sculptures of Cihuapipil-tin, goddess of the Western Paradise for the souls of women who have died giving birth. They have bare breasts, fleshless mouths, and the glyph sign for *Ce Ozomatli* ('one monkey') above their heads. **70**. Stone altar with Tlaltecuhtli carved on the bottom (cf. No. 67, above), and an animal on each side: butterfly, scorpion, owl, and spider. **71**. **Sculptures of Cihuateteo**, the souls of women who have died in childbirth, and who inhabit Ciucalco, the Western Paradise, or Cihuatlampa, the Western Quadrant, ruled by Cihuapipiltin (see No. 69, above). They were also known as mocihuaquetzque, or women warriors, because they shared the duty of fallen warriors in accompanying the Sun on its course across the sky. At noon the mocihuaquetzque met the Sun carrying the fallen warriors and led it to the Western Land, home of the dead. They were also demons of the night, frightening those out of doors with sudden noises and weird screeches.

72. **Huge stone tzompantli**. This is a funerary monument in imitation of the real thing, on which the skulls of sacrificial victims were skewered on poles inserted through specially drilled holes and stacked up in tiers. This carved example has both skulls and crossed tibiae; inside it were found two reed bundles, symbolizing the 'binding of the years' at the completion of a 52-year Aztec 'century' (see Introduction: Calendrics). Another carved example was excavated in the Templo Mayor. **73**. **Sculpture of Coatlícue**, Earth goddess (see No. 77, below). This example sits in the native fashion and wears a breastplate with two hands to represent life, and a skull crown to symbolize death. Found at Calixtlahuaca (Rte 40B). **74**. **Sculpture of Cihuacóatl**, the Serpent Woman. She was associated with the Western Paradise and patron of the Cihuateteo (see No. 71, above). A complex goddess with several guises: as Tonantzin, she was mother of Mankind; as Coatlícue, she was Earth goddess and mother of Huitzilopochtli (see No. 77, below); as Quilaztli, she brought up Ce Acatl Topiltzin, the Toltec ruler, when his own mother, Chimalman, died in childbirth (cf. No. 56, above); in Post-Conquest Mexican folklore, she became 'La Llorona' (Weeping Woman). **75**. **Sculpture of Coatlícue** (see No. 77, below). Here, she appears as a priestess with attributes of life and death as in No. 73, above. Death is symbolized by a skeletal mask set with turquoise and mother-of-pearl on the cheeks, nose, and mouth. Her breastplate has more precious stones, thought to represent sacrificed warriors. Found at Tehuacán. **76. Head of Coyolxauhqui,** Moon goddess and sister of the War god Huitzilopochtli. He beheaded her upon discovering her involvement in a plot to murder their mother (and in mythology did so every dawn to make way for the Sun). (An equally massive stone sculpture of her was discovered in 1978 by electrical engineers installing new equipment on the site of the Templo Mayor—Rte 2.) In this example she has the glyphs for 'golden discs' (coyolzauhqui) engraved on her cheeks, and wears a feather headdress, earrings, and a lip plug. Her eyes are in the shape of half-moons. Other glyphs on the lower portion of the statue are for the sacred wars and for human sacrifice—intertwined symbols for water and fire.

77. Massive stone statue of Coatlícue. Nearly 2.5m high, it was found in the sacred Teocalli of Tenochtitlán, where it was probably erected in a special temple of its own.

Coatlícue was the quintessential Earth goddess, mother of Coyolxauhqui (Moon goddess), Huitzilopochtli (War god), and the Centzonhuitznahuac (the stars). She was also known as Tonantzin, Teteoinnan (see No. 7, above), and Toci. She was contradictingly associated with the life-giving soil, agriculture, and the rainy season, and with a destructive monster guise in which she went around devouring people for no apparently good reason. Both of these qualities are amply expressed in the rich symbolism of this example.

She is depicted here with a massive monster head, covered with scales, with two beady, staring eyes, and with a wide, scaly mouth, complete with four huge fangs and a split tongue. Two great spurts of blood, in the form of snake heads—her arms—issue from each side and are thought to represent Tonacatecuhtli and his consort Tonacacíhuatl, Lord and Lady of Our Flesh (or, less graphically, Ometecuhtli and Omecíhuatl, Lord and Lady of Duality). On her neck and bosom she wears a necklace composed of charming, alternating human hands and hearts, setting off a lovely skull pendant in the middle—all symbolic of the diabolic need for blood and sacrifice to sustain the Sun. Around her waist is a scaly snake, and her skirt writhes with serpents, two rather large specimens forming the ties of her waistband and dangling below the skull of her pendant necklace—no less symbolic of the human race to which she was Mother. As if this were not enough, down her back fall 13 tresses representative of the 13 Heavens of Aztec cosmography, and of the gods who control the earth's natural forces; also of the 13 months of 20 days each in the 260-day cycle, and possibly of the usual human gestation period; and lastly, of the 13 Lords of Day in the Aztec pantheon. Another skull, counterpart to that on the front, is carved below the tresses. Beneath her skirt, her legs are covered with plumage and end in 'feet', each with four vicious talons. **78.** Sculpture of a reed bundle, symbol of the 'binding of the years' at the end of a 52-year Aztec 'century'. **79.** Case of figurines and tlemaitl, small incense burners in the shape of a spoon or 'frying pan', in which small amounts of copal incense or bits of amber were burned. **80.** Statues of agricultural deities: Xilonen and Centeocíhuatl (consort or female counterpart of Centéotl—cf. No. 41, above). **81.** Sculpture of Nappatecuhtli, an invocation of Tláloc. **82.** Sculptures of Chicomecóatl, the seven serpent goddess of maize and vegetation—by extension, of sustenance. She was also known as Chicomolotzin ('seven ears of corn'). Here, she wears a skirt and quechquémitl (cf. No. 41, above). **83.** Examples of small stone altars. **84.** Stone altar carved with astronomical symbols. **85.** Sculpture of a cactus, showing that Aztec masons could carve realistically as well as horrifically (cf. Nos. 88–91, 93, 97–100, 108, and 111, below). **86.** Ceremonial stone box carved with a Xiucóatl—a Turquoise Serpent, symbol of Xiuhtecuhtli (cf. No. 23, above). **87.** Fragments of architectural embellishments—bas-relief panels; and a ceremonial seat. **88–91.** Examples of realistically sculptured animals, incl.: sacrificed coyote or dog (shown with fleshless ribs); sacrificed jaguar (again, with fleshless ribs); another coyote, an animal associated with evil in general; and coiled rattlesnake, seemingly ready to strike (cf. Nos. 85, 93, 97–100, 108, and 111). **92. Aztec pottery**, illustrating both ordinary, handmade utilitarian vessels, and various specialized forms such as incense burners and boxes.

Aztec pottery is subdivided into four major types—*Aztec I, II, III,* and *IV*—chronologically sequential but with a significant amount of overlapping. Research in the 1970s and 1980s has shown that *Aztec III* and *IV* wares continued in use after the Spanish Conquest, in the case of *Aztec IV* wares as late as the mid-18C in rural areas, until Spanish-introduced glazed wares became more generally used amongst the Indian population.

93. Realistic serpent sculpture (cf. Nos. 85, 88–91, 98–100, 108, and 111). **94. Sculptures of Ehecatl-Ozomatli**, the Wind god in the guise of a monkey—ozomatli. Found in the Metro excavations at Pino Suárez station.
   The statue is identifiable as Ehecatl by his bird-beak mask (cf. No. 56, above). A serpent winds itself around his r. leg and his own tail is also a serpent. He was originally painted with a black body, red hands, turquoise wrists, red beak, half-red face, and turquoise eyes. As a monkey he is perhaps representing Macuilxóchitl, god of the dance and of frolicking. On the other hand, *Ozomatli* was also day 11 in the 20 Aztec days, and could be used to personify night and therefore death. Monkeys are especially common on vessels from the Gulf Coast region, and are frequently depicted in the codices (see also Nos. 96, 102, and 103, below). **95**. More Aztec pottery incl. painted incense-spoons (tlemaitl), anthropomorphic vessels, and polychrome vessels in the Mixteca-Puebla style of Cholula. **96**. Exquisitely crafted **obsidian bowl from Texcoco**, in the shape of a monkey, perhaps representing Macuilxóchitl; similar vases carved of alabaster have been found on the Isla de Sacrificios (cf. No. 38 in Room 9). **97**. Another naturalistic sculpture—coyote (cf. No. 33 in Room 12; and Nos. 85, 88–91, 93, 98–100, 108, and 111). **98**. Beautifully **sculpted diorite gourd** (calabash), a plant utilized and cultivated from the beginnings of Mesoamerican agriculture—another example of the sensitivity with which the Aztecs could sculpt (cf. Nos. 85, 88–91, 93, 97, 99–100, 108, and 111). **99. Aztec stonework**, incl.: greenstone squash; red, stone grasshopper, 48cm long; dark brown jug with green, circular and geometric decorations; seal stones; and various other figurines. Such quality is the work of the tolteca craftsmen of Aztec society (cf. Nos. 85, 88–91, 93, 97–98, 108, and 111). **100**. Small platform with a collection of stone sculptures of animals—again, tolteca work, incl.: rabbits, dogs, snakes, and insects (cf. Nos. 85, 88–91, 93, 97–99, 108, and 111). **101**. On the walls in this area are panels and diagrams illustrating the Spanish conquest of the Aztecs. **102**. Case of jewellery and ornament: gold pieces imported from the W and S of the empire, jade necklaces, items of rock crystal, and polished pyrite mirrors (an artefact manufactured in Mesoamerica since the Early Preclassic). **103. Teponaztli drum**, appropriately carved with the face of Macuilxóchitl. The hollow wooden cylinder was played horizontally, with a rubber-tipped mallet called an olmaitl. The upper surfaces of such drums were carved with two cut-out 'tongues' to produce different pitches. **104. Sculpture of Macuilxóchitl**, god of dancing, of frolicking in general, and of games, especially patolli, a board game similar to pachisi. He was identified with the calendrical name Macuilli Xóchitl ('five flower'), with Xochipilli (the Flower Prince), and with excess of any kind. His other names included Ahuíatl or Ahuiatéotl, one of the five jen of the S. Here, he is depicted emerging from a turtle shell, and associated with Xochipilli by the glyph for five flower carved on the upper part of the sculpture (cf. No. 17, below).
   105. Drum, this time the huehuetl war drum, a three-legged wooden drum covered with hide on top, but left open on the bottom. Different tone could be produced by beating it with the hands in the centre or near the rim, and by altering the tension of the head with one hand while beating with the other.

This example is carved with a cuauhtli (eagle) and a cozcacuauhtli (vulture) facing each other as if ready to dash at each other's throats—a suitable vignette for a drum meant to incite men to battle. Between their beaks are two glyphs: in front of the eagle—'war'; and in front of the vulture—'fire'. **106. Aztec musical instruments**, used in dance and ritual, incl. a wide variety of wind instruments (ocarinas, flutes, whistles, wooden trumpets, and simple conch shell trumpets) and percussion instruments (rattles, clappers, drums, and bells). **107. Sculpture of Xochipilli**, the Flower Prince. He was a youthful manifestation of the Sun god and patron of masculine fecundity; also of youth in general, poetry, and frolic, in his capacity as patron of the day *Ozomatli* ('monkey'). Similar to him was Macuilxóchitl. In another guise he was Ahuíatl, a jen of the S. Both Xochipilli and his female counterpart, Xochiquetzal, were popular with the chinampa-dwellers of Xochimilco. Here, he is depicted seated on a throne, legs crossed, and wearing a mask. Flowers, garlands, and butterflies decorate his seat. **108.** Sculpture of a rattlesnake (cf. especially No. 91; also Nos. 85, 88–90, 93, 97–100, and 111). **109.** Stone altar in the shape of a jaguar. **110.** Part of a column, carved in bas-relief with Tlaltecuhtli (see No. 67, above). **111.** Sculpture of a sacrificed jaguar (cf. especially No. 89; also Nos. 85, 88–91, 93, 97–100, and 108). **112** (on other side of screen). Stone head of an Eagle Knight wearing an eagle helmet (see No. 12, above).

ROOM 8: Oaxaca. Turn r. after leaving Room 7, then r. again. This room is divided into 12 sections to illustrate the partially contemporary Zapotec and Mixtec cultures in the Valle de Oaxaca and adjacent regions. The origin of the Zapoteca is uncertain, and there is no definitive evidence of their presence at Monte Albán until the *Monte Albán III* phase. Artefacts from the site show influences from the Olmecs of the Gulf Coast, from the Maya area of Chiapas, and from central Mexico.

The Mixteca were later arrivals in the Valle de Oaxaca, and up to the Spanish Conquest the two peoples followed a peculiar mixture of royal and noble inter-marriages, periodic conflict, and peaceful cohabitation at many sites. They shared many artistic features in ceramics and architecture.

1. Introductory display: elaborate **urn** decorated with the figures of the Mixtec goddess 'Thirteen Serpent', and behind her, a large section of wall from the Zapotec-Mixtec ceremonial centre at Mitla; both the urn and the stepped-fret work decoration on the wall are hallmarks of these peoples. **2** (on wall on l). Map of Oaxaca showing the principal sites, and a comparative chronological chart. **3** (opposite). **Monte Albán ceramics**, incl. examples from Phases I–IV, more of each of which is displayed in separate cases as the displays progress chronologically. Only one set of dates for these phases is given here; but there is wide variance in different texts.

Monte Albán I (c 700–350 BC) pottery had either no decoration, or only a few basic designs. To compensate, there was a large variety of shapes. Ceremonial greyware was already in evidence, but basic utilitarian wares were mostly monochrome browns and yellows (ranging from almost black to cream). Most designs were incised, but there were also a few painted designs of red-on-cream or brown-on-yellow. Anthropomorphic and zoomorphic shapes show Olmec influence.

Monte Albán II (c 350 BC–AD 100). Earlier forms continued, but the numbers of anthropo-morphic and zoomorphic vessels and figurines increased sharply. New forms were added, incl. tetrapod vessels and more large burial urns, embellished with face masks. Incised decoration eventually went out of fashion and was replaced by differential burnishing and by the use of fresco painting. Influences from the S, especially from Chiapas and the Guatemalan Petén region, included 'negative' painting and many of the facial features on urn masks.

Monte Albán II–IIIa (c AD 100–300) pottery was transitional, but remarkable for large burial urns embellished with masks of the gods resembling the figurine types produced in *Teotihuacán II*—evidence of early contact between the two great ceremonial and civic centres, which in due course developed into intense commercial intercourse.

Monte Albán IIIa (c AD 300–600) pottery represents the full florescence of its characteristic polished grey wares, and the resurgence of incised decoration. Influence from the S waned as contact with central Mexico, especially with Teotihuacán, intensified. Teotihuacano influence included spouted jars, tripod vessels, and the ever popular Thin Orange Ware—a hallmark of Teotihuacán and found all over Mesoamerica during the Classic Period.

Monte Albán IIIb (c AD 600–900). Greyware urns continued to be popular, but incised decoration decreased again. As Teotihuacán waned in power, so too did the influence of Teotihuacano styles. Burial urns became increasingly ornate, and vessels with jaguar feet grew in popularity.

In *Monte Albán IV* (c AD 900–1150) the Zapoteca were challenged by the Mixteca, beginning a tense rivalry. Mixtec pottery included the funerary urns so characteristic of the region, but was also especially notable for its rich polychrome vessels, incl. applied zoomorphic and anthropomorphic motifs, fretwork, floral designs, human skulls and bones, and panels of glyphs.

4. Scale model of the Middle Preclassic village site at Monte Negro, c 800 BC. **5.** Copy of a stele from Monte Albán with early hieroglyphic inscriptions of calendrical cycles and dates—*Monte Albán II* phase. The site of Monte Albán has the longest continuous and complete history of writing in Mesoamerica. **6** and **8.** Copies of stelae from Monte Albán, carved in bas-relief depicting so-called Danzantes. These figures are in fact thought to be either ball game players (by virtue of their stances and gesticulations) or war prisoners and torture victims (many of them at Monte Albán show sexual mutilation). There are more than 40 such reliefs at Monte Albán itself (see Rte 76). **7. Monte Albán I pottery**, incl. utilitarian wares, specialized burial urns, zoomorphic and anthropomorphic vessels, and figurines (cf. No. 3, above). **9. Monte Albán II ceramics**. Note especially the mask-embellished vessels, examples of fresco decoration, and tetrapod, lidded boxes (cf. No. 3, above). **10.** Flat-based vessel with traces of fresco painting. **11.** Bas-relief depicting figure with crossed arms and prominent ribs, wearing a voluted headpiece. **12. Greenstone mask** in several shades, depicting the Bat god of Monte Albán; excavated in Edificio H, and dated *Monte Albán IIIa*. (The Bat god was associated with fertility and the Maize god, Cocijo; he was important from Preclassic times in Oaxaca, and also figures prominently in Maya art. The Aztecs called him Tlacatzinacautli.)

13. Superlative examples of **Monte Albán II–IIIa phase ceramics** (l. to r., top to bottom): tripod burial urn; another urn, from the temple identified as Chicome Mázatl ('seven deer'), embellished with a bird-beak mask; male figurines, from Monte Albán Tumba 113–A, wearing zoomorphic hats and with outstretched arms; and another burial urn. **14.** Large ceramic jaguar figure (c 85cm high) seated and grinning. He was fresco painted, and wears a large knotted-scarf-like neck ornament; excavated in the W-side platform at Monte Albán. **15.** Funerary urn from Monte Albán Tumba 109, depicting the goddess 'Thirteen Serpent' with inset mother-of-pearl eyes (cf. No. 1, above). **16.** Anthropomorphic/zoomorphic funerary urn, incl. the Monte Albán god known as '5-F'. **17. Monte Albán II–IIIa ceramics**, incl. both definitive Zapotec vessels and figurines, and examples of *Teotihuacán II* vessels imported into Monte Albán (see No. 3, above). **18. Monte Albán IIIa ceramics**. Note especially: zoomorphic vessels with jaguar paws or bat claws, lidded boxes, vessels with glyph panels, anthropomorphic urns, and figurines of women wearing shawls twisted over their heads (see No. 3, above). **19.** More **Monte Albán IIIa** items: Bazán stele from Montículo 10 at Monte Albán, depicting a jaguar wearing a crown of serpents, and the gods 'Three Turquoise' and 'Eight Turquoise'. On top shelf, hollow clay cylinder with bas-relief. On middle shelf, another jaguar urn, and an anthropomorphic urn; to r. of these, clay figure of a god wearing serpent maw mask.

20. Scale model of the **Pal. of Tumba 5 at Monte Albán**, and a second scale model of a Zapotec temple. The latter shows a column-supported roof and a central Sun motif, possibly symbolic of contemporary astronomical observations. **21.** Reproduction of the **mural in Monte Albán Tumba 5**. **22.** Zapotec jewellery and ornament in jade and mother-of-pearl. **23.** Lintel stone from the Zapotec tomb at Huajuapan de León; carved with a serpent covered with panels of glyphs. **24.** Sculpture of a god with crossed arms, from Monte Albán. **25.** Steps descending to a **replica of Tumba 104** at Monte Albán.

The cult of the dead was important in Zapotec Monte Albán, and this reconstruction shows a ruler's or priest's tomb with staircase, doorjambs, and lintel of the antechamber, leading to the burial chamber. A niche in the wall contains an urn depicting a young god wearing the headdress of Cocijo (god of rain). Murals in the burial chamber depict, on l., a priest holding a bag of copal incense; on back wall, head of a deity and the glyph 'Five Turquoise'; and on r., figure wearing a plumed-serpent headdress and snake mask. The skeleton is in an extended position, as excavated, with its funerary offerings set out around it.

26 (back in main display room). Sculpture of a seated person, from Monte Albán. **27**. Mural of the Monte Albán ceremonial centre, overlooking the arms of the converging valleys of the Oaxaca system (Etla, Zaachila, and Tlacolula); depicted as the site would have appeared c AD 700. **28**. **Monte Albán IIIa–IIIb pottery**. Mostly from two tombs at Monte Albán, and a contemporary tomb at the site of Yucuñudahui. Note in particular the scene of figures paying last respects to a dead person—in the centre of the group, incl. a band of musicians. **29** (on a low platform). **Four stelae**: (a) depicting a god or ruler named with the glyph 'Eight Deer' (possibly the Eight-Deer-Tiger-Claw of the Mixtec codices, see *Tilantongo*); (b)depicting a god on a mountain and the god of fire in a frame; (c) two figures; and (d) a badly worn relief. **30**. **Monte Albán IIIb ceramics**.

31. Superlative **Monte Albán IIIb and IV** pieces, incl. urns and jars with face masks of the Maize god, a jaguar, a goat-like creature; brasero from Monte Albán Tumba 58, with the figure of Xipe Totec wearing a flayed skin, and a ceramic head of Monte Albán IV. **32**. **Stone lintel** from Monte Albán, carved in bas-relief with a line of figures approaching a seated figure, presumably a priest or ruler (a nearby painting identifies the individual figures). **33**. Stele with five figures, each with a speech symbol coming from his mouth.

34 (to an outside patio). Partial **reconstruction of Tumba 7** at Monte Albán. It shows nine skeletons with their associated funerary offerings, especially jewellery—rings, pectorals, bracelets, necklaces, and bone objects. Tumba 7 was originally a Zapotec, *Monte Albán IIIb* burial, later reopened in *Monte Albán V* for the deposition of a Mixtec burial of a rich citizen and nine companions, presumably sacrificed to accompany him. The funeral offerings included more than 500 items.

35. Stele from the site of Río Grande, carved with a head wearing an elaborate headdress and a mask. **36** (overhead). Painting of the Valle de Oaxaca. **37**. On three wall panels, reproductions of the Mixtec codices. The originals are painted on deer skins and folded accordion-like. They record genealogies, calendrical and religious themes, historic events, and conquests of the Mixteca. Recent study of the codices has come to question the Mixtec affiliation of many of them in favour of a central Mexican origin. **38** (above the codices). Copy of stone mosaic work from Mitla. **39**. Mixtec jewellery, especially goldwork, some of which has inset stones. The Mixteca were especially famous as goldsmiths in the Late Postclassic.

40. Superbly crafted mid-Postclassic **Mixtec polychrome vessel** from Tumba 1 at Zaachila, the Zapotec capital after the virtual abandonment of Monte Albán. A flaring, wide-based bowl or cup, it is red inside and highly burnished; polychrome outside, in black, browns, and white on orange, incl. stepped-fret, bands, and iconographic motifs. On its rim sits a delicately made, long-beaked hummingbird in brilliant turquoise, with large, white, round eyes, outlined in black and with black pupils.

41. Scale model of the Zapotec fortress town of Yagul. **42**. Reconstruction of Burial 6 at Coixtlahuaca. The body is wrapped in a blanket of palm fibre, tied in a flexed position, and has a mask. **43**. **Mixtec polychrome ceramics** (see No. 3, above). Note especially the polychrome vase in the shape of a deer's head, and the tripod vessel with a skeleton figure attached to one side from Zaachila Tumba 1. He has one raised arm and the other as if resting it on his hip, and represents Mictlantecuhtli, god of the Underworld. **44**. Tetrapod stone vase. **45**.

Mixtec ceramics of Late Postclassic date (see No. 3, above). **46**. Stele from Tlaxiaco, carved with a vase or urn. **47**. Mixtec metal work and lapidary art, incl. gold jewellery and breast pendants, jade and rock crystal ornaments, and carved bone. **48**. Late Postclassic ceramics, incl. musical instruments; and wooden drums. **49**. Copy of a stele at Cuilapán, with several inscriptions, incl. a year-sign. **50**. Stele from Tilantongo, an important Mixtec principality in the Postclassic, and reputedly birthplace of the legendary Eight-Deer-Tiger-Claw, one of their most successful rulers. **51**. Copies of stucco wall mouldings from Zaachila Tumba 1, depicting gods and animals participating in the funeral rites (see Rte 75).

ROOM 9: Gulf Coast of Mexico, exhibiting the ceramics, sculptures, and stelae from the entire Gulf Coast region, from the Olmec heartlands in the S to the Totonac and Huastec lands in the middle and N of Veracruz and Tamaulipas. The displays begin with several sculptures in a small subsection formed by a tall, curved wooden wall. Following these, the first major section of displays concerns the Olmecs of the S Gulf Coast. It proceeds through exhibits on the three principal Olmec ceremonial centres—San Lorenzo Tenochtitlán, La Venta, and Tres Zapotes—which succeeded each other as the focus of Olmec power from c 1500 BC to c AD 100. Recent research has shown that there were also several other important Olmec centres, one of which, Laguna de los Cerros, was probably as large and influential as San Lorenzo Tenochtitlán.

Following the Olmec exhibits the more or less contemporary Totonac and Huastec cultures, and their predecessors, are illustrated by displays highlighting some of their major sites—El Tajín, Cempoala, Tamuín, and Castillo de Teayo.

1. Immediately eyecatching is the **sculpture**, in the centre of this area, of a **man-jaguar** (or were-jaguar), a creature that features frequently in Olmec art. Definitely humanoid, it has many feline features as well, particularly in its face. This piece comes from San Lorenzo Tenochtitlán and might have been erected as the spout for a spring or a pool in one of the artificial ponds characteristic of that site (see Rte 83).

The other five sculptures in this subsection are also from San Lorenzo Tenochtitlán. To r. and l., respectively, of the man-jaguar are: **2**. Stele, lightly carved and extremely worn. Most easily distinguishable is a jaguar head to l. of the face. **3**. Another feline sculpture. **4**. Sculpture of a headless man, semi-kneeling, with a breast pendant or pectoral resembling a concave, polished pyrite mirror, carved with a six-stemmed design. He seems to have originally had articulated arms, perhaps of wood or pottery, slotted into his shoulders.

5 (on a raised area). One of the six **colossal stone head**s from San Lorenzo Tenochtitlán. **6**. Stone head, apparently from a full statue, dated c 1200–900 BC.

The next section is devoted mostly to La Venta, the second (chronologically) main Olmec ceremonial centre. **7**. Sculpture depicting a crouching man, deliberately mutilated before being buried in a pit dug at the time of the abandonment of the site. **8**. **Alvarado Stele**, showing a figure in profile standing over a bound and cowering captive who pleads for mercy. The 'victory' or 'captive victim' theme was prominent in Olmec culture and in the early cultures of Oaxaca (eg, at San José Mogote and Monte Albán). **9**. Figurines from La Venta, especially realistic in their individual faces, gestures, and sexual attributes. Such individuality is another hallmark of Olmec art (eg, in the colossal heads). **10**. Badly damaged sculpture depicting (?)the union between a woman and a feline creature. **11**. Sculpture in high relief from La Venta, depicting a face that looks emaciated in comparison to the chubby faces of most other Olmec art. **12**. Another example of a deliberately mutilated piece from La Venta. The figures are difficult to make out, but appear to depict one figure holding a 'baby face' feline creature. **13**. Characteristic Olmec lapidary work in polished jade and jadeite, incl. figurines and ceremonial axe-heads.

14. Special showcase containing a unique find, both in content and context—it was excavated in situ, just as we see it here, at La Venta. It comprises **six jade celts** erected in a crescent plan, as backdrop for **16 jade, granite, and serpentine male figures**, with elongated heads and slit-eyes. Their arrangement suggests that they are performing a ritual in which some of the figures appear to be active, as leaders and participants, while others are passive, as observers (cf. No. 8 in Room 2).

15. Sculpture from La Venta, depicting a priest or ruler in a jaguar-cum-serpent helmet. **16** (in corner). **Olmec pottery**, figurines, and jewellery. Note especially the classic Olmec 'baby face' features: oversized heads, chubby cheeks, and pouting, full-lipped mouths. These features are sometimes also given a feline snarl, perhaps alluding to the mythical union of a woman and jaguar. The jewellery is mostly of jade or jadeite, highly prized by the Olmecs, and includes a jade copy of the human-headed, duck-billed, and bird-winged statuette from San Andrés Tuxtla. The main frontal glyphs record the Long Count date of AD 162. This and the piece's general style date it to the Late Olmec period (Late Preclassic); the other glyphs on it appear to have been carved long after its manufacture. (The original is in the Smithsonian Institution, Washington, DC.).

17. **Luchador** (Wrestler). A pleasingly naturalistic stone statue of an athletic, bearded, mustachioed figure, poised, so it would seem, for a bout, or more likely for some ritual dance or movement; wearing only an athletic belt. From Sta María Uxpanapán (S Veracruz). **18**. Small case containing jade votive axeheads and other artefacts. **19**. Small case of jade, jadeite, and greenstone figurines, and vessels, showing Olmec artistic influence at the Preclassic sites of Tlatilco and Tlacopaya in the Basin of Mexico (cf. Room 4). **20**. Corner case of **jade figurines** and other items. Again, notice the prominence of 'baby faces' and feline countenances on all types of artefacts, from figurines to votive axeheads. Two particularly outstanding pieces are a jade head, and the El Tejar figurine of black, fine-grained stone, depicting a seated man. **21**. Small case containing jade, jadeite, greenstone, and other stone artefacts, incl. figurines, axe-heads, a model of a canoe, and a plaque depicting a head in profile with a pouting, infantile mouth.

22. Out of the window on r. are two sculptures, one of an Olmec 'Earth Monster'—an old theme that runs right through Mesoamerican mythology and cosmography; and, on a low hillock, another of the colossal stone heads from San Lorenzo Tenochtitlán. Comparing this example with the previous head, at the entrance to the room, one will begin to appreciate their individuality. Some scholars think that each head may in fact be a portrait of an Olmec ruler.

23 (returning to the hall, and proceeding around the window corner, to r.). Display panels on the wall illustrate the Gulf Coast region: a sites map, maps and diagrams of the geography of Veracruz and adjoining states, the hydrography, fauna and flora, and topography of the region. **24**. **Stele from Tres Zapotes** with glyphs. **25**. Pottery statue of a hunchbacked old man from Cerro de las Mesas—Huehuetéotl. He sits Indian-style, supporting a brasero on his head in which to kindle a ritual fire or burn incense.

The next sections exhibit material from the central and N Gulf Coast regions. **26**. Display panels illustrating the settlement, chronology, and development of the central Gulf Coast, c 1500 BC–AD 1500. **27**. Scale model of the site of Cempoala (see Rte 64). **28**. **Ceramics from Veracruz**, incl.: numerous anthropomorphic and zoomorphic vessels, especially popular in this region; figurines, with examples of caras sonrientes (smiling face) figurines, and evidence of the practice of skull deformation (flattening), dental mutilation (filing and blackening with tar), chest and shoulder scarification, and dyeing of hair and cheeks; many figurines also sport showy headgear, turbans, or shaved heads. There are also necklaces, earplugs, lip plugs, bracelets, and other jewellery. **29**. Large, hollow clay figurine, constructed in sections. It depicts a person wearing what appears to be an ocelotl (jaguar) skin. **30**. Stele carved with a crocodile from whose jaws issue the head and torso of a priestly figure or god, judging by his attire. **31**. Two large Totonac anthropomorphic urns, from central Veracruz. **32**. Scale model of the central ceremonial centre at El Tajín (cf. No. 34, below). **33**. Clay figurine of an old woman, squatting on her haunches. **34**. Scale model of the Pirámide de los Nichos at El Tajín (cf. No. 32, above). **35**. **Relief carving** on a stone slab, depicting a **ball player** preparing for the games with the help of an attendant. Here can be seen the various paraphernalia in play: head-dress of plumes, wide belt (or hip weight?), knee and wrist guards, and bands on the biceps; Classic Period, from Tepataxco (Veracruz). **36–37**. **Stone yugos**, **palmas**, and **hachas** associated with the ball game, carved with various intricate decorations in distinctive Totonac style.

The exact use of these items is unclear. According to some authorities the yugos, despite their weight, were worn on the hips during play, but most scholars believe that lighter, similarly shaped versions of wood and leather were used in play, while the stone examples were decorative, or only used in ceremonial processions. Still others claim that they were used to hold down the heads of sacrificial victims. However, a few closed-end examples are known, and it seems more trouble than it's worth to have to hold down a victim and at the same time get a yugo over him.

The palmas, named for their general shape, are depicted in the ball court reliefs at El Tajín as a sort of breastplate, resting on the yugos of the players. Hachas may have been used as markers or goals on some ball courts, despite the 'votive axe'-like appearance of many examples.

38. **Huastec polychrome pottery** vessels and carved stone vessels. One zoomorphic, alabaster vase depicts a monkey with features similar to the obsidian monkey in the Aztec Room, No. 96. **39**. **Stele depicting Quetzalcóatl** from Castillo de Teayo. He is identifiable by his shell-shaped pectoral and shell necklace, symbolizing the wind, and thus his manifestation as Ehecatl. He wears typical Huastec headgear, incl. conical cap, earplug, and nose ornament, and holds a bunch of maguey thorns for use in autosacrifice. **40**. **Sculpture of a youth**, from Ajalpan (Hidalgo). With its typically Huastec deformed skull and other features, this piece is evidence of the spread of the Huasteca. Such pieces may have served as standard-bearers in front of pyramids and temples (cf. Nos. 11 and 12 in Room 6, and Nos. 18 and 20 in Room 7).

41. Sculpture with attributes of Quetzalcóatl, possibly the god or a priest representing him, wearing another typical Huastec style hat, this time an elegant fan-shape. **42**. Display panels describing the Huasteca region: mountains, hydrography, topography, and flora and fauna. **43**. Broken sculpture of a human figure issuing from a bird's beak. **44**. Stele carved on one side with an old man, incl. traces of red paint; and on the other side with a bird, perhaps a symbol of the Sun. **45**. **Statue of Quetzalcóatl** wearing feathered headgear; Late Classic, c 600–900. **46**. Figurines illustrating typical Huastec body decoration and mutilation—filing and blackening the teeth, flattening the skull, and tattooing the body. **47**. Sculpture of god wearing the Huastec conical cap, from Naranjo (Veracruz). **48**. Huastec female figurines, illustrating clothing, jewellery, etc.

49 and **54**. Two long cases containing **Huastec polychrome pottery**, more figurines, and other artefacts. (Separating them, along the wall, the stele—No. 51, below.) Many of these vessels are anthropomorphic (eg, woman with a spout behind her), others are covered with simpler, geometric designs. Some are specialized vessels, such as the brasero from Las Palmillas, decorated with animals and a hunting scene. Other items include mother-of-pearl jewellery, carved bone and shell ornaments, and tools of obsidian, jade, and other stone.

50. Original (other state museums have reproductions) **Adolescent from Tamuín** (San Luis Potosí; actually found on Rancho El Consuelo). He carries a child on his back, and exhibits numerous classic Huastec features: deformed skull, mutilated teeth, extended, pierced and beplugged earlobes, and a body over half-covered with intricate tattoos—wind symbols (incl. some Maya symbols), serpents, chalchihuites (jade discs), and maize cobs. The various symbols indicate that he was a budding young Quetzalcóatl, in the guise of Ehecatl, or possibly in the guise of the Evening Star, who in Huastec mythology descended each evening into Mictlán (Huastec Underworld) with his son, the Sun—perhaps represented by the child on the statue's back.

51. Stele from Huilozintla (Veracruz), carved with a tattooed, priestly figure practising autosacrifice by piercing his tongue with a stick, the blood being eagerly lapped up by a little monster on the l.; the plumed headdress of the main figure may represent Quetzalcóatl. **52. Sculpture of Xilonen**, goddess of ripening maize. She sits Indian-style and wears a paper-plaited headpiece decorated with maize cobs—another Huastec fashion. **53. Sculpture of Xochiquetzal** (flower of the rich plume), goddess of beauty and fertility. According to one Náhuatl legend she was first wife of Tláloc before Tezcatlipoca, god of the smoking mirror, abducted her. She was the female counterpart of Xochipilli and as such was patroness of domesticity and of the Aztec day *Xóchitl*, twentieth of the 20 days. **54.** See No. 49, above. **55.** Sculpture of a goddess of planting and fertility, wearing a conical cap and holding a fan of feathers. **56.** Sculpture of a hunchbacked old man holding a phallic symbol. **57.** Sculpture of another female agrarian deity. **58.** Sculpture of another hunchbacked man, with a chest hump as well. **59.** Sculpture of Mictlantecuhtli, from Tierra Blanca (Veracruz). He wears a conical cap and has a gaunt, fleshless face and protruding ribs. **60.** Sculpture of a fertility goddess, from Castillo de Teayo (Veracruz). **61.** Stele from Tepetzintla (Veracruz), depicting Quetzalcóatl in the guise of Tlahuizcalpantecuhtli, the Morning Star; possibly depicted here as imagined in his flight to exile from Tula. **62.** Sculpture of the Pulque god, from Castillo de Teayo, dated c 9C AD. On his chest are the glyphs for *Ome Tochtli* ('two rabbit'). The pulque cult probably came to the Huasteca via the Toltecs in Hidalgo.

Return to the central patio and turn r., then r. again to enter Room 10.

ROOM 10: The Maya covers the region now comprising the states of E Tabasco and Chiapas, Campeche, Yucatán, and Quintana Roo. The room is similar in format to the Aztec Room, using information panels to illustrate the Maya subregions and lifestyles, adjoining showcases to complement them, and sculptures and stelae from various sites. Where appropriate, scale models show some of the principal structures and the techniques of their construction. In addition there is a reconstruction of the famous Tomb of Lord Pacal (Shield) from the Templo de las Inscripciones at Palenque.

The figurines, sculptures, and stelae give a great deal of information about Maya physical appearance, dress, genealogy, and social classification. Their prolific detail shows us the skirts, blouses, mantles and capes, sandals, belts, hats, animal helmets, fans and staffs of office, pectorals, bracelets, necklaces, earplugs, and other jewellery worn by the Maya of differing ranks and occupations.

1. In the centre of the introductory section is a small scale model **relief map of the Maya region**, illustrating its mountain chains and hydrography, and the subdivisions of the Highland and Lowland zones used by archaeologists. **2** and **3.** To l. and r., on the curved room dividers, panels with maps, charts, and photographs illustrate various themes: Maya geography, principal sites, ecology of the Maya region, and a cross-section of the peninsula showing its vegetational variation.

Veer l. for **4.** Sculpture from Cumpich (facing the entrance), depicting a person with a heavily tattooed face. **5** (now proceed r.). **Stela 1 from Izapa** (Chiapas); late Preclassic, c 200 BC. This depicts a figure standing on a serpent's head (?Earth) with water all around it. **6. Lintel 26 from Yaxchilán** (Chiapas); Classic, dated AD 726. It depicts the figure of a woman holding up the head or mask of a jaguar to a princely figure who has his hand extended to receive it (cf. No. 38, below). **7.** Large stucco head from Palenque; Classic, c AD 450–750. This figure illustrates characteristic Maya facial features. Moulding, sculpting, and carving in stucco, both in the round and on building facings, was a Maya speciality. **8**. Stele from Jonuta (Tabasco); Late Classic, c AD 600–900. Here, a priest is depicted, wearing an elaborate feathered headdress and phallic-looking chest ornament, kneeling and offering birds. **9**. Artefacts illustrating Maya technology, notably 'eccentric' items carved on thin sheets of obsidian (cf. No. 57, below). These are usually found in offertory caches placed beneath stelae or altars. **10**. Painting by Ernesto Alvarez depicting Maya society and class structure. **11**. Stucco head, from Comalcalco (Tabasco); mid-Classic.

12. **Lintel 53** from **Yaxchilán**; Late Classic, dated c AD 766. It shows a princely or priestly figure wearing the usual flamboyant headdress, presenting a sceptre to a smaller figure—a woman. At many large Classic Period Maya cities the aristocratic families included noble women who had important positions and powerful influence among the ruling élite (eg, Cobá, Ichpaatún, and Tancah). **13** (in middle of room). Stone disc from Chinkultic (Chiapas); Classic, dated AD 590; 55cm in diameter. It is carved with the figure of a ball player wearing characteristic gear: elaborately plumed hat, knee guards, belt, and an arm guard. The edges of the disc have a line of glyphs and there are others in the centre. **14**. Pottery cylinder sculptured with masks of the Sun god, Kinich Ahau, and with serpents, birds, and mythical beasts. These are thought to have been used at altars to hold incense or other offerings. **15**. **Classic Period Maya figurines**, many with traces of their original paint. They illustrate typical Maya features and costume: short stature, dark skins, wide heads with high cheekbones, aquiline noses, and slanted eyes. The headdress, clothing and amount and type of jewellery and other ornament denote social rank. There is also a figure of a woman with her loom and fragments of Maya cloth. **16**. **Stela 14 from Yaxchilán**; Classic, dated AD 600. This is a 'victory stele' showing a typical scene with a dominant warrior chief and a submissive captive (cf. No. 41, below). **17**. Artefacts illustrating Maya ceremony and music, incl. information panels, musical instruments, and figurines of musicians, priests, etc. **18**. Lintel 48 from Yaxchilán; Classic, dated AD 534. **19**. Figurines—companion to No. 17, above: musicians and dancers in a variety of stances. **20**. **Lintel 47 from Yaxchilán**; Classic, with several columns of hieroglyphic inscriptions.

21. Case devoted to the theme of **Maya hieroglyphic writing**, incl. figurines and copies of Maya codices. The extant Pre-Conquest Maya codices deal with calendrical cycles, ritual and ceremony, prophecy and divination, and astronomy. Although histories and chronicles no doubt existed, none have survived except as inscriptions on stelae and other sculpted monuments. Only four Pre-Conquest Maya codices have survived: Codex Dresdensis (in Sächsische Landesbibliothek, Dresden); Grolier Codex (in this Museum); the Madrid Codex (or Tro-Cortesiano; in the Museo de América, Madrid); and the Paris Codex (in the Bibliothèque Nationale, Paris). (A fifth codex was found in 1987 at Cerén, El Salvador, c AD 600, but its text could not be saved. The 'Wright Codex' is on a rectangular pottery vessel, dated c AD 600–900, in a private collection.) The Maya script is now decipherable for all intents and purposes; we can read the numerical system and the glyphs for names and places, and we know that a large proportion of the glyphs were phonetic symbols. Most Maya texts can thus be understood.

22. Maya jewellery and personal ornament: necklaces, bracelets, ear-, lip-, and nose-plugs, etc. **23**. **Lintel 18 from Yaxchilán**; Classic. Covered with hieroglyphic inscriptions. **24**. Clay figurines from Jaina, Jonuta, Nebaj, and other sites. There are ball players, figurines from Jaina burials, a princely figure sitting on a throne, and several priestly figures in rich costumes and headdresses. Some show traces of paint.

25 (in middle of room). In cruciform plan, ten small cases contain particularly exquisite examples of **Classic Maya polychrome vessels** and figurines. Included are plates from Jaina, of Late Classic date; large seashell-shaped vessel with a man emerging from the mouth of the shell; and polychrome dish painted with a hunting scene. **26**. L-plan showcase containing more mundane Maya pottery, arranged in chronological sequence to illustrate development of

Maya ceramics from its Preclassic origins to the 16C. **27**. Lintel from Yaxchilán; Classic; depicting two seated figures in the usual fancy dress. **28**. Lintel from Campeche (otherwise unprovenanced); Late Classic in detail. **29**. Lintel 32 from Yaxchilán; Classic, dated AD 756. **30**. Large urn from Chinkultic. It depicts a bird from whose beak issues a human head, and another human figure sitting on the rim of the vessel.

31. Long section of **reconstructed pyramid wall** decorated with stucco sculptures. While its medium and technique are thoroughly Maya, it also shows evidence of influence from Teotihuacán. In the centre is a large mask of the Sun god, Kinich Ahau, with amber beads in his nostrils, dentil deformation, and crossed eyes—a condition considered desirable among the Maya and deliberately induced at an early age by dangling a bauble before the eyes of babies; below him is the mask of the Rain god, Chac. On the sides of the wall are representations of the Old Fire god, Huahuatéotl, holding a brasero on his head, and the glyphs for Kin (Sun), balam (jaguar), and imix (maize, or vegetation) on his hands.

32, 33, 35, and **36**. **Scale models** of Classic Period Maya sites: Uaxactún (Guatemala), Copán (Honduras), Yaxchilán, and Río Bec (Campeche). **34**. Stele from Campeche depicting a figure richly dressed as befitted the Maya nobility, incl. the requisite flamboyant headgear. To lower r. is a second, smaller, figure, perhaps one of his subjects. **37**. **Stela 18 from Yaxchilán**. **38**. **Lintel 54 from Yaxchilán**; Classic, dated AD 756. A woman makes an offering to a priestly or princely figure in rich costume (cf. No. 6, above). **39**. **Stone panel** from the **Templo de la Cruz Foliada at Palenque**; Classic, dated AD 642. It depicts a maize plant, apparently 'deified', with priestly figures facing it on either side. On the plant itself sits a quetzal bird. One priest offers up a mask of the Rain god, Chac (near which is the date glyph).

40. Group of **three stelae** (one of them as two fragments) from **Yaxchilán**, all Classic. Stela 10, upper and lower parts; dated AD 766. The two fragments depict a sumptuously dressed warrior, kneeling, and two standing, but seemingly obeisant, figures on either side of him. Lintel 9, dated AD 687, depicts two figures identified as halac uinic (true men—civic leaders), each holding their staff of authority. Lintel 58; dated AD 756, and also depicting two figures holding staves of authority.

41. Second group of **four stone monuments** (three aligned an.‍ one alongside them). Stela 51 from Calakmul (Campeche); Classic, dated AD 731. A typical 'victory stele' depicting a halach uinic in rich costume, with one foot on a cowering enemy (cf. No. 16, above). Lintels 12 (dated AD 741), 33, and 43 (dated AD 687) from Yaxchilán; all Classic. The last shows another scene of a priest receiving an offering (cf. Nos. 6 and 38, above).

The glass doors—opposite the entrance to the room—lead outside to a full-scale display of **Maya architecture**. **42**. On l. is a copy of Stela E from Quiriguá (Guatemala); the original is Classic, dated AD 771. It depicts a priestly or princely figure. **43**. Full-scale **reproduction of the temple at Hochob** (Campeche), illustrating the Chenes architectural style, c AD 600–900. The Chenes style spread outwards from Hochob, other notable examples being at Uxmal (Pirámide del Adivino, Rte 93B) and at Chichén Itzá (Anexo Este, Rte 98): characterized by gaping, monster-mouth doorways, highly stylized and composed of a mosaic of stone slabs. In some examples, as at Hochob, the mask is thought to represent Chac, the Rain god, with his long, hooked nose. On each side of the doorway is a thatched temple with colonnettes, surmounted by wide-eyed, grimacing masks of a stellar god. The roof is crested with a double row of human figures, forming an inverted V in profile. Inside, the ceiling forms a corbel, or false, arch, made by projecting each successive layer of blocks over the edge of the previous ones until the final capstone bridges the gap above the two penultimate blocks. This reproduction is constructed of stone quarried in Yucatán. **44**. C 20m to the r. (when facing the Hochob temple) is a full-scale reproduction of the **Templo de las Pinturas at Bonampak** (see Rte 90). These copies were painted by the Mexican artist Rina Lazo.

Stairs lead down to **45**. The full-scale **replica of the princely burial of the Templo de las Inscripciones at Palenque**. At the foot of the stairs, turn r.

First is a child's burial urn and a reproduction of the tomb that contained five or six children, sacrificed to accompany the dead ruler into the afterlife. Next, in a separate case, are the beautiful mosaic mask of jade and mother-of-pearl, and several other burial offerings, incl. jade necklaces, rings, and other jewellery, and a ceremonial votive axe-head.

In a corner of the room is a scale model of Palenque, showing the Templo de las Inscripciones in relation to the other monuments. Next to it are two heads modelled in stucco, found in the lower part of the burial chamber and possibly portraits of former rulers of Palenque. The replica of the princely burial chamber—in the centre of the room—can be viewed from both ends. Inscriptions on the walls of the temple and inside the crypt itself identify the occupant of the sarcophagus as Lord Pacal (Shield), ruler of Palenque.

Continue r. at the top of the steps, to **46**. Sculpture from Oxkintok (Yucatán); Late Classic. It depicts a well-fed (?)deity—Dios Gordo—in the Puuc style, derivative of the Chenes and Río Bec styles. **47**. Sculpture of head from Kabah (Yucatán); Late Classic. The scarifications on the l. cheek are a sign of nobility, possibly making this piece a portrait of a ruler of the house of Kabah. **48**. Fragment of sculpted façade from the Templo del Adivino (Magician; on the Pirámide del Adivino) at Uxmal; Late Classic, Puuc style. It depicts the head of a priest or god emerging from the jaws of a serpent. The entire temple decoration in fact shows a mixture of styles, incl. Puuc, Chenes, Teotihuacano, and early Toltec, incorporated over the lifespan of the structure in various building phases.

49. Modern mural showing the **Maya Creation Myth** with a multitude of gods and goddesses. Related in the 'Popul Vuh' of the Quiché Maya of Guatemala, Maya creation began when there was only water and an ominous darkness. The gods got together and created the earth and its plants and animals. Man was created from some of the earth's mud, but was soon destroyed because he could not speak and was thus unable to worship his creators. The gods tried again, this time making man out of wood so that he could speak and procreate, as they wanted, but he was unable to recognize his creators and was again wiped out, except for a few survivors who were turned into monkeys. The gods made man a third time, out of yellow and white maize dough, and on the morning after, he worshipped the gods in the desired manner and was thus the ancestor of the Maya peoples.

50. Late Classic stele from Chiapas. **51**. Large fragment of the sculpted façade of the Codz Poop (rolled-up mat) or Pal. de las Máscaras at Kabah; Late Classic, Puuc in style. It depicts a Chac mask with his distinctive upturned nose. The entire palace comprises two parallel galleries of rooms, with a 46m façade covered with a frieze of Chac masks. **52**. Sculpture from Uxmal; Late Classic; showing a human head wearing a serpent-shaped hat or helmet, possibly another noble portrait.

The remaining displays illustrate Maya culture in the Postclassic Period, especially the *Maya-Toltec Phase* at Chichén Itzá. **53**. Postclassic Maya ceramics and stone vessels. Included are **Fine Orange Wares** with incised decoration, imported alabaster vases from Honduras, and Plumbate Ware vessels. The last were produced by applying a clay slip with a high iron content and firing at a high temperature, then burnishing and polishing to a high sheen; they were imported from the Highlands of Guatemala and El Salvador. A particularly notable piece is a polychrome Fine Orange Ware vase, c 13cm high, depicting an obviously important black figure with a feathered staff, wearing an elaborate, plumed headdress and a fancy belt. **54**. **Chacmool figure** from Chichén Itzá; Maya-Toltec, c late 10–12C. This example comes from the Tumba de Chacmool, also known as the Adoratorio de Venus (cf. Nos. 8 and 9 in Room

6). **55**. Scale model of the coastal site of Tulum (Quintana Roo; see Rte 102). **56**. Sculpture of a human head between the jaws of a monster, from Chichén Itzá. **57**. Ritual artefacts from Chichén Itzá, incl.: three plates or discs with turquoise, pyrite, and mother-of-pearl mosaic inlay—one of which depicts Xiuhcóatl, the Fire Snake or Turquoise Serpent (cf. Nos. 23 and 63 in Room 7); votive axe-heads; figurines; gold ornaments; and shapes known as 'eccentrics', cut out of thin sheets of obsidian and flint and often buried in caches beneath stelae or altars (cf. No. 9, above). **58**. Group of **four atlantes from Chichén Itzá**; Maya-Toltec, c AD 900–1200. They supported an altar slab in the Templo de los Guerreros (cf. Nos. 7 and 8 in Room 6, and Nos. 3 and 58 in Room 7).

59. Copy of a **mural in the Templo de los Tigres** at Chichén Itzá.

The conventional interpretation of this scene is of an army of Toltec warriors attacking a Maya village while the gods look down. Arthur G. Miller has interpreted the scene more specifically as a symbolic battle between 'Captain Serpent' and 'Captain Sun Disk', and says that the battle occurred near Seibal in the Maya Petén region. Richard Diehl suggests that the battle depicts the Itzá Maya conquest of Yucatán.

60. Large polychrome ceremonial urn from Mayapán (Yucatán); Late Post-classic, c AD 1250–1400. It depicts a tall figure of Chac, in an elaborate feathered headdress shaped as a snake. In one hand he holds a cup containing an offering of sacred water and in the other a ball of burning copal incense. **61**. Alabaster vase with mask in relief; Early Postclassic. **62**. Stela 5 from Sayil (Yucatán); Late Classic, Puuc style, c AD 800–950. It shows a richly dressed halach uinic (true man) with rectangular shield and staff of authority. **63**. Late Classic ceramics. **64**. **Sculpted Quetzalcóatl head**, the Plumed Serpent, architectural decoration from Chichén Itzá. **65**. Relief from the Casa de las Aguilas at Chichén Itzá. The entire temple has a frieze of alternating jaguars (as here) and eagles devouring human hearts.

After leaving the Maya Room, we walk past the stairs to the restaurant; the entrance to Room 11 is just beyond them.

In **ROOM 11**: **N Mexico** the exhibits illustrate that part of Mexico which was beyond the boundaries of Mesoamerica, but nonetheless influenced by Meso-american cultures in many ways, especially from central Mexico. Some sub-regions were virtually unaffected, such as Baja California, while others shared many features with the cultures of the SW USA, and shared many individual traits of the Mesoamerican Culture Complex.

Turn r. after entering. **1**. Along the wall are six introductory panels and maps showing subregions and cultural divisions—the *Desert Cultures, Plains Cultures*, and the *'Oasis Cultures'*, the effects of Spanish colonization on these groups, and a map of the principal sites. **2**. Case and panels illustrating the art and commerce of these cultures. Commerce was based on barter, exchanging mostly raw materials for finished products from central Mexico. Much 'internal' barter exchanged coastal items for the products of the central desert. **3**. Panels and diagrams explaining the N *Desert Cultures* and their subsistence—based on hunting and gathering; and a small showcase containing examples of their hunting tools and weapons. There are also some reproductions of their petro-glyphs, by Nadine Prado. 4. Replica of a hunter-gatherer burial and its offerings. **5**. Funerary offerings of weapons, tools, clothing, and basketry found in cave burials. **6**. Large case containing artefacts illustrating the daily life and tech-nology of the N: stone tools and grinding implements, fabrics, arrow and spear points, basketry rendered waterproof for boiling water and cooking, and drills for making fire.

7. Objects from Los Morales (Guanajuato); c 1C BC/2C AD (contemporary with the early development at Teotihuacán). **8**. Ceramics and other artefacts from San Miguel de Allende, El Coporo, and the Río Laja valley of Guanajuato: vessels, stone tools, pipes, and various items of bone. Some of the vessels show evidence of influence from Teotihuacán and from the W Cultures of Mexico (Room 12). Sites in this region comprised ceremonial centres of pyramid mounds, terraces, and ball courts contemporary with and influenced by the Mesoamerican Late Classic and Postclassic cultures of central Mexico, particularly the Toltecs.

9. Ceramics and stone tools from El Tunil Grande (San Luis Potosí); as with the items in Nos. 7 and 8, these show evidence of influence from central Mexico and the N Gulf Coast. **10**. Ceramics, figurines, stone pipes, tools and arrow points; plus carved stone yugos and palmas used in the ball game. The area N of Querétaro, especially the Río Verde region of San Luis Potosí, also shows considerable contact with Teotihuacán, and with the Huastec and Totonac cultures of the N Gulf Coast. Note in particular the use of stone pipes, rare elsewhere in Mesoamerica, but found in quantity here. **11** (on opposite side of room). Carved stone artefacts and fragments of architectural decoration showing Totonac influence.

12. Moving still farther N, to the States of Durango and Zacatecas, this case contains ceramics from the *Desert Cultures* showing less influence from cultures to the S and more from the cultures to the N. There are highly stylistic anthropomorphic and zoomorphic vessels and figurines, many decorated with the paint cloisonné technique—designs excised from the surface of the vessel and highlighted by filling them in with a paste of a different colour and rubbing it smooth and level with the surrounding surface. The technique was also used to decorate gourds. **13** (on wall). Map of the 'Oasis Cultures' of N Mexico and the SW USA. This region developed irrigation agriculture and permanent, settled towns during the first millennium AD. **14–16**. Three cases exhibit **ceramics** (dated c AD 400–1000) from the three subregions of the 'Oasis Cultures'— Hohokam (in S Arizona and N Sonora), Anasazi (in the 'four corners' region of New Mexico, Arizona, Utah, and Colorado), and Mogollón (in Arizona, New Mexico, and Chihuahua). These cultures overlapped to some extent in time and influence. Their highly individualistic and varied pottery decoration represents a long tradition, elements of which continue to the present day. The individual design elements and variations in decoration have been the study of archaeologists interested in kinship reconstruction and in the diffusion of styles and artistic concepts throughout the region.

The next section is concerned primarily with the site of **Casas Grandes** (Chihuahua) and its culture. The site was occupied from c AD 800 to c 1400. By c AD 1000 it had become the principal trading town and ceremonial centre of the northern region, and included multi-storeyed dwelling complexes, a huge earthen walled ball court, and several platform mounds. **17**. Photomural and artefacts representing some of the objects of its trade with the agricultural towns of the SW USA, with the Western Cultures of Mexico, and with the Toltec state, incl. ceramics showing influences from the Mogollon and Hohokam cultures, rarer objects of turquoise, greenstone, and mother-of-pearl traded from the S and from the coasts, and many other tools and utensils. **18** and **21**. Casas Grandes (or Paquimé) ceramics. The potters of Casas Grandes had their own designs, incl. a variety of anthropomorphic and zoomorphic vessels, human masks, and geometric patterns in polychrome, both applied and in paint cloisonné. **19**. Scale model of one of the multi-storeyed apartment complexes at Casas Grandes. Multi-storeyed dwellings began to replace single-storey dwellings and pit houses in the late 10C and 11C AD. They were built using adobe bricks and beam frames, up to five or six storeys, and included internal stairways, ovens, water storage tanks, and other amenities. Their appearance, and the techniques used, are thought to be partly imitative of the cliff-dwellings of the SW USA and partly the adoption of methods introduced by colonizers from Mesoamerica. **20**. Group of large, stationary block grinding stones. **21**. See No. 18, above. **22**. Two examples of more portable quern stones.

The final displays illustrate the effects of the Spanish Conquest, proselytization, colonization, and settlement of the N from the 17C to the end of the 19C. **23**. Jewellery, ornament, and other craft products from the region, in bone, shell, turquoise, and silver. **24**. Display illustrating the craft of sandpainting. **25**. Wall display on the ethnography of the region in the 18–19C.

ROOM 12: **The Western Cultures**. The final archaeological exhibits on the ground floor illustrate the cultures of W Mexico from the Río Guasave in the N to the Río Balsas valley in the S. Several cultural groups occupied the lake basins, plains, and littoral of this area. The opening displays include a section of maps and charts to emphasize this ecological diversity. The Western Cultures have many distinct features, and until c AD 600 developed somewhat in isolation of the cultures of central and S Mexico. Thereafter, however, their ceremonial centres look very Mesoamerican, being laid out around plazas and using platforms and temples built with talud-tablero facings.

Perhaps the most distinctive features of their art and architecture are the abundance of large, glossy red, hollow figurines of people and animals, their smaller, solid figurines depicting almost every aspect of their lives, and their use of shaft tombs. The Western Cultures were also among the first Mesoamerican metalsmiths, and apparently learned the craft from the merchants who plied their trade along the Pacific Coast in Central America, N South America, and the W coast of Mexico.

1 and **2** (On walls). Introductory information panels, chronological charts and diagrams, maps, and photographs of the W region. These show its geographic diversity, flora and fauna, timescales, and the principal sites. **3**. In the middle of this section is a large **terracotta figurine of a woman**, squatting Indian fashion. It comes from the 3C AD shaft tomb at Las Cebollas-Tequilitan (Nayarit), and is typical of the so-called Chinesco style—named for its vaguely 'oriental' facial features. The style is generally naturalistic, with subtle poise, carefully modelled features, and high polish. It is subdivided into several types (other examples can be seen in other showcases): the first type has just been described; a second type has distinctive heart-shaped faces with 'coffee-bean' eyes and black painting on face and body; a third type, called 'Martian', has a bizarre appearance, and brilliantly coloured geometric designs. **4**. **Ceramics from Chupícuaro** (Guanajuato). In the Preclassic Period Chupícuaro was an advanced site whose ceramics had a widespread influence in both W and N central Mexico. From its early phases of occupation there was a great variety of forms, at first in monochrome, then in bichrome and polychrome as well, using several techniques in application. Zoomorphic vessels were a speciality, incl. dogs, turtles, birds, armadillos, and others. The site was abandoned by the beginning of the Classic Period. **5**. Bichrome and polychrome Chupícuaro pottery, incl. two painted figurines. **6**. Reconstruction of a **burial at Chupícuaro**, incl. several skeletons and their tomb furniture.

7. Figurines from the tombs at **El Opeño** (Michoacán); dated c 1300 BC. **8**. Pottery and more figurines from El Opeño and from San Gerónimo (Guerrero). The El Opeño figurines, especially, show affinities to contemporary Preclassic figurines from the Basin of Mexico (eg, Tlatilco). **9**. **Figurines from Chupícuaro**. Although generally contemporary with those in the other cases of this section, these are of a distinct, flattened appearance, with thin, diagonally set eyes, applied features (known as pastillaje), and are often painted.

The figurines of the Western Cultures, from the Preclassic to the Postclassic, are extremely informative sources on the daily lives of their makers. There is a large variety of shapes, sizes, styles, and subjects; and there are often groups of related figures in ceremonial and more ordinary activities. They generally depict a short-statured, sturdy-looking people, with thick lips and almond-shaped or 'coffee-bean' eyes. Themes include mother-and-child groups, babies in cradles, groups of musicians and dancers, merchandize porters, ball players, and lots of animals. Clothing and the objects used in these activities are equally accurately depicted.

The next section is devoted to the **Classic Period**. **10**. Figurines from Colima, Jalisco, and Nayarit, the heart of the shaft-tomb region. As before, the figurines depict scenes from daily life: mother-and-child groups, women grinding maize, people—presumably of an upper class—carried in litters, musicians and acrobats, ball players, warriors, and models of temples and pyramid-platforms, and a bizarre form known as 'people strapped-to-a-bed'. **11**. More figurines from Jalisco (r.), Colima (l.), and Nayarit (centre). These examples depict styles painted white- or cream-on-red (from Jalisco); black, with elongated heads and 'coffee-bean' eyes (from Colima); and polychrome (from Nayarit).

12. Superb examples of yet another figurine type—large, hollow, glossy **red figures from Colima**. These pieces all come from shaft tombs, which helps to explain their excellent preservation. They include hairless dogs (a speciality), armadillos, turtles, fish, ducks, and other birds. Vessels made in the same glossy, red ware have tripod bases and ribbed walls. **13**. **Pottery** illustrating the technique of paint cloisonné. Pieces of negative design are excised from the walls of the vessel and a new colour of paste-like paint or pigmented clay is forced into the hollows and allowed to dry; then it is smoothed down even with the surface around it. The technique was also applied to gourds and spread to the Northern Cultures, as well as being extensively used at Teotihuacán and S of the Basin of Mexico in the Mixteca-Puebla style.

14. Colima, Jalisco, and Nayarit hollow figurines. **15**. More figurines, plus stone censers for burning copal and other resins, and masks. One notable vessel is a hairless dog body with a human head—such dual-being pieces are fairly numerous.

16. Large display of hollow figurines of humans and animals; large figure of a hunchbacked old man with a scarified face from Colima, holding a cane in his l. hand and standing on a two-headed fish; figure of a kneeling woman with almond-shaped eyes, earrings, and six nose rings; seated woman with a flattened head and short, stubby legs; scale model of shaft tomb at Etzatlán (Jalisco).

Additional showcases contain artefacts illustrating external influences on the Western Cultures during the Classic Period, from Teotihuacán and from the Olmecs; and examples of stone figurines in the *Mezcala* style of Guerrero—Late Preclassic and Classic angular-featured figurines and anthropomorphic votive axe-heads of jadeite and serpentine. **17**. **Stele from Acapulco**, carved on one side, but now extremely worn.

The final section is devoted to the **Postclassic Period**. **18**. Postclassic ceramics from Guerrero; decorated with simple geometric patterns and some incised designs. **19**. Postclassic polychrome pottery. **20**. Classic and Postclassic ceramics and other artefacts from Michoacán—the Apatzingán region. Vessels include tripod bases and polychrome decoration; bone and shell jewellery; and figurines showing influence from Toltec styles. **21**. **Scale model of the site of Ixtlán del Río**, incl. a Postclassic circular temple dedicated to Quetzalcóatl-Ehecatl. **22**. Postclassic ceramics from Sinaloa. **23**. Case of ceramics from Nayarit, incl.: monochrome and polychrome vessels, vases with appliqué masks, and flattened figurines with slanting, almond-shaped eyes.

24. Tarascan ceramics from Michoacán, incl.: full-sized and miniature vessels, highly polished tripod vessels, spouted vessels, and other forms. **25**. **Large scale model of the Tarascan site of Tzintzuntzan** (Michoacán). It shows all five of the yacatas, a specialized temple form in this culture. **26**. Tarascan stone 'throne' in the shape of a coyote. **27** (behind 'throne'). Copy of the Lienzo de Jucutacato, a 16C codex describing the migration of metallurgists from the Gulf Coast to the Tarascan territory. **28**. Items of Tarascan technology: obsidian, flint, and turquoise artefacts; shell and mother-of-pearl jewellery; pyrite mirrors; and above all, copper, silver, and gold crafts, for which the Tarascans were justly famous throughout central Mexico. **29**. Small case with more Tarascan stone and metal artefacts. Note in particular the copper mask depicting Xipe Totec, god of springtime and planting, and patron of lapidaries and smiths. **30**. Large stone **chacmool from Ihuatzio** (Michoacán). More crudely carved than the Toltec and Maya-Toltec examples, but obviously inspired by them, and in this example, with a deeply scarified face (cf. Nos. 8 and 9 in Room 6 and No. 54 in Room 10). **31**. Mural by Pablo O'Higgins showing a reconstruction of the ceremonial burial rites around one of the yacatas at Tzintzuntzan (cf. Rte 28). **32** and **34**. Two showcases containing jewellery from Apatzingán and Pátzcuaro (in No. 32), and from Lo Arado (Jalisco; in No. 34): necklaces, bracelets, rings, ear and nose plugs, and other items in silver, gold, copper, mother-of-pearl, rock crystal, turquoise, and greenstone. **33**. Stone **sculpture of a coyote** from Tzintzuntzan (cf. Nos 90 and 97 in Room 7).

Two staircases lead from the archaeological exhibits to the **Ethnographic Exhibits** on the upper floor—from Room 1 or Room 12. The recommendation is to go from Room 12 of the archaeological exhibits back across the central patio to Room 1 and begin a tour of the ethnographic collections from there, thus beginning with ethnographic Room 1.

ROOM 1: Introduction to Ethnology. Keep r. and continue anti-clockwise. This room serves a similar purpose as the introductory room of the archaeological part of the museum. Organized around the various themes with which the ethnologist concerns him- or herself, these are illustrated by examples from the various ethnic regions of Mexico. First a map shows the different physical types in Mexico, with clay figurines to illustrate their ancient lineages. Murals and recorded commentaries help to locate the different linguistic groups, and information panels explain Mexico's demographic geography.

There are examples of textiles, clothing, and dyes, with drawings of the clothing worn after the Conquest. To illustrate regional variations there are musicological displays, models of huts and houses, and a large granary surrounded by showcases containing agricultural implements and craft tools, clay pots of many different regional styles and uses, cooking utensils and regional foods, and items of furniture.

Religious beliefs, magic, and political customs are shown in photographs, and illustrated by special items of clothing, votive offerings, and other artefacts.

ROOMS 2–10. Life-size ethnographic dioramas. Each room displays the culture of related groups in a region with information panels, life-sized mannequins with authentic clothing and artefacts, models, photographs, paintings, and, in some rooms, showcases of musical instruments, pottery, and other artefacts. For each region the themes include: geography and ecology, usually in large photomurals, many in colour; demography; linguistic histories and socio-linguistic relations, where relevant; techniques of various handicrafts, especially the colourful variety of regional clothing—spinning, weaving, dyeing, basketry, sandal-making, and the uses of other natural fibres; subsistence economy, incl. hunting, fishing, and farming, with showcases of the implements used and photographs of them in use; housing and house construction, usually in full-scale models in which mannequins and artefacts are displayed in context; socio-political organization, and the accommodation of tribal practices through the viceregal period up to the present; relations with State and central governments; religious practices, incl. ancient magico-religious beliefs, magico-medicinal rites and practices, and folklore; music and fiestas, incl. examples of the instruments and special costumes used, and adaptations of European instruments and festivals.

The rooms are arranged in two wings over the archaeology rooms as follows: **ROOM 2**—*Huicholes y Coras*. **ROOM 3**—*Purépechas ó Tarascos*. **ROOM 4**—*Los Otomianos: Pames, Chichimecos, Otomí, Mazahuas, Matlazincas, Ocuiltecos*. **ROOM 5**—*La Sierra de Puebla: Nahuas, Totonacos, Otomíes, Tepehuas ó Tepehuanes*. **ROOM 6**—*Oaxaca: Mixtecos, Zapotecos, Chontales ó Tequistlatecos, Tlapanecos, Mazatecos, Chochos, Ixcatecos, Cuicatecos, Triques, Amuzgos, Chatinos, Chinantecos, Huaves, Mixes, Zoques*. **ROOM 7**—*La Costa del Golfo: Totonacos y Huastecos*. **ROOMS 8** (Highlands) and **9** (Lowlands)—*Mayas, Chontales, Choles, Tzotziles, Tzeltales, Lacandones, Tojolabales, Mames*. **ROOM 10**—*Grupos del Noroeste: Tepehuanes, Cochimíes, Papagos, Pimas, Opatas, Yaquis, Mayos, Tarahumaras, Seris*.

ROOM 11: *Indigenismo*. This final room summarizes the ethnographic exhibits and presents a synthesis of Mexican native life today. There is an exhibit on contemporary native crafts, and on the social and cultural integration of Mexico's indigenous peoples with the 'modern' world. To highlight the evolution of Mexican culture the displays are set against backdrops of photographs and paintings of Prehispanic ceremonial centres, historical scenes, and modern cities.

12 Paseo de la Reforma

This route describes modern Mexico City's main thoroughfare, from Chapultepec NE towards the centre, and also places of interest easily reached from it. Its great length (and width) and the difficulties of negotiating on foot the glorietas (roundabouts) where busy roads intersect it can be awkward and tiring except for the most determined of pedestrians. The less hardy use taxis or buses.

PASEO DE LA REFORMA in its most important, historic, and resplendent stretch runs from Chapultepec to the junction with Avs Bucareli and Juárez (c 3km). From here it continues NE (a further 3km, of decreasing interest) to the junction with Calzadas Guadalupe and Misterios. Its broad sweep takes in modern commercial buildings, hotels, department stores, embassies, cinemas; aristocratic survivals of porfirian Mexico; wide tree-lined sidewalks on which stand statues of famous Mexicans; and five spacious glorietas, planted with miniature parterres, four sustaining imposing monuments. Twelve lanes of traffic keep up an everlasting weekday rush. Visitors from the smaller-scale cities of Europe may at first feel disoriented and even overwhelmed.

A track of a sort had traversed the plain between Chapultepec and the city since the 17C. In 1864 Maximilian ordered a proper road (Calz. del Emperador) built to connect his residence a good part of the way to the Pal. Nacional. It reached as far as the present junction of Avs Juárez and Bucareli. Carlota saw to the planting of double rows of eucalyptus along its entire length, which later appeared like a tunnel arched in greenery. In 1877 it was inaugurated as Paseo de la Reforma. In 1889–99 the bronze statues (two from each of the 17 States: eg, Guadalupe Victoria by Gabriel Guerra; Andrés Quintana Roo by Epitacio Calvo) were placed on either side of the stretch between the junction and where the Independence monument is now. Ostentatious porfirian residences have mostly disappeared, to make way, especially since the mid-20C, for striking modern architecture, daringly high for Mexico and benefiting from new techniques, which give a new kind of grandeur. (The 1985 earthquake necessitated some demolition; some buildings have been repaired.)

By the main entrance to Chapultepec on the r., surrounded by the pesero terminus, is one of the 18C fountains served by the Chapultepec aqueduct. In a small garden formed between Paseo de la Reforma, as it curves W to run through the park, and C. Ródano, is the fountain popularly called *Fuente de la Diana Cazadora* (1942); its bronze statue by Juan Olaguíbel graces the paseo's first glorieta. The nearby monument to Venustiano Carranza (1960) is by Ignacio Asúnsolo.

On the other side of Paseo de la Reforma, at the corner with C. Lieja, is the low, grey-stone **Secretaría de Salubridad y Asistencia** (1926–27; Health and Welfare) by Carlos Obregón Santacilia, who recurred to native materials and designs.

These include bronze panels on the walls surrounding the inner courtyard, geometric designs carved on parts of the stonework reminiscent of prehispanic relief, and indigenous faces sculpted on some of the outer wall surfaces. Santacilia also proposed the theme for the Diego Rivera murals (1929) in the Conference Room at the top of the first flight of stairs leading up from the l. of the entrance (Mon.–Fri., 3–5). On ceiling, two large female nudes: Life and Health. On wall below Life, large hands, and sunflowers, symbol of life, in different stages of the life cycle. Below Health, hands holding wheatsheaves. On walls between, female nudes: Purity, Continence, Fortitude, Science.

On the landings of the four staircases, Rivera designed stained-glass windows, his only essay in this genre, though in the style of his murals, representing the Four Elements and man's relationship to them.

Further along (r.) is the glass-fronted **Instituto Mexicano de Seguro Social** (1947–51), also by Obregón Santacilia. Sculpture by Jorge González Camarena graces the entrance.

He also painted the mural on the formation of Mexico (1950–51) in the entrance hall—an illusion of width in a limited space. On l., beneath geological strata, Spanish armour and mask of an eagle knight; on r., a huge eagle incorporating a building under construction—the colouring of mural and its surrounds a successful blend. On the ninth floor are murals by Federico Cantú.

Beyond the first glorieta and the *Cine Diana* (l.), at the corner with Río Nilo, is the *Embajada del Japón* (1975), in creamy concrete, by Pedro Ramírez Vázquez, Manuel Rosen Morrison, and Kenzo Tange. No. 364 is the *Cédulas Hipotecarias* (1955) by Augusto H. Alvarez and Octavio B. Sánchez. In three linked sections, its 18-storey office tower combines simplicity and elegance.

Beyond, on the second glorieta, rises the **Monumento a la Independencia**, designed by Antonio Rivas Mercado and inaugurated on 16 Sept. 1910 to celebrate the hundredth anniversary of Hidalgo's call to arms.

Manuel Gorozpe was working architect; the engineers Guillermo Beltrán y Puga and Gonzalo Garita superintended construction, driving down supporting piles to a great depth. The marble sculpture is by Enrique Alciati, who also supervised the casting of the bronze statuary in Florence. On each corner of the quadrangular base, seated female bronze figures represent War, Peace, Law, and Justice. Higher up, at the foot of the column, are marble statues of Miguel Hidalgo, José María Morelos, Vicente Guerrero, Francisco Javier Mina, and Nicolás Bravo. The column (interior spiral staircase) supports a mirador above which stands the triumphant bronze winged Victory (*El Angel*). Total height (from base) is 44m. The earthquake of 1957 toppled the Angel. It was reassembled and reinaugurated in Sept. 1958. In the base rest the remains of the heroes mentioned above, and those of Ignacio María Allende, José Mariano Jiménez, and other insurgents.

Flanking Paseo de la Reforma on the r., and bounded by C. Sevilla on the W and Avs Chapultepec and Insurgentes on S and E, is the crowded ZONA ROSA, part of Col. Juárez, whose streets contain expensive shops, hotels, restaurants, and nightclubs.

Enviably placed at the NE side of the glorieta, at No. 325, is the luxurious *Hotel María-Isabel Sheraton*, by Ricardo Legorreta with José Villagrán García, opened in 1961. A little further along, at No. 305, is the *Embajada de los EUA*, constructed by R. Max Brooks and Llewellyn Pitts of South Western Architects and Engineers (Austin, Texas), and completed in 1964.

The *Embajada Británica* is behind, at 71 Río Lerma, which runs parallel to Paseo de la Reforma as far as Parque Sullivan, in COL. CUAUHTEMOC. The streets in this area bear the names of famous rivers.

The colonia's development was in progress by 1908, financed by the Kansas City Company and called Stilwell Place. Although invaded by later, taller buildings, its domestic architecture offers interesting and distinctive 'new hispanic' and transitional styles, incl. 'tipo californiano' (curved window frames, wrought-iron, tiled gables), creating a cosy atmosphere in contrast to the vastness of the Paseo.

At 35 Río Lerma is the **Museo Venustiano Carranza y de la Revolución** (Wed.– Sun., 10–4). The house was designed by Manuel Estampa and built in 1908, and was the residence of Pres. Carranza from Nov. 1919. Here may be seen mementoes of his public and private life, and the living quarters of the Carranza family.

Beyond the Monumento a la Independencia the Paseo continues to the third glorieta, where stands, at the corner with Río Rhin, the *Centro Bursátil* (Stock Exchange), opened in 1990, a blade of light glass soaring from a dark glass sheath lying next to a glass rotunda, designed by Juan José Díaz Infante. On the fourth glorieta (junction with Av. Insurgentes) stands the **Monumento a Cuauhtémoc**, imposing from a distance, more so close up.

The initial project (1878–84), to re-create an indigenous style (regarded by some as ridiculous), was by Francisco M. Jiménez; it was finished (1884–87) by Ramón Agea. The N and S sides of the lower storey of the elaborate pedestal show two bas-reliefs: Gabriel Guerra, Torture of Cuauhtémoc and Miguel Noreña, Cuauhtémoc in the power of the Spaniards. The upper storey shows the arms of Coanacoch, Cuitláhuac, Cacama, and Tetlepanquetzal. Above is the noble figure of Cuauhtémoc, by Miguel Noreña. The bronze plumed jaguars on the lowest level are by Epitacio Calvo.

Round the S side of the glorieta, No. 156 is the *Banco Internacional*, its main hall containing a mural (1965) by Juan O'Gorman. At the corner with C. Lucerna the elegant *University Club* (1905–20) was designed by José Luis Cuevas as a mansion for the Gargollo family.

Av. Insurgentes Norte runs NE. Almost immediately l. is Parque Mariscal Santa Cruz, popularly known as PARQUE SULLIVAN. At its E end looms the semicircular *Monumento a la Madre* (1949), by José Villagrán García. The central and flanking figures, in chiluca stone, are by Luis Ortiz Monasterio. A Sun. art market is held here.

N of Parque Sullivan stretches COL. SAN RAFAEL, the earliest projected (as part of Col. de los Arquitectos), by the Spanish architect Francisco Somera in 1857. Actual building began from the 1880s, and it developed over 40 years as an upper-class area. There is still some turn-of-the-century domestic architecture (eg, in Cs Serapio Rendón and Sadi Carnot).

At the junction of Paseo de la Reforma with C. París (l.) is the *Hotel Reforma* (1934; restored after 1985) by Carlos Obregón Santacilia and Mario Pani. Opposite, at No. 120, the former *Café Colón* (1888–89; by Emilio Dondé), favourite meeting-place of porfirian elegance, was where Pres. Huerta, far from elegant and 'acutely alcoholic', transacted business 'from behind a cognac bottle'. No. 116 is the airtight *Seguros la Comercial* (1958), by Héctor Mestre and Manuel de la Colina, the glass in tinted dark smoke. The *Cine París* (1953) is by Juan Sordo Madaleno and Jaime Ortiz Monasterio.

In the centre of the fifth glorieta rises the **Monumento a Cristóbal Colón**, inaugurated in 1877.

Maximilian commissioned a design from Ramón Rodríguez Arangoity. The monument was instead designed by Eleuterio Méndez. The sculpture, shipped from Paris, is by Charles Cordier. 'It will satisfy neither artist nor beholder', wrote Rodríguez Arangoity, 'the model for our Pedro de Gante was a bust of Socrates, with a bigger beard'. Below Columbus are seated the heroic figures of Juan Pérez de la Marchena, prior of La Rábida, his friend and protector; Diego Dehesa, his supporter and confessor to King Ferdinand; Pedro de Gante; and Bartolomé de las Casas.

Beyond the glorieta C. Maestro Antonio Caso (l.) leads W. At No. 45 is the building of the **Sindicato de Electricistas** (Electricians' Trade Union; 1938) by Enrique Yáñez and Ricardo Rivas.

On the staircase just inside the entrance, between the first and second floors, is a mural, 'Retrato de la burguesía' (1939–40), on the theme of capitalism and its death, by David Alfaro Siqueiros, José Renau, Antonio Pujol, and Luis Arenal, using 'duco' paint material. On l. wall, the parrot-headed mannequin, moved mechanically, represents Mussolini and holds the torch which has set fire to the classical building behind, on which is written 'Liberty, Equality, Fraternity'. Below, troops manipulate the masses. In the centre panel, a huge machine, crowned by an imperialist eagle, transforms the workers' blood into the gold coins used by the imperialist system to generate the war shown on the r. of the monster. On r. wall, a worker bearing a red banner leads the revolution which will overthrow this system. On ceiling, the sun shines on industrialization, which will build the world of tomorrow.

Further along, at No. 127, is the *Anglo-Mexican Cultural Institute*, headquarters of the British Council.

Also from the glorieta, C. Ramírez leads N to PL. DE LA REPUBLICA and the **Monumento a la Revolución**, a strange landmark, making up in mass what it lacks in attractiveness.

The international competition of 1897 to find a design for Mexico's first legislative palace degenerated into scandal. Even though Adamo Boari had won first place, Emilio Dondé, with the connivance of the Minister of Public Works, appropriated a late entry from an Italian partnership called Quaglia, and started to build. Antonio Rivas Mercado, who had won third and fourth places with two designs, gave vent to bitter indignation, and forced the government to stop the work. In 1905 the French architect Emile Bénard submitted plans for a vast neoclassical structure, with a dome inspired by St Peter's and the Gesú in Rome, which were accepted. In 1932 demolition of the neglected and rusting skeleton was about to be put in hand when Carlos Obregón Santacilia proposed a conversion. Funds were raised by public subscription and the job was finished in 1938.

What remain are the central cupola and supports, covered in chiluca stone, rising to a height of 63m. At each corner of the arched base are sculptured groups by Oliviero Martínez representing Independence, the Reform Laws, Workers' Laws, Agrarian Laws. Within the monument rest the remains of four presidents: Francisco I. Madero, Venustiano Carranza, Plutarco Elías Calles, and Lázaro Cárdenas; and of Francisco Villa.

On the N side of the plaza is the *Frontón México* (1929), by Joaquín Capilla. It is the city's main centre for the traditional game of jai-alai and attracts international-class players. It seats 4000 spectators. (Matches daily except Fri.)

The main part of Paseo de la Reforma ends at the junction with Av. Juárez, running W and E, Av. Bucareli, running S, and C. Rosales, running N. Dominating the junction is the headquarters of the **Lotería Nacional**. The earlier building (1933–39), designed by Carlos Obregón Santacilia and José Villa, and built on floating foundations by José A. Cuevas, is on the W side. The later (1968), by David Muñoz Suárez and Ramón Torres Martínez, is a building of undoubted effect, its form a prism on a triangular base, with bronze-tinted glass facing trimmed with aluminium of the same colour.

13 Avenida Bucareli. Colonias Juárez, Roma, Hipódromo, and Condesa

The area S of Paseo de la Reforma, bounded on the E by Avs Bucareli and Cuauhtémoc (and sometimes incl. places a little E of this line), the Zona Rosa apart, is not one of the city's publicized attractions. However, it will not be without interest to those who would like to know more about the capital's growth in the early decades of the 20C. It still preserves examples of the period's domestic, official, and ecclesiastical architecture, reflecting first pre-Revolution eclectic tastes, and then the mixture of post-Revolution styles, out of which were refined the functional and the modern.

PASEO BUCARELI, first known as Paseo Nuevo, was the project of Viceroy Antonio de Bucareli and laid out in 1775 on what had been marshy ground from the garita de Belén to the S (the present junction with Av. Chapultepec) to where the Lotería Nacional now stands: a wide avenue bordered by ash, poplar, and willow, its three main glorietas later graced by monumental fountains. It became a sort of upper-class recreation ground, society repairing there in carriages and on horseback. In 1852 the statue of Charles IV (see Rte 8) was placed at its N limit, and bullrings were built at both ends. Its elegance and fame diminished. In 1882 the authorities began to sell adjoining lots to speculators. From the early 20C it has formed the E boundary of Col. Juárez. Today parts appear sadly run down, yet some of its imposing early 20C buildings have struggled to escape redevelopment.

The midway glorieta holds the *Reloj Chino*, a gift from the emperor of China for the Independence celebrations of 1910, and fired at during the Decena Trágica in Feb. 1913. On the glorieta's SE side is the tezontle-covered *Edificio Gaona* (No. 80; 1923) by Angel Torres Torija, a deliberate evocation of 18C styles, with mosaic effigies of Cortés and viceroys. At the corner with C. General Prim is the classically elegant *Pal. Cobián* (No. 99), built in 1903 by Rafael García Sánchez Facio for Feliciano Cobián, now the *Secretaría de Gobernación* (Department of the Interior). No. 39 C. General Prim is one of the few Art Nouveau survivals in the city. No. 128 Av. Bucareli, the *Edificio Vizcaya* (1922), by Roberto Servín, is French-inspired; and, further S, on the corner with C. Turín, is the *Departamentos La Mascota* (1912), a huge, classically sumptuous apartment block, the first in the city, by Miguel Angel de Quevedo.

Bordered on the E by Av. Bucareli and on the S by Av. Chapultepec, and stretching as far W as Av. Lieja, is COL. JUAREZ, first projected in 1875, officially inaugurated in 1898 (with building continuing during 1901–30), planned as the desirable residential area for the porfirian aristocracy, US and other foreign capitalists, politicians, and as a diplomatic quarter.

A guidebook of 1901 referred to a 'modern colonia which transports us on wings of thought to a suburb of Paris, or better, to a corner of Switzerland'. Architects were left with a free hand to indulge their fantasies: Louis Quinze and Louis Seize, with mansard roofs; Swiss chalets; medieval castles; Art Nouveau.

C. *Donato Guerra*: No. 13 by José Luis Cuevas (1907); Nos 17–23, four houses by Manuel Cortina García (1913); at the corner with C. Abraham González, the house of Emilio Dondé (1895). At the corner of Cs *Berlín* and *Londres*, a vast mansion by Lewis and Oscar Lamm (c 1905). At the corner of Cs *Roma* and *Londres*, the church of *Sagrado Corazón* by José Hilario Elguero (1903). C. *Dinamarca*: named after the Dane, F.P. Hoeck, who erected the first house in the district. The street contained the only plaza (Pl. Washington, now a glorieta) the colonia could boast. C. *Londres*: No. 6 by Antonio Rivas Mercado (1904), well preserved, now the *Museo de Cera de la Ciudad de México* (Mon.–Fri., 11–7; Sat., Sun., 10–7; fee), containing over 80 wax figures of historical and present-day personalities, Mexican and foreign; No. 64, in neo-Isabeline Gothic, by Miguel de la Torre (1926). C. *Havre*: Nos. 64–72, five houses with mansard roofs, by the de la Lama and Zwicker partnership (1906).

No. 116 C. Londres is the *Biblioteca Benjamin Franklin* (Mon.–Fri., 9–8; Sat., 9–2), opened in 1942 under US auspices (US Information Service), a reference and lending library (for members) with a reading room and facilities for concerts, lectures, etc.

In Av. Chapultepec, between Cs Varsova and Praga, is what remains (20 arches out of 904) of the aqueduct of *Belén* (1711–79), which brought water from the springs of Chapultepec to the Salto del Agua (see Rte 7). It was dismantled in 1895–97.

The continuation of Av. Bucareli, Av. Cuauhtémoc, leads S from the Cuauhtémoc metro station to *Coyoacán* (see Rte 15). It forms the E limit of COL. ROMA. On the l. (E) it skirts COL. DOCTORES, whose N boundary is Av. Dr Río de la Loza. S of the latter, between Cs Dr Carmona y Valle and Dr Lucio, is the *Arena México*. The colonia includes important buildings in the government of the Federal District: the *Tesorería* (1963–70; restored 1988; on C. Dr Lavista, between C. Dr Lucio and Av. Niños Héroes) by Enrique del Moral; the *Procuraduría de Justicia* (1988; corner of C. Dr Lavista and Av. Niños Héroes); and the *Pal. de Justicia* (1965; corner of Av. Niños Héroes and C. Dr Navarro) by Juan Sordo Madaleno and Adolfo Wiechers. To the r., C. Romita leads into the little Pl. Romita, where stands the simple church known as *Romita* (now the parish church of San Francisco Javier), built as a barrio chapel in the 16C, rebuilt in the 18C, but preserving part of the original wooden ceiling.

We may follow Av. Cuauhtémoc S. At No. 185 (r.), between Cs Zacatecas and Querétaro, is the church of *Nuestra Señora del Rosario* (1920–30) by Manuel and Angel Torres Torija. Further S, on the l., beyond Av. Dr Pasteur, is the *Hospital General*; beyond Av. Dr Márquez, the *Hospital Infantil*; and, beyond Av. Dr Norma, the **Centro Médico**, among the most tragic casualties of the earthquake of 1985.

The latter, inaugurated in 1963 under the auspices of IMSS, was built to the design of Enrique Yáñez to include various specialist hospitals, a residential unit, a research unit, and a large circular congressional centre (designed by José Villagrán García). Rebuilding is well advanced. In the entrance area (near the corner of Avs Cuauhtémoc and Central) is a mural (1988–89) by José Chávez Morado commemorating the earthquake. Works by other artists include: David Alfaro Siqueiros' mural on the fight against cancer for the Institute of Oncology; Francisco Zúñiga's metal sculptures in the Institutes of Pneumology and Oncology; José Chávez Morado's sculptured mural in the main lecture hall; Federico Cantú's high relief 'The Legend of Quetzalcóatl' for the Institute of Paediatrics; sculptures by Ernesto Tamariz and Luis Ortiz Monasterio for the Congressional Centre.

On the r. is *Parque América* and the *Unidad Habitacional Benito Juárez* (1950–52), a low-cost federal housing project, designed by Mario Pani and Salvador Ortega Flores. Beyond the junction with Avs Baja California and Central is (l.) the *Panteón Francés de la Piedad*, with a neo-Gothic chapel (1891–92) by E. Desormes, its central spire a remarkable, almost evanescent, exercise in lightness.

COL. ROMA reaches W almost as far as Chapultepec; its N limit is Av. Chapultepec. Its streets and avenues are named after Mexican cities and States. The company Colonia Roma, formed by the brothers Oscar and Lewis Lamm from the USA, developed the area after 1903. Initial Art Nouveau influence was provided by Catalan maestros de obras working in Mexico from the turn of the century. Examples of their style (sadly diminishing) can be found in Cs Mérida, Guanajuato, Chihuahua, Colima, and Córdoba. No. 46 C. Córdoba is strongly ornamented, with twisted columns and a notable parapet. No. 130 C. Orizaba is a neo-Isabeline Gothic fortress. A later transitional style is also visible: eg, at 78 C. Orizaba, 201 C. San Luis Potosí, 109 C. Querétaro. The church of *La Sagrada Familia* (1910–12), by Manuel Gorozpe, is inspired by French Romanesque. Just S of it is the colonia's centre, PL. RIO DE JANEIRO, whence C. Durango leads E across Av. Insurgentes Sur to PL. VILLA DE MADRID (Pl. Miravalle), graced by a copy of the Fuente de la Cibeles in Madrid.

To the W and SW Col. Roma merges into COLONIAS HIPODROMO and CONDESA, developed after 1908 by Porfirio Díaz jr and Ramón Alcázar. The Jockey Club racetrack, inaugurated in 1910 by the first Mexican Derby, was built here. Transitional, functional, and art deco styles of the 1920s and 1930s, and 'tipo californiano' dwellings of 1928–35, are still in evidence, eg, in Avs México, Michoacán, Campeche, and Nuevo León. The outline of the former hippodrome may be discovered in the curve of the streets S of Av. Alvaro Obregón, between Avs Insurgentes Sur and Nuevo León, centering on PARQUE GEN. SAN MARTIN. The former racetrack is now occupied by Av. Amsterdam. The zone was remodelled by José Luis Cuevas from 1925. The striking fountain in PL. POPOCATEPETL, N of the park, is by J. Gómez Echeverría (1930). At 70 Av. Acapulco (2nd floor; at the extreme W of Col. Roma, running S from Av. Chapultepec) is the *Museo Judío Tuve Maizel* (Mon.–Fri., 10.30–2; adm. by appointment), set up by the Asociación Kehila Ashkenazi (W European Jews) and showing by means of photographs, documents, etc, the history of European Jewry, its destruction during the second world war, and the establishment of Israel.

Beyond the Panteón we may continue further S beyond Viaducto Alemán, to turn r. at Calz. Casa del Obrero Mundial. Towards the sixth turning r., Av. Monterrey, is the church of **Nuestra Señora de la Piedad** (1944–57), a contrast between the monumental and (in its concrete tracery) the delicate.

It is on the site of a small Dominican convent and chapel dedicated in 1652. The architect of the new church was E. Langenscheidt. In the apse are neo-baroque murals by Pedro Medina (1965). Some 17C sculpture from the old church has been retained; the altarpieces were removed to Churubusco (see Rte 15).

From the continuation of Avs Cuauhtémoc and Zola, further S (Pl. Etiopia), Av. Zola leads E to (corner with Av. Lázaro Cárdenas) the vast complex finished in 1954 to the designs of Carlos Lazo, Augusto Pérez Palacios, and Raúl Cacho for the then *Secretaría de Comunicaciones y Obras Públicas* (now *Secretaría de Desarrollo Urbano y Ecología*). Among the excellent sculpture are bas-reliefs (La tierra y las comunicaciones) by Francisco Zúñiga flanking the E entrance and the statue by Rodrigo Arenas Betancourt on the main esplanade. The mosaics, didactic and political in nature, are by Juan O'Gorman (N wall) and José Chávez Morado (E and W walls).

At the S end of Av. Bucareli, C. Tolsá leads E to the Arcos de Belén. At the junction with Av. Balderas is the **Ciudadela**, a grim-looking and undistinguished building, yet with important, and poignant, historical associations.

Construction of the city's tobacco factory was started during the 1790s under Miguel Costansó, but was suspended in 1797. It was finished by Ignacio Castera in 1804–07. Resembling more a fortress than a factory, it was used from the outset as a gunpowder store. In 1815 José María Morelos was held prisoner here before his execution. In 1816 it was reformed as an arms and ammunition depot, foundry, and repair shop. On 1 Oct. 1871, though a clear majority had voted for Pres. Juárez's re-election for a fourth term, a group of porfiristas took over the Ciudadela and swelled their numbers by opening the Belem prison and recruiting the cream of the astonished inmates. During the Decena Trágica of Feb. 1913 it served as the base of Félix Díaz in his revolt against government forces in the Pal. Nacional. Many innocent citizens were killed in the crossfire. On 19 Feb., Gustavo Madero and Adolfo Bassó, brother and aide respectively of the doomed president, were murdered here: Bassó, gazing at the stars while facing the firing squad, exclaimed: 'There's the Great Bear'.

Today it houses a barracks; on its W side, the *Biblioteca de México*; on its E side, the *Escuela de Diseño y Artesanía* of the Escuela Nacional de Bellas Artes. In the plaza on its N side stands a statue of Morelos (1858) by Antonio Piatti.

N of the plaza is a handicrafts market. On the opposite side of Av. Balderas, C. Pugibet leads to PL. CARLOS PACHECO. At No. 21 (the Academia Mexicana de la Historia) is the façade of the 18C *Casa de los Condes de Rábago*, removed here in 1952 from Av. Venustiano Carranza. No. 94 Av. Balderas was built for the *Comisión Nacional de Irrigación* in 1901–10 by Carlos Herrera. Further up, Av. Balderas is crossed by C. Artículo 123, No. 134 in which is the

Episcopal *Iglesia de Cristo* (services in English) built in 1895–98 in neo-Gothic style, with an appropriate high altar and stained glass—but now unaccountably in decay. No. 47 Av. Balderas is the Methodist church of *El Mesías* (1900) by Russell P. Cook. Av. Balderas runs N to meet Av. Juárez and the Alameda.

14 Villa de Guadalupe

Mexico's most venerated shrine and famous pilgrimage centre, the Basilica of **Sta María de Guadalupe**, may be reached by taking the NE prolongation of Paseo de la Reforma, continued by Calz. de Guadalupe—a distance of c 6.5km from the Lotería Nacional buildings. From the centre the metro may be taken from *Juárez* or *Hidalgo* straight to *Basílica*, nearest station, c 5 minutes walk away. Buses show the sign 'Villa'.

On the first glorieta past the intersection with Av. Hidalgo is the *Monumento a Simón Bolívar*, with its bronze equestrian statue by Manuel Centurión (1944), a gift from Venezuela to Mexico. The second glorieta (junction with Av. Lázaro Cárdenas running N to Tlatelolco; see Rte 8) holds an equestrian statue of Gen. José San Martín (1973), a gift from Argentina. The *Monumento a Cuitláhuac* (bronze statue by Ignacio Asúnsolo; 1964) stands on the third glorieta at the SE corner of Nonoalco-Tlatelolco. At the fourth glorieta, Calz. de los Misterios (see below) branches off to the l. Calz. Guadalupe now runs straight to the Basilica.

The cult of Our Lady of Guadalupe originates in the series of apparitions she vouchsafed to the Indian Juan Diego on the hill of Tepeyac (now shortened to Tepeyac) in Dec. 1531. She bade him go to the bp of Mexico, Juan de Zumárraga, to convey her wish that a church should be built on the hill in her honour. The bishop, incredulous, eventually demanded proof. On his fourth return to Tepeyácac, the Virgin bade Juan Diego to gather flowers, miraculously grown on the barren rocks, in his cloak and take them to the bishop. When the flowers had fallen to the floor before Zumárraga, the cloak was found to be imprinted with the image of Our Lady, which he recognized as exactly like that of the Virgin of Guadalupe (prov. Cáceres, Extremadura).

The settlement around the first sanctuary (rebuilt twice in the 17C) was granted the status of villa in 1789 and renamed Guadalupe Hidalgo. On 2 Feb. 1848 the Treaty of Guadalupe Hidalgo was signed here to end the US-Mexican war.

In 1737 Our Lady of Guadalupe was proclaimed patron of Mexico after the dramatic cessation of the plague was attributed to her intercession. In 1754 Pope Benedict XIV, after some persuasion, approved, by papal bull, the fixing of 12 Dec. as her feast-day. In 1895 she was crowned queen of Mexico amid great ceremony, an occasion which provoked the resignation of the outspoken Eduardo Sánchez Camacho, bp of Tamaulipas: 'the Guadalupe cult constituted an abuse, to the detriment of a credulous people, for the most part ignorant'. In 1910 and 1945 proclamations of Pius X and Pius XII named her celestial patron of Latin America and empress of the Americas.

The focus of constant activity is the basilicas, and the various other buildings of the Guadalupe complex, centred on the large PL. DE LAS AMERICAS at the foot of the hill, always thronged by the devout and the curious; ubiquitous vendors of refreshments and souvenirs are unavoidable accompaniments. It is now difficult to imagine that within living memory Guadalupe-Hidalgo was in the middle of open country and a favourite Sun. stroll from the city.

On the W side is the **Basílica Nueva de Nuestra Señora de Guadalupe**, in the shape of a hyperbola, by Pedro Ramírez Vázquez, José Luis Benlluire, and Gabriel Chávez, finished in 1975. Access is through one of seven doorways in brass and enamel. The ceiling is covered by copper sheeting. In the upper storey are seven side chapels. Above the marble presbytery hangs the sacred image beneath which pilgrims pass on a travellator. The circular building to the N is the baptistery.

On its l. is the **Basílica Vieja** (1695–1709) by Pedro de Arrieta, with a grandly Mannerist façade. The interior was heavily gone over by Emilio Dondé and

Juan Agea from 1887. Further changes were made in 1930–38. In the W aisle is the tomb of Viceroy Bucareli (1717–79) and the huge mural by José Salomé Pina of Benedict XIV greeted by Fr Francisco López, emissary from Mexico, with a copy of the Guadalupe image (1889).

At the back of the old basilica, on the W side, is the entrance to the **Museo de la Basílica de Guadalupe** (Mon.–Wed., Fri.–Sat., 10–7; fee), a valuable collection of mainly Mexican religious art.

Turn l. at foot of stairs. Juan Correa, Assumption and Coronation of Our Lady (1703). Juan Antonio Arriaga, St John Nepomuk (c 1745). Antonio Ordóñes, St Francis surrounded by angels (1787). Anon. 18C, Passion scene with the Virgin, an excellent work; Virgin and Child with two saints. UPSTAIRS. Nicolás Rodríguez Juárez, Transfixing of St Teresa (1692). ROOM 1. Nicolás Rodríguez Juárez, Our Lady of Mercy (1722). Cristóbal de Villalpando, Martyrdom of St Barbara; Baptism of Our Lady by St John the Baptist, SS Anne and Joachim in the background—a strangely conceived work; Allegory of the Holy Name of Mary, a matronly Virgin surrounded by celebrating angels, the three on r. especially fine. Baltasar de Echave Ibía, St Francis of Paula (1625). Sebastián de Arteaga, Stigmatization of St Francis of Assisi (1650), a luminous work, showing a beautiful landscape. 18C Guatemalan wooden polychrome (with estofado) nativity statues. 18C Mexican polychrome St Anne. R. 2. Devoted to St Michael. Luis Berrueco, St Michael. Juan Hernández de la Mota, Annunciation (1727). Three anon. 18C paintings, one from Puebla, of the archangel. Anon. 17C, Our Lady Queen of Angels, a charming painting—note Jacob's ladder with Jacob sleeping below. 17C statue, wonderfully colourful, of St Michael from Quito. 17C St Michael from the Philippines, polychrome ivory on a polychrome wooden base, another piece of great charm. R. 3. Devoted to Our Lady of Guadalupe. Anon. 18C, Juan Diego before the Virgin. 18C retable with medallions painted by Miguel Cabrera. Two beautiful 18C polychrome and estofado statues of Our Lady of Guadalupe.

From R. 1 we go upstairs to R. 4. Juan Correa, Allegory of the Precious Blood of Christ. José Rodríguez Carnero, Forebodings of the Virgin—a harmonious work by a praiseworthy early 18C artist. Cabrera, St John Nepomuk; St Aloysius Gonzaga. Juan Cordero, Christ and the woman taken in adultery (1853), painted in Rome, exhibited with great success in Dec. 1854 after his return to Mexico. Manuel de Arellano (fl. 1692–1721), Coronation of Our Lady. 17–18C sculpture. R. 5. An excellent display of portraits, incl. Cabrera, Padre Juan González; Abp Manuel Rubio y Salinas (1758); Abp Juan de Zumárraga. José de Alzíbar, Juan de Alarcón y Ocaña (1690–1757), abbot of Guadalupe. Anon. portraits of Abp Francisco Antonio Lorenzana and Francisco Vélez de Escalante (c 1730–1806), abbot of Guadalupe. On STAIR-CASE. Anon. 17C, Patronage of St Teresa. Juan de Villalobos (fl. 1687–1724), Allegory of the Immaculate Conception. FRONT HALL. 18C Guatemalan Virgin and Child (polychrome, estofado), encrusted with precious stones. 16C Spanish dalmatic, worked in gold. Stairs lead down to further exhibits, incl. furniture of the 18C basilica: carved wooden door of the Cap. del Sagrario; carved wooden choirstalls; altar of embossed silver; 13 scenes from the life of Our Lady (17C Flemish [?] oil on copper plate). The adjoining room contains gifts from Mexico and abroad: church furniture, Flemish tapestries; among the sculptures, a 15C (French?) ivory St Peter and a 17C Italian St Michael in ivory, bronze, and wood.

On the E side of the old basilica is the church and former convent of *Nuestra Señora de Guadalupe*, built in 1782–87 for Capuchinesses and closed in 1856. Since 1956 the church has served as centre of the local parish. Again to the E is the so-called *Parroquia de los Indios*, the 17C rebuilding of the original shrine, now semi-ruined, but preserving some remains of the original 16C structure.

At the E end of Pl. de las Américas is the **Cap. del Pocito** (1777–91), a building of extraordinary beauty, by Francisco Guerrero y Torres.

A miraculous spring of water (el Pocito), long sought for its curative powers, gushed forth on the spot where Our Lady stood when bidding Juan Diego gather flowers, but it has since dried up. Its position was beneath the entrance cupola of the chapel, for whose construction the craftsmen of Mexico City, and the architect himself, gave their services free: money for the materials was supplied by special collections among the faithful of the archdiocese. The inspiration seems to have been the treatise by the 16C Venetian theorist Sebastiano Serlio, but liberally interpreted.

A quintessence of Mexican baroque, the EXTERIOR walls display exuberant stone carving on a tezontle background. The main portal, in two storeys, is spanned by a highly individual mixtilinear arch, matched in its capriciousness by the star-shaped window, with its inner undulations in the upper storey.

Above the wall rises the curvetting parapet topped by pinnacles and covered by blue and white azulejos. Above them rise the three cupolas, again covered by azulejos, which cover the oval central, the circular front, and the octagonal rear areas. The fantasy of the detail, the frequent window punctuations in walls, parapet, and lanterns, the slender statues in niches, the little statue of Our Lady of Guadalupe before the main window—all contribute to the effect of lightness and perfect proportion.

The INTERIOR suffered inappropriate restoration in 1880–82. The paintings are by Miguel Cabrera.

Behind the old basilica on the summit of the hill is the 18C Cap. del Tepeyac (frequently restored), built on the spot where Our Lady first appeared, decorated with frescoes of the Guadalupe apparitions by Fernando Leal (1945–50). In the adjoining cemetery rest Gen. Antonio López de Santa-Anna and his second wife, doña Dolores Tosta. On the E side of the hill is the *Vela del marino*, an 18C votive offering placed there by sailors who survived a storm at sea through the intercession of Our Lady of Guadalupe. The remains of their ship have been covered by masonry.

We may return to the city centre by the CALZ. DE LOS MISTERIOS, successor to the track first traced in the 16C to link the city with the shrine, properly built in 1673–76 and lined with 15 votive monuments (1675–76) representing the decades of the Rosary; eight, not in good repair, remain: the five joyful mysteries; two sorrowful; and one glorious.

15 Mexico City: the Southern Areas

The explosive 20C growth of Mexico City has swallowed up what was once country dotted with small towns and haciendas. The urban area now reaches as far S as Xochimilco and Tlalpan, and SW into the delegaciones of Alvaro Obregón and Magdalena Contreras. Through it cuts Av. Insurgentes Sur, S stretch of Mexico's longest avenue and main axis. Complementing it to the W is the Anillo Periférico, running S from the NW suburbs and Chapultepec to Tlalpan (and being extended E). Across it runs part of the network of ejes viales, one-way and two-way three- to four-lane highways (also being extended), which, while perhaps easing traffic flow, add to the frenetic pace of city life.

This route is based on Av. Insurgentes Sur, which runs SSW from the Cuauhtémoc monument on Paseo de la Reforma. Places of interest on it, and on either side of it, will be described, as well as detours. Buses may be caught on Av. Juárez or on Paseo de la Reforma, and ply along Av. Insurgentes. The inexperienced visitor, however, may be better advised to take a taxi or enlist a friendly driver. The metro also serves points (on the *Balderas-Universidad* line; on *Zócalo-Tasqueña*; on *Polanco-Barranco del Muerto*).

Av. Insurgentes Sur goes through Col. Juárez, skirting (l.) the Zona Rosa. It meets (0.5km) Av. Chapultepec, with the arches of the Belén aqueduct (see Rte 13) 200m on the r. Occupying the centre of the glorieta is the *Insurgentes* metro station. Beyond (l.) is Col. Roma and (r.) Colonias Hipódromo and Condesa. At 3.25km we cross Viaducto Alemán, just after (l.) the building of the *Secretaría del Patrimonio y Fomento Industrial* (Ministry of National Heritage and Industrial Development). The viaducto leads W towards *Tacubaya*, see Rte 16. Beyond (4.25km; l.), at the corner with Av. Luz Saviñón, is the *Secretaría de Agricultura y Recursos Hidráulicos*, opposite the *Parque de la Lama*, where rises the vast *Hotel de México* (51 floors), begun in 1971, with a revolving restaurant at the top.

At the corner with Av. Filadelfia and in the hotel grounds is the **Polyforum Cultural Siqueiros** (daily, 10–9; fee), an immediately striking 12-sided building in celebration of the muralist David Alfaro Siqueiros. It was begun in 1964 at the expense of Manuel Suárez, owner of the hotel, to the designs of a team of architects under Guillermo Rossell.

It combines various parts dedicated to cultural activities. The *Foro de la Juventud*, with a circular stage in the manner of a Greek theatre, for plays, concerts, and conferences; the *Foro de las Artesanías*, for exhibitions of Mexican handicrafts; the *Foro Nacional*, for temporary exhibitions of modern art; and the *Foro Universal*.

The latter contains Siqueiros's monumental mural (2400 sq m) 'La marcha de la humanidad en la tierra y hacia el cosmos', a work of prodigious power, a combination of painting (pyroxylin-based paints) and relief sculpture painting, in which he was helped by over 50 painters and sculptors in his workshop at Cuernavaca. Son et lumière points up the convulsive and violently coloured work while the spectator stands on a moving platform which runs the tour of it all. The exterior faces are covered with murals by the master. On the side facing Av. Insurgentes, Siqueiros left a mural in which he represents himself, Diego Rivera, Orozco, Dr Atl, and the engravers José Guadalupe Posada and Leopoldo Méndez.

5.5km Pl. Baja California, a spacious glorieta. On the r. are the *Ciudad de los Deportes* (Sports City) and *Plaza México*, inaugurated in 1946, the world's largest bullring—maximum capacity 60,000 spectators (bullfights every Sun. at 4, Oct.–March).

Just over 1km W of Plaza México, where Av. San Antonio meets the Anillo Periférico, in C. Pirámide, are several Toltec platform structures. They have been interpreted as the palace of king Mixcóatl (or Mixcóhuatl; or Mixcoac), the 10C Toltec leader who founded the Toltec dynasty and the ceremonial centre at Culhuacán (cf. *Culhuacán* and *Tula*).

6.75km *Parque Luis G. Urbina* (*Parque Arqueológico*), 11 hectares in area, scattered around which are 51 reproductions of prehispanic sculpture, which may be viewed to the accompaniment of broadcast classical music.

Opposite the NE corner of the park Calz. Porfirio Díaz continues across Av. Insurgentes to meet Av. Matías Romero. C 2km E, across Av. Coyoacán, we come to the glorieta Rivera. Just beyond, at the corner with C. Ixcateopan (Col. Narvarte), is the church of the **Medalla Milagrosa**, a typically daring work by Félix Candela, built in 1954–55 in a style which has been called 'triangular Gothic'. The structure is a combination of warped surfaces, all of them (save for the small side chapel) paraboloids with a thickness of 4cm or less. The columns of the nave are warped like the shells they support. The slender campanile, an inspired creation, is made from warped planes.

From the glorieta Av. Cuauhtémoc runs S for c 1km to meet Av. Municipio Libre and a church 400 years older, **Sta Cruz Atoyac** (1564), once a visita of Coyoacán. The base reliefs of the atrial cross are symbols of the Five Wounds and skull and crossbones. Chief beauty is the doorway, with its tall alfíz, the frame punctuated by fleur-de-lis relief, and imposts and jamb bases carrying thick floral decoration. Apple decoration, showing Isabeline Gothic influence, stamps the cornice, aligned with the top of the alfíz frame. Only the triumphal arch remains of the original interior structure.

From here Av. Municipio Libre leads W across Av. Universidad into Av. Félix Cuevas (Eje 7 Sur) back to (2km) Av. Insurgentes. At this junction is a large branch of the *Puerto de Liverpool* department store, opened in 1962 (the business itself dates from 1847), which competes with *París-Londres* at 1235 Av. Insurgentes Sur a little way up on the opposite side.

Opposite the park, on the other side of Av. Insurgentes Sur, at the corner of Cs Manzanes and Magnolias, the 16C church of *San Lorenzo Mártir* has been partly rebuilt.

Parque Luis G. Urbina occupies part of the former village of MIXCOAC, its name perpetuated by three colonias (Mixcoac, Torres de Mixcoac, Insurgentes Mixcoac) to the W and SW, offering in the 18–19C a desirable villa campestre residence away from the city, and noted for its gardens, which supplied the city with cut flowers.

On 11 Sept. 1847 four survivors of the batallón de San Patricio, who had been captured after the battle of Churubusco (see below), were hanged in the little plaza by their US captors. On 13 Sept., 30 more suffered the same fate: these unfortunates were made to stand for several hours on a high scaffold, nooses round their necks, and to watch to the NW the storming of Chapultepec—with the promise that when the Stars and Stripes were unfurled over the castle, they would hang. In 1910, to initiate the centenary of Independence celebrations, Pres. Díaz opened the lunatic asylum of La Castañeda here, to take the place of the hospital of Divino Salvador (see Rte 8).

Along the S side of the park, Av. Millet runs to the charming old PL. SAN JUAN (now Pl. Gómez Farías). On its E side is the 17C church of *San Juan* (also named Santuario de Guadalupe), with attractive portal relief. To his house on the plaza, in July 1858, was brought the body of Valentín Gómez Farías, pioneer of Mexican liberalism. Further S, in Pl. Jáuregui (Eje 7 Sur and Av. Rodin) is the simple little church of *Sto Domingo*, part of a Dominican foundation of c 1562–78. E of Pl. San Juan, across Av. Revolución, in the colonia of Sta María Nonoalco, is the 16C barrio chapel of *Asunción Nonoalco*, with a lovely rustic three-arched entry, intricately carved, to its atrio.

At 8km Av. Insurgentes Sur reaches a busy glorieta, crossed by Av. Río Mixcoac, which runs SW to Coyoacán (see below) and Churubusco (see below). 8.5km (at No. 1587) the **Teatro Insurgentes**, by Alejandro Prieto, one of Mexico's most popular and best-equipped theatres.

It was inaugurated on 30 Apr. 1953, with a performance of the musical comedy '¡Yo Colón!', starring Mario Moreno (Cantinflas). The interior includes a revolving stage and over 1100 seats; it is also well known for its lighting effects.

The façade is covered by a Diego Rivera mural, overlaid with Italian mosaic. In the middle, two hands hold up a mask, in the centre of which the sun eclipses the moon, representing the theatre's possible quick change from reality to fantasy. Scenes from Mexican history appear as comedy and tragedy (eg, on l., Maximilian and Carlota performing a farce). In the centre, Cantinflas himself takes from the rich and gives to the poor.

At 10.25km Av. Insurgentes reaches Pl. 17 de Julio in the delegación of Villa Alvaro Obregón. Across Av. La Paz is the **Monumento a Alvaro Obregón** (1934), designed by Enrique Aragón Echegaray, the heaviness of the cube structure subtly relieved by the superimposition of the stone slabs. The sculpture is by Ignacio Asúnsolo. It and its artificial lake stand on the site of the *La Bombilla* restaurant where on 17 July 1928, during a banquet to celebrate his election to the presidency, Gen. Alvaro Obregón was assassinated by a religious fanatic, José de León Toral.

Av. La Paz leads SW to Av. Universidad and **SAN ANGEL**, once a village offering a delightful retreat from city life, now partly engulfed by its spread, although still keeping its historic and picturesque centre and winding streets of 17–18C houses—redolent of a bygone age.

Its popularity dates from c 1650, when several country houses already existed; and the regular July celebrations of its patron, Our Lady of Mount Carmel, drew many enthusiasts; but it came into its own in the 18C when the predilection of viceroys Abp Núñez de Haro y Peralta and the 1st conde de Revillagigedo established it as a fashionable resort. In 1752, Francisco de Chávarri, a rich householder, invited Revillagigedo, his family, and suite to luncheon in his orchard. 'He lavishly decorated his house', wrote a chronicler, 'and ordered two lovely arbours covered with branches and flowers set up in the orchard'. At the entrance of the viceregal retinue 'sounded a great blast of music, the musicians hidden in various caves'. After luncheon, which was of the finest, 'they lost two trays, eleven plates, and many silver spoons because the vulgar throng milled about'. That evening the guests returned to the city, their carriages accompanied by servants on horseback carrying lanterns to light the way. Part of San Angel's 19C charm was the easy informality among aristocratic visitors and villagers; though its peace was shattered by the shocks of US occupation. San Angel remained apart from the capital until as late as the 1950s.

On the E side of Av. Revolución, in PL. DEL CARMEN, is the church and former convent of **San Angelo Mártir**, its tiled cupolas visible from afar.

The discalced Carmelite foundation of San Angel was built in 1615–26, to the designs of Fray Andrés de San Miguel. The orchards brought the friars special fame. In 1697 Gian Francesco Gemelli Carreri related that 40 kinds of pear and a variety of apples, peaches, and quince made them an annual profit of 13,000 pesos. After suppression during the Reform much of the land was sold off.

The church's EXTERIOR (restored) offers a contrast between the façade, of the plainest, in the Carmelite Renaissance style advocated by Fray Andrés ('our churches should not be magnificent') and the grand cupolas, 18C additions, only one of which was completely finished. The niche holds a statue of St Anne with the infant Mary; the curving finial is a later, baroque, addition.

INTERIOR (also restored). The barrel-vaulted nave, relieved by lunettes, keeps its original 17C decoration. Remarkable are the profusion of azulejo-work on the side altars and the tile dado. The high altar is a ponderous modern echo of the churrigueresque; on either side of it are chapels containing beautiful 17C reliquary tables, designed by Fray Andrés. Above the chapel entrances are two anon. 18C paintings: St Simon Stock (l.) and St Peter Thomas (r.).

The N transept chapel of El Señor de Contreras, entered through an 18C baroque portal with a notably sturdy arch, is the work of Fray Francisco de Sta María. It was restored by 1942 after falling victim to arson in 1935. Four small paintings (from a 17C altarpiece) by Luis Juárez are placed in pairs on the small altars at the sides: Our Lady of Mount Carmel with Souls in Purgatory; Our Lady and St Joseph appear to St Teresa; Our Lady appearing to St Peter Thomas; Virgin and Child with St John of the Cross—all lamentably retouched. On l., Luis Berrueco, Our Lady of Mount Carmel protecting friars and nuns of her Order (1749). On S wall of nave, above door to sacristy, Antonio Sánchez, Triumph of the Trinity (1772).

The convent buildings are now the **Museo Colonial del Carmen** (Tues.–Sun., 9–6; fee). From S of the crossing we reach the sacristy, divided into two parts. In the first, fine gilded and polychrome panelled ceiling. Among the paintings, Juan Correa, St Teresa as pilgrim, charmingly serene. In the second, again a fine gilded ceiling. Above the elaborate marquetry chest, five paintings by Cristóbal de Villalpando, in sombre mood: in the centre, Christ scourged; on extreme l., Christ mocked; on extreme r., Agony in the Garden, with a wonderfully luminous angel and lushly sombre background; the remaining two canvases show SS Teresa and John of the Cross doing penance by self-flagellation. In the antesacristy is a hand-basin in azulejos from Puebla. Note the ribbing of the vault, also in azulejos. The tiled crypt contains the mummified remains of friars. An 18C tiled fountain surrounded by agapanthus graces the charming lower cloister; off the upper are 55 friars' cells and the Cap. Doméstica, with a late 17C altarpiece.

Further N along Av. Revolución, by its junction with Av. Desierto de los Leones, No. 1608 is the **Museo Alvar y Carmen T. de Carrillo Gil** (Tues.–Sun., 11–3; 5–7; fee), a choice collection of modern art.

The four-storey house, amplified by the architect Luis Barrios, was formerly the residence, studio, library, and clinic of Dr Alvar Carrillo Gil, whose art collection was bought by the Mexican government in 1972 and put on permanent display in 1974. The upper three floors are reserved for temporary exhibitions. The permanent collection, spaciously laid out to maximum advantage, is on the ground floor.

Outstanding early Cubist paintings by Diego Rivera are 'Mujer en verde', 'El pintor en reposo', 'Maternidad', 'Mujer sentada en una butaca' (Woman seated in an armchair), 'Volonchine' (1916–17; oils). Of the early works (1913) by José Clemente Orozco, 'Tres mujeres' (oil) and 'Baile de Pepenclies' (watercolour) are particularly enchanting. Also by him: 'Una mujer' (c 1910–13), a winsome drawing; 'El abrazo' (c 1912–13; crayon); 'La conferencia', 'El despojo', 'Muchacha' (c 1913; watercolours). Later works: 'Combate' (1920; oil); 'Pancho Villa' (1931; oil); 'Resurrección de Lázaro' (1942; oil); Portrait of Dolores del Río (1942; oil); 'Cristo destruye su Cruz' (1943; oil); 'Prometeo' (1944; oil); 'Tres mujeres' (1946; watercolour); 'Pedregal' (1947; oil).

The extensive collection of works by David Alfaro Siqueiros includes his portrait of Carmen T. de Carrillo Gil (1946; pyroxylin and masonite), marvellously emphatic. Also 'Torso femenino' (1945; pyroxylin and masonite); 'Calabazas' (Pumpkins; 1946; pyroxylin); 'Formas policromadas' (1947; pyroxylin and masonite); 'Desnudo la guitarra' (1948; pyroxylin and masonite); 'Chichén-Itzá flameante' (1948; pyroxylin and masonite), enigmatic; 'Casa mutilada' (1950; pyroxylin); 'Cuauhtémoc redivivo' (1950; oil); 'Aeronave atómica' (1956; pyroxylin and masonite); studies for the murals at Chapultepec (1956–66).

Two other artists figuring in the gallery are Gunther Gerzso (1915–), with his geometric works influenced by surrealism, and Wolfgang Paalen (1905–60), whose oeuvre is also based in surrealism, but who also shows a neo-impressionist influence. Also among the permanent exhibits are original and facsimile drawings by Rodin, Picasso, Rouault, Kandinsky, and Paul Klee.

An exploration of the old quarter between the Anillo Periférico and Av. Insurgentes Sur, incl. the modern colonias of Tlacopac, San Angel Inn, and Altavista, but comprising historic San Angel, may begin along Av. Revolución N of the gallery.

C. Tlacopac leads W from Av. Revolución into C. Madero. At the corner with C. Corregidora is the former barrio chapel of *Tlacopac* (today the church of *La Purísima Concepción*), a simple 17C Carmelite structure, in whose atrio were buried Mexican dead in the battle of Padierna and 20 soldiers executed at San Angel (see below).

C. Corregidora leads S to C. Altavista and the former hacienda of *Goycoechea*. In the 19C it was a favourite retreat of Fanny and Angel Calderón de la Barca and of Santa-Anna. José Zorrilla, who also stayed here, wrote of its patio 'shaded by a dozen eternally green orange trees ... the cedar beams with which the porches had been covered perfumed that patio'. At the turn of the century it was converted into the **San Angel Inn** (50 C. Palmas), now a famous luxury restaurant.

C. Arturo runs S to meet C. Lazcano, No. 18 in which is the 18C *Casa de los Delfines*, which continues SE to the junction of Cs Reina, Galeana, and Gral. Rivera. S of the junction is the evocative PL. DE LOS LICENCIADOS. Here the house numbered 3 displays an 18C portal, with almohadilla work, saved from the (demolished) Colegio de San Juan de Letrán by Luis Montes de Oca, Secretary of Finance (1927–32), one-time owner. Here also lived Rafael Martínez de la Torre, defender of Maximilian. The house numbered 1 is the *Casa de la Marquesa de Selva Nevada*, bought in 1814 by the 2nd marquesa, María Josefa Rodríguez de Pinillos. No. 1 C. Hidalgo, leading off the plaza, is the 18C *Casa de Posadas*. No. 43 is the 17C *Casa Blanca* (or *Casa de los Condes de Oploca*; perhaps the oldest in San Angel), showing the arms of its noble owners above the doorway.

On the other side of Pl. de los Licenciados, at 1 C. Juárez, at the corner with C. Gral. Rivera, is the *Casa del Obispo Madrid*, whose original deeds go back to 1699.

Among its tenants was Joaquín Fernández de Madrid (1801–61), titular bp of Tanagra, archdeacon of the Cathedral, and antiquary.

In PL. SAN JACINTO, a little S, is the former convent church of **San Jacinto**, founded in 1599, built c 1600–10, much restored.

The convent served as a place of rest for Dominican friars destined for missionary work in the Philippines. In Oct. 1625 Thomas Gage arrived, and stayed five months. He was amazed at the abundance of sweetmeats and conserves, quince and other fruits, provided 'to stay our stomachs in the mornings'.

The church façade is rustic in appearance. The interior contains an Our Lady of Guadalupe by Juan Correa. The convent buildings survive next door, the portería closed up.

No. 11 in the plaza is the 19C *Casa Orvañanos*. No. 15 is the **Casa del Risco** (*Casa del Mirador*; 1681). Its name derives from the famous fountain (1739), in the principal patio, put together from pieces of Talavera poblana and Chinese and Japanese porcelain. ('Risco' was the name applied to a Talavera composition.)

In Aug. 1847 householders watched, from the mirador, the battle of Padierna to the S and the advance of the US troops towards San Angel. In 1937 Isidro Fabela (1882–1964), statesman, international lawyer, and diplomat, bought it, and made a museum to contain his art collection.

The **Museo del Risco** (Tues.–Sun., 10–2) contains European and Mexican paintings, furniture, and antiques. GROUND FLOOR. 17–18C furniture, incl. ebony bargueño, with gilded inlay. Paintings include three Catalan primitives (Crucifixion, St Antony Abbot, St John the

Baptist). Among 17–19C portraits are works by Jan van Ravesteyn, Pierre Mignard, and Alessandro Longhi. FIRST FLOOR. 17C English, Flemish, and Dutch furniture. Paintings by David Teniers the Younger (Temptation of St Antony) and François Clouet (Henri II); and by 19–20C Mexican and European artists.

A plaque on the wall commemorates 71 members of the batallón de San Patricio (officially Legión de Extranjeros), 17 of whom were hanged in Pl. del Carmen on 10 Sept. 1847. Mexican prisoners were flogged and hanged from the plaza's trees; the furious locals tore the trees down.

Opening off the plaza is BAZAR SABADO (Sat., 10–7), a crowded arts and crafts market. At 15 C. Amargura, continuation of C. Juárez, is the *Casa del Mayorazgo de Fagoaga* (18C), handsomely restored.

On the W side of Pl. del Carmen is the *Casa del Mariscal de Castilla* (or Casa del Encaje; partly 17C). Above the windows are reliefs of the Seven Sorrows and of the Passion, and, below the cornice, further, lace-like, relief.

On the E side of the Obregón monument, off C. Federico Gamboa, is the beautiful little plaza of *San Sebastián Chimalistac* (17C), a former Dominican barrio chapel; it contains an anastyle altarpiece, saved from La Piedad (see Rte 13). To the N, the continuation of Av. La Paz, Av. Arenal, leads E to cross Av. Universidad. From the crossing, its projection, Av. Francisco Sosa, leads into the delegación of **COYOACAN**, today a desirable, mainly residential, suburb, but still keeping many reminders of its historic past.

It was a Tepanec city in the S Basin, on the shores of the Lago de Texcoco, probably tributary to Azcapotzalco, and later captured by the Aztecs under Itzcóatl (1426–40). It was the beginning of part of the strategic S causeway to Tenochtitlán, converging with the Ixtapalapa causeway c 2km from the shore and thence c 6.5km to Tenochtitlán. Cortés and his captains settled here while Tenochtitlán was being razed and established the city's first ayuntamiento. Here he brought as prisoners Cuauhtémoc and the lords of Tlacopan and Texcoco, and tortured them in his efforts to make them reveal the whereabouts of the treasure of Moctezuma. Here he is reputed to have strangled his first wife, Catalina Juárez Marcaida. In his will he directed that his remains and those of his family should be buried in 'his villa of Coyohuacan' and that a convent should be built wherein nuns could assist at continuous Masses for their souls—a clause left unfulfilled. During the viceroyalty Coyoacán was a peaceful place, noted for its haciendas, gardens, and streams of pure water. In the 19C it lost ground to San Angel and Tlalpan as an upper-class retreat. The 20C, however, has seen an increase in popularity. It has become the home of famous Mexicans and foreigners alike.

At the W end of C. Francisco Sosa, to the l., is the 18C chapel of *San Antonio de Panzacola*, circular and simple, but not without grace, next to a contemporary bridge. In the sacristy is a painting, attr. Vallejo, of St John Nepomuk hearing the confession of Queen Joan of Bohemia, with a striking donor's likeness. On the r. of the road is the former 17C hacienda of **Altillo**, once home of the Piña family, bequeathed in 1950 to the missionaries of the Holy Ghost and the Sisters of Charity. The central building is now a seminary.

It owes its present fame to two interesting examples of modern ecclesiastical architecture. The missionaries' chapel, *Nuestra Señora de la Caridad* (1955), designed by Enrique de la Mora and Fernando López Carmona, and built by Félix Candela, is a rhomboid, with a double-curved roof. The shell is of rough concrete, outer walls of grey quarry stone, and floor of black lava. The stained glass, by Kitzia Hoffmann, shuts out an exterior view, but bathes the interior in multicoloured, mysterious light. The same team is responsible for the *Cap. de San Vicente de Paul* (1959–60) of the Sisters of Charity, the roof shape, of three straight ferro-concrete shells, evoking their once famous head-dress.

Further along, the house at the E corner with C. Salvador Novo was home of King Carol of Romania and Mme Lupescu in 1942–43. No. 88 C. Salvador Novo is the *Museo de la Acuarela Mexicana* (Tues.–Sun., 11–6), devoted to watercolours. At the corner with C. Tlapancalco is the misnamed *Casa de Alvarado* (18C), once home of the US archaeologist Zelia Nuttall (1857–1933). Next door is the smaller *Casa de Alvaradito* (18C).

To the N are the tree nurseries *Viveros de Coyoacán*, once property of the engineer, architect, and forestry expert Miguel Angel de Quevedo (1862–1946). His house and garden (*Arboretum*) lie between C. Sosa and Av. Miguel Angel de Quevedo to the S.

No. 78 (r.) is the 18C *Casa de los Espinosa de los Monteros*. Next opens out Pl. Sta Catarina, with an 18C church. C. Francisco Sosa ends at Jardín Centenario. At the corner with C. Centenario is the so-called *Casa de Diego de Ordaz*, with a corner niche, a spacious 18C residence, unconnected with the conquistador of that name.

The extensive JARDIN CENTENARIO, crossed by C. Carrillo Puerto, once formed part of the huge atrio of the Dominican convent of **San Juan Bautista**, facing us on the E side of the plaza. Standing free on the W side is the late 16C main gateway of the atrio, its jambs carved with angel atlantes and marvellously assured, and succulent, vegetal relief.

The present church, an ambitious three-nave basilica, was begun by Fray Ambrosio de Sta María after 1560, but the vaults collapsed when the centerings were removed. The convent, by Fray Juan de la Cruz, suffered earthquake damage while under construction in 1588. Completion of the church was in the 17C. Both were rebuilt c 1798–1804 under secular clergy. In 1921 Franciscans took charge.

The façade owes more to 1804 than to 1582—the building dates carved in the alfíz rim. The INTERIOR, once a rare example of 16C basilical planning, was unspeakably converted in the 1930s into a single-nave church, full of tasteless ornament. The Cap. del Rosario, with its exquisite late 17C retable (variations on the solomonic), adorned with anon. paintings on the Rosary theme, has survived.

On the N side of the church, the gateway to a small cemetery was originally the N entrance to the atrio, reset here c 1880 and thus saved from destruction. It is a superb example of local 16C carving, with vigorously succulent fruit and vegetal motifs. S of the church is the cloister, with its huge eight-arched portería and rectangular windows above, the particular objects of careful restoration during the 1970s, when the spacious open chapel, entered through the third and fourth arches from the l., was freed from comparatively recent encumbrances. The lower cloister walk, with strong Tuscan columns and artesonado ceilings at the corners, keeps an air of antiquity; the upper is a drastic recent rebuilding. In the passage connecting sacristy and cloister are another 16C archway, the imposts carved with roses, and a contemporary holy-water stoup alongside.

On the N side of the adjoining (NE) Pl. Hidalgo is the so-called *Pal. de Cortés*, built in 1756, its walls topped with anachronistic merlons, and now housing the local office of the Federal District. The original casas reales of Cortés, which during the 16–18C had decayed to ruin, stood on the E side of the church. Salvaged pieces were probably used in the construction of the present edifice. SE of Pl. Hidalgo, along Cjón Higuera, we may reach Pl. Concepción. In its centre is the charming 18C chapel of *La Concepción*, its façade stamped with ajaraca work, which enlivens the sturdy countryfied churrigueresque. It was raised on 16C foundations, destined for the chapel of the nuns who were to pray for the souls of Cortés and his family (see above). On the S side is the 18C (restored) *Los Camilos*, a former retreat house of the Camillan fathers, complementing their foundation in the city (see Rte 7). On the W is the so-called *Casa de la Malinche*, with its bold stucco pattern, an 18C rebuilding of a house in which Cortés may have installed doña Marina.

To the S of Pl. Concepción, across Av. Miguel Angel de Quevedo, lie the former barrios of Niño Jesús and Los Reyes (now colonias), each with its simple 17–18C chapel.

N of Pl. Hidalgo lies the colonia of EL CARMEN, a turn of the century development. At 247 C. Londres (leave Pl. Hidalgo along C. Allende) is the **Museo Frida Kahlo** (Tues.–Sun., 10–6), her former home.

Frida Kahlo (1910–54) was third of the four daughters of Guillermo Kahlo (1872–1941), a photographer of distinction, and Matilde Calderón. At 16 she suffered horrific injuries in a road accident, which left her a semi-invalid for the rest of her life. In 1928 she married Diego Rivera. Her disabilities and often stormy married life never quenched her forceful personality, and her espousal of left-wing causes always kept her in the public eye.

In entrance way, large papier mâché 'judases' made by Rivera, emulating the ones burnt during popular festivities. ROOM 1 contains wooden sculptures, a series of paintings, and drawings by Frida, and pages from her diary. Also Roberto Montenegro, Portrait of Frida (1936). R. 2. Letters of Frida and Diego Rivera; her traditional Mexican costumes and jewellery; a reproduction of 'Los dos Fridas' (see Rte 10). R. 3. Works by Rivera, incl. early academic studies, drawings, Cubist paintings, and portraits, among them that of Nahui Olin (1922), a key figure in the revaluation of popular art during the 1920s. R. 4. Paintings collected by Frida and Diego Rivera, incl. small works by the landscape artists Velasco and Clausell; prints by Orozco; and paintings by Marcel Duchamp and Paul Klee. R. 5. Rivera's prehispanic figurine collection. Hence the kitchen can be looked on to: vast display of regional crafts. R. 6. Variety of craftwork. At far end, Rivera's bedroom, containing popular paintings. The walls of the staircase leading up to the first floor are covered with retablos (ex-votos) on tin sheet. At the top, Frida's studio has been left intact and also contains her death mask and funeral urn. Her bedroom contains furniture, toys, and one of the painted plaster corsets she was forced to wear because of spinal damage. Steps lead down to the garden and the prehispanic sculpture scattered throughout. There is also a small prehispanic pyramid reconstruction and a terrace decorated with stone mosaic, both designed by Rivera.

No. 45 C. Viena, parallel to the N, is the **Museo León Trotsky** (Tues.–Fri., 10–5.30; Sat., Sun., 10.30–4; notice of visit advisable), the house where Trotsky lived.

Trotsky, invited by Diego Rivera, arrived in Mexico in Jan. 1937. Here he survived an attempt on his life—the desperados led by David Alfaro Siqueiros only succeeded in killing one of their own—in spring 1940, after which the house was reinforced at government expense. In Aug., Ramón Mercader (alias Jacques Mornard, alias Frank Jacson), whom Trotsky regarded as a disciple, walked in to hack him to death with an ice-pick. After the death of his widow, Natalia Sedova, in 1962, the house remained closed until 1975, when his grandson, Esteban Volkow, opened it as a museum.

The interior is much as it was during Trotsky's lifetime: the study, where he was killed; the study of Natalia Sedova; the dining room—all full of books and mementoes. The bedroom wall still carries the marks of the machine-gun shells fired by Siqueiros and his followers. Steel-reinforced doors and shutters and the observation tower create a fortress atmosphere. In the garden is the monument beneath which lie the ashes of Trotsky and Sedova.

To the E, on the NW side of the crossing of Avs Río Churubusco and División del Norte, are the *Alberca* (swimming pool) y *Gimnasio Olímpicos*, designed for the Olympics of 1968.

To the E of Coyoacán, conveniently reached by C. Xicoténcatl across Av. División del Norte, is **CHURUBUSCO**, a pleasant suburb, now part of the delegación de Coyoacán.

It was the site of a Tepanec (one of the seven Aztec tribes) Late Postclassic lakeside settlement known as *Huichilot*, part of the Tepanec 'empire' of Azcapotzalco. Its inhabitants worshipped Opochtli, god of those living near water and inventor of fishermen's tools (symbolized by the atlatl, or throwing stick, and a bunch of arrows or darts). When the Tepaneca were subdued by the Mexica Aztecs in 1428 the settlement's name was changed to *Huitzilopochco* (place of Huitzilopochtli) in honour of the Mexica god of war.

In the 16C it was renowned for its fertility and abundant water resources, supplying Mexico City by means of a conduit. The Río Churubusco (now covered by the avenida of that name), one of the canals built to drain the Lago de México, runs W to E, and then branches NE (to join the drainage canal of the Lago de Texcoco) and SE (to the canals of the Lago de Xochimilco).

In 1847, with US troops approaching from the E, a Mexican force (c 1300, incl. the remainder of the batallón de San Patricio, with little ammunition), under Gen. Pedro María Anaya, occupied the convent to protect the retreat to Mexico of troops from Coyoacán, San Angel, and Xotepingo, and from advance points S. On 20 Aug. was fought the battle of Churubusco. The Mexicans fought with almost superhuman bravery against the far better equipped enemy (8000 strong); the issue at last decided after 3½ hours and fierce hand-to-hand combat. When the victorious Gen. David D. Twiggs asked Gen. Anaya where the Mexican ammunition was kept, he got one of history's immortal replies: 'if there were any ammunition, you wouldn't be here' ('si hubiera parque, no estarían ustedes aquí').

The 85 survivors of the batallón de San Patricio were taken prisoner and sentenced to death by the US authorities at two courts-martial held on 28 Aug., the sentences being carried out at San Angel and Mixcoac. A few escaped death on a legal technicality but were given 50 strokes of the lash and branded with the letter D on the hip. Contrary to popular belief, the batallion, which included deserters from the US army and was commanded by a Floridan, Major Francisco Rosendo Moreno, was not wholly Irish, though the majority were probably Catholics and foreigners.

C. Xicoténcatl leads to Pl. San Patricio and the former convent and church of **San Diego**, with interesting historical associations, and the only 17C Mexican convent to survive entire.

Discalced Franciscans had a novitiate and retreat here from the 1580s. In 1676–78 the convent was rebuilt at the charges of the silver merchant Diego del Castillo and his wife Elena de la Cruz. In 1918 it was taken over by INAH and has been restored. Franciscans (since 1960) have charge of the church.

In the simple W portal is a beautifully framed alabaster statue of Our Lady, flanked by the arms of del Castillo. Nestling against the tower base is the Cap. de San Antonio (1798), now the baptistery, covered with azulejos.

The vaulting of the single-nave INTERIOR (restored) was substituted c 1720 for the original artesonado ceiling. Nave and transepts are lined by anastyle altarpieces (1770–80) rescued from destruction in the nick of time and moved here from La Piedad (see Rte 13). Their bold ornamentation, multiple niche-pilasters, and spiral-enriched panelling are very impressive. The first on the r. wall includes a painting of St Dominic by Alonso López de Herrera. The high altarpiece (late 17C) has discreet solomonic columns. The entrance to the choir is a display of azulejos; the sacristy (r. of high altar) contains more. Note also, covering the end wall, Souls in Purgatory with St Michael, saints, and the Trinity (1667) by Antonio Rodríguez. On either side of the entrance, from the convent, to the r. transept gallery are the late 17C images of don Diego and doña Elena, in wood painted on gesso.

The convent buildings, E of the church, enclosing cloister and gardens, keep their beamed ceilings, sturdy portería arches, and azulejo decoration. The cannon in the atrio and by the museum entrance were brought here in 1939 from Veracruz. At the top of the main staircase, a charming azulejo-framed niche holds a 17C statue of Our Lady of Atocha (also from La Piedad).

On the upper floor is the **Museo de las Intervenciones** (Tues.–Sun., 10–6; fee). In 18 rooms are displayed arms, standards, paintings, lithographs, etc. illustrating foreign intervention and wars in Mexico throughout the 19C and into the 20C.

In the charming triple-arched upper cloister, with a tile dado, is a late 17C stone statue of a kneeling knight of Santiago (from Tacubaya).
ROOMS 1 AND 2. The 18C and Independence. Iturbide's throne and sword. Portraits of Guadalupe Victoria, Vicente Guerrero, Miguel Ramos Arizpe, Vicente Filisola, Fray Servando Teresa de Mier, Andrés Quintana Roo, and other luminaries of the period. Insurgent printing press. Objects and material relating to Masonic influence in early independent Mexico: York Rite—federalists; Scottish Rite—centralists. RR. 3–5. The Spanish and French invasions of 1829 and 1838–9 (expedition of Isidro Barradas and War of the Pastries). Exhibits include a facsimile of the Treaty of Sta María Calatrava, by which Spain recognized the independence of Mexico. Cannon from Guadalupe in Puebla. Jewels and porcelain. R. 6. The loss of Texas. Reminders of the battle of the Alamo in 1836. Colours of the New Orleans Greys, captured during the campaign. RR. 7–8. The War of 1847–48. Illustrations of the bombardment of Veracruz. Decorations for bravery conferred by the Mexican government. Likenesses of the Niños Héroes. Document confirming sale of La Mesilla by Santa-Anna for 10 million pesos in 1853. Copy of memorial to the batallón de San Patricio. Copy of the Plan of Ayutla (1855), which marked the end of Santa-Anna and liberals coming to power. R. 9. French intervention and Second Empire. Documents relating to Maximilian's accession. Portraits of his supporters, incl. Gens. Miramón and Mejía. French military relics. Sword of Gen. Mariano Escobedo. Coach used by Pres. Juárez. Keepsakes of Maximilian and Carlota. R. 10. Liberal press and propaganda. Portraits of Juárez and doña Margarita Maza. R. 11. Porfirismo. Letter of Díaz dated 1879. Photos showing contemporary repression and revolutionary movements of the 1870s and 1880s. Furniture and costumes. Reminders of the Río Blanco strike in 1906–07 and its bloody suppression. RR. 12–13. Madero and Revolution. Action photos of 1911–12, incl. Emiliano Zapata and Francisco Villa. RR. 14–18. Revolution 1914–18. Photos of US occupation of Veracruz and of the Pershing expedition of 1916–17. Photos illustrating the Constitution of 1917, especially of Articles 27 and 123, dealing with ownership of the national wealth and land (and expropriations) and the rights of workers.

From the convent we may follow C. 20 de Agosto E to Calz. de Tlalpan. At this corner are the *Laboratorios CIBA* (1953–54), by Alejandro Prieto and Félix Candela. Note the sawtooth barrel vaults over the laboratory buildings and the mosaics by José Chávez Morado, showing early Indian medical techniques, on the street façade and his murals in the entrance hall. On the other (E) side of Calz. de Tlalpan is the **Mexico City Country Club**, inaugurated here in 1907.

It results from a merger of the San Pedro Golf Club, founded in 1900 by a group of US, British, and Mexican aficionados, and the Mixcoac Golf Club, which later absorbed the Mexico Cricket Club. A few blocks N, between Calz. de Tlalpan and Av. Río Churubusco, are the *Estudios Churubusco*, largest film studios in Mexico.

From here an expedition may be made to (5km) **CULHUACAN**, reached by going S along Calz. de Tlalpan to the junction with Calz. Tasqueña and following the latter E, past the *Terminal de Autobuses del Sur* and the *Tasqueña* metro terminus (l.) across the *Canal Nacional*. Also on the l. of the road, behind the Country Club and in Col. Campestre Churubusco, is the *Universidad Ibero-americana*, founded in 1943.

N of the junction of Calz. Tasqueña with Calz. Tulyehualco is the former Augustinian convent of **San Juan Evangelista** (Sun.–Fri., 10–6; entry in C. Morelos, on the E side of Calz. Tulyehualco), noted for its 16C murals.

The district was the site, in Toltec history, where the Culhua leader Mixcóatl founded the first Toltec capital in the 10C. The Culhua were a Tolteca-Chichimeca tribe migrating from NW Mexico along with many other such groups. From Culhuacán, Mixcóatl fought several campaigns against Otomí towns to the N and S, making Culhuacán one of the more powerful city-states in the Basin. Mixcóatl was assassinated and succeeded by one of his court officials. His son, who took the name Ce Acatl Topiltzin, was forced into exile and fled N to found Tula, from which he avenged his father's murder, but was later himself overthrown by a military faction.

Culhuacán remained an important centre in the Basin and was probably reinforced by immigrants from Tula after that city's fall c AD 1170. The Culhua, in league with the Tepaneca of Azcapotzalco, drove the Mexica Aztecs from their settlement at Chapultepec in the early 14C, but were themselves subdued and made tributaries by the Tepaneca in 1367. The Mexica, anxious to establish a Toltec ancestry, accepted a Culhua prince as their first king—Acamapichtli (1372–91)—but remained tributaries to Azcapotzalco until the Triple Alliance of 1428 defeated that city. The third Mexica ruler, Itzcóatl (1426–40), took the title Lord of Culhuacán, thus excluding all others from claims to Toltec succession.

Under the Aztecs, Culhuacán remained an important provincial city, noted by Cortés' chroniclers. After the Conquest, Cortés granted it to Cristóbal de Oñate, in whose family it remained until c 1659. The convent was begun c 1562.

In the church, now a picturesque ruin, with rubble and cut-lava walls, are the column bases of nave and two side aisles. The convent (restored in 1955) is entered through a double-arched portería. In its lower storey the charming cloister has low arches on robust Tuscan columns. The beamed ceilings are set on stone corbels. Off the simple upper storey, entered through a 16C carved wooden door showing relief of the monograms of Our Lord and Our Lady, the instruments of the Passion, and the Augustinian pierced heart, are 13 friars' cells. These and the rest of the convent are decorated with murals, revealed by restoration in the 1950s. They show preference for blue tints and idiosyncratic use of perspective, but great vigour. Ornamental borders are in a layered fretwork design, typically Indian. In the portería: friars under the patronage of St Augustine. Lower cloister: country scenes; a lively frieze, interrupted by medallions of friars, horsemen, and saints; medallions of Passion scenes; vegetal motifs around doors and pillars. Upper cloister: on outer wall, saints, incl. Augustinian martyrs (lovingly done); on inner wall, Entry into Jerusalem and Adoration of the Kings.

Culhuacán lies in the delegación of IZTAPALAPA, whose agricultural areas are gradually giving way to urban development and whose vast CENTRAL DE ABASTOS (supply centre; 865 ha.) to the N is the distribution centre for foodstuffs to all parts of the Federal District. Its old centre is c 2km N of Culhuacán, reached by Calz. Tulyehualco. Its parish church of *San Lucas* (1664; heavily restored) and *Santuario del Señor de la Cuevita* (19C) figure in the famous Good Friday Passion play, which culminates on the Cerro de la Estrella.

Ixtapalapa was a provincial city-state of c 60–75,000 people on the shores of Lago de Texcoco, half on solid ground and half on chinampas. It was governed by a brother of Moctezuma II Xocoyotzin, and Cortés remarked on the sumptuousness of his palace and pleasure gardens. It was here that the great S causeway across the lake from Tenochtitlán reached the mainland. Built by Itzcóatl (third Aztec king, 1426–40) in 1429, it had 8–10m-wide canals on either side, and at its highest point rose c 1.3m above the lake. It varied in width between 15m and 20m and joined the causeway from Coyoacán c 2km from the shore, thence c 6.5km to Tenochtitlán. It was unpaved, but had a surface of rammed earth and crushed volcanic stone, and was broken by drawbridges for defence.

To the S stands **Cerro de la Estrella**, a Late Classic/Early Postclassic site settled by immigrants from Teotihuacán. It is most noted, however, as the site where the Aztecs performed the New Fire Ceremony, to mark the end and beginning of 52-year cycles (see Introduction: Calendrics).

As the cycle approached the final day, the Aztecs feared the end of the world unless the Sun rose again and the kindling of the New Fire was successful. On the designated day every 52 years all fires were extinguished and household idols, cooking implements, and the three traditional household hearth stones were discarded. Houses, yards, and streets were swept. As darkness approached, people climbed on to houses and walls, and pregnant women and children covered their faces with maguey-leaf masks for protection against demons of darkness. (Some sources say women and children were kept indoors and pregnant women hidden in huge corn-storage jars.) Children were kept awake for fear they would turn into mice if they missed the critical rite.

Priests dressed as gods climbed the Cerro, known to the Aztecs as *Uixachtlán*, and at midnight a captive was sacrificed by opening his chest cavity with an obsidian knife and extracting his pulsing heart. A fire was then kindled in the opened chest. If successful, runners spread the new flame throughout the land in relays, and auto-sacrificial ear piercing was performed by the grateful populace as penance.

General rejoicing followed, incl. renewal of discarded articles, rekindling of hearth fires, and even new buildings begun. Should the fire fail to light, however, darkness, it was believed, would engulf the earth and celestial monsters would devour mankind (see Introduction: Mesoamerican Religion).

At 11.25km Av. Insurgentes Sur reaches Av. Copilco (l.) which leads (follow signs) to **Copilco** ('place of the crown' entrance at No. 54 C. Victoria; Tues.–Sun. 9–5; fee).

It was a Middle Preclassic village settlement of c 1300–800 BC, one of several that had begun to exploit the lakeshore resources in the S Basin, practising both primitive agriculture and hunting-gathering-fishing. Long after its abandonment, due to flooding from Lago de Texcoco, the eruption of Xitle c 1 BC–AD 1 buried the site in up to 8m of lava. Excavators found remains of the Zacatenco Culture (after a contemporary site of that name on the NW shore of the lake): manos and matates for grinding, early pottery vessels and hand-modelled figurines, stone tools and weapons, the floors of the inhabitants' huts, and the caves of their burials. Skeletons were in extended position, accompanied by vessels, figurines, and stone tools.

The tunnels of Manuel Gamio's 1917 excavation have been utilized as exhibition galleries. Pictures and graphs explain local geology and the physical anthropology of the burials, relating their skeletal features to present-day Mexicans. Showcases display the artefacts and their interpretation into developmental types, incl. pottery, figurines, obsidian blades, and bone needles and ornaments.

We continue S into the area of the Pedregal de San Angel to (12.25km) the entrance (l.) to the **CIUDAD UNIVERSITARIA**, the vast main area (7.3 sq km) of the **Universidad Nacional Autónoma de México**.

On 21 Sept. 1551 Charles V authorized the first university in the Americas. The foundation ceremony took place on 25 Jan. 1553. In 1595 Pope Clement VIII expedited the bulls sanctioning the university as 'pontificia' (Real y Pontificia Universidad). In the 17C its high academic standards (Jesuit influence well to the fore) impressed Europeans. (In 1754 one Antonio López Portillo so dazzled the authorities with his learning that they awarded him four doctorates all at once.) Jesuit expulsion in 1767 cut off much promise and, despite attempts under Charles III to inject new life, decline set in. In 1865 Maximilian 'with a stroke of the pen finally put an end to the foundation of his illustrious ancestor'. From 1881 Justo Sierra pursued his campaign for a national university. In 1910, symbolically, the old university buildings were levelled and the new lay Universidad Nacional de México inaugurated by Pres. Díaz. In 1929 it gained its autonomy. It embraced various institutions throughout the city, but the venerable buildings became less and less able to meet the needs of a modern centre of learning.

In 1949 Carlos Lazo was commissioned by Pres. Alemán to develop the new site, where all faculties and institutes could be gathered together. Some 150 engineers, architects, sculptors, and painters, with c 6000 workmen, finished it, to the plans of Enrique del Moral and Mario Pani, in 1950–54.

The university city is divided into four sectors: on the E of Av. Insurgentes Sur, the *Jardín Central* (c 180 by 360m), the centre of the campus, around which are grouped faculties, schools, institutes, library, administrative offices, and ancillary organizations; adjoining to the S, the recreation and sports areas; to the SW, more university buildings; on the W of Av. Insurgentes,

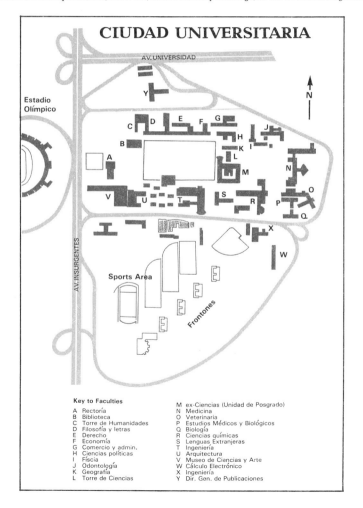

Key to Faculties

A	Rectoría
B	Biblioteca
C	Torre de Humanidades
D	Filosofía y letras
E	Derecho
F	Economía
G	Comercio y admin.
H	Ciencias políticas
I	Física
J	Odontología
K	Geografía
L	Torre de Ciencias
M	ex-Ciencias (Unidad de Posgrado)
N	Medicina
O	Veterinaria
P	Estudios Médicos y Biológicos
Q	Biología
R	Ciencias químicas
S	Lenguas Extranjeras
T	Ingeniería
U	Arquitectura
V	Museo de Ciencias y Arte
W	Cálculo Electrónico
X	Ingeniería
Y	Dir. Gen. de Publicaciones

the Estadio Olímpico, and SW of this, the residential complex and more sports facilities. Buses running along the main avenue through the grounds drop visitors off at various points within easy reach of key buildings.

The **Biblioteca Central**, the most immediately striking building, and the work of Juan O'Gorman, Gustavo Saavedra, and Juan Martínez de Velasco, stands at the NW corner of the Jardín. A tall rectangular windowless prism (air admitted by tiny openings), its four walls (300 sq m) are covered in mosaics by O'Gorman, composed of stones of a myriad colours.

An essay in complicated symbolism, each wall expresses aspects of Mexican history and culture through the ages. The N wall prehispanic Mexico, with gods, constellations, priests, rulers; the S wall the historical period and influences on it—philosophy, religion, maps, conquistadores, art and architecture, saints, missionaries; the E wall the early modern period, incl. Revolution, agrarian reform, the atom; the W wall later modern Mexico, its Independence and dependence on foreign powers. The lower two floors, the building's wide base, house the reading rooms and lending library. The upper parts of the ground-floor windows are translucent onyx panels. The higher ten floors are the storage space, natural light being dispensed with in the stacks in the interests of temperature control.

Along the N side of the Jardín stretches the *Edificio de Humanidades*. Closing off the E end the Torre de Humanidades forms part of the *Facultad de Filosofía y Letras* by Enrique del Moral, Manuel de la Colina, and Enrique Landa. On the E side of the Jardín (N end) is the edifice built as the **Facultad de Ciencias**, by Raúl Cacho, Eugenio Peschard, and Félix Sánchez.

On an exterior panel below the main part of the building (S side) is José Chávez Morado's 'El retorno de Quetzalcóatl', an Italian glass mosaic showing the Toltec god-king returning on his feathered-serpent raft to bring the benefits of learning. Accompanying him are figures from great civilizations, symbolizing the permanence of culture: ancient Egypt (gold); European Middle Ages (a friar; green); Assyria (brown); Graeco-Roman (brown and white); Orient (light green); Islam (purple). On l., broken weapons pointing up the uselessness of war; on r., the figures look to the golden fire of hope. In the background, the Pyramid of the Sun. Despite the use of brown and purple to minimize glare, the bright colours dazzle in the sunlight. The N façade of the auditorium shows another Italian glass mosaic by Chávez Morado, 'La conquista de la energía', in which man advances from ignorance and servitude towards the conquest of the atom—a beautifully proportioned and rhythmic work. On the E wall of the auditorium, in a covered space and painted with vinylite, Chávez Morado's 'Los constructores de la Ciudad Universitaria' shows builders and architects at work, and the scientists of the faculty.

Grouped around the smaller space E of the science buildings are further notable structures. On the N side the *Instituto de Física* and the **Escuela Nacional de Odontología** (Dentistry), with, prominent on its S side, Francisco Eppens's mural in glazed mosaic tile of man as a tree trunk between the wings of an eagle and the body of a serpent, his head a flame, arms extended, one hand clenched to fight, the other beseeching.

Nearby, on the S, is one of Félix Candela's hyperbolic paraboloids (built for cosmic ray research), the roof having to be not thicker than 16mm, but given rigidity by a double curvature.

On the E side is the **Facultad de Medicina**, with notable porticoes. On the façade of the W wing is Eppens's monumental allegory of Mexico, which catches the eye from afar. Amid symbols of Quetzalcóatl, Tláloc, Coatlícue, Xiuhtecuhtli, and Chalchiuhtlicue, the ancient gods, peers a full-face mestizo head, combined with Spanish and Indian heads in profile.

Further S, the auditorium of the *Escuela Nacional de Ciencias Químicas* is composed of two truncated cones coupled along a common edge, built by Félix Candela.

On the S side of the Jardín is the **Escuela Nacional de Arquitectura**, with the *Museo de Ciencias y Arte* (Mon.–Fri., 10–3.30, 4.30–7; incl. displays of handicrafts, prehispanic finds, and modern paintings) closing the S side of the Jardín on the W. On the museum's N side, and on the university city's highest point, is the **Torre de la Rectoría**, by Pani, del Moral, and Salvador Ortega Flores—15 storeys, its façades incorporating glazed tiles, glass bricks, Carrara glass, concrete, and onyx. David Alfaro Siqueiros was originally commissioned to cover four surfaces with sculpture paintings, but did not complete the work.

On the S side of the adjoining lower building is 'El pueblo a la Universidad; la Universidad al pueblo, por una cultura nacional, neohumanística, de profundidad universal', in ethyl silicate, finished in mosaic and metals. Sage, sociologist, and artist, eager with outstretched arms, offer the fruits of their learning for practical application. On the N side, a giant hand creates an image of Mexican cultural and national consciousness. He later added four crucial dates in Mexican history: 1520, 1810, 1857, 1910—and added '19--' in red: questioning when the next national upheaval would be. The cubical mass on the tower proper's E side, rather incongruously placed, shows an eagle and a condor—the union of Mexico and Central and S America.

Much to Siqueiros's annoyance, this work was later covered with Italian mosaic, which spoiled the effect of the relief.

On the W side of Av. Insurgentes Sur is the **Estadio Olímpico**, a beautiful basin, designed by Augusto Pérez Palacios, Raúl Salinas, and Jorge Bravo, used mainly for soccer, but also for athletics. The longitudinal axis is shifted some metres, parallel to the main axis of the stadium oval, thus ensuring that most seats are on the favourable W side. Over the main entrance are panels by Diego Rivera, difficult to do (mosaic inlay on concrete blocks) and therefore somewhat clumsy: one shows engineer, worker, and architect offering the university city to the Mexicans, producers of the wealth which made its construction possible; the other shows staff welcoming students.

To the S of the stadium is the University's *Jardín Botánico* (Mon.–Sat., 9–4.30).

Pedregal de San Angel, the petrified lava field left by an eruption of Xitle volcano over 2000 years ago, covers an area of c 65 sq km. It extends S to N from Tlalpan to San Angel and Coyoacán, and from E to W from Calz. de Tlalpan to Tizapán. Parts are still quarried. The resulting environment, sometimes weird, sometimes beautiful, has been put to good use by architects in the **Jardines del Pedregal**, S of San Angel and W of the Olympic Stadium (best reached by Av. San Jerónimo, which branches off the continuation of Av. Revolución from San Angel), an exclusive residential suburb.

Its development dates from 1948, the devising mainly of the architect Luis Barragán, whose expert integration of architecture with landscape has resulted in something of a fantasy land. Among other architects who designed here in the 1950s was Félix Candela, in collaboration with Raúl Fernández, Max Cetto, and Enrique del Moral.

Beyond it, to the N of Av. San Jerónimo, is the colonia of TIZAPAN, with the 18C church of *Guadalupe*, containing a churrigueresque altarpiece.

W and SW of the Jardines del Pedregal stretches the delegación of **Magdalena Contreras**, its N and NE parts rapidly transformed since the 1920s as a residential district and dotted with light industry, hydroelectric power for which is provided by the Río Magdalena, now mostly underground. Its SW area, bordering the State of México, is mountainous, well wooded and watered, and a popular target for excursions and fishing expeditions.

At its NE tip is the *Unidad Independencia*, a low-cost housing development built in the early 1960s by IMSS. Some buildings display mosaics by Francisco Eppens and Federico Cantú, and sculpture by Luis Ortiz Monasterio. Further SW, in the colonia San Jerónimo Lídice, on Av. San Jerónimo, is the 17C church of *San Jerónimo Ocotepec* whose former house is occupied by the *Escuela Superior de Guerra*, for army staff officers. Church and house were a foundation of the Hieronymites, of the Spanish congregation of the Hermits of St Jerome, a contemplative order, suppressed in 1835. Av. San Jerónimo continues SW into the SW part of the delegación, incl. the village of *La Magdalena*, now a colonia. Its parish church dates from 1769.

Unidad Independencia and the area W and SW, incl. San Jerónimo Lídice, was the battlefield of Padierna, fought on 19 and 20 Aug. 1847, when the Mexican force holding the ranch of Padierna to deny passage towards the city to Gen. Winfield Scott and his troops, advancing from the SE, was surrounded and broken. It is said that Santa-Anna, with 3000 troops, watched the battle from the heights to the N.

At 13.25km Av. Insurgentes Sur passes (l.) the **Centro Cultural Universitario**, a further development, since the mid-1970s, of UNAM, dedicated to music, drama, cinema, and higher studies. Around the *Sala Nezahualcóyotl* (1977), an impressive concert hall (the concert platform surrounded by the auditorium), are the *Teatro Juan Ruiz de Alarcón* and the *Foro Sor Juana Inés de la Cruz* (1979; plays, dance displays, concerts); and smaller halls for chamber music, films, and dance theatre. The pièce de résistance is the *Espacio Escultórico*, a huge ring of triangular monoliths surrounding a petrified lava sea, by Matías Goeritz, Manuel Felguérez, and others.

Two more important dependencies of the University are now also on this site. The **Biblioteca Nacional** (1979), removed from San Agustín (see Rte 7), and the *Hemeroteca Nacional* (see Rte 3).

At 16.5km Av. Insurgentes Sur passes under the Anillo Periférico Sur—S section of the ring highway, which to the W skirts the city to become the Mexico-Querétaro road and, to the E, runs N of Xochimilco; thence projected NE through the delegación of Iztapalapa and along the E borders of the delegaciones Iztacalco and Gustavo A. Madero; then running across the N outer part of the city to join the W stretch NW of Azcapotzalco.

The S stretch (c 17km) from the W side of the Jardines del Pedregal to the N tip of the Cuemanco canal N of Xochimilco, was called RUTA DE LA AMISTAD (Route of Friendship) to commemorate the Olympic Games of 1968, and is lined with monumental sculptures donated by the participating countries.

C 2km W, on the S side of Jardines del Pedregal, the continuation of Paseo del Pedregal crosses the Anillo Periférico on the way to San Miguel Ajusco. Beyond the junction (l.) are the premises of the *Colegio de México* (for higher studies), built in 1976 to the design of Teodoro González de León and Abraham Zabludovsky.

Just beyond the junction a turning l. leads to **CUICUILCO**.

Cuicuilco ('place of singing and dancing') was a Late Preclassic ceremonial centre on the W shores of the Lago de Xochimilco, used from c 500 BC to c AD 1, although the area was inhabited from c 900 BC. It was excavated by Manuel Gamio and Byron Cummings in 1922, and by E. Noguera, H. Moedano, and R. Heizer in the 1950s. The site was cleared and preserved as a major tourist attraction in 1967 before the 1968 Olympics.

Cuicuilco's history has five phases: *Cuicuilco I–II*—c 500–400 BC; *Cuicuilco III*—c 400–200 BC; and *Cuicuilco IV–V*—c 200 BC–AD 1.

The principal monument is a four-tiered circular platform, which may be the earliest stone-faced 'pyramid' in Mesoamerica (following earlier Olmec earthen mounds at San Lorenzo and La Venta). During *Cuicuilco III–IV* it was the most important centre in the S Basin of Mexico and a serious rival to the developing centre at Teotihuacán. The building of the platform attests to the development of socio-political forces capable of organizing and controlling large labour forces and to religious developments implied in the platform's use. At its height the town site covered c 400ha with a population estimated at 20,000. The inhabitants were agriculturalists on the threshold of urbanism, supplementing their diet by fishing and hunting in and around the lake. As a burgeoning power in the Basin of Mexico the town had trading, and perhaps political, contacts throughout the Basin and with the Gulf Coast. The emergence of social ranking is implied by the construction of the platform and in the worship practised at its altars. Excavators found smaller shrines and traces of grass and reed huts with burials under their floors (23 in one case) around the platform. Figurines, incl. ball players, similar to those in contemporary Basin of Mexico sites, such as Tlatilco and

Tlapacoya, were among the grave goods. At nearby Peña Pobre a smaller circular platform of six tiers and similar construction was found; and c 1km E of the main platform 11 other mound structures.

Evidence that showers of hot cinders warned the inhabitants of the imminent eruption of Xitle volcano, to the S, may have led to the evacuation of the area before the flow of the lava actually buried most of the site up to 8m, ending Cuicuilco's power in the Basin.

Cuicuilco

The first building phase was a round earthen platform, later partly levelled in preparation for the stone-faced platform. The present stone-faced platform comprises four superimposed circular steps built in several stages. Ramps up the E and W sides give an almost exact E–W axis.

The earliest stone-faced platform comprised two tiers topped by a slightly elliptical clay altar and stairway. The core was rammed earth faced with stone slabs set into the earth at an approx. 45 deg. angle. Subsequent phases enlarged these steps and added two more. Again the core was of rammed earth encased in stone slabs, with a final facing of river boulders. The maximum diameter is 135m and the maximum height 20m, covering 1.4ha. Successive clay altars were built one above the other on the tops of the platform and faced with red-painted plaster. Incense burners in the shape of Xiuhtecuhtli, god of fire, found in the excavations in and around the platform support the supposition that Xitle served as a model and prompted his worship.

Just S of the W ramp a small circular structure has been excavated. Large irregular stone slabs, leaning towards the centre, were embedded in the ground and capped by several more slabs (no longer in situ), leaving a small entryway on the W side. Inside, traces of red paint, applied directly to the stone, depict snake-like spirals. The use of this structure is unknown but must have been of some ritual significance. A small, stepped stone platform lies SE of the E ramp, below present ground level.

The **Museum** lies SW of the platform. At the entrance geographic charts and photographs explain the local geology and Cuicuilco's position in Preclassic Mesoamerica, particularly its relationship to earlier developments on the Gulf Coast. Proceed counter-clockwise around the two rooms.

First, display panels show the geology of the Pedregal; flora and fauna of the S Basin of Mexico; Preclassic sites in the Basin; and a comparative chronological chart of the Basin, Tabasco, and W Mesoamerica in the Preclassic and Early Classic Periods.

Room 1 has illustrations of physical types in the Basin (incl. examples of cranial deformation caused by the types of headdress worn and by bone diseases); cases of Preclassic figurines, jewellery, and a grinding stone; panel explaining the early development of Preclassic civilization; and, r., cases with Cuicuilco pottery corresponding to the five phases of the site.

Room 2 contains a case of artefacts illustrating trade within and beyond the Basin, plus panels illustrating the Cuicuilco excavations and the altar found within the top tier of the pyramid; l., panel on Preclassic technology and case with obsidian points, a grinding stone, pottery and figurines; ahead, panel illustrating religious practices at Cuicuilco.

Further l., a reconstructed burial from the ancient town (Troncomica); an early stone sculpture found at the base of the platform; and panels on burials excavated in the vicinity of the platform and on the circular stone structure at its SW base.

Ahead, an interpretative painting shows Cuicuilco about to be engulfed by lava from Xitle; on l., a case of pottery and figurines illustrating Preclassic daily life, plus panels showing excavations of Cuicuilco in 1923, 1939, and 1967. At the end are two panels (r.) on the abandonment of Cuicuilco and aerial photographs of the site.

On the other side of Av. Insurgentes Sur is *Unidad Miguel Hidalgo*, the former *Villa Olímpica*, by Ramón Torres, Héctor Velázquez, and Agustín Hernández, the base for athletes taking part in the XIX Olympiad of 1968. From here the road runs SE past the village of *Peña Pobre* to (18.5km) **TLALPAN**, centre of its delegación, largest in the Federal District. It is now a picturesque suburb, retaining many of its 18C monuments.

The former San Agustín de las Cuevas, from the 18C was a favourite country retreat, famous for its May fair. In 1815 José María Morelos was held at 3 C. San Fernando before being taken for trial in Mexico. In 1827–30 it served as capital of the State of México (a far greater area than today). Empress Carlota embellished it by planting trees. Porfirian society built grand houses with gardens. Zapatista forces sacked and destroyed many of them.

PL. PRINCIPAL preserves its original arcading and atmosphere. On the E side is the parish church and former convent of **San Agustín**, originally founded by discalced Franciscans, passing to the Dominicans c 1580. It is the result of various building stages, mainly 18C, though restored several times since, most recently in 1975. The Cap. del Rosario preserves its 18C altarpiece. Behind it, at the corner of Cs Hidalgo and Magisterio Nacional, the convent of *Capuchinas Sacramentarias* (Capuchinesses) was designed by Luis Barragán and begun in 1940. Its chapel (1952–55) is lit through stained glass by Matías Goeritz. The gold-leaf altarpiece, also by Goeritz, subtly reflects the light.

To the S, at the corner of Cs Congreso and Galeana, is the *Casa del Conde de Regla*, its façade and triple-arched portico intact. The *Casa Chata*, at the corner of Cs Hidalgo and Morelos, saved by restoration in 1941, has a beautifully proportioned baroque portal. The wooden door once belonged to the Colegio de San Pedro y San Pablo (see Rte 3). The interior is noteworthy for its two patios, its relief decoration, and its doorways.

Tlalpan has been considered an ideal location for various hospitals serving the Federal District. Among them is the **Instituto Nacional de Cardiología** (1976) by José Villagrán García, in *Huipulco*, 1.5km E. of Pl. Principal. To its main lobby have been moved the murals of the world history of cardiology painted by Diego Rivera in 1943–44, formerly in the Auditorio Nacional in Col. Doctores in Mexico City.

Below, a monochrome frieze of rectangular panels shows prehistoric medicine and the use of herbs and plants as medicines. Above, historical medicine is shown in a series of significant events accompanied by famous practitioners (inimitable, but sympathetic, likenesses) from earliest to modern times. In one corner, Michel Servet, a pioneer of early research, is burnt at the stake, victim of Calvinist intolerance. The Czech specialist Joseph Skoda has features very like those of Rivera.

The continuation W of C. San Fernando leads, on the W side of the town, to C. San Pedro Apóstol, No. 32 in which is the church of *San Pedro Apóstol*, originally of the 18C, but with substantial 19C additions. The atrial cross is carved with symbols of the Passion, and the interior contains 17–18C sculpture.

W of Pl. Principal, at 11–13 C. de la Moneda, the **Casa de Moneda**, once headquarters of the State of México, is notable for its decorative (and symbolic) battlements with their stucco relief; slender windows; and the splendid main doorway, with staged, richly decorated entablature topped by a scallop. No. 85 C. de la Moneda is another 18C house; No. 64, the *Casa del Marqués del Vivanco*, keeps part of its original façade. Nos 9, 15, 17 in the parallel C. Victoria preserve an appealing relief of the Holy Family above the simple doorway. At 15 C. Juárez (corner with C. Victoria) the so-called *Casa del Virrey de Mendoza* is now a convent. Further S, at 230 C. Juárez, the *Oratorio de Amaxalco*, now inside the house, has a richly decorated portal, charming in its rusticity.

Further W, across Av. Insurgentes Sur, at its corner with Camino a las Fuentes Brotantes (leading to *Fuentes Brotantes*, a favourite resort), is the *Cap. del Calvario*, a late 17C structure, restored in 1967, with a wooden beam roof and two 18C wooden statues: Christ scourged and Immaculate Conception. Further S, in C. Sta Ursula, leading SW off Av. Insurgentes Sur, the little church of *Sta Ursula Xitla* was saved from ruin in 1867. The Viaducto Tlalpan joins the toll road to Cuernavaca and runs from Tlalpan through (4km) *San Pedro Mártir*, which includes (C. Enseñanza) the simple little 17C church of San Pedro Verona Mártir (murals). From the highway may be seen the modern buildings (1974–78) of the **Heroico Colegio Militar**, by Agustín Hernández and Manuel González Rul, Mexico's equivalent to West Point and Sandhurst.

In the increasingly mountainous country to the S and SW, reached by the continuation of Av. Insurgentes Sur (the old Cuernavaca road) from Tlalpan, are various pueblos, formerly dependent on Tlalpan, each with its little church. At (4km) *San Andrés Totoltepec* the 17C church was restored and strengthened in 1968. 7km r. turn for (3km W) *Magdalena Petlacalco*, with a 17C church in a raised atrio, and (6km) *San Miguel Ajusco*, on the foothills of the Ajusco volcano, whose 17C church of San Miguel has a compelling portal topped by a relief of St James the Greater; Sto Tomás, in the barrio of *Sto Tomás Ajusco*, possibly dating from the 16C, has a good atrial cross with sprouting fleur-de-lis relief and an interior portal covered in pretty carving. 14km l. turn for (2km SE) *Topilejo*, where the church of San Miguel Arcángel dates from 1560, with 18C portal and cupola, the tower finished in 1812, and fine baroque altarpiece.

16 Tacubaya and Santa Fe

The area S of Chapultepec, now urbanized, was once the beautiful country town of **TACUBAYA**, associated with significant events in Mexican history.

Its mills and granaries early on supplied the capital. In 1607 Philip III commanded that the latter be moved hither, but the project was deemed too expensive. Tacubaya became famous for its haciendas, broken up in the 19C when from c 1858 a salubrious residential district developed, with notable country houses, only traces of which survive. In 1897 its historical area (bounded by Av. Constituyentes in the NW, Av. Patriotismo in the E, Av. San Antonio in the S, and Presa Tacubaya in the W) had extended far to the E, embracing present-day colonias Nápoles, Narvarte, and Doctores. Today's colonia is therefore but a small part of the original. Here in Apr. 1842 the English mexicanophile painter Daniel Thomas Egerton and his mistress, Agnes Edwards, were murdered while out for their evening stroll—'It is impossible to describe the horror with which all classes in Mexico received this dreadful tale'. In Dec. 1857 the Plan of Tacubaya, proclaimed by Gen. Félix Zuloaga, declared the new Constitution null and void, and started the war of the Reform. On 11 Apr. 1859 Tacubaya was scene of the victory of the conservatives under Gen. Leonardo Márquez over the liberals led by Gen. Santos Degollado. Márquez had the liberal officers shot, a crime which earned him the nickname 'tigre de Tacubaya'.

Although traffic makes pedestrian access difficult and shoddy new development and neglect have whittled away the older buildings, enough of the historic and porfirian remain to make a determined exploration worthwhile.

Av. Observatorio runs W to E from Av. Constituyentes to Parque Lira and is crossed at its E end by the Anillo Periférico (Av. A. López Mateos). The earliest of the 16C mills was the *Molino de Sto Domingo*, of which the granary (14 C. Sto Domingo; now a craft centre) and chapel (14 Pl. Sto Domingo; now part of a house, but preserving its façade) survive, just S of Av. Observatorio, W of the Periférico and railway line. Further W, at the corner of

C. Arzobispado, is what remains of the **Pal. Arzobispal**, built in 1737 by the abp-viceroy Juan Antonio de Vizarrón y Eguiarreta as a summer residence. It is now part of the Instituto de Geografía y Meteorología. C 1km further W, C. Sur 136 contains (since 1964) the *Hospital Inglés* (American-British Cowdray Hospital), founded in 1911 on the initiative of Lady Cowdray (Annie Cass), wife of the 1st Lord Cowdray, whose business interests in Mexico made possible a substantial endowment. On the E side of the Periférico the church of *San Diego*, now secularized, altered, and hemmed in by modern buildings, has a late 17C portal of classical sobriety.

In C. Manuel Dublán, to the S, paralleling Av. Observatorio, is *Santísima Trinidad*, a late 16C foundation (as an Indian church), and some good 19C houses. No. 40, *Casa del Agua-catito*, dates from the 17C and keeps part of the original façade. The façade and patio of the 17C *Casa del Obispo Palafox y Mendoza* (supposedly for the bp-viceroy), at the corner of Cs Dublán and Rufina, now a school, are original, but the top storey is an unhappy later addition.

PARQUE LIRA, at the E end of Av. Observatorio, was in the 19C the garden of a country house belonging to José Gómez, conde de la Cortina (1799–1860), scholar and politician. The neighbouring *Casa de la Bola* (136 Av. Parque Lira) dates from the 18C, as does the *Casa Amarilla* (No. 94). S of the park, at the corner of Av. Observatorio and C. Arq. L. Ruiz, is still preserved the neo-Gothic chapel designed by Javier Cavallari (c 1860) for a private house (now demolished). Following Av. Parque Lira SE, at the crossing with C. Mártires de la Conquista, we come to the former Dominican church and convent of *Sto Domingo*, founded c 1578 and built c 1590–1600, to the design of Fray Lorenzo de la Asunción. The atrio has been encroached upon by later buildings; the church was altered in the 19C; but the cloister survives more or less intact.

E of Parque Lira, at the junction of Avs Jalisco and Revolución, the *Edificio Ermita* (1930) is one of a notable group of art deco buildings by Juan Segura. Another by him is the block (1929) at the corner of Avs Martí and Revolución, 500m further S. No. 204 Av. Vasconcelos (continuation NE of Av. Jalisco), the *Embajada Rusa*, is a rebuilding (1912; by Mauricio M. Campos) of what used to be the house of the large hacienda of Condesa de Miravalle. Almost opposite, at 54 C. José Morán, the church of *San Miguel* (late 17C) has been much altered.

The streets going S and SW from Av. Observatorio, or SW of Parque Lira on the other side of the Periférico, connect with the Camino de Sta Fe, once the Camino Real to Toluca. It leads through hilly suburbs to (c 4.5km) **Santa Fe**.

Here in 1532, in the hills above the capital where there were abundant springs, Vasco de Quiroga founded his first model Christian community, or hospital. Its first resident curate was the Augustinian Alonso de Borja, of the same family as Pope Alexander VI and St Francis Borgia.

On view today are the church called *Asunción*, probably a 17–18C building and heir to that of the original settlement. The adjoining priest's house occupies the site of the old open chapel. At 12 C. Gregorio López may be seen ruins of secular buildings.

17 Mexico City to Xochimilco

SE of Coyoacán and E of Tlalpan, Xochimilco may be reached most quickly from the Zócalo along Av. Pino Suárez and Calz. San Antonio Abad, continuing as Calz. de Tlalpan, which runs directly S through the E central part of the city across (8.5 km) Av. Río Churubusco and (10.25km) Av. Miguel Angel de Quevedo. Eventually, at 14.25km, it forms two branches: the l. (E) branch (Viaducto Tlalpan) joining (16.5km) the Anillo Periférico (Ruta de la Amistad). Just before this junction, Calz. México-Xochimilco (less hectic) branches l. and runs SE to Xochimilco, under the Periférico. At 19.5km a r. turn for Av. División del Norte, which runs SE to (24km) Xochimilco.

The metro goes from *Zócalo* to *Tasqueña* (terminus of line 2), whence a light railway and buses run (from the southern bus terminal) to the Xochimilco marketplace.

At 3.5km Calz. San Antonio Abad meets Viaducto Miguel Alemán (to the W) which continues E as Viaducto Piedad, along the line of the former Río de la Piedad.

Viaducto Piedad leads to (3.75km; l.) the *Velódromo Olímpico*, built for the cycling events of the 1968 Olympiad. On the r. is a turn-off for the **Pal. de los Deportes**, also built for the Olympic Games, result of a collaboration between Félix Candela, Enrique Castañeda Tamborrel, and Antonio Peirí.

A circular structure (c 4000 sq m of track space), its dazzlingly effective hemispheric dome is formed by a network of iron trusses divided into 121 squares. (The co-ordinates of horizontal parallels dominate the structure.) These are closed by warped, partly aluminium, networks, which give four hyperbolic paraboloids a square. These networks are finished in wood, covered with thin copper plates. The sculpted pillars on the SE side of its plaza are called Osa Mayor (Great Bear) and are by Matías Goeritz.

Divided from it by the broad Av. Río Churubusco is the vast **Ciudad Deportiva Magdalena Mixhuca** (c 3 sq km), incl. facilities for sports of all kinds (69 football pitches, 28 baseball pitches, etc), enlarged for the Olympics, and the *Autódromo Ricardo Rodríguez*.

Hence Av. Río Churubusco goes S into the delegación of IZTACALCO, one of the smaller, and poorer; rapidly populating and industrial. Its old centre is against Calz. de la Viga to the W, after Av. Río Churubusco crosses Av. Plutarco Elías Calles, a distance of c 2.25km. One of its few interests today, at the junction of Cs Juárez, San Matías, and Asunción, is the former convent of **San Matías**, founded in the 17C as a visita of San Francisco in Mexico City. The church is a late 18C reconstruction. In the sacristy is a painting in two parts of the Adoration of the Shepherds and Kings and the Slaughter of the Innocents, by Juan Correa.

Until well into the 20C, Iztacalco and its N neighbour, *Sta Anita*, were little villages, popular targets for trippers along the Canal de la Viga.

At 8.25km we may turn off Calz. Tlalpan to join Calz. Ermita Iztapalapa (Eje 8 Sur) which goes E to IZTAPALAPA, see Rte 15. After 2.5km it reaches MEXI-CALZINGO, now a colonia, before the Conquest a Colhuaque town. Its church of *San Marcos* (at No. 475), largely rebuilt in the 18C, started as part of a small visita (before 1580), dependent on the convent of San Francisco in the capital; its portería arcade survives.

In (10.75km; r.) C. Jacarandas is the church of *Sto Cristo de la Agonia de Limpias*, a hemisphere of blue azulejos, built in the 1950s to the design of Nicolás Mariscal Barroso.

C. Jacarandas runs into Av. División del Norte, off which, c 1km further SE, C. del Museo branches r. At 150 C. del Museo is the **Museo Anahuacalli de Diego Rivera** (Tues.–Sun., 10–5; fee).

The pyramidal building houses Rivera's large private collection (c 50,000 pieces according to one source) of prehistoric artefacts, and displays over 2000 pieces from Tlatilco, Teotihuacán, and Chupícuaro; from the Western Cultures of Colima, Nayarit, and Jalisco; from Huastec and Totonac sites of the Gulf Coast; from Puebla; and from Zapotec and Mixtec sites in the Valle de Oaxaca.

The museum complex, designed by Diego Rivera in 1944, was inspired by Toltec and Maya ceremonial centres. It is built of the local black volcanic stone, and comprises a three-storey, pyramid-like building in grey-black stone on the S side of a sunken volcanic stone plaza, and platform-like talud-tablero buildings on the other three sides. The N platform has a ball-court ring goal marker set into the wall; and the whole complex is surrounded by a volcanic stone wall, thus resembling an ancient sacred precinct.

The entry is flanked by stone sculptures, and the entry arch and other arches inside are Maya-like corbel shapes. In the entry hall, stone shelves protruding from the walls support more stone sculptures. The ceilings on the ground floor are white stone mosaics and the windows are onyx sheets; ceilings on the first and second floors are coloured stone mosaics.

GROUND FLOOR. ROOM 1 (l. of entry hall). Preclassic Morelos, Guanajuato, and Michoacán. Solid and hollow figurines, pottery vessels, and cylindrical stamps in cases; stone sculptures are displayed in niches resembling niches for idols in Mesoamerican sanctuaries. RR 2 and 3 (and smaller rooms at each end of R 3). R. of entry—more objects from Preclassic Morelos, Guanajuato, and Michoacán, incl. an altar display of stone sculptures representing deities and several examples of architectural decorative elements from the region. RR 4 and 5 (l. off the end of R 3). Classic Teotihuacán. A huge wall-photo shows the main ceremonial area; cases and stone shelves display pottery and clay figurines of Classic Teotihuacano forms and decorative techniques, much of which has been found throughout a wide area of central Mexico, and demonstrates the economic power of Teotihuacán. Teotihuacano stonework is illustrated by several stone sculptures of gods and priestly figures, and stone vessels. At the end of R 4, steps descend to a tomb-like room displaying a 'house of Tláloc'. R 5, off the end of R 4, contains more Teotihuacano materials: more wall-photos, figurines, moulds for figurines, and several braseros (braziers). At the end of the room, a smaller room has stone sculptures of Huehuetéotl, god of fire.

To ascend to the First Floor, go back through RR 5, 4, 3, and 2, turn r., then l. at the first landing. (It is also possible to go straight ahead from R 5, up a different set of steps, but directions here begin from the l.-hand turning on the landing.)

FIRST FLOOR. R 6. A large gallery containing Rivera sketches and studies, mounted high up on the walls. Cases display artefacts of Mesoamerican Western Cultures, incl. red, hollow clay figurines, solid figurines illustrating daily life, and an assortment of obsidian knives and stone architectural decorative elements; also a large papier-mâché model and huge photograph of Rivera at work. R 7 (turn r. from R 6). This and two small end rooms contain figurines and pottery from Chupícuaro (Preclassic and Classic site/tradition in S Guanajuato, contemporary with Teotihuacán I and II, c 400 BC to AD 300); also solid and hollow clay figurines and models from Nayarit, Colima, Jalisco, Michoacán, and Guerrero for comparison. R 8 (l. from R 7). More artefacts of the Western Cultures. R 9 (across top of stairs). In the centre stands a magnificent stone sculpture, probably of Huehuetéotl. Around him are more superlative examples of figurines from the Western Cultures and from NW central Mexico. R 10 (l. from R 9). This and two smaller rooms at each end display Postclassic materials from central Mesoamerica, especially a fine collection of polished stone artefacts from Guerrero: polished stone face plaques and masks, ceremonial axe-heads, stone heads and figurines, and a centrepiece of a seated figure with an especially expressive face.

To ascend to the Second Floor go back through RR 10 and 9, then r. up the stairs, then l.

SECOND FLOOR—open-air galleries/balconies. R 11 (r. at top of steps). Postclassic Aztec Guerrero. Cases of the finest Aztec pottery (polychromes and incised decorations), and numerous stone sculptures representing a variety of subjects from warriors to gods. R 12 (ahead and l.). Aztec Mexico, Puebla, and Veracruz. The variety and versatility of Aztec stone sculptors, incl. skulls, serpents, gods, various animals, and busts or heads wearing jaguar skins and helmets. Cases display more fine Aztec, and Puebla, polychrome pottery. R 13 (return through RR 12 and 11, and proceed across top of stairs). Postclassic Totonac artefacts from N Veracruz: clay figurines, most notably of expressive faces, and especially the wealth of carved stone hachas, palmas, and yugos so characteristic of Totonac sculpture.

These are connected with the ball game ritual, but scholarly opinion varies as to their exact uses. Hachas and palmas may have been ball court markers and field divisions, while the stone yugos may have been ceremonial examples of lighter, wood and leather, body protection for the ball players.

R 14 (ahead off R 13). A long room containing materials from the Central and S Mesoamerican Highlands: Zapotec Mixtec Classic and Postclassic Period items from S Puebla, Tlaxcala, Guerrero, and Oaxaca in cases; and large wall-photos of Mitla (Oaxaca) and El Tajín (Veracruz).

At the top of the building (stairs from R13), an open-air balcony has more Aztec stone sculptures on the floor and on stone shelves. Set into the floor are two stone disc mosaics of (?) the sun, stars, and planets. At the head of the stairs a volcanic stone disc sculpture is mounted on the wall.

At (14.25km) Calz. Tlalpan the r. fork leads to *Tlalpan*. After 1km we may turn off r. for the **Estadio Azteca** (1963), by Pedro Ramírez Vázquez, Rafael Mijares, and Luis Martínez del Campo—Mexico's most famous sports stadium, primarily for soccer, but also for night baseball games, boxing, polo, and tennis. Spectators are protected from the elements by a cantilevered roof. The sophisticated drainage system enables play to be resumed within a minute after a downpour.

We take the l. fork for (24km) **XOCHIMILCO**, whose enormous popularity as a canal resort undeservedly overshadows one of Mexico's finest historical monuments, the church and convent of San Bernardino.

Xochimilco ('place of the flower-growing') was traditionally settled in the 12C AD by the Xochimilca, one of the seven legendary Aztec tribes. However, archaeological evidence shows that the general Chalco–Xochimilco region had been settled with villages much earlier, perhaps deliberate colonization by Teotihuacán in the Classic Period. Toltecs, too, following the upheavals of civil war, were said to have settled here. In the second half of the 15C the city became a tributary of the Mexica Aztecs under Axayácatl (1468–81) and a provincial centre.

To the Aztecs, this area was a vital source of agricultural produce, grown on chinampas, covering an estimated 10,000ha (25,000 acres). Cortés and his men set fire to many of the chinampas of Xochimilco during the siege of Tenochtitlán in order to diminish Aztec supplies.

The Xochimilca were also known for their stonework. Using imported pebbles of rock crystal, turquoise, opal, amethyst, and jadeite they worked vessels and jewellery into shape with flint adzes and copper tools. Tubular bits of copper and bird bones were used with sand and water as drills, and the finished products were highly polished with sand, finer abrasives, and finally with reed fibres. Their principal deity was Chantico ('fire in the house'), goddess of the home fire, or hearth, and patroness of goldworkers and metalsmiths in general. Her feast day was Nine Itzcuintli, the ninth day of the tenth Aztec month.

In Apr. 1521 Cortés ordered its destruction ('truly a sorrowful sight', he wrote) and the site was assigned to Pedro de Alvarado. It continued its pre-Conquest practice of supplying the capital with flowers, fruit, and vegetables. In the 18C it was still predominantly Indian, as it is today. It is the chief place of its delegación, which is wooded and mountainous in its S parts, and still mainly agricultural. The canals are the remains of the large fresh-water Lago de Xochimilco, in ancient times one with the Lago de Chalco (dried up by the late 19C) to the E, later separated from it by a dike. Water from both lakes flowed into the Lago de Texcoco.

On the E side of the vast main plaza (especially crowded at weekends) rise the imposing church and former convent of **San Bernardino**, one of the earliest Franciscan foundations in New Spain.

Fray Martín de Valencia encouraged the convent's foundation in 1525. Building proceeded in 1535–51 and from 1583 until the 1590s. Changes were made in the late 17C and early 18C. On one day during their early ministry, it is said, two friars baptized 15,000 Indians in the atrio, but had to desist when their overworked arm muscles could manage no more.

The ATRIO, entered through a double-arched gateway, has retained most of its original vastness (c 27,000 sq m). EXTERIOR. The main (W) door is singularly designed: rudimentary Corinthian columns, a round arch dotted with cherub heads pushing into the architrave, and above, an elegantly framed window supported by angel volutes, crude, unfinished, but effective, by an Indian hand. The frieze bears the date 1590; above the window, on the stone beneath the cherub chin, the date 1682; on the frieze below the cornice, 1716. The N doorway, almost medieval, but with plateresque detail, bears vivacious relief. The almost squared arch, stiffened by the Franciscan cord; the ribbon motif wrapping the line of the arched moulding in the alfíz above; the attenuated columns resting on unsuitable bases; the quirky niches on top of one another. Buttresses and merlons (with pearl motif tips) contrast with 18C cupola and tower.

The INTERIOR is remarkable for its wide single nave (21m). (The recesses along N and S walls to accommodate side altars are additions of c 1700.) It contains the finest Renaissance high altarpiece in Mexico (late 16C; restored in the 1960s and re-covered in gold leaf), a meticulously planned combination of rich estofado; polychrome sculptures, spiritual and dignified; superb reliefs; and luminous paintings. In the predella, busts of apostles, signifying the basis of Christianity. Lowest storey, upheld by doric columns supporting triangular pediments, from l.: SS Ambrose, Gregory, Jerome, Augustine. 1st storey, with ionic columns and broken pediments, from l.: SS Louis of Toulouse, Francis, Dominic, Antony of Padua. 2nd storey, with Corinthian columns and curved pediments, from l.: SS Lawrence, Michael, John the Baptist, Stephen. Top storey, SS Catherine of Alexandria and Clare.

The columns in their lowest thirds are ornamented with charming heads and foliage, the upper two-thirds fluted. Lowest storey, bishops and doctors of the Church; 1st storey, friars; 2nd storey, virgins; top storey, figures holding musical instruments. Note also the atlante figures flanking the central panel.

The central relief, of St Bernardine, is very fine. Under his cape he shelters various personages, incl. a man in gorget and mantle and a woman dressed Indian style, possibly the donors. Above, an exquisite Virgin, still and prayerful, the folds of her gown wonderfully done. In the gable, God the Father with Faith and Hope in the volutes.

The paintings, strongly attr. Baltasar de Echave Orio, are: lowest storey, Annunciation and Adoration of the Shepherds; 1st storey, Circumcision and Adoration of the Kings; 2nd storey, Resurrection and Pentecost; top storey, Ascension and Assumption; flanking the gable, SS Mary Magdalen and Mary the Egyptian.

The side altarpieces are an extraordinarily rich collection in styles from Renaissance to churrigueresque. Nearest the entrance on the N wall is a fine Mannerist example, with slender columns, a type echoed by the next but one, richer, and already showing a transition between Mannerism and baroque. Between them is an unusual baroque specimen, the columns divided into solomonic lower thirds and wavily fluted upper parts. On the S wall are two superb late baroque retables (early 18C), their supports disintegrating into twirls of luscious relief. The second from the entrance, churrigueresque, dates from 1792. Another late baroque relic is what remains of the beautifully carved choirstalls, the back supports separating the seats composed of the same type of rich relief as on the altarpieces.

From the r. side of the high altar is reached the handsome two-storey cloister, finished after 1590 (restored).

At the corner of Cs Morelos and Madero, facing the market, is the *Cap. del Rosario* (probably 18C), its façade a striking mixture of delicate ajaraca relief and blue and yellow azulejos.

The canals N and E of the town are Mexico City's favourite pleasure and picnic resort, especially animated on Sun. The main embarkation point (*Embarcadero Natívitas*) is on the E of the town (reached down C. Nuevo León; haphazard signposting). The highly decorated roofed punts (trajineras), poled by locals, may be hired for c 1½–2 hrs. (Better to join a party, for the cost is high. Hard bargaining essential. Ensure that time paid for is fully discharged.) At weekends mariachi bands add to the excitement, but several playing at once can send up a cacophony. The punts wind round the chiampas, incorrigibly, but understandably, still referred to as 'jardines flotantes'. They have now taken root in the shallow (getting shallower and more polluted) waters and have formed a pattern of islands.

From Xochimilco may be visited various villages further into the delegación, and the still rural neighbouring delegaciones of TLAHUAC and MILPA ALTA to the E and S, the latter incl. the E extension of the *Serranía de Ajusco*, with its parallel series of volcanic peaks, which straddles the Federal District and the State of Morelos.

We leave Xochimilco SW along Camino Natívitas. The road skirts the cone of Teuhtli (c 3000m). 2km *Natívitas Zacapa*, where a 16C stone cross shows a date in pre-Conquest glyphs. 6km *San Gregorio Atlapulco*, with a church and small convent (c 1600, partly rebuilt), originally a visita of Xochimilco. 11km *Tulyehualco*. 17km *San Antonio Tecomitl*, with another small former Franciscan convent, finished by 1581. Its small cloister, built of lava blocks, was repaired in 1846. The five-bay portería on the W side was probably added later as an open chapel to serve a large Indian congregation. 4km E is **Mixquic**, once an Aztec provincial city state, founded in the 13C, where the large church and ruined convent of *San Andrés* are an Augustinian foundation of c 1536, built on a prehispanic base, with liberal use of pre-Conquest materials. The church façade is dated 1620; the portería has been rebuilt (good cut-stone). 22km **Milpa Alta**, chief place of the delegacíon, with a well-known market. The Franciscan convent of *La Asunción* here was established probably in the 1530s and rebuilt in the 17C. In the church, the beautiful polychrome central panel of the original late 16C high altarpiece miraculously remains, though subjected to unfeeling restoration. Enough remains, however, for us to admire: Our Lady, surrounded by the Holy Trinity, saints, and a joyous angel choir and band—lutes, horns, pipes. Two angels engagingly follow their parts in the score with their fingers. The picturesque cloister has notable side arches resting on sturdy short columns. 26km *San Pedro Atocpan*, with the church and former convent of San Pedro Apóstol, another late 16C visita of Xochimilco. The church was rebuilt in 1660–69, but fragments of the original wooden ceiling survive. In the barrio of Misericordias the chapel of Señor de las Misericordias dates from 1560. 30km *Oztotepec* (views of volcanoes Acopiaxco and Tláloc), once also a visita of Xochimilco, to which the 17C church and little ruined convent, with a portería chapel, bear witness. The road winds W and N to (47km) *Santiago*, SW of Xochimilco.

18 Mexico City to Teotihuacán

Méx. 85 and 85D, 48km.—5km turning for **Tenayuca**.—35km Tepexpan.— 21km Ecatepec.—38km **Acolman**.—48km **Teotihuacán**.

We leave the city on Av. Insurgentes. Beyond (4.5km) the junction with Av. Río Consulado and the Monumento a la Raza, Av. Insurgentes meets another junction, from which the Eje Central (continuation of Av. Lázaro Cárdenas) runs NW to (6km) *Tenayuca*.

TENAYUCA ('walled city'; open daylight hours; fee), or at least the general district, was probably inhabited as early as the Late Preclassic Period. During the domination of the Basin of Mexico by Teotihuacán, Tenayuca, Tlacopan, Cuauhtitlán, and Temascalapa were outlying settlements of prosperous rural farming communities, with their own small ceremonial centres.

After the demise of Teotihuacán in the 7C AD an estimated 20,000 people continued to inhabit the Tenayuca-Cuauhtitlán area. As a city-state on the NW shore of Lago de Texcoco, Tenayuca received new influxes of migrating Chichimecas, led by Xólotl, in the mid- to late-12C AD after the fall of Tula. In some versions of the story of the fall of Tula, Topiltzin Quetzalcóatl, having been ousted from Tula, came S to Tenayuca before moving on to Culhuacán, where he died. According to other sources Xólotl, or his second successor, Quinatzin, moved the seat of government from Tenayuca to Texcoco c AD 1200 or a little later.
 Tenayuca was captured by the Tepaneca of Azcapotzalco in 1371, and later by the Mexica Aztecs of Tenochtitlán, as part of that city's share of the spoils after the defeat of Azcapotzalco c 1428. Tenayuca remained an important provincial city and tributary of Tenochtitlán, and was linked to Tlatelolco by a causeway across the lake.
 The site was excavated by José Reygadas Vértiz, Alfonso Caso, and Eduardo Noguera in 1925–28 and by Ignacio Marquina and Jorge Acosta in 1935. Further excavations and restorations were done in 1980 by INAH.

The main feature at Tenayuca is its **Pirámide**, presumably the dominant structure of the city's ceremonial centre.

It was rebuilt seven times, possibly at 52-year intervals to commemorate the close of calendrical cycles (ie, in AD 1143, 1195, 1247, 1299, 1351, 1403, 1455, and 1507). The final pyramid, that most prominently seen today, must have been closely similar to, perhaps even provided a model for, the Templo Mayor at Tenochtitlán. The excavations of 1925–28 were done by means of tunnels, cut into the core of the structure, beginning behind the great stairway, and revealing the superimposed stairways and facings of each of the earlier pyramids. These tunnels are now lit to enable the visitor to see the various phases of construction.
 The first pyramid was a large man-made platform, possibly incl. rows of stone coatepantli (serpents) around three sides at the base, and presumably supporting a temple. The second pyramid was larger, having incorporated the earlier platform, and rectangular (c 30m N–S and c 12m E–W). It was built largely of adobe and was c 7.5m high in four recessed tiers, each with a vertical face. A ramp c 27m wide led up the W side to the top, and was divided into two stairways, each leading to a temple, probably built of wood. This established the format and principle of a double staircase and two temples, followed by all subsequent constructions.
 The third pyramid was also rectangular (34m N–S by 18m E–W). It had a double stairway, 30m wide, and its entire orientation was shifted slightly to 17 degrees N of the setting sun, such that the sun would appear exactly opposite the pyramid on the day of its zenith, an

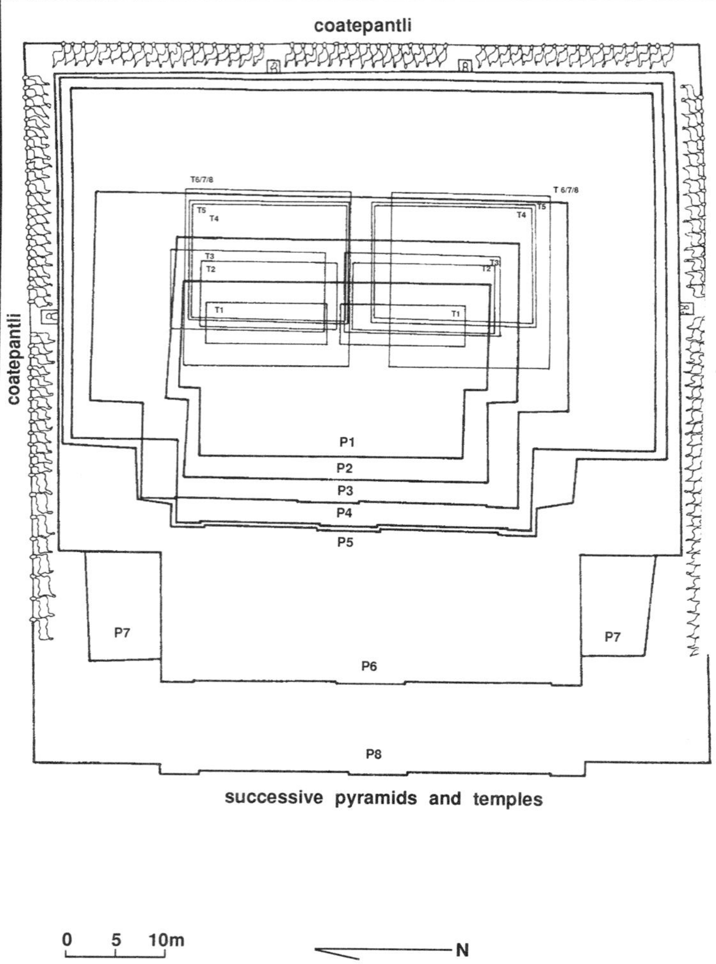

coatepantli

coatepantli

coatepantli

T6/7/8

T 6/7/8

T5
T4

T5
T4

T3
T2

T3
T2

T1

T1

P1

P2

P3

P4

P5

P7

P7

P6

P8

successive pyramids and temples

0   5   10m

N

TENAYUCA, México, D.F.

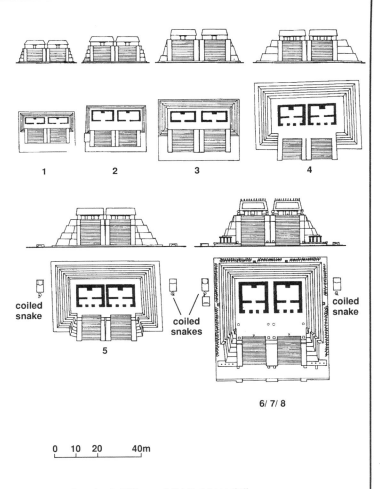

1   2   3   4

coiled snake

coiled snakes

coiled snake

5

6/ 7/ 8

0   10   20   40m

temples to Tláloc and (?) Huizilopochtli

orientation that prevailed thereafter. The fourth pyramid was still a basic rectangle (now 49m N–S by 22m E–W), with a 38m-wide double staircase, between, and divided by, massive ramps. The walls of each tier were built to incline and the overall height had reached c 12m. The fifth pyramid was a further enlargement to 58m N–S and 38m E–W at the base, with a 36m-wide double staircase. The sides of the tiers were steepened to provide a larger area at the summit for the two temples.

The sixth pyramid shows signs of Aztec workmanship, and was an enlargement to 61m N–S by 40m E–W, by 16m high. It had the usual double staircase, now 40m wide, and was found in good condition by the excavators. These stairs, after the Aztec fashion, had two inclines, the upper one nearly vertical. Buttresses were used for the first time to support the stairway in the angles between the tiers of the pyramid, thus ending the simple rectangular plan. Every fourth step of the first 50 steps was decorated with reliefs, and covered with brightly coloured stucco. Some of these reliefs may in fact have originally belonged to the fifth pyramid; they represent various symbols, incl. jade discs, belt-pins, and pendants. Two altars on the N and S sides of the top were probably of the same phase, and added to the usual twin temples.

The seventh pyramid, and remains of an eighth pyramid, were the final enlargements, to 62m N–S by 50m E–W, and 16m high; the double staircase, however, remained at 40m wide. This stairway was of two phases, the upper portion having been built along with the seventh pyramid, and the lower portion with the eighth pyramid (in other words each phase made use of part of the previous pyramid's staircase), and terminates in two carved serpent heads at the base. Around three sides of the final pyramid, but possibly associated with the original platform, is a wall of coatepantli.

Line of serpents' heads, Tenayuca

The idea of the serpent wall to surround the sacred ceremonial precinct seems to have been of Toltec origin, and the wall at Tenayuca may in fact have been inspired by the Toltecs, and in turn inspired, along with the rest of the dual pyramid design, the Aztec coatepantli at the Templo Mayor. There are 43 serpents on the N side (or 51 if the final last eight are included, which are double-headed), 50 on the E side, and 45 on the S side. They are made of volcanic stone, and were originally painted: blue on the S, black on the N and E. No two are exactly alike, even in general size.

The two temples at the top of the final constructions were dedicated to Tláloc (god of rain) and possibly to Huitzilopochtli (god of the sun and of war, and the special tribal god of the Mexica Aztecs). The walls of the final pyramid were faced with uncut stone, and the sides originally rendered smooth with painted stucco.

N and S of the pyramid are two small platforms, each supporting a coiled snake sculpture, whose crests are said to be symbolic of the equinoxes and solstices. On the W side there is a small grave on the pyramid platform, decorated in low relief by skulls and crossed bones, said to symbolize the sun. Inside the tomb, similar motifs are painted on the walls (keys with site caretaker).

A small site museum has a few displays of some early projectile points, pottery and figurines, and stone sculptures, incl. some of the missing serpent heads from the site and general vicinity. A tzompantli from the site is now in the Museo Nacional de Antropología.

The reconstructed 'Aztec' style pyramid at **Sta Cecilia Acatitlán** (reconstructed by Eduardo Pareyón and Angelina Macías) is 3km N by the Tlalnepantla road. This is a small pyramid of four recessed tiers, with a staircase, almost as wide as the pyramid itself, on the W side. Braziers flank the staircase at the top. A small temple has also been reconstructed, on the top, with an altar stone in front of the doorway. Inside there is a broken chacmool figure (one theory of its use was to hold the sacrificial, and no doubt still quivering, heart of a victim); and on a bench along the rear of the chamber, a broken statue of a god, possibly Tláloc. The original pyramid of Acatitlán may in fact have had twin temples, or at least twin shrines. It was dismantled by the Spaniards and the stone used in the nearby church.

A small museum in a 19C house shows dining room and kitchen set in contemporary displays; a tinacal, where pulque was fermented from the juice of the maguey; and two other rooms have displays of Aztec braziers, stone sculptures of the gods of maize, water, and wind, clay figurines and some zoomorphic vessels, and a display of the physical anthropology of the inhabitants of the area in the Aztec period, the last consisting of bones from a tzompantli. A small garden and patio have more Aztec sculptures and reliefs from architectural fragments.

Av. Insurgentes continues NE passing (8km; r.) the Basilica de Guadalupe. 9.5km the *Indios Verdes*, two monumental bronze statues by Alejandro Casarín (1889), originally at the entrance to Paseo de la Reforma. At 11.5km we cross into the State of México. At 12km Av. Insurgentes N crosses the Anillo Periférico. At 14km (r.) alternative (free) road 85 to Teotihuacán, which runs near the *Canal de Desagüe* and the *Caracol*, which produces salt by evaporation. Between the two roads is the colonia of *Sta Clara* (the former barrio of *Sta Clara Coatitla*), where still stands the portería arcade of a 16C Franciscan visita of Ecatepec. We continue on toll road 85D. At (21km) *Ecatepec*, now an industrial suburb on the edge of the Sierra de Guadalupe, is the 18C Casa de los Virreyes, reserved for the use of incoming and outgoing viceroys. Here on 22 Dec. 1815 José María Morelos was shot. The church of the neighbouring barrio of *Sta María Tulpetlac*, to the S, preserves its 16C doorway—arch, imposts, jambs, and alfíz covered in exquisite, if haphazard, tequitqui carving. At 24km we bear r., leaving (l.) the toll road to *Pachuca*, see Rte 62. The toll road to Teotihuacán skirts the N side of the Lago de Texcoco. 27km *Sta María Chiconautla*. The church here, a former Augustinian parish, dates from the 16C, but with later alterations. The atrial cross shows good carving.

Here, when a less stately Texcocan residence (cf. *Texcoco*) was excavated, several small patios were surrounded by porch-like antechambers, column roof-supports, and small inner rooms on either side of a larger courtyard. Such courtyard apartment residences were traditional in central Mexico at least as far back as Teotihuacán.

At 35km a r. turn leads to **Tepexpan** where a small museum displays the fossil finds of mammoths and replicas of the early human remains found here and in the general area in the 1940s and 1950s, incl. the bones of the 'Hombre de Tepexpan'.

This region was formerly on the NE shores of Lago de Texcoco. It was a marshy area, which gradually dried up as the lake shore receded, leaving a deposit of saltpetre (or laterite), known as the Becerra Formation, divided by geologists into upper and lower strata. On 22 Feb. 1947, Helmut de Terra, using a mine detector, discovered the remains of a human skeleton, promptly named 'Tepexpan Man' after the fashion of fossil hunters of the time. It was located in the Upper Becerra, corresponding to a drought period c 10,000 years ago. However, the techniques used to extract it from the ground, and the circumstances of its discovery, left much to be desired, and the fossil's age status was questioned at the time. There were no associated stone tools.

But in 1952, and again in 1959, this ancient date was confirmed when most of the skeletons of two imperial mammoths, *Mammuthus imperator*, and associated stone tools, were found on a 'kill site' at *Sta Isabel Iztapan*, c 2.5km S of Tepexpan. The tools included obsidian side-scrapers, part of a bi-facial knife, prismatic knives, flint blades, and three projectile points resembling points from the Great Plains region of the USA. Tests of the fluorine content of both the mammoth bones and the human skeleton from Tepexpan showed them to be contemporary (c 7700–7300 BC), making them some of the oldest known human remains in Mesoamerica. The 'Tepexpan Man', however, has actually proved to be a woman, 25–30 years old. Her morphological features are well within present-day parameters in Mexico (she was c 1.6m tall): dressed in skirt, blouse, and rebozo she could presumably catch the bus from Teotihuacán to Mexico without undue notice.

In the village centre (c 1km E) is the former Augustinian convent and church of *Magdalena*, founded in the 16C as a visita of Acolman. In the atrio are preserved three barrel-vaulted posa chapels; a large portería is also of interest.

38km (0.5km l.) **ACOLMAN**, an attractive pueblo, dominated by the former Augustinian church and convent of **San Agustín** (daily, 10–7; closed Thurs.; fee), a prototype in that Order's ambitious building campaign.

The Náhuatl name *Acolman* has a varied etymology. Its prehistoric name-glyph is a shoulder, arm, and hand—'translated' as 'shoulder and hand' or 'shoulder with arm'—plus the water symbol, and thus interpreted as 'place where the waters swirl'. Alternatively, the Náhuatl words acolli and mani, meaning 'big, or broadshouldered man' and 'to be or exist', are taken to support the local legend that the site refers to 'where giants were'—ie, nearby Teotihuacán, whose first pyramids were believed to have been built by a former race of giants (see below). The discovery of mastodon bones at Tepexpan and Sta Isabel Iztapan have also fostered this belief among the locals. A second legend, recorded by Fray Andrés de Olmos in Texcoco, refers to the Sun shooting an arrow into the earth; from the hole where it struck emerged the first man, who had only a head, shoulders and arms—in Náhuatl, acumaitl—'shoulder with hand'.

In the Late Postclassic, Acolman was a minor city-state allied with Tepanec Azcapotzalco. When Azcapotzalco fell to the Tenochtitlán–Texcoco–Tlacopan alliance in 1428, Acolman was also captured, and required to pay Texcoco an annual tribute of henequen mantles, huipiles, and a labour levy. Acolman's chief god was Texcatlipoca (Creator god) and a temple to him, together with a circular temple to Quetzalcóatl, existed in the town until 1580. Foundations of both temples were found during excavations in the 1920s.

The original Franciscan mission here was taken over by the Augustinians in 1539. Built on a prehispanic base, the present church was still under construction when the convent was finished in 1571. It is recorded that the Indians did not resent their labour in this great work, but complained bitterly about the additional demands made on them by local encomenderos. Floods caused by the building of a nearby dam caused considerable damage in the early 18C, and in 1735 the church was reconstructed. In 1754 the friars were dispossessed and secular priests took charge.

The mysterious stone atrial Cross (now moved beyond the W entrance to the atrio) was inspired by various European sources. The clumsy shaft relief of symbols of the Passion and the stylized hands show its Indian workmanship; but the head of Christ, Renaissance in style, is nobly done. The relief of Our Lady in the base is more primitive and may be a later work. Note the sun and moon: a blend of European religion and astrology, but with Indian associations too. The solitary posa N of the church is a rebuilding. The ATRIO's present aspect of descending terraces is a result of work carried out from 1920, to rescue the monument, then lying in 2m of mud and silt, the consequence of 18C flooding.

EXTERIOR. The W façade, completed in 1560, an expert balancing of the decorative part (once gilded) and the plain surface, is the purest example of plateresque in Mexico, the work of European craftsmen. The portal, with its double archivolt, is framed by two pairs of baluster columns, tastefully ornamented, resting on angel pedestals. Beyond the cornice the outer end in torch finials, the inner in giants holding baskets of fruit on their heads. Statues of SS Peter and Paul, in richly crowned niches, stand between the columns. Frieze, spandrels, jambs, and pediment niches are filled by more relief and sculpture in the round. Particularly engaging are the plates of fruit and pigs' trotters in the arch soffits, and on the face of the inner one, and the chain of fruit on the outer; and the frieze of horses with rumps ending in flowers, alternating with lion and angel heads. In the gable above the arch a now headless figure in a shell niche is flanked by angel musicians. In the spandrels is an Annunciation. The main design is echoed in the elegant window above. On either side, shields containing the imperial coat of arms (l.) and Acolman's name glyph (r.). A modest espadaña surmounts all. The parapet is topped by abundant decorative merlons. The irregular buttressing is a reinforcement of 1735.

INTERIOR. The rib-vaulting of the nave culminates in the form of a star (1558) in the dome of the sanctuary. Remains of the sanctuary murals, in red, ochre, and black, painted c 1580, show rows of saints, popes, bishops, and cardinals on massive thrones, divided by wide friezes; sibyls and male nudes complete the decoration. The interior pilasters date from the 18C works. The high altarpiece (c 1690) is a 20C acquisition. Two side altarpieces (baroque l.; churrigueresque r.) remain in the nave, as do two 16C stone fonts.

To the r. (S) of the church is a raised, cramped open chapel, its rudimentary arch enclosed in a plain alfíz, and the five-bay portería, where traces of original murals survive. Over the entrance to the inner room, a relief of the Augustinian emblem—a heart pierced by arrows beneath a wide-brimmed hat, from which issue tasselled cords to form a kind of strapwork surrounding the heart. The same design is repeated eight times around the central circle. To the r. is the kitchen, with an enormous hearth and a service area on its E (r.) side, to which supplies were brought by way of the atrio. On the NW (l.) side, the larder; on the N (straight ahead), the pantry, beyond which is the long refectory, on the E side of the main cloister, with a painted coffered vault and a pulpit from which a friar read aloud to his brethren while they ate. From here we gain the beautiful large cloister (restored), offering a contrast between its lower and upper storeys. The lower, two arches for every three above, without archivolts, is finely Renaissance in conception: the ball motifs surrounding the capitals an Isabeline-Gothic touch. The adventurous decoration of the upper-storey capitals is Indian work.

Off the N side of the lower walk open out three rooms, the central called the *Chocolatero*, where chocolate is supposed to have been drunk. On its l. (W) is the antesacristy, with an elaborate old chest of drawers for vestments, which gives on to the sacristy. The monumental stairway on the W side of the cloister takes us up to the upper walk. Among frescoes which decorate the walls (by a European hand, or an Indian under European supervision) is a serene, italianate Crucifixion, figures and clothing well delineated, with remarkable background detail. At right-angles to it is a Last Judgement, with a fierce representation of the suffering of the damned. The friezes above, and the enframing pilasters and pillars, are emphatically Renaissance. On the N and E sides are the friars' cells. The rooms on the W and S sides, the corridor on the N side of the smaller cloister, and the other rooms leading off it contain various 17–18C paintings and prehispanic objects found on the site. On the S side of the main cloister lower walk is the *Sala de Profundis* (chapter hall), on the W side of which a room leads to the smaller cloister, probably the earliest part to be built (c 1540), primitive with its rubble masonry, the arches not especially defined, and reinforced by trapezoidal buttressing.

From (47km) *San Lorenzo Tlalmimilopan* a road branches l. (N) to (2km) *San Juan Teotihuacán*, with the former Franciscan convent of San Juan Evangelista.

In 1557 the Augustinians started to build the convent here much against the wishes of the local Indians who downed tools and revolted, decamping from the site until their favourite Franciscans were allowed to take over.

The simple church, altered and added to in later centuries, and convent were regarded by the Franciscans as a model for their later establishments.

At 48km we keep straight ahead for **TEOTIHUACAN**, perhaps the most important and famous archaeological zone in Mexico. It is archaeologically important as one of the largest and most powerful ancient cities in Mesoamerica, and in the ancient world. It was one of the first true cities in the New World, with a large residential population pursuing numerous specialized professions as well as agricultural production; and with all the monumental architecture, and political, religious, and economic functions associated with the term 'city'. The extent of Teotihuacán's economic control, long-distance trade networks, and prospecting efforts for raw materials remained unequalled by a single city until the advent of the Aztecs and Tenochtitlán. Its proximity to Mexico City, the vastness of the entire archaeological zone, and the resources put into its preservation and reconstruction make it the most visited archaeological zone in Mexico.

Teotihuacán is an immense and complex site (see the plan on pages 300–301). While it is extremely interesting and impressive, it can also be overwhelming and exhausting, especially on a first visit in the hot Mexican sunshine. It is difficult to be too enthusiastic about such a tremendous monument to man's past, and more than one visit is strongly recommended.

Admission 8–5 (but you have until 6 to leave the site); fee. Light and Sound shows from Oct. to May, evenings Tues.–Sun. (in English—7–7.45; in Spanish—8.15–9); separate fee. Tours information obtainable in most hotels.

The following guide to the principal monuments begins at the Unidad Cultural. It proceeds around the Ciudadela at the S end of the Calle de los Muertos, progresses along the Calle visiting various monuments along it, incl. the Pirámide del Sol and Pirámide de la Luna (at the N end), and finally directs the visitor to various ruins on the perimeters of the ceremonial centre of the ancient city. (Some visitors may wish to enter at different car-parks, or may wish to go directly to the pyramids first, in order to climb them before the sun rises too high.) Finally, we return to the Unidad Cultural to visit the museum.

The Ancient City. Teotihuacán was a city planner's dream; and it is one of the few ancient cities anywhere in the world to have been completely mapped. By the height of its development, in the 6–7C AD, it covered some 22.5 sq km and had an estimated population of up to 200,000, amounting to between 80 and 90 per cent of the entire population of the E Basin of Mexico. In c AD 600 Teotihuacán was the sixth largest city in the world.

In the NE of the Basin, the spur Valle de Teotihuacán is tucked between the Patlachique range on the S and an extinct volcano, Cerro Gordo, on the N. To the E, the gradually rising valley reaches a low ridge beyond which is the shallow basin of the Llanos de Apan. Through the valley runs the Río San Juan, around which the ancient city was built. In addition, water is provided by four springs near the core of the city: three aligned NW, W, and SW of the Pirámide de la Luna, and one c 600m E of the Ciudadela compound. Nearly a dozen more have been located in other parts of the ancient city.

The city was laid out in a regulated grid plan, around two long, intersecting avenues: N–S (Calle de los Muertos) and E–W. There were two huge pyramids and more than 100 smaller temples and shrines along them, and huge compounds at their intersection, of which only the Ciudadela is well preserved. On the periphery of this ceremonial core there stood the grand palace-like residences of the priests and other élite members of Teotihuacano society. Stretching in all directions around these were thousands of smaller streets and alleys, lined in planned precision, with residential apartment complexes arrayed around central patios, with sub-floor drainage conduits and separate rooms for sleeping quarters, halls, kitchens, work areas, and small private shrines. More than 2000 of these apartments have been identified, each for a multi-family group. Various areas of the city have been recognized, by the associated pottery and other artefacts, and by the unfinished or waste materials of manufacture, as barrios for different professions: basalt workers, obsidian workers, shell workers, slate workers, potters, jewellers, plaster painters, and even a barrio occupied by foreign merchants (Barrio de Oaxaqueños from Monte Albán, c 3.5km W of the ceremonial core of the city). More than 500 such workshops have been identified and an estimated 25 per cent of the population were full-time non-agricultural specialists.

The ancient name is unknown. The name Teotihuacán is Náhuatl for 'city of the gods'. Although the site's main period of occupation and development was from c 100 BC to c AD 750, a small population lingered on in the Postclassic Period, and the Aztecs considered the site a sacred spot. To them, it had been built by an assembly of gods or giants at the beginning of the 'Fifth Sun', which was born when the god Nanahuatzin, poor and syphilitic, jumped into the sacrificial fires to reappear as the Sun, and his rich and healthy twin, Tecciztécatl, followed, to reappear as the Moon. The Aztecs themselves built a few structures to their own gods in the Ciudadela compound, covering the sculpted decoration of the Templo de Quetzalcóatl (and thus preserving it; see below). According to native chronicles collected by Bernardino de Sahagún in the 16C, the Aztecs also believed that the site was an ancient place for proclaiming kings, and that the earth-covered and overgrown mounds they could see lining the main street were their burial places. (Aztec kings themselves were cremated before statues of Huitzilopochtli [one of whose antecedents was none other than Nanahuatzin] and the ashes buried in the Teocalli at Tenochtitlán.) Such was the sacredness of Teotihuacán that Moctezuma II Xocoyotzin (1502–20), accompanied by his priests and nobles, offered frequent sacrifices there. Cortés himself passed through the ruins after the Noche Triste, but otherwise paid little attention to them.

By that time the ancient structures were well dilapidated and buried (even the Pirámide del Sol) under large earthen mounds of accumulated rubble. In its glory, however, the effect of

Teotihuacán was grand and monumental. Not only was its planned regularity maintained throughout its history, but from its foundation its orientation was set when the Pirámide del Sol was aligned to coincide with the Sun when it passed through its zenith. Large parts of the structures have had to be reconstructed, but great care has been taken to use the same materials and the architectural techniques of the Teotihuacanos have been faithfully followed. It is important to remember, too, that in spite of the general greyness of the monuments today, in ancient times they were stucco plastered and garishly painted in black, white, red, blue, green, and yellow.

Equally important is the city's lack of overt defences, although Teotihuacán was not without rivals; and paintings on the walls of élite houses depict no great scenes of battle or violence, nor of sacrificial rituals, in contrast to many other sites in Mesoamerica, some of them contemporary. On the other hand, close examination of the figurines and carved reliefs, paintings, and other artefacts does reveal a certain trend away from pure religious symbolism towards militaristic themes in the *Xololpan* (c AD 450–650) and *Metepec* (c AD 650–750) phases (see below). There are certainly numerous small artefacts, both excavated and depicted in murals, such as obsidian knives, axes, harpoons, spear-throwers, slings, and arrow tips, which could equally be hunting tools or weapons of war. A priestly figure in the mural of the Tepantitla complex holds a bunch of arrows and a tiger claw, and drops falling from knives in several scenes have been variously interpreted as water or blood. Figurines from these late phases depict helmets, shields, and perhaps padded cotton armour; and a figure on a pot lid shows a warrior with shield and spear-thrower. The great compound of the Ciudadela, although a sacred precinct, could have been used as a formidable redoubt if necessary. Thus, while not all scholars entertain the idea of a Teotihuacano political empire, it seems clear that Teotihuacanos were prepared to defend themselves and their economic interests when necessary; and that the later centuries of the Classic Period provide some evidence for the tensions that led to more militaristic pursuits in the Postclassic.

What we visit today is only the ceremonial core of the ancient city—the plazas, pyramids, temples, and élite residences—the public and fashionable buildings of 'downtown' Teotihuacán. In doing so we must bear in mind the teeming masses of its ancient population, the labour force that built this magnificent metropolis.

Excavations and Survey Projects. The first actual recorded excavation at Teotihuacán was undertaken by the priest and antiquarian Carlos Sigüenza y Góngora in 1675, when he dug a tunnel into either the Pirámide del Sol or the Pirámide de la Luna (which is disputed). The first official exploration of Teotihuacán was done in 1864 by Ramón Almaraz. His survey and small test excavations resulted in the first plan of the centre of the ancient site. More extensive excavations were carried out by Leopoldo Batres in 1884–86, and also briefly by Désiré Charnay in 1885, after he had excavated at Tula.

The long record of Mexican federal interest in the site, and its regulation of explorations, began in 1905–10, when excavations were again directed by Batres. His excavation techniques were, however, not as regular as might have been wished, even by the standards of the time, and several doubtful reconstructions resulted, as well as damage to several structures. More federally sponsored excavations were carried out by Manuel Gamio between 1917 and 1922, as part of his monumental study of the ancient and modern Valle de Teotihuacán; and these were followed by Ignacio Marquina's study of the ancient city plan. Gamio undertook excavations on the Pirámide del Sol, the Ciudadela, and the Templo de Quetzalcóatl. Less extensive excavations were undertaken in 1932–35 by S. Linné, and the excavation of Grupo I (Viking Group) was done by Eduardo Noguera and Pedro Armillas during 1942–45.

Between 1945 and 1960 several of the peripheral, élite residences were discovered and excavated, incl. the discoveries by Carlos Margain and Rafael Orellano of the murals of Tepantitla and Atetelco. Laurette Séjourné de Orfila discovered more murals at Zacuela and Yayahuala, other residential compounds; and in 1960 Jorge Acosta undertook exploration, excavation, and reconstruction of the plaza in front of the Pirámide de la Luna.

In 1962 INAH initiated the grand Proyecto Teotihuacán under the direction of Ignacio Bernal. Its aim was to complete the preservation and reconstruction of the ceremonial core of the ancient city at its most impressive, c AD 700, incl. the plazas of the two main pyramids, the main avenue, and numerous palaces and smaller temples; plus the construction of the public facilities and museum. This project was completed officially in Sept. 1964 and the site as we know it today was opened to the public. In 1971, careful explorations around the base of the Pirámide del Sol uncovered a shaft with cut steps leading down to a natural tunnel and chambers, near the subterranean centre of the pyramid. Even though of no great architectural monumentality, these indicate the early religious significance of the site.

At the same time as Proyecto Teotihuacán, a long-term project was begun by René Millon to study and map the entire ancient city. Simultaneously, a second project was undertaken by Jeffrey Parsons in the early 1970s to study the process and development of ancient settlement patterns in the E Basin of Mexico, incl. the Valle de Teotihuacán. Both projects represent the kind of survey analysis that has become of increasing importance and productivity in the archaeological work of the 1960s–1990s. Other projects of the 1960s and 1970s continued the work begun by Gamio in 1917. William Sanders, Anton Kovar, Thomas Charlton, and Richard Diehl, concentrated on the archaeology and anthropology of the Valle de Teotihuacán in the late prehistoric and early post-Conquest periods. Another project directed by Thomas Charlton studied trade networks originating in the Valley, from the very beginning of Teotihuacán right through to the early 20C, incl. the survey and excavation of historical as well as prehistoric sites. Further projects and analyses continue in the 1990s.

All these projects have shed much light on the long history of Teotihuacán and its hinterland through its greatest periods of power and glory to its decline and near-abandonment, and on the changing uses of what is called the 'Teotihuacán Corridor' of trade and communication routes in and around the Valley.

The Development of the Ancient City proceeded rapidly after the long initial and more general development of agriculture and small, permanent village sites throughout the Basin of Mexico. In the Valley itself, house clusters within compound walls have been excavated at Cuanalán, and several hamlet-sized sites were established, in the Barranca de San Lorenzo near the site, by c 900 BC.

In the earliest stages of its development Teotihuacán was in competition with Cuicuilco in the S Basin. Both sites grew rapidly, and gained control over local resources and over the trade routes to other commodities and raw materials, until the eruption of Xitle ended Cuicuilco occupation. Thus Teotihuacán was left without a serious rival. In both cases, however, the important factor is that their growths were more rapid, much greater, and at the expense of the other sites of the Basin. These remained comparatively small until after the demise of Teotihuacán, although several large cities developed simultaneously in the valleys ringing the Basin.

Six major phases are recognized in Teotihuacán's development. In each case the first phase name is also applied to the whole Basin, while the Teotihuacán names apply specifically to the site.

Patlachique or *Proto-Teotihuacán* (c 150 BC–AD 1). By c the mid-2C BC the settlement at Teotihuacán was noticeably larger than other settlements in the NE Basin of Mexico. Population had begun to gravitate to the site and to concentrate around the first constructions of ceremonial monuments. No doubt the natural grotto now beneath the Pirámide del Sol gave the site an added religious significance and attraction. Teotihuacán's control over local resources, and the redistribution of them, began to focus especially on obsidian, which was quarried at several locations to the N and E of the site. By the end of the phase it occupied c 6 sq km and had a population of perhaps 10,000. However, until the later part of this phase Teotihuacán was seriously rivalled by Cuicuilco, a city of similar size and population.

Tzacualli or *Teotihuacán I* (c AD 1–150). During this phase Teotihuacán became a religious and economic regional centre. The population continued to grow, and to concentrate even more closely in and around the city. By the middle of the 2C AD the population was 30–60,000 (some estimates are even as high as 100,000), or 80–90 per cent of the population of the entire E Basin, concentrated into an area of 17–20 sq km. The ceremonial core was by now completed, establishing the orientation and regulated grid-pattern for the 1C AD city, and its future expansion. Major constructions included the layout of the Calle de los Muertos and its E–W counterpart, the Pirámide del Sol (incl. two enlargements to reach its final base dimensions—estimated to have taken 10,000 workers c 20 years), and the Pirámide de la Luna. Although its economic control did not yet extend much beyond the Basin of Mexico, there is evidence of trade with Monte Albán and with the Gulf Coast.

Miccaótli or *Teotihuacán II* (c AD 150–250; incl. a 50-year *Transición* phase). Teotihuacán reached its maximum size, c 22.5 sq km, with a corresponding increase in population to perhaps 100,000. Major constructions included the completion of upper additions to the Pirámide del Sol, completion of the Pirámide de la Luna, and the beginning of the Ciudadela compound and its counterpart, known as the Gran Conjunto, on the E and W sides of the Calle de los Muertos. The Ciudadela included the Templo de Quetzalcóatl with its sculptures of the rain god Tláloc and serpent heads. The ceramics of this phase included the use of paint cloisonné and Thin Orange Ware (a Teotihuacano hallmark). The site's economic influence by now spread well beyond the Basin, particularly in its control of the obsidian trade and its quarries in the triangular region between Tulancingo, Pachuca, and Otumba.

Tlamimilolpa or *Teotihuacán IIa, IIa–III* (c AD 250–450). The extent of Teotihuacán reached so far S by the end of this phase that passage from the Basin to the E, into Tlaxcala and thus to the Gulf Coast, via the Valle de Teotihuacán, was effectively blocked and thus controlled. The population has been estimated as high as 200,000, based on counts of the sleeping rooms of the more than 2000 known residential compounds. This phase witnessed the continued expansion of trade and political contact, extending to the Gulf Coast and S to the Maya Petén.

Pottery and scenes on murals reflect this contact in Tajín-style scrolls, appliqué ornament, and plano-relief decorations on vases. In the opposite direction, Thin Orange Ware was traded throughout Mesoamerica, and the Teotihuacano talud-tablero architectural form influenced construction at many other sites, being both faithfully copied and locally modified.

The major constructions of this phase included the completion of nearly all the major structures to be seen today, and a massive expansion of the housing districts, to accommodate the population: the Pl. de la Luna, the Palacio del Quetzalpapálotl, the various temples and platforms around the Ciudadela and Gran Conjunto, and the principal constructions along the Calle de los Muertos. In the extensive housing boom, many of the most famous murals were painted, incl. the Mural de los Animales Mitológicos.

Xolalpan or *Teotihuacán III* (c AD 450–650). This phase was Teotihuacán's apogee. Secure in its enormous size and wealth, and the strength of its commercial control or influence, there was no need for any recognized political domination, and the existence of a political Teotihuacán 'empire' has never been seriously entertained by ancient historians. Pottery, painting, and other manufactured goods reflect the intensity of commercial and diplomatic relations with cities all over Mesoamerica. Trade and prospecting for raw and rare materials extended farther and farther to the W and N, even into the present-day USA. Fine Orange wares and cylindrical tripod vessels, decorated with burnishing, incising, painting, and plano-relief, all reached their greatest distribution.

Metepec or *Teotihuacán IV* (c AD 650–750). With little or no warning, the prosperity of Teotihuacán began to disintegrate after the mid-7C. The beginning of the decline seems to date from the time of a great fire c AD 650, which devastated part of the city. While many of its inhabitants left, those who remained (perhaps 50,000) continued to prosper for a time. Trade-goods still came in from all over Mesoamerica; and some of the finest murals were painted. But with no major public construction, the declining city never recovered. Most of the population dispersed into other, now growing, cities in the central Basin, and some moved out of the Basin altogether.

Rival centres such as Xochicalco, El Tajín, and Cholula began to fill the 'vacuum' of cohesive power as Teotihuacán declined. Parts of the central zone of the city were looted, and temples were dismantled and the materials deliberately buried. Whether the cause was external invasion or internal collapse and rebellion, a combination of these, or the pressures of economic over-extension, is uncertain. What is certain is that the site was virtually abandoned by the mid-Postclassic Period, and that its demise changed the entire course of Mesoamerican history.

Following the *Metepec Phase*, the *Coyotlatelco Phase* (c AD 750–900) is less well represented in the Valle de Teotihuacán than in the rest of the Basin of Mexico. An initial sub-phase is known (and named) at the site of Oxtoticpac, where a terraced hillside site has been excavated c 7km S of the centre of the ancient city, representing the sorry remnant of Teotihuacán's former dense population. In the 15–16C Teotihuacán remained a sacred, revered site, and a focus for settlement as a provincial centre, but was never as densely settled as in the Classic Period.

CALLE DE LOS MUERTOS (hereafter referred to as Calle). Known to the Aztecs as *Miccaótli*, it was so-named because they believed that the mounds which lined it were the burial mounds of ancient kings. The Calle is c 2km from the Pl. de la Luna (24) on the N end to the Ciudadela (1) and Gran Conjunto (2) on the S. By the *Tlamimilolpa Phase* it had been extended to the S another 2km, making the two great compounds the focal point of the grid-pattern of the city.

The width of the Calle varies between c 45 and 55m, and it rises gradually in several levelled and subdivided sections, c 27m between the two ends. The main monuments along it are the two great pyramids, and its course was established simultaneously with the orientation of the Pirámide del Sol at 15° 30′ E of astronomical N. Its main section, between the S edge of the Pirámide del Sol and the Pirámide de la Luna, is an unbroken expanse lined with small platforms. Along it there are nearly 50 lesser monuments incl. several palaces, scores of platforms for small temples or shrines, and access to several courtyards and compounds.

Although less visible today it is important to bear in mind that there was a corresponding E–W (3) street intersecting the Calle at the great compounds, and which has been mapped by René Millon. The E and W halves of this street leave the Ciudadela and Gran Conjunto at 90° and 91.5°, respectively. Although not graced with the large platforms and monuments of the Calle,

(36–37) (35)

(Cerro Gordo)

34

14

(CP)

(CP)

17

(18)
16
15

28

24

21

20

19

25

23 22

27

26

(CP)

(CP)

metropolitan Teotihuacán at its apogee

(San Juan Teotihuacán)

0   2500m

N

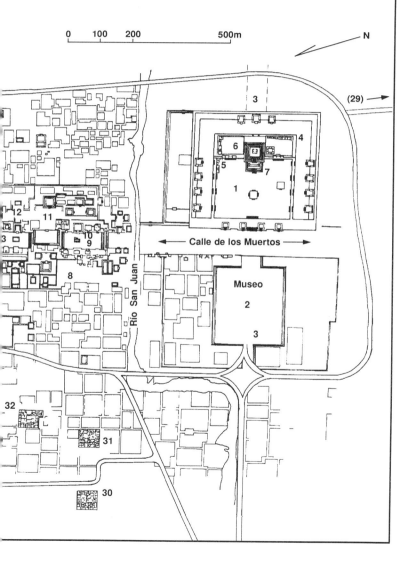

TEOTIHUACÁN
Edo. de México

```
0    100   200         500m
```

N

(29) →

3

4

6

5

7

1

← Calle de los Muertos →

12

11

13

10
9

8

Río San Juan

Museo

2

3

32

31

30

the E–W street was crowded with the walls of apartment complexes and joined by hundreds of smaller streets and alleys at right angles.

Ciudadela (1). At the central point of the ancient city this huge square compound formed a sacred precinct. It comprises a continuous platform around its perimeter, a sunken plaza, temple platforms, and a large pyramid-temple platform (4) in the E-centre of the plaza; the outer dimensions of the surrounding platform are c 410m each side. The platform along the W side, separating the compound from the Calle, is a single level, while the N, E, and S platforms are each two levels. The N, W, and S platforms each have four regularly spaced two- and three-tiered pyramids on them, with steps leading up from the platform level, facing either the sunken plaza or the Calle. The E platform has only three pyramids. A wide central staircase on either side of the W platform gives access to the entire compound from the Calle, and sets of double staircases corresponding to each small pyramid along the perimeter lead into the compound from N and S. Various other foundations of room walls and subsidiary buildings can also be seen around the interior edges of the plaza, especially in the NE corner (5).

All of these features, and the Templo de Quetzalcóatl, were carefully uncovered and restored by Manuel Gamio, José Reygadas, and Ignacio Bernal in 1917–20.

The term 'Citadel' is a misnomer given to the plaza by the Spaniards, who believed the perimeter platform to be fortress walls and the pyramid mounds to be towers.

Templo de Quetzalcóatl (6). Inside this great sunken plaza the crowning feature is the temple assumed to be dedicated to Quetzalcóatl, the Plumed Serpent, because of its decoration. The W three-fourths of the plaza (c 195m by 235m) is separated from the rear quarter by a low, narrow platform running N–S. In the centre of this rear quarter, which is raised, sits the Pyramid and Temple of Quetzalcóatl, hidden behind, and originally completely covered by, a four-tiered pyramid (7), which protrudes into the sunken plaza. This pyramid has a staircase up the W face, and on each tier traces of its original red paint can be seen.

The Temple is reached by walking around the railed platform to the S (r.) of the later pyramid, most of which has been destroyed to reveal the magnificent tablero sculptures on the tiers of the earlier pyramid. To each side of a central staircase on its W side, there are four tiers remaining of perhaps six original. These were built in the Classic Teotihuacano talud-tablero architectural style of rectangular panels (the tablero) cantilevered over sloping wall sections (the talud), in receding tiers.

Each tablero is decorated with sculptures of alternating serpent heads and Tláloc masks. The serpent heads are each surrounded by plumes, thus the 'feathered-serpent', and their scaly bodies are carved in low relief, wriggling along the tablero faces to the l. of each head; the vertebrae-like sections on the ends are their rattles. The highly stylized Tláloc masks represent the god of rain and of maize. Each mask consists of a stylized, projecting 'corn cob' mandible with two huge fangs, two protruding 'spectacle' eyes with circular 'turquoises' above them, and a coiled 'corn-cob' crown. Around the Quetzalcóatl and Tláloc heads are, in low relief, carvings of earth and water symbols, incl. shells and snails. Flanking the central staircase, the two ramps are decorated with other plumed-serpents, and on each talud there are writhing serpent bodies in low relief.

All of these sculptures were covered in a thin plaster coating and traces of the original, brilliant paints applied to this can still be seen: red jaws, white fangs, green quetzal bird plumes, red and yellow shells, white conch shells, and blue side ramps to the staircase. The eyes of the heads were originally set with obsidian, and surrounded by white shells and jadeite discs, known as chalchihuites.

Clear evidence of the temple's sacred and ritual associations was found beneath the staircase. Here the excavators discovered an offering of jadeite figurines, obsidian knives, and pottery; in the central core of the pyramid they found a layer of shells covering human bones, among which were copal resin-filled shells, and more jadeite figurines and pottery.

Opposite the Ciudadela on the W side of the Calle the **Gran Conjunto** (2) was not preserved, and its large plaza area is now occupied by modern facilities. It had dimensions similar to the Ciudadela and would have been surrounded by residential apartments and streets. Archaeologists have concluded that it served as a huge open market for the ancient city.

Returning to the Calle de los Muertos, we proceed N to the first section of structures, just N of the canalized Río San Juan.

The Calle itself is here interrupted by two transverse platform walls with steps over them into a small court, near the centre of which stands a small altar (9). Adjacent to this court Gamio uncovered two groups of buildings, in two layers, one over the other.

On both sides of the Calle there are small pyramids along the platforms. One of these (10), standing opposite the altar just mentioned, is on a level with the second staircase on the E side of the Calle, and typifies the type of shrine found all along the length of the street. Its temple had a small vestibule with two pillars, now gone. A little to the S of this the excavators found, at a lower level, a court surrounded by halls, living rooms, and traces of murals.

Just W of the Calle is the complex of **Edificios Superpuestos** (8). After passing a small vestibule on the l., with traces of three support pillars, a modern metal staircase leads down to the first level of the complex, and proceeds through it along a plank walkway. The rooms of this earlier construction were flattened and filled with earth and rubble to provide a base for the later rooms, and unintentionally preserved fragments of the earlier murals. Now partially cleared, the earlier complex comprised several patios surrounded by rooms and at least two small temples. There is first a courtyard, which at the time of its use was reached by a staircase on its E side, c 4m wide and flanked by pedestals (only partially visible now, beneath the Calle). In the NW corner is part of the terrace of a small temple with traces of a mural: red bands, green chalchihuites (representing jade discs), volutes, and scrolls, the latter resembling the styles known at El Tajín and Cempoala. Next there is a line of colonnades, followed by several rooms with walls still c 1.8m high, and a well c 11.8m deep, still containing water. In a final courtyard (before returning to the metal staircase) there is another small temple and traces of another mural.

Returning to ground level, there are more ruins (11) just off the NW corner of this section of the Calle, again comprising a complex of rooms of several building phases.

Moving N along the Calle, there is another court enclosed by transverse walls and side platforms, smaller than the previous one. To the N of this are three more similar courts, the next two of which have a number of cleared and preserved structures along both sides. Along the W sides of these are the ruins of five or six temple platforms (13) similar to those described around the earlier court.

On the E side is a larger, excavated complex known as **Grupo Viking** (12), after the American Viking Foundation, which funded the excavations. Here, in 1942–45, Noguera and Armillas uncovered two groups of buildings around separate courtyards, N and S. In the N courtyard, beneath a floor of ground lava, were found two layers of mica sheets, covering an area of c 29 sq m; each layer was c 5cm thick. The purpose or symbolic significance of these mica floors is unknown, but as the complexes of rooms were undoubtedly priests' quarters, an élite status and ritual significance seems likely. The sets of rooms are divided by a narrow alley or corridor, and other alleys or corridors lead off at right angles towards the Calle. As with the previously described examples, these structures can be seen to have undergone several alterations.

Pirámide del Sol (14) and **Plaza de la Pirámide del Sol** (15). A staircase at the N end of the final enclosed section of the Calle leads up to the wide main section running from the Pirámide de la Luna to the Pirámide del Sol.

Standing on the W side of the Pirámide del Sol, its great plaza is a raised platform c 69m sq, surrounded by a raised platform on its N, W, and S sides. In the Calle, before mounting the steps up to the plaza, are a small rectangular altar (16) and ruins of a few low platforms, all dating to the Aztec period when Teotihuacán was occupied by a small Aztec settlement and used as a place of worship.

The PL. DE LA PIRAMIDE DEL SOL (15) is flanked on the N and S by the ruins of two huge palace-like complexes of rooms, and by two temple platforms. The palaces include several oratorios and in the N complex (usually referred to as *Pal. del Sol*), fragments of murals, now removed. The S palace is in a far more ruinous state. In the centre of the plaza is another platform, which once supported a two-chambered temple, entered from the W.

The most spectacular monument at Teotihuacán, and the earliest of its major constructions, is the imposing **Pirámide del Sol** (14). It was begun in the 1C BC and, after several building stages, reached its final base dimensions sometime during the *Tzacualli Phase* (c AD 1–150). Vexingly, nearly every source one cares to consult will give a slightly different set of dimensions for it.

Platform dimensions—347m (converted from 1138ft); 351m (converted from 1150ft); or 350m each side. *Base of pyramid*—208m; 225m (converted from 246 yards); 225m; or 213m each side; or 222m by 225m (converted from 728ft by 738ft). *Height of pyramid*—55m; 74m (converted from 243ft); 65.5m (converted from 215ft); 62.5m now (originally 74.7m—converted from 205ft now; originally 245ft); or 61m (but was higher). (The sources from which these height figures are taken do not make it clear whether the height of the pyramid alone is meant; or the pyramid plus the platform. This may account for some of the variance!) *Cubic capacity*—c 1 million cubic m; 1.3 million cubic yards; or 35 million cubic ft.

It is surpassed in Mesoamerica only by the pyramid at Cholula. It is also a popular pastime to compare the Pirámide del Sol with the Great Pyramid of Cheops at Giza, in Egypt. The latter pyramid has, in fact, approx. the same base dimensions, give or take a metre or two ('Blue Guide Egypt' gives these as 440 cubits, or 230m—now reduced to 227m as the casing blocks are gone). However, Cheops is significantly higher (the same source gives 137m, originally 140m), even taking into account the discrepancies in sources for the Pirámide del Sol, and therefore of a correspondingly greater capacity. It has also been suggested that the Pirámide del Sol compares in general shape more favourably with the squatter stepped ziggurats of Mesopotamia. However, the extremely different details of each of these types, in terms of construction techniques, architectural design, materials, dates, and functions, rule out any serious consideration of inspiration from any one of these cultures to the other in the development of their respective pyramid-building traditions.

The pyramid now comprises five massive tiers of unequal height. Unfortunately the hasty and faulty reconstruction of Leopoldo Batres in the 1905–10 project has left us with an uncertain interpretation. First, whatever its present dimensions, the Batres excavations and clearing work destroyed the pyramid's outer facing; therefore its final size is actually unknown. Second, the penultimate and ultimate tiers were arbitrarily separated by Batres, so the original pyramid probably only comprised four tiers (which would, in fact, make them of approx. equal heights). Third, the stepped walls against the base of the pyramid on the N, E, and S sides were originally retaining walls, covered by the builders with a masonry layer c 7m thick, and not in fact a lower tier. Batres removed this outer masonry, exposing the inner construction.

Around the N, E, and S sides of the pyramid is a low, wide platform. The orientation axis, at 15° 30′ E of astronomical N, caused the W face to correspond exactly with the point on the horizon when the sun passes its zenith, and set the axis for all other construction at the ceremonial core, and also the basic grid-plan in later building and expansion of the city. The construction of the pyramid consists of a solid core of adobe bricks in horizontal layers, discovered in exploratory tunnels by the excavators. This core is anchored with an extensive and complex framework of pillars and tree trunks; and the sloping faces also kept stable by a framework of pillars. The whole was then sealed in a layer of earth and stone, which was in turn faced with a layer of crusted reddish tezontle, mixed into a cement-like mortar; the stones projecting in lines along the face of the pyramid are supports to counter the downward thrust of the massive weight of this coating. Some evidence suggests that the entire surface may then have been lime-washed and painted red.

The pyramid is ascended by a wide, narrow-stepped staircase up its W face, in several flights between massive ramps. At the base, two series of steps ascend the N and S sides of a smaller, projecting stepped pyramid of three tiers. This structure was added in the *Miccaótli Phase* (c AD 150–250), and is characteristic of Teotihuacano talud–tablero architecture. The top of the pyramid has a base of c 40m sq, but the exact nature of the top platform is uncertain. Here would have stood the temple, of which no trace remains.

In any ceremony, the majority of worshippers below would obviously have had a limited, mostly vicarious, participation. Some traces of an altar were discovered by excavators on the third tier of the pyramid, and tradition holds that Juan de Zumárraga, first bp of Mexico, had a large statue from the top of the pyramid destroyed in the 16C; it is said to have been 'three arm spans' in width, thickness, and height, but this may in fact have been an Aztec statue rather than a Teotihuacano one.

At the base of the pyramid, at its SW corner, the wide platform supports a palace-like group known as *Casa del Sacerdote* (Priest's House; 17). It resembles the other apartment complexes already discussed—a group of rooms around small patios and halls; traces of the plastered floor, walls, and roof support columns still remain.

Grotto (18; not open to the public at time of writing). In 1971 explorations around the base of the pyramid led to the discovery of a shaft c 7m deep, with remains of stone steps cut into its walls, at the foot of the main staircase. At the bottom of the shaft, a natural tunnel led c 100m to the approx. centre of the pyramid, to a natural grotto extended artificially into four radiating rooms with basalt slab roofs. C 30m along the tunnel there are two rooms on either side. Traces of transverse walls were discovered dividing the tunnel into 25–30 sections, and the floor was laid with plaster. In the central chambers the excavators found several slate discs (?mirrors) and some seemingly deliberately broken pottery, variously dated to the *Miccaótli Phase* by Jorge Acosta, or to the *Tlamimilolpa Phase* (c AD 250–450) by René Millon.

Speculation on the meaning of this find abounds. Nevertheless, the existence of finds in the grotto, its alteration, and the location, apparently deliberate, of the Pirámide del Sol over it, all indicate that an early sacred significance was attached to the site. Remains of stone drainage conduits, also discovered in the exploration of the tunnel and chambers, suggest there was also once a spring in the cave, adding further weight to the likelihood of early religious use of the site. In general, the religious traditions of ancient Mesoamerica, so far as we know them from Late Postclassic sources, favour the backward projection of religious connotations for cave sites, water gods, and creation myths. One suggestion is that the four chambers of the grotto are meant to represent the four quarters of the world, and perhaps relate to the corn myth in which Quetzalcóatl, having used bones from the earth to create man, transformed into an ant to search out four-coloured corn to feed his new creation.

After descending the Pyramid, we proceed across the Calle where, opposite the Pal. del Sol, there is another group of buildings around the PATIO DE LOS CUATRO TEMPLITOS (19). As its name implies, on one side of the patio (W) there is a low platform on which stand the remains of four small temples.

Proceeding N again along the Calle, at c 200m there are two features of note on the E side. The first is the so-called *Muro mal construido* ('ugly' wall) (20), a long, rough-stone wall all along the E side of the Calle for c 200m. It covers several earlier Teotihuacano buildings, and dates to a late phase of the site's occupation, post-*Metepec* (c AD 650–750), when the city was already mostly abandoned and in ruins. One theory is that it was built by Chichimecas who moved through the valley and into the Basin of Mexico in the Early Postclassic Period.

Just past the end of this wall, between two staircases, is the *Mural del Puma* (21), a large fragment, protected by a canopy. It depicts a prowling jaguar in yellow, red, and white on a plaster wall.

Moving c 100m along the Calle, and crossing to the W side, just before reaching Pl. de la Luna there are two more temples, each named after the murals inside. The first, **Templo de los Animales Mitológicos** (22), comprises a two-tiered platform, with a central stairway. Behind the platform a modern door leads to a descending stairway to the earlier and lower structure. On the surviving lower portion of the plastered walls are tiny painted animals, incl. serpents, jaguars, flying fish, and various reptiles. One interpretation is that they depict allegorical references to a 'water cult'.

Next to this temple, the **Templo de la Agricultura** (23) is so-named for its frescoes of magueys and various other plants. Unfortunately, these were discovered at the beginning of this century, before appropriate conservation techniques had been developed, and the paintings disintegrated, not, happily, before copies of them had been made by competent artists. The temple itself consists of three phases: originally it was a small pyramid and temple building; then a terrace was added along the E side (parallel with the Calle); and finally, all was covered by the present structure.

Plaza de la Pirámide de la Luna. The N end of the Calle enters the rectangular PL. DE LA LUNA (24). As with the Pirámide del Sol and its plaza, the sources give a wealth of conflicting dimensions: 203.5m by 136m (converted from 671ft by 449ft); 206.5m by 134.9m (converted from 681ft by 445ft); and 204.5m by 137m. The E and W sides of the plaza are symmetrical, with three pyramid platforms each, two slightly larger ones in the NE and NW corners, and two more behind each of these. Each pyramid has a central staircase leading up from the plaza, but nothing remains of any of the temples supported by these platforms, all of which are dated to the *Xolalpan* or *Teotihuacán III Phase* (c AD 450–650). In the centre of the plaza stands a low square platform with steps on ,all sides.

On the SW corner of the plaza the large **Pal. de Quetzalpapálotl** (Plumed-butterfly; 25) was discovered and restored, using the original materials, in 1962. So elaborate are its decorations that it must certainly have been the house of a priest or ruler.

We mount the platform staircase, which is decorated with a large serpent head, and go through the portico into the entrance hall, which has solid stone pillars supporting the roof. On the wall is a mural which at first glance appears a 'modern abstract', but in fact depicts half-eyes and the symbol for rippling water; the upper walls are red. A door in the NW corner leads to a patio lined with stout, carved stone pillars: the middle section of each pillar depicts a mythical creature called a quetzalpapálotl ('plumed-butterfly'), a favourite Teotihuacano deity; the upper and lower sections of the pillars depict various symbols representing water. All these bas-reliefs were originally painted, and had obsidian discs set into some of the symbols, a few of which are still in place. The perforations on the smooth sides of the pillars are thought to have held ropes for hanging curtains between them.

On the walls of this patio there are remains of murals, which must have made it brilliant with colour when first decorated. The most complete example is on the N side: against a red background are various geometric designs, and what appears to be the cross-section of a seashell. The small circles in the walls show where mica discs were once set into the plaster. Around the roof of the gallery, crenellations depict the Teotihuacano year-signs, completing the religious symbolism.

Opening onto the patio are three rooms: in the room to the N, the excavators found a large tecali (a marble-like stone) jaguar sculpture in the round; in the W room, a shaft was discovered which contained a tecali stele; but in the S room there was nothing of note. In further exploring the shaft in the S room, the excavators found the Subestructura de los Caracoles.

From the portico of the Pal. de Quetzalpapálotl we go S (r.) around it, then down a narrow staircase and along an ancient alley (on the r. passing the exit to the modern tunnel to the substructures, and several ruined buildings). The l.-hand building has walls remaining up to 1.5m high and a plastered central patio. Bearing r., we enter the great courtyard of the Pal. de los Jaguares (26), but pass through it for the moment to its NW corner (l. of the staircase), to the entrance of a modern tunnel. This leads to a 2–3C palace, the **Subestructura de los Caracoles Emplumados** (Plumed Shells; 27), buried to provide a base for the Pal. de Quetzalpapálotl. What remains of this structure are façades with bas-reliefs of 'feathered sea shells' of different colours and 'mouthpieces' (?musical instruments), and two pilasters decorated with bas-reliefs of four-petalled flowers, which were also painted. The temple itself rested on a low platform with a central staircase, which is decorated with green (?)parrots, out of whose yellow beaks flow streams of blue water.

From the centre of this building another narrow tunnel leads W to a small temple and altar, decorated with red circles on a white background.

We return to the courtyard via the exit of the tunnel passed on the way to the substructures. The **Pal. de los Jaguares** (26) comprises three rooms on the N, S, and W of the courtyard, and a platform on the E. The staircase to this platform is flanked by ramps, which at one time were decorated with serpent bodies, wriggling their way up to the tops as a sort of hand-hold; the rattle sections are partially buried at the foot of the ramp on each side.

On the N side of the courtyard there are three rooms, and, flanking the door to the central room, a well-preserved mural. It depicts two plumed-jaguars (jaguars wearing fancy headdresses). Each has a row of shells running down his back to the very tip of his tail, and each blows on a plumed strombus shell, which is held in one forepaw. (These instruments resemble those depicted in the Subestructura, thus identifying them as musical instruments; and the small scrolls at the ends of the shells are a Mesoamerican sound symbol.) Drops of

Jaguar painting at Teotihuacán

blood, or water, can also be seen falling beneath the shells. Above these figures is a frieze of masks—representations of Tláloc, alternating with year-signs.

In the NW corner of the courtyard, a passage leads to several more rooms of the palace. In one of these is a mural depicting pairs of human hands clutching feline-like animals, which have been caught in a net; from their mouths come the scroll symbols representing their roars. Beneath the courtyard and rooms of this palace the excavators discovered a complex system of drainage conduits and small holes emptying into sewers; examples in rooms that were obviously roofed were probably toilets.

Pirámide de la Luna (28). At the approach to the Pirámide de la Luna *Estructura A* (27), a square enclosure, is entered on the W side. Decorative panels line its walls, and inside is a small altar, presumably for religious ceremonies related to the pyramid. Dwarfing this enclosure is the monumental, projecting staircase of the pyramid, comprising five tiers of talud–tablero construction, and a twin to the projecting platform in front of the Pirámide del Sol. Behind it rises the main body of the Pirámide de la Luna (28), composed of four massive tiers with sloping walls, again similar to the Pirámide del Sol. The S, or main, face has projecting, buttress-like walls up to the third tier. Its staircase rises in corresponding stages, but the fourth landing and flight of steps have not been reconstructed.

Although this pyramid is smaller than the Pirámide del Sol, the gradual rise of the Calle gives the tops of both pyramids roughly the same elevation. Different sources again conspire to confuse the unsuspecting seeker of statistics, by giving a wealth of data: *Base dimensions*— 152m by 125m; or 149m by 140m (converted from 490ft by 460ft), plus 53m by 33m for the S projection (converted from 174ft by 108ft). *Height of main pyramid*—43m; 46m; or 45.7m (converted from 150ft). *Height of S projection*—16.8m (converted from 55ft; or 17m (converted from 56ft). *Capacity*—379,099.29 cubic m.

The pyramid had several construction stages, discovered in carefully controlled explorations of its interior. The final structure, that now reconstructed, is of the *Tlamimilolpa Phase* (c AD 250–450), and thus postdates the completion of the Pirámide del Sol by about a century. Its ceremonial significance is clearly implied in its location at the end of the Calle and by the careful symmetry of its plaza. Looking back at it when returning down the Calle, one notices how it is framed against the squat massiveness of the *Cerro Gordo*, providing an ever-present model for the prospective pyramid-builder.

Around the zone, a circuit road gives access to nine excavated apartment complexes, illustrating the housing and planning of both élite and common Teotihuacanos. There are two groups, at the NE and W central sides of the zone, and the Teopancalco complex, located S of the Ciudadela. Each of the housing complexes and the museum are described from the Unidad Cultural.

Teopancalco (29) is S of the circuit road, at the SE corner of the zone, and E of the road which goes S to Belén (where the Oxtoticpac excavations were done). In this suburb of the ancient city, archaeologists excavated an apartment complex known as the *Casa de Barrios*, incl. the discovery of a mural above an altar. It depicts two richly dressed priests, speech scrolls coming from their mouths, advancing towards a sun disc between them.

From the Unidad Cultural we go through the car park and turn r. onto the Carr. de Circunvalación; turn l. just after crossing the Río San Juan (c 750m); and after a similar distance take the r. turn, entering the Camino de Terracería, on either side of which are the various housing complexes.

Atetelco (30; 'stone wall by the water') comprises two patios of different occupational dates: the earlier Patio Blanco has been reconstructed, and consists of three porticoes with murals reconstructed from the originals (discovered by Carlos Margain and Rafael Orellano).

In the S mural are figures of jaguars and coyotes wearing feathered headdresses and with roar-and-howl scrolls, and a 'dripping heart' symbol. The central mural shows a mesh or net motif with several priestly figures, judging by their attire, with coyote, Tláloc, and bird masks.

The N mural also depicts priests, wearing feathered headdresses and clutching obsidian knives and bunches of darts. On doorjambs in the NW corner of the patio are two deformed human figures (with twisted feet).

Tetitla (31; 'place of stones') is on the E side of the road, c 360m from Atetelco. Here, a large complex of rooms, mostly in ruins, is grouped around patios separated by alleys. Nearly all the walls have murals, some of the most notable of which are Tláloc masks with disc eyes, large stepped-frets (possibly year-signs), quetzal birds with spread wings, and plumed-jaguars. In one patio there is an altar platform in the centre, with steps on one side, a miniature representation of the platforms and temples of the ceremonial zone: in the E-side room, murals depict orange panthers with vivid blue eyes; on the S walls a large symbol is repeated several times, but its meaning is unknown; and on the W side, stylistically of a later date, a mural depicts priests in long cloaks, feather headdresses with bird heads, and jadeite masks with ear-plugs; from their red fingernails fall drops of (?)blood or (?)water. More rooms to the S of the complex depict priests dressed in jaguar skins, and a painting of a temple shows its doorway and a complicated, feather-bedecked roof panel.

Zacuala (32) and **Yayahuala** (33) are located c 100m N of Tetitla. Discovered and cleared by Laurette Séjourné de Orfila in the 1960s, these complexes each comprise a large compound with multiple rooms and patios, halls and dividing alleys, and a surrounding compound-wall. Zacuala measures c 82m by 64m and Yayahuala is slightly smaller. They were obviously meant for multi-family groups, perhaps kin-groups or work-related groups; and it has been suggested that they were potentially defensible, as there are few entrances. On the floor of one room in Zacuala the occupants scratched a patolli board, the earliest known in Mesoamerica.

From the Atetelco group, we go N along the Camino de Terracería to the T-junction with San Juan Teotihuacán access road, and turn r., then l. back onto the Carr. de Circunvalación and proceed right around the zone to the Tepantitla ruins, c 300m NE of the Pirámide del Sol.

Tepantitla (34) was also discovered by Margain and Orellana. The wall paintings preserved here are some of the finest murals at Teotihuacán. They have been restored, and accurate reproductions can also be seen in the Museo Nacional de Antropología. Numerous courtyards and rooms are surrounded by a circuit wall as at Zacuala and Yayahuala. At the entrance to the first room are murals of richly dressed priests in the usual garb of feather headdresses, in this case garnished with precious stones. Around the doorway, a large mural depicts the 'Paraíso de Tláloc': to the r. of the door, Tláloc himself rises from the water (?of the lakes of the Basin of Mexico), showering rain from his outstretched hands; to each side, priests walk towards him, singing or chanting; on the sloping wall below, scores of tiny figures frolic in various postures, all apparently singing with joy (or at least chatting to their neighbours); a hill and lake are included at the base, with figures swimming or bathing; fruit trees can be seen lining the lakeshore. On the l. side of the door, the paradise theme is continued in a large open field, filled with figures playing games (?a ball game), with bats and round objects; again, all seem to be singing or talking. The entire wall is bordered in light blue, depicting Tláloc masks alternately facing front and sideways.

Through several more rooms and patios there are many more murals showing richly dressed priests with various zoomorphic attributes. Some have the glyph symbol *nahui ollin* ('four movement') on their chests, and often hold bunches of darts.

Xololpan (35) lies c 100m SE of Tepantitla, and perhaps represents a lower-class Teotihua-cano residence. There are some 40 rooms, of several building phases, incl. several burials beneath floors.

Tlamimilolpa (36) and the **Barrio de los Mercaderes** (37) lie c 0.75km E of the Tepantitla and Xololpan compounds, and are not reconstructed. Their significance is mainly scholarly, and their inclusion here is for comparison with the mainly élite residences seen so far.

They were identified and excavated during the long-term survey project to map the entire city, and their importance lies in the all too rare view they give us of the common Teotihua-cano. For it is important to remember that the teeming masses of the ancient city provided the manpower that shifted the cubic capacities comprising the great pyramids, and paved the Calle de los Muertos.

Tlamimilolpa, the largest single residential compound found so far in Mesoamerica, was a maze-like, but well-planned, compound of alleys leading to 176 rooms, 21 patios, and five larger courtyards. The rooms were windowless, and the whole was surrounded by a stout compound wall. S of Tlamimilolpa is another compound known as Barrio de los Mercaderes, after the artefacts excavated there.

The compound known as *Maquixco*, excavated c 2km W of the city, provides an example of an agricultural suburb—the food-producers for ancient Teotihuacanos. Here, the dwellings were much inferior in construction and were either individual houses or very small compounds of perhaps 10–12 nuclear families—in all, c 500–600 people in an area of c 8ha. Murals depicted only simple geometric forms, and the artefacts reflect the rural occupations and dependence of the inhabitants on city markets for manufactured goods and religious inspiration.

The **Museum** at Teotihuacán consists of one large room, subdivided by thematic displays on Teotihuacano life, and an open upper gallery. Facing the entrance is the large statue of Chalchiúhtlicue, goddess of water, found in the excavation of Pl. de la Luna—a full-sized copy of the original, which now stands in the Museo Nacional. DOWNSTAIRS. The first section has wall panels and charts showing the geology and geography of the Valle de Teotihuacán, and a comparative Mesoamerican chronological chart. This is followed by displays in cases and information panels showing the physical anthropology of the inhabitants of ancient Teotihuacán and their technology, incl. a display on ancient hunting and agricultural subsistence along the wall to the r. On the l., panels and cases depicting the physiographic conditions of the valley (climate, flora, and fauna), and then displays of Teotihuacano food and dress. The section in the far r.-hand corner has a first subdivision showing archaeological techniques, housing, and Teotihuacano socio-political organization (chiefly in panels of text, plans, and photographs); religious organization; and huge photomurals illustrating urbanization at Teotihuacán. Centrally in the far wall, a copy of one of the Tláloc sculptures of the Templo de Quetzalcóatl is mounted between more photomurals of Teotihuacano urbanization. In the centre of this area is a superb scale model (1:1,000) of the entire archaeological zone and Valle de Teotihuacán.

On the opposite side of the room is first a section with panels and display cases containing ritual objects; ancient Mesoamerican science (mathematics, writing, calendrics, and astronomy); and a statue of the goddess of death. The middle section on this side is devoted to Teotihuacano architectural techniques and decoration. Opposite is a small case showing sources of paint pigments. On a long panel dividing the room down its long axis is a full-scale reproduction of the 'Paraíso de Tláloc', plus a sculpture of Tláloc. The final section, opposite this mural, has cases containing examples of Teotihuacano sculpture, figurines, and tools. Before the stairs to the upper gallery is a full-sized copy of one of the plumed-serpent sculptures from the Templo de Quetzalcóatl.

UPSTAIRS. All around this gallery are standing panels and wall displays with large fragments of painted wall plaster, sculptures, and some cases of Teotihuacano pottery recovered in the excavations. Photographs illustrate the various stages of excavations and reconstructions in the Proyecto Teotihuacán, incl. various important discoveries and burials in situ.

Oxtotipac, Otumba, and Axapusco, 20km

From (48km; see above) the crossroads where we gain access to the archaeological zone, the road to the r. skirts the zone's S area and runs to (4km) a r. turn giving on to a passable road for (9km) **Oxtotipac**. Here the former Franciscan convent of *San Nicolás* was founded in the mid-16C as a visita of Otumba, and at most would not have housed more than three friars at a time. Facing the atrio is a cross bearing reliefs of Passion symbols. The wide jambs and archivolt of the church doorway, studded with large rosette motifs, are bordered by the Franciscan cord. Traces of original painting still remain on the façade. Floral motifs also decorate the beautiful interior triumphal arch. The high altarpiece is early baroque, as is that, though later adapted, in the l. transept. An anastyle (late 18C) side altarpiece is also in place, as is an original pulpit. To the r. of the church, the three-arched portería, with a Franciscan cord running along the cornice, and a wooden ceiling. In the tiny cloister, without arches, but with pillars upholding lintels, wood is much in evidence: in the pillar capitals, in the architrave which they support, in the brackets, and in the ceilings.

The minor road continues NE to (17km) **OTUMBA** (c 4000 inhab.; 2600 m; also reached by the main road from Teotihuacán, c 15km), an agricultural centre of great interest for its former Franciscan convent of **La Concepción de Nuestra Señora**.

The nearby quarries of the Barranca de los Estetes were a principal source of ancient Mesoamerica's obsidian. For example, analysis has shown that most of the obsidian found at Chalcatzingo in Morelos came from Otumba. Other sources include Zinapécuaro (Michoacán), Cerro de las Navajas (Pachuca), Zaragoza and Altotonga (Veracruz), Guadalupe Victoria (Puebla), and Tajumulco, San Martín Jilotepeque, El Chayal, and Ixtepeque (all in Guatemala). Of these, Guadalupe Victoria, El Chayal, Zinapécuaro, and Otumba were the most heavily exploited, and the obsidian from the last two was particularly good for making the long prismatic blades so ubiquitous and essential in Mesoamerican technology. Otumba was especially known for its grey obsidian, exploited in an extensive trade network by Teotihuacán (cf. *Calpulalpan, Pachuca, Tepeapulco,* and *Tulancingo*).

By 1531 Cortés had a residence here—an important provincial centre in the Late Aztec period. The convent, planned in 1527, was probably built during 1540–60, having four friars by 1569. The friars remained until 1756, when their parish was secularized. The town, on the Mexico-Veracruz waggon road, was graced in the 17C by a hospital and casas reales. In 1791 it was described as 'todo es ruinas, edificios caídos, y pobreza ...'. The convent remains in ruins; the church has been restored. The atrio, with cross and gate arches resting on slim, square piers, was raised on a large pre-Conquest site.

The church's W doorway, with double archivolt and thick jambs, divided by three sets of colonnettes, all laden with relief, is a charming example of Renaissance eclecticism. Above, the thin alfíz band rests on the outer set of colonnettes. The pattern is echoed in the choir window. Saved from the previous ruin are the triumphal arch, four fonts, mural fragments, and the cord running along the wall beneath the choir.

The larger middle arch of the airy portería/open chapel faces the sanctuary, framed by another fine arch decorated with relief. Entry into the ruined cloister is through a delightful portal, its massive jambs, again divided by colonnettes, and double archivolts full of tequitqui relief.

3km N, at **Axapusco**, the 16C church of *San Esteban* now shows signs of later (17–18C) modification. The churrigueresque open chapel is an even later anachronism. La Asunción del Señor at *Tlamapa*, 2km N, is another 16C visita church.

The road continuing NE from Otumba goes to (23km) *Ciudad Sahagún,* see Rte 63.

19 Tepotzotlán, Tepeji del Río, Tula

Méx. 57D, 91km.—17.5km (2km E) Tlalnepantla.—37km Cuautitlán.—41km San Lorenzo Riotenco.—43km Sta Bárbara Tlacatelpan.—44km (2km W) **Tepotzotlán**.—73km Tepeji del Río.—91km **Tula**.

We leave Mexico City along Paseo de la Reforma on the N of Chapultepec to the Petroleum Monument, there joining the Anillo Periférico (Blvd Manuel Avila Camacho) which runs NW, Lomas de Chapultepec on the l., passing (l.) the *Hospital Militar,* the *Secretaría de Defensa Nacional,* and *Hipódromo de las Américas,* Mexico's finest racecourse, opened in 1943. The headquarters of the *Jockey Club* are also here. After (9km) *El Toreo* bullring, opened in 1947, we cross into the State of México. Beyond, at the *Cuatro Caminos,* Calz. México-Tacuba and Río San Joaquín come in on our r.

C 3km to the l., reached along Calz. San Esteban, in Calz. Río Hondo, is the site of **Tlatilco**, where excavations in a brickyard in the 1940s uncovered a large Preclassic village. It was excavated briefly in 1943 by Michael Covarrubias and again by INAH in 1947; and in 1952 and 1960 by Román Piña Chan. The evidence was re-examined by Paul Tolstoy and L. I. Paradis in 1970. In the Museo Nacional de Antropología there is a reconstruction of one of the burials.

Unfortunately, despite the re-examination of the evidence, various texts give different statistics about the burials found on the site: 'over 300', 'some 500 or more', or 'an estimated 500 graves are said to have been taken out, of which 375 have been documented'. The site included four developmental phases, tied into Basin-wide archaeological phases: *Ixtapaluca* (c 1400–800 BC), *Zacatenco* (c 800–400 BC), *Ticomán* (c 400–100 BC), and *Patlachique* (c 100 BC–AD 1). As well as burials, triangular, bottle-shaped storage pits and fragments of the wattle-and-daub walls of houses were found. Some authorities claim that there is evidence for low one- and two-step platforms, possibly to support temple structures, but the evidence is unclear. The storage pits were originally for food, but once soured they were used as household rubbish dumps.

Many burials contained few or no artefacts. Others, however, were rich in pottery vessels, figurines, jewellery, clay masks, and stone tools. The pottery is some of the earliest found in the Basin, and includes a variety of shapes and decorations, both within and spanning the phases of occupation. There were flat-bottomed bowls, tecomates (collarless, spherical vessels with a narrow restricted opening), goblets, tripod vessels, long-necked bottles, and stirrup-spouted vessels. Decorations included rocker-stamping, geometric painting, slips, differential firing, and excisions filled with different-coloured paints or pastes. Pieces of especial note include the 'life–death' bowl, with a face on one side and a skull on the other; and bowls with excised 'jaguar paw' motifs, filled in with red paint or paste against a black slip (both Museo Nacional de Antropología).

Tlatilco is especially famous for its figurines, of which there is also a wide variety. One grave contained as many as 61. There are males, females, couples, figures engaged in daily activities, ball players (some of the earliest known), animals, and imaginary, monster figures. The 'mujer bonita' type is especially numerous, as are mother-and-child groups. Animals represented include peccaries, opossums, bears, armadillos, rabbits, ducks and other birds, frogs, turtles, and fish. These figurines are an important source of information on dress and domestic activities in the Preclassic and provide evidence for trade contacts and influences. Archaeologists also have fun arguing over interpretations of their 'ritual' overtones. Some pieces have the Olmec 'baby face', and from one grave came an Olmec ground stone axe-head. One authority has used these pieces, plus the 'jaguar paw' vessels and the use of white- and black- slipped pottery, to argue forcefully for Olmec presence, possibly even colonization from the Gulf Coast. Most other archaeologists, however, while not denying definite trade and contact with the Gulf, point out that the major ingredients of the Tlatilco and other Preclassic village sites in the Basin were locally made and home-grown.

Other excavated Preclassic sites in the NW Basin include *Cerro Tepalcate* ('Potsherd Hill'), which yielded stone alignments interpreted as the outlines of dwellings, and ceramics and figurines of the *Patlachique Phase*; and *El Arbolillo*, *Loma Torremote*, *Tetelpán*, *Ticomán*, *Xalostoc*, and *Zacatenco*, some of which provide names for archaeological phases in the Basin.

At 10.5km Méx. 134, the road to (63km) *Toluca*, leads off to the l.

This road leads into the district of San Bartolo Naucalpan and (c 3km W) LOS REMEDIOS, a drab suburb, but home to one of Mexico's famous pilgrimage centres, the sanctuary of **Nuestra Señora de los Remedios**.

The first sanctuary was built in 1574–76 to honour the miraculous statue of the Virgin which, so the story goes, was brought to New Spain by a conquistador and hidden near Naucalpan just before the retreat of the Noche Triste. The image was later found under a maguey tree by an Indian who took it home. But it kept flitting back to the maguey, where the first chapel was duly erected. In times of distress it became customary to carry the Virgin to the city to implore her intercession. In 1810 the royalists set her up in rivalry to the insurgents' espousal of Our Lady of Guadalupe which probably accounted for her lack of popularity during the 19C. In these days, however, devotion to her has revived.

The present sanctuary dates from a rebuilding in 1628, with 18–19C modifications. The statue itself, of Our Lady holding the infant Christ, carved in wood with estofado, 27cm high, and in detachable clothing, is placed beneath a baldachin on the high altar. Of undoubted early 16C Spanish make, it was probably a 'virgen arzonera', fitted to a horse's saddle.

In the Parque Nacional de los Remedios (c 400 hectares) the *Acueducto de los Remedios* was built in 1765, a notable feat, but it never in fact functioned.

15km *Ciudad Satélite*, a modern higher-income residential area. In the middle of the main road are the brightly coloured *Torres sin Función* (1957) by Matías Goeritz and Luis Barragán, described by the latter as 'huge modern torches'. 17.5km (r.; 2km E) **Tlalnepantla**, now an industrial suburb, its focus the former Franciscan convent of *Corpus Christi*, founded in the 1560s on the border between the Otomí settlement of Teocalhuaca and the Aztecs of Tenayuca, to mark an attempt at reconciliation between two hostile groups. In the atrio, the stone cross is carved with motifs of the Passion. The church, probably finished in the 1590s, has undergone many changes. The symbolic N doorway, however, remains intact. The central niche of the architrave contains a figure of Our Lady, flanked by medallions: a king (l.) on a crenellated band, representing Náhuatl-speaking Tenayuca; St Lawrence (r.) representing Teocalhuaca. In the pediment the Host symbolizes the unifying Church. The seven-bay portería is divided by the central arch, resting on heavier, square piers. One lot of three outside arches was possibly the convent entrance, the other the open chapel. The sacristy door is dated 1582. The 16C font carries the glyph of Tenayuca.

Blvd Avila Camacho, now Méx. 57D (toll), main highway to Querétaro, runs N. 20km *La Quebrada*; l. turn for (10km NW) *Lago de Guadalupe* (boating), (13km) *Cuautitlán-Izcalli*, and (22km) *Tepotzotlán*, see below.

At 28km we may advantageously leave the main road and bear r. to (32km) **Tultitlán**, where the former Franciscan convent of *San Lorenzo* (1569–86) has been much altered, incl. the church façade (1779). Its most imposing feature is the atrio wall, composed in part of pre-Conquest stones. Now N to (37km) **Cuautitlán**, known for lucerne cultivation and light industry.

Cuau(h)titlán was the site of a 7C BC Preclassic village on the NW shores of Lago de Texcoco, inhabited into the Classic, when multi-family apartment-like housing, similar to that at Teotihuacán, was built. Together with nearby Tenayuca its Classic population has been estimated at c 20,000. It was a Chichimec town in the Late Postclassic and we know something of its 15C history from the 'Anales de Cuauhtitlán', part of the Codex Chimalpopoca (Aztec ruler, 1415–26), written in Náhuatl at the end of the 16C.

The Chichimec rulership succumbed to conquest by Azcapotzalco in 1408, and subsequently became a provincial centre and tributary of Tenochtitlán when the Triple Alliance razed Azcapotzalco. Tribute demands included 4000 icpalli—low-backed, legless seats—for Aztec dignitaries. Cuauhtitlán's principal deity was Itzapapálotl (or Itzpapálotl = 'obsidian butterfly'), Chichimec earth-goddess and consort of Mixcóatl, chief Chichimec god.

Similar provincial towns around Cuauhtitlán were Tultitlán, c 3km to the SE; and in a string to the NNW-N-NNE: Tepotzotlán, Coyotepec, Zumpango, Xaltocán, Zitlaltepec, Huehuetoca, Jilozingo, Huepoxtla, Tequixquiac, Tlapanaloya, and Apaxco.

In 1568–69 Miles Philips and other survivors of Hawkins's fleet were brought here on their way to Mexico. 'Quoghliclan', he called it: 'where was a faire house of gray friers, howbeit wee saw none of them'. Today it is, unjustly, the butt of a popular saying, contrasting cosmopolitan sophistication with provincial dullness: 'fuera de México, todo es Cuautitlán'.

The Franciscan convent of *San Buenaventura* was founded in 1525. The atrial cross, raised high on a massive base and dated 1525 in commemoration, though probably made c 30 years later, is one of the finest of its type: Passion symbols in high relief and, on the cross-piece, portraits of the prior of the day and of Alonso de Avila, first encomendero. The present church, replacing a large original, the shell of which remains, dates from 1730. The high altarpiece incorporates four Mannerist paintings by the Fleming Marten de Vos (c 1531–1603): SS Peter and Paul; Immaculate Conception; St Michael (signed and dated 1587).

The altarpiece (early 18C ?) in the Cap. del Sagrario has lower supports resembling estípites.
On the W side of the town, on the main Querétaro road, is the *Embotelladora Bacardi* (1959–60) by Mies van der Rohe and Félix Candela, with the latter's exquisite groin vaults (30.5m sq), a thin shell applied to a large space.

The road E from Cuautitlán leads to (6km NE) *Melchor Ocampo*, where the church of San Miguel, in an atrio with an anachronistic posa chapel, and a baroque altarpiece in the r. transept, dates from 1728, and (5km E) *Tultepec*, on a hill, once with a convent dependency of the bishopric of Michoacán, then transferred to the Franciscans of Cuautitlán. A richly carved three-arched portería survives.

41km (l.) **San Lorenzo Riotenco**. Here the 18C church has a churrigueresque façade. The side portal (closed up) has a scallop shell above the arch. The interior contains two churrigueresque retables: that on the high altar (1760; dedicated to Our Lady of Guadalupe), into which symbols of Mexican nationalism have been read, is of great interest. In the predella are two eagle shields: on l., emblems of Mexico City, with, over the tower, a triumphant eagle; on r., the national arms, the eagle devouring the serpent, with a star (Our Lady of Guadalupe) above. In the centre, Juan Diego holds up the retable. Above the predella, in high relief, appear SS Jerome, Gregory the Great, Augustine, Ambrose; between them, Duns Scotus and St Teresa. Between the estípites: on l., St Rose; on r., St Philip of Jesus.

43km (r.) **Sta Bárbara Tlacatelpan**, where the 17C church contains a churrigueresque high altarpiece and two rare Mannerist (early 17C) side retables, perhaps from the old church at Tepotzotlán. The first has five paintings by Pedro de Prado (fl. 1626) showing scenes from the life of Our Lady, incl. a fine Presentation (the St Anne well done). The second incorporates four paintings (Life of St Ignatius) by Prado and a Divine Countenance, attr. Alonso López de Herrera.

From Sta Bárbara we cross (44km) over the main road (57D) to the W to (2km W) **TEPOTZOTLAN**, a straggling town with a long, narrow main street. The former Jesuit establishment is a mecca for all lovers of Mexican art and architecture—in the words of Manuel Toussaint, 'an inexhaustible fountain of treasures'.

In 1604–06 the Jesuits established their novitiate of San Francisco Javier here, alongside their college of San Martín, for Indian boys. After 1767, decay set in. In 1890 a plan was even afoot to convert the property into the Federal District penitentiary—mercifully never realized. During 1900–14 the Jesuits were again in possession, but the Revolution obliged them to leave. In 1933 church and college were declared a national monument and in 1960–64 INAH restored them for their present uses.

The church of **San Francisco Javier** dates from 1670–82, the upper part of the old walls edged with a band of ajaraca work. The façade (1760–62), though not exactly harmonious, is one of the outstanding examples of Mexican churrigueresque art, exquisite in detail and of finest craftsmanship. The figure relief and sculpture (angels, Jesuit saints, cherubs, martyrs in 18C costume) is of extraordinary elegance, as are the niches of the central panel: in the lowest storey, the infant Christ holding the globe; in the first, St Francis Xavier between double estípites; in the second (a more than usually spacious gable, separately constructed to add height), a beguilingly canopied Virgin and Child. The one completed tower, a beautiful work, is encrusted with tightly decorated estípites. (Note the lovely—however unsuitable—wrought-iron railing.) Its almohadilla base, echoed by the panel on the l. of the façade, helps point up the brilliance of the decorated parts. The little 17C tower on the N behind the façade is rimmed by four small statues. The original S door recalls the simplest Renaissance style.

The former Jesuit house and the church interior are now the **Museo Nacional del Virreinato** (Tues.–Sun., 11–6; fee), a stunning collection of the fine art of New Spain. The entrance is through the portería in the SE corner of the atrio, reached through the gateway on the l. of the church.

From the entrance we reach the W walk of the CLAUSTRO DE LOS ALJIBES (Cloister of the Cisterns); its lower storey dates from 1606, the upper probably from the 18C. The walls are lined with a series of paintings by Cristóbal de Villalpando on the Life of St Ignatius—the first, the Nativity, signed and dated

1710. On the walls of the passage prolonging the E walk are six paintings on the Life of St Stanislaus Kostka by José Padilla (1759).

From the SW corner we gain access to the church. In the entrance way are paintings of Four Doctors of the Church (1679) by Diego Calderón. The INTERIOR contains a group of retables representing the peak of the Mexican churrigueresque and overwhelming in their beauty and magnificence—further heightened and rendered almost celestial when the sun shines through the windows of clerestory and cupola. Those in the apse, forming an ensemble and dedicated to St Francis Xavier (centre), SS Luis Gonzaga (l.) and Stanislaus Kostka (r.), were designed by Miguel Cabrera and made by Higinio de Chávez; contracted for in 1753 and finished in 1755. The transept retables date from 1756: on the l. dedicated to Our Lady of Guadalupe, another exquisite work enlivened by merry polychrome angels, and possibly also by Cabrera and Chávez; to the l. of it, St John Nepomuk; on the r., dedicated to St Ignatius, Our Lady of Sorrows, and the Cross of Caravaca. The nave altarpieces, dedicated to St Joseph and Our Lady of Light, date from 1758 and have been attr. Isidoro Vicente de Balbás.

Covering the sanctuary and transept vaults are tempera paintings by Cabrera of the Glorification of SS Ignatius and Francis Xavier and the apparitions of Our Lady of Guadalupe to Juan Diego. The simple sotocoro retables hold two more works by Cabrera: Our Lady's Patronage of the Society of Jesus and the Precious Blood of Christ.

The door on the l. in front of the sotocoro leads to the chapel of the **Sta Casa de Loreto**, built in 1679–80 at the instance of Fr Giambattista Zappa who had introduced the cult of Our Lady of Loreto to Mexico and fired 'the whole town and the inhabitants of the country about' to help in its completion. In the centre is a reproduction of the Sta Casa. At its N end is the octagonal *Camarín*, Our Lady's own room, a jewel of indigenous carving, its walls lined with small churrigueresque retables (1730s), spare surfaces and pilasters laden with stucco and gilded-wood decoration, most notably negro figures sprouting from lush plant motifs. The moorish-style vaulting of the cupola, from which rises a five-storey lantern (the dove representing the Holy Ghost floating at the top), is thronged with cherubs peering down from clouds, through which shine sun, moon, and stars. All is effortlessly sustained by four archangels, who seem poised for heavenward leaps. Floor and dado are azulejo-covered.

To the l. of the Sta Casa is the **Relicario de San José**, consecrated in 1738, luxurious with gilding and polychrome, its superb little retable transitional between baroque and churrigueresque; in the centre St Joseph, patron of New Spain, surrounded by five angels. The paintings are by Juan Rodríguez Juárez and José de Ibarra.

The Sacristy, reached from the l. side of the high altar, contains 11 suave paintings by Cabrera: on the end wall, Immaculate Conception with SS Francis of Assisi and Ignatius; the ten smaller canvases show scenes from the Last Supper and allegories of the Blessed Sacrament. On either side of the choir window are two scenes from the life of St Francis Xavier, by Cabrera, and two paintings by José Padilla (1759).

On the N side of the Claustro de los Aljibes is the *Botica* (dispensary), with suitable murals and medical equipment. The other rooms opening off the cloister contain collections of 16–19C silverwork—chalices, monstrances, reliquaries, and other sacred objects, almost all from the Cathedral treasury. Especially fine is the late 16C Relicario de San Pedro y San Pablo (partly gilded, repoussé, and engraved), donated by Alonso de Villaseca.

From the E side of the cloister, stairs lead down to the PATIO DE LOS COCINAS, its octagonal fountain dated 1740. Off it open the *Anterrefectorio* and *Refectorio* (anteroom and refectory), lined with portraits of rectors; the *Cocina* (kitchen); and *Dispensa* (pantry).

From the latter we reach the two-storey CLAUSTRO DE LOS NARANJOS (orange-trees; late 17C–early 18C), once used for study, rest, and recreation. In the rooms off the cloister walks is a collection of 16–18C stone sculpture, incl. an outstanding Virgin and Child (early 17C) from San Francisco in Mexico City, with remains of polychrome decoration. On its E side is the Garden, where stands the little chapel of *Montserrat* (1695) and the reassembled fountain of *Salto del Agua* (1779; see Rte 7).

The upper-storey walk is lined with paintings of Scenes from the Life of Our Lady (early 18C) by Juan Rodríguez Juárez (nine remaining of a series of 20), among his best works. Especially good are the landscapes of the Annunciation and the Flight into Egypt, and Immaculate Conception. On the W side is the former *Biblioteca*, containing a collection of c 3000 books of the viceregal period salvaged from various institutions. The other rooms contain other notable collections. *Ivories*. 17–18C Asiatic and Mexican work. Holy Family, exquisite 18C Chinese group, the figures of Our Lady and St Joseph gently inclining towards the Child. 17–18C Philippine crucifixes, incl. one, carved along the curvature of the elephant tusk, with strongly oriental features. Virgen de la Expectación, face and hands of ivory, 18C Chinese work; silver halo, 18C Mexican work. *Taracea* (furniture inlaid with various woods, metals, ivory, tortoiseshell, and mother of pearl). *Porcelain*, mainly from China and Japan, incl. a dish commemorating the foundation of the Academy of San Carlos. *18C Furniture*, incl. lacquer work from Michoacán, Oaxaca, Guerrero, and Chiapas. Pieces in Queen Anne and Chippendale styles. *Vestments*. 16–18C Spanish and Mexican work: 17C dalmatic made in Seville for Mexico Cathedral, signed 'Marcos Maestre', woven in coloured silk and silver thread, showing scenes from the lives of Christ and Our Lady, and virgin martyrs; pluvial cope (1699), made by Antonio Rangel for the Cathedral, embroidered on crimson damask in two tones of gold; pluvial cope from Puebla, embroidered in silk and gold thread with angels and roses, and a central rose showing Christ and St Rose; gremial of Abp Zumárraga—silk and metal embroidery on velvet, made in Mexico City, probably in the 1540s. *16–17C Furniture*, incl. excellent examples in Renaissance style. Late 17C folding screen, once belonging to viceroy conde de Moctezuma (1696–1701), oil-painted and gilded; one side shows the siege of Vienna (1683), the other, hunting scenes. 17C bargueño, wood inlaid with bone decoration (European work). 18C altar of calamine (copper engraved with ormolu). *Trade with Asia*. Further pieces imported from China and the Philippines.

W of the library, reached from a corridor between the Claustro de los Naranjos and the Claustro de los Aljibes, is the single-nave CAP. DOMESTICA, once exclusively for the novices, begun c 1604–06 and refurbished in the mid-18C. The lobby at its S end includes a beautiful late 17C wooden screen with marquetry and bone inlays, crowned with the inscription 'Domine Dilexi Decorum Domus Tuae'. The painting of the Holy Family is by Cabrera; that of the Assumption and St Ignatius by an anon. 18C master. The vaulting, laden with stucco decoration, incorporates the shield emblems of the first six Orders established in New Spain, from the Franciscans (1523) to the Mercedarians (1589). In niches to l. and r. are two magnificently carved mid-17C statues, with estofado: Our Lady of Sorrows and St Joseph. Also on the l. are two retables: one (17C), gilded, with niches for statues and relics; the other (18C), with an image of Our Lady of Guadalupe, and inlaid with tortoiseshell. In the chancel, beneath the cupola, is the complex and lustrous main altarpiece (restored), churrigueresque but with a difference, ornamented with mirrors and reliquary niches, now holding small (substitute) angel figures of rice-paste. On the l. a niche contains the polychrome kneeling image (early 17C) of Pedro Ruiz de Ahumada.

Stairs lead up to the third level of the Claustro de los Aljibes, the cloister walk and rooms off it containing a superb collection of 16–19C Mexican paintings and sculpture. CORRIDOR. Carlos Clemente López (mid-18C), Fray Dionisio Vázquez refusing the archbishopric of Mexico. 18C polychrome St Francis, dramatically treated, gilded and estofado. 18C portraits of Mexican ecclesiastics, incl. Nicolás Rodríguez Juárez, Juan Ignacio María de Castorena, bp of Yucatán; Fray Gaspar de Molina y Oviedo. Juan Rodríguez Juárez, Juan Escalante y Mendoza, oidor of Mexico City. José de Ibarra, Antonio de Villaseñor y Monroy. Nicolás Rodríguez Juárez, Transfiguration. Cristóbal de Villalpando, Our Lady of Sorrows, a full-blooded treatment. José Joaquín Magón, Our Lady of Sorrows. FIRST ROOM. Two beautiful wooden estofado statues (18C) of the Immaculate Conception, one from Guatemala. Cross of the Señor de Sta Teresa, formerly in the church of Sta Teresa la Antigua. Christ carrying the Cross, 17C wooden sculpture, the suffering emphasized. Anon. 17C, the Four Sibyls, excellent and vividly coloured paintings. Eight lively 17C paintings of Scenes from the Life of Our Lady. Two 18C portraits of dead friars: Francisco de Santa Ana; Mariano Guerrero, Fray Benito de Jesús María (1797). Cristóbal de Villalpando, Flight into Egypt, tender in a lush landscape; Adoration of the Shepherds, both from a retable illustrating Scenes from the Life of Our Lady, whose other canvases are in the Pinacoteca Virreinal.

SECOND ROOM. Seven paintings by Juan Sánchez Salmerón, excellent examples of his individual, pleasing style: SS Anne and Joachim with Our Lady of the Assumption; Adoration of the Shepherds; Our Lord nailed to the Cross; Way of the Cross; St Gabriel announces the birth of Our Lady to St Joachim; Assumption; Birth of Our Lady.

THIRD ROOM. Alonso López de Herrera, Holy Face (1624), oil on copperplate. Luis Juárez, St Teresa at prayer. Pedro Ramírez, Liberation of St Peter—justly renowned among 17C Mexican baroque paintings for its combination of strength and grace. Pietro da Cortona, Holy Family. 17C polychrome and estofado statues of SS Hyacinth and Rose. Juan Salguero (mid-17C), Elijah and Elisha.

FOURTH ROOM. Four splendid paintings by Juan Correa: Expulsion from Paradise—the angel heroic against a gate of transparent crystal, set in an abundant Mexican landscape; Our Lady of the Apocalypse; St Nicholas of Bari; SS Teresa and Augustine.

FIFTH ROOM. 18C portraits. José de Alzíbar, Luis Antonio de Torres Tuñón. José de Páez, the judge Miguel Velázquez de Lorea; Jacinto Martínez de Concha.

SIXTH ROOM. 16C works. Copies of famous Renaissance portals (Huejotzingo, Yecapixtla, Acolman, etc). Santiago, polychrome and gilded wood. Assumption, polychrome and estofado. Monumental images of Our Lady and St John, polychrome and estofado, part of a calvary from the church of Sta Catalina de Sena. Virgen de la Silla (Spanish influence), from the convent of San Joaquín. Reliefs of SS Peter and Paul, from Acolman. Reliefs of the Good Shepherd and St John the Evangelist, from the Calpan retable. Our Lady of the Apocalypse, with gilded ochre background, the Virgin formal in deep blue, with medieval echoes (from Yuriria), attr. Francisco de Morales—from an original retable of 1576. Marten de Vos, St John writing the Apocalypse, the celestial Jerusalem radiant against the gorgeous colouring of the robes.

SEVENTH ROOM. 18–19C portraits of nuns, in finery for their profession and in death, a fascinating, and exclusively Mexican, phenomenon. The finest work (and an exception) is Cabrera's Sor María Josefa Augustina Dolores (Augustina Teresa de Arosqueta from Durango; 1759), a Capuchiness in her simple habit. Attr. Cabrera, Sor María Buenaventura Josefa. Anon. early 19C, Sor María Joaquina de San Rafael, daughter of an Indian cacique from Oaxaca. Among the 19C portraits, Sor María Lugarda de la Encarnación, full of character. Among likenesses of the dead, Sor Matiana Francisca de Señor San José and Sor Elvira de San José.

The road leading SW from the plaza (Méx. 77) goes to (51km) *Villa del Carbón*, an attractive place amid oak woods, known for its coal. The road passes (5km) *San Mateo Xoloc*, where the church contains an early altarpiece (c 1630–40) with contemporary paintings and an elaborate niche, Renaissance in style, containing a polychrome statue of St Matthew holding his gospel and accompanied by a little angel. 13km road NW to the *Arcos del Sitio*, the highest part of the aqueduct planned from the early 18C to bring water from the Río del Oro to the Jesuit hacienda of Xalpa, begun in mid-century, but left incomplete after 1767. The work was finished in 1854. Spanning a ravine c 440m wide, the Arcos are in four storeys, 56 arches, reaching a height of 60m. At (15km) *Santiago Cuauhtlalpan* the church, unhappily rebuilt, retains its churrigueresque altarpieces.

Méx. 57D continues directly N, the Sierra la Muerta to the W. 58km *San Miguel Jagüeyes*. At 61km we cross into the State of Hidalgo. 71km crossroads. We turn r. for (73km) **Tepeji del Río** (c 10,000 inhab.; 2175m; R,P), a friendly town on the l. bank of the Río Tepeji. Down steps from the plaza is reached the convent of *San Francisco de Asís*, founded by the Franciscans in 1558, completed by 1586. The W half of the atrio, its wall punctuated by ornamental merlons (clumsy attempts at Gothic lilies ?), was excavated from the hillside, the fill used to build a level platform for the convent. On the W side of the church is the small open chapel, below alfíz and low-slung five-centred arch dotted with rose motifs, resting on strangely ambitious ionic half-column capitals. The N doorway of the church is in well-proportioned, Renaissance style, with elegant fluted Corinthian columns enclosing the coffered arch rim and jamb mouldings. The W doorway is much less effective. The interior, a single barrel-vaulted nave, has a notable triumphal arch. In the sotocoro is a painting of the Holy Trinity, Our Lady, saints, and the souls in Purgatory by Juan Correa. In the sacristy, an Immaculate Conception (1718) by Francisco Martínez. The two-storey cloister retains traces of 16C murals framed by the Franciscan cord. The high columns and generous capitals of its lower walk leave the arches with only a minimal curve; the upper walk, with wooden ceiling, has squatter openings and rounded soffits. Here on 3 June 1861, Melchor Ocampo, indefatigable liberal ideologue and statesman, was shot on the orders of Gen. Leonardo Márquez and his body hung from a tree.

The road directly N from Tepeji del Río leads past Presa Requena to (91km) **TULA** (16,000 inhab.; 2066m; R,P), the ancient city of Tollán, the Toltec capital.

Several derivations of its name have been put forward: in Otomí it simply means 'metropolis', but more colourful renderings trace the name to the Tolteca–Chichimeca words for 'gifted artisans', or perhaps from a Náhuatl base as 'Place of the Reeds'. In any case, the Toltecs were venerated in the Late Postclassic as representing everything cosmopolitan as opposed to rustic, and generally as a race to be emulated.

In Toltec legend Tula was founded in AD 968, but archaeological evidence shows that the site was occupied as early as the beginning of the 8C AD and that the surrounding plains had been settled by village farming peoples from as early as the mid-7C BC. By AD 300, there were at least 15 towns in the vicinity, the largest of which was the site of *Chingu*, a few km N of Tula. A contemporary of Teotihuacán, Chingu covered 2.5 sq km, and seems to have been bound up in that city's economy through the export of locally mined lime. This conclusion is further supported by the fact that Chingu declined from c AD 600, simultaneously with the waning of Teotihuacán. Nearer Tula, excavations in Tula de Allende have produced materials beneath the Toltec layers, showing it to have been settled a century or two before the occupation of the hill across the river. Because of the limited nature of these excavations, however, the size of this town is unknown; nor is it known if its occupants contributed to the founding of Tula itself.

The rise and growth of Tula. Archaeologists divide Tula's history into seven phases, based on the excavation and survey evidence, and on legendary history passed down through the Aztecs.

The *Prado Phase* (c AD 700–800) is best represented at *Tula Chico*, a small settlement whose occupants had migrated from both S and N: some of their pottery resembles Coyotlatelco Red-on-Buff Ware from the Basin of Mexico; and some comes from the Bajío to the NW.

Corral Phase (c AD 800–900). By c AD 800 Tula Chico was nearly double the size of ancient Chingu. Estimates of surveys by different teams range between 3 and 5 sq km, with a population of 19–27,000. The ridgetop site of *Tula Grande* was occupied for the first time, and later in the phase a new ceremonial centre was begun there, modelled on the one at Tula Chico. For most of the phase, however, Tula Chico remained the ceremonial core of the city. The pottery of this phase continued the Coyotlatelco tradition of Red-on-Buff wares, but these were now locally made rather than imported. Obsidian tools were also abundant, but the source of the raw material is uncertain as the Toltecs did not yet control the Pachuca and Tepeapulco mines to the S.

By c 950 two major changes had occurred, neither of which is completely understood. In an uncertainly defined *Terminal Corral* sub-phase, new pottery appeared, called Mazapan Red-on-Buff. It was not altogether unrelated to the Coyotlatelco tradition, but included wavy line decoration, characteristic of the Basin. The second change was the abandonment of the Tula Chico ceremonial plaza, leaving it as an open space within the city, almost as if cursed or prohibited ground. One interpretation of this event is that the two ceremonial centres were built by rival political factions, one of which eventually gained overall control and caused the temples and palaces of its rival to be destroyed.

The *Tollán Phase* (c 950–1150) saw the full florescence of Toltec power in central Mexico and its collapse. Most of the major monuments were built at Tula Grande, and the city grew to its greatest size. From the most recent archaeological work at the site, and from legendary history, a great deal is known about the nature of the Toltec 'state', its economy, and the daily life of its inhabitants (see below).

The *Fuego Phase* (c 1150–1300). As the Early Postclassic drew to a close, Chichimec peoples were again on the move and Tula does not seem to have escaped unscathed. Tradition dates the sacking of the city in AD 1156, and the archaeological evidence shows the site to be nearly abandoned by c 1180. There was an attack on the city c 1120, causing some Toltecs to move S and settle at Cholula. There was civil strife, focused between two rival factions within the city. The defeat of one faction caused its leader to leave with many of his followers. Times had also become harder owing to a reversal of the climatic shift that had brought greater agricultural productivity to the region in the first place. Continued pressure from the Chichimeca and also from the Huasteca to the NE caused the downfall of the new ruling faction, and most of the inhabitants dispersed to other areas of Mexico.

Palacio Phase (c 1300–1521). Few people had stayed on at Tula, but *Aztec II* ceramics have been found in some 13C levels. Slowly the site was reinhabited by an overspill of the population from the Basin, and by the 15C the site covered c 8.5 sq km, with a population of perhaps 20,000. *Aztec III* and *IV* ceramics show the presence of Aztec settlers at *El Cielito*, SE of Tula Grande, where they built a palace. Other Aztecs reoccupied Tula Grande and built several structures in and around the Plaza Central. Their chief interest, however, seems to have been the looting of Toltec sculptures and other relics.

The Ancient Population and Size of Tula. Throughout the earlier phases the population of both the city and its hinterland had continued to grow. The archaeological evidence indicates that this was due both to indigenous increase and to immigration from the N and W, and from the Basin of Mexico, where much of the population of Teotihuacán was abandoning the city. Another traditional constituent of Toltec make-up was the Nonoalca, variously described in prehispanic texts as a group of multilingual bringers of the arts and sciences who settled in the S Gulf Coast region after the collapse of Teotihuacán. In the Maya 'Popol Vuh' some later migrated S into Guatemala while others moved N to join the Tolteca–Chichimeca, and were instrumental in the establishment of Tula as the Toltec capital. After the fall of Tula these descendants of this branch moved S again, into the Basin of Mexico, and joined the population settled at Chalco.

Thus Tula came to include a wide ethnic mix and a mixture of architectural and technological styles. From the NW, the site of Alta Vista provided examples of colonnaded halls and one pottery tradition; from the Basin, Teotihuacán contributed other pottery styles and the example of contiguous residential apartments; and from other regions and sites (the Huasteca, El Tajín, and Xochicalco) came models for temple plans, ball court details, and architectural decorations.

Systematic surveys to determine the maximum size of ancient Tula have produced conflicting evidence: the Proyecto Tula team concluded that the city's core was no more than 5.3 sq km, and that many areas within the suburbs were unoccupied; in contrast, Richard Diehl's University of Missouri-Columbia survey produced evidence showing the city to have been up to 14 sq km, and other texts estimate as much as 16.5 sq km. Estimates of the city's population also vary widely: the lower limit of the Proyecto Tula estimate is 18,800, while James Stoutamire of the University of Missouri-Columbia team has estimated as high as 55,000; other sources suggest perhaps 30,000 within the densely residential city limits of c 10.75 sq km, and another 30,000 in the surrounding rural zone.

Civic and Domestic Architecture. Whatever the population, much more is known about the daily life of the urban Toltecs from excavations of their residential compounds. They lived in apartment blocks, contiguous as at Teotihuacán, but different in many details. Rooms were arranged around courtyards, the main entrance to which was L-planned, forcing a sharp turn to r. or l. before entering. The rooms were built either on the ground or on low platforms, with tepetate stone foundations supporting mud-brick walls. Roofs were flat, and floors were of packed clay and sometimes plastered with lime and painted; no magnificent murals have been found, however. A small altar often graced the courtyard, and burials were dug beneath them. There were storage pits and jars set into the floors of some rooms, while others were clearly sleeping quarters, or had stone-lined caches of valuable objects set beneath the floor. Sophisticated drainage systems of ceramic tubes kept the compounds dry.

The Toltec 'State'. Some details of Tula's political and commercial activities can also be reconstructed. Home economy was based on agriculture, and one of the reasons for the settlement and growth of Tula was an improvement in the regional climate towards the end of the Classic Period. Maize, beans, and a variety of vegetables provided the main fare; meat was rare. There is some evidence of cannibalism, although how frequent is unknown. If the later Aztec example can be projected back to the Toltecs, this was limited to ritual acts. Everyday ceramics were plain or sparsely decorated, and included bowls, jars, and the ubiquitous molcajete (bowl for grating vegetables) and comal (convex ceramic griddle). Ritual vessels were more highly decorated with painted and incised designs, and included many imports. There were hour-glass-shaped braziers and shallow, long-handled 'frying pans' for burning copal incense. Imported wares included Fine Orange wares from the S Gulf Coast and the Maya, and Tohil Plumbate pottery from the Highlands of Guatemala.

Other aspects of the economy included the manufacture of ceramic drainage tubes for both home use and export, mould-made figurines, and a thriving obsidian industry. The E side of the city contained many workshops for obsidian, and during the *Tollán Phase* Tula took control of the various quarries once run by Teotihuacán.

Several trade routes were used by Toltec merchants, believed to have been organized on lines similar to the Aztec pochteca. A W route went through Michoacán into the Río Lerma–Santiago drainage, and to the NW Pacific coast. A N route went along the foothills of the Sierra Madre Occidental into Zacatecas and Durango; and Toltec prospectors penetrated far into the N in search of minerals and rare stones, as had their Teotihuacano predecessors. E trade routes went NE to the Huasteca and SE to the Gulf Coast, and thence to the Maya. Trade with the Basin of Mexico was also important, but the growing powers there seem to have blocked a direct Toltec trade route through the Basin. Instead they skirted the Basin to the E, through the Valle de Toluca, and thence into Oaxaca and Chiapas.

By contrast, the exact nature of the Toltec political state is still uncertain. At various phases of its development several other city-states were potential rivals: Teotihuacán, El Tajín, Xochicalco, and Teotenango. Toltec control was strong in N central Mesoamerica by the *Tollán Phase*; and Toltec–Maya Chichén Itzá was a S focus of power. Between these two extremes, however, there were several rival states. Tula seems to have had firm control over only the N half of the Basin, the S half being controlled by Cholula. To the W the Tarascan state was emerging at the same time as Tula, as was a Huastec confederation to the E.

Toltec Legendary History. The traditional dates of the founding and sacking of Tula, passed down to us from the Aztecs, are AD 968 and 1156, respectively. There are two principal versions of this history, neither of which agrees entirely with the archaeological evidence, and the interpretation of which is not agreed by all scholars. The Aztecs regarded the Toltecs as the epitome of civilization and were not above rewriting their own history to bolster a desire to trace their ancestry to the Toltec dynasty. There is therefore evidence for tampering with the Toltec legends as well. Some scholars also believe that events in the Toltec legends may be telescoped, or record in a formal way events or situations that occurred more than once.

One version, recorded in the 'Anales de Cuautitlán' and in the 'Relación de Genealogía', describes Ce Técpatl Mixcóatl, leader of a Tolteca–Chichimeca tribe, and founder of the Toltec dynasty. He is supposed to have settled first at Culhuacán, and from there conquered Otomí towns to the N and S. After his assassination by political rivals, a Nahua woman bore his son, Ce Acatl Topiltzin, who eventually avenged his father and led his people out of the Basin to found the new capital at Tollán. He identified himself as king and high priest, and adopted Quetzalcóatl, the Plumed-Serpent, as his patron deity. He sponsored the arts, metallurgy, sculpture, and other crafts.

His rule at Tula, however, was short-lived. A rival faction, who favoured Quetzalcóatl's heavenly rival, Tezcatlipoca, preferred the military arts and human sacrifice to potting and jewellery-making. It incited the people to conquest and plotted Ce Acatl's overthrow. Inviting him to a feast, Tezcatlipoca's supporters succeeded in intoxicating him and thus causing him to neglect his religious duties. In disgrace, he left Tula in AD 987 to go into exile. In one ending he set himself on fire and rose into the heavens to become the Morning Star; in another, he embarked to the E on a raft of serpents, prophesying to return on the anniversary of his year sign—Ce Acatl ('one reed'). (Belief in the return of Quetzalcóatl was thus passed on to the Aztecs, and exploited by Cortés in 1519 when he learned of it.)

A second version of Toltec history is based on the 'Memoria Breve de Chimalpahin'. According to this source, Tollán was ruled simultaneously by Quetzalcóatl as the religious leader and Huémac as secular leader. The former was bound by a rule preventing family inheritance, and thus incited conflict when he attempted to arrange for his natural son to take his place. The civil war that ensued resulted in the abandonment of Tula by both factions and their leaders.

Excavations. The earliest 'excavations' at Tula were actually undertaken by the Aztecs. To modern archaeologists their activities are looked upon as sheer vandalism, but to the Aztecs it was a religious quest to collect Toltec sculptures and revere their memory. The Aztecs did not completely rob the site, however, and Antonio García Cubas discovered the first fragments of Atlante statues in 1873.

The first 'modern' archaeological excavations at Tula were conducted by Désiré Charnay in the 1880s. Tula was Charnay's principal archaeological endeavour, and through his publications he can be credited with having brought the site to the attention of other scholars. Such was the impoverishment of the site due to Aztec looting, however, that many refused to believe it lived up to the supposedly glorious ancient capital of an empire. The issue was reopened in the 1930s by Wigberto Jiménez Moreno, as new discoveries relevant to the history of the Toltecs were being made at Teotihuacán and Chichén Itzá. Through careful study of the historical accounts and comparison of modern and ancient place-names and topography, he was able to prove as positively as the evidence allowed that the ceremonial centre on the hill above modern Tula de Allende was indeed ancient Tollán.

This new interest prompted INAH to organize new excavations in 1940. Under the direction of Jorge Acosta they continued for 20 years, uncovering and restoring the principal monuments to be seen today, proving to the archaeological world's satisfaction that the site was Tollán, and providing the detailed evidence for the seminal essay by Pedro Armillas outlining the archaeologico–historical phases used today.

Two new projects to study and excavate ancient Tula began in the 1960s. One was a renewed effort by INAH, called Proyecto Tula, between 1968 and 1972. Under the general direction of Eduardo Matos Moctezuma, Juego de Pelota No. 2 and parts of Tula Chico were cleared and restored, the site of Chingu was excavated, an obsidian workshop area just E of Tula Grande was studied, and several survey projects around the site were completed.

A contemporary project of the University of Missouri-Columbia was directed by Richard A. Diehl and Robert A. Benfer. They studied the remains of the ordinary residents of the city, and it is from their evidence and interpretations that knowledge of Tula's ancient housing and population comes. Their project included several excavations near the El Corral site and to the SE of it, a general survey of the entire site to establish its changing limits through the phases, and several more detailed surveys using systematic surface survey methods.

Dominating the town plaza are the former Franciscan church and convent of **San José**, built c 1550–55, possibly to a design left by the active building friar Juan de Alameda, and standing in a deep atrio, containing pre-Conquest fragments, on a platform c 3m high.

Merlons bristle along the atrio wall, c 4.25m high, and, interspersed with garitas, along the parapet of the church. The imposing strength of wall and church is heightened by the use of appropriated cut-stone ashlar masonry. The W doorway is an elegant variant of Renaissance style, with slender fluted columns and ornate capitals, coffered arch and jambs, and segmental pediment frame topped by hexagonal choir window. To the N of the rib-vaulted nave, the large side chapel is a 17C addition. To the S of the church the two-storey convent cloister retains its Gothic-style lower walk arches which rest on the column shafts without the intervention of capitals.

The Archaeological Zone at Tula comprises the principal site, known as *Tula Grande*, three outlying ruins to the NE and SE (known as *Tula Chico*, *El Corral*, and *El Cielito*), and some carvings on the rock face, across the river. There is also a small site museum.

The site is 1.5km NW of the town; signposted to car-park at main entrance, E side of site. It is also possible to walk to the site from the town plaza, proceeding NW through a residential block and across the river on a swing bridge, then r., up the dirt road to approach the site from the S, across the *Plaza Central*. Daily, 9–6; fee.

The PLAZA CENTRAL was possibly begun as the ceremonial centre for a rival political faction, in opposition to the plaza of Tula Chico, which it eventually replaced. It is 120m wide, and surrounded by the largest, if not the most grandiose, monuments at Tula. In the centre of the plaza there is a small altar platform known as the *Adatorio*.

Its poor state of health is the result of two acts of vandalism: first, it was looted by the Aztecs in search of Toltec sacred relics; second, it was virtually dismantled by Désiré Charnay, who believed it was a tomb but has left us no notes of his 'excavation'. (It can be compared, however, to the Plataforma de Aguilas at Chichén Itzá, which is a much better preserved example.) It comprises a low rectangular platform, c 8.5m sq and 1.7m high, originally with inclining sides, later made vertical, and four staircases. When excavated, a stone chacmool was discovered on it. If it was in fact similar to the Chichén Itzá example, it was probably a small, but important, courtyard altar, and may well have contained the burial of a prominent Toltec citizen.

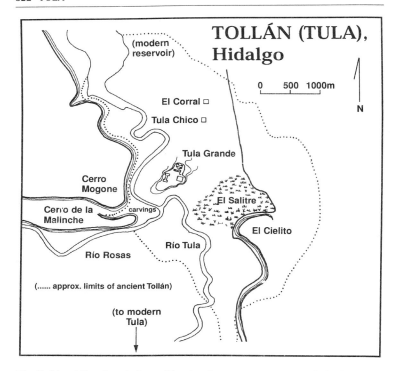

TOLLÁN (TULA), Hidalgo

The S side of the plaza is formed by structures not yet excavated: the long, low mound here may be a single platform or may cover an entire complex of buildings. The traces of a wide staircase on its S side suggest an important public building, perhaps an administration building fronting the plaza and separating it from the town below.

On the W side of the plaza is the **Juego de Pelota No. 2** and a *Tzompantli* (skull rack) platform, both of which were excavated by Eduardo Matos Moctezuma in 1968–70. The Juego de Pelota comprises an altar platform on the W side, undoubtedly used for the ritual practices associated with the ball game, and a long, I-shaped playing field, bounded by long platforms (?viewing stands) on the E and W sides; and small platforms at either end, with steps up the outer sides. Organ-cactus 'fences' are planted on the platforms at either end, outlining the plans of possible temple structures, with a stone chacmool statue in each, facing the playing field.

The Tzompantli was identified by the many teeth and fragments of human skulls found when it was excavated. It is a long, low platform with a short extension near the middle of its E side.

To the SW of the plaza, Charnay excavated a complex of ruins, which he called the *Palais Toltèque*, but these are not now easily visible.

The E side of the plaza is formed by the **Edificio Principal** (also known as *Pirámide C*). Although not as well preserved, and less spectacular, than other ruins at Tula, this was in fact the largest single structure. It was excavated in 1941–43 by Jorge Acosta and comprises a huge four-tiered pyramid with a wide, steep staircase from the Plaza Central, on its W side. The staircase is supported by an extension of the W face of the pyramid, and at plaza level, on

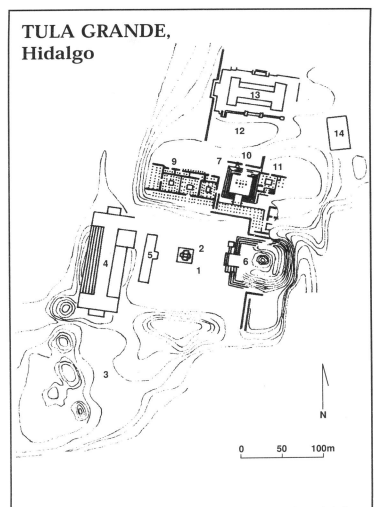

TULA GRANDE, Hidalgo

1 Plaza Central
2 Adoratorio
3 unexcavated structures
4 Juego de Pelota No. 2
5 Tzompantli
6 Edificio Principal
7 Edificio de los Atlantes/
  Pirámide de Tlahuizcalpantecuhtli

8 Templo de Quetzalcóatl
9 Pal. Quemado
10 Coatepantli
11 Pal. de Quetzalcóatl
12 Plaza Norte
13 Juego de Pelota No. 1
14 museum

the N side of this projection, are the foundations of a small Aztec building. Most of the pyramid's sides have been defaced, possibly by the Aztecs in their relentless search for Toltec relics. To the S of the pyramid, traces of walls and mounds may be the site of an adjacent palace, corresponding to the palace associated with the Edificio de los Atlantes.

The best preserved monuments form the N side of the Plaza Central. A short flight of steps at the NE corner of the plaza lead to the general platform, and to **Edificio de los Atlantes o de Tlahuizcalpantecuhtli** (also known as *Pirámide B*). At the foot of the pyramid, three rows of 14 square pillar-stumps each are all that remain of a continuous portico, which ran across the front of the pyramid and continued W along the front of its accompanying palace. Three more rows of four pillar-stumps each continue around the right angle of the platform. And four square pillars are aligned on the eighth step of the wide staircase mounting the S side of the monument.

The Edificio de Tlahuizcalpantecuhtli rises to a height of 10m in five reclining tiers, from a base of 40m sq. The four faces of the pyramid are of dressed stone and were originally decorated with carved stone panels depicting eagles and vultures devouring bleeding hearts, alternating with carved faces emerging from the jaws of plumed serpents, believed to represent Tlahuizcalpantecuhtli, Lord of the Dawn, and topped by a frieze of striding jaguars and coyotes. All of these figures were originally painted in bright colours, but almost no trace of this now remains. These tablets were also looted by the Aztecs, but they missed several on the N side, and most of the E side, which would have been covered by the Pal. de Quetzalcóatl. One interpretation of these reliefs is that they represent the cult of Eagle and Jaguar Knights, a military fraternity brought to prominence by the Toltecs and later emulated by the Aztecs.

At the top of the pyramid stand the various roof supports for the *Templo de Quetzalcóatl*, or Tlahuizcalpantecuhtli as the Morning Star.

These have been re-erected here after the Aztecs dismantled the shrine in attempting to carry off its sculptures. By digging a trench into the N side of the mound, and putting up a huge earthen ramp, they managed to lower the smaller idols and panel decorations down the slope. However, they unaccountably abandoned attempts to remove the larger columns, leaving several of them on their sides on the ramp, where they were found by the excavators.

Atlantes on Pirámide B, Tollán

First, flanking the entrance to the temple, are the sections of two round serpent columns whose heads rested on the ground and whose tails supported the lintel to the porch roof. Behind these stand the four great *Atlantes*, each 4.6m high in four sections. They represent the epitome of the Toltec warrior, wearing rectangular ear pieces, butterfly breastplates, belts clasped behind by large discs, necklaces, bracelets, and sandals decorated with plumed-serpents; each holds an atlatl (spear-thrower) in one hand, and an obsidian knife and incense bag in the other.

The Aztecs obviously got away with some of the sections, for the Atlante on the extreme l. (W) is a complete replica, as are the upper sections of that on the extreme r. Behind each Atlante stands a square column, each also 4.6m tall in four sections, and carved in low relief with the profiles of Toltec warriors. Based on comparison with examples at Toltec Chichén Itzá, the rear of the temple would originally have contained a large altar slab supported on the upraised hands of small atlantes, c 1m high. These are now in various museums.

Return now to the base of the pyramid and walk W through the square pillars of the portico. Against the base walls, beneath protective canopies, several of the front chambers of the palace (see below) have low benches with friezes in relief. These depict processions of figures—warriors and priests—wearing plumed headdresses, jewellery, and short skirts, and carrying shields and bunches of darts. Much of their red, blue, yellow, white, and black paint survives. The cornice above their heads is carved with a writing serpent.

The **Pal. Quemado** (also known as *Edificio 3*) is on the far side of a narrow alley running along the W side of the Edificio de los Atlantes. Its name was coined by Jorge Acosta, who originally concluded that its destruction by fire dated to the sacking and abandonment of Tula in the 13C. In fact, although the palace was indeed damaged by fire, we know neither when this occurred nor what caused it. The palace, like so many other monuments at Tula, can be compared to the columned halls at Chichén Itzá. It comprises three almost square rooms, each colonnaded on all four sides, leaving a skylight in the centre. These are fronted by a continuous colonnaded portico across the S side, and each is entered separately by a single doorway, on the E and W ends for the corresponding courts, and onto the Plaza Central for the centre court. Inside the central court, the walls are lined with benches carved with similar processions of figures to those just described, and the remains of a flight of steps can still be seen, leading to the now destroyed upper rooms. Chacmool sculptures were found in each court, but only the centre one survives complete. In one of these courts patterns on the floor form a patolli board, the ancient Mesoamerican game resembling pachisi. There are four smaller rooms in the rear, or N side, of these main rooms, each with column-supported roofs. A narrow portico of columns runs along their front, opening onto the Plaza Norte, and another deep, colonnaded porch forms the W side of the palace.

The rooms of the palace produced no artefacts to suggest their actual use as residences. On the contrary, they resemble no other apartment houses excavated elsewhere in Tula, and the caches of tobacco pipes and other ceremonial objects found in them suggest that they were more likely to have been used as council chambers and rooms for performing various rituals. This interpretation would probably also apply to the remains of part of the Pal. de Quetzalcóatl, partially exposed on the E side of Edificio de los Atlantes.

Standing on the N side of the Edificio de los Atlantes, the *Coatepantli* (Serpent Wall) is 2.2m high, composed of two sections: the top is carved with geometric friezes and below these are tablets carved and painted with a procession of plumed-serpents devouring human skeletons. At its E end stand the ruins of the *Pal. de Quetzalcóatl*, also known as *Edificio 1*.

Across the PLAZA NORTE stands **Juego de Pelota No. 1**, the first ball court to be excavated. It is larger than the ball court of the Plaza Central, but comprises a similar, I-shaped playing field, measuring 54m by 12.5m. It is formed by a continuous platform of several tiers on the W, down-slope, side, and has wide staircases all along the S edge of the platform. The sides of its playing field are formed by wide, gently sloping benches, and the walls above them were once set with panels, presumably carved. The empty sockets for the ring goals can also be seen. The drainage system of this ball court is so well built that it continues to function.

E of this ball court Charnay excavated a structure he referred to as 'Maison Toltèque' (officially *Edificio* 2), but very little of these ruins can now be seen.

In the patio of the site **Museum** are various sculptures of Toltec warriors, Tláloc (god of rain), and a chacmool. Inside are displays of the chronology of Tula, cases illustrating the pottery of each phase, and other Toltec objects incl. characteristic braziers, 'frying-pan' incense burners, carved slabs, and small atlante altar supports.

Tula Chico lies c 1km NNE of Tula Grande. Although unexcavated, the mounds, and evidence from surface collections here, show it to be the site of an earlier ceremonial centre similar in layout to the main site. Just SE of Tula Chico, Diehl and Benfer conducted their excavations of Toltec apartment compounds.

Located c 500m NE of Tula Chico and just across the road, the **El Corral** temple is assumed to have been dedicated to Quetzalcóatl. It is a round structure of two tiers, with rectangular structures flanking it to the E and W, the latter consisting of several rooms around an open court. The round platform is well preserved, but the staircase on its E side is mostly destroyed.

N of the stairs is a small rectangular altar, which was lined with carved stone slabs. These depict a procession of Toltec warriors, skulls, and crossed bones, and may now be seen in the site museum.

C 1.5km SE of Tula Grande is **El Cielito**, the palace built by the Aztecs in the 16C. It sits on the flat ridgetop and when excavated produced post-Conquest materials as well as late Aztec pottery, indicating that it was still used and renovated after 1521. It was unfortunately looted by treasure-hunters in the early 1970s.

The cliff face of **Cerro de la Malinche**, across the Río Tula and opposite Tula Grande, is carved with a figure thought to represent Centéotl, goddess of the waters, and Quetzalcóatl or Ce Acatl dressed as the Plumed-Serpent. Alongside these are the glyphs for *Eight Tecpatl* ('eight flint') and *Four Acatl* ('four reed'). One interpretation is that they are Toltec carvings commemorating their ruler and his consort; another is that they were carved by the Aztecs in order to give the impression of a dynastic link between their own and the Toltec ruling houses. At Chapultepec, the image of Moctezuma I Ilhuicamina (1440–68) is also depicted as Quetzalcóatl (see Rte 10), and on stylistic comparison the Malinche carvings appear to be Late Postclassic rather than Toltec.

C 15km N of Tula on a minor road, and N of Presa de Endhó, is *Tepetitlán*, where the Franciscan convent of San Bartolomé was founded in 1571 'a ynstancia y pedimento de los yndios', to whom the flaying-alive of the saint appealed as resembling the rites of Xipe Totec. The church, rededicated in 1615, faces NNE; nave and side aisles are flat-roofed, but the sanctuary is vaulted. The road continues to (29km) *Chapantongo*, where the Augustinian convent of Santiago was founded c 1569. The present church is 17C, though the lateral walls, S wider than N, may be part of the earlier edifice.

20 Mexico City to Texcoco and Tlaxcala

Méx. 190, 136, and 119. 156km.—37km (3km r.) Coatlinchán.—42km (2km r.) **Huexotla**.—44km **Texcoco**.—52km (3km N) Tepetlaoxtoc.—81km Calpulalpan.—112km Hueyotlipan.—156km **Tlaxcala**.

The broad Calz. Ignacio Zaragoza (Méx. 190) branches off from Eje 3 Oriente and runs SE, crossing (10km) Blvd Puerto Central Aereo, leading NE to the airport. At 12.5km Viaducto Piedad comes in on the r., a junction at which stands an equestrian statue of Gen. Ignacio Zaragoza, victor of the Cinco de Mayo.

At 20km Méx. 190 branches l., leaving the toll road to Puebla (Méx. 150D) on the r. At 22.5km we take the l. fork on to Méx. 136 to Texcoco. 31km (2km l.) *Sta María Chimalhuacán*, the former *Chimalhuacán Atenco*, where the former Dominican convent of Sto Domingo dates from c 1560.

In 1939 an early farming village was excavated here.The pottery dates to the last centuries BC and is similar to that of other contemporary villages dotted around the lakes of the Basin of Mexico. The name is also applied to the earliest pottery phase, incl. crude figurines, at Teotihuacán, when that site was itself a small village. In the Postclassic Period Chimalhuacán was one of the many small city-states and an Aztec provincial centre in the Basin of Mexico.

32km road r. to (1km) *San Vicente Chicoloapan*, with an abundantly elaborated churrigueresque church façade, and (7km) *Coatepec*, on the W side of the Sierra Quetzaltepec. Here the convent, once a visita of Texcoco, in a raised atrio, was founded (as Sta María de Jesús) in 1527 by the Franciscans and taken over by the Dominicans (Natividad de Nuestra Señora) c 1559. The portería leads to the single-storey cloister, a survival of the 1530s. 4km S is *San Francisco Acuauhtla*, once a dependency of Coatepec, where the 16C church doorway, carved by Indians adapting a European style, has colonnettes shaped like Franciscan cords. 37km turning r. for (3km) **Coatlinchán**, on the SW face of the peak of Huixto (3510m), where the Franciscan church and convent of *San Miguel Arcángel* were built in 1569–85. The N atrio gateway is an attractive, if naïve, work by an indigenous hand. Floral forms in low relief decorate the arch rim and monogram medallions the well-proportioned jambs. The church's elaborately decorated façade attests a late 17C (and later) refashioning. The lower-cloister arches are notable for their semicylindrical soffits, without archivolts.

42km r. turn for (2km) **HUEXOTLA** ('place of willows'), once one of the subject towns of the kingdom of Acolhuacán, of the Acolhua, one of the seven Aztec tribes.

It was established near Texcoco by refugees from Tula after that city's fall in the mid-13C, and was later a provincial centre and dependency of Texcoco in the 15C and 16C. There are three cleared areas. The most famous feature is a 4.5m high, 62m long wall, possibly defensive, built in 1409 by Ixtlilxóchitl, father of Nezahualcóyotl, and king of Texcoco before his murder in 1418 by king Tezozómoc of Azcapotzalco. Other visible remains include, on the far side of the barranca, a pyramid of four construction phases, with a stairway to the remains of a small rectangular shrine at the top; and a canal. On a nearby hill, a circular structure of three building phases is thought to have been a temple platform, probably dedicated to Quetzalcóatl. Partially excavated ruins include a group of rooms (a palace?) and a large platform area (a market-place?), all of Postclassic date.

The small, but fascinating, church and convent of **San Luis Obispo** was built c 1528–64 as a visita of Texcoco.

The convent was regarded as a model for Franciscan building: 'very, very poor, in accordance with the wishes of our father St Francis. ...The cloister shall not have two storeys and shall be but seven feet wide'. Here Fray Jerónimo de Mendieta (c 1534–1604) wrote his 'Historia eclesiástica indiana', an invaluable history of the friars' missionary efforts.

In contrast with such desirable simplicity, the building is on the highest of three prehispanic terraces, the lower two (each c 70 sq m) forming a double atrio joined by a stairway, and planted with cypresses and olives. Just N of the church are remains of a three-bay open chapel. The church itself, standing where once stood the pagan temple, was rebuilt during the late 17C and early 18C. The enchanting façade (1721–), executed in mortar, is a prime example of Texcocan indigenous work, yet spacious and sophisticated for its type. Local versions of estípites, stylishly carved with saintly heads and flower and vegetal motifs, leave ample room for entrecalles containing saints in wide niches and the florid, lacy decoration which also marks the central panel. At the E end of the nave is the original 16C pulpit. S of the church the low arches of the small evocative cloister lack archivolts; above the wooden pillars and corner piers of the unlooked-for upper storey, a 17C addition, are mixtilinear arches and a wooden cloister-walk ceiling.

To the l. of Méx. 136, near **Chapingo**, is the **Escuela Nacional de Agricultura**, founded in 1924 and occupying the former hacienda of *Nuestra Señora de la Concepción Acayac* (18C, with later 19C fin-de-siècle alterations), once property of Pres. Manuel González. Its chief attraction is a series of frescoes by Diego Rivera (begun in 1924), a commentary on the Mexican Revolution and full of symbolism, regarded as his masterpiece, which decorate the former chapel, now the Salón de Actos.

He skilfully used the architectural elements to show (on r.) the biological development of human life and (on l.) the historical and social development, both sets of panels complementing one another. On the end wall, level with the cornice, reclines a huge, opulent nude Mother Earth, in her r. hand a growing plant, surrounded by other figures representing the elements and Man, a muscular nude, about to dominate nature through modern technology; to his l., another superb female nude is water; to his r., fire thrusts out a blazing torch. At the other end, on the wall masking what used to be the choir, is another nude Mother Earth, deeply sensual, asleep, yet a figure of latent power. In the vault, a series of dark-skinned male nudes symbolize agriculture.

On the r. of the entrance a mural shows Emiliano Zapata buried beneath a maizefield.

In the entrance hall of the adjoining administration building are murals depicting the four seasons and, on the first-floor landing, Good and Bad Government; distribution of land among the peasants; the embrace of peasant and worker. Inside the administration offices are mural panels depicting the arrival of a socialist state in Mexico, transferred from the house of the director, where they were originally painted by Xavier Guerrero in 1923.

44km TEXCOCO (c 30,000 inhab.; 2778m; H,R,P), once on the E shore of the Lago de Texcoco, is known for cereals and peach orchards, and for textiles. Though bearing no reminders of its illustrious prehispanic past, it is yet a significant place, somewhat revived since 17–19C decline.

According to legend, the great Chichimec leader Xólotl led his people from the N into the Basin of Mexico after the destruction of Tula. In the mid-12C he took up residence and founded an urban centre at Tenayuca. At about the same time Texcoco was settled by migrating Otomí, who called it Katenikko. According to some sources, Xólotl himself, according to others, his second successor (Quenitzin Tlaltecatzin), moved his capital from Tenayuca to Texcoco c AD 1200 or a little later. As Texcoco grew more powerful in the Basin, the kingdom of Acolhuacán was formed, and Texcoco inevitably came into conflict with Azcapotzalco and the kingdom of the Tepaneca on the W side of the Basin (both the Acolhua and the Tepaneca were of the seven Aztec tribes). The rivalry finally reached the point of political intrigue, and king Tezozómoc of Azcapotzalco slew Ixtlilxóchitl I, king of Texcoco in 1418. Nezahualcóyotl ('fasting-coyote'), Ixtlilxóchitl's son, witnessed the murder from his hiding place in a tree, fled into exile with friends and relatives, and was offered asylum in Tlaxcala and at Huexotzingo. When he grew to manhood, itching for revenge, he returned to Texcoco to claim his inheritance and allied himself with the Mexica Aztecs under Itzcóatl; the Mexica also had old scores to settle with the Tepaneca. With a third ally, Tlacopan, they successfully attacked Azcapotzalco and ended Tepanec power for good. Out of this alliance grew the 'Triple Alliance', in which Texcoco and Mexica Tenochtitlán each took two-fifths of any spoils, while Tlacopan settled for one-fifth.

Among ancient historians Nezahualcóyotl (ruled 1431–72) has a reputation as a philosopher-king, and under him Texcoco became the foremost centre of art and learning in the Basin. He codified Texcocan law, organized a council of nobles, merchants, and commoners, and fostered art, the crafts, music, and poetry. He built a dike across Lago de Texcoco, helped develop and increase the chinampa system of agriculture on Lago de Chalco, and joined Tenochtitlán in schemes to build an aqueduct from Chapultepec, and a summer palace and pleasure park for Moctezuma I Ilhuicamina. He is famous also as a religious theorist, coming the nearest of any Mesoamerican ruler to a monotheistic religion. While being careful not to neglect the tribal gods, he preferred to worship an abstract, invisible god called Tloque Nahuaque, who had both masculine and feminine qualities. Nezahualcóyotl's own architectural works included a ten-storey temple–pyramid representing the heavens, a temple to Tloque Nahuaque, and a summer palace at Texcotzingo, incl. temples, fountains, aqueducts from mountain springs, and baths. Both Nezahualcóyotl and his son and successor, Nezahual-pilli (1472–1515) tried to stem the increasing belligerence of the Mexica; Nezahualpilli especially condemned the so-called 'Flowery Wars' undertaken to take prisoners for the sacrificial lust of Mexica priests. Enmity between Nezahualpilli and Moctezuma II Xocoyot-zin deepened when the former caused the execution of a Mexica princess for adultery; Moctezuma took revenge by persuading one of Nezahualpilli's concubines to murder his son and heir, Huexotzincatzin.

Thus at Nezahualpilli's death, two sons, Ixtlilxóchitl II and Cacamatzin (1515–20), each claimed the throne. Moctezuma II fanned the flames of civil war and supported the latter, causing Ixtlilxóchitl to support the Spanish invasion in 1519.

As a major power in the Basin Texcoco exacted tribute from many smaller city-states, incl. Coatepec, to the S. Here excavations yielded pottery showing it to have been occupied from c 2000 BC and a contemporary of Tlatilco. Other contemporary city-states of the E Basin included Chiconautla, Tepexpan, and Tezoyuca to the NW; Tepetlaoxtoc to the NE; Chiautla to the N; and Huexotla, Coatlinchán, Chimalhuacán, and Coatepec to the S and SW. The huge statue at the entrance to the Museo Nacional de Antropología was found at a quarry in the Ajusco hills of Coatlinchán.

In 1521 Cortés made Texcoco his headquarters for operations to recapture Tenochtitlán. Hence he launched the brigantines he had built in Tlaxcala. In 1523 the three Flemish Franciscan pioneers, Pedro de Gante, Juan de Aora (reputedly an illegitimate son of James IV of Scots), and Juan de Tecto, were lodged in the palace of the lords. Here Fray Pedro learned the purest Náhuatl, evincing an extraordinary eloquence which he, a stammerer, possessed neither in Castilian nor in Flemish. When the Twelve arrived in 1524, their leader, Martín de Valencia, straight away baptized Cortés's friend Ixtlilxóchitl and other nobles because they knew their catechism. In 1525 began the friars' destruction of Texcoco's 'beautiful turreted temples'. In 1582 Juan Bautista Pomar wrote of fine houses and palaces 200 years old, but decline set in. A population of 150,000 in the 1520s (the court alone numbered 20,000, getting through 400,000 tortillas a day) was severely affected by plague in 1545–48 and 1576–80. By 1626, according to Thomas Gage, it was a poverty-stricken village. In Feb.–Apr. 1827 it was capital of the State of México.

On the W side of the main plaza is the covered *Mercado*, crowded on Sun. Off the SW side we reach the former Franciscan convent, called **San Francisco**, in an atrio reduced in size.

The Franciscan Twelve were greeted by Cortés and Ixtlilxóchitl on St Antony's day (13 June) 1524 and established their first convent (*San Antonio*) in a part of the palace. The convent was translated to this site c 1527–28; in it, in 1530, Cortés reburied his first wife and buried his mother, Catalina Pizarro; and in 1536 an infant son. In 1566 his own bones were temporarily laid to rest here on their way back to Mexico. From the 16C only the portería and the lower cloister (c 1536–45) survive.

Another relic of the 16C building is the N doorway arabesque pilasters of the present church (1664–76). They run up to crude classicizing capitals, with letters of the alphabet, in order, in the panels. (The Indian craftsmen copied the Renaissance lettering from a book, thinking they were incl. an inscription, as the friars did.) On the slants are other arabesque panels next to Gothic-type colonnettes. The churrigueresque high altarpiece (1744) is by Felipe de Ureña; that in the N transept is a good baroque example. To the r. of the high altar, the huge Last Supper is attr. Luis Juárez.

On the SW side of the church juts the five-arched open chapel-portería, probably antedating the earlier 16C church and extended upwards at a later date. The part nearer the church is the chapel, its W front consisting of one large and one small arch, and limited at N and S by two pairs of small arches; the modest W opening forming the link with the second large arch—the convent entrance. The archivolt-less curves of different spans resting awkwardly on compound piers give the whole an ungainly look. The lower cloister is a refinement of the same technique, the tall arcades showing even spans and exuding a quiet elegance. Gothic traceries, rare in Mexico, survive in the S convent wall.

On the S side of the portería is the **Cap. de la Tercera Orden**, an 18C rebuilding. Rivalling the churrigueresque main retable, in the r. transept are the remains of the early 17C Renaissance retable once belonging to the earlier main church: in the predella, bas-reliefs of six apostles; more fine relief in the lower thirds of the slender fluted columns; and six anon. paintings of unusual quality—the Adoration of the Shepherds tenebrist and italianate, the others almost baroque in style. An enchanting painting of St Joseph and the Child Jesus by Juan Correa is another treasure.

On the N side of the main church stands the 18C chapel of *San Antonio*, its side doorway crowded with delightfully overstated stucco relief in popular Texcocan style.

From the plaza C. Nezahualcóyotl Oriente leads E to the 18C *Casa del Constituyente*, now the Casa de Cultura, where the constitution of the State of México was signed on 14 Feb. 1827. It houses a collection of paintings by Felipe Gutiérrez (1824–1904), a widely travelled native of the town, trained in the Academy of San Carlos. Nearly opposite, in the 18C church of *San Juan de Dios*, the State congress met on the same day in solemn celebration of the constitution.

Of Texcoco's barrio chapels the most significant are *La Concepción* (rebuilt in the 17C) and *Sta Trinidad* (18C). The former has a double-arched doorway, thick with exuberant relief. Slender colonnettes continue upwards to form the arch curves, with two pairs of felicitous angels attached—all perhaps of early 16C Portuguese Manueline Gothic inspiration. The latter has a façade with wavy pilasters and delightful upper storey: God the Father, Our Lady, and St Francis occupy delectable niches surrounded by sinuous relief and above impudent female angels.

TEXCOCO TO CHIAUTLA. 10km. We leave Texcoco to the N. 2km *Tulantongo*. Here the church of La Candelaria, in Texcocan baroque, is notable for its square choir window, framed by beautiful stone filigree work. The late 18C atrio gate shows signs of neoclassical influence. A l. turn for (5km) *San Salvador Atenco*, a good centre for the *Parque Nacional el Contador* (camping) and its many ahuehuete trees.

From Atenco we may follow the road N (which joins, after 9km, the Mexico City–Teotihuacán road, Méx. 85) to (4km; l.) **Nexquipayac**, where the doorway of the church of *San Cristóbal*, a characterful 16C work, resembles Manueline Gothic, with prominent colonnettes, alfíz, and strong foliated pattern of the archivolt. In the upper storey is a lively relief of St Christopher. 2km beyond is a turning r. for (2km) *Tezoyuca*, whose 16C church of San Buenaventura was later modified in local style; an open chapel is attached.

7km r. turn for (8km) **Chiconcuac**, a picturesque place and famous handicrafts centre (sarapes and sweaters especially). The façade of the 18C church of *San Miguel*, standing in an atrio whose wall is aggressively embossed with decorative urns, female figures, and rampant lions, is in the most expressive and ornate Texcocan baroque. 10km *Chiautla*, where the church of San Andrés is a 17–18C rebuilding of a Franciscan visita church founded in the 1570s. The three-bay atrio arcade, one of the finest in Mexico, with graceful profiles, is a 17C baroque reworking.

Further examples of popular Texcocan baroque churches are within easy reach of Texcoco. C 2km E is the outer barrio chapel of *Santiaguito*, a rustic 16C structure with added 17C decoration. At *San Simón* (c 4km NE) the lush three-storey façade, an ambitious, happy work, includes niches with saints at an angle to the portal. C 500m S is *Texompa* where, immediately to the l. of the church of San Juan, stands a striking, undulating atrial arch, with column capitals in the form of eagle feathers or cactus petals. The church's wide façade incorporates a bold choir window. In the neighbouring village of *San Sebastián* the late 18C façade and tower delightfully lighten and adapt the neoclassical. Note the garlands between the columns on either side of the starry choir window.

C 4km E of Texcoco is the former hacienda of *Molino de Flores* (1667), once property of the condes de Santiago de Calimaya. The gardens are now a national park; the chapel has a pretty baroque façade; and the pantheon contains mausolea of former owners.

At **Texcotzingo** ('laughing hill'), located in the park, Nezahualcóyotl built himself a luxurious summer palace c 1455–67, equipped with all the accoutrements of his reign, and where he could enjoy sponsoring the arts and religious contemplation he loved. The site was studied and plans drawn by W. Krickeberg in 1949, and by H. B. Nicholson in 1959. Aqueducts conducted water from as far as 27km away, baths were hewn out of the rock, long corridors of rooms, temples, courts, conference halls, a treasury, and an arsenal, were all described by eyewitnesses from Cortés' army just after the conquest. The present ruins give some idea of the cultivation of the 16C kingdoms of central Mexico.

Just N of Texcoco we turn r. (E) on to Méx. 136 to (47km) turning l. for (5km) *Papalotla*, an agreeable village whose 18C church of Santo Toribio faces a triple-arched atrio gateway (dated 1733), covered by a riot of fantastic stucco relief, a showpiece of Texcocan baroque. 52km turning l. for (3km N) **Tepetlaoxtoc**, a small town engaged in forestry. The former Dominican convent of *Sta María Magdalena*, one of the first in New Spain, was founded in the early 1530s by Fray Domingo de Betanzos (c 1480–1549), austere head of the first Dominican mission in 1526.

The 'Codex Kingsborough', written c 1553 and kept in the British Museum, is a protest by the Indians of Tepetlaoxtoc against the demands made on them by their encomendero Gonzalo de Salazar. In 1548 Abp Zumárraga is said to have confirmed 14,500 Indians here, an exertion so great (he was 72) that it brought on his death.

Of the 16C structure, reached by a broad flight of steps (reminder of a pre-hispanic sanctuary), little of interest remains. The church was rebuilt probably in the 17C. On the S transept wall is a painting of Souls in Purgatory with SS Michael, Antony, and Rose by Juan Correa. The great portal is 19C work. In the rustic cloister are traces of 16C murals (Passion scenes). In the convent garden is the retreat built for Fray Domingo, entered by an espadaña-topped portico: little chapel, tiny cloister, and cell. Here his full-length portrait, copied by Indians late in the 16C, is painted in oils on amate paper.

At 64km we cross into the State of Tlaxcala. 74km *Tecoaque*, a Late Post-classic ceremonial centre and town on the Tlaxcala-Mexica Aztec border. The structures uncovered included a central plaza, the circular base of a temple and an altar to Ehecatl, god of wind, and sunken patios surrounded by rooms with sophisticated drainage arrangements. 80km turning l. for (20km NE) *Apan*, see Rte 63. 81km **Calpulalpan** (c 10,000 inhab.; 2578m; H,P), a pulque-producing centre.

It was a 'gateway' community and obsidian distribution centre controlled by Teotihuacán. A trade route leading directly from Teotihuacán's *Av. Este* to Calpulalpan was discovered by Thomas Charlton in 1975 (cf. *Otumba, Pachuca, Tepeapulco*, and *Tulancingo*). In the 16C its lime-kilns supplied most of the needs of Mexico City.

The former Franciscan convent of *San Simón y San Judas*, founded c 1569 and started c 1580, was not completed until the 17C and has been altered in the 18C and 20C. The atrial cross, distinctively carved, is of the 16C. The church's W doorway is dated 1608 and the diaphragm arches of the roof may be a survival of the original building. Entered through an eight-bay semicircular arch portería, the cloister contains wooden supports on stone footings, and traces of 16C murals.

Méx. 136 continues SE to (112km) **Hueyotlipan** (c 4300 inhab.; 2581m), where in July 1520 Cortés and his worsted army received a warm welcome on their way from the defeat of the Noche Triste to Tlaxcala. The 17C church of San Ildefonso stands near what remains of a Franciscan convent, built c 1585 as a visita of Tlaxcala (but without a church), its cloister of coarse brick. 131km turning l. for (3km NE) *Sta Bárbara Acuicuixcatepec*, where a 16C open chapel has been transformed into a small church. 133km *Xaltocan* (2209m), with an 18C church (San Martín) in a popular adaptation of churrigueresque. 136km (l.) **Yauhquemehcan** (2515m), a small pulque and fruit producing town in a rugged and wooded landscape. The 17C church of *San Dionisio*, in dark grey stone, has a delightful façade ornamented in a local version of florid baroque. The high altarpiece is a splendidly large example of churrigueresque. At (138km) *Ocotoxco*, we meet the Tulancingo–Tlaxcala road (Méx. 119). We turn r. for (156km) *Tlaxcala*, see Rte 68.

21 Nogales to Hermosillo and Guaymas

Méx. 15, 422km.—68km Imuris (Méx. 2 to [168km] Agua Prieta).—91km Magdalena (for [153km] Arizpe).—108km Sta Ana.—279km **Hermosillo**—422km **Guaymas**.

This route follows Méx. 15, first stretch of the Pacific Highway, which, after Hermosillo, runs a few km inland from the W coast and the Gulf of California. Beyond Tepic, as Méx. 200 and Méx. 190, it continues its way to Tapachula near the Guatemalan frontier, a total distance of 3500km. The road, of varying quality, traverses the E edge of the Sonora desert and at first keeps roughly parallel with the railway from Nogales to Empalme.

NOGALES (c 75,000 inhab.; 1120m; H,R,P), an undistinguished frontier town and commercial centre, developed out of the desert during the 1880s to serve the Sonora railway (Ferrocarril del Pacífico), offically opened in 1882. It is named after the walnut groves (nogaleras) in the vicinity.

Bus station. S of the town. Services to *Tepic* (24 hrs); to *Guadalajara* (28 hrs); to *Mexico City* (42 hrs); to *Tijuana* (c 11 hrs); to *Ciudad Obregón* via *Hermosillo* (c 6 hrs); to *Guaymas*; to *Mazatlán*; etc.

Railway to *Hermosillo* and *Mazatlán*; to *Guadalajara* (48 hrs); to *Mexico City*.

US Consulate. 31 C. Obregón.

At c 42km a customs station. 68km *Imuris* (R,P), a mining centre.

From here Méx. 2 climbs sinuously NE (through the NE part of the Pimería Alta; see below) and then descends to (30km) **Cocóspera**, among the first of Fr Kino's missions (see below), in a valley divided up among farms, founded c 1691 as *Nuestra Señora del Pilar y Santiago de Cocóspera*, but in the 18C exposed to Apache raids and often rebuilt. The church, now a ruin, dates mainly from a final Franciscan renovation in 1832. The road continues to (84km) **Cananea** (27,000 inhab.; 1490m; H,R,P), on the Nogales–Agua Prieta railway and scene of a bloody encounter regarded as a precursor of the Mexican Revolution.

The exploitation of local copper deposits, the Cobre Grande mine, was begun by the Jesuits in 1760. In 1906 the Mexican miners employed by the Cananea Consolidated Copper Co. struck in protest against bad treatment and low wages compared with their US colleagues. Rafael Izábal, governor of Sonora, requested help from the US army and police. In confrontations on 1 and 2 June, 23 (incl. four US personnel) were killed and wounded.

168km **Agua Prieta** (26,000 inhab.; H,R,P), on the frontier opposite Douglas (Arizona), and a manganese-mining centre.

On 1 Nov. 1915 Villa launched an assault on the town, fortified by trenches, electrified barbed wire, and machine guns, and was utterly defeated; 3000 survivors retreated W to Naco. In Apr. 1920 the proclamation of the Plan of Agua Prieta signalled the Sonora revolt of Gens Calles and Salvador Alvarado and Col. Adolfo de la Huerta against Carranza, and in favour of Obregón.

Méx. 15 continues along the valley of the Río Magdalena to (91km) **Magdalena** (c 15,000 inhab.; 693m; H,R,P), a mining centre (manganese).

The mission of Sta María de Buquivaba was founded in 1689 by the Tyrolese Jesuit Eusebio Francisco Kino (1645–1711), evangelizer and explorer, who from 1687 established a series of mission stations in N and NE Sonora, an area of river valleys separated by plateaux and mountain ranges on the W side of the Sierra Madre Occidental, and incl. the Pimería Alta and Opatería. The latter were inhabited by Pima and Opata Indians, often at war with the

Spaniards whose frontier gradually advanced N in the 17C. In 1966 Fr Kino's remains were discovered near the Pal. Municipal and have been placed in a specially built mausoleum.

The church of *San Francisco Javier*, dedicated in March 1711, was rebuilt by the Franciscans in 1768, but damaged in 1773 by marauding Seris and Apaches. The present church dates from a renovation in the 1830s. The feast of St Francis of Assisi (4 Oct.) ends two weeks of festivities by Yaqui, Pápago, and Pima Indians.

8km NE of Magdalena is **San Ignacio de Cabúrica** where Fr Kino established the principal mission of the Río Magdalena valley in 1690. The church (c 1710–20, with later 18C modifications) has ingenuous floral stucco façade relief.

From Magdalena a mountain road runs SE into the Opatería, first missionized by Franciscans from New Mexico in the 1640s. At (45km) *Cucurpe* (P), in the valley of the Río San Miguel, the mission of Los Santos Reyes was relinquished by the Jesuits after 1767 to the Franciscans from Querétaro. The 19C church is a ruin. The wildlife of the area includes deer and wild boar. There are several nearby sites with cave paintings and petroglyphs: *La Tijera* cave in Arroyo Cerro Prieto has zoomorphic and anthropomorphic scenes; *La Pulsera* cave (c 3km NE of Cucurpe) has red painted geometric designs; and *Arroyo Saracachi* (c 3km S of La Pulsera) has a large rock shelter with painted crosses and hand prints. (Local guides are suggested.) From Cucurpe the road (for c 60km of rougher quality) continues into the Río Sonora valley SE to (110km) *Banamichi* (R,P).

From here is best reached (43km N, on an improved road along the Sonora valley) **Arizpe** (5,500 inhab.; 870m; H,R,P), at the confluence of Ríos Bacanuchi and Bacoachi, once an Opata settlement. In 1779 Teodoro de Croix, first comandante general of the Provincias Internas, made it his headquarters. In 1786 it became capital of the intendancy of Sonora-Sinaloa. In 1832–38 it was capital of Sonora. The interior of the Jesuit mission church of *Nuestra Señora de la Asunción* (built probably in the 1670s; modified c 1756 and in the 19C; restored early 1980s) contains two 18C side altarpieces and 18–19C murals. Juan Bautista de Anza (1734–88), explorer of Alta California and founder of San Francisco, lies buried here.

Hence, on a paved surface, to (120km) *Huépac*, where the Jesuit mission of San Lorenzo was founded in 1639. The church, now the parroquia, attests changes since a rebuilding in 1726, but still retains its elaborate beamed ceiling. 130km *Aconchi* (P), formerly a Jesuit mission (San Pedro), founded in the 1630s by the Portuguese Bartolomé Castaño (1601–79), whose expert musicianship proved an unfailing attraction for the Opatas. The Franciscans, who took over in 1768, incorporated their shield in the façade of the church. The road descends to (157km) *Mazocahui*, see below.

108km Sta Ana (H,R,P), in an area famous for livestock and the corn, vegetables, and fruit grown on land watered by the Río Magdalena. It is frequented by Yaqui Indians, who sell their craftware and whose dances enliven the celebration of the feast of St Anne during 17–26 July. 2km W is *San Francisco*, a ruined 18C Franciscan mission church.

A road leads W to (73km) *Altar*, see Rte 106. 48km SW by dirt road is **Trincheras**, lying between Ríos Altar, Magdalena, and Concepción (guide recommended). In an area of c 8km around Cerro Trincheras are ruins of walls, terraces, and other circular and rectangular structures resembling fortifications, but not necessarily of military character, dated c AD 1000–1300. The site was inhabited by a sedentary people in contact with the contemporary Southwestern cultures of Arizona and Chihuahua. They grew maize and also gathered food and other resources from the surrounding region. They used grooved stone grinders, stone vessels, and made red and purple on buff pottery and ceramic figurines. Both cremation and inhumation burials were practised.

150km *Benjamín Hill*. Then across a vast plain covered in mezquite via (206km) *El Oasis* (P).

279km **HERMOSILLO** (580,000 inhab.; 200m), at the confluence of the Ríos San Miguel and Sonora, seat of a university, is the modern, industrializing capital of the State of Sonora. A clean and well laid-out city containing little of historical interest, it stands in the centre of an agricultural and cattle-raising region, and is appreciated for its warm, dry winter climate. In July–Sept., however, the heat can be extreme.

Airport. 10km W of the city. Daily flights to *Chihuahua, Ciudad Obregón, Guadalajara, Los Mochis, Mexicali, Mexico City, Tijuana,* and *Tucson.*

Bus station. 2km N of the centre on Blvd Luis Encinas. Services to *Nogales* (4 hrs); to *Agua Prieta* (7 hrs); to *Los Mochis* (7½ hrs); to *Tijuana* (11 hrs); to *Mazatlán* (12 hrs); to *Guadalajara* (c 24 hrs); to *Mexico City* (c 38 hrs); etc.

Railway station. 3km N. On the Nogales–Guadalajara line: train to *Mazatlán* (12 hrs).

Hotels throughout the city.

Post Office. In Pal. Federal, corner of Cs Aquiles Serdán and Rosales.

Tourist Office. Pal. Municipal.

In 1828 the name of the villa San Pedro de la Conquista was changed to Hermosillo, in honour of the insurgent José María González Hermosillo (d. 1819). In 1831–32 it became capital of the new State of Sonora. In June 1852 it was captured and briefly held by the French adventurer Gaston de Raousset-Boulbon, in league with Arizona mining interests. Carranza set up headquarters in Hermosillo in Aug. 1913 and appointed Gen. Obregón commander of the army of the north-west. In Nov. 1915 Villa hoped to make the city his headquarters after his defeat at Agua Prieta; but his dejected besieging army was repulsed by constitutionalist forces. Since the 1960s growth has been spectacular, helped by the completion of Presa Abelardo Rodríguez to the E.

The State of **Sonora** (184,934 sq km; 2 million inhab.), second in size among the Mexican States, is bounded on the N by the USA and on the S and W by the Gulf of California. On the E the Sierra Madre Occidental, with pine and oak forests, runs N to S, its lower reaches towards the centre of the territory, forming long, wide river valleys. Four rivers—Altar, Sonora, Mayo, Yaqui—run E to W. The coastal plain varies between c 250km wide in the N and 75km in the S. Irrigation schemes and dam-building have wrought dramatic changes and agricultural advance. The NW coastal area (Sonora, Sinaloa, and Nayarit) is now Mexico's foremost agricultural region. Its traditionally hardy inhabitants have helped to make Sonora the most productively dynamic State. It is Mexico's main cotton and wheat producer. Mineral wealth awaits exploitation. The copper mines of Cananea and Nacozari are world-famous. The Sonora Desert occupies SE California and SW Arizona, as well as c three-quarters of upper Baja California and the NW and W coastal plain, from the Río Colorado to Bahía Kino, of the State of Sonora. In Mexico it is at its most forbidding (Desierto del Altar) between Ríos Colorado and Sonoita.

Spanish penetration N into what is now Sonora dates from 1533. By the late 17C, Jesuit and Franciscan missionizing, and mineral prospecting, moved the frontier N, despite frequent Indian revolts. In 1751 a major uprising of Pimas, Seris, and others caused a Spanish retreat. In the 1640s the country N of the Río Yaqui was designated Nueva Andalucía. After 1733 the same name was sometimes applied to a new jurisdiction, Sinaloa y Sonora, hived off from Nueva Vizcaya. Immediately after Independence, Sinaloa y Sonora formed a single province, but were finally separated in 1830. In the 19C Sonora was a target for filibusterers (William Walker in 1853, Gaston de Raousset-Boulbon in 1852–54, and Henry A. Crabb in 1857). In Dec. 1853 it lost over a third of its territory when Santa-Anna sold the Mesilla valley (109,574 sq km; now S New Mexico and Arizona) to the USA for $10 million.

Yaqui Indians fought bitter battles to preserve their land from US and Mexican profiteers. At the turn of the century federal troops and rurales committed atrocities against them; in 1908 many were deported to the Yucatán. The rich anti-Díaz hacendado José María Mayortena offered refuge to as many as he could on his estates in S Sonora, which assured him their support when in 1910 he raised rebellion on Madero's behalf and in 1911 became governor. After 1913 Sonora became a constitutionalist stronghold and resisted Villa's attempts to subdue it. In 1920 the Plan of Agua Prieta opened the way for a period of Sonoran predominance in national politics.

On the W side of PL. ZARAGOZA is the cathedral of *La Asunción,* a 19C neoclassical and neo-baroque mix. A similar blend is shown in the late 19C *Pal. de Gobierno* on the E side. NW of the plaza the chapel of *San Antonio,* sadly decayed, is an early 18C relic. Two more chapels, *El Carmen,* adjoining Jardín Juárez at the corner of Avs Juárez and Yucatán, and *Espíritu Santo,* at the NE end of the city, are of the 19C.

N of Pl. Zaragoza, between Blvds Transversal and Rosales, are the buildings of the *Universidad de Sonora,* founded in 1942, with a reputation for engineering. The *Museo Regional de Historia de Sonora* (Wed.–Sat., 10–6; Sun., 10–4), with craft, archaeological, and historical exhibits, is on the E side of Cerro de la

Campana (E of Pl. Zaragoza). Of particular note are the mummified body from a cave near Yécora, a find which included stone implements dated c 10–12,000 years ago; and a display showing prehistoric methods of stone- and shell-working. On the *Cerro de la Campana*, a mirador gives a good view of the city and of Presa Abelardo Rodríguez.

107km SW, on Méx. 16 through a heavily irrigated region, is *Bahía Kino* (H,P), with two villages, Kino Viejo and Kino Nuevo, developing as a resort (camping, fishing, and scuba-diving). It is one of the few remaining Seri areas and their craftware is much in evidence. 36km NW along the coast is *Punta Chueca*, a small Seri fishing village. From here, across the *Canal del Infiernillo* (currents permitting) may be reached *Isla Tiburón* (Shark Island; 1208 sq km), forbidding and remote, formerly a Seri fastness, now a nature reserve (special permission to visit needed). In May–July, the rainy season, the remaining Seris go back, but resume their wandering for the rest of the year.

FROM HERMOSILLO TO SAHUARIPA, 207km. We leave Hermosillo to the S alongside Presa Abelardo Rodríguez on Méx. 15. At 10km we turn l. and keep l. The road runs through a semi-desert area to (88km) *Mazatán* (P), then climbs the foothills of the Sierra Madre to (150km) *El Novillo* (l.), at the S tip of **Presa Plutarco Elías Calles**, completed in 1967, confining the waters of the Ríos Yaqui and Moctezuma. In splendid scenery, it has a maximum capacity of 7259 million cubic m; it irrigates 20,000 ha. and operates a hydroelectric plant of 90 MW capacity. Good fishing for bass and carp, and boating. Local wildlife includes puma, coyote, and mountain cat. 179km *Bacanora* (P), in Opata country, where a Jesuit mission existed from 1627. The church of San Ignacio has undergone many changes since the 17C. The local cactus-derived drink (bacanora) may be bought here. 207km *Sahuaripa* (H,P), a centre for shooting in the mountains (wild boar, racoon, etc.), where the church of Virgen de Guadalupe is successor to the Jesuit mission Sta María de los Angeles (later San Miguel), founded in 1627.

FROM HERMOSILLO TO AGUA PRIETA, 367km. We leave Hermosillo N on Méx. 15. At 11km we bear right across the railway line. At 19km a minor road goes N to (40km) *San Miguel de Horcasitas*, once (1753–70) capital of Sinaloa y Sonora. 49km *Topahue* natural park on the Río Sonora, wooded, with an artificial waterfall. The road continues through desert notable for sahuara cacti (which grow to a great age and a height of c 15m) and palo verde, sprouting yellowish flowers in Apr.–May. 74km **Ures** (c 5500 inhab.; 432m; H,R,P), a peaceful place in the Opatería, in 1838–42 and 1847–79 capital of Sonora. The Jesuit mission of *San Miguel*, founded in 1639, was built c 1642–55. A passable road NNW from Ures goes to (48km) *Rayón* (H,R,P), for shooting, on the Río San Miguel, and, along the San Miguel valley, to (68km) **Opodepe**, where the mission church of *Nuestra Señora de la Asunción* was founded as a visita of Jesuit Cucurpe c 1649. The present church, dating from Franciscan occupation after 1768, has suffered in preservation efforts, but has façade relief by Indian hands. From Ures the Agua Prieta road skirts the Sonora valley to (104km) *Mazocahui* (see above) and then climbs to (167km) **Moctezuma** (H,R,P), on the Río Moctezuma, known at the time of its settlement by the Jesuits (c 1644) as *San Miguel Arcángel Oposura*, and an important mission centre by 1653. Its founder, Marcos del Río (Mark van der Wecken; 1608–55), was a native of Hal in Belgium. The present church (*Nuestra Señora del Rosario*; 1730) has undergone alterations, incl. loss of a tower. The octagonal Cap. del Santísimo, at the NW side of the nave, keeps a baroque altarpiece. The silver high-altar crucifix probably dates from the early 17C.

From Moctezuma those in search of game and wildlife may penetrate further into the Sierra Madre Occidental. From *Huásabas* (47km E; good road; H,R,P) may be reached *Villa Hidalgo* (30km N; good road; H,R,P; puma, boar, wolf, racoon, hare, eagle, condor, partridge); *Granados* (c 5km S; H,R,P); and, by dirt road, *Bacadéhuachi* (c 45km SE) and *Nacori Chico* (25km further SE)—both reachable by air from Moctezuma and Hermosillo, and both with boar, puma, bear, condor. From Villa Hidalgo, a dirt road winds near the Sierra Madre and then along the valley of the Río San Bernardino through Opata territory. 66km *La Huachinera* (airstrip; R). 85km *Bacerac*. 99km *Bavispe* (P). 109km *San Miguelito*. 241km *Agua Prieta*, see above.

From Moctezuma the road ascends the valley of the Río Moctezuma, known for its game-shooting. 196km *Cumpas* (H,R,P). 244km **Nacozari de García** (c 5500 inhab.; H,R,P; railway from Agua Prieta) with copper mines, the deposits discovered in 1660. It is named after Jesús García, a railway employee and national hero who on 7 Nov. 1907 sacrificed his life by hitching an engine to two freight waggons, which had accidentally caught fire and were full of dynamite, and driving them away from the town before the tremendous explosion which killed 13 people. By his action García, whose remains were never found, saved the lives of

5000 people. 264km r. turn for (35km E) *Presa La Angostura* (fishing, especially trout, and game), built in the 1930s to confine the waters of the Río Bavispe, with a capacity of 840 million cubic m. 367km *Agua Prieta*, see above.

We leave Hermosillo S by the Carretera Internacional (Méx. 15) over the Río Sonora. The road cuts through cactus-studded desert. 338km (l.) road for (11km E) *La Pintada*, within reach of cave paintings. 415km turning r. for (18km SW) **San Carlos** (H,R,P) on Bahía de San Carlos, a burgeoning resort (deep-sea fishing, scuba-diving, yachting). The bay is set off by spectacular rock formations which shelter inlets of transparent waters. Among the beaches, *Los Algodenes*, 6.5km W, beyond the marina, also possesses fine sand, for in places desert scrub comes down to the shore. The *Tetas de Cabra* (a fair climb), at the entrance to the bay, give good views to the SE and the coastline to the NW.

422km **GUAYMAS** (158,000 inhab.), backed by jagged hills and facing the curve of its deep bay, limited on W and S by the Guaymas peninsula, is Sonora's foremost port and sea and fishing resort. The port itself is separated from the resort area of Bahía de Bocochibampo (5km NW) by a hilly promontory. There is a flourishing shrimp and oyster industry; sport-fishing facilities are second to none (especially sailfish and merlin); and the shore is renowned for its variety of sea shells. The climate, warm in winter, can become uncomfortably hot, though keeping its dryness, in summer.

Airport. 3km W of the town.

Ferry. Sailings Tues., Fri., and Sun. at 8 am for Sta Rosalia in Baja California Sur.

Bus stations. 1st Class. Corner of C. 14 and Av. Rodríguez. Services to *Hermosillo* (2 hrs); to *Tijuana* (18 hrs); to *Culiacán* and *Mazatlán* (12 hrs); to *Guadalajara* (18 hrs); to *Mexico City* (c 34 hrs); etc. 2nd Class. Corner of Av. 10 and C. 13.

Railway station. At *Empalme*, on E side of bay. Easy road connections. Trains to *Hermosillo*, *Nogales*, *Mazatlán*, *Tepic*, *Guadalajara*, and *Mexico City*.

Hotels in the town; but better at Bocochibampo and Playas de Cortés and Miramar.

Post Office. Corner of C. 20 and Av. 10.

Tourist Office. 437 Av. Serdán.

British Vice Consulate. Av. 11, Casa 3.

Guaymas derives its name from the Guayma (Huima) tribe of Indians, traditional enemies of the Seris and Yaquis, but now extinct. From 1701 a supply depot and mission was maintained by the Jesuits at San José de Guaymas; but in 1750–51 rebellious Seris drove missionary and flock out. After 1811 the port was established. In 1852 and 1854 it was the landing point of Raousset-Boulbon, whose efforts to turn over an independent republic of Sonora to the USA ended in failure and his own death by firing squad. It was because the Guaymas police refused to hand over his enemies who had tried to assassinate him that the Yaqui cacique Cajeme (José María Leyva; 1839–87) launched in 1882 one of the fiercest Yaqui rebellions against the State authorities. On 5 May 1914 the port suffered Mexico's first aerial bombardment—from a plane acquired by Gen. Obregón to reconnoitre and snuff out huertista forces. Guaymas is the birthplace of the redoubtable Plutarco Elías Calles (1877–1945), president of the republic and jefe máximo de la Revolución.

The port area centres on two adjoining plazas by the sea. Here the church of *San Fernando*, bounded by Cs 25 and 24 and Av. 15, dates from the town's 19C growth. To the S, on Av. 13, is the *Pal. Municipal* (early 20C), faced in almohadillados. The handsome building of the former *Banco de Sonora*, at the corner of C. 20 and Av. Aquiles Serdán, is of the same period.

C 10km NE is the original settlement of *San José de Guaymas* and the much-restored mission church. The feast of St Joseph (19 March) is marked by ceremonies here.

22 Guaymas to Mazatlán

Méx. 15, 799km.—128km Ciudad Obregón.—195km Navojoa (for [53km]
Alamos).—278km Estación Don.—351km **Los Mochis**.—413km Guasave.—
572km **Culiacán**.—799km **Mazatlán**.

From Guaymas a causeway across the inner bay runs to (10km) *Empalme* (H),
on the main railway line from Nogales. It is noted for its shrimps and Guaymas
oysters, abounding in the lagoons to the S, but the beach of *El Cochori* is
polluted. Méx. 15 runs SE parallel with the railway to (67km) turning r. for
(10km S) *Pótam*, a Yaqui pueblo, famous for its ceremonies on Wed., Thurs., and
Fri. of Holy Week. (Visitors may be excluded.) 77km turning r. for (6km S)
Vicam (P), another Yaqui pueblo. The road now skirts an intensively irrigated
area, between Ríos Yaqui and Mayo, to the S and SE. 99km *Bácum* (4km S),
originally a Jesuit settlement (Sta Rosa Bácum) dating from c 1620. The present
church is decorated with paintings by the Yaqui inhabitants.

Its predecessor was scene of an atrocity after the Yaqui uprising of 1867, when on 18 Feb.
1868 over 500 prisoners were locked in it. During the night soldiers fired at the church and
set it ablaze: the next morning were found 120 corpses and 50 wounded.

At (114km) *Cócorit* (3km S;P) the Holy Week rituals attract many visitors
from outside, especially for the danza de venado (stag dance), an intricate
celebration of the life and death of the animal sacred to the Yaquis. 128km
Ciudad Obregón (335,000 inhab.; 100m; airport; H,R,P), centre of a well-
irrigated agricultural region producing cotton, wheat, rice, and maize. The city,
grown from the village of *Cajeme*, has boomed since the 1950s.

The territory bounded by Ríos Yaqui and Mayo (N and S) and the Sierra Madre Occidental
was once called *Ostimuri*, a unit of Nueva Vizcaya in the jurisdiction of Sinaloa. The Jesuits
dominated here (1617–1767) and gathered their converts into the usual settlements: Yaqui in
the densely populated S; mostly Pima, Opata, and Toba in the N—inclined to revolt and
suffering epidemics and slave raids. In 1744 a Jesuit wrote of the Pimas: 'In order to reconquer
[them], it was necessary to diminish them to such a degree that, being once very populous
communities, [all three pueblos in his mission] now scarcely have 75 families'.
    C 35km N, past Laguna Naívari (Laguna Encantada), is *Presa Alvaro Obregón* (Lago de
Oviachic), fount of the region's prosperity, finished in the early 1950s and damming the waters
of the Río Yaqui. It holds 2832 million cubic m and has irrigated over 200,000 ha. It is also an
excursion and fishing centre (carp and striped bass); neighbourhood game includes deer,
hare, rabbit; in Oct.–Feb. the area abounds in duck.

Méx. 15 runs straight (SE) from Ciudad Obregón and crosses the Río Mayo to
(195km) **Navojoa** (70,000 inhab.; 38m; H,R,P), in an agricultural region and the
principal Mayo Indian centre. The original settlement, *Natividad Navojoa*, was
founded by the Jesuits in 1614. The barrio of *Pueblo Viejo* is scene of Mayo
celebrations on 24 June (feast of St John the Baptist). The Día de Muertos (Day
of the Dead; 1–2 Nov.) and the feast of Our Lady of Guadalupe are also
observed in the town, in time-honoured fashion. Its most famous native is
Alvaro Obregón (1880–1928), president of the republic, b. on the hacienda of
Siquisiva.

From Navojoa a road leads E into the foothills of the Sierra Madre. 29km *Cerro
Prieto*, with a microwave station and mirador (views). A road runs N to (19km)
Presa Mocuzari (officially *Presa Adolfo Ruiz Cortines*), damming the waters of
the Río Mayo, and developed since the late 1950s. Boats for hire and fishing
(bass and catfish). 53km **ALAMOS** (c 6500 inhab.; 410m; H,R,P), a peaceful
small town redolent of the late 18C and early 19C, which reflects the wealth
and fame it once enjoyed as a silver-mining centre.

A successful silver strike here in 1683 gave rise to the mining settlement of Nuestra Señora de la Concepción de los Alamos, also known as Real de los Frailes, which became the largest town in the NW. In the 1770s it was the residence of the governor of Sinaloa y Sonora and in 1784–87 seat of the bp of Sonora. In 1827–30 it was capital of the Estado de Occidente (Sinaloa y Sonora). During 1864–96 its Casa de Moneda turned out gold, silver, and copper coins. In 1910–40 Alamos decayed, but of late, thanks to the care and enthusiasm of US citizens who have made their homes here and to the Mexican government, which has declared it a national monument, it has been restored to its former beauty.

Facing the central cobbled PL. DE ARMAS, arcaded on three sides, is the parish church of *Nuestra Señora de la Concepción* (1763–early 19C), containing excellent ironwork. Also on the plaza, the *Pal. Municipal* was rebuilt in the late 19C. On the W side is the former house of the Almada family, prominent in the town's history, now the *Hotel Los Portales*. On the E side of the plaza is the *Museo Costumbrista de Sonora*, illustrating life in the 18–19C. S of the plaza, at 10 C. Obregón, the *Casa de los Tesoros* (now a hotel) is another well-restored casa señorial.

The *Parián* (market building) was heavily restored in 1925. The former *Casa de Moneda* is now a school. The *Cementerio* (cemetery) contains a wealth of wrought iron. On the *Cerro de Guadalupe* (W of Pl. de Armas) is the *Antigua Prisión*, from whose terrace a good view of the town and the Sierra Madre may be had.

From Alamos a minor road runs SSE along the valley of the Río Alamos to (86km) *El Fuerte* in the State of Sinaloa, see below.

From Navojoa a road runs SW through an irrigated region of haciendas and ranches to (14km) turning r. for (10km W) *Barobampo*, with rock carvings in a cave at the base of a hill behind 'Restaurante Barobampo'; 5km W (along dirt road off main road, just N of restaurant) are more carvings at another rocky outcrop. C 6.5km farther N, another track leads W off the highway to *Cerro de San José* where there are rock paintings: two skeletons are accompanied by sets of figures in white. One set includes a shark, a hand, and various geometric symbols and the other has a running deer, a (?)sun disc, a stick or club, and more geometric figures. Without associated artefacts none of the carvings or paintings can be dated.

Continuing SW along the road from Navojoa we reach (28km) *Etchojoa* (P), a Mayo village. 35km *Huatabampo* (H,R,P), much grown in recent years, with a sizeable Mayo element. 53km *Huatabampito* (R), with its fine sandy beach on Bahía de Sta Bárbara.

Méx. 15 runs SW alongside the railway through agricultural country. At 236km and 256km roads lead off r. for the small beach and fishing resorts of *Las Bocas* and *Camahuiroa*. 278km *Estación Don* (P). 15km W is *Agiabampo*, another resort, on the NE end of the Laguna de Agiabampo, which gives on to the Gulf through a narrow mouth, full of sandbanks. At 280km we enter the State of Sinaloa.

351km **LOS MOCHIS** (200,000 inhab.; H,R,P), a modern city, regularly laid out, centre of a rich agricultural and cattle-raising region, but famous above all for its sugar-cane.

Airport. c 10km SW. Daily flights to *Hermosillo, Mexico City, Guadalajara, La Paz*, and *Tijuana*.

Railway station. c 15 min. by bus or taxi, 10km E of the city. Best place to get tickets and timetables for the daily vistatrén to *Chihuahua* (see Rte 41).

Bus stations. 61 C. Obregón, between Cs Allende and Degollado, for destinations N and S. In C. Degollado, between Cs Juárez and Independencia, for *Choix, El Fuerte*, etc. 331 C. Morelos, between Cs Leyva and Zaragoza, especially for destinations N and W.

Ferry. Thrice weekly from *Topolobampo* to *La Paz* in Baja California Sur.

Hotels throughout the town.

Post Office. Corner of Cs Hidalgo and Guerrero.

It owes its development primarily to a US citizen, Benjamin F. Johnston, who started the cultivation of sugar-cane in 1903, established the first sugar mill, founded the United Sugar Company, and laid out the town in the lower basin of the Río Fuerte, whose irrigation had been started in the 1890s by a US Owenite socialist community. Damming the Río Fuerte has facilitated the growing of additional crops to broaden the area's economic base—especially the ubiquitous marigold, whose crushed petals are added to chickenfeed to deepen the colour of egg yolks.

The *Ingenio Azucarero* (sugar refinery; visits allowed), one of the largest in Mexico, is on the W side of the town. W of the crossing of Cs Leyva and Obregón is the former mansion of Benjamin Johnston; the gardens, with their international choice of flowers and shrubs, are now a public park.

16km S is the lagoon-surrounded fishing port of *Topolobampo*, ranged by high cliffs and on a spit which separates the wide and deep Bahías de Ohuira and Topolobampo (over 120sq km in area). It is known for shrimping, and is being further developed as a deep-sea port. Attractive sport-fishing may be had here. Boats may be hired to gain access to local beaches.

18km NW is *Ahome* (P), a little agricultural town where the Jesuits founded the mission of Natividad c 1605 for the Mayos of the Río Fuerte valley.

FROM LOS MOCHIS TO CHOIX, 130km. Méx. 23 runs N through the Río Fuerte valley into the Sierra Madre, keeping close to the line of the Pacific railway. 18km *Mochicahui*, in the 18C a Jesuit mission among the Mayos, is famous for its celebration of the feast of St John the Baptist (24 June), accompanied by traditional dances. 36km *San Blas* (P). 78km **El Fuerte** (15,000 inhab.; 115m; H,R,P), on the l. bank of the Río Fuerte and site of the Spanish outpost of San Juan Bautista de Carapoa, founded in 1564, re-established in the later 16C after destruction by Indians, and reinforced as a villa in 1610 by viceroy marqués de Montesclaros. In the 17–18C it was an important garrison and in 1824–26 capital of Sinaloa. The town preserves much of its old atmosphere, with its typical arcaded plaza and late 18C church. It is near the S tip of *Presa Miguel Hidalgo*, one of the artificial lakes built in 1953–56 and enlarged in 1962–64 as part of a great irrigation drive. It waters over 200,000 ha. and produces over 275 million kW hours of electricity annually. Its bass catches make it a favourite fishing spot. The surrounds offer buck-shooting. A road leads NE to (86km) *Alamos*, see above. 130km *Choix* (H), a small mining town on a tributary of the Río Fuerte.

From Los Mochis, Méx. 15 continues SE, passing the NE tip of Bahía de Ohuira, across the fertile coastal plain to (413km) **Guasave** (H,R,P), on the r. bank of the Río Sinaloa, whose name echoes the original prehispanic coastal fishermen of the area, the Guazaves, for whom the Jesuit Bernardo de Villafañe founded the mission in 1595. C 3km E are the ruins of *San Ignacio Nío*, another Jesuit mission, overwhelmed by floods in 1770.

At Guasave archaeologists excavated a settlement site and cemetery of 166 graves; the name also designates the final phase of the more general Aztatlán cultural complex. The site, excavated by G. Eckholm in 1939, included hillocks incorporated into the site and used for religious ceremonies, house foundations of stone and puddled clay, and burials, dated between c AD 1000 and 1450. The occupation is subdivided into three phases (AD 1000–1200, 1200–1350, and 1350–1450), and is thus coincident with the Yebalito phase at Culiacán. As the final phase of the Aztatlán complex it was the richest and showed considerable influence from the Mixteca–Puebla polychrome styles of Cholula and the Valle de Puebla, incl. elaborately decorated polychrome vessels, paint cloisonné, and clay pipes. There were also turquoise mosaics, iron pyrite beads, and onyx and alabaster vessels.

40km NE the small town of *Sinaloa de Leyva* was, as Villa de Sinaloa, from 1591 the Jesuit headquarters for missionizing throughout the NW, as far as N Sonora, and from 1733 capital of Sinaloa y Sonora. Its church of San Felipe y Santiago, with its singular tower, dates from a rebuilding after the floods of 1769–70.

From (456km) *Guamúchil*, on the l. bank of the Río Mocorito, a road climbs E to (17km) *Mocorito*, established by the Jesuits in 1593, with an 18C church. 515km *Pericos*, whence Méx. 24 climbs into the Sierra Madre past the N edge of Presa Adolfo López Mateos to (46km) *Badiraguato* (P), (87km) r. fork for a secondary road across the Sierra Madre to (315km) *Hidalgo del Parral* (see Rte 47), and (130km) *Mesa de San Miguel*, in the mountains near the border with the State of Chihuahua.

Along this road there are rock paintings at several villages. From (9km) *Comanita* a path leads to (4km) *La Nanchita*, where paintings can be seen c 450m N of the hamlet. At (c 12km) *La Majada de Abajo*, petroglyphs on a rock face N of the road. At *El Guayabito*, paintings on a rock wall c 450m N are near the bank of Río Pericos. At *La Majada de Arriba*, paintings along a path c 3km S of El Guayabito, on a tributary of Río Pericos, incl. humans, birds, flowers, hands, suns, spirals, stepped-frets, and other geometric designs.

533km turning l. for (25km NE) *Presa Adolfo López Mateos*, a vast reservoir (watersports, fishing, especially for bass) formed by the damming of the waters of the Río Humaya and completed in 1964.

572km **CULIACAN** (545,000 inhab.; 84m), capital of the State of Sinaloa and on the l. bank of the Río Culiacán (formed by the Ríos Tamazula and Humaya), is a modern city, with plentiful trees and flowering shrubs, and agricultural centre on the E edge of an intensively irrigated district. It enjoys a warm, semi-tropical climate. The fame of its plump tomatoes extends beyond the frontiers of Mexico.

Airport. At Bachigualato, 10km NW. Daily flights to *Ciudad Obregón, Guadalajara, La Paz,* and *Mexico City.*

Railway. On Nogales–Guadalajara line.

Bus station. Av. Andrade, S of intersection with Blvd G. Leyva Solano.

Hotels throughout the city.

Post Office. Corner of Cs Antonio Rosales and Domingo Rubí.

Tourist Office. Corner of Cs 5 de Febrero and Gral. A. Obregón.

Prehistoric material is known from in and around Culiacán. The excavated ceramics are divided into four phases: *Acaponeta* (c AD 900–1100), *La Divisa* (c 1100–1250), *Yebalito* (c 1250–1400), and *La Quinta* (c 1400–Spanish Conquest). The Acaponeta phase is closely related to widely spread Aztatlán ceramics and culture of Sinaloa and Nayarit. Aztatlán is represented by three important sites: Chametla, Culiacán, and Guasave. Early ceramics at Chametla were followed by Aztatlán with its sophisticated polychromes (using up to six colours), engraving, paint cloisonné, negative painting, and moulding. Some influence in design is evident from the Mixteca-Puebla polychromes of central Mexico (see Introduction: Mesoamerican Pottery). Copper, silver, and gold artefacts were also an important feature of this phase. The later phases at Culiacán follow and chronologically overlap Aztatlán, and the La Quinta phase was related to the Tarascan culture of the Late Postclassic (see Rte 28).

The villa of San Miguel Culiacán was finally, after two previous attempts, established on the present site c the early 1550s. Always an isolated outpost surrounded by hostile Indians, the villa and its surrounding territory were part of Nueva Galicia, governed from remote Guadalajara. The original hundred Spanish settlers were reduced to 25 by 1550, raising cattle, prospecting for minerals (silver ore in the Sierra), and enslaving those Indians they could catch. By the end of the 16C the Jesuits were missionizing in the river valley. In 1733 Culiacán became part of Sinaloa y Sonora, and was declared capital of the new State in 1830.

The State of **Sinaloa** (58,328 sq km; 2.5 million inhab.) is bounded on the N by the Gulf of California. The long, narrowish coastal plain, widening to the NE, rises to the Sierra Madre Occidental, from which run various rivers, nearly all permanent flows, chief among them the Fuerte in the N. It has been estimated that the State contains over a quarter of Mexico's surface water. The coast, with wide, spectacular bays, and extensive lagoons, salt flats, and beaches, is dotted with numerous islands. Each river valley has included, from the 1940s, intensive irrigation and hydroelectric projects.

Such was the devastation caused by Spanish irruption into the area in the 1530s that the S half was left depopulated and open to invasion by Chichimecs. In 1564–65 Francisco de Ibarra and his Basque followers began a slow conquest. In 1589–91 the Jesuits started their chain of missions and Spanish arms began to push into the N. Frequent 17C rebellions showed that often resentful Indian converts could not be contained. During 1733–1830 the area formed part of Sinaloa y Sonora. Pre-revolutionary movements made their mark, especially that headed by Heraclio Bernal, mortal enemy of foreign mining interests, in the 1870s and 1880s.

The cathedral of *San Miguel,* facing Pl. de la Constitución, is a nondescript building of c 1855. The *Correos* (Post Office) occupies the old Casa de Moneda, which minted coins during 1845–1905. N of the Cathedral, on the malecón of the Río Tamazula, is a large cultural centre which includes a *Museo de Cultura Popular* and a *Museo de Arte Moderno.*

Presa Sanalona, 32km E, is a huge artificial lake (845 million cubic m capacity), formed by the Río Tamazula. The sulphurous springs at *Imala,* a village on its W shore, with its solid little church (an 18C Jesuit mission survival), are frequented for their curative properties. Local guides will point out petroglyphs in the nearby gorge; there are also ruins on the opposite side of the lake.

Méx. 30 runs W through the area irrigated by the waters of the Río Culiacán to (37km) *Navolato* and (61km) *Altata*, a port and fishing centre, with extensive beaches, in a lagoon area; its bay is sheltered from the Gulf by a long peninsula, the Isla del Redo.

622km *Tabalá*, with a 17C Jesuit mission church. 681km turning l. (Méx. 31) for (53km N) *Cosalá* (P), briefly capital of the State in 1826–27. 769km Tropic of Cancer and change of time zone (to Central Standard Time).

799km **MAZATLAN** (300,000 inhab.), occupying a peninsula with a gently curving bay on its W side, is Mexico's chief Pacific port and a considerable commercial and industrial centre. It has also developed, thanks to its splendid setting, sandy beaches, and benign winter climate, into a popular, somewhat brash, holiday and sport-fishing (especially merlin and sailfish) resort. The beauty of its sunsets is an additional attraction.

Airports. International airport, 13km S of the town. Daily flights to *Chihuahua, Ciudad Juárez, Durango, Guadalajara, La Paz, León, Cabo San Lucas, Mexico City, Monterrey, Puerto Vallarta,* and *Tijuana*; and to *Denver (Col.), Los Angeles,* and *San Francisco*; four times weekly to *Torreón*; thrice weekly to *Ixtapa-Zihuatanejo* and *Zacatecas*.

Ferry. Daily to *La Paz* at 5 pm (17 hrs) from docks on E side of the town. Book passage in advance.

Bus station. Off Carr. Internacional, by Río Tamazula, N of the centre. Services to *Mexico City* (c 20 hrs); to *Guadalajara* (10 hrs); to *Tepic* (5–6 hrs); to *Los Mochis* (7 hrs); to *Guaymas* (12 hrs).

Railway station. On E side of the town. Ticket office at corner of Av. Angel Flores and C. Belisario Domínguez. Trains to *Tepic, Guadalajara,* and *Mexico City.*

Hotels. Numerous throughout. Less expensive in centre, away from beaches.

Post Office. On N side of Pl. de la República.

Tourist Office. In the Banamex building in Av. Olas Altas.

US Consulate. At corner of Av. Circunvalación and C. Venustiano Carranza. **Canadian Consulate.** Hotel Playa Mazatlán.

Fiestas. Pre-Lent Carnival (Thurs.–Shrove Tues.). 8 Dec.: feast of the Immaculate Conception.

In 1796 a tiny settlement existed on the coast, called Puerto de San Félix, which in 1817 counted 21 inhab. In the 1850s German traders selling agricultural equipment settled here and established the beginnings of prosperity. In 1887 hundreds of Chinese labourers, prevented from entering the USA by employers who had abandoned them, were received at Mazatlán, many to be dispersed throughout NE Mexico. (The Buddhist temple of those who stayed is in C. 21 de Marzo.) In Aug. 1914 forces loyal to Gen. Obregón captured Mazatlán from the huertista garrison after a nine months naval blockade—the first naval battle between Mexican forces. After 1920 modernization began, though Pres. Cárdenas's agrarian reforms brought political violence. Since the 1940s its growth as a resort has been spectacular.

Stretching N along the bay the beaches *Playa Norte* (popular), *Las Gaviotas, Sábalo* (distant but sheltered), with their fine white sand, are faced by modern and luxurious hotels. Paseo Claussen and Av. Olas Altas, separated by the *Cerro de la Nevería*, run alongside the beaches of the S promontory, at whose extreme S, and joined to it by a narrow man-made peninsula, is the *Cerro del Crestón*, on which rises the **Faro** (lighthouse), 157m above the water. After that of Gibraltar, it is reputed to be the second highest in the world. It marks the entrance to the docks, on the E side of the peninsula, and faces Isla Chivos, NW tip of a long peninsula stretching SE along the coast.

On the N side of Pl. de la República is the cathedral of *La Inmaculada Concepción* (1855–99), fancifully eclectic. At 35–51 C. Constitución, at the corner with C. Carvajal, is the *Teatro Angela Peralta* (1880–), the former Teatro Rubio, where, in the upstairs apartment on 30 Aug. 1883, died Angela Peralta (victim of a cholera epidemic), who had arrived at Mazatlán to inaugurate it with a series of recitals.

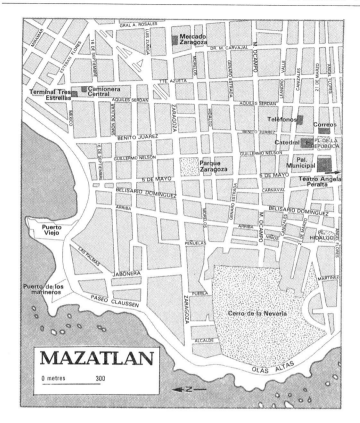

MAZATLAN

0 metres 300

23 Mazatlán to Tepic and Guadalajara

Méx. 15, 545km.—90km El Rosario.—177km Acaponeta.—284km Crucero San Blas (for [36km] San Blas).—319km **Tepic**.—406km Ixtlán del Río.— 468km La Magdalena.—488km Tequila.—545km **Guadalajara**.

Méx. 15 continues S across the coastal plain. From (24km) *Villa Unión* (P) Méx. 40 runs NE over the Sierra Madre to (295km) *Durango*, see Rte 47. 90km **El Rosario** (20,000 inhab.; H,P) on the l. bank of the lower course of the Río Baluarte, once the rich silver- and gold-mining centre of Nuestra Señora del Rosario, functioning from c 1655 and still counting for a little in the industry. The church of *Nuestra Señora del Rosario* dates from the early 18C and contains a contemporary altarpiece.

25km SW at *Chametla*, at the river mouth, Nuño de Guzmán began his murderous campaign late in 1530 and in 1535 Cortés made a base for his expedition to Baja California. Another road leads to the coast and (30km) *Caimanero*, a fishing and beach resort between the Laguna de Caimanero and the sea.

Excavations just S (no visible ruins) uncovered a Classic Period site whose distinctive pottery characterized the Early Classic of W Mexico, c AD 250–700. *Chametla Antiguo* and *Chametla*

Medio ceramics were indigenous developments and included polychrome vessels of black-and-red-on-cream, white or orange backgrounds, white-on-maroon, polished maroon, and incised designs. Spindle whorls were engraved and a distinctive figurine style was also developed. As part of the more widespread *Aztatlán Ceramic Complex*, *Chametla Reciente* vessels show outside influences (cf. *Culiacán* and *Guasave*).

Méx. 15 crosses the Río Baluarte to (112km) *Escuinapa* (H,P), an agricultural centre, which had a reputation for revolutionary fervour after 1910.

From here a road leads W to join the coast, lined S into Nayarit by lagoons edged with mangroves, freshwater lakes, marshes (replenished by seasonal flooding), and salt flats; and then S past the beautiful beaches of (14km) *Las Cabras* and *La Tambora* to (40km) *Teacapan*, an unspoilt little resort at the mouth of its lagoon.

At 165km we cross into the State of Nayarit. 177km **Acaponeta** (18,000 inhab.; 30m; H,R,P), on the river of the same name, where the Spaniards established a presidio in the 1530s in what was to become the NW extremity of Nueva Galicia. The church of *Nuestra Señora de la Asunción* and its adjoining convent (adapted to other uses) are successor to a Franciscan foundation of c 1580, burnt during the Tepehuan Indian rebellion of 1617–21, and much rebuilt since.

A minor road runs up the valley of the Río Acaponeta to (20km N) *Huajicori*, from the 1620s until 1769 an important Franciscan mission (San Sebastián Guaxicori); the late 17C church, in delightful local baroque, survives. 36km W is an entry to the vast unspoiled beach of *Novillero* (100km long), on an interminable sandbank which bars the estuary of the Río Acaponeta from the sea.

220km *Rosamorada*, famous for its Holy Week festivities. At (240km) *Peñitas* excavations uncovered a site with a sequence from the 3C to the 13C AD.

Its ceramics are similar to those of Colima in the same time period, the *Comala Phase*, and, from the later levels, to those from Chametla in Sinaloa, and to the Early Postclassic ceramics of the Basin of Mexico. A second site, *Coamiles* (Postclassic; 7km SW) yielded several monolithic slabs with geometric and curvilinear designs.

9km W is **Tuxpan** (30,000 inhab.; 725m; H,R,P), second largest town in Nayarit and on the l. bank of the Río San Pedro, in a tobacco-growing area. 255km turning r. for (8km) *Santiago Ixcuintla* (the ancient Tecpatitlán), on the Río Grande de Santiago, in a fertile plain, Mexico's principal Virginia tobacco-growing region, and (15km) **Amapa**.

Excavated in 1959 by a team from the University of California at Los Angeles, in 1960–62 by D. M. Pendergast, and in 1969 by J. B. Mountjoy, Amapa was occupied from the Late Preclassic but abandoned between c AD 400 and 600. During its earliest phases it was little more than a large village of mud and thatch houses. Climatic shift in the Classic Period brought greater regional rainfall and a northward extension of agriculture. By c 600 new occupants had adopted many Mesoamerican cultural traits. Although the major building activity dates between AD 900 and 1200, occupation continued up to the Spanish Conquest.

The site comprises nearly 200 mounds over an area of c 1.5 sq km. Many mounds would only have supported mud and thatch huts, but others were grouped into plazas of public buildings oriented to the cardinal points. The platforms were constructed of dirt cores faced with pebbles, cut stone being used only on more important buildings and staircases. An I-shaped ball court was also built, with a centre marker in the shape of a cup.

By c AD 900 metallurgy was well established. In an associated cemetery 205 metal artefacts were excavated, and c 800 pieces of pottery representing 40 different decorative types and forms (many of which can be seen in the museum in Tepic).

Metal artefacts include copper fishhooks, axes, knives, awls, tweezers, pins, needles, ear-spools, and various bells and plaques. Some pieces also show evidence of gilding or tinning, and many are claimed to be similar to pieces from Ecuador and Colombia, evidence that metallurgy spread to Mesoamerica from NW South America via Central America and the

Pacific coastal trade. The polychrome ceramics, especially orange- and red-rimmed wares, resemble forms and decoration from the Mixteca-Puebla region and from Guasave. Some graves also contained carved stone heads and clay figurines.

Wheeled toys were also made in Nayarit. One example is of a man seated on a wheeled platform—all other known examples are of animals.

This road continues through humid, marshy country to the coast at (41km) *Los Corchos* (H,R,P), a beach resort. Along it, at 17km from the main road, a r. turn leads to (8km) *Sentispac*, an unimposing small town, once capital of a flourishing pre-Conquest lordship, which became property of Nuño de Guzmán. From here a bumpy road leads NW, through an area criss-crossed by salt marshes, to (25km) the embarkation point for **Mexcaltitán** (c 2000 inhab.; R; 25 min. by launch), exquisitely set in a lagoon. Approx. oval in shape, the town-island is circled by one main street, while four straight streets cross to form the central plaza. Their high pavements ease conversion into canals when the Río San Pedro breaks its banks. The celebration of the feast of SS Peter and Paul (29 June) is a great attraction here.

At (284km) *Crucero San Blas* the road r. (Méx. 54) descends, attractively wooded, to the coast at (36km) **San Blas** (c 5000 inhab.; H,R,P), a small port and seaside resort in a natural bay, whose recent growth in popularity, especially with visitors from the USA, renders it somewhat crowded during Oct.–May. In Aug. the weather becomes very hot and ubiquitous gnats (jejéres) are a disadvantage. To the N the flat coastland is lush with mangrove swamps.

The original village (Villa San Carlos), on the shore and dating from 1767–68, was removed to a nearby hilltop in 1773. Here were settled a naval station and shipyards, part of the grand plan of exploration and conquest of all California. Hence, in 1774 and 1779 left the reconnoitring expeditions along the W coast of America as far N as Nootka Sound; and in 1778 that as far as Alaska (to spy on Russian settlements). Despite storm damage and sickness in the unhealthy climate, in 1774 San Blas was recognized as the most important naval station on New Spain's Pacific coast, not least because of the fine craft constructed in the shipyards.'The Bells of San Blas', Longfellow's last poem, was written here in 1882.

The original 18C buildings on the Cerro de la Contaduría are reached from the l. of the main road into the town. Here are the remains of the church of *San Basilio*, the fort, and the *Contaduría* (counting-house). The ruined *Aduana*, the port's customs house, is nearer the sea.

FROM SAN BLAS TO TEPIC, 74km by coast road and State road 66. The coast road branches off Méx. 54 and passes *La Aguada*, from where launches ply along canals lined by mangroves to the pool of *La Tovara*. 6km *Matanchén*, with a sandy beach, is known only from excavations. Dated c 2000 BC. The artefacts recovered included obsidian and other stone tools, shell, fish, turtle, and bird remains, but no pottery. 12km *Los Cocos*, an excellent surfing centre. 14km *Aticama*, famous for its oysters. 20km *Miramar*, at the S end of the bay. From (23km) *Sta Cruz*, a popular beach resort, State road 66 climbs through a volcanic mountain range to (74km) *Tepic*, see below.

From Crucero San Blas, Méx. 15 continues to (289km) turning r. for (5km) *Jumatán*, with a famous waterfall, and then continues a climb across the Sierra de Tepic.

319km **TEPIC** (240,000 inhab.; 915m), capital of the State of Nayarit and seat of a university, lies in the Valle de Matatipac and NW of the extinct volcano Sangangüey, amid the spectacular Sierra de Tepic. It is the centre of Mexico's most important tobacco-growing region and among its other industries counts textiles, sugar refining, and brandy distilling. It is also frequented by Cora and Huichol Indians from the sierras to the N and E, who come to sell their handicrafts. The city itself has been spoiled by haphazard development which has lost it much of its historical flavour. The tepiqueños, however, compensate for much: their kindheartedness and charm make a stay among them very agreeable.

Airport. On S side of the city, for local flights to Cora and Huichol villages in the sierra.

Railway station. At E end of Av. Allende, for trains to *Mazatlán* and *Guadalajara*.

Bus station. Av. Insurgentes Oriente. Services to *San Blas* (1½ hrs); to *Guadalajara* (5 hrs); to *Mazatlán* (5–6 hrs); to *Puerto Vallarta* (3½ hrs); to *Mexico City* (13 hrs); etc.

Hotels throughout the city.

Post Office. Corner of Cs Durango and Morelos.

Tourist Office. In Convento de la Cruz.

The city resulted from a moving of inhabitants from Ciudad de Santiago de Compostela (next to the Indian settlement of Tepique) in 1540. By 1650 more Spaniards favoured Tepic than Compostela, which had not been entirely abandoned. In Feb. 1811 the city was captured by the royalist force of José de la Cruz. A scaffold was set up in the plaza, on which were hung 20 insurgents a day, and next to it a pulpit from which, after the executions, a priest delivered a sermon against Independence. In 1822 Basil Hall found it 'a beautiful town...rendered very lively by rows of trees, gardens, and terraced walks', and the merchants eager to do business with Britain. The foundation of the Anglo-US finance and commercial house of Barron and Forbes and its establishment of a textile factory in Tepic in 1833 signalled the beginning of the influence of Eustace Barron, British consul in Tepic, and William Forbes, US consul in San Blas, in local affairs, which culminated in their expulsion in 1856.

The State of **Nayarit** (26,979 sq km; 872,000 inhab.) is bounded on the W by the Pacific. The Sierra Madre Occidental, pushing SE, rises steeply from the narrow coastal strip and cuts the State into deep gorges and narrow valleys. The volcanoes Sangangüey (2150m) and Ceboruco (2164m) rise E and SE of Tepic. Of its NE corner, the Sierra de Nayarit, the Jesuit José Ortega wrote in the early 1750s: 'It is so wild and frightful to behold that its ruggedness, even more than the arrows of its warlike inhabitants, took away the courage of the conquerors, because not only the ridges and valleys appear inaccessible, but the extended range of towering mountain peaks confused even the eye'. The main river is the Río Grande de Santiago (W course of the Río Lerma) flowing W to its delta near San Blas—its valley very fertile. Inland from the coast is a series of lagoons (refuges for wild birds), mangrove swamps, and canals, running from the N border to Sta Cruz. The coast can claim the finest beaches in Mexico.

The area of the modern State of Nayarit was part of Nueva Galicia (covering also what are now the States of Aguascalientes, Zacatecas, NW San Luis Potosí, and most of Jalisco), established in 1531 during the conquest of Nuño de Guzmán. Indian numbers further declined in pestilential outbreaks: it is estimated that the populous coastal region, some 320,000 souls when Guzmán's troops arrived, was reduced to 20,000 by 1560. The Mixtón war of 1540–41 and further Indian uprisings well into the 17C kept the authorities anxious, and the original province of Nayarit (the rugged NE corner of the present State), occupied by Cora and Huichol Indians, offered a haven to those who rejected Spanish domination. Not until the 1720s did the crown gain the upper hand, helped mainly by the Jesuits. The skeleton of the caudillo Nayarit, ruler of the region at the Conquest, was taken to Mexico City and burned on Pl. del Quemadero. The influence of Barron and Forbes in the 1850s helped sustain Manuel Lozada (1828–73), a cacique whose campaigns in defence of Indian rights and later in the imperial interest gave him considerable control in the Sierra de Alica (NE of Tepic), N into Sinaloa, and S into Jalisco. (In 1871, Porfirio Díaz, in arms against Juárez, took refuge with Lozada in the sierra.) Nayarit was raised to Statehood in 1917.

On the E side of PL. PRINCIPAL is the cathedral of *La Purísima Concepción de María*, begun in 1750; its façade and slender neo-Gothic towers date from its completion in the late 19C. On the W side is the *Pal. Municipal* (1882). Behind the cathedral, at 284 C. Zacatecas, is the *Museo Amado Nervo*, in the early 19C house where Amado Nervo (1870–1919), the modernist poet and diplomat, was born. It is furnished with mementoes, photographs, first editions, etc. On the l. of the museum C. Zaragoza leads E to C. Ures and the *Santuario de Guadalupe* (1799), the atrio gateway neoclassical and the portal recalling the plateresque. Further S along C. Zacatecas a turning l., C. Lerdo, contains (l.) the *Casa Fenelón*, now the school of medicine of the university, a notable late 19C building in afrancesado style.

From the plaza Av. México, the city's main thoroughfare, leads S. It passes (l.), at the corner with C. Hidalgo, the *Oficina Federal de Hacienda*, another 19C building, which once belonged to the house of Barron and Forbes. Further along, at the corner with C. Zapata (r.), is the early 18C **Casa de los Condes de Miravalle**, restored in 1981, now the *Museo Regional*.

It was built for Alonso Dávalos y Bracamonte (b. 1645), 1st conde de Miravalle, patron from 1697 of the Jesuit missions in Baja California, whose coat-of-arms is on the l. of the main

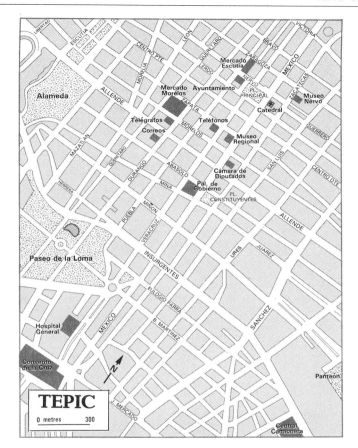

TEPIC

0 metres   300

doorway. The ground floor is devoted to the region's prehistoric Nayarit culture and Ixtlán style sculpture.

Two squatting, polychrome clay figures (one male, one female; c 80m high) from Tequilita. Clay figurines (c 5 cm) from Jalisco and Colima. Ceramic bowls and other vessels, and small figurines, from Nayarit. Double, monochrome, glossy red jar (c 45m), and mother and child figure. Monochrome and polychrome 'chinesco' figures (slanting eyes; up to 15 cm). Polychrome, squatting female figurine (c 60 cm), and glossy red, monochrome figure of an obese man (c 45 cm). Stylistic influence from Jalisco is shown in five figurines, male and female, wearing nose-, ear-, arm-, and neck-rings.

The late Classic Nayarit style (c AD 400–600) in shown in a warrior figure (c 60 cm), decorated with dots and circles in geometric patterns, black on terracotta. Ixtlán style pieces include 12 figurines (c 20–30 cm), wearing nose-rings and fan-shaped earrings, with decorations in white, red, black, and yellow showing other ornaments, clothing, and body-painting. 29 monochrome vessels with various decorations—incised geometric patterns, dark brown burnishing/polishing, appliqué, and gourd-shaped (called 'cuello de tulipa'). Seated female (c 45 cm) with flattened and fan-shaped cranial deformation, clutching her torso and wearing elaborate earrings and necklace. Ixtlán polychrome bowls and other vessels—mortuary offerings—with geometric decorations in white, black, red, yellow, and orange.

Two realistic figures (one male, one female; c 30 cm), wearing earrings and arm-rings. The male is squatting, while the female is half-kneeling and holding a bowl. Both have cranial deformation.

Warrior figure (c 35 cm), orange with white decoration. Group of six musicians (10–15 cm and 35–45 cm). Clay model of house (c 20 x 20 x 20 cm), with three figures seated inside. Group of 11 warriors holding clubs, mono- and polychrome (10–35 cm). 22 figurines (c 10–35 cm), mostly polychrome, showing everyday activities, and a square (c 15 x 15 cm) of dancers surrounding three further figures (c 8–10 cm). Warrior (c 35 cm), wearing a horned (?) headdress and what appears to be chest armour, holding a club and shield. Eight polychrome figurines (c 10–20 cm) representing pathological conditions—dwarfism, mongolism, anorexia, hunchback.

Beyond the museum opens out PL. DE LOS CONSTITUYENTES, with an obelisk in its centre commemorating the Constitutional Congress of 1917. On its W side is the handsome **Pal. de Gobierno** (1885), showing a well-proportioned development of the neoclassical; until the 1920s it served as the prison. The mural in the central cupola ('El hombre y el mal') and that at the far end ('Historia del Estado en síntesis') are by José Luis Soto (1975).

Reached from the plaza, along Av. Juárez, is the *Panteón Municipal*, with interesting 19C chapel and tomb styles.

At the far (S) end of Av. México, at the corner with Calz. del Ejercito, is the church of **La Cruz de Zacate**, originally a Franciscan visita of the late 16C, built, it is said, to house a miracle-working cross. Of the 16–17C structure are preserved arches and columns of the transepts, the stone pulpit alcove, the mixtilinear arch giving onto the sacristy, and the lovely N doorway, its archivolt framed by the Franciscan cord. The later modifications, begun in 1777, include the effective stone neoclassical high altar and transept retables. Alongside, on the S, survives the single-storey cloister. The adjoining convent in its present form (originally *Hospicio de Sta Cruz de Tepic*) was begun in 1784.

It was built as a lodging for Franciscan missionaries (Misioneros de propaganda fide) from San Fernando in Mexico City on their way N, and as a retreat from their labours. In 1767 the first friars, led by Junípero Serra, arrived in Tepic after a 39-day journey from Mexico and stayed six months before moving on in March 1768. In 1981, after complete restoration, it was taken over by the State tourist office.

SE of the convent, on the opposite side of the main road to Guadalajara, is the *Universidad Autónoma de Nayarit*, established in 1969. Murals by local artists decorate the buildings.

Permits to visit the mountain territories of the Cora and Huichol Indians (a few thousand each in number) must be sought at the Pal. de Gobierno, where advice about travel will be given. The former are to be found in the Sierra de Nayarit, along the banks of the Río Jesús María, their main pueblo being *Jesús María*, c 100km NE of Tepic and c 40km N of *Huaynamota*. The Huicholes occupy a more extensive region: in the Sierra de Nayarit as neighbours of the Coras; in E Nayarit and Jalisco, in the Río Bolaños valley between La Yesca and Mezquitic (an important centre at *Sta Catarina*, c 48km NW of Bolaños); and over into the States of Zacatecas (around *Colotlán*) and Durango (in *Huazamote*). The isolation of both peoples (especially the Huicholes of Nayarit) has enabled them to preserve their customs more effectively than most indigenous groups. Jesús María is accessible only by air from Tepic airport or from Acaponeta; the E Huichol country by air or a combination of air and muleback. Such excursions will be of interest only to the serious student of anthropology; hardly to the traveller pressed for time or of dilettante tendencies.

FROM TEPIC TO PUERTO VALLARTA, 163km. We leave Tepic to the SW and then follow Méx. 200 due S to (10km) *Jalisco* (H,P), on the E slope of the Sierra Alta de San Juan, a site reached in 1524 by the expedition of Francisco Cortés. Here the former Franciscan convent and church of San Juan Bautista, founded c 1546, were amplified in the 17C. The present church and convent owe much to 19C rebuilding. 34km **Compostela** (c 15,000 inhab.; H,P), an ancient place in the Valle de Cactlán, during 1540–60 capital of Nueva Galicia, see Rte 24. The mines of Espíritu Santo, in the mountains to the E, were discovered c 1543 and were the basis of the wealth of, among others, the Bracamonte family. Gold and silver are still mined in the region. The church, much restored, preserves 16C traces, incl. a plateresque choir window. Near *Tequilita* (c 18km SW), excavations of shaft-tombs at *Las Cebollas* recovered numerous 'chinesco' figurines dating to the 1–2C AD: highly polished, hollow ceramic figures (many of which can be seen in the Tepic museum) featuring naturalistic faces and poses, and in some cases heart-shaped faces with squint-eyes and black painting on the body and face; a third variety is called 'Martian', because of its bizarre, other-worldly aspect and bright geometric painted patterns. Beyond Compostela we turn r. and continue W to (69km) *Las Varas* (P), a tobacco-growing centre, whence a minor road runs near the coast N to (35km) *Sta Cruz*, see above. 73km turning r. for (4km) *Chacala* (R), first of a series of fine beaches along a beautiful coastline, now promoted as the Costa Alegre, stretching to Bahía de Banderas. 92km *Rincón de Guayabitos* (H,R,P). 119km *Punta Sayulita* (H,R), connected by path with (10km) *Punta Mita*, on a promontory at the NW side of Bahía de Banderas. 140km *Bucerías* (H,R). We cross the Río Ameca and from mountain to standard time (one hour ahead). 163km *Puerto Vallarta*, see Rte 25.

Méx. 15 runs SE across the cultivated plain to (351km) turning l. for (11km E) **Sta María del Oro**, where the doorway of the buttressed 18C church is ogee-arched; 5km beyond is the oval Laguna de Sta María, set in a mountain landscape. Beyond (377km) turning r. for *Tetitlán* we pass through a lava field formed by eruptions from Ceboruco, which rises on the l. The road descends into the valley of the Río Ahuacatlán. At (392km) *Ahuacatlán* the Franciscan convent of San Juan Evangelista was founded c 1550 and its atrio later planted with orange trees. Its successor church (now San Francisco) dates from the 17C and was altered in the 19C. There are some good 18–19C houses. The final battle of the Mixtón war was fought here late in 1541. 394km turning l. for (7km NE) *Jala*, where is preserved the adaptation of the open chapel of the Franciscan convent of Asunción de Nuestra Señora, founded in 1582 and rebuilt in the 1590s. The Basilica Lateranense, with a pleasing façade, is of the late 18C. The nave of the church in the neighbouring (E) pueblo of *Jomulco* has kept 16C gargoyle figures. Beyond Jala the road winds up the S slope of Ceboruco, whose last eruption occurred in 1879. 397km *Zoatlán*, with a 16C church and atrial cross. 400km *Mexpan*, with a 17C atrial cross. 406km **Ixtlán del Río** (17,000 inhab.; 1042m; H,R,P), in the Valle de Ixtlán, where the parish church dates from the 1720s, though renovated in 1801–04; the tower was replaced in the 1930s.

C 3km S of Ixtlán, a signposted road runs c 150m E to a multi-period site covering c 450 sq m. It was discovered by the parish priest in 1899, and excavated by C. Lumholtz (1902), E. W. Gofford (1950), and E. Contreras and J. Gussinger (1966). The site's chronology is still unclear.
   The visible remains comprise an L-shaped building, a rectilinear building parallel to the long arm of the former, a circular structure 30m in diameter and 4m high joined to the first by a causeway, and several grass-covered mounds around these. The circular structure, principally because of its plan, is claimed to be the platform for one or more temples dedicated to Quetzalcóatl (eg, cf. reconstruction model in the Museo Nacional de Antropología).
   These structures clearly form part of the ceremonial centre of a large site, and two small platforms on the circular structure presumably supported temples. The architecture shows some Toltec affinities and has been dated 10–12C AD.
   The ceramics and figurines indicate occupation from the 1C AD and show influences from other W regions, such as Colima. Ixtlán polychrome ceramics are known from c AD 250–550, and the site gives its name to a minor category of figurine style in S Nayarit. Lively hollow figurines (up to 70–80cm high), both plain and polychrome, from tombs on the site give an idea of everyday life, representing models of houses and temples, figures of warriors, ball-players, dancers, musicians, acrobats, drinkers, deformed and exaggerated figures, and women holding or carrying babies. The style bears some relation to the figurine traditions of Colima and Sinaloa, but, contrary to other sites, nude figures predominate.
   C 30km N of Ixtlán del Río, at *Yagila*, there is an Early Postclassic Period ceremonial site on the hillside W of the village. It comprises a sunken plaza (c 40m sq), a 10m-high, unexcavated pyramid on the N side, and a smaller platform on the S side. A basalt stele from the site, carved with several glyphs, can be seen in the village itself.
   From Ixtlán airfield light aircraft fly to Huichol and Cora villages in the Sierra Madre. 15 min. away is *La Yesca* (2830m), with narrow streets and red-tile roofs, 5km on muleback from its airfield.

Beyond Ixtlán the scenery becomes sternly grand, with barrancas and deep gorges full of tropical vegetation. At 434km we cross into the State of Jalisco and from mountain to standard time (one hour ahead). 468km **La Magdalena** (7000 inhab.; 1400m; H,R,P), a picturesque place, famous for opals, turquoise, and agate (shops and stalls in Pl. Principal). The church of the *Señor de los Milagros*, originally 16C, with a 17C cloister attached, once served a Franciscan parish of Etzatlán.

A road runs SW to (23km) **Etzatlán** (15,000 inhab.; H,R,P), in a silver- and lead-mining region, where the former Franciscan convent of *La Concepción de Nuestra Señora* is one of the few foundations to have survived Jalisco's 16C hostile Indians and natural disasters reasonably intact.

During the war of 1540–41, two friars were killed and buried in the chancel, as was Fray Andrés de Córdoba, one of the original Twelve, killed by Indians in 1567. By 1582 the Indians were reported calmer and hearing Mass, and three or four friars were serving a congregation of up to 18,000.

The church (interior drastically remodelled in the 19C) and convent, modest structures, date from c 1538 and later 16C rebuildings. In the cloister a delightful little fountain, water emitted from four cherub mouths, is probably later than the 16C. On the W side of the atrio (now the plaza) is what is left of the probable open chapel, for which the praise of 16C contemporaries ('famous and illustrious for its building') may have been reserved. It is now so altered as to be unrecognizable, though some of its columns, partly re-used in the 17–18C to form another church, remain; its original shape appears to have been mosque-like.

The area in and around Etzatlán is known for its prehistoric shaft-tombs (investigated by P. C. Furst in the 1960s); 5km N of Etzatlán, at *El Arenal* (on the Hacienda San Sebastián) is a particularly good example. The shaft is 16m deep with three chambers at the bottom. Because it was previously plundered, the dating is difficult without associated artefacts; but shaft-tombs are generally thought to be between c AD 1 and 300, based on the pottery usually found in the burials, making them contemporary with the site of Teuchitlán (below). (The contents of another of these shaft-tombs [now in the Los Angeles County Museum, California] comprised nine articulated skeletons, three more without their skulls, and 17 hollow polychrome figurines, 40 pottery dishes and bowls, quadrihedral pottery boxes with lids, shell and obsidian jewellery, and two conch-shell trumpets from the Caribbean and Pacific coasts.)

The road turns SE to (38km) *Ahualulco de Mercado*, with an early 18C church. From here (with horse and guide) may be visited the geophysical formations among the igneous rock fields of the area. C 450m beyond (50km) **Teuchitlán** a r. turn leads to the archaeological zone, also known as *Ahualulco*.

This region was explored in the early 1970s by R. Mountjoy and P. C. Weigand, who located 348 sites and excavated Teuchitlán. The sites form four groups: early hunting stations and kill sites; small villages with a central mound or altar platform and 3–6 outlying mounds; larger mound sites incl. tombs with burial offerings; and Teuchitlán itself.
The site has more than 160 mounds formed into eight mound circles, each with a large central mound with shaft tomb, a style named the 'Teuchitlán tradition'. There are platforms with structures built against the hillsides, and two ball courts, one each in the *Guachontón* and the *Loma Alta* mound circles. A rock carving in the latter group also has a carving of an I-shaped ball court with a small, square hollow believed to represent an altar for sacrifices.
The tombs in the central mounds are difficult to date precisely, as they were often re-used, and thus the contents have been mixed; but in general the site flourished during AD 1–300, although tomb construction seems to have ceased c AD 200. Occupation phases are designated *Arenal* during which the shaft tombs were dug, and *Ahualulco* between AD 200 and 300, when there is evidence of trade and influence from Teotihuacán in the form of Thin Orange pottery. The excavations uncovered household debris and specific areas of obsidian working. The mound circles have been interpreted as representing different family lineages.

63km *Tala*, the cupola of its baroque (early 18C) church striking with glazed tiles.

38km SW of Tala is **Ameca** (26,000 inhab.; 1230m; H,R,P), an agricultural and light industrial centre (especially cane sugar and derivatives) on the Río Ameca, with notable turn-of-the-century architecture. In the vicinity (guide advisable) is the *Cerro Piedra Bola*, remarkable for its huge, and unique, volcanic spherical rocks, some more than 3m in diameter.

From the site and in the general region, come distinctive Ameca Grey mould-made hollow figurines, examples of which can be seen in the Museo Regional in Guadalajara. Characteristic of the style are smoothly rounded forms, cream- or red-slipped, with elongated faces, thin noses and lips, round clay pellet eyes with filleted eyelids, and crossbanded headgear. The most frequent forms are warriors with clubs and barrel-like armour, and woman-and-child groups.

From Tala the road runs NE to join (78km) Méx. 15 SE of *Amatitán*, see below.

488km (r.) **Tequila** (12,000 inhab.; 1211m; R,P), N of the forested volcano Tequila and S of a deep canyon through which flows the Río Grande, is the main production centre of the world-famous, and potent, liquor.

Tequila, a high-quality variety of mezcal, is derived from the fermented and distilled juice from the head of the agave plant (smaller and less fleshy than the maguey), which comes in two types—azul (more common) and xiguin—and which abounds in Jalisco, Nayarit, and Michoacán. Its production and export have been associated with the families of Cuervo (since the 18C), Sauza (since 1873), Rosales, and Orendáin, and bottling plants have been opened in the USA, Japan, and Australia. Today it is Jalisco's principal industry. The name is registered internationally and the drink may be made only in those municipalities of Jalisco and Nayarit as decreed by law.

The town contains over 20 distilleries and visitors are welcome by appointment. During 30 Nov.–13 Dec. the feast of Our Lady of Guadalupe is combined with a celebration of the drink (mariachis, the jarabe, etc.).

500km *Amatitán*. 520km road (r.) for *Tala*, see above. 545km *Guadalajara*, see below.

24 Guadalajara

GUADALAJARA (4 million inhab.; 1550m), capital of the State of Jalisco and second city of Mexico, lies in the Valle de Atemajac, on the SW side of the Mexican high plateau and bordered N and E by the Río Grande de Santiago. Later 20C industrial and population growth has contributed to urban spread, and the city has thus lost its once charming provincial atmosphere. It preserves, however, some of Mexico's finest historical monuments; its regional museum contains an outstanding collection of Mexican art from the 17C; and the most famous of the murals of José Clemente Orozco enhance some of its buildings. The natives of Guadalajara, the urbane tapatíos, take pride in their city as a cultural centre; in their mariachi bands; in their own, and best-known, version of the jarabe, Mexico's national dance; and in their traditionally high standards of horsemanship, displayed in charreadas. A further attraction is the warm, dry, sunny climate.

Airport. 20km S. Daily flights to *Mexico City, Puerto Vallarta, Acapulco, Chihuahua, Durango, Hermosillo, Monterrey, Mazatlán, Tijuana, Cancún, Loreto*, and *Manzanillo*; thrice weekly to *Puebla*; and to *San Francisco, Los Angeles*, and *Houston*.

Bus station. 5km SE of the centre, reached along Av. Revolución. Excellent and frequent services to all parts. To *Mexico City* (c 13 hrs); to *Morelia* (c 6 hrs); to *Pátzcuaro* (c 8 hrs); to *Puerto Vallarta* (6–7 hrs); to *Uruapan* (c 5 hrs); to *Mazatlán* (c 10 hrs); etc.

Railway station. At the S end of Calz. Independencia. Pullman and 1st and 2nd class trains daily to *Mexico City* (12–18 hrs). Trains to *Manzanillo* (28 hrs); to *Irapuato*; to *Colima* (7 hrs); etc.

Hotels throughout the city.

Post Office. C. Venustiano Carranza, one block N of Sta María de Gracia.

Tourist Office. State, 102 Av. Morelos.

British Consulate. 1897 Calz. Jesús González Gallo. **US Consulate.** 175 Av. Progreso.

Benjamin Franklin Library. 65 Paseo del Hospicio.

Main fiesta. Virgen de Zapopan (4–12 Oct.).

The city was definitively established on its present site (its fourth), in a desolate, waterless valley, in Feb. 1542. From 1548 it was seat of a bishop of a vast diocese, stretching far beyond Nueva Galicia. In 1560 the audiencia of Nueva Galicia was moved here from Compostela. By the 1620s there were c 600 Spanish and creole inhabitants, perhaps c 700 Indians, and over a thousand slaves and free mulattoes; the city, wrote a contemporary, was full of 'marvellous churches, houses with gardens…and patios full of verdure and freshness', and the streets were 'already wide and straight'. Its chronic water shortage was alleviated in 1740, thanks to the engineer Franciscan lay brother Pedro Antonio Buzeta, whose piping arrangements from the Cerro del Colli to the W ended in a handsome public fountain. From the late 1780s Guadalajara was capital of the intendancy of the same name. But its isolation was a fact of life, even though a tenuous road communication opened up in March 1794, when a four-seater carriage, drawn by four mules, made the journey to Mexico City in 12 days, via Irapuato, Celaya, and Querétaro. From 26 Nov. 1810 until 19 Jan. 1811 Hidalgo ran his feverish government here: issuing revolutionary decrees; publishing the city's first newspaper, 'El Despertador Americano'; planning a national congress; and executing at least 200 Spaniards. In 1824 Guadalajara became capital of the new State of Jalisco. In Feb.–March 1858 Pres. Juárez made it his seat of government, after which it became a prize for the armies of both sides. In July 1914 the city fell to Gen. Obregón, after one of the crucial battles of the Revolution; in 1914–15 it was twice briefly occupied by villistas. In 1919 a revolutionary group of artists, incl. David Alfaro Siqueiros, Amado de la Cueva, and Xavier Guerrero, was formed in Guadalajara under the patronage of José Guadalupe Zuno, whose artistic bent matched his appetite for political intrigue. His later governorship (1923–26) saw positive patronage of the arts. The city's present aspect owes much to the energetic governorship of Jesús González Gallo (1947–53), who forced through much street widening and the creation of new plazas, 'persuading the reluctant tapatíos of the advantages of modernization'.

The State of **Jalisco** (80,137 sq km; 5 million inhab.) is bounded on the W by the Pacific. It is traversed from NNW to SSE by the Sierra Madre Occidental, known under various local names—a territory of exceptional ruggedness and dramatic landscape. The mountain range divides the State into a narrow forested coastal plain and a high plateau, part of the Mesa de Anáhuac (average elevation 1525m) cut into by spurs, barrancas, and minor, detached, ranges. The Sierra is largely volcanic and highest in the SW. Near the border with Colima rise the volcanoes Nevado de Colima (4330m) and, to its S, Volcán de Colima (Volcán de Fuego; 3960m). Among the State's rivers are the Río Lerma (Grande de Santiago) in the N and NE, and the Armería in the S, which keeps up a good volume throughout the year. Jalisco's economy is based on agriculture, livestock, and tequila. Newer industries around Guadalajara include electrical goods and tyre production, cement plants, and sugar refineries.

Jalisco is the heart of the region of Western Mexican Cultures, where shaft-tomb burial was practised. Many shaft-tombs have been looted, but several important sites have been carefully excavated by archaeologists: eg, Autlán, El Arenal, Etzatlán, and Barra de Navidad. El Opeño in Michoacán and Capacha in Colima are two of the earliest shaft-tomb sites.
    The ancient cultures of W Mexico developed independently, but were in almost constant contact with central Mesoamerica and, by trade along the Pacific coast, with Central America and perhaps the N of S America. Notable characteristics of these cultures are their large, hollow, glossy red clay figurines; highly burnished cream-coloured solid clay figurines with elongated heads and sharp features; and metalwork. Ceramic complexes are named after various sites, such as Ameca or El Arenal.
    The region comprised several loosely federated states, incl. from the 12C AD, Collimán, Zapotlán, Jalisco, and Tonallán (whose principal city was Tonalá, SE of Guadalajara). These were agricultural communities, who supplemented their diet by hunting and fishing. Judging from their figurines, chiefs and shamans (medicine men) both held power, and various ceremonies included dancing and acrobatics. From the later 15C there was increasing pressure from Tarascan expansion westwards out of Michoacán, and a row of forts was established along the borders. These later served as places of refuge in resisting the Spaniards, and the region was only subdued after fierce fighting and campaigning, and with the help of Tarascan allies.
    The call to Independence found a quick response in the region, with the successes of the insurgent José Antonio Torres, who invited Hidalgo to lead operations in Guadalajara. On 21 June 1823 the free and sovereign State of Jalisco, incl. Colima, Nayarit, and part of Zacatecas, was proclaimed. By mid-century liberal and reformist opinions in the State, exemplified by Santos Degollado (governor 1855–56), exercised great influence on national affairs. The conservatives were unable to consolidate their gains during the war of the Reform when the

a Rotonda
b Pal. de Justicia
c Museo del Estado
d PLAZA DE ARMAS
e PL. DE LOS LAURELES
f PLAZA DE LA LIBERACION
g PLAZUELA DE LOS MARIACHIS

GUADALAJARA

0 metres — 800

struggle for control of Guadalajara was a major factor, a pattern continued under Maximilian. The vigorous administration of the impeccably liberal Ramón Corona (1887–88) was cut short by his assassination, at the instance, it was said, of a suspicious central government. The Revolutionary wars had less effect in Jalisco, where great landed estates were not a feature, than elsewhere. In 1926–29 the Cristero rebellion, met with brutal countermeasures, raged here, and continued in a lesser way until 1932, three years after the official peace agreement.

Guadalajara's spacious, elegant centre was developed in 1947–53 and 1976–81, by Ignacio Díaz Morales. Despite demolition, significant, hitherto hemmed-in, buildings were freed; and three plazas, E, W, and N of an improved Pl. de Armas, were created.

In the centre of PL. DE ARMAS, whose buildings show a rose-golden hue in the sun, is the late 19C bandstand made in the Duval foundry in Paris. On the

E side is the handsome **Pal. de Gobierno** (1751–75; once *Pal. de la Audiencia de Nueva Galicia*), by Nicolás Enríquez del Castillo and Miguel José Conique. The elaborate portal, Conique's work, repays attention for running the gamut of styles from baroque through churrigueresque to rococo: half-columns with petatillo decoration and Corinthian capitals, emphatic voussoirs in the entrance arch, and dramatic volutes in the lower storey; the upper storey framed by richly interrupted estípites (rare in this region) and simulated drapery under the layered cornice. The clock tower (1885) is an addition by Eduardo Villaseñor.

In 1810–11 it served as Hidalgo's seat of government, and in 1858 as Juárez's. Here on 15 March an attempt by conservative soldiers (led by Lt Filomeno Bravo) on Juárez's life was foiled by Guillermo Prieto. In Jan. 1859 an explosion damaged the interior and entailed rebuilding, complete by 1872. Further restoration was carried out by Díaz Morales in 1952–60.

In the vault and on the walls of the staircase (r.) the mural (1937) by Orozco celebrates, amid a violent denunciation of contemporary injustice, an angry Hidalgo as liberator, brandishing a torch above the dead and dying in fratricidal strife. On l. wall, clericalism and militarism, which unleashed the Revolution, and a shadowy figure representing the people struggling to free itself from the embrace of snakes. On r. wall, 'Carnival of the Ideologies' represents the evils of political extremes; world leaders turned into clowns; a jungle of symbols in the war of ideas. In the Cámara de Diputados (by David Bravo; 1872) another mural (1948–49), in the vault and on part of one wall, showing Hidalgo, calmer and magisterial, quill pen and parchment in hand, as legislator freeing slaves. Below him, more legislators: Carranza, Juárez, Morelos.

Leaving Pl. de Armas to the NW we come to PL. DE LOS LAURELES, fronting which is the cathedral of **La Asunción**, unorthodox result of many years building.

The foundations were laid c 1561. After c 1594 the maestro mayor was Martín Casillas. Still unfinished, it was dedicated in 1618, and work continued throughout the 17C. Bp Felipe Galindo Chávez y Pineda (1696–1702) saw to the building of sacristy, offices, and loggia on the SE side. A further dedication took place in 1716. The façade was rebuilt after 1750; and drastic work, after earthquakes, was done in the 19C. In 1859–60 Gen. Severo del Castillo, conservative minister of war, confiscated the silver and gold treasure to coin money to pay the troops.

EXTERIOR. The three W portals retain their Mannerist style. Above the central, three niches containing statues of Our Lady and SS Peter and Paul. Above, in the large tympanum, a relief of the apostles witnessing the Assumption. The top storeys and pinnacles of the towers are a whimsical aberration, built in 1851–54 by Manuel Gómez Ibarra.

Their predecessors fell down after earthquake damage in 1818. Designs on a Staffordshire stone china (Cauldon ware; by William Ridgway; 1814–30) dinner service owned by Bp Diego Aranda y Carpinteiro (1776–1853) were the inspiration for the new. Two things may be said in their favour: they are reputed earthquake proof and their usefulness as landmarks (D.H. Lawrence's 'two lost birds side by side on a moor') have made the tapatíos rather fond of them. The cupola was rebuilt after the earthquake of 1875 by Domingo Torres. The façade was restored in 1943 by Díaz Morales.

The INTERIOR is a wonderful contrast—the only Gothic cathedral interior in Mexico. Airy ribs spring from clustered half-columns against pilaster supports. Choir and high altar were removed from the nave in 1827 (by José Gutiérrez) and relocated in the apse. This modification, together with the comparatively chapel-free side-aisles, their vaults the same height as the nave, give the whole a concentrated effect. The altarpiece of St Joseph in the l. aisle preserves an earlier tabernacle door painted by Juan Correa—St John of God and the infant Christ. In the sacristy hang an Assumption, attr. Murillo, and a St Christopher by José de Páez. In the Sala Capitular is the Church Militant and Triumphant (c 1687) by Cristóbal de Villalpando, similar to his work in the cathedral of Mexico.

To the r. (S) of the cathedral is the neoclassical *Sagrario* (1808–43), begun by José Gutiérrez and completed by Manuel Gómez Ibarra. On the N side of the plaza is the extemporaneous *Pal. Municipal* (1949–52), by Vicente Mendiola, on the site of the former archbishop's palace. The staircase murals, an indictment of the wars of the Conquest, are by Gabriel Flores.

Behind the Cathedral runs the rectangular PL. DE LA LIBERACION, Díaz Morales' most elegant precinct, with blossoming trees and two fountains. The bordering buildings are shown to great effect. On the NW corner of C. Belén and Av. Hidalgo is the *Pal. Legislativo* (late 18C; restored); on the NE corner, the *Pal. de Justicia* (restored 1952; mural by Guillermo Chávez Vega), formerly part of the convent of *Sta María de Gracia*, founded in 1573 for Dominican nuns and rebuilt in the 18C. On the opposite corner, with C. Venustiano Carranza, and facing S, is the former convent church, *Sta María de Gracia* (1752), with twin Mannerist-style portals. In the sacristy, with good rib vaulting, are four paintings (1754) on the life of St Dominic by Antonio Enríquez.

From the plaza C. Belén leads N (c 1km) to the former hospital of **Belén** (*Hospital Real de San Miguel*), built here in 1786–94 by the engineer Narciso Codina, with the chapel in the centre of the façade.

The charitable Bp Antonio Alcalde defrayed the expenses, motivated by the dreadful plague epidemics in 1785–86. In 1956–61 part of the site was enlarged by Enrique de la Mora as the *Hospital Civil*. The medical faculty of the university is also housed here. Adjoining (its entrance in C. Belén) is the *Panteón de Sta Paula*, begun by Manuel Gómez Ibarra in 1848, with interesting tomb monuments by Gómez Ibarra and Jacobo Gálvez. The chapel crypt contains the tombs of famous jaliscenses.

At the E end of the plaza rises the imposing **Teatro Degollado**, which can claim to be Mexico's finest theatre—indeed, one of the finest in the world.

It was begun in 1856 to the designs of Jacobo Gálvez. At first it was known as *Teatro Alarcón*; Governor Santos Degollado laid the foundation stone, in the former Pl. de San Agustín, on 5 March. In 1861 its name was changed in honour of the recently assassinated 'Santo de la Reforma'. The first performance was given, before completion, in Sept. 1866: Angela Peralta (with Annibale Bianchi's company) singing the title role in Donizetti's 'Lucia de Lammermoor'. The centenary was celebrated on 13 Sept. 1966 with a performance of the same opera, in which Placido Domingo took part. It holds 3000, on five layers of seats.

The classical portico is upheld by two rows of columns (16 in all) with Corinthian capitals. In the 1960s, under Díaz Morales, the exterior was entirely refaced in stone and the marble pediment relief, Apollo and the Muses, by Benito Castañeda, was substituted for one in mosaic. The refurbished interior preserves the original murals by Jacobo Gálvez and Gerardo Suárez in the proscenium arch and vault: scenes from Canto IV of Dante's 'Divina Commedia'.

On the S side of the theatre is the church of **San Agustín**, which, despite much restoration, has kept its early 17C Mannerist portal.

It was the church of the convent of Augustinian friars, assigned the site in 1573–74. The church, still building in the late 17C, preserves its old sacristy and choirstalls. The grand, grey-stone high altar is a good modern addition. The convent, with a two-storey cloister, also remains, now the university school of music.

On the N side of the Cathedral opens out PL. DE LOS HOMBRES ILUSTRES, the rotonda commemorating some of Jalisco's most famous sons, whose remains rest here; among them: Valentín Gómez Farías; Jacobo Gálvez; Manuel López Cotilla; Pedro Moreno (1775–1817), insurgent; Ignacio Luis Vallarta. The statues (except of Vallarta) are by Miguel Miramontes.

Facing the plaza on the E side is the former diocesan seminary of **San José**, a vast, thick-walled building in the ochre-coloured stone of the area, its main portal betraying classicizing features, with baroque in the solomonic columns of the niche.

It was built under the auspices of Bp Galindo Chávez y Pineda in 1696–1701 and rebuilding was started under Bp Juan Gómez de Parada (1736–51), which left it unoccupied for the rest of the 18C. In 1810 it served as barracks for Torres's revolutionary troops and prison for Spanish captives. During 1821–46 it reverted to its proper use and in the latter year served as a fortress when the city was besieged by conservative forces opposed to the liberals' wish for the return to power of Santa-Anna. In 1859 the seminary finally closed.

It houses the **Museo Regional de Guadalajara** (Tues.–Sun., 9–3.45; fee), one of Mexico's major collections, distributed in rooms around the main SW patio and four lesser ones.

GROUND FLOOR. ROOM 1, a continuous, semidivided room. 1–3. Panels introducing the evolution of the universe, the earth, and life on earth. 4. Cases containing fossils from Jalisco. 5. Wall panel—tree-of-life painting. 6. Wall photograph—glaciation. 7. Central display—mammoth skeleton (almost complete) from Zocoalco, discovered in 1962; and other fossil mammoth bones and tusks, and fossil footprints. 8. Wall panel—the Pleistocene and recent fauna of the Chapala-Zocoalco region. 9. Fossil rhinoceros skull. 10. Fossil human skulls. 11. Wall panel—the evolution of man (a little dated). A small courtyard outside exhibits fossilized trees. 12. Case of artefacts and maps showing the migration of man into the New World; early hunters of the Americas; early man in Mexico and in Jalisco (incl. early stone tools, projectile points, obsidian blade cores, grinding stones, polished stone vessels and an axe-head, and worked bone.

13. Archaeology—introductory wall panels and maps: archaeology; physiographical and cultural subdivisions of the New World; ecology and physical geography of Mexico, and of the Mesoamerican cultural area; comparative chronological chart of Mesoamerican cultures; physical geography of W Mexico, its cultural areas, and sites; detailed chronological chart for Michoacán, Sinaloa, Nayarit, Jalisco, and Colima, incl. the ceramic phases.

14. Case of *Formativo* (Preclassic Period) figurines, pottery, and polished stone axe-heads from Capacha and El Opeño in Colima and Michoacán; Sup. Formativo (Late Preclassic) figurines and painted pottery from burials at Chupícuaro; painted pottery illustrating the dispersion of Chupícuaro ceramics to central and W Mexico; hollow figurines of dogs and humans typical of the Western Mexican Cultures, and distribution map; collection of pottery, figurines, and jewellery from shaft-tombs (note especially the shell necklace, tiny pottery figurines, and stirrup jug); collection of figurines depicting scenes of daily life, religion, music, dwellings, etc. of the Western Cultures; and superlative examples of decorated pottery and large, hollow figurines from tombs in Nayarit, Colima, and Jalisco. 15. Photographs illustrating the terrain of W Mexico, and its ecological zones. 16. Cases with exceptional examples of hollow ceramic figurines dated AD 300–600 (eg, armadillos, and dog-vessel from Colima); and AD 200–400 (eg, seated-man vessel, seated-dog jug, man carrying a jug, etc. from Nayarit). 17. Scale model of a shaft-tomb (Tumba 8 at El Grillo-Tabachines, Jalisco). 18. Three cases of hollow figurines from Jalisco, dated AD 300–600 (eg, a standing and a seated man, woman-and-child group). 19. Artefacts from the Cazcana region (N of Jalisco) and pottery from Michoacán showing influences from Teotihuacán (including polychrome pottery, inscribed pottery, carved stoneware, worked shell, copper bells, clay spindle whorls, pipes, incense burners, and zoomorphic figurines; several skulls illustrate the practice of dental mutilation and cranial deformation).

20. Map—New Traditions—migrations in the Postclassic Period. 21. Postclassic sites map and case containing decorated pottery and alabaster figurines from Sinaloa, N Nayarit, and S Jalisco; figurines and pottery from Sayula and Zocoalco; technology section with obsidian blade cores, gypsum and other stone carved pieces, beaten gold and copper artefacts; obsidian points, polished stone axe-heads, jewellery, ear and nose plugs, paper beaters, shell and bone carvings, stone bead necklaces, and awls; further examples of the thriving metallurgy of the Western Cultures are shown in a map of sites where metal-

work has been found, and copper wire, bells, hooks, axes, and jewellery; and gold sheets cut into various shapes.

22. Four photographs comparing architectural structures at Tomatlán, Arreguín, Ixtlán, and Ixtepete. 23. Free-standing panel and display of carved stone pieces, incl. human figures, miniature stepped-pyramid, grinders, seat, and vessels. 24. Two cases with hollow pottery figurines, incl. seated figure (Colima, AD 1200–1500) and cylinder representing Tláloc, god of rain, from El Chanal (Colima).

R. 9–12. Ethnography: Campesinas Sociedades. A wall map shows campesino districts in Jalisco and life-sized displays, incl. ethnographic photographs, show the costume and equipment of the campesino (farmer) and vaquero (cowboy). R.10 contains photographs, local products, and industry (wooden farm cart, presses, bellows and blacksmith's tools, plus a sugar-cane press out on the veranda). R.11 concentrates on Lake Chapala—photographs, fishing boat, nets, and baskets used by fishermen; glazed stoneware and earthenware vessels; loom and spinning wheel, and local textiles. R.12 displays cultures of the Sierra Madre Occidental—map of ethnic regions (Coras, Huicholes, Mexicameros, and Tepehuanes); costumes; contemporary pottery, basketry, and wooden implements; farming tools; weaving tools, incl. woven pictures; and musical instruments. A smaller, separate room contains artefacts and costume of the Nahua of S Jalisco.

FIRST FLOOR. ROOM 2. 17–18C PAINTINGS. Sebastián López de Arteaga, Marriage of Our Lady, a favourite subject. Baltasar de Echave Orio, Stigmatization of St Francis—spare, stark, and effective. Luis Juárez, St Teresa of Avila, a typically luminous work, the emphasis on brown and gold shades. Francisco de León, Our Lady of Solitude (1727). Pedro Ramírez, Scourging of Christ (1678), with vigorous anatomical detail. Cristóbal de Villalpando, Joseph saved from the well—heavily restored; SS John and Peter before Christ's tomb; Assumption, with unusually sombre effects; Triumph of the Church (after Rubens)—an opulent work full of life and gorgeous colour. Nicolás Rodríguez Juárez, St Sebastian; Four Evangelists (oils on copperplate); Virgin and Child. Juan Rodríguez Juárez, Education of the Virgin (1720), a marvellous combination of tenderness and elegance, St Anne taking pride of place (note the two young donors, Ana María and Isabel María Castijón). Among the 17C anon. works: St Antony, a strange and charming work; Our Lady of Antigua Guatemala, with a byzantine effect; Allegory of the Carmelite order, with a profusion of flowers and fruit.

R.3. THE 18C. Miguel Cabrera, Virgen de la Merced; St Joseph's Patronage of the Colegio de San Ildefonso (Mexico City); Crucifixion and Jesuit saints; St Raymond. Francisco Antonio Vallejo, Our Lady of the Distressed. Nicolás Enríquez and Antonio Sánchez, Scenes from the Passion, surprisingly vigorous works. Sebastián Salcedo, Ecce Homo (1774). José de Alzíbar, St Augustine; St Thomas Aquinas. José de Páez, Death of St Rosalia; Holy Family. Francisco de Cuentas, Virgin and Child (1710). Diego de Cuentas, Our Lady of the Apocalypse; Holy Trinity and seven archangels; Bp Felipe Galindo Chávez y Pineda (c 1632–1702). Miguel de Mendoza, Annunciation.

R.4. JOSE DE IBARRA. St Dominic preaching—the best work, very expressive; St Paul writing—easy and graceful; St Dominic inspired by Our Lady; Apparition of Our Lady to St Dominic; Marriage of Our Lady; Virgin and Child; Blessed Alonso Rodríguez.

R.5. 18C ANON. POPULAR DIDACTIC AND ICONOGRAPHIC PAINTING, primitive in style. Anon 16C, SS Lawrence and Stephen. Anon. 18C, Our Lady of Guanajuato; Christ of Zacatecas. Mariano Guerrero (late 18C), Fray Benito de Jesús María. Characterful late 18C portraits of nuns: Sor Mariana Teresa del Santísimo Sacramento and Sor María Vicente de Sto Domingo; and priests: Juan José Román y Bugarín and Juan José Martínez de los Ríos. José Aguilar, Holy Trinity and Saints. José López, Our Lady of Victory. Antonio de Torres, Our Lady of Guadalupe.

R.6. THE 19C AND 20C. 19C POPULAR PAINTING, incl. works by José María Estrada (c 1810–62), a native of Guadalajara, whose endearing portraits give an unrivalled insight into character and costume. Note especially the portraits of a young Franciscan friar, in which ingenuousness of technique heightens gentleness and expressiveness in the sitter; Agustín José Rico; José María Cano; Cesareo de la Rosa. Among works by his contemporaries:

Abundio Rincón, Priest from Cocula; Fray Francisco Rodríguez, startling in its colouring. Félix Zarata, Josefa Flores (1850). Among anon. works: Niña del periquito, the clumsiness of the figure contrasting with the sweetness of the face; Trinidad Villa, a typical woman of Jalisco, with a touch of caricature; Hacendado, tough and miniatory.

19C PORTRAITS. Juan N. Herrera, Unknown man, a first-rate example of the leonese painter whose portraits are probably the finest of their period. Felipe S. Gutiérrez, Countryman, a handsome indigenous type. Petronillo Monroy, Old Man. Germán Gedovius, Portrait of Luis Quintanilla.

ACADEMIC PAINTING IN GUADALAJARA, incl. anon. portrait of Antonio Castro Montes de Oca. THE LATER 19C. Carlos Villaseñor, House of Alonso de Alba (Jalapa). Luis de la Torre, Ocotlán; Laundresses. Félix Bernardelli, Old man. Works by Francisco Sánchez Guerrero, José Vizcarra, Othón de Aguinaga. IMPRESSIONISM. Landscapes and seascapes by Joaquín Clausell.

20C WORKS. Roberto Montenegro (early works), Portraits of Lola Olmedo, Diego Rivera, Rafael Ponce de León, Francisco de la Torre, Jesús Reyes Ferreira. Gerardo Murillo (Dr Atl), Bathers; Moonbeam on the wave; landscapes: Iztaccíhuatl; Acapulco; Dawn on the mountain. Rafael Ponce de León (a satiric artist), various works, incl. portraits of Diego Rivera and Roberto Montenegro. José Guadalupe Zuno, A Dog's Life (lithograph); Conquest (mural), depicting the horrors of the campaign of Nuño de Guzmán. Sketches by Diego Rivera; engravings by Carlos Orozco Romero.

The CENTRO BOHEMIO circle of jaliscense painters is represented by further works by José Guadalupe Zuno and Orozco Romero (Señora María Marín, calm and luminous), Carlos Stahl, José Luis Figueroa, Ixca Farías (Casa de barrio—vibrant colour and simplicity), Jesús Guerrero Galván (Self-portrait), Juan Antonio Córdoba (The artist's wife), Amado de la Cueva (Lupe Marín). Other artists represented include Diego Rivera, Cubist portrait; David Alfaro Siqueiros, Self-portrait (1918); Juan O'Gorman, Portrait of José Clemente Orozco (1943); Francisco Díaz de León, Pottery-seller.

R.7. HISTORY OF JALISCO I. Historical documents and facsimiles; vestments and fragments saved from convents; arms and armour; portraits of bps of Guadalajara and governors of Jalisco. A section on Hidalgo includes insurgent and royalist news-sheets. R.8. HISTORY OF JALISCO II. From the Constitution of 1857. The collection includes furniture, portraits (incl. Santos Degollado), arms and armour; household and business relics; material relating to the university.

R.13 (the former chapel choir) contains some of the museum's European paintings. School of Jan Gossaert (Mabuse), Madonna. Jan (Velvet) Breughel, Noah's Ark; Noah's Sacrifice. Juan Pantoja de la Cruz (1551–1608), doña Isabel Clara Eugenia. CHAPEL. School of Zurbarán, SS John, Simon, Elias, Jerome. School of José de Ribera, St Andrew. Luca Giordano, Birth of Our Lady; Presentation in the Temple; Assumption. Albert Bouts, Triptych of the Nativity.

Directly W of the Pal. Municipal stands the church of **La Merced**, dedicated in 1721 for the convent of Mercedarian friars, its three-storey façade Mannerist, with basic relief. In the middle storey, the central image of Our Lady is flanked by those of St María de Cervellón (a founder of the order of Mercedarian nuns) and St Mariana de Jesús (María de Paredes, the 'lily of Quito'). The tower was badly finished in the early 20C.

On the W wall of the sacristy is an enormous canvas (1709) by Diego de Cuentas: the Descent of Our Lady of Mercy to declare her intentions on the foundation of the order to SS Raymond of Peñafort and Peter Nolasco and King Jaime of Aragón.

Hence we follow C. Sta Mónica N to the church of **Sta Mónica** (c 1720–40) with the most sumptuously baroque exterior in Guadalajara, on which local craftsmen (a little behind the times) imposed their highly individual development of the style.

It was the church of a convent of Augustinian nuns, founded, with Jesuit support, from St Mónica in Puebla in 1720, and destroyed as a result of the Reform laws.

EXTERIOR. The two portals, facing E, are flanked by solomonic columns supporting variations of the Corinthian capital. In the lower storey the columns are almost stifled by the luscious vines and bunches of grapes, enlivened by little birds. The vegetal and strapwork decoration of the upper storey columns offers a more restrained contrast. Between the columns are extraordinary, recessed caryatid pilasters, echoing the column decoration. In the wide friezes genial angels hold the frames of heraldic devices: the two-headed eagle and a mitre above a heart pierced by arrows. On the pedestal supports on either side of them are caryatids trapped in more vine decoration. Windows and niches, at the E end, continue the same richness and entablatures are good and emphatic. In the NE corner stands a statue of St Christopher holding the Christ child, most likely contemporary with the church despite its archaic style.

INTERIOR (refurbished in questionable taste). The original and elaborate Gothic vaulting is in marked contrast to the exterior. Coro bajo and coro alto are also still in place, though unhappily interfered with. The engaged columns of the latter's entrance doorway from the convent echo the exterior decoration.

From this corner we may turn r. (E) along C. Reforma to reach, at the intersection with Av. Alcalde, the classicizing church of *San José* (1880–90) by Manuel Gómez Ibarra. It was built on the site of the Dominican convent, destroyed during the Reform. Av. Alcalde leads N to the *Santuario de Guadalupe* (1777–81), its façade in no recognizable style and its portal framed by two decorative buttresses, with espadañas above. Turning l. (W) along C. Reforma we reach (4th intersection) C. González Ortega. On the r., at its corner with C. Garibaldi, is the church of *San Diego*, simple yet effective, begun in 1730.

It belonged to the *Colegio de Niñas de San Diego*, founded c 1703 by Madre Ana de San Joseph and finished in 1752. The college, just N of the church, is now a school.

One block further, at the corner of Cs Reforma and Contreras Medellín, is the church of **San Felipe** (1766–1802), built for the Oratorians, finished by Pedro José Ciprés, but further altered after 1904 by its new Jesuit custodians. Its ornate façade, incorporating niches, lambrequin motifs, and columns lavishly ornamented a third of their height, and beautiful tower attest the neostyle, soberer baroque of the late 18C. Two blocks S along C. Contreras Medellín, between Cs Independencia and Juan Manuel, is what remains of the convent of *Las Capuchinas*, founded in 1761. The church, its exterior disclosing a retiring charm, preserves the coro bajo, with its spiked grille, to the l. of the high altar.

Following C. Contreras Medellín further S and crossing Av. Hidalgo, we come to the church of **Jesús María**, part of a convent of Dominican nuns founded in 1722. For all its simplicity, the double portal is delightful.

EXTERIOR. The lower storeys of the doorways are a throwback to strict Renaissance style. The upper storeys are in the form of galleries between whose arches appear figures in high relief: Our Lady of Light and roughly carved little angels flanked by SS Francis and Dominic (l.); the Holy Family flanked by SS Anne and Joachim (r.). At the foot of the buttress between the doorways is a relief of Our Lady of Solitude. A statue of St Christopher stands in a niche at the corner.

INTERIOR. The coros alto and bajo, with thick grilles, have been kept intact. The convent, now reoccupied by nuns, lies W of the church.

Two blocks S, at either side of Av. Juárez, are the church and part of the former convent of *El Carmen*, founded in 1724. The former, an early 19C rebuilding, is severely neoclassical.

E of Jesús María, along C. Morelos, between Cs Donato Guerra and Melchor Ocampo, is the church of *Sta Teresa*, with severe twin portals, once belonging to a convent of Carmelite nuns founded in 1690–95. Again the coros alto and bajo have survived, the former with an excellent abanico.

From here we may return to the centre. On reaching the SW corner of Pl. de los Laureles the turning r., C. Colón, leads to Plazuela de la Universidad and the former chapel of the college of **Sto Tomás de Aquino**, now the telegraph office.

The Jesuits established their college in 1590, but building did not finish until 1688. Among its teachers was Francisco Javier Clavijero (1731–87), pioneer of Mexican culture. After the Jesuit expulsion the Real Universidad Literaria de Guadalajara was inaugurated here in March 1794. The chapel, all that remains of the college buildings, was given a neoclassical portico in 1827 by José Gutiérrez.

The interior contains murals (1924–26) by Amado de la Cueva and David Alfaro Siqueiros depicting working-class solidarity forged during the Revolution. De la Cueva's death in a motor accident served as excuse for interrupting the work. It remained unfinished. The workers' figures are schematic; red stars decorate the cupola.

Av. 16 de Septiembre runs S from Pl. de los Laureles to (l.; beyond C. Prisciliano Sánchez) JARDIN DE SAN FRANCISCO, facing which is the church of **San Francisco**.

At one stage in the 16C the Franciscans were accused (exaggeratedly) of building so quickly that their church 'was going up and falling down in places at the same time'. The present church dates from 1678–92 and the convent was finished in 1746. During the Reform most of the convent was destroyed and in 1867 the rest was expropriated. In 1934 the remaining property was sold for 11,000 pesos; in Apr. 1936 arsonists wreaked havoc with the church.

Its remaining beauty is the baroque façade, solomonic columns combining well with dignified statues. In nave and choir hang 16 paintings of saints (1698; painted for San Francisco in San Luis Potosí) by Juan Correa (needing restoration).

On the other side of the avenida is the chapel of **Nuestra Señora de Aranzazu** (1784), only survivor of the convent dependencies. The two retables, with fine polychrome statues and relief, are the only churrigueresque ones to survive in Guadalajara.

Av. 16 de Septiembre continues S (c 1.5km) to the railway station. (C. Mexicaltzingo, a turning r. halfway along, leads to the parish church of *San Juan Bautista Mexicaltzingo* [1789].) It runs alongside PL. JUAREZ, laid out in 1960 by Julio de la Peña, in its centre a 33m high stele rising behind a bronze statue of Pres. Juárez. The bronze screen with reliefs commemorating the war of the Reform is by José Chávez Morado.

On the other side of Pl. Juárez, along Calz. Independencia, is PARQUE AGUA AZUL, another development of the early 1960s and a popular resort. Among its various attractions is the *Teatro Experimental*. Further N, between Calz. Independencia and Av. 16 de Septiembre, before the roundabout, are the *Casa de Cultura* and the *Biblioteca Pública del Estado* by Julio de la Peña, with murals by Gabriel Flores and José Servín.

From the roundabout Calz. Independencia leads back to the centre. Beyond the second roundabout, with a monument to Ramón Corona (c 1897) by Jesús Contreras, C. Cuauhtémoc leads r. into the barrio of *Analco*. At the corner with C. 28 de Enero is the church of *San Sebastián* (late 17C), on the site of a Franciscan visita chapel. The main and lateral portals exhibit a charming popular baroque. The patio of the adjoining building provides a refuge for the cloister arches from the convent of Sta Mónica, with superb floral relief. The neighbouring church of *San José de Analco*, facing the plaza two blocks NE, and site of the earliest outlying parish, dates in its present form from the later 19C.

Backing on to the rear of the Teatro Degollado a huge fountain representing the foundation of Guadalajara faces Paseo Degollado. Hence a stepped walkway, fountains running its whole length, leads to PL. TAPATIA, bordered by modern arcades and opened in 1982. In its centre a fountain sinuously commemorates the immolation of Quetzalcóatl.

From here we have a wonderful view of the vast **Hospicio Cabañas** (called by Díaz Morales 'the Escorial of America') in which are combined the geniuses of Manuel Tolsá and José Clemente Orozco.

It was founded as an orphanage by Juan Cruz Ruiz de Cabañas y Crespo (bp 1796–1824), remarkable for his charity and energy in promoting public works, in 1801. The plans were drawn up and sent from Mexico City by Tolsá, at whose suggestion José Gutiérrez came from the capital in 1804 to supervise construction. Inauguration took place in 1810. In 1811–21 the Hospicio was used as barracks; it reverted to its intended use in 1827. The chapel was built during 1840–43 under Manuel Gómez Ibarra. Various cultural institutions are now lodged here.

The building, which includes 23 patios, is a true demonstration of grandeur born from simplicity. Behind the classically balanced portico rises the exquisite cupola, raised on slender columns, the finials around its parapet adding an extra elegant touch. The wall panels, lunettes, pendentives, vaults, drum, and

Hospicio Cabañas, Guadalajara

cupola of the CHAPEL, reached through the patio directly beyond (E) the portico, are covered with frescoes by José Clemente Orozco (1937–39), a profoundly moving meditation on the history of Mexico, in which every facet of man is explored.

The *Transept* themes treat prehistoric, barbaric Mexico. In the vault of the W transept Huitzilopochtli, god of war, fangs dripping with blood, and scenes of Aztec sacrifice; in the E transept vault, allegory of the clash of indigenous and Christian religions (the heads of Christ crowned with thorns and of Quetzalcóatl). At the ends of nave and transepts, pairs of figures—Franciscan friars, Indian warrior and conquistador, Cervantes and El Greco, etc.— and the caravels of Columbus (E transept wall) symbolize the imposition of Western civilization. The six *Vaults* of the *Nave* and the wall panels between them contain the most significant parts. In the first vault S, Philip II supports the Cross, on which is perched the crown. Next, Spaniards on two-headed horses crush Indians. S of the cupola, a Franciscan holding a swordlike cross with an Indian convert at his feet and a strange hybrid being, half-human half-machine, whispering in his ear and tracing the first letters of the alphabet. N of the cupola, Cortés, a sternly dignified figure, against a scene of conflict, a hybrid genius whispering in his ear. Next, conquering Spaniards. Last, a horse, half-animal, half-machine, treads girders which crush human beings. The *Wall Panels* come in complementary pairs. First, the Dictators, and columns of marchers waving banners; the Militarized Masses; Despotism, a jackbooted faceless overseer lording it, armed with a knout, over tiny subjected figures. Opposite are Demagogues, incl. false prophets dressed as clowns; Sorrowing Humanity, which moves into the third panel where is the serene Bp Ruiz de Cabañas blessing three orphan girls and three women kneeling before him. Beyond the cupola, in the N stretch of the nave: first, apocalyptic horsemen—the Tragic; the Religious, with Guadalajara as the city shown; the Conquered, a group of heroic armoured figures. Opposite the Tragic appears the Unknown, symbolizing Spain poised for victory over hooded, sorrowing Mexico; then the Scientific, a huge wheel rolling over the remains of Aztec civilization; last, the Baroque, expressed in architectural forms.

In the *Pendentives*, powerful, striving male nudes symbolizing the Revolution. In the panels of the lower *Drum*, representations of the arts and crafts. Effectively separated from these panels by the drum windows framed by columns comes the supreme achievement: three reclining figures, enigmatic, dark against a red background, intertwined and framing a fourth, flying upwards—the man in flames, signifying the triumph of the spirit over materialism.

On the S side of Pl. Tapatía is the *Mercado Libertad*, projected by Alejandro Zohn and inaugurated in 1958, whence we may cross Av. Javier Mina by bridge to reach the church of *San Juan de Dios* (1726), its portal including a triple niche with statues of Our Lady of Solitude and SS Joseph and Antony of Padua. The adjoining arcade is all that remains of the convent (to which the church belonged) of the Brothers of St John of God, founded in 1608.

Between Avs Javier Mina and Obregón, at the side of the church, is PLAZUELA DE LOS MARIACHIS, in fact a narrow arcaded street, famous centre for performances by Mariachi bands, a speciality of Guadalajara.

Beyond the church of El Carmen the wide Av. Vallarta, continuation of Av. Juárez, continues W through Parque de la Revolución. Between C. Escorza and Av. Tolsá (l.) is the headquarters of the **Universidad de Guadalajara**, a handsome building of 1914–18, originally designed as Pal. Legislativo, by D.A. Navarro Branca.

The University authorized by decree of Charles IV in 1791 and inaugurated as the Real Universidad Literaria de Guadalajara in 1794 suffered frequent closures during 19C and early 20C upheavals. A new university of Guadalajara was opened in 1925 by Governor Zuno, only to be closed again, during a crisis of educational ideas, in 1932. In 1935 Governor Everardo Topete launched the Instituto Socialista de Altos Estudios, which in 1937 became the Universidad de Guadalajara.

At the invitation of Governor Topete in 1936 the dome and end wall of the main lecture hall (*Paraninfo*) were painted by Orozco—'one of the gloomiest visions of the present ever painted'. On the end wall, blind skeletal suffering masses, their arms raised in gestures of despair (top r.) and others (bottom r.), more threatening, face their leaders who huddle to the l., armed with saw, dagger, and books of theory; the r.-hand leader attempts to harangue, his r. leg braced and back pockets filled with gold. The flames signify revolt. In the l. panel, flames in the background, two workers who collaborate with the bosses and their soldier ally, with hideous ape-like faces, armed with clubs and bayonet, at their feet rifles and books of theory they are paid to put into practice. On the r., three starved figures, one begging, another a child lying dead.

The cupola offers a relatively serene contrast. Man (five-headed) as scientist, mathematician, philosopher, architect, and artist plans the realization of the true being; the Teacher, his head raised, handsome and serene, offers assurance; opposite him, the Worker (Orozco himself) stands upright above curved metallic forms representing the machine; the Rebel, a rope round his neck, feet pointing upwards, his head at the Worker's feet, holds a red flag which forms a background to the Teacher's head.

Behind the university and facing a pleasant plaza is the **Cap. Expiatorio**, an unexpected neo-Gothic church, begun in 1897 by Adamo Boari.

By the mid-1920s it was only half built and Abp Francisco Orozco y Jiménez prevailed upon an at first reluctant Ignacio Díaz Morales to complete it. The EXTERIOR stands complete with three rich portals, galleries, fine rose window, and slender spire echoed in the buttress finials. The three-aisle INTERIOR is notable for its roses, five on each side, and in the apses beautiful stained glass which continues up into the lacy spire with wonderful effect.

On the N side of Av. Vallarta, Av. Tolsá continues N as Av. Murguía to (c 2km) the district of *Mezquitán*, once an Indian barrio, now part of the city and site of the *Panteón* (late 19C). The parish church of *San Miguel* (c 1800) has a two-storey façade ringing the changes in various 18C styles.

3.25km further W along Av. Vallarta, through a well-to-do residential district, we come to the double arch ordered up in 1941 by Governor Silvano Barba González. Just beyond it on the left, at 27 C. Aceves, is the **Museo José Clemente Orozco** (Tues.–Sat., 12–4; Sun., 10–2), in his house and studio, containing a collection of his sketches and drawings, and some portable murals painted on masonite with pyroxylin.

In *Las Fuentes* (in the SW extremity of the city; 8km from the centre) is a partly restored late Preclassic, Classic, and Postclassic pyramid (on a dirt road, singposted). The settlement, *Ixtepete*, dates from c AD 100, and later showed Teotihuacano influence (during the phase which produced the second pyramid referred to below). Several cremation burials in urns were also found, differentiating Ixtepete from the shaft-tomb tradition practised farther W. After c AD 1000 it was on the fringe of Tarascan influence and was occupied up to the Spanish Conquest.

The principal, restored monument is a pyramid of six superimposed building phases. The original pyramid measured 16m x 20m and was 1.8m high; the final structure was 42m x 38m x 6m high, with staircases near the four corners. A similar site of the same date, and also on the fringe of the Tarascan state, was Tuxcacuesco in S Jalisco.

7km SE of the city centre is **Tlaquepaque**, in prehispanic times centre of an autonomous state, then an outlying village, now a suburb caught up in the urban sprawl of Guadalajara. Its fame rests on its crafts—ceramics, weaving, glass, silver, papier-mâché figures—and over-commercialization has not improved it. There is a *Museo Regional de la Cerámica* (Mon.–Sat., 10–12) in C. Independencia. The parish church of *San Pedro*, on the N side of Jardín Hidalgo, further E along C. Independencia, was finished in 1813, but preserves good baroque detail.

6km E of Tlaquepaque, reached along Calz. de las Torres, is **Tonalá**, site of the early villa of Guadalajara in 1533–35. In the 1570s Augustinian friars were established here. The church and convent of *Santiago*, modified in later centuries, incorporates parts of the older buildings. The town is now a famous ceramic and crafts centre, given impetus by US artists.

8km NW of the city centre is **Zapopan**, now a suburb, a renowned pilgrimage centre, filled to overflowing on 12 Oct. for the feast of Our Lady of Zapopan. On the high altar of the basilica of *Nuestra Señora de Zapopan*, dedicated in 1730, is kept the venerated image of the Virgin, said to have belonged to Fray Antonio de Segovia (1485–1570), first Franciscan missionary in Nueva Galicia, and to have miraculously aided him in ending the Mixtón war in 1541.

In the sacristy is a painting of the death of St Francis Xavier (with two delightful little girl donors) by Francisco de León (late 17C). Another painting by him, Baptism of Christ, is in the lower convent cloister. Among the other paintings owned by the convent is an Apostolate by Diego de Cuentas and a series (1764) on the life of St Francis Solano, a 16C Franciscan, by José de Páez, painted for the convent of San Fernando in Mexico City and brought to Zapopan in the 1920s. Six canvases, of extraordinary quality despite having been allowed to deteriorate, out of the eight original, remain.

At *El Grillo*, cut through by the city bypass in the Zapopan district, there is a mound group S of the highway and some burial sites (looted long ago) on the N side.

Av. Gigantes runs E of the city centre past (4km; r.) *San Andrés*, with an 18C church (good carving on portal and interior rib-vaulting), to (7km E) *Tetlán*, site of an early Franciscan doctrina, established in 1531–32, and in the 1530s a private fief of Nuño de Guzmán. The present church dates from the 18C, but reminders of the original foundation, incl. posa chapels, survive. Its stone pulpit, with saintly figures in high relief, is an early 17C work.

25 Puerto Vallarta to Guadalajara

PUERTO VALLARTA (c 70,000 inhab.), magnificently set in the centre of the coastal curve facing the huge Bahía de Banderas, has developed since the 1950s from a small, comparatively anonymous and remote, fishing village into a resort of international fame. The atmosphere, however, is still pleasantly relaxed; over-commercialization has been avoided and growth controlled. It is much patronized, particularly by visitors from the USA, during Dec.–Apr., and enjoys a warm climate throughout the year.

Airport. 11km N. Frequent flights to *Guadalajara, Mexico City, Manzanillo, Tijuana, Mazatlán, La Paz;* and to *Tucson, Phoenix, Los Angeles, San Francisco,* etc. Bus service from airport through the town to Playa del Sol.

Ferry. Twice weekly to *Cabo San Lucas* (Tues. and Sat.; 18 hrs) at 4 pm from ferry terminal, c 8km N of town centre.

Bus stations. In or off Av. Insurgentes, S side of Río Cuale. Services to *Mexico City* (c 15 hrs); to *Guadalajara* (7 hrs); to *Mazatlán* (9 hrs); to *Tepic* (3½ hrs); etc.

Hotels. Cheaper hotels in the town S of Río Cuale; older establishments in the town N of the river; more expensive hotels away from the town centre along the beaches.

Post Office. C. Morelos, just N of Pl. Principal.

Tourist Office. In Pal. Municipal (entrance in C. Juárez).

The town, rising from the sea front towards the wooded hills to the E, its whitewashed adobe houses characteristically roofed in red tile, is divided by the Río Cuale. The main commercial centre is on the N side. On the N side of Pl. Principal is the *Pal. Municipal*, and, one block E, the church of *Nuestra Señora de Guadalupe*, dating from the 1940s; the top of its tower is shaped like a crown. In the hills behind the town nestle the more luxurious houses, many belonging to US citizens. The central beach, *Playa del Sol* (or *Playa de los Muertos*), S of the river mouth, tends to be crowded. The more secluded, and

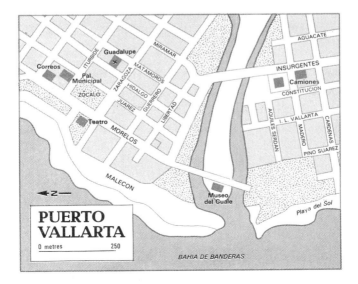

cleaner, beaches stretch further S (*Las Amapas* and *Las Estacas*) and to the N (*Las Glorias, Las Palmas, Playa de Oro, Playa del Chino*). On the island in the middle of the river is the *Museo del Cuale*, a small archaeological and crafts exhibition.

The beach at (11km S) *Mismaloya* (reached by bus or boat) is still comparatively remote. *Yelapa*, on the S side of the bay, is reached by boat (one hour beyond Mismaloya), a remote tropical haven, with ideal sandy beaches.

A.   Via the coast road and Autlán de Navarro

Méx. 200 and Méx. 80, 521km.—209km junction with Méx. 80.—322km Autlán de Navarro.—443km Cocula.—497km Sta Cruz de las Flores.—521km **Guadalajara.**

The road skirts Bahía de Banderas and runs sinuously inland through a barranca and tropical growth lined with waterfalls to (44km) *El Tuito*. It then passes through a wild mountainous area eventually to descend and gain the coast. 152km *Chamela* (H,R,P), a fishing centre and developing resort on Bahía de Chamela, dotted with small islands and with excellent beaches. 168km *Careyes* (H), beautifully isolated, with beach and cliffs amid tropical palms. 192km *El Tecuán* (r.), (197km) *Tenacatita* (r.; H,R), and (204km) *La Manzanilla*, unspoiled resorts (r.) with fine beaches and good fishing. 209km junction with (l. turn) Méx. 80.

The r. turn continues to (6km) **Melaque** (2000 inhab.; H,R,P), on the W of Bahía de Navidad, popular for its sandy beach, deep-sea fishing, and water sports. Méx. 80 runs N across the divide separating the valleys of the Ríos Purificación (W) and Cihuatlán (E), and near the boundary of Nueva Galicia (W) and New Spain (E). 247km *La Huerta* (P). 271km (r.) *Los Tecomates*, with cave paintings, probably Postclassic. 273km turning l. for (24km; rough road) *Purificación* (P), site of the villa once capital of the southernmost jurisdiction of Nueva Galicia. 277km (r.) *Casimiro Castillo*, with Postclassic cave paintings. Continuing NE along the valley of the Río Purificación we come to (322km) **Autlán de Navarro** (c 26,000 inhab.; H,R,P), in the Sierra del Perote. Parts of the Franciscan convent of *La Transfiguración*, founded in 1546, still exist, though modified.

Near Autlán excavations produced pottery, shell and clay bracelets, clay figurines of four types and obsidian tools, but no metal artefacts. The ceramics have been divided into three phases from c AD 1000 to the Spanish Conquest. A few structural remains can still be seen, but they are not well preserved.

324km road (r.) via (11km) *El Grullo*, a picturesque place, to (60km) *Venustiano Carranza*, on the Río Jiquilpan, whence roads N to (36km) *Tapalpa* (see Rte 25B), NE to (42km) *Sayula* (see Rte 25B), and SE to (40km) *Ciudad Guzmán*, see Rte 25B.

Méx. 80 winds through the mountains to (358km) *Unión de Tula*, in a prosperous agricultural area irrigated by the Río Ayuquilla, whose waters are harnessed by the Presa de Tacotán, 14km NW. From (373km; l.) *San Clemente* a road runs W to (15km) *Ayutla*, a mining centre in the Valle de Ayutla. Hence a mountain road (not easy) runs NW through the highest part of SW Jalisco's volcanic range, well forested, to (87km from San Clemente) *Talpa de Allende* (H,R,P), where the Santuario de la Virgen del Rosario (19C) is focal point for Candlemas celebrations (25 Jan.–2 Feb.).

Méx. 80 runs E to (388km) *Juchitlán* and then N to (405km) *Tecolotlán* (R,P), 15km W of which is *Tenamaxtlán*, where the church of Santiago has a portal dating from 1708. We descend to a broad plateau. At 439km the road l. runs NW to (34km) *Ameca*, see Rte 23. We turn r. for (443km; r.) **Cocula** (15,000 inhab.; H,R,P), where the former Franciscan convent of *San Miguel* (1630–48) is the fourth edifice built by the friars on the site. It survived as a Franciscan *doctrina* until after Independence. 482km (r.) *Acatlán de Juárez* (thermal springs 1km NE). 497km **Sta Cruz de las Flores**. Here the church (1692–1712), which once served a hospital run by the Franciscans from Tlajomulco, has an extraordinarily ornamented rustic baroque façade, done in the workable brownish limestone of the region and cramming in a gamut of forms and motifs. Already in ruins by the early 20C, its survival has been assured by works in the late 1960s, which pleasantly, though incorrectly, rebuilt the interior. At *Tlajomulco* (2km SE), once chief place of a jurisdiction on the S boundary of Nueva Galicia, the façade of the 18C church of Santiago, successor to the Franciscan convent of San Antonio (1567–98), harks back to an earlier style. At (505km; r.) *Sta Anita* the church (also 18C) retains delightfully exuberant relief: in the façade a Holy Family group (incl. God the Father, the Holy Ghost, SS Anne and Joachim) amid floral and vegetal decoration and in the pendentives of the cupola. 521km *Guadalajara*, see Rte 24.

B. Via Colima

Méx. 200, Méx. 110, Méx. 54, and Méx. 80, 598km.—215km Melaque.— 272km **Manzanillo**.—330km junction with Méx. 110.—370km **Colima** and Méx. 29.—454km **Ciudad Guzmán** and Méx. 54.—559km Acatlán de Juárez and Méx. 80.—598km **Guadalajara**.

From Puerto Vallarta to (215km) *Melaque*, see Rte 25A. Méx. 200 runs inland from Melaque. At 220km a road curves back to the coast at (5km) **Barra de Navidad** (H,R,P) facing a long spit of land extending into *Bahía de Navidad*. Its beach of white sand has ensured its popularity as a holiday resort, much favoured at weekends by people from Guadalajara. In season it has begun to attract holidaymakers from further afield.

Barra de Navidad was occupied in the Late Classic–Early Postclassic (c AD 650–1000) and was a seasonal fishing site. Excavations yielded obsidian and utilitarian pottery associated with a large mound, 18m in diameter and 8m high (which can still be seen).
    The bay was discovered by Juan Fernández de Híjar in 1535, and a small port and shipyards were established. It was the embarkation and disembarkation point of famous expeditions. In 1539 Francisco de Ulloa called here on his way from Acapulco to Baja California. In Nov. 1542 left Ruy López de Villalobos' unsuccessful expedition to the Spice Islands; in June 1543 that of Juan Rodríguez de Cabrillo to Alta California. In Aug. 1587, the shipyards having already been closed down by royal command, the two surviving ships of the circumnavigating Thomas Cavendish arrived, before going on to capture the Philippine galleon off Cabo San Lucas.

At (228km) *Cihuatlán* we reach the Río Chacala and the border between the States of Jalisco and Colima. Hence Méx. 200, lined with groves of tropical fruits, runs S and then SE towards the coast and its various beautiful bays and lagoons. 255km *Miramar*, E of the Laguna de Miramar (H,R) and on the W side of Bahía de Santiago.

SW of the laguna *Playa del Oro*, investigated by D. M. Pendergast, V. Lombardo, and M. V. Wise 1960–62, yielded remains of a coastal village occupied during the Classic Period. The Pottery has been divided into four types, and the figurines into four groups of 17 types.

259km *Santiago* is on the E side of the bay. 261km *Salagua* (ancient Tzalahua, capital of the Colima tribe; H,R), on the W of the adjoining Bahía de Manzanillo, separated from Bahía de Santiago by the Las Hadas peninsula, on which is the luxurious *Las Hadas* hotel complex, designed by José Luis Ezquerra, erected at the expense of Antenor Patiño, the Bolivian tin millionaire, and opened in 1974.

It faces its own beach, site of a prehistoric town, admirably situated on the W of the bay. The road skirts the bay and runs inland around the Laguna de San Pedrito. 272km **MANZANILLO** (55,000 inhab.), superbly situated on the SE of its bay, is Mexico's chief port for trade with the Orient and a burgeoning and popular seaside resort. The town proper is the head place for the dependent resorts along the bays and beaches to the N and NW.

The indigenous settlement of Tzalahua was chosen by the Spaniards as an ideal site for a shipyard, which they called Santiago de Buena Esperanza, now Salagua. In 1579 the settlement was raided by Francis Drake. In 1825 by Act of Congress it was ordered fitted up 'for foreign trade and coastal traffic', but its establishment was uncertain and the site was highly insalubrious. In 1846 the population was only 51, but two years later the port was refounded. From here in Apr. 1858 Pres. Juárez embarked for Panama on his way to Veracruz. Port modernization has proceeded apace during the 20C, the Pemex wharf having been in service since 1952.

The old town, with its narrow streets, surviving wooden houses, and wide central park (called Zócalo) is not without attraction. To its E stretches the salt-water Laguna de Cuyutlán, 30km long.

Airport. c 45km N, on Méx. 200. Daily flights to *Guadalajara, Mexico City*, and *Cabo San Lucas*, and to destinations in the USA.

Railway station. E of the main plaza, at the E end of C. Juárez. Daily service to *Guadalajara* (over 8 hrs). The railway runs at first S along a neck of land at the W end of the Laguna de Cuyutlán.

Bus station. E end of C. Hidalgo, c 15 min. walk from centre. Services to *Guadalajara* (6 hrs); to *Mexico City* (19 hrs); to *Tijuana* (36 hrs); to *Colima* (2 hrs); etc.

Hotels. Cheaper (and only one top-class) in town centre. For holidaymakers a variety of hotels, suites, apartments, bungalows strung along the bays from Playa de Oro, E of the Juluapan peninsula, which closes the W end of Bahía de Santiago; Playa de Miramar and Playa Santiago on the same bay; Playa las Hadas and Playa Azul on Bahía de Manzanillo; and Playa San Pedrito, NE of the port and by the headland which closes the Laguna de San Pedrito.

Post Office. Corner of Cs Juárez and 5 de Mayo.

Tourist Office. In Salagua (near Hotel Pacífico Azul).

The **Islas Revillagigedo**, in the Pacific c 800km due E of Manzanillo, are of volcanic origin and form part of the State of Colima. *Socorro*, the largest, is 17km in diameter; the others are *San Benedicto* (c 5 sq km), *Sta Rosa* (or *Clarión*; c 25 sq km), and *Roca Partida*.

The archipelago was touched upon by Hernando de Grijalva in 1533 and in the 1570s by Drake. In the mid-19C a brief Australian and Canadian colonization took place. A Mexican expedition of 1957 found a population of 8000 sheep, the colony's legacy. Among other resources are sulphur, guano, and fish. Today the islands are a Mexican naval base. Permission to visit them (24 hrs by ship from Manzanillo to Socorro), from the Secretaría de Marina in Mexico City, must be sought.

Méx. 200 continues along the N side of the Laguna de Cuyutlán. (The railway runs along its S side facing the sea shore.) At 314km a road runs S to (7km) *Cuyutlán*, famous during Apr.–May for the ola verde, a huge wave of green water, up to 10m high, which rolls in against the beach, whose black sand, a feature of the coastline here, retains an uncomfortable heat in the hot weather. 320km *Armería*. 330km turning r. on Méx. 200 for (5km) **Tecomán** (45,000 inhab.; H,R,P), an important agricultural centre on the coastal plain, within reach of an unsophisticated and secluded coastal stretch running SE from the mouth of the Río Armería. *Boca de Pascuales* (12km SW) is the best-known village resort.

From Tecomán, Méx. 200 continues SE to (26km) *Cerro de Ortega*, near the border with the State of Michoacán. Hence the newly completed and spectacular highway (the coast as yet undeveloped) connects with (214km) *Playa Azul*, see Rte 29.

From the Tecomán turning Méx. 110 goes inland through low mountains which interrupt the coastal plain. 370km **COLIMA** (111,000 inhab.; 458km), capital of the State of Colima, in a broad, fertile valley through which run the Ríos Armería (W) and Coahuayana. To the N, enhancing its spectacular situation, rise the volcanic peaks Nevado de Colima and Volcán de Colima (active since 1957), which has played a miniatory part in Colima's history. It is a city of great charm, surrounded by luxurious vegetation, which spills over into its parks and gardens, and retains many of its distinctive 18–19C one-storey houses. Its people, the colimenses, are known for their hospitality. Through the city runs the Río Colima, a tributary of the Armería. Its climate is semi-tropical, the heat tempered by mountain breezes, with summer and early autumn rains.

Railway station. S of the centre, reached from Jardín Quintero along C. Medellín. Trains to *Guadalajara, Ciudad Guzmán*, and *Manzanillo*.

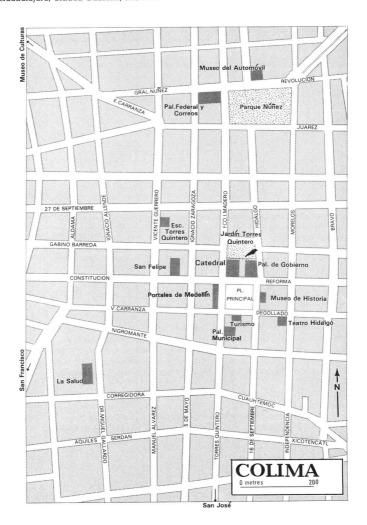

Bus station. C. 3km E of centre, off Av. Niños Héroes. Buses to *Manzanillo* (2 hrs); to *Ciudad Guzmán* (1½ hrs); to *Guadalajara* (3½ hrs); *Mexico City* (12 hrs); etc.

Hotels throughout the town.

Post Office. Corner of Av. Madero and C. Gral Núñez.

Tourist Office. 20 Portal Hidalgo.

The villa of San Sebastián de Colima, moved to its present site in 1525, suffered a series of natural disasters during the 16–17C. In 1658 fire destroyed most of it. In March–Nov. 1792 Miguel Hidalgo was parish priest here, exiled by a kindly bishop to distance him from his enemies in Valladolid. Among the most serious visitations were two earthquakes in 1818, an eruption of the volcano in 1869, and a hurricane in 1881. The building of the narrow-gauge railway between Guadalajara and Manzanillo in the 1880s made the city less inaccessible. The Volcán de Colima last erupted in 1941.

The State of **Colima** (5455 sq km, incl. the Revillagigedo islands; 423,000 inhab.), third smallest Mexican State, is mostly a narrow coastal plain. The Nevado de Colima is entirely, and the Volcán de Colima mostly, in Jalisco. The soil is generally fertile and productive. Coffee of the Caracolilto variety grown in the N mountain slopes is claimed as the best in Mexico. The total yearly fish catch amounts to c 12 per cent of the national.

Colima is noted for early Preclassic Period ceramics, known mostly from shaft- or chamber-tombs such as Los Ortices, Chanchopa (N of Colima), Morett, and Playa de Tesoro. The chronological sequence is incomplete, however, and more recent excavations at El Chanal (see below) may help to fill in the gaps. The present chronology is summarized as follows (but with a gap in knowledge between early Campacha ceramics and later phases): *Campacha* (or *Capacha*): c 2000–1000 BC; *Ortices*: c 500 BC–AD 300; *Comala*: c AD 300–600; *Armería/Colima*: c AD 500–1100; *Periquillo/Chanal*: c AD 1100–Conquest.

The Classic and Postclassic Period centres of Armería, Comala (S of Colima), El Chanal, Las Animas, Los Ortices, Periquillo, Tecomán, and Colima itself (known as Cajitlán or Cajital) were probably allied in a loose federation. They were successful in defending themselves against the Tarascans on their E borders, and against the Spaniards for several years, until a Spanish and Tarascan alliance defeated them in 1523.

Artistically the region is most known for its large, hollow, glossy red ceramic figures, especially for the information these give us of everyday life. Favourite subjects were dogs, put in graves to lead the buried person's spirit into afterlife, people in various activities, and a wide variety of other animals. There were also bright orange ceramics with black-speckled surfaces, solid figurines (also depicting scenes of everyday life—dancers, musicians, warriors, ball players, mothers nursing babies), and a long line of other ceramic forms, incl. incense burners in various shapes (flower baskets, two-headed snakes, gods), flutes, whistles, and ocarinas. Many vessels in red or brown had small, black painted birds or snakes modelled on the rims or sides.

Most of these artefacts, together with metalwork and obsidian tools, come from excavated shaft-tombs, whose distribution ranges across Jalisco and Michoacán.

In 1523 Gonzalo de Sandoval, aided by Tarascan allies and with reinforcements from Mexico, reduced the territory as far W as Cihuatlán. In 1524 Francisco Cortés was sent as governor and started a campaign N as far as Tepic. During the 17C the region suffered volcanic eruptions, earthquakes, and hurricanes—dangers which have continued to threaten until the present. Under the 1857 constitution Colima became a State. The Revolution left it largely untouched, but the savagery of the Cristero rebellion had a profound effect. In 1941 an earthquake had catastrophic results. In 1959 an earthquake and cyclone devastated the coastal region. In 1981 the State elected a woman governor, Griselda Alvarez, the first in Mexican history.

The tree-shaded PL. PRINCIPAL (Jardín Libertad), framed by 19C portales, was laid out in 1877–80; the bandstand, bought in Germany, dates from 1891. On the E side is the cathedral of **San Felipe**, built as the parish church in 1820; by 1873 described as being in 'the ravages of ruin'; re-erected by the builder-architect Lucio Uribe in 1882–94.

It fell down in the earthquake of 1900 and was again rebuilt, only to lose its tower (since reconstructed) in the disastrous earthquake of 1941.

The adjoining **Pal. de Gobierno** (1877–1904; modernized in the 1940s) is also by Uribe. The main staircase is decorated with murals (1952) on historical and patriotic themes by Jorge Chávez Carrillo. On the N side the fancifully neo-

Gothic *Portales de Medellín*, another Uribe contribution, date from 1860. The adjoining (on the E) JARDIN TORRES QUINTERO is another agreeable plaza.

From the cathedral Av. Madero runs E to C. 27 de Septiembre. Here we may turn l. to reach C. Guerrero and (l.) the *Escuela Gregorio Torres Quintero* (1955), its entrance way containing more murals by Chávez Carrillo, on educational and cultural themes. Continuing N along C. 27 de Septiembre to the crossing with C. Manuel Gallardo we come to the *Instituto Universitario de Bellas Artes* (1981), incorporating a museum of local crafts and folklore (Mon.–Sat., 10–1.30).

Further E along Av. Madero, No. 237, facing PARQUE NUÑEZ, is the *Pal. Federal* (c 1910) by Ramón López de Lara. Facing the E side of the park, at 79 Av. Revolución, is the *Museo del Automóvil* (part of a garage—Refaccionaria Zaragoza; adm. on request), a fascinating, if casual, display of vintage cars collected by Francisco Zaragoza.

The rest, and major part, of the collection, incl. 19C carriages, more vintage cars, and old furniture, is to be seen at the *Casa del Campo del Carmen*, the former main house of a hacienda 2km NE of Villa de Alvarez, immediately NW of Colima.

By taking C. Gral. Núñez N from the NE corner of Parque Núñez and then C. Emilio Carranza NE to its junction with Calz. Pedro A. Galván, we reach the **Museo de las Culturas de Occidente**, opened in 1980 (9–1 and 2–6). There are two floors of open displays, semidivided into thematic and chronological areas.

On entering we proceed to the r. and around the displays counterclockwise; numbers below correspond to the floor plans; the materials on each floor are generally summarized as follows:

Ground Floor. Introduction, ecology, and geography of Colima; cultural evolution of Colima and the Western Mexican Cultures, in numerous chronologically arranged semidivisions; Mesoamerica in general and Colima's place therein.

Upper Floor. Thematic displays of Colima's prehistoric cultures; social organization; technology; costumes and traditions; art; external relations and outside influences.

GROUND FLOOR. 1. Introduction to museum, and floor plan. 2. Panel—archaeology of Colima; two cases with hollow figures of dogs (standing and dancing), ball player, spiral shell, man carrying jugs—from Tumba 5, Colima. 3–4. Maps and descriptions of the ecology of Colima—l. = climate, flora and fauna, chart of geologic periods; r. = geology, physiography, climate. 5. Hollow figure of dog. 6. Hollow figure of zoomorphic jug. 7. Two panels—preceramic Western Cultures of Mexico. 8. Map of cultural subdivisions.

9. *Complejo Capacha*—map of sites and description of phase. 10. Four cases with Capacha ceramics—painted jars, zoomorphic vessels (armadillo, parrot, deer, snake, dogs). 11. *Complejo Ortices*—map of sites and description of phase. 12. Five cases of *Complejo* ceramics—painted and moulded jugs, zoomorphic and painted vessels, figure of seated mother-and-child.

13. *Complejo Comala*—map and description of phase. 14. 16 cases of Comala materials. To r. of panel—hollow figure of man with monkey on his shoulders; l. side of room—zoomorphic vessels (dog with corn cob, armadillo, turtle), five cases of vessels with inscribed decoration and two cases containing vessels with applied animal motifs; r. side of room—hollow figures of man blowing conch shell, man with snake, man with fish-head, man with flute, solid figurines, moulded face-vessels, plus three cases of smaller hollow anthropomorphic and zoomorphic figures, masks, flutes, and other vessels.

15. *Complejos Colima y Armería*—map of sites and description of phase. 16. To r.: cases of Armería materials—group of dancing figurines, hollow anthropomorphic and zoomorphic figures. 17. To l.: cases of Colima materials—seated woman holding dish, painted pottery, hollow figure of man with lizard and conch shell, moulded and painted vessels, incl. tripod vessels and anthropomorphic motifs.

18. *Complejos Chanal y Periquillo*—map of sites and description of phase. 19. To l. and r.: cases of Chanal and Periquillo materials—Chanal copper and gold work, hollow figures and painted pottery, Periquillo hollow figures; three further cases of Chanal painted tripod and zoomorphic vessels.

20. Spanish contact—Juan Rodríguez de Villafuerte, from 1523. 21. Provincial divisions of Colima after the Conquest.

22. Four panels: introduction to Mesoamerica; Mesoamerican cultural areas; comparative chronological chart; map and chronological chart of the *Western Cultures*.

UPPER FLOOR. 23. Description and floor plan—'Expresión Cultural Temática de Colima'. 24a. r., Funerary customs (Colima shaft-tombs). 24b. r., Distribution of shaft-tombs in Mesoamerica and S America. 25. r., Family and social organization, work and play. Then, turning l. along the galleries, a further ten cases illustrate these themes with hollow figures, solid figurines, flutes, etc. (eg, hollow figure of man with tump-line and jug, seated mother-and-child figurines, musicians, figurines of people eating). 26. l., Religion; r., four cases with effigy ceramics.

27. General technology. 28. Ceramic technology. 29. l., r., and centre, Examples of vessel forms. 30. r. and centre, Ceramic *attributes* (eg, tripods, handles, effigies). 31. Panel and three cases: *incised and excised decoration*. 32. Turning l. along the galleries—r., panel and cases showing *painted decoration*.

33. l., Stone-working technology (obsidian blade cores, pressure flaked knives and points, ground stone axe-heads, etc., quern stones and clay figurines of women grinding; other polished stone items). 34. r., Importance of the conch shell for jewellery, etc. 35. l., Metalwork—axe-heads, cleavers, face.

36. r., Houses and other architecture illustrated by contemporary clay models from excavated sites.

37. Turning l. along the galleries, six more cases with clothing and adornment—jewellery and solid clay figurines wearing contemporary dress. 38. l., Physical features of ancient Colima populations. 39. r., and centre, Ancient warfare—examples of weapons and of hollow figures of warriors.

40. l., Floral and plant themes in moulded ceramic vessels. 41. Ahead r. and centre, Faunal themes in zoomorphic vessels and figures (parrots, other birds, snakes, lizards, frogs, deer, armadillos, dogs and other animals). 42. Turning l. along galleries, l. and r., the importance of the dog in Colima cultures.

43. l., External relations with and influences on the Colima culture from greater Mesoamerica.

44. r., Exceptional examples of Colima art in superb effigy and zoomorphic figures.

No. 70 Av. Torres Quintero, the continuation W of Av. Madero, was Hidalgo's house in 1792. Opposite, a little further W, is the *Presidencia Municipal* (restored 1977–79). Still further W may be reached the church of *San José* (semi-ruined), begun in 1904 by Hermenegildo López. At 36 C. 5 de Mayo, the parallel street to the N, is the house occupied in March–Apr. 1858 by Pres. Juárez when on his way from Guadalajara to Manzanillo and Panama during the war of the Reform. The church of *La Salud* (1871; to be restored), in C. Dr Miguel Galindo (N), between Cs Nigromante and Corregidora, is by Lucio Uribe and has a neo-romanesque doorway.

On the S side of Pl. Principal, at the corner of Cs Independencia and Degollado, the *Teatro Hidalgo* was built by Uribe in 1871–83.

Andador Constitución leads N from the NE corner of Pl. Principal into C. Constitución. The church of *San Felipe de Jesús*, on the r. between Cs Guerrero and Zaragoza, Hidalgo's parish centre, and rebuilt in the late 18C, contains a good baroque altarpiece. Two blocks further N, C. Maclovio Herrera (l.) leads NE to Av. Pino Suárez and the JARDIN SAN FRANCISCO. In the shadow of the modern church are the sparse ruins of the pioneering Franciscan convent of *San Francisco*, founded in 1554, but a victim of earthquake and arson until rebuilt for the fourth time, not to last, by 1650.

A secondary road runs NW through *Villa Alvarez*, frequented for its Feb. bullfights, to (7km) *Comala*, picturesque with its white houses and red roofs, and (35km) the foothills of the volcanoes. Footpaths make an ascent relatively easy.

6km N of Colima, and just E of Comala, the site of **El Chanal** (c AD 1100–Conquest; excavated by V. Rosado Ojedo in 1948, and in the 1970s by Thomas Sears of Southwestern Texas State University) has given its name to the Late Postclassic pottery of the Colima region. It comprises a tiered pyramid 3m high, on top of which is a representation of Tláloc, god of rain. Bas-relief carvings on the steps depict divinities, animals, and calendrical signs. The pottery sequence from the site exhibits changes from the general scheme of the sequence for the Colima region, eg, with distinctive ceramic censers c 25cm tall, some of which can be seen at the Museo de las Culturas de Occidente in Colima.

From Colima we continue NE on Méx. 54 (spectacular views) to (388km) *Cuauhtémoc*. 390km *Quesería* (R,P), with views of the two volcanoes. 401km *Tonila*, with more good views. We cross from Colima into Jalisco. 433km (l.) **Atenquique** (R,P), an incongruously polluted paper-producing centre, in beautiful surroundings on the E edge of the *Parque Nacional del Volcán de Colima*.

From here a road leads NE via (5km) *Tuxpan*, where is preserved the atrial cross (all that remains) of the Franciscan convent of San Juan Bautista, founded in 1536, to join (15km) Méx. 110. This now continues N to (20km) *Vista Hermosa* and then NE through the W part of the

Sierra de Michoacán, watered by the Río Tuxpan. 31km *Tamazula de Gordiano* (1285m), once known for silver-mining, now a watering-place, and centre of a sugar-producing area. 75km *Mazamilta* (7500 inhab.), a scenic place, its white-walled, wooden-balconied, and red-tiled houses adding to its character. The road continues over the border into Michoacán to (125km) *Jiquilpan*, see Rte 27.

454km **CIUDAD GUZMAN** (70,000 inhab.; 1504m; H,R,P), the most sizeable town in Jalisco after Guadalajara, is the centre of an agricultural and stock-raising region. (Pig-breeding is a speciality.)

A Franciscan convent, a pioneer (and dangerous) venture by Juan de Padilla, was founded in 1532, a centre for his missionary work among a mixed Indian population. The feast of St Joseph is commemorated here during 12–23 Oct. with traditional dances, religious processions, etc. The earthquake of Sept. 1985 struck here with some force.

The *Cathedral* (1866–1900; the towers a later addition), begun to the design of Domingo Torres, occupies the site of the Franciscan convent of Nuestra Señora de la Asunción (see above). *San Antonio* is a late 19C buttressed neo-Gothic effort, with good tower, steeple, and crenellations. The circular church of *El Sagrado Corazón* (restored) keeps a 17C portal. The *Museo de las Culturas de Occidente* contains a small collection of hollow figurines, other ceramics, stone and metal artefacts, and skeletons from Colima and Jalisco burials.

Our road (Méx. 54; in preference to the faster road to *Acatlán* on the E side of the Laguna de Sayula) continues N to (480km) **Sayula** (18,000 inhab.; 1353m; H,R,P), SW of the drying-up Laguna de Sayula (salt, sodium, and magnesium deposits) and once chief place of the so-called province of Avalos, named after its first 16C encomendero, Alonso de Avalos, cousin of Cortés. The former Franciscan convent of *San Francisco* dates from the 1570s and was rebuilt in the 17–18C. The cloister has been restored. 492km turning l. (a winding road) for (32km W) **Tapalpa** (5000 inhab.; H,R,P), on the E slopes of the Sierra de Tapalpa, with cobbled streets, and a favourite excursion from Guadalajara. The 18C parish church, substantially modernized and finished in fine tilework, is connected to the Cap. de la Soledad (1700) by a flight of steps. At (499km) *Amacueca* the Franciscans braved earthquake damage to continue building the convent of San Francisco (1533–c 1580). The surviving church and convent buildings date in the main from a late 18C rebuilding after more earthquake damage in 1749. 522km *Zacoalco de Torres* whose church, rebuilt in the 17C, is the successor to the Franciscan convent (San Francisco) founded in the 1550s. 559km *Acatlán de Juárez*. From here to (598km) *Guadalajara* see Rte 25A.

26   Guadalajara to Lake Chapala

Round trip, 134km.—30km (4km SW) Cajititlán.—52km **Chapala**.—134km **Guadalajara**.

The Chapala toll road (Méx. 23; Calz. González Gallo from the city) runs SE past the airport. 26km turning l. for (11km) the *Salto de Juanacatlán*, a spectacular waterfall on the Río Grande de Santiago, 18m high and more than 150m wide; its enormous force (especially during the rainy season) has been harnessed by a hydroelectric plant, which can deprive it of life during dry periods. 30km turning r. for (4km SW) **Cajititlán**, on the N shore of the Lago de Cajititlán, has two 18C churches, their exteriors in local heavy hewn stone. *Los Reyes*, with a simple façade and graceful tower, has a strikingly vaulted interior, the ribs of the apse dotted with musical cherubs in relief. The charming gilded altarpiece, with statues of the three kings, harks back to an early 17C style. The sanctuary of *Guadalupe*, a singular edifice, has a characterfully curved pediment. On the SW side of the lake the 18C church at *San Lucas* displays a popular baroque exterior, crammed with ingenuously exuberant relief. 35km turning r. for (8km) *San Juan Evangelista* on the S shore of the lake, the church here another good example of local 18C baroque; the interior arches are decorated with Passion and Marian motifs.

52km **CHAPALA** (16,000 inhab.; 1520m; H,R,P), with an ideal climate on the N shore of the Lago de Chapala, is a favourite holiday resort and excursion centre from Guadalajara and other nearby towns.

The **Lago de Chapala** is Mexico's largest natural lake (86km E to W; 25km at its widest N to S), receiving the waters of the Ríos Lerma and Zula on the E and N and drained by the Río Grande de Santiago (which leaves it where the Río Zula meets it) on its N side. The unceasing demands of industry have lowered its water level (which should be an average c 30m), constantly threatening its cleanliness, its fish, and its bird life. But efforts to right the balance have of late been successful. To the N it is bordered by the Sierra de Atotonilco; to its S by the Sierra de Pajacuarán; and on its W by the small Sierra de Rosario. Its surrounding villages have become a favourite place of retirement, mainly for US and Canadian citizens.

Its main islands (basalt formations) are *Chapala* (or *Los Alacranes*), 6km SE of the town of Chapala; *Maltaraña*, at its E end; and *Mezcala*, S of the village of San Juan Mexcala, c 20km E of Chapala on the N shore. This latter (1680 by 756m) was in 1812–16 a stronghold of a thousand or so diehard insurgents. Remains of their fortress may still be seen.

From Chapala the road skirts the NW shore to (60km) *Ajijic*, an attractive fishing village, favourite residence of foreign artists and writers—the example possibly set by D.H. Lawrence, who here wrote 'The Plumed Serpent' (1926). Shops cater for craftware-hunters. In 1530 the Franciscans founded a convent here, San Andrés Axixique.

Several sites around Chapala have been excavated, and a laboratory and museum have been established here to study and display some of the finds—mostly from graves—incl. ceramics, figurines, and metal artefacts.

68km *San Juan Cosalá*, with thermal baths. 78km *Jocotepec*, another crafts centre (sarapes). Beyond here the road forks. To the l. Méx. 15 runs SE along the S side of the lake via (49km) *Tizapán el Alto* to (90km) *Sahuayo*, see below. We turn r. on Méx. 15, at 99km joining Méx. 80 beyond *Acatlán* for (134km) *Guadalajara.*

27 Guadalajara to Jiquilpan and Ciudad Guzmán

Méx. 80, Méx. 15, and Méx. 110, 286km.—58km junction with Méx. 15.—156km **Jiquilpan** and Méx. 110.—286km **Ciudad Guzmán.**

56km (l.) *Jocotepec*, see Rte 26. At 58km we turn l. on Méx. 15 along the S shore of the Lago de Chapala through lovely scenery to (91km) *Tuxcueca* and (107km) *Tizapán el Alto*. We cross into the State of Michoacán. 130km *Cojumatlán de Régules*. 147km turning l. for (31km NE) *La Barca* (see Rte 28); turning r. for (1.5km) *Sahuayo*, in a region which provided many fighters both for Independence and for the Cristeros in 1926–29. Its church of Santiago was rebuilt in the 19C, but keeps a baroque portal.

156km **JIQUILPAN** (20,000 inhab.; 1654m; H,R,P), a picturesque, rather jumbled-looking town and centre of the milk industry, stands on the r. bank of the Río Jiquilpan, which unites with the Río Jaripo to drain into the Lago de Chapala.

Called Guanimbe by its prehispanic Tarascan inhabitants, it and its region were subjugated by the Spaniards by the late 1520s. Its most famous natives are Gabino Ortiz (1819–85), liberal orator, politician, and writer, and Pres. Lázaro Cárdenas del Río (1895–1970), whose family home has been converted into a small museum.

On the attractive central plaza is the church of *San Francisco*, rebuilt relic of a Franciscan convent founded c 1540 and secularized in the 1770s. It preserves a 17C portal. The municipal library, **Biblioteca Gabino Ortiz**, reached near the rear of the church, occupies a former barrio chapel. The interior is decorated with murals by José Clemente Orozco.

The work, an allegory of menaced Mexico for whom outdated ideals will not suffice, was undertaken in 1940 at the expense of Pres. Cárdenas—a gift to his home town. The rectangular panels of the side walls are predominantly in black and white, splashed with the red in the revolutionary banners. They represent the cruelty of the oppression of the masses and of the revolutions which claim to liberate them: a captive Indian behind his oppressor's horse; an execution scene; horses trampling powerless humanity; mindless revolutionary masses, all mouths and screaming of slogans.
   On each side of the entrance are two jaguars climbing a giant cactus; above them, two ghastly parodies of Liberty stretch a snake-like ribbon above the door. In the pointed apse is an Allegory of Mexico, its violent colour in contrast with the side panels. A dignified Indian woman sits astride a jaguar prowling through cacti; she is menaced by a second, voracious, jaguar, egged on by a derby-hatted figure (l.). To the r. are three, heavily satirical, female figures—Law, Liberty, and Justice. The red, white, and green of the Mexican flag blend with the whole.

From Jiquilpan, Méx. 15 goes E to (59km) *Zamora*, see Rte 28. Méx. 110 runs W to (130km) *Ciudad Guzmán*, see Rte 25B.

28 Guadalajara to Pátzcuaro

Méx. 23, Méx. 35, Méx. 15, and Méx. 41, 309km.—35km Sta Rosa and Méx. 35.—84km Ocotlán.—114km La Barca.—171km **Zamora** and Méx. 15.—239km Zacapu.—282km Quiroga and Méx. 41.—290km **Tzintzuntzan**.—309km **Pátzcuaro**.

We leave Guadalajara on the Chapala road (Méx. 23, toll; well surfaced; comp. Rte 26). At (35km) *Sta Rosa* we turn l. on Méx. 35 towards the Sierra de Atotonilco. 43km *Atequiza*. 50km *Atotonilquillo*, with thermal springs. At (67km) *Poncitlán* remains of the church of the Franciscan convent of San Pedro y San Pablo, founded c 1540, are incorporated in the parish church. Near here, at the ranch of San Miguel, the conservative forces of Gen. Miramón won a victory over the liberals under Santos Degollado on 14 Dec. 1858, which eased their entry into Guadalajara. 84km **Ocotlán** (52,000 inhab.; 1527m; H,R,P), on the Mexico–Guadalajara railway and at the confluence of the Ríos Zula and Grande de Santiago, is the largest of the Chapala lakeside towns. Its parish church of *Nuestro Señor de la Misericordia* (1849–70) is by Francisco Salcedo. 94km *Jamay*, at the E end of the lake, with a neo-baroque monument (1875–79) to Pope Pius IX. 114km **La Barca** (20,000 inhab.; 1540m; H,R,P), near the mouth of the Río Lerma and, in the 16C, itself on the lakeside and called Chiquina-huitenco.

Late in 1826 G.F. Lyon stopped here, but had to vacate his inn room because it was full of bats. Although he found the village 'in ruins', a local lady assured him it held two public balls every week; and occasional bullfights, 'in one of the last of which three ladies had entered the Plaza de Toros, and distinguished themselves very highly'.
   The house known as *La Moreña* belonged to Francisco Velarde (1820?–1867), known as 'El burro de oro', an official shot after the fall of the second empire, despite having offered a million pesos for a reprieve. The town stands at a road junction: 29km N is *Atotonilco el Alto* (see Rte 36); 67km E *La Piedad*; 32km SW *Sahuayo*.

We cross the Río Lerma, the boundary between Jalisco and Michoacán, and continue to (127km) *Vista Hermosa* and then SE to (142km) *Ixtlán de los Hervores*, in an area of natural hot springs with curative properties. 171km

ZAMORA (c 90,000 inhab.; 1567m; H,R,P) is a commercial and agricultural centre set in a fertile valley through which winds the Río Duero, tributary of the Lerma.

The villa of Zamora was founded in 1574, although a handful of Spaniards had settled in the area in the 1540s to run large cattle haciendas and wheat farms. It was to become one of the province's principal market towns. In 1829 its strong conservative element backed moves to make it capital of an independent territory: 'this city is one of the most faithful, most zealous, most passionate defenders of the Church'. It showed marked loyalty to Maximilian and the republicans did not win it without a fight, on 4 Feb. 1867, when imperialist troops inflicted heavy casualties on them before being forced to retire to Jacona. Thereafter conservative religious movements found a ready sympathy here. From 1913 the city was much fought over and maltreated by revolutionary factions, and championed the Church during the conflicts of the 1920s.

Facing W across Pl. Principal stands the **Cathedral**, which, despite an unfortunate building history, is still a striking mixture of classicism and neo-baroque, with a beautiful façade, slender classicizing and rusticated towers, graciously enframed upper storey, and miniature balustrade.

Projected by Fr José María Cabadas, it was begun in 1838 to the design of Nicolás Luna. By 1871 emergency work was needed to shore it up. In 1879 the towers, by Romualdo Mares, were finished, but began to topple eight years later. In 1911 the top storey of the S tower fell and had to be repaired. Further restoration has been needed since. In the sacristy is a painting of St Jerome by Luis Juárez.

To the N, on C. Hidalgo, is the church of *San Francisco* (1791). In C. Ocampo, a little to the S, is the so-called *Catedral Inconclusa*, a ghostly pile in unabashed neo-Gothic, begun in 1898, abandoned by 1920. The church of *El Calvario* (1830), at the N end of C. Hidalgo, is another work by Luna.

The region S of Zamora, not all easy of access, will repay those interested in discovering some typical Tarascan villages, known for their traditional crafts. Roads often rough.

FROM ZAMORA TO PERIBAN DE RAMOS, 79km. We leave Zamora to the SW. 3km **Jacona**, a prehispanic Tarascan outpost, moved from its original site at Tangamandapio (14km W) in 1555. The former Augustinian convent of *San Agustín*, begun in the 1560s, was not completed until the 17C and has since been modified. The church has a platseresque portal; the convent is now a school.

Just W of Jacona at the foot of Cerro Curutrán and c 5km S are the two sites called **El Opeño**. The area was a Preclassic village site, as yet little explored except for surface finds and the execution of two groups of chamber tombs. There are no structural remains above ground and little is known of the prehistoric community that supported the cemeteries.

The S tombs (excavated by Eduardo Noguera in 1938) comprise five stone-lined tombs each 1m deep, cut into the tepetate (volcanic rock) and entered by side-shafts with cut steps. There were both single and multiple burials, and *Tumba 3* contained nine skulls separated from their sorted and separately stacked long bones. The tombs themselves were elliptical in plan and contained notch-stemmed arrow points, a greenstone figurine, jade earplugs, and pottery and ceramic figurines of both local and foreign styles. There were vessels resembling those from Tlatilco in the Basin of Mexico, figurines similar to types C–D from Ticomán–Cuicuilco, also in the Basin, and pottery similar to Chupícuaro styles. Some vessels had negative painting (see Introduction: Pottery), referred to as Opeño Negativo.

The tombs W of the town (excavated by José Arturo Olivos; reported in 1974) were also entered by steps cut into side-shafts. One tomb, at 4.45m, was considerably deeper than the others. The burial chambers were sealed by stone slabs. One tomb contained the bones of ten individuals and the other two adult males, and there was evidence of repeated entry and re-use. Pottery included Opeño Negativo, red-and-buff-on-cream vessels similar to Chupícuaro ceramics, wares resembling those from Tlatilco, and sherds of vessels similar to the Colima Capacha style. There were also 16 C–D type figurines in the side-shaft of one tomb, incl. ball-players with knee pads, and what appear to be bats. Other figurines were made of kaolin-like clay and seem to have been deliberately broken before deposition. A basalt yuguito (miniature ball-player's waist yoke), obsidian projectile points, a greenstone pectoral with a carved St Andrew's cross, and Caribbean seashells indicate general contact with central Mesoamerica, the Basin of Mexico, the Gulf Coast, and possibly the Olmec. Even some of the tools for digging out the tombs were left. A radiocarbon measurement for one of the tombs gives a date of c 1500 BC, and they are thus considered the antecedents of the shaft-tombs of Jalisco, Colima, and Nayarit.

Other shaft tombs (c 500 BC–AD 250) have been excavated at Los Ortices and Chanchopa, S of Colima.

The road directly W leads to (56km) *Jiquilpan*, see Rte 27.

Our road continues SW through the Sierra de Patamban (part of the W Michoacán volcanic divide) to (32km) **Tarécuato**, where stands the former Franciscan convent of *Sta María de Jesús*, founded in the 1540s. The wide jambs and imposts of the church portal show the Isabeline Gothic apple motif. The atrial cross and its base are covered with Passion symbols. The austere Danish Franciscan Jacobo Daciano lived here during 1548–66; in 1556 he is said, while in ecstasy, to have had at its precise moment a vision of the death of Charles V. 35km (r.) minor road for (45km NW) *Jiquilpan*. 44km *Tingüindín*. 68km *Los Reyes de Salgado*, a market town on the Río Itzícuaro and centre of a sugar-producing region, connected by railway to Guadalajara, its main market. It has an 18C church. 79km **Peribán de Ramos** (H,R,P), on the SW slope of the Cerro Tancítaro, with a woodcarving tradition. The former Franciscan convent of *San Francisco* was founded c 1546 and the church preserves its plateresque portal.

From here roads lead S and SE over the mountains via (78km) *Nuevo San Juan Parangaricutiro* to (91km) *Uruapan* (see Rte 29); S to (84km) *Apatzingán* (see Rte 29); and N and W through pine forests to (37km) *Angahuan*, see below.

FROM ZAMORA TO ANGAHUAN, 78km. We follow Méx. 15 SE as far as (16km; r.) *Tangancícuaro*, S of the *Lago de Camécuaro*, a favourite resort whose surrounding area is a national park. From here we turn S off the main road along a rough road to (32km) *San José de Gracia* and (36km) *Ocumicho*, whence we wind NW to *Patamban*—all pueblos with traditional crafts. 62km **Charapán** (R), on the SE slopes of the Sierra, a picturesque place with its wooden houses roofed in shingle (tejamanil). The large barrel-vaulted church is successor to the Franciscan convent of *San Antonio*, dating from the 1570s. 10km E is *San Felipe de los Herreros*, where the Augustinian convent was founded in 1595; the church dates from the late 17C. 78km **ANGAHUAN** (2000 inhab.; H), a quintessential Tarascan village. It was from the 1540s a visita of the Franciscans at Uruapan before being turned over to the Augustinians at Sirosto c the late 1570s. The church, dedicated to **Santiago**, has the date 1562 on the façade and 1577 on an interior inscription. Beneath the jutting eaves of its shingle roof the truly remarkable W doorway shows medieval and Mudéjar influences on Indian taste. Although the copious vegetal and fruity relief of its several series lacks finesse, one cannot fail to be struck by the abundance: the rustic candelabra, little angels, and fruits of the jambs, the dense but separated ornament of the three alfices, and the decoration of the arch rim. In the middle storey are ingenuous reliefs of the saint and four seraphim. At a tangent to the arch, an inscription: 'Sancto Jacovo Apostolo Mayor'.

The interior contains other treasures: in the presbytery an intricately carved coffered ceiling (probably 17C); all around the higher part of the wall a frieze enclosing imitation cufic lettering, incl. the date 1577 at the end on the gospel side; and, in the baptistery, the original 16C font. At the foot of the belfry to the l. of the church is an open chapel, its double-arched gallery, entered from the church, once the preserve of choir and instrumentalists.

Opposite the church is the former visita hospital, a small chapel in front and facing E. The portal, restored in 1941, includes an alfíz which takes in the inscription 'Bispera del Glorioso Santiago. Año de 1570 se acabó este hospital por mandado del Señor Canónigo Juan de Velasco'.

C 12km S of Angahuan is the volcano **Paricutín**, born on 20 Feb. 1943 before the eyes of Dionisio Pulido, a peasant farmer who was ploughing his field. A stream of lava began to pour from a fissure to inundate a wide area (c 20 sq km) of countryside. During its first year of activity it had risen to a height of 450m. The neighbouring village of Parangaricutiro was completely buried, except for the higher parts of its early 17C convent church of San Juan; the village of Paricutín itself disappeared completely. The volcano ceased to vomit in March 1952, by which time it had rid itself of a thousand million tonnes of lava. The immediate effect was disastrous, but settled volcanic ash has made a fresh layer of fertile soil. During its active life a tourist industry developed around it, which accounts for various hotels in the area. There remain the defunct cone and crater, and an enormous field of stark lava. The ruins of *San Juan Parangaricutiro* (formerly known as *San Juan de las Colchas*—St John of the Counterpanes, a craft chosen by Vasco de Quiroga; comp. below) are easily reached on foot (3km).

For a visit to the volcano (c 7 hrs there and back; stout shoes needed) guides and mules, essential (charges not unreasonable) for crossing the jagged lava terrain, may be hired in Angahuan. A final climb from the volcano foot to the cone takes c 30 min., and remains of bubbling activity may still be seen.

From Angahuan the road continues W (difficult going) to (82km) **Tzacán** (or *Sacán*). Here are the former Augustinian church and small convent (the latter in ruins) of *San Pedro*

(16–17C), with a small hospital alongside, with fascinating tequitqui window relief. Hence we may go on to (108km) *Sirosto*, with remains of the Augustinian convent of Sta Ana, founded c 1576, but much shaken by earthquakes and adapted, and (115km) *Peribán de Ramos*, see above.

From Zamora Méx. 15 continues SE to (187km) *Tangancícuaro*, see above. At (197km) *Chilcota* is the small convent of Sta María, a short-lived (c 1553–70) Augustinian foundation. The church portal, with heavy alfíz and old carved door, has a rudimentary charm. 203km *Huancito*, famous for ceramic ware. 207km *Carapán*. From here Méx. 37 leads S to (75km) *Uruapan*, see Rte 29. At 211km Méx. 37 leads N, an attractive hilly stretch, to (72km) *La Piedad*, see Rte 36. 239km **Zacapu** (c 50,000 inhab.; 1980m; H,R,P), on the N slope of the Sierra de Nahuatzén and on a branch railway from Irapuato to Apatzingán, stands to the E of the Lago de Zacapu. In the neighbourhood are numerous thermal springs. The former Franciscan convent of *Sta Ana* was first built c 1548 by Fray Jacobo Daciano; a second, on the foundations of the first, by Fray Pedro de Pila c 1586. The church portal, typical of the region, is in a spare plateresque, with twin-arched window over the doorway arch and shell motifs gracing the upper storey. The cloister preserves ancient wooden columns.

Zacapu is of Tarascan origin, and Tarascan finds have been excavated in the vicinity. At *Mal País* (c 1km NE of Zacapu) a small Tarascan ceremonial centre, with yácata tombs, was excavated by Carl Lumholtz, revealing both cremation burials in cinerary urns and mass graves. Secondary burial has also been argued on the basis of slit incisions on some of the bones, seemingly made after the flesh had decayed away, and presumably when the graves were re-dug. Whether or not the mass burial represents a princely entombment with servants for an afterlife remains uncertain.

On the former island called *El Potrero de la Isla*, in the lake of a volcano 1km W of Zacapu, Alfonso Caso excavated several more Tarascan tombs.

N from Zacapu a road descends via (21km) *Panindícuaro*, NW of the Cerro Brinco del Diablo, to (43km; r.) *Villachuato*, at a road junction. Hence a road leads W via (7km) *Angamacutiro* and (35km) *Penjamillo* (fishing in local lakes) to join (46km) Méx. 37, 24km S of *La Piedad*. The road E of Villachuato runs via (18km) *Puruándiro* and (63km) *Huandacareo*, both with curative thermal springs, to (82km) *Cuitzeo*, see Rte 32.

At (246km) *Naranja de Tapia* is a 16C church, once part of a Franciscan visita of Valladolid. The portal, with alfíz and double-arched window, displays tequitqui relief. Méx. 15 crosses the N heights of the Sierra de Michoacán to the N shore of the Lago de Pátzcuaro and (271km) **Sta Fe de la Laguna** where Vasco de Quiroga founded in 1534 one of his two remarkable 'hospitals' called Sta Fe, comp. Rte 16.

Here several thousand Tarascan Indians resided in family units, according to the precepts of Thomas More's 'Utopia', living on the produce of their labour. An orphanage, old people's home, hospital for the sick, and school for vocational and humanistic studies were included. The musical Tarascans quickly achieved high standards in plainsong and polyphony, accompanying themselves on instruments of their own making. By 1570 their numbers here had dwindled to 500. Nothing of the settlement remains, except a restored (hospital ?) chapel, called *Casa de Don Vasco*. The church of *San Nicolás*, where don Vasco's staff, hat, and chair are treasured, is a 17C foundation.

282km **Quiroga** (10,000 inhab.; 1995m; H,P), the former *Cocupao*, famous for the crafts of Michoacán. The small church and former convent of *San Diego* date from the early 17C. The single-storey cloister houses a museum in don Vasco's memory.

From Quiroga, Méx. 15 continues to (45km) *Morelia*, see Rte 31.

We continue S on Méx. 41, skirting the E shore of the lake, to (290km) **TZINT-ZUNTZAN** (3000 inhab.), once the venerated capital of the Tarascans, full of their religious sites.

The ancient Tarascans spoke a language not closely related to any other Mesoamerican language. One scholar has demonstrated some similarities to Andean Quechua, a similarity that strengthens the suspicion that Western Mexico had contact by sea with S America; and to the Zuñi language of the SW USA. Not all scholars accept these conclusions, however.

The 'Relación Michoacán', written by a Franciscan friar c 1538, chronicles the development of the Tarascan state and customs. Tarascan origins are uncertain, but it is thought that they may derive from earlier cultures represented at the sites of El Opeño and Apatzingán in S Michoacán. Tarascan unification was formalized, at least in their traditional history, by the leader Curátemi, in the 12C, when he and his people moved into the region of the Lago de Pátzcuaro after the fall of Tula. At the same time, they mingled with the local Yanaceo-Chichimec group, taking on the latter's warlike character, but retaining their own language and other customs. They had three principal centres: Pátzcuaro, Tzintzuntzan, and Ihuatzio, around the shores of the lake. According to legend, king Tariácuri of Pátzcuaro, just before his death c 1400, divided his kingdom among his son and two nephews: to his son, Huiquingare, he gave Pátzcuaro; to one nephew, Tangajoan, he gave Tzintzuntzan; and to his other nephew, Hiripan, he gave Ihuatzio. Tzintzuntzan eventually became the most powerful, annexing Pátzcuaro after the death of Huiquingare.

Tangajoan extended his empire and maintained an E frontier with the Matlazinca of Teotenango and Calixtlahuaca. He was succeeded by Zuanga, and then by Tzitzisphandácuere (more conveniently known as Tzitzi, or as Characu—'heir-prince'), who further extended the empire to the S and W to include most of present-day Michoacán and parts of Guerrero and Jalisco.

He defended his frontiers with a line of wooden forts and garrisons organized into squadrons armed with bows, obsidian-bladed clubs, slings, and spears. So powerful was his influence, that the principalities of Zacatollan, Colliman, and Zapotlán, in Jalisco, and of Tonallán near Guadalajara, all paid him tribute.

In the latter half of the 15C he formed an alliance with the Pirinda Matlazinca faction of Tzinacantepec, Tecaxic, and Xiquipilco, against the other Matlazinca and the Aztecs, the latter at this time extending their empire beyond the W rim of the Basin of Mexico. At Tajimaroa he successfully halted this advance by defeating the Aztecs in 1479 and recovering the town, which had only previously been captured by Axayácatl.

Tzitzi was succeeded by Zuanga, his son and the fourth ruler of that name, who successfully defended the frontiers of his empire against two more attempts at conquest by the Aztecs under Moctezuma II Xocoyotzin. Zuanga died in 1519 in an epidemic begun in central Mexico by the black slave of the conquistador Pánfilo de Narváez. He was succeeded by Tangajoan II Tzintzicha, and under the latter Tarascan territory was explored by Cristóbal de Olid in 1522. (The Spaniards had asked the Tarascans for aid against the Aztecs in the siege of Tenochtitlán, but their reply had been to kill the Spanish emissaries. When Tenochtitlán lay in ruins the Tarascans apparently felt they had little option but to surrender, lest they suffer a similar fate.)

Tzintzicha made a formal surrender to Cortés, appearing before him in ragged clothing as a Tarascan mark of submission, and later was converted to Christianity. Perhaps for this reason the Aztecs called him Caltzontzin ('broken sandal').

The Tarascan empire was carefully guarded and administered. There were lines of forts on the frontiers, and regular raids were undertaken, in particular to Ixtapan for salt. A complex bureaucracy included tax collectors and census takers, and even spies operating as traders in much the same way as did the Aztec pochteca.

Principal Tarascan deities include Curiacaueri, the Sun and Fire god, and his consort, Cuerauáperi. These two thrived on the blood of sacrificial victims, necessitating, as with the Aztecs, the perpetual Tarascan wars, as well as self-sacrifice by ear-, lip-, and tongue-piercing. Other gods formed a complex pantheon for various functions, similar to other Mesoamerican pantheons (eg, the ruler Tariacuri was deified as the Wind god).

The Tarascans practised ritual burial. The dead king was washed, richly clothed and bejewelled with a feather headdress, robes and cloaks, gold bells, turquoise bracelets, gold ear-plugs, and greenstone lip-plugs. The new king selected men and women to serve the old in his afterlife: chambermaids, jewellery keepers, a cook and servers, washers, caretaker of the royal wardrobe, hairdresser, garland weaver, chair carrier, woodcutter, shoemaker, incense man, oarman, doorman, feather worker, silversmith, weapons keeper, doctor, musicians, dancers, storyteller, and even a mountain climber. These were sacrificed at a midnight burial, following a solemn procession from the palace to a temple burial tomb known as a yácata (see below). The funeral bier and bodies were cremated, and the king's ashes bound up with the funeral offerings and deposited in an urn with a golden mask and shield. This was placed on a wooden couch in a decorated tomb, along with fine cloaks, robes, and jewellery. The sacrificial victims were buried collectively in the 'patios' behind the temples, according to the 'Relación', and it is these that have been excavated at Tzintzuntzan, while the locations of the royal tombs have yet to be found.

The Tarascans were noted craftsmen as well as warriors. They worked in wood, copper, bronze, gold, silver, feathers, and stone; Tarascan women were famous rug-weavers. Their pottery was brilliantly polychrome, and included the technique known as 'negative painting'. Artefacts from excavations include copper and gold bells and jewellery, polished obsidian and turquoise bracelets, lip- and ear-plugs, and carved stone chacmool figures.

To the Aztecs, the Tarascans were merely Chichimeca, that is, barbarians. They spoke a language unfamiliar to Aztec ears and were thought to come from the legendary cave of Chicomoztoc (see *La Quemada*). The Tarascans practised several Chichimec customs, notably tobacco-smoking in clay pipes, and the preparation of food several days in advance, possibly a habit left over from more nomadic times. On the other hand their craftsmanship was famous, and they carved stone chacmool figures resembling those of the Toltecs, whom the Aztecs regarded as the ultimate source of everything civilized. Moreover, Fray Bernardino de Sahagún actually refers to them as Toltecas in his 'Historia'. There is some evidence to suggest that they had at some time been in contact, even if indirectly, with the metal-working traditions of S America.

Tzintzuntzan ('place of the hummingbird') was one of three principal Tarascan civic and ceremonial centres, founded by their leader Curátemi in the 12C AD. The ancient city has been estimated to have had a population of 40,000 at the time of the Spanish Conquest.

It was excavated by Alfonso Caso (1937–38), Jorge Acosta and Daniel Rubin de la Borbolla (1939–41 and 1944), Hugo Moedano (1941), and by Román Piña Chan, incl. restorations (1960s). The modern town is equally famous for the anthropological studies of George M. Foster and his students from the University of California at Berkeley.

Both town and lake were known in Náhuatl as Michoacán (place of fish). Vasco de Quiroga fixed upon it for his see of Michoacán. On taking possession in 1538, however, he decided to transfer it to Pátzcuaro. Yet the old city continued to dispute with Pátzcuaro the title 'ciudad de Michoacán'. Plague in 1643 devastated it, the population falling from 20,000 to 200.

The convent of **San Francisco** was rebuilt in the 1570s, on foundations of the 1530s, by Fray Pedro de Pila, and further modified in the 17–18C. Already falling into ruin by the 19C, the small church (restored) was fire damaged on Maundy Thursday 1944. The enormous atrio (183m to a side) keeps probably the oldest olive trees in the Americas, their thick gnarled trunks in two rows. The church faces E. Its portal is a handsomely ornate version of local plater-esque and dominated by shell motifs. Its double-arched window (ajimez) is beneath a classical pediment. To the fore of the convent, the façade of the walled-up polygonal open chapel is similarly decorated. The cloister retains part of a once elaborate wooden ceiling. On the N side of the atrio, and in its own small atrio, is the hospital chapel (1619; restored), its portico (facing N) decorated with shell and sun and moon medallions.

On the hill of *Yahuarato* at the E end of the lake c 1km N of the modern town, several groups of ruins include the *Casa del Sacerdote*, the *Casa de Aguila*, a storage building, and, the principal attraction, the huge platform and plaza with its five temples, known as *Yácatas*. The face of the main platform and two of the Yácatas have been completely restored; the others are in ruins and from them the visitor can learn some of the details of their construction.

Fronting a huge plaza, a long, stepped platform c 425m by 251m is ascended by a similarly proportioned stairway c 91m wide. On the rear side (nearest the stairs) are five temple platforms of a plan unique to the Tarascans.

Each Yácata, numbered *I–V*, was composed of 12 inclined steps of c 1m in height each, recessed c 30cm. The front portion of each platform was rectilinear and connected by a short perpendicular extension to the main, circular part, which supported the temple. Steps from the main platform led to the tops of the rectilinear part of each Yácata, giving access to the temples. *Yácata V* measures c 140m by 22m, with the maximum diameter of the circular temple platform being 29m. Each Yácata was built up of flat stones retained by stepped walls carefully fitted and bonded with a mud-based mortar, and faced with fitted slabs of volcanic stone, some of which are carved with hieroglyphic signs.

At the base of Yácata V, two collective-burial tombs were found, probably of the servants meant to accompany the king in death. Other burials were found elsewhere on the site, but no apparent royal burial. Burial offerings, however, included gold, silver, copper, and bronze jewellery, obsidian earplugs, featherwork, lacquer-ware vessels, and turquoise mosaics.

Tzintzuntzan is seen to advantage on festival days: 1 Feb., feast of Christ the Redeemer, instituted here by Vasco de Quiroga; and during Holy Week, especially Maundy Thursday, when the Passion is re-enacted.

296km turning r. for (2km) **Ihuatzio**, with a 16C barrio church, on the N bank of a sizeable inlet at the SE end of the lake. It was the third principal town established by Curátemi, founder of the Tarascan empire.

2km up the hill from the village there is a large late Postclassic plaza (c 400 x 300m; excavated in the 1930s by Alfonso Caso and Rivera Paz). Two partially restored, rectangular pyramid-platforms form the W side; terrace ruins and mounds form the other sides. The excavations uncovered the plans of three yácatas similar to those at Tzintzuntzan, and the chacmool figure found is in the Museo Nacional de Antropología.

309km **PATZCUARO** (40,000 inhab.; 2174m), tranquil near the S shore of the Lago de Pátzcuaro, evokes the past of the historic Tarascan heartland. Its narrow cobbled streets, distinctive adobe single- and two-storey houses with overhanging red-tile roofs, and delightful leafy plazas give it an individual stamp and atmosphere unequalled elsewhere in Mexico. Its understandable popularity with visitors both from abroad and from all parts of the republic still has not spoiled it.

Railway station. 3km N of the centre, reached along Av. de las Américas. Trains to *Uruapan, Morelia, Mexico City* (fastest c 10 hrs; slower c 13 hrs).

Bus station. S of the town, on the Circunvalación (Av. Zaragoza). Frequent services to *Uruapan* (1½ hrs); to *Morelia* (1½ hrs); to *Guadalajara* (6½ hrs); to *Mexico City* (c 8½ hrs); to *Zamora* (c 2 hrs); and for most smaller towns in Michoacán.

Hotels throughout the town.

Post Office. C. Obregón, leading N from Pl. Bocanegra.

Tourist Office. Corner of Cs Ibarra and Mendoza.

Fiestas. *Good Friday*, culmination of Holy Week ceremonies: impressive procession. *8 Dec.*, feast of Nuestra Señora de la Salud: dances and procession. Pátzcuaro begins to fill early in preparation for the Day of the Dead on Janitzio (see below).

Pátzcuaro ('place of stones', or 'material for cues [temples]'), was one of the three principal Tarascan civic and ceremonial centres. It was their first capital, established by Curátemi in the 12C, but was later overshadowed by the site of Tzintzuntzan. The prehispanic city is now covered by the modern town.

Pátzcuaro is also known for anthropological studies done here by George M. Foster and his students from the University of California at Berkeley.

In July 1522 Huitzitzilzi and Cuinharangari (known as don Pedro), brothers of Tangajoan II, cordially received the expedition of Cristóbal de Olid. In 1524 Cortés, who established good relations with all three, distributed lands in Michoacán among his followers, but reserved to himself the Lago de Pátzcuaro and its surrounding area, which, however, was seized by the first audiencia in 1529. In 1525 the king had ceded his rights to the Spanish crown. In 1530 the region fell victim to the massacres and depredations of Nuño de Guzmán, who burned the king alive and in one month caused chaos, depopulation, and the flight of the remaining Indians. Pátzcuaro, once a barrio of Tzintzuntzan and famous for its pre-Conquest featherwork and as a retreat for the ruling house, was reconstituted by Vasco de Quiroga (c 1470–1565), nobleman and lawyer, chosen by Charles V to bring peace to the maltreated Tarascans. He took holy orders at the age of 68 and from 1538, as bp, he created here a major Indian and (to a lesser extent) Spanish settlement as the political centre of the 'ciudad de Michoacán', equivalent to the heart of the Tarascan kingdom. It flourished and expanded until in the 1540s it embraced 70 barrios and c 70,000 inhab. The Tarascans were admired even by the Spaniards for their sympathetic character: 'brave...intelligent...peace-ful...affectionate'. Don Vasco, encourager of crafts and industry, kindly, resourceful, sometimes crotchety, but strong-minded, won their undying affection and left the region stable and prosperous; he is still venerated here as Tata Vasco. In 1541 Viceroy Mendoza ordered the 'cibdad de Mechuacan' to be moved to Valladolid, but Quiroga continued to refer to Pátzcuaro as 'city of Michoacán'. By the 1750s it had become a largely mestizo town.

In 1815 Iturbide occupied Pátzcuaro and had the insurgent governor shot. In 1818 Gertrudis Bocanegra, who lost husband and son in the Independence struggle, was shot for refusing to reveal the names of partisans.

The smaller of the two main plazas, officially PL. GERTRUDIS BOCANEGRA (more often called *Pl. San Agustín* or *Pl. Chica*), is pleasantly shaded. In its centre is a statue of the heroine. On its W side is the *Mercado*, concentrated and

colourful, the vendors from the villages of the Pátzcuaro region. On the N side is the former church of **San Agustín**, part of the Augustinian convent founded in 1576, with an early 17C Mannerist portal. It has been beautifully and simply converted into a public library, *Biblioteca Gertrudis Bocanegra*.

The superb mural (1942) on the N wall is by Juan O'Gorman—a clear and direct view of the Conquest of Michoacán and its bad and good effects: Thomas More and Vasco de Quiroga stand out; Morelos (lower r.) about to begin the liberation. The convent buildings were drastically converted into a theatre, now a cinema.

From the plaza C. Ramos leads W to the *Santuario de Guadalupe* (1833), built at the charges of Feliciano Ramos, a former slave who recovered his liberty and made his fortune running a team of muleteers.

From the E side of the plaza Cs Régules and La Paz lead to the Basilica of **Nuestra Señora de la Salud**, also called the *Colegiata*, including all that remains of Vasco de Quiroga's projected cathedral of the see of Michoacán.

His project for a cathedral big enough to hold 30,000 Indians was begun c 1543–44, and was a continual source of controversy. It was, originally and ambitiously, designed with five naves to converge on a sanctuary, within a 180-degree angle, so that the huge congregation might have a view. After 1565 a new plan, by Claudio de Arciniega, was adopted: one nave only and with a wooden roof. The incomplete structure continued its chequered career of damage and repair into the 19C. (In 1842 Fanny Calderón de la Barca found a notice on the door: 'for the love of God, all good Christians are requested not to spit in this holy place'.) The interior decoration, by Claudio Molina, dates from 1898–99. Only parts of the walls of the original structure remain.

The INTERIOR is entered through a handsomely carved windbreak. On the high altar (1907) is a venerated image of Nuestra Señora de la Salud, made from caña de maíz, possibly by order of Vasco de Quiroga c 1540 for his hospital of Sta Marta.

The original clothing, forming part of the image, was cut away in 1690 ('by night', we are told, because of the protests of an indignant parishioner who 'watched like a hawk') so that new and sumptuous adornments of brocade and jewels could be fitted on the mutilated figure. In 1962 a madman levelled ten rifle shots at the statue, but did not succeed in damaging it. He was saved from lynching by a furious crowd thanks to the intervention of the parish priest.

The two large 18C paintings, Holy Family (r. wall) and Assumption (l. wall), are by Ignacio Velasco. The remains of doña Juana Pérez Pavón, mother of José María Morelos, rest to the l. of the high altar.

In the sacristy are paintings by Manuel de la Cuerda (mid-18C). The treasury contains the chalice used at the first communion of Queen Victoria Eugenie of Spain in 1906 after her reception into the Church, presented to the Colegiata by the queen-mother, María Cristina.

S of the basilica, at the corner of Cs Lerín and Alcantarillas, is the site of the **Colegio de San Nicolás**, the present building dating from the 18C.

The Real Colegio de San Nicolás Obispo was founded c 1540, and built where had been the residence of the Tarascan royal house, by Vasco de Quiroga as a seminary to train Spanish boys eventually to staff his cathedral and to give Tarascan boys a Christian grounding and thorough knowledge of Spanish. Among its early pupils was Antonio Huitziméngari, son of Tangajoan II and godson of Viceroy Antonio de Mendoza. In his will don Vasco bequeathed to his foundation landed property, his horse, a picture of St Ambrose, and 626 books. In 1573–80 it was run by the Jesuits, in the latter year removing to Valladolid. In 1588 they got possession of the site and expanded their teaching activities to it.

It now houses the **Museo de Artes Populares** (Tues.–Sun., 9–1, 3–5; fee), containing a collection of Michoacán craftware from the 17C to the present day: palm fibre figures from Ihuatzio; textiles from Angahuan; pottery from Tzintzuntzan, Santa Fe, and Puruándiro; lacquerware from Uruapan, Quiroga, and Pátzcuaro; embroidery from Tzintzuntzan; clay masks, worn at religious fiestas; ex-votos; 19C wax figures; 18C crucifixion in caña de maíz; etc.

On the S side of C. Alcantarillas stands the church of **La Compañía**, occupying the site of don Vasco's first, temporary, cathedral.

This was handed over to the Jesuits in 1573 and was burned down in 1583. Its present severe and solid aspect dates from the 17C. Behind the high altar in a reinforced coffin rest the remains of don Vasco. Attached to the church is the former Jesuit college of San Ignacio, founded in 1576, but much rebuilt.

Further S along C. Lerín is the church known as *El Sagrario*, built during 1693–1717 to house the image of Nuestra Señora de la Salud. It was renovated and enlarged in 1845 and 1874, and reconsecrated in 1893. Behind it, on the S side of C. Colimilla, is the so-called **Casa de los Once Patios**, now converted into a crafts centre.

It dates from 1747 and was built for a convent of Dominican nuns from Sta Catalina in Valladolid. It covers part of the site of the hospital of *Sta Marta*, a foundation (1540) of Vasco de Quiroga. Fanny Calderón de la Barca was disappointed in the nuns: 'common-looking women, and not very amiable in their manners'.

From the W end of C. Colimilla, C. José María Cos leads N to PL. VASCO DE QUIROGA, wide and beautiful, planted with venerable and sturdy ash trees, and bordered by inimitable two-storey buildings (16–18C; carefully restored), all toughly built, with flat or gently sloping tiled roofs and charming patios. On the W side is the *Pal. Municipal*, the former *Casas Consistoriales*. Adjoining it, on the corner with C. Ponce de León, is the *Casa de los Marqueses de Villa-hermosa de Alfaro*, built for Jerónimo de Soria y Velázquez, oidor decano of the audiencia, created marqués in 1711. On the NE side is the *Casa de Antonio Huitziméngari* (also known as *Casa del Gobernador*), preserving marked 16–17C features.

Don Antonio (d. 1562), son of Tangajoan II and chief cacique of Pátzcuaro, was appointed governor of the province of Michoacán in 1545, which he ruled in despotic fashion, very well in with the Spaniards and even considered Spanish. His son, don Pablo, last legitimate male descendant of Tangajoan, installed himself in the Jesuit college and died of the plague in 1576 while attending its victims. The king's legitimate descendants through the female line married into the Spanish nobility, thus forming a mestizo royal branch. A descendant of one of these alliances was Pres. Pascual Ortiz Rubio (1877–1963).

On the E side is the *Casa del Gigante* (late 18C), built for Col. Francisco García de Menocal, a native of Havana and founder of a prominent Michoacán family. It is so-called for a huge painted warrior statue (probably contemporary with the house) on the first floor.

From the SW corner of the plaza C. Romero leads S to the church of *San Juan de Dios*, founded in 1670 alongside the hospital of the Brothers of St John of God, and restored in 1841. C. Ponce de León leads E off the plaza past (r.) the *Real Aduana*, an 18C house with fine baroque ornamentation and once the customs house where goods brought to Acapulco in the China fleet were declared on their way to Mexico City. A little further (r.) is JARDIN REVOLU-CION, from which, on the l. side of C. Codallos, may be seen the Indian barrio hospital chapel called *El Hospitalito* (c 1545).

On the l. in C. Terán, beyond the crossing, is the former Franciscan convent and church of **San Francisco**. Building started in 1576–77; the church, despite its Romanesque look, was completed in 1638.

Church and convent were fired by the town's republican captors in 1867; their present aspect dates partly from a rebuilding in 1892. A notable survival is the convent doorway, a plater-esque variation, with pronounced impost capitals and dated 1577. This gives on to the charming cloister with its Mudéjar-style pillars.

In the church is a venerated crucifix in pasta de caña (paste of cornstalk pith on a skeleton of dried maize leaves), which in July 1656 was seen to make various movements. A small cell in the thickness of the wall contains a painting (St Francis appearing to a dead pope) attr. Alberto Enríquez (Fray Francisco Manuel de Cuadros), a Peruvian executed for heresy in 1678.

C. Terán continues E to (3km) the *Cerro del Estribo*, an extinct volcano giving wonderful views of town and lake. On the way (l.), surrounded by a 16C cemetery, is a chapel known as *El Calvario* (1666), culmination of a Way of the Cross which draws many of the faithful during Holy Week.

NW of the town, reached along C. Serrato S of the Colegiata, which joins the old road to Morelia, is the chapel called *El Humilladero* (1553). The pedestal of its wayside cross is carved with the city arms which incorporate a plan of don Vasco's cathedral.

The **LAGO DE PATZCUARO** (2050m), inextricably associated with the history of the Tarascans, its grey-green waters set in a matchless landscape, its shore dotted with picturesque, timeless villages, is one of the loveliest lakes in the world. Five islands, three of them inhabited, are strung out on it. From SW to NE it measures some 20km and at its widest 14km; its depth ranges from 8 to 50m. It is fed by various rivers descending from the mountains, principal among them the Guzní and the Chapultepec.

The embarkation point (muelle) is on the S bank, c 4.5km N of Pátzcuaro, beyond the station. Here a frequent motor-boat service plies to the principal island, *Janitzio* (c 700 inhab.; 30 min.), a quaint place, but overwhelmed by curious tourists, especially on 1 and 2 Nov., for the celebration of the Día de los Muertos. This is an essentially private, intense, and moving commemoration of the Holy Souls; but now, alas, heavily commercialized. The islanders keep up their fishing traditions in flat-bottomed boats and their displays with their distinctive nets—varacuas (trawl nets); cherémicuas (narrow nets); and guaramútacas and tiruhspétz-cuas (scoop nets)—are a carefully fostered attraction. Looming over the island is a vast and unsuitable monument in reinforced concrete representing José María Morelos, the work of Guillermo Ruiz, begun in 1933. A spiral staircase leads up to the head (good view). Murals by Ramón Alva de la Canal.

N of Janitzio lie the islands of *Tecuén*, *Yunuén*, and *La Pacanda*, the latter inhabited, and, to its SW, *Jarácuaro*, the largest and lowest, with a 16C church.

FROM PATZCUARO TO ERONGARICUARO, 22km, a good excursion around the S side of the lake, leaving Pátzcuaro to the N, past the monument to Tangajoan II. Opposite (3.5km) the railway station is the headquarters of CREFAL (Centro Regional de Educación Fundamental para la América Latina), founded in 1951, under the patronage of UNESCO—and on the initiative of its then director-general, the Mexican diplomat Jaime Torres Bodet (1902–72)—the Organization of American States, and the Mexican government to promote education programmes throughout Latin America. In 1960 it adopted the designation Centro de Educación para el Desarrollo de la Comunidad en América Latina, though it retained its former acronym. The house, a former residence of Gen. Lázaro Cárdenas, was donated by him to the centre. At 4km we take the turning l., the road to Uruapan. 12km (r.) *San Pedro Pareo*, its 16C church with a typical local plateresque portal. 22km **Erongarícuaro** (c 4000 inhab.; 1980m; R,P), a picturesque town, with some 17C houses, which during the Second World War provided a haven for André Breton and other surrealists. On the N side of the peaceful colonnaded plaza is the former Franciscan convent of the *Asunción de Nuestra Señora*, built c 1563–86 and recently well restored. The doorway, delightfully chunky and sturdy, is an outstanding example of local plateresque. The semicircular arch, with pronounced voussoirs, and resting on markedly low imposts, is enclosed by an alfíz decorated with five large shell motifs. The double-arched window (ajimez) above, in a quadrangular frame and decorated with shells and medallions, has an even larger shell as its central motif. On the E side is the triple-arched open chapel in the form of a portería, the arches resting on paired columns and giving an excellent view of the central apse. The convent entrance—the small door in the l.-hand bay, its arch set off by an ingenuous alfíz limited by baluster columns—gives on to the small two-storey cloister. The church is notable for its flat-beamed ceiling and for the beams of its choir.

The parish church of the neighbouring pueblo, *Huiramángaro*, preserves its 16C plateresque high altarpiece (modified).

FROM PATZCUARO TO TACAMBARO AND VILLA ESCALANTE, 55km and 19km. We follow Méx. 120 S towards (15km) *Opopeo*, from where Méx. 41 runs E to (39km) *Cruz Gorda* and then S to (55km) **Tacámbaro** (c 16,000 inhab.; 1577m; H,P), beautifully situated amid orchards and pine and cedar forests, and on the r. bank of the Río Tacámbaro, a tributary of the Río Balsas, which descends down the S slopes of the Sierra de Curucupaseo.

Off the main plaza is the former Augustinian convent of *San Jerónimo*, the result of several building campaigns. Founded in 1538–39 and built mainly in 1553–56, the church was rebuilt in 1667 and the entire convent in 1706 and 1730. Further alteration took place in the 19C.

From Opopeo, Méx. 120 goes W to (19km) *Villa Escalante*, the former Sta Clara de los Cobres, an attractive place, established by Vasco de Quiroga as a community of coppersmiths, their source the old mine of Inguarán (c 80km S), and still a major copper-fashioning centre. The industry is celebrated with a copper fair every 11–16 Aug. The road runs S to (47km) **Ario de Rosales** (18,000 inhab.; 2050m; H,P), another agreeable town, on an elevated plain surrounded by gorges; c 15km S is the volcano *Jorullo*, a phenomenon of June–Sept. 1759, in the Sierra de Inguarán, the S foothills of the Volcanic Divide, and still active in a minor way. The road descends into the tierra caliente to (97km) *La Huacana* and hence winds past (113km; r.) *Presa Zicuirán* (fishing) and (l.) *Presa del Infiernillo* to (145km) *Cuatro Caminos*, see Rte 29.

FROM PATZCUARO TO MORELIA, 58km. We leave Pátzcuaro NE on the old road (State highway 14) to Morelia. 6km *Zurumútaro* has kept its 16C church of San Pedro, a reminder of its former status as subject pueblo to Pátzcuaro. At 16km a poor road runs S to (4km) **Tupátaro**, another former subject pueblo. Here the simple 16C adobe church of *Santiago Apóstol* (restored; open for Sun. Mass—otherwise visitors must seek out the caretaker) contains a marvel of Mexican art: a wooden ceiling composed of 47 exquisite painted panels. At the sides, archangels hold symbols of the Passion. In the centre, scenes from the lives of Jesus and Mary. Towards the altar, more scenes from Our Lord's life. One of the cross-beams bears the date 1772. The gilded churrigueresque high altar incorporates six paintings on the same theme. 33km **Tiripetío**, whose convent of *San Juan Bautista* was once the most important Augustinian foundation in New Spain and a famous craft and intellectual centre.

It was built in 1539 at the invitation of Vasco de Quiroga and under the supervision of the friars Juan de San Ramón and Diego de Chávez who had arrived here in 1537. The sumptuous bold-buttressed church was up by 1548. In the atrio the processional ways were 'streets of orange-trees and cypresses'. Artisans came from Mexico City and from Spain to instruct the Indians in building techniques, and Indians in turn were sent to the capital to learn. Tiripetío became a trade school for Michoacán, its craftsmen (to the town's detriment) called far afield. In 1540 it gained added prestige from the foundation of its college-seminary (*Colegio de Estudios Mayores*), the first in New Spain, by Fray Alonso de la Veracruz, who thus formalized a dedication to instruct the Tarascans: 'from its first day its doors had been generously opened to Tarascan talent'. The church was badly damaged by fire in 1640 and radically repaired in the 19C. The convent buildings were completely restored from 1938.

45km (r.) *Santiago Undameo* (the former *Necotlán*), at the S end of *Presa Cointzio*. The small Augustinian convent was founded in the 1590s. The church dates from the 1630s. 58km *Morelia*, see Rte 31.

29 Pátzcuaro to Lázaro Cárdenas

Méx. 14 and Méx. 37, 327km.—62km **Uruapan** and Méx. 37.—120km Cuatro Caminos (for [31km W] Apatzingán).—315km Playa Azul (for [12km E] **Lázaro Cárdenas**).

12km *San Pedro Pareo* (see Rte 28), whence we bear SW from the lake. At 21km road S for (6km) *Zirahuén*, a fishing village on the NE of the *Lago de Zirahuén* (4km at its widest), famous for its blue waters, with opalescent tinge, amid pine forests. 33km *Tingambato*, in the Sierra de Nahuatzén. The Augustinian convent of Santiago flourished here from the 1580s. Its church, all that is left, dates from a mid-17C rebuilding.

It was a Classic Period site occupied c AD 500–1000. Excavations by Román Piña Chan uncovered a large ceremonial centre complete with talud-tablero architecture and a ball court. There are platforms around a main plaza, with staircases leading up to multi-chambered structures, but, incongruently, no central Mexican ceramics (cf. *Amapa* and *Teuchitlán*).
   A rough road leads S, crossing the railway line, to (8km) *San Angel Zurumcapio*, with a 16C church and atrial cross displaying homely relief. The road may be followed SW to (20km) *Ziracuaretiro* (1500m) and thence to (38km) *Uruapan*.

62km **URUAPAN** (c 240,000 inhab.; 1634m), is a charming, semi-tropical city on the S slopes of the Sierra de Uruapan which descends to the tierra caliente. It is famous for its lacquerware. Its superb avocados have an international reputation.

Airport. C 8km SE of the centre, reached along Av. Latinoamericana. Flights to *Mexico City* and *Guadalajara*.

Railway station. E of the centre, on Paseo Lázaro Cárdenas. Two services (early morning and evening) to *Pátzcuaro, Morelia*, and *Mexico City*.

Bus station. 3km NE of the centre, on Morelia road. Frequent services to *Mexico City* (9½ hrs); to *Morelia* (2½ hrs); to *Colima* (5½ hrs); to *Zihuatanejo* (c 8 hrs); to *Pátzcuaro* (c 1½ hrs); to *Guadalajara* (5 hrs); to *Angahuan* (c 1¼ hrs); etc.

Hotels throughout the city.

Post Office. 36 C. Cupatitzio.

Tourist Office. 23 C. 5 de Febrero.

Fiestas. Frequent: Palm Sunday; 22 July (St Mary Magdalen); 25 July (Santiago); 4 Oct. (St Francis of Assisi); 12 Oct. (Discovery of America—Día de la Raza); 24 Oct. (Festival of Choirs and Dancing)—an exceptional event, in which competitors must be of Tarascan extraction; high standards of Tarascan musicianship are maintained.

In 1524 its territory was granted to Francisco de Villegas, whose descendants stayed in possession until the late 17C. C 1532–33 Fray Juan de San Miguel founded the Franciscan convent and laid out a spacious town divided into nine barrios. In 1540 the dispersed local Indians, who had fled Nuño de Guzmán, were gathered in to form a congregación. In 1639 the Franciscan Alonso de la Rea wrote that the town's planning 'could not have been bettered by the aristocracy of Rome'. On 20 Nov. 1767 Gálvez condemned ten leaders of the Indian community who had dared to protest against the expulsion of the Jesuits to be hanged. Their homes were destroyed, their severed heads fixed on high poles where their houses had been, and their widows and children banished for life. In Oct. 1865 the imperialist Gen. Méndez brought several distinguished prisoners to Uruapan and had them shot.

At the W end of the lively PL. PRINCIPAL (or *Jardín Morelos*) is the church of *San Francisco*, part of the convent, rebuilt in the 1560s, but fire damaged in 1813 and drastically restored. Next to it is a small historical museum. At the E end is the former hospital known as **La Guatapera**, built by Fray Juan de San Miguel (d 1555), its sloping tiled roof and charming patio giving a rustic effect. It is chiefly memorable for the doorway of its chapel—an Indian blending of plateresque and Mudéjar.

It recalls the Angahuan portal (comp. Rte 28), and was probably fashioned by the same craftsmen, but is less adventurous. Jambs, imposts, round arch, and restricted alfíz are decorated like a tapestry. Above (l.) is a shield bearing the Franciscan symbol of the Five Wounds; on the r., an empty shield probably once bearing the royal coat-of-arms. The central niche contains a statue of the founder by his admiring Indians. All has been restored after fire damage in 1851 and 1944. The hospital is now a handicrafts museum (daily, 9–1.30; 3.30–5.30), with a collection of 16C lacquerware. Behind it is the church of *La Inmaculada* (19C).

The nine barrio chapels planted by Fray Juan still stand and still keep marks of antiquity: *San Miguel* (C. Lerdo de Tejada) N of the plaza; *San Juan Bautista*, further W along the same street; *La Trinidad* (C. Reforma), SE of the plaza; *La Magdalena* (between Cs Francisco Sarabia and Morelos), E of the plaza; *San Pedro*, directly S of the centre, across the Río Cupatitzio, its arch voussoirs in the form of striking floral relief which descends beyond the imposts into the jambs.

N of the hospital is the picturesque *Mercado de Antojitos* (savouries), known for the region's culinary specialities. W of the plaza, reached along C. Pino Suárez, is *Parque Nacional Eduardo Ruiz*, full of luxuriant tropical vegetation, and an imaginative ramification of the Tepalcatepec Commission (see below). Beneath the crag called Rodillo del Diablo (Devil's Knee) rises the Río Cupatitzio which flows S to the waterfall of Tzaráracua (60m; 12km S), in beautiful surroundings, a favourite excursion.

From Uruapan Méx. 37 runs N to (16km) turning l. for (19km) *Angahuan*. 21km *Capácuaro*, a characterful place, where the church of San Juan Bautista (a parish church since 1603) dates probably from the late 16C. 30km turning l. for (15km W) *San Felipe*, see Rte 28. 36km **Paracho de Verduzco** (10,000 inhab.; 1567m; H,P), a quaint and peaceful Tarascan town in the Sierra del Paracho and N of the extinct volcano (3324m) of the same name. Paracho's traditional craft (chosen by Vasco de Quiroga—see Rte 28) is the making of guitars. The Corpus Christi celebrations here have a great reputation for their music and dancing. 40km *Aranza*, with a typical church, San Jerónimo, focus of a secular parish founded by don Vasco in the early 1560s. 48km *Cherán*, another Tarascan town (interesting Corpus Christi celebrations). 8km SE is *Nahuatzén*, in beautiful scenery on the W slopes of the Sierra de Nahuatzén. The road runs W and N to (75km) *Carapán* on Méx. 15, see Rte 28.

The road W from Uruapan winds over the sierra to (13km) *Nuevo San Juan Parangaricutiro*, where the inhabitants of the overwhelmed San Juan Parangaricutiro and Paricutín (see Rte

28) were resettled in 1944. Hence we may go S through spectacular mountain and forest scenery to (57km) *Tancítaro*, at the foot of the volcano Tancítaro (3845m), above the Sierra de Apatzingán, the highest peak in Michoacán, in a national park. *Peribán de Ramos* (see Rte 28) is 28km N.

From Uruapan, Méx. 37 runs S alongside the Río Cupatitzio, its waters harnessed since the late 1940s by hydroelectric works. 71km (r.) the *Tzaráracua* falls and dam. At (89km) *Barranca Honda* (bridge 87m high) is a view of the basin of the Río Tepalcatepec, focus of the Comisión del Tepalcatepec, initiated in 1947 and affecting 18,000 sq km of Michoacán and Jalisco between the Meseta Central and the Sierra Madre del Sur. In 1960 it was absorbed into the Balsas Commission, see below.

Archaeological knowledge of the Tepalcatepec Basin is meagre. A cultural sequence, beginning in the Classic Period, includes molcajetes, pots with ring stands, the use of resist-painting decoration, polished pyrite mirrors, and copper objects. These are isolated and slightly different from the more familiar Jalisco–Colima region metallurgy and ceramics.

97km *Gabriel Zamora*, the former Lombardía, and (116km) *Nueva Italia de Ruiz*, the centres of two haciendas developed, in a then unhealthy region, from 1902 by Dante Cussi (1848–1928), an Italian immigrant.

Helped by his three sons, he transformed the area under a series of irrigation works completed, despite enormous difficulty, by 1915. By 1938, when the government expropriated 61,500 hectares, they had shown the way to future development: especially ricefields, maize, lemon orchards, and livestock. They sold their remaining land to the new ejidos.

120km *Cuatro Caminos*. The road E goes to (125km) *Villa Escalante*, see Rte 28. The road W (Méx. 120) goes through the tierra caliente to (31km) **Apatzingán** (160,000 inhab.; 682m; H,R,P), after Uruapan the most important town in the Tepalcatepec river basin, and focus of prodigious agricultural production.

Here on 22 Oct. 1814, after defeat at Valladolid, Morelos and his demoralized Congress proclaimed the liberal constitution of Apatzingán (Decreto Constitucional para la Libertad de la América Mexicana), never put into practice.

The *Casa de la Constitución* on Pl. Principal is arranged as a museum and contains some of Morelos's possessions.

Before reaching Apatzingán, at 19km, a road turns r. for (17km N) *Parácuaro*, near which is the unexcavated, unrestored site of *Los Molcajetes* ('grinding bowls'). Spread over several sq km are terraces supporting building foundations formed around plazas. On the grounds of the Ejido Los Bancos, some engravings have been found on a rock-shelter on the bank of the Río Capiri, incl. a highly stylized human figure and various motifs. Because of the lack of associated, datable artefacts, the date of the carvings is unknown.

Méx. 37 continues S through the tierra caliente and into the CUENCA DEL BALSAS, alongside the W stretch of **Presa el Infiernillo**.

This vast artificial lake, formed by the Ríos Balsas and Tepalcatepec, extends c 90km N–S and c 120km along its E–W arm, through which runs the Michoacán–Guerrero border. Average width is c 4km. It stores 12,000 million cubic m of water and has a generating capacity of 672MW, mainly for Mexico City.
    The Río Balsas Commission was set up in 1960 to develop c 113,200sq km. The largest Mexican river flowing into the Pacific, it rises in the Valle de Puebla as the Atoyac and runs mostly W, at first as the Mezcala, through Guerrero. From Ciudad Altamirano it flows W, forming the Guerrero–Michoacán border. At El Infiernillo it joins the Tepalcatepec and then plunges S through the Sierra Madre del Sur.

Méx. 37, from now on a winding road, begins its crossing of the Sierra Madre del Sur. At (193km) *La Lobera* a road leads SE to (43km) *El Infiernillo* at the SW end of the lake. Hence we continue on an increasingly sinuous course, with spectacular views, towards the coast. 256km *Arteaga* (H,R,P). 315km **Playa Azul** (c 8km S; H,R,P), part of an open stretch of beach reaching c 40km to the W, not overdeveloped and relatively unsophisticated; but a little too close to the industrial activity to its E for comfort. Wonderful sunsets, but strong currents. The latest stretch of coast road (Méx. 200), scenic and awaiting development, runs W along the narrow coastal plain between the Pacific and the slopes of the Sierra Madre to (214km) the border with the State of Colima, see Rte 25B.

12km E is **Lázaro Cárdenas** (c 60,000 inhab.; H,R,P), at the delta of the Río Balsas, created on the initiative of Gen. Cárdenas where once had been the fishing village of *Melchor Ocampo*. It has been in development since 1964 as Mexico's largest Pacific coast deep-water port and is dominated by its portentous iron and steel works, the *Siderúrgica Lázaro Cárdenas–Las Truchas* (SICARTSA), supplied by Michoacán's iron ore deposits, and by hydroelectricity from *Presa La Villita* (Río Balsas; 14km N).

30 Lázaro Cárdenas to Zihuatanejo and Acapulco

Méx. 200, 363km.—120km Ixtapa.—128km Zihuatanejo.—265km Tecpan.—363km **Acapulco**.

The coast road (Méx. 200) makes a spectacular run, first along the Pacific coast into the State of Guerrero. The foothills of the Sierra Madre reach sometimes to the shore and form parallel mountain ranges, between which precipitate rivers empty, during summer rains, into the sea. Since the 1950s a hitherto remote area has become the focus for the development of seaside resorts, some of it intensive.

The road runs inland to (14km) *Presa la Villita*, a large artificial lake damming the waters of the Río Balsas. The road doubles back to the coast and skirts Bahía de Petacalco. At (85km) *La Salitrera* Méx. 140 begins a winding course across the sierra to (166km) *Ciudad Altamirano*, see Rte 31. Méx. 200 continues to (120km) *Ixtapa* and (128km) *Zihuatanejo*, two burgeoning, but very different, resorts.

IXTAPA, planned from the 1960s and started up in 1975, is an expensive seaside development disposing of over 20km of beach, some picturesque coves, an 18-hole golf course, and the latest in hotels. It stretches from Punta Ixtapa, on the NE, along the sweep of a wide bay in which are several islands.

A road has been forged through the mountains of Guerrero linking it and Zihuatanejo with Mexico City. Its featurelessness will only make Ixtapa agreeable to those who wish to laze in the sun and enjoy water sports—and the pampering provided by luxurious accommodation. Behind the hotels a new residential area is growing.

ZIHUATANEJO (c 10,000 inhab.) is a much more attractive place, offering more variety in accommodation, prices, and recreation. Its nucleus is the old fishing village and port on the sheltered Bahía de Zihuatanejo. Its site, ringed by mountains, is spectacular. Palms, mangoes, and other tropical growths abound.

At Zihuatanejo excavators found hundreds of open metal rings—often hooked together in bunches—bells, pieces of sheet gold, and the slag from metal-smithing. Also on the coast, the *Barnard Site*, c 35km SE, was excavated by Ellen and Charles Brush in 1968, and yielded polychrome pottery (especially malacates—spindle whorls), and more metal artefacts. On analysis, many of the artefacts proved to be bronze, apparently deliberately produced by adding tin to the copper. These, and the polychrome pottery with loop-supports, resemble materials from Costa Rica and Nicaragua. The Barnard Site was only briefly occupied at the beginning of the 10C AD, and the finding of these materials among the general household refuse of the site indicates that metal tools were not necessarily purely luxury items (cf. *Amapa*).

On 31 Oct. 1527 the expedition of Alvaro de Saavedra Cerón (three ships—two soon lost—and a hundred men) set sail from here on its dangerous voyage to the Moluccas and Philippines, reaching the N coast of New Guinea. As late as the 1950s it was an isolated and utterly unspoilt place specializing in the shipping of bananas grown in the hinterland, although patronized by aficionados in search of peace and quiet. Its new-found popularity, and careful development, date from the 1960s.

Airport. 16km SE. 3–4 flights daily to *Mexico City* (50 min.); one flight daily to *Guadalajara*. Flights to destinations in W USA. Bus service to Ixtapa and Zihuatanejo.

Bus stations. 54 Paseo del Palmar and 2km E on Méx 200. Frequent services to *Lázaro Cárdenas* (2½ hrs); to *Acapulco* (c 4 hrs); to *Mexico City* (c 12 hrs); to *Guadalajara* (c 12 hrs); to *Tijuana* (c 50 hrs); to *Morelia* (c 7 hrs); to *Manzanillo* (c 16 hrs); etc.

Boat service from the quay to the *Isla de Ixtapa* (15km out to sea), a good day excursion. The island has small restaurants, a wildlife reserve (incl. parrots), and three beaches.

Hotels. Less expensive than in Ixtapa, and more homely. Along the beaches and further inland. Fully booked in season, especially at weekends. Less crowded midweek, Dec.–March.

Post Office. Near corner of Av. Morelos and C. Guerrero.

Tourist Office. Opposite Hotel Stouffer Presidente in Ixtapa.

At the entrance to the bay is a small island, *Roca Negra*. The beaches lining the bay are separated by rocky outcrops, the more remote best reached by taxi, or by boats which ply from the quay. The main beach, *Playa Zihuatanejo*, faces the town centre, and can become crowded. To the E is *Playa Madera*, small and secluded. *Playa de la Ropa*, on the SE side of the bay, is spacious and excellent for watersports. Above it is a pseudo-Parthenon, built by a recent chief of police from the illegal proceeds of his term of office; but which he has never been allowed to occupy. The subject of many wry Mexican jokes. On the S is the most remote of the beaches, *Las Gatas* (best reached by motorboat), ideal for a day's outing.

Méx. 200, marvellously set between mountains and lagoons and the Pacific, continues to (145km; r.) *Barra de Potosí* (noticeable surf), another resort in the making. From (167km) *Petatlán* (H,P) the road approaches the seashore and passes various non-resort beaches on the edge of the well-cultivated coastal plain. 210km *Papanoa* (c 5000 inhab.; H,R,P), popular with surfers, with a 15km stretch of strand around a beautiful bay. The road runs inland again to (265km) **Tecpan** (c 10,000 inhab.; 120m), native place of the Galeana family who played a prominent part in the war of Independence and were said to be descended from an English sailor shipwrecked on this coast. Hermenegildo Galeana (1764–1814), hero of various actions against the royalists, was one of Morelos's staunchest supporters. At (285km) *San Jerónimo* a road runs S to (9km) *Paraíso Escondido* (R) at the W end of the Laguna de Mitla. From 290km a new road N and NE crosses the sierra to (263km) *Chilpancingo*, see Rte 82. 331km *Coyuca de Benítez* (vast lagoon). The road runs N of the Laguna de Coyuca.

363km **ACAPULCO** (c 880,000 inhab.), one of the world's most famous and most powerful seaside attractions, is superbly set in the curved and sheltered Bahía de Acapulco, its sea a vivid blue, at a point where spurs of the Sierra Madre del Sur reach to the coast. Its variety of beaches, ranging from small and sheltered to large and pounded by Pacific rollers; its hot summer and temperate winter climates; its facilities for every kind of water sport; its luxury hotels and restaurants; and its vibrant, even frenetic, nightlife help to explain its unrivalled magnetism. It is also Mexico's best Pacific harbour and one of the world's finest anchorages.

Its importance as a port gives the inner part of town a less attractive aspect. The authorities, however, have undertaken general refurbishing and there are controls on further development.

Airport. 30km SE. Frequent flights to *Mexico City*; to *Oaxaca, Guadalajara, Mérida, Villahermosa*, etc.; and to *New York, Philadelphia, Toronto*, etc. Bus service to city centre (1 hr).

Bus stations. Corner of Avs Cuauhtémoc and Massieu, and 47 Av. Ejido. Frequent services to *Mexico City* (7 hrs); to *Tasco* (5 hrs); to *Cuernavaca* (6 hrs); to *Zihuatanejo* (5 hrs); to *Lázaro Cárdenas* (6 hrs); to *Puerto Escondido* (8 hrs); to *Chilpancingo* (3 hrs); etc.

Taxis. Constant service. Agree prices in advance. Limousines (up to five passengers sharing) from airport.

Hotels. Innumerable, ranging from very expensive (along Costera Miguel Alemán and the airport road beyond the bay to the S and E) to inexpensive (in the old town on the W side of the bay). Reasonably priced in older, family hotels above Caleta and Caletilla beaches S of the old town on W side of bay. Advance booking advisable, especially during Nov.–Apr.

Post Office. 125 Costera Miguel Alemán.

Tourist Offices. 187 and 4455 Costera Miguel Alemán.

British Consulate. At Hotel Las Brisas. **US Consulate.** At Club del Sol Hotel (corner of Costera Miguel Alemán and Av. de los Reyes Católicos). **Canadian Consulate.** At Club del Sol Hotel.

Cruises. Yachts leave from the piers on the W side of the bay for trips round the bay, to La Quebrada, and to Puerto Marqués. Glass-bottom boats run from Playa Caleta to Isla Roqueta.

Calandrias (horse-drawn carriages) may be hired for jaunts along Costera Miguel Alemán.

Acapulco, meaning 'conquered (or destroyed) place', was one of many small city-states conquered by the Aztec king Ahuitzotl (1486–1502) in his campaigns to reach the Pacific

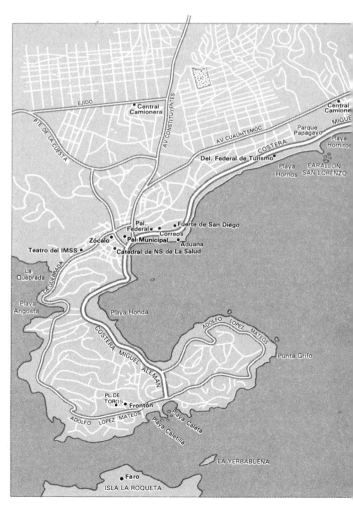

coastal ports. It was an important trading port throughout the Postclassic Period and also important in the diffusion of ideas from Central America and N South America, in particular metallurgy.

The excavated site of *Puerto Marqués* (late Incipient Agriculture Period) yielded fibre-tempered, pitted pottery (Pox Ware) similar to pottery from the Purrón Phase in the Valle de Tehuacán (2300–1500 BC) (cf. *Coxcatlán*). Figurines of a slightly later date include Olmecoid 'baby-face' forms. The region around Acapulco has also yielded pottery and figurines, of still later date, showing influence from Classic Maya styles: SE at *La Sabana* (near Ciudad Perdida) and NW along the coast at *San Jerónimo* (see above). Other partially excavated sites (no visible ruins) with similar finds include *Tecpan, Petatlán* (where there are some nearby cave paintings as well), and *Papanoa*.

A shipyard was established at the present site c 1528 and some sort of settlement may have existed by 1532 when the expedition of Diego Hurtado de Mendoza set sail from here to the

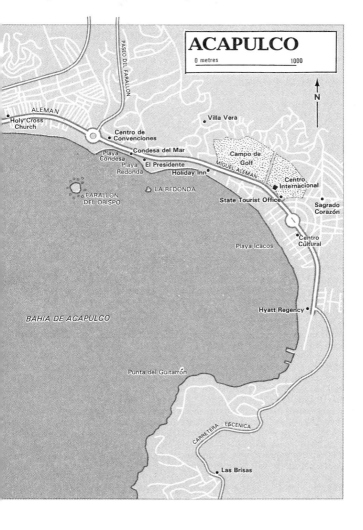

south seas. This was followed by those of Francisco de Ulloa to the N along the coast of Nueva Galicia, in search of the fabled lands of Quivira and Cíbola (1539), and of Domingo de Castillo, who made the first known map of the W coast (1540). The fleet of Miguel López de Legaspi set sail from Puerto de la Navidad in Nov. 1564 to explore the Philippines and to try to find the eastward passage back. On 3 Oct. 1565, one vessel, the 'San Pablo', beat its way back through the newly found eastward passage. On arrival at Acapulco only two of the depleted crew had the strength to stand up: the captain, Felipe de Salcedo, and the pilot, the aged Augustinian friar Andrés de Urdaneta.

Acapulco was the only port of departure and arrival of the yearly Pacific Galleon (Nao de China); it also received ships from Chile and Peru. In 1633 the Pacific fleet was fixed at four galleons, later reduced again to one (600–800 ton weight). Its arrival at Acapulco was occasion of rejoicing and a great market. It departed for the E full of merchandise from New Spain and the W. In 1615 and 1624 the Dutch, in hope of capturing a galleon, took the port. In 1742 Commodore George Anson in the 'Centurion', on his four-year voyage round the world, lay in wait outside the bay to intercept the galleon, the 'Covadonga', but was frustrated. (He later boarded and sacked it off the Philippine coast.)

Acapulco's decline dated from the 1780s, with the new route from the Philippines direct to Spain via the Indian Ocean and along the African coast. In 1846 the French traveller Gabriel Lafond de Lurcy wrote: 'the climate is frightful; a sky of bronze, a stifling heat, and no motion in the air'. Although in the 19C it functioned as a coal port, it remained isolated for more than a century. Its revival dates from the 1920s. Since the 1940s, however, thanks to the unflagging encouragement of Pres. Alemán (1900–83), who made his home here, its progress has been phenomenal.

The ZOCALO is the centre of the old town on the W of the bay. On it is the cathedral of *La Soledad*, oriental in aspect, built in the 1930s. From the E side of the Zócalo we come on to COSTERA MIGUEL ALEMAN and view the sweep of the bay. Here are the docks and piers from which local cruises leave.

A little to the NE (l.) is the **Fuerte de San Diego** (9–4.30; Sun., 9–3; closed Tues.), Acapulco's only historic monument, in the shape of a star, with bastions (baluartes) at each of the five points.

The first fort on the site (1615–17), by the Dutch engineer Adrian Boot, was damaged by earthquake in 1776. It was rebuilt in 1778–83 to the initial designs of Miguel Costansó, later modified by Ramón Panón. With the redirection of the Manila Galleon, however, its main purpose had already disappeared. In Jan. 1811 Morelos made his first attempt to capture it. On 5 Apr. 1813 he again laid siege, which ended on 19 Aug. when the Spanish garrison capitulated.

From the Zócalo, Calz. Quebrada climbs up to the cliffs of *La Quebrada*, on a narrow inlet near the Mirador hotel. From the cliffs, divers (clavadistas) launch themselves into the sea from a height of c 50m, timing their drop for exactly when the swell is at its deepest. At night they dive holding torches. A mirador (fee) a little further on offers a good view opposite the spectacle.

The continuation of Calz. Quebrada, Av. López Mateos, winds round the promontory, past the bullring, the Coliseo Arena (boxing and wrestling), and the jai alai frontón, to the two sheltered beaches *Caletilla* and *Caleta* (favoured by Mexican families) facing *Isla Roqueta* (more beaches). Near the NE tip of the islet is an underwater shrine to Our Lady of Guadalupe (seen from the glass-bottom boats which ply from Playa Caleta). On the E side of the promontory, in a sheltered series of small bays, are *Playas Larga, Honda*, and *Manzanillo*, still popular, part of the older Acapulco and first lighted upon during the 1930s.

Beyond the Fuerte de San Diego, Costera Miguel Alemán, main thoroughfare of the newer Acapulco, sweeps round the bay, a distance of 8–9km, before it merges on the E side with Carretera Escénica. Between it and the beaches are some of the more expensive hotels. The first beach, *Playa Hornos*, between the docks and the Hyatt Continental hotel, is popular in the late afternoon and with surfers. *Playa Condesa*, just E of the centre of the bay, is the most popular and crowded, fronting the Acapulco Continental, Condesa del Mar, El Presidente, and Holiday Inn hotels. The bar of the *Presidente*, by Juan Sordo Madaleno and

José Wieckers Escandón, finished in 1959, is decorated with designs by Salvador Dalí, meant for a nightclub, never built.

On the E curve of the bay is *Playa Icacos*, less crowded. To its N, behind the Holiday Inn, is the **Centro de Espectáculos, Convenciones y Exposiciones de Acapulco** (called *Centro Acapulco*), inaugurated in 1973, incl. expensive shops and restaurants; the *Teatro Ruiz de Alarcón*; the open-air *Teatro Nezahualcóyotl* for performances by the Ballet Folklórico and the vertiginous Voladores de Papantla; and a small *Museo Arqueológico* (guided visits 11–1; 4–6).

From the E side of the bay Carretera Escénica runs S past the naval base and the luxurious *Hotel Las Brisas*, in fact a cluster of pink villas (with a fleet of pink jeeps for guests to manoeuvre themselves about), round the headland to *Puerto Marqués*, a fashionable beach on yet another bay. Beyond is *Playa Revolcadero*, with strong surf, overlooked by hotels *Pierre Marqués* and *Princess*, its style recalling an Aztec pyramid.

Beyond La Quebrada (c 12km) is the beach of *Pie de la Cuesta*, not recommended for swimming because of strong undercurrents and danger of sharks, but possibly the best place to view the marvellous sunsets. N of Acapulco rises the *Cerro del Veladero* (900m), a worthwhile 3-hr steep walk, famous for its lemon trees and beautiful views.

31 Morelia

MORELIA (430,000 inhab.; 1941m), capital of the State of Michoacán, is beauti-fully set in the wide and fertile Valle de Guayangareo, watered by the Río Grande de Morelia. It is a stately and serene university city, full of dignified old buildings in rose-coloured trachyte which gives it a special hallmark and harmony. It is famous for its intellectual, literary, and musical traditions, and for its chocolate and confectionery. As befits the cradle of various distinguished Mexicans, the city is a national monument and all new building must conform to traditional style.

Airport. 27km NE of the centre. Flights to *Mexico City, Guadalajara*, and *Zacatecas*.

Bus station. Av. Eduardo Ruiz, between Cs León Guzmán and V. Gómez Farías. Services to *Pátzcuaro* (1½ hrs); to *Mexico City* (6 hrs); to *Celaya* (3 hrs); to *Acámbaro* (c 2 hrs); to *Querétaro* (c 4 hrs); to *Guadalajara* (5 hrs); to *Guanajuato* (4 hrs); etc.

Railway station. NW of the centre, in Av. de los Sindicatos, at the end of C. Guadalupe Victoria. Trains to *Uruapan, Pátzcuaro*, and *Mexico City*.

Hotels throughout the city.

Post Office. 369 Av. Madero Oriente, in Pal. Federal.

Tourist Office. 79 C. Nigromante, in Pal. Clavijero.

Fiestas. 30 Sept.: to honour birthday of José María Morelos.

A royal decree of Oct. 1537 provided for the founding of Valladolid. In 1541 Viceroy Antonio de Mendoza ordered the shifting of the 'city of Michoacán' from Pátzcuaro to Guayangareo. This in opposition to Vasco de Quiroga who was not impressed that, in the viceroy's opinion, the site fulfilled the seven Platonic conditions for an ideal city. 'A high bleak plain', he called it, 'a desert, windy, and barren of people, far from food and water'. His Spanish neighbours began to move to the new villa. In 1545 it became the 'city of Valladolid'. It always claimed the title 'city of Michoacán', which Pátzcuaro (and Vasco de Quiroga) refused to relinquish. During the 18C growth was spurred on by outstanding bishops: Juan José de Escalona y Calatayud (1729–37) whose building activities were matched by his extraordinary charity; benefactions equalled by Antonio de San Miguel (1784–1804), called 'padre de los pobres', who lavished the bishopric's substantial income on the building of the aqueduct—'the sensible way to give alms is to promote public works'—and of workers' housing, and was indefatigable in his efforts to relieve the suffering caused by famine and epidemics in 1785–86 and smallpox in 1798, when he fearlessly ministered to the sick and dying.

The city counted as a cultural and intellectual centre. The great Jesuit philosopher Clavijero; the theologian José Pérez Calema; San Miguel himself, admirer of Adam Smith; the forceful churchman Manuel Abad y Queipo, admirer of Rousseau; and, professor of theology and rector of San Nicolás, Miguel Hidalgo—all represented the 'Ilustración

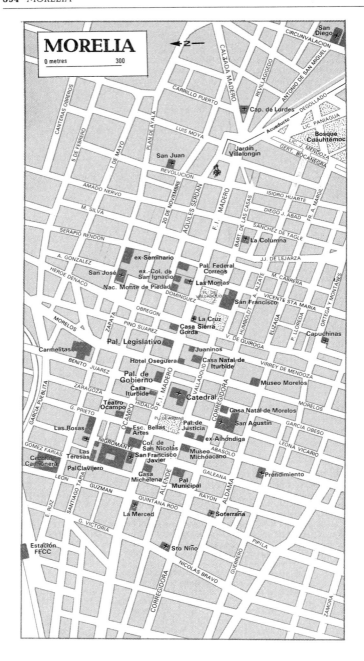

MORELIA

0 metres | 300

San Diego
CIRCUNVALACION
ANTONIO DE SAN MIGUEL
REVILLAGIGEDO
CALZADA MADERO
CARRILLO PUERTO
CANTERAS OBREROS
DEGOLLADO
LIC. PANIAGUA
Cáp. de Lurdes
Acueducto
Bosque Cuauhtémoc
LIC. J. MENDOZA
GERT. BOCANEGRA
Jardín Villalongín
LUIS MOYA
PLAN DE AYALA
5 DE FEBRERO
6 DE FEBRERO
1 DE MAYO
San Juan
REVOLUCION
AMADO NERVO
ISIDRO HUARTE
M. SILVA
20 DE NOVIEMBRE
AQUILES SERDAN
MADERO
F. I.
DIEGO J. ABAD
FR. A. MARGIL
SERAPIO RENDON
SANCHEZ DE TAGLE
BART. DE LAS CASAS
La Columna
A. GONZALEZ
ex-Seminario
JJ. DE LEJARZA
HEROE DENACO
San José
ex.-Col. de San Ignacio
Pal. Federal Correos
Las Monjas
M. CABRERA
Nac. Monte de Piadad
DOMINGUEZ
PAL. DE VALLADOLID
San Francisco
STA. MARIA
VICENTE
ORTEGA Y MONTAÑES
OBREGON
ALZATE
MORELOS
ZAPATA
PINO SUAREZ
La Cruz
Casa Sierra Gorda
V. DE QUIROGA
HUMBOLDT
ELIZAGA
P. LLOREDA
Capuchinas
Pal. Legislativo
Juaninos
Carmelitas
Hotel Oseguera
Casa Natal de Iturbide
VIRREY DE MENDOZA
BENITO JUAREZ
Pal. de Gobierno
Casa Iturbide
VALLADOLID
Museo Morelos
MORELOS
ZARAGOZA
G. PRIETO
GARCIA PUEBLITA
Teatro Ocampo
F. I. MADERO
HIDALGO
Catedral
CORREGIDORA
Casa Natal de Morelos
CAMPO
Esc. Bellas Artes
PLD ARMAS
Pal. de Justicia
San Agustín
GARCIA OBESO
Las Rosas
NIGROMANTE
Col. de San Nicolas
ex-Alhóndiga
ABASOLO
LEONA VICARIO
GOMEZ FARIAS
Las Teresas
San Francisco Javier
Museo Michoacano
Central Camionera
Pal Clavijero
Casa Michelena
Pal Municipal
GALEANA
Prendimiento
ALLENDE
ALDAMA
LEON
GUZMAN
SANTIAGO TAPIA
RAYON
QUINTANA ROO
La Merced
Soterraña
E. RUIZ
G. VICTORIA
Estación FFCC
PIPILA
Sto Niño
NICOLAS BRAVO
GUERRERO
CORREGIDORA
ZAMORA

Michoacana'. In 1809 a group of creoles plotted in Valladolid the Independence of New Spain, but their plans were nipped in the bud. It is said that the young Agustín de Iturbide joined them only to betray them. During 15–20 Oct. 1810, Hidalgo (excommunicated by Abad y Queipo) and his troops occupied the city (Allende had to use cannon to bring to heel a rampaging mob whose spoils were later publicly auctioned); he returned briefly in Nov. before proceeding to Guadalajara. In Dec. 1813 Morelos attacked Valladolid, but was beaten off with heavy losses by Iturbide. After the signing of the Plan of Iguala, Iturbide entered Valladolid in triumph on 20 May 1821 after a ten-day siege. In 1824 the city became capital of the new State of Michoacán; four years later its name was changed to Morelia in honour of its most famous son. In 1842 Fanny Calderón de la Barca admired 'the wide and airy streets, the fine houses, the handsome public buildings...the climate is delightful', and in 1860, to Mathieu de Fossey it was 'without doubt the best built little town in the republic'. The imperialists, at first under Gen. Márquez, occupied Morelia in 1863–67. In 1928–32 it was headquarters of Gen. Lázaro Cárdenas, whose chief task was to repair the damage caused by the Cristero rebellion.

The State of **Michoacán** (59,864 sq km; 3.8 million inhab.) includes some of the republic's most beautiful country: its mountains, lakes, fertile valleys, and largely unspoiled coastline providing an unforgettable landscape. The N area bordering on Jalisco and Guanajuato occupies the W of the great central plateau (Mesa Central; Mesa de Anáhuac). Two huge mountain ranges cross it in the centre and S. The first forms part of the central volcanic range (Sierra Volcánica Transversal) and runs E to W across the State, branching out into many lesser ranges. It dips S of Uruapan into the tierra caliente, beyond which, in the S and SE, rises the Sierra Madre del Sur, a barrier between it and the Pacific. Michoacán counts three great river systems. The Río Lerma, with numerous tributaries, in the NE and N marking the border with Guanajuato and Jalisco before discharging into the Lago de Chapala. The Río Balsas in the S, forming the border with Guerrero, its basin an area of large-scale irrigation, centred on Presa el Infiernillo, which also captures the Río Tepalcatepec running SE from Jalisco through the tierra caliente. The lakes of the N and central regions, the numerous reservoirs, and abundant natural springs make Michoacán's water resources among the most abundant in Mexico. Hydroelectric works generate power for a wide area beyond the State itself.

By 1570 Michoacán, an enormous territory then, comprising the present State and parts of today's San Luis Potosí, Guanajuato, Jalisco, Guerrero, and Tamaulipas, formed one of the five largest of the 40 provinces of New Spain. In 1786, with the reorganization of the government, the present area fell within the intendancy of Valladolid. It played an important part in the pre-Independence and Independence movements, and some of the most famous protagonists in the drama were natives or intimately connected with it. In 1824 Michoacán became one of the 19 States of the new federal republic, its area to be modified by later boundary changes. Melchor Ocampo (late 1840s) and Santos Degollado (1857–58), who provided a refuge for the liberal government forced out of Mexico City, were notable radical governors. In 1863–67 the imperialists, supported by Church and aristocracy, had some success and their able general, Ramón Méndez, fought his battles here. Violence after the Revolution and during the Cristero rebellion was brought under control by Lázaro Cárdenas (governor 1928–32).

The ample PL. DE ARMAS is deeply shaded by laurel trees (*Jardín de los Mártires*) and framed on three sides by the portales of its various houses. The W arcade is known as *Portal de Matamoros*, scene of the execution of Mariano Matamoros in Feb. 1814; those on the S as *Portal de Aldama* and *Portal de Allende*; those on the N as *Portal de Iturbide* and *Portal de Hidalgo*. In the latter, in May 1812, the insurgent priest José Guadalupe Salto, his body mangled by torture, was executed. Along the N side of the plaza runs AV. MADERO, former *Calle Real*, Morelia's main thoroughfare and bordered by some of its finest buildings.

On the E side rises the cathedral of **La Transfiguración de Cristo**, pride of Morelia and beautifully set off in the space created by this plaza, by Pl. Melchor Ocampo on its far (E) side (both 19C developments), and by the atrio enclosed by metal railings. Of immense dignity and harmony, despite long gestation and amalgam of styles, it had great influence on the building of other churches both in the city and in the surrounds.

The plan, approved c 1660, of this third cathedral on the site, is by Vicente Barroso de la Escayola (Vicenzo Varrocio Escallola), an Italian architect. Building began in 1672–74; some advance was made after 1683, under Barroso (with Pedro de Guedea). Later architects (after Barroso's death in 1694) were Juan de Silva, Juan de Cepeda, and Lucas Durán. Dedication took place in 1705; the main façade was still in progress in 1717; the façades and towers were finished in 1744 under José de Medina. Various annexes were done in 1765, but the interior took several more years to complete. In 1858 it was stripped, on the orders of Governor Epitacio Huerta, of almost all its silver, gold, and other wealth: altar decorations; railings; pulpits; and precious stones, worth half a million pesos. In 1880 and 1898 further drastic modifications were made.

EXTERIOR. Although the bulk of the building is low, an illusion of height is given by the superb towers (c 61m), the clerestory of the nave, and the numerous finials above the upper balustrade; and of lightness by the marvellous pinkish-brown trachyte fabric. Dominating features are the overall use of the pilaster and not the column, and of tableros (rectangular panels of varying shapes standing out from, or hollowed into, the façades). The atrio railings (1854) and gates are by Domingo Garfías. The bases of the towers, their huge urn motifs betokening the neoclassical, stand forward of and emphasize the main (N) façade. This is in three vertical sections, with a sense of hierarchy, the main-door storeys higher than those of the two side doors. On a firmly classical base are developed Mannerist, baroque, and tentatively churrigueresque variations. Either side of the main door the niches contain statues of SS Peter (l.) and Paul; above them, medallions of SS John and Matthew. The lambrequins under the ionic pilaster capitals, the niches, and the pilaster bases are a churrigueresque touch, repeated on the towers. The second storey contains the Adoration of the Magi (l.), the Transfiguration (centre), and the Adoration of the Shepherds (r.) in high relief; SS Michael and John the Baptist occupy the niches; above them, SS Mark and Luke in medallions. Note how the oval windows cause the cornice gently to curve and thus break the horizontality. The upper storey is a more adventurous flourish: curvetting cornices, volutes, and stepped mouldings, and two estípites. The central relief represents the Seven Sorrows; in the more elaborate niches are SS Barbara and Rose.

The E and W doorways resemble the main side doorways. The former has a central relief of Our Lady of Guadalupe, the latter of St Joseph holding the infant Christ, guarded by the Holy Ghost, and attended by delightful angels. Next to the E tower is the *Sagrario*, manifested by its cupola; further along the E wall, the *Cap. de las Animas*, a late 18C addition, with a mixtilinear doorway. Next to the W tower is the *Sala Capitular*, a 19C addition. The main, tiled cupola (1715) is the work of Juan Antonio de la Cruz. At the SW end, forming an angle with the W wall, is the *Mitra* (late 18C; offices of the bishopric), with a charming cloister and squat cupola, its drum supported by slender buttresses, above the main stair.

The INTERIOR, with nave and side aisles, once magnificently furnished, but still bathed in warm light through slender window panels of translucent marble, was drastically altered in 1843–44 when the baroque side-altars were removed to make way for the present ones, in neoclassical style, by Luis Zapari; and the present high altar, whose silver tabernacle is one invaluable 18C survival, was put in place. In 1880 the whole was redecorated in shades of gold and brown, and in 1898 the choir and the Altar del Perdón, once, Spanish-style, at the N end of the nave, were removed, thus freeing the latter from obstruction. The huge old organ (1732), high at the N end, also removed from the nave, displays magnificently carved casing complete with estípite supports graced by angel musicians. At the S end of the E aisle is the altarpiece of the Señor de la Sacristía, a venerable image in caña de maíz, said to be the gift of Philip II. In the Sagrario (off E aisle, N end) a painting of the Virgin and Child is attr. Cabrera. Off the E aisle is the *Cap. de las Animas*, containing a mural (1766): an allegory of Our Lady of Guadalupe, Souls in Purgatory, and the Mendicant Orders, shedding an interesting light on 18C society in New Spain.

Off the S end of the W aisle is the former sacristy. In the space leading from it to the atrio are two paintings: Our Lord and the Doctors in the Temple, and the Circumcision (anon.; both probably early 17C); and St Mary Magdalen (early 18C).

At the N end of the Portal de Matamoros, at the corner of Av. Madero, is the *Hotel Virrey de Mendoza*. This and the next-door house at No. 346 Av. Madero Poniente were made into a sumptuous residence by Vicente Romero y Valle in 1779, incorporating materials originally earmarked for the Cathedral. From

1831 it belonged to the Gómez de Soria family who sold it in 1938, when it was reconditioned as a hotel.

On its S side, 48 Portal de Matamoros, now a cinema, dates from the 17C, but was much altered after 1773 and its sale to Juan Manuel de Michelena. On 14 Oct. 1864 a ball in honour of Maximilian was given here by the then owner, Vicente Sosa.

On the opposite side of Av. Madero, C. Guillermo Prieto leads N. No. 57 (l.) was, it is supposed, the residence of Manuel Abad y Queipo (1751–1825), where he issued sentence of excommunication against Hidalgo. On the l., at the corner with C. Melchor Ocampo, is the *Escuela de Bellas Artes*, a house built in 1737 for Miguel Romero López de Arvizu, precentor of the Cathedral. The central balcony, above the grandiose main doorway, shows the arms of the Espinosa, Contreras, and Justis families, all connected with 18C owners. Diagonally opposite in C. Prieto is the *Teatro Ocampo*, built in 1828–29, rebuilt in 1869–70 by a Polish engineer, Jan Bochotnicki, using material salvaged from the Cap. de la Tercera Orden of San Francisco, and modernized in 1962.

One block further N, at the corner with C. Santiago Tapia, we come to a pleasant garden plaza adorned by statues of Vasco de Quiroga and Cervantes. On its N side, complete with its upper-storey arcade, is the former **Colegio de Sta Rosa María**, earliest conservatory of music in America.

It was founded in 1743 by Bp Francisco Matos Coronado for orphan girls in the former convent of Sta Catalina. The present building, dating from 1746–56, owes its construction to Bp Martín de Elizacoechea. Here the boarders, who had to be legitimate and of 'pure blood', and who later included the daughters of Isidro Huarte (see below), received the general education then considered suitable for girls, under the supervision of Dominican nuns, and special instruction in music from masters from the Cathedral school. In 1862 the college was closed. After being put to various uses (in the early 1880s it was at the same time both a hospice for poor women and an infantry barracks), since the 1940s it has housed a music school founded by the composer Miguel Bernal Jiménez (1910–56), also an expert in plainchant and polyphony. Among the pupils are the Niños Cantores de Morelia, also first formed by Bernal Jiménez, a famous boys' choir.

On its W side is the church of **Las Rosas**, built to accompany the college and dedicated in 1757.

EXTERIOR. The twin portals facing S and divided by a decorative buttress exhibit interesting, and winning, detail. The lowest storeys are marked by characteristic pilasters and tableros. Above the cornice are horizontal panels containing reliefs of St Rose holding the infant Christ, flanked by an angel and a saint (l.) and the Holy Family (r.). The second-storey windows are framed by stubby ionic pilasters and caryatids sprouting tails of foliation. The topmost storey, below stepped gables, contains delightful, if ingenuous, medallions of SS Firminius and Francis Xavier (l.) and SS Martin and Teresa of Avila (r.) beneath God the Father and the Holy Ghost.

The INTERIOR has been dulled by 19C renovation, but the small coro bajo has been preserved, its arch filled by attractively patterned wrought iron. The two side altarpieces and high altarpiece span churrigueresque and anastyle. The latter is a work of great delicacy, covered in foliated relief, with retiring, lacily ornamented pilasters instead of estípites in the lower central section. In the sacristy is a painting of the Holy Trinity (c 1750) by Francisco Martínez.

Opposite the church is the **Teatro Rubén Romero**, until 1767 the domestic chapel of the Jesuits, on the N side of their monumental headquarters, and during 1824–57 of the discalced Carmelite nuns. In 1962 it was transformed, with new façade and staircase, to its present use. Next door is the former convent of *Las Teresitas*, founded in 1824 for discalced Carmelite nuns in what had been the Jesuit *Casa de Ejercicios*. From here C. Gómez Farías runs N to the *Central Camionera*, on the site of the *Beaterio de Carmelitas*, founded by Ana María del Tránsito y Silva c 1765 as a retreat for pious women professing the Carmelite rule. On the eve of its suppression in 1861 the community numbered 'thirteen ladies who wore the habit, and more than 60 girls and servants, all living in greatest poverty'. The surviving chapel, now forming part of the station, dates from the early 19C.

From Las Rosas, C. Nigromante runs S to Av. Madero. Almost all its r. (E) side is taken up by the grand **Pal. de Clavijero**, renowned for the noble simplicity of its lines, begun in 1660 as the house and college of the Jesuits. The fine main portal ends in a baroque gable.

After their expulsion in 1767 it continued as a seminary. In Nov. 1810, 84 Spaniards were held here before being executed on Hidalgo's orders. In Dec., 170 more Spaniards took refuge within its walls. They were saved from the attentions of a murderously inclined mob by the quick thinking of Canon Jacinto Llanos y Valdés, who appeared displaying a monstrance holding the Blessed Sacrament and thus cowed the rioters who immediately dropped their weapons. After Independence the first sessions of the new State congress were held here. Today it is given over to offices of the State government. The impressive principal patio has seven arches a side fronting the lower walks. The pilasters are marked by tableros of varying shapes. In the former college garden (to the W) is the *Mercado de Dulces Regionales*, for sweets and desserts.

At its S end is the former church of **San Francisco Javier** (or *La Compañía*; 1660), fronting C. Nigromante. Its broad façade has fluted pilasters. Its SE tower bears the honorary date 1582, commemorating the arrival of the Jesuits. Today it houses the public library.

On the opposite side of C. Nigromante is the imposing **Colegio de San Nicolás de Hidalgo**, once the glory of Valladolid, now heir to one of Mexico's most famous seats of learning.

On its removal from Pátzcuaro in 1580 the Colegio de San Nicolás merged with the Franciscan Colegio de San Miguel. In 1767–70 Miguel Hidalgo was a pupil here; in 1773 he returned as a member of the teaching staff; in 1787 he was named treasurer, secretary, and vice-rector; and in 1790–92 held the rectorship. In 1791 José María Morelos became a pupil, 'exalted above almost all his fellows'. In 1799 the composer José Mariano Elízaga (1786–1842), the 'Mexican Mozart', was appointed organist. In 1810–46 the college was closed, but in 1847 was reopened by Melchor Ocampo (whose heart and books are its honoured possessions) as the Colegio Primitivo y Nacional de San Nicolás de Hidalgo. Its new-found prestige owed much to the work of the new secretary, Santos Degollado. In 1869–72 the simple 17–18C edifice was remodelled in a mixture of afrancesado and neoclassical by the Belgian architect Guillaume Wodon de Sorinne. Further restoration took place in 1931 and 1969. Since 1917 it has formed part of the University of Michoacán.

The boldly framed windows and fluted pilasters of the façade (the main on Av. Madero) contrast with the rubble masonry of walls and parapet. The interior is grouped around four patios of diminishing size, and has kept much of its original character.

On the S side of Av. Madero Poniente, opposite the S side of the church of San Francisco Javier, No. 398, at the corner with C. Galeana, is an interesting house first mentioned in 1649 and lived in by capitulars of the Cathedral until 1792; then renovated by its hacendado possessor Angel Vélez y Morantes, and in the 19C. No. 414, **Casa Michelena** (late 17C) has a handsome façade and spacious patio.

It was rebuilt by Canon Antonio Belaunzarán y Rodríguez, who bought it in 1790. In Oct. 1810 it lodged Hidalgo. In 1822 it was acquired by José Mariano Michelena, first Mexican minister in London, who lived here until his death in 1853. From 1880 it housed the Monte de Piedad. It is now the *Escuela Preparatoria Melchor Ocampo*.

No. 454, now *Casa del Estudiante*, dates from the 1780s.

Hence in 1812 José Guadalupe Salto was taken to his execution on a stretcher. During the Calles regime it sheltered Catholic prisoners destined for execution.

No. 508, much altered, dates from 1750–60 and still gives an idea of its fine original windows. No. 485, opposite, dates from 1744. In the next turning S, C. Quintana Roo, is the church and former convent of **La Merced**, interesting for its portals.

The Mercedarians arrived in Valladolid c 1604 when Pedro de Burgos and Alonso García bought a house on the site. The church was not finished until 1736. The former convent is now a school.

The N portal, with Tuscan pilasters and broken pediment, is in the Renaissance tradition, but is probably 18C work. The main, unfinished, E façade is a surprising contrast: the vigorous, crude estípites of the lower storey have centrepieces so cubelike that any idea of an inverted pyramid is almost lost. The magnificent wooden doors combine Mudéjar panelling with Renaissance and baroque foliation, and saintly (Peter Nolasco and Raymond Nonnatus) relief. The interior was redone, neoclassically, by Teofano López in 1908.

Following C. Quintana Roo S, we meet C. Allende.

One block W in the next turning S, C. Corregidora, is *El Sto Niño*, a privately built church (early 18C).

At the corner with C. Galeana (r.) is the handsome **Pal. Municipal**.

It was begun in 1781 as the *Real Factoría del Tabaco* on the authority of Roque Yáñez, manager of the royal revenues. Here in 1810 Hidalgo signed a decree abolishing slavery. In 1846 Governor Melchor Ocampo chose it as his residence. The exterior has fine windows and balconies. A notable feature of the patio is the lack of column support for the corner arches, which adds a light touch, much in contemporary taste.

Further along, on the SW corner of Cs Allende (No. 305) and Abasolo, is the **Casa Huarte**.

It dates, in one-storey form, from the early 18C. In 1772 it was bought by Isidro Huarte, political mentor of Agustín de Iturbide. He largely demolished it to raise the present two-storey edifice, ready in 1775. Here he lived with his second wife, Ana Manuela Muñiz y Sánchez de Tagle, and their children. His third daughter, Ana María (1786–1861), was to marry Iturbide in 1805. In 1851 it passed to Manuel María Malo, who made it into one of the most luxurious residences of the day. Maximilian stayed here in Oct. 1864. 'He was deliriously acclaimed by so many people', wrote Malo's wife, Francisca Román. She also wrote of her feelings when Maximilian appointed her lady in waiting to the empress: 'it filled me with satisfaction; and I was much talked about and envied in this city'. After various uses it was made over to the Museo Michoacano in 1939 and extensively restored in 1975–78.

The **Museo Michoacano** (Tues.–Sat., 9–7; Sun., 9–3; fee) is the State's most complete archaeological and historical collection.

The staircase faces the main doorway across the central patio. Its double entrance arch, without central support, is crowned by a statue of St Antony, with a winged cherub beneath its pedestal. On the rear side is carved a complex floral motif incorporating the date 1775. In the courtyard are several stone sculptures from the site of Ihuatzio (Rte 28): two chacmools, representing Curitz-caheri (Tarascan high priests); two quadrupeds representing messengers from paradise, and a feline in Teotihuacano style from Los Alzati; a stele with inscribed glyphs of the morning star (Venus)—'messenger of the sun'—and Ozomatli, the sign for the 20th Náhuatl day, signifying 'monkey'.

On the staircase walls is a mural by Alfredo Zalce, 'Cuauhtémoc and History' (1951), an emotive, deeply-felt work by Michoacán's most famous muralist. His theme: that the conquest of Mexico did not stop with Cortés, but has been continuing ever since; with would-be oppressors and exploiters threatening Mexico. In the centre, Cuauhtémoc confronts Cortés, with La Malinche, seen as a whore, and forces of reaction (l.); the insurgents (a protective Hidalgo and resolute Morelos) are on the r. Behind Cuauhtémoc, a monster eagle with horrific claws appears in the fumes of an atomic explosion and confronts a metallic serpent. On the r. wall, liberal and revolutionary figures, incl. Melchor Ocampo, Juárez, Madero, Zapata, Carranza, and Cárdenas; and the Niños Héroes. On the l. wall, the opposition of the peasantry to armed repression.

We mount to the upper floor. SALA DE ARQUEOLOGIA. On the wall is a second mural by Zalce, 'Fray Alonso de la Veracruz' (1952), showing the illustrious Augustinian missionary, who founded the convent at Tiripetío, teaching his Tarascan pupils.

The room contains artefacts and panels illustrating the prehistoric cultures of Michoacán. Photographs and maps show the general ecology and regional geography of the State. Displays illustrate specific sites. Diagrams of the shaft-tomb burials at El Opeño, and cases containing lithic tools, pottery, and figurines from Chupícuaro. Exhibit of the excavations at Loma de Sta María. Tarascan smoking implements, the purpose of which was to feed the gods with food (smoke), which went up to heaven. Caracol- and conch-shell adornment, from both the Gulf Coast and the Pacific, illustrating the ancient participation of Western Mexican Cultures in long-distance trade; included are necklaces, bracelets, pectorals, rings, bangles, and earspools; jadeite and other stone jewellery, and shell musical instruments, spoons, punches, and other tools. From the 'Military Period' (from c AD 1000) are stone axe-heads and obsidian work, at which the Tarascans excelled, plus objects for ritual sacrifice, and ornaments of turquoise and gold, and other metal artefacts.

The SALA DE ETNOGRAFIA illustrates the changes to Michoacano society since the Spanish Conquest. There are various maps and explanation panels, and the room is semi-divided into displays on life-sized frames, of costume and accompanying artefacts from various regions of the State.

SALA DE LOS SIGLOS XVI Y XVII. 16C treatises: Treatise on the Sacraments (1527), with Alonso de la Veracruz's own annotations; his 'Speculum Coniugiorum' (1572 edn). Fragments of 16C codices: 'Códice de Chilchota'; 'Códice de Carapan', enumerating for the benefit of the Spaniards the rights of Indian landowners. Portraits of 16C Franciscans and Augustinians. 17C anon. paintings. Arms and armour. Crucifixes. SALAS DEL SIGLO XVIII. 18C furniture and portraits, incl. portraits of nuns, among them Sor María Francisca de los Angeles, one of the founders of Sta Rosa in Querétaro. SALA DE LOS SIGLOS XVIII Y XIX, with its original beamed ceiling. 18–19C furniture and paintings. Its main attraction is a famous and colossal anon. painting (10m long) which shows the translation of the Dominican nuns of the convent of Sta Catalina to their new premises in the C. Real on 3 May 1738. It offers a fascinating and lively picture of contemporary religious and social life: all Valladolid taking part in the great event. The nuns, escorted by priests, process two by two into their new church. Behind the last pair, a priest holds the Blessed Sacrament beneath a canopy. Behind him come the civil authorities, preceded by macebearers and representatives of the city aristocracy. Their richly dressed womenfolk watch from balconies. Members of all the religious orders, displaying statues of their patron saints on litters, also watch. In the foreground Indians celebrate with music and dance.

Among 19C furniture and paintings here and in the adjoining small room are the candelabrum ordered from Paris by Manuel María Malo to adorn his house for Maximilian's visit; works by Félix Parra (El Cazador) and Manuel Ocaranza (La Flor Envenenada); and miniatures of 19C statesmen and insurgents. The ground-floor rooms contain paintings by the local artists Mariano de Jesús Torres (b. 1838; illuminating and delightfully ingenuous views of Morelia) and Félix Parra (1845–1919; sketches and watercolours). Temporary exhibitions are also held here.

The house opposite, No. 98 Portal de Matamoros, dates from the 1720s and was from 1779 the home of the parents of Hidalgo's ally, the intendente José María Anzorena. It was transformed in the mid-19C.

At the SW corner of Pl. de Armas is the **Pal. de Justicia**, the former casas consistoriales (seat of viceregal local government), dating from 1682–95, but largely rebuilt, in handsome eclectic style, by Wodon de Sorinne in 1883–95. The beautiful baroque arches of the main patio, lacking corner supports on the lower floor, were left untouched in the rebuilding. No. 237 C. Allende (1730–32; but much altered), alongside, was the birthplace (1772) of José Mariano Michelena. An annexe on the S side of the Pal. de Justicia once served as the city gaol, built c 1750, though much restored. In 1774 its rebuilding was decreed: 'since it is public knowledge and well known that it has become so badly secured that criminals may easily climb out—as has happened on not a few occasions'. The same decree ordered the erection of the *Alhóndiga* (public grain store), next door at the corner of C. Abasolo with C. Corregidora (No. 694). It was converted into a prison in 1874, but is now a kindergarten.

Two blocks S along C. Abasolo is *El Prendimiento*, a small 18C church, thoroughly restored in neo-Romanesque style early this century.

On the S side of the Alhóndiga, C. Abasolo skirts the W side of the plaza which was once the atrio of the Augustinian convent and is now occupied by a food and drink market, the *Mercado Hidalgo*. On the E side are the church and former convent buildings of **San Agustín**.

Founded as *Sta María de Gracia* in 1548–50 by Alonso de la Veracruz at the licence of Vasco de Quiroga, the convent was not properly completed until the 17C, although the church façade is of the plateresque type well established in Michoacán. The interior was done over, 'con buen gusto', and new altars put in, under Rafael Peña, in 1835–40. The choir contains four paintings of scenes from the Life of St Augustine (c 1682) by Diego Becerra. Note the assured detailing of the clothing and jewels of the gentlemen carrying the saint's corpse in the Burial of St Augustine. The convent buildings were misused as a tenement after the friars had been expelled during the Reform. Restoration took place in 1930. In use as a student hostel, they keep some 16C work, especially the windows.

On the S side of the presbytery are the sacristy and antesacristy, through which may be reached the old sacristy, now converted into a chapel, with an antechapel, its original 16C vault painted with 17C frescoes of the Passion and of the Trinity, and incorporating the signs of the zodiac, rediscovered in 1933. Among the collection of 17–18C paintings in this ensemble are Alonso de la Veracruz teaching (antesacristy; anon., probably 18C, but in earlier style); and a Calvary (chapel), Christ condemned, and Christ stripped of his garments (both antechapel), interesting and naive works (1732–36) by the Indian artist Manuel Xavier Tapia.

On the W side of the plaza, the *Hotel Central*, built as a hostelry by the Augustinians, dates from c 1810.

E of the church, at the corner of Cs Corregidora and García Obeso, is the **Casa Natal de Morelos**, dating from 1650, the house where José María Morelos was born on 30 Sept. 1765.

His mother, doña Juana Pérez Pavón y de Estrada, was surprised by labour pains while walking in the street and was taken into the nearest house for the birth. In the 19C it was converted into a hospice by the Augustinians, and its new use caused alterations which lost it its primitive character. It is now a library and cultural centre.

One block further E, C. Corregidora meets C. Morelos Sur. To the S, at No. 323, is the **Casa Museo de Morelos** (Tues.–Sun., 9–1, 4–6), built in 1758.

It was sold in 1801 for 1830 pesos by Juan Martínez to Morelos, who added the second storey in 1805–06. His sister, Antonia, and her husband, Miguel Cervantes, lived here until the insurgent successes of 1810–11 provoked attacks on and dismantling of the building, and caused them to flee. They returned after Independence. Their grandson, Francisco Pérez Dueñas y Cervantes, sold the house to the State in 1910.

Its present aspect dates from remodelling in 1838–40 and restoration in 1934. The museum contains mementoes of the hero, incl. the bandage that covered his eyes at his execution in 1815.

C. Soto Soldaña continues E from the house, crossing C. Virrey de Mendoza, No. 192 in which (l.) has a good 18C portal, to C. Vasco de Quiroga, which runs S to Pl. de las Capuchinas. On its S side stands the church called **Las Capuchinas**, its slender Mannerist portal panel finished off with pronounced floral relief around and above the gracefully curving gable—slenderness repeated in the tower, notable for rich mouldings and balconies, even though too tall for the body of the church.

It belonged to a convent of Poor Clares of the strict rule dedicated to *Nuestra Señora de Cosmaloapan* and founded by nuns from the convents of Sta Clara and Corpus Christi in Mexico City in 1737. The nuns returned briefly during the second empire after having been expelled in 1863. In 1883 a hospital was installed in the convent (E side of the church; what remains is now a school), but 'the prevailing wind from the south wafted infection towards the city centre'.

The INTERIOR has kept its beautiful churrigueresque altarpieces. The two on either side of the nave, similar in design, contain paintings of the Life of Our Lady (W wall) and the Passion (E). The niches of that in the W transept have lost their original statues.

Returning along C. Vasco de Quiroga we come to PL. VALLADOLID, occupying the site of the atrio and cemetery of the former convent of **San Francisco**, which stands on the E side.

First called *San Buenaventura*, it was established in 1546, but only completed, with a subvention of 400 ducats from the Crown, at the beginning of the 17C after the original church had been demolished. After 1565 it was the chief house of the Franciscan friars of the province of San Pedro y San Pablo de Michoacán. It was repaired (in fact, sadly interfered with) in 1828 and in the 1880s Wodon de Sorinne started to make a hotel of it, but soon abandoned the idea. Some restoration took place in 1948. In 1967–68 the plaza, hitherto spoiled by intrusive market buildings, was cleared. The convent was restored in 1970.

The W façade of the church, with shell and floral motifs around the arch rim, is in the temperate plateresque mode favoured in the region. (It is dated 1610, so is something of an anachronism.) Much of the interior is of the 20C, but the choirstalls date from 1746. The convent buildings are entered by the five-arched portería and show interesting 16C medievalizing work, especially the ogee windows and little service doorways on the S side. They are now a flourishing **Casa de Artesanías**, where Michoacán handicrafts may be admired and bought.

From the N side of the church C. Fray Bartolomé de las Casas goes E past No. 310 (r.), attractive one-storey house preserving 18C elements, to *El Señor de la Columna*, an 18C chapel, its interior refurbished in 1938.

On the W side of the plaza C. Valladolid leads back to Pl. de Armas. No. 79 is the house in which Iturbide was born on 27 Sept. 1783.

It dates from the 17C, but was much altered in the 18C and again in 1965. In 1768 it was bought by José de Arregui y Gastelú, canon of the Cathedral, great-uncle to Iturbide. His exhausted mother, Josefa Arámburu, in labour for four days and almost given up for dead, invoked the intercession of Fray Diego de Basalenque, an early 17C prior of San Agustín, and the child duly arrived. A little further W, at 63 C. Allende, on the S side of the Cathedral, is the site of the city's first hospital, called *Hospital Real del Nombre de Jesús*, founded in the later 16C, which remained here until 1700. The present edifice keeps an 18C style, though only the main patio has been preserved.

From the N side of Pl. de Armas we follow Av. Madero Poniente eastwards. Facing the plaza, in the Portal de Hidalgo, are Nos. 251 and 241, the *Hotel Valladolid*, both adapted 18C houses. No. 229, the *Hotel Casino*, and its adjoining house on the corner with C. Ignacio Zaragoza, were the property from 1735 and 1685 respectively of members of the Peredo family, but both were transformed in the mid-19C.

At No. 84 C. Zaragoza the old house where the *Hotel de la Soledad* now stands was acquired by the Alvarez de Eulate family in 1735. They re-erected the lower floor, but got no further. By the 1750s the house was an inn. Modernization began in 1944.

No. 171 Av. Madero, now the **Casa Herrejón**, occupies the site of the house built in the late 16C for Pedro de Villela, one of Valladolid's earliest inhabitants. It was rebuilt for Manuel de la Bárcena (1769–1830), one of the Council of Regency in 1821 and archdeacon of the Cathedral. It was later lived in by Pelagio Antonio de Labastida y Dávalos, future abp of Mexico, when rector of the seminary in the 1850s. No. 157, once house of Mariano de Berrospe, regidor (councillor) perpetuo de Valladolid, dates from 1726, although the façade, with heavily fanciful upper-floor window framing, was completely altered in the early 20C.

The stretch of the avenida facing the Cathedral is known as *Portal de Galeana*.

No. 117 is the much-altered **Casa Iturbide**, once house of the Iturbide family, now a bank.

The original dwelling on the site went up in 1622. In the 18C it became property of the Carmelite friars, who rebuilt it. It was later bought by José Joaquín de Iturbide, father of Agustín, who modernized it in 1785. In Aug. 1821 Ana María Huarte was acclaimed here by the authorities and joyful crowds. A concert was given in her honour, when 'the music of the divine Elízaga amazed and transported the spirits of his audience'. Agustín's sister Nicolasa sold it in 1837 and in the later 19C it passed to Joaquín Oseguera, who altered the façade to suit contemporary taste and modernized the rest (José Evaristo Ramos; 1895).

On the opposite corner with C. Benito Juárez rises the imposing **Pal. de Gobierno**, formerly *Seminario Tridentino*.

The college, mainly for training secular priests, was built in 1760–70. Among its pupils were Morelos, Iturbide, Michelena, José Sixto Verduzco, Vicente Santa María. A later pupil was Melchor Ocampo. In Apr. 1859 Gen. Márquez was fêted here by the students; in retaliation Governor Huerta expelled them and turned the building into a barracks. After 1867 it became seat of State government and headquarters of the fire brigade.

EXTERIOR. In the S façade, spare ornamentation enhances grand simplicity. The centre panel rises from the main doorway, framed in layered mouldings, its vegetal lintel key an attractive addition, to the elegant window, covered by a mixtilinear lintel, and to the stepped pediment, topped by a large finial. Three vertical sections on either side of the doorway, marked off by pilasters, show, with their bold cornices and balconies, the increase in embellishment up to the parapet, with its repeated finials. At each corner, buttresses support singularly exotic open towers, which add an Oriental touch.

INTERIOR. From the main entrance we have a clear view through the three patios. The corridor arches of the principal patio are supported on high pilasters with lambrequin motifs in the spandrels. The grand effect complements that of the façade. On the E side is the great staircase, its walls covered by a mural (1953), optimistic in vein, by Alfredo Zalce, its theme the history of Mexican Independence, the Reform, and the Revolution.

The central figures of the insurgents are shown in a compact mass: Hidalgo and Morelos again to the fore, their followers in ranks behind, fanning outwards. To the r. of Morelos are Guerrero and Iturbide; to the latter's r. and behind, Guadalupe Victoria and Melchor Ocampo. The dominating figure is Pípila, hero of the siege of the Alhóndiga at Guanajuato, who supports them all as he fires the building.
On the N and S walls of the upper corridor are more murals by Zalce on the history, geography, and economy of Morelia and Michoacán. The staircase gives on to the *Sala de Recepciones*. In it are seven portraits of figures in the history of the State by Cuevas del Río, painted in the 1940s; and one of Lázaro Cárdenas by Agustín Cárdenas.

C. Benito Juárez runs N, crossing C. Melchor Ocampo to meet C. Santiago Tapia. In the latter, on the r. at the corner with C. Zaragoza, No. 271 is the *Hospital del Sagrado Corazón* (or *Hospital Dr Manuel Arriaga*), built in 1754–55 as the *Carceles Eclesiásticas*—the prison for ecclesiastical offenders. Mariano Matamoros was held here before being marched barefoot through the streets to his execution. Beyond in C. Juárez, on the l., No. 223 is the former *Pal. Episcopal*, an austere two-storey edifice begun in the 1680s, finished in 1734. A rebuilding started in the 1850s was left unfinished. Humboldt stayed here in 1803. It is now the offices of the *Secretaría de Salubridad y Asistencia*.

At No. 240 (r.) is the **Museo de Arte Colonial** (Tues.–Sun., 10–1, 3–5), containing a representative choice of mainly religious art from the 16–19C, once in the city's convents and churches. R.I. 18C oil paintings, incl. a tender St Joseph and Child, from Las Rosas, by Cabrera. 18–19C crucifixes. R.II. 18–19C religious texts. Miguel Herrera (mid-18C), Presentation of Our Lady; Cabrera, Allegories of Our Lady of Mount Carmel; J.C. Padilla (late 19C), Our Lady of Light (in a beautiful gilded frame). RR.III–IV. Three Kings (16C) in caña de maíz. José de Alzíbar, Bp Antonio de San Miguel. 16–19C wooden crucifixes. R.V. 18C polychrome carved wooden candlesticks. CENTRAL HALL. Juan de Sámano (18C), Our Lady of the Column; Cabrera, Allegorical portrait of Bp Juan Palafox.

At the N end of C. Juárez on the r., on the N side of Pl. de la República, are the church of **El Carmen**, with its four cupolas, and its adjoining convent, both much altered by time, but still keeping a few early treasures.

The convent was founded in 1593, the fourth in New Spain for discalced Carmelite friars. The church was finished probably in 1619 and the convent rebuilt during the 1730s. It occupied a large area, its gardens reaching as far N and W as the present Cs García Pueblita and Guillermo Prieto. In 1839 the church was altered 'con magnificencia y buen gusto', in the heart-sinking terminology of the time, by Prior Manuel del Corazón de Jesús. The convent was rebuilt in 1855. In 1859–60 it was closed down and three new streets were driven through its grounds (Cs Mártires de Tacubaya, García Pueblita, and the N prolongation of Juárez). Since then it has served as seminary, bus station, and student hostel.

EXTERIOR. The main W doorway shows tableros and lambrequin motifs under the pilaster capitals. The S doorway (dated 1619) is elegantly Mannerist. The lower pediment breaks to make room for the niche holding a statue of Our Lady of Mount Carmel and the infant Christ. In the SW corner is an espadaña bolstered by buttresses—20C additions. Of the cupolas, a form much favoured by the Carmelites, that on the N side is the latest (19C).

INTERIOR. The look of the nave is not improved by insufficient light, a result of 19C modifications. The 18C image of Our Lady of Mount Carmel on the high altar is the only piece of sculpture to have escaped the changes. Off the N transept is the antesacristy, which gives on to the small cloister. On its N side the doorway into the sacristy is a beautiful 17C survival, of generous proportions, its jambs and flat arch decorated with floral, lozenge, and triangular relief; its key an exquisite cartouche enveloping a cross. Off the S transept is the *Cap. Sabatino*, dating from 1659. Among the church's paintings are four by Luis Juárez, probably dating from the late 1630s: Virgin and Child with St John of the Cross (r. transept; retouched); Coronation of St Teresa (sacristy); Elijah and St Angelus (antesacristy).

Since 1978 the charming convent buildings have been a cultural centre.

From the E side of Pl. de la República we take C. Morelos Norte S to gain Av. Madero. No. 82 (l.), on the corner with C. Aquiles Serdán, was built in 1770 to the design of Diego Durán. In 1839 it was bought by José de Ugarte, three times governor of the State—in 1844, 1845, and 1854–55; partisan of Santa-Anna; and military commander of Michoacán under Maximilian.

Next door, at the corner with Av. Madero Oriente, No. 21 is the former house (now a bank) of the García Obeso family, acquired by Gabriel García Obeso in 1781 and restyled in 1783. Here took place the first meetings, promoted by his son, José María, of the conspirators of Valladolid in 1809. No. 63 next door, the *Hotel Morelos*, was the birthplace in 1782 of the insurgent Juan Nepomuceno Foncerrada y Saravilla, fruit of an illicit union of two of Morelia's most respectable families. Opposite, the *Hotel Oseguera* (No. 24) was built in 1704 by order of Bp Juan de Ortega y Montañés as a hospital ('for one hundred sick') to be run by the Brothers of St John of God (juaninos). It still preserves 18–19C elements.

At the corner of Av. Madero Oriente and C. Pino Suárez is the **Pal. del Poder Legislativo**, which houses, among other offices, the State chamber of deputies.

It was bought in the late 18C by the intendente José María Anzorena y Foncerrada. Its present fin-de-siècle aspect dates from a remodelling in 1897, after which it became the property of Governor Aristeo Mercado. For a time it contained the university library. No. 94 opposite, a handsome house, is of the late 17C, modified in the 18–19C. On its S side, in C. Virrey de Mendoza, is the 18C *Cap. de los Juaninos*, formerly attached to the hospital.

One block further E in Av. Madero Oriente, at the corner with C. Alvaro Obregón, is the *Dirección de Educación Federal y Estatal* (Education Department), formerly the **Casa del Conde de Sierra Gorda**.

It belonged to the cultured Mariano Timoteo de Escandón (d. 1814), 3rd conde, who arrived in Valladolid in 1775 as canon of the Cathedral and rose to archdeacon. Temporarily in charge of the diocese in Oct. 1810, he lifted Hidalgo's excommunication and granted him 114,000 pesos from the Cathedral treasury, in return for a useless receipt. The house's 18C lines were modified at the end of the 19C, and before the Revolution it was briefly destined as the episcopal palace.

Diagonally opposite is the little church of *La Cruz* (1680–90; renovated 1970). Next to it, No. 226 Av. Madero Oriente, its principal patio rebuilt this century, keeps a baroque doorway. Opposite, at the corner of C. Belisario Domínguez, No. 261 (early 18C) was built probably by Juan de Silva for the Roque de Lecuona family, and was rescued from decay in 1954.

C. Belisario Domínguez leads N to the church of **San José**, on the grand scale, with classical and churrigueresque borrowings.

It was started under Bp Pedro Anselmo Sánchez de Tagle in 1760; the interior, not finished until later in the century, was brought up to date in 1875–76. The towers were not raised until 1945. In 1849 it was destined for the Carmelite nuns from Las Teresitas, but never used by them.

EXTERIOR. The façade, facing W, is well viewed from C. Emiliano Zapata. Three levels of bold pilasters, with tablero and fluted shafts, and capped by doric, ionic, and corinthian capitals, form recesses for tableros. Flanking the window and the third-storey relief of St Joseph are discreet estípites. The beautiful S portal, facing C. Belisario Domínguez, with a niche holding a statue of St Joseph within a broken pediment, harks back to Mannerism.

INTERIOR lighting has not been improved by stained-glass windows (1940). The 18C confessionals were originally in the Cathedral. In the N transept is a St Michael by Cristóbal de Villalpando and a Dream of St Joseph, attr. Cabrera.

At an angle to the S doorway is that of the *Casa Cural* (258 C. Belisario Domínguez), a one-storey priest's house, now parish offices. The 18C portal has a mixtilinear gable.

N and E of the church, along C. Plan de Ayala, is the building begun in 1849 as the new convent for the Carmelite nuns from Las Teresitas. The Reform intervened, and it became an infantry barracks instead. It is now the Belisario Domínguez primary school. Further to the E is the former second home of the *Seminario Tridentino*, a grand and handsome building, a combination of neo-classical and French, by Adolphe Tresmontels, finished in 1884. It is now the *Escuela Preparatoria Pascual Ortiz Rubio*.

S along C. Belisario Domínguez, at the corner with C. Aquiles Serdán (No. 298), is the *Nacional Monte de Piedad*, formerly part of the Dominican convent of *Sta Catalina*, finished in 1738. Next door (224 C. Aquiles Serdán) the *Colegio de San Ignacio*, once part of the same convent, was acquired by the clergy after the Reform as a school for poor boys, but closed in 1930.

Beyond C. Belisario Domínguez in Av. Madero Oriente rises the church called **Las Monjas**, once the church of Morelia's principal convent of nuns.

It belonged to the Dominican convent of *Sta Catalina de Sena* (known informally as *Las Catarinas*), built at the orders of Bp Escalona y Calatayud during the 1730s and ready in 1738, when the nuns moved from their former premises (see above). The community, numbering 28, was expelled for good in 1867.

EXTERIOR. Main feature of the S façade is the striking double portal, for all its late date betraying a mixture of earlier styles. The lower storeys are firmly classical; two pairs each of fluted columns, supported by bases marked by tableros and supporting Corinthian capitals, flank semicircular arches with tentative flowery relief above and in the spandrels. Above the cornice, horizontal tablero panels. The upper storeys are much more adventurous, borrowing freely from the plateresque: the elegant windows shown off by exaggerated frames; the columns ending in idiosyncratic Corinthian capitals; the roses on either side of the frames and the pedestals and shell canopies in the entrecalles are strong Renaissance echoes. The rich entablature and cornice are also bases for tasteful semi-octangular gables, in the midst of which are beautifully framed niches enclosing statues of SS Dominic and Catherine of Siena crowned by broken pediments—neo-Mannerist touches. The slender baroque tower is excitingly different, its upper two storeys, surmounted by solomonic columns, culminating in a pyramid set off by complementary finials and, for climax, a statue of St Dominic.

The single-nave INTERIOR was refurbished in eclectic style in 1884. The choirs, however, remain. The arch of the coro alto is filled by three rows of wooden balusters; that of the coro bajo by a delicate wrought-iron grille in three rows, patterned with volute motifs and a Dominican cross beneath the key.

Next door, on the site of the former convent of Sta Catalina, is the handsome *Pal. Federal* (c 1884–85), raised at the order of Abp José Ignacio Arciga by Adolphe Tresmontels for a girls' school, the *Colegio de Guadalupe*, in the care of Carmelite nuns.

Av. Madero Oriente continues E to JARDIN VILLALONGIN, flanked on the N and E by the arches of the **Acueducto**, robust and well-proportioned, which run SE along Av. Santos Degollado.

It was the rebuilding (1785–89) of a 17C aqueduct on the initiative of Bp Antonio de San Miguel as part of a programme of public works during economic depression. It served 30 public fountains. Some of its 253 arches were removed in 1976.

Av. Santos Degollado skirts the NE side of BOSQUE CUAUHTEMOC, the city's main park. Also from Jardín Villalongín, above Av. Santos Degollado and past the *Cap. de Lurdes*, an 18C chapel, rebuilt in 1893–1907 and formerly known as the *Cap. del Rincón*, runs Calz. Fray Antonio de San Miguel, laid out as Calz. de Guadalupe in 1732 and shaded by ash trees. It leads to the **Santuario de Guadalupe**, its interior a surprising departure from Morelian sobriety.

It dates from 1708–16. In the 1730s Bp Escalona y Calatayud built next to it a house to serve as a residence for bishops-elect and as a retreat centre for priests of the diocese. In 1761–62 both church and house were granted to the discalced Franciscans (dieguinos) and renamed *San Diego*. In 1811 some of the Spaniards executed on Hidalgo's orders were buried in the church; in 1862 the remains of José Mariano Michelena were interred here. The adjoining mansion was opened in 1877 as an exhibition centre; it then became a hospital; it is now the *Escuela de Jurisprudencia*.

The church's EXTERIOR shows all the hallmarks of Morelian classicism, with decorative relief reserved for the gable. Note the volutes offsetting the crown of the slender tower. The INTERIOR is a dazzling tour de force of polychrome on a base of baked clay, mostly done in 1907–13 by Joaquín Horta Menchaca, but never completely finished. In the pendentives, medallion reliefs of the story of the Guadalupe miracle. The high altar (1830s or 1840s) is by Nicolás Luna. In the plaza on the other side of the calzada is an equestrian monument to Morelos (1913).

FROM MORELIA TO TASCO, 472km. At 27km on Méx. 15 (see Rte 34) we turn S on State road 49, passable and spectacular, which runs through the Sierra de Mil Cumbres—in fact through the main volcanic range—and following, or keeping near, the valley of the Río Cuitzamala, which drains S into the Río Balsas. 43km *Tzitzio*. 119km *El Limón* (strange rock formations). At 124km we meet Méx. 6 from Zitácuaro (see Rte 34) and descend to (139km) *Tiquicheo* (440m; P). The road now climbs W to (172km) *Quenchendio*.

From here a minor road winds into the mountains to (17km) *Carácuaro*, where Morelos was parish priest in 1810 and from where he set out to meet Hidalgo at Indaparapeo. From here he later set out with 25 men to raise his standard in the S. The little parish church of San Agustín (c 1760) and Morelos's house may be seen. 8km further NW on the same road is *Nocupétaro*, where he also served as parish priest at the church of Sta Catarina.

The road (Méx. 49) then descends into the wide valley of the Río Balsas, the tierra caliente, S to (199km) **Huetamo** (9,000 inhab.; 318m; H,R,P), on the Río Huetamo, a tributary of the Balsas, and famous for its melons.

Huetamo was a Postclassic Tarascan town, but in the vicinity there have been found artefacts and architectural traces of Teotihuacano, Maya, and Xochicalco influence. In the region around *Zirándaro* (c 30km S) more than 100 sites have been found and 19 have been excavated. The area was an important source of metals (tin, copper, gold, and silver) and jade, and was one of the gateways for the diffusion of metallurgy into Mesoamerica (see *Zihuatanejo*, the *Barnard Site*, and *Colima*).

217km *San Lucas*. Just before (252km) **Ciudad Altamirano** (13,000 inhab.; 250m; H,P) we cross into the State of Guerrero. It is the starting point for the road (SW) crossing the Sierra Madre del Sur to the coast at (181km) *Zihuatanejo*. The town boasts lush tropical vegetation.

5km SW along Méx. 134, **Coyuca de Catalán** was one of many small Late Postclassic Western Culture city-states. From protohistoric sources we know that it was governed by Hiripan, then by his son, Ticatame, who was forced to accept the overlordship of the king of Tzintzuntzan in the 15C.

At the nearby site of *San Miguel Amuco*, the discovery of an Olmec stele in 1967 reveals Preclassic Olmec presence—a standing figure wears a cape and holds a bundle of what appear to be reeds.

From Ciudad Altamirano to *Toluca*, see Rte 40B.

The road (Méx. 140) continues SE to (273km) *Tlapehuala*. 291km *Poliutla*, where the 18C church of San José preserves an interesting set of altarpieces, churrigueresque and earlier.

C 5km S is *Los Monos* (Monkeys). The remains comprise pyramids on platforms and a ball court, all 7C and 8C AD. On the walls of some of the pyramids and platforms are carvings of monkeys.

Beyond (306km) *Arcelia* (H,P) the road leaves the Balsas valley and climbs again into the central volcanic range to (324km) *Almoloya*, with an 18C church, and (373km; 2km S) **Teloloapan** (c 20,000 inhab.; 1620m; H,P), on the river of the same name. 7km S is *Acatempan*, scene of the historic meeting (the 'abrazo de Acatempan') between Vicente Guerrero and Agustín de Iturbide on 10 Jan. 1821, at which the latter persuaded Guerrero to join the movement for Independence and which paved the way for the Plan of Iguala. At *Oxtotitlán* (21km further S) a double corbel-arched Maya-like tomb was reported. The Grutas de Oxtotitlán (discovered in 1968; 2km E) contain cave paintings showing Olmec influence. Méx. 140 winds through the mountains to (436km) *Iguala* and (472km) *Tasco*, see Rte 82.

32 Morelia to Irapuato

Méx. 43, 132km.—35km **Cuitzeo**.—56km Moroleón.—64km (3km E) **Yuriria**.—112km Salamanca.—132km **Irapuato**.

We leave Morelia to the N. At 9km Méx. 120 diverges to the r. (NE) for (40km) *Zinapécuaro*, see Rte 33. 10km (1km l.) **Tarímbaro**, where the convent of *San Miguel*, founded by 1570, was completed by the 1580s and served also as the Franciscan friars' main infirmary. The open chapel is in the rare shape of a ribbed semi-dome apse, a coffered archivolt resting on wide fluted pilasters. A bench runs round this curve. At 27km a dirt road (l.) runs to (7km W) **Copándaro**, where the Augustinian convent of *Santiago* was founded in 1550–51 by Fray Alonso de la Veracruz and built in 1560–67, winning praise for its elegance. The church façade is in simple plateresque. The triple-arched portería/open chapel leads into the charming little cloister, with two sets of paired arches in the upper storey corresponding to one wide three-centred arch below. 8km further W is *Chucándiro*, with a former Augustinian convent dating from the 1640s. The road descends to cross the **Lago de Cuitzeo** by the Calz. de Cuitzeo (4km long), inaugurated in 1882.

The lake, 48km from W to E and 4km at its narrowest from N to S, is a shallow volcanic basin giving off sulphuretted hydrogen. It is in full desiccation, its salty waters having been drained in the 1940s, which makes it a mud flat during the rainy season and a dust flat in dry weather. A narrow tongue of land, c 10km W to E, juts out into the lake, dividing it almost into N and S halves. Salt production has been a local industry from prehispanic times.

35km **CUITZEO** (16,000 inhab.; 1800m; H,R,P), on the N bank of the lake, is a place of some charm, its old houses in bright colours. In its centre is the convent of **Sta María Magdalena**, among the finest of the Augustinian foundations in New Spain.

The old Tarascan town, an outpost on the Chichimec frontier, was burned in 1530 during the depredations of Nuño de Guzmán. The new was laid out by the Spaniards along straight lines. The convent was in large part built during 1550–79, perhaps to the design of Pedro del Toro, although the façade is attr. Fray Francisco de Villafuerte. Work continued in the 1590s under the friars Gerónimo de Morante and Dionisio Robledo. The N tower (1612) is by Fray Gerónimo de la Magdalena.

EXTERIOR. The façade is a superb example of academic plateresque, in three distinct storeys. Close observation, however, reveals the Indian hand that carved it—with considerable freedom. The doorway arch is semicircular, with a double archivolt, the outer rim containing angel and floral relief; in the jambs, reliefs of flowers and the Augustinian emblem, the pierced heart. The inner rim alternates flower and heart. As their lowest third section the slender baluster columns have the Augustinian shield imposed on the wings and claws of headless eagles, with strange bird-vegetal creatures sprouting on either side. The upper frieze combines triglyphs and stylized angels, and the continuations of the columns are pod-like candlesticks. In the centre of the alfíz formed by cornice and window-ledge is the pierced-heart emblem framed by stylized gourd plants. The window, Romanesque in inspiration, is flanked by colonnettes; angels are cramped in the spandrels (contrasting with their lighter colleagues below); ledge and cornice are prolonged, with seeming pointlessness, on either side. Above, the niche holds a rigidly formal Magdalen. Accompanying shields, crowned Indian style, contain urns and pelicans (though differently arranged). Above is another strangely prolonged cornice. At the top, within the gable, more symbolism: the Augustinian heart in the breast of a double-headed eagle. Discreetly above all, the mitre and crozier of St Augustine of Hippo. On either side of the main column capitals two cartouches borne up by cornucopias attest (l.) the patron saint and (r.) possibly the Indian, or mestizo, craftsman responsible for the work: FR IO METL ME FECIT— Francisco Juan [Jerónimo] Metl (?) made me.

INTERIOR. The walls were built thick so that stone vaults could be substituted for the original ones. The N windows are higher than the S: the former able to illuminate the vaulting; the latter, the lower sections of the nave and the side altars—the original 17C examples lost to indifferent neoclassicism. The rib-vaulting in the apse (rare in 16C Mexican churches) is particularly good.

The six-arched PORTERIA/OPEN CHAPEL is arguably the finest in its detail in Mexico. The slim fluted columns resting against elegantly moulded pilasters end in foliate capitals supporting an entablature. The arch nearest the church leads to a fine doorway giving on to the cloister. Of the remaining five, the centre one faces the delightful apse of the open chapel with its fluted jambs, delicate ribs marked by floral bosses, and pendant. On the N (l.) wall, a late 16C mural of the Last Judgement.

The CLOISTER, dotted with decorative merlons on the outside, has solid buttressing and elegant upper double arcade, its columns and archivolts showing finesse. Both galleries have good barrel and rib vaulting; the doorways into the convent beautiful moulding. Traces of the original frescoes may be seen in the galleries and on the staircase walls. Along the upper parapet is a series of fantastic gargoyles, each different and providing a Gothic touch. From them spouts the water into the generous cistern beneath the cloister, long preferred by the townsfolk.

The road W from Cuitzeo goes via (19km) *Huandacareo*, with thermal springs; (36km) *Villa Morelos*, the former Huango, where remain the sacristy (now serving as a church) and atrial cross of a grandly projected (1550), but never finished, Augustinian convent of San Nicolás; and (64km) *Puruándiro*, also with thermal springs, to (82km) *Villachuato*, see Rte 28.

Continuing N on Méx. 43 we cross (44km) into the State of Guanajuato. 56km **Moroleón** (c 30,000 inhab.; H,R,P), an industrial town. Its neo-Gothic *Templo Expiatorio* was finished in 1913. 64km road-fork.

The turning r. leads to (3km E) **YURIRIA** (c 20,000 inhab; 1750m; H,R,P), on the S shore of the Lago de Yuriria, at the SW extremity of the Bajío.

The ancient *Yurirapúndaro* (in the old language of Michoacán meaning Lake of Blood, from the red flowers which floated on it) was at the Conquest a mainly Tarascan settlement in an area subject to Chichimec raids until the end of the 16C. It suffered during the war of Independence. In 1812 Iturbide dislodged a pro-insurgent faction and had them summarily shot: 'those miserable wretches are now contemplating their error in hell. Perhaps others may profit by their example'. In 1815 the town was devastated by the marauding band of the sanguinary insurgent Antonio Torres, parish priest of Cuitzeo.

The **Lago de Yuriria**, 17km from E to W and 7km maximum from N to S, occupies the lower part of a basin surrounded by volcanic hills. In 1548 it was artificially connected to the Río Lerma during works initiated by Fray Diego de Chávez. It serves as a reservoir for the S area of the State and abounds in catfish.

Facing the ample PL. PRINCIPAL is the former Augustinian convent of **San Pablo**, a foundation of unsurpassed grandeur, described in the 1620s by the chronicler Juan de Grijalva as 'the most superb building imaginable...surpassed only by the spirit of him who made it' and in 1950 by Manuel Toussaint as 'uniting, like no other, the characteristics of the age: sword and cross; strength and art'.

Work possibly began c 1556, with the main building campaign in the mid-1560s. The maestro mayor seems to have been Pedro del Toro, and the friar Gerónimo de la Magdalena also worked on the construction. After 1625 buttresses were added to the church; and the interior was gilded under the direction of Francisco de Cantillana. The upper-storey cloister was vaulted after 1650 by Fray Juan López. The portería, rebuilt c 1680, is by Cristóbal Medrano. In the later 16C the Chichimecs, contrary to general belief, attacked the convent only once, and then only gained the atrio. They mistook the statue of St Nicholas in the S portal for a real person and shot arrows at it. In 1815 Antonio Torres set fire to the church to melt down the gold from its altarpieces: the men of the town had fled; their sturdy womenfolk stayed behind and put the fire out, at great risk to themselves.

EXTERIOR. The W façade, alongside the square, strong crenellated tower (more appropriate to a castle than a church), is a work of staggeringly ornate plateresque ('tropical plateresque'), probably by Indian sculptors. It is a

Church of San Pablo, Yuriria

coarsened development of the façade at Acolman (comp. Rte 18), but this does not detract from the wonderful effect of a compulsion to cover all available surfaces. In the lower storey the inner pair of baluster columns show relief of sirens with female heads, but the bodies of birds. Between the columns, on corbel bases, stand statues of SS Peter and Paul, formally rigid, under heavy cubical, crownlike baldachins. The double archivolt of the doorway is divided into coffered voussoirs: shells in the inner arch; platters of food in the outer. Above the projecting cornice four canephorae continue the line of the columns; cornucopias appear next to the outside figures. The niches above the door are occupied by jaunty musicians. What would, in a purer style, be empty space above the cornices is filled by profuse sprays of strapwork and foliation, springing, on either side of the window, from medallions in which are angels carrying bow and arrow. Above the window, the image of St Augustine. The S portal, though more restrained, shows similar motifs. Here the columns, fluted in the lower storey, baluster composing the niche of St Nicholas, create a heavier effect.

Although the convent was not conceived as a fortress, the massive bearing walls, topped by ornamental merlons, were built to withstand all kinds of shock and to sustain the heavy vaults. The buttresses provide further strengthening. The N wall, adjoining the cloister, has baffled exits which may have served as confessionals.

INTERIOR. The extrados of the nave barrel vault swells the roof. What appears as a transept is virtually another nave of the same height giving a Greek cross form, rarest of occurrences in convent churches. The beautiful and intricate rib vaulting here and in the apse projects into a series of external flat domes. The pulpit is another 16C survival, along with the fragment, with decorated, fluted columns, of a wooden relief (without polychrome and estofado) from a retable burned in 1815: Eternal Father (c 1576) by Juan Rodríguez.

The grandness of the four-arched PORTERIA may well betoken its original use as an open chapel. It leads into the CLOISTER, a major achievement and recalling medieval grandeur: buttresses, square for the lower gallery, in pointed profile for the upper, stand well forward of the tall arches of the former and the corresponding openings above. The rib vaulting in the lower arcade, springing from an emphatic entablature, is first-rate in its precision and the best possible examples of composite half-columns seem to support the archivolts. Tiercepoint vaulting covers the majestic open staircase. A museum containing prehispanic and 17–18C pieces is located in four rooms off the lower gallery.

Méx. 43 continues N to (90km) **Valle de Santiago**, in a region crossed (NNW to SSE) by small volcanoes, their craters occupied by lakes. Within the *Centro Regional de Guanajuato* a small museum contains displays describing the local geography, in particular the volcanic activity of the remote past. Cases contain fossils, and ceramics from the Preclassic and Classic Periods, and there is a stele from Pantoja depicting Quetzalcóatl (the Plumed Serpent). 112km *Salamanca*, see Rte 36. 132km *Irapuato*, see Rte 36.

33 Morelia to Acámbaro

65km.—12km **Charo**.—42km Zinapécuaro and Méx. 120.—65km **Acámbaro**.

We leave Morelia to the NE along Calz. Madero to gain a secondary road for (12km) **CHARO** (c 4000 inhab.), in the Sierra de Ozumatlán, a site described by Fray Diego de Basalenque as 'like a painted Flemish landscape'. The former

Augustinian convent of **San Miguel** occupies a commanding position on the Monte San Miguel.

It was founded in 1550 and by the end of the 16C an impressive convent had been built. The church was well ahead by 1605, but work on it continued during the 17C. In 1858 an earthquake badly damaged it. The present tower dates from 1901–06. Here the 4th prior, Diego de Basalenque (1577–1651), wrote his history of the Augustinian Order in Michoacán. In 1729, a later prior, Matías de Escobar, wrote another famous chronicle of the province, 'Americana Thebaida'.

EXTERIOR. The church façade, finished in 1603 under Fray Francisco de Acosta, is well-proportioned and combines plateresque and Mannerist modes, with delicate relief, discreet use of tableros, and statues of Augustinian saints. In the pediment, above an ajimez window, a relief of St Augustine protecting his friars under his mantle, a familiar theme. On the l. of the doorway, St Nicholas of Tolentino, patron of the dying and of the souls in Purgatory.
On the N side of the church is the portería/open chapel. To the l. is the stone confessional, decorated with the shell motif of Michoacán, traditionally placed here by Fray Diego de Basalenque. The CLOISTER walls were decorated with murals on Augustinian themes commissioned by the first prior, Fray Pedro de San Jerónimo, in the 1570s. They in large part survive, restored in the 1950s.

On the walls of the anteportería (the short passage into the cloister) are four scenes from the Passion. On the r., Agony in the Garden and Taking of Christ. In the latter, Judas kisses Christ, and St Peter flees in the background. On the l., Christ mocked and Christ scourged. In the grotesque above the first, two figures (angels?) uphold a panoply of the Five Wounds; in the grotesque above the second appears a figure of the Child Jesus beneath an open cloak.
The murals continue on the walls of the single-storey cloister, which preserves its original beamed ceiling. Another Passion scene, an Ecce Homo, appears on the l. of the doorway into the church on the S wall. Christ, crowned with thorns, His hands tied, appears between St John the Evangelist (l.) and Isaiah. The grotesque above is composed of angels, fishes (symbols of evil, which attack the boats of the faithful), and dolphins (symbols of resurrection and salvation). Intertwined with them are portrait medallions of friars.
Along the E wall is the most significant, though much deteriorated, mural: 'La Thebaida Agustiniana'—Thebaid, the name given to the Valley of the Upper Nile, where in the 3C the first anchorites flourished. The Augustinian Order was founded in the 13C from the group-ings of hermits who followed the rule of St Augustine. Michoacán was considered the new Thebaid. The scene is of different groupings of hermits at Thegaste, birthplace of the saint.
On the N wall are two genealogical trees: of Augustinian friars, seven branches of a rose tree sprouting from St Augustine's breast; and of nuns of the Order, sprouting from St Monica's; on the r. of the latter, four female saints.
Scenes of martyrdom complete the mural series. On the S wall, of a bishop stoned by a group of young men and of a saint in a boat pierced by arrows shot by two young men and flanked by three women praying and three men. Above the W wall doorway appear four Augustinian martyrs tied to a column; in the medallion of the grotesque the nun in a white habit probably represents St Monica. On the r. of the doorway, the beheading of Augustinian saints, with the Crucifixion in the background; on the l., a procession of martyrs about to be boiled alive in a cauldron—one of them appears to have fainted in terror.

22km *Indaparapeo* was scene of a famous meeting between Hidalgo and Morelos on 20 Oct. 1810. The latter asked to serve as chaplain in Hidalgo's army, but instead was ordered to lead the revolt in the S. 31km *Queréndaro*, famous for its avocados, SW of Presa Mal País. 37km turning l. for (42km) **Zinapécuaro** (1920m) on the W slopes of the Sierra de Ucareo, once a Tarascan stronghold against the Chichimecs, and favoured by Viceroy Antonio de Mendoza in 1540 as a Spanish outpost. It has, since the Middle Preclassic, been noted for its obsidian quarries, supplying central Mesoamerica and the valleys of Oaxaca. The former Franciscan convent of *San Juan Bautista* was built on a hilltop, its main gate reached by a narrow stair crowded in by houses. Church and convent, rebuilt c 1630, display notable stucco sgraffito patterns.
The road (Méx. 120) leads NE through the Sierra de Ucareo. At 50km a track leads E to (c 8km) **Ucareo**, where in the 1550s the Augustinian prior Juan de Utrera began the convent of *San Agustín* on so sumptuous a scale that he was

accused of designing it 'not according to the requirements of the place, but to those of his art', and begged by Viceroy Luis de Velasco to proceed on much modester lines. The church was fired in 1750 and the site ravaged by earthquakes in the 1870s. In the restored church, with beam and tile ceiling, is a churrigueresque high altarpiece. The small one-storey cloister also has a wooden-beam ceiling. Underneath it survives the original cistern. 65km *Acámbaro*, see Rte 40A.

34 Morelia to Toluca

Méx. 15, 247km.—99km Ciudad Hidalgo.—118km Tuxpan.—146km Zitácuaro.—247km **Toluca**.

We leave Morelia to the E along Méx. 15. The road runs through the mountainous *Sierra de Mil Cumbres*, the part of the central volcanic range which slopes S towards the Río Cutzamala, a tributary of the Río Balsas. Its oak and pine forests have suffered immoderate felling. At 27km State road 49 runs S to join (97km) the Zitácuaro–Iguala road, see below. 54km *Puerto Garnica* in the *Parque Nacional Cerro de Garnica* (views). 69km *Mil Cumbres* mirador. 75km l. turn for (31km N) *Zinapécuaro*, see Rte 33. 99km **Ciudad Hidalgo** (former *Tajimaroa*; c 30,000 inhab.; 2360m; H,R,P).

It was the scene of bloody fighting over several years in Aztec attempts to expand to the W. The town was inhabited by Otomí, on the border of Matlazinca territory (to the S). In 1479 the town was finally taken by the Aztecs under Axayácatl (1468–81), but later, a renewed Tarascan attack defeated the Aztec garrison and retook it.

Moctezuma II Xocoyotzin attempted twice to expand Aztec borders to the W, and the town was fiercely contended in the early 16C, ending in a stalemate (the proverbial 'Mexican stand-off'?). The Tarascans built heavy fortifications around the town, which acted as a frontier outpost and merited the admiration of the Spaniards when they arrived on the borders of Tarascan territory shortly after the capture of Tenochtitlán (cf. *Xiquipilco* [*Jiquipilco*], and the *Matlazinca*).

The parish church is a remodelled survivor of the Franciscan convent of *San José*, founded c 1550. Built in 1598, it faces E, thus accommodating itself to the plaza of the pre-Conquest town. The atrial cross, with an obsidian disk (see below) at the intersection, is starkly carved with symbols of the Passion: four Franciscan shields of the Five Wounds and blood flowing from the nails which pierce it. The portería probably served as an open chapel before the church was built. Around the basin of the font, once fountain of the plaza, carved with cherubs and shells, is an inscription representing the alphabet twice over. 103km road N for (30km) *Maravatío*, see Rte 40A.

Méx. 15 continues S along the valley of the Río Tuxpan. 118km **Tuxpan** (c 5000 inhab.; 1750m; H,R,P) is famous for its gladioli. The church of *Santiago*, by Pedro de Arrieta, dates from the late 17C. It contains a huge mural of Souls in Purgatory interceded for by saints in heaven (1708), its central figures an intense St Teresa and a magnificent St Michael, by Cristóbal de Villalpando. 129km turning r. for (6km W) *San José Purúa* (20,000 inhab.; 1869m; H,R,P), in a beautiful landscape, famous for its thermal springs. At (137km) *San Felipe de los Alzati* the atrio (now a cemetery) of the 17C visita church survives, its wall decorated with rosettes representing the Host. The atrial cross, on the corners of whose base are four smaller crosses in flower shape, has an obsidian disk at its intersection. Remains of the Postclassic Matlazinca town include two pyramids of three tiers each, with central stairways and a few carvings on their walls.

24km N along Méx. 44 is **Angangueo** (10,000 inhab.; 2628m), a mining town, its deposits of silver, lead, and zinc worked until 1953 by the American Smelting and Refining Co. Its neo-Gothic church of La Purísima Concepción by José Rivero y Heras dates from 1882.

146km **Zitácuaro** (c 40,000 inhab.; 1781m; H,R,P), on the W slopes of the Sierra de Zitácuaro, is an important distribution centre for the products (livestock, timber, fruit, coffee, vegetables) of a vast region and also known for its ceramics.

In Aug. 1811 the Congreso Nacional Gubernativo y Suprema Junta Nacional Americana, the first, short-lived, body set up to direct the insurgent effort, was established here under Ignacio López Rayón. But he and its other leaders, among them José Sixto Verduzco and José María Liceaga, soon fell out. In Jan. 1812 Calleja sacked, evacuated, and fired the town: 'infiel y criminal villa'.

A plaque at the corner of Cs Rayón and Victoria marks the site of the Pal. Nacional, where meetings of the Congress took place. The Parroquia was built c 1639, on the site of the Franciscan convent church of San Juan (founded in the 1570s), to house a miraculous image of Our Lady, brought from Spain in the 16C.

From Zitácuaro Méx. 6 descends S and SW near the valley of the Río Zitácuaro via (6km; r.) the large Presa del Bosque (boating, fishing, bathing) and (50km) Tuzantla, a picturesque little town on a fertile plain amid tropical vegetation, to join (99km) Méx. 49 for (300km W) Iguala, see Rte 82.

At 178km Méx. 15 crosses from Michoacán into the State of México and into the Bosque de Bosencheve (3000m), a national park stretching NW; the Laguna del Carmen is N of the road.

From here a mountain road (State road 57; magnificent scenery, but not always safe in the rainy season) runs SW to (7km) San José Villa de Allende, quiet and clean, a tree nursery centre. 18km turning l. for (10km E) Donato Guerra, with a spectacular waterfall to its N. 31km **Ixtapan del Oro** (2000 inhab.; 1800m), an attractive place in a coffee-, mango-, and banana-growing region. Its gold mines are now worked out. 2km NW is the so-called Salto de Chihuahua, a famous waterfall.

The road winds spectacularly S to (55km) a road junction. 6km W (r.) is Nuevo Sto Tomás de los Plátanos, built on a height (2000m) after the capturing of the waters of the Río Ixtapantongo in Presa Ixtapantongo submerged the old village, whose church bell-tower can be seen above the waters. This river and the tributaries of the Río Temascaltepec have been harnessed for hydroelectric works (chain of dams and artificial lakes), from Tingambato (47km SW) to Valle de Bravo.

At Ixtapantongo hydroelectric plant there are Toltec rock paintings in the Barranca del Diablo: c 15m high and 50m long, they depict Toltec gods, warriors, and ceremonies, and seem to be superimposed on earlier pictures.

We turn l. and the road comes to (58km) Colorines, on the shore of a small artificial lake, with abundant jacaranda trees and bougainvillea. The road skirts the N shore of Presa de Valle de Bravo (officially Presa Miguel Alemán), largest of the series of lakes, formed after 1949 by the flooding of c 4900 hectares of rich agricultural land supporting a dense population, which had to move to higher sites. The Sta Bárbara dam supplies electricity to the Federal District.

74km turning r. for (5km S) **Valle de Bravo** (12,000 inhab.; 1870m; H,R,P), the former Avándaro, on the E shore of Presa Miguel Alemán, a pretty town, now the more traditional part of a large recreational complex focusing on the lake (water sports). This, the various waterfalls in the area, the golf course at the new Avándaro (3km SE), and the numerous hotels (some very expensive) are favourite, sophisticated, weekend resorts from the rigours of Mexico City. The semicircular yacht club, an exercise in architectural ingenuity, rises and falls with the level of the lake.

92km Amanalco de Becerra, with a 17C church. 140km junction with Méx. 15, see below. 142km (r.) Zinacantepec, see Rte 40B. 147km Toluca, see Rte 40B.

Méx. 15 continues E to (187km; r.) turning S for (34km) Valle de Bravo, see above. 195km turning l. for (2km N) Villa Victoria, to the SE of a large lake (water sports). 247km Toluca, see Rte 40B.

35 Toluca to Mexico City

A. Via La Marquesa

Méx. 15, 51km.—14km Lerma.—30km junction for Sierra de las Cruces.—
32km La Marquesa.—51km **Mexico City**.

Méx. 15 leaves Toluca due E. 14km *Lerma*, in the Río Lerma's (rising c 30km S)
once rich and fertile basin. The parish church dates from 1693.

2km S, at *San Pedro Tultepec*, once an island in the middle of the now defunct Laguna de
Lerma, the 17C church preserves the original timberwork of ceiling and choir, and a baroque
altarpiece.

At 17km a turning r. leads to (2km) *Ocoyoacac*, in the 16C granted to Isabel de
Moctezuma and her heirs. The church of San Martín has a churrigueresque
high altarpiece; embedded in the floor are old coins, ex-votos left by parish-
ioners. The carnival plays here on 15 Jan. use 16C Castilian. At c 27km we
enter the *Llanos de Salazar*, a high plateau. Its centre is the village of *Salazar*,
starting point for climbs in the surrounding mountains. The summit of the *Cerro
de Campana*, to the NW, may be reached by track in 2 hrs. At 29km a road runs
S to (16km) *Xalatlaco* (see below) and at 30km another N through the *Sierra de
las Cruces*.

Its high point, the *Monte de las Cruces* (so-called because of the numerous crosses planted
here to mark murders by bandits), was the scene on 30 Oct. 1810 of an insurgent victory over
1500 royalist troops in extended line. The insurgents, hopelessly indisciplined and ill-
equipped, numbered c 80,000, incl. crowds of hungry, tattered camp followers, clutching
improvised weapons. Having lost their two cannon to fierce Indian bands, at 5.30 in the evening
the royalist commander, Col. Torcuato Trujillo, formed a column of survivors and cut a way
through to Cuajimalpa and thence to Mexico City, where the greatest consternation reigned.
Viceroy Venegas refused Hidalgo's demand that he hand the city over and no sympathetic
rising took place. Desertions from the insurgent army continued apace. News of Calleja's
advance from Querétaro and his own lack of artillery profoundly discouraged Hidalgo.
Acrimony between himself and Allende, who wanted to attack the capital, further imperilled
the insurgent cause. On 2 Dec. he began the retreat from Cuajimalpa towards Ixtlahuaca.
   At *Huixquilucan*, 8km along this road, the church of San Antonio has a portal (early 18C)
in popular baroque style, full of vegetal relief. At *Dos Ríos*, a little further on, the road enters
the Valley of Mexico and reaches (27km) *Mexico City* and the Anillo Periférico by the
Hipódromo de las Américas.

32km *La Marquesa*, especially visited at weekends. An obelisk commemorates
the battle of Las Cruces. Monuments honour Santos Degollado and Gen.
Leandro Valle, commandant-general of the Federal District, two great figures
of Mexican liberalism killed after a conservative ambush near here on 15 June
1861. Méx. 15 enters the Federal District and runs NE. At 40km a road winds
S into (5km) the *Desierto de los Leones*, today a national park and resort amid
the scent of pine and fir. It is also notable for the ruined convent of **Nuestra
Señora del Monte Carmelo**, built in 1606–11 for Carmelite contemplative friars
and occupied by them until the late 18C. In 1914 Pres. Huerta authorized the
conversion of part of the convent as a restaurant; it later became a zapatista
hiding-place. The cloisters and gardens evoke a peaceful past. We reach (51km)
Mexico City along Av. de los Constituyentes.

B. Via Tianguistenco

90km. Méx. 55 to (12km) Mexicalzingo.—26km Tianguistenco.—31km Xalatlaco.—90km **Mexico City**.

We leave Toluca to the SE along Méx. 55. 4km **Metepec** is famous for its many-coloured decorative pottery: especially delightful árboles de la vida (trees of life), on which perch, or from which hang, human figures, birds, fish, animals, fruit; and Christmas cribs. Facing the main plaza is the former Franciscan convent of *San Juan Bautista*, founded in the 1550s as a doctrina of Toluca. The church was rebuilt in the 18C and acquired its two-storey façade, an outstanding example of popular baroque. It resembles a folding screen, its slender engaged pilasters soaring in the upper storey to emphasize the impression of height and covered in the same delicate tapestry-like relief as the spaces between them. In the two-storey cloister (1555–65) traces of murals of the life of St Francis remain. 12km *Mexicalzingo*, beyond which we turn l. for (15km) *Chapultepec*, where the church of San Miguel (1692) contains good timberwork and a baroque altarpiece. An anachronistic open chapel is attached.

24km turning l. for (13km N) *Lerma* (see Rte 35A) and r. for (18km SW) *Tenango de Arista*, see Rte 79. S on the Tenango road is (3km) *Almoloya del Río*, beneath the N slopes of the volcano Holotepec and on the E bank of the now dried-up *Laguna de Almoloya*, source of the Río Lerma; and (7km) *Texcalyacac*, where a nave altarpiece (r.) in the church of San Mateo contains five paintings of the Guadalupe story by Juan Correa.

The course of the **Lerma**, with the largest basin (124,000 sq km) in the country, runs 515km through the States of México, Michoacán, and Guanajuato to the Lago de Chapala. The Lerma Aqueduct (*Sistema Lerma*), built during 1941–51, is both a stupendous feat of engineering and an ecological disaster. It cuts through the mountains from Almoloya to Chapultepec in Mexico City (c 56km) and has not only diverted the river waters at their source, but also captured riparian springs in the Valle de Toluca to supply water (7500 litres a second) to the capital. The engineers' greatest challenge was the Sierra de las Cruces, tunnelled for 15km. The water power is also harnessed to supply electricity. The result has been the shrinking of the Lago de Chapala and the drying-up of the Lerma basin.

At (26km) **Tianguistenco** (R,P) the main façade of the parish church of *Nuestra Señora del Buen Suceso* (1755), paid for by José de la Borda (comp. Rte 82), is in imposing neostyle baroque. The elaborate columns in three distinct sections provide the main supports. Between those of the lower storey rise two slender twisted columns on richly carved high bases whose corinthian capitals break through the cornice to support slanted bases for strange repetitions of the bases below, decorative slanted blocks laden with lambrequins. Above the high doorway, which adds to the soaring effect, the relief shows the papal tiara and the keys of St Peter. An unusual feature is the reliefs of the tower bases, a vigorous St Christopher on the l. The N doorway makes similar use of paired columns. Just to the N of Tianguistenco is *Capulhuac*, with the 17C church of San Bartolomé.

28km (r.) *San Lorenzo Huehuetitlán*, where the church incorporates an early 17C open chapel. 31km *Xalatlaco*. The neighbouring village of *Santiago Tilapa* boasts a 16C chapel with tequitqui relief and wooden ceiling. From Xalatlaco the road continues E through the forested Sierra de Ajusco into the Federal District. 65km *San Miguel Ajusco*. From here to (90km) *Mexico City* via Tlalpan, see Rte 15.

36 Guadalajara to Mexico City via Irapuato and Querétaro

Méx. 90, Méx. 110, Méx. 45, and Méx. 57D, 593km.—97km Atotonilco el Alto.—165km La Piedad and Méx. 110.—251km **Irapuato** (hence the toll road, Méx. 45D, runs directly to [365km] **Querétaro**) and Méx. 45.—271km **Salamanca**.—312km **Celaya**.—371km **Querétaro** and Méx. 57D.—423km San Juan del Río.—593km **Mexico City**.

We leave Guadalajara to the SE and take the toll road (Méx. 90) via (13km) *Tonalá*, see Rte 24. 35km *Zapotlanejo*, a picturesque town on the S edge of Altos de Jalisco and 5km from the l. bank of the Río Calderón, which runs into the Río Grande de Santiago from the Sierra de Tepatitlán, to the NE.

A few km upriver at the *Puente de Calderón* Hidalgo's huge, undisciplined host was smashed by the small army of Brig. Félix Calleja on 17 Jan. 1811, a defeat which spelt doom for the insurgents.

From (66km) *Tototlán* a road runs S to (26km) *Ocotlán* and the Lago de Chapala, see Rte 26. 97km *Atotonilco el Alto* (H,R,P) on the r. bank of the Río Zula. Its parish church was designed at the turn of the century by Adamo Boari. 29km S is *La Barca*, see Rte 28.

Roads NE and NW lead into Los Altos, see Rte 50. 31km NE is *Arandas* (1290m), known for its mariachis and pretty women. Its church is neo-Gothic.

Beyond (147km) *Degollado*, with a notable neo-Gothic church (c 1861–70), we cross briefly into the State of Guanajuato and then (157km) the Río Lerma into the State of Michoacán. 165km **La Piedad** (c 50,000 inhab.; 1656m; H,R,P), at an important road junction, and famous for its dairy products. The celebrated bridge over the Río Lerma (1832) was built under the direction of José María Cabadas (comp. Rte 28) while parish priest here.

53km SW is *Zamora* (see Rte 28); 153km S is *Uruapan* (see Rte 29); 112km N is *León*, see Rte 50.

Méx. 110 continues E into the State of Guanajuato to (201km) **Pénjamo** (15,000 inhab.; 1705m; R,P). The remains of doña Ana María Gallaga (1731–62), mother of Miguel Hidalgo, rest in the parish church, the place of her wedding to don Cristóbal Hidalgo y Costilla (1713–90) on 15 Aug. 1750. 213km turning l. for (7km N) **Corralejo**, in the Sierra de Pénjamo, now a small agricultural town, formerly the hacienda of San Diego Corralejo, birthplace of Miguel Hidalgo on 8 May 1753. His father, don Cristóbal, was steward of the hacienda; his mother's uncle, Antonio Gallaga, leaseholder of the dependent ranch of San Vicente. The ruins of house and chapel built by don Cristóbal survive. In the parish church at (222km) *Abasolo* (the former *Cuitzeo de los Naranjos*) Miguel Hidalgo was baptized on 16 May 1753. 238km Méx. 80 from *Tepatitlán* (172km E) joins Méx. 110.

251km **IRAPUATO** (250,000 inhab.; 1700m; H,R,P), on the river of the same name, in an agricultural and cattle-raising region, the W part of the fertile Bajío. It is especially famous for its strawberries (fresas), sold throughout the town and on its outskirts, and exported in quantity to the USA. A strawberry fiesta is held every 2 Apr. The façades of its 18C churches, in singular local baroque, are its chief architectural beauty.

During the war of Independence it was headquarters of Col. Agustín de Iturbide in his fight against the insurgents. (He called it 'strategically best placed to dominate the Bajío'—words echoed a century later by Gen. Alvaro Obregón: 'those troops who hold Irapuato will have the destiny of Mexico in their hands'.) His second daughter, Josefa, later princess at Maximilian's court, was born here in 1814. The first 24 strawberry shoots were brought from France by Nicolás Tejada in 1852, and planted out of curiosity. The first strawberry ice creams, cause of unalloyed delight, were sold in 1858.

The town centre was revitalized by restoration in the 1960s, and in large part turned into a pedestrian precinct. On the W side of PLAZUELA HIDALGO is the **Parroquia** (*La Soledad*), begun c 1681. Its regular baroque façade is covered by vegetal relief, the palm leaves on the columns particularly noticeable. On the E side stands the church of **San José** (mid-18C), its façade the most characterful in Irapuato, more popular and interesting in style, with its four pairs of heavy estípites and prolonged top storey, studded by a relief of the Crucifixion and with an upper statue of the patron saint framed by two types of baroque column. The delightfully canopied niches add to its sturdy distinction.

From the S side of the plazuela we turn r. along C. Santos Degollado to meet JARDIN HIDALGO. On its E side are the churches of *La Tercera Orden* and, further back, *San Francisco*, both later 18C, the latter damaged by fire in 1985. On the W side is the **Pal. Municipal** (1800–10; by Esteban González), strongly neoclassical, formerly the *Colegio de Niñas*, founded and staffed by nuns of the Company of Mary from the convent of La Enseñanza in Mexico and suppressed at the Reform. Its patio is claimed to be the largest in the republic.

It was built in the atrio of the church of *La Soledad* (dedicated in 1710; S doorway in C. Ramón Corona), whose interior is notable for its trilobular arches upholding the octagonal base of the cupola.

On the N side of the Pal. Municipal, in C. Fernando Dávila, is the church known as **El Hospital** (*Nuestra Señora de la Misericordia*; c 1710–33). Varied solomonic columns mark the two lower storeys of its S façade and the topmost niche. This is in the centre of a felicitous semicircular gable covered by a crinkled canopy and flanked by reliefs of the sun and moon, symbols of the Immaculate Conception. An inscription bears the name of the indigenous sculptor: 'Crispín Lorenzo…1733'.

At its W end C. Fernando Dávila joins C. Revolución. Following this street and taking the third turning l., C. 5 de Febrero, we reach, at the corner with C. Allende, the early 19C house built for the Hernández family and used in the last years of the viceroyalty as local headquarters of the Inquisition. C. Allende leads to C. Guerrero: c 150m to the l. is the church of *San Francisco de Paula* (San Francisquito; c 1800–05), with a good neoclassical portal. The house at the corner with C. Ocampo (continuation of C. Allende) was built early in the 19C for the Zuloaga family.

From Irapuato Méx. 45 runs N to (33km) *Silao* and (65km) *León*, see Rte 50. The toll road, Méx. 45D, runs directly E to (114km) *Querétaro* (see Rte 37), keeping well N of the more interesting, and inevitably slower, Méx. 45.

We continue SE to (271km) **SALAMANCA** (200,000 inhab.; 1720m; H,R,P), in the E part of the Bajío and long an important agricultural centre. Recent industrial development has polluted the waters of the Río Lerma on which it stands. This is chiefly owing to the Pemex oil refinery, to which oil is piped from Poza Rica in the State of Veracruz. Salamanca possesses, however, two of Mexico's most significant historical monuments.

Originally called *Sirandaro* (or Barahona) it was founded in 1602, and during the 18C shared in the prosperity of the Bajío as a flourishing cotton-weaving centre. The first serious battle of the war of the Reform was fought here on 9–10 March 1858: a conservative force under the young one-armed Gen. Luis G. Osollo defeated the liberals under Gen. Anastasio Parrodi. From Salamanca in Oct. 1876 José María Iglesias issued his proclamation against the re-election of Pres. Lerdo de Tejada, claiming the presidency for himself (see Rte 37). Two heroes of the war of Independence were born in Salamanca: the guerrilla Albino García, shot in Celaya in 1812; and Tomasa Estévez (1788–1814), a 'mujer seductora', who seduced royalists to desert.

In the town centre, at the corner of Cs Allende and Sánchez Torrado, is the former parish church of **San Bartolo** (c 1730), its façade a work of tremendous character and vigour, drawing on the baroque and churrigueresque, with a reminder of the plateresque, and attesting the ebullience of indigenous Mexican craftsmanship.

The entrance arch, seeming at first sight semicircular, is in fact subtly polygonal. Bulbous columns, the upper halves fantastically solomonic, the lower in a zigzag pattern, form the lowest storey supports, broad estípites those of the upper storeys. The lower storey niches are framed by screw-like columns ending in canephorae; on either side of the elaborate niche supports, masked heads end in leafy spirals. On either side, in turn, of the lower storey edge stands a human figure dressed in jerkin and boots, a shell motif behind the head. The shape of the central window surprises by its strangeness. Covering all and climaxing in the huge semicircular pediment is an abundance of juicy, vegetal, floral, fruity, and snakelike relief and angel supports (especially in the middle storey niche frames). Above the entrance arch a rich cordlike motif combines with the lower line of the frieze to form an anachronistic alfíz.

At the corner of Cs Revolución and Andrés Delgado is the former Augustinian convent of **San Agustín**, started in 1614–17, completed and remodelled in the mid-18C. The plain exterior of the church is in direct contrast to the dazzling gold and polychrome of the INTERIOR. 19C 'good taste' accounted for the high altar (1832). The ten altarpieces of nave and transept-like bays were mercifully spared. The two latter, dedicated to St Joseph and St Anne, are by Pedro Joseph de Rojas, works of daring brilliance and fantasy, prodigiously projecting, done in the late 1760s.

This craftsman, resident in Querétaro, signed a contract in May 1768, by which he undertook to have the retable of St Anne, without statues or gilding, ready in ten months: and to have it ready 'at the door of his house on waggons, to be taken to Salamanca, where he must himself go to set up and gild the said retable to its final conclusion'.

The style of both altarpieces combines anastyle baroque and rococo. The supports flanking the sumptuous niche pilasters take on a unique form, almost lost in the wealth of rococo motifs, seraph heads, angels, cherubs. Imposts become cherubs; capitals baskets of flowers. Both are enlivened by tableaux, embellished with lovely estofado, illustrating scenes from the saints' lives. That of St Joseph, richer and more spontaneous of the two, shows the Flight into Egypt; the Marriage of Our Lady and St Joseph; the Death of St Joseph, attended by Our Lord and Our Lady; the Dream of St Joseph; and the Finding of the Child Jesus in the Temple. That of St Anne shows the Presentation (top l.) and St Anne and Our Lady (top r.). The emphatic crowns and the beautiful central canopies heighten the theatrical effect.

Features of the four main nave altarpieces, probably a little later in date, are the ornamental niche pilaster, the background mat-like (petatillo) and mesh effects, and the wealth of rococo motifs. On the r., the altarpiece of St Nicholas of Tolentino shows scenes from his life set forward from fanciful niches on platforms upheld by angel heads. The group showing him hearing the pleas of a beggar, his clothes picturesquely patched, and two kneeling children is particularly fine. The retable next to it frames the church's side doorway. Opposite are the altarpieces of St Thomas of Villanueva, with a gorgeous horizontal middle section of the richest lattice-like relief, and of St Rita of Cascia, patron of the impossible, with relief scenes from her life in medallions, placed against flattened pilasters, subdued by thrusting relief.

The pulpit dates from the late 18C. The outside of the staircase shows a painted scene of the progress of the blessed into heaven. Striking inlay decorates box and canopy. An extra-fanciful touch is the doorways to the sacristy, topped by gorgeously sculpted umbrella-like canopies. The paintings in the choir are by Juan Baltasar Gómez (1768).

The adjoining former convent, on the left of the church, consists of the 17C cloister, called claustro chico, and a larger cloister (c 1771), its arches springing from the sturdiest of pilasters embellished with heavy lambrequin and inverted-volute relief. After the battle of Salamanca the convent served as a 'hospital de sangre'—a terrible sight according to a priest who ministered to the wounded and the dying. It was later taken over as the town gaol.

The altarpiece of St Anne by Pedro Joseph de Rojas in San Agustín, Salamanca

From Salamanca Méx. 43 runs S to (51km)*Yuriria*, (77km) *Cuitzeo*, and (112km) *Morelia*, see Rte 32.

We leave Salamanca to the SE on Méx. 45. 312km **CELAYA** (163,000 inhab.; 1810m; H,R,P), at key road and railway junctions, is in the centre of the Bajío, the fertility of whose soil (enhanced by irrigation works on the Río Lerma to its S) has assured the town's economic importance, added to of late by the growth of manufacturing and chemical industries. It is a pleasant and clean place and is famous for its cajeta (a light, coffee-coloured thick syrup based on goat's milk and sugar, and coming in various flavours), now being mass-produced in hardened form for countrywide distribution.

The villa of Celaya was founded in Jan. 1571 in an effort to reinforce the Spanish presence against Chichimec raids and as a garrison settlement to safeguard vital lines of communication between Mexico and the silver mines at Zacatecas. By the 18C it had settled into great prosperity, especially as a cotton-weaving town, an industry which persists. On 21 Sept. 1810 Hidalgo, at the head of a disorganized army soon swelling to 50,000 strong, entered Celaya. At a ceremony the following day he was, 'by popular vote', appointed captain-general and Ignacio Allende lieut.-general. On 6–7 and 13–15 Apr. 1915 it was scene of decisive defeats for Francisco Villa's forces at the hands of Alvaro Obregón. The latter planned defence meticulously, using barbed wire around his positions, and Villa's frantic cavalry charges were mown down by Obregón's artillery and machine guns: 4000 villistas killed, 5000 wounded, 6000 prisoners; 138 constitutionalists dead, 227 wounded. Carranza thus gained the upper hand and was able eventually to return to Mexico City.

Celaya's most famous native is the self-taught architect (and, in a minor way, painter, sculptor, and poet) Francisco Eduardo Tresguerras (1759–1833), one of Mexican history's great characters. The town, which appointed him maestro mayor de obras públicas, bears the imprint of his work. When Joel Poinsett arrived here in the autumn of 1822, Tresguerras lay in wait for him, 'and brought a manuscript, which he insisted on reading. It was an essay on taste, and contained some severe sarcasms on his own countrymen'.

The **Bajío**, a fertile, low-lying plain, is known as 'the granary of the republic', producing vast amounts of Mexican staple crops. It comprises that part of the Mexican high plateau limited on the N by the S foothills of the Sierra de Guanajuato; on the S by the N spurs of the Sierra Volcánica Transversal; on the E by the approx. line Querétaro–Amealco; on the W by the Sierra de Pénjamo and the valley of La Piedad. From SE to NW flows the Río Lerma, its course forged by the natural drainage of a series of lakes which has left rich layers of volcanic soil and lacustrine deposits. The artistic wealth of the Bajío towns mirrors 18C economic vitality.

On the E side of PL. PRINCIPAL, densely planted with laurel and cypress, is the modern *Pal. Municipal*, successor to the Ayuntamiento where Hidalgo's appointment as capt.-general was forcibly ratified by those few members who turned up for the ceremony.

On the W side (112 Portal Corregidora) the *Casa de José Mújica* (c 1808; modified c 1880) is probably by Tresguerras, as is the house on the NW corner (Portal Enrique Colunga).

A block E is the elongated C. Independencia, formerly PL. DE ARMAS, at its centre the *Monumento a la Independencia*, a composite column supporting an eagle, a serpent, and other symbols, by Tresguerras. It was first conceived (1792) as a tribute to Charles IV, but transformed to accommodate the new order. On its E side is the church and former convent of **San Francisco**, founded as *Nuestra Señora de la Concepción* in 1570.

Its first rebuilding dates from the 17C and its second from 1715. But its present aspect seems to owe much to the intervention of Tresguerras early in the 19C. The establishment included a hospital and seminary—Colegio Real y Pontificio de la Universidad, subject to the University of Mexico—opened in 1624 and closed down in 1859.

The church portico, with curved pediment above an elaborate frieze and statue of Our Lady above on a pedestal, attests Tresguerras' own interpretation of the neoclassical (although alterations were made c 1895). The cupola, all green and gold tiles, is similar to that of El Carmen; the drum is laden with neoclassical motifs; the three-storey tower recalls 17C baroque. The altars of the interior (1819) are also by Tresguerras, as are the choirstalls.

In the convent atrio he built a series of chapels to accompany the Stations of the Cross, the last (surviving in its original state) to serve as his own tomb. In this, called *Nuestra Señora de los Dolores*, he gave free rein to a predilection for rich decoration which he had somewhat to sublimate in his public life. The façade, delicately ornamented around a neoclassical base, is touchingly graceful. He directed that it should be filled with his favourite possessions. His death from cholera caused his burial away from the town centre and his remains were not removed here until a year later.

On the S side of the atrio is the 18C chapel of *La Tercera Orden*. The high altar (c 1820), its pediment broken in a novel way, and plainer side altars are also Tresguerras' work. The doorway of the former convent (finished in 1733), now a school, is marked by pilasters enclosing slender tableros. Clever use of tableros in the pilasters facing the patio, harmonizing with the moulding of the arches, is also a feature of the two-storey cloister, along with cherub relief in the spandrels of the lower-storey arches and angel faces in the ornate upper capitals.

The *Mercado Morelos*, S of the plaza, was built to the design of Lewis Long in 1903–06.

One block N of Pl. Principal is the great church of **El Carmen**, the masterwork of Tresguerras, one of the most famous, yet highly individual, contributions to the Mexican neoclassical.

The previous, baroque, church on the site was burned down in 1802. Reconstruction, probably using the previous foundations and parts of the walls, cost 225,000 pesos. It was completed in 1807. Restoration took place in 1852–55 and in 1963–66.

EXTERIOR. The church is cruciform in plan. The portico, facing E, surmounted by an elegant two-storey tower capped by a pinnacle, projects from the nave and is a model of proportion. The beautiful, glistening cupola, with green and yellow tiles, rests on a drum borne up by paired columns; the lantern, surrounded by a balustrade, is a fittingly tasteful finish. The side (S) door, a more intricate composition, is still a marvel of balance, combining neoclassical motifs and reminders of the baroque.

INTERIOR. Both unity and grandeur are achieved: the superb high altar; the six side altars, all white and gold, pairing in different designs, and the pairs of altars in the transept; the strongly marked cornice; the pilasters; the gallery above; and the vaulting are vividly neoclassical—but not without extra baroquish flourishes. The *Cap. de los Cofrades*, on the S side, contains frescoes by Tresguerras: the Last Judgement (1803), the Raising of Lazarus, and the Burial of Tobias. In the sotocoro of the N transept is a magnificent painting by Nicolás Rodríguez Juárez, Triumph of the Church (1695), saved from the previous church. On the l. the Church is shown as a queen, her carriage, crushing the heretics Pelagius, Nestor, Arian, Calvin, and Luther, drawn by pontiffs, bishops, and doctors of the Church towards a triumphal arch, in front of which wait SS Teresa and John of God, and Elijah. The Holy Trinity watches from above.

Behind the sotocoro is a charming small cloister. A monument to Tresguerras (1951) faces the church on the S side of C. del Carmen.

One block S of Pl. Principal, at the corner of Av. Allende and C. Democracia, is the former Augustinian convent and church of **San Agustín** (1609). The convent buildings, with excellent interior doorways, variously carved, house the *Casa de Cultura* (temporary exhibitions). SW of Pl. Principal, in Av. Juárez, is the attractive late 18C *Casa del Diezmo*, combining the town's historical archive, the tourist office, and a small local museum. Still is use over the Río Laja, E of the town, is the bridge called *Puente Tresguerras* (1804–06), designed by him, another elegant work, with basket arches and projecting voussoirs.

Celaya is also on Méx. 51, running N to (52km) *San Miguel de Allende* (see Rte 58) and S to (35km) *Salvatierra*, see Rte 40A. At 27km along the road to San Miguel is **Comonfort** (the former *Chamacuero*), where the church of *San Francisco*, dating probably from the 1640s (modified), contains a collection of superb 18C altarpieces. Outstanding are two anastyle examples in the transepts, dated 1792, donated to celebrate the birth of María Manuela Taboada, future wife of the insurgent Mariano Abasolo, by her father. The style is notably queretano, with wonderfully free cornices; one incorporates flowing design around beautifully framed oval paintings.

C 6km NW of Comonfort is *Orduña*, where a yácata (platform like those at Tarascan Tzintzuntzan, Rte 28) have been excavated. A similar has been discovered at *Cañada de la Virgen*, c 50km NW.

From Celaya we may continue E along the toll road (Méx. 45D) or through typical Bajío country on Méx. 45 via (341km; r.) *Apaseo el Alto*. 371km *Querétaro*, see Rte 37.

We leave Querétaro to the S to join Méx. 57D, the toll road to Mexico City, which runs at first E to (392km) turning l. for (37km NE) *Bernal*, near the *Peña de Bernal*, a famous craggy eminence (350m) dominating the plain, and (65km) *Tolimán* in the Sierra Gorda. Its 18C church is successor to the Franciscan convent of San Pedro, founded in 1583. 412km turning r. (Méx. 120) for (112km SW) *Acámbaro*, see Rte 40A.

423km turning l. for **San Juan del Río** (c 25,000 inhab.; 1890m; H,R,P; famous agricultural fair, 3rd week in June), a pleasant town rendered more peaceful since the toll road has diverted traffic from its centre. It preserves streets of 17C–early 19C houses. In Pl. Independencia the parish church of *Los Españoles* (now *Nuestra Señora de Guadalupe*) was given its classical portal in the late 18C. The adjoining church of *Sagrado Corazón* was formerly reserved for Indians (Cap. de los Naturales). At the corner of Av. Benito Juárez Poniente and C. Zaragoza the church and convent of *Sto Domingo* were built for the Franciscans in the 17C, but later taken over by the Dominicans. No. 62 Av. Juárez, church of the former *Beaterio de Nuestra Señora de los Dolores*, built for pious ladies following the strict rule of St Clare in 1766, and with a tranquil cloister, preserves a beautiful fanlike coro alto grille; on the l. wall of the presbytery is a cratícula. At No. 136 in the same street are the church and former hospital of *San Juan de Dios*, established by the Brothers of St John of God in 1662. At the W entrance to the town the stone bridge (1720) was designed by Pedro de Arrieta.

The town is in a wine-producing region and is the main centre in Mexico for semi-precious stones (opals from the Trinidad and Esperanza mines). Other stones from all over Latin America are polished and set here. Avoid street vendors.

432km *Palmillas*. At 436km Méx. 55 (r.) runs S into the State of México.

At 31km is a turning l. for (4km E) **Aculco** (c 6000 inhab.; 2309m), a pretty town famous for its cheeses. The former Franciscan convent of *San Jerónimo* was built in the 17C to serve a small parish (secularized in 1759). The church has a façade of great charm, though interfered with in the 19C and in 1914 after an earthquake in 1912. The lowest-storey column bases display good vegetal relief. In the top storey is a lovely relief of Our Lord appearing to St Rose to ask her to be his spouse ('Tu esclava soy Señor mi Jesús'), watched over by God the Father and the Holy Ghost. In the atrio are three posa chapels supported by little bulbous columns. The sacristy contains a Last Supper by Cabrera. In the environs of Aculco on 6 Nov. 1810 the insurgent forces, with Hidalgo indecisive after his failure to push home his attack on Mexico City, suffered a devastating defeat, their first important setback, at the hands of Calleja, who had descended on them from Querétaro.

474km turning l. for (27km N) *Amealco* (see Rte 39) and r. for (3km S) *Calpulalpan*, where on 22 Dec. 1860 an improvised liberal army under Gen. Jesús González Ortega, and incl. Ignacio Zaragoza and Leandro Valle as junior commanders, decisively defeated the conservatives under Gens. Miramón and Márquez. The battle marked the end of the war of the Reform and the downfall of Miramón; the liberals made their triumphal entry into Mexico City on 1 Jan. 1861. 504km turning r. for (87km SW) *Toluca*, see Rte 40B. 533km turning l. for (21km N) *Tula*, see Rte 19. 551km (r.) *Tepotzotlán*, see Rte 19. 593km *Mexico City*.

37 Querétaro

QUERETARO (385,000 inhab.; 1834m), on the river of the same name, and on the E edge of the Bajío, is one of the most beautiful and irresistible of cities, its narrow streets and plazas redolent of the country's past. As a treasure house of the fine arts it has few rivals and the sunlight gives a luminosity which heightens the enchantment. It is also 'the city of history par excellence', indelibly associated with stirring events that have shaped modern Mexico. Its recent industrial growth has brought funds in part used to restore and beautify the historic centre, part of it, agreeably, accessible to pedestrians only.

Railway station. Av. Héroe de Nacozari, on N side of river, NW of junction of C. Corregidora and Av. Mariano Escobedo. Trains to *Mexico City* (Aguila Azteca [see Rte 53]; c 5 hrs), to *León*, to *Guadalajara*, to *San Luis Potosí*, to *Aguascalientes*, etc.

Bus station. On S side of Alameda. Services to *Mexico City* (3 hrs); to *San Miguel de Allende* (1 hr); to *San Juan del Río* (1 hr); to *Irapuato* (2 hrs); to *Guadalajara* (7 hrs); to *Pachuca* (4½ hrs); to *León* (3 hrs); to *Celaya* (1 hr); to *Acámbaro* (2 hrs); to *Morelia* (c 4 hrs); to *Guanajuato* (c 3½ hrs); to *San Luis Potosí* (3 hrs); etc.

Hotels throughout the city.

Post Office. 7 C. Arteaga.

Tourist Office. 17 C. Pasteur.

Fiestas. 12 Sept. (feast of Sta Cruz de los Milagros); 15 Sept. (Grito de Dolores); 16–24 Dec. (Christmas celebrations).

On 25 July 1531 the forces of two christianized Otomí caciques, Fernando de Tapia and Nicolás de San Luis Montañez, with Spanish help, defeated (in a battle traditionally held to have been fought without weapons) a combined Otomí, Tarascan, and Chichimec army to found a colony here, 'Santiago de Crettaro', established by 1537–38. C 1548 the prehispanic site (c 8km SE), also called by the Spaniards Crettaro, was re-established here. The opening of the road to the mines of Zacatecas gave Querétaro strategic importance as a bastion against Chichimec raids. In 1656, on payment of 3000 gold pesos, it was granted the title of city, 'muy noble y muy leal ciudad de Santiago de Querétaro', confirmed by Philip V in 1712. In 1680 Carlos de Sigüenza y Góngora was present at the dedication of the church of La Congregación and was so impressed by what he saw that he began his 'Glorias de Querétaro', in praise of 'the third city of New Spain'. In the 18C Querétaro consolidated its wealth: a great commercial centre, thriving on the fertility of the Bajío soil. Wealth was reflected in the flowering of queretano ultrabaroque which may be seen and enjoyed especially in the churches of Sta Clara and Sta Rosa, and in the domestic architecture: patios of fantastic multifoil and mixtilinear arches, and beautiful wrought-iron balconies.

In 1803, wrote the local historian José María Zelaá e Hidalgo, 'the city comprises not only the vulgar multitude but also great and noble families, among whom Castilian grandees, knights of the military orders, and rich landed gentlemen are not found wanting. The demeanour of its inhabitants is genteel; their apparel both splendid and bought at suitable cost; but without extravagance or indecency. The principal persons use their coaches, which today number above six and sixty, to shed lustre and magnificence on this city'. In 1804, it is recorded, Querétaro contained 18 factories and 327 obrajes (small workshops) turning out a variety of textiles, mostly by forced labour. The owners admitted they had to lock the workers in.

By 1808, under the guise of literary gatherings, a group of conspirators, headed by the corregidor Miguel Domínguez, a popular figure, and his wife Josefa Ortiz, a woman of character and courage, and Epigmenio González, had begun to plan for Mexican Independence, and their meetings were attended by Miguel Hidalgo, Ignacio Allende, Juan Aldama, Mariano Abasolo, and others. With the outbreak of the war of Independence the corregidor and his wife were arrested, but soon released: the former continuing in office; the latter continuing her involvement with the insurgents, which brought about her denunciation to the viceroy as 'incorrigible, a veritable Anne Boleyn' and, in 1813, her incarceration in Mexico City. The city was fortified by the Spaniards until taken by Iturbide, after the proclamation of the Plan of Iguala, in June 1821. In 1848 the treaty of peace to end the US-Mexican war was signed here. In 1853 Guillermo Prieto eloquently commented on the prevailing decadence: 'Querétaro is a dethroned king, sunk in poverty…surrounded by the remains of erstwhile opulence…it is a paralysed giant'. During the 1850s it was the base of operations of Col. (later Gen.) Tomás Mejía, Otomí cacique and staunch Catholic conservative, in arms against the Plan of Ayutla and bitter critic of the Reform.

On 19 Feb. 1867 Maximilian arrived in Querétaro, where there was much personal sympathy for him, to start the empire's decisive stand against the republicans, but the city, surrounded by hills from which the besiegers could fire, was badly situated for the imperialists. Their principal commanders were not united. The republican force, under Gen. Mariano Escobedo, was gradually reinforced to 40,000 men with 80 pieces of heavy artillery, in contrast to the imperialists' 7000 and 40 pieces. By 9 March the republicans had surrounded the city. Theatre and churches were raided for lead to melt down for shot and the garrison was reduced to eating domestic animals. Gen. Miramón's skirmishes against the republicans were never pressed home and a break-out, on 23 March, by Gens Márquez and Vidaurri to the S to seek reinforcements from Mexico City did not bring the desired result. On 15 May the republicans entered Querétaro. Maximilian made a last stand on the Cerro de las Campanas, but was soon forced to surrender. His trial, along with those of Miramón and

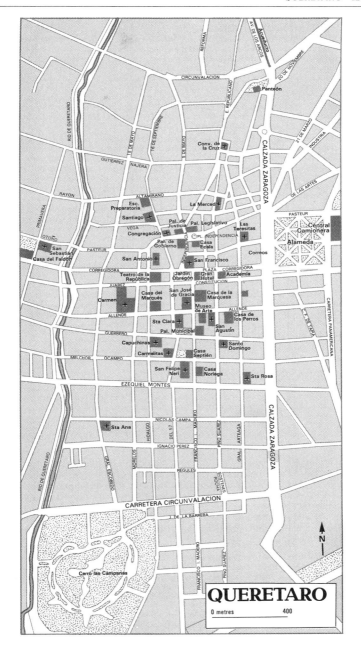

QUERETARO

0 metres 400

Mejía, took place on 13 June. Sentence was delivered the following day. On 19 June the three were shot on the Cerro de las Campanas.

In Dec. 1876 at the hacienda of La Capilla, on the W outskirts, a series of meetings between José María Iglesias and Porfirio Díaz obliged the former to yield to Díaz's claims, and ushered in the porfiriato. In the period 1876–1910 Querétaro won back its prosperity. In Dec. the Constitutional Congress met here, its debates culminating in Feb. 1917 in the proclamation of the political Constitution of the republic. At a convention called by Plutarco Elías Calles in Querétaro during 1–4 March 1929 was established, to unify the forces of the Revolution, the Partido Nacional Revolucionario, precursor of the Partido Revolucionario Institucional (PRI). Since the 1960s spectacular industrial growth has taken its toll of the city's neighbouring land and the outer reaches have spread into the Bajío. The suburbs are also serving to house overspill population from the Federal District.

The State of **Querétaro** (11,769 sq km; 984,000 inhab.) is in the centre of the republic, between the Sierras Madre Occidental and Oriental. In the N is the Sierra Gorda; in the S the Sierra Queretana. In the S are rolling plains and fertile valleys, part of the E Bajío, whose rich soil is often 3–4.5m deep. In the extreme W runs the Río Lerma. Mineral wealth, still not fully exploited, includes gold, copper, lead, marble, and tin, but the chief products have been opals and mercury. Industry, of increasing importance in the 1970s, is mainly around the capital, an excellent communications centre.

At Spanish penetration the area was part of the province of Xilotepec, called provincia de los Chichimecas, an ancient Otomí kingdom. Until the end of the 16C it was the scene of frequent warfare between Spaniards and their Otomí allies and Chichimecs. The latter continued, from their fastnesses in the Sierra Gorda, to give trouble until well into the 18C. In 1793 the city and its surrounds were created a separate entity, unique in New Spain, under a corregidor de letras (the appointment reserved for the king alone). At the second constitutional congress in 1823, which established the federal system, Querétaro was saved for Statehood thanks to the brilliant pleadings of the congress vice president, Félix Osares.

The ALAMEDA, N of the bus station and on the S side of Calz. Zaragoza, was laid out during the porfiriato after the original park of 1793 had been laid waste in 1867. The central statue of Hidalgo dates from 1897. From its W side we may take C. Corregidora two blocks N to PL. DE LA CONSTITUCION, laid out in 1967 to commemorate the 50th anniversary of the Constitution; on its S side is a statue of Venustiano Carranza. Behind is the **Academia** (now, more correctly, **Instituto) de Bellas Artes**.

It was inaugurated in 1804 by Miguel Domínguez as a school sponsored by the Third Order of St Francis to provide an elementary education free of charge for poorer boys. In 1808 an academy of drawing was added and the first floor begun. Here in 1848 the Mexican Congress met to discuss the disastrous treaty which was to end the war with the USA. In 1880 a conservatory of music was established; in 1910, much adapted, it became the Academia de Bellas Artes. From Nov. 1916 the Constitutional Congress met here to formulate the new Constitution. From the early 1950s it has been the Institute of Fine Arts within the University of Querétaro.

On the N side of the plaza is the *Gran Hotel* (by Cipriano Bueno; 1890–93), built on part of the atrio of the convent of San Francisco. On its other side opens the attractive PL. PRINCIPAL, officially JARDIN OBREGON. Its fountain dates from 1882 and its bandstand (popular concerts on Thurs. and Sun. evenings) from later in the 19C.

On its SE side are the church and main cloister of the former convent of **San Francisco**, all that remains of a huge Franciscan establishment once comprising various additional churches and chapels.

The first foundation, called *Santiago*, was built c 1550–60. The present church was finished after 1658 by José de Bayas Delgado; the convent between 1683 and 1698. Their dependencies, stretching over the area now occupied by the two plazas, were wantonly destroyed during 1849–63. The convent was used as a military hospital in 1867 and then allowed to fall into ruin. Its present aspect owes much to restoration in 1934 and in the 1960s.

EXTERIOR. The well-proportioned W portal, with its classicizing motifs and statues of SS Peter and Paul, Antony and Bonaventure, is firmly Mannerist; but a primitive, vigorous relief of St James (Santiago Matamoros) incorporated into the top storey is a survivor from the original church. The tower is dated 1676. The clock is an addition of 1883.

INTERIOR. The neoclassical high altarpiece dates from 1809. Its statue of the Immaculate Conception is by Mariano Arce (early 19C). In the Sacristy is an intensely moving Pietà, also by Arce. The sotocoro vault shows geometric relief. In the choir is an elaborate baroque lectern; the choirstalls (1796) are by Tresguerras.

The convent is entered just to the S of the church. It now contains the **Museo Regional de Querétaro** (Tues.–Sun., 10–1; 3–6; fee). A feature of the fine main cloister is the sturdy bulbous columns of the upper storey, fluted in their upper two-thirds and with a zigzag pattern in their lower third. Note also the relief of the lower-storey vaults.

GROUND FLOOR. ROOMS 1 and 2. 1. Two necklaces from the sites of Las Ranas (San Joaquín) and Tulum (Quintana Roo), of jade or jadeite, rock crystal, and obsidian. Besides their craftsmanship these two pieces demonstrate the lengths of Mesoamerican long-distance trade and the redistribution of the relatively rare materials of which they are made. 2. Projectile points and other obsidian tools from several local sites: Puebllto, San Bartolo, and San Juan del Río; Maya tools from Tulum; basalt club, dated c 200 BC, from Las Ranas; ceremonial axe-head of gargantua from Toluquilla. 3. Stone sculpture in elaborate headdress, earrings, etc. 4. Miscellaneous figurines from Maya Tulum, dated c 200 BC–AD 1400, notably a woman-and-child group and a four-legged creature (feline?) with incised geometric patterns and black paint. 5. Miscellaneous ceramics: red and cream monochromes, black monochromes with incised decorations, and small ceramic and stone masks. 6. Fragment of a chacmool sculpture. 7. Human skull, illustrating the practice of cranial deformation, common in many Mesoamerican cultures. 8. Miscellaneous bone and shell jewellery, especially necklaces of beads. 9. Hollow ceramic figurine, depicting a seated figure with features in high relief and wearing an elaborate headdress. 10. Clay crucible for melting minerals, from La Sierra (c AD 400); masks and an animal figurine from Arroyo Seco (Huasteca; c 100 BC–AD 200); stone seal from Playa Azul (Michoacán); stone masks; three figurines depicting pregnant women, two of clay and one of stone; human tooth set with greenstone; five 'petrified' shells from Lacandona de Chiapas; seated clay figurine with white-on-red painted decoration (c AD 400–600). 11. Three 'smiling face' figurines or masks, from Late Classic-Early Postclassic El Tajín. 12. Stone slab of the Chichimeca, c 3m by 1m by 15cm, with bas-relief carving of geometric patterns.

UPPER FLOOR. The rooms devoted to 19C history include autograph letters of Miguel Domínguez and of Allende to Hidalgo. Idealized portraits of insurgents. Busts of Josefa Ortiz and objects belonging to her. Lock panel, through the keyhole of which she communicated her warning to Pérez. Urn in which her ashes were taken to Querétaro. Fragment of the Plan of Iguala (1821). Standards of the Querétaro battalion used in action in Texas in 1835–36. José Reyes Meza's painting (1968) of Maximilian's surrender to Gen. Mariano Escobedo on 15 May 1867. Relics of the siege of Querétaro. Maximilian's knife and writing desk. Documents of the trial and inkstand used at it. Table on which his corpse was embalmed. Coffin used to move his body.

Paintings in the SALA MAGNA (W side) include Luis Juárez, Education of the Virgin (1615), very expressive. Juan Correa, Pietà; St Joseph and the Child Jesus, both rich in colouring, and the latter in landscape detail. Cabrera, Christ laid in the tomb (1757); 18 paintings of the life of St Ignatius done for the Colegios de San Ignacio y San Francisco Javier. José de Ibarra, Dogma of the Immaculate Conception; Circumcision.

Facing the NE corner of Jardín Obregón is JARDIN DE LA CORREGIDORA, in its centre a monument to Josefa Ortiz, designed by Carlos Noriega, its iron parts cast in Berlin, and unveiled in 1910. Behind it, alongside Av. Hidalgo, are the church and former convent of **San Antonio**, started in 1613 for discalced Franciscans, but transformed c 1700.

The W portal was finished in 1628 and modified in the 18–19C. The *Cap. de la Sta Escala*, to its r., dates from 1809. Among the earlier works of art preserved in the interior are a statue of

St Francis (1606) by Francisco Martínez and a painting of Christ carrying the Cross (1723) by José García. The octagonal Sacristy is crowned by a cupola shaped like a cone, the lantern forming its cusp. Lantern base, windows, relief arches, octagonal frames, and other rectilinear and polylobular elements produce a uniquely and startlingly fine play of forms. Geometric relief characterizes the sotocoro vault. In the upper gallery of the cloister is a Way of the Cross, the stations done in azulejos.

On the N side of the church C. Pasteur Norte runs N to the Río Querétaro. To the r., by a pink bridge, we may cross into C. Otoño. At the corner of C. Otoño and Av. Primavera is the church of *San Sebastián* (1718) facing a pretty plaza. On its W side is the *Casa del Faldón* (c 1778), full of character and interest. It is the result, so the story goes, of a bitter dispute between the alcalde Pablo de Tapia and the regidor Fadrique de Cázares. The latter was banished from the city after angrily tugging the alcalde's coattails (faldón) during a struggle for precedence in a Corpus Christi procession and chose the district (Otra Banda—the Other Side) for a house of exile, with a mirador from which he could observe life across the river.

From behind the church the evocative, stepped PASEO DE LA CORREGI-DORA, with one-storey 18C and early 19C houses faced in pastel shades and tezontle, leads to the church of **La Congregación**, its towers, with their pyramidal spires, a well-known landmark.

It was built for the secular priests of the Congregation of Our Lady of Guadalupe, and dedicated on 12 May 1680, amid great celebrations, incl. poetic contests, bullfights, and fireworks. Juan Caballero y Ocío (1644–1703), an illustrious benefactor of Querétaro (whose monument [1981] stands in front of the church), provided the funds and the architect was José de Bayas Delgado. Like all queretano churches of the 17–18C, its exterior was once painted in geometric and foliate motifs—'with such harmony', wrote Zelaá e Hidalgo, 'that it at once engages the attention of all who pass by'.

EXTERIOR. The railings enclosing the atrio, beautifully elaborated at the corners, are good specimens. The three-storey W portal is a highly individual derivation from Renaissance models. In the lowest, fluted pilasters flanking the doorway are shortened by extended bases, whose tops form the imposts of a pentagonal arch enclosed by another, semicircular. Spandrels (the stone cut to emphasize the triangular shape), frieze, and capitals show varied relief decoration. In the first storey, layers of moulding give the window a pronounced eared frame. Flanking it are two unexpected hermae (the earliest appearance of such figures in queretano architecture) supporting the entablature. The gable was probably altered c 1737 to accommodate the image of Our Lady of Guadalupe; and two framing estípites (rare examples in queretano ecclesiastical architecture) added to bring it up to date. The cupola was rebuilt larger by an Indian mason, José Guadalupe, in 1736.

The INTERIOR, with good rib vaulting, was altered, not ineffectively, in the 19C to suit neoclassical taste. The painting of Our Lady of Guadalupe on the high altar is attr. Baltasar de Echave y Rioja, and the organ case to Ignacio Mariano de las Casas. One small altarpiece of the late 18C survives in the Sacristy. Here also is a Crucifixion by Mariano Arce. The adjoining house of the Congregation contains paintings by José García (1723). Note the beautifully carved wooden ceilings.

AV. 16 DE SEPTIEMBRE, another fascinating street bordered by 18C and 19C mansions, continues E to (at the corner with C. Próspero C. Vega) the parish church of **Santiago**, formerly belonging to the Jesuits.

The first Jesuit church and college on this site, *San Ignacio*, date from 1618–25. They were rebuilt c 1700, thanks again to the generosity of Juan Caballero y Ocío, who endowed a further college, *San Francisco Javier*, on an enlarged site. The college was rebuilt in 1755 to the design of Ignacio Mariano de las Casas. On 27 June 1767 the community gathered in the refectory to hear the notice of expulsion, after which they fell on their knees and sang the Te Deum. Through the efforts of the secular priest José Antonio de la Vía, in 1771 the church was reopened as the parish church of *Santiago* and the colleges as the *Colegios Reales de San Ignacio y San Francisco Javier*; they functioned as a famous boys' school until closure at the Reform. In 1863 they were re-established as the *Colegio Civil* and in 1951 became the nucleus of the new University of Querétaro. The *Escuela Preparatoria* of the university is now housed here.

EXTERIOR. The church portal, facing S, is typically queretano, a delicate elaboration of motifs on a Mannerist base. The frieze of succulent vegetal relief encloses cherub heads. In the upper storey the statues of SS Ignatius and Francis Xavier stand forward of niches so compact as to be too small for them, between ionic columns and delightful hermae supports. The W wall is supported by flying buttresses and the espadañas add a rustic touch.

INTERIOR. Other typical queretano touches are the octagonal, cross, and circular reliefs of the sotocoro vault. The sacristy portal which gives entrance to the college buildings shows fine relief of foliage and rocailles. The main CLOISTER, of rare beauty, with enlivening flying angel and vegetal relief, and prominent cherubic keystones above the lower-storey arches, dates from 1755. Note too the inner doorways: the jambs with a variety of superimposed fluting; from them spring mixtilinear arches with ruffled arch faces—striking Mudéjar touches. The staircase shows an interesting play of arches, one of them seemingly without support.

From La Congregación, C. Pasteur leads up to PL. DE LA INDEPENDENCIA, the former PL. DE ARMAS, choicest of queretano plazas, small, intimate, and peaceful. In its centre is a fountain monument to Juan Antonio de Urrutia y Arana, 2nd marqués de la Villa del Villar del Aguila (1670–1743), great benefactor of Querétaro and builder of the aqueduct.

It dates from 1842. During the siege of 1867 the plaza was a favourite retreat of Maximilian and thus became a special target for republican cannon. A ball shattered the statue, which was replaced in 1892 by the present likeness, the work of Diego Almaraz y Guillén, who also modified pedestal and fountain.

On the N side is the **Pal. de Gobierno**, gracious and historically significant, finished in 1770 by Martín José de la Rocha as the *Casas Reales*, part of its ground floor to serve as the city gaol.

It was the residence of the corregidor, and thus in time of Miguel Domínguez and Josefa Ortiz. Here took place various literary gatherings, which cloaked deeper conspiracies for the independence of New Spain. In late Aug. 1810 the plotters were discovered and denounced to the authorities. The corregidor locked his wife in her apartments for her own safety and, obliged to dissimulate, searched the houses of the brothers Epigmenio and Emeterio González. She, however, whispered news of the discovery through a keyhole to the under-gaoler Ignacio Pérez, whom she had summoned by a pre-arranged signal, and urged him to fly to San Miguel el Grande to warn Ignacio Allende. ('Pérez, go this instant and tell Allende and Hidalgo what has happened tonight'. 'Señora, I have neither help nor resources'. 'Go, and do what you can'.) Pérez immediately set out, arrived at San Miguel at dawn on 15 Sept., and, not finding Allende, who was already in Dolores, confided the message to Juan Aldama, Allende's friend, who galloped off, arriving at Dolores in the early hours of the 16th. Hidalgo resolved to start the uprising there and then. In 1821 Iturbide transacted business here after his defeat of the Spanish garrison. In Nov. 1857 Col. Tomás Mejía, having again won the city, mounted the main staircase and showed himself to the people from the central balcony on horseback. Maximilian and his commanders held councils of war here in 1867. The palace is the birthplace of Manuel Gómez Pedraza (1789–1851), president 1832–33.

In the NE corner (C. Pasteur and Av. 5 de Mayo) of the plaza is the *Pal. de Justicia*, restored in the 1970s, built in the late 18C as the residence of Juan Antonio del Castillo y Llata, husband of Josefa Escandón, later 4th condesa de Sierra Gorda. Opposite it, on the E side of the plaza, the *Pal. Legislativo*, another restored 18C house with beautiful ironwork balconies, was built for Timoteo Fernández de Jáuregui. Prominent in the middle of the W side is the **Casa Ecala**, the most striking civil exterior in the city, an assured display of lordly baroque.

It was built c 1780 for the aguacil mayor y regidor (chief constable and city councillor) Tomás López de Ecala who, it is said, vied with his neighbour Domingo Hernández in the beautification of their adjacent houses. The façades were pushed further and further into the plaza until the authorities intervened to stop the race when López de Ecala was in front.

The four broad low-slung arches of the arcade are more complex, thanks to their multiple moulding, than they at first sight seem. They spring from capitals adorned with scrolls, motifs repeated higher up. The effective continuation of the lines of the supporting pilasters up to the parapet divides the façade into four sections, which emphasize the marvellous detail. Above the arches runs a slender frieze punctuated by short lambrequins, but invaded by the beautifully elaborate and moulded balcony bases, seemingly held up by the keystones. The wrought-iron railings (by Juan Ignacio Vielma) are exquisite works of art—note the double-headed eagle worked into the centre. The windows, elegantly framed, but with subtly different mouldings, are topped by detached stone pediments, finished off above by a flourish of volutes. The jutting, emphatic effect is completed by the parapet, beneath which runs a frieze of blue and white azulejos marked off by a twisted stone rope interrupted by gargoyles. The S section is graced by a stone canopy (now around a window), which once framed the family coat-of-arms, erased in 1862.

Two inimitable traffic-free streets (andadores) lead off the W side of the plaza. From the NW corner we may reach Jardín Obregón along Av. 5 de Mayo (the former C. del Biombo); from the SW corner Paseo de los Insurgentes Queretanos (the former Cjón de Cabrera) leads to Pl. de la Constitución.

C. Pasteur continues S from the E side of the plaza. The second turning l., Av. Independencia, leads to the E quarter of the city past (r.) the church of *La Merced* (1850–70), to PL. DE LOS FUNDADORES (statues of Fernando de Tapia; Nicolás de San Luis Montañez; Fray Jacobo Daciano, reputed founder; Juan Sánchez de Alanís, who laid out the city in 1537), inaugurated in 1982, fronting which are the church and convent of **La Cruz**, a place of great historic importance.

The site, once called Loma de Sangremal, is by tradition where the battle of 25 July 1531 took place. The Franciscans maintained a small establishment here (for retreats), rebuilt c 1654–66 and called *San Buenaventura*. In 1683 the Franciscan missionary founders of the Colegio Apostólico de Propaganda Fide de la Santísima Cruz de los Milagros acquired the buildings and laid out ample gardens to E and W, now occupied by the plaza and the Panteón (see below). From here, under their first superiors, Fray Antonio Linaz (1635–93) and Fray Antonio Margil (1657–1726), the friars founded their sister colleges in Mexico City (San Fernando), Pachuca, and Zacatecas, and started their evangelization of Sonora, Texas, the Californias, Guatemala, and Nicaragua. In 1750–58 the convent was the base for Fray Junípero Serra during his labours, material as well as spiritual, in the Sierra Gorda (see Rte 38).
  In June 1821 it was the scene of the last gallant stand of the Spanish commander, Domingo Luaces, defending the city against the forces of Iturbide. Maximilian made his headquarters here in 1867. On 14 March, Gen. Escobedo launched his first attack and captured the convent outbuildings. The convent itself was the target for heavy artillery fire. That evening the imperialists counterattacked, inflicting 2000 republican casualties and suffering 600 of their own. On 24 Apr., Maximilian narrowly escaped death when a 12-pounder ball came through the window and landed at his feet. At dawn on 15 May, the republican forces, forewarned by the emperor's aide Col. Miguel López that the imperialists intended to try to break out on 16 May, breached the convent walls and precipitated the imperial surrender.

Church and convent preserve their 17–18C lines, and were substantially restored in the 1960s. The high altar incorporates the stone cross hewn in the 16C, and said miraculously to have grown since then, to commemorate the victory of Christianity in 1531.

Just to the N of the church is the chapel of *El Calvarito* (1712). In its sacristy is a font at which, it is said, the first queretano Christians were baptized in 1531. Behind the church is the *Panteón de la Cruz*, dating from 1847. It contains the tomb monument of Josefa Ortiz, whose remains were removed here from Mexico City in 1894. Those of her husband were also brought here from Mexico in 1922.

From the Panteón we have an excellent view of the **Acueducto**, one of the great and enduring public works of New Spain, built in 1726–38 as part of the overhead and underground mechanism to pipe water from La Cañada (8km E) to the fountains of the city. Built of stone and rubble masonry, it consists of 74 arches and is 1280m long. Over half its total cost of 131,099 pesos was borne by the marqués de la Villa del Villar del Aguila, who visited the works twice a day, 'climbing the scaffolding, scaling walls, and, very often, with his own hands, passing rubble, stone, and brick to the masons'.

From Pl. de los Fundadores we may return to the centre along Av. de la Reforma. Just before its junction with C. Corregidora is the church and former convent of **Las Teresitas**, for discalced Carmelite nuns, its shallow neoclassical portico held up by six pillars with ionic bases and capitals.

Its initial design was by Manuel Tolsá and work began in 1803. It was then taken over by José Damián Ortiz de Castro, and finished, with certain modifications, by Tresguerras in 1806. The founders were María Antonia Gómez Rodríguez de Pedroso, marquesa de Selva Nevada, and three other nuns who accompanied her from Mexico City, under the escort of Abp Lizana y Beaumont. Maximilian was imprisoned in the former convent in May 1867. Cayetano Rubio, a rich and kindly businessman, arranged for all his meals to be sent to him. From it Gen. Ramón Méndez was taken to be shot. It is now divided between diocesan offices and a conservatory of sacred music.

The church INTERIOR is in cold contrast to other queretano nuns' churches, resembling, in the words of Francisco de la Maza, 'a salon for diplomatic receptions'. Its indifferent murals are by Tresguerras himself. At the N end is the coro alto, the last in New Spain, also with murals by him.

On the N side of Jardín Obregón, facing the attractive C. Angela Peralta, is the **Teatro de la República**, started in 1845 to the design of Camilo San Germán and finished, as *Teatro Iturbide*, under the English engineer Thomas Surplice in 1852.

On 13 June 1867 the court martial, composed of seven junior officers, to try Maximilian, Miramón, and Mejía, assembled here and on the night of the 14th delivered its sentence of death. On 1 Dec. 1916 the opening debate of the Constitutional Congress was held here.

A little to the N, at the junction of Cs Juárez and Morelos, are the church and former convent of **El Carmen**, founded for discalced Carmelite friars in 1614. The cloister (1627), simple and single-storey, is probably the work of Francisco de Chavida. Reconstruction of the convent was finished in 1756 and the new church, by Juan Manuel Villagómez, was completed in 1759. The portal harks back to Mannerism.

The interior, redecorated under Vicente Juárez in 1875, is made more spacious by the side niches (unusual for the period), which once held altarpieces. Note too the estípites in the cupola.

From the theatre AV. HIDALGO, a street full of interesting old houses (18C–early 19C), runs W. No. 7, at the corner with C. Allende, is the **Casa del Marqués**, built in the early 18C for the marqués de la Villa del Villar del Aguila, with excellent stonework detail and lionlike balcony supports. Diagonally opposite is the mid-18C **Casa del Conde de Sierra Gorda**, once home of José de Escandón (1700–70), 1st conde de Sierra Gorda, whose military campaigns against the Chichimecs of the Sierra Gorda enabled the Franciscan missionaries to continue their work of conversion; and whose campaigns further N were instrumental in settling Nuevo León and Nuevo Santander. The beauty of its patio is enhanced by the characteristic multifoil arches. An extra dash is added by the blending of rococo and Mudéjar in the upper gallery.

At No. 29, on 30 May 1848, the treaty of peace, amended by the US Senate, between Mexico and the USA was ratified by Pres. Manuel de la Peña y Peña, owner of the house, and Foreign Minister Luis de la Rosa for Mexico and jurist Nathan Clifford and Ambrose H. Sevier, chairman of the Senate foreign relations committee, for the USA.

At the corner with C. Guerrero is the church and what remains of the former convent of **Las Capuchinas**, founded for Capuchinesses as *San José de Gracia* in 1721, its construction finished in 1771. The two portals are in well-proportioned classicizing style. The convent, now headquarters of the regional PRI, was the last prison of Maximilian, Miramón, and Mejía.

As the carriages taking them to execution on the morning of 19 June 1867 rolled away, Mejía's wife, Agustina Castro, clutching their new-born son, flung herself at his carriage and tried to cling to it. People wept as the cortège proceeded to the Cerro de las Campanas, and abuse was shouted at the escorting soldiers.

From the W end of Av. Hidalgo we may take C. Nicolás Campa two blocks N to the church of *Sta Ana* (1856–75). Hence we may continue by Av. Gen. Escobedo to the **Cerro de las Campanas**, the hill on which Maximilian made his final stand on 15 May 1867 before his surrender to Gen. Escobedo, and on which he, Miramón, and Mejía were shot. The place of execution is marked by a memorial chapel, built at the charges of the Austrian imperial house and blessed by the bp of Querétaro, Rafael Sabas Camacho, on 10 Apr. 1901, in the presence of representatives of the Austrian, Belgian, German, Norwegian, and Swedish governments, and of Señora Concepción Miramón de Fortuño, daughter of Gen. Miramón. The compensating monument to Pres. Juárez on the summit was unveiled on 15 May 1967. On the S slopes of the hill are various faculties of the *Universidad Autónoma de Querétaro*, founded in 1949.

From Las Capuchinas we follow C. Guerrero S to C. Balvanera, along which (r.) is the church of *Las Carmelitas* (1800–02), once part of a convent for discalced Carmelite nuns and school for poor girls. Hence we may go along C. Ocampo S to reach Av. Madero. To our r. is the cathedral of **San Felipe Neri**, its extraordinary façade, full of fascinating detail, in a style (neostyle) once described as 'the last card of the Mexican baroque'.

It was begun in 1786 as the church of the Oratorians, finished in 1800, and solemnly blessed by Fr Miguel Hidalgo, great friend of the community, in 1805. After considerable damage during the Reform years, it was renovated in 1894. Its latest restoration was in 1994.

EXTERIOR. The stonework is effectively set off against the tezontle base. The six columns, with Corinthian capitals, of the lower storey stand well forward of the wall and rest on high pedestals decorated with ornate lambrequins. Those in the centre on each side display three distinct sections, the garlands at the tops of the lowest sections adding a neoclassical dash, and rise higher than their companions to break the entablature. Their slanted bases emphasize their singularity. The spandrel-like relief above the pentagonal doorway arch shows rococo design and on the arch rim rests the drooping centre of another, wavy entablature which supports a lovely central relief of St Philip Neri sheltering members of the Oratory under his cloak. This second entablature, from which hang large lambrequins and undulating floral pendant motifs, forms a striking backdrop to the outer, and to the columns. In the upper storey the paired small columns, on either side of relief medallions, already neoclassical, of SS John the Baptist and Joseph, rest on bulbous bases and support a more orthodox entablature. Above, the curved pediment, traversed by a garland, reins in the baroque and rococo of the lower storeys. In it are two medallions: of SS Joachim and Anne with the Child Mary. Above it, a medallion of the Holy Trinity. The broken entablature is repeated in the uncompleted tower; below it, an assertive, much plainer, lambrequin. The E portal echoes the façade in some respects, its rococo motifs (and angel capitals on engaged columns and quaint wavy mouldings) thrown more into focus in a restricted space. Note the excellently carved festoons and angel heads on the door.

Chief beauty of the restrained single-nave INTERIOR, with neo-baroque altarpieces, is the sculptural group by Mariano Arce, of St James the Greater and SS John and Paul (1815; modified in 1873). The adjoining former Oratorian house was well restored, as the *Pal. Conin*, in 1979–81.

Opposite the cathedral is the *Casa Noriega*, a fine 18C mansion, with a pretty courtyard, which has served as Casa del Diezmo and town hall. Diagonally opposite, at the corner of C. Ocampo and Av. Madero, is the former **Casa Septién**, built in the late 18C for Antonio Septién y Castillo, member of an influential Bajío family.

Benito Juárez stayed here in 1863 and 1867, and during 1947–81, after substantial restoration, it served as Pal. del Gobierno.

Further E along Av. Madero we cross C. Guerrero. On the corner to our r. is the *Pal. Municipal*, built in the early 19C as an inn, later (until 1914) the *Pal. Episcopal*. It faces JARDIN GUERRERO, to the E of which is the church of **Sta Clara**, all that remains of one of the grandest convents in New Spain, once comprising the two blocks bordered by Avs Hidalgo and Madero, and Cs Allende and Guerrero.

It was founded in 1601, thanks to a legacy of Diego de Tapia, son of Fernando, so that his daughter Luisa could embrace the religious life as an urbanist Poor Clare, among nine nuns from Sta Clara in Mexico City. The nuns were solemnly translated to their new premises in July 1633. The present church was contracted for in 1662 with José de Bayas Delgado. In 1810 Josefa Ortiz was briefly imprisoned in one of the cells after the Grito de Dolores. The dismemberment of the convent began in 1856.

EXTERIOR. The twin doorways, typical of nuns' churches, facing S and crowned by statues of SS Francis and Clare, reflect the Mannerism of the late Renaissance. The cupola, remodelled in the 18C, is covered with azulejos. It hardly prepares us for the aisleless INTERIOR, completely renovated in the later 18C to create an effect of dazzling splendour, a matchless combination, distinctively queretano, of gilding and polychrome—churrigueresque and ultra-baroque.

On his visit here in Aug. 1777 the Galician Franciscan friar Juan Agustín Morfi recorded his disapproval: 'a church got up in costly fashion, but without that good taste which is desirable in this type of work'. The priest who had charge of the church in 1880 obviously agreed with him and resolved on 'improving' change. He began by tearing out the high altar before the government in Mexico City intervened to stop further damage.

The five altarpieces, done probably in the 1770s, along the N and S walls are each markedly different in the prodigiousness of their designs and in the virtuosity of their gilding, supplemented by metallic reds, greens, and blues and by a profusion of polychrome. The central one on the N wall brings the estípite into the repertory of queretano ultrabaroque: four large, bulbous examples, laden with festoons, garlands, medallions, and angel heads; an entablature above broken into by overflowing rococo ornamentation; and estípites again appearing in the topmost storey. In its companions, each with its special basket-weave background, obvious supports are all but suppressed in vast ornamental masses. On either side of the altarpiece facing the SW doorway are two huge pilasters, bases for irrepressible decorative variations. Their fronting statues stand on clouds before rectangular frames filled in by pleated curtains. The cornice above is laden with flamboyant aureoles enclosing large hearts. From the huge central volutes hang spheres. More festoons, garlands, angels, and rococo relief threaten every space and even dwarf the central figures of the Trinity.

The neighbouring pulpit is a lovely work, its baldachin almost oriental in inspiration; its slim base aglow with garland relief.

Also flanked by two niche pilasters, the altarpiece facing the SE doorway, next to the choir, has remarkable projecting relief—scrolls, shells, lambrequins, palms, fronds combining with massy clouds, cherubs, symbols of the Passion, elegant drapery, and the charming conceits of the base to give a luxurious setting for the Cross placed against the light of the window.

On the S side, between the two doorways, the altarpiece is full of quivering brilliance, but more affected in style than the rest; though the twin openings below contain lovely rococo relief. The side pilasters of the retable on the l. of the SW doorway and nearer the high altar, are masked by the vast scale of their superimposed volutes and circular shell reliefs. The stepped mouldings, enhanced by rococo designs, of the central panel and the cornice above, broken on either side by scrolls which serve as supports for the upper statues, are of masterly elegance. The whole is enclosed by an enchantingly individual lace-like fringe, a suitable feminine finish, like that of the retable-like entrance to the Antesacristy opposite. This is framed by beautifully elaborated mouldings and guarded by angels surrounded by a wealth of volutes. Above, pillow-like cantilevers form the base of the tribune (for the mother superior), its grille densely and exquisitely worked in volute patterns and framed by short thick columns swathed in garlands and fringes. In the Sacristy are paintings of the Communion of St Bonaventure by Juan Correa and of the Last Supper (1783) by Manuel Pérez de la Serna.

CHOIR. Intact at the E end of the church is one of the chief artistic glories of the hispanic world: the coros alto and bajo.

EXTERIOR. On the N (l.) side of the coro bajo is the low cratícula, through which the nuns received communion. Flanking the grille are polychrome New Testament figures. The grille itself is simple enough, its outer crossbars forming rectangles, reinforced from behind with wooden balusters and heavy iron bars. Its frame is decorated with elaborate shell motifs; from its lintel flutters a delicate fringe, under which hang five gilded and fanlike drapes. Above, in the wide frieze, are three luxurious gilded frames holding three female reliefs (the centre one a sweet nun, but not a Poor Clare) signifying Poverty, Chastity, and Obedience. The simplicity of the coro alto grille is emphasized by its sumptuous framing and the undulating discreetly coloured pelmet running across its top and fastened to its crossbar by rosettes. Filling the arch is the lustrous abanico, a tapestry of gilded acanthus, set off by a lazily unfolding gilded and tinted curtain. In its centre is a Crucifixion attr. Mariano Perusquía (c 1800).

INTERIOR. In the coro bajo is the stone kneeler on which the nuns knelt to receive communion. Two charming retables are laden with rococo relief. The paintings (anon. late 18C didactic works) reminded the nuns of saints familiar and rare, and of the apparitions of Our Lady of Guadalupe. From here we may descend to the Crypt (1760) built by Ignacio Mariano de las Casas. When the 14 graves were filled, the bones of the longest-buried were removed and deposited in the ossuary in the centre of the floor. The coro alto preserves an ultrabaroque main retable, with four niche pilasters and entablature enveloped by rococo relief. Above the doorway to what was the antecoro are three Scenes from the Life of Our Lady (1731) by Tomás Javier de Peralta.

At the corner of the garden in front of the church stands the **Fuente de Neptuno** (1797; altered 1846), harmoniously understated, by Tresguerras.

It is in fact a curiously eclectic work. Reminiscences of the classical appear in the guttae under the capitals. The balusters are Renaissance in style, as is the general tone of the whole. The side medallions of the frieze are baroque; the pilasters a mixture of various types; the capitals appear to be Tresguerras' own invention. The statue of the god is a modern replacement (1988) of an earlier work (Christ or John the Baptist ?).

A little further E, at the corner of Av. Madero and C. Allende, is the church of **San José de Gracia**, attached to the former *Hospital Real de la Limpia Concepción*.

The earliest hospital in Querétaro, founded in 1586, functioned under the name of San José de Gracia. In 1624 it was put under the charge of the Hermanos de la Caridad (Brothers of Charity of the Order of St Hippolytus) who in 1652 started to build a large new establishment: the church, finished in 1726, and the hospital in 1765. After the siege of 1867 the hospital was transferred to the convent of Sta Rosa de Viterbo. Its former premises (note the fine stone doorway in C. Allende) have been restored as the telegraph office.

Opposite the church is the so-called **Casa de la Marquesa,** finished in 1756 for Francisco Antonio de Alday by the queretano master builder Cornelio. Later it was the residence of doña Josefa Paula Guerrero Dávila Fernández del Corral, marquesa de la Villa del Villar del Aguila. The noble exterior, with its beautifully carved original door, contrasts with its exotically fanciful principal patio, strongly Mudéjar, and its delightful play of multifoil arches and wrought-ironwork—the epitomy of the 18C baroque reaction against earlier, sober styles.

Following C. Allende S we come on the r. to the former convent of **San Agustín**, its patio a composition of stunning richness and virtuosity, a final baroque statement of the traditional Augustinian love of display.

Convent and church were begun in 1731, possibly supervised by the friar Luis Martínez Lucio and funded by Juan Julián Díez de la Peña. One Francisco Ledo appears to have acted as master builder. The intervention of the young architect Ignacio Mariano de las Casas in the later stages is a possibility. In 1762 Juan Manuel Villagómez claimed to have been the architect. The convent was finished in 1743; the church dedicated in 1745. After various profane uses during 19C political upheavals, in 1889 the convent was reconditioned as federal palace and post office.

CLOISTER. The effect of the lower storey is singular enough. Grafted on to the square pillars are hermae standing on a single foot, the heads placed above prominent scroll effects and between them the arch spandrels full of fruity relief. The originality and quality of the upper storey are of the highest order. Pillar bases and archivolts are clad in tableros. From the pillar faces rise fantastic atlantes, their vegetal trunks ending in flourishing volutes; their arms extending through the spandrels into the frieze and agitating a wealth of ribbon and foliage relief.

Each figure is different, but its appearance depends on its position. In the lower storey the feet of the hermae in the centre of each side and at the corners point straight; the feet of the eight other hermae are turned towards those in the centre. The corner hermae have the wrinkled faces of old men; the four in the centre of each side are young and beardless; all the remaining eight (feet pointing inwards) wear turbans. In the upper storey the atlantes in the centre and in the corners have three fingers raised with thumb and first finger forming a circle; all the others raise all four fingers. The former indicate that all is built to perfection; the latter adopt an attitude of admiration.

The desire to establish symmetrical contrasts is shown by the pairs of birds and animals (ducks, winged horses, lions) which accompany the atlantes. On N and S the upper-floor foliage relief is precisely detailed; on E and W such schematic care is ignored. In the arch keystones appear Augustinian saintly figures and symbols.

A superb undulating cornice and frieze crown the whole and complete an effect of grand vivacity.

The grand staircase holds surprising touches in the three arches which give on to the upper floor. The key of the central arch is decorated with intertwined ribbon relief, amid which appears the name S. AGUSTYN, while a realistic little angel seems to be in effortless flight.

The church EXTERIOR bears hallmarks of 18C Mexican baroque, but with arresting, angular, differences. Its variety of geometric shapes, slanting and broken lines, and relief produce an effect of constant movement in the Bajío sun. In the lowest storey of the wide, tall façade the engaged columns are semi-octagonal, with quaintly ornate capitals, and swathed in fillet relief, a variation of the solomonic. Between them, niches hold statues of SS Augustine and Francis. The triple-layered entrance arch, of the greatest finesse, is 16-sided, with saucy cherubs embedded in the spandrel foliage. In the middle storey the columns, of similar style, flank statues of SS Monica and Rita. The central feature of the top storey is a monumental Crucifixion, with a relief of vine laden with grapes in the background (symbolic of the Precious Blood), in an astoundingly lovely ornate frame flanked by atlantes, one arm raised in token support of their capitals. On either side, statues of Our Lady of Sorrows and St Joseph (the Holy Child he once held has disappeared). The beauty of the friezes, cornices, niches, and capitals serve to heighten the general opulence. Another Augustinian saint, Nicholas of Tolentino, occupies the niche of the side doorway. Fascinating detail continues into the octagonal drum of the cupola (also octagonal, with polylobular windows), where stand somewhat insouciant angel musicians, their costumes quite likely inspired by prints of court ballets at Versailles, in which the young Louis XIV took part. Waist-down parts of similar figures can be seen among the unusual effects of the square, unfinished tower.

Main feature of the INTERIOR is the beautiful stone sculpture of nave and cupola. In the capitals of the pilasters which separate the sections of the nave play cherubs similar to those in the portal spandrels. Each arch has a keystone decorated with a special motif: cherubs, roses, the monogram of Jesus, Our Lady of Sorrows, St Monica. In the arch opposite the altar is a monstrance and in the frieze above a pair of peacocks, symbols of eternal life. In the niches where rises the cupola are statues of SS Peter, Paul, Andrew, and James the Greater; the other apostles stand between the windows of the drum.

The convent is now home to the **Museo de Arte** (Tues.–Sun, 11–7; fee). A tour begins on the UPPER FLOOR, with exhibits illustrating the history of San Agustín. It continues through the periods of Mexican art. *Mannerism.* Attr. Baltasar de Echave Orio, Agony in the Garden. Luis Juárez, Ascension (1610), notable for beautiful colouring and the lively expressions of the watchers. Anon. (16C), SS Elizabeth and John the Baptist. Basilio de Salazar (early 17C), Our Lady and the Franciscan Order. Baltasar de Echave Ibía, St Mark. *Baroque.* Antonio Rodríguez, three paintings of saints (Benedict, John of Matha, and Columban) carrying croziers (good landscape). Cristóbal de Villalpando, nine paintings of the apostles, after Rubens, taken from engravings, by N. Ryckemans, of the originals in the Palazzo Rospigliosi in Rome. The use of chiaroscuro and the rich golden brown of St John's robe are especially striking; the painter's signature is on the chalice. Attr. Juan Correa, Death of St Joseph. Nicolás Rodríguez Juárez, St Gertrude; the Child Jesus with Our Lady and SS Joseph, Anne, and Joachim; St Francis Xavier; St Antony; St Antony curing the sick. Juan Rodríguez Juárez, Flight into Egypt, a masterwork, very Mexican in its evocation of tenderness and affection, all pointed up by beautiful colouring. Diego Sanabria, St Anne (1716). Pedro Calderón (early 18C), Annunciation, the stillness of the Virgin well observed. Francisco de León, St Gertrude. Attr. Luis Berrueco, Our Lady and Angels. Good anon. works include: St Anne (late 17C); Agony in the Garden (early 18C); and Mystical Marriage of St Rose; Visitation; Christ with Globe; St Bernard and the prophet Elias; St Catherine and ministering angels; Flight into Egypt; Christ scourged (all 18C). 17–18C polychrome Crucifixions and sculpture (incl. a notable 18C St Augustine) salvaged from convents during the Reform.

Nicolás Correa, St Dominic receiving the rosary from Our Lady and the infant Christ (late 17C), one of the very few surviving paintings by this master. Cabrera, Head of St John; Head of St Paul. José de Ibarra, Ecce Homo (1733). Miguel Antonio Martínez Pocasangre, flight into Egypt, an 18C naive work. Anon. 18C, Dolorosa; St Vincent Ferrer; St Isidore.

Cabrera, St Bernard; St Ildefonsus (1741); St Augustine (1757); Our Lady appears to an archbishop. Francisco Antonio Vallejo, Immaculate Conception (1767); Death of St Francis Xavier. José de Alzíbar, St John Nepomuk (1782).

The rooms on the GROUND FLOOR shown anon. European paintings and 19C Mexican works: Juan Urruchi, Joseph and Potiphar's wife; Juan Manchola, Good Samaritan and Return of Tobias (1857); Alberto Briviesca, Our Lady returns from Calvary; Joaquín Ramírez, Foundation of Tenochtitlán; Luis Portu, Still Life; Pelegrín Clavé, Ana Bustos (1880); José Jara, Boy fishing (1886); Ramón Sagredo, Ismael abandoned (1856); Primitivo Miranda, Death of Abel (1844).

Also in C. Allende, further S on the r. beyond the crossing with Av. Pino Suárez, is the **Casa de los Perros**, a delightful single-storey 18C house attr. Ignacio Mariano de las Casas (1719–c 1784–86), who, tradition has it, lived here. The façade brackets are in the shape of crouching dogs. The patio is decorated with grotesque animal and human gargoyles, incl. Pegasus, Minerva, a dolphin, Perseus with the head of Medusa, etc. Its fountain is supported by three winged sphinxes. Hence we turn l. (W) along Av. Pino Suárez to the church and convent of **Sto Domingo**.

Dedicated to *San Pedro y San Pablo*, the convent was built in 1692–97 with generous aid from Juan Caballero y Ocío, and served as a base for missionary work in the Sierra Gorda. Except for brief intervals it has always belonged to the Dominicans.

The church façade, with hermae flanking the window, is simple and classicizing, while the high tower has a singular stamp. The façade of the adjoining **Cap. del Rosario** (erected in 1760 next to the earlier, 18C chapel as a shrine for a statue of Our Lady of the Rosary), by Las Casas (with later variations by Francisco Martínez Gudiño), is a strange queretano surprise, with its elaborate shallow lower-storey niches, and exotic hermae, with whiskers, folded wings, and plumed helmets in the upper.

Its small interior space is dominated by the unusual cupola, with its large lantern, interior relief, and windows in the four corners of its base. Beneath it stood the statue.
  The 18C atrial cross, carved with Passion symbols, was moved here from the Panteón del Espíritu Santo in the early 1950s.

From Sto Domingo we go S to join Av. Gen. Arteaga and turn r. to reach the *Cap. del Espíritu Santo*, one of the various examples which survive on the edge of the historic centre. A little further on we come to a tree-shaded plaza and, on its S side, the church and former convent of **Sta Rosa de Viterbo**, a jewel of late 18C queretano art.

The original foundation of 1669 was as a beaterio for the three pious Alonso Herrera sisters who wished to live under the rule of St Francis, soon to be joined by other kindred spirits; the community went on to found a school for girls, the *Col. Real de Sta Rosa de Viterbo*, which got royal approval in 1727. Building on the present site, to the design of Las Casas, began in 1731 and the church was dedicated in 1752.

EXTERIOR. The twin portals, facing N, recall the Mannerism of the previous century. In the niches are SS Rose and Francis. The capricious buttresses, in the form of giant volutes, and stamped with grotesques and topped by unusual plump finials, were added in 1759, it is said by Francisco Martínez Gudiño to strengthen the fabric, but were probably designed by Las Casas himself; and were in turn probably inspired by engravings of the S German baroque. The slender tower has an E European look; Las Casas, a skilled clockmaker, also contributed its clock. After 1785 Tresguerras worked to improve tower and cupola, and added the balustrades. The elevation of the octagonal cupola is emphasized by its high drum, with supporting columns tightly bound by ashlar rings, and airy lantern.
  The INTERIOR is a blaze of gilding and polychrome in queretano churrigueresque and ultrabaroque; light flooding in through the windows incorporated by the altarpieces and above the tribunal to produce wonderful effects. The altarpieces, confessionals, and choir date probably from the 1770s. The altarpiece on the S wall nearest the choir is remarkable for its graceful estípites, flanked on either side by highly ornamental medallion frames. Between capitals and entablature the enormous globular ovals are a distinctive contrast in volume. Next to it is the tribunal, seemingly pressing down on and swelling sideways a small altarpiece, its side medallions enveloped in rich vegetal and cherub relief. The volute flourishes add a rococo touch. The altarpiece of Our Lady of Guadalupe, nearest the high altar, and that of St Joseph (opposite) are marvellous blendings of churrigueresque and rococo, spaciously designed within outer and inner estípites, crowned by canopies drawn aside by angels. The inner shrines are also framed by canopies, which enhance their refinement. Most beautiful of all are the medallion paintings (by Cabrera) of the entrecalles, framed by softly curving palm wreaths. The pulpit, inlaid with silver and ivory, is exquisite, the outside of its staircase studded with gilded birds.

The high altar (1849), an unfortunate substitution, is by Laureano Montañez. The Sacristy, to its l. (S), contains interesting treasure, incl. a quaint series of polychrome seated statues of Christ and the twelve apostles (18C), possibly once used for a tableau of the Last Supper. The hand-basin, an ornamented and crowned grotto, draped in crimson and gold relief, is accompanied by little crowns to serve as towel-rails. In a gilded semicircular frame is the huge painting, possibly by José de Páez, of the Hortus Conclusus (enclosed garden), full of conventual symbolism.

Under the gateway sits Our Lady, the Good Shepherdess. Above, the Crucifixion, the flock of the faithful at Christ's feet, an angel collecting His blood in a chalice, the cross the Tree of Paradise. Nuns tend the garden, with a fountain of life prominent on the r. Also attr. Páez is the portrait of Sor Ana María de San Francisco y Neve, a gifted and beautiful nun. That of the convent's early benefactor, Juan Velázquez de Lorea (1670–1732), is by Cabrera.

The CHOIR, at the E end of the church, is another stupendous combining of ultrabaroque and rococo. The grille of the coro bajo is revealed by angels drawing aside the drapes on either side. Above and flanking it are paintings, of Christ, Our Lady, and the Apostles in exquisite frames, producing an effect of charming disorder, appropriate to the rococo. Below, on the r., the craticula; on the l., the doorway, both laden with baroque relief and fitting symbols. Above the grille of the coro alto rises the abanico, a work of surpassing beauty, in eight sections and full of delicate rococo relief. In its centre, on a sumptuous pedestal and against a shell-like halo, is a young Christ, framed by pearl-grey clouds sprinkled with stars.

The interior of the coro bajo contains the organ (1759) built by Las Casas; a painting by Tomás Javier de Peralta of a procession through the city to beg Our Lady's intercession against plague (1742); and a not unpleasing altarpiece in mid-19C 'republican baroque'.

The adjoining convent buildings, during 1867–1963 the *Hospital Civil*, are now a school of graphic arts set up under the auspices of the OAS and the Italian government. The upper cloister walk is notable for its bilobular arches. The staircase, in five ramps, is entered under three arches, that in the centre without support. Above the staircase the vaulting is adorned by circular, star, and lozenge relief.

38   Querétaro to Tamazunchale

Méx. 57D, Méx. 120, and Méx. 85, 380km.—52km San Juan del Río and Méx. 120.—72km Tequisquiapan.—249km **Jalpan**.—270km **Landa de Matamoros**.—331km Xilitla.—345km junction with Méx. 85.—380km **Tamazunchale**.

From Querétaro to (52km) *San Juan del Río*, see Rte 36. We leave San Juan del Río to the NW on Méx. 120. 72km **Tequisquiapan** (15,000 inhab.; 1377m; H,R,P), in the Valle de Tequisquiapan and on the N of its large lake formed by the Río San Juan, lies near the S foothills of the Sierra Gorda. It is frequented, especially at weekends, for its thermal springs and good hotels. Its comfortable climate, whitewashed buildings, and cobbled streets add to its appeal. The church of *Sta María de la Asunción* dates from the early 19C; the outlying chapel of *La Magdalena* from the 16C. 101km *Cadereyta*, once a mining villa (founded in 1627); the church of San Pedro y San Pablo (18C) contains a gilded baroque altarpiece. The road runs through the valley of the Río Extoraz and then climbs into the rugged Sierra Gorda. 127km *Vizarrón*. 139km turning r. for (24km E) *San Joaquín*.

Near San Joaquín, **Toluquilla** (c 12km SW of Vizarrón) and **Las Ranas** (c 10km W of San Joaquín) were either colonies of or heavily influenced by the Huasteca of the N Gulf Coast. They were occupied in the 11–12C AD, and both comprise alignments of terraced platforms, buildings, and ball courts on narrow mesas, looking down on the plains. The high talud profiles with jutting cornices, particularly on the ball court walls, are similar to the style at El Tajín; and half a basalt yugo, associated with the ball game, from Las Ranas was carved in the style characteristic of N Veracruz: a profiled head and intricately interlaced scrollwork. It has been suggested that the two sites were the Huasteca's first line of defence against attack from Chichimec tribes from the N Highlands.

Toluquilla includes several pyramid platforms and circular ruins aligned with and clustered around two ball courts. Similarly, at Las Ranas there are two alignments on ridges at approx. right angles, with five ball courts, several platforms and pyramids, and extensive terracing at the SW end of one ridge.

179km turning l. for (14km W) *Peña Miller*, birthplace of Tomás Mejía (1820–67). 209km *Pinal de Amoles*, another mining centre. A particularly wild stretch brings us to (249km) **JALPAN** (c 5000 inhab.; 770m; R,P), first of the Franciscan mission centres of the Sierra Gorda.

The **Sierra Gorda** (better known today as *Huasteca Queretana* or *Sierra de Querétaro*), an offshoot of the Sierra Madre Oriental, rises like a barrier from the plains of Querétaro and Hidalgo. It reaches into NE Guanajuato and S San Luis Potosí. Its slopes descend into various river systems. It is a region of violent contrasts: desolation and aridity set off by fertile valleys, a symptom of patchy watering; forests of oak and conifer.

The Augustinians established missions among the Chichimecs (Pame-speakers and Jonaces) of the area c 1550, but were driven out by their would-be charges. In 1573 the lost Englishman John Chilton was succoured by Indians with water from a Venetian goblet, got, they told him, from Jalpan after they had killed the friars and fired the premises. In 1743–44, José de Escandón began systematic pacification and founded five missions. In 1750 Franciscans from San Fernando in Mexico arrived at Jalpan and began the successful consolidation of the missions, which flourished until 1770 when they were secularized. By 1814: 'all has come to naught. The Indians returned to their hide-outs and those beautiful churches have become the haunts of animals'. The churches remain, their façades incorporating symbolism and didacticism. Their interiors were despoiled during 19C wars.

The façade of the church of **Santiago** (1751–58; repaired in 1895 after earthquake damage), the work of Fray Junípero Serra, helped by Fray Francisco Palóu, is riotously covered in vegetal, floral, and fruit relief. Its simple entrance is recessed (abocinada) below a beautiful squarish shell-like canopy, below which are niches, flanked by solomonic columns, holding statues of SS Peter (l.) and Paul. On either side of the portal, two pairs of estípites are continued into the top storey, the inner pair as elaborate finials. In the entrecalles, statues of SS Dominic (l.) and Francis; in their bases, unique combinations of the Habsburg and Mexican eagles: double-headed and devouring the serpent. Above the door, the Franciscan shield of the Five Wounds. Enclosed in the rich cornice is another Franciscan shield: two arms, one clothed one bare and wounded, nailed to the Cross—symbol of Christ's approval of the Franciscan Order by giving St Francis the stigmata. In the entrecalles of the first storey, niches hold statues of Our Lady of Guadalupe (l.) and Nuestra Señora del Pilar (who appeared to Santiago in Zaragoza). The cornice gives way for the choir window, its curtains drawn back by tiny cherubs. Around the upper part of the frame is the Franciscan cord. The clock is a barbarous substitute (1838) for the original statue of Santiago. The tower makes liberal use of the solomonic column. The simple convent buildings survive next to the church.

35km NW along the Río Jalpan valley is **CONCA**, second of the missions, founded on 25 Apr. 1744. The church of **Santiago** (1754–58; altered in 1892), smallest and stoutest of the five, is the work of Fray José Antonio de Murguía. The robust carving of the buttressed façade is at its thickest in the top storey.

The doorway is attractively mixtilinear. Between the swelling fluted engaged columns flanking it are statues of SS Francis (l.) and Antony. The first-storey solomonic columns are entwined with vines and bunches of grapes; between them, statues of SS Ferdinand of Castile (l.) and Roch, symbolizing victory over heresy, and charity. In the centre, the shield of the two arms, sword and sceptre beneath them, bordered by the Franciscan cord, amid thick vines and foliage, a crown above. The choir window, two angels drawing aside its curtains, breaks the cornice and the dense vegetal relief of the top storey, a huge semicircular pediment, its central figure a St Michael. Resting on the pediment, the Holy Trinity.

From Concá the road continues NW to (76km) *Río Verde*, see Rte 61.

From Jalpan Méx. 120 climbs to (270km) **LANDA DE MATAMOROS** (2000 inhab.; 1025m), a mining pueblo on the Río Tancuilin, a tributary of the Mocte-zuma. The church of **Sto Domingo y San Francisco** (1760–68) has perhaps the most interesting façade of the five, crammed with uplifting relief detail and marked by sturdy estípites on all three storeys, the lowest sheltering small niches. In the entrecalles large ornate niches (rib-vaulted in the first storey) shelter more saints. The simple portal is covered by a rudimentary alfíz, almost lost amid the relief which sinuously invades every surface. In the lowest storey, between the estípites, the saints are Dominic (l.) and Francis; in the small niches (l. to r.) Giacomo de la Marca, Bernardine of Siena, John Capistran, and Bl. Albert of Sarteano—great Italian Franciscans. Above the arch and breaking the cornice is a charming group: an apocalyptic Immaculate Conception attended by two angels swinging thuribles, and cherubs holding back a curtain. Pots of flowers enhance the ensemble. SS Peter and Paul stand on either side of the first storey. On either side of the octagonal window are the two Franciscan shields: the two arms and the Five Wounds. Beneath them sit Duns Scotus and María de Agreda (1602–65), champions of the Immaculate Conception; the latter, pen suitably poised, correspondent and adviser of Philip IV and author of 'Mística ciudad de Dios'. On either side of the top storey are SS Stephen and Vincent of Zaragoza. In the centre above the window, St Lawrence flanked by medallion reliefs showing the Entry into Jerusalem and the Scourging of Christ. In the pediment, St Michael slaying a dragon. The adjoining portería leads to what remains of the convent.

From (280km) *La Lagunita* a minor road (not easy) climbs SE to (16km) **TILACO**. Here the atrio, complete with posa chapels, survives. The church of **San Francisco de Asís** (1754–62) is the work of Fray Juan Crespí. The façade is wholly delightful in its gaiety and spontaneity. Flanking its recessed portal, in shell form, are solomonic columns and between them gracefully framed niches holding SS Peter and Paul. In the frieze cheerful sirens support the first storey estípites and stepped mouldings rise in the centre to form a circular two-arm shield with the Holy Ghost as its key. The first storey niches hold the Immacu-late Conception and St Joseph. The centre panel is full of enchanting detail. Two angels draw aside the window curtains, overhung by a pelmet; lower down, another pair of angels brandish vine branches. Above the window, St Francis provides occasion for an elaborately fanciful surround, resembling a box in a theatre. Its front is adorned with an arcade of small estípites and tasselled fringes above and below. Attending the saint are two pairs of angels, holding the canopy above him and playing guitar and violin on either side. Crowning all is a huge, fountain-like urn. The portería of the convent has been walled up and the cloister much altered.

285km turning l. for (19km N) **TANCOYOL**, where the church of **Nuestra Señora de la Luz** (c 1760–66; badly damaged during the Revolution) stands in an atrio with a surviving posa chapel. Its first three storeys display three pairs of estípites on each side. Its central arch, now empty, once contained the statue of Our Lady of Light. The lowest storey saints are Peter and Paul (mutilated), their niches ogee-arched, their pedestals pointing down to wonderfully elegant vegetal relief spreading out like a fan. In the first storey, SS Joachim and Anne (sympathetic likenesses, the latter holding the Virgin). Above them, SS Antony (mutilated) and Roch. Above the window, a relief of the stigmatization of St Francis. On either side of the top storey, the crosses of Calatrava and Jerusalem, emblems of the Dominican and Franciscan orders. The relief next to the outer estípites envelops angels holding symbols of the Passion. The open chapel to the r. of the church is the only one of the five to remain intact.

Beyond (310km) *El Lobo* we cross into the State of San Luis Potosí. 331km **Xilitla**, known for its coffee production, in the well-forested Sierra de Xilitla, part of the Sierra Madre Oriental, watered by tributaries of the Río Moctezuma to the S. The Augustinians established the small remote convent of *San Nicolás* here c 1550, raided by Chichimecs in 1576 and burned by them in 1587. A small chapel survives. At 345km we meet Méx. 85 running N to (71km) *Ciudad Valles* on the San Luis Potosí–Tampico road. We turn SE to (380km) **Tamazunchale** (c 12,000 inhab.; 206m; H,R,P), on the r. bank of the Río Moctezuma and in a fertile region of luxuriant tropical growth, and famous for its birdlife. A 16C chapel survives.

39 Querétaro to Actopan

Méx. 57D, Méx. 45, and Méx. 85, 191km.—61km Palmillas and Méx. 45.— 99km Huichapan.—143km junction with Méx. 85.—151km **Ixmiquilpan**.—191km **Actopan**.

From Querétaro to (61km) *Palmillas*, see Rte 36. From here we turn E off the highway into the State of Hidalgo to (87km) a turning for (22km E) *Amealco*, with the 17C Franciscan visita church of Sta María. 93km *San José Atlán*, with a 16C Franciscan visita church, once a dependency of Huichapan, in an atrio with simple posa chapels and an atrial cross. 99km **Huichapan** (c 4000 inhab.; 2000m; H,P), where in 1531 the Franciscans established a parish for the Otomí Indians, although the permanent convent and church of *San Mateo* were not finished until 1585. The present church dates from extensive rebuilding, in the 17C and especially in 1753–63, the work of Antonio Simón. In the atrio, now an extension of the main plaza, is the 16C atrial cross, one of the finest and largest in Mexico, densely carved with Passion symbols: note the crown of thorns around the centre, framing the image of Christ's face on Veronica's veil; below it, the column of Christ's scourging, with the cock that crew for St Peter perched on top. The church's spacious façades are marked by regular churrigueresque, the surfaces enlivened by sprouting tree and floral relief. The two churrigueresque retables in the interior also date from the latest rebuilding. A niche holds the funerary statue, rescued from an imposing monument, of Manuel González de León (d. 1750).

Other 16C survivors are the cloister and possibly the chapel attached to the N wall of the church; a relief in its façade recalls the hut where the first Mass was offered in 1531. The chapel of *San Francisco*, S of the church, dates from the 17C (good portal relief).
   From Huichapan a road runs N and then NE to (32km) *Tecozautla*, where the former Franciscan convent of Santiago Apóstol, with its three-nave church, dates probably from the 1630s.

135km turning r. for (5km S) **Alfajayucan**, an Otomí pueblo. Here the Franciscans founded their convent of *San Martín* c 1559 in an area 'perilous with Chichimecs'. By the time it was completed on another site in 1586, the area was peaceful enough for Spaniards to graze their sheep. The church (portal recalling Romanesque; interior reordered in the 19C) and convent block (N side of church) accompany a five-arched portería/open chapel. The fresco decoration in the pretty wooden-ceiling cloister, by a European hand, is dated 1576 and signed SMD. The atrial cross is now in the cloister.
   At 143km we meet (l.) Méx. 85.

It leads N to (10km; r.) **Tasquillo**, where the 16C church of *San Bernardino*, with a rustic façade, was once a visita of Alfajayucan. Three posa chapels (possibly 16C) are outside the square of the atrio, planted with walnut and ash trees, its wall studded with merlons. The atrio S gate is where the fourth posa should be. 34km turning l. for (7km W) **Zimapan** (c 5000 inhab.; 1800m; H,P), where a mining camp was set up c 1575 to work the silver of the surrounding sierra. Andrés Manuel del Río (1764–1849) pioneered modern methods of extraction here and the mines contributed much to the wealth and scientific knowledge of

New Spain on the eve of Independence. The façade of the church of *San Juan Bautista*, begun c 1750 by José Casimiro Izaguirre, is in russet stone churrigueresque. Its multifoil arch is flanked by thick clustered estípites which contrast with the more regular types of the upper storey. The rhomboid transept window is a humorous conceit.

From the Zimapan turning Méx. 85 winds interminably over the Sierra Madre Oriental via (109km) *Jacala* (1300m), with an interesting church (1774), and (171km) *Chapulhuacán* (1500m), with a solid church (San Pedro) begun by the Augustinians in the early 1540s, to (202km) *Tamazunchale*, see Rte 38.

We continue, keeping r. along Méx. 85, to (151km) **IXMIQUILPAN** (c 6000 inhab.; 1682m; H,R,P), predominantly Otomí, on the Río Tula.

At the Conquest it was main centre of an Otomí state, which the Spaniards controlled by the mid-1520s. In the 1550s half its territory came to Gil González de Avila, executed in 1566 for his part in the plot to place Martín Cortés on the throne of New Spain. The Augustinians founded their convent in 1550. Ixmiquilpan is headquarters of the federal government's aid programme to better the lot of c 65,000 Otomís in the surrounding country, whose barrenness makes their lives hard.

The convent of **San Miguel Arcángel**, with one of the largest convent churches, higher than the atrio (arranged so as not to disturb the ancient Otomí plaza), was planned and built by Fray Andrés de Mata, and completed in the 1550s.

'There are four religious here', he wrote in 1571. 'I am the prior and of the least account. I know the Otomí and Mexican tongues, and thus am able to help the Indians. Another of the company is Fray Joan de la Madalena, professed many years since and of high esteem. He speaks the Mexican tongue, in which he confesses and preaches...'

EXTERIOR. The church, its parapet bristling with merlons, is less grandiose than his work at Actopan (comp. below). The W portal is well-proportioned plateresque. The coffered relief of the double archivolt is of cherubs, flowers, and bowls of fruit; on either side, pairs of fluted engaged columns, whose composite capitals support a frieze of cherub and winged-horse relief. The balance is maintained by the admirable choir window with its classical pediment. The upper part of the tower is a delicate response to the mass of the base.

INTERIOR (70m long; 14m wide). The nave is covered by a barrel vault, ended by a triumphal arch. The presbytery and the semihexagonal apse are uplifted by exquisite rib vaulting, whose extra height adds to the effect. On the S side are the baptistery, and three side chapels, rare in a convent church (two alongside the N cloister walk). The vaulting of the sotocoro is also excellent.

Efforts in the 1950s to rid the church of the worst of its later accretions revealed a didactic frieze (c 2m high; now fragmentary) running fairly low the length of the walls, the first discovered example of scenes showing Indian warriors in a 16C church in New Spain. Probably the work of indigenous hands under Augustinian direction, it is painted in tempera: Indians fighting evil and its awful possibilities. Warriors combat monsters, dragons, centaurs—amid motifs resembling acanthus stalks and leaves, sometimes ending in fantastic heads and forming a border for each scene. In most cases the figures are shown in profile, with leaves sprouting from their mouths to denote speech, or even song. Warriors wear the copilli (headdress of an Indian noble; probably a concession to the caciques) or tiger heads.

In one scene (S wall of sotocoro), on the l. a warrior wearing a copilli menaces with buckler and club; across his breast he wears a sash from which hangs a human head; from his belt hang ornamental leaves. Opposite him, an archer; and between them a third, fallen, warrior who still clutches his banner. On the extreme r., two Indians spring from the leaves, one trying to shield himself from danger. Another scene (S wall, near altar) shows a dragon, adorned with acanthus, his body covered in scales, his headgear of feathers. From his mouth, full of sharp teeth, darts his tongue, which curls into a volute. An Indian, felled by the monster, holds in his l. hand a club and in his r. hand a stone, which he strives to hurl at his adversary.

Another, and well-preserved, scene (S wall of presbytery) shows a monster centaur with a human face, his head adorned with quetzal feathers, his long neck with acanthus. In his r. hand he holds three arrows (coincidental with the Augustinian emblem). From the strap around his middle hangs a human head. Before him runs a warrior wearing a copilli, brandishing a club, and with his l. hand grasping a prisoner by the wrist. He also carries hunting equipment. This scene is almost repeated in the middle of the S wall of the nave. The frieze shows signs of the mistaken work of recent hands.

Higher up, at the springing of the vault, runs another, better preserved, frieze, similar in style, full of satyrs, half-men, half-fish, small boys, etc. More friezes, happy and sinister, run around side-chapel and baptistery walls.

In the sacristy are more murals (probably 17C), in grisaille, of the Passion. Entry into Jerusalem (N wall), in which palm-wavers are seen through the legs of the ass on which Our Lord rides, begins the series. On E wall, Agony in the Garden; on W, Christ appearing to Mary Magdalen—with animal and landscape detail.

The open chapel stands S of the church between the double-(Gothic) arched portería and the convent wall, somewhat lessened by both. The elaborate CLOISTER, buttressed outside its lower storey, is typical of Augustinian taste. The lower arches run a different rhythm to the upper; but the superimposition of the upper bays is subtly done. In the lower walk is good ribbing. In the upper are five medallion murals in tempera, incl. a Virgin and Child; and the Child Jesus with the Augustinian pierced heart emblem. Note the frieze of small boys on fantastic horses, shields, and Augustinian saints.

Some 18C houses are also of interest. The 18C chapel of *El Carmen* has a churrigueresque façade and contemporary altarpieces. The enormous rubble masonry bridge over the Río Tula dates from 1655.

The road NE from Ixmiquilpan leads to (18km) a turning for (4km N) *Cardonal*, in a region famous since the 16C for lead mines. The Augustinian convent of Purísima Concepción dates probably from the early 17C. The atrial cross mixes Indian (primitive Passion symbols) and European (inscription). The road winds spectacularly E across the Sierra de Pachuca to (46km) *Tolantongo*, with underground warm-water river baths and thermal springs, S of the Laguna de Metztitlán. Banana plantations and subtropical vegetation contrast with the aridity further W.

FROM IXMIQUILPAN TO MEXICO CITY VIA ATOTONILCO TULA, 139km. We leave Ixmiquilpan SE on Méx. 85, at 7km forking r. to follow a minor road which runs S through the Valle del Mezquital; the road keeps the upper Río Tula on its r. From (31km) *Progreso* (P) a road runs E via (12km) *Tepatepec* to (28km) *Actopan*, see below. 35km *Mixquiahuala*, a mainly Otomí town near the r. bank of the Tula, where the church of San Antonio (formerly San Nicolás; briefly an Augustinian visita handed over to secular clergy in 1568), rebuilt in the 17–18C, preserves an exquisite portal (c 1570). 45km turning r. for (6km W) *Tezontepec*, where the Augustinian doctrina of San Pedro was founded c 1554; it is memorable for the decorative battlements of its atrio, in which the posas, with entry and exit openings, survive. 47km **Tlahuelilpa**, where the Franciscan convent of *San Francisco*, once a visita (with a resident friar) of Tula, dates probably from the 1560s. It has a pretty church (small and lovely chancel arch and wooden ceiling); a single-storey cloister (though decayed), whose low arches, with layers of moulding and copious relief in the archivolts, generously fluted columns, and richly carved capitals, vary with each arcade; delightful inner doorways; and above all an enchanting raised open chapel, an original design by a local master. Its arch is composed of nine oval medallions showing reliefs of flowers and instruments of the Passion. From the central medallion emerge two angels holding the Franciscan shield enclosed by a crown of thorns. Above are five plaques, incl. St Francis and two friars. The whole is enclosed by an alfíz bordered by the Franciscan cord.

A road runs SW to (14km) *Tula*, see Rte 19.

From (51km) *Tlaxcoapan* a road goes E via (14km) *Ajacuba*, with thermal springs, to (68km) *Pachuca*, see Rte 62. 54km **Atitalaquia**, with the remarkable

Convent of San Francisco, with open chapel, Tlahuelilpa

church of *San Miguel* (mid-18C), relief fragments from its late 16C predecessor grafted into its walls. In its three-storey W façade, carved in rosy stone, stand out bold, plump, well-ornamented estípites enclosing saintly statues in felicitously sculpted niches. The holy water stoups at the foot of the lower entrecalles are a rare feature. Above the doorway the cornice is particularly strong, as is the choir window, framed in jutting patterned stone. In the top storey the statue of St Michael is flanked by pilasters carved with sinuous relief. The N doorway is in simpler style.

C 2km SW, at **Tlamaco**, on the l. bank of the Río Salado and known for its stone quarries, the barrio chapel of *San Jerónimo*, originally a visita of Tula before being transferred to secular clergy in 1563, is a lovely relic. Its portal consists of a low three-centred arch, the archivolt rich in fruity and foliate relief. Above it rises a triangular spiral moulding, which culminates in the name of Mary, soaring into an oblong alfíz. To its l. is a small triple-arched open chapel.

57km **Atotonilco Tula** (P), where the former Franciscan convent of *Santiago* dates from c 1560. Church parapet and atrio walls are enlivened by merlons. The W doorway is artlessly plateresque—yet delightfully whimsical—with statues and flanking pilasters combined, and quaint, steeple-like niche covers. Flapping seraphim crowd the archivolt and bold relief the jambs. The rose window is a beautiful and rare example, with elaborate tracery. The nave triumphal arch is decorated with rose relief.

We cross into the State of México. At (61km) **Apaxco** (c 7000 inhab.) the 16C church of *San Francisco* has a characteristically carved portal. Adjoining is an open chapel, raised on steps and jutting out like a bay window, discriminatingly designed if coarsely done. The columns of its central arch rest on pedestals which form sills for its side arched openings.

Above the arches are reliefs of angels: at the sides carrying the five-wound emblem; at the centre, flanking a ruined royal coat-of-arms beneath a crown placed above a crown of thorns encircling the monogram of Christ. The three sides of the façade are framed by a pattern of vines. Along the top runs a cornice moulding carved with figures of seraphim, above which is set the Franciscan cord. Over the central arch is a statue niche and an espadaña.

70km *Tequixquiac*, with a 16C church and museum (open on request) of finds unearthed in the opening of the Tequixquiac tunnel (see Rte 62).

Around Tequixquiac are gravel beds and sands rich in fossils. In them the bones of mammoths, extinct horse, bison, extinct camelids, ground sloth, and mastodon have been found. Associated with some of these were 20 man-made tools, some in situ, incl. obsidian side- and end-scrapers, blades with fine pressure flaking, and bone awls. In 1870 a camelid sacrum was found by the Mexican naturalist Becerra, which had been carved into the face of a dog or coyote (now in Museo Nacional de Antropología); dated c 10–13,000 BC. At the opposite end of the prehistoric time scale, Tequixquiac was one of the many administrative centres and concentrations of population in the Aztec Basin of Mexico.

82km turning l. for (2km) *Zumpango*, see Rte 63. The road skirts the Lago de Zumpango. 96km *Melchor Ocampo*. Hence to (102km) *Cuautitlán* and (139km) *Mexico City*, see Rte 19.

Méx. 85 (very winding) continues SE through a wide valley. 158km road fork r. for (50km) *Atotonilco Tula*, see above. 172km *Yolotepec*, once the parish of San Juan Yolo, a dependency of Actopan. The church is strongly buttressed, its parapet and atrio wall lined with merlons. 180km *Lagunilla*.

5km N is the *Gruta de Xoxafi*, with two main underground galleries. 8km NE is *Santiago de Anaya*, the former Santiago Tlachichilco, where the former open chapel (16C?) has interesting, if flat, Indian coffering and carving in its façade.

191km **ACTOPAN** (c 7000 inhab.; 2069m; H,P), where the former Augustinian convent of **San Nicolás de Tolentino** combines a Renaissance spirit with a primitive local vigour to produce an incomparable masterpiece on a grand scale. Its extensive frescoes constitute the most important corpus of early religious art in the Americas.

The region, populated by Otomís, with a Pame-Chichimec minority, came under Spanish control in 1521–22. In the mid-17C part of the encomienda was assigned to the heirs of Moctezuma. The convent was paid for (or at least patronized) by the caciques Juan Inica Actopa and Pedro Izcuitloapilco, planned by Fray Andrés de Mata, and built in the 1550s, probably with the later help of Fray Martín de Aceibedo. Its vast atrio (once 290 by 183m) has been mainly taken over by the plaza.

EXTERIOR. The W doorway of the church is in outline plateresque, also recalling Romanesque, and may be seen as two portals, one inside the other. The play of light and shade is notable. The four pairs of fluted columns are raised on double bases, which emphasize their height and slenderness. Between the columns are slim niches. The coffering of the doorway arch and jambs is repeated in the large, triple-layer, false-perspective arch above the tympanum, splaying like a fan—an inspired effect. In the coffers is flower, food, and angel-head relief. Resting on the cornice, the choir window is held in by baluster columns. The upper part of the Mudéjar tower, beautiful and effective, is opened by large arches; above them are rows of smaller arches; at the top are sets of garitas and merlons. Buttresses support the side walls and apse; garitas are placed at intervals along the parapet, merlons in the spaces between them.

INTERIOR. In contrast to the barrel-vaulted nave, the two E bays beyond the triumphal arch display fine rib vaulting, as do the polygonal apse and the sotocoro at the W end. Gothic vaulting also covers the sacristy (S of presbytery), which contains a monumental font, a statue of St John the Baptist on its lid, and is enlivened by floral frescoes and a mural frieze, incl. pelicans and grotesques.

The CONVENT, now a museum (10–6; fee), is entered through a triple-arched monumental portería, perhaps the most imposing in Mexico. The arches are flanked by four tall pilasters reaching up to composite capitals and, beyond the cornice, to torch finials. Generous coffering is repeated in the archivolts and the three rows of the soffits resting on thick fluted jambs and pillars. Above is an enclosed gallery, also triple-arched.

The outstanding series of murals begins here. In the lunette (l.) St Augustine, book and church in hands, protects his friars under his mantle; St Bernard of Montjoux, reformer of the Order, is on the l., in white habit. In the lunette (r.), the ship of the Order arrives at the port of Paradise; in the bow, St Monica and nuns unfurl the standard of the crucifix; in the stern, St Augustine controls the helm, another saint the sail. From Heaven, God the Father and the Holy Ghost aim arrows of wisdom at St Augustine, while on the shore is raised the Cross (a palm tree), whence Christ diffuses His love. Around the Cross are shown themes conducive to salvation. The vault is covered in strikingly decorative and intricate strapwork painting, with medallions of saints.

On the W side of the lower cloister is the Sala de Profundis. On the upper part of its N wall is another mural devoted to the Order of Hermits (Tebaida augustiniana). In the centre, an old pear tree. All around, friars in their cave cells, praying, visiting, receiving heavenly visitors. On the l., one friar washes Christ's feet.

Each Gothic arch of the lower walk of the noble cloister matches two semicircular, supported by Tuscan columns, in the upper. Between the lower arches, buttresses marked by elongated concave tableros. The lower walk is covered by handsome rib vaulting, the upper by wooden beams. Along the walls run painted friezes, of Augustinian friars, flowers and vegetal motifs, young male nudes riding fantastic animals and perched on the tops of shields. On end walls of the upper walk are more murals: Last Judgment, Agony in the Garden, Ecce Homo, and God the Father.

In the SW corner is the kitchen, the finest of its time, with an enormous chimney, and connected by stairs to the cells of the upper floor. Along the S side is the magnificent refectory—fit for the finest banquets—its superb barrel vault, lined with deep octagonal coffering, painted with Renaissance patterns in bright orange and black on a white ground. Note the polygonal pulpit, from where the lector read to the eating friars, and the stoup. The mural of Calvary shows the crosses of the two thieves as gnarled trunks. Flanking the door are Jesus falls on the way to Calvary and Last Supper, the apostles encircling the table. Two cypresses frame these murals, at the foot of which are SS John and Matthew writing their gospels.

On the E side of the cloister is the Sala Capitular. Next to it is the antesacristy, leading into the sacristy.

In the NE corner begins the grand staircase, its walls covered with murals, in black on a white ground with small splashes of higher colour, a gallery of illustrious Augustinians, and other luminaries connected with the Order, shown enthroned or working at their desks. Each wall proper is divided into three rows of three paintings (with further paintings below on S, N, and E), framed by semicircular arches on baluster columns, all richly ornamented. Dividing the rows are friezes of grotesques. Above each holy head is a long curly tag of identification. In the lowest storey (S) may be seen Fray Martín de Aceibedo accompanied by Juan Inica and Pedro Izcuitloapilco. Among the Augustinian divines at their desks are Fray Gerónimo of Naples (W top l.); Alonso de Toledo, abp of Seville (W top middle); and Guillermo de Vecchio, bp of Florence (W top r.). St William, duke of Aquitaine, stands in front of a parapet and a more distant landscape. The upper lunettes allow more elaborate treatments. In one may be seen St Nicholas of Tolentino amid hills and crags. In another, St Monica praying in a landscape.

From the upper gallery access may be had to the tower and choir, decorated with murals. The refectory looks on to the garden. On its E side are further buildings with a long arcade, once stables, now containing displays of Otomí art. Throughout the convent there is an amazing variety of window shapes: triangles, circles, ellipses, rhomboids, which emphasize its uniqueness.

On the N side of the church is the open chapel, below the stupendous BOVEDA DE ACTOPAN, a barrel vault 17.3m across, wider than the church, surpassing all vaults in the hispanic world except those in the cathedral at Gerona. The slender archivolt is more like a decorative border and is carried by the voussoirs behind. The interior surface is painted with crimson and black coffering (restored)—after Sebastiano Serlio's design copied from a mosaic in Santa Costanza in Rome. Murals (rare in this type of building) show Old Testament scenes and the horrors of Hell.

From Actopan, Méx. 85 continues S to (199km) *El Arenal*, where the seeming open chapel to the N of the sanctuary of the *Señor de las Maravillas* (1806–10) is probably an early 19C addition to accommodate pilgrims come to venerate a miracle-working image. Then we run gradually SE to (227km) *Pachuca*, see Rte 62.

40 Querétaro to Toluca

A. Via Salvatierra and Acámbaro

Méx. 45, Méx. 51, and Méx. 55, 315km.—59km Celaya and Méx. 51.—96km **Salvatierra**.—129km **Acámbaro**.—210km **Tlalpujahua**.—249km junction with Méx. 55.—315km **Toluca**.

From Querétaro to (59km) *Celaya*, see Rte 36. We leave Celaya on the S across the Bajío to (96km) **SALVATIERRA** (c 20,000 inhab.; 1750m; H,R,P), unspoiled and charming, in the Valle de Salvatierra. It stands on the Río Lerma whose waters intensively irrigate the surrounding agricultural area.

In Feb. 1644 Viceroy García Sarmiento de Sotomayor, conde de Salvatierra and marqués de Sobroso, decreed the founding of San Andrés de Salvatierra. On Good Friday 1813 it was the scene of Iturbide's bloodiest victory, over the insurgent Ramón López Rayón who had held the town. He wrote afterwards, for the viceroy's benefit, that he had hit upon 'the best way to sanctify this day. It is not easy to calculate the number of excommunicated wretches who in consequence of the action descended to the deepest abyss; but from the accounts of the commanders and the corpses I saw, I infer they numbered three hundred and fifty'. In addition, he had 25 survivors shot. In the 1870s Salvatierra revolted against the further secularizations of the Reform, pushed ahead by Pres. Lerdo de Tejada, with ensuing violence.

On the E side of PL. DE LA CONSTITUCION, planted with laurel and palm trees, is the imposing early 19C *Pal. Municipal*. Next to it stands the parish church of *Virgen de las Luces*, begun in the 1740s; finished in 1808. Its façade combines ineffective churrigueresque and neoclassical. The S tower dates from 1962–65. On the high altar is the venerated 16C statue of Our Lady of Salvatierra ('nuestro tesoro y encanto'), probably of Spanish origin. The adjoining *Santuario de Guadalupe* (c 1750) was put up to house the image while the parish church was being built.

From the plaza C. Juárez runs S to PL. DE LOS FUNDADORES, where is the church of *El Carmen*, an imposing pile in the simple style (with espadaña) preferred by the Order, and begun in 1644 under the architect and lay brother Andrés de San Miguel, who died here later the same year.

In the side chapel (N) is a painting of Our Lady of Mount Carmel's patronage over the Order by Miguel Placencia (1773–74).

Reached along C. Madero, W from Pl. de la Constitución, is the Franciscan convent of **San Buenaventura** (now known as *San Francisco*), founded probably in the 1630s. Its atrio, now a garden, is gained over a little bridge. The present church, with its conspicuous tower, dates from c 1750. Adjoining it is the former chapel of *Tercera Orden* (now called San Antonio), rebuilt in 1740. Off the convent patio, planted with geraniums and bougainvillea, is a museum dedicated to Franciscan martyrs of the Cristero war.

On the W side of town (reached by C. Guillermo Prieto) is the huge stone *Puente de Betanes* (1644) over the Lerma, planned and started by Fray Andrés de San Miguel. It was fortified by López Rayón in 1813 and the scene of Iturbide's victory.

Further S, past *Mercado Hidalgo*, along Cs Guerrero and Altamirano (second turning r.), is the church of *Las Capuchinas*, part of a convent founded in 1790 and finished in 1798. Its two W doorways face a pleasant plaza.

30km W of Salvatierra is *Yuriria*, see Rte 32.

We continue SE through the valley of the Lerma to (129km) **ACAMBARO** (c 42,000 inhab.; 1945m; H,R,P), whose central hospital-convent group and surviving 18C domestic architecture make it a place not to be missed by the discriminating traveller.

The Franciscans laid out the new town on a grid plan and established a parish, between c 1526 and the early 1530s. In 1586 Fray Alonso Ponce, in New Spain on an inspection tour of Franciscan convents, arrived at Acámbaro to a heartwarming Tarascan welcome: 'muchas bailes y danzas…mucha música de trompetas…todo el pueblo mostró mucho contento, devoción y alegría, con la llegada del padre Comisario, al cual ofrecieron después mucho pan de Castilla, fruta y gallinas'. The Franciscans remained even after secularization in 1757. They were deprived at the Reform, but have now returned to their old parish. At Acámbaro on 21 Oct. 1810 Hidalgo was proclaimed generalísimo and Allende capt.-general of the insurgent forces.

The main Av. Hidalgo runs N to S through the town centre. Beyond Jardín Independencia on the W side is PL. PRINCIPAL; on the E are the former **Hospital Real de los Naturales** and the Franciscan convent of **Sta María de Gracia**, the former founded in 1532, the latter most likely in 1526.

Hospital and its church face W on the N side of the convent. The church portal is one of the most beguiling manifestations of 16C Mexican art, an intriguing mixture of Isabeline Gothic, Mudéjar, plateresque, with symbolic relief. It is enveloped by a large alfíz described in a circular moulding which springs from Gothic brackets, its concave interior punctuated by Isabeline apple motifs; in its upper part, beyond the cornice, it is enriched by rings. The doorway is a remarkable conjunction of thick jambs, in fact huge decorative tableros, and round arch, narrower than the jambs (a naive touch ?). On either side are two engaged and tapering fluted columns. In the jambs, medallions of SS Peter and Paul are perched upon by angels, bodiless, imperious figures, winged and plumed. Beneath are large tassel motifs ending in heads of pelicans, symbol of the Precious Blood. At both ends of the archivolt, framed by the Franciscan cord, plateresque medallions contain Passion symbols; in between, a lovely relief—vines entwined with roses, and ending in pine-cones (tree of life). Repeated rose and star reliefs, in upper and lower storeys, emphasize attributes of Our Lady. The window frame is marked by Gothic flowers and the crucifix below it squared off by the cord. Of the two ajimez windows in the tower base, the one facing W has kept its quaint relief and primitive charm. Also of the 16C is the holy water stoup beside the W door. This door and the lateral N door (the former dated 1792; the latter earlier 18C) present divine and saintly relief and coffering.

On the S side of the church is the hospital, rebuilt after the 16C and mutilated with the construction of the convent. Its portería arches remain.

Convent and church (facing N) were rebuilt in 1734–49. On the E side of the simple church portal, the portería leads into the cloister. Particularly striking are the arcade decoration of the upper storey, the bulbous columns at the foot of the staircase, and the jollily rustic statues of saints important to the Order above the capitals.

N side—SS Paschal Baylon, Antony of Padua, Bernardine of Siena. E side—St Dominic, the Immaculate Conception, St Francis. S side—SS Isabel of Portugal, Clare, Elizabeth of Hungary. W side—SS Roch, Louis IX, Isidore. In the corner angles the pine-cone represents the tightly-knit Christian community. Above them, monograms of Our Lord and Our Lady and (NW and SW) Franciscan cross emblems. Note the plump fleur-de-lis (signifying chastity) finials on the parapet.

At the corner of Cs Morelos and Abasolo is a **Museum** (9–1 and 4–6; fee) exhibiting pieces from the ceramic traditions of Mexico from the Late Preclassic Period into the Postclassic (c 800 BC to AD 1200). Most of the collection is from the Preclassic–Early Classic site of Chipícuaro in S Guanajuato.

Now covered by the waters of Presa Solís, the site was excavated in 1948–49 by INAH. Nearly 400 graves were found, with abundant grave goods, incl. thousands of complete vessels and figurines now distributed among museums and private collections throughout the world. Interspersed among the burials, the excavators found hundreds of rectangular basins of packed mud, filled with fine ash, which have been interpreted as the sites of fires during the burial ceremonies. There were both adult and child burials, but not all were 'normal'. As well as full skeletons, there were burials of skulls on their own, decapitated skeletons, and skeletons with cut and perforated skulls stacked on their knees. There were also burials of dogs. Unfortunately, little evidence was found of the village supporting this cemetery, except a few stone alignments and fragments of clay floors.
    The ceramics include vessels, figurines, and a variety of musical instruments from throughout Guanajuato and Hidalgo, and from the Valle de Teotihuacán. The influence of Chupícuaro designs also spread far into N, W, and central Mexico. There were two principal phases: *Chupícuaro Brown Ware* (c 200 BC–AD 1), dominated by brown wares decorated with polychrome geometric designs, and some black-based polychrome wares; and *Chupícuaro Black Ware* (c AD 1–300), dominated by black-slipped vessels and black polychromes, red-rimmed red wares, and red-on-buff wares. As their names and types imply, the two phases form a developmental continuum with considerable overlap. Both phases also had small, mould-made figurines with diagonally set, long, thin eyes, and larger, hollow figurines painted black-on-cream. One sub-type, featuring 'figures-strapped-to-a-bed', indicates connections with the chamber-tomb-building cultures of W Mexico. Musical instruments included ocarinas, flutes, whistles, and rattles.
    Further S along the ascending Av. Hidalgo is the church of *San Antonio* (mid-18C; good tower) and three 18C chapels (of 14 once in use) for Stations of the Cross processions. At the S end, from Pl. Soledad, and on the E side of Av. Hidalgo, begins the aqueduct, finished in 1781.
    In Jardín Independencia, on the N side of Pl. Principal, the church of *Guadalupe* (c 1749–92; altered early 19C) contains, in its sacristy, an interesting anon. 18C painting of the genealogical tree of Our Lady of Guadalupe and, between presbytery and sacristy, an 18C fountain adapted as stoup, with crude relief. In Jardín de Nigromante (once part of the convent atrio), just N of the hospital church, the 18C fountain-base, called *Los Toritos*, is ornamented with humorous relief.
    Finest of the old houses is the *Casa Sámano* (476 Av. Hidalgo, just NW of the convent), finished in 1772. Its exterior, except for the doorway, has been much changed; its patio is graced by lobular arches.
    On the N side of town, a few streets from the hospital, is a bridge over the Río Lerma dating from the early 19C (after 1810); on each side of its entrances are monuments (c 1760–80) of popular religious type. A little to its E are remains of another (18C; associated with Hidalgo).
    From Acámbaro to the *Lago de Cuitzeo* and *Morelia*, see Rte 32.

The road E from Acámbaro crosses well-cultivated country on the S side of the huge *Presa Solís*, fed by the Río Lerma, and enters the State of Michoacán. 168km *Maravatío*, with a 17C parish church and 30km N of *Ciudad Hidalgo*, see Rte 34. Our road continues SE through the pine- and oak-forested mountains on the N slopes of the volcanic divide to (210km) **TLALPUJAHUA** (c 7000 inhab.; 2578m; H,R,P), a quaint place with steep and winding cobbled streets, in the Sierra de Tlalpujahua, a mining region.

Silver mines were established here in 1558 and 30 houses of miners and merchants were reported in the new real de minas in 1570–71. Tlalpujahua was the birthplace of the five insurgent brothers López Rayón: Francisco, Ignacio (1773–1832; secretary of Hidalgo), Ramón (1775–1839), José María, and Rafael; and was an insurgent stronghold during the war of Independence. In 1937 a fire destroyed part of the town, incl. the sanctuary of *El Carmen*, of which the tower survived.

A reminder of the late 16C is the little church of *La Cofradía*, built as Santísima Trinidad. The former Franciscan hospice, founded c 1600, also survives—a little church and single cloister. The town's chief beauty is the large parish church of **San Pedro y San Pablo** (now more often called *El Carmen* after the burned-out sanctuary).

EXTERIOR. Its mid-18C baroque façade (with churrigueresque touches) shows highly distinctive features: prismatic solomonic columns swathed in strong, slanted mouldings, with siren and mask relief in the bases; tableros and estípites surrounding the choir window; and a beautiful, curved pediment forming an outer frame for more delights—a double niche (rare occurrence) enclosing statues of SS Peter and Paul flanked by ornate estípites and symbolic lozenge reliefs, and topped by a relief of a monstrance displaying the Host and the finial statue of St John the Baptist. The Sacristy, probably once a church on to which the present church was grafted (note the fine buttresses to support the new building), dates from the 17C.

The INTERIOR was redone, in bad taste, early this century. The 17C painting of Our Lady of Mount Carmel on the high altar was salvaged from the sanctuary. In the sacristy is a triptych: anon. 18C paintings of the Passion.

The house of the López Rayón family, now a museum, contains interesting relics of Ignacio López Rayón and exhibits illustrative of the mines.

At 212km we cross into the State of México, keeping l. at (214km) a road junction for (218km) **El Oro de Hidalgo** (c 7000 inhab.; 2730m; H,P), on the E slopes of the Sierra de Tlalpujahua, the former *Real de Oro*, which from 1787, when its silver and gold began to be exploited, until 1940 knew great prosperity. Reflecting that prosperity are the *Pal. Municipal* (1906–10), in the afrancesado style so marked a feature of the porfiriato, and the ostentatious *Teatro Juárez*, which enjoyed its heyday during the same period. The *Museo de Minería* illustrates the local industry. We continue E to (249km) *Atlacomulco* (see Rte 40B) on the Querétaro–Toluca road. 315km *Toluca*, see Rte 40B.

B. Via Acambay

Méx. 57D and Méx. 55, 190km.—61km Palmillas.—111km Acambay.—131km Atlacomulco.—197km **Toluca**.

From Querétaro to (61km) *Palmillas*, see Rte 36. At 65km we bear r. on Méx. 55 to (92km) the turning l. to *Aculco*, see Rte 36. The road climbs gradually to (111km) **Acambay** (c 7000 inhab.; 2500m; R,P), in the valley called 'de los mil espejos' after the many little lakes formed during the June–Sept. rains, which reflect the sun. Views from the nearby heights. The *Casa de Cultura* contains a museum showing local archaeological finds.

Huamango, c 5km N, is an unexcavated Otomí ceremonial centre at the top of a steep hill E of the road. There are two pyramid bases, one of three tiers of small, flat stones, a stucco floor and a N-facing stairway; the other also has a N-facing stairway, very dilapidated. Around the levelled plaza are traces of other platforms and walls.

131km **Atlacomulco** (6000 inhab.; 2526m; H,R,P), an ancient centre of the Mazahua Indians 2km E of the r. bank of the Río Lerma, at a road junction. It is the birthplace of Isidro Fabela (see Rte 15). The house where he was born, on the main plaza, now the *Casa de Cultura*, is a small museum (9–2; fee) illustrating his life and achievements.

The road E runs to (97km) *Mexico City* via (50km) *Villa del Carbón*, see Rte 19. An interesting excursion can be made by turning l. (N) 20km along this road, following a mountainous road through the Sierra de las Cruces N and NE to (35km) **JILOTEPEC** (c 6000 inhab.; 2525m), an Otomí town N of forested mountains.

At the Conquest the cacique of Jilotepec, a seat of Otomí power, was related to Moctezuma II Xocoyotzin and was an enthusiastic convert to Christianity, carrying his proselytizing activities to the Chichimecs to the N. By 1533 the town and its province had been given in encomienda to the conquistador Juan Jaramillo de Salvatierra, husband of Doña Marina (Malinche; Cortés's interpreter). On her death he married Beatriz de Andrada, who, on Jaramillo's death, disputed the inheritance with doña María, daughter of doña Marina, and married Francisco de Velasco, brother of the viceroy.

Off the main PL. AVILA CAMACHO, and fronting a large atrio, is what remains of the Franciscan convent of **San Pedro y San Pablo**, founded in 1529. The atrial cross is raised on a grand base. The church dates from c 1590–1600. The jambs and three-centred arch of the attractive portal are covered with rosette relief and flanked by fluted pilasters. It and the choir window are described by a discreet alfíz. In the single-nave interior, with a beamed ceiling resembling artesonado, the ogee triumphal arch is a fine and rare example, graced by rosettes and chain moulding. The baptistery retains its fine 16C stone font. On the S side of the church, the cloister is a poor 19C rebuilding, but in its centre is a 17C cross covered in Passion relief. On the N side, amidst a 20C school building, are the remains of a once famous open chapel, described in 1585 as 'muy grande y sumptuosa', possibly endowed in the 1550s by doña Beatriz, who had generously contributed to the erection of its vaster model, San José de los Naturales (comp. Rte 7). Parts of the side and back walls survive. There were seven aisles, each five bays deep, once covered by a wooden roof. Three arches, embedded in the wall, survive. The tower is a 19C addition.

At the entrance to the town, on the old road to Tula, is the **Cruz de Doendó**, finest of Mexican wayside crosses, its sloping base, which once contained a chapel, attesting Indian workmanship.

7km N, at *Soyaniquilpan*, the 16C church of San Francisco has a depressed arch and liberal use of Isabeline Gothic apple relief in alfíz and window frame of the portal. The triumphal arch marking off the presbytery holds good relief. The road W from Atlacomulco goes to (120km) *Acámbaro*, see Rte 40A. Another road (Méx. 44) branches SW from the Acámbaro road after 4km to (14km) *San Felipe del Progreso*, another Mazahua town (weaving and silverwork). Hence we may follow a mountain road to (67km) *Angangueo* and (101km) *Zitácuaro*, see Rte 34.

146km (3km NW) *Jocotitlán*, at the foot of the Cerro de Jocotépetl (3928m), covered in pine forests. The parish church, La Purísima Concepción, dates from the early 17C. 160km *Ixtlahuaca*, with a 17C parish church (good portal) and 16C atrial cross—and a famous market every Mon.

19km E is *Xiquipilco*, or Jiquipilco, a Postclassic N Matlazinca town, near the E borders of Tarascan territory (cf. *Calixtlahuaca* and *Teotenango*). It was the site of fierce battles: first, in 1464, between Matlazinca factions—the Toluca and Teotenango–Tenancingo factions were defeated by the Pirinda faction of Xiquipilco and Tecaxic, and their Tarascan allies; and later in 1475, when the Aztecs put down a Matlazinca revolt.

From Ixtlahuaca, Méx. 55 runs S to cross the Río Lerma.

197km **TOLUCA** (c 450,000 inhab.; 2680m), capital of the State of México, is at the highest altitude of any city in the republic. The Nevado de Toluca (4558m) is a volcano c 22km SW. The Lerma, tapped to supply water to Mexico City, skirts the territory from SE to N. Today Toluca is an industrial centre and has what is probably the country's largest weekly market. Late 18C and early 19C architecture (houses crowned by quaint stone crosses and barrio chapels in the outer areas) survives. Toluca is a centre for excursions to the archaeological and historical sites in the E and SE of the State. The ring road Paseo Tollocan continues on the E to Mexico City.

Airport. c 10km NE. Flights to *Acapulco, Guadalajara,* and *Monterrey.*

Bus station. C. Berriozábal, 2km SE of the centre, across Paseo Tollocan from the E end of Av. Venustiano Carranza. Frequent services to *Mexico City* (1 hr); to *Cuernavaca* (3½ hrs); to *Guadalajara* (9 hrs) and local services to *Calixtlahuaca*; to *Metepec*; etc.

Hotels throughout the city.

Post Office. Av. Hidalgo, on E side of Jardín Zaragoza.

Tourist Office. Edificio Oriente, Av. Lerdo de Tejada (facing Pl. Garibay).

The Valle de Toluca has been inhabited since the Preclassic Period, from c 1700 BC. The principal occupation and the rise of powerful principalities, however, began in the 7C AD when Matlazinca and Chichimeca groups migrated into the plain. They were a powerful trading intermediary and rival of the Tarascans on their W, and of the Toltecs and later Aztecs to the N and E.

Toluca ('those who bow their heads') was a Matlazinca city and a rival to the powerful ridge-top city of Teotenango (see Rte 80), overlooking modern Tenango de Arista, to the S. In

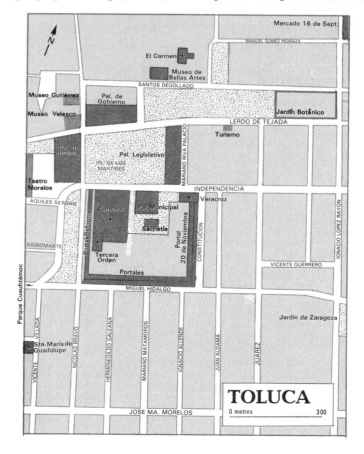

the 15–16C Matlazinca civil wars, the Toluca allied themselves with the Aztecs when the latter invaded the valley.

Jurisdiction over the villa of Toluca, the valley, and an area extending W to Michoacán was claimed by Cortés and his heirs. During the viceroyalty, the villa and reduced area around it were governed by a corregidor named by Cortés's descendants. In the 1830s the Cuban poet José María Heredia settled here and published various periodicals. Its Instituto Literario, founded in 1827 and precursor of the University of the State of México, achieved great prestige during the 19C. Among its distinguished alumni were Ignacio Manuel Altamirano and Andrés Molina Enríquez, author of 'Los grandes problemas nacionales', the most eloquent analysis of social problems under the porfiriato.

The State of **México** (21,451 sq km; c 11.3 million inhab.) is crossed E to W by a volcanic system (Tarasco Náhuatl) which divides into two very different parts: the S penetrating the hot Valle de Balsas; the N occupying the highest part of the Valley of Mexico (Valle de Anáhuac), heartland of Aztec Mexico, a circular lacustrine plain and intermontane basin from which most of the lakes have disappeared. Three of Mexico's highest volcanoes are in the State: the Nevado de Toluca and, in the extreme E, the legendary peaks of Popocatépetl and Iztaccíhuatl. The Río Lerma rises near Almoloya del Río in the centre and runs NW; the Balsas and its tributaries cross the S. The Federal District forms an enclave in the territory. Despite dense population and heavy industry, there are beautiful mountainous country and dramatic landscapes. Agriculture is encouraged by fertile lava-based soils and plentiful rainfall.

After the Conquest considerable areas of the modern State of México were held in encomienda by Cortés. The intendancy of México, created in 1786, occupied c 120,000 sq km. In 1824, with the loss of 11,500 sq km, it was converted into a State, with the Federal District an enclave in the area. In 1849–69 Guerrero, Hidalgo, and Morelos were carved out from its territory. The years 1942–45 saw the governorship of Isidro Fabela, who laid the basis for industrial advance.

The city centre is the wide PL. DE LOS MARTIRES, over a century in the making, with further modernization after 1950. Its statue of Hidalgo (E side) was sculpted at Florence in the 1870s by Augusto Rivalta. On the S side is the cathedral of **San José**, a grandiose and controversial edifice, long in building and still unfinished.

It occupies part of the Franciscan church and convent of *Nuestra Señora de la Asunción*, founded in the late 1520s, largely finished by 1585, almost completely destroyed by 1874. The new parish church was begun, to the design of Ramón Rodríguez Arangoity, in 1870, and continued after his death in 1884 by Luis G. Anzorena, but abandoned soon after. In the 1940s Vicente Mendiola was commissioned to complete it. The towers were put up in his absence and without his authority. It became cathedral when the bishopric of Toluca was created in 1950, and was consecrated in 1978. Rodríguez Arangoity's classicizing concept, much influenced by his training in Rome and Paris, has thus been diluted by time and other hands.

EXTERIOR. The central section of the façade, neoclassically inspired, is graced by statues of apostles and doctors of the Church, and pairs of Corinthian columns supporting the pediment, which contains a relief of the Resurrection. Of the towers, Mendiola said in 1980: 'I am still asking [the bishop] to allow me to put [them] right'.

In the INTERIOR, lit through clerestory and choir windows, the nave is marked off by clustered pilasters. At the end of the W aisle is a refreshing contrast—the baroque façade of the chapel of *La Tercera Orden*, a mid-17C survivor of the old convent. Solomonic columns, arch, octagonal window frame, and niche jambs abound in luxuriant relief, and the lower (r.) niches hold statues of SS Francis and Louis IX of France. Its simpler W doorway (in Portal Reforma) gives access to the interior where, in the baptistery, remains of an arcade from the 16C convent may be seen. It also contains a Pietà by Nicolás Rodríguez Juárez.

On the N side of the plaza is the *Pal. de Gobierno*, designed, in a sparely elegant classical style, by Rodríguez Arangoity and begun in 1869 under J.F. Valdés. It was amplified and altered from the late 1940s by Vicente Mendiola. On the W is the *Pal. de Justicia* (1869–70), also by Rodríguez Arangoity. On the E, the *Pal. Legislativo* (late 1960s), by Mendiola, which he called 'not precisely classical, but frankly provincial—Mexican'.

To the E of the cathedral, on Av. Independencia, is the much-altered *Pal. Municipal* (1873–83), another design of Rodríguez Arangoity, and, beyond it, the church of *Vera Cruz* (begun in 1753; dedicated in 1797), with a recessed façade and the discreetest estípites, built for the lay brotherhood of the True Cross.

Behind the Pal. Municipal survives the former sacristy (1729) of the destroyed convent church, saved in the early 1970s. A small plaza has been cleared for it. Its quatrefoil interior, tastefully restored, contains reminders, constructed according to contemporary drawings, of the three retables made for it by Felipe de Ureña—the first completed churrigueresque examples in New Spain.

From the W side of Pl. de los Mártires, behind the Pal. de Justicia, we may reach the *Teatro Morelos*, built, with distinctive arcading, in the 1960s, its neighbouring raised plaza enlivened by an equestrian statue of the hero.

At the corner of Av. Lerdo de Tejada and C. Bravo (NW corner of Pl. de los Mártires) is the *Museo Velasco*; a little further up C. Bravo is the *Museo F.S. Gutiérrez*—both with works by the 19C painters. From the NE side of Pl. de los Mártires, C. Licenciado Verdad leads to the former convent and church of **El Carmen** (1699–1720), once belonging to discalced Carmelite friars, established in Toluca by 1690, and secularized in 1861. The convent building now houses the **Museo de Bellas Artes** (Tues.–Sun., 9–1, 2–5), containing Mexican paintings of the 17–20C.

17–18C Works. José Juárez, Martyr. Attr. Juan Correa, Virgen de la Merced. Nicolás Enríquez, two paintings of the Immaculate Conception. Miguel Cabrera, St John Nepomuk; Holy Trinity. José de Páez, Holy Family.

19C Works. José María Velasco, Volcanoes from the Cerro del Ocotlán. Edouard Pingret, Lady in blue; Festive Scene. Leandro Izaguirre, Gentleman. Santiago Rebull, Portraits of a lady and gentleman. Germán Gedovius, Portraits. Felipe Gutiérrez, Male Nude; Portrait of Matilde Zúñiga; Flight into Egypt (a charming throwback); Episodes from the war of the French Intervention (good landscape). Leandro Sánchez Montano, Lady with a book. Isidro Morales, Autumn (genial and colourful). Fabián L. Cuenca (naive painter), Bazaine leaves Mexico. Mateo Herrero, Garden landscape.

The collection of 20C works is extensive and includes interesting examples of Rufino Tamayo; Alfredo Zalce; José Clemente Orozco (Rape); Francisco Zúñiga (Desolation); Roberto Montenegro; Diego Rivera (two drawings); David Alfaro Siqueiros; Fernando Castro Pacheco (Portrait of a woman); Ignacio Aguirre; Jorge González Camarena; Trinidad Osorio (Flowerseller); Antonio Serrano (Still Life); etc.

The church has benefited from restoration (1967) and the demolition of encroaching buildings to make way for a new plaza to its S. With its peaceful raised atrio, it now presents a combination well viewed from Pl. de los Mártires. Its portal is severely classical; its elegant tower was finished in 1814. The interior was heavily remodelled in the 1850s and work has continued well into the 20C, as is only too apparent from the overdecoration. On the E side, the *Cap. de la Tercera Orden* (1700–02; enlarged in the early 1790s) was done up in neoclassical style c 1857. Its walls are lined with paintings (1722) by Francisco Martínez: Holy Family waited upon by angels; Our Lady of Mount Carmel helping souls in Purgatory; St Teresa receiving Communion; etc.

Further E, along C. Santos Degollado, is the building erected for the MERCADO 16 DE SEPTIEMBRE in 1933. It is now the *Jardín Botánico*, with an international display of flowers, plants, and trees. The stained-glass windows were designed by Leopoldo Flores Valdez. On the W end, their most spectacular component, 'El hombre sol', reminds one of the tradition of the world re-created by fire.

The cathedral precinct is framed on E, W, and S by the PORTALES erected in 1832–36, at the instance of José María González Arratia, a developer who bought out the Franciscans, owners of the site. On the S side of Portal Madero (S) Av. Hidalgo runs W to the ALAMEDA (Parque Cuauhtémoc), another of González Arratia's legacies to his city. In C. Vicente Villada, a turning l., is the church of *Sta María de Guadalupe* (formerly San Juan de Dios; once part of the convent of the Brothers of St John of God), dating from c 1700, with a rustic baroque façade. A little further S, C. Villada crosses Av. Morelos, which we follow W (r.) to the church of *La Merced* (started late 17C), church of the convent of Mercedarians. The murals of the life of Our Lady in the transept (1785) are by Pedro José de Rojas. Part of the convent remains.

C. Villada continues S. On the l., is the large classical building (1850s) of the *Instituto Científico y Literario*, since 1956 part of the University of the State of México. Beyond Av. Gómez Farías we reach *Jardín Matlazinca*, on the Cerro del Calvario, giving a good view of the city. Here is the *Museo de Ciencias Naturales* (cosmography, geography, biology, geology). The church of *San José* (called El Ranchito), on the E side of C. Villada, dates from 1885–94.

C 5km SW of the centre is the **Centro Cultural Mexiquense** (Tues.–Sun., 10–6), a spacious cultural complex, incorporating modern buildings and the former hacienda of La Pila. The first (circular) building l. is the *Museo de Arte Moderno*, for exhibitions by modern artists. To the l. of the entrance is a mural in volcanic stone by the Japanese artist (resident in Mexico) Luis Nishizahua.

In the former main house of the hacienda (second building on r.) is the *Museo de Artes Populares*, which includes a representative selection of the crafts of the State of México. Reached through its Patio de las Palomas is the *Museo de la Charrería*, with exhibits illustrating the history and crafts of Mexican horsemanship.

Opposite the Museo de Artes Populares is the *Biblioteca Pública* (designed by Pedro Ramírez Vázquez), in its entrance lobby a mural, in painted clay, inspired by prehispanic art, by Nishizahua.

At the end of the precinct is the *Museo de Antropología e Historia*, covering the State's ecology, archaeology, and post-Conquest history.

We leave Toluca on the Querétaro road (Méx. 55) and turn l. at (7.5km) **CALIXTLAHUACA**. The site ruins (open daily; fee), signposted, are scattered on the hillside between the modern villages of Calixtlahuaca and Tecaxic.

As the location of the ruins implies, there were in fact two ancient towns: *Calixtlahuaca* (*calli* [house] and *ixtlahuaca* [field or plain]; thus a field or plain of houses), and *Tecaxic*. Most of the ruins have been covered by the modern villages and the fields between them, but surface survey and excavations throughout the 1930s, principally by José García Payón, have provided evidence for the area's occupation between c 1700 BC and AD 1510.

The occupation of the two towns is divided into five phases:

1. c 1700 BC–c 200 BC—earliest occupation.
2. c 200 BC–8C AD—continued occupation; strong Teotihuacano influence during the 4–8C AD; first Templo de Quetzalcóatl-Ehecatl constructed.
3. c AD 900–1200—strong Toltec influences; second stage of Templo de Quetzalcóatl-Ehecatl.
4. AD 1200–1474—Calixtlahuaca was a Matlazinca town and their chief ceremonial centre; third stage of Templo de Quetzalcóatl-Ehecatl.
5. AD 1474–1510—Aztecs invaded the Valle de Toluca, captured Tecaxic and other Matlazinca towns, and established a garrison at Calixtlahuaca; fourth stage of Templo de Quetzalcóatl-Ehecatl completed.

Little is known of the people of the first phase, and only a few traces of the walls of their dwellings have been found. Their presence is mainly attested by pottery and figurines of several styles and dates. Occupation was continuous into the second phase and the ceramic sequence shows considerable influence from Teotihuacán in the 4–8C AD. The first temple dedicated to Quetzalcóatl is the only building surviving from this phase.

In the third phase the ceramics indicate Toltec influence, perhaps presence. The Templo de Quetzalcóatl, now apparently worshipped in his guise as Ehecatl, the Wind god, was reconstructed, superimposed over the previous temple. The first stage of a large complex of rooms on platforms was built down the hill from the temple. During this period Tecaxic may have paid tribute to Tula, and the Toltecs appear to have used the Valle de Toluca as their main trade route into S Mexico (see Introduction: Early Postclassic). Although most traces of the ancient town have been obliterated by the modern villages, ceramic scatter indicates that dwellings and public buildings occupied terracing along the hillsides between Calixtlahuaca and Tecaxic, and in the adjacent valley.

In the fourth phase the town became the capital and principal ceremonial centre for several Matlazinca towns and villages in the Valle de Toluca. The Templo de Quetzalcóatl-Ehecatl was reconstructed again. Contact with the Basin of Mexico was strong, especially with the Tepaneca of Azcapotzalco, possibly in a political and economic alliance.

Post-Conquest Spanish and Aztec sources describe the Late Postclassic conflict between various Matlazinca factions in the Valley, and between the Tepaneca and the Mexica Aztecs in the Basin of Mexico. After the conquest of Azcapotzalco in 1428, and the Aztec dominance of the Basin, the Mexica invaded the Valle de Toluca in 1473–74 under Axayácatl. They received help from the Matlazinca faction in Toluca, under king Chimaltecuhtli, and captured several towns, incl. Calixtlahuaca-Tecaxic, and made them pay heavy tributes. Rebellion in 1475 caused the return of Axayácatl, allegedly leading an army of 32,300. A fierce battle took place near Xiquipilco, in which a personal combat was fought between Axayácatl and the rebel leader Tlilcuetzpalin. Although Axayácatl was wounded, the Aztecs were victorious and are said to have taken over 11,000 captives for their sacrifice in Tenochtitlán. Along with other rebellious towns, Tecaxic was left in ruins, but was still occupied, and an Aztec garrison was established in neighbouring Calixtlahuaca.

Despite these measures Tecaxic rebelled again in 1482, along with several other Matlazinca towns, massacred the Aztec garrison, and attacked other Aztec colonies in the Valle de

Toluca. King Tizoc marched with an army from Tenochtitlán, defeated the rebels, destroyed the temples of Tecaxic and erected a commemorative stone monument with carved skulls (see below), and took thousands more captives.

Tecaxic rebelled yet again in 1510 and was put down by Moctezuma II Xocoyotzin, who razed the town for good, caused the inhabitants to flee into Michoacán and take refuge among the Tarascans, and established an Aztec colony in Calixtlahuaca to take Tecaxic's place on the tribute register. It was during this phase that most of the monuments now visible were built, incl. the fourth and final stage of the Templo de Quetzalcóatl-Ehecatl and later stages of the room complexes at the base of the hillside.

From at least the Toltec phase Calixtlahuaca-Tecaxic was built to be defended. Excavations uncovered evidence of water-collection channels and cisterns, and of grain stores, but there was no convenient place in the town's hillside location for a central ceremonial plaza. Most of the common dwellings, now obliterated or buried beneath fields, would have been scattered in the valley bottom. Remains now visible are of the fourth and fifth phases of occupation, mainly restored ruins on several terraces cut into the hillside of *Cerro Tenesinó* between the two modern villages. Seventeen principal structures have been excavated, but not all of them have been restored:

> *Estructura 1*—Preclassic and later rebuilt pyramid.
> *Estructura 2*—Matlazinca-Aztec pyramid.
> *Estructura 3*—Templo de Quetzalcóatl, of the second to fifth phases.
> *Estructura 4*—Templo de Tláloc, Aztec.
> *Estructuras 5* and *6*—two three-tiered Aztec pyramids.
> *Estructura 7*—a platform NE of Estructura 4.
> *Estructuras 8* and *9*—mounds to the S of Estructuras 5 and 6.
> *(Estructuras 10, 11,* and *12* are known only from their excavation.)
> *Estructuras 13, 14,* and *15*—Aztec mounds and traces of ruins at the summit of Cerro Tenesinó, E of Estructuras 8 and 9.
> *Estructura 16*—low, rectangular platform at the base of Cerro Tenesinó.
> *Estructura 17*—calmecac of Toltec-Aztec date at the base of the hill.
> *Altar de los Cráneos*—Aztec monument erected by Tizoc, E of Estructura 4.

On the outskirts of modern Calixtlahuaca, *Estructuras 16* and *17* are on the S side of the road to Tecaxic. *Estructura 16* is a large, low, rectangular platform, all that remains of a ball court. A few metres further on, *Estructura 17* is known as the *Calmecac*, an Aztec (possibly Toltec) 'college' for the training of selected youths, preparing them for government, military, and religious offices.

Pupils were selected from all classes of Aztec society, but the majority were from the upper classes (see Introdution: Late Postclassic Period). Although it is not certain that Estructura 17 was a calmecac, it seems likely, given the history of Matlazinca rebellion, that such an institution was established with the Aztec garrison in order to indoctrinate Matlazinca youths and to train the sons of the Aztec colony.

It comprises a large rectangular enclosure (measuring 40m x 28m) oriented N, S, E, and W, with surrounding platforms and staircases leading to room complexes. The NE side is formed by a low rectangular platform with a tri-partite staircase leading to a building on top. The NW side is similarly formed by a low platform with traces of three rooms on top, with a higher platform behind these. On the SW side there are two nearly square platforms separated by a walled entryway into the plaza. Each has a wide central staircase and traces of rooms on top. The SE side of the enclosure is formed by a labyrinthine complex of more than 30 intercommunicating rooms, courts, stairways, and small platforms at varying levels.

Pottery associated with various rooms and walls has provided evidence for distinguishing between several building phases during Toltec and Aztec occupation. The complex was burned in 1510 when Moctezuma II Xocoyotzin destroyed the town.

From Estructura 17 several of the other principal ruins can be seen dotted on terraces among maguey fields on the hillside. To reach these we walk up through the fields (with due respect for the crops), first to a small plaza with the Templo de Tláloc.

Calixtlahuaca: plaza group (structures 4–7–2)

The **Templo de Tláloc** (*Estructura 4*) forms the W side of a small plaza complex of structures built in red and black tezontle. There are parts of three sloping tiers, and a fourth tier on the down-slope side. The second tier, forming the base of the platform at plaza level, is 27m x 20m and supports a pyramid 19m x 18m; the entire structure is 12m high, with traces of another tier on top. A 7m wide staircase ascends the E side in two flights, flanked by ramps, with two square pedestals, presumably for braziers, at the foot.

At the N side of the plaza, *Estructura 7* is a low, square platform, 17 m sq, with a wide staircase facing the plaza. The S side of the plaza is open except for the *Altar de los Cráneos* erected by Tizoc, opposite the Templo de Tláloc. It is cruciform in plan, with a rounded E arm, and c 9m wide E–W. Only 1.86m of its walls remain and its original height is uncertain. The 496 protruding pegs and carved skulls may have displayed real skulls of sacrificial victims, a warning to the rebellious Matlazinca.

At roughly the same level, on a spur several hundred metres NE, is the **Templo de Quetzalcóatl-Ehecatl** (*Estructura 3*). Built of volcanic andesite, the present structure is the last of four superimposed temples, parts of which can be seen in several openings left in the restorations.

The first temple was a circular pyramid of c AD 300. It was 10m in diameter, 5.5m high in five tiers, and had a 2.5m wide staircase on its E side. The second temple, using the first as a foundation, was also circular. It comprised four tiers, and was 16.5m in diameter, 7.5m high, and had a 3.4m wide staircase up the E side. The third temple, of the 13C or 14C, continued the circular plan, comprised four tiers, and was 17.3m in diameter, 9.75m high, and had a 6.5m wide staircase on the E side. Around the overhanging, vertical faces of each step ornamental serpents' heads were carved, and originally painted in bright colours. This temple was destroyed by earthquake in 1475.

The final temple, of the Aztec phase, was circular and 22m in diameter, but also incorporated a gently sloping projection on the E side, supporting the staircase with a low platform to either side. The full height of the final structure is estimated to have been c 12m.

The staircase is 8.4m wide in two flights. Two stone pedestals for braziers stand at the base and a rectangular stone altar site in the centre of the landing between flights. The terrace wall retaining the N side of the temple platform was also strengthened and increased in height during the various phases of construction, and a ramp with steps was added at the time of the second temple.

Each of these temples was dedicated to the feathered serpent, Quetzalcóatl, in the guise of Ehecatl. An Aztec style statue of Ehecatl-Quetzalcóatl was recovered during excavation of the foundations on the S side of the platform, and can now be seen in the Museo del Estado in Tenango del Valle. It depicts a human wearing the duck-billed mask symbol of Ehecatl, a loincloth, and sandals.

For the more energetic there are more structural remains up the hill slope and on the top. Some 275m E of the Templo de Quetzalcóatl-Ehecatl are two platforms, *Estructuras 1* and *2*. The first is of roughly hewn stone slabs and was rebuilt at least twice between the 3C and 6C AD; the final enlargement of red basalt was destroyed in the earthquake of 1475. The second is also of red basalt and postdates the Aztec conquest of Axayácatl in 1475–76.

Farther up the hill, c 180m, are *Estructuras 5* and *6*, two three-tiered platforms of rough masonry, a few blocks of which have some very worn carvings. This complex may have been a temple dedicated to Mixcóatl, god of fire, the night sky, and hunters, two statues of whom were found in the excavations.

Farther S up the hill are the shapeless mounds of *Estructuras 8* and *9*, and at the summit, the mounds of *Estructuras 13, 14*, and *15*, and remains of the terrace retaining wall, 48.5m long and 12m high. A statue of Coatlícue, Aztec Earth goddess and mother of the Moon, found in the excavations at the summit is now in the Museo Nacional de Antropología.

The **Nevado de Toluca** (four-wheel drive vehicle essential) is reached by leaving the city to the SW on Méx. 134 (the road to *Temascaltepec* and *Ciudad Altamirano*; see Rte 31). At 21km we turn l. on the road to *Sultepec*, and at 29km meet the dirt road (not advisable in the rainy season or in severe winter weather) that leads (c 20km) to within a kilometre of the summit. An unhurried ascent is recommended; the thin mountain air will try the novice visitor. The volcano is now extinct. Within the crater are two lakes, *Lago del Sol* (400 x 200m; 4209m) and *Lago de la Luna* (200 x 75m; 4216m). To the N is the *Pico del Aguila* (4564m), climbed by Humboldt in Sept. 1803; to the S, the *Pico del Fraile*. Both are recommended only to experienced climbers. The views N and E to the valleys of Toluca and Mexico; W and S to the mountains of Michoacán and Guerrero, and the tierra caliente, are wonderful.

In Oct. 1838, Heredia, with an English friend, Mr Sowkins, arrived at the summit at 11 o'clock in the morning. 'The sky above our heads', he wrote, 'perfectly serene, was of a beautiful dark blue, peculiar to that region. The sunlight was faint, as if two-thirds of the sun's disc would be eclipsed. The waning quarter-moon shone like silver. My blood coursed through my veins and I felt an overwhelming desire to launch myself through the air'.

After the turning at 29km to the Nevado, the main road runs S and enters a region known as the Provincia de la Plata, famous since the 16C for its mines (silver, some gold, copper, lead, zinc) to (67km) a turning r. for (11km SW) **Sultepec** (8000 inhab.; 2336m; H,P), an attractive place in mountainous country, established as a real de minas in 1569. The former convent of *San Miguel* (discalced Franciscans; dieguinos) was founded in the 17C. Its church has an agreeable baroque façade and has preserved a contemporary high altarpiece and a painting of St Rose by Joaquín Villegas (1779). A small *Museo Regional* illustrates the history of the area. The road continues SE to (110km) **Zacualpan** (c 4000 inhab.; 2050m; H,P), another old real de minas in a well-forested region. The church of *La Concepción* dates from the early 17C.

FROM TOLUCA TO CIUDAD ALTAMIRANO, Méx. 134, 224km. The road (often serpentine in its upper reaches) traverses spectacular mountainous terrain in the SW of the State of México, especially in the municipality of Tejupilco, before descending into the Balsas river system. 21km turning l. for *Sultepec*, see above. 69km **Temascaltepec** (c 6000 inhab.; 1770m; H,R,P), an old real de minas in the Sierra de Temascaltepec. The region's mines (gold, silver, lead) have been exploited since the 16C (after Independence, for a time by British companies). The town's attractiveness is enhanced by its whitewashed houses with typical balconies and cobbled streets. Its parish church (dating from the 16C) possesses a contemporary image of Christ crucified, said to have come from Spain and to be endowed with miraculous powers. To the NE, the *Peñón de Temascaltepec* rises to 2620m. The road N runs to (24km NW) *Valle de Bravo*, see Rte 34. The road ascends and then descends to (103km) **Tejupilco de Hidalgo** (6000 inhab.; 1455m; modest accommodation, R,P), in the Valle de Tejupilco, another picturesque place, with a lovely shaded Pl. Principal. At *Las Juntas*, on its outskirts, are the ruins of the house where don Cristóbal Hidalgo y Costilla was born. C 12km S, on Hacienda de Guadalupe, in 1959 archaeologists found stone slabs carved with simple geometric bas-reliefs, judged by their style to be of Preclassic date. Several mounds in the immediate vicinity indicate a rural site. At *Ixtapan*, c 3km SW of the hacienda, similar reliefs, undoubtedly from the same site, have been found on stones incorporated into the walls of the village church. From Tejupilco the road, running NW, skirts the mass of the Cerro Valiente. 125km *Estanco*, starting point for excursions in the pine-forested mountains of the extreme W of the State, as far as the *Cañada de Nanchtitlán* (c 36km W). Méx. 130 descends into the State of Guerrero (at 162km) and the tierra caliente. 224km *Ciudad Altamirano*, see Rte 31.

Reached by taking the Valle de Bravo road W from Toluca and turning l. (S) at 8km is (9km) **Zinacantepec**, where the Franciscan convent of *San Miguel*, founded in the 1550s, was not finished until late in the 16C, or early in the 17C. Its atrio is entered through a double-arched side entrance. The church walls show traces of stucco sgraffito; its interior shows groin vaulting. The original stone pulpit and earthenware holy water stoup are in place. By the high altar are two 16C statues from a retable, brought here from Tepeaca, the one of St Augustine having lost its estofado. In the chancel, murals of the life of St Francis. In the sacristy an anon. Pietà (1626).

On the S side of the church is a classic combination of portería and open chapel. Its central arch, higher than the other four, faces the elevated altar, with a painted mural retable: St Michael the centrepiece, surrounded by Franciscan saints; Our Lord and angels above; God the Father in the pediment. It has been retouched by a recent hand, as have the other murals, incl. the Genealogical Tree of St Francis (perhaps early 17C) above the doorway into the cloister, he reclining, the tree sprouting from his breast; St Francis speaking to animals; St Francis receiving the stigmata. At the S end of the portería is the baptistery, containing a gorgeous global font (1581), modelled in terracotta and showing four medallion reliefs: Annunciation; St Martin; St Michael and Satan; Baptism of Christ; and a band of horn of plenty, acanthus, and serpentine relief. The cloister, with plain, effective, arches, retains traces of a grand timber ceiling. The roof is punctuated by zoomorphic gargoyles. A room off the upper walk contains two paintings (Penance and Death of St Nicholas of Tolentino) attr. Juan Correa.

41   Ciudad Juárez to Chihuahua

Méx. 45, 375km.—134km Villa Ahumada.—375km **Chihuahua**.

CIUDAD JUAREZ (1.4 million inhab.; 1144m), largest city in the State of Chihuahua and fourth largest in Mexico, on the S bank of the Río Bravo (Río Grande) and forming one large conurbation with El Paso, Texas, offers all the advantages and disadvantages of a frontier city. It is, however, more dignified than some, with its wide boulevards and pleasant parks. It is a catchment area for visitors, on brief stays, from the USA.

Airport. 17km S. Flights to *Chihuahua, Torreón, Mexico City, Acapulco, Tijuana, Monterrey*, etc.

Bus station. E side of city, at the corner of Av. López Mateos and C. Triunfo de la República. Frequent services to *Chihuahua* (5 hrs); to *Jiménez* (8 hrs); to *Torreón* (12 hrs); to *Parral* (10 hrs); to *Durango* (16 hrs); to *Mexico City* (26 hrs); etc.

Railway station. S end of Av. Lerdo (Av. Ramón Corona) and E side of Av. Cervecería. Daily train to *Mexico City* (36 hrs) via Chihuahua, Torreón, Zacatecas, Aguascalientes, León, Silao, Celaya, and Querétaro.

Hotels throughout the city.

Post Office. Corner of Avs Lerdo and Ignacio Peña.

Tourist Office. Corner of Av. Malecón and C. Francisco Villa.

US Consulate. 924 Av. López Mateos. **British Consulate.** 185 C. Fresno.

Lienzo charro. Near junction of Avs Plutarco Elías Calles and Triunfo de la República.

Bullfights. Generally on Sun., Apr.–Dec., in the Pl. Monumental at the E end of Av. 16 de Septiembre. Also at the Pl. de Toros Balderas between Avs Lerdo and Juárez.

Fiestas. 10 Aug.: St Lawrence. 4 Dec.: St Barbara.

The city originates in the Franciscan mission (1659) of Nuestra Señora de Guadalupe del Paso del Norte. In 1865–66 Pres. Juárez had his government here. It was renamed Ciudad Juárez in 1888. The well-publicized meeting between Presidents Porfirio Díaz and William H. Taft took place here in Oct. 1909. An early blow for the Revolution was struck on 10 May 1911 when the forces of Pascual Orozco and Francisco Villa took the city by storm. On 21 May the treaties of Ciudad Juárez, signed by representatives of Díaz and Madero, marked the end of the porfiriato. Henceforth it was to be a vital port of entry during the Revolution, and one of Villa's prime targets. In July 1963 a US-Mexican convention ceded to Mexico the territory of El Chamizal between El Paso and Ciudad Juárez.

The older part of the city may be reached along Avs Juárez and Lerdo, which run S from the Sta Fe and Stanton St bridges. In the *Aduana Fronteriza* (customs house; late 19C), near the junction of Avs Juárez and 16 de Septiembre, were signed the treaties of 1911. It later became Villa's headquarters. Further W along Av. 16 de Septiembre, facing the old Pl. de Armas, is the small adobe *Misión de Guadalupe* (1663), attached to the 19C cathedral of *Nuestra Señora de Guadalupe*. The older building has kept its fine original woodwork: beams of unusual narrowness and delicacy, and supports. No. 527 Av. 16 de Septiembre was Juárez's house in 1865–66.

On the NE side of the city and S of the Puente de Córdova is the *Centro Pronaf* (Programa Nacional Fronteriza, inaugurated in 1961 to develop the frontier region), which includes a commercial centre, convention and exhibition halls, and the *Museo de Arte e Historia Natural* (Tues.–Sun., 10–7), which caters also for temporary shows. In *Parque Chamizal*, to the N, beyond Av. Malecón, is the *Museo de Arqueología* (daily, 9–6.30; fee), in a low, circular building designed by Pedro Ramírez Vázquez—a good introduction to Mexican archaeology and crafts, incl. finds from Casas Grandes.

We may leave Ciudad Juárez to the E along Carretera Panamericana (Méx. 45). After 11km Carretera Juárez Porvenir (Méx. 2) branches off SE along the frontier to (68km) *Práxedis G. Guerrero* and (89km) *El Porvenir*. NE of El Porvenir a bridge crosses the Río Bravo to *Fort Hancock* in Texas.

Méx. 45 continues S alongside the Chihuahua railway line and across the N part of the Mexican High Plateau, through semi-desert and savannah, and rangelands. The climate is hot and extremely dry. At 21km Méx. 2 runs W across the desert to (158km) l. turn for (40km) *Laguna de Guzmán*, where traces of Archaic hunter-gatherers (c 8000–5000 BC) have been found, in an area also referred to as the Cochise Culture; and then via (223km) *La Ascensión* to (277km) *Nuevo Casas Grandes*, see Rte 42. 51km *Samalayuca*, in a spectacular area of sand dunes (c 80km long and 24km wide) which change position continually in the wind; a wind which also raises diaphanous curtains of white sand which appear golden in the sun.

To the W, as we continue S, is a vast enclosed basin in full desiccation because of chronic lack of rain and intense evaporation. A similar fate has hit the smaller *Laguna de los Patos*, to the E before we reach (134km) **Villa Ahumada** (c 10,000 inhab.; 1181m; H,R,P), known for its cheeses.

15km W, near the ranch of *El Carrizal*, on 21 June 1916 took place a battle between Mexican and US cavalry after the Mexican commander, Gen. Félix U. Gómez, had sought to prevent the Pershing expedition's progress southward. Gómez was killed, but the US advance was halted.

From (219km) *El Sueco* (P) State road 10 runs W to (114km) *Buenaventura*, on Méx. 2, 82km S of *Nuevo Casas Grandes*. 345km turning r. for (30km W) *Parque Nacional Cumbres de Majalca*, amid pine and oak forests and strange rocky landscape.

375km **CHIHUAHUA** (780,000 inhab.; 1430m), capital of the State of Chihuahua, lies on a plain to the E of the Sierra Madre Occidental and on the r. bank of the Río Chuvíscar—'a city lost in a territory of epic dimensions'. Today it derives its wealth mainly from lumbering in the Sierra Madre and from the area's cattle ranches. Its handsome wide avenues and plazas, and inner suburbs developed in the later 19C in conspicuously quaint fin-de-siècle style, help its reputation as a civilized city. But its centre has been ravaged by piecemeal redevelopment. Associations with the insurgents and with Francisco Villa add to its interest.

Airport. 16km NE. Daily flights to *Ciudad Juárez, Hermosillo, Mazatlán, Mexico City, Monterrey*, and *Torreón*.

Railway stations. Av. División del Norte, well NE of the centre, for trains to *Zacatecas, Mexico City*, and *Ciudad Juárez*. Just off C. Méndez (SW of the Penitentiary) for the Chihuahua al Pacífico railway. Vistatrén (air conditioned and more enjoyable) daily, leaving at approx. 7 am. The journey takes c 14 hrs. Travellers are advised to check timetables and book seats in advance. Ticket office opens at 6.30 am and is open at intervals during the day.

Bus station. NW of the centre, between Cs. 10 and Progreso. Services to *Ciudad Juárez* (6 hrs); to *Zacatecas* (14 hrs); to *Hidalgo del Parral* (6 hrs); to *Mexico City* (20 hrs); to *Durango* (11 hrs); to *Torreón* (8 hrs); etc.

Hotels throughout the city.

Post Office. Corner of Calle 7 and Av. Juárez, in Pal. Federal.

Tourist Office. Corner of Calle 31A and Av. Reforma.

In 1709 an administrative centre for the various settlements in the area, called *San Francisco de Cuéllar*, was founded. In 1718 its name was changed to *San Felipe el Real de Chihuahua*. In Apr. 1811 the principal insurgents were brought to San Felipe for trial, and executed in batches in May and July, Miguel Hidalgo being the last to suffer on 30 July. In 1909 Abraham González organized in Chihuahua the National Anti-re-electionist party. The city was much fought over during the Revolution. After Villa had tried to capture it for the fourth time in autumn 1917, the constitutionalist commander, Gen. Francisco Murguía, hanged 256 captured villistas in batches from the trees along Av. Colón. On 26 Nov. 1919, Gen. Felipe Angeles, Villa's second-in-command, was executed here.

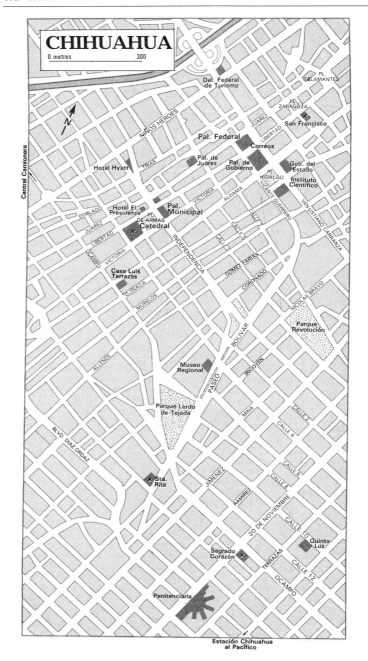

CHIHUAHUA

0 metres — 300

Del. Federal de Turismo

PL. TALAMANTES

PL. ZARAGOZA

San Francisco

NIÑOS HÉROES

JUÁREZ

LIBERTAD

Pal. Federal

Correos

Hotel Hyatt

TRÍAS

Pal. de Juárez

Pal. de Gobierno

Gob. del Estado

PL. HIDALGO

Instituto Científico

VICENTE GUERRERO

ALDAMA

VICTORIA

VENUSTIANO CARRANZA

DOBLADO

Hotel El Presidente

PL. DE ARMAS

Pal. Municipal

Catedral

JUÁREZ

LIBERTAD

CALLE 3

CALLE 5

INDEPENDENCIA

VICTORIA

OCAMPO

Casa Luis Terrazas

GÓMEZ FARÍAS

CORONADO

OJINAGA

MORELOS

NICOLÁS BRAVO

Parque Revolución

Central Camionera

ALLENDE

BOLÍVAR

Museo Regional

PASEO

IRIGOYEN

MINA

CALLE 2

CALLE 4

Parque Lerdo de Tejada

BLVD. DÍAZ ORDAZ

CALLE 6

Sta. Rita

JIMÉNEZ

RAMÍREZ

CALLE 8

CALLE 10

20 DE NOVIEMBRE

Quinta Luz

Sagrado Corazón

TERRAZAS

CALLE 12

OCAMPO

Penitenciaría

Estación Chihuahua al Pacífico

The largest Mexican State, **Chihuahua** (247,087 sq km; 2.2 million inhab.), occupies the N part of the Mexican High Plateau (Altiplanicie Mexicana); its surface largely an elevated plain sloping towards the Río Bravo del Norte, which (E and NE) forms the frontier with the USA. Its W and S parts are broken by the Sierra Madre Occidental, whose spurs form fertile valleys. Deeply eroded canyons (barrancas) at higher levels have heavy rainfall which is carried off in torrents towards the Gulfs of California and Mexico. On the E side of the Sierra Madre various streams sink into the desert in enclosed depressions (bolsones) where flood waters form lakes which evaporate into mud flats or salt marshes (salinas). The plateau experiences extremes of temperature. The E third of State territory is sparsely populated desert. The Bolsón de Mapimí, in the SE, once considered irredeemable, has been shown to be fertile. The principal river, Río Conchos, flows N and NE through the State. The area between just N of Madera in the W and Guadalupe y Calvo in the S is Mexico's most important commercial forest. Irrigation in the NW has made the district between Nuevo Casas Grandes and Buenaventura an abundant producer of corn, wheat, oats, and fruit. Mining (lead, zinc, silver, gold, iron) yields 22 per cent of national production. The State's main reputation is for livestock—c 16 million hectares of pasture.

In the remote mountainous region W of Chihuahua (mostly inaccessible by road) numerous cave sites of the early inhabitants of the region have been located and a few excavated (Cf. *Casas Grandes*). Most of today's State of Chihuahua fell within the territory of Nueva Vizcaya (New Biscay), denominated in 1562 to comprise all lands to the N of Nueva Galicia. Its first governor, Francisco de Ibarra, after a series of campaigns, established a Spanish presence in most of it. Mines were opened, cattle brought in, and wheatfields planted, but conflict with Indian tribes was unavoidable. During and after the uprisings of 1616–18, 15,000 Tepehuanes are said to have perished in battle and by hanging. During the 17C Franciscans and Jesuits extended their missionary efforts to the N, the former keeping to the plain, the latter concentrating on the Indian tribes of the sierra. The Indians could not be reconciled, and constantly raided and pillaged. In 1647–97, the wild Tarahumaras of the W and SW revolted four times and were crushed, but at terrible cost to the victors. From the late 17C a new menace appeared in the Apaches, who swept down from the N to begin two centuries of on and off warfare. Outside their few towns, the reales de minas, and the string of garrisons established by the crown, the Spaniards had laid out vast haciendas and farms, employing hundreds and maintained in perilous conditions.

The territory of the new State, established in 1824, was frequently menaced by Indian raids, especially in 1848–52. US invasion in 1847–48 was resisted under the leadership of Angel Trías, an able, rich, and popular liberal governor. The years after 1854 marked the rise of Luis Terrazas (1829–1923), the only regional cacique who retained his power base throughout the French intervention, the purges of the Juárez restoration, and the porfiriato. By 1910 he and his son-in-law, Enrique C. Creel, headed a clan, its huge landholding a veritable kingdom. Their monopoly of power dashed the hopes of advancement of outsiders and their seizure of the lands of smallholders at a time of unemployment, strikes, and drought at the turn of the century made the anti-re-electionist and revolutionary movements in Chihuahua the strongest in Mexico. From 1911 the State was power base of Abraham González, Pascual Orozco, and Francisco Villa. The latter recruited the major part of his División del Norte here. From here he mounted his raid (Feb. 1916) on Columbus, New Mexico, provoking the Pershing expedition which spent 11 months bogged down in the State while Villa did as he pleased.

On the SW side of PL. DE ARMAS stands the cathedral of **Nuestra Señora de Regla y San Francisco de Asís**, one of the great religious buildings of N Mexico, a final and powerful expression of baroque.

The original plan for a new parish church, by Joseph de la Cruz, was sent to Spain for royal approval in 1726 by Bp Benito Crespo y Monroy. In 1727 a grander edifice was decided upon when work had already begun. In 1734 La Cruz died and was buried 'opposite the pulpit'. The façade was finished in 1741 under Antonio de Nava; the cupola in 1742–43; and the graceful towers, probably by Bernardo del Carpio, in 1757–58. By 1760 the exterior was complete. The acute economic crisis which hit the area in mid-century prevented progress on the interior and funds were diverted for campaigns against the Apaches and Comanches. Work was resumed in 1789 under Nicolás Morín; the bells were founded by Juan Antonio Gómez in 1798.

EXTERIOR. The surfaces of the main, N, façade, in three storeys, are covered in bold relief. The columns, six in each of the lowest and first, two in the second, are most attractively varied in design: the lowest divided into two equal parts by a concave ring, bases and tops in vegetal relief patterns, central sections fluted, and crowned by Corinthian capitals; the first divided into three unequal parts and swathed in large leaves and festoons; the second divided into two unequal sections by a convex ring, fluted in the lower parts, adorned with spiralling festoons and fluting in the upper. In the centre of the bold, imaginative central vertical section is an octagonal choir window, its keystone a bust of St Joseph holding the Child Jesus. An elegant pentagonal arch within an outer, semicircular, forms the upper part of the doorway; a papal tiara forms the keystone and angels flutter in the spandrels. An elaborate version of an eared frame in the top storey holds the central relief of St Francis. The niches hold statues of the 12 apostles.

The side portals are piled with relief, especially in their charmingly curved upper storeys. On the W portal, the finial is a statue of St Michael. Beneath him, in the sumptuous first-storey niche, stands St James the Greater as pilgrim. In the lower storey are St Benedict (l.) and a young apostle (r.). In the arch key, St Joseph holds the infant Christ; above them, God the Father. St Michael also appears as the finial on the E portal. The saint in the central niche is probably St Philip the Apostle. In the lower niches, two unknown saints. In the arch key, Our Lady holding the infant Christ.

At an angle to the E portal is that of the *Cap. de Nuestra Señora del Rosario*, topped by a relief, delightful even in its rigid formality, of Our Lady of the Rosary between SS Dominic and Rose, and offering hope to the souls in purgatory. Behind the E tower is the so-called *Pozo de Animas*, probably an ossuary; in its upper part is a relief of St Francis as intermediary for the souls in purgatory.

The INTERIOR (redecorated in 1939–40) is notable for the rich entablature above the engaged and clustered pilasters supporting the side arches. The high altarpiece (1790–92), started by Nicolás Morín and finished by his son Ignacio, is one of the very few 18C stone examples in Mexico.

In 1939 a new central part was put in. In 1939–40, its pediment was more ornately remade. It preserves its slender estípites. In the niches are wooden statues of St Philip (repainted, but original) and Our Lady of Regla (a later substitution). At the S end of the aisles on either side of the cupola are the altarpieces of St Joseph (1793; E) and Our Lady of Sorrows (c 1813; W). The two side altars further N were set up in 1826.

Of great interest are the sculptural details of the pendentives of the cupola and the nave arch keys. In the former, amid plentiful acanthus, reliefs, earthy and strong, of doctors of the Church: SS Gregory the Great, Jerome, Ambrose, and Augustine. The keys of the arches which support the drum represent four advocations of Our Lady: of Regla (S), of the Rosary (E), of Guadalupe (N), and of Sorrows (W). In the spandrels of the sotocoro arch (N end) are Faith (l.), her eyes bound, holding a chalice and cross, and Hope (r.), her robe rippling in the wind, holding an anchor. Representing Charity in the key is St Lawrence. Above, the key of the choir arch shows St Joseph facing the choir and Our Lady facing the nave. In the first nave arch are St Michael, supported by four cherub heads (facing choir), and St Gabriel (facing high altar). Next comes Moses, backed by St John the Baptist. Facing the latter and backing Our Lady of Guadalupe is St Francis; SS Ignatius and Dominic (W and E) back Our Lady of Sorrows and Our Lady of the Rosary. Above the window facing St Dominic appears St Philip Neri, and opposite St Ignatius, St John Nepomuk.

Further examples of fine relief are the doorways to the sacristy (the Host in the pediment; SW end) and treasury (SE end). In the sacristy is an anon. 18C Way of the Cross. In the cube of the E tower is the gilded wooden altarpiece of the Señor de Mapimí (c 1752). The *Cap. del Rosario* dates from 1757–60.

Behind the Cathedral, C. Victoria runs SW. Turning l. at the junction with C. Ocampo we reach (corner with C. Aldama) the ostentatious former residence of Luis Terrazas, built at the turn of the century, now a cultural centre.

C 12 blocks further SW along Cs Victoria and Matamoros is the *Santuario de Guadalupe* (1793–c 1825). The statues of SS Ignatius and Francis Xavier on either side of its curved pediment are from the church of Loreto (see below). From here may be seen the *Acueducto* (1751–92), still in use for part of the city's water supply.

The bandstand in the centre of Pl. de Armas was a gift from Belgium to Luis Terrazas. On the NW side is the glass-fronted *Hotel el Presidente*. In the middle of the NE side, on the site of the old *Casas Consistoriales*, stands the **Pal. Municipal** (1906–07), with suitably grand first-floor windows and balconies, and imposing Sala de Cabildos, designed by an English architect, John Waite, in collaboration with Enrique Esperón and Alfredo Giles. The façade was remade in 1964 after fire damage. Its two flanking buildings, now banks, date from the same period.

From the N corner of the plaza Av. Juárez runs NE. At the end of the third block, on the l., is the **Casa de Juárez**, a small one-storey late 18C house, residence of Benito Juárez during 1864–66.

It is now a museum, the living quarters tastefully and sparingly arranged; facsimile letters and documents, and photographs, in the other rooms providing a commentary on the president's life and times.

Further along on the r., between Avs Venustiano Carranza and Vicente Guerrero, is the **Pal. Federal** (1910), built on part of the site of the church and college of **Loreto**, former headquarters of the Jesuits.

The college dated from 1718, the church from c 1752–61. After the expulsion in 1767 they served variously as military hospital, Casa de Moneda, prison, and barracks, until demolition in 1878. One small part has been left intact as a national shrine: the prison cell in which Hidalgo was kept for 98 days on bread and water before his execution. Adm. Tues.–Fri., 10–2; 4–7; Sat.–Sun., 10–2.

Also built on the site of the college is the handsome, eclectic **Pal. de Gobierno**, which backs on to the Pal. Federal across C. Libertad and faces PL. HIDALGO.

It was built (1882–92) to the designs of Pedro Ignacio Irigoyen and Enrique Esperón. It was restored after fire damage and the third storey added in 1941–47. At the far side of the main patio a perpetual flame marks the spot where Hidalgo was executed. The indifferent murals (1960–62) are by Aarón Piña Mora.

In the centre of the plaza is a monument to Hidalgo, unveiled in 1889, at each corner statues of Aldama, Jiménez, Allende, and Morelos. On the NE side is the extension to the Pal. de Gobierno, opened in 1978; on the SE side the *Instituto Científico y Literario* (1926–28), founded in 1827 and the nucleus of the University of Chihuahua, founded in 1954.

From the front of the Pal. Federal, C. Libertad runs two blocks NE to PL. SAN FRANCISCO and the church of **San Francisco**, part of a Franciscan convent founded in 1715.

The church was finished probably in 1741; the convent (a fragment surviving on the NE side of the church) was still building in 1736, but was partly demolished in 1878. Some of the insurgents were held here in 1810.

On its NW side is the *Cap. de San Antonio*, where Hidalgo's decapitated body lay buried in 1811–23. The squat tower (1740) is by Nicolás Muñoz. In the transepts the two 18C altarpieces are (r.) churrigueresque and (l.) anastyle.

In PL. TALAMANTES, to the N, a monument (1910) commemorates the liberal dead in the battle of Talamantes (Jan. 1860), a conservative victory during the war of the Reform.
From the Pal. Federal, Av. Venustiano Carranza runs NW. At its junction with Av. División del Norte is a monument (1957) to Francisco Villa by Ignacio Asúnsolo.

From the SW side of Pl. Hidalgo, Av. Vicente Guerrero goes S, merging with PASEO BOLIVAR (keeping some late 19C mansions). Along Calle 7 (3rd turning l.) we may reach PARQUE REVOLUCION, where stands the *Mausoleo de Francisco Villa*, a neo-Gothic folly intended as his tomb. It remains empty. Villa's corpse, minus the head, rests in Mexico City.

Further along, at the corner with Calle 4, is the **Quinta Gameros**, among the finest examples of fin-de-siècle eclecticism in Mexico.

It was begun in 1907 for the mining engineer Manuel Gameros by the Colombian architect Julio Corredor Latorre and largely finished by 1910, too late for the family to settle in. In 1914 it was Carranza's residence and, during later Revolutionary years, prison, and barracks for Villa's troops. Since 1961 it has been the **Museo Regional** (Tues.–Sun., 10–1, 3–5; fee), in which fabric and interior furnishings hold more interest than the local collections (Desert

Cultures tradition of N Mexico and W parts of the USA, and of the agricultural peoples of the SW USA).

Particularly striking are the four corner mansard towers and the slender cupola; the windows, varied in style and inspired by Art Nouveau, laden with carved stone decoration, incl. female faces in the arch keys; and the classic female statues between the columns of the entrance balcony.

INTERIOR. In music room, drawing room, dining room, bedrooms, and bathroom have been arranged the furniture and fittings designed by José Luis Requena for his house at 43 C. de la Veracruz in Mexico City (now demolished)—the finest Art Nouveau interior in Mexico. Sofa and chairs in the drawing room are Louis XV-inspired. In the dining room, carved mahogany furniture; sideboards covered in marble; oil paintings (Spring and Autumn) by Ramón Cantó on gold leaf in the side doors.

Next on the r. along Paseo Bolívar is *Parque Lerdo de Tejada*. Opposite, along Calle 10, we may go SE six blocks to No. 3014, the **Museo Histórico de la Revolución** (Mon.–Sat., 9–1, 3–7; fee), in the house called *Quinta Luz*, built from 1914 by Francisco Villa.

It was lived in for many years by Villa's legal widow, Luz Corral (1893–1981), who maintained it as a museum. Here are found mementoes of Villa and, especially interesting, Luz Corral. Pictures, arms and armour, letters, household objects, costume, etc. illustrate the story of porfirismo and the Revolution. A prize object is the bullet-riddled Dodge car (1919) in which Villa was assassinated at Parral in 1923.

Two blocks past Parque Lerdo is the little church of *Sta Rita* (1729), repaired in 1971 after flood damage. Six blocks SE along Calle 6 we reach Av. 20 de Noviembre. To the l. is the church of *Sagrado Corazón*, ugly manifestation of pre-Revolutionary piety. To the r. is the *Penitenciaria*, the city prison, by Alfredo Giles, inaugurated in 1908.

21km E, reached along a turn-off from Méx. 45, is **Aquiles Serdán** (c 10,000 inhab.; 2284m; R,P), settled originally as the mining camp of *Sta Eulalia* in 1707–08. The church of *Sta Eulalia*, begun in 1760, shows similarities of detail with the cathedral of Chihuahua and has a S doorway with plentiful relief. The arch key is a figure of St Luis Gonzaga. In the upper storey, encompassed by inverted volutes, the niche holding the statue of St Joseph is framed by sturdy twisted columns; above, a statue of St Raphael. The plainer main, W, doorway, by Nicolás Morín, dates from c 1790.

FROM CHIHUAHUA TO OJINAGA, 210km. We leave Chihuahua along the road to Parral (Av. Independencia; Méx. 45) running SE, at 5km turning l. along the airport road. At 13km we join Méx. 16 (l.) which runs along the valley of the Río Chuvíscar. 22km **Villa Aldama** (10,000 inhab.; 1262m; R,P), the former mission of *San Jerónimo*. The parish church of *San Jerónimo* was built by the Franciscans towards the mid-18C. The church of *Sta Ana* originated in the rival Jesuit mission of Chinarras, founded in 1716, close to that of the Franciscans. The road continues NE through desert to (141km) *Coyame*, known for the distillation of sotol, an alcoholic liquor, and within easy reach of underground caves (apply locally for a guide). 172km *El Peguis*, a viewpoint over a canyon into which the waters of the Río Conchos cascade. 210km **Ojinaga** (c 20,000 inhab.; 841m; H,R,P), the former 18C military post of Presidio del Norte, where the Río Conchos meets the Río Bravo, across the frontier from Presidio in Texas.

42 Chihuahua to Nuevo Casas Grandes

Méx. 16, State road 23, and Méx. 23, 430km.—49km General Trías.—104km Cuauhtémoc and State road 23.—350km Buenaventura and Méx. 23.—430km **Nuevo Casas Grandes**.

The most direct route is by Méx. 45 directly N of Chihuahua, by the road W (Méx. 10) from (156km) *El Sueco* to (270km) *Buenaventura*, and thence NW to (352km) *Nuevo Casas Grandes*. The route given below, although 100km longer, takes in various places of interest to the SW and W of Chihuahua.

We leave Chihuahua to the SW on Méx. 16, the road running between mountain ranges. At 30km a minor road turns off to the l. along the valley of the Río Sta Isabel to (35km) *La Joya*, where the church of Sta Ana keeps its original

17C wooden ceiling and interior surface paintings. This road continues to (56km) *Satevó*, where the Jesuits set up the first mission in the Chihuahua area among the Tarahumaras c 1640. Méx. 16 continues to (49km) **General Trías** (c 1200 inhab.; 1430m; R,P), on the Río Sta Isabel. The church of Sta Isabel dates from 1845. At 61km a minor road runs S to a region watered by affluents of the Río San Pedro.

It reaches (21km) *Belisario Domínguez*, the former San Lorenzo, founded in the mid-1640s as a Jesuit visiting station among the Tarahumaras. The church dates from the 18C. At (36km) *Tutuaca* the road forks. The l. fork (SE) runs to (55km) *Sta María de las Cuevas*, a Jesuit mission during c 1690–1753; their church retains its interior decoration. *Cueva de los Comanches*, c 10km S (guide necessary), has zoomorphic and anthropomorphic paintings, reputedly by Comanche Indians. The r. fork (SW) climbs to (62km) *San Francisco de Borja*, another mission (1678–1767), with a 17C church.

104km **Cuauhtémoc** (c 40,000 inhab.; 2100m; H,R,P), known for stock-raising and dairy products. The hard work and skills of the Mennonite community have created a region of unexpected fertility.

The Mennonites originated in a breakaway religious group founded in the 16C by the Dutchman Menno Simonis. Like-minded groups were established in German-speaking Europe. In the 1870s, after persecution, they left for N America and settled in Saskatchewan. They came to Mexico after 1921. Mexican tolerance assures respect for their pacific traditions. Their fair colouring, low German dialect, and quaint costumes of the women make them noticeable. They have colonies in Chihuahua, Coahuila, Durango, and Zacatecas.
C 24km S is *Cusihuiriáchic*, once a regional headquarters of Nueva Vizcaya, with the largest non-Indian settlement, and a source of silver ore since the 1680s. The 18C church of *Sta Rosa* keeps a contemporary altarpiece with paintings by José de Alzíbar.

FROM CUAUHTEMOC TO MADERA AND LAS CUARENTA CASAS, 221km. State road 16 continues W, parallel with the railway, to (44km) *La Junta*, whence a road goes S to (103km) *Creel*, see Rte 43. We continue NW along the valley of the Río Papigóchic, an affluent of the Río Yaqui, to (64km) **Ciudad Guerrero** (c 5000 inhab.; 2000m; H,R,P).

It had a brief existence (1649–52) as Villa Aguilar, with a Spanish garrison and a Jesuit chaplain (killed in 1650), before being laid waste in a Tarahumara revolt. The valley was resettled by Spaniards in the 1670s, and disputed as mission territory between Jesuits and Franciscans. Until 1859 it was known as Villa de la Encarnación. 7km S is *Presa Abraham González* (fishing).

82km *Sto Tomás*, a Jesuit mission during 1697–1767; their little church contains three baroque altarpieces. 109km *Matachic* and (124km) *Temósachic* (P at both), two more former Jesuit missions, were the scene of an uprising against the Díaz government, bloodily suppressed in Apr. 1893.

From Matachic a road runs SW deep into the sierra to (c 50km) *Tosánachic*, a quaint pueblo with wooden houses, intensely cold in winter, gradually to wind S and SE to (c 150km) *Basaseachic*, see Rte 43.

178km **Madera** (c 12,000 inhab.; 2079m; H,R,P), a pleasant town, prosperous because of its forestry industry. Hence a reasonable road continues down the valley to (c 215km) *Vallecito*. C 6km N is the archaeological site of **Las Cuarenta Casas** (signposted) in the arroyo El Garabato. It is architecturally similar to Casas Grandes and culturally related to the farming cultures of the Southwest USA. There are several groups of apartment-like structures in a series of caves. Investigations by INAH (1980–81) found remnants of wall paintings in some, and established that different rooms were used for ceremony and for residence. The principal period of occupation was c 1060–1205, with occasional re-use up to c 1340, corresponding to the occupation phases of Casas Grandes.

3km beyond Cuauhtémoc State road 23 diverges N towards spectacular mountain ranges, and then W to (182km) *Bachíniva*, on the Río Sta María, a former

Franciscan mission among the Tarahumaras and Conchos from the early 1660s. Their church of Sta María Natívitas, much altered, remains. At 247km a road diverges E to cross the Sierra de Sta Catarina towards the valley of the Río Sta María.

After 25km we reach *Namiquipa* (P), a small pueblo founded by the Franciscans in the 1660s. The original Concho inhabitants were replaced by Tarahumaras by the end of the 17C. The road winds N to (70km) *Presa el Tintero* (sailing and fishing).

259km (l.) *San José de Bavícora* (P), to the W of a large drainage basin, *Lago de Bavícora*, and in a region which the Jesuits turned prosperous by cattle-raising in the 18C. 270km *Gómez Farías*. 303km *Ignacio Zaragoza* (H,P), from where the road climbs E and then NE to (350km) *Buenaventura* (H,P), in a well-watered section of the valley of the Río Sta María. Hence Méx. 23 gradually descends to (430km) **Nuevo Casas Grandes** (c 20,000 inhab.; 1473m; H,R,P), centre of a mining and agricultural area in the Valle de San Diego, and 6km NW of Casas Grandes (Paquimé).

A Franciscan mission was founded at Casas Grandes in 1640 and pack trains crossed the area on the route between Parral and Sonora. C 1661 a Spanish colony settled, and a more permanent Franciscan mission, but all was destroyed in a rebellion of Suma Indians in 1684. By the mid-18C Casas Grandes was again settled by non-Indians. Warned out of the USA in Feb. 1911, Francisco I. Madero, at the head of 500 hurriedly assembled troops, attacked the town on 5 March, only to meet defeat by a reinforced federal garrison: the first military action in his revolt against Díaz.

From the plaza of old *Casas Grandes* it is 1km walk to the site-house (9–4.30; fee).

CASAS GRANDES was on the S reaches of the group of cultures known as the Southwestern American Oases Culture, in N Mexico, Arizona, New Mexico, and parts of Colorado and Utah. Archaeologists distinguished three main cultural variants, which developed more or less independently during the first millennium AD: *Hohokam* (in Arizona and N Sonora), *Mogollon* (in the mountains of SE Arizona and SW New Mexico), and *Anasazi* (in the high plateau of Arizona–New Mexico). These cultures shared many characteristics in architecture, farming techniques, social structure, and religious ceremony, but are distinguished by regional variations in these practices and by separate ceramic traditions.

Casas Grandes (excavated principally by Charles DiPeso for the Amerind Foundation and INAH in 1961 and in 1966) was occupied between c AD 800 and 1400, and several phases of development are evident in its architecture.
    In its earliest phase, *Viejo*, it resembled the SW cultures—there were groups of pit-houses and kivas (subterranean ceremonial chambers). In the next phase, *Medio*, single-storey adobe house clusters were built and irrigation agriculture developed, incl. canals and subterranean drains. Burials were made beneath the house floors. In time these single-storey houses were replaced by massive adobe and beam communal complexes, of up to five storeys high, with internal stairways, ovens, water storage tanks, heating systems, and windows—an architectural style resembling the cliff-dwellings built farther N—together with architecture indicating Mesoamerican influences.
    From c AD 1000 Casas Grandes (*Paquimé*) became an important trading centre partly in response to direct contact by traders from the W cultures of Mexico and perhaps by Toltecs exploring for mineral sources (although more recent tree-ring dating evidence suggests that Paquimé's fluorescence may have been a little later). The trade route extended along the E slopes of the Sierra Madre Occidental to Paquimé, then N into Arizona and New Mexico as far as Chaco Canyon. In exchange for salt, alum, peyote, incense, raw copper, and quartz the Mesoamericans traded finished artefacts in mother-of-pearl from the W coast, turquoise, and copper (especially copper bells). There were special compounds for various tradesmen. With the trade came Mesoamerican ideas, interpreted and transformed by the Paquimeans: I-shaped ball courts of earth, plazas and circular stone ceremonial houses, truncated pyramids, and platform effigy mounds; human sacrifice; Mesoamerican style birds in ceremonial art, masked dancers, eagle-men, stylized plumed serpents, feathers, crosses, and sun symbols. Pottery styles, however, remained in the SW traditions and continued in the locally

distinctive polychrome styles of black painting on white backgrounds with red lines in geometric designs.

The population continued to increase and extended over c 2 sq km. Burials in elliptical stone-block tombs, c 1.5m long, were scattered over a wide area around the site.

By c AD 1260 the overstretched economy had begun to wane, and together with regional drought caused construction to cease, maintenance to be neglected, and a general decline in trading contacts. Burials began to be placed in dried-up canals of the irrigation system. By 1400 flimsy dwellings were the only construction, followed by burning and razing. Although still occupied, the site was much impoverished when Spanish missionaries arrived in the 17C.

The ruins of Casas Grandes consist mostly of the foundations of walls and structures, but some central buildings have been reconstructed and many others strengthened and preserved. INAH has organized the various ruins into 16 different *Unidades*. They comprise a central plaza around which are clusters of compartmentalized dwellings, to the N and E (*Unidades 6–8*, and *12–16*), and circular and rectangular buildings on a platform with adjacent circular mound at the NW corner of the plaza (*Unidad 5*).

To the W are platforms and two truncated circular pyramids (*Unidades 9–10*), and a smaller plaza and building complex (*Unidad 11*).

To the NW are the principal *Juego de Pelota*, with a large square, truncated pyramid abutting its S end, a rectangular platform along its W side (*Unidad 3*); and an outlying circular mound (*Unidad 4*).

To the N are remains of a cruciform platform with small circular platforms at the end of each arm (*Unidad 2*), and farther N, another small plaza and building complex (*Unidad 1*) with several outlying pits.

In the *Hotel Piñón* at Nuevo Casas Grandes (605 Av. Juárez) is a collection from Paquimé (enquire at desk)—mostly ceramic pieces and domestic stone artefacts. The pottery includes anthropomorphic and zoomorphic pieces with incised decoration characteristic of the general SW cultural region of the USA and N Mexico. The stone material includes several manos and matates for grinding, and a few pieces of polished stone for personal adornment.

Other archaeological ruins, and interesting geological formations, in the vicinity of Nuevo Casas Grandes are approachable only with a guide in a four-wheel drive vehicle or on horseback (enquire at Casas Grandes). Near *Colonia Juárez*, a Mormon settlement c 24km SW, where there is a 10C settlement reminiscent of the Mogollon towns of the SW USA. Among caves in the limestone rocks rectangular rooms were built of mud, with willow-branch ties between the wooden frame-posts and stepped passages between rooms. There are metates (grinders) and large granary ollas (c 3.65m high) at the cave mouths or above them.

At *Cerro de Moctezuma*, c 15km SW of Casas Grandes, the ruins of a circular building, 15m in diameter, have a wall 2m thick. Inside the circle is a square structure divided into four rooms. Of these and several other similar ruins in the region little is known except their general SW cultural affinity.

C 60km SW of Nuevo Casas Grandes is *Pacheco*, 11km N of which (by path) is the ejido *Ignacio Zaragoza*. Here is an archaeological zone known as *Cueva de la Olla*, preserving remains of dwellings built to afford shelter, with adobe walls and traces of paintings.

43 Chihuahua to Creel

Méx. 16 and State road 16 as far as Basaseachic, 387km.—104km Cuauhtémoc.—148km La Junta.—174km El Divisadero.—216km Tomóchic.—271km road for Basaseachic.—387km **Creel**.

This route leads into exceptionally rugged terrain in the Sierra Madre Occidental, home of the Tarahumara Indians, and, from the late 17C, an area of intrepid Jesuit missionizing. It includes various *Barrancas del Cobre*, famous deep canyons cut into the lava plateau and containing riverbeds, affluents of the Río Fuerte. The slopes of these giant geological faults, still not properly mapped, are covered in forest and wild plants, the green especially marked in the rainy season. In the dry season the rock formations show pronounced grey and ochre colouring; in the evening sun the ochre deepens to golden hues. Those attempting journeys by motor vehicle (four-wheel drive) are warned that distances are great, population centres few, petrol stations rare (sometimes it is obtainable from private household tanks), and that the greatest care should be taken on remote and difficult mountain roads and tracks.

From Chihuahua to (104km) *Cuauhtémoc*, see Rte 42

Here a minor road runs S past (r.) the *Laguna de los Mexicanos* to (55km) *Carichic* and thence across the sierra, marked by branches of the Río San Ignacio, to (108km) *Bocoyna*, see below.

148km *La Junta*. From here the spectacular mountain road continues S to cross the valley of the Río Papigóchic. At 165km a road runs S to (65km) *San Juanito*, see below. 174km *El Divisadero* (views over the valley). 216km *Tomóchic* (P), a Jesuit mission during 1689–1767, on the river of the same name. It was the scene of much unrest in 1891–92 when the hard-pressed Indians, provoked into resisting aggression by State troops, were besieged and bloodily defeated in Oct.; no males remained alive. Beyond (271km) the road SE to *San Juanito*, we may reach *Basaseachic* by keeping r. and continuing NW for c 5km. Here, amid grand scenery designated a national park, the *Cascada de Basaseachic*, formed by the streams Durazno de Tello and Basaseachic, with a single jump of 310m, is one of the natural wonders of N America. The torrent sweeps through the *Cañón de la Candameña* SW to form the Río Moris before joining the Río Mayo in Sonora.

From Basaseachic it is possible to continue NW across the Sierra Madre Occidental via (50km) *Yepachic*, (84km) *Maycoba* (State of Sonora), and (116km) *Yécora* (P) to (140km) *Sta Rosa*, from where we may continue via (199km) *Tonichi* and (239km) *Tecoripa* to (357km) *Hermosillo*, see Rte 21.

From the turning at 271km we go SE to (356km) *San Juanito* (H,R,P) before continuing S to (375km) *Bocoyna*.

Hence we may diverge SE by gravel road to (20km) *Sisoguichic*, a Jesuit mission during 1677–1767, which keeps its late 17C church.

387km **CREEL** (5000 inhab.; 2200m; H,R,P; airfield for flights to remote settlements in the canyons), an excursion centre on the Chihuahua al Pacífico railway, very cold in winter.

FROM CREEL TO BATOPILAS, c 150km. The road (not of the best), through the *Parque Natural Barranca del Cobre*, keeps generally to the mountainsides and cuts transversely across canyons and ravines, zigzagging down into them and climbing up to reach the next peak. For appreciable stretches it also keeps to the course of a stream. The views are captivating. Advice on its possibilities will be given at Creel. Depending on conditions, the journey takes 7–9 hours.

The road runs SE, passing, at 8km, the *Lago de Arareco*, to (20km) *Cusárare* (l.), with a late 17C Jesuit mission church, lined with 12 paintings of scenes from the life of Our Lady by Miguel Correa (fl. 1716–18; son of Juan), and a small museum devoted to Tarahumara crafts. A 30m waterfall and cave paintings may be seen (guide recommended). At 41km we cross the stream called *Basíhuare*, whence the grandeur of the canyon can be appreciated. At c 50km we cross the Río Urique (at 1965m). The old bridge, constructed in 1907, still stands alongside the new concrete one. From here the Urique canyon opens out to the W, eventually to reach a depth of 1400m. The village of *Urique*, in the depths of the canyon c 40km W as the crow flies, is accessible by track from El Divisadero or Bahuichivo on the Chihuahua al Pacífico railway, by track from Batopilas (see below), or by occasional aircraft from Creel.

At 64km, not long before *Samachic*, a difficult road runs SE to (33km) *Aboreachic* and (74km; 3km S) *Guachochic*, and thence to (262km) *Parral*, see Rte 47. We keep to the r., the road narrowing (much care needed) for (88km) *La Bufa*, with views of the Batopilas canyon. The sinuous descent into the canyon (c 14km), an almost incredible experience, is often very narrow and in part apt to small floods from the waters of a cascade. After the descent the road follows the Río Batopilas between two rock walls.

150km **Batopilas** (c 700 inhab.; 462m; R,H), a quiet subtropical village, untouched by progress, inhabited mainly by Tarahumaras. In 1708 rich silver deposits were discovered here and during 1732–50 Batopilas was the chief place of one of the administrative divisions of

Nueva Vizcaya. In 1880, Alexander Robert Shepherd, onetime governor of the District of Columbia (USA), founded the Consolidated Batopilas Silver Mining Co. and made his home here. The ruins of his house may still be seen.

44 The Chihuahua al Pacífico Railway

This line, affording one of the great railway journeys of the world, and one of the greatest engineering feats, stretches from Ojinaga to Los Mochis on the Pacific coast. The original idea, in 1872–73, belonged to a US engineer, Albert K. Owen, who planned a railroad from Norfolk (Va) to Topolobampo. In 1900 the Kansas City, Mexico and Orient Railroad Co. was set up and in 1902 the first lines were laid in the State of Chihuahua. (Francisco Villa worked as a contractor.) Work was stopped by the Revolution. In 1928 the Ojinaga–Chihuahua stretch was finished; by 1930 the line Chihuahua–Creel. In 1940 the Mexican government began another construction campaign—boring through mountains, building tunnels, and raising bridges over the canyons—completed in 1961. The line was officially opened on 23 Nov. 1961 by Pres. López Mateos. It had cost in all $100 million. Its total length (Ojinaga–Los Mochis) is 921km. There are 36 bridges and 96 tunnels. Chihuahua is 268km from Ojinaga.

The railway runs SW, at 293km entering a cultivated high plateau (altiplano). 319km *General Trías*. Then NW to (349km) *San Andrés*, birthplace of Luz Corral (see Rte 41). After 369km we begin an ascent, past (r.) the *Laguna de Bustillos*, now contaminated by the cellulose, plywood, and viscose plants at (382km) *Anáhuac*. We pass through Mennonite country to (400km) *Cuauhtémoc*. 426km *Pedernales*, an early stronghold of Francisco Villa. 451km *La Junta*, whence a branch line runs NW and N to *Ciudad Juárez*. The railway climbs into pine-forested country, centre for the lumbering industry. 471km bridge over the Río San Pedro; we run S to (531km) *San Juanito*. 562km the fourth tunnel, the second longest (1260m). 565km *Creel*. 583km *Los Ojitos* (2460km), highest point on the line.

585km the line begins a sharp descent, called *El Lazo* (loop), forming a circle and crossing over itself. 622km **El Divisadero**, where the train stops for c 15 min. for a magnificent view over the Urique canyon. 637km *San Rafael* (refuelling; water taken on). 639km *La Laja* bridge. 657km *Rocohuaina* bridge (119m). 662km *Cuiteco*, renowned for sweet apples. 669km *Bahuichivo*. From 704km the line descends in curves and loops; three levels of the line can be seen. 705km *La Pera* tunnel (937m). 708km *Témoris* (1026m), a former Jesuit mission (Magdalena Témoris), founded in the 1670s. We leave it across the Sta Bárbara bridge (218m) over the Río Mina Plata. 728km *Tacuina*. 743km State border between Chihuahua and Sinaloa, the line descending towards the coastal plain. 748km *Chínipas* bridge over the Río Chínipas, affluent of the Río Fuerte. It is the highest on the line (102m above ground). 755km last and longest tunnel (1818m). 781km bridge over the Río Fuerte, longest on the line (499m). 791km *Loreto*. 839km *El Fuerte*. To the N, *Presa Miguel Hidalgo*. 882km *San Blas* (32m). We cross the Pacific railway between Nogales and Guadalajara. 921km *Los Mochis*.

45 Chihuahua via Zacatecas to Torreón

Méx. 45, Méx. 49, Méx. 40, Méx. 45, and Méx. 54, 849km.—84km Delicias.—153km Ciudad Camargo.—224km Jiménez and Méx. 49.—417km Bermejillo.—459km Gómez Palacio (for [5km E] **Torreón** and [152km E] **Parras**) and Méx. 40.—577km **Cuencamé** and Méx. 49.—779km junction with Méx. 45.—796km **Fresnillo**.—839km junction with Méx. 54.—849km **Zacatecas**.

We leave Chihuahua to the SE. 13km turning l. for (8km E) *Aquiles Serdán*, see Rte 41. The road, running near the historic railway line, fought over, wrecked, and rebuilt during Revolutionary years, traverses monotonous desert and range country, broken now and then by hills and canyons. Beyond Chihuahua we run through the *Cañón de Bachimba*, where Pascual Orozco's army, in revolt against Pres. Madero, was finally defeated by Gen. Victoriano Huerta on 3 July 1912.

In March 1913, Abraham González, maderista governor of Chihuahua, was thrown from a train here, to be crushed under its wheels and buried at the side of the track, on the orders of Pres. Huerta's substitute governor.

After c 50km the road enters an intensely cultivated region, made fertile by the harnessing of the waters of the Ríos Conchos and San Pedro, and the building since the 1940s of new dams. 75km *Meoqui* (P), which shares in the local agricultural prosperity. 84km **Delicias** (70,000 inhab.; 1170m; H,R,P), founded in 1925, the centre of the region, producing above all cotton, wheat, and wine.

Within easy reach are two vast man-made lakes (fishing, sailing): *Presa Rosetilla* (12km E) and *Presa Francisco I. Madero* (15km SW). *Villa de Rosales* (9km W), with a 19C aqueduct, is a centre for fishing expeditions, by and on the Río San Pedro.

Méx. 45 accompanies the Río Conchos and irrigation canal S to (153km) **Ciudad Camargo** (35,000 inhab.; 1653m; H,R,P), the former *Sta Rosalia*, an agricultural and mining centre at the confluence of the Ríos Florido and Alto Conchos. It is the native place of David Alfaro Siqueiros (1896–1974).

A road runs SW to (29km) the *Lago de Toronto*, formed by *Presa la Boquilla*, source of much of the water which irrigates the region to the N. The lake is rich in fish, supplying the nearby towns, and ideal for sailing. A turning c 20km along this road leads to (c 3km N) **San Francisco de Conchos**, former centre for the Franciscan missionary effort in the region and founded c 1604. The Tepehuán Indians did away with the friars and destroyed the original church in 1645. The present church dates from the mid-18C.
    Ciudad Camargo is connected by road to (259km NE) *Ojinaga*, see Rte 41.

From Ciudad Camargo there is a choice of two roads S, between which run the railway and the Río Florido to the E, although a longer run (81km to just E of *Jiménez*) is better for travellers straight to *Torreón*.

Here we are already in the **Bolsón de Mapimí**, a vast steppe-like depression, haphazardly fertile, depending on rainfall and the formation of alluvial deposits, in the N high plateau, extending from the NE corner of the State of Durango, between the Ríos Nazas and Aguanaval, through Chihuahua and Coahuila.

We keep to Méx. 45, on the W, through semi-desert to (224km) **Jiménez** (250,000 inhab.; 1381m; H,R,P), in a cotton-growing and cattle-raising region (Hereford cattle in evidence), on the Río Florido.

Until 1774 it was known as Guajuquilla, a military post, and thereafter as Sto Cristo de Burgos. It flourished as a supply centre for neighbouring haciendas. The parish church and Pal. Municipal are 19C edifices.
    Méx. 45 continues to (79km SW) *Hidalgo del Parral*, see Rte 47.

We take Méx. 49 running SE. At 288km a turning l. leads to (14km N) *Los Remedios*, a former hacienda, with thermal springs (rock paintings in the vicinity). At 295km we reach the State border with Durango. 322km *Ceballos* (P).

From here a track goes NE to the *Cerro de San Ignacio*, at the foot of which is the so-called *Zona del Silencio*, where the State borders of Chihuahua, Coahuila, and Durango meet. The journey is difficult, to a place of extreme desolation, so extra provisions, water, and petrol are essential. Since the 1970s the area has been the subject of geophysical research. It has an absorption of solar energy well above the average; an unusually high incidence of meteorites; and a mass of magnetite in the subsoil, which renders radio communication and the use of compasses impossible. Here has been established (since 1975) the Estación de Estudios de la Reserva de la Biosfera, one of several such, under the auspices of the UN.

From Ceballos it is possible to reach (114km SW), by a difficult road across an arid region, Méx. 45, the Hidalgo del Parral–Durango road (see Rte 47) 46km NW of *La Zarca*.

Méx. 49 continues SE into the Región Lagunera, see below. From (417km) *Bermejillo*, Méx. 30 runs W to (23km) **Mapimí** (5000 inhab.; 1367m; R,P), on the N slopes of the Sierra de Mapimí, centre of a mining region (gold, silver, copper, and lead) since c 1589 and at times in the 17C a Jesuit mission periodically attacked by Tepehuán Indians. The 18C church of *Santiago Apóstol* has a baroque façade with good relief. At No. 2 C. Zaragoza, Pres. Juárez lodged during his flight N in summer 1863. The town was also a stopping-place (24 March–2 Apr. 1811) for Hidalgo and his fellow captives on their way to trial and execution in Chihuahua.

C 11km SE is the mine of *La Ojuela*, re-exploited from 1892 by the Compañía Minera de Peñoles, which introduced the hanging bridge (326m long) over a deep ravine and which obtained remarkable production during the 1920s.

The road continues W to (120km) *La Zarca*, on the Durango–Hidalgo del Parral road, see Rte 47.

459km **Gómez Palacio** (110,000 inhab.; 1195m; H,R,P; cotton and grape fair, 20 Aug.–5 Sept.; melon fair, late July–early Aug.), on the l. bank of the Río Nazas and in the fertile Laguna region.

It was founded in the 1880s on lands donated by a Spanish philanthropist, Santiago Lavín, and, with the arrival of the railway, soon became a flourishing manufacturing centre—part of its prosperity based on the dynamite and explosives factory (Compañía mexicana de explosivos), c 15km N near Brittingham station. Its capture by villista forces on 26 March 1914 was the prelude to Villa's second descent on Torreón.

The *Museo de Antropología e Historia* contains a local collection and, in the Las Rosas district (corner of Cs Berlín and Rosas), the *Casa de Cultura* contains a gallery of modern art and an interesting photographic display of the Revolution.

The neighbouring town of *Ciudad Lerdo*, 3km SW, founded in 1867, is a notable fruit-growing and horticultural centre. Part of its terrain, along the banks of the Río Nazas, has been converted into the *Parque Nacional de la Laguna*. A monument commemorates the Mexican aviator Francisco Sarabia who made a record flight from Mexico City to Washington, D.C., in 1937.

FROM GOMEZ PALACIO TO SALTILLO VIA TORREON, 281km. We leave Gómez Palacio to the SE and cross the Río Nazas into the State of Coahuila. 5km **TORREON** (500,000 inhab.; 1148m; H,R,P; airport), in the Región Lagunera and a prime industrial (mining, smelting, cotton goods) and agricultural (dairy products, wine, wheat) centre.

Leonardo Zuloaga, owner of a ranch here, c 1850 built an adobe tower (torreón) from which to view the progress of the Carrizal dam on the Río Nazas. In 1883 land was ceded for a key railroad station where the Central line (Ciudad Juárez–Mexico City) was to link with the International line (Durango–Piedras Negras, with a connection to Monterrey). Around the station grew the new town, officially founded in 1893. During the Revolution, Francisco Villa captured it four times: in spring 1911 his unruly troops massacred 200 of the Chinese community; in Oct. 1913 he plundered the banks and gave some of the proceeds to the poor; in Apr. 1914 he forced out a federal garrison.

The **Región Lagunera** (or *La Laguna*) spans the NE corner of Durango and the SW extremity of Coahuila. It lies in the basins of the Ríos Nazas and Aguanaval, and owes its name to the former hacienda of San Lorenzo de la Laguna, once property of the marqueses de San Miguel de Aguayo, and famous for its vineyards. By the mid-19C cotton production was under way and in 1895 and 1909 regulations were issued for the controlling and diverting of the rivers, to benefit smallholders. From 1936 Pres. Cárdenas settled 30,000 families here, thus forming the first large state-run farm, with a bank to provide funds. In 1946 Presa Lázaro Cárdenas, a dam at El Palmito, where the Ríos del Oro and de Ramos converge to form the Río Nazas, was completed. Both it and the later Presa de las Tórtolas have greatly increased the area under cultivation. Even so, periodic water shortages and intense summer heat can cause crises.

The older part of the regularly laid-out town is on the W side of C. Múzquiz, continuation of Blvd. Miguel Alemán, along which we enter. At the corner of Av. Juárez and C. 5 de Mayo is the original *Torreón*. Further SW, facing the plaza, is the church of *San Juanito*, the first to be built, with a coffered ceiling. In the more modern part, to the E of Pl. de Armas, are the *Pal. Municipal* and the **Teatro Isauro Martínez**, the latter strange and medievalizing, dating from the late 1920s, the work of Agustín Tarazona. The interior decoration combines whimsicality and sumptuousness, with pronounced oriental influences. Still further E, in BOSQUE VENUSTIANO CARRANZA, is the **Museo Regional de la Laguna** (Tues.–Sun., 10–5; fee). It consists of three rooms, each subdivided into displays illustrating: the archaeology of N-central Mexico; Mesoamerica in general, comparing and contrasting the two regions; and the ethnography of N Mexico.

The entrance begins with the local archaeology. (Numbers refer to the numbers on the floor plan.) ROOM 1. Archaeology of N-central Mexico. 1. The introductory panel (r.) discusses the subsistence of hunter-gatherer peoples, incl. a map of the sites where early remains have been found. Examples of stone projectile points, and displays illustrating the ancient climate, flora, and fauna of 14,000–9,000 years before the present, plus photographs of some of the cave sites (eg, Cueva de Candelaria). 2. Physical anthropology display showing the physical types of the region. 3. The nomadic economy of hunter-gatherers, incl. hunting weapons and methods of transport. 4. The primitive religious practices of hunter-gatherers, incl. discussions on decorative items and ritual tools, the ritual use of peyote, and ritual sacrifice. 5. Cave art, both painting and engraving, and tools of nomadic daily existence (bone punches, stone arrow tips, etc.). 6. Primitive methods of textile-making, incl. examples from the region around the Cueva de Candelaria. 7. More artefacts used in daily activities, plus materials showing influences from elsewhere in Mexico, especially from the Toltecs. Most notable is the carved stone disc, called Tezcacuitlapilli, depicting Toltec warriors. 8. On the other side of the passageway into the next room, a display illustrates the culture of the agricultural peoples of Durango and Zacatecas. Ceramics, pipes, and textiles; plans, descriptions, and photographs of Chalchihuites and La Quemada in Zacatecas, and of Casas Grandes in Chihuahua.

R.2. Mesoamerica. 9. The first three displays discuss and illustrate the concept of Mesoamerica, the early domestication of plants, and the changes this brought. Preclassic artefacts. 10. The Classic Period, in particular, the rise of Teotihuacán in the Basin of Mexico. 11. Two photomurals of the monuments at Teotihuacán. 12. Teotihuacano ceramics, most notably, vases decorated with the paint cloisonné technique in which sections of the surface of the pot are excised, filled with a different coloured paint, and smoothed down even with the original surface; and figurines. 13. Copy of one of the Teotihuacán murals. 14. Two Teotihuacano stone sculptures. 15. Another copy of a mural from Teotihuacán. 16. Large-scale plan of the site of Teotihuacán. 17. Teotihuacano materials. 18. A small case contains Early Postclassic materials of the Toltecs, most notably, some examples of Plumbate Ware pottery (characteristic of the Toltecs, but ultimately derived from the Highlands of Guatemala); and a large knife of volcanic stone. 19. In the corner of the room stand four stone sculptures, incl. Tláloc (god of rain), a warrior, and a serpent. 20. Continuing into the Later Postclassic, photomural of the site of Tenayuca in the Basin of Mexico. 21. Copies of the Codex Boturini (or Tira de la Peregrinación: migration of the Mexica Aztecs into the Basin and their settlement first at Culhuacán, then at Chapultepec, and finally on Tenochtitlán Island. 22. Examples of Aztec ceramics. 23. Gulf Coast cultures. A map shows the principal sites. 24. Four cases containing mostly Classic and Postclassic Period artefacts from the Totonac culture and its predecessors. 25. Final wall of the room. Two cases containing artefacts of the Olmec culture and a discussion of the architecture at La Venta. 26. Three displays illustrating Classic and Postclassic artefacts from W Mexico, incl. characteristic glossy red ceramics in the shapes of plants, and large hollow figures of warriors, etc., plus some examples of copper bells. Discussion of shaft-tombs.

R.3. Ethnographic displays, incl. examples of the costume of Guerrero, Oaxaca, and Chiapas; plus various pottery and other associated artefacts.

From Torreón, Méx. 40 continues E. 28km *Matamoros*. At (58km) *Emiliano Zapata* a minor road runs SE to (24km) *Viesca*, on the S shore of the dried-up Laguna de Viesca, now starved of the waters of the Río Aguanaval, which used to empty into it, but exploited for clay and saltpetre. A plaque commemorates the house where Hidalgo and his companions were held on 3 Apr. 1811. The road continues E to (77km) *Parras*, see below.

Méx. 40 goes N to (75km) the junction with Méx. 30.

This road runs at first N via (19km) *San Pedro de las Colonias*, on the W of the Laguna de Mayrán, through a series of sierras enclosing drainage basins to (205km) *Cuatrociénegas*, see Rte 55.

From here we turn r. through the depression, once the large *Laguna de Mayrán* into which the Río Nazas emptied until its waters were diverted for irrigation. 152km turning r. for (27km S) **PARRAS DE LA FUENTE** (27,000 inhab.; 1687m; H,R,P; grape festival, 4–15 Aug.), the charming centre of an area rejoicing in vineyards and fruits. Its brandy and traditional sweets, made from milk, figs, and nuts, are additional attractions.

In the 19C it became the power base of the immensely rich Madero family, its fortunes dramatically improved by Evaristo Madero (1828–1911), an archetypal hacendado patriarch, governor of Coahuila in 1880–88, owner of vast estates in Coahuila and Zacatecas, and father of 14 legitimate children. His illustrious grandson, Francisco Indalecio Madero (1873–1913), future president, was born here. Francisco, with the help of his wife, Sara Pérez, set an example of benevolent paternalism, establishing model estates, providing generous funds for the education of orphans, and improving living conditions, which earned them the undying love of their tenantry.

At the entrance to the town is the so-called **Hacienda de Urdiñola** (adm. by appointment), possessor of what are claimed to be the oldest vineyards in America. Its *Museo del Vino* preserves the 19C fixtures considered the most advanced of their day. The parish church of *Sta María de las Parras* dates from the late 17C. The former Jesuit college of *San Ignacio* houses a library of ancient books. In C. Almeda del Rosario is the house in which Francisco I. Madero was born.

Méx. 40 continues through hot desert to (281km) *Saltillo*, see Rte 55.

From Gómez Palacio, Méx. 40 runs SW. 462km *Ciudad Lerdo*, see above. 530km turning r. for (25km NW) *Presa Francisco Zarco* (water sports) on the Río Nazas. 550km turning l. for (46km NW) *Nazas* (H), on the r. bank of the river, intensively irrigating a region producing quality cotton. The house in which Juárez lodged on his flight N in 1863 may be visited.

This road continues W along the valley of the Río Nazas to (94km) the Durango–Parral road, see Rte 47.

577km **Cuencamé** (5000 inhab.; 2800m; M,R,P), settled as a real de minas in 1601, still a mining centre. Its parish church, *San Antonio de Padua* (1728), contains one churrigueresque and one anastyle altarpiece.

From Cuencamé, Méx. 40 continues SW to (23km) *Yerbanís* and a turning r. for (22km NE) **Peñón Blanco**, where the agreeable *Pal. Municipal* dates from 1836. The surrounding part of the Sierra de Durango is a paradise for climbers, botanists, and wildlife enthusiasts. C 1½ hrs drive from here, along a rough road, is the huge, white granite rock (highest point, c 2700m) which gives the place its name. It rises in the ranch of *La Joya* (for adm., seek permission in the pueblo; best time to travel, Oct.–March, the dry season), which borders on other unusual rock formations. The area is also noted for its cacti, agaves (incl. the lechuguilla, which flowers once, when the plant reaches c 6 years), and other semi-desert plants, and fauna (coyotes and pumas). 55km *Ignacio Allende*. 67km *Guadalupe Victoria*, in a flourishing agricultural region. To the S and SE is the *Malpaís*, a desolate volcanic badlands. Beyond (88km) *Francisco I. Madero* we continue SW for (114km) *Durango*, see Rte 47.

We continue SE on Méx. 40 to (642km) the State border with Zacatecas, beyond which, at 652km, roads lead off l. to *Juan Aldama* (thermal springs) and r. to *Miguel Auza*, an unpretentious spa. The road goes through rolling plains and past isolated hills. 699km turning l. for (18km NE) *Nieves*, on the r. bank of the

Río Nieves, a tributary of the Aguanaval, in an area interesting for its fauna. 719km **Río Grande** (15,000 inhab.; 1870m; H,R,P), a cattle-raising centre since the 1580s. The former hacienda of *La Pastelera* keeps its 18C church. 15km SW is *Presa el Cazadero* (boating and fishing). At 764km we reach the Tropic of Cancer and at 779km Méx. 45 from Durango, see Rte 47.

796km **FRESNILLO** (c 72,000 inhab.; 2250m; H,R,P) is a comparatively quiet town in an area traditionally significant for mining and cattle-raising.

It began, probably in the late 1560s, as a mining settlement in hostile Chichimec country. In 1833 a cholera epidemic forced closure of the mines, but by 1842 improved steam-powered machinery had been imported from England to reactivate them. Deposits of silver, gold, copper, lead, and zinc are still worked, though their importance has declined.

On the N side of Pl. Principal the parish church of **La Purificación**, with a handsome classicizing portal (facing E) and admirable tower, dates probably from restorations in 1728–80. Atrio wall and notably eclectic gateway were begun in 1901 by Luis G. Muñoz, who also did the high altar (1933). The former *Colegio de Minería* (1855), by Diego Velázquez de la Cadena, has a splendid neoclassical portico. Also of interest is the church of *El Tránsito* (1705–11), two blocks SE of the plaza, for its ceiling beams and finely wrought wooden choir balcony. C 5km N is the earlier mining settlement of **Plateros**, founded as *San Demetrio* c 1566. Its church (late 18C), with a delightful façade panel, contains a miraculous image of the Sto Niño de Atocha, and many votive offerings, attesting its importance as a pilgrimage centre.

At 839km Méx. 45 is joined by Méx. 54 from Saltillo, see Rte 55. 849km *Zacatecas*, see Rte 46.

46 Zacatecas

ZACATECAS (150,000 inhab.; 2496m), in the Sierra de Zacatecas, an arid landscape, is capital of the State of the same name and seat of a university. It extends through a narrow canyon and is dominated to its N by two peaks (cerros): La Bufa and El Grillo. Its narrow, irregular cobbled streets lined by pink-stone houses, marked by windows and balconies enclosed by elegant wrought-iron railings; its small, quiet plazas; the fabric of its churches, which 'aspires to garnet red'; and, above all, its magnificent cathedral—all are reminders of its heyday, when the fabulous riches of its mines were a mainstay of the Spanish economy. The altitude, and often bitter winds, can make it a cold place in winter, and in the early morning and evening. The zacatecanos are more reserved and dour than is usual in Mexico: perhaps a reminder of their Basque ancestry.

Airport. 25km W. Flights to *Mexico City, Mazatlán*, and *Tijuana*.

Bus station. On S outskirts along Carr. Tránsito Pesado. Local buses connect with city centre. Frequent services to *Mexico City* (9 hrs); to *Guadalajara* (5 hrs); to *San Luis Potosí* (3 hrs); to *Durango* (5 hrs); to *Chihuahua* (c 12 hrs); etc.

Railway station. S end of Calz. González Ortega. Trains to *Mexico City* (15–16 hrs) via Aguascalientes, León, Irapuato, and Querétaro. To *Ciudad Juárez* (9½ hrs) via Chihuahua.

Hotels throughout the city.

Post Office. C. Allende.

Tourist Office. Corner of Av. Hidalgo and Cjón del Santero.

Silver ore was discovered here probably in 1546 and the first miners' settlement established, just to the N of the present city, in 1548–49 when an expedition in search of silver backed by the Basques Juan de Tolosa, Diego and Miguel de Ibarra, and others. The first silver mine, San Bernabé, was struck in June 1548; and then another, called Albarrada de San Benito de

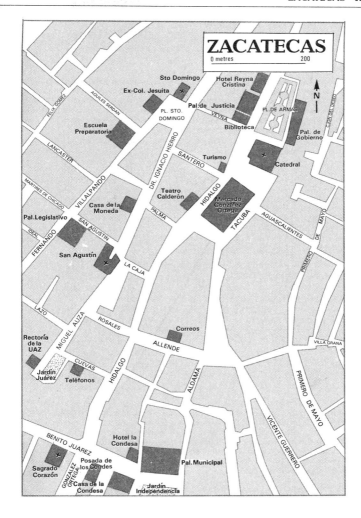

Vetagrande. By the late 1560s the mining area extended several leagues N to Pánuco. By 1732 the mines were gradually flooded and deserted. In 1767 José de la Borda decided to revive the industry and save himself from ruin. At his death in 1779 he had spectacularly succeeded and had paid off his debts. By the end of the 18C, it is said, Zacatecas had supplied one-fifth of the world's silver. In 1824 it became capital of the new State. The English travellers H.G. Ward and G.F. Lyon (1826–) had reservations about it: Lyon was received by the governor's wife, who chain-smoked during the audience, and found the people fractious, especially on Sun. In 1842 an English company, Manning and Marshall, took control of the mint for 14 years at a rent of 2000 pesos a year, this in addition to English exploitation rights in the Vetagrande mine. On 23 June 1914, Francisco Villa and his División del Norte, a force of 23,000, attacked Zacatecas, relentlessly firing down from the northern heights. The huertista garrison, 12,000 strong, was crushed. The next morning, wrote Villa, 'as I contemplated the battlefield and the streets, the magnitude of the holocaust was visible. Those who came out to meet me…had to leap over the corpses...Beside the enemy dead many of my soldiers lay sleeping in pools of blood'.

Zacatecas was constructed on its present lines in the 18C, especially after 1715, but comparatively few ecclesiastical and civil buildings from that period survive. Its present aspect, however picturesque and harmonious, dates mainly from the 19C. The city underwent a major facelift during 1962–68.

The State of **Zacatecas** (1.3 million inhab.; 75,040 sq km) lies wholly on the great central plateau, with an average elevation of 2350m. It is traversed to the W by lateral ranges of the Sierra Madre Occidental and numerous isolated ranges in other parts. There are no appreciable rivers. It is primarily a stock-raising region, especially in the N and NW. Although mining no longer dominates, there are still deposits of silver, gold, mercury, copper, iron, zinc, lead, bismuth, antimony, and salt.

The area of the present State fell entirely within Nueva Galicia. An expedition by Pedro Almíndez Chirinos got as far as Cerro de la Bufa in 1530. Colonists, however, were constantly at war (c 1561–90) with the Zacatecos and Guachichiles, who were forced to retreat northwards. Their places were taken by more docile Indians from areas to the S and from central Mexico, who went to work on the haciendas and in the mines. Foundations of great fortunes were made: Fernando de la Campa y Cos, conde de San Mateo de Valparaíso from 1727, owned vast haciendas; the Fagoaga family from Sombrerete, marqueses del Apartado from 1772, amassed huge additional wealth from new strikes in the 1790s. In 1824 the State of Zacatecas came into being and the mining industry, in decline after the war of Independence, slowly recovered thanks to foreign investment. Díaz's revolt against Juárez (Plan de Noria) was finally defeated by Juárez's loyal general, 'that prodigy of drunkenness and energy', Sóstenes Rocha, on La Bufa on 2 March 1872.

PL. DE ARMAS (officially Pl. Hidalgo) is more long than square. On its E side is the **Pal. de Gobierno** (1727), a mansion built for Joseph de Rivera Bernárdez (d. 1743), 2nd conde de Santiago de la Laguna. Its interior murals (1970) by Antonio Rodríguez are on anti-Spanish, liberal themes. On the W side is the *Pal. del Poder Judicial*, the former *Pal. Rétegui* (early 19C), former home of Manuel Rétegui, who made a fortune after 1772 in the Fresnillo mines and then restored the Malanoche mine in Zacatecas. Its interior arch shapes are fanciful. Next to it is the *Hotel Reyna Cristina* (c 1855), with beautiful balcony ironwork.

On the S side is the cathedral of **Nuestra Señora de la Asunción**, possessor of perhaps the most famous, undoubtedly the most stupendously rich, façade in Mexico: a unique tour de force, which may be seen as the culmination, freely exotic, of Mexican baroque.

It succeeded two previous churches on the site. It was begun, as the parish church, in 1729 and dedicated, still incomplete, in 1752. Its architect was probably Domingo Ximénez Hernández. But, as Clara Bargellini reminds us, the parts played by other masters—'from Joseph Sánchez to the mason Marcos de la Cruz'—were important; so were the interventions of Bp Nicolás Carlos Gómez de Cervantes; and those of 'Joseph Rivera Bernárdez, patron of fine art and historian; Miguel Bermúdez and Joseph de Ribera Villalobos, priests; and the people of the city'. In 1859, to raise funds for the liberal cause, Gen. González Ortega removed most of the treasure. It was consecrated cathedral in 1862.

EXTERIOR. The three-storey W façade, in the shape of a shield and worked in rose-ochre stone which changes colour with the light, resembles a tapestry of finest ivory. The columns and spaces between them are covered in rows of pearl, fruit, feather, shell, cherub (among the most endearing in all Mexico), angel, and foliage relief. In the second storey, the relief surrounding columns, niches, and cornice is a dense encrustation of clouds and vines. All is encompassed by a gently curving frame, whose sections, ascending one against the other and ending in two plump volutes, attest its careful composition. Enthroned on high, above the topmost cornice, is God the Father, strangely flattened against the all-pervading relief. Attending Him are angels (beguiling figures) playing horns and viols, and holding censers. Beneath, in the second storey, the six short columns enclose niches of Christ in the middle, His l. hand holding the globe, His r. hand raised in benediction, and four apostles. The innermost column shafts are composed of jolly little angels; those of the middle pair show caryatids seeming to strain to support so much ornamentation. The

Cathedral, Zacatecas

niches of the dominant first storey hold four more apostles, their majestically worked pedestals as long as the statues themselves.

The central rose window is of unsurpassed grandeur, bordered by fantastic relief so luxurious that it threatens to overflow into the central space. The keystone is a monstrance containing the Host supported by an angel (oriental in aspect) standing with wings folded; immediately above, the Holy Ghost in the form of a dove. On either side, happy cherubs swing thuribles; further down, and all the way round, more cherubs climb over bunches of grapes and blow horns in celebration. At the four corners outside the circle are reliefs of doctors of the Church: SS Jerome and Gregory above; SS Augustine and Ambrose below. The grille is a recent (1964) reconstruction.

In the centre of the lowest storey is the double-arched main doorway, mixtilinear underneath, semicircular above, the keystone a relief of the Immaculate Conception. The voussoirs of the archivolt form a stunning composition of winsome cherubs dancing attendance on her. In the niches on either side are statues of four more apostles. The six columns, solomonic in their upper two-thirds, are sumptuously decorated and seem to continue beyond the jutting cornice, and forward of two friezes, the lower partly of delightful angel relief, divided by a row of shells.

The S lateral doorway (finished 1775) is within a disciplined baroque tradition, but still extraordinarily rich. Into the doorway arch and jambs are cut geometrical patterns. On either side, the solomonic columns are exuberant with vine and grape relief; above, the entablature completes the fine lower- storey proportions. The upper storey is more exotic, the central niche of the Virgin and Child (Nuestra Señora de los Zacatecos) placed on a base lavish with acanthus relief, repeated in the spaces between the columns where it surrounds medallions of saints. Above the latter, parting the foliage, appear children above whose heads splay shell motifs. The inner columns are in the form of strange, slender, intricately worked caryatids.

The N doorway (finished 1777) is fascinatingly archaic (recalling 16C precedents), but inventive. On either side of the door, the columns end in smiling winged caryatids who raise their arms above what seem like contemporary wigs to steady, not support, crownlike Corinthian capitals. In the spandrels, angels carry instruments of the Passion. Grapes in the columns are pecked at by plump birds. Above the cornice, and on an ample base, is a Crucifixion (or rather three symbolic images) against generous drapery. Christ on the Cross is painfully tensed and the figures of Our Lady and St John, ingenuously out of scale, stand on pedestals upheld by cherubs. The frame is a beautiful entablature above and estípites on either side marked by grotesque masks. In the strongly moulded pediment above is the Holy Trinity, unusually represented: God the Father, the Holy Ghost, and two angels holding the Mandylion. Breaking the smoothness of the wall on either side are two kneeling angels.

The slender, graceful towers exhibit highly original column and pilaster relief. The capitals also obey no known order. The N tower was not completed until 1904, by Dámaso Muñetón. In 1844 the old cupola was replaced by the present one, a not too successful copy of the grand neoclassical dome of the church of Loreto in Mexico City.

The INTERIOR is in stark contrast with the exuberant exterior. Of the original decorations survive the keystones of the arches, which show the Evangelists, saints, symbols of the Litany of Our Lady and of the Passion; and the exquisitely carved interior frame of the rose window.

From the plaza Av. Hidalgo runs N to join C. Juan de Tolosa which leads on the r., past the *Fuente de los Conquistadores* (1946), to C. Abasolo and the ruined church and convent of **San Francisco**.

It was founded from Guadalajara in 1558 and the first convent, built by 1567, was the centre of a missionary effort within and beyond Nueva Galicia. A fire in 1648 destroyed the church and much of the convent. Rebuilding was completed in 1732–36. It suffered damage (more than most) during 19C upheavals and revolutionary assaults, and the application of buttresses had little effect. By 1925–27 its collapse had begun.

The surviving façade is a well-spaced baroque, the solomonic columns of the first and second storeys entwined with thick relief, a feature also of the octagonal choir window. Also remaining are the cupola and the presbytery vault. The small cloister preserves Gothic-style vaulting.

Further N on the l. in C. de Jesús, the church of *Jesús*, begun in 1887, contains a 16C image of Nuestra Señora de la Candelaria. Beyond, in C. Mexicapan, the church of *Mexicapan*, built in the 19C on the site of a late 16C chapel, recalls the name of the city's earliest Indian barrio.

From the SW corner of Pl. de Armas the typical, narrow Cjón de Veyna leads to PL. DE STO DOMINGO. On its N side is **Sto Domingo** (1746–49).

It was formerly the church of the Jesuits, second on the site and called *La Compañia*. The Dominicans were put in possession after the expulsion of 1767.

The wide anachronistically baroque façade, discreet in its ornamentation, unfolds like a screen between the two, surprisingly low, towers. Neoclassical interior remodelling spared the superb gilded side-aisle altarpieces, eight in all, predominantly churrigueresque, alive with polychrome statuary and medallions. In the octagonal sacristy are eight Scenes from the Passion by Francisco Antonio Vallejo.

On the W side of the plaza is the former **Colegio de San Luis Gonzaga**, once the college and seminary of the Jesuits.

It was founded in 1616 and rebuilt at the same time as the church. After 1767 it passed to the Dominicans. In 1795 it was royally confirmed as the Real Colegio de San Luis Gonzaga. After its closure in 1832 it was converted into the city gaol and suffered drastic changes. During 1953–79 it was gradually restored to its former beauty.

The elegant doorway is marked off on either side by estípites. Above the undulating arch, the three medallions once displayed the royal arms. Punctuating the broad façade, the small window openings, alternating with others even smaller, could be shuttered against the severities of the climate. Delightful cherubs form the keys of the patio arches.

It now houses the **Museo Pedro Coronel** (Wed.–Mon., 9–1, 2.30–6), an unsatisfyingly eclectic collection of prehistoric objects, paintings, prints, etc., donated to the city by this local painter. Also housed here is the notable *Colección Mertens de Arte Huichol*, not yet on permanent display.

A few steps away in C. Fernando Villalpando is the former *Rectoría de la Universidad*, now *Escuela Preparatoria No. 1*, an 18C house, once property of the family of the conde de San Mateo de Valparaíso. By following C. Fernando Villalpando SW, past (l.) the newly appointed *Pal. Legislativo*, we come (r.) to ALAMEDA GARCIA DE LA CADENA, a favourite park laid out in 1831–42 and rescued from neglect from 1943. On its S side, in Av. Torreón, are the offices of the *Unión Ganadera Regional* (Stockbreeders' Association), a mid-18C house, another property of the conde de San Mateo de Valparaíso. Immediately striking are the upper-storey portico and the stately doorway, above which is the family coat-of-arms. On the Alameda's NW side is the *Hospital del IMSS*, behind which is the entrance to the *Mina el Edén*, from which visitors may ride on a small train into the heart of the *Cerro del Grillo* (Cerro del Bosque), and the beginning of shafts first excavated in the 16C.

From Pl. de Sto Domingo, C. Dr Ignacio Hierro, an outstandingly picturesque street full of late 18C and 19C houses, runs S. Note the fine balconies which enhance the façades of Nos. 514 and 401–405. No. 307 is the former *Casa de Moneda* (early 19C; now *Tesorería del Estado*), the local mint during 1810–1905, with a good courtyard.

At the corner of Cjón San Agustín are the former church and convent of **San Agustín**, carefully restored to some of their old splendour.

The first Augustinian convent was built in 1576; the second, substitute, establishment in 1614. The church (mostly later 18C) was not dedicated until 1782. The friars were forced out in 1859. In 1863 church and convent were bought by Gen. Jesús González Ortega, who turned the latter into an hotel and the former into a mixture of bar, billiard hall, and gambling den, having reduced the five beautiful altarpieces to firewood. In 1882 the church was bought for 25,000 pesos by the Presbyterian Missionary Society of the USA, who completed the destruction of the interior and razed the churrigueresque façade. Bp Refugio Guerra of Zacatecas excommunicated all who had a hand in it. Restoration of the side portal took place in 1949–51; of the rest, where possible, in 1967–69—after the sorting-out of a mass of original masonry, dismantled and converted to other uses during years of desecration.

EXTERIOR. The N portal, of unusual slenderness, is a bewitching revelation of late 18C zacatecano art. On either side stand two ornamental niche pilasters resting against five more engaged pilasters and blending above into architrave, frieze, and cornice—a vigorously jutting frame for the centrepiece. The doorway shows curve and countercurve. Above it, acanthus relief ascends in increasing density to form the base of the main theme: the young St Augustine reclining beneath a fig tree in the garden of his house in Milan and presented with the Epistles of St Paul to aid his conversion. He is dressed in 16C doublet and hose, and rests his head on his r. hand. On the r., the portal of the house, the door with oblong coffered panels, Spanish-style; surrounding it, Italian cypresses. Above it, the messenger angel, who has delivered the book, commands: 'tolle et lege' (take and read). On the l., angel musicians; in the centre, the sun disperses the clouds and benignly warms the scene.

The reassembled stonework of the INTERIOR gives a fair idea of the richness and elegance of the original. The entrances to the chapels are extraordinarily fine: the delicate relief of archivolts, jambs, and anachronistic alfices, flanked by slim estípites. More densely beautiful is the entrance to the sacristy, more intricate relief following the curve of the narrow doorway arch, and flanked by exquisite pairs of estípites and niche pilasters supporting cornices on which rest emphatic volutes. In the r. transept has been placed a striking painting by Juan Correa, Our Lady of Seville (Nuestra Señora de la Antigua) with SS Joseph and Teresa—the central figures of Our Lady and the infant Christ in a golden background.
The exterior of the adjoining convent, now occupied by the bishopric, was inevitably amplified, though not unpleasingly, in the 1860s. The CLOISTER is a superb example of pulsating Augustinian grandeur. Ogee arches in the lower storey are matched by inversions in the upper. Movement is supplied by wavy mouldings which spring from the lower to the upper pilasters. Each corner of the upper walks, and the staircase, is topped by a cupola, five of the eight supported by convent and church.

Beyond San Agustín opens out the evocative PL. MIGUEL AUZA, beyond which we reach JARDIN JUAREZ, lined by attractive houses, on its E side the *Pal. Municipal* (early 19C), now the university rectory. From it Cjón de Cuevas leads to AV. HIDALGO, the city's principal street; on the l., the PORTAL DE ROSALES (1827), known for its shops and restaurants. We turn r. (S), eventually to join Calz. González Ortega, which leads S to Paseo Ortega, a park alongside which runs a stretch of the *Acueducto*, well built in the late 18C–early 19C to bring water from the S to Pl. Villarreal and blocked up by 1921. The equestrian statue to Jesús González Ortega, by Jesús Contreras, was unveiled in 1898. On the W side of the park is a mansion, in porfirian style, built as the governor's residence, which now houses the **Museo Francisco Goitia** (Tues.–Sun., 9–1.30; 3.30–6).

It contains a permanent collection of paintings by 20C zacatecano artists, chief among them Francisco Goitia (1882–1966), born near Fresnillo, who enlisted during the Revolution in the forces of Francisco Villa. His war sketches formed the basis for much of his subsequent work.

By continuing along Calz. González Ortega towards the main railway station we reach the little-known church of **Guadalupito**, begun by Refugio Reyes in 1891.

It contains a venerated 16C statue, the Cristo de Guerreros, and an unexpected cache of important paintings: Juan Correa, Marriage Feast at Cana (1698); the Risen Christ appears to Our Lady (1698; presbytery); Annunciation and Flight into Egypt (two charming ovals in the transept; strong attributions). In the sacristy, six scenes from the Life of Our Lady (1706) by Cristóbal de Villalpando, once property of Francisco García Salinas (1786–1841), an outstanding governor of the State. Juan Correa, St Peter of Alcántara (in need of restoration); St Joseph and the Child Jesus (an attribution, reported stolen). In the antesacristy, Juan Correa, Communion of Our Lady.

On our way back into the centre we may pause at the crossing with Av. Juárez. To the l. is the neo-Gothic church of *Sagrado Corazón* (1823). To the r. we reach JARDIN INDEPENDENCIA, the former PL. VILLARREAL, in effect the city's main plaza. On its N side is the former *Alhóndiga* (late 18C), which did service as Pal. Municipal before becoming the *Biblioteca del Estado*. On its S side is the *Portal de las Flores* (1909); on the W, the 18C *Casa de la Condesa de San Mateo de Valparaíso* (Ana María de la Campa y Cos; see Rte 7).
From here C. Aldama goes N into the beautiful trapezoidal C. TACUBA. At its N end is the former *Mercado González Ortega* (1886–1903), a handsome building on a slope, now readapted for shops and restaurants, the upper floor facing C. Hidalgo, the lower C. Tacuba. Opposite in Av. Hidalgo is the *Teatro*

Calderón (1891–97), an unusually light example of porfirian eclecticism, by George C. King.

From the grounds of the Motel del Bosque on the NW side of the city, reached by taking C. Genaro Codina from Pl. de Sto Domingo and turning l. through Cjones García Rojas and Mante, a cablecar (teleférico) crosses to the historic CERRO DE LA BUFA. The views over the city are magnificent. On it is the chapel of **Nuestra Señora de los Zacatecos** (*Virgen del Patrocinio*; 1727–28; modified 1790), built at the charges of the conde de Santiago de la Laguna. The baroque façade, of extraordinary gracefulness, is faced with varied tableros. On either side of the charming central niche, holding a relief of the city's patron, are round windows enclosing images of the sun and moon. Also here are an observatory (1906) and, at the foot of the crag, the *Mausoleo de los Hombres Ilustres*, resting place of famous zacatecanos. The descent may be made on foot to reach the area behind the cathedral.

On the E side of the city, on the road to Guadalupe (see below), are the modern buildings of the *Universidad Autónoma de Zacatecas*. Among its attractions are an anthropological museum and a mining museum.

5km E of Zacatecas, and virtually a suburb, is **Guadalupe**, named after the church and convent of **GUADALUPE**, the latter now partly converted into an important museum of historical art (Tues.–Sun., 10–5; fee).

The Colegio de Propaganda Fide de Nuestra Señora de Guadalupe de Zacatecas was founded in 1707 to train Franciscan missionaries for work in Coahuila, Texas, and other neighbouring parts. Church and convent were dedicated in May 1721. It was one of eight such colleges in New Spain, each autonomous under a friar guardián. Its founder and first superior was Fray Antonio Margil (1657–1726) from the older foundation at Querétaro (see Rte 37). Later, missions were started in Nuevo Santander, and after 1767, the friars took over former Jesuit missions in the Tarahumara. In the early 19C they were in charge of missions in Alta California. In 1859 the college was closed down. It is estimated that 3880 missionaries had been trained there. The Franciscans are again in possession of the church.

Church. EXTERIOR. The baroque façade, in reddish stone, is arrestingly full of movement and lively relief. The lower-storey columns divide into three parts: the lowest show small boys amid climbing plants; the middle solomonic coiling; the upper mat-weave (petatillo) pattern. In the niches are statues of SS Francis and Dominic. Above the pentagonal arch is a beguiling relief composition. On the l., St Luke paints Our Lady's portrait; below him appears St John in ecstasy; in the centre, Our Lady of Guadalupe upheld by St Francis; on the r., St Bonaventure and María de Agreda (see Rte 38). Above the cornice, the upper-storey columns show variations of zigzag and vegetal swathing. In the centre is God the Father attended by cherubs and musical angels, embedded amid a riot of cloudlike acanthus. Beneath Him, a dove symbolizes the Holy Ghost, and, to the dove's r., a small boy falling from the cloud and holding a small cross symbolizes the infant Christ. On either side of the columns, two reliefs show the Annunciation. The original tower is on the r. The pseudo-moorish tower on the l. is a 19C aberration.

The INTERIOR was remodelled in neoclassical style in the 19C. The sacristy contains a fine triptych mural (1720) by Antonio de Torres: St Francis and the Angel with a flask and St Bonaventure receiving communion, on either side of the Last Supper (the Apostles' expressions beautifully done).

On the l. of the church is the CAP. DE NAPOLES (*Cap. de la Inmaculada*), the most interesting, perhaps the outstanding, ecclesiastical work of the later 19C in Mexico. It was built, on the plan of a Greek cross, during 1850–95 to the projections of the friar Juan Bautista Méndez; the final decoration was entrusted to another friar, Jesús del Refugio Sánchez.

Four small apses round off the arms and the centre is covered by an elegant cupola. Its design base—with fluted pilasters, Corinthian capitals, frieze, jutting cornice, and altarpieces—recalls the neoclassical. The superimposed decorative detail, in shades of gold against the white of the surfaces, is gorgeous neo-baroque. Beneath the ciborium on the high altar is the statue of the Immaculate Conception (said to have been made in Naples) donated to the college by Queen Isabel Farnese in the 1740s.

Convent. On the r. of the church the convent is gained through a triple-arch portería. Hence a corridor gives on to the principal cloister (CLAUSTRO DE SAN FRANCISCO), its walls lined with 24 paintings (earlier 18C; ingenuous in style) of scenes from the Life of St Francis. The arch openings are screened by wooden lattices. From the cloister a passage leads to the main staircase, its walls hung with enormous paintings. Nicolás Rodríguez Juárez, St Christopher. Cabrera, Founders of the Colleges of Sta Cruz (Querétaro) and Guadalupe sheltering beneath the cloak of St Francis—first on the saint's l., Antonio Margil; last l., a fine portrait of an unknown friar and, behind him, a supposed self-portrait of the painter; Virgin of the Apocalypse. José Ríos Arnáez (mid-18C), Triumph of the Holy Name of Jesus. Above the access arch, Ibarra, St Joseph, with portraits of the donors José Joaristi, alcalde of Zacatecas, and his wife Dionisia Fernández de Lis (1751). A few more steps lead to the long corridor of the CLAUSTRO DE LA ENFERMERIA, lined with friars' portraits and original furniture. Off it open various rooms. The so-called SALA DE LAS DAMAS includes anon. paintings of female saints (SS Marina and Catherine) in 17C costume. Another room contains four small paintings by Juan Patricio Morlete Ruiz, once belonging to altarpieces: SS Gregory the Great, Augustine, Jerome, and Ambrose. In two more rooms are paintings by Antonio de Torres. In the first, Slaughter of the Innocents; Rebecca offers water to the servant of Abraham and his camels; Triumphal Entry of David and Saul; Beheading of John the Baptist. In the second, Eight Scenes from the Life of Our Lady (1719), incl. Christ baptizing His Mother—all full of interesting detail.

The doorway of the CAP. DE LA ENFERMERIA, a graceful baroque work, is full of appealing relief, incl. angels and cherubs, with God the Father in the centre of the frieze. The interior is covered by a charming cupola. In the pendentives, three scenes of the Miracle of Guadalupe. At the sides, scenes from the Life of St Antony of Padua. On the altar, expressive statues, with good estofado, of SS Anne and Joachim (18C) and Juan Correa, Our Lady of Zacatecas, a late work, with, in the bottom l. hand corner, a delightful portrait of the young donor, supposedly the condesa de San Mateo de Valparaíso. Attr. Correa, St John of God.

Also leading off from the top of the main staircase is a short corridor whose walls are lined with 14 oval paintings of Scenes from the Life of Our Lady by Cabrera. The first cell on the l. was that of the guardián. The adjoining cell, formerly reserved for illustrious visitors, contains part of the library (adm. by special permission), once reaching 35,000 volumes. Here also are kept eight scenes from the Way of the Cross and one of Our Lord carrying the Cross by Juan Correa, and three more (1787), complementary, on the same theme by José de Alzíbar.

From this corridor steps lead to the CHOIR. The backs of the rear seats of the black wooden stalls contain medallion paintings of apostles, saints, and Marian emblems. Above perch wooden statues, done with estofado, of founders of religious orders. The seat of honour is occupied by a lifesize statue of St Francis (whose r. hand, it is said, once obliged those who approached for a blessing with a sign of the Cross, triggered by an ingenious mechanism) and above it a relief of Our Lady of Guadalupe. The anon. rear wall painting shows Philip V on a white charger as defender of the Church and Christianity in Palestine, shown as a woman in mourning, prisoner of the Turks. Opposite, above the grille, a charming Virgen Pasaviense, another anon. 18C work.

Adjoining the choir is a small room once occupied by the organ-blowers. It now contains two rare 18C examples of feather mosaics: St Peter and St Francis; a 17C ivory crucifix from the Philippines; 18C choirbooks, the leaves done by hand on parchment; 16C crucifix from Michoacán, in caña de maíz.

The upper walk of the principal cloister is lined with 29 paintings, popular in style and with curious detail, of the Passion by Antonio Enríquez (mid-18C), the uneven quality betrays collaborative hands. Off it, a small cell, possibly once the pharmacy, contains four major paintings by Cristóbal de Villalpando, signed and dated 1706.

The first, Holy Family ('Cinco Señores'), shows the young Christ with Our Lady, St Joseph, and SS Anne and Joachim. The second, Mystical City of God, has St John and Sor María de Agreda seated before a vision of the new Jerusalem, above which Our Lady of the Apocalypse is received into Heaven by the Holy Trinity. The third, Tree of Life, shows Adam and Eve kneeling on either side of the Cross, entwined with bunches of grapes; beneath the arms, SS Michael, Gabriel, and Raphael; above, l. and r., SS Christopher and Hyacinth, carriers of Christ; below, symbols of the world, the flesh, and the devil. In the fourth, Annunciation, the Holy Trinity (with Christ as the sun) is shown above Our Lady and St Gabriel, figures of supreme elegance and grace; surrounding them, a theatre of countless angels.

The cell next door contains: Luis Juárez, Visitation and Presentation; Basilio, St Francis supported by angels (perhaps the only surviving work by a 17C master).
    From the adjoining CLAUSTRO DE LOS OBISPOS a staircase leads to the former library, hung with 14 scenes, vigorous if crude, from the Passion (1749) by Gabriel José de Ovalle, a local painter; the vivid, distorted faces of Christ's enemies especially arresting. Also by him, Immaculate Conception; Death of Our Lady. Attr. Cabrera, Holy Family at table in the open air; Franciscans and Dominicans at table, attended by angels; Marriage Feast at Cana. José de Alzíbar, Our Lord's protection of Pope Pius VI and King Charles III (1783).

Beneath the small staircase which leads down from the Claustro de los Obispos is a small cell, once occupied by Fray Antonio Margil, containing belongings of the early missionaries, incl. a large cross lined with cloth, carried by Fray Antonio on his journeys.
    6km N of Zacatecas is *Vetagrande* (c 1000 inhab.), now something of a ghost town. Some of its 18C buildings still exist, though ruined.

47 Chihuahua to Zacatecas via Durango

Méx. 45, Méx. 49, and Méx. 54, 990km.—224km Jiménez.—303km **Hidalgo del Parral**.—428km turning W for (50km) Sta María del Oro and (175km) Tepehuanes.—706km **Durango**.—756km Nombre de Dios.—831km **Sombrerete** (for **Chalchihuites**).—920km junction with Méx. 49.—980km junction with Méx. 54.—990km **Zacatecas.**

From Chihuahua to (224km) *Jiménez*, see Rte 45. From here Méx. 45 runs W through comparatively fertile valleys watered by rivers running into the Río Florido. 239km turning l. for (12km S) *Villa López*, founded c 1603 as the Franciscan mission of San Buenaventura Atotonilco. 256km turning l. for (4km S) *Salaices*, from which the *Cueva del Diablo* (3km NW; stalagtites and stalagmites) may be reached. 279km turning l. for (6km S) **Valle de Allende** (5000 inhab.; 1552m), the former *Valle de San Bartolomé*, a Franciscan mission centre from the 1560s and an attractive place, known for its gardens and fruits. Its parish church, now called *Nuestra Señora del Rosario*, was restored and finished by Nicolás Morín in 1788–92. The heads of Hidalgo and Allende were put on show here (commemorative plaque in the centre) before being taken to Guanajuato.
    303km **HIDALGO DEL PARRAL** (c 120,000 inhab.; 1661m; H,R,P), on the Río Parral amid arid mountains, is an old mining town which preserves some interesting buildings from its wealthy past.

In the 1560s the first real of the Parral district, at Sta Bárbara, was founded. In 1631 the discovery of further lead-free deposits led to the founding of the real of San Joseph del Parral. In 1634, a second real, San Diego de Minas Nuevas (the modern Villa Escobedo, a few km NW), was settled, and the region became one of the most productive in New Spain. The Jesuits had a house here. The news in Apr. 1652 that the Indians of Parral had risen in rebellion and killed and eaten a Jesuit caused a sensation in Mexico City. During 1632–1739 Parral was the unofficial capital of Nueva Vizcaya. In 1920 Francisco Villa retired to the 25,000 hectare hacienda of Canutillo, paid for by the government, S of the town in Durango. On 20 July 1923 he was assassinated while on a visit to Parral.

On the N side of PLAZUELA HIDALGO is the parish church of **San José** (1673–86), the work of Simón de los Santos. It has a wide single nave and low cupola, and has kept two churrigueresque side altarpieces. Near the high altar is the tomb of Juan Rangel de Biesma, founder of the real de minas. Across the river (to the E) is the *Teatro Hidalgo* (late 19C; fired in 1928). Also across the river (to the SE) from Av. Independencia stands the church of *Nuestra Señora del Rayo* (c 1690–1710). Near the junction of Av. 20 de Noviembre and the wide C. Flores Magón is *San Nicolás*, another simple 17C church, with a wooden beam roof and original paintings. C. Flores Magón ends near PL. GUILLERMO BACA, where stands a statue, Buscador de Ilusiones (seeker after dreams; 1957) by Ignacio Asúnsolo, commemorating the early prospectors. On the W side of the plaza is the church of *San Juan de Dios* (formerly *La Soledad*; 1712), containing a churrigueresque altarpiece and contemporary paintings in the sacristy. On the N side are the modern *Santuario de Guadalupe* and, by the NE corner, the *Casa Stallfurth*, a late 19C house, but restrained in style, and *Villa de Grado*, once property of Villa, where his body was carried after his death.

From the W side of the plaza a narrow street leads to the **Casa de Alvarado**, a fabulous porfirian folly built for the magnate Pedro Alvarado.

Alvarado (1866–1937), a native of the town, became a multi-millionaire through his ownership of the Palmilla mine, which at peak production yielded a vein of extraordinary richness. A public-spirited and benevolent man, if politically naïve, he is said to have offered to pay off the national debt. After countless benefactions, he died in relative poverty.

A little to the r., before reaching Puente de Guanajuato, is another grandiose late 19C residence, the *Casa Greense*, with a profusely ornamented doorway flanked by marble columns. Across the bridge, before reaching Pl. Juárez, a venerably bent tree whose roots have raised the pavement marks the spot where Francisco Villa, his secretary Miguel Trillo, and three bodyguards were shot.

The **Museo y Biblioteca Francisco Villa**, on the corner of the street, occupies a house rented by Villa's assassin, Jesús Salas Barraza, because Villa always slowed down there while driving past on his way back to his ranch, and in which Salas installed eight gunmen to wait for the favourable moment. The museum contains a helpful collection of photographs.

Beyond the Villa de Grado is C. Héroes de Nacozari, on which we may turn l. for three blocks, then r. up the hill to reach the church of *Nuestra Señora de Fátima* (1953). Products of local mines, incl. gold, silver, zinc, and copper, are incorporated in the church structure and the benches.

12km NW of Parral is *Villa Escobedo* (the former *Minas Nuevas*), abandoned in 1929, now in ruins, its old plaza and streets recalling its wealthy past.

The road to (28km) *Sta Bárbara* runs SW from Parral. It is a peaceful place, in the sierra of the same name, and still maintains mining activity. *San Francisco del Oro* (11km to its NW), settled with a gold and silver bonanza in 1658, never achieved the importance of Parral, Minas Nuevas, and Sta Bárbara in former times, but has outstripped them during the 20C.

From Hidalgo del Parral to *Pericos*, see Rte 22.

The road W from Hidalgo del Parral to (326km) *Creel* (see Rte 43) through the wooded Sierra Madre Occidental is reasonably paved as far as (188km) *Guachochic* in the Tarahumara region. It passes through the broad Valle de San Pablo, in which is situated (95km) *San Pablo Balleza*, in beautiful cattle-raising country. In the 17C the area was opened up by pioneering Jesuits.

Méx. 45 continues to (327km) *Villa Matamoros* (P). At 357km we cross into the State of Durango. 386km turning r. for (3km SW) *Canutillo*, the former hacienda of Francisco Villa. A small museum contains mementoes of him. 428km turning r.

This road leads W to (50km) **Sta María del Oro** (7000 inhab.; 1871m), a mining town (silver, gold, copper), the former *Real del Oro*, which reached its heyday in the 18C when ores with a high gold content were discovered. The region is mountainous and wooded, with oak and holm oak. Hence we may continue W into the heart of the Sierra Madre, watered by tributaries of the Río Nazas, dense with pine and oak, to join (at c 115km) Méx. 23, the Guanaceví–Tepehuanes road, near *San Ignacio del Zape*, where four Jesuit missionaries were killed in a massacre perpetrated by Tepehuán Indians in 1616. 33km NW is *Guanaceví* (c 3000 inhab.), already a mining area by the 1590s, still with unexploited mineral deposits. From the junction at c 115km the road runs S to (c 175km) **Tepehuanes** (4000 inhab.; 1787m; P), on the Río Tepehuanes, founded in 1597 as Sta Catarina de los Tepehuanes and moved to higher ground in 1690 after a flood. It is still the principal centre of the Tepehuán Indians, early resisters of Spanish colonization.

From Tepehuanes the road runs SE to (c 227km) **Santiago Papasquiaro**, founded as a Jesuit mission in 1597, on the Río Santiago (Papasquiaro). It was the birthplace of the gifted brothers Revueltas: the composer Silvestro (1899–1940); the muralist Fermín (1903–35); and the writer José (1914–76).

From Santiago Papasquiaro an excursion may be made to the remote and exceptionally rugged W region of the State of Durango on the Pacific slope of the Sierra Madre. A new, but difficult, road runs W, via (45km) *Ciénega de Salpica* and (95km) *El Ojito de Camellones*, to (c 160km) **Topia**, settled as the real de minas of *Vera Cruz de Topia* with Franciscan missionaries in the 1560s. 10km S, difficult of access, is *Canelas* (c 1500 inhab.), from 1725 a mining community, now a notable orange- and coffee-producing centre.

From Santiago Papasquiaro, Méx. 23 runs SE past (l.) the *Lagunas de Santiaguillo* and *Guatimapé*.

On the shores of Santiaguillo, primitive implements of the Cochise Desert Tradition have been excavated. Of much later date, in the semi-desert S of Santiago Papasquiaro (c 2 days on horseback with a guide) it is possible to visit the unexcavated site of *Sotolitos*. An elongated structure may be a ball court, and surface pottery indicates contact with, or possibly even the most known S extension of, the Hohokam culture of the SW USA.

330km *Canatlán*, known for its exquisite apples. At 344km we join Méx. 45 for (398km) *Durango*, see below.

Méx. 45 skirts a bleak plain marked by deeply eroded watercourses to (475km) *La Zarca* (P); 119km E is *Bermejillo*, see Rte 45. 40km SW is *Presa Lázaro Cárdenas*, fed by the waters of the Ríos Ramos and Nazas. Méx. 45 enters the E slopes of the Sierra Madre. At 559km a road leads E via *Nazas* to (94km) Méx. 40 from Gómez Palacio to *Durango*, see Rte 45. 607km turning l. for (60km S) *Francisco I. Madero*, see Rte 45. 5km along this road is San Juan del Río (P), chief place of a region settled by the Spaniards in the 1570s among Tepehuán and Zacatecos Indians. At 652km we join Méx. 23 from *Tepehuanes*, see above.

706km **DURANGO** (c 380,000 inhab.; 1889m), capital of the State of Durango, lies in the SW corner of the Valle de Guadiana, a broad high valley located between E spurs of the Sierra Madre Occidental. To the S is the Sierra de Durango. It is the centre of a cattle-raising and farming region, and of industries which include cotton, woollen, and flour mills, tobacco factories, and sugar refineries. Its historic past is reflected in some fine ecclesiastical and civic buildings. Fabulous high-altitude light (the sky an invariable intense blue) and surrounding landscape have made it one of the world's great film-making centres. The climate is temperate, but winters can be severe. The duranguenses have a tradition of hospitality and kindness to strangers.

Airport. 26km NE. Flights to *Guadalajara, Mazatlán, Mexico City, Monterrey*, etc.

Bus station. 3km E of the centre, reached along Av. Felipe Pescador. Services across Sierra Madre Occidental to *Mazatlán* (7 hrs); to *Torreón* (5 hrs); to *Fresnillo* (3 hrs); to *Zacatecas* (4½ hrs); to *Chihuahua* (11 hrs); to *Hidalgo del Parral* (7 hrs); etc.

Railway station. N of the centre, reached along C. Constitución.

Hotels throughout the city.

Post Office. 213 C. Constitución.

Tourist Office. 408 C. Hidalgo Sur.

Fiestas. 8 July: Founder's Day.

In 1552–53 the prospector Ginés Vázquez del Mercado, on an expedition in search of silver, came upon the huge mound of iron, just N of the present city, now called Cerro del Mercado. He retired furiously disappointed. In 1554 the site, called Guadiana, a name which stuck informally for many years, was visited by Francisco de Ibarra and in 1563 Franciscan friars established a congregation of Tepehuanes at Analco (see below). Ibarra founded the villa of Victoria de Durango later that year. From the first it was the official seat of government of Nueva Vizcaya, although the governors resided at Parral during 1632–1739 and later sometimes at Chihuahua. In 1788 it became capital of the intendancy of the same name. The British chargé d'affaires, H.G. Ward, recorded a visit to Durango in 1826 which delighted him. He particularly admired the women for their 'bustling activity…there is no part of the Republic in which…the little comforts of life [are] so well understood'. In spring 1913 Durango was sacked by Tomás Urbina, Villa's associate; in 1914–15 it was twice more occupied by villista forces.

Famous duranguenses include Pres. Guadalupe Victoria (Miguel Fernández Félix; 1786–1843), b. at Tamazula in the W of the State, but educated in Durango; Francisco Zarco (1829–69), politician and journalist; Francisco Villa (Doroteo Arango; 1878–1923), b. on the hacienda of Río Grande, near San Juan del Río; the contralto singer Fanny Anitúa (1887–1968); and the actress Dolores del Río (1906–83).

The W and SW of the State of **Durango** (1,350,000 inhab.; 123,181 sq km) are in the Sierra Madre Occidental. Canyons more than 1400m deep, known as quebradas, mark its W flank. Even today parts of the extreme S remain an unexplored wilderness. The main river, the Río Nazas, flows E from the Sierra Madre through the NE. When swollen by spring rains it is a vital source of water and permits commercial crops of finest cotton, wheat, maize, tobacco, sugar cane, and fruit. Mining has been a traditional mainstay. Durango holds first place in the republic as a producer of gold, second for iron, fourth for silver. Just N of the capital, the Cerro del Mercado (c 215m high), helmet-shaped, is a mass of nearly pure haematite iron ore. Vast tracts of forest make Durango second only to Chihuahua in timber production.

In 1562 Francisco de Ibarra began a series of campaigns to bring under Spanish control what was to be called Nueva Vizcaya, extending from Mezquital, S of Durango, to N of Chihuahua, and from the W coast to the E as far as Saltillo. From the 1570s onwards there were frequent Indian uprisings, the most bitter the Tepehuán revolt of 1616–18, eventually crushed in a welter of carnage and enslavement. In the 18C the Apaches moved down from the N and indulged in pillage and raiding until well into the 19C. Franciscan and Jesuit missionaries gathered unwilling converts into crowded settlements which became hotbeds of European diseases; whole tribes were decimated. From 1911, the State became a key battleground, losing a large part of its livestock to marauding revolutionary bands. From 1926 the Cristero movement was strong here.

On the N side of the central PL. DE ARMAS stands the cathedral of **La Inmaculada Concepción**, another of the great churches of N Mexico, testimony to local 18C civic and episcopal pride.

It is the successor to three earlier churches on the site and was begun in 1695 under Mateo Núñez of Guadalajara, followed in 1698 by Simón de los Santos, to whom is owed the basic structure. In 1702 Joseph de la Cruz took over as architect. By 1721 he had completed most of the l. (W) tower, main portal, r. tower base, lower storeys of side portals, sacristy, and other dependencies. The side portals were finished in 1764 by Pedro de Huertas. The E tower was finished in the late 18C. On a visit in Oct. 1777 the Galician Franciscan friar Juan Agustín Morfi commented: 'the choir is infested by ants which, at certain times of year, do not permit anyone to remain there'.

EXTERIOR. The main (S) façade and the high flanking towers present a dignified composition. In its lower storey the portal (by Nuñéz or Los Santos) is Renaissance-inspired; in its upper (by La Cruz) a cross between Mannerism and baroque. The fluted columns of the lower storey, their capitals veering towards, but not quite, Corinthian, enclosing rigid statues of SS Peter and Paul, contrast with the solomonic columns of the upper and the livelier images of SS John the Baptist, Joachim, Anne, and Joseph. The wall and friezes are faced with what resembles more a graphic design than relief. The gable is attractively broken; on either side are figures of archangels, who also appear above the side but-

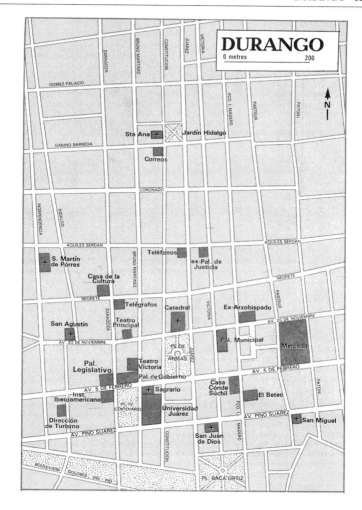

DURANGO

0 metres — 200

N

Labels on map: GOMEZ PALACIO, ZARAGOZA, BRUNO MARTINEZ, CONSTITUCION, JUAREZ, VICTORIA, FCO. I. MADERO, PASTEUR, PATONI, GABINO BARREDA, Sta Ana, Jardín Hidalgo, Correos, CORONADO, INDEPENDENCIA, HIDALGO, AQUILES SERDAN, AQUILES SERDAN, S. Martín de Pórres, Teléfonos, ex-Pal. de Justicia, NEGRETE, Casa de la Cultura, BRUNO MARTINEZ, PASTEUR, Telégrafos, Catedral, Ex-Arzobispado, AV. 20 DE NOVIEMBRE, San Agustín, Teatro Principal, VICTORIA, ZARAGOZA, AV. 20 DE NOVIEMBRE, Pál. Municipal, Mercado, PL. DE ARMAS, Pal. Legislativo, Teatro Victoria, Pal. de Gobierno, AV. 5 DE FEBRERO, Inst. Iberoamericano, AV. 5 DE FEBRERO, Sagrario, Casa Conde Súchil, El Bateo, PATONI, Dirección de Turismo, PL. IV CENTENARIO, Universidad Juárez, FCO. I. MADERO, AV. PINO SUAREZ, San Miguel, AV. PINO SUAREZ, CONSTITUCION, San Juan de Dios, BOULEVARD, DOLORES DEL RIO, PL. BACA ORTIZ

tresses and around the lateral cupolas, added in the late 19C by Benigno Montoya. Diminishing in girth as they soar upwards, the towers, the highest yet built in Mexico, are tipped by an elegant combination of cupola and lantern of crowded columns. Of far greater interest, full of movement and exuberant relief, are the side portals, displaying to great effect advancing 18C tastes. In their lower storeys the columns, enclosing statues of the four evangelists, are boldly solomonic in their upper two-thirds. In their upper storeys, the fluted backgrounds of the upper column sections are swathed by spiralling sashes. Estípites appear on either side of the window, a churrigueresque touch, echoed by the lambrequin motifs in the column bases. The saints of the E doorway upper storey are Barbara and Hedwig; St George appears in the W doorway upper storey (r.); his companion (l.) is unidentified.

The wide INTERIOR (central nave, side aisle, and side chapels) fell victim to a drastic, romantically overwhelming, reconditioning in 1841–44 when Bp Antonio Laureano López de Zubiría ordered the removal of 'everything baroque'. He put up the high altar, one of the better examples of baroque-tinged neoclassical, but left, in the apse, the beautiful choirstalls (1737), embossed with saintly figures in relief. In the first chapel r. is a fine anon. late 17C Descent from the Cross.

In the sacristy are four paintings (Adoration of the Shepherds, Adoration of the Kings, Resurrection, Ascension) by Juan Correa (1686), survivals from the original high altarpiece. The SALA CAPITULAR contains portraits of the bps of Durango, among them three of great importance: José Juárez, Bp Pedro Barrientos Lomelín (1656–58); Juan Patricio Morlete Ruiz, Bp Vicente Díaz Bravo (1770–72); and José de Ibarra, Bp Antonio Macarulla Minguilla de Aguiláin (1774–81).

From the Cathedral, C. Juárez runs N to JARDIN HIDALGO. On its W side is the church of **Sta Ana**, begun in the 1730s as a chapel and amplified from c 1774, with traditional twin side portals facing E, possibly for a convent of Capuchin nuns. Set back between buttresses tipped by half-columns, the doorways are an anachronistic mixture of Mannerism and subdued baroque. Together with the fine tower they create a strong impression.

To the E of the Cathedral along Av. 20 de Noviembre is the *Pal. Municipal* (at the corner with C. Victoria), built in the late 19C as residence of the mining magnate Pedro Escarsaga. Its staircase murals (1950–52), by Felipe Hernández, Manuel Rodríguez, and others, illustrate the history of Durango. The one-storey building at the corner with C. Madero, one block further (l.), is the former *Arzobispado*, renovated and decorated c 1885 by Gregorio Díaz and Benigno Montoya.

To the W of the Cathedral along Av. 20 de Noviembre we pass the *Teatro Principal* (late 19C) to reach the church of *San Agustín*, part of the Augustinian convent founded in the 17C, but much enlarged since.

The neo-Gothic altarpiece (late 19C) is by Benigno Montoya, who also designed the chapel, with neo-Gothic decoration, of the seminary now called *San Martín de Porres* in C. Independencia, further on to the r.

Opposite the Teatro Principal we may take C. Bruno Martínez S past (r.) the *Teatro Victoria*, inaugurated in 1800 as the private theatre of Juan José de Zambrano (see below), but altered inside and out later in the 19C, and reconditioned in 1980. Just beyond we reach PL. IV CENTENARIO, laid out, to celebrate the 400th anniversary of the city's founding, in 1963; in its centre a monument to Juárez by Francisco Montoya de la Cruz. On its N side is the wide and handsome **Pal. de Gobierno**, built in the late 18C as the residence of Juan José de Zambrano (1750–1817), regidor and mining millionaire, and converted to its present use after Independence.

On the E side is the main building (mid-18C) of the **Universidad Juárez**, occupying the former headquarters of the Jesuits.

They established their college in 1596. After their expulsion in 1767 it became the diocesan seminary. In 1860 it became officially the *Colegio Civil*, and later *Instituto Juárez*, which developed into the university, inaugurated in 1957.

On the ground floor has been reassembled a portal (late 16C) of the former Franciscan convent of *San Antonio* (once occupying the block directly E of the Pal. Municipal), wantonly destroyed during the brief governorship of Gabriel Gavida in 1917. On its N side is the former Jesuit church, now called *El Sagrario* (1757).

From the NE corner of the plaza we may take Av. 5 de Febrᵉ⌐o E, to the corner with C. Madero. Here is the finest house in the city, if not in all N Mexico, the **Pal. del Conde del Valle de Súchil**.

It was built (c 1770), probably by Pedro de Huertas, for José Soberón del Campo y Larrez, 1st conde del Valle de Súchil, a rich hacendado. In 1777, Juan Agustín Morfi stayed here: 'of the houses [of the city] it is reputed to be the best; but it has no other merit than extravagance'.

Its portal, flattened to take account of the corner (puerta chata), is framed by tableros. On either side of the barely raised entrance arch are two pairs of engaged pilasters: the inner composed of tableros; the outer straight and undulatingly fluted. They uphold the wide balcony, its backdrop a gorgeous composition of perfectly proportioned estípites, whimsically mixtilinear window arch, and a background of floral and scroll relief. The niche holds a statue of Our Lady. The two-storey patio reveals further delights: lower columns engraved in a zigzag pattern continued in the arch soffits, floral spandrel relief, friezes of lozenge shapes, and, in the upper storey, small estípite caryatids punctuating the balcony.

Almost opposite in C. Madero is *El Bateo*, a time-honoured saddlery, founded by Leonidas Rodríguez in 1903. To the S we may follow Av. Pino Suárez W to the church of *San Juan de Dios*, formerly attached to a hospital run by the Order of St John of God, now destroyed. The church dates from 1739 and keeps a contemporary portal as well as a later, neoclassical, one. On the r. of the high altar is a painting of Our Lady of Mount Carmel and St John saving souls in purgatory, by Francisco Martínez.

Further along Av. Pino Suárez, the turning l. along C. Zaragoza leads across Blvd Dolores del Río to **Analco**, where the earliest Franciscan mission was founded in 1558. The church (*San Juan Bautista*) was rebuilt, and excellently, in the mid-19C in a mixture of neo-Gothic and neoclassical, with a touch of Renaissance. The tower is by Benigno Montoya.

Two more churches, on the NW side of the city, contain more work by the local architect Benigno Montoya (1862–1929). The sanctuary of *Guadalupe*, dating from 1772, contains a neo-Gothic high altar (1884–85) and other gothicizing work by him. Its adjoining convent, now a school, dates from 1910. The church of *Nuestra Señora de los Angeles* (at the corner of Av. Aquiles Serdán and the Madero glorieta), begun in 1809, was finished by Montoya in 1890–97.

From *El Nayar* (c 11km S of Durango) it is possible to reach the **Schroeder Site**, a Classic–Postclassic Period ceremonial centre occupied between c AD 550 and 1350. Culturally it is known as the Guadiana branch of the Chalchihuites Cultural Complex (see below). When prospectors from Teotihuacán ceased to exploit the mines around Alta Vista (S of the site), by c AD 500, much of the local population engaged in the quarrying seems to have moved N to Schroeder, where they built a new ceremonial centre, incl. a ball court. The site was especially active between AD 500 and 700, and, according to one authority, was responsible for spreading the ball game complex (ie, the game and its ritual and religious overtones) to the Hohokam culture of the SW USA; contacts between the two regions were certainly strong during this and later times. A second active phase ensued from c AD 900, showing strong contacts with rising Toltec centres to the S.

82km SE of Durango, reached by passable road through rugged territory along the valley of the Río Mezquital, is **Mezquital** (1450m), in a remote area sparsely populated by Tepehuanes, known for its wildlife; but missionized by Franciscans from the 1580s. There are mineral springs in the vicinity.

We leave Durango to the E on Méx. 45. 756km **Nombre de Dios** (c 7000 inhab.; 1734m; P), in attractive surroundings, known for its mezcal (a rougher type of tequila).

It was founded in 1563 by order of Viceroy Luis de Velasco and, with its surrounding territory (c 600 sq leagues), formed an enclave of New Spain, responsible to the viceroy, until 1787. The Holy Week ceremonies here attract many local participants. Remains of the Franciscan convent of *San Francisco* (c 1566) survive.

788km *Vicente Guerrero* (P). 15km S is *Súchil*, an abandoned mining town in an area of cattle ranches and wheat farms settled by the Spaniards in the late 16C. We cross into the State of Zacatecas. At 811km (l.) a road leads N into the *Sierra de los Organos*, with basalt formations like organ-pipes.

831km **SOMBRERETE** (c 15,000 inhab.; 2351m; H,R,P), in the Valle de Sombrerete, with cobbled streets enhancing its provincial atmosphere and reminders of its mining past.

It was founded in the 1560s as the real de minas of Villa de Llerena in an area of small mining settlements, the earliest (c 1555) at San Martín, c 8km NW. In 1646 the discovery of rich ores started a boom which lasted until the end of the 17C. In the 18C the Fagoagas (marqueses del Apartado from 1772) achieved local ascendancy; their wealth increased after a tremendous

Portales at Sombrerete

silver strike in the Pabellón mine in 1791. The town suffered considerable earthquake damage in 1925. Deposits of gold, silver, copper, and lead in the vicinity do not attract the same activity as in former days.

On the l. of the street which leads to the town centre from the Durango–Zacatecas road, on the E side of its ample plaza, is the impressive church of **Sto Domingo**, built in reddish limestone by the Dominicans (1735–61), when they shared parochial duties with the Franciscans, at the charges of Fernando de la Campa y Cos, 1st conde de San Mateo de Valparaíso. Its façade shows a baroque lowest storey in contrast to the churrigueresque middle storey, full of exuberant relief, especially in the quatrefoil choir window upheld by a lushly carved pedestal in which stand out playful boyish figures. The top storey is notable for its strange caryatids. The interior contains paintings of saints by Francisco Arellano.

To the r. of the street to the town centre we may reach Pl. San Francisco and the Franciscan convent of **San Mateo**, founded in 1576. There remains the simple two-storey cloister. The church is a mid-18C rebuilding, with estípites in its façade and solomonic columns in its tower. The adjoining *Cap. de la Tercera Orden*, a pleasing oval, belongs to the 19C and has a neoclassical front. NW of San Francisco, on a height, is *La Soledad* (1740; rebuilt 1948–51), with another characterful baroque façade. Next to it is the church of *La Vera Cruz* (before 1684), with a wooden roof.

Sombrerete's main street, formerly CALLE REAL, is lined with 18–19C domestic architecture. At its SE end begins a series of portales and stands the original secular parish church, *San Juan*

Bautista (finished 1777), with a baroque façade, just before we reach Pl. Principal. It contains an interesting font and, in the chapel to the l. of the entrance, an altarpiece of 1685.

51km SW is **Chalchihuites** (10,000 inhab.; 2231m; H,P), with severe winter frosts, another old mining town. The Casa Raveles is a noticeable porfirian essay in ostentation.

Chalchihuites is also both a complex of sites and a culture. As a culture it is the farthest N extent of the Mesoamerican cultural whole, although individual traits such as the ball game and certain religious symbolisms extend farther N (cf. *Casas Grandes*).

In the Classic Period climatic change brought greater rainfall farther N and a consequent extension of Teotihuacano interest. The indigenous Chalchihuites farming peoples were exploited by Teotihuacanos prospecting for exotic stone and the result was a chain of hilltop fortresses over 100km across S Zacatecas and W Durango, overlooking farming settlements in the plains below. Archaeologists divide the cultural area into *Río Suchil* in Zacatecas and *Guadiana* in Durango, each further subdivided, chiefly on the basis of pottery variations, into numerous phases between c AD 200 and 1350. The best known sites are *La Quemada* (or *Chicomoztoc*, Rte 49) and *Chalchihuites*.

Teotihuacanos, and later Toltecs, prospected to the N in search of hematite, chert, flint, jadeite, turquoise, and cinnabar (in Querétaro). Large churned-up gravels, talus slopes, pits, and tunnels up to a few km into the hillsides attest to the extent of their mining operations. The indigenous pottery is distinguished by geometric and zoomorphic red-on-buff decorations on tripod- and plain-based vessels, and by cloisonné decoration on tripod bowls (black polished surfaces, incised with animals and geometric designs, filled with red paint)—all features which influenced ceramic developments in central Mexico in the Classic Period. The region was less important to the Aztecs, as it became drier in a reverse climate shift (see also the *Schroeder Site* near Durango, above).

As a 'site' **CHALCHIHUITES** ('precious stones') comprises a string of groups of mounds and plazas over some 19km. These were surveyed and excavated by Manuel Gamio (1908–10), Eduardo Noguera (1930 and 1960), J. Charles Kelly, and Philip Weigand. In the hills to E and W are quarry sites with complexes of rooms at ground level, presumably for the quarrymen (eg, at *La Polvareda* to the E, at *Hacienda el Vergal* to the W, at *San Rafael* to the SW, and at *Mezquital* to the N). C 8km SW of the modern town are the fortress ruins of *El Chapín*, *Cerro Colorado*, and *Pedregal Moctezuma*.

The largest group of excavated ruins are at **Hacienda Alta Vista**, SW of Chalchihuites. The site was first occupied in the late 1C BC but was most active under Teotihuacano control from c AD 350 into the 7C. There are some 750 mines in the vicinity. The site was abandoned sometime after AD 900.

The site comprises a complex of courtyards formed by platforms with house walls and other structures built in mud and stone. The largest platform group measures 36.5m each side (1332.25 sq m). A smaller group, known as the *Salón de las Columnas*, covers 400 sq m, comprising four rows of seven columns each, unevenly spaced and each c 2.8m thick, made of stone and adobe bricks covered in baked mud. Other excavated structures are small courtyards surrounded by pyramidal bases, a palace, elegant burials (one group of which was in a series of crypts), a tzompantli (skull rack), and numerous workshops. The whole site was linked by a labyrinth of rooms, inner patios, and passageways.

A particular Alta Vista speciality was turquoise-working: material was traded in from sources as far N as New Mexico, and more than 17,000 pieces were excavated. Turquoise-working seems to have been especially important after the decline of Teotihuacano control and mining. The architecture at Alta Vista is thought by Richard Diehl and other archaeologists to have set the precedent for much Toltec architecture in the 10C and 11C, especially at Tula itself.

The road runs E through a mountainous region, interspersed with plains watered by tributaries of the Río Aguanaval. 872km road l. for (5km N) **Sain Alto** (c 5000 inhab.; 2901m; H,R,P), on the l. bank of the Río Sain Alto, a small town once known for ore-processing; now a stock-raising centre. The local mines yield mercury. At approx. 892km we cross the Tropic of Cancer and at 920km join Méx. 49 at *La Chicharrona*. 937km *Fresnillo*. 990km *Zacatecas*, see Rte 46.

48 Durango to Mazatlán

The W section of Méx. 40, 319km. A famous and spectacular drive over the Sierra Madre Occidental into the State of Sinaloa and to the Pacific coast at Mazatlán. Of all the mountain roads of Mexico, it offers the finest views. It is the only highway to cross the Sierra and was opened in 1960. Slow speeds are essential and inevitable along stretches which wind round the edges of deep canyons.

From Durango we begin a climb through grazing lands on which are raised thoroughbred racehorses. After c 64km begins the steeper ascent into the Sierra Madre. 101km *El Salto* (10,000 inhab.; 2610m; H,P), a lumbering centre (pine and oak). At c 125km we reach the highest point on the road (2745m) and begin the descent to (146km) *La Ciudad* (P). 3km E (track) is the entrance to the *Parque Natural Mexiquillo*, a wild region of mountain, forest, capricious rock formation, and a famous waterfall. From the mirador *Buenos Aires* a view may be had of the *Espinazo del Diablo* (devil's backbone). At 169km we reach the *Espinazo del Diablo* (1170m), a narrow spine of land c 9km long with 500m drops on either side. From the mirador we have the widest and most breathtaking view of the Sierra.

At (201km) *El Palmito* (R,P) we cross into Sinaloa and from standard to mountain time. (Watches should be set back one hour.) The road winds through picturesque terrain, especially so in Feb.–March when flowering amapas trees cover the landscape in pale rose, past (242km; l.) **Copala**, in the 17–18C the chief place of a jurisdiction of Sinaloa and mining centre, and preserving much of the atmosphere of its past. Its 17C parish church of *San José* has a baroque altarpiece. We descend to the coastal plain. 272km **Concordia** (5000 inhab.; 100m; R,P), the former *San Sebastián*.

Francisco de Ibarra established headquarters here in 1564–65 and made it the unofficial capital of Nueva Vizcaya. In 1616–17 the colonizing Spaniards of the area were besieged here by wild and rebellious Xiximes.

The church of *San Sebastián* facing the small plaza, alongside small white-washed houses, is of the earlier 18C, its façade finely chiselled, its tower offset on the r. by a statue of St Barbara topping a thick column, its central window surmounted by a statue of St Sebastian, and its mixtilinear gable sheltering a relief of Our Lady of Guadalupe. By the sacristy doorway are statues (now headless) of two benefactors, Francisco Javier Vizcarra, 1st marqués de Pánuco, and his son.

295km *Villa Unión*, the historic Mazatlán, developed since the 1570s as a mulatto community. 319km *Mazatlán*, see Rte 22.

49 Zacatecas to Guadalajara

Méx. 54, 312km.—23km Malpaso and roads E to (26km E) Jerez and S to (196km) Bolaños, and S to (66km) Teul.—42km turning for (3km) **La Quemada**.—151km Jalapa.—312km **Guadalajara.**

We leave Zacatecas to the SW across a bleak plain to (23km; 1km r.) *Malpaso*.

Hence a minor but decent road runs W to (26km) **Jerez de García Salinas** (c 25,000 inhab.; 2027m; H,R,P), an historic place on the r. bank of the Río Jerez. Although it boasts no major monuments, its early 19C houses, with their typical patios, create a tranquil and pleasing atmosphere.

As the villa Xerez de la Frontera it was founded in 1569, by order of Viceroy Martín Enríquez de Almansa, to help safeguard lines of communication between Mexico City and Zacatecas. By 1584 only 12 Spaniards remained, the rest having been killed by Chichimecs. Famous natives include Francisco García Salinas (1786–1841), an enlightened governor of Zacatecas (1828–34), pioneer of public education and of vaccination; and Ramón López Velarde (1888–1921), the post-Modernist poet. Its spring fiesta, beginning on Holy Saturday, is a famous celebration.

The parish church of *La Inmaculada Concepción* dates from the 18C; the church of *La Soledad* from the mid-19C; its atrial gateway, railings, and pillars are an excellent combination. The *Escuela de la Torre* (1894–95) by G. Dámaso Muñetón is a major example of neo-Gothic. López Velarde's birthplace has been converted into a museum. The *Teatro Hinojosa*, a romantic 19C construction, is in the form of a horseshoe.

The road continues SW through the Sierra de Jerez to (54km) *Tepetongo* (2210m) with a 19C neo-Gothic church, and at 59km crosses into the State of Jalisco. 100km **Colotlán** (c 6000 inhab.) in the foothills of the Sierra de Zacatecas and on the l. bank of the Río Colotlán, from the late 16C chief place of a province disputed between New Spain and Nueva Galicia, and settled in part by Tlaxcaltecans loyal to the Spaniards. The parish church of *San Luis*, in red volcanic stone, is a 19C rebuilding. The chapel of *San Nicolás* preserves a baroque portal.

In 1826 G.F. Lyon lodged at Colotlán in a ground-floor room of the ayuntamiento adjoining the gaol, but crowds kept gazing in. He was accosted by a prisoner's stock of English: 'I say John English—ha ha! my boy'.

At 117km, on the border of Zacatecas and Jalisco, the road divides. The r. fork runs W in Jalisco via (15km) *Totatiche* (R,P), with a 17–18C church, and (37km) *Villa Guerrero* (R,P), and then S to (79km) **Bolaños** (c 1000 inhab.; 845m), on the Río Bolaños, a tributary of the Río Santiago (Lerma) and in the beautiful, precipitous Sierra of the same name, an isolated and semi-deserted place of great historical importance.

The silver mines (Minas de Tepeque) of the central Bolaños river valley were being worked by Spaniards, incl. Toribio de Bolaños, in the 1540s, but abandoned in the next decade, when Indians drove them out. By the 1620s miners had returned. A rich vein was discovered at Tepeque (renamed Bolaños) in 1744. During 1747–61 occurred an incredible bonanza, and viceroy conde de Revillagigedo I established a treasury office here in 1752. A revival took place in 1775–83 thanks to Antonio Bibanco from Castile. In 1798 the mines were flooded and the town practically finished.

The narrow winding streets are lined by 18C buildings. The parish church of *San José* (1753), apart from its curvetting cornice, recalls an earlier style in its three doorways and upper window. The so-called *Casa de Moneda* is well preserved and even shows delicate estípites; the former *Casa Real* (residence of the corregidor established here in 1754) is now the Pal. Municipal. C 1km S the church called *La Playa* (after the satellite mining camp of that name which sprang up in the 1740s) has signs of mid-18C work, with an upper relief of Our Lady of Guadalupe. The hanging bridge over the river is another reminder of the past.

At (86km) *Chimaltitán* (P) the former Franciscan church and convent of Santiago was founded in 1616. The cloister is now in ruins.

The l. fork at 117km runs directly S to (158km) *Guadalajara* via (22km) *Tlaltenango*, (35km) *Tepechitlán*, and (66km) **Teul de González Ortega**.

In the region between the Ríos Bolaños and Juchipila in N Jalisco and S Zacatecas, several important sites have been found and excavated. Many show Mesoamerican influence in pottery and architectural features, revealing them to be on the NW frontiers of Mesoamerica, along with the more well-known sites of La Quemada and Amapa. Known mostly from excavations, these sites were contemporaries of, and show influences from, Chalchihuites, to the NE. They include *Banco de las Casas, Las Ventanas, Totoate* (dated c AD 200–900), and *Teul*. The last, excavated in 1961, is the best known.

Occupied in the Late Classic and Postclassic Periods, Teul is dated by its figurines, which include types similar to those from the better studied region of S Nayarit (eg, Amapa). There is a ball court and ruins of other monumental structures. Teul is mentioned in the 16C by Pedro Almíndez Chirinos, who described the site as a fortress and religious city inhabited mainly by priests looking after the temples.

Another site, slightly later than Teul, is *Huistla* in the desiccated basin of Laguna de la Magdalena, near Magdalena (78km NW of Guadalajara), occupied c AD 900–1100.

From Malpaso Méx. 54 continues SW to (42km) the turning l. to (3km) **LA QUEMADA**, perhaps the farthest northern extension of agriculture in the Mesoamerican culture area, during the brief Postclassic Period of climatic shift. It was strategically located on Teotihuacano trade routes to the N, later used by the Huicholes of Jalisco and by the Toltecs. The site also figures in some versions of ancient Aztec tribal legend.

The Chichimeca. La Quemada is closely linked to the rather loosely defined Chichimecas, nomadic tribal groups in N central Mexico. Chichimeca means 'descendants of the dog', a not-very-flattering title probably given to the nomads by city-dwellers, who were periodically menaced by nomad migrations/invasions. One scholar has claimed that the ending -meca is a corruption of metl—the maguey plant—and thus refers to peoples who originated in the N plateau where the plant is common.

The Chichimecas were ancestral to many of the peoples who become known to us in the Postclassic Period through Aztec and Spanish chronicles in central Mexico, such as the Acolhuas, Otomís, Tarascans, Tenochas, Tepanecas, and other tribes of the Basin of Mexico. Among the deeds sometimes attributed to Chichimec movements are the destruction of Teotihuacán in the 7C AD, the sacking of Tula in the mid-12C AD, and the establishment of several important ceremonial centres in the Basin of Mexico, such as Colhuacán, Tenayuca, Texcoco, and Aztec Tenochtitlán itself.

The ruins at La Quemada have been known since the 17C. Fray Antonio Tello, in his 'Historia de Nueva Galicia' (c 1650), describes some ruins several leagues from Jerez, which must be La Quemada; and for no apparent reason refers to them as Tuitlán. In the 18C Juan de Torquemada and Clavijero describe ruins S of Zacatecas, and propose the theory that they belonged to the ancient Mexican tribes migrating from the N into the Basin of Mexico. Clavijero specifically refers to the site of Chicomoztoc, which in Aztec legend was the city where the seven Nahua tribes lived for nine years before dispersing to the S.

We know little of the inhabitants of the site, but can piece together several plausible histories from the evidence of both legend and excavation. G.F. Lyon described and drew a plan of the site in 1826, as did C. de Berghes in 1833 for the Vetagrande mines. The first excavations were by Leopoldo Batres (1903); later excavations were by Eduardo Noguera for the Archaeological Department of the Ministry of Education, by Ignacio Marquina, P. Armillas, and García Vega (1951–52), and by Hugo Moedano, Agustín García, and Carlos Margain for INAH. Beginning in 1955, restoration work on the Pirámide Votiva and other structures was carried out by José Corona Núñez. In 1961, test-borings into the terraces of the site recovered pottery of both Classic and Postclassic date.

La Quemada overlooks the Valle de Malpaso on the natural 'terrace' of the Cerro de la Quemada, at c 1950m above sea level, and c 150m above the valley. The names La Quemada (Burnt Place) and Chicomoztoc (Seven Caves) are relevant to legendary sources about the site; and there are in fact several caves in the surrounding hills. Other than the massive defensive acropolis structures, there is little at the site to reveal its ancient inhabitants. The 1961 borings indicate that it was occupied for c 1000 years in the Classic and Postclassic to about the middle of the 13C. The extant structures date from its heyday, c AD 900–1000. The site is of a militaristic, utilitarian nature, with no decorative frills. Any perishable structures of the peoples who farmed the valley, which presumably spread down the hillside S of the site, are gone. Some of the structures on the site resemble the apartment-like complexes of the cultures of the US Southwest, while others are of Toltec design (Tula is 450km SE). La Quemada straddles the important N trade route for hallucinogenic peyote, salt, feathers, and shells, the protection of which, and to provide a deterrent to Chichimec tribes, are probable reasons for its location. Sometime after c AD 1000, perhaps after the fall of Tula in the mid-12C or perhaps as late as c 1250, the site was burned and abandoned.

In legend Chicomoztoc was the origin of the seven nomadic Nahua or Mexican tribes— Acolhua, Chalca, Mexica, Tepaneca, Tlahuica, Tlaxcalteca, and Xochimilca—who peopled the Basin of Mexico and adjacent valleys. Even the Zapotecs and Mixtecs of Oaxaca claimed origin from the seven caves in some legends. In legend Chicomoztoc was located in the ancient land called Azatlán, variously located in Michoacán, Jalisco, or Zacatecas, where men issued from the interior of the earth through the mouths of caves. The destruction of the site is usually attributed to the Chichimeca, and often associated with the collapse of Tula, as well as with the fall of the similar fortress site of Chalchihuites, and the retraction of the N limits of Mesoamerican agriculture after the climatic reversal. It is possible that troops from La Quemada themselves participated in the sacking of Tula. Alternatively, Huichol mythology records the destruction of a fortress that dared to interfere with their N trade connections, especially with the peyote trade.

La Quemada stretches N–S c 1300m and is c 80m across at its centre, but nearly 350m at its N terrace. While the E slope is passable, the W side of the site is mostly vertical and virtually impregnable. A 30m wide causeway was built to approach from the S, rising gradually to the acropolis, over 150m higher. There are two other, narrower ways leading up from the W end of the main causeway. The site ruins include three principal groups of structures, the first on the S slope, below the main acropolis, and the other two on the acropolis itself.

At the E end of the causeway are two small pyramids flanking the entrance to the first terrace and its groups of structures. Both are in poor repair but the S one measures c 18.65 m sq at the base and rises nearly 4m. Passing between these, to the r. is the first group of structures, known as the **Catedral**. Here, a long terrace, bound by retaining walls, supports a courtyard and a columned hall reflecting Toltec influence (or the reverse?). The court measures 66.7m x 63.7m, but little of its retaining wall remains. Around the court is a raised platform; and across the court an entryway leads to the *Salón de las Columnas*, c 39.5m x c 31m, with walls 2.6m thick surviving up to 3m high.

Within the walls are 11 columns built of flat feldspar stones, originally plastered over, standing up to 4.5m high. These once supported a roof, leaving the central hall open to the sky. The building has been variously interpreted as a council chamber or ceremonial temple.

Returning across the courtyard, proceed N, up the wide platform to the acropolis and the second group of structures. On the W, the hillside drops away abruptly, while on the E a rampart wall, 9m high, is in poor repair. At the N end of this causeway, on a platform formed by retaining walls on the E, S, and W, and on the N by the retaining wall of the next level, is a small pyramid. To the N of it a stairway leads up (6m) this last retaining wall to the next level, to a rectangular courtyard fronting a five-chambered building, of unknown purpose. To the E, at a lower level, stands the Pirámide Votiva (described below).

W of this group, a second flight of steps leads to the third level, retained by a wall c 7.5m to 9m high. Bearing slightly W, a passageway leads to two courts, N and S, surrounded by walls. Built of uncut stone slabs, these walls and circumvallations stand up to 10m high and are up to 3m thick. Each court comprises a pyramid on the N side (one of them survives up to five tiers) and the ruins of multi-roomed buildings and subterranean passages, once possibly corbel-arched, on the other sides; some of these walls stand up to 4.5m high and represent the best preserved examples at La Quemada.

Flights of steps to the N, beyond the N pyramid, lead to a rocky ridge falling sharply away to the E, with some traces of ruins; and to a corridor of badly ruined pyramids and traces of retaining walls W of the ridge. Down the W slope are four more terraces. To the N side of the rocky ridge is a retained platform with a pyramid, from the N side of which a narrow causeway leads up, between a gateway, to the final redoubt, and the third group of structures. This group also comprises pyramids and courtyards, but they are in a much worse state of preservation than the others. Most notable is the circumvallation of uncut, feldspar slabs, 3m thick and 10m high with sloping sides.

Returning to the W of the causeway, near the Salón de las Columnas, a narrow path around the S tip of the cerro leads onto an esplanade, at the end of which sits the steep-sided **Pirámide Votiva**, the best preserved and restored structure at La Quemada. Built of stone slabs, it apparently reached an apex, rather than serving as a platform with a truncated top, for a temple. It is c 16.5 m sq at the base of the first tier, and the total height of this plus the pyramid proper is c 10.5m. The actual use of the pyramid, despite its suggestive name, is uncertain.

In the vicinity of La Quemada there are traces of other ruins, perhaps outposts to the main fortress. Most notable is a hilltop site at *Cerro del Cuecillo*, E of Chicomoztoc, where a small pyramid similar to those at La Quemada can be seen.

55km *Villanueva*, on the Río Malpaso and in an agricultural region. 95km (2km r.) *Tayahua*, with an 18C church, in the valley of the Río Juchipila, along which the road now continues. To the W is the Sierra de Colotlán, to the E the Sierra Fría. 105km (2km r.) *Presa el Chique*, an artificial lake harnessing the waters of the river. 121km *Tabasco* (1600m; P). 151km *Jalpa* (1800m), with an 18C church. From here Méx. 70 runs NE via (42km) *Calvillo* to (93km) *Aguascalientes*, see Rte 50.

The valley narrows towards (189km) *Juchipila* (1350m; P), where the church (mid-17C) once belonged to the Franciscan convent of San Francisco, founded in the 1540s. Their accompanying hospital building (much modified) still exists. Beyond (205km) *Moyahua* the river branches off SW from the road through the narrow, deep Cañón de Juchipila, through which the remnants of Hidalgo's defeated host made their way on 20 Jan. 1811 after Puente de Calderón. The road now crosses the Sierra de Nochistlán, covered in pine-oak forest, which reaches 2500m to the NW, into Jalisco. 263km *Ixtlahuacán del Río* (P).

27km E is *Cuquío*, where at 10 o'clock in the morning of 18 Jan. 1811, the worsted Hidalgo arrived with a few followers. He dismounted and said to those standing by: 'Alas, but do not worry, for soon we shall return'. He then ordered a breakfast of eggs.

312km *Guadalajara*, see Rte 24.

50 Zacatecas to Guanajuato

Méx. 49, Méx. 45, and Méx. 110, 324km.—27km junction with Méx. 45.— 138km **Aguascalientes**.—181km Encarnación de Díaz.—225km **Lagos de Moreno**.—268km **León**.—300km **Silao** and Méx. 110.—324km **Guanajuato**.

We leave Zacatecas via Guadalupe on Méx. 49 which goes through semi-desert country (plentiful cacti). On the r. is the Laguna Zacatecana. At 16km a road l. to the hacienda of *Tacoaleche*, the main 19C two-storey house now a school. 22km *Troncoso* (r.), with a better-preserved 19C group of buildings of another hacienda.

At 27km the road forks. Méx. 49 continues E to (162km) *San Luis Potosí*, see Rte 57. We continue SE to (48km) *Ojo Caliente* (2114m), with thermal springs. 64km *Luis Moya* (2030m), after which we keep SW on Méx. 45 and enter the State of Aguascalientes, traversing a broad plain to the E of a series of steep-edged plateaux. It is irrigated (several artificial lakes) by the waters of the Río Aguascalientes and its tributaries. 98km *Rincón de Romos* (1927m; P), in a well-irrigated and rich agricultural district, and traditionally known for the raising of fighting bulls.

The road running E just beyond Rincón de Romos climbs into the Sierra de Tepezalá, the State's principal mining region, now on the upturn after years of decay. 15km *Tepezalá* (2116m), founded as a garrison in 1573, but with 17–18C buildings being rescued from ghost-town status. The road then winds up to (27km) *Asientos* (2315m), the former real de minas of Asientos de Ibarra, with a church perhaps dating from a rich strike in 1770.

107km (5km r. across the Río Pabellón) **Pabellón de Hidalgo**, on the edge of Presa San Blas. Here in the hacienda of *San Blas*, on 25 Jan. 1811, Hidalgo surrendered command of the insurgent forces to Allende. The main house has been converted into the *Museo de la Insurgencia* (furniture, portraits, murals, documents, etc., commemorating the war of Independence). The chapel contains an anastyle altarpiece (1782 ?).

108km turning r. to (14km W) *San José de Gracia*, a few km E of *Presa Calles*, the first large artificial lake planned (1929) in Mexico as part of major irrigation works. It is also popular for regattas and with fishermen and swimmers. 130km turning r. for (6km NW) *Jesús María* (P), a small spa (thermal springs).

138km **AGUASCALIENTES** (440,000 inhab.; 1908m), capital of the State of Aguascalientes and a city as charming as its name, lies in a broad valley watered by the Río Aguascalientes and known for its thermal springs. It is also the centre of a rich agricultural region. Local industry includes cotton and textile factories, potteries and distilleries. The city stands above a network of tunnels (no adm.) of uncertain (some say prehistoric) origin. It is clean and well-run, and enjoys a warm, dry, and sunny climate.

Airport. 26km S of centre, reached along Blvd José María Chávez. Flights to *Mexico City, Guadalajara, Tijuana*, etc and to *Los Angeles*.

Bus station. S of centre, on Av. Circunvalación. Services to *Guadalajara* (5½ hrs); to *San Luis Potosí* (3 hrs); to *Zacatecas* (3 hrs); to *Guanajuato* (3½ hrs); to *Mexico City* (7 hrs); etc.

Railway station. 1km N of centre, reached along Av. Madero. Trains to *Mexico City* (6½ hrs), to *Ciudad Juárez* (c 20 hrs), and to *San Luis Potosí* (6½ hrs).

Hotels throughout the city.

Post Office. C. Hospitalidad.

Tourist Office. Pal. de Gobierno.

Fiestas. 25 Apr.: St Mark. 15 Aug.: Grape Festival.

Asunción Aguas Calientes was founded in 1575, a settlement on the Mexico–Zacatecas road. In 1857 the city became capital of the new State. In Oct.–Nov. 1914 the Convention of Aguascalientes assembled in an effort to resolve the differences between the revolutionary factions. On 2 Nov. it named Eulalio Gutiérrez, who had a reputation as 'a dynamiter of bold and inventive capacities', as provisional president. It then disintegrated into open warfare between Carranza's constitutionalists and the forces of Villa and Zapata.

The city's present look still owes much to Refugio Reyes (1862–1943), from Saucedo in Zacatecas, a self-taught architect who as a boy had helped men constructing the Teatro Calderón in Zacatecas. His work is eclectic and never less than interesting.

The State of **Aguascalientes** (682,000 inhab.; 5471 sq km) occupies part of the Mexican high plateau and extends from spurs of the Sierra Madre Occidental in the W to fertile plains in the E and SE. Tributaries of the Río Aguascalientes, which feeds the Río Verde far to the S, have been harnessed for irrigation in the N central part of the State. Valleys in the N and W are devoted to agriculture and cattle-raising; ranches raise Mexico's most renowned fighting bulls; and since the 1950s there has, thanks to irrigation, been increased production of vegetables and fruits, among them the grapes from which are made excellent wines and respectable brandy. Since the 1960s mining activity in the NE (deposits of zinc, copper, gold, silver, lead, and antimony) has received a new impulse.

After 1589 haciendas produced maize, cattle, horses, and mules for the Zacatecas mines. In 1835 Santa-Anna, having defeated the rebellious government of Zacatecas, granted Aguascalientes independence as a federal territory. (The story goes that at a ball given in his honour at the house of Pedro García Rojas he was struck by the beauty of his host's wife, Luisa Martínez Villa, and begged a kiss. She obliged and forced the issue by telling him that she had done

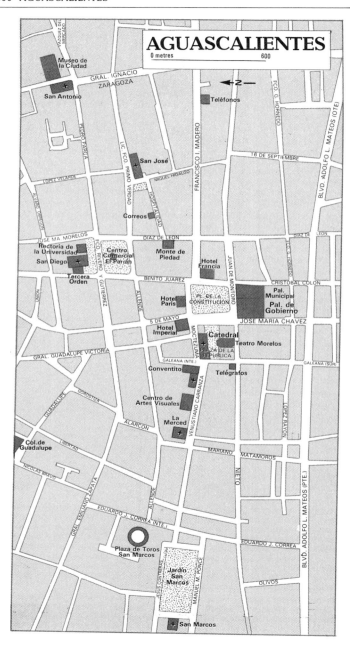

AGUASCALIENTES

0 metres — 600

Museo de la Ciudad

San Antonio

GRAL. IGNACIO ZARAGOZA

Teléfonos

VAZQUEZ DEL MERCADO

PEDRO PARGA

LIC. FCO. PRIMO VERDAD

FRANCISCO I. MADERO

FCO. G. HORNEDO

BLVD. ADOLFO L. MATEOS (OTE)

San José

16 DE SEPTIEMBRE

LOPEZ VELARDE

ALVARO OBREGON

MIGUEL HIDALGO

HOSPITALIDAD

Correos

JOSE MA. MORELOS

DIAZ DE LEON

DIAZ DE LEON

Rectoría de la Universidad

San Diego

Centro Comercial El Parián

Monte de Piedad

Hotel Francia

FCO. RIVERO Y GUTIERREZ

Tercera Orden

BENITO JUAREZ

JUAN DE MONTORO

CRISTÓBAL COLON

FCO. HORNEDO

UNION

ALLENDE

Hotel París

PL. DE LA CONSTITUCIÓN

Pal. Municipal

Pal. de Gobierno

5 DE MAYO

JOSE MARIA CHAVEZ

Hotel Imperial

Catedral

MOCTEZUMA

PLAZA DE LA REPUBLICA

Teatro Morelos

GRAL. GUADALUPE VICTORIA

GALEANA (NTE)

GALEANA (SUR)

Conventito

Telégrafos

GORISTICA

Centro de Artes Visuales

VENUSTIANO CARRANZA

LOPEZ RAYON

GUADALUPE

ALARCON

La Merced

Col. de Guadalupe

LIBERTAD

NICOLAS BRAVO

MARIANO

MATAMOROS

NIETO

ALLENDE

GRAL. EMILIANO ZAPATA

EDUARDO J. CORREA (INTE.)

BLVD. ADOLFO L. MATEOS (PTE.)

Plaza de Toros San Marcos

EDUARDO J. CORREA

Jardín San Marcos

JESUS CONTRERAS

MANUEL M. PONCE

OLIVOS

San Marcos

it in gratitude for his promise to give Aguascalientes autonomy.) But it was not until 1857 that independence as a sovereign State was confirmed.

The city centre is the commodious PL. DE LA CONSTITUCION, repaved and remodelled in 1985. The central exedra (1948) half envelops a column erected in 1807, at first in honour of Charles IV; after Independence, the bust of Ferdinand VII which crowned it was knocked down. On the SW side stands the **Pal. de Gobierno**, among the finest civic buildings in Mexico.

It was begun c 1665 as the residence of the Rincón Gallardo family, for whom the marquesado of Guadalupe was created in 1810. Its N section, and first patio, is essentially 18C work. It was restored and extended S, to include a second patio, c 1900.

EXTERIOR. The pinkish stone of windows, doorways, balconies, and parapet frieze stands out against a background of red tezontle. On either side of the central doorway and balcony, a striking combination, with whimsical arch and mouldings based on scroll patterns, are placed the simple ground-floor doorways and richly framed upper-storey balconies, on prominent pedestals and topped by family and allied coats-of-arms, occasions for more ornamental flights. At the SW angle, however, the effect is more concentrated: the doorway lintels are heavy with lambrequin designs and combine with a generous balcony which rounds the corner, makes room for an even more elaborate window, and is topped by the conspicuously jutting canopy of a corner niche.

INTERIOR. The patios, uniting lightness and grandeur, are divided by a monumental staircase. The arches, semicircular below, basket above, repeat the scroll motif in their soffits and in the low column and pilaster capitals; while the double archivolts are attractively grooved. In the S patio, on the S wall of the lower storey and N wall of the upper, are murals (1961–62) by the Chilean Oswaldo Barra, full of vitality, illustrative of the city's customs and history.

Next door is the **Pal. Municipal**, a much-altered 18C building (amplified in 1980). In the first patio are two bronze reliefs, cast in France, by Jesús Contreras (late 19C): Camaxtli, god of the chase, and Centéotl, god of abundance.
   On the W side of the plaza is the cathedral of **Nuestra Señora de la Asunción** (1704–38). Its façade, in relatively straightforward baroque, shows plentiful foliage in low relief; panels and niches holding statues of doctors of the Church framed by solomonic columns, their spirals smooth against the shafts; and, in the top storey, a relief of the Assumption. Above, is a curving and broken gable, a fantasy out of keeping with the rest.

The INTERIOR, deplorably gone over during the 19C and painted dull brown, contains 17–18C paintings. In the Baptistery (immediately l.), Baptism of Christ by Francisco Martínez. In the S (l.) aisle: Cabrera, Our Lady of Guadalupe; above entrance to Cap. del Santísimo, Juan Correa, Immaculate Conception. Above high altar, Andrés López, three scenes from the Life of St John Nepomuk (1792); to l., Cristóbal de Villalpando, Assumption; to r., Manuel Osorio, Holy Family (1720). In the N (r.) aisle, above door to antesacristy, Luis Berrueco, Visitation.
   In antesacristy, Cabrera, Sacred Hearts of Jesus, Mary, and Joseph. In Sacristy, José de Alzíbar, Death of St Joseph; Marriage of Our Lady. Cabrera, Agony in the Garden. In the offices of the bishopric on the first and second floors, Cabrera, Our Lady of the Rosary; St Barbara; St Catherine; St Gertrude; St Teresa of Avila.

On the N side of the plaza is the *Hotel París* (1914; which has served as Pal. Legislativo) by Refugio Reyes, who also designed the much-favoured *Hotel Francia* on the E side.
   On the S side of the Cathedral, Pl. de la República leads past the **Teatro Morelos** (by José Noriega, 1882–85; remodelled 1964), where from 10 Oct. to 13 Nov. 1914 was held the momentous Convention of Aguascalientes:'…delegates sat clutching their rifles and revolvers, signifying applause by crashing rifle butts on the floor. Speeches were punctuated by pistol shots'.
   At the W end of this plaza we enter C. Galeana Norte and turn r. At the corner with C. Venustiano Carranza is the *Casa de la Cultura*, a restored 18C building, once a convent. Next door on the r. along C. Venustiano Carranza is the church

of *San Ignacio* (familiarly known as *El Conventito*; 1848), with neo-Gothic touches. Further along (r.; No. 111) is the *Centro de Artes Visuales* (Mon.–Sat., 10–2, 5–9), an early 19C house restored for temporary art exhibitions, summer schools, etc. Opposite, No. 118 (*Museo Regional de Historia*—Tues.–Sun., 10–2; 5–8.30; fee) is by Refugio Reyes.

Next on the r. is **La Merced**, formerly the church of the Mercedarians; since 1906 of the Dominicans.

It was begun in 1650, but work went slowly. The façade, with its firm estípites, dates from 1773. Its great charm is the reliefs of the Holy Trinity in the capacious gable and of Our Lady of Mercy attended by saints above the window. The atrio entry and neo-Gothic tower are of the late 19C.

C. Venustiano Carranza leads W to JARDIN SAN MARCOS, laid out in 1831–48; the encompassing balustrade dates from 1842. It is bordered by 19C–early 20C houses. Celebration of the fair of St Mark (18 Apr.–5 May) is centred here.

At its W end is the church of **San Marcos** (1752–67), its façade the plainest semblance of churrigueresque. The sacristy contains an Adoration of the Magi (1775) by José de Alzíbar, probably his finest work.

Just S is the *Casino de la Feria*, incl. a monumental arena (palenque) for cockfights, with seats for 4000.

On the E side of Jardín San Marcos, C. Eduardo J. Correa Norte runs N past (l.) the *Pl. de Toros de San Marcos* (1896), one of Mexico's time-honoured bullrings, which has now given place to the plaza (1974) in Av. López Mateos Poniente (SW of Jardín San Marcos). Continuing N across C. Emiliano Zapata and (r.) along C. Nicolás Bravo, we come to the church of **Guadalupe** (1767–89), with a churrigueresque façade.

The size of its lower storey gives room for raised, elegant estípites and entrecalles of unusual length, so laden with relief that they seem to drip decoration. The central panel continues uninterrupted by the cornice; elegance also marks it, from the delicate multifoil pattern of the door archivolt through the window canopy to the clock-tower finial. The adjoining convent was assigned to teaching nuns of the Company of Mary (see Rte 4) in 1807.

From the convent C. Guadalupe runs SE to C. Guadalupe Victoria, where we turn r. to join C. Rivero y Gutiérrez. Turning l. along this street we come to (l.) the church of **San Diego**, facing S across a small garden, with, on its W side, the *Cap. de la Tercera Orden*.

The foundation (c 1647) was for the Carmelites, but was taken over by discalced Franciscans (dieguinos), who finished the work in 1682.

The chapel façade seems a throwback to a simple Renaissance style, but was renovated in 1896. The saintly images in the niches add an ingenuous touch. Among the interior paintings, the Child Jesus appearing to St Antony, by Juan Correa.

Behind the high altar of the church is the circular *Camarín de la Virgen*, built in baroque style in 1792–97, but with neoclassical additions. In the Sacristy are three Scenes from the Life of St Francis (1681), in one canvas, by Juan Correa; St Philip of Jesus by Nicolás Rodríguez Juárez; and Souls in Purgatory (1719) by Antonio de Torres.

On the r. of the church is the former convent, transformed in 1846 into the Instituto Científico y Literario and in 1973 into the rectory of the new University of Aguascalientes. Opposite, and occupying the whole block, is the *Parián*, a covered market.

C. Pedro Parga continues E to the church of **San Antonio**, most ambitious work of Refugio Reyes, for which he yielded to eclecticism's fullest flights.

It was built, in ochre stone from Ciénega Grande, in 1896–1908. Its style is a marvellous mixture of neo-baroque (cupola volutes), classical (columns, friezes, festoons, and balustrades), and moorish (central tower). The cost was enormous. The organ came from Germany; the statues from Italy; various ornaments from Paris; and the bells from the USA. The medallion paintings (Life and Passion of Christ) are by Candelario Rivas.

Opposite the church in C. Zaragoza (No. 505) is the **Museo de la Ciudad** (Tues.–Sun., 10.30–2; 4–7.30).

It was originally destined (1914) as the *Escuela Normal para Maestros*, but altered in 1915–16 in neoclassical style by Refugio Reyes to house the *Escuela Normal del Estado* (until 1974).

The museum's permanent collection centres on the works of native artists. In rooms C, D, and E are paintings, studies, and sketches by Saturnino Herrán (1887–1918), who used prehispanic themes and costumbrismo for inspiration. ROOM C: Sepia sketches and studies in crayon (incl. portrait of his wife). Among oil paintings: 'El Jarabe'; 'La criolla del mango' (1916); 'La criolla del rebozo'; 'La criolla de la mantilla' (1917); 'El gallero' (1914); portrait of Gonzalo Arguelles Bringas (1917). ROOM D: charcoal and crayon studies for his most famous work, 'Nuestros Dioses' (1914–17). ROOM E: more oils, incl. 'La ofrenda' (1913), another fine work; 'El Quetzal' (1916); 'El trabajo' (1908), his first signed work; 'Alegoría de la Construcción'.

ROOM B contains paintings, sketches, watercolours, engravings, and typographic designs by Gabriel Fernández Ledesma (b. 1900). The SALA DR J. DIAZ DE LEON contains another, and utterly charming, of the city's paintings by Juan Correa, portraying the young St Clare, about to renounce the world, importuned by a suitor.

A little to the E, facing C. Vázquez del Mercado, is the *Castillo Douglas* (1917), designed for a family of Scots descent by Refugio Reyes.

We may make our way back to the centre along Cs Pedro Parga and Rivero y Gutiérrez, turning r. along C. Benito Juárez, on the W side of the Parián. At the SW corner of Cs Juárez and Allende is the *Casa de la Gardenia* (now the *Biblioteca Jaime Torres Bodet*; 1916) and at No. 3 C. Juárez (NE corner of the plaza) the former *Banco de Zacatecas* (1906), both by Refugio Reyes.

Two more works by him may be seen in C. Juan de Montoro, which runs into the SE corner of the plaza—No. 103 (the *Juzgado de Distrito*; District Court) and No. 215, a private house.

By following C. Díaz de León S across Blvd López Mateos to C. Abasolo we reach the church of **El Encino** (1773–96), its atrio facing a peaceful garden.

The EXTERIOR, in stone of pinkish ochre, is in subdued churrigueresque, its graceful composition, full of decorative detail recalling tapestry work, belying its original function as a barrio chapel. The façade gently curves, marked off on either side by engaged columns. The two pairs of tall estípites add to the effect of slenderness and emphasize the central panel, with the door arch allowing plays of volutes and the oval, four-lobed recessed window.

The INTERIOR contains a monumental Stations of the Cross (14 canvases) painted in Mexico City in 1798–1800 by Andrés López, helped by his brother Cristóbal. Grief, urgency, dignity, and the suffering of the exhausted Christ are brought home with drama and verve, against a sombre background of massive buildings. In the Baptistery, Baptism of Christ by Juan Correa.

On the r. of the church the former presbytery has been adapted as the **Museo José Guadalupe Posada** (Tues.–Sun., 10–2, 3.30–7), containing some of the output of the graphic artist (1852–1913) whose bitterly satirical works against the porfiriato played a part in bringing it down. The collection includes the plates from which his early works were printed.

W of Aguascalientes, Méx. 70 runs into the Sierra Madre past (15km; r.) *Presa Abelardo L. Rodríguez* to (45km) turning l. for (4km S) *Malpaso* (small lake). 51km **Calvillo** (6000 inhab.; 1704m; P), in the Valle de Huéjucar (famous mountain views). The town, full of simple 18C buildings, and surrounding area are Mexico's primary producer of guavas. The road continues SW to (93km) *Jalpa*, see Rte 49.

The E extension of Méx. 70 from Aguascalientes crosses the Sierra de Comanja to (53km) turning r. for (4km S) **Ciénega de Mata**, from the 17C, as *Concepción Ciénega de Rincón*, part of the vast estate of the Rincón Gallardo family. The main hacienda buildings (incl. a baroque chapel and collections of arms, maps, and other mementoes) are not open to the public, though permission to visit may sometimes be granted. Méx. 70 continues to (86km) **Ojuelos** (c 10,000 inhab.; 2284m; R,P), a fascinating town, grown from a 16C garrison on the Mexico-Zacatecas road, in the NE extremity of Jalisco. The area of the fort, maintained c 1570–90, and later adapted as a hacienda compound (the pretty chapel was added in the 18C), has been restored, with its tower and central plaza.

The 18C town centre preserves its old marketplace (*Parián*, now known as Pl. Hidalgo)—the arcade has an oriental flavour; its charming little parish church; and coaching inns.

Méx. 70 continues NE to (168km) *San Luis Potosí*, see Rte 57.

We continue S on Méx. 45 to (158km) *Peñuelas*. The hacienda here (18C chapel) was scene of a battle on 15 June 1860 when the liberal Gen. Jesús González Ortega defeated the conservative Gen. Silverio Ramírez, who held it with superior forces. This victory enabled the liberals to take Aguascalientes and put the Bajío at their mercy. 165km the State border with Jalisco. At 167km the road forks.

The r. fork gives on to a road which runs through the broad valley of the Río Aguascalientes into NE Jalisco, a region known as *Los Altos*, between the Sierras Arandas, Tepatitlán, and Comanja. It is characterized by clean, well-kept towns with leafy gardens; a population attached to its social and religious creole traditions; and its many haciendas. 43km **Teocaltiche** (H,R,P), settled in the mid-16C as an Indian village belonging to the crown. The contemporary hospital (now a cultural centre) and chapel survive, founded by the Franciscans whose small convent (no longer existing) was taken over by seculars in 1551. The parish church dates from the mid-19C.

Cerro Encantado (no structure remains), c 10km SE of Teocaltiche, when excavated yielded artefacts common to shaft-tomb sites, but no such tombs. In one burial there was a pair of mushroom-horned figurines—male–female pair, dated by associated radiocarbon samples to AD 100–250. Pottery from the site resembles that from the Chalchihuites region.

From Teocaltiche a road runs W and then S on the E side of the Sierra de Nochistlán to (54km) *Yahualica*, then S to join (115km) Méx. 80 just SW of *Tepatitlán*, see below.

The alternative route from Teocaltiche is SE through Los Altos, country drained by tributaries of the Río Verde, to (82km) *Jalostotitlán* (1730m), with a neo-baroque parish church. From here we join Méx. 80 SW to (135km) **Tepatitlán** (26,000 inhab.; 1860m; H,R,P), a key agricultural and stock-raising centre, and a centre of Catholic fervour during the Cristero war. The locals have a reputation for fair hair and good looks. The towers and portico of the grand 19C parish church of *San Antonio* were added in 1911–25 by Martín Pozos. The sanctuary of *Guadalupe* (1875–93) is by José María Pozos. Hence Méx. 80 runs SW across a region of plateaux to (176km) *Zapotlanejo* and (209km) *Guadalajara*, see Rte 24.

Méx. 45 continues S to (181km) **Encarnación de Díaz** (1864m; H,R,P) on the Río Encarnación. The parish church on the main plaza (adorned with bizarrely shaped topiary hedges) dates from the 18C, while the church of *Jesús, María y José*, with its huge cupola, is a typical 19C creation.

225km **LAGOS DE MORENO** (c 50,000 inhab.; 1940m; H,R,P), on the Río de San Juan de los Lagos, stands at crossroads and on the Mexico–Ciudad Juárez railway. The old centre is charming and peaceful, with attractive 18–19C houses.

Sta María de los Lagos was founded in 1563, c 5 leagues W of the Comanja mines and as a strongpoint on the Mexico–Zacatecas road. In 1604 Alonso de la Mota y Escobar wrote that its situation was 'the finest in the kingdom'. But after 1882 the railroad put its stagecoach and muletrain provisioning business into decline. Among famous natives are the insurgent Pedro Moreno (1775–1817), after whom Lagos was renamed in 1829; and the poet José Rosas Moreno (1838–83).

The river S of the centre is crossed by an 18C bridge; on the N side is the ALAMEDA, bordered on the S by Paseos Ribera and Pedro Moreno, elegant porfirian reminders. On the N side of PL. PRINCIPAL is the majestic parish church of **La Asunción de María**, in rosy stone, raised on a platform approached on all sides by broad flights of steps.

It is a work of the mid to late 18C, started by the parish priest Diego José Cervantes (d. 1766) and continued by his successor, Juan José Aguilera (d. 1797).

EXTERIOR. The tall graceful towers (completed in the 19C) add to the impression of great height. Set back from their bases, the façade centrepiece is a work of inexpressible refinement, combining late baroque and rococo, resembling a slender folding screen, and alive with down-turned spiral, lambrequin, and plaited capital motifs. On either side of the main door (which bears the date 1777), and at a slant to it, are two ornamental niche pilasters, their saintly images set well forward. Above their cornices are rocaille-type niches, shallow and like mirrors. The cornice above the choir window breaks in its centre to form a rippling support for the pedestal of the statue of Our Lady. Crowning all is a beautiful scalloped arch. The side doorways are in similar style, with prominent medallion relief. At the rear, the sacristy portal is remarkably eclectic, its arch, in ogee form, flanked by solomonic columns; its wavy cornice is broken by a scallop; above it, an intricate relief enveloping monograms.

The altarpieces of the INTERIOR are unworthy 19C substitutions. The drum of the cupola and the pendentives below have kept their original estípite supports, sculptured images, and relief. The sacristy, at the N end, is entered through two finely carved doorways.

Two blocks E of Pl. Principal, facing its little plaza, is the restored church and convent of *Las Capuchinas*, founded in 1756; the church walls decorated with striking mortar relief. Opposite is the *Teatro Rosas Moreno* (begun in 1887, restored in the 1960s), imaginatively grand, with a neo-Renaissance façade marked by bold cornices, the work of Primitivo Serrano Flores.

On the N side of Pl. de la Merced, W of Pl. Principal, are the church and convent of *La Merced*, founded in 1685, but unsuitably rebuilt.

Lagos boasts two notable 19C churches: *El Calvario*, its slanting façade loaded with classicizing finish, but the towers neo-baroque, was consecrated in 1873; *La Luz* was built during 1868–1913.

Méx. 80 runs through Lagos NW via (68km) *Ojuelos* where it joins Méx. 70 to (150km) *San Luis Potosí*, see Rte 57. In the opposite direction it goes SW to (195km) *Guadalajara*, see above.

46km along the latter road is **San Juan de los Lagos** (c 30,000 inhab.; 1740m; H,R,P), a pleasant town and one of Mexico's main pilgrimage centres.

It was founded in the late 16C as San Juan Mezquititlán and owes its fame to a miracle-working statue of Our Lady made of caña de maíz brought here by Fray Miguel de Bolonia in 1623. Pilgrims come from far and wide at all times of the year; the principal celebrations culminate on 8 Dec. (feast of the Immaculate Conception) and 2 Feb. (Candlemas). The conspirators of Querétaro (see Rte 37) originally planned to start the active movement for Independence here on 8 Dec. 1810, with a call to arms by Ignacio Allende. The discovery of their plans forced Hidalgo to bring the date forward. During the war of the Reform the liberal Gen. Miguel Blanco stripped the basilica of treasure, worth 100,000 pesos. He left a valueless receipt for 40,000.

Facing the main plaza is the basilica of *Nuestra Señora de San Juan de los Lagos*, in typical pinkish stone, begun in 1732. The façade, narrowed by the soaring towers, is baroque, but with classicizing niches in the gable. Our Lady's statue, the face grave yet tender, is on the high altar in a silver tabernacle. In the Camarín de la Virgen behind the high altar are six oil paintings on copperplate, often attr. Rubens; but in fact the work of a Spanish studio, and ordered in the 1750s.

Méx. 45 continues SE into the State of Guanajuato to (268km) **LEON** (c 930,000 inhab.; 1885m), an ever growing industrial city on the Río Gómez and on the W side of the Bajío. It is one of the world's most important leather-working centres and its factories turn out shoes of high quality (and reasonable prices) both for home consumption and for export.

Airport. On the road to Silao, c 15km S of the centre. Flights to *Mazatlán, Mexico City, Monterrey*, and *Puerto Vallarta*.

Bus station. 2km W of Pl. de la Constitución, reached by C. Culiacán on N side of Blvd Adolfo López Mateos. Services to *Guanajuato* (2 hrs); to *Uruapan* (2 hrs); to *Irapuato* (3 hrs); to *Salamanca* (4 hrs); to *Lagos de Moreno* (1 hr); to *Mexico City* (6 hrs); to *Aguascalientes* (4 hrs); to *Querétaro* (3 hrs).

Railway station. S side of city, reached along Av. Venustiano Carranza. On the Mexico–Ciudad Juárez line.

Hotels throughout the city.

Post Office. Corner of Cs. Pedro Moreno and 5 de Mayo.

Tourist Office. SW side of Pl. de la Constitución, in C. Juárez.

Fiestas. 20 Jan.: St Sebastian, coinciding with agricultural and industrial fair.

Villa de León was founded in 1576, on the Mexico–Zacatecas road. Floods occurred in 1637, 1649, 1749, 1762, and 1803. In 1817 Francisco Javier Mina successfully attacked it. In July 1888 a flood killed 252 people, destroyed over 2500 houses, and caused an exodus, which lost León its place as Mexico's second most populous city. On 1–5 July 1915, in one of the decisive battles of the Revolution, Obregón's forces defeated the remnants of Villa's División del Norte. In 1926–28 the forces of Gen. Daniel Sánchez combating the Cristeros subjected the city to terror: priests and laymen were shot. In 1937 was founded here the Unión Nacional Sinarquista, a fascist movement. Its followers demonstrated in 1946 against alleged fraud in municipal elections and occupied the Pal. Municipal. A massacre ensued when the army fired into the crowd: nearly a hundred were killed or wounded.

The portales of PL. DE LA CONSTITUCION (or *Pl. de los Mártires*) date from 1828. On the N side, the *Casino* (1905) and *Hotel Francés* (c 1870) occupy the site of the old *Casas Consistoriales*. On the W side is the handsome **Pal. Municipal**, a reconstruction (1859–68) by Juan F. Contreras of the Colegio de Nuestra Señora de la Luz. Next door (r.) is the parish church of **El Sagrario** (late 18C), built by the Franciscans, who had charge after 1589. The façade was finished in 1836; the N doorway is a relic of their 17C church. At its W end is the *Cap. de la Tercera Orden* (mid-18C). The convent buildings were demolished in 1953.

On the N of the church opens PL. DE LOS FUNDADORES. On its N side the arcade dates from the late 18C; on the E, the *Hotel México* is a converted 18C building.

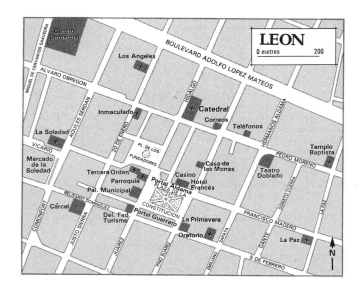

From the SW corner of the plaza we may reach, along C. Josefa Ortiz, the neoclassical church of *La Soledad*, begun in the late 18C, its doorway of the early 19C. The altars date from 1806. Next door is *Mercado de la Soledad*.

Parallel to the W side of the plaza, C. 20 de Enero runs N to join Av. Alvaro Obregón. At the corner is the neo-Gothic church of *El Inmaculado Corazón de María* (1890–1906), with a soaring spire. Further up across Av. Obregón on the l. we come to **Nuestra Señora de los Angeles**, most distinguished of leonese churches, finished in 1808.

Its convex façade, a unique and daring late baroque work, a fantasy of mellifluous curves, is marked by ambitious composite pilasters stamped by ornate medallions, as frames for saintly reliefs in the lowest storey and mirror-like in the first and second. In the gently sloping entrecalles spread elegant empty niches. From the capitals sprouts swelling relief. The cornices are wonderfully bold, the lowest protecting the ground-floor level like a canopy. Above the doorway rises the central panel, full of sinuous relief and moulding, with its own elaborations on the lambrequin motif. The sculptures of the INTERIOR are by Sixto Muñoz (c 1830).

Av. Obregón runs E. At the corner with C. Hidalgo rises the cathedral of **Nuestra Señora de la Luz**, many years in building.

It was begun by the Jesuits as their new church (*Compañía Nueva*; their old church, *Compañía Vieja*, was finally destroyed in 1901), in 1760, and left half-finished after their expulsion in 1767. Work was pushed forward after 1864 by León's purposeful bishop, José María Díez de Sollano y Dávalos (1820–81), a paragon among 19C Mexican prelates. Its finishing architect was the Englishman Lewis Long, who made his home in the city. It was finally consecrated in 1889.

EXTERIOR. The side doorway facing C. Hidalgo is a survival from the Jesuit foundation. The S entries to the atrio (1878–80) are sumptuously neo-baroque, while the main S façade is neo-Mannerist. The l. (W) tower dates from 1876, the r. tower from 1878. The cupola, designed by Manuel Gómez, was in progress in 1862.

The INTERIOR has an abundance of classicizing motifs. The high altar dates from 1902; the murals are by Candelario Rivas. In the chapel of *San José* (1891–92) Long audaciously combined Mudéjar and classical elements. In the *Sala Capitular* are eight portraits of canons by the leonese portraitist Juan Nepomuceno Herrera (1818–78).

Further along in C. Pedro Moreno, on the opposite corner to the *Correos*, is what remains of the 18C *Casa Obregón*. At the next corner in C. Pedro Moreno stands the *Teatro Doblado* (1869–90; restored) by José Noriega.

C. 5 de Mayo goes S back to Pl. de la Constitución past (r.) the **Casa de las Monas** (1870), by Manuel Guedea Coraza, an attractive blend in neoclassical style, which served as Pal. de Gobierno when León became temporary State capital in 1914–16. Francisco Villa lodged here in 1915.

At the SE corner of the plaza is *La Primavera* (finished in 1908), an early department store by Lewis Long. A little further along Av. 5 de Febrero is *San Felipe Neri* (*Oratorio*; 1835–39), the Oratorian church. In the sacristy is a portrait by Herrera of the first provost of the congregation in León, José Manuel Somera y Landeta (d. 1846).

23km SW of León is **San Francisco del Rincón** (c 40,000 inhab.; 1760m; H,R,P), a spa town which contains a museum dedicated to the works of Hermenegildo Bustos (1832–1907), a highly individual and self-taught portraitist, born at *Purísima de Bustos* 3km W. C 30km SW of San Francisco del Rincón are the ruins of *La Gloria*, a Postclassic fortress-like group of structures on a ridge somewhat similar to La Quemada in Zacatecas.

To the NE of León a road winds through the Sierra de Guanajuato to (94km) **San Felipe** (*San Felipe Torres Mochas*—'stubby [ie, unfinished] towers'; 12,000 inhab.; 2130m; H,R,P), set in the mountains where rises the Río Laja, on the central plateau.

The villa of San Felipe was founded in 1562. In 1793 the parish was assigned to Fr Miguel Hidalgo. He found the place congenial and his house became a flourishing cultural centre, informally called 'La Francia chiquita' (France in miniature, where, among other things, French revolutionary ideas were discussed). 'The life the said priest leads here', an observer informed the Inquisition, 'they assure me that in general it is a constant diversion. He either studies history, to which he has dedicated himself, or gambles, or diverts himself with music, for he has hired a complete orchestra whose members are his table companions; and he treats them like his family'. He left in Sept. 1803 for Dolores.

The unfinished parish church of *San Felipe*, originally part of a Franciscan convent founded c 1583, dates from the late 17C. Also unfinished is the church of *La Soledad* (early 18C) where Hidalgo also officiated. At No. 9 C. Hidalgo is *La Francia Chiquita*, Hidalgo's house, now a small museum (Tues.–Sun., 9–2, 4–6).

From San Felipe, Méx. 51 runs 62km NW to *Ojuelos* (see above) and 53km SE to *Dolores Hidalgo*, see Rte 52.

The road (Méx. 37) continues NE to (128km) the former hacienda of *Jaral de Berrio*, once property of the Berrio family, and scene of one of Mina's successful assaults, in July 1817. The huge main house was built in the mid-19C. Hence we may continue into the State of San Luis Potosí to (192km) *San Luis Potosí*, see Rte 57.

300km **SILAO** (31,000 inhab.; 1770m; H,R,P), on the W edge of the Bajío.

On 10 Aug. 1860 occurred here one of the decisive battles of the war of the Reform. The liberals under González Ortega, after three hours of furious fighting, defeated the conservatives under Miramón and Mejía, and put the latter's famous cavalry to flight.

The church of **Santiago**, its second tower unfinished, has a regular baroque façade (1730), culminating in a great relief of St Christopher. The sanctuary of *Guadalupe* (1818–48) is suitably imposing. At the corner of Cs 5 de Mayo and Francisco I. Madero is the house where Francisco Javier Mina was held prisoner before being shot in Oct. 1817.

Méx. 45 continues SE to (33km) *Irapuato*, see Rte 36.

We continue E on Méx. 110. At 308km a road runs N to (12km) the *Cerro del Cubilete* (2480m), on which stands a 20m high bronze statue of Christ the King.

The cornerstone of the monument, very near the geographical centre of the republic, was laid amid scenes of ostentatious piety in Jan. 1923 in the presence of the apostolic delegate and four abps and eight bps in full pontificals and riding on palfreys. 50,000 attended. Two days later an angry Pres. Obregón expelled the apostolic delegate. The statue, by Fidias Elizondo, was finished c 1929.

324km *Guanajuato*, see Rte 51.

51 Guanajuato

GUANAJUATO (c 70,000 inhab.; 2050m), capital of the State of Guanajuato, is dramatically wedged in the Cañada de Marfil at the junction of three ravines, in that part of the Sierra de Guanajuato known as the Sierra de Media Luna. It is a city of incomparable beauty and fascination, a 'lovely vision', a hostage to the intricate geography of its setting. From the limited ramifications of its main thoroughfare, numerous narrow streets and alleys, interspersed with tiny irregular plazas and lined by quaint old houses painted in bright colours, twist and turn, rise and fall, against the ravine slopes. The climate is benign throughout the year, with moderate summer and early autumn rains.

Guanajuato attracts visitors from far and wide; but remains largely unspoiled, holding firmly to its traditions. A high proportion of its domestic architecture, popular and official, and distinguished for its balconies and railings, dates from the 18C and early 19C. Its churches, built in a period of mining riches, are among the high points of Mexican churrigueresque.

Bus station. In SW outskirts. Services to *San Miguel de Allende* (2 hrs); to *León* (1 hr); to *Dolores Hidalgo* (1 hr); to *San Luis de la Paz* (2½ hrs); to *Guadalajara* (7 hrs); to *Morelia* (4 hrs); to *Querétaro* (4 hrs); to *Mexico City* (6 hrs); etc.

Railway station. W end of town, in C. Tepetapa. Slow services to neighbouring towns.

Hotels throughout the town.

Post Office. 25 C. Ayuntamiento.

Tourist Office. 14 Pl. de la Paz.

Fiestas. 23 June: Presa de Olla. 7–14 Nov.: Las Iluminaciones.

Entremeses Cervantinos. During spring university students perform one-act interludes (entremeses) by Cervantes, Lope de Vega, Francisco Quevedo, Calderón, and other 16–17C playwrights. Pl. San Roque, candlelit for the occasions, is the main venue.

Festival Internacional Cervantino. First staged in 1972, this festival, held in May both outdoors, in the various plazas, and in the theatres, brings acting companies, dance groups, orchestras, and musicians from all over the world.

In prehistoric times the region around Guanajuato was inhabited by the Otomí, who are now confined mostly to a few isolated mountainous areas. Their name, meaning 'bird-arrows', hints at their semi-nomadic lifestyle in the Preclassic and Classic Periods. As late as AD 900 many still lived in cave sites and practised a hunting and gathering economy; others settled into agricultural towns in the central plateau of the region during the Classic Period, and may have taken part in the downfall of Teotihuacán in the 7C. In one legend they are referred to as the Otontlaca, and related to the general mass of the Chichimec tribes. They moved into the N Basin of Mexico following the Chichimec invasions/migrations under the leader Xólotl, and their own leader is said to have married Xólotl's daughter. The principal Otomí town in the Basin was Xaltocán, later subdued by the Tepaneca of Azcapotzalco, and later still by the Mexica Aztecs. Another Otomí group settled at Cuauhtitlán and eventually extended their domain into the Toluca, Mezquital, and Anáhuac valleys during the 8C AD. In the 10C some Otomí were incorporated into the Toltec hegemony. In the late Postclassic the Otomí in the NE of the Basin of Mexico came under Tarascan rule and their principal town was called Cuanaxhuata ('hill of frogs'). Characteristic features of the Postclassic Otomí included body tattooing and blackening of the teeth similar to Huastec fashion. Their principal deities were the gods of fire and of the moon; mushrooms were used as hallucinogens in divination ceremonies.

In 1546 Rodrigo Vázquez started a ranch 'near the source of a river which men called Guanaxuato'. In 1552 mineral deposits were discovered. In 1557 a real de minas was founded—'Santa Fe, Real y Minas de Quanaxhuato'; in 1558 the opening-up of the Mellado and then the Rayas veins laid the foundations of future wealth and by 1570, 600 Spanish miners occupied the camps of Sta Ana and Sta Fe. In 1741 a decree of Philip V gave Guanajuato the status of city by reason of 'the advantageous conveniences which its abundant mines of gold and silver offer which make [it] singular and estimable above all those discovered'. In 1760 Antonio de Obregón y Alcocer, 1st conde de Valenciana (1720–86), opened the Valenciana mine. After 1769 its output was enormous and by 1774 it was producing 800–1000 loads of ore a week. The reforms of Gálvez provoked serious riots in 1766–67; nine troublemakers were hanged, nearly 200 imprisoned, and a paramilitary force was formed to patrol the streets: 'to control the insults of a populace as numerous as it is vicious and insolent'. By the end of the 18C Guanajuato was the world's leading silver producer, with a population of 78,000. The yield of its chief mines—Rayas, Mellado, Cata, Sirena, Tepeyac, Valenciana—situated within a distance of 1985m along the central lode, the Veta Madre, running a fairly straight line SE to NW of the city, equalled the entire production of Peru. The upheavals of 1810 and the abandonment of the mines led to decay and depopulation. Iturbide's spell as army commander in the Bajío in 1815–16 aggravated the decline. A guanajuatense priest, Antonio Labarrieta, denounced his cruelty and theft of 1,300,000 pesos from the Casa de Moneda. The city gaol, it was reported, was crowded with women relatives of insurgent leaders. In 1858 Juárez assumed the presidency here before moving on to Guadalajara. During the porfiriato prosperity returned, with investment in the mining industry. The Revolution spelt renewed decline. Since the 1940s there has been a tentative mining resurgence.

The Río Guanajuato, covered by vaulting and bridges, its flow obstructed by sediment, flooded disastrously in 1760, 1770, 1772, 1780, 1794, 1804, 1867, 1873, and 1905. In 1908 the waters were diverted into a tunnel beneath the level of the riverbed. The former course, c 2900m long, was forgotten. Between 1951 and the mid-1960s, however, the authorities cleared the silt and accumulated rubbish, installed drainage, and built a subterranean avenue, the present C. Belaunzarán and Av. Hidalgo, which has helped to keep the centre clear of major traffic.

Guanajuato has kept the quaint old names of its narrow streets and alleys—eg, Salto del Mono (Monkey-jump), La Cervatana (Blowpipe), El Ramillete (Nosegay), Cinco Señores, Cuatro Vientos, La Casualidad (Chance), and, most famous of all, El Beso (The Kiss), so narrow that kisses can be planted through opposite upstairs windows.

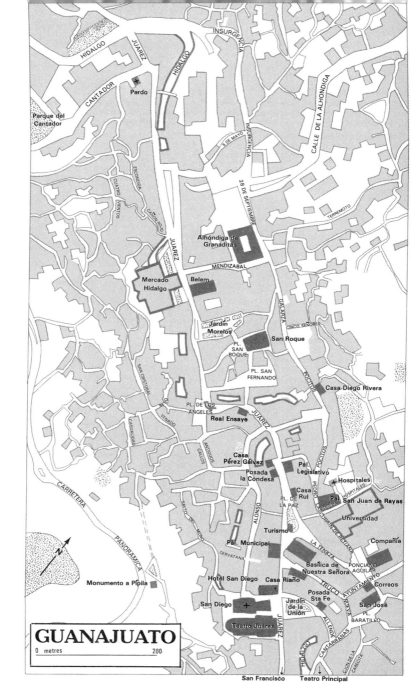

GUANAJUATO

0 metres   200

The State of **Guanajuato** (c 3.8 million inhab.; 30,589 sq km) lies mostly on the High Plateau. Its SE region touches the volcanic axis and the NE the Sierra Madre Oriental. The Bajío covers its S half, which makes it one of the most developed agricultural areas of the republic. Various tributaries of the Río Lerma, which forms the border with Michoacán, drain it. Mining, though not on the intense scale of the past, has revived somewhat: silver and gold, and tin, opals, lead, mercury, and copper.

The partition of the Bajío lands among encomenderos, the founding of Silao, Celaya, and León, and the pacification of the Chichimecs—all underlined the region's vital role in the economy of New Spain, independent of Mexico City, and ensured a mainly creole and mestizo population. In 1786 Guanajuato became one of the nine intendancies. The intendant Juan Antonio de Riaño (1792–1810), humane and kindly, won widespread praise as one of the best administrators in New Spain, his family circle imbued with the ideas of the French Enlightenment. The war of Independence had its beginnings here and the years 1811–15 saw Iturbide's pitiless campaigns—'his bloody sword stained to the hilt'—against guerrillas. In 1817 took place the brief but brilliant incursion into the territory of Francisco Javier Mina, the Spaniard who had espoused the cause of Independence. In 1824 Guanajuato became a State, although it was periodically to lose this status. In 1885 Díaz installed Manuel González, the corrupt former president, as governor, who ruled until his death in 1893: all the bandits in the State, he declared, had been killed except himself. The Revolution, the Cristero war, and the Sinarquista movement left a legacy of violence.

The three-sided JARDIN DE LA UNION, planted with Indian laurels, is favoured in the evenings, for strolling, lingering at the outdoor cafés, and listening to band concerts. On its W side is the *Posada Santa Fe* (late 18C), reconditioned in 1942. On the S is the church of **San Diego**, its façade an unusual churrigueresque.

It belonged to the convent of discalced Franciscans founded in 1667. Church and convent were rebuilt after flood damage in 1780–84. The conde de Valenciana defrayed half the cost. On 25 Nov. 1810 the priest José Belaunzarán stood before the doorway, crucifix in hand, and remonstrated with Manuel Flon (conde de la Cadena), Calleja's second-in-command, against the latter's order that anyone found in this street should have his throat cut. He was partly successful, though Flon next day ordered summary executions in the Alhóndiga (see below).

EXTERIOR. The façade, gently concave, is, within a certain irregularity, a model of proportion and delicate detail. Its lower storey is marked off by slender fluted columns. The central supports are finest ornamental niche pilasters, the niches framed in rococo relief. Estípites, with central medallions, stand either side of the doorway. In the upper storey, caryatids rest on inverted cones swathed in spiral moulding.

The INTERIOR was overtaken by neoclassicism, though the sacristy doorways date from the late 18C rebuilding. In the sacristy the altarpiece of Our Lady of Solitude contains paintings (c 1750) by Nicolás Enríquez. The cupola drum was made exceptionally high at the expense of the pendentives, cut off below the keys of the presbytery and transept arches.

Next door to the church is the **Teatro Juárez**, a well-meaning but incompatible display of grandeur.

The design was entrusted in 1873 to José Noriega, but work was suspended for lack of funds. In 1891 it was resumed under Antonio Rivas Mercado. On 27 Oct. 1903 occurred the 'sumptuous inauguration...an aristocracy full of refinement and authentic elegance filled the salon, attired and bejewelled like any court of Europe...During the performance the foremost spectacle was the audience, fragrant with delicate perfumes, full of beautiful women, exquisitely dressed and splendidly bejewelled. Señor General don Porfirio Díaz came, accompanied by his select Cabinet and members of the diplomatic corps. With indescribable sumptuousness they staged the opera "Aida", so well suited to grand theatrical display. Outstanding were the beautiful and sublime artists Grissi and Pozzi and the singers Logobardi and Ottoboni...'

The EXTERIOR, with its great portico, its two rows of fluted columns, and upper balustrade, is more afrancesado than neoclassical. Along the balustrade are statues, in blue-green stone (supplied by W.H. Mullen, of Salem, Ohio), of eight of the Muses. (There was no room for the ninth.) The INTERIOR, entered through the sumptuous foyer and graced by a grand staircase, is decked out in various styles. The decoration of the auditorium is lavish with endless patterns of arabesques and flowers; the boxes are lush with scarlet upholstery; the front curtain was designed by Labastá, from the Opéra Comique in Paris. The carpets, seats, sculptures, and candelabra in the smoking room (fumador) and bars were imported from France; the stained glass from Italy.

From Jardín de la Unión we may take the narrow C. de la Paz W. No. 4 is the birthplace of the historian Luis González Obregón (1865–1938). No. 12 is the former *Casas Reales*, now *Pal. Municipal*. Here resided Juárez during 12 Jan.– 12 Feb. 1858 and here he assumed the presidency. No. 14, house of his friend Bernardo Chico, was where Hidalgo lodged in Sept.–Oct. 1810.

Here opens out PL. DE LA PAZ, slimly triangular, lined by handsome 18–19C houses. On the r. is the basilica of **Nuestra Señora de Guanajuato** (1671–95).

EXTERIOR. The façade spans Mannerism and baroque. The side doorways are more fully baroque. A strange later addition, the clock tower with homely estípite supports, is by Agustín Durán y Villaseñor. The INTERIOR, neoclassically altered during the 19C, preserves a charming rococo organ and paintings, attr. Juan Rodríguez Juárez, in the pendentives of the cupola. Usually displayed on the high altar, but disguised in added accessories, is the venerated statue of Our Lady of Guanajuato, an exquisite mid-16C (possibly Sevillian) work, carved in wood, polychrome, and with superb estofado; a gift from Philip II in 1557. It stands on a gorgeous late 18C silver pedestal partly repoussé (note the tiny estípites), the gift of Vicente Manuel de Sardaneta y Legaspi, 1st marqués de San Juan de Rayas, and owner of the Rayas mine. The sacristy, with a rococo doorway, contains three paintings (1777) by Francisco Antonio Vallejo: Last Supper, St Andrew Avellino, and St John Nepomuk.

At the corner with C. Truco, S of the church, is the *Casa Riaño*, of the intendant's family. The statue dedicated to Peace (1895–98), in front of the church, is by Jesús Contreras.

Continuing on the S side of the plaza, No. 48 is the birthplace of Lucas Alamán (1792–1853). No. 62, turning a bend at the W end, is the **Casa de Pérez Gálvez**, faced in terracotta.

It was first property of the conde de Valenciana and then of Antonio Pérez de Andújar y Gálvez Crespo y Gómez, conde de Pérez Gálvez (1805), husband of Gertrudis Obregón, the conde's elder daughter. It keeps its original door with bronze knockers in the form of masks.

Opposite, at the corner with Cjón de la Condesa, is the neo-Renaissance former **Pal. de Gobierno** (No. 77; 1897–1903) by Lewis Long, in greenish grey stone (loza), famous here. No. 75 is the celebrated **Casa Rul**.

It was built, probably before 1802, for Diego de Rul y Calero (conde de Casa Rul in 1803), who married María Ignacia Obregón, younger daughter of the conde de Valenciana. Its attribution to Tresguerras remains unproved; it could be the work of José Gutiérrez or José del Mazo y Avilés. Humboldt, who stayed here in 1803, wrote: 'one could be proud of it in the best streets of Paris or Naples'.

The purity and refinement of its neoclassical façade are admirable. The upper storey is perfectly balanced: deeply fluted ionic columns and pilasters, long windows covered by jutting central curved and outer triangular pediments, and Greek pattern friezes. The central pediment encloses family coats-of-arms. The stunning octagonal patio is in rose-brown stone.

From the W end of the plaza, Av. Juárez bends S. Immediately to the l., C. Alonso, a particularly fine street (No. 12 in which is the old *Mesón de San Antonio*), runs back E. On the l. in Av. Juárez is the former **Casa del Real Ensaye** (18C; Royal Office of Assay, where mined silver and gold quality was tested), with balconies (fine wrought-ironwork) and windows at various levels, and a baroque doorway.

The coat-of-arms on the façade, a later addition, is of the Busto family, marqueses de San Clemente from 1730, their wealth derived from the Mellado and Cata mines. When the Jesuits were expelled in 1767, five grandsons of the 1st marqués were among them.

We next reach PL. DE LOS ANGELES. Beyond (r.) is JARDIN MORELOS, a home of parakeets, built on the site of *Mercado Reforma* (1875; by José Noriega), whose gateway and colonnade survive. Further on is the church of **Nuestra Señora de Belem** (finished 1775; now called *Inmaculado Corazón de María*), formerly belonging to the Bethlemites, its façade the most restrained churrigueresque, and with a curvetting cornice. Its neo-Gothic altars date from 1898.

The restored former hospital (which fell down in 1876 when a second storey was added) and convent (No. 79), built in 1727–75, are now university faculties.

Opposite is the vast, iron-framed **Mercado Hidalgo** (1904–10), by the French architect Ernest Brunel. The entrance main arch, overborne by a series of archivolts, recalls that built by Eiffel for the Exposition Internationale of 1878 in Paris.

In C. Mendizábal, opposite the market on the l., is what remains of the principal house of the hacienda of *Dolores Granaditas*; its first floor rests on huge stone arches, beneath which were workshops where silver was processed.

From the market we may follow Av. Juárez W to Paseo del Cantador (l.). A little way down on the l. is the church of *Nuestra Señora de Guadalupe de Pardo* (1757). On it has been grafted the façade of **San Juan de Rayas**.

The latter church, once at the entrance to the mine outside the city, became ruinous. The churrigueresque façade (mid-18C) was rescued and reset-up here in 1946. In the central panel the mixtilinear entrance arch contrasts with the inverted curve of the cornice and the gracefully framed choir window. Inside the flourish of the gable curls drapery to show off a relief of John the Baptist baptizing Christ.
  Paseo del Cantador runs S to JARDIN DEL CANTADOR, full of pines and exotic flowers and shrubs.

At the corner of Cs Mendizábal and 5 de Mayo looms the fortress-like **Alhóndiga de Granaditas**, which, in the words of David Brading, 'erected to ensure a cheap supply of grain for the people of Guanajuato, in effect became the mausoleum of Spain's colonial empire, and the birthplace of an independent Mexico'.

The original plans, urged on by Riaño, were drawn up by Agustín Alejandro Durán y Villaseñor and modified at the Academy of San Carlos. José del Mazo y Avilés was (from 1797) supervising architect and work was finished in 1809.
  At news of Hidalgo's revolt, Riaño fortified the Alhóndiga and on 24 Sept. 1810 transferred here c 470 badly armed troops and the municipal treasury and archives. A number of Spanish and creole citizens, with wives, children, and valuables, took refuge within. On 28 Sept. the insurgents laid siege. Riaño was killed. The defenders lost heart, intimidated by missiles pounding the building and the blood-curdling shrieks of the attackers. The main door was forced when the heroic Juan Martínez (Pípila), holding a flagstone to cover his head and back, and a pine-torch in his r. hand, crawled forward to set it alight. Through it rushed the insurgent horde. A massacre ensued: c 200 defending soldiers and 105 civilians were slaughtered and 3 million pesos fell to Hidalgo. On 24 Nov., when Calleja's avenging troops were approaching the city, the mob brushed aside the revolutionary guards and forced its way in to perpetrate even more horrible slaughter. Of the 247 Spanish and Mexican prisoners, only 30 escaped to seek sanctuary in the convent of Belem. On 26 Nov., the victorious royalists packed the Alhóndiga with their own prisoners; Flon ordered 30 of them shot. In Oct. 1814 the heads of Hidalgo, Allende, Aldama, and Jiménez were put in iron cages which were attached by hooks to each corner of the building. There they remained until 28 March 1821, when Gen. Bustamante ordered them down.

Exterior austerity is broken by neoclassical portals on N and E. The cool patio is notable for the pillars in smooth guanajuatense stone. Today the Alhóndiga houses the **Museo Regional de Guanajuato** (Tues.–Sat., 10–2, 4–7; Sun., 10–4; fee).
  On the E entrance staircase is a mural (1955) by José Chávez Morado. Its theme is slavery in New Spain and its abolition, and it shows the exploitation

of the Indians, the Inquisition, evil collaborators, and the final throes of Spanish power. Its heroes are Bartolomé de las Casas, and Hidalgo succouring the maimed and oppressed. In the *Recinto de los Héroes* on the ground floor, Chávez Morado's second mural here (1966) honours Guanajuato, with a centre-piece showing the encaged head of Hidalgo.

A tour of the museum begins on the upper floor. The two archaeological rooms begin with a collection of artefacts known as the 'Field Collection' (after their donator in 1976). Included are figurines and sculptures from various regions. Gulf Coast—geometric, animal, and bird designs. Guerrero—animals (coyotes, jaguars, serpents, butterflies) and supernatural beings. Central Mexico—from c 1000 BC, hunting and fishing tools from hunter-gatherer cave sites; and birds, serpents, and rabbits. Pacific Coast—animals, especially a fine duck figurine. Viceregal period artefacts include various natural patterns (leaves, rosettes, stars, trees, discs).

The second room contains a display concentrating on Chupícuaro (Rte 40A). Artefacts and information panels explain the location and ecology of the site, its division into two main chronological phases (300 BC–AD 100 and AD 100–300), burial patterns, and figurine styles. Cases of artefacts include examples of figurines; monochrome bowls and plates of c 300 BC; black- and red-slipped vessels, some with incised, stippled, or raised decorations, and some in anthropomorphic forms; vessels, jars, and masks, in both red-and-cream mono-chromes and polychromes, with applied decorations; and La Estela, a Nahua plaque symbol in the figure of a flower (c 60cm x 30cm). The special display of figurine styles is notable for depicting heavily ornamented types, incl. much information on female dress and jewellery fashions.

The history of Guanajuato from 1750 to 1917 is illustrated by firearms, folk art, portraits, documents, coins, medals, uniforms, photographs, etc. Especially well illustrated are 18–19C mining, and the dangers faced by miners; 18C haciendas; the reforms of José de Gálvez and their effects on Guanajuato; the flood damage of July 1905; and Guanajuato in Revolution. A highlight of the collection is the vintage photographs of late 19C guanajuatense types.

On the ground floor is the ethnographic collection, with pottery, early sculpture, lamps, ironwork, tinsmiths' work, embroidery, textiles, glassware, equestrian equipment, etc., from Guanajuato, Silao, Celaya, Dolores, Moroleón, etc.

Facing the N side of the Alhóndiga are the CERRO DEL CUARTO and the picturesque barrio del Terremoto. We follow C. Pocitos E. On the r., Cjón de la Galarza leads to Cjón San Roque (r.), along which we reach the enchanting PLAZUELA SAN ROQUE, scene on spring evenings of the entremeses cervan-tinos (see above). Here is the church of **San Roque** (1726), charming in its rustic classical simplicity, its stonework taking on the lightest of pink tinges in sun-light.

C. Pocitos passes (l., No. 47) the **Casa de Diego Rivera** (Mon.–Sat., 10–2; 4–7; fee), birthplace in 1886 of the renowned painter. It contains a small collection of his early impressionist and cubist works; watercolours for the 'Popol Vuh'; and a sketch for the controversial mural done for the Rockefeller Center in New York in 1933.

No. 7 C. Pocitos is the former **Pal. de los Marqueses de San Juan de Rayas** (c 1763), now containing the **Museo del Pueblo de Guanajuato** (Tues.–Sun., 10–2, 4–7; fee).

Temporary exhibitions of the work of local artists are held here. Among the permanent collection are engravings by José Chávez Morado and studies by Pablo O'Higgins, Alfredo Zalce, David Alfaro Siqueiros, and Diego Rivera. Portraits by Hermenegildo Bustos; 19C rustic religious art. Local ceramics. Among 18C paintings is the detailed portrait of Mariana Reynoso. On the upper floor is the Chapel (1776), with a churrigueresque façade. It is decorated with a Chávez Morado mural on the history of Guanajuato.

Next, reached up a monumental stairway, are the buildings of the **Universidad de Guanajuato** (1953–55), by Vicente Urquiaga, in a clashingly out-of-line pseudo-historical style.

In a narrow street to the l. of Cjón de los Hospitales, which runs along the N side of the stair, is the *Cap. de los Hospitales* (1560–65; for Tarascan Indians; much altered). Its atrial cross is original. Cjón de los Hospitales runs N to join C. Peñasco. By turning r. along the latter we join Calz. de Guadalupe which climbs up to the church of *Guadalupe* (1732–33).

On the r. of the university, raised above C. Lascuraín de Retana, is the church of **La Compañía**, its portals among the earliest examples of churrigueresque.

In 1732 the Jesuits founded their school, *Santísma Trinidad*, converted in 1744 into a college. Their church, planned by the Bethlemite Fray José de la Cruz, was built in 1747–65, under Felipe de Ureña. It attracted lavish donations; miners contributed labour without pay: 'Fortunate city, in whose centre sparkles, like a diamond set in silver, this church...'.
In 1785 church and college were taken over by the Oratorians (*San Felipe Neri*). In 1828 the college became the Colegio del Estado. From it the university was created in 1945.

EXTERIOR. The main (S) façade shows three fine portals. The lower storey of the central portal is flanked by three free-standing estípites on either side of the doorway, above which, dissolving the cornice, is a relief of the Holy Trinity, delightfully framed. The upper storey contains two pairs of estípites and marks the beginning of two more, which ascend into the gable. Enclosing the upper parts, and in contrast to their delicate ornamental curves, a strong moulding descends from the gable like an alfíz. In the lower storeys of the side portals, wide pilasters form the backing for large ornamental niches, and ornate window openings are placed beneath the jutting, rising cornice. In the upper storeys, the two estípites uphold a fancifully curling gable. The W tower was never finished. The E tower has a remarkable bulbous spire, soaring above the many-columned bell-tower. The E portal, though plainer, has good relief, and, in the upper storey, caryatid supports.

The cupola (1869–84), insistent, though unharmonious, landmark in three diminishing layers, dates from a remodelling of the church by Vicente Heredia and Herculano Ramírez and hints at neo-baroque. The first cupola collapsed in 1808.
Interesting original survivals of the INTERIOR are the sacristy portal and the pulpit. In the sacristy is a painting of SS Ignatius and Francis Borgia with Our Lady, by Cabrera (1765).
In the college patio, now the Escuela Preparatoria, with classicizing arcades, has been reassembled the churrigueresque portal (late 18C) from the church at Marfil.

From La Compañía we follow C. del Sol past the *Correos* and the simple little church of *San José* (19C), then turn l. and l. again into the pretty PLAZUELA DEL BARATILLO, with a fountain donated to the city by Maximilian. From its SE corner we may follow C. Cantarranas. A turning l., Subida del Teatro Principal, leads to PLAZUELA DE MEXIAMORA, another typical spot, surrounded by low houses in popular style. At No. 12 was born Benito León Acosta (1819–86), the first Mexican aeronaut.
We continue past (l.) the *Teatro Principal* to PLAZUELA DEL ROPERO. On its S side is the *Casa Santa de Loreto* (1846–54), a circular chapel designed by Cleto Salinas. At No. 6 C. Sóstenes Rocha, off its S side, is the house of Juan Antonio de Riaño, reached by a flight of steps added in 1878, along with the ramp and bridge, when the level of the street was lowered to allow carriages to pass.
Adjoining Plazuela del Ropero on the W is the former PL. DE SAN FRANCISCO (C. Manuel Doblado). Here is the church of **San Francisco**, with a well-marked churrigueresque façade.

It is the rebuilding (1792–1828) of the church of *San Juan* (1729), taken over by the Franciscans in the 1750s. The estípites and entrecalles of the lower storey, already an anachronism, are beautifully proportioned; the relief above the arch is enclosed by an elaborate motif resembling a giant lambrequin.
To the S and E of Plazuela del Ropero, and reached along Cs Sóstenes Rocha and Felipe Carrillo Puerto, Calz. Puertecito, and C. San Sebastián, is the barrio of *Pastita*, now a choice residential suburb, graced by the PARQUE DE LAS EMBAJADORAS. Here also is the church (1782) and cemetery of *San Sebastián*.

C. San Sebastián merges into PASEO DE LA OLLA, which leads to *Presa de la Olla* (c 6km from Jardín de la Unión), an artificial dam laid out in 1742, in front of which is PARQUE FLORENCIO ANTILLON, with a statue of Gen. Sóstenes Rocha. The area round about still retains its porfirian mansions, incl. that now used as *Pal. de Gobierno*, on the r. just before the park. Behind Presa de la Olla is *Presa San Renovato* (1838).

From the SE corner of Presa de la Olla we may gain the CARRETERA PANORAMICA (a 22km drive) which winds round the city on the edges of the ravines (magnificent views). To the W (r.) it goes to the *Monumento al Pípila* on the Cerro de San Miguel, from where the panorama of the city is resplendent. To the NE (l.) it goes to *La Cata*.

5km N of Guanajuato, along the road (Méx. 110) to Dolores Hidalgo, is *La Valenciana*, what remains of the little town which grew up in the heyday of the Valenciana mine. On an eminence above it is the church of **San Cayetano**, in rose-tinted stone, one of the crowning works of the Mexican churrigueresque.

It was built during 1765–88, partly at the charges of the conde de Valenciana, but the labourers in the mine were expected to give part of their exiguous daily wage towards its cost—in all 391,000 pesos. On completion each donated a piece of ore the size of a fist. The parish priest of Guanajuato is said jealously to have protested at its magnificence. One tower was therefore left unfinished to placate him. The conde intended it and its accompanying house for the Theatines, a congregation of clerks regular, but they never took possession.

EXTERIOR. The façade, facing S, is a miracle of refinement, its multitude of rococo motifs and symbols covered with rare fastidiousness. On either side of the central vertical panel pride of place goes to the interestípites, with niches in both storeys: in the lower stylishly piled on top by delightfully irregular pulvinated friezes supporting cone motifs, scrolls, and saints in elaborate medallions; in the upper by multilayered finials. The flanking estípites are unusually slender, barely tapering. The exceptionally high lower storey gives room for a dense pattern of floral, fruit, and vegetal motifs, shells, medallions, human figures, angel heads, jagged moulding, and a central relief of the Trinity. Above the window, the cornice is broken into by more dense relief and its curve provides a base for long pedestals supporting archangels. In the topmost curvetting cornice is a statue of the patron saint.

The recessed W portal is a masterpiece of concentrated relief, the two side supports combining the feature of estípite and ornamental niche pilaster. Two minute estípites flank the central relief of St Joseph.

The single-nave INTERIOR is notable for the almohadilla carving of arches and pilasters; the ingenious relief of the choir arch spandrels; the even more ingenious, curiously rippling and purely decorative, tezontle vaulting; the pulpit, encrusted with rare woods, ivory, and tortoiseshell; the stone doorways; and the estípite supports of the cupola. All pale before the three magnificent altarpieces, pride of the Mexican churrigueresque, full of polychrome detail, each keeping to a different design. The high altar, dedicated to St Cajetan, shows contrasting estípites: slender ones flanking the lower-storey niches (note the emphatic volutes); strong ones on the outside. On the l. is the altar of Our Lady of Guadalupe, richest of the three, in which the angels and cherubs who mass at the very top—so far forward they seem about to leap—have to vie with the thick estípite and niche pilaster relief, and wealth of decorative moulding, to be seen. On the r., the altar of the Assumption, perhaps the finest, with a profusion of fine gilding interrupted only by polychrome angels' heads, angelic busts, and four small saints in the middle of four large, swelling estípites which again dwarf the small, slim supports on either side of the central niche.

The *Valenciana* mine, reopened in 1967, is across the road and higher up than the church. The shaft (6m wide and 525m deep) is still worked.

Branching off to the r. from the beginning of the Dolores road is a winding rustic road to (c 2km) *La Cata*, another old mining centre, which saw bonanzas from 1724 (11 years) and from 1790, but whose shaft was flooded in the early 19C.

Here the church of **Sto Señor de Villaseca**, fronting the charming Plazuela del Quijote, dates from the 17C, although rebuilt c 1725; its magnificent churrigueresque façade (incomplete) was added sometime after 1760.

EXTERIOR. Between the slender estípites, bulking slightly in the middle and sharper than usual in their lower parts, the ornamental niche pilasters are decorated with little medallions, of ingenuous charm, which show scenes from the Passion and its symbols. Similar motifs may be seen above the arch, in its intrados, and above the cornice. The arch key shows three figures: the theological virtues. The space above the arch is a gorgeous outburst of foliation, cherubs, stepped mouldings, and wavy volutes; in the middle, a lovely medallion of the Holy Trinity—above it, angels part curtains, descending from a papal tiara.

INTERIOR. Apart from the many ex-votos, its chief interest is the three reliefs in the sotocoro: the Last Supper, which forms the key to the vault; and the Resurrection and Ascension in the spandrels of the nave arch.

C 1km further along this road is the site, high and solitary, of the Mellado mine, with remains of its dependent village, incl. a tranquil little plaza and 18C church.

Reached along Calz. Tepetapa, c 0.5km beyond the railway station, is the *Panteón Civil*. Next to it is the so-called *Museo de las Momias* (daily 9–6; fee), where a macabre, and distasteful (and overrated), few minutes may be spent looking at mummified corpses, preserved in salty soil and dug up after relations failed to keep up crypt fees. At 2.5km is a turning for (4km) **Marfil**, a refining village in Guanajuato's 18C heyday and in the latter 19C a favoured residential suburb, now a ghost town whose restoration owes much to an Italian-American enthusiast, Giorgio Belloli.

In the former hacienda of *San Gabriel Barrera* (late 17C; daily, 9–5.45) one can admire 18–19C furniture from Europe and China. The chapel contains a 17C altarpiece.

52 Guanajuato to San Luis de la Paz

Méx. 110, 103km.—54km **Dolores Hidalgo**.—103km San Luis de la Paz.

Méx. 110 winds over the Sierra de Guanajuato (magnificent views) to (54km) **DOLORES HIDALGO** (c 40,000 inhab.; 1989m; H,R,P), a quiet, charming place; scene of the most momentous event in Mexican history.

It began in the late 1560s as a congregación, Pueblo Nuevo de los Dolores. On 3 Oct. 1803 Miguel Hidalgo y Costilla succeeded his brother José Joaquín as parish priest here. He left spiritual affairs to his curate, devoting himself to scholarship and encouraging agricultural improvements (incl. the planting of mulberry trees for silkworm cultivation) and the establishment of light industries, and travelling to Guanajuato, San Miguel el Grande, Querétaro, and Valladolid. His resentment of his, and creole, lack of preferment and hatred of all things Spanish brought him to prominence as a leading conspirator against the weakened viceregal government. On 16 Sept. 1810 he was rushed into proclaiming Mexican independence here ('Grito de Dolores'). In 1824 the town was renamed Villa de Hidalgo. In 1948 a federal decree approved its subtitle: 'cuna de la independencia nacional'.

PL. DEL GRANDE HIDALGO is bordered by one-and two-storey 18C houses; in the centre a monument to Hidalgo (1887) by Gabriel Guerra. On the N side is the *Pal. Municipal* (late 18C; restored), birthplace of the insurgent Mariano Abasolo (1784–1816). On the staircase the mural (1977) by Samuel Menache honours Independence. Next door is the church of **Nuestra Señora de los Dolores** (1712–78), as important for its façade as for its historical associations.

On the front steps at dawn on Sun. 16 Sept. 1810 Hidalgo, attended by friends, servants, and a swelling crowd summoned by the ringing of the church bells, stood to give the Grito de Dolores, which possibly ended with: 'Long live the Catholic religion, long live Ferdinand VII, long live our country, long live our holy patron, Our Lady of Guadalupe, and may she reign for ever in this continent of America...death to bad government'.

EXTERIOR. The façade is a highly individual churrigueresque, dense and compact. In the lower storey, ornamental niche pilasters appear on the outside, estípites in the centre; slender engaged supports, a cross between estípites and baluster, on the inside. The entrance arch, decorated with a loop motif, its intrados like a shell, is encompassed by a low alfíz, which encloses horn of plenty relief in the spandrels. In the upper storey are two sets of niche pilasters; again estípites occupy the entrecalles. In the central panel are the choir window, flanked by estípites, and above it, flanked by tentative niche pilasters, a winsome statue of Our Lady in contemporary dress. Crowning all, a Crucifixion.

The ample INTERIOR bears all the signs of 19C spoliation, although two fine altarpieces survive: in the W transept, that of Our Lady of Guadalupe, fully churrigueresque and gilded; in the E transept, that of St Joseph, ungilded, more advanced in style, superbly carved. On the first altar in the W aisle is a good polychrome St Michael. Among the sacristy paintings is a St John of the Cross (1730) by Antonio de Torres.

No. 6 C. Zacatecas, off the NW corner of the plaza, is now a small *Museo de la Insurgencia*. It was formerly the town gaol. From it on 16 Sept. 1810 Hidalgo and his associates, threatening the mayor with a pistol, sprang the prisoners and enlisted them in the insurgent ranks.

On the W side of the plaza is the **Casa de Visitas** (1786), an imposing mansion built to house the representative of the viceregal government, its grandeur emphasized by the elaborate cantilevers of its balconies and its rare arches decorated by scroll-like carvings.

From the SW corner of the plaza we reach, at the corner of Cs Hidalgo and Morelos, the single-storey **Casa de Hidalgo**, now a museum (Tues.–Sat., 10–6; Sun., 10–5; fee).

It was built in 1779 as the *Casa del Diezmo*. In 1804 Hidalgo moved his residence and parish offices here. On the night of 14 Sept. 1810 he was joined by Ignacio Allende, alarmed at the news filtering through from Querétaro, but their hours of urgent talks resolved nothing. At 2 o'clock in the morning of 16 Sept., Juan Aldama arrived from San Miguel, bearing the warning of Josefa Ortiz, and sought out Allende. Together they entered Hidalgo's bedroom. He immediately rose and exclaimed: 'gentlemen, we are lost; we have no choice but to go and seize gachupines'. They decided to make first for the jail, but Hidalgo turned back to wake a manservant: 'Juan, let's go; it's time—arise'. In June 1863, Juárez lodged here on his flight N and in Sept. 1864 Maximilian paid a visit, addressing the people from a window.

The main rooms, furnished with late 18C anon. paintings, 19C lithographs, furniture (not all of it associated with Hidalgo or his family), ceramics, etc., are grouped around a rectangular patio. To the r. of the entrance lobby is the parlour (perhaps also used by Hidalgo as his private office); to the l. his official office, followed by his bedroom, the parish office (on the corner), the main sitting room, the bedrooms used by his brother Mariano (1756–1811) and his sisters, the dining room, and the kitchen. The large hall beyond the kitchen was originally built to store the grain brought in from the country as tithes.

Among the objects displayed are: in the parlour, three late 18C chairs from the Oratory at San Miguel; table from the Hacienda de Burras, near Guanajuato, used by Hidalgo when writing a surrender demand to Riaño; proclamations of Viceroy Venegas against the insurgents; fragments of the skulls of Hidalgo, Allende, and Morelos, kept in a velvet-covered box. In his bedroom, personal objects of Hidalgo, incl. his spectacles. In the parish office, pages from the baptismal register; vestments used by Hidalgo. In the sitting room, typical 18C furniture (the chests modern copies); family letters; copies of letters of Allende to Hidalgo, of Venegas to Riaño, of Morelos to Hidalgo asking leave to raise rebellion in the S. The hall of the tithes is full of objects donated from all parts of Mexico to the museum in homage to 'the Father of the Fatherland'.

From the house C. Puebla leads E past (l.) the little church of *La Tercera Orden* (late 18C; restored 1956), with a curious SE tower, facing a pretty plaza, to (r.), at the corner with C. Distrito Federal, the church of *Nuestra Señora de la Saleta* (1875–96) by Ceferino Gutiérrez (see Rte 58), showing neo-Gothic enthusiasm.

From Dolores, Méx. 51 runs NW to (53km) *San Felipe*, see Rte 50.

Méx. 110 continues to (60km) the junction with Méx. 51 running SE, along the valley of the Río de la Laja, to (20km) *Atotonilco* and (35km) *San Miguel de Allende*, see Rte 58. We continue NE to (94km) the junction with Méx. 57, the San Luis Potosí–Querétaro road, see Rte 58. 103km **San Luis de la Paz** (c 12,500 inhab.; 2025m; H,R,P), known for its wine production, on the N slopes of the Sierra Gorda.

It began in 1590 as a Jesuit mission, of Otomís, Mexicans, and Tarascans, in Chichimec territory. By the mid-17C it had a small garrison of four Spanish soldiers and a captain. In Sept. 1817 it fell to Francisco Javier Mina during his brief campaign.

The chapel of *Sta Cecilia* (18C) incorporates estípites in its façade. The neo-Gothic sanctuary of *Guadalupe* dates from 1880–97.

A road goes S to (11km) **Pozos**, attractive in its dilapidation, founded in the 1590s as a mining camp. The nearby shafts had fallen into disuse by 1743. Of late, a restoration programme has begun and some of the old houses are used as weekend residences.

The road continues to (39km) **San José Iturbide** (H,P), founded in 1769 as *San José de Casas Viejas*, changed in honour of Iturbide in 1849. Its huge parish church (1873–78), by Ramón Rodríguez Arangoity, is a superb tribute to classical revival (tempered with afrancesado elements). The nearby notary's office possesses three interesting portraits: of Rodríguez Arangoity by Felipe S. Gutiérrez (1883); of his collaborator, the mason Valentín López; and of the parish priest, Nicolás Campa.

E of San Luis de la Paz an increasingly steep and difficult road, only to be attempted by the toughest of vehicles, climbs into the Sierra Gorda to (68km) **Xichú** (2000 inhab.; 2304m), founded as a real de minas (San Francisco Sichú de los Amues) in the 1590s. It revived during the second world war when its lead was exported to the USA for the munitions industry. The mine was closed after 1945 (though its mineral potential, incl. gold, silver, molybdenum, and sulphur, is still considerable) and today the local economy is centred on tomato production and timber from surrounding forests. The little town, with three main streets and lovely gardens, is delightfully picturesque.

53 Nuevo Laredo to Monterrey

Méx. 85, 230km.—24km junction with Méx. 2 for (250km SE) Reynosa and (341km SE) Matamoros.—131km Sabinas Hidalgo.—230km **Monterrey**.

State road 1, 272km.—65km Anáhuac.—168km (5km r.) Bustamante.—175km Villaldama.—272km **Monterrey**.

NUEVO LAREDO (436,000 inhab.; 171m; State of Tamaulipas), on the Río Bravo, port of entry from Laredo (Texas), is an uninteresting modern town, developed from 1848–49.

Airport. 14km S. Flights to *Mexico City* and *Guadalajara*.

Bus station. 3km S of international bridge. Services to *Mexico City* (17 hrs); to *Monterrey* (4 hrs); to *Tampico* (13 hrs); to *Querétaro* (14 hrs); to *San Luis Potosí* (12 hrs); etc.

Railway station. Av. César López de Lara, between Avs Gutiérrez and Arteaga. Daily train (Aguila Azteca) to *Mexico City* (26 hrs) via *Monterrey* (5 hrs); *Saltillo* (8 hrs); *San Luis Potosí* (15½ hrs); and *Querétaro* (21 hrs).

Hotels throughout the town.

Post Office. Corner of Avs Reynosa and Dr Mier.

Tourist Office. By international bridge.

US Consulate. Corner of Avs Allende and Nayarit.

Fiesta. 11 Sept.; agricultural fair.

From Nuevo Laredo there is a choice of two roads to Monterrey. The main Pan American highway (Méx. 85) runs SW across a plain, generally dry, and given over to cattle-raising.

At 24km Méx. 2 branches off l., skirting the frontier and *Presa Falcón*, which straddles it.

This huge artificial lake (capacity 5100 million cubic m), which harnesses the waters of the Río Bravo, was a joint US-Mexican undertaking, inaugurated in 1953. On the Mexican side it irrigates c 220,000 hectares in Tamaulipas and Nuevo León as far as Monterrey.

125km turning l. for *Nueva Ciudad Guerrero*, a new town laid out in 1953 to replace Guerrero, submerged by Presa Falcón. 147km *Ciudad Mier* (H,R,P), settled in 1753 as *El Cántaro*, with an 18C church. Near (185km) *Ciudad Camargo*, in a cotton-producing area, remains of the former settlement, called *Villa Nueva de Camargo*, established in 1846 and destroyed in 1856 during an attack by Santiago Vidaurri (see below), may be seen. The town connects across the Río Bravo with *Río Grande* in Texas. To the S lies *Presa Marte R. Gómez* (Presa Azúcar; capacity 1080 million cubic m), formed by the damming of the waters of the Río San Juan in 1959. 214km turning l. for *Gustavo Díaz Ordaz*, with a toll bridge to *Ebano* in Texas. 250km **Reynosa** (450,000 inhab.; 37m; H,R,P), a noisy, widely dispersed town, with oil refineries and a gas plant, from which gas is piped to Monterrey. A toll bridge joins with *Hidalgo* and *McAllen* in Texas.

FROM REYNOSA TO MONTERREY, 225km. Méx. 40 runs straight SW, into the State of Nuevo León (at 32km) to (92km) *General Bravo* on the Río San Juan. 104km *China* (R,P), ideal base for fishing in lakes formed by the damming of the Río San Juan. From here Méx. 89 runs SW to (89km) *Montemorelos*, see Rte 54. Méx. 40 continues W to (192km) *Cadereyta Jiménez* (H,R,P), founded as a villa in 1637. Its church of San Juan Bautista (19C) succeeds a Franciscan foundation of 1640. 37km S is *Villa de Allende*, see Rte 54. We approach Monterrey through

(220km) the suburb of *Guadalupe*, once a Tlaxcaltecan barrio of Monterrey. In its parish church is a venerated image of Christ brought to the town in 1715. 225km *Monterrey*, see below.

From Reynosa, Méx. 2 traverses a low-lying, intensively irrigated region, famous for cotton cultivation. The system channels the Río Bravo to the lagunas of El Culebrón, Cárdenas, and Palito Blanco, which form huge storage basins. It dates from the presidency of Lázaro Cárdenas (1934–40) when colonies of Mexicans were repatriated from the USA and settled in the new towns of the area. 266km *Ciudad Río Bravo* (H,R,P). 341km *Matamoros*, see Rte 59.

Méx. 85 crosses into the State of Nuevo León and approaches the E slopes of the Sierra Madre Oriental. 105km *Vallecillos* (274m), a former mining centre (from 1766). 131km **Sabinas Hidalgo** (c 25,000 inhab.; 313m; H,R,P), on the r. bank of the Río Sabinas, an active town, founded as a mining camp (Santiago de las Sabinas) in 1693. The 18C church of *San José* contains the only surviving churrigueresque altarpiece in the State. 29km W is *Villaldama*, see below. The road continues S, eventually climbing through the *Cuesta de Mamulique* in the Sierra de Picachos. 195km *Ciénega de Flores*, an attractive town. 230km *Monterrey*, see below.

The alternative, longer, more difficult, but more interesting route leaves Nuevo Laredo to the W. It crosses into Nuevo León as State road 1 and reaches (65km) *Anáhuac*, a modern town connected by road with (67km NW) *Presa Don Martín* (capacity 250 million cubic m) in the State of Coahuila, built in 1932 and damming the waters of the Ríos Salado de los Nadadores and Sabinas. It is a popular fishing spot. 110km *Lampazos de Naranjo* (340m), birthplace of Santiago Vidaurri (1808–67; see below), at the NW extremity of the Sierra de Lampazos, which rises on the l. of the road. At 132km turning r. (W) via (18km) *Candela* across hilly country to (113km) *Monclova*, see Rte 55. 168km turning r. for (5km) **Bustamante** (7000 inhab.; 457m; H,R,P), known for its groves of walnut trees, founded in 1686 as San Miguel de Aguayo with a colony of Tlaxcaltecans. The 19C church of *San Miguel* contains a venerated statue of Our Lord of Tlaxcala, the gift in 1715 of Ana María de García, a noble but poor Tlaxcaltecan widow.

A rough road leads to (4km S) *Albergue El Palmito*, a mirador, with a marvellous view of the Sierra de Gomas. From here a path leads to (2km) the *Grutas de Bustamante* (visits recommended only for enthusiasts), with stalagtite and stalagmite formations, but still awaiting proper exploration.

175km **Villaldama** (7000 inhab.; 469m; P; thermal springs), founded in 1690 as the real de minas of San Pedro Bora de Leones, from which silver with a high lead content was extracted. Today it is famous for its oranges, a speciality of the wider region. The church and ruined hospice of *Nuestra Señora de Guadalupe* were a Franciscan foundation from Guadalupe, Zacatecas (1716). Among other ruined buildings (19C) are a strange church, mixing neo-Gothic with neo-classical, and the *Teatro Morelos*. We continue through the Sierra de Gomas to (272km) *Monterrey*.

MONTERREY (3 million inhab.; 600m) capital of the State of Nuevo León, leading industrial, and third most populous, city in Mexico, enjoys as fine and dramatic a setting as any in the republic. It lies on the flood-plain of the Río Sta Catarina, and on its E and W sides rise the fantastically shaped summits of two mountain chains, the Cerro de la Silla (1740m) and the Cerro de las Mitras (2380m highest point). Headlong recent growth has done away with much of the older city. Industry in the outskirts causes pollution, held in by the neighbouring heights. Monterrey's natives (regiomontanos) have a reputation for a friendly and businesslike approach and for thrift.

Airport. 22km NE. Flights to *Cancún, Chihuahua, Durango, Guadalajara, León, Mazatlán, Mexico City, San Luis Potosí, Tampico, Toluca, Torreón* and to *Chicago, Dallas, Houston, Los Angeles, San Antonio;* etc.

Bus station. Corner of Av. Colón and C. Amado Nervo. Services to *Mexico City* (12 hrs); to *Nuevo Laredo* (3 hrs); to *Reynosa* (4 hrs); to *Saltillo* (2 hrs); to *Matehuala* (5 hrs); to *San Luis Potosí* (8 hrs); to *Torreón* (6 hrs); to *Ciudad Victoria* (4½ hrs); to *Zacatecas* (7 hrs); etc.

Railway station. NW of bus station, at corner of Calz. La Victoria and C. Nieto. Aguila Azteca (see above) to *Mexico City* (21 hrs). Evening trains to *Mexico City* via Saltillo and San Luis Potosí in c 15 hrs.

Hotels throughout the city.

Post Office. In Pal. Federal, corner of Av. Washington and C. Zaragoza.

Tourist Office. Corner of Av. Matamoros and C. Zaragoza.

US Consulate. 441 Av. de la Constitución Poniente. **British Consulate.** 104 Privada de Tamazunchale, Garza García (Col. del Valle).

Fiestas. 20 May: accompanying agricultural and commercial fair. 12 Dec.: Our Lady of Guadalupe.

In 1596 the old settlement of San Luis Rey de Francia was refounded as the city of Nuestra Señora de Monterrey, after viceroy conde de Monterrey, but without his authority. The incoming governor in 1752 found nowhere to stay and a population of well under a thousand. In Jan. 1811 the insurgent José Mariano Jiménez set up his headquarters here, but was soon arrested and executed. In 1824 Monterrey became capital of the State of Nuevo León. It was fortified in Sept. 1846 to resist attack by Gen. Zachary Taylor's US troops, the Mexican garrison under Gen. Pedro Ampudia ('burly, grumpy, cruel, with little eyes') putting up a game resistance. In Apr.–Aug. 1864 the city was Juárez's seat of government before falling to

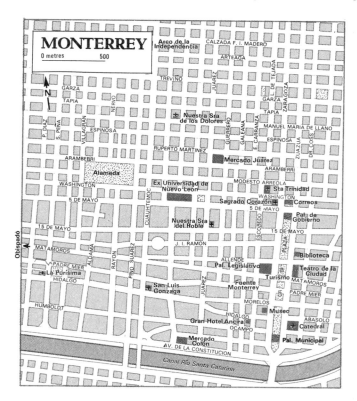

the imperialist troops of Gen. Armand Castagny. Gen. Escobedo won it back for the republic in Apr. 1866.

Industrialization began during the porfiriato, backed by capital from the USA and Europe, attracted by tax exemptions granted by Governor Bernardo Reyes. In 1890 the Cuauhtémoc brewery was established by José Schneider; in 1892 David Guggenheim set up the smelting plant Gran Fundición Nacional Mexicana; by 1911 the Compañía Fundidora de Fierro y Acero de Monterrey (iron and steel), founded in 1903, was turning out 60,000 tons of steel a year. In Apr. 1914, the city fell to Pablo González, Carranza's general. Villista forces, under Gen. Felipe Angeles, occupied it in 1914–15. The 1920s and 1930s saw steady growth and some political and social upheaval. Industrial development continued to attract immigrants in search of work. The closing of Fundidora Monterrey in 1986 was a symptom of Mexico's economic crisis.

The Río Sta Catarina (its bed often dry, but still able to flood) was canalized in 1949–52. Water shortage is a feature of life in Monterrey. The climate is unusually extreme. Summers can be uncomfortably hot; in Jan.–Feb. below freezing temperatures and snow are not uncommon.

The Sierra Madre Oriental traverses the territory of **Nuevo León** (64,555 sq km; 4 million inhab.) from N to SE. The SW tip bordering on San Luis Potosí forms part of the Meseta del Norte section of the High Plateau. To the E and N of the Sierra Madre the State's broadest and flatter area inclines in its SE amid subtropical valleys towards the Gulf of Mexico; comprises low hills and plains in its centre; and forms semi-desert and sandy cactus-covered wastes in its N part. Various rivers, erratic except during occasional torrential rains, run E and NE across the State to join the Río Bravo or flow into the Gulf. Industrial production, concentrated in or near Monterrey, is second only to that of the Federal District.

In 1599 viceroy conde de Monterrey recognized the New Kingdom of León, partly settled since 1579, an area much larger than the present State. Cattle-raising, mining, and new settlements were encouraged by Martín de Zavala (governor 1626–64). But the hunting-down and cruel treatment of Indians as slaves, even though forbidden by royal decree, was nowhere more scandalously blatant. In the 18C Nuevo León lost territory to Texas, Nuevo Santander, and Nueva Galicia. Native Indian groups all but vanished. In 1825 the new State came into being, slightly larger than the attenuated former kingdom. Santiago Vidaurri (governor 1855–64) was thought capable of detaching Nuevo León and Coahuila from the federation. In 1864 his breach with Juárez became irreversible and he accepted office under the empire. Great advances were made under Gen. Bernardo Reyes (governor 1885–87, 1889–1900, 1902–09) who combined suppression of political unrest with social reform and encouragement of economic development. 'General Reyes, así se gobierna' (this is the way to govern), an admiring Díaz told him. Development since the 1940s has been phenomenal.

The historic centre has undergone an overwhelming change, with the demolition of 40 blocks S of Av. 5 de Mayo to join the two main plazas in one huge elongated GRAN PLAZA (1982–86), the brainchild of Governor Alfonso Martínez Domínguez, to the design of Benjamín Félix, Ramón Naredo Hernández, and Oscar Bulnes.

At the S end is PL. ZARAGOZA, where rises (S side) the heavy *Pal. Municipal* (1976), on concrete stilts. In front of it is an equestrian statue of Gen. Ignacio Zaragoza. On a traffic island on its S side is a sculpture by Rufino Tamayo, 'Homenaje al Sol'. On the E side is the cathedral of **La Inmaculada Concepción**, result of many years of building.

The first parish church was begun in 1635 and in ruins by 1710; the second was then begun, but remained a shell until 1796 when the French architect Jean-Baptiste Crouzet took charge. He had largely finished by 1800. Various touches were added and changes made throughout the 19C. It was dedicated in 1833. During the siege of 1846 it suffered bombardment and served as a gunpowder store. The archdiocese of Monterrey was created out of the bishopric of Linares in 1898. The 2nd bp of Linares (see Rte 54) moved the residence to Monterrey in 1783.

EXTERIOR. The W façade is an interesting and subtle mixture of styles, betraying a certain improvisation. Only one tower (S) was completed; its companion on the N is an espadaña. The smooth columns, with Corinthian capitals in the upper storeys, are a nod to the prevailing neoclassical. In the spandrels of the doorway arch are quaint angel reliefs in medallions; above the arch, hovering cherubs flank the papal insignia—strange echoes of the plateresque, continued in the niches with their pronounced archivolt and jamb relief. The pediments in the upper storey, broken to bend backward in volutes, are Mannerist reminders. Rich frieze and top-storey relief and mixtilinear gable are firmly in the N baroque tradition. The S doorway, with curious relief and peculiarly swathed (and shaped) columns, is perhaps of the mid-18C. On the N side is the *Sagrario* (1874–1890s).

INTERIOR. Around the high altar are murals (1942–45) by Angel Zárraga: in the vault, figures representing sanctity; on the walls, New Testament scenes and saints—their style recalling the early Italian Renaissance.

Opposite the cathedral is the *Condominio Acero Monterrey* and next to it the arcaded building formerly the *Pal. Municipal*, finished in 1853, and now housing the **Museo de Historia de Nuevo León** (Tues.–Sun., 10–6; fee).

Four long rooms on the upper floor contain exhibits illustrating State history from prehispanic times. Although the exhibits are not as precisely labelled as they might be, there is a helpful commentary for the 19C and the revolutionary period.

Behind it is PL. HIDALGO, with a statue of Hidalgo (1893), now centre of the ZONA ROSA, a pedestrian precinct with shops, cafés, and restaurants. At the SW corner of this plaza is the *Gran Hotel Ancira* (c 1900–10), a time-honoured institution, once called 'the last of the grand Mexican hotels for gentlemen'. Francisco Villa is said to have shattered precedent by bringing his horse into the lobby during his visit early in 1915.

Just NW of the cathedral stands the *Faro de Comercio* (c 70m high), a prismatic, orange, reinforced concrete tower (by Luis Barragán) which throws out a laser beam by night to illuminate the key points in and around the city. Further N (in the area of the Gran Plaza bounded on the N by Av. Padre Mier) are a fountain to honour commerce and a statue to honour the workers of Nuevo León. Beyond Av. Padre Mier is the *Fuente de la Vida* (by Luis Sanguino). On its W side is the State Congress and on its E the *Teatro de la Ciudad*. On the N side of the theatre is the *Biblioteca del Estado*. The *Parque Hundido* has become a favourite peaceful haven. Still further N is the *Explanada de los Héroes*, an ample plaza, with statues of Hidalgo, Morelos, Mariano Escobedo, and Juárez.

At the far N end of the Gran Plaza complex stands the **Pal. de Gobierno** (1895–1908), bold and imposing, built in reddish granite from the quarries of San Luis Potosí to the design of Francisco Beltrán.

Its classically inspired portico is supported by eight fluted columns ending in Corinthian capitals. The central finial is topped by a winged Victory. At either end of the parapet are two bronze groups, forged in Salem (Ohio), of a child encircling a lion with a garland of roses. The interior embraces five patios. The Salón de Recepciones (Salón Verde) preserves original paintings by the Italian Anibale Guerini. On 20 April 1943 a critical wartime meeting took place here between Pres. Manuel Avila Camacho and Pres. Franklin D. Roosevelt.

Behind the Pal. de Gobierno, on the other side of Av. 5 de Mayo, is the *Pal. Federal* (1929), with a high tower, considered a skyscraper in its day, and incorporating the *Correos*. On the W side of its facing plaza is the church of *El Sagrado Corazón* (1874–91; tower added after 1940).

W of the Gran Plaza, at the corner of Av. 15 de Mayo and C. Juárez, is the basilica of *Nuestra Señora del Roble*, designed by Mariano Peña, dating in the main from 1854–84, altered in the 1970s, and containing a venerated 17C image of Our Lady.

The most convenient way to the Cerro del Obispado, to the W of the city centre, is along Av. Hidalgo, which crosses C. Cuauhtémoc by the neo-Gothic church of *San Luis Gonzaga* (1909). Further W we come to PL. DE LA PURISIMA, graced by a fountain (1865) by Mateo Matei placed originally in Pl. de Armas (Pl. Zaragoza). On the W side is the famous church of **La Purísima**, a revolutionary design in reinforced concrete by Enrique de la Mora, finished in 1946.

EXTERIOR. The four parabolic arches have been integrated in the Latin cross form and the choir is behind the high altar. The tower, simple and effective, stands free. Above the entrance are a large Crucifixion and the Apostles, in bronze, by H. Hoffmann; the relief of Our Lady at the top of the tower is by Adolfo Laubner.

The INTERIOR, through doors of onyx, is cluttered with featureless ribbing, but boasts works by distinguished artists in the side recesses and along the back wall; Jorge González Camarena, Christ Crucified and St Philip of Jesus; Federico Cantú, St Jean-Marie Vianney and Our Lady of Guadalupe; Benjamín Molina, the Four Evangelists; Guerrero Galván, St Thérèse of Lisieux.

From the NW corner of the plaza, Av. Padre Mier leads up to the CERRO DEL OBISPADO (Cerro del Chepe Vera), on which stands the **Obispado** (former palace of the bishop), now the **Museo Regional de Nuevo León** (Tues.–Sat., 10–1, 3–6; Sun., 10–5; fee).

It was built, with churrigueresque details, in 1787–90 by order of the 2nd bp of Linares, José Rafael Verger, to give work to the poor after snows in Aug. had ruined the harvest. He died here in 1790. It was attacked and stormed on 22 Sept. 1846 by US forces. In 1871, a powder magazine exploded and did away with part of the N wing. In 1903 it served as a hospital during an outbreak of yellow fever. In Jan. 1915 it was stormed again by villista forces. In pagan post-revolutionary days it briefly housed a cabaret.

The eight permanent exhibition rooms take us through the history of Nuevo León from prehispanic times to the Revolution. R. 4, the former chapel, contains anon. historical paintings and sculpture. In R. 6 is the printing press bought in England and given to the Bostonian Samuel Bangs in 1816 by Monterrey's most famous native, Fray Servando Teresa de Mier (1765–1827), to turn out propaganda on behalf of the expedition of Francisco Javier Mina (see Rte 51). On his capture by the viceregal authorities in 1817, Bangs was brought to Monterrey and compelled to print, without payment, on their behalf. Also exhibited are guns (belonging to three nuevoleonese soldiers) used at the execution of Maximilian.

The central Av. Cuauhtémoc runs N past (r.; in the parallel Av. Juárez) the former main building (now a high school) of the *Universidad de Nuevo León*, begun in 1933, but closed in 1934 after riots; and reopened in 1943. To the l. is the wide ALAMEDA DE MARIANO ESCOBEDO, which includes an aviary, an aquarium, and a serpentarium.

Further up (r.; in C. Méndez, at the corner with Av. Manuel María de Llano) is the Redemptorist church of *Nuestra Señora de los Dolores* (1909) and its accompanying *Santuario del Perpetuo Socorro* (1930). Beyond the *Arco de la Independencia* (l.) Av. Universidad (continuation of Cuauhtémoc) passes (l.) the **Cervecería Cuauhtémoc** (1890), now including a museum complex (Tues.–Fri., 9.30–5; Sat.–Sun., 10.30–6). The *Salón de Fama* tells the story of Mexican baseball; the *Museo Deportivo* illustrates a wider variety of popular Mexican sport. The *Museo de Monterrey* includes a permanent art collection (Orozco, Rivera, Siqueiros, Rufino Tamayo, Carlos Mérida, etc.) and is also used for temporary exhibitions. The *Museo de la Cervecería* is devoted to the development of brewing in Monterrey.

In the so-called gardens complimentary beer is offered to visitors. Suffice to say that Monterrey beer (the Bohemia and Tecate brews) is among the world's finest.

In the NE part of the city, at 1000 Calz. Roberto Gaza Sada, is the **Centro Cultural Alfa** (Tues.–Sun., 3–9.30; fee), contained in a startlingly slim modern building shaped like a telescope and including a *Museo de Ciencia y Tecnología* and a Planetarium.

18km SW, off Méx. 40 to Saltillo, is the **Mesa de Chipinque** plateau (H,R), part of the Serranía de Chipinque, a wide mountain range to the S of the city (highest point 2200m). The area is much favoured by the regiomontanos, who have seen its development as a resort where they can escape the heat of the city.

FROM MONTERREY TO CIUDAD MIER, 156km. Méx. 54, through an arid mountainous region. 19km *Apodaca*, with a noticeable 19C church. Across the Sierra de San Gregorio to (96km) **Cerralvo** (R,P), an attractive place, founded in 1577 as the mining settlement of San Gregorio, resettled in 1625, and confirmed as the villa of Cerralvo in 1638. The *Pal. Municipal* on the leafy Pl. Hidalgo is a late 19C building. In the *Casa de las Cureñas* (18C) silver was processed in the latter days of the kingdom of Nuevo León. The *Parque Nacional El Sabinal* is noted for its shady savin-lined walks.

From (115km) *General Treviño* a road runs N to (13km) *Agualeguas*, a fishing and bathing resort. We cross into Tamaulipas for (156km) *Ciudad Mier*, see above.

54 Monterrey to Ciudad Victoria

Méx. 85, 288km.—82km Montemorelos.—133km **Linares**.—288km **Ciudad Victoria**.

We leave Monterrey on Méx. 85 to the SE. The road runs through the Cañón de Huajuco—the Sierra de la Silla on the l. and the Sierra de las Mitras on the r. 36km (r.) *Villa de Santiago* (once known as Santiago Guajuco; R,P), with a 19C church and near *Presa Rodrigo Gómez* (called familiarly Presa de la Boca; sailing and fishing). From (39km) *El Cercado*, in a wooded landscape, a minor road runs SW into the *Parque Nacional Cumbres de Monterrey*. Its most famous feature is the waterfall known as *Cola de Caballo* (25m), the water splaying out like a horsetail. The road descends into warmer, subtropical zones, notable for fruit- and vegetable-growing.

59km *Villa de Allende*, in a fertile region, which occupies second place in the State for orange production. 82km **Montemorelos** (30,000 inhab.; 432m; H,R,P), Mexico's foremost orange producer, on the Río Morelos, affluent of the Río San Juan, with an attractive central plaza.

From here Méx. 35 runs NE via (19km) *General Terán* to (89km) the Monterrey–Reynosa road, see Rte 53. Another road runs SW into the Sierra Madre Oriental to (45km) *Los Rayón*, in a tobacco-producing area, and, through a landscape marked by circular depressions thought to have been caused by meteorites, to (70km) **Galeana** (7000 inhab.; 1655m; H,R,P), founded in 1678 as a mission by Franciscans from Zacatecas. Its church of *San Pablo de los Labradores* was begun in 1752 and recalls the name of the mission. The Sierra de Galeana is among the most dramatically mountainous in the State. 5km S is the *Laguna de Labradores* (sailing and fishing), its bed composed mainly of alabaster. C 14km W is the *Cerro El Potosí* (3800m), highest peak in the State. This road winds S through the Sierra Madre to (273km) *Matehuala* and (465km) *San Luis Potosí*, see Rte 57.

Méx. 85 continues S through farming country to (121km) *Hualahuises* and then E to (133km) **LINARES** (50,000 inhab.; 684m; H,R,P), a place of great charm, on the l. bank of the Río Pabillo, affluent of the Río de las Conchas.

It was founded as the villa of San Felipe de Linares (after viceroy duque de Linares) in 1711–12. In 1777 it became the seat of a bishop, although Monterrey was to become the episcopal residence. A new diocese was confirmed in 1962. It is today the State's second city after Monterrey.

On the main plaza is the cathedral of **San Felipe** (late 18C), in spare but effective style harking back to the Renaissance, with an espadaña and tall tower, a later addition. The handsome *Pal. Municipal* (late 19C) and the porfirian *Casino* also front the plaza. In the adjoining plaza is the church of *La Misericordia*, built from 1715 by the Franciscans.

From Linares Méx. 60 runs SW into the Sierra Madre via (44km) *Iturbide* amid spectacular scenery to (64km) the Montemorelos–Matehuala road 8km S of Galeana, see above.

At 162km we cross into the State of Tamaulipas. Beyond (182km) *Villagrán*, founded c 1755 as the mining camp of Real de Borbón, the road runs alongside the Río Purificación. From (250km) *El Barretal* Méx. 85 runs S to (288km) *Ciudad Victoria*.

CIUDAD VICTORIA (255,000 inhab.; 321m), capital of the State of Tamaulipas, on the Río San Marcos and in a henequen-producing region, is a tranquil modern city with shaded avenues and plentiful greenery. The victorenses' reputation for friendliness adds to the pleasant atmosphere.

Airport. 18km SE. Flights to *Mexico City*.

Bus station. NE of the centre, reached along Av. Carrera Torres. Frequent services to *Monterrey* (4½ hrs); to *Tampico* (4 hrs); to *Matamoros* (4½ hrs); to *Ciudad Valles* (4½ hrs); to *San Luis Potosí* (5 hrs); to *Querétaro* (9 hrs); to *Mexico City* (12 hrs); etc.

Railway station. W of the city centre, at the end of Av. Hidalgo. Daily trains on the Monterrey–Tampico line.

Hotels throughout the city.

Post Office. In Pal. Federal, C. Juan B. Tijerina.

Tourist Office. 272 C. Rosales (C. 16).

It was founded in 1750 as Villa de Sta María del Refugio de Aguayo. In 1825, renamed Ciudad Victoria in honour of the president, it became capital of the new State. During 1827–29 Samuel Bangs (see Rte 53) had his press (Prensa Libre de Bangs) here. On Christmas Day 1846 the city fell to US troops. After the Revolution it became the power base of Emilio Portes Gil (governor 1925–28; president 1928–30) whose Partido Socialista Fronterizo was ancestor of the PRI.

The E and centre of the State of **Tamaulipas** (2.4 million inhab.; 79,829 sq km) are on the coastal plain of the Gulf of Mexico, interspersed by volcanic ranges: in the N the Sierra de Tamaulipa Nueva (Sierra de San Carlos); in the S the Sierra de Tamaulipas (Sierra de Tamaulipa Vieja). The frontier with the USA is the Río Bravo. There is a remarkable coastline of barrier beaches, behind which are lagoons, changing size and salt content according to season. On the coast the climate is hot and humid during Apr.–Aug. Rainfall is especially heavy in late summer and autumn. Hurricanes can hit in Nov.–Feb. Industry is based on oil and gas, and petrochemical works. Among the crops of the central and S zones, sorghum and fruit are the highest-yielding.

In 1519–23 Francisco de Garay, governor of Jamaica, tried to establish a colony in the S of the present State, inhabited by the civilized Huastecs. The outrages committed by his troops provoked murderous retaliation. Cortés sent Gonzalo de Sandoval to pacify the N Huasteca by terror. In 1528 Nuño de Guzmán introduced his own terror, raiding N for slaves. Spanish cattlemen in the 17C and early 18C invaded and despoiled Indian lands, Indians having to be killed to keep sheep safe. In 1748–49 the viceroy ordered the definitive occupation of the region, to be called Nuevo Santander, under the military government of José de Escandón, who worked hard to establish the province, then extending almost as far N as the Río San Antonio in Texas. In 1824 the State of Las Tamaulipas was included in the federation. It lost the zone N of the Río Bravo after the treaty of Guadalupe Hidalgo. Porfirio Díaz showed especial favour to his tamaulipeco friends, some of whom became bywords for oppression of their labourers and were condemned even in the glare of the porfiriato. During the Revolution a movement in the Sierra Madre led by Alberto Carrera Torres adhered to the ideals of Zapata.

Av. Hidalgo, the city's main commercial thoroughfare, cuts through from E to W. In its centre is PL. DE ARMAS, with, on the S side, the *Pal. de Gobierno* (1948), containing murals (unfinished) illustrating State history by Ramón García Zurita. On either side of its front stair are bronze statues of Juárez and Carranza. The cathedral of *La Concepción* (E side) is one of the plainer 19C (altered since) ecclesiastical structures. On the N side is the *Centro Cultural Tamaulipas* (finished 1986), incl. a theatre, art gallery, and library. The *Pal. Municipal*, a little further W, in Av. Madero, dates from 1860. At the E end of Av. Hidalgo is PL. HIDALGO. On its N side is the *Teatro Juárez*, part of the *Universidad Autónoma de Tamaulipas*, founded during the governorship of Norberto Treviño Zapata (1957–63). A small historical museum is attached. In the neighbouring Rectoría is the **Museo de Antropología e Historia** and the *Instituto de Investigaciones Históricas* (Mon.–Fri., 9–1, 2–7; Sat., Sun., 9–1).

It contains exhibits illustrating the prehispanic Huastec culture and the history of Nuevo Santander and Tamaulipas. Among the historical pieces are the carriage of José de Escandón, 1st conde de Sierra Gorda, and the testament of Agustín de Iturbide.

Off the NE corner of the plaza is the modern *Pal. Federal* and, behind it, on C. Matamoros, the *Instituto Tamaulipeco de Bellas Artes*, for cultural events. A sprinkling of 19C houses graces the streets surrounding Pl. de Armas.

FROM CIUDAD VICTORIA TO SAN LUIS POTOSI, 347km. Méx. 101 climbs SW across the Sierra Madre Oriental. The region it traverses is known as región ixtlera, after the aloe plant (its fibre much tougher than henequen) much cultivated in it. 68km *Jaumave* (735m; R,P). 94km *Villa de Palmillas* (1300m; R), founded as the Franciscan visita of San Andrés de las Palmillas in the 17C. The church, now called Virgen de las Nieves, dates from the later 18C (contemporary altarpiece). 141km **Ciudad Tula** (7600 inhab.; 1173m; H,R,P), chief town of the region, which enjoyed a prosperous heyday during the porfiriato. It is the birthplace of doña María del Carmen Romero Rubio y Castelló (1864–1943), the influential 2nd wife of Porfirio

Díaz. At 180km Méx. 101 joins Méx. 80. 56km SE (l.) is **Ciudad del Maíz** (8000 inhab.; 1240m; H,R,P), in the Valle del Maíz, with an attractive old plaza, and a good excursion centre. It was scene of one of Francisco Javier Mina's victories (see Rte 51) over royalist forces, on 8 June 1817. From Ciudad del Maíz a poor road runs S to join (75km) Méx. 70, the San Luis Potosí–Ciudad Valles road, see Rte 61. From the junction with Méx. 80 we turn r. for (238km) *Huizache*, where we join Méx. 57 to (347km) *San Luis Potosí*, see Rte 57.

From Ciudad Victoria, Méx. 70 runs directly E, S of Presa Vicente Guerrero and then N of the Sierra de Tamaulipas, to (121km) **Soto la Marina** (5000 inhab.; 25m; H,P), in an area abounding in wildlife. Here on 15 Apr. 1817 arrived the expeditionary force of Francisco Javier Mina. On 12 July 1824 Agustín de Iturbide, having sailed from Southampton in England on 11 May, accompanied by his wife, two of his children, and his Polish friend Carlos de Beneski de Beaufort, reached land here. He was arrested by Gen. Felipe de la Garza, conducted to Padilla, and shot. Beyond the town the broad Río Soto la Marina flows E to its mouth at Barra Soto la Marina, near the fishing village of *La Pesca*. The road continues N of the river, a further 48km.

The road S of Soto la Marina, Méx. 180, runs between the Sierra de Tamaulipas and a wooded range of hills facing the coast to (114km) *Villa de Aldama*, see Rte 60.

From Ciudad Victoria to *Ciudad Mante* and *Ciudad Valles*, see Rte 60; to *Matamoros* and *Reynosa*, see Rte 59.

55 Piedras Negras to Saltillo and Zacatecas

Méx. 57, Méx 54, 806km.—123km Nueva Rosita.—134km Sabinas.—248km Monclova.—441km **Saltillo** and Méx. 54.—806km **Zacatecas**.

PIEDRAS NEGRAS (c 62,000 inhab.; 220m; H,R,P) is a busy frontier town in Coahuila across the Río Bravo from Eagle Pass in Texas. It was founded in 1850, and during 1880–1911 was known as Ciudad Porfirio Díaz.

Hence Méx. 2 runs N along the frontier via (46km) *Jiménez* and (89km) *Ciudad Acuña*, with a frontier crossing from Del Río in Texas, to (112km) **Presa de la Amistad** (area 30,000 hectares), built as a result of Mexican–US collaboration in 1965–69, providing irrigation and hydroelectric power over a wide area either side of the frontier. It is also a popular fishing and boating resort.

Méx. 57 runs SW from Piedras Negras. At 9km Méx. 2 runs S to (44km) *Villa Guerrero*, on the site of the Franciscan mission of *San Bernardo*, founded in Querétaro during 1698–1703. The ruins (chapel, sacristy, and baptistery) may still be seen. 42km *Nava* (R,P), a charming place (fruit-growing). From (54km) *Morelos* Méx. 29 runs N to (104km) *Ciudad Acuña*, see above. We turn SE to (62km) *Allende*, and then SW to (123km) **Nueva Rosita** (c 52,000 inhab.; 430m), a principal town in the Coahuila mining region (coke production), from where the miners in 1950 organized a march (caravana del hambre) on Mexico City in protest at their pay and conditions, which resulted in the nationalization of the US companies. The murals in the *Escuela de Minería y Metalurgia* are by Armando León and Pablo Plata.

FROM NUEVA ROSITA TO BOQUILLAS DEL CARMEN, 235km. State road 2. For the adventurous only, who should set out well provisioned and with a four-wheel drive vehicle in good condition and equipped with spare parts. Local advice should be sought. 25km *Palau*, another mining centre, from where a road runs SE via (33km) *Barroterán*, a mining town, to (43km) *El Sauz*, see below. 35km **Melchor Múzquiz** (26,000 inhab.; 504m; H,R,P), established in 1736–37 as the garrison of *Sta Rosa María* (or *Sacramento*), renamed in the mid-19C after its most famous native, Melchor Múzquiz (1790–1844; president 1832). Today it is an important mining town (lead, silver, zinc as well as coal) with a pleasant main plaza and a new and an old parish church (*Sta Rosa de Lima*), dating from the 19C and late 18C. To the S, W, and NW of the town extends the Sierra Hermosa de Sta Rosa.

Beyond Melchor Múzquiz we penetrate the Coahuila desert, often covered in grey-coloured vegetation. To the W rises the Sierra La Encantada; to the E the Sierra del Carmen, and, beyond it, the Serranías del Burro, which occupy the extreme NE of State territory. At 86km, in the Valle de los Guajes, a track (r.) goes to the *El Infante* ranch, known for its game. The plain gives way to low hills and mountain slopes; dramatic rock formations and extended rock walls, coloured red, violet, magenta, and yellow. Near (235km) *Boquillas del Carmen* the sierra is covered with pine and oak. To the E rise the *Pico del Carmen* (2263m) and the *Pico Etéreo*. There is a small customs post for crossing over the Río Bravo into Texas.

From Nueva Rosita, Méx. 57 runs SE to (134km) **Sabinas** (26,000 inhab.; 240m; H,R,P), a coalmining town on the Río Sabinas.

It was captured on 26 July 1920 by Francisco Villa. He then wired Pres. de la Huerta in Mexico City and offered to surrender in return for a hacienda to which he could retire. On 28 July he signed his capitulation here.
    66km SE is *Presa Don Martín*, see Rte 53.

From Sabinas, Méx. 57 runs S via (156km) *El Sauz* to (248km) **Monclova** (c 245,000 inhab.; 585m; H,R,P), on the l. bank of the Río Monclova, in an area famous for cattle and walnuts, but renowned above all for its iron and steel works, Altos Hornos de México.

It was settled as Santiago de Monclova in 1689. After their capture near Baján, Hidalgo, Allende, Aldama, Abasolo, Jiménez, and other insurgents were held here before being transferred on 26 March 1811 to Chihuahua. On 18 Apr. 1913, the Convention of Monclova disowned the usurpation of Huerta and confirmed the appointment of Carranza as First Chief. The Altos Hornos, established in 1942, is the most important iron and steel complex in the republic.

The town's two old churches, *Santiago* (18C), at the corner of Av. Carranza and C. Hidalgo, and *San Francisco* (begun in the late 17C), in Pl. Juárez, have been much modified. The *Hospital Real*, at the corner of Cs Ermita and Aldama, dates from the 18C.

113km E of Monclova (State road 30) we may reach the Nuevo Laredo–Monterrey road.
    The road NW runs to (21km) *San Buenaventura*. Thence Méx. 30 goes W, amid rocky landscapes, to (83km) *Cuatrociénegas* (8000 inhab.; 740m; H,R,P), in the basin of the Río Nadadores and in a wine-producing area (Grape Fair in second half of June). It is the birthplace of Venustiano Carranza (1859–1920). The house where he was born is now the *Museo de la Revolución*: six rooms contain facsimiles, dioramas, photographs, etc. illustrating his life and career. The parish church of *San Luis*, soberly eclectic, dates from the mid-19C.
    From here Méx. 30 undulates through outlying sierras of the Sierra Madre Oriental to (262km) *San Pedro de las Colonias* (H,R,P) and thence W to (334km) *Torreón*, see Rte 45.

From Monclova Méx. 57 runs S to (263km) *Castaños*, on the l. bank of the Río Nadadores, amid orchards and walnut groves. At 273km the road forks.

From here, the l. fork, Méx. 53, goes SE through desert into Nuevo León to (98km) *Los Pedernales*. 104km poor road l. for (42km) *Los Fresnos* in the Cerro Chiquihuitillos (prehispanic cave paintings). 107km *El Zapote* and (119km; 3km r.) *Mina* are two more centres for exploring cave paintings. 131km *San Nicolás Hidalgo*. 169km *Monterrey*, see Rte 53.

308km turning l. for (11km NE) **Baján**, a village near a small range of hills called Las Murallas. It was at *Acatita de Baján*, on 21 March 1811 that Hidalgo, Allende, Aldama, Abasolo, and Jiménez, on their way from Saltillo to Monclova and making for the USA, 'disorientated by lack of sleep, dying of hunger and thirst, and dozing in their carriages', were captured by a force led by Ignacio Elizondo, captain of the Monclova militia. An obelisk 6km SE commemorates the event.
    At 341km a road l. leads to (6km E) *Guadalupe* where on 6 March 1913 was signed the Plan of Guadalupe which disowned Huerta and appointed Carranza as First Chief. Méx. 57 runs through a lonely landscape, full of typical vegetation, to (441km) *Saltillo*.
    SALTILLO (379,000 inhab.; 1600m), capital of the State of Coahuila, stands in the upland Valle de Saltillo surrounded by rugged peaks, W extensions of the Sierra Madre Oriental. It is a major industrial centre, famous for its serapes, which come from its textile mills, and for its pottery and silverware. The warm,

sunny, and dry climate attracts many visitors, as does the cathedral, one of the outstanding ecclesiastical buildings of N Mexico. The saltillenses have a reputation for 'honesty and courtesy'.

Airport. C 10km N. Flights to *Mexico City*.

Bus station. Periférico Sur, between Cs Hidalgo and Morelos. Bus No. 9 connects with Pl. de Armas. Services to *Monterrey* (2 hrs); to *Ciudad Victoria* (4 hrs); to *Zacatecas* (5 hrs); to *Piedras Negras* (9 hrs); to *Concepción del Oro* (2 hrs); etc.

Railway station. W of the centre, in Av. E. Carranza. Daily train (Aguila Azteca) to *San Luis Potosí* (7½ hrs), *Querétaro* (12½ hrs), and *Mexico City* (18–19 hrs). To *Monclova* (5 hrs) and *Piedras Negras* (10½ hrs). Monterrey–Mexico City line: to *Monterrey* (2½ hrs), *San Luis Potosí* (6 hrs), and *Mexico City* (13½ hrs).

Hotels throughout the city.

Post Office. C. Guadalupe Victoria Poniente.

Tourist Office. In Centro de Convenciones, on Blvd de los Fundadores, 6.5km E of the centre.

Fiestas. 6 Aug.: Sto Cristo de la Capilla. 13 Aug.: Annual Fair begins.

The villa Santiago del Saltillo was founded in 1577. In 1591 colonists from Tlaxcala (71 families and 16 bachelors) were settled next door at San Esteban de Nueva Tlaxcala. In March 1811 Allende and Hidalgo retreated N from here in the hope of getting aid from the USA. In 1824 Saltillo became capital of Coahuila and Texas, a status it was periodically to lose to Monclova. In 1846 occupying US troops were received with great hostility. In 1864 Juárez made his headquarters here. Carranza's departure from Saltillo with a small force in Feb. 1913 marked the beginning of the constitutionalist Revolution. What was to become an all-powerful influence with Mexican labour, the Confederación Regional Obrera Mexicana (CROM), was founded in Saltillo in 1918.

The State of **Coahuila** (2 million inhab.; 151,571 sq km), third most extensive of the republic after Chihuahua and Sonora, lies mainly within the N regions (Meseta del Norte) of the High Plateau, across which, from SE to NW and from E to W in the S, stretch two ramifications of the Sierra Madre Oriental, in turn divided into numerous ranges. To the W of the NW-inclining Sierra Madre is the Bolsón de Mapimí, a broad interior drainage basin marked by ephemeral lakes and oases (incl. the Laguna district), sustained by rivers rising in the Sierra Madre Occidental. To the E and NE the terrain gradually slopes towards the Gulf coastal plain. Irrigation, intensive in the Laguna, also benefits districts of the N and centre. Mining takes place in the centre, N, and NE. The iron and steel industry has come up against Mexico's economic crisis.

The N, and more substantial, part of the present State (also called Nueva Extremadura) was from the 17C disputed between Nueva Vizcaya and Nuevo León. The S part formed the province of Parras and Saltillo, subject to Nueva Vizcaya. The first Spanish exploration was by Alvar Núñez Cabeza de Vaca in 1535. From the 1690s until 1722 Texas and Coahuila were under the same jurisdiction. After the war (1561–89) against Spanish settlers, Chichimecs fled to the area, but were hunted down for slaves; the Bolsón de Mapimí was a last redoubt for small tribes, which dwindled away. By the 1730s Apaches were invading, harassed by Comanches from the N, the former resisting attempts to herd them into missions. Among the huge estates was that of José de Azlor y Virto de Vera, 2nd marqués de San Miguel de Aguayo (1677–1734), in 1719 appointed governor of Coahuila and Texas. In an expedition of 1721–22, at his own expense, he assured Spanish domination of Texas. In the 1840s Carlos Sánchez Navarro bought up the interests in the State of Baring Brothers, the London finance house, owners of the Aguayo estate, which by 1850 came to 81,000 sq km. In 1824 Coahuila and Texas were recognized a State, but Texas was lost in 1836. In 1856 Santiago Vidaurri annexed Coahuila to Nuevo León, which, with his governorship of Tamaulipas, gave him enormous power in the N, an act reversed by Juárez in 1864.

On the E side of PL. DE ARMAS, still evoking the past, stands the cathedral of **Santiago**, a great undertaking which reflects a period of economic prosperity.

It was started in 1745, the project of the parish priest Felipe Suárez, 'whose ideas', wrote Agustín Morfi dyspeptically in 1777, when the work was still unfinished, 'exceeded the generosity and devotion of his neighbours'. It opened for worship in 1800. The tower was completed in 1897.

EXTERIOR. The W façade joins late baroque and churrigueresque, a composition of robust beauty, laden with vigorous relief-scrolls, fruit, foliage,

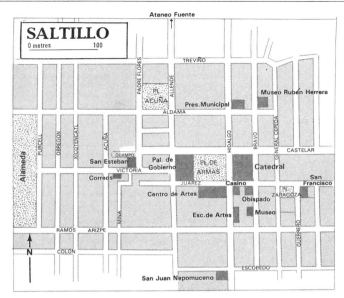

cherubs, saintly figures, shells. The supports, superbly cut and defined, stand well forward. In the lower storey, two pairs of solomonic columns; in the upper, two pairs of estípites, among the finest in Mexico. On either side of both storeys rise baluster-like columns remarkable for their girth and strength, enveloped in relief, but on the r. truncated by the base of the tower. The doorway is covered by a great, deep shell, itself covered by a second arch. The shell motif is repeated in the niches between the supports and in the gable, which is crowned by energetic scrolls, more than a decorative flourish. The baroque S doorway repeats solomonic columns, volutes, and the deep shell motif above doorway (this time with a pentagonal arch), whose soffit of varied tableros contrasts with the gay relief of its face) and niches. The cupola is reinforced by four buttresses. Solomonic columns appear at intervals in the drum; estípites in the lantern.

INTERIOR. In the interior of the cupola is a curious frieze of reliefs of saints; more figures, between solomonic columns, are interspersed between the windows of the drum. Polychrome reliefs of saints fill the pendentives. The nave columns are decorated as if for an exterior portal. In the transepts are two beautiful gilded altarpieces which echo the style and motifs of the exterior. That in the r. transept, both baroque and anastyle in design, displays in its lower storey two pairs of solomonic columns flanking spacious niches encompassed by unusually wrought volutes. The central tabernacle, upheld by slenderer columns, is topped and flanked by a riot of volute patterns—motifs repeated in the upper storey. The fine central painting here, of the Holy Family, is by José de Alzíbar. The l. transept altarpiece, covered in rococo patterns, is done with great delicacy, with hints of the churrigueresque in its upper parts, but with slender variations of the ornamental niche pilaster flanking the four levels of ornate niches in the outer sections. The pulpit is covered in gold leaf.

On the N side of the cathedral is the *Cap. de Cristo*, opened in 1762, to contain an image of the Crucifixion brought to Saltillo in 1608 by the Basque Santos Rojo.

Facing the cathedral is the *Pal. de Gobierno*, rebuilt in the later 19C after the original went up in an explosion in 1856. Of the same period is the *Casino*

(1874), S of the cathedral at the corner with C. Hidalgo. Opposite is the *Centro de Artes Visuales*, an early 19C house (with a fountain of 1885) containing a museum of modern art (works by Gerardo and Federico Cantú, Pablo O'Higgins, and others) and rooms for temporary exhibitions.

Almost opposite the Casino is the *Alianza Francesa*, and, further up on the l., the *Escuela de Artes Rubén Herrera*, part of the University of Coahuila. Further S, at the corner with C. Escobedo, is the well-designed church of *San Juan Nepomuceno* (late 19C), which contains an interesting altarpiece painting by Antonio Sánchez (1775; side chapel). In nave and sanctuary are vast canvases by Gonzalo Carasco, contemporary with the church.

From the SE corner of the plaza, C. Juárez leads past the former *Obispado* (r., corner with C. Bravo) where Juárez lodged in Feb.–Apr. 1864. In C. Bravo (r.) is the 18C building once occupied by the *Liceo de las Artes*, its portal a replica of that of the church of Landín (see below). It is now the *Museo de las Culturas*. C. Juárez continues to PL. ZARAGOZA. On its E side is the church of *San Francisco* (1787).

Its adjoining convent was (1867–1933) the premises of the Ateneo Fuente (see below). The Baptist church was rudely built in the atrio alongside it in 1885.
    To the W of Pl. de Armas, in the space marked off by Cs Guadalupe Victoria Poniente, Melchor Ocampo, and Padre Flores, is the church of **San Esteban**, built in the final years of the 16C as the church of the barrio of San Esteban de Nueva Tlaxcala. It has undergone various changes: in the 1920s it was roofed in cement and the high altar was changed from the S to the N end. Further W along C. Victoria we reach the shady ALAMEDA, notable for statues in memory of two famous saltillenses by Jesús Contreras (late 19C): Gen. Ignacio Zaragoza (1829–62), in bronze, and an allegory dedicated to the poet Manuel Acuña (1849–73).
    To the N of Pl. de Armas, C. Hidalgo reaches C. Aldama. To the r. before the crossing is the rebuilt 18C house where Hidalgo lodged in March 1811; to the r., after the crossing, the *Presidencia Municipal*, an adapted 18C building (murals by Elena Huerta). Behind it is the *Biblioteca Pública*. Opposite the library, at 342 C. Bravo Norte, is the *Museo de Arte Rubén Herrera* (Wed.–Mon., 9–12, 3–6), containing works by this painter (1888–1933), who directed the academy of painting in the city.
    In the N part of the city, at the crossing of Av. Venustiano Carranza and C. González Lobo, is the *Ateneo Fuente*, finished in 1933 in the new semi-functional style. Founded in 1867, it attained prestige as the leading high school in N Mexico. It is now part of the University of Coahuila, and contains a museum of natural history and a *Pinacoteca* (9–1; incl. works by Juan Rodríguez Juárez and Saturnino Herrán). The huge portal of the *Instituto Tecnológico* opposite, where Av. Venustiano Carranza meets C. Universidad, is a modern throwback to late 18C exuberance. Along Av. Lázaro Cárdenas, in the SE suburbs may be reached the ruined 18C church of **Landín**, once belonging to a ranch of that name. Its richly decorated portal survives.
    From Saltillo to (276km) *Torreón* (E on Méx. 40), see Rte 45; to (83km) *Monterrey*, see Rte 56; to (452km) *San Luis Potosí*, see Rte 56.
    An excursion may be made E of Saltillo, along a road penetrating the Sierra Madre and offering beautiful views, to (17km) *Arteaga*, in the Valle de Arteaga. 5km E, the *Valle de los Lirios* is another beauty spot.

From Saltillo, Méx. 54 goes S, between two mountain ranges, via (457km) the hamlet of *La Encantada* to (463km) the junction with the road (r.) for (66km NW) *La Rosa* on the Saltillo–Torreón road, and (122km W) *Parras de la Fuente*, see Rte 45.

An alternative, and historic, road runs parallel to the W, nearer the railway line. Along it, 8km slightly SW of Saltillo, is the hacienda of **Buenavista**, associated with the battle of 22–23 Feb. 1847 when the US troops of Gen. Taylor met those of Santa-Anna, who had advanced, amid hellish conditions, from San Luis Potosí. Taylor had withdrawn his men (c 7000, but with superior artillery) to Buenavista, N of the pass called *La Angostura*, halfway between it and La Encantada. Santa-Anna disposed of c 14,000, whom he had paid out of his personal fortune. The battle took place in La Angostura. By the afternoon of 23 Feb., Santa-Anna had ordered a retreat, on the grounds that his men were exhausted, that he had nothing for them to eat, and that many might desert during the night. Mexican casualties were 694 dead and 1039 wounded; US casualties 267 dead and 456 wounded.

470km *Agua Nueva* was the furthest point of Taylor's advance before he fell back to Buenavista. The road continues S across desert into the State of Zacatecas to (553km) the junction with a road W to (4km) *Concepción del Oro* and (27km) *Mazapil.*

Concepción del Oro (15,000 inhab.; 2070m), attractively situated in the sierra of the same name, is a mining (lead, zinc, copper, gold) town with typical one-storey houses. 4km NW is *Bonanza*, once a satellite mining camp of Mazapil. **Mazapil** (5000 inhab.; 2340m), in the Sierra de Mazapil, is another old mining town, where Spaniards from Zacatecas first settled in 1569, attracted by silver deposits. The 18C church of *San Gregorio Magno* has a rustic baroque façade and four contemporary altarpieces. The area was part of the vast landholding of the 2nd marqués de San Miguel de Aguayo (see above), who transferred here in 1712 from Pamplona in Spain. His house in Mazapil survives.

Méx. 54 goes S into the S High Plateau. At (608km) *San Tiburcio* a road runs E to (117km) *Matehuala*, see Rte 56. 806km *Zacatecas*, see Rte 45.

56 Monterrey to San Luis Potosí via Saltillo

Méx. 40, Méx. 57, 535km.—83km Saltillo and Méx. 57.—337km turning NW for (56km) Real de Catorce.—343km Matehuala.—535km **San Luis Potosí**.

Méx. 40 leaves Monterrey to the W. On either side ranges of the Sierra Madre. 18km turning l. for (2km SW) the *Cañón Huasteco*, a zone of high, massive rock formations topped by a forest of firs. 25km turning r. for (16km N) *Villa de García* (697m), a picturesque little town.

9km NE, at the foot of the Cerro el Fraile, are the **Grutas de García**, one of the most spectacular cave systems in the Americas, reached by a funicular (10–5; 700m; 10 minutes for the ascent; guide). The caves, now illuminated, contain an endlessly fascinating succession, on the grand scale, of stalagtites and stalagmites.

71km *Ramos Arizpe* (P), in attractive surroundings. 4km N are the ruins of the hacienda of **Sta María**. Its 17C church, with a timber ceiling and gilded altarpiece, has survived. Here on 17 March 1811 Hidalgo offered his last Mass. 83km *Saltillo*.

We leave Saltillo on Méx. 57 due E and then S into the Sierra Madre, descending into Nuevo León and desert country. At (215km) *Entronque San Roberto* (P) a road leads E to (98km) *Linares*, see Rte 54. Beyond (285km) *Sta Ana* we cross into the State of San Luis Potosí. 337km turning r. (NW) for (19km) *Cedral*.

Beyond Cedral the road runs W to (11km) turning l. along a winding road for (26km S) **Real de Catorce** (700 inhab.; 2750m; H), in a valley of the Sierra de Catorce, a ghost town, born of a silver-mining boom, and approached through a tunnel (2.3km long), a disused early 20C mining gallery.

Silver ore was discovered here in 1778 and the camp, first called Alamos, by 1780 had developed into the town of Purísima Concepción de los Catorce. In 1795 its population was 14,750. By the early 19C it held third place among silver producers in New Spain and in 1803 its output is said to have been worth 3.5 million pesos. The Casa de Moneda functioned in 1863–69 for the coining of silver. Its shafts were largely flooded at the outbreak of the Revolution, which provoked wholesale emigration.

Although threatened by restoration and development as a tourist centre, the town still preserves its uncannily quiet, desolate air. The inhabitants live among crumbling buildings in hope of a new silver strike. On the E of Pl. Principal the parish church of *La Purísima Concepción* (1780) is the target for pilgrims during the first week in Oct. The walls are covered in ex-votos; the sacristy contains contemporary paintings. To the E of the church, the *Casa de Moneda* is in fact a three-storey early 19C house. To the NW of the plaza, the *Palenque de Gallos* (restored) was built in the mid-19C like an amphitheatre for cockfights; the *Pl. de Toros*, to its N, dates from the same period (excellent views). In C. Lanzagorta is a small parish museum (10–4; fee) containing objects from the mines' heyday.

343km **Matehuala** (c 50,000 inhab.; 1615m; H,R,P), in the wide Valle de Salado, is at an important road junction and well placed for visits to Real de Catorce. It was the scene of a famous battle on 17 May 1864 when the imperialists under Mejía defeated the republicans under Manuel Doblado, which assured peace in San Luis Potosí for two years.

The road E from Matehuala runs into S Nuevo León, to (49km) *Doctor Arroyo* (P) and then NE into the Sierra Madre to (106km) a junction for (10km E) *Aramberri* (1077m). 21km S of Aramberri is *General Zaragoza* (1371m) in a beautiful mountain landscape, well-wooded, crossed by streams, tributaries of the Río Blanco. The main road (State road 61) continues N to (203km) *Galeana*, see Rte 54.

363km road r. (SW) through the Sierra de Catorce to (63km) **Charcas**, historically a remote outpost in the Sierra de Charcas, since the 1570s a mining and ore-processing centre. In the baptistery of the parish church of *San Francisco*, a 16C foundation, but altered with the years, is a Baptism of Christ (1690; in need of restoration) by Juan Correa.

He also painted an ambitious Genealogy of St Francis in the sacristy of the church of San Sebastián at *Venado*, 21km S. To him also are attributed paintings of saints in the pendentives of the sacristy cupola and of the Last Supper in the same place.

426km *El Huizache* (R,P), whence Méx. 80 runs SE to (112km) *Ciudad del Maíz*, see Rte 54. 458km turning l. for (15km E) **Guadalcázar** (c 2000 inhab.; 1673m), in the Sierra de Guadalcázar, founded as a real de minas in 1616 and still a mining centre. It has two 18C churches and a so-called *Casa de Moneda* of the same period. 481km turning l. for (c 6km) the hacienda of *Peotillos*, in its present form dating from 1863. Its predecessor was scene of a battle on 15 June 1817, when a force of 300 led by Francisco Javier Mina soundly defeated 2000 royalist troops. 488km *Villa Hidalgo*. On the l., the Sierra de Juárez. 535km *San Luis Potosí*.

57 San Luis Potosí

SAN LUIS POTOSI (500,000 inhab.; 1877m), capital of the State of the same name, stands on a plateau in the Valle de San Luis, its commercial and industrial importance founded on its traditional mining wealth, the products of neighbouring haciendas, and on textiles and brewing. It is a splendid city with a confident air, generated by the diligent and courteous potosinos. San Luis has held on to a fair portion of its rich artistic and architectural heritage, exemplified by its cathedral, its churches, its old houses with their beautiful windows and balconies, and, above all, by the incomparable treasures of San Francisco and El Carmen.

Airport. 23km NW. Flights to *Mexico City, Guadalajara*, and *Monterrey*; and to *Chicago*.

Bus station. C 4km E of centre, reached along Av. Universidad and S of Glorieta Juárez. Frequent services to *Mexico City* (6 hrs); to *Guadalajara* (6 hrs); to *Querétaro* (3 hrs); to *Zacatecas* (3 hrs); to *Aguascalientes* (3 hrs); to *Monterrey* (8 hrs); etc.

Railway station. N side of Alameda Juan Sarabia. Aguila Azteca via *San Miguel de Allende* (2¾ hrs), *Celaya* (3½ hrs), *Querétaro* (5 hrs), to *Mexico City* (10–11 hrs); to *Monterrey* (8–9 hrs); to *Tampico* (13 hrs); to *Aguascalientes* (6½ hrs).

Hotels throughout the city.

Post Office. 235 C. Morelos.

Tourist Office. 325 Av. Venustiano Carranza.

US Consulate. 1430 Av. Venustiano Carranza.

Fiestas. 20 Jan.: St Sebastian. 25 July: St James the Greater (Santiago). 25 Aug.: St Louis IX. 29 Sept.: St Michael. 12 Oct.: Virgen de los Remedios.

San Luis Minas de Potosí (after the mines of Potosí in present-day Bolivia) was founded in 1592. Haphazard exploitation by adventurers began. By 1620 the mines appeared exhausted, but by the mid-17C prosperity returned, thanks to the discovery of new veins, especially of silver. In 1767, during a period of social unrest, serious rioting, in protest at the expulsion of the Jesuits, brought the visitor-general, José de Gálvez, to restore order. His report attested to 'sacrileges, and atrocious offences against Divine Majesty, and execrable blasphemies with which the rebels insulted the benevolence of our august sovereign…and on that day [26 June] they added other most grave crimes, for they opened the prison and set free many villainous criminals'. He put the rioters on trial, brought an energetic executioner from San Luis de la Paz, executed 32, banished 33, and imprisoned 109 for life. In 1786, after Gálvez's reforms, San Luis became capital of a vast intendancy and in 1824 capital of the new State. In 1835 and 1846 it was headquarters of Santa-Anna, recruiting armies for his campaigns against the Texans and the US invaders.

The anti-Díaz cause found a champion in Camilo Arriaga, who summoned a national liberal convention to meet in the city early in 1901. In 1910 Francisco I. Madero, charged with inciting rebellion, was brought here and held under supervision until he jumped bail in Oct. to flee to Texas. From San Antonio he issued his Plan of San Luis Potosí declaring Díaz's re-election void. Jesús Carranza's capture of San Luis in July 1914 precipitated the downfall of Pres. Huerta. In 1915 Tomás Urbina, Villa's henchman, was in brief, fierce control until defeated by the carrancistas. Persecution flared up in 1926 when all churches were closed and ten priests only allowed in the city.

The State of **San Luis Potosí** (2 million inhab.; 63,068 sq km) is mostly a plateau extending from the N plains to the S area of the High Plateau and inclining to the E. In the E is the Sierra Madre Oriental, its slopes covered by forests of oak and pine, and, beyond it, the fertile

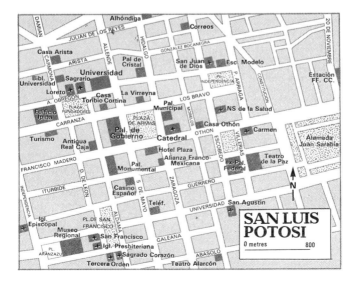

SAN LUIS POTOSI
0 metres   800

Huasteca. Except in the far SE, where rise streams which feed the Río Moctezuma, the State has no significant rivers and rainfall is light. Cattle-raising has increased in importance: the livestock of the Huasteca is of finest quality. Mineral wealth is still a mainstay, eg, at Guadalcázar, where ores yield gold, copper, zinc, bismuth, and silver.

Spanish penetration into the area dates probably from the 1550s. Apart from the N districts of Charcas, Catorce, and Salinas, which were part of Nueva Galicia, the territory formed the N extremity of the kingdom of New Spain. The intendant of San Luis Potosí (from 1786) ruled a huge territory (616,000 sq leagues) extending N into Nuevo León, Nuevo Santander, Coahuila, Texas. In 1810 Félix Calleja, commanding the San Luis brigade, organized 4000 cavalry, 1200 infantry, and 1500 Indians, and struck S, to defeat Hidalgo. In 1817 Francisco Javier Mina won victories at Ciudad del Maíz and Peotillos. The boundaries of the State were fixed in 1824. In 1858–64 it was one of the principal theatres of the war of the Reform and the French Intervention. The 1920s saw the rise of Saturnino Cedillo as State boss. In 1938 he led a conservative, pro-clerical revolt, the only, hitherto, post-Revolutionary internal uprising, against Pres. Cárdenas, who quickly scotched it. The governorship of Gonzalo A. Santos (1943–49) ushered in a further period of caciquismo, to last until 1959 when local protest forced the resignation of his governor ally. Prompted by continuing unrest, Pres. López Mateos ordered in federal troops to restore order.

PL. DE ARMAS (*Jardín Hidalgo*) is bordered by historic buildings, in its centre a bandstand (1848).

Here the pro-Jesuit rioters of 1767 were executed, Gálvez watching from a balcony, 'his valiant soul', as a contemporary priest put it, 'full of terrible grief at the sight of the still warm corpses hanging from the gallows'.

On its W side stands the *Pal. de Gobierno*, clean-cut and neoclassical, built in 1799–1816 as the *Casas Consistoriales* by Miguel Costansó and repaired in 1817–27 by Jean-Baptiste Crouzet. It was enlarged in 1847, renovated in 1950, and further enlarged on the S side in 1966 and on the W in 1971–73.

Here in 1867, Juárez, courteously but firmly, refused appeals for the lives of Maximilian, Miramón, and Mejía from those who came, some clamorously, to importune him: 200 ladies from San Luis; Princess Salm-Salm, who fell on her knees and clasped Juárez's; the wives of Miramón and Mejía; and Maximilian's defending counsel, Rafael Martínez de la Torre and Mariano Riva Palacio. In the *Sala Juárez* on the first floor is a diorama which shows the meeting between Juárez and the princess and the table at which he ratified the death sentence.

On the N side of the plaza is the so-called *Casa de la Virreyna* (1736; now a restaurant). Its façade was destroyed in the late 19C.

It belonged to Manuel de la Gándara, uncle of Francisca de la Gándara (1786–1855), the only Mexican-born vicereine, who married Félix Calleja in 1807. Next door, at the corner with C. Hidalgo, the former *Pal. Solana* (late 18C) was thoroughly remodelled (top floor added) by Molina and Compiani c 1896.

On the S side is the *Hotel Plaza*, a house rebuilt in the early 19C, which opened in 1860 as the *San Luis*, the city's first hotel of repute. On 18 June 1858, Luis Gonzaga Osollo, ablest of the conservative generals, praised for his noble character and good works, died here of typhoid at the age of 30.

On the E rises the cathedral of **La Expectación de la Virgen**, with an original, audaciously designed, baroque exterior.

It was built in 1701–29 and consecrated in 1730. In 1855–66 modernizing changes were made to the interior. In 1896, two Italian architects, Claudio Molina and Giuseppe Compiani, were commissioned by Bp Montes de Oca to do it up 'in byzantine style'. Their excesses were toned down by further modifications in 1955.

EXTERIOR. The W façade, its effect heightened by the light-brown stone and the patterns and features in which it is fashioned, is shaped in seven planes. In the two outer sections the wall projects into trapezoids, making three surfaces on either side. Solomonic columns, covered in vine shoots, frame the forward niches; classical pilasters those at the sides. A contrast is the shapes cut into the bases between and below the cornices: tableros in the lower storey, rhomboid in the upper. The storeys are, unusually, of equal height. Only the thickness of columns and pilasters diminishes in the upper.

In the niches stand marble statues of the apostles, ordered from Italy by Bp Montes de Oca—smaller copies of those by pupils of Bernini in St John Lateran at Rome. The original statues now stand at the edge of the roof on N and S sides.

In the central section, the graceful multifoil doorway arch is topped by a charming key, a relief of the infant Christ backed by a shell and surrounded by more delicate relief which overflows into the spandrels. The three-storey towers, with three types of solomonic column, harmonize beautifully with the façade. The N tower, an exact copy of the S, in grey stone, was finished in 1910.

The S doorway, at first sight simple, is in fact deceptively rich. A Christ child (?) relief forms the key to the pentagonal arch. The shafts of the remarkable columns are divided into three sections, marked off by rings. Thick foliate relief in the lowest encloses playful cherubs; in the centre, a spiral pattern; in the upper, a petatillo pattern. The composite capitals, their decoration repeated on either side at the top of the backing pilasters, continue the ornate effect. Rhomboids, emphatic in the column bases, are repeated, lightly, above the cornice which juts over the vine and flower frieze.

INTERIOR. The vaulting of nave and side aisles rests on huge composite pilasters. Survivals of the decoration of 1896 are the gilded coffering of the cupola and the painting of the vaults; scraping off paint from pilasters and arches has released the stonework and reintroduced spaciousness. The neo-classical side altars (with a neo-Gothic in the N aisle) replaced their baroque predecessors in 1855–56. Beneath the high altar is a copy of a recumbent statue of St Sebastian by Antonio Giorgetti in the church of San Sebastiano on the Appian Way, bought in Rome by Bp Montes de Oca. The statue of Nuestra Señora de la Expectación above is attr. Mariano Perusquía. In the chapel at the W end of the S (r.) aisle is the green and white marble tomb of Bp Ignacio Montes de Oca y Obregón (1840–1921), built at his orders in 1896. His bust is by Giulio Tadolini, a Roman sculptor.

Montes de Oca, a quintessential creole aristocrat, studied for the priesthood at Oscott College (Warwickshire) and served briefly as curate in Ipswich before returning to Mexico in 1865 as chaplain to Maximilian. In 1885 he became Bp of San Luis Potosí. He died in exile in New York. At 17 he spoke seven languages; Card. Wiseman declared that he was worth seven men.
On the wall behind the third altar is an Immaculate Conception by Juan Patricio Morlete Ruiz. Beyond it, the entrance to the SACRISTY, containing paintings: José de Páez, Seven Sacraments, Death of St Joseph; Morlete Ruiz, St Rose; Nicolás Rodríguez Juárez, Scourging of Christ, St Dominic, St Nicholas; Juan Rodríguez Juárez, Angels with the Lamb, St Lucy.

Alongside the cathedral is the **Pal. Municipal**, remodelled in 1873 from the *Viejas Casas Reales*, sacked and ruined in 1767, in full decay by the 1820s. It was acquired in 1892 by Bp Montes de Oca and magnificently furnished by him, but was sacked by the revolutionaries in 1914.

The former episcopal library, now the council chamber, was decorated in 1892–97 by Erulo Eroli.

From the NW corner of the plaza we take Av. Venustiano Carranza, passing (r.) the remains of the *Casa de Toribio Cortina* (18C), once belonging to a royalist commander wounded in 1810.

It was destructively adapted as the *Cine Othón* in 1930 when the widow of the eponymous poet (see below) worked here selling tickets. The balconies on the r. were spared.

Beyond it we reach the spacious PL. DE LOS FUNDADORES, site of the city's foundation. On its W side is the huge *Edificio Ipiña* (1906–23), by Octaviano L. Cabrera Hernández, built for José Encarnación Ipiña (1836–1913) and today housing part of the university.

Friend of Juárez, whose expenses he defrayed in 1863, hacendado, and benefactor, in 1911 Ipiña was appointed interim governor and gave the revolutionary chief Cándido Navarro a large sum of money to head off wholesale pillage.

On the N side of the plaza are the former church, chapel, and college of the Jesuits. In the centre is the church called **El Sagrario** (formerly *La Compañía*). Its façade (late 17C) has contrasted columns: fluted in the lower storey, covered with jagged rings in the upper. The 18C interior was restored and updated in 1840, and redecorated in the late 19C by Jesús L. Sánchez.

The façade of the adjoining chapel of **Loreto** is exquisitely baroque.

EXTERIOR. The intrados of the arch, jambs, frieze, swelling twisted columns, outer border, and curved doorway pediment are covered in filigree relief of marvellous delicacy. Vine shoots wind round the columns and bunches of grapes hang bold across the bulbous sections. Jambs and borders are filled with flowers on whose stems stand exotic birds spreading their fanlike wings. The relief creeps upwards to frame the niche containing the statue of Our Lady of Loreto, flanked by a pair of beautiful octagonal windows, studded with decorative keys. On either side, the cosmetic buttresses, of rectangular and triangular panels, support the semicircular outer pediment.

The gilded high altarpiece combines baroque and churrigueresque.

On the other side of the church is the old building of the **Universidad Autónoma de San Luis Potosí**, the former Jesuit college, begun in 1653.

The present structure, with its wide, handsome, late neoclassical façade, belongs largely to a rebuilding in 1882, but the fine patio preserves the original lower-storey arcade. Various offices of the university (founded in 1923) remain here, incl. the faculty of science and an archaeological and ethnographical museum. Also preserved here are manuscripts and books from the Jesuit library.

Behind the chapel, in C. Damián Carmona, is the *Biblioteca de la Universidad* (1922), heavily neoclassical. Further along, at No. 210, is the house where Mariano Arista (1802–55) was born.

From the roof of the *Hotel Panorama*, opposite the Edificio Ipiña, a panoramic view of the city may be had. Av. Carranza runs W to (c 2km; l., at the corner with C. Juan de Oñate) the **Casa de Cultura** (Tues.–Sat., 10–2, 6–9; Sun., 10–2), a mansion begun in 1909 for the Meade family, in a charming garden. Temporary art exhibitions are held here. The permanent collection includes 17–18C Mexican religious sculpture and 18–19C paintings (Juan Correa, José de Ibarra, José de Alzíbar).

Behind the Pal. de Gobierno, at the corner of Av. Madero and C. Aldama, is the former **Real Caja**, only remaining baroque civil building in San Luis, with a puerta chata.

It was built in 1764–68, possibly by the treasurer Felipe Cleere, as the local treasury and tax office. In 1938 it was reconditioned as the State treasury. Today it houses the university school of engineering.

The well-proportioned portal displays beguiling detail, in the framing of door and window, and in the contrast of upper- and lower-storey columns, both sets with corinthian capitals, but the upper wrapped with spiralling festoons which make them appear solomonic. The coat-of-arms above the window is that of Bp Montes de Oca. The niche below the intricately curving gable holds a favourite statue of the Immaculate Conception. Framing the sides are tall, slender engaged columns laden with winding leaf relief. Elegance is the hallmark of the octagonal patio, where the arches are upheld by pilasters of unusual spareness. On the r. of the entrance is the beautifully carved doorway to what was once the chapel.

Diagonally opposite stands the glowering **Pal. Monumental** (1899–1903) by the French Canadian Henri Guindon, on the site of the *Casa de Moneda*, destroyed in 1893. It was a property of the influential Meade family, bankers and hacendados of English descent. Here stayed Francisco I. Madero as their guest during his detention. Hence he escaped in Oct. 1910 to San Antonio. It was altered and amplified in 1950–73. Opposite, in C. Aldama, are the premises of *La Lonja*, since 1868 a meeting-place of potosino society, with ballroom and restaurant.

From the NE corner of Pl. de Armas, C. Hidalgo goes N. On the l., at the corner with Av. Obregón, is the *Pal. de Cristal* (1909), also by Guindon, for Eduardo Meade. Three blocks further, on the r., opposite *Mercado Hidalgo*, is the old

Alhóndiga (1771–75). Its interior was transformed after 1912; the exterior arcade remains intact.

The district to the N includes the site of the former barrio of *Tlaxcalilla*, home of the Tlaxcaltecans settled there in 1592. A survival is the church and cloister of **Asunción**, founded in 1605. The church, modified since, contains a painting of Our Lady of Guadalupe (1761; l.; in nave) by José Pardo. The sacristy contains three scenes from the Way of the Cross by Antonio de Torres and a St Casimir by Antonio Sánchez; a Crucifixion and Descent from the Cross are doubtfully attr. Baltasar de Echave Ibía.

From the Pal. de Cristal, Av. Obregón continues E. On the l., at its corner with C. Escobedo, is **San Juan de Dios**, once attached to the hospital (founded in 1611; suppressed in 1827) of the Brothers of St John of God.

Two of them, Luis Herrera and Juan de Villerías, instigated the potosino uprising, in support of Hidalgo, in Nov. 1810. The church was rebuilt in 1908 by Octaviano L. Cabrera Hernández; only the walls and side portal remain of the original. It is now run by the Dominicans. The *Escuela Modelo* (1907; also by Cabrera Hernández) occupies the site of the hospital. It faces JARDIN DE SAN JUAN DE DIOS, laid out anew in 1976, with a monument to Independence (1911).

C. Escobedo goes S and crosses Av. Carranza. On the l. is the *Cap. de Nuestra Señora de la Salud* (1742–43). In its sacristy is a painting of Our Lady of Guadalupe (1802) by Andrés López.
C. Escobedo next crosses C. Othón. The r. turn leads back to Pl. de Armas past (r.) the *Casa de Othón*, where the poet and dramatist Manuel José Othón (1858–1906) was born.

Several of his manuscripts, photographs, and other mementoes are displayed here; the furniture, though contemporary, bears no relation to him.

The l. turn leads into PL. DEL CARMEN, developed in 1973, with a bronze fountain by Joaquín Arias. On its E side stands **El Carmen**, a church celebrating the exaltation of 18C Mexican art.

The merchant Nicolás Fernando de Torres (d. 1732) bequeathed part of his fortune for the foundation of a convent of discalced Carmelites. A hospice was set up in 1747; the convent in 1768–71. The church was built in 1749–64. In the 1820s Tresguerras worked on the interior, removing some 18C work. Further changes were made by Molina and Compiani from 1898.

EXTERIOR. The W façade is a novel and extravagant baroque and churriguerresque mix. Solomonic columns and estípites, covered with figural and foliate forms, stand forward against a feast of all manner of ornament: revealed by carved drawn-back drapery in the pediment and at the sides. In the lower storey the pedestals are decorated in strapwork relief. The columns are uniquely worked in three separate sections. The first above the bases show cherub head and shell relief; the second petatillo patterns; the third are solomonic, their recessed parts entwined by leaves, with a chain in the centre to fix them to the shaft, while the bulbous parts are covered by ornamental strips which discreetly hide the spiral movement. Beyond the outer columns the borders repeat these strips. The lively flanking pilasters are also in three sections. Elaborate plug-like motifs which sprout from the flowery voussoirs of the doorway arch are a Manueline inheritance put to a baroque use. In the key, a Carmelite emblem: an arm gripping the flaming sword of Elijah. In the niches, topped by more strapwork relief, are statues of the prophets Elijah and Elisha, venerated by the Order. The inner estípites of the first storey are bordered by acanthus relief. The window framing is superb, flanked by double estípites; the lavish outer border culminates in an ogee arch pushing into the entablature, a delightful conceit, breaking with contemporary taste and harking back to the 16C. In the niches stand SS Teresa and John of the Cross. In the compressed second storey, estípites give place to the curtain, whose thick folds are upheld by wingless cherubs. The central niche holds Our Lady of Mount Carmel; on either side, SS Mary Magdalen dei Pozzi and Angelus. As a topmost finial against the sky stands a statue of St Michael.

The carved wooden doors (c 1765–70) have garlands and rocaille patterns inside geometric panels, and reliefs of Our Lady and St Joseph holding the infant Christ. The tower (finished in 1768), its upper storey octagonal, is thick with solomonic half-columns; at its tip—a weather vane—is a statue of St Teresa embracing the Cross. From the N portal arch also sprout plug motifs. Its lower-storey solomonic columns are thick and sensual. In the upper-storey niche, St Joseph.

Although the INTERIOR has lost a once total churrigueresque splendour, enough has survived to dazzle. At each side of the end of the nave before the crossing are a unique pair of churrigueresque altarpieces (c 1762), carved in soft whitish-cream local stone, gold leaf finely picked out on it, ascending to fill the arch and frame the window. The estípites of their three storeys are of varied design and the entrecalles are elaborate ornamental niche pilasters, the niches holding polychrome saints.

The interior of the cupola is most richly ornamented. At the angles of the octagonal drum are polychrome statues of saints of the Order and the four evangelists in sumptuously framed niches. From the angles spring decorative ribs terminating in cherub heads embedded in a kind of cornucopia forming a ring around the lantern base.

In the middle of the N (l.) transept, covering the entrance to the Camarín, is the overwhelming PORTADA DE LOS ARCANGELES—a final statement of churrigueresque and anastyle, after which 'nothing remained but repetition or death'.

It was built, c 1787–92, by local craftsmen, 'architects who can make altarpieces in stone and mortar so that they appear like wax'. Its fabric is mortar, burnished to resemble porcelain, originally coloured white, brown, and gold. It is in three storeys and three vertical sections.

The mixtilinear doorway arch is flanked by simple pilasters. Above it is the wide anastyle central section, which holds two niches, the lower enclosing a relief of angels incensing the Blessed Sacrament, the upper containing a Carmelite badge in relief—cross and three stars. Doorway, niches, and window are topped by stepped moulding, volutes, and scrolls of increasing sumptuousness. Repeated stepped and spiralling curves in the upper centre bring the whole forward so as to unsteady the admirer. In the side sections the three pairs of elegantly slender estípites are almost unbelievably elaborated with relief. Far more emphatic are the similarly elaborated ornamental niche pilasters between them and reducing them, but also echoing the central curves and mouldings, and providing a background for statues of archangels.

In the door frame are two paintings by Alzíbar: Dormition (l.) and Coronation (r.) of Our Lady. On the E wall of the transept is a narrow anastyle altarpiece (1770s), with polychrome statues of SS John the Baptist and Michael.

Behind the portada is the CAMARIN DE LA VIRGEN (devastated by fire in 1957; exactly restored by 1959), its apse formed to accommodate its beautiful curving churrigueresque altarpiece covered by a scallop canopy. The complex central parts of the estípites shelter saints in high relief. The spaces between them allow room for niche pilasters with central statues of SS Anne and Joachim. Gilding trails round the side walls and gracefully into the cupola, enhanced by figures in gilded mortar.

The HIGH ALTAR (1827–28), unfortunate contrast, is by Tresguerras. He also designed the sculpture (done in mid-century by Sixto Muñoz) and did the frescoes in the predella. The tabernacle door is covered with silver repoussé work (1780): Lamb of God and God the Father.

On the S (r.) wall of the sanctuary is a painting, Triumph of Our Lady, attr. Antonio Sánchez (fl. 1769–72). Lower down on the N (l.) side is the tomb of Nicolás Fernando de Torres and his wife, Gertrudis Maldonado Zapata, whose remains were brought here in 1784. The modern pulpit shows churrigueresque influence.

In the S transept a finely carved stone portal leads into the sacristy. In the niche above it is the image of Our Lady of Mount Carmel brought to San Luis by the founding friars. On either side, pastels (St Teresa transfixed and St Peter; 1801) by José Luis Rodríguez Alconedo. On the E wall the narrow anastyle altarpiece matches that in the N transept. Above it is an anon.

Portada de los Arcángeles, in El Carmen, San Luis Potosí

painting of St Teresa (1792). To the l. and r. of the inner sacristy door are two paintings by Alzíbar: Nativity and Immaculate Conception. Above it, Our Lord and the Doctors in the Temple by Francisco Morales (1818–84). In the SACRISTY are eight paintings of scenes from the life of Elijah (1764) by Francisco Antonio Vallejo; and here and in the adjoining room, other paintings by him and by Antonio Sánchez. In the CHOIR are more Vallejo works: Scenes from the life of St Teresa.

S of the church, the offices of the Secretaría de Salubridad y Asistencia occupy part of the former convent. The rest has been destroyed.

Further S, facing C. Villerías, is the **Teatro de la Paz** (1889–94; by José Noriega), with a classical portico. The interior decoration is by Jesús L. Sánchez.

A performance of Donizetti's 'Lucrezia Borgia' inaugurated it. It was also the scene of Camilo Arriaga's First Liberal Congress in 1901.

Opposite is the grandiose mansion (c 1892) which houses the **Museo Nacional de la Máscara** (Tues.–Fri., 10–2, 4–6; Sat.–Sun., 10–2), a collection of masks and costumes from different parts of Mexico.

At the E end of C. Guerrero we reach ALAMEDA JUAN SARABIA. In its centre is a monument to Hidalgo (c 1823) by Pedro Patiño Ixtolinque. On its S side is the church of *San José* (1885). On the N side C. Othón continues E. Just beyond the railway bridge, on the l., facing Plazoleta Ramón López Velarde, is the *Cap. de San Cristóbal de Montecillo* (1730–47).

From the W side of the Alameda, C. de la Constitución runs S to JARDIN LERDO DE TEJADA, in the former barrio of San Sebastián, founded in 1603 for Otomí and other Indians. On the S side is the church of **San Sebastián** (1708–c 1745). In its baroque façade the lower-storey solomonic columns are elegantly swathed; those of the upper storey have richer decoration. Note too the use of geometric patterns cut into the stone. Félix Calleja and Francisca de la Gándara were married here on 26 Jan. 1807.

On the S side of the Museo de la Máscara we may take C. Guerrero to its crossing with C. Escobedo, and then turn l. for the church of **San Agustín**.

It belonged to the Augustinian convent founded in the early 17C, of which only the three-storey façade remains. The beautiful tower dates from 1750–70. The interior was modernized in 1840 (high altar by Ciriaco Iturribarría; statue of Our Lady by Sixto Muñoz) and painted in 1890 (repainted and regilded in 1930). The holy-water stoup in the antesacristy and access portal into the sacristy are good 18C work.

The first turning W of San Agustín, C. Morelos, leads two blocks S to the corner with C. Abasolo. Here is the **Teatro Alarcón** (1827), by Tresguerras.

The curiously flattened façade gives straight into the auditorium, partly destroyed by fire in 1900. The first operatic performance in San Luis, Bellini's 'Il pirata', was put on here in 1828.

From the SE corner of Pl. de Armas, C. Zaragoza (former C. de la Concepción) leads S to the Santuario de Guadalupe (c 3km).

In the first block on the r. remains the fine balcony of the late 18C house (revamped to accommodate a shop) said to have been occupied by Calleja: the window jambs in the form of caryatids, without forearms, their bodies undulatingly pleated and ending in lion's claws; the keys in rococo relief. Opposite is the old shop *Al Libro Mayor* (late 18C).

On the r., at the corner with C. Iturbide, is a contrasting mansion (1891), eclectically porfirian, now the *Alianza Franco-Mexicana*.

Beyond C. Rayón is JARDIN COLON, site of the convent of *La Merced*, demolished in 1861–62. From here Av. Juárez, with a pleasant central promenade (Calz. de Guadalupe), runs S to the Santuario. At its beginning stands the circular **Caja del Agua**, a fine neoclassical monument.

It was built, in 1827–31, as the terminal fountain of works piping water to the city from the S, under the direction of Juan Sanabria. It is probably by Tresguerras. The workmanship is superb. Note the covered urns on the four buttresses; the basins, above them two spouts in the form of a flower; the garland pattern and festoons; and the pineapple finial above the oval ventilating openings.

The **Santuario de Guadalupe** (1772–1806), c 1.5km further S, is a mixture of late 18C styles by an enthusiastic amateur, Felipe Cleere.

EXTERIOR. Attention focuses on the portal panel, facing N, set back between three pairs of columns in each storey, which owe much to neostyle baroque. In the lowest storey their fluted shafts, ending in ionic capitals, are clasped by vegetal rings; in the second and third storeys they end in Corinthian capitals and are girded by garlands. The doorway arch undulates in rocaille patterns. Above, the choir window is influenced by neoclassical, but the statue of St Michael, on a sumptuous pedestal, is baroque, as is the relief of Our Lady at the top, sheltered by a huge crown. Rich relief fills in column bases, the spaces between the columns, and the friezes, while a rhomboid pattern helps to frame statue and titular relief. Framing the central panel are more, varied and engaged, columns, double at the outer edge with doric capitals and, on the inside, continuing with a reticulated pattern, their tops supporting the sloping upper line. The slender towers were completed in 1806. The carving of the side (W) doorway is rococo.

The INTERIOR has polygonal arches. The image of Our Lady of Guadalupe on the high altar was painted by Jesús Corral at the order of Pres. Bustamante in 1838.

C. 5 de Mayo runs S from the SW side of Pl. de Armas. At the SW corner of the first crossing, with C. Iturbide, is the *Casino Español*. From its roof in 1840 the would-be aeronaut Juan Balbontín made an unsuccessful attempt in a contraption of his own devising. Further down, No. 610 was the birthplace of the insurgent Mariano Jiménez (1781–1811).

Turning r. along Av. Universidad we arrive at PL. DE SAN FRANCISCO, its S part once the atrio of San Luis' grandest convent. Its present aspect, however agreeable and shady, owes much to 19C destruction and 20C development. On its W side is the church of **San Francisco**.

A provisional convent on the present site was begun c 1600 and was still standing in 1651. The new convent was in progress by 1686 and still building in the mid-18C; its area limited by the present Av. Universidad on the N, C. Comonfort on the S, C. Independencia on the W, and C. 5 de Mayo on the E. Its dismemberment began with the Reform, when a new street, C. Galeana, was bulldozed through from E to W.

EXTERIOR. Facing E, the rosy stone façade shows early potosino baroque. The lower storey is more Mannerist; the upper baroque, with rhomboid-pattern bases for the solomonic columns. The polygonal arch is described in an outer, semicircular. Franciscan emblems (crossed arms and five wounds) are pediment reliefs. The ingenuous statues represent SS Bonaventure and Antony (lower storey); St Francis (upper centre); and, above the pediment, a bishop and two friars. Solomonic columns also characterize the massive N tower (1704–07), in baleful contrast with the small S bell-tower (the Sevillian clock in the base dating from 1759), with medievalizing ogee arches. The cupolas (mid-18C) have exterior ribbing separate from the joining of the vaults, an effect peculiar to San Luis.

INTERIOR. The nave altarpieces are dull 19C substitutions of baroque originals. Those of the high altar and transepts are invented antiques in stone (c 1950). On the r. of the nave is the original 16C stone font 'in which the Franciscans baptized the aborigines of the territory'.

In the S transept stands a stele carved with the symbol of Tamoanchán. In post-Conquest native chronicles this is described as a terrestrial paradise or mythical land of man's origin. It was prominent in Toltec and Central Highland mythology, but seems to have been of Huastec origin. In one saga, Quetzalcóatl, the Feathered-serpent, brought bones from the Underworld, ground them up, and mixed them with some auto-sacrificial blood from the gods of Tamoanchán, thus forming mankind. The site of Xochicalco in Morelos was also sometimes referred to as Tamoanchán, the home of the bird-serpent; and the mythical land was also known as a resting-place for the souls of children. The word itself is Maya: ta = prefix for 'of', moan = a mythical bird of the 13th heaven, and chan = an archaic form of can, meaning 'snake' or 'sky'; thus 'land of the feathered-serpent'.

Among the paintings is a series (1718–22), originally in the cloister, by Antonio de Torres depicting the life of St Francis. In the sotocoro: Temptation of St Francis; Pope Innocent III dreams of St Francis; Souls in Purgatory. In the passage to the side doorway (r.): St Francis with Our Lord; Innocent III sanctions the Order of Friars Minor; St Francis enters Assisi in triumph; 17C anon. (possibly Spanish), Virgen de la Candelaria—not shown to advantage here. On either side of high altar, St Francis with Our Lord and Our Lady in Glory; St Francis taken up to Heaven. The series continues in nave and transepts (Birth of St Francis; St Francis leaves his Parents, etc.).

The CHOIR has its late 18C stalls and organ, and more paintings by Torres (in their original place): Christ and Our Lady with SS Francis and Dominic; SS Bonaventure and Thomas Aquinas; and, in the pendentives, SS Jerome, Ambrose, Augustine, and Gregory the Great.

The SACRISTY (after 1750) is behind the high altar and transepts. Its estípite supports, octagonal cupola, and walls, lunettes, and pendentives filled with paintings give it an independent sumptuousness and emphasize its space.

The paintings include: Pedro López Calderón, St Philip of Jesus (to l. of door from N side of high altar). Cabrera, St Francis receiving the Holy Child from Our Lady; Birth of Our Lady; Death of St Clare. Torres, Flight into Egypt. Facing one another on main walls: Francisco Martínez, St Francis and an angel with a flask; Communion of St Teresa, with members of the family of Joseph de Erreparaz. By door from S side of high altar: Martínez, St Teresa transfixed. Over entrance to antesacristy (former Sala de Profundis), a beautiful stone relief, unique for an interior, revealed by two cherubs drawing back a curtain, of St Francis receiving the stigmata, while Brother Leo washes and binds the wounds—two separate happenings in one scene. Above r., the apocalyptic Christ floats away above the lush landscape, complete with waterfall, the skull, and the lamb. The polychrome of the saint's habit is full of gold; that of his companion is green, with gold flecks.

Above it, Cabrera, Funeral of St Clare; on either side, Torres, Dream of St Joseph; Our Lady and St Joseph. The paintings in the pendentives are attr. Cabrera. In the ANTESACRISTY (1755), Cabrera, Death of St Clare; St Clare with the Host; and Torres, Incorruptibility of St Francis; St Francis with Christ and Our Lady; Descent from the Cross; St Francis receives the stigmata. Note also the elaborate holy-water stoup.

To the l. (S) of the church portal is the three-arched former portería of the convent. Next door, the *Iglesia Presbiteriana* (1894), reminder of reformist insensitivity. From here we may turn into C. Galeana and the entrance to the **Museo Regional Potosino** (Tues.–Fri., 10–2, 3–6; Sat.–Sun., 10–1; fee), in a surviving part of the convent. Its main attraction, on the first floor, is a jewel of churrigueresque art, the chapel of **Aranzazu** (1760–1800).

It was a private chapel for novices. The entrance façade, carved in stone, displays delicate detail: triple engaged estípites on the inside, double on the outside; in the key of the mixtilinear arch, the Aranzazu emblem—a tree, a bell, and a dog, crowned by an angel head; above, a foliated band. The upper storey combines rococo motifs. The huge swelling estípites acting as supports in the polychrome INTERIOR, heavily gone over in more recent times, produce an overwhelming effect. The side altars are also churrigueresque. The charming painting of St Rosalia is by Cabrera.

Outside the chapel are four paintings of scenes from the life of Our Lady (1732) by Pedro López Calderón; a 17C Crucifixion in caña de maíz from Salvatierra; and, to the r., the sedan chair of Bp Montes de Oca. The archaeological and ethnographic collections concentrate on the Huastec, Otomí, and Río Verde cultures. Two wall maps locate sites in the State in different periods.

The display includes cases containing Huastec, Otomí, and Totonac stone tools, pottery, clay and stone figurines, clay pipes, metalwork, and bone and shell jewellery. Carved stone sculptures include Totonac yugos (exact use not certain, but associated with the ball game, probably ceremonial); human figures possibly depicting a fertility goddess, woman-and-child group, the Maize goddess, Quetzalcóatl in his usual Huastec guise as the Wind god Ehecatl, and a copy of the famous 'Huastec Youth' from Tamuín (original in the Museo Nacional de Antropología). Barrel-shaped wooden drum from Guadalcázar—a Náhuatl teponaztli. This was played in a horizontal position with a rubber-tipped mallet, and could produce at least two pitches from the two cut-out 'tongues' in the side.

On the ground floor, a collection of local historical artefacts, incl. a 16C stirrup in the form of a cross, from Arabia, imported from Spain.

Behind the museum, Plazoleta de Aranzazu is on the site of the convent stables, whose arches remain. Also visible is the apse window of the chapel, flanked by double estípites.

To the W, on the other side of C. Independencia, is the *Iglesia Episcopal* (1898) by Russell P. Cook. To the N of San Francisco, on the other side of Av. Universidad, is the *Museo Regional de Arte Popular y Casa de Artesanías* (Tues.–Sun. 10–2, 4–6), exhibiting and selling arts and crafts from all parts of Mexico. At the SE corner of the plaza is the *Agora de FONAPAS* (19C), now a cultural centre, in which the art historian Francisco de la Maza (1913–72) was born.

Diagonally opposite are two chapels, dependencies of the convent. At the corner of Cs Galeana and Vallejo is *Sagrado Corazón* (1728–31; *Cap. de los Remedios*). Next door is *La Tercera Orden* (1694), its façade a design of pilasters and ovals. Its neoclassical high altar is a superior example. In the transepts are two paintings by Antonio de Torres: Annunciation and Marriage of Our Lady. In the sacristy, St Hedwig by Juan Correa.

Two blocks further S on C. Vallejo is the *Pal. de Justicia* (1972) by Francisco J. Cossío. It occupies the site of *Nuestra Señora de los Dolores* (or *Las Recogidas*), an institution, somewhere between prison and convent, founded in 1772, for women fallen on hard times, 'prostitutes...but also honest widows, abandoned melancholics, girls who had gone astray'. The only part remaining, the chapel, probably rebuilt in the mid-19C, now forms the lobby of the new building.

Two blocks S again, on the S side of JARDIN MIGUEL BARRAGAN, is the church of *San Miguelito* (1733), once belonging to the barrio of Santísima Trinidad. Its wide front is marked by a pleasing baroque portal. On the E side of the jardín is the *Mercado Tangamanga* (1948), planned by Roberto Valle.

From San Luis Potosí Méx. 70 runs SW via (82km) *Ojuelos* to (168km) *Aguascalientes*. From Ojuelos, Méx. 80 runs S, via (150km from San Luis) *Lagos de Moreno*, (196km) *San Juan de los Lagos*, (269km) *Tepatitlán*, and (310km) *Zapotlanejo* to (345km) *Guadalajara*, see Rte 50.

FROM SAN LUIS POTOSI TO ZACATECAS. Méx. 49, 191km. The road runs on to the NE slopes of the Sierra de San Luis. 22km (l.) **Mexquitic** (2062m). Here the Franciscans founded their first mission in the San Luis Potosí area: a hospice in 1583 and in 1590 the convent of *San Miguel*, which survives. 31km road N for (100km) *Charcas*, see Rte 55. We enter the State of Zacatecas. 74km rough road S for (30km) **Pinos** (c 4000 inhab.; 2419m) in the Sierra de Pinos. It was founded as a real de minas in the 17C and flourished until the late 18C. The parish church of *San Matías* dates from the 1680s. In the baptistery, a Baptism of Christ by José de Páez (1764). *San Francisco* (19C) contains a churrigueresque altarpiece. We re-enter San Luis Potosí for (99km; r.) *Salinas*, in a major salt-producing area. To the S is the *Peñón Blanco* (2670m). 124km turning r. for (21km N) *Villa de Ramos*, scene of a mining bonanza in 1608 which lasted several decades and re-established in the 1760s. The church preserves a baroque portal. 168km *Troncoso*, see Rte 50. 191km *Zacatecas*, see Rte 46.

58   San Luis Potosí to San Miguel de Allende and Querétaro

Méx. 57, 202km.—141km diversion for (30km SW) **San Miguel de Allende** (and [15km NW] **Atotonilco**).—202km **Querétaro**.

Méx. 57 runs SE through the Valle de San Luis, between the Sierra de San Luis (W) and the Sierra de Juárez (E). At 25km, Méx. 37 (r.) runs SW via (22km) *Villa de Reyes*, to the W of the Sierra de San Miguelito, to (73km) *San Felipe Torres Mochas* and (167km) *León*, see Rte 50. 47km (r.) *Sta María del Río* on the Río Sta María. The silk rebozos manufactured here have a wide reputation. At 82km we cross into the State of Guanajuato. A minor road branches r. for (57km SW) *Dolores Hidalgo*, see Rte 52. At 116km we cross Méx. 110 for (9km E) *San Luis de la Paz*, see Rte 52. 141km diversion r. for (30km SW) *San Miguel de Allende*.

SAN MIGUEL DE ALLENDE (c 50,000 inhab.; 1872m) spreads attractively along a slope overlooking the broad Valle de San Miguel, watered by the Río de la Laja and its small tributaries, in the NE part of the Bajío. Its status as a national monument has ensured the preservation of an exceptional concentration of historic churches and narrow streets full of 18–19C mansions. Its beauty and ideally warm climate have attracted a strong foreign (mainly US) community and students attend various language schools.

Bus station. C. Canal, c 1km W of centre. Frequent services to *Atotonilco* (c ½ hr); to *Dolores Hidalgo* (1 hr); to *Guanajuato* (2 hrs); to *Querétaro* (1 hr); to *Mexico City* (c 4½ hrs); to *San Luis Potosí* (c 2½ hrs); to *León* (c 3 hrs); to *Morelia* (c 4 hrs); to *Guadalajara* (c 6 hrs).

Railway station. 2km W of centre. Aguila Azteca via *Celaya* (45 mins.) and *Querétaro* (2¼ hrs) to *Mexico City* (7–8 hrs).

Hotels throughout the town.

Post Office. 16 C. del Correo.

Tourist Office. Pl. Allende, next door to Parroquia.

US Consulate. Corner of Cs Canal and Hernández Macías.

Fiestas. 1st Fri. in March: Señor de la Conquista. Good Friday; Palm Sunday; Corpus Christi. Sun. after feast of St Antony (13 June). 29 Sept.: St Michael.

Despite Chichimec hostility, Spanish settlers extended their cattle haciendas into the area; and in 1549–50 the Mexico–Zacatecas road was pushed through. To protect it, the villa at San Miguel was founded in 1555 under Angel de Villafañe, and came to be known as San Miguel el Grande. By the 18C it was a flourishing centre of manufactures: its harnesses, stirrups, spurs, swords, knives, and, above all, woollen textiles, were used throughout New Spain. Birthplace of Ignacio de Allende and Juan Aldama, San Miguel became one of the centres of conspiracy against the weakening viceregal government and in favour of Independence. From here, on the night of 15–16 Sept. 1810, Aldama made his famous ride to Dolores to warn Allende and Hidalgo that the authorities had decided to act against the plotters. On 8 March 1862 San Miguel was renamed 'de Allende' after its most illustrious native.

On the S side of the central PL. ALLENDE is the startlingly out-of-place parish church of **San Miguel Arcángel**.

The original church, started in 1690 to the design of Marcos Antonio Sobrarías, was partly demolished to make way for a new N section (1880–), a pseudo-Gothic fantasy by a local Indian mason, Ceferino Gutiérrez (reputedly illiterate), who was inspired by postcards and drawings of French cathedrals.

Recent restoration has rescued the original stonework of the INTERIOR. In the l. transept is a 16C Crucifixion, in caña de maíz, made in Pátzcuaro. On either side of the high altar are two paintings by Juan Rodríguez Juárez, Adoration of the Kings and Presentation in the Temple, part of a series on the life of Our Lady, continued in the Sacristy (Annunciation, Visitation, St Joseph and Our Lady begging shelter at the inn, Pietà); and r. aisle chapel (Assumption).

Behind the high altar is a *Camarín* (early 19C), tastefully done and attr. Tresguerras. Beneath it is the crypt. Among the tombs is that of Anastasio Bustamante.
To the r. of the church is a statue representing Fray Juan de San Miguel (1942). To the l., the church of *San Rafael* (early 18C, with 19C gothicizing alterations, incl. the tower), also called *Sta Escuela de Cristo*, after a pious society founded in 1742, whose chapel it became.

At the SW corner (with C. Umarán) of the plaza is the **Casa de Allende**, a first-rate example of a San Miguel house, begun probably in the mid-18C and reflecting late baroque taste; perhaps finished c 1800, with neoclassical touches.

Above the main doorway, its upper parts vigorously projecting, is a curved pediment supported on either side by embellishing volutes, from which spring large ornamental vases. The balcony window, in contrast, is Renaissance inspired. Of exceptional interest are the projections of windows and balconies, covered in thick festoons, triglyphs, and lambrequin motifs. It was the birthplace of Ignacio de Allende y Unzaga (1769–1811), later generalísimo of the insurgent forces, son of the Basque immigrant Domingo Narciso de Allende and Ana María de Unzaga. A Latin inscription below the cornice reads HIC NATUS UBIQUE NOTUS (Here was born he who is known far and wide). The house contains the *Museo Histórico* (Tues.–Sun., 10–3.30).

No. 4 in C. Umarán, which goes W, is the so-called **Casa de los Perros**, the corbels of its main balcony in the shape of dogs. It was built in the mid-18C by Juan Antonio de Umarán y Arenaza, grandfather of the insurgent Juan de Umarán. No. 28 was the birthplace of Ignacio Ramírez (1818–79), known as 'El Nigromante' (Magician), liberal politician, writer, formidable intellectual influence in 19C Mexico, and briefly minister of justice under Juárez (1861) and Díaz (1876–77).

No. 5 C. Cuna de Allende, another 18C house, was the birthplace of another insurgent, Luis Malo, shot at Monclova in March 1811. In C. Cuadrante (r.) No. 18, with fine windows and balconies, is the so-called *Casa del Inquisidor* (1780). In 1815 its tenant was an official of the Inquisition, Victorino de las Fuentes. Opposite is the *Casa de la Inquisición* (offices and gaol), of the same period, with a delightfully, if ingenuously, sculpted corner niche enclosing a cross in greenish stone studded with azulejos. From here we may go S along C. Hernández Macías, across the bridge over the Arroyo del Valle de Maíz, into

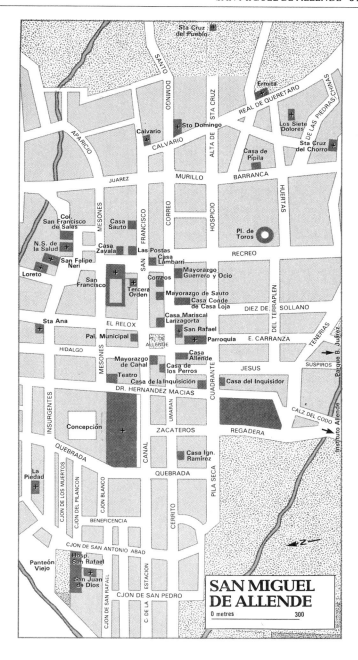

SAN MIGUEL
DE ALLENDE

0 metres   300

Calz. Ancha de San Antonio, the Celaya road. On the l. No. 4 is the high-walled **Instituto Allende**, a language and arts and crafts centre.

It was once the country residence of Manuel Tomás de la Canal (see below), and begun in 1735. In 1809 it was bought by the discalced Carmelite nuns from Querétaro (Las Teresitas) who entrusted its reconditioning to Manuel Tolsá, suspended in 1810. After restoration, it was opened in 1951 as the Institute, and incorporated into the University of Guanajuato. It offers courses in languages, painting, sculpture, photography, silverwork, pottery, etc. Temporary exhibitions are regularly held. Concerts and plays are put on in the students' theatre.

Above the main doorway the niche holds a statue of Our Lady of Loreto. In the chapel are preserved part of the original murals and 18C furniture and paintings, incl. a Face of Christ by José de Ibarra. On a rise on the other side of the road is the unfinished chapel of *San Antonio* (mid-18C).

We may turn N along Cs de la Regadera and Zacateros to the, disproportionately large, church and former convent of **La Concepción** (known familiarly as Las Monjas).

The foundation (1754), for Conceptionist nuns, owed much to the generosity of María Josefa Lina de la Canal, daughter of Manuel Tomás. Building, to the plans of Francisco Martínez Gudiño, began in 1755, but was unfinished at the dedication in 1765. The tower went up in 1842; the cupola in 1891.

Most notable feature of the EXTERIOR is the superb cupola, in best neoclassical style, the work of Ceferino Gutiérrez, who used that of Les Invalides in Paris as his model. The huge, cold INTERIOR still preserves the coros alto and bajo; in the latter, behind the heavy grille, is a fine, gilded anastyle altarpiece, gift of the conde de Casa de Loja. High on the walls of nave and transepts are a series of paintings of scenes from the life of Our Lady by Juan Rodríguez Juárez, culminating in an Assumption above the coro bajo grille; and (r. wall) two paintings (Our Lord and Our Lady) attr. Cabrera. The high altar dates from c 1895.

The monumental cloister is now the *Centro Cultural Ignacio Ramírez*, where arts and crafts and music and dance courses are held throughout the year, but most popularly in summer. The upper-storey walls are enlivened with murals by local artists and others (incl. David Alfaro Siqueiros).

In the W part of town, reached along C. Canal and then r. up Cjón de San Antonio Abad, are the church of *San Juan de Dios* and former hospital of *San Rafael*, with a lovely patio, both founded in 1770; behind it is the town cemetery.

At the corner of Cs Hernández Macías and Mesones, on the r. of La Concepción, is the neoclassical *Teatro Angela Peralta* (late 19C).

C. Canal leads E back to Pl. Allende. No. 17 is the birthplace of José María de Jesús Díez de Sollano y Dávalos, 1st bp of León and son of the 4th conde de Casa de Loja (see Rte 50). No. 14 is an enchanting old house; above the door, a medallion of the Trinity. At the corner with the plaza and spanning almost all the street block, is the **Casa del Mayorazgo de Canal**, the most magnificent in San Miguel.

It belonged to the family established in the town by Manuel Tomás de la Canal y Bueno de Baeza (1701–49), its greatest benefactor; and was begun by his son, José Mariano de la Canal y Hervás, and finished c 1800 by his grandson, Narciso María Loreto de la Canal y Landeta.

The main portal is grandly neoclassical, with Corinthian columns and curved pediments; but not without late baroque touches: the lambrequin motifs in the doors, the lower frieze and spandrel relief, and the inner niche detail. Even the triglyphs and metopes of the upper frieze, which runs beneath the cornice of the whole building, are uniquely sumptuous.

The niche holds a statue of Our Lady of Loreto, the family's patron, standing on the Holy House. Flanking it are the coats-of-arms of Canal (l.) and Hervás, the family of Manuel Tomás's wife, María de Hervás y Flores (d. 1749). Tucked into the upper pediment is a cross of Calatrava, symbol of the order of knighthood to which Manuel Tomás belonged. The patio, with its high arcades, reflects authority. The bull's-eye windows repeat a recurring exterior motif.

On the corner of the plaza and C. del Relox is the so-called *Casa de la Conspiración* (18C; remodelled in the later 19C, though preserving its old patio), scene of conspiratorial meetings against the viceregal government before 1810. No. 1 C. San Francisco, diagonally opposite, one of the earliest surviving houses, dates probably from the later 17C. No. 10 (l.) is what remains of the house of the brothers Juan and Ignacio Aldama, allowed to deteriorate and in the 1960s converted into a cinema. No. 15 (l.; late 18C), with a lovely patio, was built for María Antonia Petra de Sauto y Jáuregui.

From the SE corner of the plaza we take C. del Correo. The house immediately on the l. and fronting the plaza is the **Casa del Mariscal Lanzagorta**, with beautiful and strongly marked balconies. Its portal is a porfirian reconstruction after fire damage. The insurgent Francisco Lanzagorta Incháurregui (d. 1811) lived here. On the corner with C. Díez de Sollano (r.) is the *Casa del Conde de Casa de Loja* (late 18C). In the pediment of the high doorway the shield contains the quarterings of the Landeta, La Hera, Boniete, Saravia y Rueda, and Jáuregui families.

No. 12 C. del Correo is the *Casa del Mayorazgo de Sauto*, converted after Independence into the town's first post office. (On the r. of the doorway the original post-box may still be seen.) Today's *Correos* occupies its later extension, which stretches to the corner with Cjón Josefa Ortiz. No. 17 (r.) is the *Casa Guerrero de Ocío* (1797), built by the marqués de Jarral de Berrio and once property of Antonio Agustín Guerrero de Ocío Vázquez y Cuervo, who in June 1822 married María Josefa Carlota de Allende, niece of Ignacio.

Turning l. into Cjón Josefa Ortiz we come (r.) to the *Casa Lámbarri* (mid-18C). Opposite (28 C. San Francisco) is the former *Casa de las Postas*, stage for diligences on the Mexico–Zacatecas road. At No. 38 C. San Francisco, further up, died Gen. Anastasio Bustamante (1780–1853).

Along C. San Francisco we may reach places of interest in the E part of the town. At the corner with C. Calvario is the chapel of *El Calvario*, last stage of the public Way of the Cross which begins at 5 C. Juárez and whose stations are marked in niches on the walls of houses. At the next corner in C. Calvario is the church of *Sto Domingo* (begun in 1737; renovated in 1847), almost medieval in appearance, with solid buttresses and unfinished espadaña. It adjoined a small convent of Dominican nuns. Hence the enclosed choir at its far end.

C. Calvario climbs SE to merge into C. Real de Querétaro, with good views of the town, past (l.) the *Ermita de Nuestra Señora de Loreto* (rebuilt in the mid-18C), one of several little outlying chapels. No. 90 C. Barranca, down the hill at the W end, is the birthplace of Juan José de los Reyes Martínez y Amero (Pípila; 1782–1863 [?]), hero of the siege of the Alhóndiga in Guanajuato (see Rte 51).

Facing Cjón Josefa Ortiz, and at the N end of the small JARDIN DE SAN FRANCISCO, is the church of **San Francisco**, its façade, in rose-coloured stone, one of the best examples of Mexican churrigueresque.

The Franciscans founded their convent in San Miguel c 1606. This, their second church on the site, initially dedicated to San Antonio, was begun in June 1779 and finished in Apr. 1799. Local families contributed towards the cost and prize money from bullfights was also donated.

EXTERIOR. In each of the two storeys, separated by a barely perceptible cornice, backed by tableros in the centre, are two pairs of estípites and, between them, ornamental niche pilasters—all of a refined slenderness and embellished with the most delicate and charming vegetal, floral, fruit, cherubic, and childlike detail as well as scroll, lambrequin, and shell effects. In the medallions appear reliefs of Franciscan saints. Above the doorway arch, itself crinkled to allow for a pattern of cherub heads, is a relief of the Immaculate Conception. Above the window, reliefs of the Crucifixion and, on either side, Our Lady and St John. The finial is a statue of St Francis. The unfinished side portal displays a similar slenderness and delicacy. The tower, neoclassical in its lines, has been attr. Tresguerras.

The INTERIOR, doubtfully attr. Tresguerras, is strongly neoclassical. Among the antesacristy paintings is a Death of St Francis by Juan Rodríguez Juárez. In the sacristy, seven paintings of the Archangels, their value diminished by clumsy repainting, by Juan Correa. The convent (1606–38) shows much alteration, but fragments of the original murals (incl. a Crucifixion in passage between the two cloisters) remain.

On the W side of the jardín is the church of *La Tercera Orden* (1713), a rustic affair, recalling, in its portal, the late 16C.

Beyond San Francisco, along C. Juárez, No. 5 in which was the house of Leobino Zavala, a 19C man of letters, we cross C. Mesones, with attractive old houses, into a broad plaza taken over by the town's principal market and lined on its N side by a series of buildings associated with the Oratorians: 'a religious city in miniature within the secular city'. On the extreme r. opposite, and fronted by an unsuitable modern bronze statue of Allende, is the former **Colegio de San Francisco de Sales**, founded in 1753.

Nearly all the conspirators of 1810 studied here, and later pupils were the future Bp Díez de Sollano and Ignacio Ramírez. At the outbreak of the war of Independence, Allende ordered the imprisonment here of Spaniards arrested at Dolores and San Miguel.

At its W end is the church of **Nuestra Señora de la Salud** (c 1770–80), built at the expense of the Oratorian Luis Felipe Neri de Alfaro.

EXTERIOR. Its convex and captivating portal (puerta abocinada), accompanied by a stubby little tower, shelters under a giant conch. (The dark stone was once painted in bright colours.) Its two storeys display two pairs each of winningly unsophisticated estípites and between them statues in niches (shell motif repeated above them) of the Immaculate Conception (centre) and SS Anne and Joachim (above) and the Sacred Heart and St John the Evangelist (below). The spandrels of the neo-Mudéjar arch are filled with abstract designs; above the key, a royal crown; above the central upper niche, a papal tiara. The twin windows, topped by scroll relief, are an unusual departure. Above, and enveloped in the great conch, a small conch encloses a miniatory Eye of God.

The INTERIOR contains interesting paintings. Among them a Crucifixion by Tomás Javier de Peralta; Our Lady of Guadalupe by Antonio de Torres; St Francis Xavier by Cabrera. In the sacristy, Our Lady of Grace by Juan Baltasar Gómez.

Facing the adjoining plaza to the W is the Oratory of **San Felipe Neri**, the main Oratorian church and still in the Congregation's possession.

The Congregation was founded at San Miguel in 1712 by Fr Juan Antonio Pérez de Espinosa from Pátzcuaro, who had so moved the sanmiguelenses as guest preacher during Lent that they begged him to stay. The church (1712–14) is an adaptation of a mid-17C church (*Ecce homo*) which belonged to the mulatto community.

EXTERIOR. The baroque façade maintains a sturdy singularity. Pairs of columns stand well forward of the niches which hold statues of SS Peter and Paul (lower storey) and SS John the Baptist and Philip (upper). Columns and surfaces are covered with exotic leafy relief, that on the lower-storey columns making them look solomonic. Above the arch, an alfíz; in the spandrels, breezy angels. The pediment, in the form of a fan, is broken by a temple-like niche holding a statue of St Joseph and the Child Jesus. The E side doorway, its niche enclosing a sweet statue of Our Lady of Grace, and recalling a 16C style, is a relic of the earlier church.

The INTERIOR betrays neoclassical and later busyness, although the organ is a delightful rococo survivor. On the nave walls hangs a series of 33 paintings by Cabrera, darkened by time, detailing the life of St Philip Neri; in the r. transept, Our Lady of Guadalupe, also by Cabrera. Among the paintings in the sacristy are an Immaculate Conception by Juan Rodríguez Juárez and a Crucifixion (1772) by Andrés de Islas. A door off the sacristy gives access to a gallery of portraits of distinguished Oratorians and benefactors, incl. Manuel Quijano (1783) and José Pereda, both lawyers of the Real Audiencia in Mexico City, by José de Alzíbar; Fr Nicolás A. de Guadalupe by Juan Baltasar Gómez; Fr Alejo Antonio de Larragoiti by Matías Velasco.

From the l. transept we enter the **Sta Casa de Loreto**, inspired by the Santa Casa, Our Lady's house miraculously flown from Nazareth to Loreto in Italy. It was built in 1736 at the charges of Manuel Tomás de la Canal.

On either side of the entrance are two pairs of solomonic columns, after those of Bernini supporting the Baldacchino in St Peter's at Rome. In a glass case edged with silver on the high altar (remodelled in the 19C) is the venerated image of Our Lady of Loreto. In facing niches on the side walls are the funerary statues, gently and movingly done, of Manuel Tomás and his wife, María Hervás y Flores. His is carved from a single piece of wood. Both date from the later 18C (after their deaths in 1749) and were restored in 1834 when the faces and hands were repainted and the lamps they hold and frames added. Behind the altar is the octagonal CAMARIN (Our Lady's chamber). Its vault of four crossing arches is characteristically Mudéjar and its four surviving altarpieces are uniquely and most delicately elaborate and inventive, covered in dense golden foliate decoration, which spills over into the pilasters between them. They are dedicated to SS Anne, Joachim, Mary Magdalen, and John Nepomuk, whose images stand in glass cases; the smaller images, some under fetching little canopies, are beautifully worked in ivory. The wall of its little sacristy is covered by a painting by Andrés López: in its centre, Our Lord appearing to St Margaret Mary; on the outsides, the Sacrifice of the Old Law and The Last Supper. On the r. side of the church is the Oratorian house, *Claustro Felipense*. In the refectory is a painting of St Francis Xavier by Nicolás Rodríguez Juárez.

C. Insurgentes goes W past (No. 21) the *Academia Hispano Americana* to the church of *Sta Ana* (1847) and the former *Beaterio* attached to the church, now the public library, with the best collection of books in Castilian and English outside Mexico City.

15km NW of San Miguel de Allende, reached along Méx. 51 and then by a turning l., is **ATOTONILCO** (5000 inhab.; 2140m), a pilgrimage centre.

The sanctuary, with an adjoining Casa de Ejercicios (house of spiritual exercises), was founded in 1740 as a place of retreat by Luis Felipe Neri de Alfaro. The church was finished in 1748 and the various chapels added later in the 18C. On 10 Apr. 1802 Ignacio de Allende was married here to María de la Luz Agustina de las Fuentes. On his march from Dolores to San Miguel in Sept. 1810 Hidalgo stopped here and appropriated a banner bearing the image of Our Lady of Guadalupe from the sacristy, thus adopting her as patron of the insurgent cause.

The sanctuary of **Jesús Nazareno** consists of a single nave with six chapels opening out on either side, each of different design, which emphasizes the irregular layout. In the INTERIOR, walls, vaults, and cupolas were covered with frescoes, a good part of which have been uncovered thanks to the removal of whitewash. They are in an ingenuous, didactic 18C style, the work of Miguel Antonio Martínez de Pocasangre, who probably also painted the panels (punishment of vice and reward of virtue) of the interior door. To the l. (entrance under the choir) is the *Cap. del Sto Sepulcro* (1760–63), exceptional for its frescoes of the Passion; the poems, by Fr Alfaro, inscribed on the walls; and, in the presbytery and transepts, three cave-like openings crowned by lifelike scenes of the Nailing of Our Lord to the Cross, the Crucifixion, and the Descent from the Cross, which have been called 'the most monumental sculptural groups produced in New Spain'. To the r., under the choir, is the *Cap. de Belén*. Of especial interest is the *Cap. del Rosario*, the vault of its cupola covered in frescoes (showing great splendour within the popular style) of Loreto in Italy, Devotion to the Rosary, and the Battle of Lepanto. The main altarpiece, combining sweetness and elegance, is adorned with anon. paintings behind panels of Venetian glass. At the entrance to its camarín are portraits, in tempera, of the parents of Fr Alfaro: María Velázquez de Castilla and Esteban Valero de Alfaro. Here is a delightful and unique little reliquary-retable, sadly decayed. In the *Sacristy* is a St Antony of Padua (spoiled by repainting) by Juan Correa and a portrait of Fr Alfaro by Andrés de Islas.

156km turning l. for (5km) *San José Iturbide*, see Rte 52. We cross into the State of Querétaro. 202km *Querétaro*, see Rte 37.

59 Matamoros to Ciudad Victoria

Méx. 180, 313km.—139km San Fernando.—217km Santander Jiménez.—
237km Presa Vicente Guerrero.—313km **Ciudad Victoria**.

MATAMOROS (357,000 inhab.; 12m), on the frontier opposite *Brownsville* in
Texas, is an overgrown industrial city and part of an important cotton-growing
district. As frontier towns go, it is a not unpleasant place which offers some
introductory pointers to the Mexican way of life.

Airport. 17km S. Flights to *Mexico City, Monterrey, Ciudad Victoria,* etc.

Bus station. C. Canales, c 1.5km SE of Pl. Principal. Services to *Ciudad Victoria* (4½ hrs); to
Tampico (7½ hrs); to *Mexico City* (18 hrs); to *Chihuahua* (16hrs); to *Veracruz* (18 hrs); etc.

Railway station. C. Hidalgo, between Cs. 10 and 11. Service to *Monterrey* (c 7 hrs).

Hotels throughout the town.

Post Office. 214 Calle 6.

Tourist Office. Puerta México, in the customs building by the international bridge.

US Consulate. 232 Calle 1.

It grew out of Nuestra Señora del Refugio, formed in 1794, a villa in 1812, on the site of the
ranch of San Juan de los Esteros Hermosos. It was given its new name and called 'heroica e
invicta' in 1851. It was at the centre of events at the outbreak of the US-Mexican war. During
3–8 May 1846 it was bombarded by Gen. Zachary Taylor's batteries from Fort Texas
(Brownsville); on 8 May, Gen. Mariano Arista, commanding the Mexican garrison, was
defeated at the nearby village of Palo Alto; on 17–18 May, Taylor's troops finally marched in.
On 26 Sept. 1864 Gen. Mejía occupied it and held it for the empire against the republican
troops of Gens. Negrete and Escobedo until 23 June 1866, with only 1800 men. 'It was', he
said afterwards, 'the key to the empire'.

On PL. PRINCIPAL the cathedral, built in 1826, has been much altered. The
city's main historical monument is the **Casa Mata**, at the corner of Cs
Guatemala and Santos Degollado, SE of Pl. Principal. This is the old fort
defended by Arista's and Mejía's troops in 1846 and 1864–66. It now houses a
museum (closed Mon.), with exhibits illustrating the Revolution and indigenous
crafts. At the corner of C. 5 and Av. Constitución the **Museo del Maíz** (Tues.–
Sun., 9.30–5) traces the importance of maize in Mexican history and civilization.

C. 35km E, on the coast at the mouth of the Río Bravo, was the town of *Bagdad*, which grew
during the US civil war when contraband goods were supplied through it to the Confederates.
A hurricane in 1880 buried it beneath sand, and it was officially declared 'disappeared'. Today
locals continue to prospect for buried treasure.

Méx. 180 runs SW, skirting, at some distance inland, the flat, sandy lagoon-
filled coast of the Gulf of Mexico. 139km **San Fernando** (7000 inhab.; 55m; R,P),
on the Río Fernando, which begins its flow into the **Laguna Madre**, c 25km E.
This, a stretch of water c 2000 sq km in area, and c 220km in length, which
reaches from c 24km S of Matamoros in the N to c 16km N of Soto la Marina in
the S, is separated from the sea by strips of sandbank (3km at their widest). The
waters are salty; in summer their salinity is greater than that of the Gulf itself.
Turtles, oysters, and fish abound, but development of the salt industry threatens
new departures for the area. The road skirts the Sierra de Tamaulipa Nueva.
217km **Santander Jiménez** (4000 inhab.; H), founded as the villa of Nuevo
Santander in 1749 and capital of the colony of Nuevo Santander until c 1801.
Its quaint pink-tinged church of *Cinco Señores* contains a small mid-18C altarpiece decorated with gold leaf. The mid-18C *Pal. de los Condes de la Sierra
Gorda* still stands. At 237km we turn r. to skirt the N shore of **Presa Vicente
Guerrero** (364.5 sq km; officially *Presa de las Adjuntas*), formed in 1970,
abounding in bass. It submerged the town of *Padilla*, founded in 1749, where
the first State congress met in 1824–25. Some of its buildings emerge at low

water. Here, after his untimely return to Mexico (see Rte 54), Agustín de Iturbide was executed on 18 July 1824. His body was buried in the churchyard, before being reinterred in Mexico City. 266km *Nueva Ciudad Padilla*, built from 1971. 286km *Güemes*. 313km *Ciudad Victoria*, see Rte 54.

60 Ciudad Victoria to Tamazunchale

Méx. 85, 338km.—137km Ciudad Mante.—231km **Ciudad Valles**.—282km Ciudad Santos (for Tancanhuitz).—338km Tamazunchale.

Méx. 85 climbs SE, soon crossing the Tropic of Cancer, and skirting the E slopes of the Sierra Madre (spectacular views), to (58km) *Llera de Canales*, an attractive little town surrounded by orange, lemon, and avocado groves, to the E of *Presa El Módulo* (fishing).

Méx. 81 branches off SE with the Sierra de Tamaulipas to the E (l.) to (89km) *Villa de González* (R,P). From here Méx. 80 runs due W to (60km) *Ciudad Mante*, passing, to the S, the **Bernal de Horcasitas** (1111m), a mass of basalt, dramatically shaped like a stout fortress raised on a pedestal-like circular base, approx. 6km in diameter. It is surrounded by jungle greenery (stinging nettles abound), home of deer and leopard, various reptiles, and noisome insects. An ascent is not recommended. From Villa de González, Méx. 80 continues SE to (104km) *Manuel*, whence a road runs NE to (36km) *Villa de Aldama* in a region of cenotes (freshwater deposits; here called aguadas) and (81km) *Barra del Tordo*, a fishing village on the bank of the Río Carrizal estuary, 2km from the sea. From Manuel, Méx. 80 goes SE to (161km) *Altamira*, within sight of the coast and offshore oil installations. 185km *Tampico*, see Rte 61.

83km *El Encino*. 8km NW is the source of the Río Sabinas, a deep pool of clear water c 15m in diameter. At 104km a road branches r. for (11km W) *Gómez Farías* and (4km SW) *El Nacimiento*, in an area of springs and rich vegetation. From (123km) *El Limón* a road runs W to (43km) *Ciudad Ocampo*, founded in 1749 as *Sta Bárbara*, in beautiful surroundings.

It is the site of a cave, excavated in 1958 by Richard MacNeish. Artefacts included stone points and scrapers, and the debris from their manufacture (c 5–3000 BC); and in later levels, fragments of woven and twilled mats and baskets dated 2500–2250 BC. Several other camp sites, surface finds, and temporary sites were also located in MacNeish's survey of the Sierra Tamaulipas (cf. *Tehuacán* Valley).

137km **Ciudad Mante** (c 75,000 inhab.; 83m; H,R,P), on the Río Mante, in the centre of a sugar-producing region and with two of the most productive refineries in Mexico.

60km E is *Villa de González* (see above). At 29km along this road, a minor road turns 18km S to *Presa Ramiro Caballero*, formed by the dammed waters of the Río Guayalejo.

At (164km) *Villa de Antiguo Morelos* a road (Méx. 80) branches off W to (86km) *Ciudad del Maíz* (see Rte 54) via (30km) *El Naranjo*, 16km NW of which are the waterfalls of *El Salto* (50m). Méx. 85 continues S, to the W of the Sierra del Abra, into the State of San Luis Potosí.

231km **CIUDAD VALLES** (c 172,000 inhab.; 95m; H,R,P) on the l. bank of the Río Tampaón (or Río Valles), on the NW edge of the Huasteca, was founded as the villa of Santiago de Valles in 1533, though its site may have been moved more than once in its early years. It is today an important commercial centre for the region's produce—sugarcane, fruit, coffee, cattle, etc. The *Museo Regional*

Huasteco contains artefacts from and information on local sites, on the site of Tamuín in particular.

Ciudad Valles is on Méx. 70, the San Luis Potosí–Tampico road, see Rte 61.

S of Ciudad Valles the coastal plain gives way to outlying sierras of the Sierra Madre Oriental. 280km turning r. for (4km W) *Aquismón*, a Huastec pueblo in the Sierra de Tampache. 11km W, by a tortuous path, is the *Sótano de las Golondrinas*, one of the deepest caverns in Mexico (370m vertical drop). 282km (3km E) *Ciudad Santos*, a centre for Huastec crafts, 8km S of which is *Huehuetlán*, another archetypal Huastec pueblo.

C 14km NE of Ciudad Santos is *Gen. Pedro Antonio de los Santos*. Near the town are two archaeological sites, both Huastec civic and ceremonial centres: **Tancanhuitz** and **Tamposoque**. Tancanhuitz comprises at least a dozen platforms and mounds in a certain planned symmetry, oriented NW–SE. These have the usual cores of earth and clay, with facings of stone slabs, and include circular, rectangular with rounded corners, and square-fronted/circular-backed plans. Most are of at least two tiers, and one large circular platform is four tiers (12m diam., 3m high), with a ramp up the SW side. In general, such circular platforms are more common among the Huastecs than elsewhere in Mesoamerica (cf. *El Tamuín* and *Ebano*).

The ruins at Tamposoque also show a symmetrical layout and variety of ground-plans. Here, one immense platform (actually a terracing of the low slope rising E) has a staircase roughly one-third of its width on the W side, flanked by two circular platforms with steeper steps up their W sides. At the top of the main staircase, between the two platforms, are the ruins of a small, rectangular altar platform. Towards the rear of the terrace (to the E) are two large, square-fronted/circular-backed platforms, each with steps up the squared front, and another small rectangular (?)altar between them, although the two fronts are in staggered alignment. On the W part of the site, in front of the main terrace, there are three more monuments: two small circular platforms, one (on the N) with steps on the E and W sides, and the other (on the S) with only one set of steps up its N side; W of these two, aligned directly in front of the wide staircase of the main terrace, is a low rectangular platform with steps up its E side.

At 303km Méx. 85 is joined (r.) by Méx. 120 from *San Juan del Río*, see Rte 38. 338km *Tamazunchale*, see Rte 38.

61 Tampico to Ciudad Valles and San Luis Potosí

Méx. 70, 395km.—59km Ebano.—108km **Tamuín**.—230km turning l. for (37km) Lagunillas and Sta María Acapulco.—395km **San Luis Potosí**.

TAMPICO (622,000 inhab. [incl. *Ciudad Madero*]; 12m), Mexico's chief port for exports, its third fishing port, and one of the centres of the oil and petrochemical industries, is set at the estuaries of the Ríos Pánuco and Tamesí in an area of lagoons and fine beaches, still not entirely spoiled by industrial development. The inland region offers opportunities for shooting and fishing. The city itself, though inevitably affected by the oil industry and port activity, still has some liveliness and tropical atmosphere.

Airport. 15km N of the city. Flights to *Mexico City*; *Guadalajara*, *Veracruz*, and *Monterrey*.

Bus station. C. Zapotal, c 4km NW of Pl. de Armas. Services to *Ciudad Victoria* (4 hrs); to *Matamoros* (7½ hrs); to *Mexico City* (c 10 hrs); to *San Luis Potosí* (c 8 hrs); etc.

Railway station. C 1km SE of Pl. de Armas. Trains to *San Luis Potosí* (19 hrs); to *Monterrey* (11 hrs).

Hotels throughout the town.

Post Office. Pl. de la Libertad.

Tourist Office. 101 C. Andrés de Olmos.

US Consulate. 2000 Av. Hidalgo.

San Luis de Tampico was founded in 1554–60 on the r. bank of the Río Pánuco near its mouth, where now is Villa Cuauhtémoc in the State of Veracruz. In Sept. 1568 John Hawkins, escaping N in the 'Minion' from his defeat at San Juan de Ulúa, was forced through lack of supplies to offload c 100 crew here to fend for themselves in an unknown and hostile land (see Rte 72). The quixotic expedition of the Spaniard Isidro Barradas, sent from Havana to reconquer Mexico, occupied Tampico in July 1829, only to be defeated in Aug. by Santa-Anna. Its oil associations began in 1898 with the Waters Pierce Oil Co., which installed a refinery for imported oil. In 1900 began the exploration of the US magnate Edward L. Doheny, founder of Standard Oil, who at nominal cost bought quantities of oil-rich land in the region. In 1907 Weetman Pearson founded his Mexican Eagle oil company, which in 1909 made a strike near Tuxpan. Exploitation of local coastal riches (Faja de Oro) began during the first world war. An unprecedented boom was ended by a series of catastrophic fires late in 1921. In Apr. 1914, while the town was besieged by constitutionalists and the Fifth Division of the US fleet stood off the coast to protect the oil installations, a US whaleboat sailed up the canal to collect petrol. Its crew were briefly detained by Mexican federals. Although their commander apologized, the US government used the incident to humiliate Huerta and as an excuse to occupy Veracruz. The resurgence of the oil industry since the 1930s has seen the growth of the satellite town *Ciudad Madero*, c 5km NE. Tampico is connected by pipeline to Ciudad Victoria and Monterrey.

The city fills a tongue of land formed by a S bend of the Río Pánuco. Its area is reduced by a large (polluted) lake in its centre, connected to the river by a channel on the SE side. On the S side of the lake is the old city centre, still keeping grand and humble buildings from the early boom. It is grouped around PL. DE ARMAS, a place of some distinction, with its palm, oriental elm, and other trees, and especially animated in the evenings. On the N side is the cathedral of **San Luis**, finished in 1931 and built with money donated by Edward L. Doheny and his wife. Its exterior is a variation of neo-Gothic; its interior notable for the strange swastika-patterned floor, supplied from Monterrey.

The higher W parts of the city extend along the banks of the Río Tamesí and touch the *Lago de Chairel* (yacht club) in the State of Veracruz.

The neighbouring **Ciudad Madero**, conspicuously well laid out, is reached NE from the centre of Tampico along Av. Obregón. Installed in the precinct of the *Instituto Tecnológico* of the University of Tamaulipas, in Av. 1 de Mayo, is the **Museo de la Cultura Huasteca** (Mon.–Fri., 10–5; Sat., 10–3).

The Huasteca, ancient and modern. The various displays illustrate the Huasteca as a tribe and region. The ancient Huasteca stretched along the coast from Río Bravo in the N to Río Cazones in the S, and extended inland to the sierras in the States of Tamaulipas, Nuevo León, Veracruz, San Luis Potosí, NE Querétaro, and N Hidalgo.
  The earliest occupants of this area lived in cave sites in Tamaulipas, where early evidence for the development of agriculture has been found (see Rte 60). Thereafter, the cultural evolution of the area is divided into several phases.

Pavón (c 1100–850 BC), during which the earliest pottery included red and white monochrome wares, mostly olla cooking pots and flat-bottomed cups. *Ponce* (c 850–600 BC). Monochrome black ware and incised decoration were added to the ceramic repertoire, and there is evidence of artistic links with the Olmec Gulf Coast and the Maya Petén (Guatemala; also linguistic links, see below). *Aguilar* (c 600–350 BC), during which tripod vessels became important and the pottery, in a variety of colours (orange, brown, red, coffee, white), indicates the beginnings of contact with central Mexico. *Pánuco I (Chila Blanca*; c 350–100 BC). A continuation of Aguilar, with red-on-coffee coloured ceramics and figurines with characteristic 'coffee bean'-shaped eyes. *Pánuco II (El Prisco)* (c 100 BC–AD 200). Continuation of Pánuco I; increasing popularity of zoomorphic and anthropomorphic figurines. *Pánuco III* (c AD 200–700). The site of El Tajín expanded and had close contacts with Teotihuacán. Characteristic was the appearance of hollow, rectangular supports on vessels. *Pánuco IV* (c 700–1000). Contact with Teotihuacán waned and El Tajín became the most powerful city in the region. Totonac influence from that city became stronger, but distinctive Huastec features continued to prevail in the Pánuco area, especially at sites such as Tamuín (below) and Las Flores (below). *Pánuco V* (c 1000–1250). Toltec contacts grew stronger and contacts with the central Veracruz-Puebla region, especially with Cholula, developed. The cult of Quetzalcóatl developed and clay moulds for figurines appeared in the region. *Pánuco VI* (c 1250–1521). Aztec and Mixtec ceramic influences were taken up, but a characteristically Huastec black-on-white (or buff) ware also remained strong.

In 1467 the Huasteca successfully defended themselves against Aztec expansion, although the Aztecs eventually garrisoned the town of Tochpan (Tuxpan) and Castillo de Teayo, and forced the Huasteca to pay tribute. Records for Tuxpan list the following annual payment: 6948 loads of coats (mantles); 800 loads each of shirts, loincloths, and chillies; 20 sacks of feathers; two jade necklaces; a turquoise necklace and two turquoise mosaic discs; and two military costumes. During the Late Postclassic the Huasteca broke up into several jealously guarded independent kingdoms, united only in their hatred of the Aztecs.

Spanish chronicles describe the Huasteca as generally naked, given to sexual licence (incl. what were perversions to Spanish eyes) and drunkenness.

The Huasteca, more generally, had early kinship links with the Maya before the various Maya groups migrated S and E into Yucatán, Chiapas, the Petén, and highland Guatemala. From c 1400 BC they were separated from the Maya homelands by groups occupying the Middle Gulf Coast region. Guatemalan Maya chronicles refer to Huastec ancestry, a relationship manifest in a linguistic link surviving in a Huastec-Maya dialect still spoken in two isolated areas: SE San Luis Potosí (around Tancanhuitz and Ciudad Valles) and N Veracruz (around Tantoyuca, Tancoco, Chontla, and Amatlán). Some Huastec cultural influence spread as far as the SE USA, but it was more influential in central Mexico, especially in the religious sphere.

The cult of Quetzalcóatl, manifested as the Wind god Ehecatl, was an early Huastec development. The characteristic circular temple-platform was earlier and always more common in the Huasteca than in other parts of Mesoamerica. Huastec dwelling houses were also circular, and their pottery was predominantly of spherical forms. Other Huastec deities were also taken up in central Mexico, incl. Tlazoltéotl, Xilonen, Teteoinnan, and Xochiquetzal.

Other predominating features of prehistoric Huastec culture were their predilection for cranial deformation (perhaps another Maya link) and their participation in international politics. Heads of babies were shaped after birth, teeth were filed and blackened, and hair dyed yellow. There is some evidence that migrating Huastecs participated in the founding of Teotihuacán, and that later, they were partly responsible for the fall of Tula when the daughter of the last Toltec ruler, Huemac, sought a Huastec consort. Another source states that the founder of Tenayuca was married to a Huastec princess.

Circular structures, or rectangular with rounded corners, were characteristic of Huastec architecture and are thought to have inspired similar buildings in central Mexico and in the Maya area. Normally rare elsewhere in Mesoamerica, circular structures are known from many excavations in the Huasteca, and predominate at Ebano (San Luis Potosí), Las Flores (near Tampico), Tancol (Veracruz), and Pavón (Veracruz). At Pavón one structure, an asphalt-surfaced cone, is of Late Classic date, while the earlier levels at the site have given its name to the earliest, *Pavón, c 1100–850 BC*, ceramic phase in the Huasteca. The Huasteca colonized as far W as *Buena Vista Huaxcama* in San Luis Potosí, taking advantage of the good farming conditions extended by the climatic shift in the Late Classic Period, bringing greater rainfall to the region.

Present Huastec houses are rectangular, with rounded corners, mostly in scattered rancherías, rather than in organized villages with plazas. Most dwellings are a single room, with only the most essential furniture and cooking utensils; mats for sleeping on, three-legged benches, baby cradles suspended from the rafters, and a small altar for a favourite saint to protect the household and its occupants.

Local religion is a mixture of Catholicism and ancient rites, incl. zimanes (sorcerers) and hypnotists, consulted for both physical and spiritual problems, such as the evil eye and the jalcud (being taken over by the spirit of another). Religious feasts include Catholic celebrations plus several prehistoric ones. The most spectacular is that of the voladores, shared with the Totonac culture (see Rte 64). Another ancient rite is the planting of a baby's umbilical cord simultaneously with a banana tree. Later the fruit is eaten by the child and those who live in the same household. Ancient burial customs are rapidly dying out, but where practised include burying the dead with special supplies by their feet (sandals, machete, coin, ceramic bowl, jícara craft for crossing rivers, and corn and other food).

The museum is a single, semi-divided display room: 1–3. Panels, Huastec cultural groupings; definition of the Huasteca; Huastec topography, climate, vegetation, and geography. 4. Huastec physical characteristics through figurines. 5. Prehistoric Huastec technology, incl. axe heads, grinding stones, masks, figurines, polishers, paper-pounders, knives, arrow points, pyrite mirrors, loom weights, and bone and antler tools. 6–8. Huastec cultural chronology and examples of ceramic vessels and figurines (incl. an articulated example) for each phase. 9. Sculpture of Huastec Youth (1.45m; copy of the original found at El Tamuín, now in the Museo Nacional de Antropología). It includes characteristics described above: filed teeth and relief-work depicting Ehecatl and Maya glyphs (eg, Anau = Lord), and various symbols (incl. water and corn ears). He carries a child on his back, and is assumed to be Quetzalcóatl. 10. Panel and photomurals of Huastec El Tamuín. 11. Huastec jewellery in jade, turquoise, shell, and other stones. 12. Totonac stone yugo, a sort of waist belt or girdle for the ball game; in stone they were probably for ceremonial and burial purposes rather than actual play. 13. Artefacts and information relating to Huastec religion. 14, Artefacts and information on Huastec warfare: bows, arrows, atlatls, knives, copper hatchets, maces, obsidian-set clubs, and cotton armour (cf. No. 21). 15. Huastec architecture at Tancanhuitz, El Ebano, El Tamuín, and Las Flores. 16. Colour photographs of El Tamuín. 17. Stone slab from Texupezco (Veracruz), carved with water symbols. 18. Figurines showing the dress of Huastec women. 19. Ethnographic examples of Huastec textiles. 20. Stone sculpture of a deity with animal (tiger?) headdress. 21. Stone sculpture of a Huastec warrior carrying a spear- or dart-thrower, and wearing a loincloth and earplugs. 22. Stone sculpture, probably of Teteoinnan, Tlazoltéotl or Ixcuinama (goddess of fertility), with a 'halo'. 23. Sculpture of a deity with conical headpiece, flanked by motifs for life and death. 24. Huastec cultural influences to and from neighbouring cultures: Totonac, Olmec, and Maya. 25. Huastec uses of bitumen to blacken their teeth, stain their skins, paint figurines, and to make beads and necklaces.

N of Ciudad Madero is *Playa Miramar*, a favourite local beach, not as polluted as some might suspect, but to be approached with caution.
From Tampico to *Tuxpan* and *Poza Rica*, see Rte 64.

Méx. 70 leaves Tampico to the W and enters the State of Veracruz, the Huasteca region, and the floodplain of the Río Pánuco, an area marked by lagoons, and by oil storage tanks and refineries, a reminder that it was the earliest Mexican oilfield. At 35km, Méx. 105 branches S for (345km) *Pachuca*, see Rte 62. Just before (59km) **Ebano** (P) we cross into the State of San Luis Potosí.

At Ebano, or *El Ebano*, excavations in 1937 uncovered possibly the earliest known circular structure in Mesoamerica, and perhaps the earliest architecture of the Huasteca. If correctly dated to the *Pánuco I* phase (as early as 400–100 BC), it would predate the circular pyramid at Cuicuilco. It comprises a circular, dome-shaped clay structure, 27m in diameter and 3m high, and may have supported a wooden altar or other structure on top. The clay is beaten down and has been burnt, but whether deliberately or by accident is uncertain. As with later Huastec temples it was probably dedicated to Ehecatl, the Wind god (cf. *Tamuín*).

108km **Tamuín** (7000 inhab.; 275m; H,R,P), on the l. bank of the Río Tamuín. C 6km E of the town a road S runs to (6km) *Rancho El Consuelo* (working ranch, please close gates after entering). On this land is **El Tamuín**, one of the largest Huastec sites known and one of their principal civic and ceremonial centres. It sits on a high bluff above the river and was occupied between c AD 800 and 1500. Excavations were done by INAH under the direction of R. Orellano, but unfortunately there has been no restoration work, nor a complete plan of the site.

The zone is extensive (c 16–17ha), but the principal monument is a large platform of three levels. It comprises an earth and rubble core, 14m long and 4.5m high, faced with river pebbles, an unusual practice in Mesoamerica. It supports several structures, the chief of which are a temple and two altars, all connected to one another by a low mini-platform. These present temple ruins face E and were the third such structure to be superimposed over an earlier temple; the earliest of which was erected in the 9C AD. Inside, its walls bear the remains of frescoes, varyingly preserved: according to different sources, these are described as red on white, red on plaster (which they certainly are), red and green, or red and yellow.

The best evidence is, of course, before your very eyes, and the reader is left to judge for him- or her-self whether the particular play of light under which he or she views these paintings makes them appear with white, off white (?yellow), or a pale shade of green background.

They depict various geometric key patterns, and a gathering of 11 figures in red, five seated and six standing, all richly dressed and carrying fans, symbols of rank, spear-throwers, and other ornamental objects. Experts disagree as to whether these are gods, or priests dressed as and worshipping gods; but one figure appears to hold a severed human head by its hair and one is thought to represent Quetzalcóatl.

The execution of the scene is so compact that it is difficult to distinguish between one figure and another, a practice shared in the Huastec art of carving ornamental figures on small shells. More generally, the style resembles that of the 'Mixtec' codices, while the theme itself reflects Toltec influence, with whom the Huasteca certainly had important trading contacts.

The two associated altars are in the shapes of two truncated cones with adjoining tips (resembling a Late Postclassic brazier) and of a single truncated cone. It was in the excavation of these that the famous stone sculpture known as the 'Huastec Boy' (or 'Adolescent'), was found (now in the Museo Nacional de Antropología).

The platform has a staircase which the excavators concluded to be later in date, and to the N and S of which they found several tombs. These were lined with river pebbles, presumably from the same source as those which faced the platform, and had stucco-covered walls. They contained bodies of both males and females, in foetal positions, facing E, but only the S group included funeral offerings.

There are several similar, but less well-known sites in the vicinity: *Tantoque* (or *Tantoc*) on the outskirts of Tamuín, in El Aserradero; *Tamposoque*; and *Tancanhuitz* (Rte 60). Tantoque is similar to El Tamuín, with small platforms and terracing faced with pebbles; its various ruins are grandly known as the *Pirámides del Sol y de la Luna* or *Pirámide Mayor y del Tizate*. There are numerous other minor mounds.

121km (3km S) *Taninul*, with sulphur baths and a Huastec stepped pyramid. 138km *Ciudad Valles*, see Rte 60. Beyond Ciudad Valles the road crosses outlying sierras of the Sierra Madre Oriental before descending, then climbing again into the Sierra Madre proper. 192km turning r. (N) for (7km) *Tamasopo* (c 1000m), beautifully set in the valley of the Río Tamasopo (waterfalls in the vicinity). 230km turning l.

This road (not easy) winds S into the N part of the Sierra Gorda across the Río Verde, home of the Pame Indians. 30km turning l. for *Sta Catarina* (1387m), their main pueblo, and chief of 15 distributed in the sierra. 37km *Lagunillas*. To the S, on a plateau, is **Sta María Acapulco**, founded as a Franciscan mission on the Chichimec frontier c 1620, destroyed in 1663, refounded c 1749, and still an important Pame religious, political, and cultural centre. Of great interest, on the higher part of the plateau, is the church, on the E side of an atrio. Built of rubble masonry, visibly buttressed, covered by a wooden roof reinforced with palm leaves, and resembling a barn, it dates from a little after 1750.

EXTERIOR. The W façade shows traces of polychrome and is divided into three vertical sections composed of niches holding statues worked in clay over wooden interiors and covered in stucco. In the first level appear SS Peter and Paul; in the second, a nun and a friar battling with a dragon; in the third and fourth, figures in Franciscan habits.

INTERIOR. The nave is covered by a wooden barrel vault, divided into eight sections. Five of these preserve paintings of saints from the mendicant orders and other saintly figures. Also miraculously preserved are the pulpit and altarpieces. That behind the high altar, in exuberantly rustic churrigueresque, covered in gilding and polychrome, is dedicated to the

Assumption. The paintings show scenes from Our Lady's life. The three side altarpieces, though contemporary, are simpler in style. On the N side of the nave are the little baptistery, the antesacristy, and, communicating with the chancel, the sacristy.

On the W side of the atrio is the three-room *Casa Cural* (priest's house). Going round the plateau is a Way of the Cross (14 stations), focus of Holy Week celebrations.

271km *Río Verde*, a market town whence a road runs SE to (71km) *Concá* and (106km) *Jalpan*, see Rte 38. 103km NW is *Guadalcázar*, see Rte 56. 276km turning l. for (11km S) the *Lago de la Media Luna* (35m deep). Across the Sierra de Juárez to (357km) the *Valle de los Fantasmas* (curious rock formations). 395km *San Luis Potosí*, see Rte 57.

62 Tampico to Pachuca and Mexico City

Méx. 70, Méx. 105, Méx. 85 (and Méx. 85D), 474km.—35km junction with Méx. 105.—50km Pánuco.—166km Huejutla.—217km Tlanchinol.—252km **Molango**.—283km Zacualtipán.—305km Metzquititlán and (4km SE) Sta María Xoxoteco.—315km road NW for (23 km) **Metztitlán**.—346km **Atotonilco el Grande**.—370km Mineral del Monte.—380km **Pachuca** and Méx. 85.—402km Méx. 85D for (468km) Mexico City.—429km road E for (14km) **Zumpango**.—474km **Mexico City**.

From Tampico to (35km) turning l. for *Pachuca*, see Rte 61. Méx. 105 now goes S to cross the Río Pánuco for (50km) **Pánuco** (c 14,000 inhab.; 20m; H,R,P), centre of one of Mexico's foremost oil-producing regions and on the r. bank of the river.

The site of Pánuco produced a large collection of important finds of the Huastec culture, and gave its name to the Late Postclassic phase of this region (c AD 1200 to the Spanish Conquest). The villa of San Esteban del Puerto de Pánuco was founded early in 1523 after Cortés had defeated the Huastecs, who had risen against the followers of Diego Camargo; soon after, Cortés frustrated the attempt, accompanied by wholesale violence against the Huastecs, of Francisco de Garay to colonize the area. Further Huastec revolts were put down late in 1523 and in 1525–26. In 1527 Nuño de Guzmán arrived as governor, and ruled it and its province independently until it was incorporated into New Spain in 1533.

88km *El Higo* (P), where a road branches r. to cross the Río Moctezuma into the State of San Luis Potosí and to (90km) *Ciudad Santos*, see Rte 60. Méx. 105 runs parallel with the Río Tempoal to (117km) *Tempoal* whence Méx. 127 runs SE to (138km) *Tuxpan*, see Rte 64. We cross into the State of Hidalgo at (166km) **Huejutla** (8000 inhab.; 170m; H,R,P), chief town of the Huasteca region of NE Hidalgo.

The former Augustinian convent of *San Agustín* (restored), now the cathedral, was completed by 1570 after the friars had set up here in 1544 under their Portuguese provincial, Fray Juan de Estacio. The lie of the land made construction difficult, so the church had to be given a N–S axis; the atrio, now the main plaza, runs at a lower level along the W side of the convent. Two posa chapels once occupied the NW and SW corners. The elevated open chapel is uniquely placed at right angles to the axis on the church's W side, with its altar on the E.

54km NW is *Tamazunchale*, see Rte 38. From c 14km along this road it is possible to reach (c 4km N) *Huichapan*, where a circular monument, 34m in diameter of receding tiers, and two rectangular, round-cornered temples have been excavated; at nearby *Vinasco* several late Postclassic stone-lined, covered tombs have also been excavated (ask for directions in Huejutla).

217km **Tlanchinol** (c 2000 inhab.), in mountainous, wooded country. It was known in the 16C as Tlanchinolticpac and its convent of *San Agustín* was built c 1548–68. It was seen by John Chilton in 1572: 'Clanchinoltepec…with eight or nine friars of the Order of Saint Augustine'. The atrio wall incorporates an elaborate espadaña; within the atrio the posa chapels (three in the fragilest of states, one whole) are barrel-vaulted. The church's tile roof was put in in 1852, displacing ancient thatching. It lost its westernmost section during the 18C, from which dates the present façade. On the old church bell is the date 1571.

C 18km E is *Huazalingo* (970m) where the little parish church of La Ascensión, sustained by thick, picturesque buttresses, dates probably from the early 18C. It preserves its original gilded altarpiece.

Méx. 105 winds S to (244km) **Lolotla** (1700m), where the Augustinian church of *Sta Catarina* was built in 1538 and a convent established in 1590. The present parish church, a restoration of the original, preserves much attractive relief: in the doorway, echoed above around the choir window, and in the gable (St Catherine and the head of emperor Maxentius, vanquished by her wisdom and constancy). Outstanding are the dragonlike figures in the voussoirs of the doorway arch and beside and above the cross which surmounts it.

252km **MOLANGO** (c 3000 inhab.; 1650m; H,P), beautifully set in an alpine landscape on the slopes of the sierra, its houses red-roofed and white-walled. (Today large deposits of manganese ore are worked.) Rising above the town, on a man-made eminence composed of tons of earth and stone, incl. the remains of the pre-Conquest sanctuary of the god Mola, is the former Augustinian convent of **Sta María** (later known as *Nuestra Señora de Loreto*).

It is probably the oldest conventual establishment in the Sierra Madre Oriental and was built during the 1540s under the direction of the remarkable Fray Antonio de Roa who 'when he said Mass his tears were so abundant that his sacristans had to give him three successive handkerchiefs'. He would also, wrote a pious chronicler, preach to the Indians in extreme pain after walking on red-hot coals and through fire, warning them that hellfire was much worse.

The atrio, at a lower level than the convent and approached by ramps (with stairs on the W side), is constricted by the site. On the wall is an espadaña (rebuilt after earthquake damage). The wide W doorway of the church, enclosed by an alfíz upheld by baluster colonnettes, shows Romanesque characteristics adapted by Indian hands. Half-columns, arch-rim mouldings, and jambs are covered by energetic foliated decoration; intrados of the arch and jamb interior faces by little angels carrying crosses. Above, a Gothic rose window, with fine tracery, illuminates the choir. The N doorway, with depressed arch, is also covered in vegetal, flower, and fruit relief.

The wooden ceiling of the interior is a modern replacement of various previous replacements since the 16C, results of fires. A unique, double-arch tribune is set in the S wall of the presbytery, the bases and capitals of the arches ornamented with pearls of Castile, the parapet with vegetal and apple relief. The portería, which may have been an open chapel, leads to the semi-ruined cloister, Renaissance in style, the lower storey only surviving, its clustered columns supporting semicircular arches.

A minor road winds E to (12km) **Xochicoatlán** (1790m), where the Augustinian convent of *San Nicolás* was set up in 1572. The church suffered in a fire in 1849, and has been much restored. The sacristy doorway and lavabo are among the survivors. Remains of the convent can be made out to the S of the church. The road continues SE to (29km) *Tianguistengo* (1687m; H), where the church of Sta Ana is probably an early 17C Augustinian foundation.

At (259km) *Malilla*, from c 1570 a visita of Molango, the little church, still in its original trapezoidal atrio with a restored (1976) cross, has an ingenuously wide entrance arch emphasized by low imposts and decorated with tequitqui relief. 283km **Zacualtipán** (12,000 inhab.; 2000m; H,P), known for apples and peaches. The church of the Augustinian priory of *Sta María*, founded in 1578, has been restored as the parish church of *Jesús Nazareno*, its doorway arch full of relief and covered by a huge, wide alfíz. A local curiosity is the monolithic *Casa del Soldado* (18C), carved out of two large rocks. On the larger is a relief of a soldier in tricorne hat.

C 10km S, at *San Bernardo*, the church, once a 16C open chapel, has a unique double-arch doorway and an ingenious relief of the saint above. 13km W of Zacualtipán is **Zoquizoquipan**, with an early 17C Augustinian church, once visited from Metztitlán, standing in a raised atrio containing four tiny posas (also 17C), each with its own espadaña. Above the church façade is another espadaña. Both church and atrio wall are covered with merlons. Each of the four low entrance arches to the atrio display interesting relief. The atrial cross shows human arms only along the horizontal; the vertical is occupied by Passion symbols.

305km *Metzquititlán* (1421m), with a 16C chapel, built by the Augustinians. 4km SE along a dirt road is **Sta María Xoxoteco**, where stands a 16C Augustinian church (restored; perhaps originally an open chapel), its interior painted with a remarkably forceful series of didactic murals (c 1540–56; recently freed from a mortar covering) which depict the cycle of temptation and punishment of sin, and other scenes which combine everyday and religious themes.

S (choir) wall: Calvary (deteriorated, further spoiled by the embedding of the wooden choir beams in the later mortar wall covering). N (presbytery) wall, invaded by a slab of recent blue paint: in the tympanum, Last Judgment (barely preserved); below l., the Creation, with a magisterial God the Father with Adam, Eve, at the moment of her creation, and animals; below r., the Tree of Knowledge, with a serpent coiled round the trunk and Adam and Eve on either side, and the Expulsion from Paradise—Adam and Eve fleeing an avenging sword. On E and W walls, between the lower and upper friezes and the springing of the vault, unfolds a vast scene of the tortures of Hell, complete with demon torturers, men and women undergoing torments, instruments of torture, and arms, legs, heads, and entrails cut off and out, and dismembered (particularly graphic on the E wall). Superimposed on the suffering of the damned are rectangular tableaux illustrating everyday happenings, with religious content, which point a moral. W wall from entrance: Pulque Drinkers—two seated figures in a landscape, served by a third figure l., each accompanied by a demon who seems to breathe words of temptation in his ear. Chastisement (two scenes one above the other)—in the upper, a Spaniard beats an Indian; in the lower, a hideous demon with hooves and hanging breasts draws an Indian away from a miniatory Spaniard—illustrations of the necessity of punishment to prevent relapses into paganism and falling into the hands of Satan. E wall, above sacristy door: higher up, the Sacrifices—on either side of a pagan shrine appear figures representing error and ignorance (l.) and an Indian and a Spaniard (r.), two notably more civilized figures, hands joined in prayer, looking towards the letters IHS, symbol of the Blessed Sacrament; lower down, a charming marriage scene, the accompanying devils probably underlining the necessity of avoiding temptation and of proper preparation for matrimony. The adjoining scene, culmination of the horrors of Hell, shows a man strung up to be flayed by two demons while a third seems to encourage the others from below.

At 315km a road begins a winding course NW along the valley of the Río Metztitlán.

At 14km (r.) is *Jihuico*, a village on a mountain slope. Approached up a steep incline is the church of Sta María Magdalena, developed towards the S in subsequent ages, and to accommodate an espadaña, from a 16C open chapel. On the outside, high up around the N, W, and E walls, is a frieze of lozenge-shaped Christian symbols in relief.

23km **METZTITLAN** (c 5000 inhab.; 1600m; P), in the Vega (fertile plain) de Metztitlán, a break in the wild sierra. From the Río Metztitlán on its S to the convent high on its N side it 'makes one of the handsomest townscapes surviving from the century of the Great Conversion'.

Metztitlán ('country of the moon') was an Otomí capital contemporary with and independent of the Aztecs; its city-state included parts of present-day Puebla, Tlaxcala, Hidalgo, and Veracruz. The Aztec King Tizoc (1481–86) attempted to capture the town in 1481, but failed, and thereafter Aztec campaigns were concentrated to their N and W. In 1568 a band of English survivors from John Hawkins's fleet (comp. Rte 72) were allowed to rest at Metztitlán while being taken, haltered and bound, to Mexico. One of them, Miles Philips, recalled the convent, 'a house of blacke friers: and in this towne there are about the number of three hundred Spaniards...The friers sent us meat from the house ready dressed, and the friers, and the men and women used us very courteously, and gave us some shirts...Here our men were very sicke of their agues, and with eating of another fruit called in the Indian tongue, Guiaccos, which fruit did bind us so sore, that for the space of ten or twelve dayes we could not ease ourselves'.

John Chilton visited in 1572: 'Mestitlan...standeth upon certaine hie mountaines, which are very thicke planted with townes very holesome and fruitfull, having plentifull fountains of water running thorow them'.

The monumental former Augustinian convent of **Los Santos Reyes**, raised on a high promontory above the town, creates a dramatic effect.

The Augustinians established a parish here in 1537 and built their first convent, lower down to the W of the present site, in the 1540s. It was partly destroyed in a flood. Their second convent dates from the 1550s. Room was made for the ATRIO by piling tons of earth against the top of the slope. In the SE corner is a posa chapel, and what was possibly another faces the S door of the church. To the l. of the church's N end stand two open chapels, a unique arrangement, possibly to honour two separate Indian confraternities; or the smaller perhaps a posa. The atrial cross shows a crown of thorns and drips of blood where the nails have been driven.

EXTERIOR. The church portal is a pallid plateresque: between the engaged columns, which have a ribbon motif around their shafts, are statues of SS Peter and Paul, crownlike canopies above their heads. In the entrance archivolt, a relief pattern of cherub heads and rosettes; in the jambs, platters of fish and apples and pears. Above the cornice, niches holding statues of the Christchild and attendant musical children. An original espadaña crowns the façade. The side doorway (W) is in severe Renaissance style.

The high and long INTERIOR (56.60m from door to apse wall) is covered by barrel vaulting in the nave, ribbing beyond the triumphal arch, and coffering in the apse. Some of the original murals in the sotocoro, and running, frieze-like, around the nave, have been brought to light: bands of bird and flower patterns enclosing a broader band of angels, Augustinian emblems, grapes, floral and vegetal motifs. The side retables include fine 17C baroque pieces. The high altarpiece (contracted in 1696) is a magnificent work of art, one of the high points of Mexican baroque, a collaboration between two of the greatest artists of the time, the sculptor Salvador de Ocampo and the painter Nicolás Rodríguez Juárez.

In the form of a screen, it stands on a high base, above which the generous predella gives room for reliefs of the four evangelists and SS Bernard and Benedict interspersed with mobile little angels who stand out from the column bases. The main body divides into three horizontal storeys and three vertical sections separated by solomonic columns swathed in fruit and foliate relief. On either side of the central section are niches, slanted towards the centre, holding statues of saints. The outer sections are occupied by paintings (sadly faded) of scenes from the lives of Our Lord and Our Lady (on l. from above: Ascension, Circumcision, Adoration of the Shepherds; on r., Assumption, Presentation of Our Lady, Birth of Our Lady). To the centre panel in the lowest storey belonged a tabernacle and sculptures of four doctors of the Church and St Augustine (the latter now kept in the convent). The centre panel ends in an arch, within an all-enveloping shell (partly damaged), above the top storey, in which stands the broken pediment, a Mannerist touch, of the top-storey panel. In the pediment, God the Father looks down on the Crucifixion, Our Lady and St John standing beneath the Cross. On either side stand SS William of Aquitaine and Clare.

The centrepiece is a stunning relief of the Epiphany: the figures bringing a blend of expressiveness, dignity, and elegance, the folds of the robes exquisitely done. (Note how Our Lady's cloak and St Joseph's l. hand reach beyond the frame—r.) On either side, SS John of Sahagún and Monica. Below them in the lowest storey, SS Nicholas of Tolentino and Thomas of Villanueva.

To the r. (E) of the church is the three-arched PORTERIA. Of its original murals have been rescued a Tree of Redemption (the Crucifixion; S wall), its branches forming medallions of the Sacraments, springing from the Fountain of Life at which takes place a baptism; and an Immaculate Conception (E wall), surrounded by the symbols of the Litany of Loreto.

From the portería we reach the grand two-storey CLOISTER. In the lunettes at each corner of the lower-storey walk are paintings of the four evangelists and four doctors of the Church. The ceiling of the refectory, on the E side, is likewise painted, with narrow mock ribbing and italianate patterns in the spaces between. On the N side is the grand staircase, its walls showing more murals, of the Triumph of the Virtues of Chastity and Patience. The upper cloister walk preserves six corner lunette paintings: the Arrest of Our Lord, Sacrifice of Isaac, Road to Calvary (these two in better condition), the Bronze Serpent, Crucifixion, and Resurrection.

In the barrio of Coatlán, to the W, remains part of the cloister of the earlier Augustinian foundation, known as *La Comunidad* (1537–39). In the town centre is the house called *La Tercena* (c 1540), with a loggia, probably where the tribute of the Indians was collected.
From the W side of Metztitlán a narrow road zigzags through the sierra to (3km) **Atzolcintla**. High up on the l. is the 16C open chapel of *San Juan*, once used by the friars from Metztitlán, and now incorporated in a cemetery. Sturdy and square, its parapet is surrounded by merlons, interrupted by an espadaña on the W. Below, within a huge alfíz, its frame marked by rosette reliefs, is the wide arch (since filled in with rubble masonry) through which the Indians could gain a view of Mass celebrated within. Along the archivolt runs a fleur-de-lis relief pattern springing from a jar motif above each impost, whose bases are carved fruit and leaf patterns.
The road winds N to cross the Río Metztitlán near (45km; l.) the *Laguna de Metztitlán*.

Méx. 105 continues across the Sierra de Pachuca to (346km) **ATOTONILCO EL GRANDE** (c 5000 inhab.; 2138m; H,P), on the N slopes of the sierra, with a picturesque PL. PRINCIPAL, on which the *Pal. Municipal*, with a mirador, dates from the 17C. Its chief interest is the former Augustinian convent of **San Agustín**, founded in 1536 and built during the 1540s and 1580s, the enterprise of Juan de Sevilla (d. 1563), prior for 20 years.

The church portal, facing W, exhibits a faded plateresque, probably because of the damage it has suffered. In the lower storey, two pairs of fluted columns and between them lines of coffering enclosing stylized roses. In the spandrels are medallions containing busts of SS Peter and Paul. Above, a frieze of cherubim. On the S side is a lateral tower decorated with merlons. Between heavy buttresses on the N wall a raised open chapel is unusually placed to face away from the church.
INTERIOR. The great barrel-vaulted nave narrows beyond the triumphal arch into the presbytery. Sotocoro and presbytery are covered in rib vaulting (1586). On the S side, two delightful ogee arches grace the doorways to the baptistery and the side chapel known as *Sto Entierro*; their flattened fruit and foliage relief continuing into the jambs.
The CLOISTER has striking arcades composed of semicircular arches without archivolts, their imposts high; the upper columns embedded in the parapet, which gives them a stunted look. The heavy square buttresses which interrupt the arcades are insensitive 19C additions. In the lower cloister walk are 16C mural paintings of Passion scenes (Crucifixion, Descent from the Cross, Entombment), discovered in 1951. Though inevitably faded, they show high technical ability and imagination, and are surrounded by frieze frames composed of capital letters and religious symbols. On the wall of the staircase leading to the upper cloister, another mural shows St Augustine in full pontificals and a complimentary inscription above him; on his r., Socrates, Plato, and Aristotle; on his l., Pythagoras, Seneca, and Cicero.
9km NW of Atotonilco is *Sta María Amajac*, known for its thermal springs.

358km turning l. for (9km E) *Huasca de Ocampo* (2050m).

3km NE is the former hacienda of *San Miguel Regla* (now a hotel; open only to guests), built by the mining magnate Pedro Romero de Terreros (see below), who died here. The 19C hacienda of *San Juan Hueyapan* (rooms for rent and horses for hire) lies 8km E. 7km NE is *Sta María Regla*, a quaint village in an area of basalt rock formations.

370km (l.) **Mineral del Monte** (c 20,000 inhab.; 2670m; R,P), a town of narrow winding streets, its various levels connected by flights of steps.

A mining camp, Asunción Real del Monte, existed here in 1569, part of a richly endowed silver-mining area, where deposits had been discovered in 1552. Between 1738 and 1781 the Vizcaína mine, with an output of 20 million silver pesos, made its owner, Pedro Romero de Terreros, 1st conde de Regla (1710–81), the richest man in New Spain. The mines functioned in 1824–28 under English management, the Compañía de los Caballeros Aventureros en las Minas de Pachuca, but the enterprise failed, with a loss of 5 million pesos. 350 Cornish miners (with their families) were among those brought over to work. Three shiploads of machinery were dragged over the mountains from Veracruz: the boilers and heaviest implements borne on gun carriages, pulled by horses and mules from the Royal Arsenal at Woolwich, an operation directed by engineers and stevedores from Birmingham and Southampton. The journey took a year, men and beasts perishing on the way. Houses with high sloping roofs and chimneys are a reminder of Cornish taste (as is a Mexican variation of the Cornish pasty, flavoured with chilli). The English plant was bought up by the Compañía Real del Monte y Pachuca, founded in 1849 by Manuel Escandón and Antonio and Nicanor Béistegui, which in 1850 uncovered the great Rosario bonanza.

The church of *Vera Cruz* (rebuilt early 18C) contains small baroque side altarpieces. In its antesacristy is a portrait of Bp Palafox (dated 1749) by Antonio Pérez de Aguilar. The original parish church of *Asunción* dates from c 1578. Occupying a whole block is the house known as the *Maestranza*, built to house the offices, stores, and machine shops of the Compañía Real del Monte y Pachuca.

371km turning r. onto a winding, spectacular mountain road to (21km) **Mineral del Chico** (c 12,000 inhab.; 2850m), another mining settlement, founded c 1565, its narrow winding streets leading from a large central plaza. Some of its quaint houses end in pointed roofs; others have rhomboid façades, obeying the demands of the terrain. The *Parque Nacional el Chico* is set among pinewoods and capricious rock formations.

380km **PACHUCA** (c 161,000 inhab.; 2600m), capital of the State of Hidalgo, grew to prominence as the centre of a world-famous silver-mining region. Although today little visited by foreign travellers, it retains interest for its historical associations. Its layout is irregular and streets are steep and narrow. The climate can be chilly, for NE winds prevail during eight or nine months of the year.

Bus station. In SW outskirts, reached along Av. Juárez and Blvd Felipe Angeles. Services to *Mexico City* (2 hrs); to *Querétaro* (4½ hrs); to *Tampico* (c 5 hrs); to *Tula* (1½ hrs); to *Tulancingo* (1 hr); to *Metztitlán* (1½ hrs); to *Epazoyucan* (½ hr); to *Mineral del Monte* (½ hr); etc.

Hotels throughout the town.

Post Office. Corner of Av. Juárez and C. Jaime Nuño.

Tourist Office. 1590 Av. Juárez.

British Vice Consul. 1209 Av. de la Revolución.

Cerro de las Navajas, near the city, was an important obsidian quarry in ancient times, exploited by Teotihuacán and others. Several trade routes were used to distribute it, known collectively as the 'Teotihuacán Corridor'. Silver deposits were discovered to the SW in 1552; c 1553–55, after finds on the hacienda of Purísima Grande near Pachuca, Bartolomé de Medina started the experiments which led to the patio process of ore reduction by quicksilver amalgamation: start of silver production technology in New Spain. In the late 17C it was said that 'the Turks of Jerusalem would not accept any silver bar unless it bore the name of Pachuca (which they called Pachocha), a term which was synonymous with wealth'. In 1879 John F. Finerty found the Cornishmen who had settled here 'as kindly a lot of fellows, barring a few insular prejudices, as anybody could desire to meet'. In 1906 the Compañía Real del Monte y Pachuca sold out to the US Mining, Smelting and Refining Co., which in 1947 was sold to the federal government. It operates under its old name. The Pachuca mines (nearly 2000km of tunnels through the mountains) still turn out 10–15 per cent of the world's silver. The export of manganese to the USA is considerable.

The N and E parts of the State of **Hidalgo** (1.8 million inhab.; 20,987 sq km) are among the most mountainous (average altitude 2399m) in Mexico; the Sierra Madre Oriental and its dependent sierras occupy most of the area from SE to NW. In the NE is the Huasteca hidalguense, low hills and tropical lowlands, which is also one of the State's cattle-raising areas. The S and W parts are relatively flat, semi-arid tableland. Elsewhere rainfall tends to be higher than average for Mexico. Its mines—silver, gold, lead, copper, zinc, manganese, cadmium, mercury—are the State's chief resource.

In 1869 the free and sovereign State of Hidalgo was created. In 1877–95 Rafael Cravioto, a tyrannical Díaz crony, was governor, who nevertheless encouraged economic development. The Cristero rebellion paradoxically coincided with the governorship of Matías Rodríguez (1925–29), a man of outstanding probity, 'honesty, goodwill, kindliness...in public office to serve others rather than himself'. Under him, Hidalgo resembled 'a refreshing oasis'. Pres. Calles, reviewing the qualities of the State governors, described him as 'the best of them all'.

Pachuca and other municipalities are today marked to receive overspill population from the Federal District.

In the centre of the main PL. INDEPENDENCIA is the **Torre del Reloj** (clock-tower; 1905–10, by Tomás Cordero), the niches of its second storey graced by female statues in Carrara marble, representing Independence, Liberty, the Reform, and the Constitution. The main bell is a smaller replica of Big Ben in London. On the W side the *Hotel Grenfell* (c 1840) is a former coaching inn.

A short distance W of the plaza, in C. Bravo, is the *Foro Cultural Efrén Rebolledo*, once the house of Rafael Cravioto, now a cultural centre. To the N, at the corner of Cs Allende and Julián Villagrán, is the Methodist church of *Divino Salvador* (begun in 1892), a Cornish legacy.

C. Hidalgo, parallel with the E side of the plaza, goes N to PL. DE LA CONSTITUCIÓN, with a monument to Hidalgo (1888). On its N side is the parish church of **La Asunción**, rebuilt in 1648–1719, with a simple façade. In the baptistery is a painting of Souls in Purgatory (1680) by Juan Correa. On the E side, offices of the Compañía Real (early 19C). Behind the church, reached along C. Venustiano Carranza, is the former **Cajas Reales**, retaining the aspect of a Spanish fortress.

It was built in 1670–75 for the storing of the royal tribute, 'His Majesty's quinto'—a fifth part of the silver from the neighbouring mines. In 1728 from here 240,000 pesos-worth was sent to Mexico despite difficulties of extraction and the beginning of a decline. In 1812 the insurgents raided the treasury and made off with 220,000 pesos. Maximilian stayed here on his visit in Aug. 1865 when he inspected the mine shafts. It is now headquarters of the Compañía Real.

S of Pl. de la Constitución, reached along C. Morelos, is Pl. Gral. Anaya, where stands (N side) the house (c 1898) built in afrancesado style for Francis Rule, an English magnate; it is now the Ayuntamiento. At the S end of C. Hidalgo is the so-called *Casas Coloradas*, built for the 3rd conde de Regla at the beginning of the 19C.

From the SE corner of Pl. Independencia, C. Matamoros goes SW to the large PL. JUAREZ in which is a bronze statue of Juárez (1957), by Juan Leonardo Cordero. On its W side is a rebuilding of the neoclassical *Teatro Bartolomé de Medina* (1887), which has been used as Pal. Legislativo. On the N is the modern **Pal. de Gobierno**, which is notable for its interior mural (completed in 1974) by Jesús Becerrél, painted at the behest of Pres. Luis Echeverría and to honour the UNO. (Echeverría, who appears in the centre, later hoped to become Secretary-General of the organization.)

Boldly coloured and with surrealistic touches, the work illustrates the UN's duties towards mankind: progress illustrated on the l.; war and repression on the r. Among famous faces are Columbus, Cuauhtémoc, Sor Juana Inés de la Cruz, Juárez, Fidel Castro, Pres. Gerald Ford, Queen Elizabeth II, and Indira Gandhi.

From Pl. Juárez we may take Av. Xicoténcatl E, across the bed of the Río de las Avenidas, then C. Arista to the church and former convent of **San Francisco**.

It was founded for discalced Franciscans in 1596 and the church was finished in 1660. Between 1734 and 1808 the convent functioned as a Colegio de Propaganda Fide. In 1924, during the delahuertista rebellion, the church was dynamited, which has entailed extensive restoration. The painting in the choir is by Francisco Martínez (1735). In the sacristy are four 18C oils of the life of St Francis; in the antesacristy finely carved lavabos. Behind the high altar is the *Cap. de la Luz*, containing the tomb of the 1st conde de Regla and a churrigueresque altarpiece.

The ample convent buildings and modern dependencies today house the *Centro Cultural Hidalgo*, and include the **Museo Regional de Hidalgo** (Tues.–Fri., 10–2, 4–7; Sat.–Sun., 10–5; fee) illustrating the archaeology, ethnography, and history of the region. The lobby mural is by Roberto Cuevas del Río. In the larger cloister, added in the 18C at the expense of the 1st conde de Regla, is the *Archivo Fotográfico Casasola*, compiled by Agustín V. Casasola (1874–1932) and illustrating the history of Mexico from the final years of the porfiriato to the post-revolutionary era. It forms the basis of a huge collection, amounting to more than 600,000 negatives, the most famous and complete in the republic. Some of its prize exhibits are shown in rooms off the upper cloister walk. Temporary displays are also mounted. (Archive open Mon.–Fri., 8–3; photographic museum Tues.–Sun., 10–2, 4–6.)

High above the W side of Pl. Independencia, in C. Abasolo, is the former hospital of *San Juan de Dios* (1725–58), built next to the church of Guadalupe. Restoration from 1869 to house the State's literary institute and school of arts (since 1961, the *Universidad Autónoma de Hidalgo*) incorporated church (now an auditorium) and hospital into one building.

From Pachuca to *Texcoco*, see Rte 63.

FROM PACHUCA TO POZA RICA, 203km via Méx. 130. We leave Pachuca to the SE. 7km (2km E) *Pachuquilla* was founded in the 16C as an Indian community and as residence of the Indian regional governor. There remains the 16C portico chapel of Sta Magdalena, with two series of arcades. 15km turning r. to *Epazoyucan*, see Rte 63. 38km turning r. for (64km SW) *Teotihuacán*, see Rte 18. 46km **Tulancingo** (70,000 inhab.; 2200m; H,R,P), the pleasant second city of Hidalgo, famous for its cider, on the r. bank of the Río Grande de Tulancingo. It was at one corner of a triangular area of prehistoric obsidian extraction (Tulancingo, Pachuca, and Otumba). Exchange routes started at Tepeapulco, went through Tulancingo, and then to the Gulf Coast. Tulancingo was also on the legendary route of one branch of the Nonoalca in their migration N to settle among the Tolteca–Chichimeca and to help found Tula. The church of the former convent of *San Juan Bautista*, founded by the Franciscans c 1528, was pulled down to make way for the present neoclassical cathedral (1788–1807), designed by José Damián Ortiz de Castro. A side chapel contains a Marriage of Our Lady and a Holy Family by Juan Sánchez Salmerón. The two-storey cloister (restored) dates probably from the 1570s. In the atrio is the restored *Cap. de la Tercera Orden* (1575), with its original alfarje ceiling. The former convent gardens are now a park.

7km N is Mexico's satellite transmission station (no adm.). 3km N is **Huapalcalco**, ideally located to regulate the Classic Period obsidian trade of Teotihuacán. Excavations by César Lizardi Ramos and Florencia Müller Jacobs uncovered Preclassic, Classic, and Postclassic structures, of which the most notable are: *Grupo VI*, a platform with buildings of various phases with Teotihuacano style talud-tablero facings; a pyramid with a mural of geometric motifs, 10m long and 0.9m high, dated by associated material and by its style to the 2C BC (now covered for its protection); and *Estructuras V* and *VI*—Toltec, Early Postclassic Period.

9km NW, at **Acatlán**, are the ruins of the Augustinian convent of *San Miguel*, the church built c 1554, the cloister by 1569. In the atrio are three domed posas. The church has walls over 3m thick, far in excess of what was needed to support the vaults. Through the portería, once also used as an open chapel, access is gained to the simple two-storey cloister.

11km SE is *Natívitas*, where the church of Sta María (1689) contains baroque altarpieces and a painting of St Rose of Viterbo by Pedro Calderón (1729).

58km turning l. for (12km N) *Metepec* (P) and (45km NE) *Tenango de Doria*, in wooded, well-watered, and mountainous country. The latter is known for the embroidery work produced by the Otomí Indians of the region. At 63km turning l. for (28km NE) *Pahuatlán* in the State of Puebla and in a region mainly populated by Otomís. In the neighbouring pueblo of *San Pablito Pahuatlán* timeless Otomí religious rituals are still practised. 69km **Acaxochitlán** (c 4000 inhab.; 2270m; P), picturesque, where wines and sweets are produced from the fruits grown here in abundance. The road passes between two artificial lakes, *Omitemetl* (N) and *Tejocotal* (S), before crossing (at 83km) into the State of Puebla. 74km the road forks. The turning r. goes S to (131km) *Tlaxcala*, see Rte 68. We keep l. for (99km) **Huauchinango** (25,000 inhab.; 1497m; H,R,P), in a fertile subtropical region blessed with above average rainfall. 109km (r.) *Nuevo Necaxa* (H,R,P), a resort near pine forests. *Presa Necaxa* (1200m) has been used to generate hydroelectric power since early this century. 121km *Xicotepec*, in a fruit-growing area. The valley (fine views) between (146km) *Rafael Avila Camacho* and (203km) *Poza Rica* (see Rte 64) is another fertile fruit-growing and cattle-raising area watered by the Río San Marcos.

From Pachuca we take Méx. 85 through the S slopes of the Sierra de Pachuca and across the plain of Huaquilpan. At 402km (l.) begins the toll road (Méx. 85D) for (468km) *Mexico City*. We continue on Méx. 85. 421km *Tizayuca*, with a 17C parish church and 16C atrial cross. We then enter the State of México. At 429km a road runs E, along the N edge of the Valley of Mexico, via (3km; r.) *San Lucas Xoloc*, where the 18C church façade is a good example of uncrowded churrigueresque, to (14km) *Zumpango*.

ZUMPANGO (c 15,000 inhab.; 2258m; R,P) is on the E side of the *Laguna de Zumpango*.

This lake, now much reduced, is one of the few remaining in what was once a lake region, menacing in heavy rain, in the N of the Valley of Mexico, but now depleted by drainage. The *Gran Canal*, the fundamental engineering work to drain off the waters which had helped to precipitate the periodic flooding of Mexico City since prehispanic times, was started in the 1880s and inaugurated in 1900. It runs from the E of the capital NW, between the lake and town of Zumpango (47.5km). The waters then pass into the Tequixquiac tunnel (c 14km NW), 10km long, before emptying into the Río Tula, and thence, via the Ríos Moctezuma and Pánuco, to the Gulf of Mexico. Refinements to the drainage system have removed some of the canal's significance.

The parish church of **La Purísima Concepción**, dating probably from the late 1720s, has a concave façade (puerta abocinada), a rare specimen within the Mexican baroque, showing traces of the polychrome which once covered it. The supports of its two storeys are wavy fluted columns; between them, the eight niches of the lower storey and the four of the upper contain statues of saints (most likely the Apostles); above the niches, Marian symbols. In the arch key is an image of St Sebastian; and, above the recessed rose window, the Immaculate Conception. Covering all is a shell-like canopy. In the NE corner of the atrio is what remains of an open chapel which also served as a religious theatre, perhaps a survivor of the original late 16C church.

Another 18C church, **Nuestra Señora de Loreto**, contains a series of 14 paintings of the Passion, with Christ represented as the Sacred Heart, crude but vigorous works painted in 1773 by Francisco Báez (1726–91) and donated by one Pedro Nolasco Leonardo.
From Zumpango to (57km) *Mexico City* and (82km) *Ixmiquilpan*, see Rte 39.

435km *Tecamac*, where the 16C church of Sta Cruz (much modified), in a large atrio, contains baroque altarpieces. Méx. 85 continues to (446km) *Sta María Chiconautla* and (474km) *Mexico City*, see Rte 18.

63 Pachuca to Texcoco

Méx. 130, Hidalgo State road 115, and Méx. 136, 123km.—15km State road 115.—20km **Epazoyucan**.—51km **Tepeapulco**.—87km Calpulalpan and Méx. 136.—123km **Texcoco**.

15km turning r. (State road 115) for (20km) **EPAZOYUCAN** (5000 inhab.; 2300m), in maguey-covered country. The former Augustinian convent of **San Andrés** stands on a terrace c 4m above the atrio, which in turn stands c 4m above the town.

The friars arrived in 1540 and built their first church in seven months; the present convent building went up during the 1550s and 1560s. It is probable that a pre-Conquest monument, perhaps to Tláloc, was destroyed and the rubble used either on the original site or on a new one to make new platforms. In 1556 Abp Montúfar complained that the friars were expending 6000 pesos on a retable. The fountain facing the church has the inscription: 'se acabó esta fuente en 17 de Abril de 1567'.

The spacious ATRIO is approached by a unique curved double stairway. Posa chapels, three only and wooden-roofed, away from the wall, stand at the NW, SW, and SE corners; a chapel similar to the posas is attached to the N edge of the church, and must have been used as an open chapel. All four are crested with fleur-de-lis motifs, their arches and supporting pilasters decorated with arabesque relief. The CHURCH, reinforced by wide buttresses, has a plain façade, Renaissance in contour, the doorway, with part-fluted and part-twisted columns, encompassed by an alfíz, whose outline descends from the choir window frame. The interior contains a huge choir balcony resting on a sotocoro marvellously composed of close-set wooden beams. In the baptistery is a mural (early 17C ?) of the Baptism of Christ; in the sacristy, more murals (late 16C ?), of the Passion, incl. a Last Supper.

The two-storey CLOISTER (restored) is notable for its semicircular arches with concave mouldings; from the imposts rise elaborately curled vegetal motifs. In the recesses at each corner of the lower walk, and above the SE doorway, are the most effective of the murals surviving from 16C New Spain, discovered in 1922 by Federico Mariscal. They show scenes from the Passion and betray various European influences. They can be dated c 1556.

The Ecce Homo and the Crucifixion show Flemish influences (eg, in the stylization of the clouds and the attenuation of the figures—note the bearded figure in the former). The colouring has seemingly been added at a later date. The Way of the Cross, urgent, crowded, and dramatic, is reminiscent of the Spanish primitives. The Descent from the Cross, full of religious feeling, is Giottesque in inspiration. Above the SE doorway, and complementing the above scenes, is a Death of Our Lady, most moving of all, also italianate; the depiction of the hands of Our Lady and the bystanders most expressive. A large head of Christ appears in the well of the staircase leading to the upper gallery.

25km **Sta Mónica**, where the portal of the 16C chapel is an ingenuously original example of the flights of fancy of contemporary Indian workmanship. The staggeringly wide arch, jambs, and imposts are enclosed in an emphatic alfíz. All surfaces are covered in vegetal and floral relief, with plenty of room in which to develop. The cord defining the arch is, unusually, square in section. In the spandrels, instead of medallions, are potted plants.

31km turning r. for (8km SW) **Zempoala** (c 5000 inhab.; 2532m), in a desert-like region covered in maguey. The former Franciscan convent of *Todos Santos* dates probably from the 1570s. Its deep atrio now presents a desolate appearance. To the N of the church stands a singular and spacious open chapel, perhaps the first structure built on the site. What remains is in the form of a large semi-hexagonal apse enclosing a smaller version, once fronted by an ample rectangular three-aisled nave, a building meant to dominate. The simple façade of the buttressed church incorporates a slim tower; the well-proportioned W doorway, decorated with almohadillas on arch and jambs, is bounded by fluted columns. The interior has superb rib vaulting, one of the few completely thus vaulted in New Spain. The semi-ruined cloister, three arches a side resting on sturdy little columns, exudes an intimacy out of step with the mass of the rest of the complex.

In the town centre stands a *Rollo*, a thick basalt column, symbol of the Crown's authority delegated to the viceregal corregidor, as is evident from the inscription in the base of the pyramidal top whose four faces bear reliefs of the Spanish royal arms and on which is perched a diadem. Beneath the inscription, four lion gargoyles. The column base is upheld by jaguars.

The other great attraction of Zempoala is the *Aqueduct*, built in c 1541–57 under the direction of the friar Francisco de Tembleque, to carry water to Otumba (45km S), over a system of 156 arches, 67 of which remain.

32km *Sta María Tecajete*, with a picturesque hacienda, its early 19C buildings still intact (no adm. without previous permission). 34km turning l. for (9km NE) **Singuilucan** (2525m), where the Augustinians built the convent of *San Antonio* in the 1540s. The present church, built in the second half of the 18C, displaces the original. It contains a large churrigueresque high altarpiece (1776) and baroque altarpieces in the transepts. In the sotocoro, an interesting 18C painting showing a procession of a local religious brotherhood in honour of the Señor de Singuilucan, a miraculous image of Christ on the Cross which used to be kept in the church.

The adjoining portería gives access to the two-storey buttressed cloister, with its stout walls, narrow bays, and decorated jambs, off which the former refectory is now a chapel, with a baroque altarpiece and 17–18C anon. paintings.

37km *Sto Tomás*, known as Tzlistaca in the 1520s. Its church, begun in the 16C, preserves a portal full of fanciful relief carved by Indian hands. 51km **TEPEAPULCO** (formerly *Tepopolco*—'near the big mountain'; c 3500 inhab.; 2350m), in a flat maguey-producing area. It was the site of a small Classic Period ceremonial centre, clearly an outlying settlement of Teotihuacanos. The Franciscan convent of **San Francisco** was founded in 1528–29 and built probably during the 1530s and 1550s.

The friars ordered the destruction of many teocallis, incl. a large one dedicated to Huitzilopochtli; and with the combined earth and rubble the Indians raised the large atrio 7.75m above the town, reached by an imposing stairway. The convent, reached by another stairway, is raised another 4.5m above the atrio, possibly on or near the mound of a pagan sanctuary. The combined atrio and precinct around the convent have a total length of 305m, the church thus occupying a splendid setting. It was repaired in 1627 and has undergone various changes since, incl. the cupola and towers, which give an 18C look. In 1558–60 Bernardino de Sahagún compiled here the 'Primeros memoriales' for his 'Historia general de las cosas de la Nueva España'.

One of the atrial crosses, both displaced from their original sites, is carved with three mysterious little figures, perhaps the Trinity, or Christ and the two thieves. The church doorway is exquisitely and densely ornamented in the jambs, arch, and pilasters which continue upward to form the alfíz rim. Within the alfíz, crowned by a little niche, is a relief panel showing St Francis receiving the stigmata. The present interior barrel vaulting dates from 1854 when the old timberwork was dismantled; the bad paintings on the nave walls date from 1924. Between baptistery and sacristy, embedded in the wall, is a stone cross displaying reliefs of the Passion. To the r. of the church, the portería was also the open chapel, the largest arch put before the convent door, instead of before the altar, set before a narrow arch. The cloister walls are painted with murals, simple in style, incl. a Mass of St Gregory, with Franciscan cord frames added at a later date. Adjoining the convent, the water cistern known as *Caja de Agua*, built after 1541 and still in use, is fed by springs c 25km away. A small museum in the town shows ceramics and other artefacts from Teotihuacán, and Toltec and Aztec ceramics and lithics, incl. monolithic sculptures.

Reached by road 2km N and then 1.5km E are the ruins of a multitiered pyramid (only the lower three tiers remain) with a staircase, facing a modest plaza with other unrestored ruins around its perimeter. The site was presumably intimately involved in the distribution of obsidian from the Otumba quarries (see Rte 18; cf. *Calpulalpan*, *Pachuca*, and *Tulancingo*).

3km W is **Ciudad Sahagún**, an industrial town developed on the site of the pueblo of *Irolo* and established by presidential decree in 1952 to bring economic improvement and employment to one of the poorest areas on the fringes of the Federal District. Iron and steel plants and railway workshops provide most of the jobs and apartment blocks, schools, and market areas were laid out on modern lines. 5km N of Ciudad Sahagún is **Tlanalapan**, where the church of *San Francisco* (restored) was built in the 16C by the friars of Tepeapulco. Its W portal is a sumptuous work, Romanesque-inspired, by Indian hands: triple jambs and double archivolt within an alfíz. The round mouldings of the arch continue in the supports, while medallion, disc, and undulating plant motifs cover the constituent parts.

The road runs SE to (67km) **Apan** (c 10,000 inhab.; 2493m; H,P), a town of Toltec origin (presumably established to exploit obsidian sources in the nearby hills and barrancas) on the SE side of the Lago de Apan and known for its production of pulque, from the ubiquitous maguey, in quantity. The parish church of *Sagrado Corazón de Jesús* (built before 1746) replaces the original church of the Franciscan convent of Asunción de Nuestra Señora, founded c 1569, little of which remains. Its W portal shows hallmarks of early 18C baroque, with a good relief of the Ascension, polygonal arch, and typical columns, one-third relief, two-thirds fluted. The high altarpiece is an outstanding churrigueresque work, full of large and small estípites, the latter used to support the niches. The portería and convent were probably rebuilt in the 17C. Traces of 16C murals have been brought to light.

A small museum in Apan has artefacts from the region, incl. Tepeapulco and Huapalcalco.

From Apan the road goes SW into the State of Tlaxcala. At (87km) *Calpulalpan* (see Rte 20) we join Méx. 136 going W to (123km) *Texcoco*, see Rte 20.

64 Tampico to Veracruz

Méx. 180, 497km.—189km Tuxpan.—247km Poza Rica.—256km turning for El Tajín.—249km Papantla.—423km Villa Rica.—457km turning for (3km W) **Cempoala**.—457km La Antigua.—497km **Veracruz**.

We leave Tampico by the toll bridge across the Río Pánuco on Méx. 180, the slow coast road which traverses the tropical lowlands. In (14km) *Tampico Alto* a yellow building (next to church) is a small museum containing displays of Huastec pottery and figurines, and a row of stone sculptures, mostly Huastec. 109km *Naranjos*. At 112km a road goes E to (37km) *Tamiahua*, a fishing centre on the S extremity of the vast Laguna de Tamiahua. At 144km we join (r.) Méx. 127 which goes to (95km NW) *Tempoal*, see Rte 62. We continue SE to (189km) **Tuxpan** (c 55,000 inhab.; 14m; H,R,P), near the mouth of the Río Tuxpan, a port which has seen better times and which today has been invaded by oil-storage tanks, termini of the oil pipeline from Poza Rica. It still attracts visitors, however, for its fishing and beaches of fine, white sand, beginning at *Barra de Tuxpan*, 12km E. Main attraction in the town is the MALECON, the river-front parade, c 2km long. A small *Museo Regional de Antropología e Historia* shares the same building as the Tourist Office (mural by Teodoro Cano) on the W side of Parque Juárez.

Modern Tuxpan is on the site of Postclassic *Tochpan* (or *Tuzapan*; 'place of the rabbit'), a trading port at the mouth of the Río Vinasco. The Aztecs established a garrison here to protect their trading interests and to keep an eye on the Huasteca to the N, with whom they had fought and from whom they exacted a tribute, and the Totonaca, whom they had subjugated just before the arrival of the Spaniards.

Méx. 180 crosses the Río Tuxpan by a toll bridge. 223km (r.) *Tihuatlan* (P). 229km turning r. for (23km NW) **Castillo de Teayo** where a three-tiered pyramid stands by the town plaza.

The site and region were studied in the 1950s and 1960s by José García Payón and Alfonso Medellín Zeñil, who found Toltec remains underlain and overlain by Huastec remains. The pyramid forms part of what must have once been a ceremonial centre, founded, according to the excavators, c AD 815. The Toltecs invaded the area in the 12C. While some scholars interpret the structure as Huastec–Toltec, others interpret it as Totonac–Aztec, built to counter Huastec expansion to the S.

The pyramid is built on a low platform, in three levels with sloping walls, similar to stepped pyramids at Tula and Calixtlahuaca. It is 576 sq m at the base and 13m high, with a monumental staircase covering most of one side. At the top is a small, thatched temple.

Around the pyramid base are stone sculptures and stelae with representations of Tláloc, Centecocíhuatl, Chalchiutlícue Xochiquetzal, and Xochipilli. A statue of Xipe Totec (with head missing) in a flayed human skin, found in the La Cruz barrio, and a stele showing Quetzalcóatl are now in the Museo Nacional de Antropología.

C 34km W, at *Metlaltoyuca*, a small Huastec ceremonial centre was uncovered on a plateau called Casco de Piedra; five platforms around a plaza, a ball court, and a circular structure, presumably a temple dedicated to Ehecatl.

247km **Poza Rica** (c 499,000 inhab.; 55m; H,R,P), at an important road junction, is an industrial city born of the 1920s oil boom. From 1925 until c 1965 its oilfields yielded c 65 per cent of national production. Two pipelines bring crude from here to Salamanca and to Mexico City.

From Poza Rica to *Pachuca*, see Rte 62.

Méx. 180 leaves Poza Rica to the SE. 256km turning r. for *El Tajín*, see Rte 65. 269km **Papantla** (38,000 inhab.; 298m; H,R,P), splayed out in a region of low hills and dense tropical vegetation, and between the basins of the Ríos Cazones and Tecolutla, is a town of narrow, winding streets and one-storey houses with tile roofs. It is the social, cultural, and commercial centre of the Totonac Indians, whose distinctive costumes—the men in loose white shirts and pantaloons—add to its picturesqueness. It is the hub of Mexico's foremost vanilla-producing district.

The dome of the bandstand in the centre of the main Parque Israel C. Téllez is decorated with a mural by Teodoro Cano, as is the entrance to the *Pal. Municipal*, on the W side—works of the 1960s.

On Sun. evenings in the atrio of the parish church is performed the famous dance of the Voladores, an ancient Totonac fertility rite. It used to be reserved for Corpus Christi celebrations, but its practice has been extended as its original purpose has taken second place to the supposed demands of tourism. Its fascination, however, has not been lost. Four young men (not above 30 in age) and their musician leader climb up a pole (c 15m high) to a platform at the top. The Four bind themselves in ropes attached to the top of the pole and launch themselves head down into space, gradually and rhythmically spiralling downward while describing wider circles until they touch the ground. Their last-minute aim is to land on their feet. Meanwhile the musician, keeping his balance at the top, girates while blowing a reed-pipe and tapping a small drum. Voladores put on displays in other parts of Mexico, purely as a spectacle.

Méx. 180 continues E to (299km) *Gutiérrez Zamora* on the Río Tecolutla. 11km E, on the coast at the river mouth, is *Tecolutla*, a pleasant, slightly faded resort, but within reach of ideal palm-fringed beaches. (Beware of sharks.) At 319km Méx. 180 reaches the coast. From (340km) *Barra de Nautla* Méx. 131 runs inland.

It goes SW across the plain watered by the Río Nautla and its tributaries. 16km **San Rafael** (c 6000 inhab.; H,R,P) was settled in the 1830s by French colonists from Burgundy and Alsace.

Their prosperity was founded on vanilla and citrus fruit cultivation, and on farming. Their bilingual descendants are in evidence today.

40km **Martínez de la Torre** (27,000 inhab.; 151m; H,R,P), commercial centre of the region.

From here a road (intricately winding) runs SE to (36km) **Misantla** (419km), on the site of a Totonac ceremonial centre, contemporary with El Tajín. Several groups of structures survive and have been partially excavated: *Los Idolos*, of four linked plazas surrounded by 20 mounds; *La Lima*; and *Tapapulum*. The pyramid mounds were decorated with large basalt carvings of tortoises, felines, sea shells, and warriors, executed in the 13–mid-15C, when the Totonacs were resisting Aztec attempts to conquer them; they eventually lost.

Misantla was twice fired by the royalists during the war of Independence, in 1815 and in 1817, when Guadalupe Victoria made a stand here after his defeat at Nautla. He was again defeated and became a lone and suffering fugitive in the mountains of Veracruz, a life to which Fanny Calderón de la Barca later referred when describing him: 'honest, plain...lame and tall, somewhat at a loss for conversation...amiable and good-natured...capable of supporting almost incredible hardships'. The church of *La Asunción* (later 18C) has a churrigueresque façade. We may continue through the Sierra de Chiconquiaco to (92km) *Naolinco* (1605m), with waterfalls, c 5km N. Then the road winds through a lovely tropical landscape to (118km) *Jalapa*, see Rte 71B.

Méx. 131 continues to (55km) *El Jobo*, with an 18C church. In 1829 Pres. Guadalupe Victoria retired to his hacienda here at the end of his term of office. 61km **Tlapacoyan** (504m; H,R,P), on the N slopes of the Sierra de Teziutlán, and known for apples, bananas, and lemons.

From here a road winds tortuously up through the Sierra de Teziutlán to (35km) **Altotonga** (12,000 inhab.; 1885m; H,R,P), in a coffee-, sugar-, and fruit-producing area, and then on to (64km) *Perote*, see Rte 71C.

Beyond Tlapacoyan, Méx. 131 crosses into the State of Puebla. 94km **Teziutlán** (c 40,000 inhab.; 1990m; H,R,P), in the sierra of the same name, a beautiful wooded region, producing much fruit. Its steep streets are lined by one-storey houses. On the central plaza, evocative of 18C provincial life, is the cathedral of *Sta María* (restored). *El Carmen* is another 18C church.

Chignautla (5km W) is worth a visit for its late 17C church of San Mateo, its façade combining baluster and solomonic columns.
From Teziutlán to *Tlatlauquitepec* and *Puebla*, see Rte 71B.

Méx. 180 continues along the coast to (343km) **Nautla** (c 3000 inhab.; H,R,P), a little port and fishing centre, called Almería by the conquering Spaniards.

Nautla was a Totonac town and province, conquered by the Aztecs under Ahuitzotl. While Cortés was in Tenochtitlán, the second hostile incident between Aztec and Spaniard occurred (the first was at Quiahuitzlán). Cortés had left his lieutenant, Juan Escalante, with 150 men as a rearguard in Veracruz. Quauhpopoca, Aztec governor of Nautla province, requested an escort of four soldiers so that he could come to pledge allegiance to the Spaniards. However, when the four arrived, Quauhpopoca had two of them murdered on the spot; the other two managed to escape. Escalante led a punitive force of 50 Spaniards and thousands of Totonacs against the Aztec garrison, and in the battle Escalante, his horse, and six other Spaniards, plus many Totonacs and Aztecs, were killed. So wrote Cortés. Bernal Díaz, however, claims that Escalante was killed when he interfered with Quauhpopoca's attempt to collect tribute from the Totonacs, by that time already allies of the Spaniards.
The incident provided Cortés with an excuse to request an audience of Moctezuma, seize him, and imprison him in the Palace of Axayácatl in Dec. 1519. Thus began the series of battles leading to the conquest of the Aztec empire.

Beyond (369km) *Vega de Alatorre* the foothills of the Sierra Volcánica Transversal come down to the coast. 410km *Palma Sola*, c 7km NW of Mexico's first (and controversial) nuclear power station, on the S side of Laguna Verde. 423km **Villa Rica**, a site of great significance.

After his landing at Chalchicueyecan on 21 Apr. 1519, Cortés and his party marched up the coast via Cempoala and, on 18 May, founded Villa Rica de la Vera Cruz on a plain half a league from the hilltop fortress of Quiahuahuixtlan (Quiahuiztlán). Here, to give his activities a semblance of legality, he established the ayuntamiento (the first in New Spain) of Villa Rica, and here returned after cementing alliances with Cempoala and other neighbouring states. Alonso Hernández Puertocarrero and Francisco de Montejo were dispatched to Spain with a missive for the emperor. In 1525 the settlement was moved to La Antigua (see below) and in 1599 to Cortés's original landing place. Foundations of the original Spanish church and remains of a fort (on the Cerro de la Cantera) may be seen.

424km **Quiahuiztlán**. On the *Cerro de los Metates* nearby, stood the Totonac town where Cortés had his first hostile encounter with Aztecs.

Arrogant calpixque (tax collectors) ordered the inhabitants to refuse to receive the Spaniards. Cortés, equally arrogant, had them arrested, thus initiating the conflict between the Aztec and Spanish empires. The site was contemporary with Cempoala, whither Cortés then proceeded.

The scattered ruins here comprise two groups of specialized tombs in the shape of miniature temples. One group is at the end of a platform formed by an artificially modified ridge. The platform includes a staircase and balustrades, and is partly bordered by merlons. The second group of tombs is on the hilltop.

The tombs include secondary burials as well as primary, and may have been 'family masolea', although only the élite, with their considerable burial offerings of jewellery and the best ceramics, were included.

A small conduit ('psychoduct') often leads to the temple-shrine above the burial; animal sculptures were also frequently found next to the tombs, and are thought to be the *tonales* ('animal souls') of those inside. Both features appear to reflect the Maya and general Gulf Coast belief that the distinguished dead must be kept abreast of events after their deaths.

457km turning r. for (3km W) **CEMPOALA** (or *Zempoala*), possibly a corruption of Náhuatl Cempohuallan ('twenty waters'), the largest city and capital of the Totonacs, who undoubtedly called it *Totonacapan*. Noted by archaeologists as early as 1891, when excavations and a plan were done, it was declared a national site in 1920 and more extensive excavations were carried out by José García Payón in 1939–41.

These excavations, and explorations in the general vicinity, produced artefacts of every period from stone points to effigy figurines, to polychrome pottery, showing long occupation in the area. A few km W of Cempoala the site of *El Trapiche*, also excavated by García Payón, had layers contemporary with Cempoala, but in its earliest strata there were ceramics with white rims and rocker stamping similar to ceramics at La Venta and Tres Zapotes. There is some evidence that Cempoala was settled after c AD 650 by refugees from Teotihuacán, and excavations at nearby *Ranchito de las Animas* and *Cerro Montosa* produced Teotihuacano and Cholula-Puebla pottery. By c AD 800 the Totonacs had taken over the site, begun the constructions now visible, and made it their capital.

The **Totonacs**, linguistically of the Macro-Mayan group, originally settled in the mountainous region of E Puebla. They gradually expanded eastwards into central and N Veracruz during the 9C and 10C AD, a movement accelerated by pressures from the expanding Toltecs. In Veracruz, Totonac ceremonial centres were established at Ahuilizapan, Cempoala, Colipa, Cuetlachtlán, Cuauhtochco (Huatusco), Jalapa, Misantla, Papantla, and Quiahuitzlán. As they established their hold over this territory they incorporated many earlier cities, the most important of which was El Tajín. Most of what we know of the Totonac state, however, is much later, from Aztec and Spanish chronicles.

Cempoala superseded El Tajín as the Totonac capital, although it has never been proven that the Totonacs were the founders of El Tajín; and the two sites overlap in time. At its height in the 15C and 16C Cempoala and its hinterland may have had as many as 250,000 people, with 80–120,000 in the city itself. (Estimates for other Totonac cities are 120,000 for Jalapa, 24,000 for Colipa, and 60,000 for Papantla.) However, when Cortés and his men saw the city in 1519, only recently conquered by the Aztecs, they estimated only 30,000 inhabitants.

Strong commercial contacts with the Aztecs had been established by the middle of the 15C and in 1458 Moctezuma I Ilhuicamina (1440–68) invaded the region and forced the Totonacs to pay tribute. In 1463 (some sources say 1469) a rebellion was put down and garrisons placed in several Totonac cities, incl. Cempoala; 6000 prisoners were taken for sacrifice, whom the Totonacs had to free by a tributary ransom. Thus, when Cortés landed at Chalchicueyecan, the smarting Totonac chief Quahtlachona (or in Náhuatl, Chicomacatl) was quick to invite the Spaniards to Cempoala. They dubbed him, because of his apparent rotundity, 'the Fat Cacique', and were duly received on 15 May 1519. There, Cortés and his men witnessed the Totonac practices of human sacrifice, especially of children, cranial deformation, tattooing and other ornament, and rock-walled burials beneath the cane and thatch houses.

Cortés persuaded the Totonacs to join him against the Aztecs and they attacked a local Aztec garrison. Returning to Cempoala, Cortés caused the city's idols to be destroyed, nominally 'converted' the Totonacs, confirmed them as allies, and sank the remainder of his fleet to begin his march inland with Totonac porters and warriors on 16 Aug. 1519.

On 29 May 1520, Cortés attacked the force of Pánfilo de Narváez in the Templo Mayor precinct, managed to capture Narváez himself, and persuaded most of his forces to join the expedition against Tenochtitlán.

It was a member of the Narváez force who spread the first smallpox amongst the Indians of Mexico. The disease spread in epidemic force, causing devastation of native populations, which had no built-up immunity. This, and the damage to the site's temples in the fighting, led to the decline and eventual abandonment of the city in the 17C. Much of the site is still in thick vegetation, and the modern town, founded in the 19C, sits on parts of the ancient city.

Cempoala covered as much as 8.5 sq km, with perhaps as much as 120,000 sq m occupied by the principal architecture. The main monuments visible today are within an area of c 4300 sq m. The site is strategically situated in a bend of

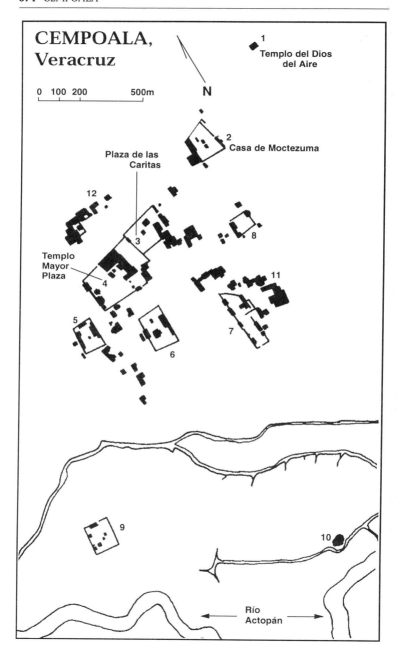

CEMPOALA, Veracruz

0 100 200   500m

N

1 Templo del Dios del Aire

2 Casa de Moctezuma

Plaza de las Caritas

12

3

Templo Mayor Plaza

4

8

5

6

11

7

9

10

Río Actopán

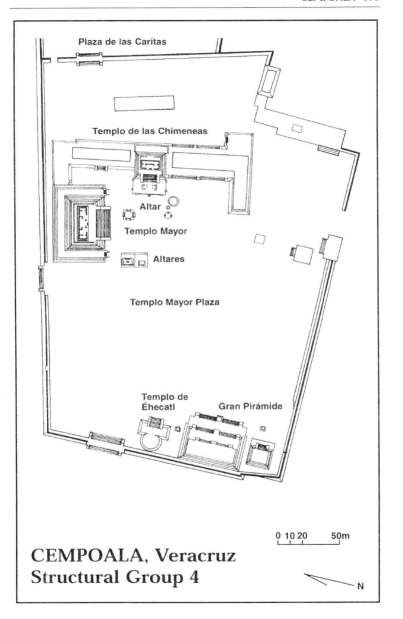

Plaza de las Caritas

Templo de las Chimeneas

Altar

Templo Mayor

Altares

Templo Mayor Plaza

Templo de
Éhecatl

Gran Pirámide

0 10 20   50m

CEMPOALA, Veracruz
Structural Group 4

N

the Río Grande de Actopan (or Río Chachalacas), providing for highly productive agriculture and defence.

Walls divided the city into at least nine major precincts. Within these were raised pavements against flooding, and platforms with houses, temples, pyramids, and other structures. The Spaniards remarked on the fresh water supply system to every household.

There are 12 main structural groups visible today, and many unexplored mounds amongst the vegetation around the site. At least ten T-shaped burials were also found excavated.

Entering the main precinct (Structural groups 3 and 4) we are surrounded by the walls of the TEMPLO MAYOR PLAZA, with the separate walls of the CARITAS PLAZA to the E. In the centre of the N side is the **Templo Mayor**, of 13 receding tiers up the front and 11 at the back. The crenellated platform on which it stands measures 66.7m x 39.5m and rises 1.8m above the plaza. The top tier is 10.6m above this. Steps mount the platform on either side and a monumental staircase covers most of the face of the pyramid. At the top, crenellations run around three sides with a temple within them, comprising a porticoed front, main central room with an interior compartment against the back wall, and two smaller rooms to each side.

Altares. In front of the Templo Mayor and just off its SW corner are two altar platforms. The first has steps each side while the latter has steps up the E side with two rectangular altars on top. The latter platform is sometimes referred to as the altar of 'eternal fire', the keeping of which was a sacred practice recorded by Spanish chroniclers.

The platform supporting the Templo Mayor continues to its E, then at a right-angle S into the plaza and at a second right-angle W. In the middle of the S extension sits the **Templo de las Chimeneas**, so-called after remains of columns on the lower platform in front of the temple pyramid. The pyramid has six slanting tiers and the remains of a double-entrance temple, divided into front and back rooms. Off the SW corner of the extended lower platform are remains of two circular altar platforms, one with remnants of steps in three places.

In the SW corner of the plaza stands the **Gran Pirámide** (*Templo del Sol*), flanked by two smaller pyramids. Three superimposed platforms, each with double staircases and wide landings, support remains of a temple. This is a pyramid built in the 16C only shortly before Cortés and his men visited the precinct. To the N is a smaller platform with steps and a circular rear, a shape similar to the Templo de Ehecatl (below), and suggestive of a similar function; and to the S is a square platform with steps and two other much smaller platforms. Three smaller square and rectangular altar platforms cluster in the SE of the plaza (S of the main platform extension).

Templo de las Caritas. To the E of the Templo Mayor plaza is a smaller walled precinct. Near the middle of the N wall is a two-tiered platform with a staircase to a single-room temple. The temple is so named, 'of the Little Faces', because the interior walls were formerly plastered and painted with the alternating signs of the Sun, Moon, and Evening Star (in symbols similar to those used in the Mixtec codices), with rows of inset clay skulls above them. (Traces of the red, blue, and yellow paint are still visible.) This temple is also called the *Templo de Astronomía*, after symbols depicting the 52 masks of the 52-year cycle (see Introduction: Calendrics).

All these monuments were once covered in white stucco, which, when seen from a distance, the Spaniards fancied was covered with silver!

C 500m E of the two precincts described above is a third precinct containing the **Casa de Moctezuma**, a square, two-tiered platform with staircases. On top, crenellations on three sides enclose a single-room temple with painted stucco decoration inside and out.

In the village itself the rectangular-circular **Templo del Dios del Aire** (*Templo de Ehecatl*, god of wind) comprises a five-tiered platform on a wide, low platform. A steep staircase leads up to crenellations around a circular temple. A low extension platform at the foot of the staircase supports a rectangular, open, columned temple, a later addition to the original structure. Before this extension are remains of a square altar platform with steps up each side, and a circular incense-burning platform with steps on the N side.

In the village, across Parque Cuauhtémoc, the *Casa de Cultura* contains displays of Totonac, Cholulteca, and Aztec pottery (polychrome plates, bowls, cups, and incense burners); examples of Totonac 'laughing faces' and other figurines; matates, obsidian knives and other stone artefacts, flat and cylindrical seals, lip ornaments, and spindle whorls; slates with Náhuatl and Totonac words and fragments of painted stucco; and the 1891 plan of the site (scale 1:3000), and photographs. Yugos, hachas, and palmas excavated from the site are now in the Museo Nacional de Antropología.

3km E on the coast *Chachalacas* is a favourite resort with visitors from Jalapa and Veracruz.

From (462km) *José Cardel*, Méx. 125 runs W to (13km) *Puente Nacional*, whence Méx. 140 goes NW to (59km) *Jalapa* (see Rte 71B) and Méx. 125 continues W and then S to (117km) *Córdoba*, see Rte 71A.

470km (r.) *La Antigua* (c 7000 inhab.; R,P), on the l. bank of the Río Huitzilapan, now a quiet place dedicated to fishing. Villa Rica de la Vera Cruz was removed here in 1525. The chapel called *La Ermita* is reputed to have been built on Cortés's orders. Behind the *Parroquia* (rebuilt in the 18C), on the main plaza, are the ruins of a house popularly supposed to have belonged to Cortés.

497km *Veracruz*, see Rte 72.

65 El Tajín

EL TAJÍN, the Totonac word for 'lightning', 'thunder', or 'hurricane' (and the Totonac god of rain), was the legendary sacred city of Hurakán. It is the largest and most important site in N Veracruz.

9–6; performances of the *voladores* on Sat. and Sun. at 11; fee.

From its abandonment in the 13C AD the site was 'unknown' until its rediscovery in 1785 by Diego Ruiz, of the garrison in Papantla; 16C chronicles mentioning Papantla give no indication of an awareness of El Tajín. A sketch by Ruiz of the Pirámide de los Nichos appeared in 'La Gaceta de México' for July of that year. Humboldt visited El Tajín in 1804; and Carlos Nebel visited in the early 1830s, and included lithographs of the Pirámide de los Nichos in his published sketches of Mexico (1836). It was declared a national monument in 1934, and the first clearing and restoration began under the directorship of José García Payón in 1938.

Despite early discovery and much study and restoration, most of the mounds remain unexplored and the absolute chronology of the various groups of constructions is not entirely clear. The archaeological zone at its largest controlled some 9.5 sq km; the civic zone itself was c 80ha and the main ceremonial area c 6000 sq m, with more than 200 mounds. Infra-red photographs of the zone and surrounding region have revealed traces of a large-scale ancient irrigation scheme, and an estimated 3000–3500 people lived in the central zone and up to 13,000 in the entire city.

The central zone is limited by two arroyos, running N–S and converging just S of the site's centre. Two sections can be distinguished: *El Tajín* proper in the S and *Tajín Chico* in the N, divided by the retaining wall of the artificial terracing of the latter. El Tajín proper, generally earlier than Tajín Chico, is built on ground level and primarily oriented on the cardinal points. Tajín Chico is oriented on a NW–SE axis. Slopes around the central zone are covered with terraces and mounds, mostly unexplored and covered in vegetation. The main entrance to the ancient city has not been located.

Several chronological schemes for the site have been proposed. There were three principal phases of occupation and building activity (some sources combine the second and third; see below). Early agricultural sites (c 1000 BC) have been found at El Ojito and Tampico, less than 50km away, but the First Phase (*Tajín I–IV*) at Tajín itself was from c 100 BC to the 6C AD.

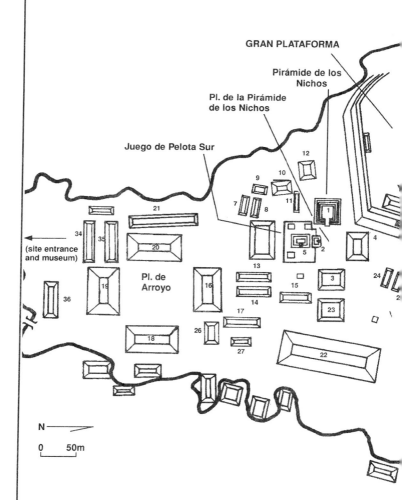

EL TAJÍN, Veracruz

GRAN PLATAFORMA

Pirámide de los Nichos

Pl. de la Pirámide de los Nichos

Juego de Pelota Sur

(site entrance and museum)

Pl. de Arroyo

N

0   50m

Numbers and letters apply to mounds and structures described in the text:

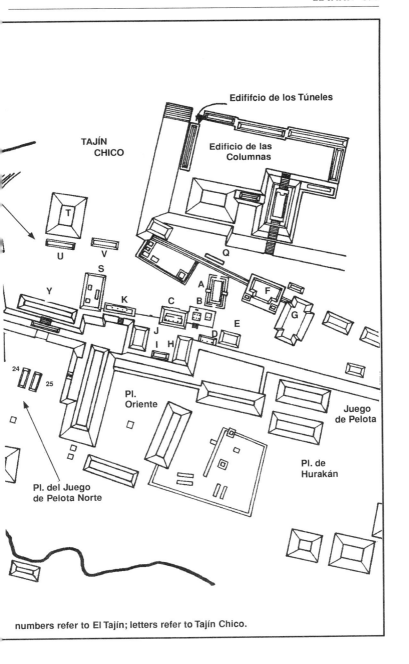

Edififcio de los Túneles

Edificio de las Columnas

TAJÍN CHICO

T

U V

S

Y K

A

C B

F

J

I H

E D

G

Q

24 25

Pl. Oriente

Juego de Pelota

Pl. de Hurakán

Pl. del Juego de Pelota Norte

numbers refer to El Tajín; letters refer to Tajín Chico.

The Second Phase (*Tajín V*), during which Tajín succeeded Remojadas, near Veracruz, in influence in the Gulf Coast, occupied the 6C to 8C AD; and the Third Phase (*Tajín VI–VIII*) from the mid-8C to the early 13C. The city was at its most powerful in the second and early third phases.

Tajín I (c AD 100–200): the first agricultural settlers, probably from the Huasteca, built the first structures, none of which have survived except as traces of foundations found in excavations; ceramics were related to those of *Teotihuacán II*.

Tajín II (c AD 300–400): the first pyramid was constructed in the S zone, without niches; it now lies beneath the Pirámide de los Nichos. Ceramics in this phase were related to those of *Teotihuacán III*.

In *Tajín III* and *IV* (c AD 400–650) the S zone was more fully occupied, incl. the building of the first, short-lived, ball court, and a huge platform and buildings in Tajín Chico. Late in phase IV or early in phase V, the Pirámide de los Nichos and the Juego de Pelota Norte (but without its sculpted panels) were built. There was strong Teotihuacano influence during phases III and IV, leading some to suggest that El Tajín was either a military ally of, or even dominated by, Teotihuacán. On the other hand neutron activation analysis of the Luster Ware pottery at Teotihuacán shows that it was made in El Tajín from a local clay source.

In *Tajín V* (c AD 650–800) the city became the dominant centre in the Gulf Coast region and the Totonac capital, or at least a principal Totonac city. With the demise of Teotihuacán, El Tajín was one of several contemporary regional centres to reassert itself (cf. Cholula and Xochicalco). The Pirámide de los Nichos and the Juego de Pelota Norte were the most important constructions; in the latter, sculpted panels were added later in the phase or early in *Tajín VI*.

In *Tajín VI* (c AD 800–1000) Monumentos 2 and 5 were built, in the same plaza as the Pirámide de los Nichos, and new buildings were added to the great platform of Tajín Chico, incl. the substructure of Monumento A.

In *Tajín VII* (c AD 1000–1100), Monumentos A, B, C, and D were built in Tajín Chico.

Finally, in *Tajín VIII* (AD 1100–early 13C), the Juego de Pelota Sur, with carved panels, and the Edificio de las Columnas were built (although some sources place the construction of the Juego de Pelota Sur earlier, c AD 900).

El Tajín was abandoned between AD 1200 and 1230. According to different sources, the population was forced to disperse, by Huastecs coming from the N, or by Otomís, Chichimecs, or Toltecs from the W. Its authority was succeeded by the Totonac city of Cempoala, to the S. In the 16C, Papantla was an Aztec outpost.

El Tajín, especially from phase V, was cosmopolitan in outlook. Its sculpture and architecture show Olmec and Izapan influence, later Teotihuacano and Maya styles, and later still Toltec styles. At the same time it developed its own sculptural and architectural tradition, which remained primarily within the immediate region, but can be detected at sites in the Basin of Mexico, at Xochicalco, at Mitla, and as far S as Honduras.

The relief carvings on the pyramids and ball court panels show especial predilection for toads, jaguars, serpents, and humans. A distinct technique of double outlines was used in scrollwork, spirals, and interlacing ribbons, and in figures on architectural friezes, yugos, hachas, and palmas (ball game equipment), and pyrite mosaic mirrors. There are depictions of sacrificial rites, death, and militaristic themes, incl. what appear to be 'Eagle Knights' (a widespread military order or cult in the Late Postclassic Period). Dot and bar numerals and hieroglyphic inscriptions on basalt and andesite frequently refer to 'Thirteen Rabbit', possibly the name of a famous ruler of the city. El Tajín architecture exhibits several distinct features, especially in certain combinations: the heavy use of niches; fretted friezes on 'flying', or projecting, cornices (Tajín's version of talud-tablero); strictly functional stairways (rather than monumental); and the use of the corbel arch (borrowed from the Maya) in combination with flat roofs of single slabs of concrete made with a mixture of lime, crushed pumice, ground seashells, and fragments of wood and pottery, poured into temporary wooden frames. Such slabs, between 33 and 90cm thick, enabled Tajín architects to cover areas up to 75 sq m at c 5m wide.

El Tajín was one of the earliest sites to practise the ball game as a ritual, and was probably one of the centres for the development of the voladores ritual. One interpretation of the carved panels in the Juego de Pelota Sur, and of depictions on yugos, hachas, and palmas, is that they represent the myth of the sun god descending into the Underworld, to be reborn as the maize god and god of fertility. Altogether there are 11 ball courts at El Tajín, two with carved panels and all with stone-slab linings quarried from sources on the Río Cozones, 35km away.

The site entrance is at the S end, near the museum. The S zone, at ground level below the GRAN PLATAFORMA, comprises five plazas, called, S–N: Pl. del Arroyo, Pl. de la Pirámide de los Nichos (a double plaza), Pl. del Juego de Pelota

Norte, Pl. Oriente, and Pl. de Hurakán, the last two being E of the Gran Plataforma of Tajín Chico.

PL. DEL ARROYO is formed by several platform mounds: *Monumento 16* on the N, *18* on the E, *19* on the S, and *20* on the W. *Monumento 36* lies S of 19; *Monumento 21* is to the N of 20; and *Monumento 17, 26,* and *27* are on the NE corner of the plaza. In the SW corner the parallel *Monumentos 34* and *35* are the sides of a small ball court.

PL. DE LA PIRAMIDE DE LOS NICHOS. Moving N, we begin to encounter the more famous monuments of El Tajín at the double plaza overlooked by the Pirámide de los Nichos. Just S and E of the plaza, *Monumentos 13* and *14* form the sides of another ball court, with *Monumentos 15, 23,* and *22* (a huge rectangular mound) farther to the N and E. *Monumento 15* has five tiers, the first two with panels of niches and a staircase. *Monumento 23* is 17 m sq in five tiers, also with a wide staircase.

To the W of these mounds is the justly famous **Juego de Pelota Sur**. It had three building phases: first, a court with rough, uncut stone walls; second, dressed stone walls were added and covered with stucco; finally, the stone side-panels were carved with the scenes described below. The playing field is 60m long, 23m wide, and has walls of stone blocks up to 11m long.

Built late, in *Tajín VIII,* the most famous features are the six carved panels of ritual scenes. Beginning with the *NE Panel* (1.56m–1.98m) we see the ritual sacrifice of a ball player. The scene is complex but careful observation will reveal six figures in the centre and to the r. Two central, standing figures, dressed in ball-player gear (note the yugos around their waists) are holding down (l. figure) and sacrificing with an obsidian knife (r. figure) a third figure, also wearing ball-player gear. On the far r. a seated figure presides over the sacrifice with a staff of authority in his r. hand. Above the sacrificial victim is a skeleton-like, masked figure symbolizing death descending on the victim. On the far l. a second skeletal figure is seated on a pot and also symbolizes death.

The *N-Central Panel* (2.08m x 3.16m) depicts a pulque ceremony. There are four figures: on the l. a human holds a jar under his r. arm and points with his l. hand at a second figure, reclining in the position of a chacmool on another jar, presumably containing pulque. Above these are two more figures, Tláloc (god of rain) above the centre and Quetzalcóatl to the r. Tláloc is recognizable by his spectacle-eyes, the lightning symbol in his r. hand, and a sceptre of authority in his l. Quetzalcóatl is seated and characteristically wears a conch-shell pectoral. On the r. of this central frame is a sequence depicting the growth of the maguey plant. Above the central scene a border frame of two grotesque, reclining figures joins at the foreheads and noses to make a mask-like face looking straight at the viewer (cf. S-Central Panel, below).

The *NW Panel* (1.98m x 1.56m) depicts a ball court scene. Structures carved in the lower corners represent a ball court. Two players, in their protective gear, stand in the court facing each other, one with crossed arms and the other holding an obsidian knife in his l. hand. Between them is the intertwined ollin symbol signifying movement. On the l. wall of the ball court is a presiding figure with a sceptre of authority; on the r. wall a half-kneeling figure with a coyote head, the animal charged with leading sacrificial souls into the next world. On the far r. of the panel is the skeletal figure of death.

The *SW Panel* (1.72m x 2.02m) depicts an initiation ceremony. Here there are six figures: in the centre a man in ball-player gear lies on a bench with crossed arms and looks up at a figure hovering over him, dressed as an eagle or vulture, presumably a priest. This figure's arms are spread in imitation of wings, and he wears the heraldic sun god symbols, patron of the ball game ritual. Above these two is the skeletal figure of death-descending. To either side of the reclining youth, two other men play musical instruments—a teponaxtle 'drum' and a rattle. On the far l., rising from a pot, is the now familiar figure of death in a resplendent headdress.

The *S-Central Panel* (2.66m x 3.01m) seems to show an allegorical scene of the pulque ceremony. In the central portion are two figures, one squatting and one wearing a fish-shaped helmet. The former has spectacle eyes and a protruding canine, identifying him as Tláloc; he holds between his knees the special acocote (pulque) gourd, from which the other figure drinks. A rabbit-figure (buck teeth clearly shown) is suspended in the upper r. corner of the central frame; while in the upper l. corner, mostly flaked away, is another figure, probably also Tláloc, as it holds the symbol of lightning (just to the l. of the squatting Tláloc's head; cf. the Tláloc in the N-Central Panel). On the l. side of the central frame is a maguey plant in flower; and above the central scene are two reclining figures joined at their foreheads and noses, virtually identical to those in the N-Central Panel.

The *SE Panel* (2m x 1.64m) appears to be the initiation of a priest. The initiate stands in the centre looking at a seated figure, who offers him a handful of (?)darts, which themselves appear to ascend into the sectioned tongue of a mask-like face between and above the two figures. A third figure sits behind the initiate, with a raised r. arm. To the r. of this scene the familiar skeletal death figure rises from a globular pot.

W of the Juego de Pelota Sur a small group of mounds forms a miniature plaza with *Monumentos 9* and *10* on the W and *Monumentos 7* and *8* forming another ball court on the S, and *11* on the N. *Monumento 12* is to the NW.

However, directly N of the Juego de Pelota Sur stands PL. DE LA PIRAMIDE DE LOS NICHOS proper. It is formed by *Monumentos 2* and *5* on the S side, by the Pirámide de los Nichos on the W side, by *Monumento 3* on the E, and by *4* on the N.

Monumento 5 is a pyramid of two tiers, c 10m high and 31m sq at the base. A double staircase on the N face of the lower tier has three niches in the centre, 13 niches on the E, S, and W faces, and a Tajín style 'flying' cornice. The upper tier also has niches and a 'flying' cornice. At the base of the upper stairway is a 1.56m-high sculpture of an emaciated human figure with feather headdress, circular ears, ear plugs in the shape of lightning symbols, raised r. arm, and l. arm across its chest, holding a curved stick. It is unlike any other sculpture at El Tajín and the curved stick is reminiscent of Huastec art.

Monumento 5 had five building phases altogether. It sits on a large platform of 3124 sq m, with five equidistant staircases on the E side, and two 9m-wide staircases on the N side (flanking Monumento 2). Embedded in the NW side of this platform is a small quadrangular building in two tiers with a N-side staircase.

The first phase was a pyramid built on ground level; the second was on the platform just described; the third added four separate corner structures (of which only the SE survives); the fourth added a platform to buttress the upper tier; and the fifth added cut-stone facings and the two groups of niches.

Monumento 2 was faced with river boulders, which when removed revealed the substructure of an earlier pyramid and staircases, now preserved. *Monumento 3* is 34m sq and comprises seven tiers, each faced with moulded panels in 40cm sections. A wide staircase has six central projections (altars?), each with three niches. *Monumento 4* is dilapidated and is one of the oldest structures at El Tajín. It had four construction phases beginning c 100 BC, before the plaza existed, and a rubble core distinct from any other at the site.

The majestic **Pirámide de los Nichos** (*Monumento 1*) is 35m sq at the base and rises to 18m in six tiers of 3m each; and to 25m if the height of the temple at the top is added. The sixth tier is solid, and built from the ground up, with each lower tier built around its predecessor, leaving a ledge around the base of each stage. The core is a rubble of river cobbles, faced with slabs of sedimentary rock.

A stairway (10m wide) leads up the E side and has four central projecting altar-like constructions, each with three niches, and the remains of a fifth. Eleven xicalcoliuhqui (stepped frets) adorn the side ramps. The vertical face of each tier of the pyramid is broken by regularly spaced niches, varying in depth between 0.68m and 1.09m, and composed of receding frames of stone slabs.

These continue around all four sides of each tier, and behind the staircase, with 22, 19, 16, 13, 10, and 7 niches each side, in ascending order for each tier (and thus, multiplying by four, 88, 76, 64, 52, 40, and 28 niches, respectively in each tier). Adding these 348 niches to the 17 niches around the temple on top gives a total of 365, presumably corresponding to the days of the year (see Introduction: Calendrics). (The reader should here be warned that a well-known source on ancient American art and architecture states that there are 364 niches, but includes a plan showing 343, but adding up to 379 if one accounts for those which lie hidden behind the staircase for each tier!) The walls of the temple were each decorated with five sculpted panels (now in the site museum) depicting the heavens, gods, and various sacred animals.

The present pyramid replaced the earlier, six-tiered, pyramid with the river pebble core. Along the E face of the structure is a series of regularly spaced stone cubes with centre-holes, possibly to hold poles for banners.

N, beyond Pl. de la Pirámide de los Nichos, is an open ground, PL. DEL JUEGO DE PELOTA NORTE. In its centre stands the **Juego de Pelota Norte—** *Monumentos 24* and *25*. It is 25m long and 6m wide, and constructed, like the Juego de Pelota Sur, of carved stone blocks. Likewise there are six panels of scenes, but these are so dilapidated that the subjects are no longer discernible. However, on one of the N-side panels a human figure can be distinguished, possibly Tajín—the hurricane god; and on the S-Central Panel a seated person can be seen, wearing a bat mask and holding a bag decorated with feathers, plus the ollin symbol. Only vestiges of other figures or symbols can be seen on the remaining panels. On the N side of the plaza a large projecting mound, from the upper terrace of Tajín Chico, forms the S side of PL. ORIENTE.

Continuing N, through Pl. Oriente, just off its NW corner is another large *Juego de Pelota*, forming the SW corner of PL. DE HURAKAN. Its other sides are formed by unexplored mounds.

The huge artificial platform (7m high, 300m wide, and 1500m long) of the N zone is **TAJIN CHICO**, and comprises two irregular plaza areas. The first, along the S and E edges of the platform, comprises numerous lettered *Estructuras: A—K, Q, S—V*, and *Y*. Most of these are unexplored or only partially explored, but several have been preserved and restored.

The platform itself was constructed of earth levelled from a hill now occupied by the Edificio de las Columnas. The work covered buildings of the earliest phases at El Tajín, and was retained by a 7m terrace wall with a row of niches along the top.

A small irregular plaza is formed at the S end of the terrace by *Estructuras S, T, U, V,* and *Y.* To the N of these a second plaza is formed by *Estructuras A, B, C,* and *K,* with *D, H, I,* and *J* to the E. Farther N still *Estructuras E, F,* and *G,* plus unlettered mounds, form more plazas.

Estructura A is a rectangular platform of 750 sq m, with 'flying' cornices and niches on the first tier, plus two groups of buildings. The first comprises two rooms at each corner, forming a second tier with another cornice, and windows in the NE and NW rooms. The second group is in the centre of the platform. The platform 'stairway' is in fact false, the original functional part actually lying beneath the corbel arch. On the cornices and stairway ramps are various decorations with swastikas and fretted friezes typical of El Tajín.

Estructura B is another civic building, a platform of 357 sq m and 6.5m high (excluding the roof-support wall on top). There are two superimposed storeys. The ground floor is on the S, entered from the W, and with six column roof-supports. The first floor comprises a room on the N with two columns and another six-columned room sitting above the ground floor.

Estructura C covers 2220 sq m in three tiers, up to 7.5m. There are dwellings on the top with façades to the W and E. Stepped fretwork on the lower two tiers gives the impression of niches, and there are other familiar frieze decorations on the third tier of dwellings, incl. altar-like projections with true niches on the E stairway. The roof was a single slab of concrete, covering 150 sq m, some fragments of which remain in the upper room. The W staircase was added later, covering some of the earlier niche-like decorations.

Estructura D is behind (E of) Estructura B. It covers 72 sq m, with walls 2m thick, enclosing a chamber of 26 sq m. There are three pillars on the E façade to support a poured concrete roof, plus the now familiar cornicing, stepped fretwork, and niches. The present chamber succeeded an earlier one, as with most buildings of Tajín Chico.

To the N *Estructuras E, F,* and *G* are unrestored rectangular platforms forming another small plaza.

A quadrilateral platform forms the W side of the main plaza, with *Estructura Q* at the next level up, to the W. It is 108 sq m, with two rows of columns to support a slab roof, and a projecting cornice.

A trail from Estructura Q leads up to the *Edificio de las Columnas*, possibly of Toltec inspiration. It rests on a platform 45m above the plazas of Tajín Chico and covers some 33,600 sq m. It was entered by staircases on the E and W, with a 21m long, 7m deep terrace along the E façade. On the E side are six decorated panels similar to the 'Greek Cross', with vestiges of the original paint still visible; a cornice and niches are above these. The lower steps also have cornices, friezes of stepped frets, and niches. Seven columns, each 1.1m in diameter, fronted the building and are now on display outside the site museum. Two large blocks of the slab roof, which these supported, can be seen lying on the platform. The columns were carved with calendrical figures, sacrifices, and warriors, incl. what are believed to be 'Eagle Knights' of the military order or cult.

Annexed to the S side is the *Edificio de los Túneles*, with two vaulted passages on its W side, leading to a temple at the summit of the hill. The results of further exploration of this complex are eagerly awaited.

At the entrance to the site there is a small **Museum** with various ornamental fragments from the buildings. These include the carved stone slabs from Monumento 4. One depicts two intertwined serpents forming the symbol ollin (movement), surrounded by 16 petals. Two figures holding fans flank them, and two more priestly figures, carrying copal incense bags, form the edges. Near the waist-level of the figure r. of centre is the Maya dot and bar glyph for '19' (three bars 15 plus four dots 19). The decorated wall panels from the Temple of the Pirámide de los Nichos, and the carved columns from the Edificio de las Columnas are also here.

THE SOUTH-EAST AND THE ISTHMUS

66 Mexico City to Puebla

Méx. 190, 140km.—27km **Tlapacoya**.—29km turn for Ixtapaluca.—61km Río Frío.—91km San Martín Texmelucan.—106km **Huejotzingo** and (8km SW) **Calpan**.—120km **Cholula**.—140km **Puebla**.

The quickest way between the two cities is by the toll road (Méx. 150D; 127km). The more interesting, and slower, way is by the old road (Méx. 190), which keeps near the toll road for most of the distance, but allows for interesting stops on the way and a more agreeable final approach to the city of Puebla.

We leave Mexico City to the SE along Calz. Ignacio Zaragoza, the airport on the l. In *Peñón de los Baños*, the colonia just N of the airport, is a rock outcrop. At one time it was a site of hot springs on an islet in Lake Texcoco, where the Aztecs carved several bas-reliefs of calendrical symbols and glyphs.

S of the airport was the island of *Pantitlán*, where in May, when the first rains were expected after the dry season, Aztec priests performed a ritual including the sacrifice of children to Tláloc, ritual bathing, and imitations of the movements and cries of aquatic birds, in order to induce rain and initiate the growing season.

At (17km) *Los Reyes*, now a teeming and overburdened satellite town on the border between the Delegación of Ixtapalapa in the Federal District and the State of México, the toll and free roads diverge.

A r. turn at the sign for an archaeological zone leads to a little-visited 13–15C Aztec ceremonial plaza. The site's principal pyramid has been restored, and has a W-facing staircase between solid side-ramps; traces of other, earlier buildings are also still visible.

19km turning l. for (21km N) *Texcoco* see Rte 20. 22km turning r. for (8km SW) *Tláhuac*.

Tláhuac (ancient *Cuitlahuac*), chief place of the easternmost delegación of the Federal District, was once an Aztec provincial city-state, founded during the Toltec period in the 13C, and on a dike which separated the now drained Lagos de Xochimilco and Chalco. The former convent of *San Pedro*, ceded by the Franciscans to the Dominicans in 1554, is a mixture of the building work of both Orders. It contains a painting of Our Lady of the Rosary, among clouds, surrounded by the 15 mysteries in medallions. Famous contemporary personages (Pius V, Philip II, etc.) appear beneath her. Two 16C statues, SS Peter and Gregory the Great, survive from an original retable.

At 27km, beyond *Ayotla*, turning r. for **TLAPACOYA**.

Tlapacoya and the Chalco region have been inhabited from the time of man's entry into the Basin of Mexico. Work by José Lorenzo has located many sites, incl. the excavation of early hearths associated with stone tools of both local and imported materials; and heaps of discarded animal bones, representing habitation sites as early as c 19,000 BC. In 1956, excavations by Beatriz Barba de Piña Chan in Tlapacoya itself uncovered traces of a Preclassic ceremonial centre. In the 1970s Paul Tolstoy, L. I. Paradis, and Christine Niederberger traced the development of the settlement in more detail.

At **Zohapilco**, just S of the present village, Niederberger excavated remains of hearths, dietary remains, tools, and the wastage from their manufacture, dating from c 5500 BC. In later levels tiny maize cobs were found, along with the bones of a varied meat diet—deer, rabbit, gopher, dog, mud turtle, birds, and even human bones in a context suggesting cannibalism. NW of Ayotla, excavations at a village site yielded pottery dated c 1400–1150 BC, the *Ayotla Phase*; and traces of other early village sites have been excavated at Xico and Chalco, to the SW and S, respectively, and can be compared to the better-known sites of Copilco, Ixtapaluca Viejo, and Tlatilco.

The Preclassic village at Tlapacoya, a 'gateway' community at the SE entrance to the Basin, yielded some of the earliest pottery in the Basin. In later levels the ceramics show influence from the Gulf Coast, incl. rocker-stamping with three different Olmec glyphs, dated c 1070–940 BC. A wide range of pottery, obsidian knives, bone needles, etched seashells, spiral-woven baskets, jadeite beads, zoomorphic figurines (especially of hollow dogs), and some of the earliest known figurines of ball players, reveal a comfortable village life through several phases of occupation. Pottery ranged from simple incised blackware vessels, to highly burnished redware figurines.

The present remains at Tlapacoya are of structures built in the 2–1C BC. By that time the site had become an important ceremonial centre, and a large earthen platform was constructed against the hillside. Although not quite as early as the mound at Cuicuilco, it went through several phases of additions between c 400 and 200 BC, and was eventually retained by a stone wall against the hillside, and faced with stone. In its final form it included six recessed tiers, and in characteristic Mesoamerican fashion a new staircase was built for each new temple on top, as the platform grew. The overall impression is thus one of superimposed platforms, cut by staircases, to produce 13 platform areas. In the final phase of occupation three tombs were cut into the top platforms and covered with monolithic slabs. When excavated, the skeletons showed cranial deformation and dental mutilation, perhaps another indication of Gulf Coast influence. But as Teotihuacán and Cuicuilco began to dominate the Basin of Mexico in the 1C BC, Tlapacoya's function as a ceremonial centre waned. It became a neglected backwater but was nevertheless inhabited right through to the 16C, when it was a noted Aztec centre for weaving.

At 29km *Ixtapaluca* the turning r. goes to (8km S) *Chalco*, see Rte 74. The turning l. is for (4km N) **Ixtapaluca Viejo** (also known as *Acozac*—'in the yellow water'). The site is on a hill above the golf course (l. of road).

The remains of this small Postclassic ceremonial centre include a stepped temple-pyramid, dedicated to Quetzalcóatl in his guise as the Wind god, Ehecatl, a ball court, and traces of several other platforms and rooms. The ball court measures c 35 x 8m, with boundary walls c 2m high. The main pyramid is c 12m high, and from the top there are good views of the valleys of Mexico and Texcoco to the NW. In the Aztec period Ixtapaluca was a city-state and provincial centre of the empire.

Ixtapaluca is also the name of a Preclassic ceramic phase (c 1400 BC–c 800 BC) in the Basin of Mexico, especially represented at the sites of Tlapacoya and Tlatilco. The site and phase were linked closely to other Basin sites (E and SE of Tenayuca) excavated by George Vaillant in the 1930s. Ixtapaluca was followed by *Zacatenco*, a mid-Preclassic village site and phase (c 800–400 BC); its graves produced decorated ceramics and figurines, mostly of females, which enabled Vaillant to work out a chronological scheme based on a seriation of the types. The mid-Preclassic village site at El Arbolillo in the Guadalupe hills to the N gave its name to a sub-phase of Zacatenco. *Ticomán* (site and phase; c 400–100 BC) followed Zacatenco. The Zacatenco–Ticomá phase site of Loma Torremate (N rim of Basin) was a large nucleated village by c 500 BC with 400 to 475 individual households in compound-clusters (total population of c 2500), a precursor to the ceremonial precincts of classic Mesoamerican city-planning.

33km turning l. for (7km N) *Coatepec*, see Rte 20. The road gradually climbs into the *Sierra Nevada*, extending c 100km from S to N and forming a barrier between the Valley of Mexico and the Valley of Puebla. This volcanic range includes some of the republic's most spectacular peaks: to the S, the two great volcanoes *Popocatépetl* and *Iztaccíhuatl*, and, to the N, *Telapón* (3996m) and *Tláloc* (4150m). 47km *General Manuel Avila Camacho*. Beyond here the road passes through the so-called *Llano Grande* (*Bajo* to the N; *Alto* to the S), a break in the steep climb, well wooded (horses for hire) and signposted, extending S to *Amecameca* (see Rte 74) and N across Méx. 190 beyond the Tláloc volcano.

Atop Tláloc volcano, c 9km N of Río Frío, traces of walls surround the flattened summit. Two quadrangular structures stand at corners and from the courtyard a paved street runs between walls for nearly 300m. Around the enclosure are several mounds, incl. a circular one assumed to have been the platform for an Aztec temple to Quetzalcóatl. (Reaching the summit requires a 4km climb between Tláloc and Telapón.)

61km **Río Frío** (R,P), an historic stopping point on the old Mexico-Tlaxcala road. We cross into the State of Puebla.

91km **San Martín Texmelucan** (c 52,000 inhab.; 2278m; H,R,P), in the Valle de San Martín, a bustling town known for its cheese and textiles, and at an important road junction. In the main C. Libertad, at the junction with C. Hidalgo, is the former convent of *Sta María Magdalena*, founded by discalced Franciscans in 1615, but not finished until the 18C. A tile tablet on the church façade bears the date 1782.

The INTERIOR is furnished with five churrigueresque, and one baroque, retables, ranging from grand to very simple. On the high altarpiece, a lovely central statue of the Magdalen. The side altarpieces and the walls are adorned with paintings by Juan de Villalobos and other contemporary painters. The sumptuous organ (1794; rebuilt 1919) bears, at the upper extremes, musical cherubs, mermaids, and below the loft, which forms a tribune above the doorway to the Cap. de la Tercera Orden, mermen. In the sacristy, Lamentation over the dead Christ (1691) by Juan Correa. The Cap. de la Tercera Orden contains a churrigueresque altarpiece and paintings by Juan de Villegas, Pedro Rafael Salazar (naive), and others.

In the convent is a series of paintings of scenes from the life of Our Lady by Juan Tinoco (some signed and dated 1702).

Along C. Hidalgo we reach the long PL. DE ARMAS, on its far side the 18C parish church of *San Martín*. The adjoining chapel of *La Purísima Concepción* contains a superb, wide churrigueresque high altarpiece in white and gold: in the centre, a statue of St Joseph with SS Catherine and Rose on either side. In the church sacristy, a fine painting of St Sebastian by Juan de Villegas.

To the N of San Martín Texmelucan, on Cerro Xochitécatl, stand the grass-covered platform mounds of *Moyotzingo*. Pottery from surface collections dates to the Middle Preclassic, or earlier. The streaky-finish pottery is related to pottery from Morelos and the Valle de Tehuacán.

From San Martín Texmelucan to (22km) *Tlaxcala*, see Rte 68.

Méx. 190 continues SE with the E slopes of Iztaccíhuatl on the r.

106km **HUEJOTZINGO** (c 22,000 inhab.; 2280m; P) is an unspoiled town, full of characteristic (mainly 18C) old houses with jutting gargoyles. Its large market adds to its agreeableness. The apple orchards which surround it produce a famous cider.

Huexotzingo was a Postclassic city-state of considerable power. It claimed similar Chichimeca-Náhuatl-speaking ancestry as Tlaxcala, to which it was allied. Its power increased in 1359 when it conquered neighbouring Cholula. In the early 15C it befriended and harboured, along with Tlaxcala, the boy Nezahualcóyotl of Texcoco, when his father was murdered in 1418, and helped the Texcocans and the Mexica Aztecs to defeat Azcapotzalco in 1428. It opposed the Triple Alliance of Texcoco, Tenochtitlán, and Tlacopan, especially when Tenochtitlán began to dominate the Basin of Mexico at the expense of the other two.

Huexotzingo sometimes hampered Aztec trade by blocking their use of the E trade route from Tlatelolco to Izúcar de Matamoros, and was defeated by Moctezuma I Ilhuicamina (1440–68) in bitter fighting over the city of Chalco. Many Chalcan refugees, however, fled to Huexotzingo to continue their resistance against Aztec rule, encouraging and abetting the long standing hatred between Tlaxcala-Huexotzingo and the Aztecs. In 1519, wrote Bernal Díaz del Castillo, the caciques of 'Guaxocingo', allies of the Tlaxcaltecans, tried to dissuade Cortés from continuing to Tenochtitlán. Nevertheless, they provided him with scouts. In 1524 he laid claim to Huejotzingo and its province. In July 1524 the first Franciscan chapter meeting in Mexico decided to make it the centre for the evangelization of a vast area, incl. Cholula, Tepeaca, and the Mixteca, to the E and S. The old site, in sheltered ravines at the foot of Iztaccíhuatl, had been a place of refuge for the Indians who had fled the depredations of the conquistadores, and a convent of four friars was set up there in the same year. In the early 1540s the hitherto dispersed settlement was gathered into its present site a league or so below on the plain, a move supervised probably by Fray Juan de Alameda; a second translation of population from the old site was completed by 1610. 16C and early 17C plagues claimed many lives. In 1560 the population was estimated at 50,000; by 1612 c 5000 were left. In Oct. 1625

Thomas Gage, on his way from Veracruz to Mexico, was entertained till midnight by the singing and dancing of the Indian pupils of the Franciscans.

Dominant on the E side of the main plaza is one of the glories of New Spain and one of its first four conventual foundations, the former Franciscan convent of **San Miguel Arcángel**. A Mexican interpretation of various European, and Mudéjar, architectural and ornamental styles has created a monument of boundless interest.

A church in the old settlement was described (for the benefit of Nuño de Guzmán and to discredit the clergy) in 1529 as being 'as sumptuous as that of San Juan de los Reyes in Toledo'. Building in the present town started in 1544. By 1555 atrio wall and gates, posas, portería, and church N doorway were in place; the convent went up in 1548–60; the church dates from 1550 to 1571. During less sensitive times early this century part of the convent was converted into a gaol; the posas were degraded as execution sites.

The square ATRIO is entered up steps through a handsome triple-arched gateway in the W wall or a double arch in the N wall. At each corner are four identical square POSA chapels, harmonious survivals, topped by pyramidal roofs, two arched doorways, slightly recessed from the wall, in each. The doorway jambs are composed of clustered columns of varying thickness, from whose imposts spring the several layers of the archivolts, with a flattened chain relief prominent among them. The column capitals and bases are decorated with pearl of Castile motifs. Above each doorway is an alfíz framed by the Franciscan cord ending in a penitential knout. In the spandrels, and within the alfíz, are flying angels in high relief, their robes ruffled in the wind, holding symbols of the Passion. (Those on the SE posa were chipped away by troops during the

The north doorway of the convent church of San Miguel, Huejotzingo

Revolution.) Above the arch centres are shields carved with the monograms of Jesus and Mary, and, above them, resting on the alfíz cord and invading the frieze, are crowns. Aligned along the frieze are four more shields carved with the Franciscan emblem of the Five Wounds. Each posa, except the SW, retains a line of palmette motifs along the parapet and a surmounting cross.

The posas were dedicated to the Assumption, St John the Baptist, SS Peter and Paul, and St James; a confraternity identified with each cared for its own posa. The NE is dated 1550.

EXTERIOR. The W doorway of the thick-walled and deeply buttressed church is a striking display of Gothic and Renaissance. A sinuous cusped ogee arch, with seven medallions (symbolic of the Seven Joys of Our Lady?) above in an alfíz bordered on top by the Franciscan cord, rectilinearly laid out, and thin engaged classical columns at the sides, is surmounted by a second storey, in which the window is framed by another Franciscan cord and flanked by two shields bearing the Five Wounds and three nails, and again flanked by the cord. The arch capital and horizontal mouldings at either side show sets of pearls of Castile.

Even more striking is the N doorway (called Porciúncula—the name of St Francis's hut), a fascinatingly exotic mixture of ornamental influences, both medieval and Renaissance. Above it rises a bold alfíz, its border dotted with rosettes, which encloses two spandrel shields carved with the Five Wounds emblem. The arch itself is a remarkable flourish, strongly reminiscent of Portuguese Manueline Gothic: in the centre of the layered archivolt appears the chain of the Order of the Golden Fleece; from the outer rim radiate succulent palmettes and leafy sprouts; from the intrados hangs a series of tuber motifs. The arch imposts are upheld by massive jambs worked in arabesques; wedged into their capitals and bases are more pearls of Castile. Standing forward of them are two engaged columns, decorated with such vigour as almost to overwhelm the central fluted sections. The flowering capitals end in a kind of pineapple form, above acanthus leaves. Immediately beneath and in the bases swell thick bulbous rings worked in basket-weave pattern; the shields attached to the shafts bear the keys of St Peter; the Cross; the Crown of Thorns; the Nails; and the Franciscan cord.

The walled-up opening above it may have been the beginning of an open chapel, abandoned because of economic stringency in the 1580s. Around the parapet the merlons are, unusually, triangular in shape, but levelled at the tip, with narrow slits down the middle.

INTERIOR. Traces of the original murals remain, especially the black and white frieze running under the choir and along the walls of the nave. In the choir, above the door, are remains of a Calvary mural. The vaults of choir, nave, and presbytery show beautiful, and rare, ornamental plaster ribbing—interlacing patterns of tiercerons and liernes—springing from eight half-columns set into the walls (note the playful angelic capitals). The opening under the choir balcony (r.) is to the confessional, into which a friar could glide from the convent side. By the W door are two fine stone holy-water stoups. The rotund pulpit on a slender column, and girded by the cord, is another 16C survival. Of the 17C and 18C nave retables (an interesting, if random, collection) that dedicated to the Trinity (l.; nearest the high altar) is Renaissance in spirit and has excellent relief. On the r. the doorway into the sacristy is surrounded by a frame studded with sharp Mudéjar relief—floral motifs enclosed in a reticulated pattern.

The high altarpiece is an artistic treasure, one of the very few 16C examples to survive in Mexico. It is Mannerist in conception, its arrangement obeying a well-thought-out historical and theological order.

It was contracted in 1584, not by the friars but by the town authorities, with the painter Simón Pereyns: 'Simón Perines...maestro de dicho arte'. Another famous painter, Andrés de la Concha, also figures in the contract, to take Pereyns's place should he fall ill or die. Other assistants were mentioned, incl. 'two Indian ladies...millers...to provide tortillas and sustenance'. The work was to cost 6000 pesos and its making produced enormous local interest. The sculptor, Pedro de Requena, began work in Jan. 1585. The gilder, who spoke no Castilian but was esteemed for his expertise in estofado, was the Indian Marcos de San Pedro.

The work is divided into four storeys and seven vertical courses; the central section and the two side sections holding the paintings set deeper than the four holding the polychrome figures. Each cylindrical column of the lowest and first storeys (doric capitals in the lowest, ionic in the first) is ornamented in its lower part by reliefs of little boys. In the second and third storeys each column is of the baluster type: the lower third showing cherub, fillet, and fruit relief; an almost spherical part above decorated with angel heads; and above that a baluster formed of acanthus below, a smooth middle section, and a seraph next to the capital. The frieze divisions between the tiers are covered in seraph, shield, drapery, and fruit relief. At the top of the outside courses, to l. and r., pediments composed of volutes are loaded with fruit. Next to them, one course in on either side, are two beautifully worked frames for oval paintings, surrounded with fruit and supported by mancebos.

In the predella are bas-reliefs, outstandingly expressive, of the apostles and paintings of SS Mary Magdalen (l.; Pereyns's signature [XIMO PERINEZ FCT 1586] in the lower part) and Mary the Egyptian (r.). The sculpture above is renowned for its stillness and dignity; the figures are sparing in gesture and appear lost in thought. The paintings are typically Mannerist, the draughtsmanship good, the figures detached.

Lowest storey. The statues (l. to r.) are of doctors of the Church: SS Augustine as bishop (holding the Sacred Heart); Gregory the Great (wearing tiara and holding the Church); Peter Damian; and Ambrose. The paintings are the Adoration of the Shepherds (l.: the shepherds Flemish in inspiration) and the Adoration of the Kings. 1st storey. SS Bonaventure (Franciscan preacher), a majestic figure, and Jerome (doctor of the Church), flanked by SS Antony and Bernardine of Siena (Franciscan preachers). The paintings are the Circumcision (l.) and the Presentation in the Temple. 2nd storey. SS Lawrence (martyr), Bernard, Dominic (founders of Orders), and Sebastian (martyr). The paintings are the Resurrection (l.) and the Ascension. 3rd storey. SS Antony Abbot and John the Baptist. In the ovals, the Scourging of Christ (l.) and Christ carrying the Cross. In the tympanum, a relief of God the Father. The central relief shows St Francis receiving the stigmata; his friar companion stays reading while the saint undergoes his agonizing bliss. The figure above is an irrelevant replacement for the statue of St Michael, now destroyed. The space below once contained the tabernacle.

CONVENT. The double-arched PORTERIA, S of the church, is an imposingly firm and monumental work, fascinatingly decorated. One archivolt shows two bands of the same chain which runs round the posa arches; the other an individual voussoir flower. The central support has been described as possibly 'the biggest freestanding baluster in the world'—an ingenious piece of imaginative carving. In the vestibule of the *Cap. de la Tercera Orden*, beyond the portería, is a mural of the Annunciation. In its N wall is the entrance to the confessional (see above). The CLOISTER is unassuming, but, with its orange trees, of undoubted charm. Original black and white and coloured murals, of excellent quality (restored in places), still remain on the walls. Of especial significance, in the NE corner, is that showing Our Lady of the Magnificat surrounded by metaphorical attributes (Tower of David, Gate of Heaven, Star of the Sea, City of God, Enclosed Garden, etc.); on her l., the Dominican St Thomas Aquinas, standing above a crown, a sign of his kinship with the emperor Frederick II; on her r., the Franciscan Duns Scotus, wearing the biretta, sign of his chair at Oxford: a reminder of their differences over the doctrine of the Immaculate Conception.

Further examples, by the same expert hand, are in the SALA DE PROFUNDIS (E side). Above the doorway is a famous portrayal of the Apostolic Twelve, the first 12 Franciscans to arrive in New Spain, on their knees on either side of the Cross, symbol of their evangelizing work. The W wall is lined with paintings of saints in an ornamental arcade between two thick bands of grotesques. At its S end St Francis appears in a landscape, in which are played out four scenes from his life.

Dressed as a 16C nobleman receiving the call from God and preaching to the birds (r.); receiving the stigmata and carried off in a chariot of fire (l.). The adjoining arches contain SS Bonaventure and Antony; SS Clare and Helena; SS Catherine and Barbara. On the S wall, above the lavabo, appear SS Peter and Paul upholding the Church, and Christ washing the apostles' feet. In the little room to the N are murals of three archangels.

Off the upper cloister open the friars' cells. (The permanent community numbered four in 1572; eight in 1681.) On the N side of the upper cloister walk, with traces of murals, the arches of a series of niches are elaborately carved and their soffits lined with medallion relief.

Just to the N of the main plaza, reached along Av. 5 de Mayo, is the church of **San Diego** (c 1598–1600), its fabric most likely containing elements from an earlier 16C church. Its simple façade bears signs of 18–19C updating.

INTERIOR. Against the side walls are matching fragments of two Renaissance altarpieces, possibly from the convent of San Miguel, one containing a late 18C painting by Manuel Caro of St Diego as shepherd with God the Father (16C) in the pediment. Among the other paintings in the church are a St Francis by Juan Sánchez Salmerón (under choir); Miracles of St James, by Juan de Villalobos and José Rodríguez de Carnero (late 17C; r. of nave); and, in the presbytery, Death of St Joseph by Juan de Villegas (1711) and Death and Coronation of the Virgin by Miguel de Carranza (late 18C). The sacristy preserves a coffered ceiling, probably from the earlier 16C building.

8km SW, reached by a winding country road (or by a longer route; see below), is **CALPAN** (c 8000 inhab.; 2510m), amid walnut groves at the foot of Popocaté-petl. Here the former Franciscan convent of **San Andrés**, a combination of fascinating architectural detail and dating from 1548, creates a powerful impression, its posa chapels having the most ornate indigenous carving in Mexico.

The atrio, at a lower level than the plaza, is enclosed by a battlemented wall, entered through a triple-arched gateway on its W side or through a larger in the N side, by the NE posa. The posas, though related, are differently designed and date from the 1550s. Each is pushed back out of its corner, which gives added effect.

The first (NE) posa, dedicated to the Assumption, is laced with tequitqui carving (rosettes in a band moulding connecting the arches, a grotesque pattern with monograms framing the alfíz, and tasselled flowers around arches and niche) and sculpted with three reliefs: in the niche, Our Lady with the Seven Swords—huge to emphasize her suffering—of the Seven Sorrows; an Assump-tion amid seraphim; and an Annunciation. The pyramid roof is topped by a crown of thorns. The second (NW), dedicated to St Francis, shows him kneeling on one corner; at another is probably the donor, Diego de Ordaz Villagómez. The borders include a chain; the N spandrels crudely carved angels; the medal-lions, monograms of Jesus and Mary, the name Francis, and the Five Wounds. The angles of the bulging square dome are edged with the Franciscan cord. The third (SW), dedicated to St Michael, has a marvellous relief of the Last Judgment and another of the three archangels. Its top is a pyramidal spire edged with torus moulding and crowned by a papal tiara. The fourth (SE) resembles the first, the carving less skilled; any figures were either not carved or destroyed. It is dedicated to St John the Evangelist and has symbols of the Evangelists.

The W façade of the church manifests medieval and Renaissance ornament. The doorway is beautifully proportioned; in the spandrels (two angels holding a flourish of a shield containing the Five Wounds, a motif repeated in the arch and jambs), the sculpture resembles that of the posas. The striking columns and mouldings probably belong to a later period. The whole is topped by a scallop shell, with maguey decoration alongside the window, unhappily lengthened in the 19C. Below the window, a relief of St Andrew holding his cross. To the S is the original two-arched portería, which may have contained an open chapel. The arcade above it is a later addition. The two-storey cloister is a recent restoration.

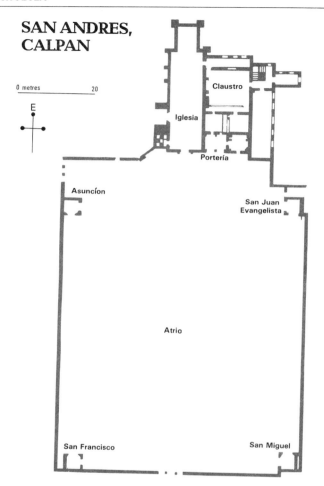

SAN ANDRES, CALPAN

0 metres 20

E

Claustro

Iglesia

Portería

Asunción

San Juan Evangelista

Atrio

San Francisco

San Miguel

110km turning r. for (15km W) *Calpan*, see above.

120km **CHOLULA** (c 40,000 inhab.; 2150m; H,R,P), on the E slopes of Popocatépetl, is fascinating not only for its prehispanic remains but also for its convent and many churches.

By its size alone Cholula (ancient Cholollan) was clearly a site of major importance through the Classic and Postclassic Periods. Excavations were done by José Reygadas Vértiz in the 1930s, by Ignacio Marquina in the 1960s, and since 1967 the German Tlaxcala-Puebla Project has carried out excavations around the base, revealing more of the ancient city's plazas, temple platforms, houses, and sculptures.

Ancient Cholula was occupied from the Middle Preclassic, but there is some evidence of a short-lived abandonment in the Early Postclassic, in favour of Cerro Zapotecas, 3.5km W. By the time of the Spanish arrival its pyramid was the largest single structure ever built in the New World. Cholula began as a farming centre. Its pottery shows evidence of Olmec influence from La Venta in the Gulf Coast region. By c 600 BC it was a small city-state-like centre, rivalled by several similar centres in and around the Basin of Mexico, incl. Teotihuacán. Its first pyramid was built at this time, dedicated to Quetzalcóatl. The original pyramid went through at least four major enlargements and many minor additions and alterations, possibly corresponding to the 52-year calendrical cycle (see Introduction: Calendrics).

In the Classic Period, Cholula, although still an important centre, became somewhat overshadowed by the growth of Teotihuacán. New construction of the pyramid reflected the influence of Teotihuacán in the style of talud-tablero architecture adopted by its builders, and by the murals painted on the walls. Its territory included the Ñuiñe, between Puebla and the Mixteca Alta, and it may have acted as a buffer zone and trading middleman between the interests of Teotihuacán and Monte Albán. There was also contact with Gulf Coast El Tajín, whose style influenced Cholula ceramics and sculpture in particular.

With the collapse of Teotihuacán, from c AD 650, Cholula reasserted itself as one of several rival states in central Mexico, incl. Xochicalco, El Tajín, and later Cempoala and Tula. Between AD 650 and 800 the Olmeca-Xicalanca (sometimes called the 'Historic Olmec', and unrelated to the Preclassic Olmec) moved into the region, took over Cholula (also establishing a capital city at Cacaxtla in Tlaxcala), and undertook further enlargements to the pyramid. Other new settlers may have come from Teotihuacán. Simultaneously it seems that many Cholultecos, perhaps as a defensive movement, moved to Cerro Zapotecas. There they built a complex of temple pyramids on terraces, a ball court, and an elaborate irrigation system.

In the 12C Cholula was again overshadowed by the Toltecs, possibly under direct rule from Tula. The pyramid shows Toltec influence in a new style of talud-tablero refacing and in the use of skulls and skeletons as decorative motifs. In Toltec legend Cholula was one stage in the journeys of Topiltzin-Quetzalcóatl, when a rival faction forced him into exile from Tula, and he travelled S and E vowing one day to return to claim his rightful power. At the end of the 12C refugees settled in Cholula after the destruction of Tula by migrating groups from the N. In 1359 Cholula was conquered by Huexotzingo and, just before the arrival of Cortés, by the Aztecs under Moctezuma II Xocoyotzin (1502–20), who maintained a summer palace there. By this time the population had reached an estimated 100,000, and Cortés described the city as having some 400 towers (pyramids?), temples, and shrines.

In addition to its importance as a place of pilgrimage, Cholula was an important Aztec market, in particular for silver- and gold-work, and for distinctive polychrome pottery called Mixteca-Puebla Ware, of which Cholula was the centre of production and which incorporated influences and traits from several cultures over several centuries. Mixtec-Puebla (or Mixtec-Cholultec) culture was the result of the influx of peoples from three groups: the Nahua, the Mixtec, and the Chocho-Popoloca (Olmeca-Xicalanca), plus immigrations at various times of Teotihuacanos, Toltecs, and others, and a 'recognizable' culture is traditionally dated from the time of the Cholulteca ruler Huemoc (1098–c 1150).

Produced from the 10C, Mixteca-Puebla ware underwent several phases of development and spread throughout central and S Mexico. In vivid colours, extremely fine and precise delineations of lunar and solar discs, symbols for fire and water, human hearts, war, the calendrical day-signs, serpents, jaguars, deer, and other animals, were depicted on the vessels. It has been found at sites as far away as the Gulf Coast at Isla de Sacrificios, from which Cholula received Fine Orange Ware vessels in return. A second important Mixteca-Puebla product was codices. Although recent studies have begun to question the original 'translations' of these painted texts, and their blanket attribution as 'Mixtec', they remain invaluable as ethnographic evidence for ancient historians.

When Cortés arrived with his army and was welcomed 'with many trumpets and kettle-drums', he soon sensed nothing but hostility. He ordered the leading citizens to be confined in the temple of Quetzalcóatl and on 18 Oct. 1519 began a massacre, which lasted all day and accounted for between 5000 and 10,000 deaths. The ancient buildings were mostly reduced to rubble. In 1630, to the Peruvian Bernabé Cobo the deserted suburbs seemed more extensive than those of Seville. Cholula was the first Mexican town to proclaim the second empire, the Chololtecans putting up 500 floral arches to decorate the road to Puebla.

It is an excellent centre for visiting the churches not only in the town itself, but also in the neighbourhood, whose cupolas are a feature of the landscape. Many are set in atrios with handsome gateways. They contain popular paintings of the 17–19C, often movingly spontaneous. Their façades and interiors are often alive with exuberantly decorative stone, tile, and plasterwork, in which local craftsmen have no peers. The tradition continued into the 19C, when a delight in rich decoration could rise above prolongations of the neoclassical, and thrives today.

PL. MAYOR (*Pl. San Pedro*) is the widest (so the Chololtecans claim) in Mexico after the Zócalo in Mexico City. On the W side is the former *Casas Reales* (1646), with an arcade of 46 arches. Today it houses the *Pal. Municipal*. Facing it on the plaza is an early 17C octagonal fountain graced by a delightful figure of St Raphael.

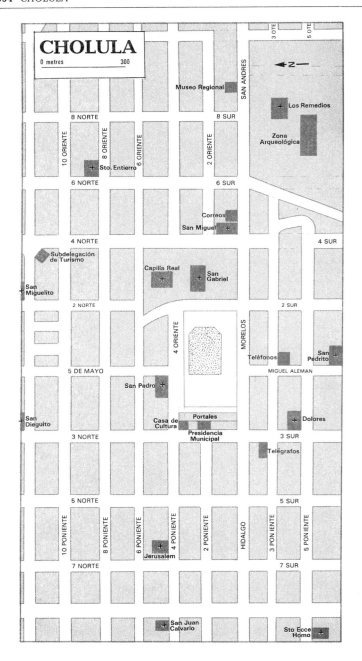

CHOLULA

0 metres   300

Museo Regional

SAN ANDRES

3 OTE
5 OTE

N

Los Remedios

Zona Arqueológica

8 NORTE   8 SUR

10 ORIENTE
8 ORIENTE
6 ORIENTE
2 ORIENTE

Sto. Entierro

6 NORTE   6 SUR

Correos

San Miguel

4 NORTE   4 SUR

Subdelegación de Turismo

San Miguelito

Capilla Real   San Gabriel

2 NORTE   2 SUR

4 ORIENTE

MORELOS

Teléfonos   San Pedrito

5 DE MAYO   MIGUEL ALEMAN

San Pedro

Portales

San Dieguito

Casa de Cultura   Dolores
Presidencia Municipal

3 NORTE   3 SUR

Telégrafos

5 NORTE   5 SUR

10 PONIENTE
8 PONIENTE
6 PONIENTE
4 PONIENTE
2 PONIENTE

HIDALGO

3 PONIENTE
5 PONIENTE

Jerusalem

7 NORTE   7 SUR

San Juan Calvario

Sto Ecce Homo

On the N side is the church of **San Pedro** (1640), built for seculars in defiance of the Franciscans, with a handsome three-storey tower. The cupola is an 18C addition.

The INTERIOR was modernized in the 19C and further embellished (by Pedro H. Leonor) in 1940. In the r. transept is a St Michael by Cristóbal de Villalpando. In the sacristy, a Christ scourged, with SS John, Peter, Philip Neri, and Charles Borromeo (1652) by Diego de Borgraf. The St John on Patmos in the baptistery is attr. Villalpando.
   Opposite the church is a 17C house, the stone imposts of its principal doorway worked in the form of two eagles from whose open beaks spring two eagle knights.

On the E side is the former convent of **San Gabriel**, chosen by the Franciscans as a model for their larger houses.

It was founded c 1529. The church was built in 1549–52 and the convent finished c 1580. It became a centre for learning. The French Franciscan Jean Focher, from the University of Paris, taught canon law here from c 1545, and later in the 16C, 30 friars dedicated to 'the study of the arts' (and administering surrounding parishes) were in residence. In Aug. 1640, it is recorded, the 'young and sprightly' viceroy marqués de Villena and duque de Escalona was entertained here 'with a religious comedy...and songs, dances, and merrymaking'. On 8–9 June 1864, Maximilian and Carlota assisted at the wedding in the church of an Indian couple, the empress showing particular favour to the bride.

A handsome double gateway leads into the ATRIO on the N side of the church. At the corners, except the SE, are three posas with classical pediments and merlons. Raised above the atrio, the CHURCH is surrounded by square buttresses, their heads combining with the parapet crenellation to give a fortress-like appearance. The corner buttresses are aslant with the façade. The plateresque W doorway is surprisingly plain, but is surmounted by a rose window. The N doorway is in beautifully proportioned plateresque, the arch

Convent of San Gabriel, Cholula

imposts, the rings of the outer columns (shaped like candlesticks), and the fine entablature emphasizing its horizontality. The inner arch layer is the Franciscan cord.

The INTERIOR underwent 19C modernization, but has preserved rib-vaulting, the timber ceiling of the spacious choir, and a richly carved stoup. On the r., under the choir, is a Burial of Christ by Antonio de Santander. In the sacristy, a St Michael, attr. Luis Berrueco. Behind the apse is the *Cap. de la Tercera Orden* (early 19C).

In the lower walk of the restored CLOISTER are black and white murals (1580s ?), incl. three scenes from the life of St Francis: as a young layman before Christ crucified, removing his clothes before the Bp of Assisi, receiving solemn approval of his Rule from Pope Honorius III; Coronation of Our Lady; in the frieze, grotesques containing portraits of friars (late 16C–early 17C; retouched 19C). In upper walk, St Sebastian and Mass of St Gregory (a glimpse of contemporary vestments and ornaments).

To the NE of the church, facing and raised above the atrio, is the so-called **Cap. Real**, once a vast chapel (52 x 58m), open at the W end, for the natives.

It was built probably in the early 1560s, on the model of San José de los Naturales (see Rte 7), but the vaults collapsed c 1581: nine lightweight, brick barrel vaults side by side over nine parallel naves; the vaults resting on stone arcades, each with seven arches carried on slender columns—a daring feat, probably beyond the skills of the builders. Its reconstruction, planned by Luis de Arciniega, was finished by 1608; but the new wooden roof rotted and restoration was not completed until 1731.

The side and back walls, the piers of the nine front arches, the merlons and candelabra finials above, the plain square towers at each end, and water spouts (now useless) to drain the eight gutters between the old vaults, survive from the original building. The present Mosque-like roof, with the densest constellation of domes in the W world, supported by strong pillars, is the result of the early 18C rebuilding.

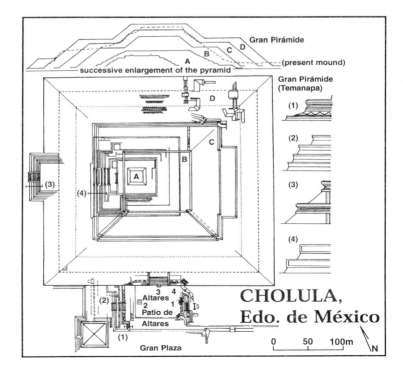

Gran Pirámide

successive enlargement of the pyramid

(present mound)

Gran Pirámide (Temanapa)

CHOLULA,
Edo. de México

0   50   100m

Gran Plaza

Behind the convent, at the corner of Calz. San Andrés and C. 4 Norte, is the church of **San Miguel** (1632; remodelled c 1832), with an atrial cross (1690). It contains four paintings of angels (three in their original frames) by José Rubí de Marimón (late 17C). In the choir, St Francis receiving the stigmata, attr. Cristóbal de Villalpando.

Further E along Calz. San Andrés we may gain access to the ZONA ARQUE-OLOGICA (10.30–5; fee).

The **Gran Pirámide** (*Pirámide Tepanapa*) appears today as a large hill. Extensive excavations at its base have uncovered some of the plazas, platforms, and temples of the city around it, but the only practical way to examine its interior was to tunnel into it. Over 6km of tunnels have been cut to explore the various phases of its construction, and of other plazas and temples at the bases of the earlier pyramids, which were covered in the enlargements. The visitor can walk through some of these to see the constructions and several murals painted in red, black, blue, and yellow.

The first pyramid (*Estructura A*) was 17m high, in five tiers, 120 m sq at its base, and decorated with red, blue, and yellow paintings of mythological creatures.

In the Classic Period an enlargement (*Estructura B*) covered the first pyramid in Teotihuacano style talud-tablero facing and murals of geometric designs, seashells, and insects (grasshoppers?, butterflies?) in black, red, yellow, and blue.

In the 3C AD a structure built against the W side of this pyramid was decorated by a mural called *Los Bebidores* (Drinkers), discovered in 1965. Lifesize and c 46m long, it depicts a general scene of celebration, perhaps of a successful harvest, indicative of Cholula's prosperity: men drinking, a dog, a bee, and two old women. The men are nude or clad only in waistbands and jewellery; some wear ceremonial masks.

On the S side of the pyramid the GRAN PLAZA was built, flanked by two terraced platforms (reconstructed) on the E and W sides of the *Patio de Altares*. Diagonal steps (unique to Cholula) lead from the patio to each platform. The patio contains four altars, one before each set of platform steps, a third before steps up the S side of the pyramid itself, and a fourth in the NE corner of the patio. Some of the terrace faces are carved with Teotihuacano quadrilateral fretwork; others are painted with bold geometric designs and starlike patterns. *Altares 1* and *3* are upright and have borders of scrolls resembling El Tajín masonry decoration; *Altar 2*, on its side, is carved with plumed serpents; *Altar 4* is plain. A deep trench excavated at the SW of the plaza shows stratified deposits from the Classic Period through to the Spanish Conquest, incl. some skeletons under glass.

In the 8C, a third major enlargement (*Estructura C*) covered the pyramid with a nine-tiered structure and a series of courts and plazas (*Estructura D*), built on the NW corner of it. The final pyramid was at least 55m high (the actual summit has long since been destroyed), covering an area of 12.25ha (350m x 350m), the whole precinct covering some 16–17ha.

The sanctuary of *Nuestra Señora de los Remedios* (mid-17C) offers a well-known silhouette. It was rebuilt by 1874 after an earthquake in 1864. The atrial cross is dated 1666.

Further along Calz. San Andrés is the **Museo Regional** (Tues.–Sat., 10–5), which includes models of the various phases of enlargement. We shall never know the full size of the Gran Pirámide, however, as the Spanish and local population utilized the site as a convenient stone quarry in local building. The museum also has an exhibition of Teotihuacano and Cholulteca pottery, in particular illustrating the long sequence of occupation from c 600 BC to the Spanish Conquest.

The church to the E of the archaeological zone is *San Juan Aquiahuac* (17C), its façade with a truncated first storey and tiny niches—a popular version of Mannerist.

Churches in the South Quarters

C. Miguel Alemán goes S from the plaza. At the corner with C. 7 Oriente is *San Pedrito* (17C; altered), with a notable high altar (mid-19C), in republican baroque, and pulpit. The barrios of *Tecámac* and *Mexicalcingo*, further S, each have their church: *San Pablo* (9 blocks S of the plaza), with a 17C tower separated from the church, rebuilt in the 19C; *San Pedro* (5 blocks further S), also rebuilt in the 19C, with a good stone pulpit. Along C. 3 Sur we may reach the *Cap. de los Dolores* (corner with Av. 5 Poniente), simple and preserving 16C fragments in the entrance stair and a wooden ceiling. It contains a Flight into Egypt (first half of 18C) by Francisco Solano. Three blocks S is the sanctuary of *Tzocuilac* (1807–11), its façade a mixture of solomonic baroque and neoclassical. Two blocks SE is *Sta María Axixitla*, with a doorway of 1755. It contains a beautiful late 17C polychrome statue of the Immaculate Conception. Two blocks W is *Santísima Trinidad Axixitla*, with an atrial cross of 1666, an engaging façade recessed behind a great arch, and works by the late 18C Tlaxcaltecan painter Miguel Lucas de Vedolla, incl., in the presbytery, SS Michael and Gabriel.

South-East Quarters

Calz. San Andrés goes E to SAN ANDRES CHOLULA. We turn r. along C. 5 de Mayo to reach, at the corner with Av. Reforma, the church of **San Andrés**, founded in 1585, not finished until 1670. Its three-arched atrial gateway is surmounted by a statue of St Michael.

EXTERIOR. The superb three-storey façade, in grey stone, is Mannerist, with a variation of pilasters and almohadillas in arch and window rim. In the niches between the lower-storey pilasters are statues of SS Bernardine and Antony. Within perfect recessed circles in the spandrels are delicately chiselled flowers. In the gable is a statue of the martyrdom of St Andrew, shone upon by the Holy Ghost.

INTERIOR. On the r., by the choir, is a baroque altarpiece, its predella (a later addition) full of rococo ornament; the paintings (Annunciation and Visitation; 1706) are by Pascual Pérez. Also here is a Last Judgment by him. On the l. of the nave opens out the *Cap. del Sagrario*, with abundant gilded ornaments and a churrigueresque altarpiece. Among the paintings are a Trinity, Dream of Jacob, and Our Lady of the Rosary, by Pérez, and a Crucifixion (1691), with Puebla as the New Jerusalem, by Antonio de Santander.

The little chapel of *Santísima Trinidad*, two blocks SE, contains a baroque altarpiece and passable paintings.

Three blocks E and one N, on Av. 2 Poniente, is the church of *Santiago Xicotenco* (early 18C) with, in the l. transept, a baroque altarpiece dedicated to the Passion.

Four blocks S and one W of San Andrés, on Av. 11 Poniente, is *Sta María Cuaco*, with 18–19C exterior detail. Also on Av. 11 Poniente, two blocks E, is *Sto Niño* (early 18C). On the r. corner buttress sits an angel, his throne decorated with flowers and shoots. Five blocks S of San Andrés is **San Pedro Colomoxco** (late 17C), its stumpy pyramidal tower the showiest in Cholula, laden with stucco angels, the four evangelists, spirals, and leaves—painted in different colours. In the façade little atlante angels serve as footstools for the coarse images of SS Peter and ✝Paul on either side of the choir window. Above, in the curved gable, are star-flower reliefs. In the presbytery is a late 17C retable.

On the E side of San Andrés Cholula is the **Universidad de las Américas**, a US foundation (1940; as Mexico City College, for US students), transferred here in 1970. Its student body is now international.

West and North-West Quarters

Following Av. 4 Poniente from the NW corner of the plaza we come first to the church of *Sta Cruz de Jerusalén*, built by the Franciscans in the 18C; altered to accommodate a 'baroquish neoclassical' façade, finished c 1840. In the cupola pendentives are paintings by Julián Ordóñez (d. 1856), the best poblano muralist of his day. Two blocks further is *San Juan Calvario* (early 18C). In its sacristy is a Burial of Christ by Lorenzo de Leyva, ingenuous, but freely done.

Reached along C. 2 Norte from the NE corner of the plaza, at the corner with Av. 12 Oriente, is **San Miguelito** (early 18C), its atrio arch dated 1776. The high altar contains a painting of Our Lady of Light by Luis Berrueco; on either side of the presbytery, two large paintings by Gerónimo Gómez: Our Lady of the

Apocalypse and Bath of the Child Mary. In the sacristy are three paintings by Juan de Villalobos: Beheading of John the Baptist; Workshop of St Joseph; and St Michael; and a History of the Good Robber (c 1730), with plenty of detail, by Marcos Serrano.

Three blocks N is the church of *El Niño Perdido*, where the chief treasure is a fascinating, though much spoiled, late 17C painting of Our Lady of the Rosary, in a mandorla, surrounded by 15 medallions, one for each mystery, and attended by saints and gentlemen (donors ?) wearing ruffs.

Following Av. 12 Oriente W from San Miguelito into Av. 12 Poniente past the little church of *San Dieguito* (late 17C ?) and then taking C. 3 Norte one block N, we reach **Santiago Mixquitla** (1678; not 1578, as carved into the extrados of the arch), with a Renaissance façade in grey stone. The coats-of-arms on the façade are (l.) a substitution (1820s) of that of Mexico for Castile and (r.) that of the local encomendero.

Two blocks NW of San Juan Calvario, on a slight hill, is *Guadalupe*, begun in 1842; ten blocks N of San Juan Calvario is *San Matías Cocoltla* (1689).

Reached along C. 6 Norte, at the corner with Av. 8 Oriente, is the church of **Sto Sepulcro** (17–18C), with an austere façade. Two baroque altarpieces occupy the end walls of the transepts. The high altar, much interfered with, contains paintings by Cristóbal de Villalpando, unforgivably retouched. Further N along C. 6 Norte, at the corner with Av. 20 Oriente, is **Jesús Nazareno Tlaltempan** (finished in 1681), its tower, finest in Cholula, in three monumental parts—an impression of wonderful lightness. In the sotocoro are paintings by Francisco Solano: Last Judgment (1739) and Holy Family. On the nave walls hang scenes from the life of Christ (Woman taken in adultery, Curing the blind man, Curing the sick, Last Supper) attr. Cristóbal de Villalpando. That of Christ and the Samaritan woman in the l. transept (badly treated) is undoubtedly by him. Here also is a Crucifixion by Rubí de Marimón.

Among churches in the neighbourhood. C 4km N *Sta Bárbara de Almoloya* (late 17C; redecorated in 1936–49) containing interesting paintings: in the sotocoro, a Last Judgment by Juan Sánchez Salmerón and a set of six, attr. Cristóbal de Talavera (d. 1731), on the sorrows of Our Lady. 4km NE *San Juan Cuauhtlancingo* (1722). On its façade, reliefs of the martyrdoms of SS Catherine and Barbara, and two stone heraldic lions. On the high altar, fine statues showing estofado. C 4.5km SW *San Gregorio Zacapechpan* (late 17C). In the façade a Habsburg eagle and two rampant lions on either side of the patronal statue. The interior contains three churrigueresque altarpieces. C 2km S of San Gregorio is *Los Reyes Tlanechicolpan* (18C), with two churrigueresque altarpieces (high altarpiece later modified) and (in the nave; r.) two charming Holy Family scenes, attr. Miguel Castillo.

The most agreeable, but longer, road into Puebla is S along Méx. 190 to (125km) **Sta María Tonantzintla**, still a rustic place. On the l. of the main road near the entrance to the town is the *Instituto de Astronomía*, with the second of the republic's observatories, inaugurated in 1942.

The little church of **Sta María** offers one of the most amazing examples of poblano popular baroque, the work of expert Indian craftsmen.

It started as a small 16C chapel for local Indians. Its present aspect dates from c 1690–1730, although restoration has detracted from 18C colour harmonies.

The EXTERIOR is a delightful, compact interpretation of early baroque, just over the border with classicism, covered in red tiles; the sturdy pilasters, playful multifoil arch, perfectly proportioned choir window with its small balcony, niches, parapet, and graceful tower dotted with blue, yellow, and white glazed decoration. The cupola, covered with yellow tiles, is studded with star motifs.

INTERIOR. Sotocoro, nave and transept vaults, cupola, clerestory, surfaces above the arches of the crossing, and presbytery are covered in a staggering profusion of polychrome, gilded stucco. From among the all-pervading lavishness of flowers, leaves, scrolls, fruits, and garlands appear the heads and figures of cherubs and little angels, Indian boy heads helmeted and plumed, and giants, eyes wide and staring; in pendentives sit saints and apostles; in the sotocoro is a cherubic orchestra circling the Virgin and Child sitting on clouds; in the cupola ('an *Indian* paradise') saints and angels ascend between slender, twirling pillars to a centrepiece of the Holy Ghost. The two churrigueresque nave altarpieces (c 1760) are dedicated to SS Antony (r.) and John Nepomuk. The apse walls are covered by a rich gilded baroque retable. The high altarpiece is a modern reproduction. In the l. transept, a baroque retable and a charming painting of Our Lady of Tzocuilac (1752) by Francisco Muñoz de Salazar; in the r. transept, a baroque altarpiece covers the end wall. On its l., paintings of scenes from the life of St John Nepomuk (1764), by Miguel Castillo.

127km **San Francisco Acatepec**, where the church of **San Francisco**, on a hill above the rolling countryside, is another delicious creation by local craftsmen.

It was started probably in the late 17C; the façade dates from c 1750–60. On New Year's Eve 1939 it was fired by arsonists, but has been lovingly restored thanks to funds provided by Irineo Pantle and his family.

The azulejo work of the EXTERIOR, in the words of José Moreno Villa, 'approaches delirium and admiration comes near to stupefaction...Here we are in a capricious dream world. All is colour and brilliance'. The façade, like a folding screen faced from top to bottom in blue, yellow, and green glazed tiles, as though it were made of china, stands forward of a backing wall of predominantly red glazed and unglazed tiles, which merges with the bases of the tower and slanting espadaña. Its three storeys are separated by emphatic cornices, curvetting in their centres. The estípites in the first and second attest to the popularity of churrigueresque, while the lowest storey, with its columns, covered in dark blue and white tiles, is both baroque and Mudéjar-inspired for the semblance of an alfíz enclosing the shell motif above the doorway. The starlike topmost opening, surrounding a mixtilinear ring which encloses a statue of St Francis, is a work of exquisite refinement, a point of departure for the elegant descent of the upper cornice. Above it, a relief of the Trinity. The tower, its twisted columns swathed in golden tile bands, is a lovely mass of stucco relief and glazing.

The gilded polychrome stucco of the restored INTERIOR crowds into the vaults, and especially the choir, like bands of thick velvet. The solomonic columns of the high and side altarpieces (reconstructions) are almost lost amid lush relief and cherubic figures. Another manifestation of resourceful local baroque is the doorway to the baptistery, with provincial heads amid the stucco swirl.

130km **San Bernardino Tlaxcalancingo**, where the 18C church of *San Bernardino* formed part of a Franciscan visita convent (1671). (The atrial cross is dated 1707.) Its façade is another charming composition of glazed and unglazed tiles, inset with four ceramic tableros adorned with large flower-pots. On the lower l. side another tablero bears a sun image and an inscription: 'this church was glazed in 1782'. The interior is full of gilded relief on a white background. In the nave (r.) a baroque altarpiece with paintings by Francisco Tores Baldés (late 17C). 140km *Puebla*, see Rte 67.

67 Puebla

PUEBLA (officially **Heroica Puebla de Zaragoza**; historically **Puebla de los Angeles**; c 960,000 inhab.; 2162m), capital of the State of Puebla, lies on a plain in the Valle de Puebla, its W outskirts crossed by the Río Atoyac. To the W lies the Sierra Nevada, with its two great volcanoes, and to the NE the volcano La

Malinche. Puebla is known for its textiles, leather goods, and alabaster; its special cuisine and sweetmeats; its automobile plant; and, above all, for its internationally famous pottery (loza de Talavera) and glazed tiles (azulejos), everywhere conspicuous on houses and churches. It is a creole city, conservative and Catholic, once second only to Mexico. Despite neglect and dense traffic, much of interest remains to fascinate the visitor—the cathedral, an extraordinary abundance of churches, museums, and characteristic old houses. A stay of at least a week will be needed for those who wish to study them properly.

Natives of Puebla are called poblanos. The city is laid out on a grid, tilted NW–SE, its centre point the NW corner of Pl. de Armas, whence radiate the four main thoroughfares: C. 5 de Mayo NE and C. 16 de Septiembre SW; Av. Reforma NW and Av. Maximino Avila Camacho SE. All streets within the right-angle formed by Reforma and 5 de Mayo are called Poniente (west) and are designated by even numbers; those within the right-angle of 16 de Septiembre and Reforma are also called Poniente and designated by odd numbers. Streets within the right-angle 5 de Mayo and Maximino Avila Camacho are called Oriente (east) and are designated by even numbers; those within the right-angle of 16 de Septiembre and Maximino Avila Camacho are also called Oriente and are designated by odd numbers. The present system was brought in in 1917.

Airport. 25km NW, S of Huejotzingo. Flights to *Mexico City* and *Guadalajara*.

Bus station. Blvd Norte (between Blvd Carmen Serdán and Camino a la Pedrera), on NW side of the city. Frequent services to *Mexico City* (2 hrs); to *Cholula* (15–20 mins); to *Huejotzingo* (45 mins); to *Atlixco* (1 hr); to *Tepeaca* (1 hr); to *Tlaxcala* (1½ hrs); to *Cuernavaca* (3½ hrs); to *Playa del Carmen* (26 hrs); to *San Cristóbal de las Casas* (20 hrs); to *Tuxtla Gutiérrez* (18 hrs); to *Mérida* (22 hrs); to *Veracruz* (6 hrs); to *Orizaba* (c 2½ hrs); to *Córdoba* (c 3 hrs); to *Jalapa* (c 4 hrs); to *Teziutlán* (c 4½ hrs); to *Oaxaca* (7–8 hrs); to *Campeche* (20 hrs); etc.

Railway station. Av. 80 Poniente, at N end of C. 9 Norte. Daily trains to *Mexico City* (6 hrs); to *Oaxaca* (12 hrs); to *Jalapa* (7–8 hrs); and to more local destinations.

Hotels throughout the city.

Post Office. Corner of C. 16 de Septiembre and Av. 5 Oriente.

Tourist Office. 3 Av. 5 Oriente.

Fiesta. 5 May: commemoration of the battle of Cinco de Mayo.

The original foundation of Ciudad de los Angeles (16 Apr. 1531) was moved to a more elevated site on the W bank of the Río San Francisco and in March 1532 officially called Ciudad de Puebla de los Angeles. The first glassmaker, Rodrigo de Espinosa, set up his workshop in 1542; in the mid-16C the technique of glazed pottery, incorporating Flemish and oriental elements, was introduced here and an export market to central and S America established. By the early 1600s Puebla's 35 textile factories and architects, masons, sculptors, silversmiths, and painters, who were to achieve a great reputation, contributed to economic boom and the city's growth and splendour. In 1539 the bishopric of Tlaxcala, oldest in New Spain, was moved to Puebla. The most famous incumbent was to be Juan Palafox y Mendoza, illegitimate but of noble birth, protégé of Olivares, and appointed visitor-general of New Spain in 1639 (and viceroy in June–Nov. 1642). His eagerness for moral and spiritual regeneration, zealousness in the royal service, and championing of the secular clergy endeared him to the creoles, but earned him the implacable enmity of the Jesuits and mendicant orders, whom he gradually brought to heel. He referred to Puebla as his 'spouse' and his 'Rachel'. By the late 18C, though the ceramic industry was in decline, there was an economic revival and during 1790–1805 Puebla was annually despatching over a million lb of cloth to Mexico. It was, according to Humboldt, 'more populous than Lima, Quito, Santa Fe, Caracas', and still, after Mexico, Guanajuato, and Havana, the most considerable city of the Spanish colonies. Its rich convents and the refinement of its upper classes added to its prestige. One distinguished family was that founded by James Furlong, an exiled Catholic from Belfast, who in 1772 married the poblana Ana Malpica. Their eight sons were to play a prominent part in local government and in the church during the 19C.

 In 1823 the English traveller William Bullock was enormously impressed. 'It is', he later wrote, 'from the splendour of its churches, and other religious edifices, and in the richness of their endowments, that Puebla must take the first rank in the Christian world. In the profuse ornaments of the altars, the sacred vessels and vestments, the expensive carving and gilding of the interior of the churches—in the pompous religious processions and other ceremonies, it yields to no city in America or Europe'. In 1841 Fanny Calderón de la Barca called it 'the Philadelphia of the Republic'.

REPÚBLICA

3 NORTE

BLVD. ZARAGOZA

40

38

36

34

2 NORTE

5 DE MAYO

Fuerte de Loreto

Museo del Estado

32 ORIENTE

30

San Antonio 28

HÉROES

DEL

5

DE

26

Fuerte de Guadalupe

San José

ORIENTE

San Juan de Dios

2 NORTE

16 ORIENTE

14

4

Dolores

6 NORTE

MAYO

CALZADA DE LOS FUERTES

12

ORIENTE

PASEO S. FRANCISCO

22 ORIENTE

20 NORTE

Casa Velasco

6

San Cristóbal

14 NORTE

16

18

Casa
Alfeñique

Teatro

San Francisco

14 ORIENTE

6 NORTE

Barrio del Artista

2 ORIENTE

Parián

Ecce Homo

niversidad

San Roque

MAXIMINO ÁVILA CAMACHO

La Luz

2 ORIENTE

SUR

14 SUR

3 ORIENTE

20 SUR

Analco

PUEBLA

0 metres   400

On 5 May 1862 (the Cinco de Mayo) a Mexican force under the young Gen. Ignacio Zaragoza won a famous victory here over the French expeditionary force led by Gen. de Lorencez. In 1863, from 16 March to 17 May, the French and the Mexican imperialists (30,000 strong) under Marshal Elie Forey, laid siege. Despite fierce resistance from the 21,000 Mexican republicans, especially during the assaults on the forts of Sta Inés and San Javier (during which Forey said that the artillery and rifle fire reminded him of that at Sebastopol), their situation, without expected reinforcements, became hopeless. Before their final surrender they succeeded in breaking up their cannon. On 5 June 1864 Maximilian and Carlota were received 'with extraordinary honours'. On 2 Apr. 1867 Porfirio Díaz took Puebla from the imperialists and took it again in 1876 after his overthrow of Pres. Lerdo de Tejada. In Nov. 1910 the attempted arrest and death of members of the Serdán family marked the beginning of intense revolutionary activity and a decade when the city was hotly contested by constitutionalists and zapatistas. The post-revolutionary years have seen a rapid growth in area and population, and much destruction and careless redevelopment. It is a tribute to Puebla's resilience that so much has survived.

The State of **Puebla** (4 million inhab.; 33,919 sq km) extends to the E of the Sierra Nevada, to the W of the southernmost slopes of the Sierra Madre Oriental, and to the N of the Sierra Madre del Sur. The S area bordering on N and W Oaxaca forms part of the Mixteca. The central region, crossed by the Sierra Volcánica Transversal, divides into: that to the NE belongs to the plateau of Anáhuac; that to the SW includes the valleys of Puebla and Valsequillo, watered by the State's most important river, the Atoyac, which flows SW, eventually to form the Río Balsas in the State of Guerrero. In the far NE the State territory reaches the Gulf lowlands. Puebla is primarily an agricultural State, producing mainly for home consumption. Industry, particularly visible along the motorway between Puebla and Mexico, has developed since the 1970s. Mineral reserves (gold, silver, and especially the variety of alabaster, or onyx, known as tecali) are considerable.

In the path of the advance of the conquistadores from the coast to Mexico, the area was largely conquered by 1522 and parcelled out in encomienda. Deforestation followed; European fruit and vegetables and cane sugar were introduced; and a flourishing textile industry developed. The intendancy of Puebla (incl. the present State), a vast area stretching from the Pacific to the Gulf, was created in 1786, its affairs from the 1790s enlivened by the energetic intendant Manuel Flon (conde de la Cadena; comp. Rte 51) who, it was claimed, by 1803 had eliminated public disorder and cleaned up the capital.

In 1824 the State of Puebla was created. During the 19C city and State, because of their strategic position, were inevitably prey to the movement of armies and war. The years 1892–1911 spanned the harsh governorship of Mucio P. Martínez, who made a fortune through his ownership of a dozen illicit gambling houses and monopoly of the State pulque supply, but under whom the psychiatrist and educationist Rafael Serrano pioneered educational reform, organized probably the finest college of education in Mexico, and set up a school in every village. In 1929 popular indignation forced the reopening of Catholic churches and schools closed by an anticlerical government.

The city centre is the handsome PL. DE ARMAS, shaded by tall trees, graced by the beautiful *Fuente de San Miguel* (1777) by José Antonio de Santa María.

In Sept. 1847 a Mexican force under Santa-Anna bombarded US troops, left behind by Gen. Winfield Scott after his capture of the city in May to guard sick and disabled comrades, who had secured their positions in the plaza. The approach of US reinforcements forced Santa-Anna to retire. The plaza's present layout dates from 1869–97.

On the W side is the *Portal de Iturbide*, on the E the *Portal de Morelos*. On the N side, above the *Portal de Hidalgo*, rises the grandiose *Pal. Municipal* (1897–1901), by the English architect Charles J. S. Hall.

On the S side is the great cathedral of **La Inmaculada Concepción**, the work of many years and various hands, which still retains a remarkable stylistic unity.

The first cathedral, built in 1536–39 (where now stand the Sagrario, the Cap. de los Reyes, and the Sacristy), was not fully demolished until the 18C. The second was begun in 1575 to the plan of Francisco Becerra. In 1589–1601 the maestro mayor was Luis de Arciniega. In 1626 work was suspended, and in 1634 changes to the original project were put in hand by Juan Gómez de Trasmonte, although nothing much was done. On his arrival in 1640 Bp Palafox found it in a sad state: 'the pillars were built but halfway; all was open to the heavens; without implements or materials of any kind, or assets with which to buy them; they had started neither arch nor vault; nor had they any hope of continuing. Fugitives from the law had fled there for sanctuary. In the chapels were dwelling Indians, some married, others in a state of sin'. He set about finishing the work, appointing the Aragonese Mosén Pedro García Ferrer as its director and ordaining that the nave should be raised above the side aisles to permit more light. With the interior finished, consecration took place on 18 Apr. 1649, amid splendid ceremonial, in which 1200 clergy took part. Palafox departed from Veracruz on 10 June 1649. The main (W) façade was finished in 1664; the N tower in 1680; the N portal in 1690; the S tower in 1768. The interior was thoroughly renovated in the early 19C. In 1823 William Bullock attended Tenebrae in Holy Week: he 'never witnessed such a splendid scene'. In spring 1824 the British chargé d'affaires, H.G. Ward, recorded a visit with his wife: 'the curiosity excited by the first appearance of an English woman was so ungovernable, that the great marketplace, through which the carriage had passed, transferred in a moment by far the largest portion of its inmates to the Cathedral, where the crowd soon became so great, that, although no incivility was intended, it was quite impossible for us to remain'.

An excellent view of the EXTERIOR can be got from the NE side, from where the lines of nave, aisles, and transepts; the huge azulejo-covered dome supported by volutes; and the many finials can be clearly seen. The front is set well back in the large atrio, enclosed by fine wrought-iron railings. These, and the angel figures along the pilasters, date mainly from 1878–93, although on the S side may be seen a late 18C section. The three portals of the W façade, begun by Francisco Gutiérrez and finished by Vicente Barroso de la Escayola, are predominantly Mannerist but with baroque touches. In the two lower storeys the paired columns bear doric and ionic capitals; the upper storeys contain single columns with Corinthian capitals, supporting, in the lower side portals, curved pediments. Standing out against the darkened surface are statues and reliefs in white stone. In the central *Puerta del Perdón* the statues, by Juan de Solé González (1662), represent SS Peter and Paul (on either side of the door) and SS Joseph and James the Greater (first storey). The reliefs show symbols of the Immaculate Conception (lilies arranged in a vase; below) and fortitude (the oak tree; above). Crowning the gable is the coat-of-arms of Charles V. The central reliefs of the side portals show St Rose kneeling before Our Lady and the infant Christ (l.) and St Teresa (r.), both attr. De Solé González. Renaissance classicism is the hallmark of the towers (70m high), designed by Luis Gómez de Trasmonte and Rodrigo Díaz de Aguilera; the N tower was built under Carlos García Durango; the S under Manuel Vallejo, who may have added the little tiled cupolas, which lighten their austerity.

The N portal, with the same combination of orders, though with pilasters instead of columns in the middle storey and a central window in an eared frame, is a richer work, by Diego de la Sierra. The indifferent statues represent the four evangelists, the medallions above them four kings of Spain: Charles I (Emperor Charles V), Philip II, Philip III, and Philip IV. Above the beautiful upper circular window, again the royal coat-of-arms. The cupola, designed by García Ferrer, was built under Jerónimo de la Cruz. The building of walls, arches, columns, and pilasters was supervised by Agustín Hernández.

The INTERIOR consists of a broad nave, two side aisles, two outer rows, each of seven side-chapels, and an ample transept. Square pillars with Tuscan half-columns attached on each side support the round arches of the side aisles, upholding low domical vaults, and the barrel vault of the elevated nave, lit by the round windows of the clerestory. The floor is paved with coarse marble-like stone, laid down in the late 18C. The effect is of spaciousness and harmony, but at the expense of antiquity.

From c 1819 José Manzo y Jaramillo reorganized the interior. He replaced the baroque altarpieces with neoclassical ones; redecorated the whole in gold and white, incl. the vaults; and gilded the column bases and capitals.

The CHOIR is in the centre of the nave. Facing the Puerta del Perdón against the W side is the Altar del Perdón (1796). In the floor in front of the altar, the tombstone of Bp Domingo Pantaleón Alvarez de Abreu (1743–68) and another destined (vain hope; he died, and was buried, in Spain in 1659) for Bp Palafox. The wrought-iron screen on the E side of the choir, commissioned in 1697, painted and gilded, with a cherub-head frieze, is by Mateo de la Cruz. The

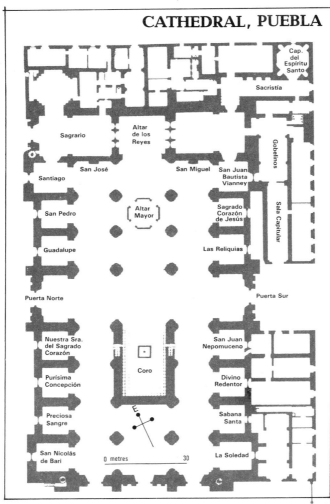

CATHEDRAL, PUEBLA

Cap. del Espíritu Santo

Sacristía

Sagrario

Altar de los Reyes

Gobelinos

San José

San Miguel

San Juan Bautista Vianney

Santiago

Sala Capitular

San Pedro

Altar Mayor

Sagrado Corazón de Jesús

Guadalupe

Las Reliquias

Puerta Norte

Puerta Sur

Nuestra Sra. del Sagrado Corazón

San Juan Nepomuceno

Coro

Purísima Concepción

Divino Redentor

Preciosa Sangre

Sabana Santa

E

San Nicolás de Bari

0 metres   30

La Soledad

balustrade, also of wrought-iron, which winds round it above the cornice, and that of the corridor which crosses the transept, date from 1691. The stalls, inlaid with rosewood, ebony, mahogany, and other rare woods and ivory, were done by Pedro Muñoz in 1719–22. Also of the 18C are the side organs, garnished by images of exuberant angel musicians. On the N exterior wall are four paintings (Allegory of the Blessed Sacrament, Assumption, Appearance of Our Lady of Mercy to King James I of Aragón and St Raymond, Miracle of St Leocadia in the presence of St Ildefonsus), by José de Ibarra (1732). On the S wall, two scenes from the life of St Ignatius by Juan Rodríguez Juárez, and two further paintings, honouring Our Lady and the infant Christ, by Ibarra. The design of the rich N and S choir portals is attr. Diego de la Sierra.

The angel reliefs in the pendentives of the cupola are by García Ferrer.

The sumptuous neoclassical HIGH ALTAR (1797–1818), designed by Manuel Tolsá and completed by Manzo, using alabaster, marble, and jasper, represents also the combined efforts of Simón Salmón (gilding); Pedro Patiño Ixtolinque, José Zacarías Cora, and José María Legaspi (sculpture); the mason Pedro Pablo Lezama; José Ramírez (stucco); Manuel Caamaño (bronze and silverwork); and Joaquín Inocencio (carving). In the crypt beneath it are the tombs of 12 bishops of Puebla, incl. the first, Julián Garcés (1526–42).

Beyond, in the apse, is the CAP. DE LOS REYES, with its famous altarpiece (1646–49), its design traditionally attr. Juan Martínez Montañés, made by Lucas Méndez. The tabernacle and niches of the grand first storey provide the earliest use of the solomonic column in New Spain.

In c 1820 it was reconstructed by Manzo, who kept to the original shape and preserved the paintings and alabaster columns, but substituted white plaster with gilded ornament for carved and gilded wood. Polychrome and gold wooden statues were discarded for neoclassical ones, representing Louis IX of France, Ferdinand III of Castile, Edward the Confessor; Elizabeth of Portugal, Margaret of Scotland, Empress Helena.

The superb paintings are by García Ferrer. In the lowest storey: the Nativity (l.), combining wonder and tenderness, the shepherd on the r. leaning on his crook a likeness of Bp Palafox; Adoration of the Kings (r.). In the centre, the grand Assumption surrounded by angels. In the spandrels, two angels. Above, Coronation of Our Lady. Almost unrecognizable under added robes in the tabernacle is the Virgen de la Defensa, an exquisite late 16C polychrome wooden statue from Andalucía.

Adorning the cupola is a masterfully swirling painting by Cristóbal de Villalpando, Apotheosis of the Blessed Sacrament, begun in 1688. In the centre, beneath the monstrance containing the Host, kneels Our Lady; above her, the Holy Trinity; covering the rest of the dome, the archangels, an angelic orchestra, and Old and New Testament figures. In the pendentives, four biblical women: Judith, Ruth, Esther, and Jahel.

The side altarpieces (1686–87), redone by Manzo, preserve eight excellent paintings (1702) of scenes from the lives of SS Francis Borgia and Francis de Sales by Juan Rodríguez Juárez.

At the E end of the aisles, neoclassical altars of San José (l.) and San Miguel (r.), with sculpted saints attr. José Villegas Cora (d. 1785). In the transepts hang four paintings. On the N side, St Christopher, by Antonio de Lara (c 1760), and St Michael, by Luis Berrueco; S side, Patronage of St Joseph, by Miguel Jerónimo Zendejas, and Life of St Philip Neri, by Cabrera.

The superb gilded ironwork grilles of the SIDE CHAPELS were done by Juan de Leyva Pavón (1722–26). SOUTH (r.) AISLE, *Cap. de la Soledad*. On the side walls, Crucifixion and Descent from the Cross (1679), two vigorous and colourful paintings by Rodrigo de la Piedra. *Cap. de la Sabana Santa*, containing a copy of the Holy Shroud, exhibited on Maundy Thursday. The poor paintings are by Manzo. The *Cap. del Divino Redentor* contains, on the r. wall, a huge and dramatic painting by Cristóbal de Villalpando, Moses showing the bronze serpent to the Israelites in the Desert, combined, above, with the Transfiguration (1683), both parts full of telling detail. *Cap. de San Juan Nepomuceno*. Paintings of the saint's life by Miguel Jerónimo Zendejas (late 18C). *Cap. de las Reliquias*, lined with bronze reliquaries. *Cap. del Sagrado Corazón*, containing the tomb of Gen. Miguel Miramón (1832–67), the remains brought here in 1895 by his widow, doña Concepción Lombardo. *Cap. de San Juan Bautista Vianney*, with main altar paintings by José Joaquín Magón.

Of the chapels in the N aisle, that of *Guadalupe* contains a Holy Family, an uneven early work by Villalpando; and Apparitions of Our Lady of Guadalupe by Antonio de Lara. On the aisle outer pillars, the 14 oval paintings of the Stations of the Cross, beautifully framed, are by Cabrera.

Beyond the *Cap. del Apóstol Santiago*, at the NE corner of the cathedral, is the SAGRARIO (late 17C), its portal (c 1690) by Diego de la Sierra, who also designed its adjoining (E side) little chapel with octagonal cupola (1703–24). Among the paintings in the latter is the last work of Miguel Jerónimo Zendejas, painted in 1815 at the age of 90, Agony in the Garden.

On the r. (S) side of the Altar de los Reyes is the SACRISTY, containing fine chests of drawers (17–18C) for the storing of vestments and treasure. Huge canvases on the N wall, by Baltasar de Echave y Rioja, show the Triumph of the Church (centre), the Triumph of Religion (r.), and the Triumph of Faith (l.). On the S wall, José Joaquín Magón, Patronage of Our Lady. On E and W walls, Luis Berrueco, Christ washing the apostles' feet and Last Supper. The passage on the S side of the sacristy gives access (r.) to an anteroom adorned with four Gobelins tapestries (said to be the gift of Charles V, but dating in fact from the 17C). The adjoining SALA CAPITULAR contains portraits of the bps of Puebla and an Immaculate Conception (1672) by Francisco Rizi. By turning l. from the sacristy passage, we reach, at the SE corner of the cathedral complex, the octagonal *Cap. del Ochavo*, built in the late 17C, its altar panels containing three small paintings by Villalpando: Paradise; the Flood; and Martyrdom of St Catherine (1689).

On the S side of the cathedral, the block enclosed by Avs 5 and 7 Oriente and Cs 16 de Septiembre and 2 Sur contains a series of foundations which, thanks to 18C regularization, give the appearance of one huge building: at the C. 16 de Septiembre end, between Avs 5 and 7 Oriente, the former **Pal. Episcopal** (No. 1), residence of the bps of Puebla (incl. Palafox) since 1619; extended in the late 17C by Bp Manuel Fernández de Sta Cruz (to include a gaol for refractory priests and so that he could pass through to the adjoining colleges 'to observe the pupils at their studies'); and completely refashioned in 1792. Next along Av. 5 Oriente are what were the *Colegio de San Pedro*, the *Colegio de San Juan*, and the *Colegio de San Pantaleón*.

The Colegio de San Juan was opened in 1596 for the education of 12 boys who served as acolytes in the cathedral and transformed by Bp Palafox into the *Seminario Tridentino*. Its premises were restored in the 1740s. The Colegio de San Pedro, for 30 pupils from the ages of 11 to 17, was established in 1644 as a preparatory school for the seminary. Both came to be regarded as one institution, the **Real y Pontificio Colegio** or **Seminario Tridentino**, which was dispossessed by the Reform. The Colegio de San Pantaleón was founded in the mid-18C and opened in 1762 as an extension of the seminary. In Av. 7 Oriente, at the rear of the Colegio de San Juan, are the former premises of the *Colegio de San Pablo*, a theological college founded in the late 17C, rebuilt in the mid-18C, and finally closed down after the fall of Maximilian.

On either side of the window above the doorway of the Colegio de San Pedro (No. 3; says 5; 1648), designed by García Ferrer, are coats-of-arms of Bp Palafox; in the niche above, a statue of St Peter. The former Colegio de San Pantaleón, at the corner of Av. 5 Oriente and C. 2 Sur, is now the *Pal. de Justicia*, which has made use of good original furniture.

Reached through the Colegio de San Juan (No. 5) is the most venerable library in Mexico, the **Biblioteca Palafoxiana** (Tues.–Sun., 1–5), containing a priceless collection of books and incunabula.

Palafox donated to the seminary his library and various personal possessions: 'five thousand volumes, more or less, with their shelving…two globes, celestial and terrestrial, a yard and a half high…'. Other works were added to it, incl. the collection of Bp Francisco Fabián y Fuero (1765–73), who fitted out its new premises and under whom it was inaugurated: 'so well furnished and complete that the kingdom holds nothing to compare with it; even in Spain, save for the royal collections, there is no library like it'. Later bishops added their own books to it. In 1836, it counted 12,536 volumes, mostly in Latin, but also numerous works in Spanish, French, Italian, Japanese, and indigenous tongues. The sumptuous entrance portal and the retable which adorns the reading room date from Bp Fabián's refurbishment.

Since 1974–76 the Colegio de San Juan and the Colegio de San Pedro have been restored as the *Casa de Cultura*, for art exhibitions, craft classes, cultural events, and the State tourist office.

Behind the NE corner of the cathedral, at the corner of C. 2 Sur and Av. 3 Oriente, is the house known as **Casa del que mató el animal** (house of him who killed the animal), with its surviving Renaissance portal (late 16C), its jambs and lintel crowded with fascinating relief, evocative of late 15C French or Flemish tapestry. In each of the bases, three rosettes; in the jambs, hunting scenes, the huntsmen holding dogs (after rabbits) on leashes; in the capitals, birds pecking at plants; in the lintel, a pomegranate frieze.

Calle Cinco de Mayo

C. 5 de Mayo runs NW from the NW corner of Pl. de Armas. In the first turning l., Av. 2 Oriente, No. 3 is the Renaissance portal of the **Alhóndiga**, established in 1626.

Above the window, the city's coat-of-arms in relief. The public grain store to which it belonged, rebuilt in the 1770s, became in 1824 the State congress, where on 26 Dec. 1832 Manuel Gómez Pedraza was sworn in as president. On 7 June 1864 a ball was held here in honour of Maximilian and Carlota. It was demolished in 1899, but the portal has survived further changes to the site.

At the corner of C. 5 de Mayo and Av. 4 Poniente (l.) is the early 18C house built for Juan de San Martín Valdés (d. 1749), mayor of the city in 1740–42, displaying his coat-of-arms above the doorway. Next on the l. is the church, and what remains of the convent, of **Sto Domingo**, a foundation almost as old as the city.

In 1533 the first bp of Tlaxcala, the Dominican Julián Garcés, granted the Dominicans two blocks for their convent, originally called *San Miguel*. The present church, begun in 1571, was finished in 1611, mainly the work of Juan de Rivas and Pedro López Florín. Thomas Gage stayed in the convent in Sept. 1625, and was impressed by its wealth, and the many convents of friars and nuns—'an idle kind of Beggars', he called them.

Only a part (recently restored) of the original enormous ATRIO survives, entered through the one remaining gateway (early 17C), a handsome construction, Mannerist in style, its interior covered in 18C tile decoration. To the r., at right-angles to the church, is the portería of the late 16C convent, the arches filled in; the upper wall facing covered in rich 17C mortar relief. On the l. may be seen the beautiful multicoloured cupola of the Cap. del Rosario (see below), divided by ribs of polychrome tile; over each window a statue of an enamelled blond angel wearing a blue sash.

The church façade, in grey stone, with an alabaster relief of St Dominic in the gable, is one of the finest examples of Mannerism in Mexico. The tower dates from 1801. The stucco relief (c 1632) which covers the INTERIOR vaulting, by Pedro García Durango and Francisco Gutiérrez, is the starting-point of a style developed throughout the century in the Puebla area. Each transept contains one rich baroque and one churrigueresque altarpiece, the latter beautifully cut and full of rococo motifs, and high on the r. (N) wall is a painting of the Death of St Dominic attr. Alonso López de Herrera. The high altarpiece, though spoiled by repainting in 1947–48, is a superb essay in early baroque, influenced by Renaissance example.

The columns are of different types, solomonic in the lowest storey, covered in relief and approaching the baluster in the first and second. In the top storey the supports are interrupted by angel atlantes. In the centre panel the statues are of SS Dominic and Francis; above them, a lovely relief of Christ and Our Lady in majesty receiving the two saints, overlooked by God the Father and the Holy Ghost. The whole, by Pedro Maldonado, dates from 1688–90, and probably uses the statues, by Lucas Méndez, from an early 17C predecessor. The exquisite pulpit (16C in style) is of creamy alabaster, inlaid with black stone and mother of pearl. The side chapel of Our Lady of Guadalupe contains two traditional likenesses of the Virgin and a St Nicholas, all by Juan Correa.

Entered from the S (l.) transept, through a gilded classical portal, is the **Cap. del Rosario**, one of the overwhelming achievements of luxurious Mexican baroque, the very height of the poblano stuccoist's art.

It was raised in 1650–90, described at its inauguration as 'the eighth wonder of the world'. The decoration, begun by Francisco Gutiérrez, seems to have continued into the 1730s.

The INTERIOR is best seen in the afternoon when light floods in through the dome and transept windows. Walls, arches, vaults, pendentives, drum, and dome are engulfed in a thrusting jungle of stucco ornament, covered with gold leaf and polychrome—saints, angels, cherubs, fruit, vines, and all-pervading strapwork. In the three vaults of the nave are oval reliefs representing Faith, Hope, and Charity. In the eight divisions of the dome are female images: Divine Grace (facing the nave) and the Seven Gifts of the Holy Ghost—Wisdom, Understanding, Counsel, Fortitude, Knowledge, Piety, and Fear of the Lord. At the summit appears the Holy Ghost. In the drum stand 16 female martyr saints; in the transepts, the four evangelists; and, flanking the side windows, SS Anne and Joachim and Elizabeth and Joseph. The dado is of coloured tiles, covered by a frieze of cherub heads and the fleur-de-lis Dominican symbol. The central baldachin, which shelters the statue of Our Lady of the Rosary, is by Francisco Martín Pinto (though later altered, not for the best): columns of tecali alabaster (later substitutions) in the lower storey, gilded solomonic columns in the upper, where dancing angels heighten its evanescent effect as it soars up to a finial statue of St Gabriel. A delightful angelic orchestra plays in the small choir vault. At the far (S) end are two lovely reliefs: Birth of Our Lady and Presentation of Our Lady in the Temple, which combine a gentle modesty with a baroque need for effect.

Note, in the first, the contrast between the maids on the r. with the baby and the heavenly musicians above.
    Lining the walls is a series of nine paintings of scenes from the life of Our Lady by José Rodríguez de Carnero, sombre in the nave, luminous in the transepts.
    To the E of the chapel, and gained from the S door of the church, is the *Cap. de la Tercera Orden* (mainly 17C). With its entrance in Av. 4 Poniente is another chapel, *Cap. de los Mixtecos* (1696), built for Indians from the Mixteca.

Just beyond Sto Domingo, at 409 C. 5 de Mayo, are the **Galerías Pintoricas y Museo José Luis Bello** (Tues.–Sun., 10–5), an art collection brought together by José Luis Bello y Zetina, grandson of José Luis Bello y González (see below). The house is an adaptation of part of the convent.

The various rooms contain interesting 19C furniture (some of it from England), French and Bavarian porcelain, Baccarat glass. The paintings include works by European and Mexican masters. Luis de Morales (1510–86), Crucifixion. Murillo, St Francis. Zurbarán (?), St Peter. El Greco (?), Elias the prophet. Diego de Borgraf, Death of St Francis Xavier. Juan Tinoco, St Mark; Isaiah. Cabrera, St Joseph and the infant Christ. Manuel Caro (1751–1820), St Luis Gonzaga. José Luis Rodríguez Alconedo, idealistic portrait of Francisco Pizarro, conqueror of Peru.

Next door opens the *Mercado La Victoria* (1912). Av. 6 Oriente, one of the most attractive streets in Puebla (and full of sweetshops), runs E to (r.; on the corner with C. 2 Norte) the buttressed church of **Sta Clara** (1714), formerly part of a convent of urbanist Poor Clares, founded in 1607, closed and sold off during the Reform.

The nuns were famed for their confectionery, especially the camotes de Sta Clara, still sold in this street. Empress Carlota is said to have been very fond of them and in lucid moments during her mad old age in Belgium would beg anyone going to Mexico to bring her back some.

Opposite (No. 206 Av. 6 Oriente) is the **Museo Regional de la Revolución Mexicana** (Tues.–Sun., 10–4; fee), the house of Aquiles Serdán.

Aquiles Serdán Alatriste (b. 1876), president of the pro-Madero Anti-Re-election Club in Puebla, soon drew the hostile attention of the State authorities, especially after his meetings in the USA with Mexican exiles planning an insurrection to begin on 20 Nov. 1910. On 18 Nov. he shot dead the chief of police leading a search party into the house. 400 troops and a hundred police then laid siege, the family and friends within (18 men, incl. Aquiles and his brother Máximo, and three women—his wife, his mother, and his sister Carmen) responding with gunfire, and Carmen Serdán appearing on the balcony, rifle in hand, in an attempt to harangue the onlookers, too cowed to move. Máximo was mortally wounded and Aquiles eventually killed when his hiding-place in a cellar was discovered. Bullet marks may still be seen outside and in. The museum contains an interesting archive of photographs illustrating the career of Aquiles Serdán and the battles of the Revolution. A votive lamp burns above Aquiles' hiding-place.

Further along the street on the l. (corner with C. 4 Norte) is the church of **San Cristóbal**, its façade facing E.

It was built in 1676–87, possibly to the design of Carlos García Durango, to accompany a home for foundlings, established in 1604. During the early 18C it was the custom to parade the children in public to show how well they were looked after and in hope of attracting adoptive parents. In 1846–75 the popular Sisters of Charity were in charge. The orphanage still exists next to the church, which lost its towers in 1856 when conservative forces besieged the city.

EXTERIOR. The façade, in grey basalt, is admirably compact, with more than an echo of Mannerism, full of vigorous relief. The arch key is two children, symbolizing the church's function. On either side, two pairs of sturdy columns, with wavy fluting (a very early use) and Corinthian capitals, uphold a jutting cornice, above which rise four plinths; on the inner pair stand angels holding shields. The central marble relief is of St John writing the Apocalypse, accompanied by appropriate symbols. The side portal is more firmly Mannerist.

The INTERIOR has not lost its sumptuous covering of stucco relief (interspersed in the cupola with polychrome saints in high relief). It contains the finest work of José Villegas Cora and José Zacarías Cora (uncle and nephew; 18C), incl. SS Anne and Joachim (high altar), by the former, and St Christopher (r. of main door) by the latter. The pulpit, fixed to the wall without floor support, is of clear greenish alabaster.

From the NE corner of Mercado Victoria, Av. 8 Oriente leads one block to cross C. 2 Norte. Just N of the crossing is the church of *Sta Teresa* (1608–26), built for a convent of discalced Carmelite nuns.
    To the l., along Av. 10 Poniente (corner with C. 5 Norte), surrounded by an atrio, is the church of **La Merced** (1659; much altered in the early 19C), once the church of the Mercedarians.

On the N side of the atrio survives the baroque convent frontage, decorated with mortar relief. The church façade is handsomely Mannerist. In the lower storey, statues of SS Cosmas and Damian; in the upper, the founders SS Peter Nolasco and Raymond of Peñafort. The central relief shows Our Lady of Ransom with the latter two saints.

At the next crossing on C. 5 de Mayo, the house at the NW corner with Av. 12 Poniente is the *Casa de Gavito* (early 19C) built for Juan Manuel Gavito Rubio, regidor in 1815. We turn l. along Av. 12 Poniente, to C. 3 Norte and the church and former convent of **Sta Rosa**, which has a special fame.

Originating c 1670 as a place of retreat for female Dominican tertiaries, Sta Rosa achieved convent status in 1740 when the church seems to have been dedicated. The convent was finished c 1748. The story goes that on a day in the early 1680s viceroy conde de Paredes and marqués de la Laguna and Bp Fernández de Sta Cruz visited the community in their previous house (a little S along the same street). The cook, Sor Andrea de la Asunción, on this occasion excelled herself and invented, on a base of chillies, chocolate, and almonds, the famous mole poblano sauce. In 1869, after the Reform, the convent became a lunatic asylum. In 1926 the kitchen was converted to its present use.

Chief interest of the typical church, with its twin portals, is the spacious coro alto, covered in oil paintings, the Assumption in the vault probably by José Joaquín Magón, and containing a mid-18C altarpiece. The restored convent, with two peaceful cloisters, the main covered in tiles, the second whitewashed, houses a **Museo de Artesanías** (Tues.–Sun., 10–5; fee) and includes the marvellous kitchen resplendent with coloured tiles where the nuns elaborated their variations of the mole poblano. C. 5 de Mayo continues N. At the corner with Av. 16 Oriente, enclosed in an atrio, is the ample church of **San Juan de Dios** (1667–81), formerly belonging to the hospital of the Brothers of St John of God.

The façade relief shows the saint washing Christ's feet. The interior preserves good pendentive reliefs and an outstanding late churrigueresque high altarpiece (1775), full of rococo motifs, which has lost its original gilding and has an ivory-like quality. In the central panel, a noble polychrome St John. In 1867 the hospital, on the N side of the church, became the public gaol.

Opposite in C. 5 de Mayo are the church and former convent of **Sta Mónica**. The latter's strange history has given it a singular fame.

It originates in a misguided foundation of 1606 for noble married ladies whose husbands were away on business. The intended occupants, however, preferred to stay at home, so in 1609 it became a compulsory house of correction for prostitutes. In the late 17C the latter were moved to other premises and a college for girls, 'virgins, noble, virtuous, and poor', established, and rebuilt in 1680. In 1688 it was transformed into a convent for Augustinian nuns. The church was dedicated in 1751. The nuns were expelled at the Reform and the convent was turned into a factory for the manufacture of gas (from pine resin) for street lighting. But they secretly returned and continued their sequestered life known only to devout supporters. In 1934 they were denounced to the authorities, who turned the premises into a museum, enriched by works of art from Sta Catarina and Las Capuchinas.

The INTERIOR has kept the COROS ALTO and BAJO with their screens and cratícula, larger than usual, at the side of the coro bajo. Covered in azulejos on the wall of the coro alto is a niche containing the heart of Bp Fernández de Sta Cruz. His portrait, by Juan Tinoco, hangs on the end wall. From the coro bajo we may view the crypt, with an ossuary in the corner which did not suffice; by the grille is another, with tile inscription: 'In this place are buried the bones of the dead religious of this Convent, who did not fit in the ossuary. August 1st 837'.

Entrance (not the old convent entrance) to the **Museo de Arte Religioso** (Tues.–Sun., 10–5; fee) is at No. 203 Av. 18 Poniente. The rooms through which the tour passes have been much altered since the 18C. The so-called prioress's office is followed by three rooms containing ornaments, needlework, chaplets (for ceremonial occasions), banners, cult objects, etc. The PICTURE GALLERY is hung with paintings, incl. an Annunciation and Presentation of Our Lord in the Temple by Juan Correa; the rest mainly 18C and of varying quality, by poblano artists. After a group of cells we reach the long, narrow CAP. DOMESTICA, where a cross, a crown of thorns, and a rope against each seat are a reminder of penances undergone by the community; lining the walls are paintings by Juan de Villalobos and Antonio de Espinosa (late 17C). In the sacristy are fine lace and embroidery. From here we gain access to the coro alto and coro bajo (see above), whence a series of dark lower rooms is gained. Next, a small flower-filled patio, a tiled kitchen, and, up a staircase, the upper walk of the beautiful main cloister, its walls and arches faced with glazed and unglazed tiles, the patio filled with fruit trees, flowers, and shrubs. Various rooms opening off the cloister contain the most important works of art, and wooden boxes, chests, coffers, etc., which held the nuns' personal possessions; porcelain; lacquerwork; trinkets; drinking cups; etc. Among the sculpture are an enchanting relief of St Paschal Baylon in ecstasy in his well-equipped kitchen, while angels keep an eye on his cooking-pot and bean stew; a St Anne with Our Lady and the infant Christ, traditionally attr. Juan Martínez Montañés; an anon. St Joseph, showing fine estofado; pieces by José Villegas Cora.

Diagonally opposite Sta Mónica, in the block bounded by C. 5 de Mayo, Avs 18 and 20 Oriente, and PL. DE SAN JOSE, is the parish church of **San José**, an assembly of main church and various chapels raised above street level, 'so imposing', in the opinion of Manuel Toussaint, 'that it almost appears like a small cathedral'.

The first church on the site, completed in 1595, still exists, as a lobby chapel to its successor, begun c 1628. Nave and presbytery were completed by 1653. Side aisles and vaults were finished by 1693. The Cap. de Jesús (S side of church) was built in 1693–1706, the masterwork of Diego de la Sierra. The chapels on the N side are *Sta Ana* (c 1780), *Los Naturales* (1827), and *Divino Preso* (17C; once called *Cañón Dorado* or *Jesús Nazareno*).

EXTERIOR. The walls are faced in red tile. To the l. rises the lovely cupola of the *Cap. de Jesús*, covered in light blue, yellow, and orange tiles, the dome surrounded by a balustrade with elaborate corner finials. Facing E, the church façade is in simple enough baroque, but rendered sparingly delightful by the blue and gold tiles which cover the lower-storey columns and upper-storey pilasters, which flank a relief of the Virgin and Child.

INTERIOR. In the portico are two huge canvases: Crucifixion and Descent from the Cross, by Pascual Pérez. To the l. opens the large *Cap. de Jesús*, its interior recalling an early 17C style; the transept columns, the middle parts showing zigzag fluting, the upper and lower intricate relief, are masterfully conceived and cut. In its sacristy is a Way of the Cross attended by priests, by José Rubí de Marimón.

The side aisles are crowded with one baroque and six churrigueresque altarpieces; the two churrigueresque which close the aisles contain paintings (Our Lady with SS Anne and Joachim, and Flight into Egypt) by Diego de Borgraf. The Sacristy, perhaps the most beautiful in Puebla, is grandly furnished and contains four large anon. 17C paintings of scenes from the childhood of Christ.

A continuation along Av. 18 Poniente from Sta Mónica and then up C. 3 Norte leads to Plazuela de los Mártires de Tacubaya and the church of **San Antonio**.

It was founded, as *Sta Bárbara*, in 1591 for discalced Franciscans (dieguinos), the friars taking over a small Franciscan house established in the early 1580s. One of the first novices of the new foundation was Felipe de las Casas (see Rte 7), who soon gave up his vocation. The present church and cloister date from an 18C rebuilding or modernization, during which was discovered the little 16C chapel of Sta Bárbara, incorporated as a camarín in the apse. The convent garden, on the E side, was converted into the *Panteón de San Antonio* (1854–80), its main portal designed by José Manzo.

The church façade, attractively covered in glazed and unglazed tiles, is pierced by a strongly classical portal panel, probably a survival of the early 17C church, with a sweetly engaging alabaster relief of St Barbara. The baptismal font is a jewel of the poblano tileworker's art.

From here we may reach the corner of C. 5 Norte and Av. 30 Poniente, which brings us to the church of *Nuestra Señora del Refugio* (1747–52), in the old barrio of *Las Caleras*, once known for its lime kilns (hornos de cal).

Avenida de La Reforma

Going W on Av. de la Reforma from Pl. de Armas, we come to (r.) the church of **La Santísima Trinidad**.

It belonged to a convent of Conceptionist nuns established here in 1619 for 14 female first cousins of the Rivera Barrientos family, under the tutelage of two (already professed) aunts. The church was inaugurated in 1673; the classical main portal (1670–72) is the work of the mestizo masons, father and son, Juan and Juan Antonio Jerónimo. In 1931 it was refaced in stone, which gives the exterior a frigid quality.

The INTERIOR has suffered the inevitable 19C regularization. Its outstanding feature is the roomy choir, although the coro bajo grille and dividing wall have been torn out in modern times to lengthen the nave. Along its E wall is a painting of the Last Supper and Washing of the Feet (1720) by Manuel Marimón. Still, most happily, surviving is the CORO ALTO, with its great grille and abanico, the latter the oldest surviving and one of the finest in Mexico: in gilded wood with white fillets; its strapwork pattern is Renaissance-inspired, yet treated with baroque freedom; in the centre shines a bounteous sun, above it the arms of Bp Diego Osorio Escobar y Llamas, benefactor of the convent. In the sacristy is a St Leocadia by Diego de Borgraf and Scenes from the life of Bl. Beatrice da Silva, the Portuguese founder of the Conceptionist Order, by Rubí de Marimón (1722).

No. 315 Av. de la Reforma was already known c 1760 as *Casa de Temazcal* (public bath house).

From Santísima Trinidad C. 3 Norte leads to the church of **Sta Catarina** (l.: corner with Av. 2 Poniente), typically simple and austere, formerly belonging to the earliest nuns' convent (Dominican rule) in the city, founded probably in the 1550s and established in 1603. The present church, begun c the mid-17C, was not finished off until 1750, when the cupola and the richly tiled tower, with a Mudéjar touch, were completed. The dark interior preserves five baroque, and one churrigueresque, altarpieces.

At the W corner of the block (Av. 2 Poniente and C. 5 Norte) is the *Methodist Church* (1923).

C. 3 Sur leads to the **Museo de Arte José Luis Bello y González** (r.; corner with Av. 3 Poniente; Tues.–Sun., 10–5; fee).

This collection, begun by José Luis Bello y González (1822–1907), native of Veracruz who later became a textile magnate in Puebla, was bequeathed equally among his four sons, two of whom, Rodolfo and José Mariano (1869–1938), assiduously added to their shares. The house belonged to José Mariano who, on his death, left his combined collection to the Academy of Fine Arts of Puebla. The exhibits occupy 14 rooms and connecting passages (interesting 19C stained glass).
     GROUND FLOOR. The walls of the first, *Salón rojo*, are hung in red tapestry; in one corner, a niche of Puebla-ware glazed tiles. 19C furniture inlaid with bone and ivory. *Sala Agustin Arrieta*. Four still lifes and The Beggars by Arrieta (1802–74). 17–18C chests. *Sala de Cobres*. Mexican and Spanish copper kitchenware (18–19C). 19C painted Mexican crockery. *Sala de Calamines*. 19C ornamental pieces made of calamine. The painting, Christ presiding at a love feast, is a fair example of the work of the academic artist Gonzalo Carrasco (1860–1936), who later became a Jesuit. The *Sala de Talaveras* contains a comprehensive collection of resplendent 17C talavera ware, incl. a retable of St Paschal Baylon in his kitchen and a superb fireplace, on which stands a retable of the Crucifixion.
     FIRST FLOOR. *Sala de Marfiles*. Superb collection of 17–18C ivories from the Philippines (triptych of the Holy Family), China, Japan, Europe. There follow interesting 16–19C pieces of wrought iron—Spanish stirrups; Mexican, Spanish, and Arab spurs; intricately wrought locks and keys. *Sala de Porcelanas Chinas*. Chinese porcelain, enamels, and watercolours on rice paper. The *Sala de Cristales*, entered through a Baccarat glass door, contains good collections of cut glass and Sèvres, Limoges, and Meissen porcelain. There follows the *Sala de Ornamentos Religiosos*, with rich vestments and church plate, mostly of local 17–18C make. In the *Sala de Música* the musical instruments include a rare early 19C upright piano and monumental 18C Mexican organ. On the walls of the *Pinacoteca* are paintings (St Francis, Two Urchins) attr. Murillo, and 19C Mexican and Italian works.

Further along Av. 3 Poniente (l.) in a small atrio is the church of **San Agustín** (1612–29), part of the Augustinian convent built towards the end of the 16C.

The buildings were badly damaged during 19C military action, especially the siege of 1863; and the church was rebuilt in 1870. Immediately to its S the remains of the cloister are enveloped in later dwellings.
     In the severe classical façade, fashioned by the stonecutter Antonio Alonso, is a relief of the Vision of St Augustine, flanked by statues of SS Monica and John of Sahagún; below, SS Nicholas of Tolentino and William of Toulouse. The interior lacks interest, except for two paintings: Juan Tinoco, St Rosalia; José Joaquín Magón, Our Lady of Light (delightful rendering of the donor).
     The house in Av. 3 Poniente on the N side of the church, popularly known as the *Casa de las Cabecitas*, preserves its late 16C plateresque doorway, flat-arched, with five voussoirs, pearls of Castile in the imposts, and two medallions showing the heads of the original owners.

From here we may regain Av. de la Reforma (one block N) and turn l. The block between Cs 7 and 9 Norte is occupied by the main and ancillary parts of the building once known as the **Hospicio**.

It began in 1622 as the *Colegio de San Ildefonso*, founded by Bp Alonso de la Mota y Escobar as a centre for higher learning, and placed in the care of the Jesuits. In 1609 they bought four houses in the block opposite (between Cs 7 and 9 Sur) to found another college (in 1701), for philosophy and theology students, called *San Ignacio*, in 1790 merged with the Colegio Carolino (see below). After 1767 the San Ildefonso premises were altered to accommodate the *Hospicio de Pobres*, an asylum for the poor, later destined for military use during the siege of 1863. In 1894 the present façade was built. The present incumbent is the *Beneficencia Pública del Estado*, housing various good offices of State welfare.

Sandwiched between it and San Marcos is the 17C church of *San Ildefonso*. Opposite the Hospicio is the *Pal. de Gobierno* (c 1900), an elegant greyish-blue-faced building.

At the corner of Av. de la Reforma and C. 9 Norte is the church of **San Marcos** (1675), its façade quaintly redone in 1797 in an overall tile pattern interspersed with polychrome panels of saints. The tower is dated 1836.

From San Marcos we may go up C. 9 Norte. Turning r. along Av. 4 Poniente we come (r.) to the *Cap. de los Dolores* (1723–38), with a popular baroque façade (lively relief). At the corner of Av. 4 Poniente and C. 7 Norte is the church of *Belén* (1692–1700), formerly belonging to the Bethlemites (comp. Rte 8). The classical portal (by José Joaquín de Torres) was added in 1797; the delightful relief, of tecali alabaster, of the Nativity in the atrio is 17C work. Further up C. 9 Norte, beyond Av. 8 Poniente (r.), is the 18C *Cap. de San Ramón*, containing an Immaculate Conception by Luis Berrueco and, in the presbytery, an anon. 18C Our Lady and the Child Jesus with saints.

In Av. 10 Poniente (r.) No. 710, on the N side, was the china factory (locería) of the Zayas family from the 17C—relief above the door; in the 19C it was the most important in the city.

On the l. beyond Av. 10 Poniente is the church of *El Sagrado Corazón de Jesús* (1854–60), built at the urging of the Mercedarian friar José María Huerca to accompany a new convent of Mercedarian nuns (now the police academy). Undaunted by the general instability and military occupation, he went ahead with the companion church on the S side, *Sagrado Corazón de María* (1860–66), now swallowed up by workshops attached to the academy. The first contains the tomb of Governor Miguel Cástulo Alatriste, shot by the conservatives in 1862, grandfather of Aquiles Serdán.

To the r., No. 708 Av. 12 Poniente is the former *Locería de Cabezas*, a typical two-storey house faced with azulejos, the china factory founded by Juan Cabezas in the 1780s.

From here we may reach two more churches in the NE part of the city: *San Pablo de los Frailes* (1678), once attached to a hospital for Indians run by the Dominicans, secularized in 1880 to serve as a railway workshop (Av. 18 Poniente; l.); and *Sta Ana* (1681; restored after fire damage in 1898), at the corner of Av. 26 Poniente and C. 13 Norte.

Going W along Av. 10 Poniente we come to JARDIN JUAREZ, on the E side of which is the church of *El Señor de los Trabajos*, formerly known as *San Pablo de los Naturales*, founded c 1550, rebuilt since then, and altered in the 19C, known for an early 17C painting of Christ carrying the Cross, now on the high altar. Av. 10 Poniente skirts the area to the N occupied by the terminus of the *Ferrocarril Mexicano*, the railway station of the line to Mexico City inaugurated by Pres. Juárez on 16 Sept. 1869. The simple pink-faced station, classically inspired, may be seen on the W side of the Jardín. Beyond, at the corner with C. 17 Norte, is the church of *San Miguel*, an outlying barrio chapel dating from the late 16C, but much altered.

Beyond San Marcos, Av. de la Reforma reaches the N side of PASEO BRAVO, a park bounded on W and E by Cs 13 and 11 Sur and on the S by Av. 11 Poniente; projected in the 1830s; and laid out and extended throughout the 19C. Facing it in Av. de la Reforma is the church of **Nuestra Señora de Guadalupe** (1694–1722), its FAÇADE stating a contrast between the Mannerism of the central portal panel and the delightful play of tiles surrounding it. Within the high arch the tiles run in zigzag bands, orange, blue, green, yellow, and white; in the spandrels are tile angels. In the tower bases are panels relating the legend of Our Lady of Guadalupe, while the towers themselves, slender and elegant, combine baroque solomonic columns with classical pediments. The side chapel cupola is particularly striking, covered in dense relief, the dome divided into segments.

The INTERIOR was tastelessly redecorated in 1922. Only the side chapel (*San Antonio*) preserves its original stucco work. This is densely done, abounding in floral motifs. Especially enjoyable are the archangels in the pendentives (lamps once hanging from their outstretched arms), the figures between the windows of the cupola drum, and the angels in the spandrels of the basket choir arch.

At the NW corner of the Paseo is the former church of *San Javier* (1743–51), once accompanying a Jesuit college for the instruction of Indian boys, adapted and enlarged from 1844 as the penitentiary, largely destroyed in 1863, and rebuilt in 1891 under Eduardo Tamariz.

Two blocks W of the Paseo, in C. 17 Sur, is the church of *San Sebastián*, centre of an Augustinian parish from 1546 and still in the care of that Order; heartsinkingly rebuilt in the 1940s. S of the Paseo, in C. 15 Sur, between Avs 17 and 19 Poniente, is *Santiago* (1644; restored early this century), in a pleasant atrio whose entrance gate, now isolated with the demolition of the atrio wall in 1917, dates from 1689.

Calle 16 de Septiembre

From the SW corner of Pl. de Armas, C. 16 de Septiembre runs S, the Cathedral on the l. No. 125 C. 5 Poniente (r.) is the so-called **Casa de las Cigüeñas** (house of storks; 1687), after the relief above the doorway, built for Juan de las Peñas and his wife, Magdalena de Mora y Medrano.

The first block of this street was the old *Calle del Correo Viejo*, the first post office in the city (founded in 1580) functioning here until 1822 in the second house on the S side (unbelievably destroyed). At the corner with C. 3 Sur is the house of Juan de Zárate y Vera (alcalde in 1769–70).

No. 505 C. 16 de Septiembre (r.) is the **Casa del Deán** (1580), the oldest surviving house in the city.

It was built for the dean of the cathedral, Tomás de la Plaza, third to hold the office (1564–89), and remained the property of the descendants of his niece, María Izguerra, until the 20C (the Pérez Salazar family).

Pure Renaissance classicism marks the portal, above which is the inscription PLACA DECANUS. The interior (Sun., Wed.–Sat., 10–5; fee) contains two rooms of murals on a secular theme, unique in Mexico: the Triumphs of Petrarch, complete with sibyls, curvetting steeds, detailed landscape (little forests, villages, ships on lakes), and friezes of grotesques.

On the corner of C. 16 de Septiembre and Av. 7 Poniente is the church of **La Concepción**, in its exterior a typical buttressed nuns' church (1617–1732), part of a convent for Conceptionist nuns founded in 1596. The INTERIOR, single-nave without transepts, still preserves the coros alto and bajo, their two vaults noticeably larger than those of the nave. The coro bajo grille is formed by circles joined at their tangental points. On one side, the cratícula, and, between it and the grille, a little revolving cupboard, its curved sides covered in azulejos, through which petitions could be passed to the nuns from the outside world. The coro alto grille is divided into three sections by columns. Above is the abanico, its effect spoiled by a poor painting fitted into it during the 19C. The interior contains a series of superb churrigueresque retables and a painting by Juan de Villalobos of Our Lady protecting the Conceptionist Order. At the NE corner with C. 3 Sur is the house once belonging to Nicolás Ramírez de Arellano (c 1768).

Turning l. along Av. 7 Oriente, past the Colegio de San Pablo (see above), we come, at the corner with C. 2 Sur, to the church of *El Hospitalito* (rebuilt 1707–21). Above the portal, the coat-of-arms of Pope Innocent XIII. No. 708 C. 2 Sur is the much rebuilt former **Hospital de San Juan de Letrán**.

Founded in the 1530s, in the 1640s it was converted by Palafox into a *Colegio de Niñas Virgenes*; and from the 18C included a *Colegio de San José de Gracia* (for married women). Its further conversion, by Pedro Ramírez Vázquez, as the **Museo Amparo** (Wed.–Mon., 10–5; fee), was completed in 1991.

It is named after Amparo Rugarcía (1911–75), wife of the poblano banker Manuel Espinosa Yglesias. The museum, superbly arranged, displays representative pieces from Mexico's prehistoric, viceregal, and republican past, and the present day.

GROUND FLOOR. Mural, 'Hacia un nuevo humanismo' (1990), by Pedro Diego Alvarado, grandson of Diego Rivera, and Rivera's own portrait of Amparo Rugarcía (1952). Collection of replicas of cave art and rock paintings from Europe, Oceania, and America.

UPPER FLOOR. The ancient Mesoamerican displays comprise seven interconnecting rooms. The displays are thematically and geographically arranged to show four distinct regions: Gulf Coast (Olmec, Totonac, and Huastec cultures); West Mexico; Isthmus of Tehuantepec and Maya regions; and Central Highlands (Toltecs, Aztecs, Zapotecs, Mixtecs). A chronological chart, with brief cultural references, serves to orient the visitor and help relate the various exhibits to one another.

Sculptures illustrate Maya art and their theocratic social organization, incl. blocks of architectural sculpture. Exquisite Maya ceramics. Cases and sculptures illustrating the Aztec migration into the Basin of Mexico. A room devoted to West Mexico has solid and glossy red hollow figurines of animals and people, wearing elaborate headdresses.

Copies of murals from Teotihuacán (c AD 400–650).

From the Gulf Coast are several smooth, carved Olmec figures with their typical half-closed eyes and pouting lips. Huastec bone collar (c AD 1200–1325) and carved Totonac yugo with skull and characteristic Totonac scrollwork (c AD 600–900). From the Isthmus, fragment of frieze from the Río Usumacinta zone (c AD 400–600). A Mixtec stone lintel is dated c AD 1000–1500.

Thematic displays include production techniques, with ceramic and stone figures and vessels from Classic Period Teotihuacán, Monte Albán, El Tajín, and Zacatenco. Various pieces, in cases or individually displayed, show modelling techniques and polychrome painting, eg, jaguar from Colima and conch from the Gulf Coast.

Jewellery and ornament include Olmec and Maya, Totonac, Zapotec, Mixtec, and Aztec pectorals, necklaces, earspools, and other items. Also masks from Teotihuacán, Oaxaca, and Guerrero.

Symbolism includes Classic Period Maya carved stucco heads, Aztec obsidian skulls, clay flutes, and ceramic figures of dancers. Display of skull deformation, with accompanying displays of tzompantlis.

The rooms devoted to the viceregal and later periods contain 17–18C Mexican, Guatemalan, Ecuadorian, and Peruvian painting and sculpture (incl. Diego de Borgraf, St Francis; Vallejo, Holy Family; 18C anon from Quito, SS Justin and Rufina; polychrome figures, especially from Querétaro), and furniture. 18C Mexican church silver. Ceramics and azulejos from Puebla. Paintings by Pedro Gualdi, Clausell, Landesio, and Dr Atl.

Further along Av. 7 Oriente (l.) is **San Jerónimo** (1635), once part of a convent of nuns (not, however, of the Jeronymite Order; comp. Rte 7) and a college (*Jesús María*), 'for the daughters of gentlemen and the most illustrious personages in the city', founded c 1613–17. The INTERIOR was thoroughly gone over in the mid-19C in neoclassical style, more successfully than usual; a change that left the magnificent frontage of the coros alto and bajo (W end) largely untouched. The grilles and abanico are composed of variations on the oval; the grille of the coro alto hides the original (17C). At either end of the cornice are busts of two of the convent's benefactors: Juan García Barranco, the founder, and José Carmona y Tamariz (d. 1677). Between them, angelic figures representing the nuns' four vows: poverty, obedience, chastity, and the enclosed life. In the centre, the sacrificial lamb. Above, in the abanico, an anon. 18C painting of Our Lady with six nuns and a novice.

A few steps further from San Jerónimo (corner of Av. 7 Oriente and C. 4 Sur) is the CALLEJON DE LOS SAPOS, an agreeable pedestrian precinct known for its stalls where are sold antiques, antiquarian books, and old newspapers and magazines. Proceedings are often accompanied by mariachi bands.

At the corner of C. 16 de Septiembre and Av. 9 Oriente are the church and former convent of **Las Capuchinas** (1703), founded for Capuchinesses from Mexico City. The elegant portal is a blend of Mannerist and baroque. In the niche, a statue of St Anne; below it, a relief of two crossed arms (Christ and St Francis), a Franciscan symbol. The INTERIOR keeps its deep coro alto, the small grille, studded with spikes, fixed into the wall. Above it, an anon. late 18C painting of the Holy Trinity. In the sacristy, Scenes from the Passion by Rubí de Marimón. The little convent cloister survives.

Opposite, Av. 9 Poniente leads to PL. DE LA CONCORDIA, faced by two important churches. On the E side is **La Concordia** (1670–76), built for the Oratorians to the design of Carlos García Durango, with its broad classical façade in dark granite lightened by white marble statues (SS Peter and Paul flanking the doorway; St Philip Neri, a late 19C addition, unsuitable in the deep window).

In the broad nave hang huge paintings of scenes from the life of St Philip Neri by Miguel Jerónimo Zendejas (late 18C); in the side chapels, four semicircular paintings (1693) by José Rodríguez de Carnero (SS Margaret, Barbara, and Joseph, and Sorrows of Our Lady) and three scenes from the life of St Philip attr. Pascual Pérez. The pulpit (late 17C) is a beautiful alabaster piece which escaped 19C neoclassical regularization. In the sacristy, Patronage of Our Lady, attr. Juan Tinoco, and portraits of Viceroy Bucareli with priests of the Oratory (1802) and Salvador Biempica y Sotomayor (bp of Puebla 1790–1802), by Manuel López Guerrero.

Adjoining the church is the *Casa de Ejercicios* (entrance in Avs 9 and 11 Poniente), established in the early 19C and badly damaged, like the church, in the siege of 1856. From the Av. 11 Poniente entrance may be gained the so-called *Patio de los Azulejos* (restored), the finest in Puebla, the noble architecture set off by great buttresses, the walls faced with coloured tiles, but in a style unusual for the city. The former Oratorian house (1677–99; restored), with its fine cloister (the work of Diego de la Sierra) to the S of the church, is now a primary school. It was in his office here that Joaquín Furlong (provost 1814–52) printed for Iturbide the Plan of Iguala (1821).

On the other side of the plaza is the church of **Sta Inés** (1663), formerly belonging to a convent of Dominican nuns founded in 1620. In the simple façade, an image of St Agnes in painted earthenware. The INTERIOR was refashioned in 1842 in the usual neoclassical style, though the coros alto and bajo were respected. In the abanico, Triumph of the Church by Antonio Padilla (c 1842; the church shown as a maiden clothed in pontificals); the paintings surrounding the coro bajo grille are also by him, as is the scene from the life of St Agnes (1848) in the presbytery.

C. 16 de Septiembre continues S for two blocks. To the l. along Av. 13 Oriente, at the corner with C. 2 Sur, is **La Soledad**, built for a convent of Carmelite nuns, finished in 1731, dedicated in 1749.

Outstanding features of the EXTERIOR are the beautiful cupola and tower, covered in black and white azulejos, and the beguiling relief of the classical façade. It shows Our Lady surrounded by happy little angels holding her attributes listed in the Litany of Loreto: above, Sun of Justice and Mirror of Justice; l., Gate of Heaven and Mother of Divine Grace (a fountain); r., Tower of Ivory and House of Gold. José Manzo's 19C modernization of the INTERIOR spared the four magnificent baroque altarpieces in the transepts, the two against the end walls among the largest, latest, and most elaborate examples of solomonic baroque that exist. Also spared are the tribunals on either side of the high altar and the original alabaster pulpit, with angel figures in the base—one crudely destroyed by the modern access stair. On either side of the entrance, two huge canvases (1748) by Pablo Joseph de Talavera commemorating the convent's foundation, and crammed with lively detail. The small sacristy preserves four early 18C retables.

On the r., in Av. 13 Poniente, is the chapel of **Los Gozos** (1736–45), its façade, in outline Mannerist-inspired, incorporating seven reliefs illustrating the Seven Joys of Our Lady. From lower l. upwards: Annunciation, Visitation, Adoration of the Kings; centre, above a relief of the Assumption, Nativity; from upper r., Finding of the Child Jesus in the Temple, Resurrection, Ascension.

Continuing along C. 16 de Septiembre we pass the church of *La Mansión* (l.; 1825–27) to arrive at PLAZUELA DEL CARMEN (officially *Jardín Cuauhtémoc*), with, on its S side, the church, chapels, and convent of **El Carmen**.

They belonged to the discalced Carmelite friars, established in Puebla in 1586 when they took possession of a small chapel and three houses on this site. The present buildings date from 1625–34. After the Reform the convent became a barracks; the last friars left in 1891.

The ATRIO is entered through a gateway, at the corner of C. 16 de Septiembre and Av. 17 Oriente, recomposed in recent times with azulejos, a glazed panel of Our Lady of Mount Carmel above. Shaded by cypresses, the atrio takes on a romantic atmosphere in half-light when the azulejos with which the façades,

Church of La Soledad, Puebla

walls, cupolas have been (more than once, and perhaps to excess) refaced assume softer hues.

Fronting the atrio on the l. are the façades of the Cap. de la Tercera Orden (with semi-hexagonal arch), one of three on the N side, and of the church proper (facing W), and, at right-angles to them (facing N), of the portería of the convent; above the doorway, in an elaborate stellar pattern, the symbol of the Carmelite order—the anchor signifying hope, the three stars, poverty, chastity, and obedience.

Among the many paintings which line the walls of church and chapels are Patronage of Our Lady of Mount Carmel (chapel, immediately l.) and Stigmatization of St Mary Magdalen dei Pazzi by Pascual Pérez; Holy Trinity by Cristóbal de Villalpando (nave, r.); a series of saints by the 18C poblano painter Mariano Morlete; and Martyrdom of St Anastasius by Juan Correa (nave; l.).

Avenida Maximino Avila Camacho

We go E along Av. Maximino Avila Camacho from the NE corner of Pl. de Armas. At the corner with C. 2 Norte is the former *Pal. de Gobierno*, now the *Tesorería Municipal*, large, eclectic, and porfirian. Next door on C. 2 Norte is the **Casa de los Muñecos**, its front faced with large tile human figures in grotesque poses against tile patterns in red, white, and blue.

It was built in the late 18C for the regidor and alcalde Agustín de Ovando y Villavicencio, who never lived in it, but rented it out. In 1792 it was described as 'two new houses, of three storeys, which he fashioned and completely rebuilt in the Calle de Mercaderes, looking towards the west'. According to the popular version the muñecos (dolls) satirize the aldermen (regidores) who objected to Ovando building his house higher than the (old) ayuntamiento. An academic view is that they represent figures from classical mythology (eg, Hercules on r. above portal) in the first storey and, in the second, the Tlaxcaltecans liberated from prehispanic terror and superstition.

No. 209 Av. Maximino Avila Camacho belonged (late 18C) to María Josefa de Mendívil, wife of Rafael Mangino (see Rte 1), and was a hotel from the mid-19C. In C. 4 Norte (l.; corner with Av. 2 Oriente) are the church and former hospital of **San Pedro**, one of the earliest foundations in the city.

The hospital was established probably in 1544–45, at first for male patients only, from the 1640s for females as well. In the late 19C the Sisters of Charity took it over. It was moved to other premises, in C. 13 Sur, in 1917. The church, dedicated in 1679, has a plain Renaissance-style façade. The hospital (being built in 1605; improved c 1685 by Diego de la Sierra; further transformed in the 18C) has survived better than most. It is now the *Pal. de Deporte*. In the centre, above the portal, beautifully framed, is a relief of the arms of the bishopric of Tlaxcala-Puebla—a jar containing lilies. The imposing two-storey patio shows bulbous columns.

To the r. the Avenida opens out into a small plaza with, on the E side, **La Compañía**, the most important 18C church in Puebla.

The Jesuits dedicated their first church, called *Espíritu Santo*, in 1600. Their second, designed by José Miguel de Santa María, was built in 1746–67 (the year of the Society's expulsion), except for the towers, concluded in 1804–12.

EXTERIOR. The wide façade, an exercise in studied grandeur, entered by five ample archways, covers an entrance portico and offers a fascinating mixture of styles: sober Renaissance (which keeps the whole within bounds), baroque, and rococo, with a hint of churrigueresque, covered in carefully applied, rich vegetal and strapwork relief—hallmark of the poblano style. Another singular feature is the ornamental brackets disposed throughout as capitals of the pilasters. The bases of the lower pilasters are decorated with lambrequin reliefs and angels with vegetal wings. Much movement is achieved in the centre panel: a curiously emphatic trefoil arch and, above it, the central window, its classical pilasters supported, as it were, by delicately elaborated relief patterns. In the lowest storeys of the towers are slight estípites. Note how, despite the cornices, the vertical lines of the pilasters continue into the towers. The dome (rather than cupola), another curiosity, is divided into four parts by moulding strips; the lines of the windows below give the appearance of a drum. The statues (SS Ignatius and Francis Xavier below SS Luis Gonzaga and John Berchmans) were added in 1899. Above the lower niches are reliefs of SS Peter and Paul.

The INTERIOR was modernized in the mid-19C and further unfortunate changes were made in 1926–31. But we may still admire the three entrance doorways from the inside, the central flanked by estípites mounted on sturdy pilasters, and the extraordinarily high arches of the nave supported by half-columns clustered round the pillars. The SACRISTY, occupying the width of the church, remains from the first foundation and is decorated with expert relief. Among the paintings are a huge Triumph of the Society of Jesus by José Rodríguez de Carnero and good examples of the work of Juan de Villalobos: St John the Baptist, St John the Evangelist, Holy Family, Our Lady with SS Anne and Joachim, Communion of St Luis Gonzaga.

In the ANTESACRISTY is the alabaster tombstone of Melchor de Covarrubias (d. 1592), buried in the old church, whose generous legacy enabled the Jesuits to build their church and college. Another tombstone, in the same material, commemorates Catarina de San Juan (1606–88; buried in the presbytery of the old church), a native of Delhi and of noble birth, snatched in childhood by Portuguese traders and brought as a servant to Acapulco and then to Puebla. She became a mystic and was regarded by the people as a saint, which occasioned a novena of sung Masses after her death and a biography in three volumes written by her confessor, the Jesuit Alonso Ramos. In 1691 the Inquisition, anxious to scotch growing veneration for her memory, banned it.

The remainder of the block encompassed by Cs 4 and 6 Sur and Avs Maximino Avila Camacho and 3 Oriente is occupied by the former Jesuit college, now part of the **Universidad Autónoma de Puebla**.

It was founded, as *Colegio de Espíritu Santo*, in 1578, and was to become the main Jesuit college in Puebla, for creole and Indian boys. In 1790 it became known as *Colegio Carolino* (after Charles III); from 1875 *Colegio del Estado* (with various later name changes reflecting the political climate); and in 1937 the University of Puebla was founded here. The present buildings, with two patios, the main one along dignified classical lines, date from the 18C. The part to the E of the church is occupied by the *Biblioteca Lafragua*, the college library founded by José María Lafragua (1813–75).

Opposite, in Av. 3 Oriente (No. 403), is the former **Colegio de San Jerónimo**, another Jesuit foundation, established in 1583 as a preparatory (Colegio de Estudios Menores) to the Colegio del Espíritu Santo, and in 1790 merged with the Colegio Carolino (see above). Its most illustrious pupil was Francisco Javier Clavijero. After 1790 its 18C buildings became a tobacco factory and then customs offices before (in 1905) being sold for conversion into dwellings. It is now part of the university.

Opposite the university building, at 406 Av. Maximino Avila Camacho, is the **Pinacoteca Universitaria**, a house once known as the *Casa de las Bóvedas* (house of vaults) and showing daring architectural novelties.

It was built in 1684–85 for the prebendary Diego Peláez Sánchez by Diego de la Sierra, altered in the 18C, and in 1813 became home to the *Academia de Primeras Letras y Dibujo*, later to become the *Academia de Educación y Bellas Artes*. Its collections and functions are now absorbed by the university.

Of outstanding interest are the beautiful windows, classically based but uniquely elaborated, of the first floor of the façade, and those of the first floor of the W side of the patio. The interior arcade is of unequal arches upheld by composite pillars and columns, in which, on the first floor, a zigzag pattern is all-pervasive, and forms arches to frame the vaulting. The staircase is plentifully decorated, and on its N side are three-lobed arches with floral relief in the spandrels and diamond shapes incised in supports and soffits.

Temporary art exhibitions are now mounted in the various rooms of the building. On the upper floor are exhibited paintings from the permanent collection. They include: José Juárez (after Rubens), Holy Family with St John the Baptist. 17C Dutch school, Christ and the Samaritan woman (attr. by some to Sebastián López de Arteaga). Diego de Borgraf, Immaculate Conception. Juan Tinoco, Apostolate, an ambitious and effective series of 12 paintings of the Apostles. Cristóbal de Villalpando, St Francis; St Ignatius. Pascual Pérez, Our Lady presenting the infant Christ to a tonsured saint. Luis Berrueco, St Rosalia. 17C Neapolitan school, St Sebastian (attr. by some to Guido Reni). José Luis Rodríguez Alconedo, Teresa Hernández Moro (1810); Self-portrait; Lady and child (three pastel drawings).

Beyond the university in Av. Maximino Avila Camacho is *San Roque* (1662–72; rebuilt after heavy damage in the siege of 1834), attached to the ample former mental hospital run by the Brothers of the Order of St Hippolytus, and still catering for demented women until well into the 19C.

Av. Maximino Avila Camacho continues E, across Blvd Héroes del 5 de Mayo, to COLONIA ANALCO, the barrio 'on the other side of the river' (San Francisco), originally for Indians from the Mixteca, in the early 17C augmented by Spanish and Tlaxcaltecan immigrants. On the E side of PL. DE ANALCO (between Avs 5 and 7 Oriente), in a spacious high atrio which gives good views of the city, is the church of **San Angel de Analco** (1618–19), still with remains of antique splendour, incl. its various cupolas, archangel reliefs in the principal pendentives, and wrought-iron baptistery (r.; 1780) and side chapel (l.; 1767) gates, despite inevitable 19C alteration and subsequent interior decoration. Among the paintings is a Death of St Francis Xavier by Diego de Borgraf. On the N side of the atrio, alongside Av. 5 Oriente, is the 18C chapel of *Sto Tomás*.

To the NE, prominent at the corner of Av. 2 Oriente and C. 14 Norte, is the church of **La Luz** (c 1730–1805), finished off in neoclassical style, with a handsome portal and pyramidal tower finials. Façade and tower bases are faced with unglazed tiles, interspersed with glazed panels showing images of saints. The INTERIOR, one of the better examples of neoclassical, contains a series of paintings of Scenes from the Life of Our Lady (1737) by Miguel de Mendoza.

Four blocks further E, and one S, on Av. Maximino Avila Camacho, is the chapel of **Sta Bárbara** (1789; recently restored), its picturesque exterior bristling with pinnacles and faced with azulejos, which also decorate the interior skirting. The little churrigueresque high altar is adorned with mirror motifs.

Along C. 20 Norte, running N from Av. Maximino Avila Camacho, is the chapel of *Los Remedios* (early 18C; with modern additions), with an interesting façade, a mixture of rustic Mannerism and baroque.

From San Roque C. 6 Norte runs N, passing the **Parián**, a handicrafts market (four lines of booths bordered by Avs 2 and 4 Oriente and Cs 6 and 8 Norte).

At the corner of Av. 4 Oriente and C. 8 Norte (l.) is the famous **Casa del Alfeñique** (c 1790), so-called for the delectable excesses of its upper window frames, parapet, and finials.

It is named after a speciality of 18C Puebla, alfeñique, a sweet made from almond paste and sugar, 'as fragile and translucent as porcelain'. It was built for the ironmaster Juan Ignacio Morales; the architect was probably Antonio de Sta María Incháurregui. In 1896 the then owner, Alejandro Ruiz Olavarrieta, gave it to the State of Puebla.

It now houses the **Museo Regional del Estado** (Tues.–Sun., 10–5), an interesting collection illustrating the history of city and State.

GROUND FLOOR. Prehispanic artefacts found locally. 16C codices painted on cotton fabric. 16C Spanish armour. Adaptation of the 16C royal banner of the city in a mother-of-pearl holder. 16C wooden crucifix. 16C manuscripts and armorial documents. Portrait of Bp Palafox. Historical documents include Mexico's Act of Independence signed by Iturbide on 28 Sept. 1821. Carriage of Bp Francisco Pablo Vázquez (1831–47). Carriage of Porfirio Díaz (1890).

UPPER FLOOR. Medals, photographs, portraits (the young Díaz; Ignacio Zaragoza) illustrating the 19C wars. 19C photographs of poblano types. 19C costumes. Penitential instruments used in the convents of Puebla. Portraits of Iturbide and Ana María Huarte. 17C wax miniature of St Peter by Javier Salinas. Jesús Romero, portraits of Mucio P. Martínez and Gen. Mariano Escobedo. Anon. 16–18C paintings. 19C costumbrista paintings. Anon. portrait of Manuel Maneyro (1807–86), Mexican consul in Rotterdam, Bordeaux, and Geneva. Portraits by Felipe S. Gutiérrez (Manuel Gómez Pedraza, the painter José Obregón).

Av. 4 Oriente is lined with particularly fine 18C houses, notably No. 408.

Opposite, C. 8 Norte, expanding at its N end into a plaza, becomes the **Barrio del Artista**, incl. some 40-odd picturesquely roofed booths, where local sculptors and painters exhibit and sell their works.

The booths here and to the S were set up c 1832, for the sale of second-hand clothes, and called *Parián de los Tornos*. They were attached to the textile factory owned by Francisco Puig, where were spinning wheels (tornos de hilar) on which his merchandise was turned out.

Further up C. 6 Norte we come (r.) to the handsomely restored **Teatro Principal**, facing a small plaza.

The sixth theatre in the city, it was built, to hold 1600 spectators, in 1759 and opened, as the *Coliseo* (or Coral de Comedias), in 1760. During the war of Independence it was temporarily

(1812–14) closed: 'for it would be an offence against God to stage plays in times such as these'; and the city's artillery was kept here. After its reopening, bullfights were held in it, but it became so run down that it had to be closed again for repairs (1817–20). In 1902 fire almost destroyed it. Rebuilding, and reinauguration in 1940, took place under Governor Maximino Avila Camacho. On the W side of the theatre, at 409 Av. 8 Oriente, is the *Casa del Alguacil Mayor*, a 16C house modified c 1700 for Pedro de Mendoza y Escalante, alguacil mayor (chief of police) from 1702, but preserving its 16C patio. Further W along Av. 8 Oriente, Nos 214–16 are the former *Mesón de Cristo*, a time-honoured inn established in the 16C, rebuilt in the 18C.

To the E of C. 8 Norte runs the broad BLVD HEROES DEL 5 DE MAYO, built over the Río San Francisco. To the N of the theatre, on Av. 10 Oriente, is the *Puente del 5 de Mayo* (1743–44; amplified in 1878), successor to the first bridge over the river (1555). On its N side is the *Cap. del Puente (Cap. de Nuestra Señora de los Dolores*; 1704), the interior redone in 1833.

The Eastern Quarters

On the other side of the boulevard we reach the church and former convent of **San Francisco**, the city's second (after Sto Domingo) great religious foundation. The alterations that time has wrought on it have in some ways added to its interest.

The Franciscans were established in the barrio known as El Alto to the E of the city by 1535. They had begun building in earnest by 1550, largely completing the church in 1567–70 and the convent, with a hospital attached, c 1585. The choir, by Francisco Becerra, dates from c 1575. Sacristy and antesacristy were finished in 1631 and the NE chapel c 1665; the tower was built in 1730–67; the present façade dates from 1743–67. The convent buildings, on the S side of the church, suffered after being converted into a military hospital and barracks after 1867.

EXTERIOR. The façade, designed by José Buitrago, is remarkable for the slender verticality of its grey stone portal panel, placed against a wall of unglazed orange-red tiles set between the oblique interior facings, also covered by tiles, of the corner buttresses and divided by bands of coloured azulejos. Set into the wall and facings are lovely rectangular compositions of azulejos: vases of flowers which blossom out to fill the whitish backgrounds. The three levels of the centre panel are marked by estípites of varying length and style, enclosing niches in which stand statues of saints. In the first storey, a relief of St Francis receiving the stigmata. Above the gable, a statue of St Michael. The N doorway, the oldest in Puebla, and also in three storeys, is an individual blend of plateresque and native styles: flat arch above the door and jambs covered in relief; first storey framed by lower and upper cornices and side pilasters also covered in relief; second storey composed of narrow triangular pediment enclosing the coat-of-arms of the bishopric of Tlaxcala, all within an alfíz formed by a top cornice and quaint twisted columns. At right-angles to the doorway, walled-up and barely recognizable, is the open chapel, with three bays and a stone pulpit still attached to one of the piers.

Now freed from its ponderous 19C additions, the enormous NAVE has recovered its pristine beauty. Original survivals are the ornamental plaster ribbing of the vaults and the beautiful late 18C choirstalls, their backings showing estípites and their seats and surrounds full of rococo motifs. In the chapel opening out to the l. of the presbytery, before the altar, is the tomb of Sebastián de Aparicio (1502–1600).

He became a lay brother here in 1574, was later beatified, and is closely connected with the building of the first roads in New Spain. He supervised waggon traffic between the capital and Veracruz, and opened the road to Zacatecas in 1542. He also astonished the Indians by yoking bullocks to wheeled vehicles. Above the tomb is a venerated image of Our Lady: La Conquistadora, lovable and homely, 42cm high, polychrome with estofado, probably 15C Flemish, already in the convent in 1582.

Nave and transept walls are lined with appealingly naive 18C anon. paintings of Bl. Sebastián's life, accompanied by verse narrative.

To the r. of the presbytery is the antesacristy, which contains a large painting of the spiritual lineage of St Francis (1731) by Cristóbal de Talavera and a Martyrdom of two saints by Luis Berrueco.

The church of San Francisco counted as the first station of a *Via Crucis*, planned in the 17C to commemorate the 14 stations of the Way of the Cross. The 2nd and 3rd stations (in and just outside the atrio) have disappeared. The 4th and 5th (*Los Finos Amantes* and *El Cirineo*) are by and opposite the N side of the atrio. The rest are spaced out along C. 12 Norte (*La Verónica*, *El Platero*, *Las Piadosas*; 6th, 7th, and 8th stations), ending in a precinct called *El Calvario* at the N end of the street alongside Calz. de los Fuertes, which contains the remaining six stations and another chapel, *Nuestra Señora de los Desamparados*; on the r. of the terrace are remains of a small house once reserved for retreats, incl. a fountain of azulejos, surrounded by an arcade.

On the E side of San Francisco, at the corner of C. 14 Norte and Av. 8 Oriente, is the chapel of *Sto Ecce Homo* (1742). Further NE, at the corner of C. 16 Norte and Av. 14 Oriente, is the church of *La Valvanera* (1763). The church of *La Misericordia* (1678; lately restored as *Nuestra Señora de Fátima*), at the corner of C. 18 Norte and Av. 24 Oriente, in fact two adjoining chapels, postdates an early chapel reserved for blind Indians. Two blocks E is the chapel called *Xonaca*, after a barrio founded in 1618 for Tlaxcaltecans. Its handsome portal is dated 1642; the tower 1783.

In Av. 16 Oriente, opposite the chapel of Verónica (see above), is the church of *La Cruz* (1693–1744), in an attractive atrio. Among its paintings are Our Lady of Light (1717) by Luis Berrueco; Adoration of the Kings and Adoration of the Shepherds (1778) by a later Cristóbal de Talavera; and St John Nepomuk by José Joaquín Magón. Further N in C. 12 Norte is the chapel of *San Juan del Río* (c 1675–87), with an excellently carved Mannerist portal.

N of Paseo de San Francisco, the park on the other side of Av. 14 Oriente from the church, Calz. de los Fuertes winds upwards to the eminence on the NE side of the city, now laid out as the CENTRO CIVICO 5 DE MAYO between two small fortified hills, the *Cerro de Loreto* (W) and the *Cerro de Guadalupe* (SE).

The road passes (l.) the baseball stadium to reach the **Fuerte de Loreto**, built in 1815 as part of the city's defences against the insurgents and modernized in 1862. It enclosed the *Cap. de Loreto* (late 17C–early 18C) which in turn covers the *Casa de Loreto* (comp. Rte 19), entered through richly worked baroque outer and inner portals. The fort was restored from 1933 and now houses a *Museo Histórico de la No Intervención* (Tues.–Sun., 10–5), illustrating the military history of Puebla. We pass a monument to Ignacio Zaragoza (1962) before reaching the civic centre, started in the 1960s to the plans of Guillermo Rossell and Abraham Zabludovsky. Among the buildings are the hemispherical *Auditorio de la Reforma*, a planetarium, the *Museo de Historia Natural* (Tues.–Sun., 10–5), and the **Museo Regional de Puebla** (Tues.–Sun., 10–5).

In the first section diagrams and maps illustrate Mesoamerican archaeological periods and regions, along with finds from the Early Preclassic site of Totimehuacán, and a 3C BC skeleton and jewellery from a burial at Zinacantepec. Next, given pride of place, is an Olmec jadeite statue, found in the 19C in the Acatlán region. It is Middle Preclassic in date (c 800–500 BC), and has incised glyphs. Its presence in Puebla demonstrates the spread of Olmec influence in central Mexico, by diffusion, trade, and perhaps even colonization.

Several cases display finds from the Classic Period (here dated c 200 BC–AD 900). 1. Teotihuacano pottery. 2. Thin Orange Ware vessels, abundant throughout Mesoamerica in the Classic, and whose source of clay is still uncertain but may have been the Ixcaquixtla region of Puebla. 3. Mural reproduction of *Los Bebidores* (Drinkers) from the site of Cholula (2C AD). 4. Artefacts from Cacaxtla, incl. figurines of priests showing Gulf Coast influences, and reproductions of part of the polychrome paintings. 5. Finds from Cerro de Xochitecatl, near San Miguel del Milagro, incl. especially the preponderance of female figurines, thought to reflect the presence of a fertility cult, and showing influences from both the Gulf Coast and from Teotihuacán. 6. Finds from Cholula and Teotihuacán illustrating religious ceramics with zoomorphic designs.

Further displays illustrate the Postclassic (here dated AD 900–1521). 7. Ceramics from Tlaxcala–Puebla, incl. polychrome vessels decorated with religious themes and calendrical motifs in the widespread Mixteca–Puebla style. 8. Chacmool sculpture from Tlaxcala; one interpretation of their use was to hold the hearts of sacrificial victims. 9. Musical instruments used for festivals and religious rites. 10. Mask depicting a god. 11. Incense burner (*sahumerio*) decorated with mythical themes. 12. *Tepanaztle*, Náhuatl name for a musical instrument made from a hollowed-out log, struck in a horizontal position; the upper surface had two cut-out 'tongues', which produced different pitches when struck by a rubber-tipped mallet.

Aztec stone sculptures, illustrating the skill of stonemasonry in the Late Postclassic. 13. Large stone slab with the engraved date *chicome tecpatl*—'seven flint'. 14. Sculpture of Chicomecóatl or Centeotl: the former was the 'seven serpent' goddess of vegetation and maize, usually depicted holding ears of maize-corn; she was also manifested as Chalchiúlicue and Xilonen, goddess of fertility. The latter was god of the maize-plant, son of Tlazoltéotl, Earth goddess. 15. Zoomorphic representation of Cóatl, the 'snake', and fifth of the 20 Náhuatl day signs; 'viper of Pascabel'. 16. Sculptures of the gods of war, Huitzilopochtli, and of spring, Xipe Totec. 17. Expressive sculpture of a howling dog or coyote. 18. Cuauhtle-huánitl, the ascending eagle, or Tonatiuh, the young warrior deity and god of the sun. 19. The Tetecúhtin, governing lords of Cholula, independent governors within the Aztec hierarchy (facsimile of the cloth painting of Tlaxcala). 20. Various sculptures of dogs from Tepeaca, rendered in grey basalt. 21. Fragment of a stone fountain, illustrating the versatility of indigenous stonework.

POST-CONQUEST PUEBLA is illustrated by photographs and models illustrating the 16C evangelization of the region; 18C furniture (incl. late 18C ornate cedarwood chair from Totimehuacán), paintings (incl. Luis Berrueco, Profession of St Clare; anon. late 18C, Patronage of Our Lady of Guadalupe, showing Bp Alvarez de Abreu with nuns), and documents. Tiles, ironwork, lacquerware, porcelain, fans, and religious sculpture throw light on local industry, crafts, and trade with the Orient during the 17C and 18C. The final sections deal with the Independence and Reform periods, and 19C French influence in Puebla; and local customs and types.

The **Fuerte de Guadalupe**, reached from the civic centre along Av. Ejercito de Oriente, was started in 1817–18 and reinforced in 1862. It displaced the chapel of Nuestra Señora de Belem (1759–63), ruinous by the early 19C, and a new church, *Nuestra Señora de Guadalupe* (1804–16), remains of which may still be seen.

The heights were occupied by US forces during May 1847–June 1848. They were also scene of the battle of 5 May 1862 when the Mexican army, c 4000 strong, under Gen. Ignacio Zaragoza beat the French expeditionary force under Gen. comte de Lorencez, whose aim was to win the forts of Loreto and Guadalupe, held by Gen. Felipe Berriozábal and Zaragoza respectively. The Mexicans beat off three attacks by a column of Zouaves and companies of chasseurs and infantry, as well as a separate assault on the fort of Guadalupe. During the siege of 1863 the forts were held for the republicans by Berriozábal.

By going S along C. 11 Sur into Blvd Valsequillo (State road 708) we may reach (9km) **San Francisco Totimehuacán**, the site of a Toltec ceremonial centre when the Toltec leader Mixcóatl ruled the city of Culhuacán in the S Basin of Mexico. The bases of three pyramids have been excavated here, one each to Tonatiuh (the Sun god), Mextli (Náhuatl for the Moon), and Quetzalcóatl (manifested as the morning star). There are other, unexcavated mounds as well.

Near the town, the German Puebla Project has excavated part of a Preclassic Period site at *Tepalcayo*, abandoned by the 2C AD, at the beginning of the Classic. The Franciscan convent of San Francisco, founded c 1569 but unfinished, was busily gone over by its new recollect occupiers in the 18C. 18km (2km r.) *Africam Safari*, a zoo (34 hectares) on the E side of *Presa Manuel Avila Camacho* (Laguna de Valsequillo). Much earlier remains have been found here: crude stone tools and an elephant pelvic bone with cut marks. Although not precisely datable, these may be as old as 28,000 BC. (The carbon used in the dating measurements came from the same geologic formation, but not from the same outcrop as the tools and pelvis.) 37km *Tecali*, see Rte 73.

C 10km NE, at the foot of Cerro de la Malinche, on the road (State road 322) towards San Miguel Canoa, is the archaeological site of *Manzanilla*. Here there are unrestored terraces and the mounds of a small ball court with two stairways; and c 675m E of these, more ruins, incl. a larger ball court and about a dozen mounds. All are thought to date to the Classic Period on the basis of the pottery from surface collections.

68   Puebla to Tlaxcala

Méx. 119, 33km.—21km Zacalteco.—24km turning for **Cacaxtla**.—27km Tepeyanco.—33km **Tlaxcala**.

We leave Puebla to the N on Méx. 119, the road passing under the Mexico City–Córdoba motorway and crossing into the State of Tlaxcala to the W of the volcano *La Malinche* (4461m). 15km turning r. via (1km) *Papalotla* to (4km) *Mazatecochco*, where the church of San Cosme has a churrigueresque altarpiece. 17km *Xicohtzingo* (2000m), with an 18C church (Sto Toribio), which keeps a lateral baroque altarpiece. 21km **Zacalteco**, where the church of *Sta Inés*, rebuilt in the 17C with delicate façade relief, preserves some of its original 16C fabric (from the days when it was a visita of Tepeyanco) and a fine baroque high altarpiece.

7km E is **Acuamanalá** where the façade of the 18C church of *San Antonio* is a typical example of exuberant rustic churrigueresque. The interior contains baroque altarpieces; the cupola of the sacristy is enlivened with polychrome relief. Just beyond Zacalteco a minor road runs NE to (3km) *Huactzingo*, where the church of San Juan is an 18C adaptation of a 16C open chapel and contains a baroque high altarpiece. *Teolocholco*, 2km further E on this road, has an 18C church (San Luis).

24km turning l. for (11km W) *Natívitas*, where the 17C church of Sta María, with a churrigueresque altarpiece, belonged to a Franciscan visita convent founded c 1570.

4km N of Natívitas (road signposted) is **CACAXTLA** (Tues.–Sun. 10–5; for the murals, 10–1 only; fee), part of a complex of ruins in SW Tlaxcala, incl. Cacaxtla, Xochitécatl, Atcoya, Atlachino, Mixco, Tenanyecac, and Huilacapixco. Occupation of this zone was long and continuous, from c 2000 BC to the abandonment of Cacaxtla c AD 850.

Excavated by the German Puebla-Tlaxcala Project and INAH since 1971. In 1975 looters discovered some polychrome murals in one of the principal buildings, which they reported to a local priest, who reported them to INAH.

The earliest occupation comprised a subsistence-farming village. Later developments included the erection of ceremonial buildings, the manufacture of figurines representing Huehuetéotl (old Fire god), and a general population increase. Irrigation farming was developed between c 800 and 300 BC, stimulating further population increase and the manpower to construct stone-faced platforms and temples to Huehuetéotl and Tláloc (Rain god). Extensive commercial activities are indicated by finds of trade items from the Valle de Tehuacán, the Gulf Coast, Chiapas, and Guatemala, as well as from the nearby Basin of Mexico.

Between 300 BC and AD 100 Cacaxtla was a prominent regional civic and religious centre for the worship of Huehuetéotl and Tláloc. Its nearest rivals were Cholula (S) and Teotihuacán (NW), and the latter's influence was prominent between AD 100 and 600. Other local centres developed at Sta Anita Nopalucan and at Xochitécatl. From c AD 600 the decline of Teotihuacán was accompanied by population movements and disruption to the trade networks established in more settled times.

By c AD 650 Olmeca-Xicalanca, or Historic Olmec, peoples had moved into the region, captured Cholula, and taken over Cacaxtla as their capital. From here they could dominate the Valle de Puebla from the Tlaxcala plateau. Fortification ditches and terraces were built at Cacaxtla, at Xochitécatl, and at Atlachino, c 1.5km NE. Cacaxtla's prosperity is reflected in the palatial residences, suburbs, and temples built on its terraced hillsides, many with stucco relief decoration and murals on their interior walls. The site was abandoned c AD 850 during a second period of disruptions and population movements, and not reoccupied until the 16C, when it became a redoubt in Tlaxcalteca resistance to the Aztecs.

Cacaxtla's present visible ruins comprise several complexes of terraces, platforms, porticoed buildings, and murals. Most of these represent the prosperous phase before the occupational hiatus, and are the end result of numerous alterations and reconstructions. Many earlier public buildings were entirely of stone, but later constructions often incorporated adobe reliefs as well.

There are three distinct areas: the *Gran Basamento*, and the *Pl. de las Tres Pirámides* to the S, and *Los Cerritos* to the E. The first is a complex of rooms on platforms, and sunken patios around a large plaza—*Pl. Norte*, 25m x 35m, with stairs at the N and S ends. Each is described in succession, as we move around the plaza counterclockwise (see plan).

NE corner—**1 Edificio A**. This is a porticoed building with outer and inner tripartite rooms. There are five murals, one on each side of the doorways between the two rooms, one on each side of the door jamb, and a long mural on the far wall of the inner room. The murals in this building are estimated to be c 75 years later than those in Edificio B (see below). To the r. of the doorway **(A)** entering the outer room is a bird-man in black, holding a ceremonial bar ending in a stylized serpent head. To the l. of his face is a glyph with footprints, reminiscent of Teotihuacano style, and a feathered eye, reminiscent of Xochicalco style. On the r. door jamb **(B)** is the figure of a dancer, also in black. L. of the doorway **(C)** is a figure dressed as a serpentine-jaguar, again in black, carrying a quiver which drips water. And on the l. door jamb **(D)** is a figure wearing a long-nosed mask. The deterioration of the mural **(E)** on the far inner wall is, unfortunately, almost complete, and only a few parts of figures can be recognized.

N side—**2 Edificio B**. This is a long, rectangular room of at least five phases of construction, fronted by six pillars. A mural, originally 22m long, was discovered behind the stone *taluds* and on either side of the staircase leading up to the pillared front of the later building. It depicts a battle scene between vividly painted, life-sized jaguar-men, wearing poncho-like skins, short skirts, sandals, leggings, belts, and ornaments, and bird-men, wearing great bird-beak helmets. The jaguar-men are victorious, with most of the bird-men already down on their backs beneath the raised spears of the victors. Painted in bright blue, red, black, and white, this scene represents a rare example of central Mexican eclectic art, showing dynamic detail and perspective in its sense of motion, spilled blood and internal organs, and overlapping, writhing bodies. Equally interesting, the murals of both Edificios A and B show close similarities to Maya art styles in the dress and elongated faces of the figures, perhaps indicating strong economic and diplomatic ties between the two areas.

N of the plaza—**3 *Patio Hundido*** and **4 *Montículo Y***. N of Pl. Norte, behind Edificio B, are two late phase constructions. The first is a rectangular, sunken patio or small plaza with indentations and stairs on each side. In front of the N indentation is a small pavement for incense burning and two receptacles for burials and offerings. N of this is a two-tiered platform with the ramp for a staircase up the S side, but the stone has been robbed for local building.

NW corner. The **5 *Pasillo de los Tableros*** is a small, stone-panelled passage along the W side of Edificio B. **6 *Edificio C***, only partially explored, is similar in plan to Edificio A. One of its later modifications was **7 *Las 'Conejeras'*** ('rabbit warrens'), an adobe-lined hole in the centre of one wall; but its use is unknown.

W side—**8 *Edificio E***. This is a small, three-chambered building with a central room entered through a portico with two carved pillars, and N and S wing-rooms.

SW corner—**9 *La Celosía*** (lattice window). This is a lower room, c 3m deep, with pillars and lattice decoration in one window.

S side—**10 El Palacio**. This is a complex of rooms around the N, S, and E sides of a small patio, with an altar. In the NE corner there are several more rooms around a second, smaller patio, whose walls have decorative rhombuses in bas-relief. On the E of the main patio is a room with four pillars and faint traces of polychrome paintings on the stucco walls, no doubt once another vivid mural.

W and S of El Palacio and plaza. **11 *Edificio F, Portico F*** and **12 *Cuarto de las Escaleras*** form a small complex of porticoed rooms S of El Palacio. In the Cuarto de las Escaleras there are steps at the N end, at each side of which were found

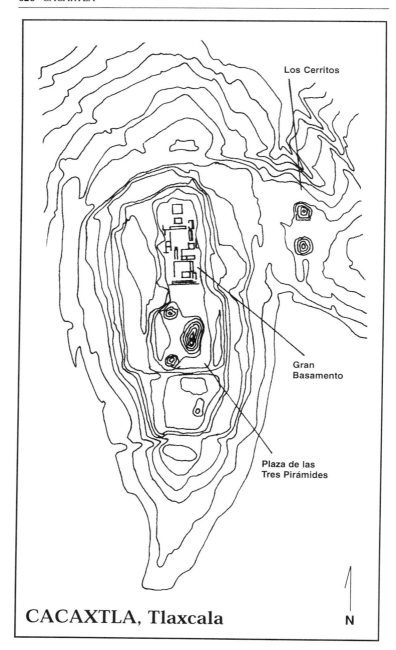

Los Cerritos

Gran
Basamento

Plaza de las
Tres Pirámides

CACAXTLA, Tlaxcala

N

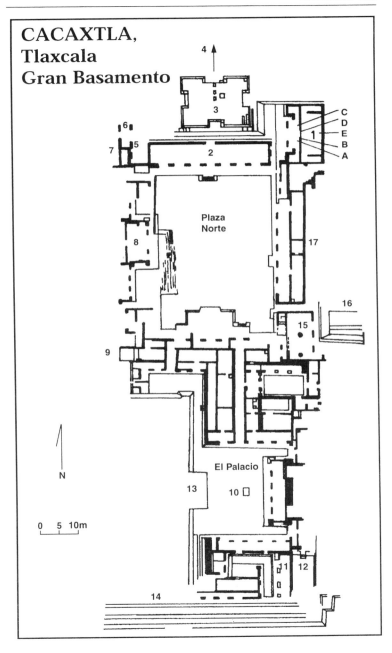

CACAXTLA,
Tlaxcala
Gran Basamento

traces of murals, unfortunately almost totally deteriorated; only the legs and feet of a few figures remain. The **13** *Taludes del Sur* form the S steps of the terracing of the hillside. **14** *Conjunto Dos* is an as yet unexplored complex, probably another series of rooms around a patio.

(From the Cuarto de las Escaleras return along the E side of the El Palacio complex.)

E side. The **15** *Edificio de las Columnas* is a rectangular substructure with pillars on its E and W sides. In the middle of the E room are the bases of two columns, each more than 1m across. The **16** *Taludes del Este* correspond to the Taludes del Sur, and are the terracing of the E hillside.

E side. **17** *Edificio D* is a long, rectangular room with a five-pillar portico and a tripartite inner room.

To the S of the Gran Basamento is the PL. DE LAS TRES PIRAMIDES, where three platforms clearly form another plaza group.

E of the Gran Basamento is a terraced spur-hill on which sits *Montículo B*, a three-tiered pyramid-platform with a staircase on its W side, leading up to a temple with several pillars at the top, and a second, unexcavated mound. Next to Cacaxtla, the small Formative Period site of *Xochitécpatl* was opened in 1995.

From Natívitas we may continue S and then W to (18km) turning r. for (4km N) **San Miguel del Milagro**, a picturesque village in the foothills of the Cerro San Miguel. Here the diverse sanctuary of *San Miguel*, built at various times since the 17C to commemorate an apparition of the archangel to the Indian Diego Lázaro in 1631, is a popular pilgrimage centre, especially on the feast of St Michael (29 Sept.). In the gable of the façade, a charmingly ingenuous relief of a hovering St Michael and an adoring Diego Lázaro. In the interior, a beautiful alabaster pulpit, resembling a folding screen, upheld by a wingless polychrome angel, his robe embroidered in gold. 19km *Xochitecatitla*, whose chapel of San Miguel contains a superb churrigueresque altarpiece. From here the road runs NW to (29km) *San Martín Texmelucan*, see Rte 66.

27km **Tepeyanco** (3000 inhab.; 2213m), in a rural landscape, the W foothills of La Malinche. The former Franciscan convent of *San Francisco*, recently rescued from complete ruination, was founded in 1554 and built probably during the 1560s.

Its large atrio, at a lower level than the town plaza, is entered through a main gate of three rounded arches on slender square piers on the S side; or through a side entrance, again triple-arched, on the N side, convenient for the open chapel. The posas are later (most likely 17C) rebuildings. An espadaña is raised above the atrio wall. The church's roof was raised and vaulted before 1600. On its N side are remains of a rib-vaulted open chapel, probably dating from the 1540s, and in use before the church was built. It was later considerably enlarged by a new five-arched portico (fragments of which survive), 9m forward from the previous frontage.

Of great interest is the 18C parish church of *San Francisco*, its façade, set off against the chunky low tower, a delicate composition of glazed and unglazed tiles marked by stucco pilasters and a three-lobe doorway crowded with relief. The interior contains baroque altarpieces originally in the convent church, and an elaborate churrigueresque high altarpiece whose slanted estípites create an impression of great depth.

28km *Acuitlapilco*, a small village with an 18C church (Sta María) and the so-called Casa de Cortés, where the local sculptor Carlos Monroy has created a fanciful evocation of historic Tlaxcala in polychrome mortar and tiles. The road passes (r.) the shallow Laguna de Acuitlapilco.

33km **TLAXCALA** (c 30,000 inhab.; 2252m), capital of the State of Tlaxcala, stands, in rather bleak country straddling the continental divide, at the foot of the NW slopes of La Malinche and astride the Río Zahuapan. Its reputation as a backwater, partly explained by its singular history, has endowed it with a peaceful atmosphere and a cleanliness which render exploration of its celebrated historical buildings doubly agreeable. The climate is warm, with a pleasant summer freshness, and healthy.

Bus station. Av. Ignacio Zaragoza, SW of the centre. Services to *Mexico City* (c 4 hrs); to *Puebla* (1½ hrs); to *Huamantla* (1 hr); to *San Martín Texmelucan* (45 mins); to *Apizaco* (½ hr);

to *Tlaxco* (45 mins); to *Zacatlán* (2 hrs); to *Texcoco* (2½ hrs); to *Tulancingo* (3 hrs); to *Pachuca* (4 hrs); etc. Buses connect with city centre.

Hotels. Some in city centre; the more expensive on N side of the city along Av. Revolución (continuation of Av. Juárez).

Post Office. 20 Pl. de Armas.

Tourist Office. Corner of Av. Juárez and C. Lardizabal.

In 1519 Cortés and his army entered Ocotelulco (across the river, N of the present city), lordship of Maxixcatzin, military leader of the federation of Tlaxcallan. 'When we entered the town there was not a space in the streets and on the roofs for all the Indian men and women with happy faces who came out to see us'. Building of the new Spanish city, already termed 'leal ciudad', was begun in 1536 and in 1563 its title was advanced to 'muy noble y muy leal'. From 1545 the representative of the Spanish crown resided here, his title of governor confirmed in 1587. In 1568 John Chilton passed through and described 'Tlaxcalla, a city [he must have meant the federation] of two hundred thousand Indians. The Indians both of this city, and of the rest, lying about Mexico, goe clothed with mantles of linnen cloth made of cotton wooll, painted thorowout with works of divers and fine colours'. The 17C saw progressive decline, affecting both the textile industry and the population, which fell from

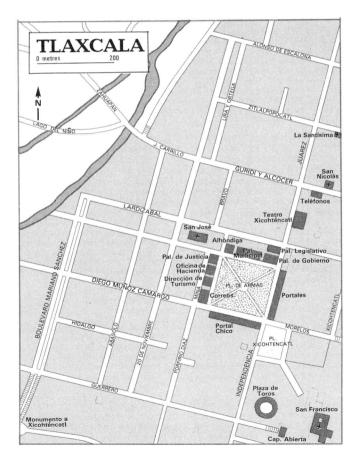

11,000 to 4000. Liberal-conservative rivalry was finally decided in Apr. 1867 when the mainly Austrian imperialist garrison surrendered. From 1974 the city has benefited from a programme of urban renewal.

The State of **Tlaxcala** (675,000 inhab.; 4016 sq km) is a region of valleys, some broad and fertile, and plains lying across the continental divide. The Río Zahuapan crosses it from N to S to unite with the Río Atoyac. It is almost exclusively an agricultural State, producing alfalfa, maize, barley, and potatoes; pig-breeding is the principal livestock activity.

The modern State of Tlaxcala corresponds almost exactly to the area of the prehispanic Tlaxcallan, whose bond with the Spaniards was to leave a permanent mark on its history. It was a loose federation of independent states hostile to the triple alliance (see Rte 20). Among these lordships, four—Tepeticpac, Tizatlán, Quiahuixtlán, Ocotelulco —achieved a kind of pre-eminence, with the lord of the latter, Maxixcatzin, as military leader. The lord of Tizatlán, Xicoténcatl II (b. 1484), decided to fight the Spanish incursion, but was defeated in two battles early in Sept. 1519. The Tlaxcaltecans then sued for peace, and received Cortés politely at Ocotelulco on 23 Sept. Various Spanish-Tlaxcaltecan marriage alliances were arranged (incl. those between two sisters of Xicoténcatl and the brothers Pedro and Jorge Alvarado) and the four lords (so tradition has it) accepted baptism. In Oct. an alliance was forged, by which the Tlaxcaltecans joined forces with the Spaniards on their campaigns against Cholula (see Rte 66) and Tenochtitlán, and on further voyages of conquest. The Spaniards found refuge in Tlaxcala after the retreat from Tenochtitlán in July 1520 and it served as a base for retaking the Aztec capital. Their loyalty ensured the Tlaxcaltecans special privileges, as wards of the Spanish crown. They had their own government alongside that of the Spanish governor and many were settled as reliable colonists throughout the Spanish empire. Charles V's decree of 9 Sept. 1525 fixed the seat of the vast (titular) bishopric of Yucatán at Tlaxcala.

Ancient privileges were whittled away and estates were taken by Spanish colonists. Traditional loyalty to the Crown asserted itself during the war of Independence. In 1857, Tlaxcala achieved statehood, confirmed in 1868–74. In 1885–1911 Governor Próspero Cahuantzi, friend of Díaz, held sway, his government well run, with justice impartially administered, but founded on terror, especially towards peasants and workers. The revolutionary years saw the struggle of the idealistic Domingo Arenas, supporter of Zapata, against the constitutionalists.

The city centre, the renowned PL. DE ARMAS, surrounded by historic build-ings, is a peaceful, shaded haven, dense with venerable ash trees. Its once main octagonal fountain (1646), now non-functioning and pushed a little NW, was a gift from Philip III, but not put in place until 25 years after the king's death. On its E side are the 28 arches of portales (16C, but frequently restored); on its S side the seven arches of the contemporaneous *Portal Chico*, a former merchant's house. On the N corner of the W side is the erstwhile *Pal. de Justicia* (now the State congress), the former **Cap. Real**.

It was built first from 1528, under Fray Andrés de Córdoba, destined for the exclusive use of indigenous nobles; and rebuilt in the 18C. In 1796 it was damaged by fire and in 1800 ravaged during an earthquake; its subsequent rebuilding and conversion date from 1974. The doorway incorporates two 16C bas-reliefs, probably taken from the Casas Reales, showing coats-of-arms of Charles V, the second, and wider, supported by two Wild Men holding branches, figures of European myth carried to America.

The continuous building complex on the N side of the plaza marks the seat of government of city and State, and of historic Tlaxcala.

It was begun probably in 1545–55. The doorway sections—chief remaining beauty—may belong to a new building campaign c 1578. In 1692 bread rioters fired it and in 1711 an earthquake inflicted more damage. Repairs were then put in hand. By 1761 it was again in a bad state and renovation took place in 1762–63. The interior was restored during 1885–1911. In 1928 the façade was faced with brick-like reddish tiles; the windows robbed of their historic simplicity; and the 18C balcony railings replaced. There has been further restoration since 1974.

On the W side is the former **Alhóndiga**, which has kept its characterfully chunky 16C doorway: low-strung arch and imposts and jambs dotted with large relief rosettes. In the centre is the **Pal. Municipal** (the former *Casa Consistorial*, meeting-place of the representatives of the four principal lordships of old Tlaxcala).

The Alhóndiga at Tlaxcala

The central EXTERIOR section keeps marvellously contrasted 16C work. In the lower storey three basket arches rest on sturdy pilasters, their capitals and bases decorated with relief worked by Indian hands. Around the three upper-storey windows curve contrasted arches (in the centre, semicircular; at the sides, convex and multifoil), their extradoses filled with foliage relief.

On the E side is the **Pal. de Gobierno** (the former *Casa Real*), which also preserves its original portal, though only in the lower part. The extrados of the convex, multifoil arch, the clustered pilasters, and imposts are covered in intricate floral relief, a prime example of Indian technique (tequitqui) set against fanciful, in this case Portuguese-inspired, European forms.

The patio walls are decorated with murals on the history of Tlaxcala by Desidero Hernández Xochitiotzin (1966).

Beyond the NW side of the plaza is the cathedral of **San José**, its façade a cheerful combination of reddish brick, tile, and stucco, characteristic of the region, in neostyle baroque.

The first parish church was started in 1526. This, its successor, was built in the late 18C, damaged by earthquake in 1867, and restored under Alexander von Wuthenau from 1868.

The EXTERIOR is faced in slanted, oblong brick and tilework, against which is set the white stucco of columns, pilasters, cornices, and gable. Wide pilasters form the basic supports for the cornices, broken in the lower storey to form the pedestal for the image of St Joseph, backed by the choir window, another oblong. The columns, standing forward of the inner and outer pilasters of the lower storey and of the upper storey, are elegantly decorated with garlands, angel heads, fluting, and twining bands; below the capitals of the central pilasters are saintly images resting on lambrequin motifs. The undulating gable is an adventurous finish.

The INTERIOR contains good churrigueresque side altarpieces in the nave and in the r. transept. In the sanctuary chapel (l.) is a beautiful baroque altarpiece.

From the SE side of Pl. de Armas we reach PL. XICOTENCATL, with a monument to Xicoténcatl (1978). Again from the SE side begins an avenue lined by
ash trees which ascends to the three-arched gateway of the upper atrio of the
former Franciscan convent of **La Asunción de Nuestra Señora**.

In 1536–37 the friars' third (and present) foundation at Tlaxcala was begun and nearly
completed by 1540, with repairs and lesser works in hand for some years afterwards. The
church was finished in 1564, but in the early 17C was raised and given its wooden ceiling.
The side chapels date from the 17C. On 29 Dec. 1640, in obedience to the dictates of Bp Palafox
(comp. Rte 67), a party of laymen and secular priests entered Tlaxcala on horseback to take
over the parish from the friars, who fought a fruitless rearguard action by barricading
themselves in the convent.

The convent had two atrios. The lower, on the W side, has disappeared under
the bullring and C. Independencia. The UPPER ATRIO is the result of demolition and levelling of the slope of the hill. Its simple three-arched W gate, with
fluted columns, is at the top of a ramp leading from the lower atrio. Just through
the gate (restored), facing a small patio, is a chapel, in the 16C known as
Nuestra Señora del Rosario, a flattened hexagon in plan, its ogee arches supported by hexagonal pillars. Above runs a cornice upheld by brackets in which
the ogee motif is repeated. In the wall above the arches are remains of original
painting. Above the cornice is the Franciscan cord motif. The interior shows a
striking rib vault. The purpose of the two tower-like blocks at either side,
probably later 16C constructions, is not clear. The upper storey, which gives on
to the upper atrio, probably gave access to the clergy and choir (?).

A 16C historian records that Mass was offered here on feasts of the Assumption and Corpus
Christi. It probably antedates the main complex of the upper atrio.

The upper atrio is enclosed by a rough stone wall, probably part of the fabric
of a pre-Conquest sanctuary on the site. In the NW corner is the peculiarly
placed bell-tower, joined to the convent by a secret passage along the top of the
N gateway. At the SW corner is a surviving posa (c 1547; restored), clumsy in
design, with a rib vault and pyramidal top. Embedded in the wall opposite the
church is a room probably also used as a posa or chapel.
    The church (without vaulting) resembles a barn, its doorway of the plainest
Renaissance type. The INTERIOR is covered by the famous raised ceiling
(restored; by the Sevillian López de Arana) of carved and inlaid wood, the most
beautiful example of alfarje to survive, a tribute to the strength of Mudéjar
technique in New Spain. Its ornate central horizontal panel and crosspieces are
studded with gilded stars. The nave is lined with six Renaissance and baroque
altarpieces (the 2nd r. dated 1664). The pulpit (16C), of carved stone, so
tradition insists, was the earliest in New Spain.

The high altarpiece, though small, is a fine baroque example of the mid-17C, one of the
earliest to show distinctively lush solomonic columns and vertical gadroons in the curves.
Note the contrast between the lowest-storey columns and the swelling effect of those of the
upper two storeys. The anon. paintings show scenes from the life of Our Lady and the
conversion of the four chiefs of Tlaxcala. The first chapel r. preserves its lovely gilded wooden
gates and fan-like top, and contains a baroque altarpiece (elegant variations of the solomonic;
note the thick vertical festoons in the twists of the upper-storey columns and the cherubs
resting amid the tropical lushness of the lower-storey twists), dedicated to Our Lady of
Guadalupe.
    The CAP. DE LA TERCERA ORDEN (c 1654; towards presbytery on r.) is entered through
an original wooden doorway. On either side are two 16C stone reliefs of the Annunciation.
Baroque and churrigueresque altarpieces line the walls. The l. side chapel (*San Antonio*)
contains an altarpiece of 1717, finely decorated, with a delightfully popular character, and
paintings of the life of the saint. The beautiful high altarpiece, serene yet sophisticated, and
those of the two immediate side walls, resemble a complete, expanded work; the paired
solomonic columns reveal compactly rich spirals. The central statue of St Francis shows him
sustaining three globes (his three Orders), his stigmata symbolized by semi-precious stones.
In the l. transept the earliest altarpiece of all exalts the Third Order. That opposite, in the r.

transept, contains paintings dated 1700. The font is claimed as the one used for the baptism of the four chiefs.

In the sacristy is a painting of St Francis appearing to St Teresa (1677) by Diego de Borgraf. The triple-arched portería leads into the small cloister, which retains part of its old timber ceiling. The convent is now the **Museo Regional** (Tues.–Sun., 9–5; fee).

GROUND FLOOR. Six stone sculptures: four with bas-relief carving; one represents the Tlaxcalan god Camaxtli (14–15C) and is possibly from Tlaxcala city. Chacmool from San Juan Mixco—reclining on back, 'helmeted' head turned over l. shoulder, and flattened abdominal area—possibly for ritual offerings.

FIRST FLOOR. 1. Mastodon tusk and fragments of bones of other prehistoric mammals. 2. Part of trunk of petrified tree. 3. Stone quern. 4. Tzompantec phase (c 1500–c 1200 BC)—ceramic vessels and figurines, and obsidian blade tools. 5. Tlatempa phase (c 1200–c 800 BC)—ceramic bowls (incl. two with tripod bases), obsidian blades, anthropomorphic stone head (c 20 cm), clay figurines and masks.

6–7. Texoloc phase (c 800–c 300 BC)—ceramic vessels with incised decoration; clay figurines (c 5 cm); human skull with occipital flattening; figure of Huehueteotl supporting bowl on head and shoulders.

8–11. Tezoquilpan phase (c 300 BC–AD 100)—five clay masks (c 3–4 cm); stone quern; 11 bowls (three with tripod bases, two with incised geometric decoration, and one with a moulded mask on the side).

12–13. Tenanyec phase (c AD 100–c 650)—eight ceramic vessels with incised geometric decorations, fluting and burnishing; ten polychrome figurines; baby in basket; miscellaneous stone artefacts, incl. axe and adze heads.

14–15. Texcalac phase (c AD 650–c 1100)—bone artefacts, incl. needles and carved teeth; obsidian blades; stone figurine (c 15 cm) from Cacaxtla; ceramic bowls and two anthropomorphic jugs; polychrome urn (c 50 cm) from Cacaxtla, ornate decoration, incl. central figure wearing bird headdress, skirt with caracoles, sandals, and jewellery, plus two supporting human figures.

16–18. Tlaxcala phase (c 1100–1519)—ceramic polychrome bowls and jugs; eccentric or caricatured clay human and animal figurines; two stone sculptures of a realistic human head and a seated god.

Reached along C. Obregón, to the S of San Francisco, is the 17C church of *Nuestro Señor del Vecino*.

From the NE side of Pl. de Armas we may take C. Juárez past (immediately l.) the *Pal. Legislativo* (1901), now the police headquarters, and (r.) the *Teatro Xicohténcatl* (late 19C). In C. Guridi y Alcocer (r.) is the church of *San Nicolás* (17C) and beyond, in C. Zitlalpopocatl (r.), the church of *La Santísima* (18C). C. Juárez continues NW into Blvd Guillermo Valle. To the r., beyond C. Alonso de Escalona, are the ruins of the *Hospital de la Encarnación*, built by the Franciscans for 140 patients in 1537. Beyond (r.) is the chapel of *San Dieguito* (16C).

On a hill on the E edge of the city (c 3km from Pl. de Armas), reached along C. Guridi y Alcocer, is the sanctuary of **Nuestra Señora de Ocotlán**, a masterpiece of popular churrigueresque.

It was begun, probably c 1670, to succeed a small 16C chapel built to commemorate an apparition of Our Lady to a Tlaxcaltecan Juan Diego (comp. Rte 14) in 1541. Its present appearance dates mainly from the 1720s, the work of an Indian, Francisco Miguel (d. 1740), and a team of craftsmen with the encouragement of the priest Manuel Loayzaga, and completed c 1750. It was refurbished in 1852–54 and in 1939–40.

EXTERIOR. The façade, a 'fantasy of dazzling stucco framed in red tile', shows remarkable effects of light and shade. (Frequent whitewashings necessary, especially after the rains.) The centrepiece, recessed below a giant shell canopy, and the twin towers are gorgeously florid; the white estípites, interestípites, and pinnacles overflow with fruit, rosettes, and cherub, prophets' and saints' heads. Placed within the interestípites, at the tops of the upper estípites, and above the window are the seven archangels, ready to soar aloft on uplifted wings. The choir window, shaped like a star, is most elegantly draped, a background for the central statue of Our Lady, gracefully posed, resting on a statue of St Francis supporting three globes. The towers have greater girth than the bases; although their grace and agility give the opposite impression.

The overwhelming feature of the INTERIOR is the churrigueresque retables, a mass of gilding, beneath the dome. They are preceded by a triumphal arch from which another giant shell motif comes forward into the nave. The covering of every surface and the continuation of the gilding into the pendentives and cupola give the impression of one resplendent unity. Polychrome statues of saints and angels occupy the niches, and above the high altar more angels seem to climb into the vault. In the centre of the l. altarpiece is a moving Pietà. The high altar includes silver- and gold-work by Antonio Fernández and José de Isunza.

In the antesacristy are five large canvases of the apparition of Our Lady of Ocotlán, St Lawrence, and two Franciscan themes (1781) by Manuel Caro. The Sacristy contains five Passion scenes by José Joaquín Magón (The Last Supper dated 1754); the table is one of the best examples of its type. Behind the high altar is the octagonal CAMARIN DE LA VIRGEN (1718–22; special permission to view needed), a jewel of late baroque and a mass of gilding and polychrome stucco. It is covered by a richly stuccoed dome, upheld by archangels, in which sit Our Lady and the Apostles at Pentecost, with the Holy Ghost poised above their heads in the centre. The ribs of the vault are framed by bands covered in stucco; in each section saints emerge from the floral ornament. Each side is divided off by lush solomonic columns. The paintings of scenes from the life of Our Lady are by Juan de Villalobos (one dated 1723). It all moved Viceroy Revillagigedo II to declare that 'he had seen much in Europe…but never had seen greater beauty than in this image of Our Lady, nor finer carving in any retable, nor a nicer elegance in any other chamber than in her camarín'.

5km beyond Ocotlán to the E is **Sta Ana Chiautempan** (10,000 inhab.; 2288m), the State's chief textile centre, famous for its serapes. The cloister of the former Franciscan convent of *Sta Ana*, finished c 1585, still stands, its atrio shaded by tall ash trees. It is now a seminary. The church was not finished until the 17C. In the presbytery, two paintings attr. Juan Correa, Adoration of the Shepherds and Baptism of Christ.

FROM TLAXCALA TO SAN MARTIN TEXMELUCAN, 22km. We leave Tlaxcala to the NW, crossing the Río Zahuapan to join a branch of Méx. 136 running SW. On the r. of Méx. 136 is *Totolac*, now a suburb of Tlaxcala, with a few remains of the small Franciscan convent of San Juan, founded in 1545. 4km turning r. for (1km S) **Panotla** (4000 inhab.; 2233m), where the façade of the church of *San Nicolás*, all white mortar resembling exquisite ivory and set back beneath an opulently decorated arch, is a bewitching churrigueresque fantasy.

The three-lobed arch, the quatrefoil window with a curtain elegantly pinned around it, the angel figures, the plentiful rococo relief, the beautifully modelled estípites, the sculpted saints—all create, in Toussaint's words, 'a vertigo of mysticism and art'. At the base of the tower appears an inscription with the date 1769. The atrial cross bears a Náhuatl inscription and the date 1728.

14km turning r. for (1km NW) **Mariano Matamoros** (formerly *San Felipe Cuixtlán*; then *Ixtacuixtla*), where the little Franciscan convent of *San Felipe* was functioning by 1585. The former open chapel survives, rebuilt and with an added cupola; the portería, once used as an extension of the open chapel, to make it a bay deeper, has been incorporated in the later parish church, five bays wide and two deep. An original alfíz can still be made out. The convent church, a late 16C addition, became a ruin after the friars left in 1640. 22km *San Martín Texmelucan*, see Rte 66.

FROM TLAXCALA TO PUEBLA VIA HUAMANTLA, 102km. Tlaxcala to *Apizaco*, see Rte 69. From Apizaco, Méx. 136 goes across the NE slopes of the La Malinche volcano. At 26km a road goes S to (4km) *San Andrés Ahuashuatepec*, its late 18C church faced with glazed and unglazed tiles. 2km NE is *Tzompantepec*, the façade of whose church of San Salvador is one of the richer manifestations of 18C popular churrigueresque. 46km **Huamantla** (22,000 inhab.; 2553m; H,R,P), centre of a region which produces maize, potatoes, and pulque, and called 'Heroica' after a reverse inflicted on US troops in Oct. 1847 by a local force under Eulalio Villaseñor. The former Franciscan convent (originally *San Luis*, now known as *San Francisco*) was founded in 1569, although the church was not finished until the 18C. The façade of the parish church, *San Luis*, is a fine example of the transition from Mannerist to baroque. The simple statues in the five niches are of alabaster. The interior contains a churrigueresque high altarpiece and two baroque side altarpieces. Of great interest is the church of *La Caridad* (mid-18C), the estípites of its façade crowned by archangel figures, repeated in the lively relief above the doorway and surrounding the unusually shaped window—all against a facing of tiles. The days leading up to the feast of the Assumption (15 Aug.) see active preparation of carpets of flowers to cover the streets.

The road runs S into the State of Puebla beyond (58km) *Zitlaltepec* and then (Méx. 129) SW, under the Mexico–Veracruz motorway, to (76km) *Acajete*, with three popular baroque 18C churches, and, (88km) **Amozoc** (14,000 inhab.; 2331m), a town known for its silver- and iron-ware. Facing the plaza, the former Franciscan convent of *Asunción de Nuestra Señora*, founded in 1580–85, rebuilt in the 17C, has had a chequered career since. Opposite, the parish church also dates from the 17C (interesting gilded altarpieces). 102km *Puebla*, see Rte 67.

69 Tlaxcala to Tulancingo

Méx. 119 and Méx. 130, 176km.—4km **Tizatlán**.—23km Apizaco.—49km Tlaxco.—78km Chignahuapan.—94km Zacatlán de las Manzanas.—176km **Tulancingo**.

Beyond the Río Zahuapan we turn r. (NE) along Méx. 119. 4km turning l. for **TIZATLAN**, now a village, but at the Conquest one of the principal lordships of Tlaxcallan (see Rte 68).

Tizatlán itself was once capital of the Tlaxcaltecan city-state ruled by Xicoténcatl II (b. 1484) just before the arrival of Cortés.

Evidence of the earliest inhabitants of Tlaxcala, however, is more scarce: a flint Clovis point has been found at Apizaco, and surveys by Angel Barcía Cook throughout the Puebla–Tlaxcala region have located as many as 275 village and town sites by the Late Preclassic Period. Cook's work shows that the region was technologically advanced at an early date and that much of the Teotihuacano traditions of talud-tablero architecture and stucco plasterwork originated with Tlaxcalteca masons. Many of the early town sites had fortifications, and N Tlaxcala maintained close contact with Teotihuacán throughout the Classic Period.

In the Postclassic several kingdoms or principalities arose after the demise of Teotihuacán. The most powerful of these was the kingdom of the Tlaxcalteca, which had three principal cities—Cholula, Huexotzingo, and Tlaxcala–Tizatlán; and a number of lesser smaller centres, such as Ocotelulco and Quiahuixtlán. N of Tlaxcala was the contemporary kingdom of Meztitlán, and to the S there was a loose federation of hill tribes known as Yopotzinco, where one of Tlaxcala's long-term rivals was the fortress city of Tepexi el Viejo.

The city-state of Tlaxcala was traditionally founded in 1328 (another source states 1348) by the Tlaxcalteca or Teochichimeca, one of the seven traditional Aztec tribes from the caves of Chicomoztoc (cf. *La Quemada*). The Tlaxcalteca originally settled in the S part of the kingdom of Alcohuacán (Texcoco), until they were driven out of the Basin of Mexico by three of the other seven tribes: the Alcolhua of Texcoco, the Tepaneca of Azcapotzalco, and the Mexica, at that time of no fixed abode. Some of the Tlaxcalteca settled in the Chalco region in the SE of the Basin, far enough from their persecutors not to be bothered about, but close enough to remain a thorn in their sides; but most of them moved W and founded the city of Tlaxcala–Tizatlán. The area was already populous, and included another group, the Otomí, who had moved there in the Early Postclassic. Together, the Tlaxcalteca and the Otomí kept up a policy of harassment against the growing power of the Mexica, an enmity that never diminished. The principal Tlaxcaltecan deity was Mixcóatl–Camaxtli, after the legendary Toltec leader, Mixcóatl.

In the 15C the Mexica Aztecs established complete control over the Basin and began their conquests to the E and S. By the beginning of the 16C they had reached the Gulf Coast and established garrisoned trading colonies along the principal trade routes, thus effectively cutting off Tlaxcaltecan access. The kingdom was virtually under siege for 30–40 years until the arrival of the Spaniards, during which time it suffered severely from a dearth of salt and other basic items, and its people became known in the chronicles as poorly dressed and Spartan-like. Moctezuma II Xocoyotzin made a final attempt at conquest in 1502 but failed, and thereafter left the lozenge-shaped region as an enclave surrounded by lands under Aztec control; and in any case the kingdom represented no great economic prize, since the Aztecs already had control over all the main trade routes.

The Pal. of Xicoténcatl was excavated by Alfonso Caso in 1927 and 1935. In addition to finds described below, he found fired clay bricks, more evidence of Tlaxcaltecan technology, as fired bricks are known only at four other prehispanic Mesoamerican sites: Tula where their use is uncertain; and Comalcalco (Tabasco); Santa Rita Corozal (Belize); and Zacualpa (Guatemala).

At the coming of Cortés, its old lord, Xicoténcatl I, had handed over rule to his son Xicoténcatl II. The town was Cortés's headquarters during his preparations for the siege of Tenochtitlán and continued to be a place of great consequence alongside the new Spanish city across the river, for the rest of the 16C.

The ruins at Tizatlán include several monuments and some polychrome murals. A main platform has steps leading to two rectangular altars with symmetrically arranged pillars. To the W of these are a wall ruin, possibly part of a temple.

Polychrome murals remain on altars on the main platform, in yellow, ochre-red, blue, and black, and fragments of painted plaster survive in several other ruins. The paintings are said to represent the wars between the Tlaxcalteca and the Mexica, and in general style they resemble the Codex Borgia. On the W altar, two sides are identically decorated in friezes of blue, red, and yellow on a black background, depicting a skull, a left hand, a heart, and an unidentified circular object, each four times. On the S wall of the altar are two gods: on the r. is Tezcatlipoca, identified by his 'smoking mirror', in which he is able to see all that happens on earth and can thus apportion rewards and punishments accordingly; his body is black, identifying him with Camaxtli, the Tlaxcaltecan god of war; he wears a plumed headdress, a square nose ornament, and a circular pectoral with four gold balls hanging from it; he clutches an atlatl (spear-thrower), and a blue incense pouch, together with two sticks painted yellow, blue, and brown to represent aloe spines, used in torture rites by priests and nobles. The l.-hand figure is Mictlantecuhtli, Lord of the Underworld, shown as usual as a skull and skeleton.

The E altar is also decorated on three sides. Two walls have doubled rows of 13 and 13½ coloured squares, respectively, inside which various figures are painted, many of them repeated: there are 27 serpent-like creatures, 6 symbols of dripping water or blood, 5 human skulls, 3 black squares with red centres, a human heart, and a red circle surrounded by smaller circles. Along the bottoms of the rows runs a border of stepped frets and inverted U-shapes. The significance and meanings of the designs are wrapped in religious symbolism and thus insufficiently understood. On the third wall of this altar are two scenes: on the l. a nude goddess swims in a blue tank, surrounded by a jaguar, an eagle, and three gods; and on the r. an unidentified animal swims in a blue tank surrounded by two geometric figures and three gods.

Thanks to restoration from 1981 the Franciscan open chapel of **San Esteban**, one of the most important historical monuments of New Spain, has recovered much of its old clarity.

It dates possibly from 1539 and may be the chapel specially built in six months for Easter that year by the Indians: 'which, when finished, was a magnificent room: they call it Bethlehem'— significant word because 'Tlaxcala' and 'Bethlehem' have the same meaning—'house of bread'. 'They painted the outside', continued Toribio de Benavente (Motolinía), 'in four days...On one space they painted the works of the first three days of the creation of the world, and on another space the works of the other three days. As for the other two spaces, on one is the tree of Jesse, with the lineage of the Mother of God above it, done very beautifully, and on the other space is our father St Francis...The chapel has well made arches and two choirs, one for the singers and one for those who play instruments...'. The chapel became the sacristy of the later church (1770), but restoration works have given it back some independence.

The three central arches of the five-arched front curve outwards in a half-hexagon before a raised sanctuary. On either side of the nave are two high choir galleries, all roofed by wooden beams sustained by double ornamental brackets divided by a Franciscan cord moulding. The spaces between the brackets are occupied by painted panels. Around the triumphal arch is an original painting (gone over by a later hand) of God the Father surrounded by angels playing instruments and swinging thuribles. Its soffit also keeps its painted decoration. On the S wall of the apse a mural fragment showing Paradise, with Adam and Eve, and Hell has been revealed; on the N wall, another, indistinct, mural fragment.

10km (l.) *Belén Atzitzimititlán*, with a 16C church (modified). Just beyond (12km) the turning r. to (3km E) *Amaxac de Guerrero* (church of San Bernabé; 1607) and (5km) *Sta Cruz Tlaxcala* (church of Sta Cruz, with three large baroque altarpieces), we branch r. for (14km) **Sta María Atlihuetzia**, where the ruined Franciscan convent and church of *Concepción Purísima* date from c 1555–85. The trapezoid open chapel, with rib vaulting, dates from 1538–44; the three-arched portico was added in the 1550s. The parish church of *Sta María* (early 18C), with a baroque façade, contains one of the most ambitious baroque high altarpieces in Mexico, its solomonic columns laden with elaborate relief. 18km *Ocotoxco*, see Rte 20. 23km **Apizaco** (30,000 inhab.; 2408m; H,R,P), largest town in the State and its most important industrial centre, also well-known for the manufacture of multi-coloured walking sticks (bastones). The parish church of *San Andrés* dates from the 17C.

From Apizaco, Méx. 136 runs SE to (23km) *Huamantla*, see Rte 68.

Méx. 119 continues N into the Sierra Tlaxcalteca to (49km) **Tlaxco** (8000 inhab.; 2600m; P), in a wooded mountain landscape. The 18C parish church of *San Agustín* contains a churrigueresque altarpiece. We cross into the State of Puebla. At 76km a road runs SE to begin a winding and difficult climb over the Sierra Madre Oriental to (163km) *Teziutlán*, see Rte 64. 78km **Chignahuapan** (6000 inhab.; 2260m; H,P), in the NE slopes of the Sierra de Puebla, known for silver and lead extraction. The 18C church of *Santiago Apóstol* contains baroque transept altarpieces. 94km **Zacatlán de las Manzanas** (15,000 inhab.; 2000m; H,R,P), a typical town of the sierra, the eaves of its houses affording shelter from rain which falls throughout the year. Its name reflects the varieties of apples grown in the region, along with pears and plums. A yearly apple fair is held here (8–21 Aug.).

Its principal monument is the former Franciscan convent of *San Pedro y San Pablo*, founded in 1555. The large, three-aisled basilican church, a later building or remodelling, has a W portal in strict Renaissance style. An inscription above it carries the date 1564, while another, on the S tower, mentions 1562 and 1567. The INTERIOR is still striking in its purity, even though altered in later times, probably in the 19C. Nave and side aisles, at a lower level, are covered by flat wooden beam ceilings, and separated by slender fluted columns, from which spring semicircular arches. Above the nave arches the painted medallions fill in for original clerestory windows. A series of projections at the angle of ceiling and nave wall probably once supported a second, ornate alfarje, ceiling beneath the present one. Best feature of the convent is the thick squat columns of the lower cloister.

At 96km a road branches r. for (40km) *Ahuacatlán* (1330m), with the 17C church of San Juan (rich baroque façade and high altarpiece).

Hence (only for the adventurous) we may follow the road E via *Tepango de Rodríguez* and *Zapotitlán de Méndez* to (c 105km) *Hueytlalpan*, where the Franciscans had founded the convent of San Andrés by 1546. Here Andrés de Olmos (d. 1571), wrote 'Arte para aprender la lengua mexicana'. The church, vaulted and three-aisled, probably dates from the original works in the 1550s and 1560s.

Méx. 119 continues NW to join Méx. 130 at (139km) the border with the State of Hidalgo. 176km *Tulancingo*, see Rte 62.

70   Puebla to Izúcar de Matamoros

Méx. 190, 68km.—31km **Atlixco**.—45km turning for (14km W) **Huaque-chula**.—52km Tepeojuma.—68km **Izúcar de Matamoros**.

We leave Puebla to the SW. 13km *San Francisco Acatepec*, see Rte 66. Here we join Méx. 190 which skirts the E slopes of Popocatépetl. 31km **ATLIXCO** (c 75,000 inhab.; 1881m; H,R,P), in the Valle de Atlixco, at the foot of the SE slopes of Popocatépetl, is set in an agricultural and stock-raising area, long known for its fertility, where light industry has also developed since the 19C, lately joined by automobile plants. Its historic core preserves a group of Mexico's most interesting religious foundations, famous for the local brand of baroque relief.

At the time of the Conquest the valley of Atlixco (or Atrisco) was considered 'the most famous valley in New Spain: all can be irrigated; all is irrigated; and thus they harvest in it an infinity of wheat'. According to Motolinía: 'for many years this valley has been a kind of paradise, because it has all the means to be considered so. Verily paradise means a place of orchards and gardens, where there is an abundance of water, roses, and fruits—as there is here. They call it "Val de Cristo"'. In 1579 Spanish settlers established Villa de Carrión, soon more familiarly known as Villa de Atlixco—a status changed to city in 1843. In the early 19C, commented Humboldt, Atlixco was 'celebrated for the beauty of its climate, the fertility of its countryside, and for an abundance of tasty fruit'. In May 1847 the State government of Puebla, in face of US attack, transferred here, but from midnight on 19 Oct. US troops under Gen. Lane cannonaded the city from the Cerro de San Miguel. No resistance was offered and the victors went on a pillaging spree. The French troops who occupied Atlixco in Apr. 1863, however, made the strongest impression on the atlixquenses. As a local historian put it: 'Everyone noted their conduct, admired their manners; even their most insignificant gestures were commented upon. Every opportunity was sought to hear them speak and even though their language was not understood, no chance of starting up a conversation with them was missed'.

The city centre is the ZOCALO, small and intimate, planted with jacarandas and tulip trees, and laid out in the early 19C, now endowed with a tiled moorish bandstand. On the E side is the *Pal. Municipal*, probably dating from the early 17C, but repaired in 1926–31 and remodelled in 1960–63.

Next door is the **Parroquia** and (on the N) its adjoining **Sagrario**, an imposing mass which dominates what was the nucleus of the original Spanish villa.

It is the second church on the site. The nave dates from c 1620–50; the chapels were added at the end of the 17C. The Sagrario was added c 1720; the sacristy in the mid-18C; the tower c 1770. A good part of the paintings and furniture of the interior were originally in the church of El Carmen (see below).

EXTERIOR. The gable crowning the W façade bears a relief of the royal arms of Spain. Estípites flank the openings of the tower. From C. de la Constitución can be got a good view of the majestic cupola, with its tile decoration: yellow suns and yellow and blue strips. In the niches of its lovely little pinnacle are appealing statues; the finial is an image of St Joseph and the child Jesus. The W doorway, strangely simple, was modernized in 1839. In the gable of the Sagrario façade (more sumptuously baroque than the church, with adventurous mortar relief; now closed up) is a monstrance upheld by a two-headed eagle, two playful lions, and two little angels.

The INTERIOR was redone, in white and gold, in 1839. In the transepts are two excellent anastyle retables (some original statues missing), with slanted ornamental niche pilasters. In the r. transept the neostyle retable of Our Lady of Guadalupe. The 17C baroque pulpit displays delicate marquetry work. The Stations of the Cross are from the studio of Cabrera. In the r. aisle the 3rd chapel contains a painting by Luis Berrueco of Our Lady of Mount Carmel protecting Carmelite religious. In the 4th chapel is another work by Berrueco, Our Lady of Joy, and Vision of St Teresa by Luis Juárez (which demands better treatment). The 1st chapel l. aisle contains a St Francis Xavier (1744) by Miguel de Herrera. In the sacristy are two more paintings by Luis Juárez, Education of Our Lady and Marriage of Our Lady (with excellent detail), and Sacred Heart adored by angels (1858) by the local painter Francisco Morales.

C. de la Constitución leads E from the plaza. The red-tiled building (l.) at the corner with C. 2 Norte was the *Casa de Ejercicios*, a late 18C foundation to provide education, on Jesuit lines, for boys. At the end of C. de la Constitución, bounded by C. 4 Norte and C. Nicolás Bravo, is the former church and convent of **El Carmen**.

Founded for discalced Carmelite friars in 1589 and built in 1600–20, this, the most splendid and richest of Atlixco's foundations, was closed finally in 1867. The church is now an army store. Even in their maltreated state (made worse by a gimcrack white façade along C. 4 Norte) the buildings, surrounded by an impressive atrio wall, have not yielded their old grandeur. The central façade, flanked by buttresses, is Mannerist, marked by imposing pilasters (with almohadilla divisions in the lower storey) and, in the upper storey, angels upholding the imperial crown; the emblem of the Carmelite Order; and a niche (now empty), with images of SS Peter and Paul on either side.

At the corner of Cs 4 Norte and 6 Oriente is *El Dulce Nombre de María*, an 18C chapel; and further N in C. 4 Norte (r.) the church of **San Félix**, rebuilt in the late 18C and changed since then.

On the high altar is an imposing early 17C wooden statue of an enthroned and blessing St Felix (Pope St Felix I, patron of the town), the estofado expertly done. On the r. of the nave, a small reliquary retable (from El Carmen; c 1618). Among the paintings, an 18C Apostolate, St Peter represented as pope, the rest as bishops, by an anon. poblano painter. In the sacristy, an 18C painting showing the church in its original form.

In Av. Independencia, at the corner with C. 6 Oriente, is the church and former convent of **Sta Clara**, the façade aligned with the street.

It was the only convent of nuns in Atlixco, founded in c 1617–18 for urbanist Poor Clares, the founding sisters—'blessed and fertile plants'—coming from San Juan de la Penitencia and Sta Clara in Mexico City. The church was rebuilt in the later 18C; the convent was suppressed at the Reform.

The twin classical portals, now somewhat mutilated, are separated by four of the nine buttresses which line the S side of the church. The INTERIOR preserves some of its rich decoration and works of art, above all an exquisite wooden polychrome relief of St Clare (not displayed) protecting members of her Order. In the presbytery, two vast paintings (both in two panels; both needing thorough restoration) by Luis Berrueco: Assumption and Coronation of Our Lady. The two-storey 17C cloister, notable for its fine mouldings, still exists to the N of the church.

Across C. Libertad, C. 6 Poniente meets C. 3 Norte. To the l. in the latter is the former convent and church of **La Merced**, a Mercedarian foundation of 1613.

EXTERIOR. The façade is a jewel of early 18C atlixqueño baroque, in greyish (creamy in the sun) stone, once coloured blue, rose, and white. Two pairs of solomonic columns in each storey form the supports; between them niches sheltering a king and a bishop (lower storey) and SS Raymond of Peñafort and Raymond Nonnatus (upper storey). The mortar relief covering columns and surfaces, though lacking in delicacy, is extraordinarily vigorous and intense. Vines and bunches of grapes completely cover the lower-storey columns, while those of the upper storey are swathed in double bands enclosing floral and foliate motifs. In the trilobe arch of the doorway runs a pattern of palmettes; in the narrow jambs, an original semi-geometric pattern; in the spandrels, little angels; in the frieze and narrow bands between door and column, drooping vines. The arch key is a dove, the Holy Ghost; above, interrupting the frieze, appears an infant Christ among grapes and vines. Centrepiece of the upper storey is a niche containing the statue of Our Lady of Mercy resting on an intricate console of volutes and strapwork, her mantle held up by angels to protect a king, a knight, a pope, and a cardinal. Above the niche flutter two smiling angels, who develop into a complex of scrolls and flowers; on either side of the shell-like choir window are two winged sirens in feather headdresses, their tails elaborately curled. Above the window another ornamental flourish envelops a grotesque head which breaks the upper cornice and serves as base for the statue of St Joseph and the infant Christ in the space provided by a broken pediment. The S doorway obeys an earlier, Mannerist, style.

INTERIOR. Among the 18C pieces still kept in the narrow high nave is a beautiful wooden pulpit, partly gilded, encrusted with ebony, rosewood, and mother of pearl. The huge painting of the Patronage of Our Lady of Mercy, a major work by José Joaquín Magón (1763), is important for the light it sheds on contemporary lay costume (lower r.). In the sacristy, a 17C anon. (probably Spanish) Martyrdom of St Catherine; Triumph of the Immaculate Conception by Juan Tinoco; and a gilded polychrome Our Lady of Mercy (late 17C).

On the l. of the church is the triple-arched portería. One of the cloister's interior doorways, decorated with flowers and birds in relief, is an early work, possibly taken from one of the decayed houses demolished to make room for the convent c 1620.

From the SW corner of the Zócalo, Av. Hidalgo leads W to the chapel of **La Tercera Orden** (late 17C–early 18C; for members of the Third Order of St Francis), its almost pyramid-like façade another characteristically energetic piece of atlixqueño baroque (but not without Mannerist echoes), full of vine, flower, fruit, mask, and angel relief. In the lower storey niches appear images of SS Peter and Paul and Francis and Antony. The upper storey, topped by an espadaña, resembles a mixtilinear alfíz. On either side, mixtilinear medallions bear images of SS Bonaventure and Bernardine; above them, sirens with fantastic tails. The columns and choir window frames show basket-weave patterns. In the top niche, a statue of Bl. Luchesius of Poggibonsi, the first tertiary. The side doorway is another sumptuous, and earlier, work.

The INTERIOR contains interesting altarpieces. The 1st l., a modern reconstruction of incompatible fragments, incorporates columns from an early 17C work; the 2nd is of the sturdy churrigueresque kind. The ambitious baroque high altar, an exaltation of the Third Order, is interspersed with statues of 12 tertiaries around the central figures of St Ferdinand and Our Lady of Guadalupe. Presbytery and crossing walls are hung with seven paintings of the Life of St Francis by Lorenzo Zendejas (late 18C). In the l. transept, a small churrigueresque retable, the central part of a large original.

Beyond the chapel we fork r. into Av. 16 de Septiembre to reach the former church and convent of **San Francisco**, on a terrace on the side of the Cerro de San Miguel.

Originally dedicated to Sta María de Jesús, it was founded c 1538 in the centre of the Indian town of Acapetlahuacan—not only 'to escape the mosquitoes and noisome creatures which pullulated in parts of the humid valley', but also to keep control over the Indians—and built during 1540–70 along lines indicated by Fray Juan de Alameda, with additions c 1610–20. The convent and its Indian parish, which the Franciscans managed to hold on to, was finally secularized in 1755.

The terrain limits the size of the atrio, which sufficed for the small number of Indians to whom the friars administered. Its curved wall was modified in the 18C.

EXTERIOR. The church has an inevitably fortress-like appearance. There is an upper outdoor walkway just inside the parapet to ease movement otherwise made difficult by the extrados of the vault, and a SE tower with squinch support. The SW tower is an early 18C substitution. The façade, between two corner buttresses, displays a mixture of Isabeline Gothic and plateresque. Jamb bases and shafts (note the Franciscan cord), and capitals, intricately worked with late Gothic mouldings, support a flat arch. Slender inner columns and the cornice enclose an alfíz studded with 12 ornamental motifs. The outer twisted columns may (but not necessarily) be late 17C additions. In the upper panel, which frames the choir window, are 11 tequitqui medallions showing anagrams of Christ.

The INTERIOR is covered by superb rib vaulting, in the first two sections from the W end less complex than in the third and the apse, which is narrower than the nave. The monumental high altarpiece was probably once that of the church of El Carmen and, though adapted to accommodate an early 19C tabernacle, is of extraordinary quality. The four enormous solomonic columns, grandly proportioned and finely cut, of the lower storey show an Italian influence. Its seven paintings of Scenes from the Life of Our Lady are by Francisco Martínez (1732). Of the two holy water stoups, one, possibly once part of a late 16C fountain, is decorated with basket-weave relief; the other, with a frieze of angels and foliage entwining monograms of Christ, dates from the 17C.

The entrance to the CONVENT is opposite the main arch of the five-arched portería. The other four arches may well have been an open chapel. The cloister, three arches to a side, is probably older than the church.

In the lower cloister walk are murals (in poor condition) depicting the Capture of Christ (W wall) and the Scourging of Christ (E wall). In the spandrels of the arches runs a frieze of grapes and flowers. The murals of the upper walk are of great interest, coloured in blue, red, green, and ochre. The first is of a medieval city, through which runs a river; the second is a Latin cross, its arms ending in trefoil shapes, set against a tapestry of Greek crosses, and, behind, a landscape; the third shows a doorway framed by an arch, at the sides of which are two more arches through which may be seen a landscape.

On the W side of San Francisco the *Cap. de la Soledad* dates from the mid-18C. On the top of the hill, the simple church of *San Miguel* (18C) is a popular pilgrimage centre on the feast of St Michael (29 Sept.).

Following C. 11 Sur S from Av. Hidalgo, we come on the l. to the church and hospital of **San Juan de Dios**, founded in 1731 by the Brothers of St John of God (juaninos). The church, finished in 1789, stands in an atrio entered through a three-arched portico (the centre arch covered by an elaborate representation of the imperial coat-of-arms). Among the paintings are a Death of St Teresa (1720; from El Carmen), an excellent work by Ventura de Torijano, and Our Lady of Light and St Barbara (either side of high altar), by Luis Berrueco.

The enchanting CLOISTER, now part of the municipal hospital, its once brilliant red, grey, white, and blue tilework now attractively faded, has an enclosed upper walk and a central fountain, its basin supported by a statue of Heracles choking the Nemean lion. To the hospital belongs a series of paintings by Luis Berrueco and Pablo Joseph de Talavera (1743), illustrating scenes from the life of St John of God; they include a scene where the saint disciplines himself to try to convert three musical courtesans.

S of the Zócalo on the r., at the corner of Av. Independencia and C. 3 Poniente, are the church and convent of **San Agustín**, founded by the Augustinians in 1590, dedicated to St Cecilia, built during the 17C, and finished by 1698. The conspicuous church tower is plentifully decorated with mortar relief; in the upper part of the base, an ornate cartouche contains the Augustinian emblem of the Sacred Heart. The principal doorway, facing N, is Mannerist, and with good relief in the lower storey.

Of the original INTERIOR decoration there remains only that of the choir arch spandrels. In the centre of the r. wall is a Baptism of St Augustine (with architectural detail) by Nicolás Rodríguez Juárez. The two flanking paintings on a St Augustine theme, also by him, have been heavily retouched. The adjoining chapel, dedicated to Our Lady of Guadalupe, contains fine baroque stucco decoration in the interior of the dome and, at the entrance, two important paintings by Juan Correa: Adoration of the Kings (badly needing restoration) and Flight into Egypt. The restored cloister suffered when converted into dwellings after the Reform and has lost its character.

A country road goes W from Atlixco to (15km) **Tochimilco**, on the SE side of Popocatépetl, an attractive pueblo among camphor trees, where the Franciscan convent of the *Asunción de Nuestra Señora* was founded c 1560.

The unfinished doorway of the buttressed church, faced with rubble masonry, veers towards the classical, with a steep pediment capped by a choir window and its apple motif fringe, of N Italian type. At the level of the chemin-de-ronde is a line of merlons. The interior is beautifully rib-vaulted with pointed arches, and shallow lateral arcades lightening the thickness of the nave walls; the sanctuary is noticeably narrower than the nave. A fragment of a 16C altarpiece shows St Francis receiving the stigmata, in a landscape, with a patient companion. On the S side of the church, the three-bay, low portería supports an elevated open chapel, handsomely restored, once reached by a winding stairway in the SW corner buttress, which also served the canopied stone pulpit. On the S side of the tower base, a mural of St Christopher. The two-storey cloister has notable basket arches. Off the SW corner of the church is a 16C fountain (still working), its octagonal basin receiving water from eight surrounding columns and eight heads in the central pillar, which is topped by a coat-of-arms. Of the contemporary aqueduct, 14 arches remain.

Méx. 190 continues S to (45km) turning r. for (14km W) **HUAQUECHULA**, where the 16C writer Francisco Cervantes de Salazar said he'd found 'the best oranges, pomegranates, and figs in the world'. It boasts one of Mexico's most imposing Franciscan foundations, the convent of **San Martín**, built mainly in the 1530s and 1550s, most likely on the urging of Fray Juan de Alameda (d. 1570), who was buried in the sanctuary. (Among masons' marks at the side and rear of the church are the dates 1569 and 1570.)

The atrio, its wall topped by large merlons, is at a lower level than the adjoining terrain. Buttresses bulk out the grandeur of the EXTERIOR, and the two oblique at the NW and SW corners shelter the doorway, a lovely indigenous version of plateresque, marked off by slender baluster columns, decorated with relief above the arch imposts, fluted below, and a double cornice of projecting modillions, the relief repaying examination. Arch rim, spandrel edges, and jambs (within and without) are covered in delicate, foliated bevelled relief, that in the jambs surrounding candelabra. In the spandrels angels bear shields of the five wounds, a Franciscan emblem. Above, in a short-armed alfíz, is a relief of St Martin. The circular window, espadaña, and tower are incongruous later additions. In the jambs of the delightfully squat, uniquely inspired, N doorway are reliefs of SS Peter and Paul, intriguing Indian versions of contemporary Flemish figures, hats jauntily cocked. In the alfíz above the fluted basket arch, Christ sits in majesty between four angels blowing trumpets for the Last Judgment.

INTERIOR. Notable rib-vaulting covers the ample nave. The pulpit is a work of spellbinding charm, with levitating angels in the panels, a movement emphasized by splayed wings, rippling hems, and firmly horizontal feet. Six side altarpieces include baroque and churrigueresque specimens. As the baluster columns make clear, the high altarpiece is a rare 16C Renaissance example.

It was renovated in 1675, when it doubtlessly lost its original sculpture, and 17 paintings by Cristóbal de Villalpando (the six largest, Scenes from the Life of Our Lady; three in the top storey, Ascension, Crucifixion, Assumption; and eight Franciscan saints), his earliest known work, were added. In 1792 it was painted white, to lend it a neoclassical look; in 1886 the parish priest had the canvases repainted, thus contributing to their deterioration. Twelve paintings (sadly spoiled) of the Life of St Francis by Luis Berrueco (some figures in 16C costume and with appealing touches) line presbytery and sacristy walls.

The elevated open chapel above the portería, with its beautifully wide moulded arch covered by an alfíz (another excellent restoration), contains an intricate rib vault, possibly the finest in Mexico to have survived. The lower cloister arches, from the earlier 16C building campaign, borne up by buttresses, contrast with the more open upper arcade, probably of 1569.

At (52km) **Tepeojuma** (5500 inhab.; 1560m) the large church of *San Cristóbal* was started by the Dominicans probably in the 1540s. Of the original foundation, only the walls of the crossing, transepts, and apse still stand. The fourth bay, converted into a sanctuary, is now set apart from the rest of the nave by a screen with three arched openings. On the exterior, note the ionic capitals which adorn the crossing piers on the nave side. 60km *La Galarza*, with its Bacardi distillery.

68km **Izúcar de Matamoros** (c 45,000 inhab.; 1326m; H,R,P), at the S end of the Valle de Atlixco and known for honey, cheese, butter, fruit, as a centre of the sugar industry, and for its ceramics. It was the principal settlement of the prehispanic Itzocan, especially important in the Late Postclassic period as an Aztec market on the trade route from Tlatelolco to points S and E, and fell to the Spaniards in Sept. 1520.

With its raised atrio, the former convent of *Sto Domingo*, first of the chain of Dominican foundations between Puebla and Guatemala, was established c 1530. Its present aspect dates from a rebuilding c 1551–56. One posa remains, near the church's NW corner. The large church, one of the widest single nave (70.5 x 23m) barrel-vaulted examples in Mexico, was finished in the early 17C; the façade is of 1612. It retains its vast choir balcony, covering a third of the nave, and two original raised stone lecterns, drastically interfered with in later ages, which served for the reading of the epistle and gospel. N of, and flush with, the façade is a high wall with oddly placed windows, enveloped by a filled-in arch, once the start of the barrel vault of an open chapel. Above it is another room accessible from the choir balcony, perhaps a musicians' gallery for outdoor Mass. In the N side chapel are a Last Supper and Washing of the Feet (1681) by Baltasar Echave y Rioja. Detached from the church, on its N side, is the two-storey convent, now a school. The lovely cloister rib vaulting springs from compact corbels.

The 18C church of *Santiago*, with rustic exterior mortar relief and azulejo work, contains three churrigueresque retables.

C 12km E, at *Las Bocas*, at a cliff base on the E end of the valley, was an Olmec site contemporary with San Lorenzo Tenochtitlán in Veracruz, Tlatilco in the Basin of Mexico, and partly Chalcatzingo. Hollow 'baby face' figurines with jaguar paw-and-hand motifs from the site date it between c 1200 BC and c 700 BC. Las Bocas controlled one end of the valley while Chalcatzingo controlled the other.

C 15km NW, reached by Méx. 160 and a rough road branching NW, is *Tepapayeca*, where the Dominicans established a visita, Sta María, in the 1530s. The lovely little one-storey cloister survives, with delightful relief, especially the angels in the column capitals. The church contains 17–18C altarpieces.

From Izúcar to (163km) *Mexico City* and (344km) *Oaxaca*, see Rte 74.

71 Puebla to Veracruz

A. Via Fortín de las Flores

Méx. 150D and Méx. 150, 313km.—160km **Orizaba** and Méx. 150.—176km Fortín de las Flores.—184km Córdoba.—313km **Veracruz**.

We leave Puebla along Blvd Zaragoza to join the motorway N of the *Unidad Deportiva Cuauhtémoc*. It runs on the S side of the La Malinche volcano and gradually SE, through the Sierra de Tepeaca and into the Valle de Tecamachalco beyond (49km) the junction for *Acatzingo* and the road NE (Méx. 140) to *Perote, Jalapa*, and *Veracruz*, see Rte 71C. Beyond (103km) the turning for *Esperanza* (r.) we cross into the State of Veracruz, the Pico de Orizaba on the l., through the Sierra Negra.

160km **ORIZABA** (175,000 inhab.; 1284m) is a busy industrial city forming, with the neighbouring towns of Ciudad Mendoza, Nogales, and Río Blanco (on its W side and largely bypassed by the motorway), part of a conurbation in the valley of the Río Orizaba, at the foot of the SE slopes of the Pico de Orizaba. Its principal manufactures are beer, cotton goods, and cement, and its position on the verge of one of the republic's most fertile regions ensures its pre-eminence as distribution centre for coffee, fruits, and exotic flowers. Its temperate climate is marked by persistent drizzle (chipi-chipi) and more steady summer, early autumn, and winter rain, which has earned it the nickname 'ciudad pluviosilla'.

Bus stations. 577 Av. 6 Oriente and 425 Av. Zaragoza Poniente. Services to *Veracruz* (3½ hrs); to *Mexico City* (4½ hrs); to *Córdoba* (1 hr); to *Jalapa* (4 hrs); to *Puebla* (c 2½ hrs); etc.

Railway station. S of centre, corner of Av. 10 Poniente and C. 10 Sur. Trains to *Mexico City* (9 hrs) and *Veracruz* (3½ hrs).

Hotels throughout the town.

Post Office. Corner of Av. 2 Oriente and C. 7 Sur.

Tourist Office. 1 C. Norte.

In prehispanic times the valley of Orizaba was called Ahuializapan, referred to by Cortés in his 'Tercera carta de relación' in the derived version of Aulicaba. The Spanish settlement began as a stopping-place on an alternative, but more direct, route from Mexico to Veracruz and the cultivation of sugar cane began to flourish after 1540. In 1580 the largest refinery in the viceroyalty, in what is now the neighbouring town of Nogales, was sold to Rodrigo de Vivero, whose son, also Rodrigo, was created conde del Valle de Orizaba in 1627; his descendants' domination of the region was to be absolute. A special assembly of notables convened at Orizaba, which had served as French headquarters during the march inland in 1862, in Oct. 1866 persuaded the vacillating Maximilian not to abdicate and return to Europe, and thus prepared the way for the final showdown at Querétaro.

In 1906 the workforce of the Orizaba region formed the Gran Círculo de Obreros Libres. A strike and a harsh settlement imposed by Pres. Díaz provoked riots, and the sacking of the factory shops to which the workers were permanently indebted. The culmination took place on 7 Jan. 1907 in Río Blanco and Nogales when a multitude of workers, with their wives and children, were fired upon and mown down by troops, and their leaders shot. In 1914 a carrancista newspaper, 'La Vanguardia', commenced publication in Orizaba under the editorship of Dr Atl; José Clemente Orozco drew political caricatures. In 1915 the city became headquarters of the Casa del Obrero Mundial, an early trade union group with anarchist overtones, which later, under Atl's influence, was to adhere to constitutionalism.

On the N side of the central PARQUE CASTILLO is the many-domed parish church of **San Miguel**, begun c 1710, finished probably c 1780, and modified since. It lost its churrigueresque altarpieces in the early 19C. The high altar dates from 1808. Works by the 19C local painter Gabriel Barranco decorate the interior.

Just to the NW in Av. Madero is the *Pal. Municipal*, in green and yellow prefabricated steel, originally the Belgian pavilion at the 1889 Paris exhibition, shipped to Mexico in parts and reassembled here in 1894. On the S side of Parque Castillo the *Teatro Llave*, a more orthodox 19C building, was badly damaged by the earthquake of 1973.

Av. Colón leads E from Parque Castillo, passing the church of *El Calvario*, dedicated in 1833, next to a short-lived convent for Carmelite nuns (1839–67). To the S, C. 2 Oriente reaches PARQUE LOPEZ. On its N side is *Sta María de los Siervos* (early 20C), with an italianate neo-Romanesque façade. On the E side are the church and former convent of **El Carmen**, begun by the discalced Carmelite friars in 1735–36, badly mauled during 19C upheavals, rebuilt in 1886–88. Its atrio wall is marked by inverted arches, volutes, and urn finials. The church façade is simply churrigueresque. In the lower storey, images of SS Joseph and Teresa; in the gable, of St John of the Cross.

Behind El Carmen, at the corner of Blvd Miguel Alemán and C. 13 Sur, is the church of *Los Dolores* (18C; but frequently reconstructed).

Further E, facing the park between Cs 2 and 4 Oriente and 23 Sur, is **La Concordia** *(San Felipe Neri)*, former church of the Oratorians, begun c 1725–29, finished in 1741.

The adjoining house, to the S of the church, was built in 1767–74. After 1860 it served as hospital, until its ruination in the earthquake of 1973. The church was repaired after an earthquake in 1865.

The churrigueresque façade and octagonal tower base are decorated with lovely stucco relief, each estípite differently fashioned—an unusual feature. Two archangels surmount the inner estípites of the upper storey. In the gable two cherubs flutter either side of the Sacred Heart beneath drawn curtains. The interior preserves two churrigueresque side altarpieces (reconstructed) dedicated to the Immaculate Conception (N) and St Joseph (S).

Further E, at the corner of Cs 6 Oriente and 43 Sur, and adjoining the *Panteón Municipal*, is the little church of **Sta Gertrudis** (mid-18C), with another outstanding churrigueresque façade, packed with stucco relief. The towers were casualties of the earthquakes of 1819 and 1973.

Following Av. Colón W of Parque Castillo we come to the *Centro Educativo Obrero*, the interior with a mural by Orozco showing revolutionary scenes, a reminder of his stay in the town. Just beyond we take C. 6 Sur to the corner with Blvd Miguel Alemán, where stands the church of **San José de Gracia** and the former *Colegio Apostólico de Propaganda Fide*.

A royal decree of 1797 licensed the Franciscan missionaries of San Fernando in Mexico (comp. Rte 9) to establish a further foundation here; the first friars arrived in 1799. Despite the short time before their final suppression in 1834, the community managed to send missions to Tehuantepec and Tabasco. The original architectural plans for the church and convent were made by José Gutiérrez, criticized and worked over by Miguel Costansó, and finalized by 1802 by Manuel Tolsá; but even then do not seem to have been followed. On the E side is the church of *La Soledad*, originally of the 18C, ceded to the Franciscans on their arrival.

To the S, at the junction of Av. Madero Sur and C. 10 Oriente, is the church of *San Juan de Dios* (1763; much rebuilt), formerly belonging to the Brothers of St John of God. Visits may be arranged to the Moctezuma brewery (*Cervecería Moctezuma*) on the W side of town (enquiries at the Tourist Office).

The always snow-capped **Pico de Orizaba**, or **Citlaltépetl**, an extinct volcano, at 5747m is the highest peak in Mexico. Eruptions took place in 1545, 1559, 1613, and 1687. Historic climbs were made by the Frenchman Henri Galeotti in 1839, by US officers from Gen. Winfield Scott's army in 1848, by the French climber Alexandre Doignon in 1851, and by the Mexican Martín Tritschler, who planted the national flag on the summit in 1873. Its rocky parts are principally of hornblende and trachite, with great veins of obsidian.

Méx. 150 continues across a rich coffee-growing area (the triangle Orizaba–Fortín–Córdoba) to (176km) **Fortín de las Flores** (c 20,000 inhab.; 990m; H,R,P), famed for its profusion of flowers, encouraged by a benign climate and plentiful rainfall during May–Dec. In the grounds of the *Hotel Ruiz Galindo* (corner of Av. 1 and C. 7) is the *Hacienda de las Animas*, once favoured by Maximilian.

From Fortín a road runs N, touching the E slopes of the Pico de Orizaba, through a scenic coffee- and fruit-growing region, to (23km) *Coscomatepec de Bravo* (R,P) and (42km) **Huatusco** (c 15,000 inhab.; 1340m), amid abundant greenery, a delightful spot, known for its white-walled houses with red-tile roofs and the *Teatro Solleiro* (1889).

It was the Totonac city of Quauhtochco, conquered by the Aztecs between 1450 and 1472; excavations also uncovered traces of Preclassic occupation. The temple pyramid visible today was constructed by the Aztecs in the 15C, incl. façades studded with 'nailhead' stones, possibly meant to represent stars. Associated ceramics included *Aztec III* Black-on-orange, Cholula lacquer-finish polychromes, and Mixteca–Puebla polychromes made from local clays. Figurines included representations of many central Mesoamerican deities.

Less well known and inadequately explored is *Comapan* (c 20km NE), a 15C fortress and cemetery site on an escarpment. The defences are stone-revetted terraces as well as free-standing walls, plus unexcavated ruins of temples and residences.

52km turning r. on Méx. 125 to reach Méx. 140, the Jalapa–Veracruz road, at (111km) *Puente Nacional*, once an obligatory stopover for travellers from Veracruz to Mexico. The bridge over the Río La Antigua was completed, as Puente del Rey, in 1811, to the plans of Diego García Conde.

A small Totonac temple site has been excavated near here. There were two platform structures to support temples, one rectangular and one circular, the latter probably dedicated to the Wind god, Ehecatl.

Jalapa (see Rte 71B) is 52km NW; *Veracruz* 54km SE.

184km **CORDOBA** (c 200,000 inhab.; 984m; H,R,P), with a warm moist climate, is a distribution centre for the coffee, fruit, and tobacco in which the region abounds. The houses of its old centre, not unattractive in its decay, with stout wooden doors and balconies, are reminiscent of Andalucía.

The Spanish villa of Córdoba was founded in 1618 and intended to defend the area against any future uprising by negro runaways. (In a revolt of 1607–11 marauding negro bands, led by the chieftain Yanga, had been active on the slopes of the Pico de Orizaba and attacked travellers on the Mexico–Veracruz road.) In the 1740s, 2000 negro slaves laboured in its 33 sugar-cane mills (trapiches). On 27 Aug. 1821 the newly arrived 63rd and last viceroy, Juan O'Donojú (a tragic figure—two of his nephews had just died of yellow fever in Veracruz and he was himself to die of pleurisy in Mexico City on 8 Oct.), signed here with Iturbide the Treaties of Córdoba recognizing Mexican Independence.

On the SE side of PL. DE ARMAS, the town centre, is the parish church of *La Inmaculada Concepción de Sta María*, a late 17C foundation refurbished in neoclassical style. Its bells can be heard for miles. On the opposite side, the handsome late 19C *Pal. Municipal*. At No. 111 C. 1 (NE side) is the *Casa Cevallos* (1687) where the Treaties of Córdoba were signed. The *Museo de la Ciudad de Córdoba*, at No. 303 C. 3 (SW of the plaza), in a renovated late 17C house, shows local archaeological finds, historic documents, etc.

Of the other churches *San Antonio* is a discalced Franciscan foundation (1686). The *Teatro Pedro Díaz* dates from the later 19C.

From Córdoba, Méx. 150 runs to (201km) *Yanga* (with an unexcavated archaeological zone), as San Lorenzo ceded to negro settlers after the truce with Yanga (see above). 206km (l.) *Las Palmillas* has a small museum with Totonac figurines and other artefacts.

The road descends through the final foothills of the Sierra Madre Oriental towards the tropical lowlands of the Gulf. 210km *Cuitláhuac* (R,P). From (242km) *La Tinaja* Méx. 145 goes S to (36km) *Tierra Blanca*. The road runs alongside the Río Atoyac and reaches the coast just before (301km) *Boca del Río*, a fishing village at the mouth of the river, and then goes N to (313km) *Veracruz*.

B. Via Teziutlán

Méx. 150, Méx. 129, Méx. 125, Méx. 129, Méx. 131, and Méx. 140, 401km.—
48km Nopalucan.—54km San José Chiapa.—79km Oriental and Méx.
125.—91km Villa de Libres.—131km junction with Méx. 129.—191km
Teziutlán and Méx. 131.—242km Perote and Méx. 140.—295km Jalapa.—
401km **Veracruz**.

The road runs E to (14km) *Amozoc* (see Rte 68), then NE (Méx. 129) around the
E foothills of La Malinche to (38km; l.) the road to (18km N) *Huamantla*, see Rte
68. 48km **Nopalucan**, where the interior of the 17C church of *Santiago* dazzles
with six gilded altarpieces. In the nave, two churrigueresque (l.; 1776) and two
solomonic (r.)—the second l. dedicated to St Joseph, with paintings by Francisco
Muñoz de Salazar; the second r. with paintings by Francisco Javier de Salazar
(1737). In the transepts, two solomonic—on l., dedicated to the Passion, with
paintings by Juan de Villalobos; on r., with paintings by M. Santiesteban.

54km **San José Chiapa** (c 3000 inhab.), with marble quarries, is where Bp
Palafox, at the height of his dispute with the Jesuits, the Inquisition, and viceroy
conde de Salvatierra, took refuge while the city of Puebla was given over to the
rejoicings and revenge-takings of his opponents (June–Nov. 1647). (The Jesuits
staged a procession on St Ignatius' day, a triumphal float bearing the image of
the saint and a grotesque of the bishop; but St Ignatius' head fell off.) The
chapel of *San José*, in an atrio, was built in 1768–70 by Bp Fabián y Fuero to
commemorate his predecessor.

Its façade, wide and startlingly handsome, is marked by two estípites running its full length
and bearing the arms of Palafox himself and those of the marquesado of Ariza (his father's
title), and four miniature ones above the doorway. The interior, despite tasteless early 20C
decoration, contains two rare works of art. The pulpit, with its estípite base, is a perfect
combination of marquetry and alabaster. Entirely of alabaster, the exquisite high altarpiece
(1769) displays solomonic columns, a final play of the baroque, and statues showing encarnación technique in faces and hands, and veins of opalescent green in their clothing. In the
central Crucifixion, the figure of Christ shows signs of paint only in hair and beard, eyes and
lips. The painting of the Holy Family beneath is an anon. 17C Spanish work. The tabernacle
door bears a relief (the lamb lying on the book of seven seals) of gilded alabaster.

From (72km) *Tequixquitla* in the State of Tlaxcala, Méx. 136 goes W to (30km)
Huamantla, see Rte 68. 79km *Oriental* (2345m) in the plains known as Llanos
de San Juan. 91km **Villa de Libres** (the former *San Juan de los Llanos*), where
the 17C parish church of *San Juan* contains an interesting set of 18C altarpieces. Those lining the nave are a veritable display of solomonic columns and
incorporate caryatid supports. In the predella and support bases of one adjoining the transept (1737), appear souls in Purgatory. The high altarpiece, full of
movement, with good relief and statuary, and niches of varying shapes, on a
base decorated with projecting leafy relief, dates from 1728. Méx. 125 continues
N. At 131km State road 575 begins a run N through the Sierra de Zacapoaxtla.

It reaches (17km) *Zacapoaxtla*, picturesquely situated, and (32km; l.) *Nauzontla* before going
on to (51km) **Cuetzalán del Progreso** (6000 inhab.; 1022m; H[simple], R,P), delightfully vivid,
with narrow, winding streets and red-roofed houses, in a warm, humid region with frequent
rains. It is especially animated on Sun., when the local Nahua and Totonac Indians set up
their market and wear traditional dress. An ethnographic museum in the Pal. Municipal
includes finds from local sites, and a plan and photographs of the site of *Yohualichán* ('house
of night'). This is accessible along a dirt road (6km NE). It includes several monuments with
staircases, around a central plaza measuring c 60m by 70m; four wide terraces up the hillside;
and architectural embellishment similar to that at other major Totonac centres, such as El
Tajín and Misantla. It was occupied between c AD 200 and 800.

Méx. 129 branches NW to (145km) **Tlatlauquitepec** (c 6000 inhab.; 1930m; H,P),
on the r. bank of the Río Tlatlauqui, where the Franciscan convent of *Sta María*,
set up before 1548, was handed over to secular control in 1567.

It partly survives, but has been frequently altered. The church interior was thoroughly gone over in pretentious neoclassical during the 19C, but has kept its old wood and tile roof.

The road weaves a tortuous course to (186km) *Chignautla* and (191km) *Teziutlán*, see Rte 64. From Teziutlán, Méx. 131 runs E to join, at 213km, the road from Tlapacoyan to *Perote*, see Rte 71C. 242km *Perote*. Hence we may take Méx. 140 via (295km) *Jalapa* to (401km) *Veracruz*, see Rte 72.

C. Via Perote and Jalapa

Méx. 150, Méx. 125, Méx. 140, 299km.—38km junction with Méx. 125.— 49km Acatzingo.—93km Zacatepec and Méx. 140.—140km Perote.—193km **Jalapa**.—283km turning for Remojadas.—299km **Veracruz**.

We leave Puebla to the E on Méx. 150, the road to Tehuacán. 14km *Amozoc*, see Rte 68. 31km *Tepeaca*, see Rte 73. At 38km we turn l. on to Méx. 125, which runs NE under the motorway to Orizaba and across the Sierra Volcánica Transversal. 49km **Acatzingo** (2160m; P), its central plaza scene on Tues. of a famous market. On its E side, in an atrio, entered through a gateway composed of three pointed gothicizing arches, stands the solid church now known as *Nuestra Señora de Guadalupe*, once part of the Franciscan convent of *San Juan Evangelista* (c 1558–60).

Its W façade is an exercise in academic Renaissance style, doorway and choir window admirably combined. A walkway inside the parapet helps circulation around the roof, bulbous with the rise of the vaults. The interior is remarkable for its high rib vaulting, even higher above the chancel. The font, carved with flying angels wearing Indian masks, bears the glyph '4 rabbit' (1574).

An octagonal 16C fountain stands before the 18C parish church of *San Juan*, its winning little side doorway using solomonic columns. In the fine slender pulpit are panels of alabaster (tecali). The side *Cap. de Nuestra Señora de los Dolores* (1750–75), entered through a beautifully worked grille, contains noteworthy baroque altarpieces. The matching examples in the transepts, using caryatids, as well as solomonic columns, as supports, incorporate paintings of the Passion by José Joaquín Magón. The high altarpiece, set on a convex base, with four writer saints in the predella, is graced by a rich silver frontal, a rococo tabernacle also of silver and flanked by twin anthropomorphic supports, and by magnificent sculpture, the folds of the robes most effectively done. At the top is a Pietà guarded in the other central niches by the seven archangels; at the sides stand the four evangelists. The paintings on either side of the altar are by Gaspar Muñoz de Salazar (1750). Covering the nave walls, with their skirting of azulejos, are four huge canvases of the Passion by Miguel Jerónimo Zendejas (1775–78), probably the best of this controversial painter's output. The pulpit is a lovely combination of polychrome wood and alabaster. The adjoining chapel of *La Soledad* contains three more baroque altarpieces.

At 53km a turning r. (State road 568; somewhat rough) to (11km SE) **Quecholac** (2250m), in the SW slopes of the Sierra del Monumento.

Once known as Quechula, in the mid-16C it was a well-to-do city of the Popoloca Indians, rich in cattle and grain, and is still a good example of that period's urban layout.

Pl. Principal, formerly part of the atrio of the Franciscan convent, was built on a vast pile of rubble thrown up by the wrecking of the prehispanic religious site. S and E of the plaza are some 16C houses. Facing it is the former church of the convent of *La Magdalena*.

The Franciscans established a parish, dependent on Tepeaca, here in the 1540s, with a huge, three-aisled basilican church, possibly paid for by the Indians themselves and finished in the 1570s. In the 17C a new parish church was built within the walls of the 16C nave.

Entrance to the shortened atrio is through a three-arched gateway in fanciful popular baroque, part of the 17C building campaign. Of the later church, only the façade, sanctuary, and nave supports survive, the remodelled older structure having reasserted itself as the place for worship. The five baroque retables, one most effectively left ungilded, with gorgeous caryatid supports, are a very late development of the style; that dedicated to the Souls in Purgatory (with a huge appropriate painting) dates from 1780. Another, reticulated in its composition and with crinkled cornices, dates from 1817.

The convent buildings have disappeared, though the ancient doorway of a house in the street behind the church may have been part of them: solid jambs, roundel ornament, intricately curving arch, and alfíz.

Méx. 125 continues NE to (57km) turning r. for (3km) *San Pablo de las Tunas*, where the church of San Pablo, rebuilt probably in the late 17C, preserves a 16C doorway and font. Its chief treasure is the wide, churrigueresque high altarpiece, with ingenuous touches, the statues in the wide entrecalles standing beneath drawn drapes. At (74km) *San Salvador el Seco*, with an 18C church, a road (Méx. 144) goes SE through the W foothills of the Pico de Orizaba via (12km; l.) **Aljojuca**. Here the nave of the 17C church of *San Jerónimo*, its façade updated in the mid-18C to conform to the churrigueresque, is lined with altar-pieces, in white and gold, combining both solomonic columns and estípites.

The road continues to (29km) *Ciudad Serdán* to join at 47km the Puebla–Orizaba road, see Rte 71A.

83km turning r. (State road 394) for (8km SE) *San Nicolás de Buenos Aires*, with an 18C church (good baroque altarpiece). From (93km) *Zacatepec*, Méx. 136 and Méx. 125 run WNW and NW to (44km) *Huamantla* and (28km) *Villa de Libres* respectively, see Rtes 68 and 71B. To the W is the *Laguna Totolcingo*, with marshy surrounds, the haunt of wild duck. We continue NE on Méx. 140 through the Llanos de San Juan and, beyond (l.) the *Laguna de Alchichica*, into the State of Veracruz.

140km **Perote** (c 25,000 inhab.; 2460m; H,R,P), an unattractive town to the NW of the Cofre de Perote. To the N, on Méx. 131 to (25km) *Altotonga* (see Rte 64), is the *Fortaleza de San Carlos* (1770–77), built as an armaments and provision-ing store and as a stronghold from which aid could be got to Veracruz in case of attack. 'It has more the appearance of a prison than the usual abode of man, there being scarcely a window or chimney to be seen', observed William Bullock in 1823. In 1843, a victim of epilepsy and in hope of a cure, Guadalupe Victoria spent his last days here. After Mexico's declaration of war on Germany in June 1942, German subjects were interned here. It is now a prison.

The *Cofre de Perote* (4282m; so called because its peak is squared off like a chest), final E peak of the Sierra Volcánica Transversal, is what remains of a volcano, formed by andesites of hypersthene and augite pouring out over the sierra. Its slopes show deep ravines left by lava flows. Its summit is reached by a reasonable road, suitable for most vehicles all year round, running SE from the town through a pine forest for c 26km to a height of 4000m; then on foot for c 2 hours. No special equipment or preparation necessary, though warm clothing is strongly recommended. In winter the heights are snow-covered.

From Perote, Méx. 140 winds through the E slopes and pine forests of the Sierra Volcánica. 185km *Banderilla*, where the Jardín Lecuona contains what is reputedly the finest display of tropical flowers (gardenias, camelias, and especially rare species of orchids, etc.) in Mexico.

From here Méx. 127 winds N to (118km) *Martínez de la Torre*, see Rte 64.

193km **JALAPA** (c 378,000 inhab.; 1425m), capital of the State of Veracruz, is set in a valley on the E slopes of the Sierra Volcánica, overlooked by the Cofre de Perote to the W and with the Pico de Orizaba towering above wooded hills to the SW. Its climate is mild and subject throughout the year to a drizzle (chipichipi) for days at a time. Hence a profusion of flowers and the suitability of its surrounds for coffee- and tobacco-growing. The narrow cobbled streets and old houses (painted in pastel and brighter shades) contribute to the picturesqueness of its old centre, even though it possesses no major historic monuments. Its parks, laid out in the 19C, are an added attraction. The women of Jalapa (jalapeñas) are celebrated for their beauty.

Bus station. 2km E of the centre, in Av. 20 de Noviembre. Services to *Mexico City* (6½ hrs); to *Veracruz* (2½ hrs); to *Puebla* (3 hrs); to *Perote* (1 hr); to *Córdoba* (2 hrs); etc.

Hotels throughout the town.

Post Office. 70 Av. Zamora (Pal. Federal).

Tourist Office. 191 Blvd Manuel Avila Camacho.

By the mid-17C Jalapa was already a haven for natives of Veracruz, moving inland in search of more security. After 1720 it was known as Xalapa de la Feria, when it flourished as a commercial centre (until 1776); for only here could the goods brought from Cadiz by the fleet arriving at Veracruz be sold. As an obligatory stopping place on the Veracruz–Mexico road, it was much admired by travellers. 'A more healthy and delightful spot does not exist upon the face of the globe', declared Bullock in 1823. His volume of 'Ackerman's Fashions' was 'in prodigious request' and the jalapeños loved looking at his prints of London's public buildings, their wonder difficult to square with their conviction that the English were not Christians. In Apr. 1847 the advancing US troops of Gen. Scott successfully outflanked and beat, in a bloody climax, Santa-Anna's army at Cerro Gordo (c 30km E); the fall of Jalapa, Perote, and Puebla followed and the way to Mexico City was open to the invaders. During the battle, soldiers of the 4th Illinois Regiment captured Santa-Anna's wooden leg and are said to have used it as a baseball bat while playing at Jalapa. The town's status as State capital, a distinction hitherto disputed between it, Veracruz, and (briefly) Orizaba, was finally confirmed in 1885. Among famous natives are Antonio López de Santa-Anna (1794–1876); Sebastián Lerdo de Tejada (1823–89; president 1872–76); the historian José María Roa Bárcena (1827–1908); and Juan Díaz Covarrubias (1837–59), one of the 'martyrs of Tacubaya' (see Rte 16).

The old one- and two-storey houses of Jalapa, which help to give the place its charm, date mainly from the 18C and 19C: jutting tile roofs upheld by sturdy wooden beams; balconies of wrought iron also upheld by jutting beams; windows covered by wrought-iron grilles (sometimes with a decorative touch worked in); patios, full of tropical plants and flowers, with (in the two-storey houses) arcades on two sides, and closed galleries on the other two. Good examples are on Av. Revolución and at the corner of Cs Insurgentes and Xalapeños Ilustres. Less and less of this domestic architecture survives. In the town centre may also be seen the old business and commercial houses, grouped around two patios.

The State of **Veracruz** (c 7 million inhab.; 72,815 sq km) extends c 700km NW to SE along the Gulf and averages c 50km in width. More than 40 rivers rising inland terminate here, carrying rich soils and creating sandbars at the deltas. In the tropical E lowlands the climate is hot and humid. Behind the coastal strip the land rises, in the W central part amid lush vegetation and tropical rainforest (with, in places, a mean annual precipitation of 1500mm), to the E slopes of the Sierra Madre Oriental and to those of the Sierra Volcánica Transversal, whose principal and final peaks are the Pico de Orizaba and the Cofre de Perote. In the SE, the swampy jungle of the N Isthmus, rainfall is much heavier. It is a rich State, for its commerce, manufactures, agriculture, and oil and sulphur production and processing in its N and S regions. Tropical agricultural products include sugar (highest production in the republic) and coffee of exceptional quality.

The area of the present State was point of departure for the rapid Spanish exploration and conquest of New Spain. Here followed a swelling number of soldiers, clergy, merchants, artisans, public officials, prelates, and viceroys from Spain to open up the waggon road to Mexico. In May–June 1520 an outbreak of hueyzáhuatl (probably smallpox) began on the coast and reached Tenochtitlán by Sept., the first of many outbreaks which were to ravage the native population, reducing it from c 22 million to less than 2 million by 1580. In the tierra caliente behind Veracruz alone the Indians were all but wiped out. Negro slaves were introduced to work on cattle and sugar haciendas, their descendants helping to give the State its distinctive racial mix. The first Mexico–Veracruz road was under construction by 1531–32; by 1585 two highways, furnished at intervals with hospitals, connected coast and capital. The intendancy of Veracruz, established in 1786, constituted one of the 12 new divisions of the reorganized viceregal government. During the Independence struggle and early combative years of the republic, Veracruz was power base of three prominent leaders, Nicolás Bravo, Santa-Anna, and Guadalupe Victoria. The new State of Veracruz (the intendancy minus the district of Tampico, which went to Tamaulipas created in 1824 had the last-named as military governor. To add to post-revolutionary disorder, the rebellion of Veracruz's military governor, the violent Guadalupe Sánchez, in support of Adolfo de la Huerta against Pres. Obregón in 1923, ushered in a period of forced loans, arbitrary arrest, torture, and murder.

Development of the oilfields along the coast began in earnest in 1907 with the setting-up of Sir Weetman Pearson's Compañía Mexicana del Petróleo El Aguila, SA. Promotion of land reclamation projects, hydroelectricity, modern farming methods, and industry in the basin of the Papaloapan river system and the rehabilitation of the port of Veracruz found its impulse in the governorships of Miguel Alemán (1936–40), Jorge Cerdán (1940–44), and Adolfo Ruiz Cortines (1944–48).

The central PARQUE JUAREZ was once the atrio of the Franciscan convent of *La Natividad de Nuestra Señora*, begun in 1541, damaged by earthquake in 1546, sacked and burned by Indians in 1572, repaired by 1580; half of the buildings slid into the valley in 1886; the rest were promptly demolished. Traces of the walls survive.

In 1625 Thomas Gage was a guest and professed great indignation at the all-night gambling of his friar hosts.

On the E side of the park is the *Pal. de Gobierno*, on the site of the viceregal casas consistoriales, demolished in the early 1850s. It was begun in 1854–55 and probably finished c 1870. It contains murals by José Chávez Morado. In it was incorporated the *Pal. de Justicia*, built during the enlightened governorship of Teodoro A. Dehesa (1892–1911). On the N side of the park stands the *Pal. Municipal* (late 19C). A few steps E along C. Enríquez brings us to the wide *Parroquia* (Sta María), started in the mid-17C, finished by 1773, and given its neo-Gothic façade in the mid-19C. A side chapel immediately to the r. of the entrance contains an Our Lady of Mount Carmel (1766) by Cabrera and likeable 18C paintings of the Life of Our Lady.

From the NE corner of the park Av. Revolución climbs to the church of *Nuestra Señora del Calvario* (18C; the distinct r.-hand tower dating from 1871). It contains two churrigueresque altarpieces, with rococo touches, originally in the Franciscan convent. E of the centre, in C. Cuauhtémoc (reached along C. Xalapeños Ilustres), is *San José* (1770), where Santa-Anna was baptized.

In the NW part of the city, reached from the centre (4km; c 45 minutes walk) along Avs 20 de Noviembre and Xalapa, is the **Museo de Antropología de la Universidad Veracruzana** (Tues.–Sun., 10–5; fee).

The various galerías and salas are entered down steps. Patios have further displays. (NB—at the time of visit, the *La Mojarra* stele was not yet on display; see Tres Zapotes, Rte 83.)

ENTRANCE HALL. First of several Olmec colossal basalt heads, this example with a feathered headdress (no. 8 from San Lorenzo Tenochtitlán/Texistepec; 12 tons; Middle Preclassic c 1150–900 BC). GALERIA 1 (l.) Glass case containing a Totonac carved stone *palma* (associated with the Mesoamerican ball game) representing eagle devouring feline figure (c AD 700–900). Wall panels explain museum's layout and ancient Mesoamerican chronology. Olmec colossal basalt head, headdress formed of two paws each with three claws (no. 5 from San Lorenzo Tenochtitlán; 8 tons; Middle Preclassic).

GALERIAS 2, 3, and PATIO OLMECA. Basalt sculpture of asexual human figure (Monumento 1 from Soteapan, Zapotitlán; c AD 100–600). Andesite sculpture of an animal with humanoid features and long fangs (Monumento 1 from Coatzacoalcos; c 600–100 BC); carved basalt 'altar' showing human figure emerging from cave (Monumento 28 from Laguna de los Cerros; c 1150–900 BC). Basalt sculpture of bird's wing or hand (Monumento 13 from Laguna de los Cerros; c 600–100 BC). In the patio are a carved basalt stele showing seated figure in cave-like setting, a characteristic Olmec scene (Monumento 14 from San Lorenzo Tenochtitlán; c 1150–900 BC); colossal basalt head known as 'El Rey', with the symbol for jade in his headpiece (no. 1 from San Lorenzo Tenochtitlán; 24 tons; c 1150–900 BC); Stele 1 from Actopan, El Viejón, showing two figures, the l.-hand one holding a maize plant (andesite; c 600–100 BC).

GALERIA 4 and SALA OLMECA 1. Basalt figures of assistants to Rain god supporting sky (Monumento 2 from Portrero Nuevo; c 1150–900 BC); basalt 'altar' with human figure emerging from cave (Monumento 5 from Laguna de los Cerros; c 1150–900 BC); basalt jaguar deity, with a 'St Andrew's' cross on back of headdress (Monumento 1 from San Martín Pajapan; c 600–100 BC); Olmec basalt figure wearing banded headdress, known as 'El Príncipe' (Monumento 1 from Sta Cruz del Milagro; c 600–100 BC); seated figure with hands under legs, with high, bun-like hairdo (Monumento 1 from Cuauhtotolapan Viejo; c 600–100 BC); Stele 2 from El Mesón with human figure wearing elaborate headdress, and geometric symbols beneath (basalt; c 600–100 BC).

Colossal basalt head no. 4 from San Lorenzo Tenochtitlán. This example wears a headdress comprising four parallel horizontal strips and eight vertical strips and discs (4.5 tons; c 1150–900 BC). Another, similar basalt head, no. 3 from San Lorenzo Tenochtitlán, wearing headdress of four parallel horizontal bands like twisted cords (6 tons; c 1150–900 BC).

Basalt seated figure whose mouth comprises two opposing serpents and whose hands hold a type of 'knuckleduster' (Monumento 10 from San Lorenzo Tenochtitlán; c 1150–900 BC); another basalt figure (fragment of torso) with 'knuckledusters' (Hueyapan de Ocampo; c 1200–900 BC); basalt human head with serpent fangs (Monumento 5 from Estero Rabona; c 900–100 BC); fragmentary basalt human figure with arms held diagonally to his l., wearing trunks, sash, and cape (Monumento 11 from Laguna de los Cerros; c 900–100 BC); basalt human figure wearing broad sash and cape with double band (Monumento 6 from Laguna de los Cerros; c 900–100 BC).

Another colossal head, no. 9 from San Lorenzo Tenochtitlán, with prominent smile (3.5 tons; c 1150–900 BC); seated figure holding bar, known as 'El Escriba' (San Lorenzo Tenochtitlán; c 1150–900 BC); fragment of seated figure wearing loincloth, cape, and pectoral with an 'X' (San Lorenzo Tenochtitlán; c 900–100 BC).

In centre of Sala 1, glass case holding small Olmec sculptures.

Two basalt figures from Laguna de los Cerros—Monumento 19 wears cape and straps across chest, trunks, and knotted belt; and Monumento 2 (4 tons) from Coatzacoalcos, with serpent mouth, holding 'knuckledusters', and wearing pectoral with cross; also, basalt fragment of seated person, from Laguna de los Cerros (all three c 900–100 BC).

GALERIA 5 (Olmec). Three basalt sculptures: dead person with tongue of fire (Monumento 5 from Cerro de las Mesas; c AD 100–600); male figure wearing loincloth and knotted belt, and holding rod of authority (Medellín; c AD 100–600); 'altar' fragment with figures (Monumento 4 from Laguna de los Cerros; c 1150–900 BC).

GALERIA 6 and SALA OLMECA 2. Basalt figure of old man, 'old Fire god' (Cerro de las Mesas; c AD 600–900); volcanic stone 'eagle box' thought to be for the hearts of sacrificed victims (Hueyapan de Ocampo; c AD 100–600).

Jadeite figure of adult holding child in arms—the child wears death mask and has two 'Xs' engraved on chest (Monumento 1 from Las Limas; c 900–100 BC); jade head with almond-shaped eyes (S Veracruz; c 900–100 BC).

Colossal basalt head (no. 7 from San Lorenzo Tenochtitlán; c 1150–90 BC).

In centre of Sala 2, glass case with Olmec masks, hachas (thought to be associated with ball game), and jade pieces. To r., in corner, several basalt sculptures, incl. Monumento 1 from Laguna de los Cerros, with mouth of two serpents and symbol for 'four movement' in r. eye.

Monumento 1 from Isla de Tenaspi, known as 'Homshuk'—human countenance with features possibly alluding to a creation myth (Classic Period).

To l., grouped in corner, six Classic Period stelae, all basalt: Stele 8, Cerro de las Mesas (3 tons)—Xólotl, twin of Quetzalcóatl, with hieroglyphic date AD 792; Stele 6, Cerro de las Mesas (2 tons)—Quetzalcóatl or Huaman, wearing plumed serpent headdress and with hieroglyphs for AD 727; Stele 5, Cerro de las Mesas (2.5 tons)—Wind god, Ehecatl–Quetzalcóatl; Stele 4, Cerro de las Mesas (2.5

tons), showing figure with digging staff; Stele 3, Cerro de las Mesas (2 tons)—priestly figure wearing jaguar mask; Stele 1, Piedra Labrada (1.5 tons), with symbols for 'five serpent' and 'five crocodile'; Stele from Cerro de la Piedra (2 tons)—priestly figure in walking posture, carrying 'votive axe' in l. hand.

Towards centre of room, two Classic Period basalt figures: from Papaloapan (3 tons), of male figure with planting staff; and Monumento 7, Cerro de las Mesas (1.3 tons), of warrior with lance and shield.

Along wall, case of Olmec ceramics. Preclassic and Classic Period sculptures: basalt box with symbols of jade (chalchihuitl) from Laguna de los Cerros; basalt jaguar 'throne' from Piedra Labrada; earthenware funerary urn from Catemaco; fragments of basalt columns from Piedra Labrada; Monumento 2, Cerro de las Mesas (basalt; 2 tons)—mask of the god of rain; Monumento 1, Medias Aguas (sandstone; 2 tons)—mask with serpent features.

GALERIA 7 (Totonac). Two basalt sculptures of obese persons (Nopiloa and Soledad de Doblado; both c AD 100–600); basalt figure of Cipactli, the earth monster (Monumento 1 from Soledad de Doblado; c AD 100–600); seated basalt sacrificial figure, symbolizing fertility (Manlio Fabio Altamirano; c AD 100–600); basalt chacmool figure from Cotaxtla—glyphs indicate the date AD 1467, the year the Mexica Aztecs reconquered province of Cotaxtla.

GALERIAS 8, 9, and PATIO TOTONACA 1. Volcanic stone figure of Ce Tochtli, with the calendrical symbol 'one rabbit' (1.2 tons; Xicoxhimalco; 15C); basalt serpent sculptures, one from Coatepec; basalt figure of Tlaltecuhtli, earth monster in form of toad; vessel in shape of jaguar head (Xalapa; c AD 100–900).

In patio: Monumentos 1 and 2 from Mirador Pilapa—deer with headdress, Late Classic, and jaguar and sun, Preclassic, both basalt; basalt jaguar ready to spring, probably once with obsidian insets in eyes (18 tons; Nopiloa; c AD 100–600); volcanic stone 'eagle box' with face in niche (1 ton; Misantla; c AD 100–600); head of dead person (Misantla; Classic Period); obese person with relief of fish on chest (Manlio Fabio Altamirano; Classic Period); two basalt sculptures of Xipe Totec, sacrificial god and god of fertility (2.5 and 1.7 tons; Aparicio; both Classic Period).

GALERIA 10. Central Veracruz and Remojadas Preclassic ceramics.

GALERIA 10 and SALA TOTONACA 1 (Remojadas). Basalt sculpture of ribs of human torso (1.2 tons; Misantla; c AD 100–900); basalt dog (unprov., Classic); basalt rabbit (Espinal de Sta Bárbara; Classic).

Main Sala has cases of Remojadas ceramic male and female figurines, incl. 'smiling face' figurines, jewellery, ceramic vessels, and musical instruments. Sculptures around the room include an earthenware Xipe Totec; basalt face engraved within a face; basalt countenance representing 'duality'; earthenware Mictlantecuhtli, god of death; basalt monkey and toad—all Classic Period Totonac. Postclassic Aztec serpent sculpture with coiled tongue.

GALERIA 11. Postclassic Totonac vessels.

GALERIA 12. Model of El Tajín; basalt lintel with earth monster devouring corpse (Xicochimalco; Postclassic).

SALA TOTONACA 2 (El Tajín and Las Higueras). Figure with elaborate plumed headdress (El Tajín; Classic); basalt 'Descending god' (Sta Ana; Classic); sculptures of ball player from El Tajín, and of warrior (central Veracruz). Far end of room, murals from Las Higueras.

Centre of room, fragments of columns from El Tajín and Yecuatla (Classic Period); Mictlantecuhtli; Tláloc frieze; three sandstone stelae from El Tajín representing Tláloc and Cipactli, priest holding up copal incense bag, and the tree of life (all c AD 100–900). Behind these, sandstone figure of Chicomecóatl, goddess of corn and fertility; she is sacrificed seated on a throne, seven serpents spring from her neck, and she holds a glove; other objects associated include hacha and palma.

Further cases in this Sala and in GALERIA 13 contain other El Tajín and Totonac artefacts, incl. ceramic vessels with animal heads.

GALERIA 14 and SALA TOTONACA 3 (El Zapotal). Basalt disc for holding standard (Soteapan, Piedra Labrada; Classic Period). Basalt cadaverous figure from Cotaxtla, probably representing death (Postclassic).

The main room (before steps to Galería 15) contains standing, open-mouthed El Zapotal figures, with elaborate headdresses. Along walls and in centre, human and animal figurines and ceramic vessels from El Zapotal, Ríos Blanco, Papaloapan, and related Classic Period sites in central Veracruz.

GALERIAS 15 and 16 conclude the Totonac displays with further figures and panels on Totonac life, and begin the story of Mexica Aztec conquest into Veracruz. Numerous seated and standing figures, incl. priestly figures in elaborate dress, and cases of ceramic vessels and jewellery.

PATIO TOTONACA 2 contains sculptures: Classic Period torso from Misantla, Idolos (basalt; 3 tons); basalt tortoise from Misantla, Idolos (2 tons; late Classic/early Postclassic); basalt rabbit from Jamapa (0.5 ton; Classic); basalt jaguar ready to spring, from Misantla, Idolos (3 tons; late Classic/early Postclassic); basalt monolith from Maltrata, with figures in a 'royal' scene, incl. warrior and richly clad noble (20 tons; Classic).

GALERIAS 17, 18, and SALA HUASTECA. Postclassic Huasteca culture of central and N Gulf Coast. 'Osteological culture', incl. skull deformation and tooth filing. Family life, incl. agricultural practices, common vessels, clothing and personal decoration, dance, models of houses and humans. Model of Castillo de Teayo.

In centre of room: 'Piedra del Maíz', sculpture representing god of rain and goddess of maize-corn; the goddess offers Tláloc maize plants, and in her l. hand holds serpent with symbol of a ray or sunbeam (sandstone; 7.5 tons; Castillo de Teayo).

Other sculptures (Postclassic unless otherwise stated): Tláloc figure from Tuxpan (sandstone; 1.2 ton). Sandstone Aztec figure of Ome Cipactli, from Chicontepec, with the calendrical inscription 'two crocodile' (AD 1467). Sun deity from Ozuluama (sandstone; 1.2 ton); on back is sacrificial figure with exposed heart and claws or talons instead of feet and hands. Male sacrificial figure with exposed heart (sandstone; 1 ton; Tempoal). Sandstone female figure representing the moon from Amatlan-Naranjos. Human figure representing the sun (sandstone; 1.5 ton; Ixcatepec, Palmas Altas), and another lunar representation in form of woman (sandstone; 0.7 ton; Ixcatepec, Palmas Altas). Sandstone figure of Mictecacihuatl (goddess of death) from Chicontepec (1 ton).

Continuing along wall. Sandstone figure of corpse. Figure of Ehecatl–Quetzalcóatl from Huasteca Veracruzana (sandstone; 1.3 ton). Sandstone figure in dancing pose, from Tuxpan. Sandstone figure with arms crossed in submission (Huasteca Veracruzana; Preclassic). Figure carrying infant (volcanic stone; Huasteca Veracruzana; Classic). Woman wearing fan-shaped hat (sandstone; Huasteca Veracruzana; Classic).

Continuing along next wall, and into room. Sandstone figure of woman with headdress and skirt-like garment, from Tempoal. Figure of Cihuateo with rectangular headdress (sandstone; Chontla, Magosal). Sacrificial figure holding knives and with exposed heart (sandstone; 1.3 ton; Tempoal). Male captive with calendrical symbol in headdress (sandstone; 1.4 ton; Huasteca Veracruzana). Sandstone figure of Tlazoltéotl (goddess of wrongdoing; also moon deity) from Izcatepec, Palmas Altas. Sandstone figure of a woman wearing fan-shaped headdress; on her front, rectangular band with three circles representing jade, value, and birth. Two more sandstone sculptures of Tlazoltéotl, from Tampico Alto. Another sandstone female figure with circular symbols of preciousness.

In small patio just outside final room: sandstone male and female figures from Tempoal; he wears typical maxtlatl (loincloth), while she has mutilated breasts.

2.5km S of Jalapa along the road to Coatepec is the *Jardín Botánico Francisco Javier Clavijero* (Tues.–Sun., 8–4; fee), which in a 5 hectare area gives an unrivalled display of the plant life of Veracruz.

From Jalapa, Méx. 140 descends SE to (245km) *Puente Nacional* (see Rte 71A) and (283km) turning r. for (25km SW) *Soledad de Doblado*, a few km NE of which was the site of prehistoric **Remojadas**. A large and important site known mainly from excavated materials; it flourished between c 500 BC and the demise of Teotihuacán in the 7C AD. Thereafter the important, influential centres of the Gulf Coast shifted to El Tajín (Rte 65) in the N and to Nopiloa (Rte 84) in the S.

Remojadas is famous for its distinct style of 'smiling face' hollow figurines, mass produced from moulds, distributed throughout the Gulf region and traded into the Central Highlands. The men, women, infants, ball players, and warriors depicted have several Maya-inspired features, but are otherwise distinctive. Facial features and other details are often picked out with black asphalt paint, found at local sources. One interpreter has suggested that they depict a forced gaiety, perhaps from hallucinogenic drinks, prior to being sacrificed. However, a similar group of 'smiling face' figurines from Nopiloa and El Zapotal, whose relationship to the Remojadas group is uncertain, were buried guarding graves of Middle to Late Classic date.

Remojadas is also famous for its animal figurines mounted on wheels or on platforms with wheels. This region was the centre of manufacture and distribution, although not in abundance, throughout the Gulf Coast region and into central, S, and W Mesoamerica. A group of 50 was found in a tomb at Lambityeco (Oaxaca); and from Nayarit came a unique seated man on a wheeled platform. Most archaeologists regard these items as toys, although one super-diffusionist has claimed that they are imitations of Chinese bronze carts!

299km *Veracruz*, see Rte 72.

72 Veracruz

VERACRUZ (c 567,000 inhab.), Mexico's principal E coast port and main entrepôt and communication centre, once gateway to New Spain for travellers from Europe, is a welcoming, relaxing, yet busy city, with a tropical climate, tempered by cold (and sometimes dangerous) N winter winds, and strong Caribbean flavour. What it lacks in significant historical monuments, it makes up for in a pleasurable atmosphere, to which contribute the lively veracruzanos (the mestizos known as jarochos), with their addiction to conversation, café life, and the all-pervading music of marimba bands.

Airport. 4km S of centre. Flights to *Mexico City*, *Villahermosa*, *Tampico*, *Morelia*, *Uruapan*, and *Mérida*.

Bus station. 1698 Av. Salvador Díaz Mirón (c 3km S of Zócalo). Services to *Mexico City* (8 hrs); to *Córdoba* (2½ hrs); to *Orizaba* (3½ hrs); to *Jalapa* (2½ hrs); to *Papantla* (5 hrs); to *Poza Rica* (4½ hrs); to *Villahermosa* (8 hrs); to *Coatzacoalcos* (5½ hrs); to *Campeche* (15½ hrs); to *Mérida* (18 hrs); to *Puebla* (5 hrs); to *San Andrés Tuxtla* (3 hrs); to *Santiago Tuxtla* (2½ hrs); etc.

Railway station. Pl. de la República. Trains to *Mexico City* (12½ hrs) and to *Tapachula* (24 hrs).

Hotels throughout the city.

Post Office. Pl. de la República.

Tourist Office. Pal Municipal.

British Vice Consul. 145 Av. Morelos. **US Consul**. 388 Av. Víctimas del 25 de Junio.

Fiesta. Carnival (week before Lent). Famous celebrations.

The first, ephemeral, foundation (Apr. 1519) of Villa Rica de la Vera Cruz, near the present Ulúa, after Cortés's landing at Chalchicueyecan, was moved in May to Quiahuahuixtlán, and then to La Antigua (8 leagues S; see Rte 64) in 1525. Cortés' 'army' included 508 men, c 100 sailors, 16 horses, and 14 cannons. Moctezuma II Xocoyotzin had been kept informed of the Spaniards' progress down the coast of Yucatán through the trading ports. As soon as Cortés landed Moctezuma despatched a delegation of five high officials to meet him, and sent rich gifts, incl. a turquoise mask set with quetzal bird plumes.

Cortés' arrival had been prophetical. For some ten years prior to the first Spanish landings Moctezuma had had a series of omens which, although difficult to interpret, seemed to foretell the end of his rule and the fall of his empire. The Aztecs not unnaturally connected Cortés with the Toltec historical legend of the disappearance into the E of Ce Acatl Topiltzin Quetzalcóatl (see Introduction: Early Postclassic and Mesoamerican Religion; and *Tula*).

The Aztec emissaries proceeded to dress Cortés, whom they believed to be the god, in Quetzalcóatl's garb while Cortés, on his part, impressed them by firing off his cannon and challenging them to combat. Terrified, they refused the challenge and returned to Moctezuma with their report. Cortés also received delegations from other cities (eg, Cempoala and Quiahuitzlán) and then began the long march inland to Tenochtitlán.

Vera Cruz Nueva was established at the present site, opposite Ulúa, in 1599–1600. Some 200 Spanish and mestizo residents moved S from the fortress of San Juan de Ulúa, outnumbered by the 600 negro slaves of the few Spaniards at the fortress of San Juan de Ulúa, on the island which had served as the only official port on the Gulf coast of New Spain. Here arrived the annual fleet (flota) which brought European goods, as well as incoming viceroys, ecclesiastics, and government officials, to New Spain. It returned to Spain laden with goods from Asia, brought across by land from Acapulco, and American merchandise and silver. Around Veracruz was built a wall, and batteries and fortifications were to give further protection.

Travellers attested the unhealthiness of the place, incoming Europeans particularly in danger from a rampant form of yellow fever, called vómito negro, which decimated the population in 1648 and was to rage ferociously in the 18C and 19C. In 1638 Veracruz became headquarters of the Armada de Barlovento, established to protect Spanish shipping in the Gulf and Caribbean against pirate incursions, but its ideal strength (12 galleons and two men-of-war) was often not met. In May 1683 the port was taken and sacked by a combined Dutch, French, and English pirate force under the notorious Lorencillo (Laurent van Graff), Nicholas van Hoorn, and Nicholas Grammont, which subjected the inhabitants to six days of terror and rape. Nearly all were locked in the parish church, with the threat that it would be blown up if they didn't declare all their possessions. The invaders are said to have made off with 4 million pesos-worth of money and goods; 400 veracruzanos were killed or died of suffocation. From 1746 new ramparts (incl. eight bulwarks) were built to encircle the town and protect the port. By the early 19C, 250 ships were entering and leaving yearly; annual exports were worth 34 million pesos; and customs revenue was a major prop for the viceregal, and later Mexican, administrations. For all its red and white domes, cupolas, convents, hospitals, and churches, William Bullock called Veracruz 'but a painted Golgotha, the head-quarters of Death, for I believe it to be one of the most unhealthy spots on earth!' In the 1830s the English traveller Charles Joseph Latrobe recorded current advice against the vómito: 'throw yourself upon the mercy of God'. And in 1879 John F. Finerty met an English resident whose parents, wife, three children, two brothers, and sister had all died of it.

During 1838–39 a French fleet blockaded the port and captured the fortress of Ulúa (the Pastry war), Santa-Anna losing a leg in the action. In 1847 the US expeditionary force under Gen. Winfield Scott landed here. In 1859–60 it was Juárez's headquarters during the latter part of the war of the Reform, resisting two attempts by Miramón to take it, and from here Juárez expedited the Reform laws. When Maximilian and Carlota arrived in May 1864, their welcome was of the sparest, the town authorities, along with the regent Juan Nepomuceno Almonte, having taken refuge in Orizaba to escape the vómito. In Dec. 1866–March 1867 the French troops who had been the basis of imperial power embarked from Veracruz, leaving Maximilian and his remaining supporters at the mercy of the republicans.

In the 1890s rebuilding and modernizing the harbour were entrusted by Pres. Díaz to Weetman Pearson, a task finished by 1902. In May 1911 Díaz embarked for Europe aboard the German merchant ship 'Ypiranga'. During Oct. 1912 Félix Díaz, his nephew, revolted in Veracruz against Madero, who was to pay dearly for the Supreme Court's reprieve of his enemy. In Apr. 1914, to prevent the same vessel discharging a consignment of arms destined for Huerta's forces, US troops came ashore to meet vigorous resistance from the cadets of the Mexican naval academy and the townsfolk, which forced a brief US retreat. But after a fresh bombardment, Veracruz fell to the invaders. About 200 Mexicans, chiefly naval cadets, and 21 US sailors and marines were killed. The US occupation lasted until Nov.—the US authorities undertaking a drastic cleaning-up exercise, using their troops and Mexican workers as a labour force. Proper drainage and a strict sanitary system introduced; the lighting system repaired; water supply improved; streets paved; and the vulture scavengers, a feature of Veracruz since its foundation, disappeared. In Dec., Carranza established his government here. With the end of the Revolution the port endured years of decay and labour anarchy, a victim of unruliness and violence among the port workers. Recovery has been in large part due to able State government.

Bounded by reefs and small islands, the harbour has few natural advantages. A modernization programme began in 1946 to replace and expand unloading and cargo-handling equipment, and warehousing facilities. The dry dock was finished in 1951. The city beaches

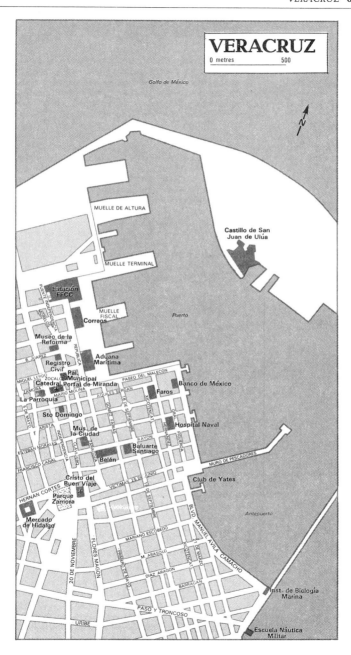

are polluted. Those wishing to avail themselves of more salubrious surrounds will have to go to Mocambo beach near Boca del Río, c 8km S.

The city centre is the inimitable ZOCALO (*Pl. de Armas*), dotted with laurel and palm, especially lively on Sun. evenings when veracruzanos stroll, hawkers ply their trade, cafés resound with animated talk, and marimba and mariachi music fills the air. On the E side is the *Pal. Municipal*, built in the 17–18C, and much altered subsequently, most recently in 1971. On the S side, the undistinguished parish church of *La Asunción* (1723–24). Its Baccarat candlesticks were ordered by Maximilian, arrived after his death, were put up for sale, and bought by a family called Velasco who donated them to the church. On the W side is the café **La Parroquia**, a favourite meeting-place (its atmosphere will fascinate discerning foreign visitors), famous also for its coffee—and the art of pouring it. Also on the S side of the plaza is the *Portal de Miranda*, with its small shops and wooden balconies, an evocative corner of old Veracruz.

Behind the Pal. Municipal we may reach PL. DE LA REFORMA and the port area. On the far side are the *Aduana Marítima* (customs building) and, further N, the *Correos*, both by Salvador Echagaray (1902). To the l., opposite the Aduana, are the *Registro Civil* (register office; restored 1972) and, opposite, at the corner with C. Juárez, the former church of *San Francisco* (1775; restored 1983–84), once part of the Franciscan convent which Juárez made his headquarters in 1859–60. It houses a *Santuario de la Reforma* (9–1, 4–6) honouring the Reform (statues of Juárez and his principal supporters).

From the S end of Av. de la República, Paseo del Malecón runs E to the building known as *Edificio Faros* (c 1902; built by Salvador Echagaray), facing a small park.

It was Carranza's headquarters in 1914–15 and is now occupied by the Mexican navy. The public are allowed free access to the **Museo Histórico de la Revolución** on the upper floor, which includes Carranza's bedroom, contemporary photographs and documents in facsimile, and relics of the First Chief, among them the table on which his autopsy was carried out.

From the W side of the Zócalo we may follow Av. Independencia S. To the l. in C. Aquiles Serdán is a relic, now enclosed by a modern building, of the Dominican convent of *Sto Domingo* (1656).

It was in its predecessor, after his arrival in New Spain in Sept. 1625, that Thomas Gage was entertained, sumptuously, by the prior—'young and light-headed...a gallant and amorous young spark...his tables covered with carpets of silk; his cupboards adorned within with several dainties of sweetmeats and conserves'.

Further along C. Aquiles Serdán, to the l., excavations in 1984 at No. 425 Av. Zaragoza turned up remains (late 16C to 18C) of the Augustinian convent of *San Agustín*, occupied by the friars after 1767 and the expulsion of the previous owners, the Jesuits.

In the opposite direction (S) along Av. Zaragoza we come, at No. 397, to the **Museo de la Ciudad** (Tues.–Sun., 10–6; fee), housed in a mansion built in 1852. It contains both archaeological and ethnographic collections. A wooden map at the entrance shows the principal archaeological sites and regions.

Preceramic sites, dated c 3000–2000 BC, were found and excavated in the 1970s on the central and S Gulf Coast. Such sites as *Sta Luisa* on the Río Tecolutla near Papantla, *Palma Sola* and *El Viejón* are basically middens with the few tools and food remains of fishing and collecting peoples, contemporary with Abejas Cave and other sites in the Valle de Tehuacán.

The display cases and information panels relate Veracruz sites to general Mesoamerican prehistory and include Olmec, Huastec (in the N part of the State), and Totonac (central and N Veracruz) collections. El Tajín and Cempoala are well represented, and there is an excellent pottery collection, a small sample of 'smiling face' figurines from Remojadas, and a mural of the Rain god Tláloc on granite. A dome in the museum is illustrated by Alberto Beltrán with the legend of the 'Twelve Old Men of El Tajín'.

Another major display shows finds recovered (diving began in 1975) from a shipwreck off the coast, at San Juan de Ulúa, comprising part of Cortés' original treasure. These include a gold necklace and other jewellery, and several gold ingots apparently cast in Coyoacán.

The next turning l., C. Francisco Canal, leads past the former convent of *Nuestra Señora de Belem* (18C), once belonging to the Bethlemites (see Rte 8) and functioning as hospital during the severest of late 18C epidemics. Further along, past Av. Gómez Farías, is the **Baluarte de Santiago** (1635, reconditioned 1779), only remaining part of the fortifications of old Veracruz, existing by the 1630s, rebuilt from 1746, and demolished at the end of the 19C. It contains a historical museum (10–7; fee).

Av. Independencia ends at PARQUE ZAMORA. On its E side is the church of *Cristo del Buen Viaje*, originating in the early 17C, but much rebuilt since then.

The island known in history as *San Juan de Ulúa* (also called the Gallega reef), on the N side of the port, is now joined to the mainland by the N breakwater constructed in 1902. It is conveniently reached by bus from the Aduana Marítima.

From soon after the Conquest the island was the only recognized port on the Gulf coast (see above), and a fortress was begun probably in the 1580s. In Sept. 1568, off course and in dire straits during his third slaving voyage, the English buccaneer John Hawkins arrived here to refit his seven ships (incl. the 'Jesus of Lubeck', the 'Minion', and the 'Judith', under Francis Drake) and take on badly needed supplies. The time was inopportune owing to the imminent arrival of the fleet from Spain bearing the new viceroy, Martín Enríquez de Almansa. In the ensuing Spanish surprise attack, Hawkins, though his guns destroyed the principal Spanish fighting ships, the 'Capitense' and the 'Almirante', was worsted, but managed to get clear in the 'Minion', while Drake and the 'Judith' escaped. For lack of provisions Hawkins was forced to offload about a hundred survivors on the coast further N (see Rte 61). The hard fate of these men, and of the 30 or so taken prisoner at Ulúa, is a grim episode in Mexican history. Some died of wounds and ill treatment, some were killed by Indians; others fell into the hands of the Inquisition (see Rte 1), or were shipped back to Spain to be sentenced to death or to be worked to death as galley slaves. A handful got back to England.

The fortress, rebuilt and strengthened in 1746–71, served both as bastion and, until the outbreak of the Revolution, as prison, the cramped, vermin-infested dungeons regularly flooding at high tide so that wretched captives were forced to crouch up to the chin in salt water. In 1821–25 it was the last redoubt of Spanish forces on the American continental mainland, reinforced from Havana until the decisive Mexican blockade undertaken by order of Pres. Guadalupe Victoria.

The **Fuerte de San Juan de Ulúa**, now administered by the Mexican navy, is open to the public (daily, 9–5; fee) and recent works have rescued it from the worst effects of neglect and disrepair. Visitors, however, should proceed gingerly if they wish to descend to the inner fastnesses and the cells, where such prisoners as Fray Servando Teresa de Mier and fellow insurgents (see Rte 5) languished.

Boat trips may be taken from the docks to **Isla de Sacrificios** (5km SE), so-called because the Spaniards on their expeditions in 1518 and 1519 found evidence of human sacrifice there.

It was in fact a sanctuary and place of sacrificial offerings, many of the objects from which now grace Mexico's museums. The Postclassic ceramics excavated here have been named after the island and divided into four phases: Phase I (c AD 900–1000) comprised the last vestiges of the 'smiling face' tradition of pottery whistles; Phases II–IV (c 1200–Spanish Conquest) are distinctive for their polychromes, which show influences of Mixteca–Puebla styles, and Plumbate Wares. Fine Orange Wares were exported from the island in exchange for these, and are found, for example, at Cholula.

In 1683 it was chosen by Lorencillo as a place to hold some of the richer citizens to ransom. In 1823 Bullock found it 'a mere heap of sand, with only one wretched Indian family living upon it...strewed with the bones of British subjects who have perished in this unhealthy climate, and whose remains are not allowed to be buried in consecrated ground'.

73 Puebla to Oaxaca

Méx. 150, Méx. 131, and Méx. 190, 342km.—31km **Tepeaca** (for [13km W] **Cuautinchán,** [11km SW] **Tecali,** and [63km S] Tepexi el Viejo).—52km **Tecamachalco.**—114km Tehuacán and Méx. 131.—237km Cuicatlán.—311km San Pablo Huitzo and Méx. 190.—342km **Oaxaca**.

We leave Puebla to the E on Méx. 150. Beyond (14km) *Amozoc* we keep r. for (31km) **TEPEACA** (c 25,000 inhab.; 2257m; H,R,P), a straggling town set in a ravine on the E slopes of the Sierra de Tepeaca.

In July 1520, after the Noche Triste, Cortés established headquarters at the prehispanic hilltop site of Tepeyacac, renaming it Villa Segura de la Frontera. Here he wrote his second 'carta de relación' to Charles V, describing the pacification of the region and the new settlement itself. In 1543 it was moved E to its present site by the Franciscans.

The town centre is the ample PL. PRINCIPAL, crowded on market days (Thurs. and Fri.). In it is the unique octagonal **Rollo** (1559), symbol of the villa's status and power to dispense justice. It stands, like a Moorish tower, on a pedestal carved with four zoomorphic reliefs, is two-storeyed, and is pierced by eight twinned windows (ajimez). Local tradition assigns it to Fray Sebastián de Trasierra. The clock tower is a 19C addition. On the E side of the plaza rises the former convent of **San Francisco**, almost awe-inspiring in its mass, an imposing prototype for 16C Franciscan convents in New Spain.

It was started during the 1540s; the church was finished in 1580, the convent buildings in 1593. Despite the military character of its appearance—12 prominent buttresses, and parapet crenellation—the notion that the church was built to serve also as a fortress cannot be maintained. The atrio is entered through a sturdy triple gateway, the tiled tympana above it additions of c 1750.

EXTERIOR. Small in relation to the size of the façade, the W doorway is a simple rectangular panel defined by rectangular mouldings, the arch mildly ogee in form. The tiny alfíz is marked by a line of pearls of Castile which also fringe the doorway itself and curve round the choir window arch. Similar motifs are placed in profusion on the buttress heads, which resemble sentry boxes (garitas), and ornamental merlons which line the parapet. At the levels of the double lower and upper windows, chemins-de-ronde wind round the building, perforating the buttresses: the lower deep within the wall, the upper clearly visible and with access to balconies in front of each buttress. Behind the parapet is a wall walk bordering the domes of the vaults. The N doorway is simply classical.

INTERIOR. The high rib-vaulted nave is bathed in light from 20 windows evenly disposed at two levels above the shallow bays which line the walls—the latter an exceptional arrangement. One of the S wall bays shows a mural of the Miracles of St Francis, attr. Simón Pereyns or Francisco de Morales, both in Tepeaca at some time in 1566–68. The sanctuary, narrower than the nave, is raised on a high platform.
    Through the twin-arched portería, once possibly also an open chapel, we may gain the cloister by a doorway whose alfíz, basket arch, and thick jambs are lightly covered in rosette, roundel, and pearl relief. The cloister, with its depressed arches on thick clustered half-columns below and pilasters above, has been much restored. To the r. of the portería is a chapel, a later addition, with a portal (1726) profusely decorated in popular baroque.

13km W of Tepeaca is **CUAUTINCHAN** (c 2000 inhab.), a timeless village on a fertile plain amid camphor trees, girded by mountains, and irrigated by water from Presa Valsequillo to the W. Its commanding monument is the former convent of **San Juan Bautista**.

The Franciscans set up a visita of Tepeaca here in 1530. In 1554 the Dominicans got possession and ousted the Franciscans. The natives, bitterly resentful, locked the small original establishment, hid the keys, and stayed at home, refusing to harbour the Dominicans. In the end, the bp of Puebla relented and the Franciscans returned in triumph. The new convent was built in 1560–93.

The undulating atrio wall is topped by merlons. The nobly impressive church, with a wall walk behind the parapet, chemin-de-ronde piercing the buttresses at window level, and semicircular apse (a rare example), has a simple Mannerist portal and choir window panel, which has been compared with those of 16C Florence. INTERIOR. All eyes are drawn beyond the triumphal arch to the apse, covered by a lovely fan vault. The high altarpiece, a great three-storeyed triptych, though small in relation to the space in which it is placed, is one of the rare 16C Renaissance examples still to be found in Mexico.

It was possibly the work of Pedro de Brizuela, a native of Burgos in Spain, and the painter Nicolás de Tejeda de Guzmán, made c 1560–70 for a chapel in the church of San Francisco in Puebla. The paintings are among the very earliest surviving in Mexico. The lowest storey supports are four slender columns with ionic capitals; the upper storeys each hold four baluster columns, sign of the plateresque, with similar capitals; above, supporting the pediment, are two more. The friezes which divide the different levels show a repeated motif of three seraphim with baskets. Of the 23 paintings, the eight in the main body of the retable are of Scenes from the Life of Our Lady; in the pediment, God the Father; in the predella, the Apostles; at the sides, Saints, among them SS John the Baptist and Mary Magdalen, SS Lawrence and Catherine of Alexandria, SS Ambrose and Augustine, and St Dominic. They are uneven in quality, but the Annunciation, Adoration of the Shepherds, and Resurrection, and the Apostles are superior work.

A small side altar, dedicated to St Diego of Alcalá, containing four paintings of scenes from his life, is a slightly later Mannerist work. Among the convent's other treasures is a famous 16C wooden polychrome statue of St Anne with Our Lady and the infant Christ, showing superb use of estofado (renewed perhaps in the 17C).

To the r. of the church, continuing the line of the façade, are an open chapel and four-arched portería which gives access to the ruined cloister, still with traces of original murals (eg, an Annunciation).

FROM TEPEACA TO TEPEXI DE RODRIGUEZ, 58km. The road runs SW through the Sierra de Tepeaca to (11km) **TECALI** (c 5000 inhab.; P), on a plain, a town once famous for its neighbouring quarries of translucent yellowish alabaster, which has catered for sublime works of art and the most ordinary of knicknacks.

Founded by the Franciscans c 1554, the convent of **Apóstol Santiago** was built in 1569–79. Though now partly ruined, its basilican church (nave and two side aisles) still retains much to admire.

The portal is the prototype of academic Mannerism—also called Renaissance purism—in Mexico. Two pairs of columns, fluted in their upper two-thirds, with rich capitals, sustain an entablature and triangular pediment. The semicircular arch and jambs are marked by diamond and pear motifs in relief. Above the pediment, choir window and gable are set off by the clean lines of plain pilasters; the side doorways are also suitably restrained. The thin tower has something of the medieval. Within the walls of the roofless interior, rows of slender high columns support a magnificent double arcade, separating nave and aisles. Beyond the triumphal arch the boxed chancel is the same width as the nave. On the N side, the cloister has been partially restored.

The neighbouring parish church of **Señor Santiago** (1728) contains two 16C plateresque altarpieces originally in the basilica and framing paintings by the same anon. artist. The larger (r. transept; 1570s or 1580s), in three storeys, once served as high altarpiece. The pilasters, with ionic capitals, and friezes which divide the storeys and vertical panels, are adorned with lovely fruit, seraphic, festoon, and other relief. In the middle of the predella is a little tabernacle, flanked by two pairs of baluster columns. The predella paintings show four doctors of the Church—Gregory the Great, Ambrose, Jerome, Augustine—resting in landscapes, among the earliest examples of the genre in Mexico. In the lowest storey, Annunciation (primitive, but good) and Visitation (note the architectural detail and landscape background), and St Francis and St Dominic. Middle storey, Adoration of the Shepherds and Adoration of the Kings, and St Clare and St Catherine of Siena. In the top, Baptism of Christ (again, in a good landscape), and St Stephen and St Lawrence, and, at the sides, Faith and Hope. Above, in the pediment, God the Father.

The smaller altarpiece, now in the nave, is dedicated to St Francis. Bordered by elegant relief, its side pilasters are wide enough to contain four paintings (two Franciscan saints, two doctors of the Church) and the curving pediment holds an allegorical painting of St Francis, while the large and fascinating central painting shows him stigmatized amid scenes from his life.

The high altarpiece and two others in l. transept and nave are three excellent churriguer-esque examples, the statues of saints and angels standing between the estípites under pavilion canopies, from which flow drawn curtains and around which curves ingeniously twisted moulding.

From Tecali, State road 708 runs SE, flanking the Sierra de Tentzo, to (26km) *Atoyatempan*, in the valley of the Río Atoyac, amid an irrigated landscape, with waterfalls formed by the Río del Aguila in the vicinity.

3km S are the *Cascadas de Acatzizintla*, especially worth seeing at the end of the rainy season (May–Sept.), which flow into the Río Atoyac.

Beyond Atoyatempan we join State road 455 which runs S to (36km) *Molcaxac* (c 2000 inhab.; 1847m).

From here a poor road descends SW through an eroded, hilly region, which becomes increasingly desolate (limestone extraction offers precarious possibilities for the inhabitants), to (20km) **Huatlatlauca**, on a plateau flanked by two ravines. Here the convent of *Los Santos Reyes*, originating in a mission founded by Franciscans, was taken over by the Augustinians in 1567. The buildings date probably from the late 1570s, an ensemble pleasingly rustic in style. In its lower storey the church portal is tentatively Mannerist; in its upper a triple ingeniously wavy arcade rests on baluster columns beneath a wide alfíz. The interior guards the most spellbindingly beautiful timber ceiling in Mexico, polychrome beams and elaborate side supports carved with angel, animal, fruit, floral, and vegetal motifs. The sotocoro is a cypress beam carved with elements inspired by local flora. Remains of the small open chapel are in evidence. The two-storey cloister, entered through the buttressed portería (arches without archivolts) contains outstanding murals on Augustinian themes. Several small barrio chapels (17–19C) also survive in the town.

By track, c 15km NW, at *Huehuetlán*, is the former Dominican convent of Sto Domingo (c 1569), much modified.

From Molcaxac we may continue S (a hilly region draining into the Río Atoyac) to (58km) **Tepexi de Rodríguez** (c 13,000 inhab.; 1746m; P), in the S Mixteca, the former Tepexi de la Seda, with plenty of shade. Of the former convent of *Sto Domingo*, founded by the Franciscans in 1550, and ceded to the Dominicans in 1567–68, there remain only a few rooms. The church is a recent reconstruction.

5km W (pathway) the site of **Tepexi** ('rocky place') **el Viejo**, excavated by Shirley Gorenstein in the 1970s, was a Late Postclassic hilltop fortress. It is described in Preconquest chronicles as part of the S Puebla kingdom of *Quauhtlinchán*, and thus a reasonable history of the site can be reconstructed in combination with the excavation results.

In 1438 Quauhtlinchán was conquered by Tlatelolco, which made marriage alliances with the rulers of several S Puebla towns, incl. Tepexi. It remained relatively autonomous, however, fighting constantly with other towns to the N and S of it, incl. Tlaxcala, over the control of tributary villages. This state of affairs was broken in 1503 when Moctezuma II Xocoyotzin marched into the Valle de Puebla at the head of an army, following the tradition of his ancestors of initiating their reign with a military triumph and superlative sacrifices to the gods. Tepexi was captured and thereafter remained a tributary to the Aztec garrison town of Tepeaca, c 70km N. In 1520 it was captured by Cortés and its old rivals, the Tlaxcalans.

The excavations uncovered the fortress precinct and four other groups of ruins. The flat ridgetop was expanded and retained by massive outer walls up to 15m high; the defensive circuit wall, incl. a gate and what seem to be guardhouses, were up to 5m high, and covered with smooth plaster to prevent scaling. Within the walls, the foundations of pyramid-platforms and other buildings around plazas were found. Tombs were also located within the walls, but the excavators found these long since looted. The ceramics show occupation between c AD 1300 and 1520, and included mostly local wares, plus smaller amounts of Mixteca–Puebla polychromes. The greater town occupied more than 62,000 sq m (6.2ha) and a population estimate of 6–12,000 for the 15–16C town agrees closely with the Spanish census of 1565, of 10–11,000 (cf. *Guiengola* and *Yagul*).

From Tepexi de Rodríguez, State road 455 continues S through the Mixteca to (76km) *San Juan Ixcaquixtla*, known for ceramics, and then, tortuously, to (140km) *Acatlán*, on Méx. 190, the Mexico–Oaxaca road (see Rte 74).

From Tepeaca we continue SE on Méx. 150 to (35km) turning r. for (4km S) *Mixtla*, with an 18C church (churrigueresque façade), and (38km) the junction with Méx. 125 to Acatzingo (see Rte 71C).

52km **TECAMACHALCO** (c 21,000 inhab.; 2055m; H,R,P), in the Valle de Tecamachalco, where stands, facing an enormous atrio, the former Franciscan convent of **Asunción de Nuestra Señora**.

The first Franciscan mission here, among the Popoloca Indians, dates from 1541. From 1543 its superior was Fray Andrés de Olmos. The church was built during 1551–57; the convent finished in 1585. An inscription on the tower base dates it to 1589–91. In 1569, 9000 Indian families were said to live in the town, with a hundred Spanish families residing at its centre. The Franciscans were dispossessed in 1640.

EXTERIOR. The beautifully proportioned W doorway, although (most unusually) expertly integrating with the choir window, still displays a variety of shapes and lines: Isabeline Gothic in the outer window arch, in the cusped ogee doorway arch, and in pearls of Castile which run between the pronounced mouldings of alfíz, doorway arch, and imposts; Mudéjar in the wide, low alfíz. The jambs contain concave tableros; the outer moulding ends in sober concave flourishes, faint precursors of baroque volutes. A flurry of merlons crowns the parapet above, echoed in those of the tower. The contemporary N doorway, with similar mouldings and pearl pattern, has a more spacious alfíz, its interior composed of dark tezontle panels, and beautiful trefoil arch rim of foliated relief.

INTERIOR. The rib vaulting of the wide nave is of thin, fine brick. Bases and capitals of the triumphal arch are formed like elaborate baskets. Sinuousness is also a feature of the top of the sacristy doorway—two convex curves on either side finishing in a centre point. Top and jambs are a kind of ribbon between inner and outer mouldings and dotted with rosettes.

Fixed into the spaces between the ribs of the sotocoro vault are the oval medallion paintings which have given Tecamachalco its abiding fame.

They were done in 1562, on fibrous papel de amate, and using a technique resembling tempera, by a local Indian chief, called Juan Gersón. (His name was no doubt given him on baptism by a friar who admired the works of the French theologian and chancellor of the university of Paris, Jean Gerson [1363–1429]), some of which were published in New Spain from 1544.) In them may be seen the efforts of an indigenous painter, steeped in a rigid prehispanic tradition, to come to terms with more flexible and expansive European ideas.

They treat episodes from the Old Testament and the Apocalypse, inspired, the Holy Office notwithstanding, by the engravings of Dürer and the Wittenberg Bible, which unavoidably influenced the illustration of 16C Catholic bibles.

The mid-point panels of the four sides of the bay show the symbols of the Evangelists; that of St Matthew (W side) hidden by the windbreak. Seven of the eight panels nearest the central boss contain Old Testament scenes from Genesis and Ezekiel. From N side clockwise: Cain kills Abel; Noah's Ark and the Flood; the Tower of Babel; Sacrifice of Isaac; Jacob's Ladder; Vision of the Throne of God and the 24 Ancients (this scene from Apocalypse 4:1–10); Ariel, the Altar of Burnt Offerings (Ezek. 43:13–18); the City of God (Ezek. 40:2–49). The 16 medallions between the ribs at the corners of the vault depict scenes from the Apocalypse.

At the W end two scenes (Vision of Christ amid the Seven Golden Candlesticks and Fall of Babylon—1:12–18; 18:1–21) are hidden by the windbreak. From E end clockwise: Cry of the Slain and Distribution of White Robes (6:9–11); the Four Horsemen (6:1–18); Choosing of the Elect and Holding of the Four Winds (7:1–12); St John eats the Book (10:8–11); Falling of the Stars (6:12–16); the Angels bound in the Euphrates (9:14–15); the Woman clothed with the Sun and the Great Dragon (12:1–6); Sounding of the Fourth Trumpet (8:12–13); Beast of the Sea and Beast of the Earth (13:1–18); Binding of Satan (20:1–3); Vision of the Lamb on Mt Sion (14:1–7); the New Jerusalem (21); the Plague of Locusts (9:1–11).

The raised open chapel is above the portería for the r. (S) of the church which gives access to the ruined cloister, of which only the lower-storey arcades survive, with three low arches a side.

In the baptistery of the 18C parish church of *San Sebastián* are four huge paintings on baptism by José Joaquín Magón.

Méx. 150 continues SE through the Valle de Tecamachalco, the Sierra de Tecamachalco on the l. Beyond (76km) *Tlacotepec* (P) we enter the Valle de Tehuacán.

93km *Tepanco*, where the church of San Juan Bautista (early 18C) has a good baroque façade and contains five contemporary altarpieces—the high altar ungilded. 114km **Tehuacán** (c 68,000 inhab.; 1676m; H,R,P; airport), a spa city, chief distribution centre for the products of the E Mixteca. It is known also for its dry, healthy climate; an abundance of flowers and trees; grapes, oranges, and especially pomegranates; nearby deposits of silver, lead, and tecali alabaster; and above all for its mineral water (Agua Peñafiel and Garci Crespo are best known), from warm springs in the outskirts, bottled for distribution throughout the republic and N America.

The Spaniards first established farms in the valley, originally inhabited by Náhuatl and Popolocan speaking Indians, in the 1530s. Their first settlement, c 10km SE, was moved in 1567 to the present, healthier site. Its importance as a spa has faded somewhat since its heyday in the 19C, although the more elderly infirm remain faithful.

Facing PL. PRINCIPAL is the *Pal. Municipal*, finished in 1959, an engaging mixture of neo-Mudéjar and neo-baroque, faced with red and blue azulejos. The late 18C cathedral of *La Purísima Concepción* has a neoclassically based, with baroque and neo-plateresque touches, portal. In Av. Reforma Norte is the church of *El Carmen* (1748–83); its cupola, covered with azulejos, is a conspicuous landmark. The adjoining convent (No. 210) houses the *Museo del Valle de Tehuacán* (Tues.–Sun., 10–5), which contains displays of some of the more than 10,000 Preclassic, Classic, and Postclassic artefacts from survey work, controlled surface collections, and excavations directed by Richard MacNeish and Edward Sisson in the valley's 456 registered sites. These include obsidian and bone tools, basketry and cotton netting from the earliest sites, ceramics from their earliest appearance in the region through to Classic and Postclassic Mixtec and Cholula polychromes, maps, diagrams, site plans, and information panels illustrating the evolution of societies in the valley. The museum also highlights the importance of maize cultivation (cf. *Coxcatlán*).

Of the other historical buildings near the city centre, the hospital of *San Juan de Dios*, begun in the 1790s, functioned as a municipal hospital until recently; the church known as *El Calvario* (1770; decayed) is influenced by rich poblano baroque.

At **Tehuacán el Viejo**, c 10km SE (see above), the ruined church of the Franciscan convent of *La Concepción de Nuestra Señora* (c 1535–40) may still be seen. Here in the 1560s the Indians, much attached to their resident friar, walled him in to prevent his being replaced by a secular curate. He escaped, so they kidnapped another Franciscan and ran off with him to the mountains. The authorities yielded when the captors swore they would rather be hanged than turn in their prize for a secular.

Tehuacán Viejo was the site, now virtually obliterated, of a prehistoric settlement, similar to many villages and towns distributed throughout the valley from Preclassic to Postclassic times. Just SW of the town is the cave of *El Riego* where MacNeish found evidence for some of the earliest primitive agriculture in the New World (see also *Coxcatlán*).

From Tehuacán, Méx. 150 runs NE to (75km) *Orizaba* and (95km) *Córdoba*, see Rte 71A.

Méx. 125 goes S and then SW to (25km) *Zapotitlán Salinas*, with an 18C church (baroque altarpiece), where sea salt deposits, formed thousands of years ago, are exploited. We cross into the State of Oaxaca, just before (60km) *Santiago Chazumba*, with a 17C church containing a churrigueresque altarpiece. 82km turning r. for (4km NW) *Tequixtepec*, with remains of the Dominican convent of San Pedro y San Pablo, founded in 1576. The present remains of a Mixtec site include some sculptures and stelae with calendrical glyphs, scattered in the plaza and on some of the private properties of the village.

At 118km we join Méx. 190, the Mexico–Oaxaca road, 2km E of *Huajuapan de León*, see Rte 74.

From Tehuacán we continue SE, through the narrowing Valle de Tehuacán, watered by the Río Salado, on Méx. 131 (State road 908). The Sierra de Zongolica lies to the E. 126km turning r. (State road 815) for (9km S) *San Gabriel Chilac*, with an 18C church (baroque altarpiece). 135km *Ajalpan* (P). 154km *Coxcatlán* (P).

The cave of **Coxcatlán** (SE of the modern village) and other sites in the Valle de Tehuacán (*Abejas, Purrón, El Riego*) are significant for excavations by Richard MacNeish in the 1960s, in his search for the origins of New World agriculture.

The excavations produced 10,000 artefacts (some in the Museo del Valle de Tehuacán) and 26,000 ancient corncobs, one of which was 5600 years old and ancestor to domesticated maize. There were cave burials of c 6000 BC, with offerings in baskets, cremations, and signs of cannibalism—all evidence of early ritual practices. Later remains included evidence of the use of cotton for knotted netting by c 2000 BC.

The chronology of the sites spans c 7000 to c 1500 BC, divided into phases: *Ajuereado*—c 7000–c 6500 BC; *El Riego*—c 6500–c 4800 BC; *Coxcatlán*—c 4800–c 3500 BC; *Abejas*—c 3500–c 2300 BC; and *Purrón*—c 2300–c 1500 BC. The last phase included evidence for some of the earliest Mesoamerican pottery.

Hundreds of small communities were established throughout the valley in the Classic Period and inhabited up to the Spanish Conquest. The Purrón Dam, a structure begun c 700 BC, had its last construction phase c AD 300, and subsequently silted up and was abandoned, causing breaks in occupation until c AD 800. In the Postclassic, intensive agriculture with canal systems and dams supported a population estimated between 60,000 and 120,000, living in dispersed communities. Typical of these Classic-Postclassic sites was *Coxcatlán Viejo*, where Edward Sisson excavated houses of farmers and salt traders clustered around modest temple plazas with tombs and cremation burials in coarse-ware jars. Many houses comprised several rooms with patios, plastered walls, water storage basins and drains. In one house a truly ancient 'heirloom' was found, so far unexplained—a 2400-year-old Olmec greenstone figurine.

Just before (177km) **Teotitlán del Camino** (P), we enter the State of Oaxaca.

Teotitlán del Camino was known to the Aztecs as the centre of a region of principalities or city-states between Oaxaca and Tlaxcala. It is uncertain whether it was under Aztec rule: one argument claims that it was, because Teotitlán was not included in the invitation lists to witness ceremonial sacrifices in Tenochtitlán, as it would have been if it were a potential enemy, and not yet conquered; on the other hand, it did not pay tribute to the Aztecs, but had a special position in the Aztec trade network from Tlatelolco via Izúcar de Matamoros.

Teotitlán was also a centre for the observation of the planet Venus. Called *Citlálpol* (Great Star) by the Aztecs, Venus was important throughout Mesoamerica, and other observation sites were located in the Maya zone. Special priests called tonalpouque (counter of the days) were responsible for making accurate records and for the preparations for ceremonies on special days. There was a Venus cycle of 584 days, and an eight-year cycle of exacly five Venus periods. The celebrations at the end of an eight-year cycle were held in honour of Xochiquetzal, goddess of flowers, beauty, love, and domesticity, and first consort of Tláloc. On the day of her festival all seasonings (chilli, salt, and lime) were abstained from, and dancing took place dressed in costumes representing various animals and plants, as well as a sinuous snake dance. A special cycle was celebrated every 104 years, when all the most important calendrical cycles coincided: two 52-year cycles, 64 Venus cycles (or 13 eight-year cycles), 146 260-day cycles, and the 365th day of the solar year.

From here leaves a winding mountainous road through the S heights of the Sierra de Zongolica, a region inhabited by the Mazatec Indians.

39km turning l. (N) for (11km) *San Francisco Huehuetlán*, whose 17C church contains six baroque altarpieces. 51km *San Mateo Eloxochitlán* (c 2000 inhab.; 1800m), a predominantly Mazatec village. 68km **Huautla de Jiménez** (c 23,000 inhab.; H,R,P), a principal Mazatec town. Traditional pagan rites involve the ingestion of a species of mushroom which brings on hallucinations and a 'meeting with the Divine'.

From Teotitlán del Camino, Mex. 131 continues S past (188km) *San Juan de los Cues* and (202km) *Sta María Tecomavaca* to (237km) **San Juan Bautista Cuicatlán** (c 8000 inhab.; 595m; R,P) in the NW foothills of the Sierra de Ixtlán, a region inhabited in part by the Cuicatec Indians. Beyond it, the road runs through the valley of the Río Quiotepec, gradually climbing to (307km) **San Francisco Telixtlahuaca** (c 5500 inhab.; 1720m; R,P), on the r. bank of the Río Atoyac and in the NW of the Valle de Etla, with an interesting church (1732–36). 311km **San Pablo Huitzo** (once known as Guaxilotitlán), where the former Dominican convent of *Sta Catalina* dates from the 1580s. Two posa foundations may be seen at the NW and SE corners of the atrio. The church, restored and rebuilt, has a notable recessed W doorway and deep nave bays; the S wall and barrel vault are additions of the 1950s. A ruined single-storey cloister survives, S of the church.

At San Pablo Huitzo we join Méx. 190, the road from Mexico City, which goes SE to (342km) *Oaxaca*, see Rte 75.

74 Mexico City to Oaxaca

Méx. 190, Méx. 115, Méx. 160, and Méx. 190, 507km.—38km Chalco.—50km **Tlalmanalco**.—60km Amecameca.—72km Ozumba.—88km turning r. for (1km) **Atlatlauhcan**, (6km) Totolapan, (16km) Tlayacapan, and (23km) Oaxtepec.—92km turning l. for (5km) **Yecapixtla** and (15km) Ocuituco.—101km **Cuautla** and Méx. 160.—121km Amayuca (for [6km SE] **Chalcatzingo**, [16km S] **Tepalcingo** and [50km SW] Jolalpan).—163km Izúcar de Matamoros and Méx. 190.—312km Huajuapan de León.—354km Tamazulapan del Progreso.—364km Tejupan (for [22km NE] **Coixtlahuaca**).—376km Yucura and Méx. 125 (for [13km SW] **Teposcolula**).—389km **Yanhuitlán**.—397km San Mateo Yocucuí (for [7km SW] **Tiltepec**).—399km (for [25km S] Tilantongo and Monte Negro).—491km Nazareno Etla.—493km San José Mogote.—507km **Oaxaca**.

Mexico City to (29km) turning r. for *Chalco*, see Rte 66. This turning (Méx. 115) runs SE, beneath Méx. 150D (the motorway to Puebla) to (38km) **Chalco** (c 18,000 inhab.; 2270m; H,R,P), once situated on the E shore of the *Lago de Chalco*, the most important lake in the Valley of Mexico for its passenger and cargo traffic, gradually drained during the 19C. It spanned N to S from Ayotla to Ayotzingo and Mixquic, and W to E from Tláhuac to Chalco, an area now crossed by canals and what remains of chinampas.

Farming communities have lived here since the Preclassic and Chalco was one of many moderately-sized ceremonial centres on the S rim of the Basin of Mexico. In the Postclassic it was the capital of the Chalca, one of several Chichimec tribes who moved into the Basin in the 12C AD. Another prominent group, the Nonoalca—allegedly from Tula—also settled at Chalco (and in the Chontalpa region and Guatemala).

Chalco was linked by canals to Xochimilco and may have had the first chinampa agriculture in the form used by the Aztecs, and from here it spread throughout the Basin lakes. The Chalca dynasty was eliminated in 1392 by the rulers of Azcapotzalco, and as a provincial centre Chalco was annexed to Tenochtitlán by Moctezuma I Ilhuicamina (1440–68) when the Triple Alliance of Tenochtitlán, Texcoco, and Tlacopan razed Azcapotzalco.

Architects were brought from Chalco by the Mexica to build the first stone pyramids and temples at Tenochtitlán, but many Chalca fled SE to Huexotzingo rather than suffer Aztec rule. When Cortés arrived in the Basin, the Chalca became his allies. Nothing remains above ground of the former ceremonial centre.

Xico, on the former shores of Lake Chalco and c 4km W of the town, was the site of the find of a human infant jaw, probably contemporary with the Tepexpan find (Rte 18) dated c 7500 BC.

Much later, the town was a place where immigrants from the waning Teotihuacán settled in the Late Classic–Early Postclassic, along with nearby Cerro de la Estrella and Portesuelo. A Late Classic stele found here closely resembles the style of the more famous Xochicalco stelae. By the mid-13C it was a small Toltec ceremonial centre; and in the 15C it was one of the many semi-autonomous city-states paying tribute to the Aztecs.

The former church and convent of *Santiago el Mayor*, completed in 1585, was altered in the 17–18C. The present façade (c 1780) still shows a Franciscan cord moulding and contains a stone font (1542) at which Juana de Asbaje (see Rte 7) was baptized. Atrio, portería, and cloister still retain 16C work.

From Chalco a road goes SW to (9km) *Mixquic*, see Rte 17. At 4km along it a road branches l. for (5km) **Sta Catarina Ayotzingo** (2305m), where the Augustinian convent of *Sta Catarina* was founded in the 1580s. The church, rebuilt in 1720, contains a striking baroque altarpiece. In the restored convent building are two paintings, Our Lady with SS Anne and Joachim and Adoration of the Shepherds, sadly faded and interfered with, attr. Simón Pereyns.

5km E of Chalco, at *San Gregorio Cuautzingo*, the 16C church doorway is decorated in decidedly Indian style, colonnettes providing a frame for flat floral relief.

We continue on Méx. 115 to (42km) crossroads. 1km S is *Cocotitlán*, where the church of San José (1778) contains two notable baroque altarpieces. 50km **TLALMANALCO** (8000 inhab.; 2312m; P), once an Aztec provincial centre in the S Basin, in the chilly wooded foothills of Iztaccíhuatl and on the l. bank of the Río Tlalmanalco (or Río Compañía), which, further NW, runs canalized along the E and N sides of the Chalco basin to the Lago de Texcoco.

The Franciscan convent of **San Luis Obispo** was founded in the 1520s on the site of an Aztec ceremonial centre.

Fray Martín de Valencia (c 1474–1534), renowned apostle of the Indians and superior of the apostolic Twelve, died at Ayotzingo and his body was brought back here for burial in the first church on the site. But by 1567, to the consternation of the friars, his remains, a magnet for the devout and guarantee of the convent's fame and prosperity, were found to have disappeared. The present church, with the simplest of classical portals and choir window, and primitively vaulted, dates from 1582–91.

INTERIOR. To the r., near the entrance, is a baroque altarpiece (1694), made by Tomás Juárez, with three (Christ meets His Mother on the Way to Calvary; St Veronica wipes His Face; Capture of Christ) of its original five Passion paintings by Juan Correa. On the l. wall, two early 17C altarpieces. The magnificent high altarpiece is full 17C baroque, its solomonic columns laden with luscious vines. In the niches, outstanding statues of saints (among them, St Joseph in the centre of the upper storey, flanked by SS John the Baptist and Antony of Padua; beneath them, SS Anne and Joachim) showing finest use of estofado. In the topmost frame (a mid-18C addition with flanking estípites), a lovely relief of the Visitation. Also in the apse, two paintings, beautiful though faded, by Baltasar de Echave Orio, Adoration of the Shepherds and Presentation in the Temple (from the original high altarpiece). In the sacristy, a painting of Christ on the Cross by Luis Juárez.

To the N (l.) of the church are the well-kept ruins of the OPEN CHAPEL, unequalled by any other, 'a sumptuous and dramatic setting for the liturgy' which would appeal to the Indians.

It was built probably in 1560–64, but was left unfinished. Its extraordinary richness is possibly based on recent Spanish and Portuguese ideas—mainly plateresque, with liberal neo-Gothic, Indian, and Mudéjar intermixings, and Romanesque traces—to create an original synthesis. A modern interpretation sees in its complex symbolism a psychomachy, based on the 'Psychomachia' by the early Christian poet Aurelius Prudentius Clemens (348–after 405), describing the struggle of Faith, supported by the cardinal virtues, against Idolatry and the corresponding vices for the soul of man.

SAN LUIS OBISPO, TLALMANALCO

Capilla Abierta

E

Iglesia

Claustro

Portería

Atrio

0 metres   20

Planned as a huge trapezoid, its immediately striking features are the five-arched portico and the chancel arch, resting on wide jambs and framed by a generous alfíz. The crowded relief lavished on archivolts, capitals, pilasters, imposts, jambs, and alfíz frame represents a variety of arabesque; human, devilish, animal, and cornucopia motifs; and, above the portico capitals, a series of individual portraits, which may represent local caciques or the sculptors themselves. The corbels above support the beginnings of further clustered columns, perhaps preparation for another series of arches. The chancel arch spandrels bear medallions of the stigmata. On the l. diagonal side wall of the chancel, a stairway leads up through the masonry to what must have been a stone pulpit; on the corresponding r. wall are traces of a second pulpit: one for the Epistle, another for the Gospel.

The handsome seven-arched portería to the S of the church probably also served as portales de pelegrinos, used by pilgrims on visits to a favourite shrine. Through it we reach the convent buildings, begun in 1582, most likely finished in the 1590s. In the lower cloister walk frescoes of Fray Martín himself and St Clare survive along with other decorative work.

60km **Amecameca** (c 25,000 inhab.; 2470m; simple H,R,P), another former Aztec provincial centre, dramatically placed at the foot of Iztaccíhuatl. On the E side of Pl. Principal is the former Dominican convent of *La Asunción de Nuestra Señora*.

The Franciscans attempted to settle here in 1534–37, but the Dominicans persuaded the Indians that they were more respectable than the ragged friars minor, and so, in 1547, took over the place, when the convent was begun. The church was finished in 1554, and then substantially altered in the 17C; the tower dates from 1680.

Against the r. wall is the beautiful baroque altarpiece (1720s) attr. Francisco Peña Flores, with relief scenes from the Life of St Joseph. The cloister is intriguing for its low arches, carefully yet clumsily put together, supported by thick unusual versions of Corinthian capitals, atop stout hexagonal pillars—echoes of the Romanesque.

2km E, c 90m above the town, is the *Santuario de Sacramonte*, started by the Dominicans in the 1580s and added to in subsequent centuries, an important pilgrimage centre built to house a venerated image of Our Lord. It is also the entrance to a cave which was the retreat of Fray Martín de Valencia in the early 1530s.

Amecameca is a good centre for those wishing to ascend to the *Parque Nacional de los Volcanes* and to climb the twin snow-capped volcanoes: **Iztaccíhuatl**, which presents three peaks from N to S—*La Cabeza* (head; 5146m), *El Pecho* (breast; 5280m), *Los Pies* (feet; 4740m); and **Popocatépetl** (5452m), the southernmost eminence of the Sierra Nevada. Iztaccíhuatl's last eruption occurred in July 1868; that of Popocatépetl in 1862, though there was considerable activity in 1920–28. The maximum diameter of its crater (in the form of an ellipse) is 850m, with a depth of 250–300m.

On the flanks of Iztaccíhuatl at c 260m, an Early Preclassic village site called *Coapexco* was excavated in the 1970s. Artefacts dated c 1150–1100 BC were found over an area of c 50ha, with over 50 concentrations of materials indicating domestic structures in an area of 8000 sq m. Pottery and clay figurines resemble those from San Lorenzo Tenochtitlán (Rte 83); and serpentine beads, iron-ore, and mica fragments were imported from the Gulf region (cf. *Copilco, Ixtapaluca Viejo, Tlatilco*, and *Tlapacoya*).

Those wishing to make the climb are urged first to contact relevant organizations in Mexico City or at least to make enquiries at Amecameca. The best time is late Oct.–early March. Acclimatization period against altitude sickness recommended. Warm clothing is essential against bitter cold. Gear may be hired at Amecameca.

A road, beginning 2km S of Amecameca, runs E through the saddle between the volcanoes via (5km) *San Pedro Nexapa* to (23km) *Paso de Cortés* (R), the pass through which Cortés made his final descent towards Tenochtitlán on 3 Nov. 1519 (small monument). The view today, of a vast metropolis often overhung by a cloud of contamination, is very different from that described by 16C chroniclers: the 'Venice of America', seemingly floating on transparent waters. Hence the road continues S to (29km) *Tlamacas* (3897m; H), headquarters for climbing Popocatépetl, or a memorable excursion for those not intending to go further. From here a path ascends to the shelter called *Las Cruces* (c 3 hrs; no special equipment needed) at 4480m, where snow cover begins. A further ascent (3 or 4 hrs), this time with crampons, ice axe, goggles, brings the climber to the lowest point of the crater, called *Labio Inferior*.

Méx. 115 continues S to (68km) *Popo Park* (simple H, R), an excursion amid pinewoods with views of the volcanoes. 72km (l.) **Ozumba** (c 10,000 inhab.; 2500m; H,R,P), where stands the former Franciscan convent of *La Purísima Concepción*, a 16C foundation, altered in the 17–18C. The atrial cross is of the Jerusalem type favoured by the Franciscans.

The triple-arched portería contains 16C murals (ruined by overpainting in oils in 1848). From l.: the first three Franciscans to arrive in New Spain—Pedro de Gante, Juan de Tecto, and Juan de Aora; Cortés (kneeling before Fray Martín de Valencia) and his party welcoming the Apostolic Twelve; Martyrdom of the Tlaxcaltecan boys (young Christians killed by their relatives for destroying idols); Cortés whipped for arriving late at Mass, an occurrence (possibly apocryphal) supposed to have been circulated by him as a warning to the Indians.

The church façade and tower (both 1697) combine baroque and classical elements, a relief of God the Father between the topmost volutes. Note the sturdy wooden doors (c 1740–50), with foliate designs in panels. The crowding solomonic columns of the sumptuous baroque high altarpiece (1730), by Francisco Peña Flores, enclose statues of saints and are full of vegetal and fruity relief. That in the l. transept, a later work by the same artist, combines solomonic columns and estípites; in the predella, appealing reliefs of the apostles. In the r. transept is a fine 18C tribune. Off it opens the *Cap. de la Tercera Orden*, which contains another altarpiece (1724), perhaps also by Peña Flores.

An Aztec pyramid c 30m high is all that remains of the ceremonial plaza of yet another administrative centre.
  2km SE is *Atlautla*, where the 17C church of San Miguel contains a baroque high altarpiece.

1km S is **Chimalhuacán-Chalco**, amid avocado and zapote trees. Here the atrio gate of the Dominican convent of *San Vicente Ferrer* (c 1530–60) overlooks the main road. The church, of stout aspect, is reinforced by pairs of flying buttresses on its N side, probably 17C additions. The basket arch of its fascinating W doorway, with Mudéjar and Isabeline Gothic qualities, is in an alfíz, its area studded with star and strapwork relief; two medallions containing the Dominican fleurs-de-lis; two coats-of-arms of Charles V; and a niche containing a statue of the patron saint. The archivolt is vigorously ornamented with arabesques. Good jamb, pilaster, and capital carving completes the strong definition.

The font in the baptistery bears the date 1542 and is inscribed with the name of Pope Paul III. On both sides of the chancel end of the nave are remains of 17C altarpieces. The effect of the intimate little cloister, three arches wide, has been spoiled by the addition of an upper parapet masking the column shafts.

74km *Tepetlixpa* (P), with the 16C church of San Esteban (later modified; baroque altarpiece). 79km *Nepantla* (P), birthplace (12 Nov. 1651) of Juana de Asbaje (see Rte 7). Part of the house of her birth has been reserved as a small museum (9–2; fee). We continue into the State of Morelos. 88km turning r.

We may diverge here for an interesting and scenic roundabout route through the Sierra de Totolapan, in the S foothills of the Sierra de Ajusco. 1km **ATLATLAUHCAN** (c 2000 inhab.), dominated by the former Augustinian convent of **San Mateo**, a prime example of grand simplicity, founded c 1570, dating substantially from 1570–1600, declared a national monument in 1945, and restored in 1975.

The huge tree-shaded ATRIO is bordered, at a lower level, by a processional way just inside its wall, its parapet lined by the merlons which are the hallmark of the whole complex, separated off from the main area by a low wall on the other side. At the SE and SW corners are two surviving posa chapels, their domes crowned by a colonnette and ball; heavy piers topped by merlons support their plain arches—the whole Mudéjar in effect. The CHURCH, severe in aspect, with its strong buttresses, merlons, espadañas, and substantial tower on the N side, is adjoined, also on the N, by the OPEN CHAPEL, whose three arches, topped by merlons and a two-storey espadaña, give on to a trapezoidal barrel-vaulted interior. Part of the original vault painting remains: gilded arabesques with red borders against a blue background surrounding a golden sun, a silver moon, and white stars in which are planted seraphic heads.

On the S is the portería, its two unequal arches freed during restoration, which leads into the two-storey CLOISTER, where the rubble masonry adds to a sturdy primitiveness, already exhibited in the plain arches of unequal width in the lower storey and the small bays of the upper, even smaller on the N and W sides. The exterior walls are reinforced by buttresses with pentagonal sections and tapered heads. The lower-storey vaults are stunningly painted in hexagonal and octagonal coffering, alternating with rhomboids and triangles; at the corners in strapwork, vegetal motifs, and the Augustinian emblem of the Sacred Heart. Several small 16C oratories survive in the town barrios, built to serve during ceremonial processions.

C 4km E at *Texcalpan* is a 16C open chapel (San Juan), complete with merlons and espadaña, interior murals, and two 18C retables.

The road continues NW to (6km) **Totolapan** (c 3000 inhab.), in the Valley of Morelos, where the convent of *San Guillermo* was founded by the Augustinians in 1536 after their disgrace at Ocuituco (see below) and mainly finished by 1545. Much of its early building was paid for by Cortés. In the atrio, its walls bristling with ornamental merlons, traces of a processional way and two posas survive, one without its roof, the other with stubby merlons poking up from the edges of its cube and from its pyramidal roof. The solid walls of the crenellated church are supported by perforated buttresses; its interior was modernized c 1972. The sacristy contains paintings by Francisco Antonio Vallejo. Projecting c 2m in front of the church, the portería also served as an open chapel, its altar covered by a transverse barrel vault. The buttresses and bays, and rubble masonry, of the cloister are typical of Morelos convents. Among rediscovered murals is a delightful Holy Family, in one of the cells off the upper cloister walk.

C 1km E, at *Tepetlixpita*, on the other side of the main road, crowded in by later buildings, is a former open chapel, San Agustín, put up by the friars to serve a dependent barrio.

8km turning r. for *Ahuatlán* and *Nepopualco*, both c 2km NW, the former reached by a turning r. before the entrance to the latter, both with ruined 16C open chapels, the latter on the N side of the parish church, with a trapezoidal apse and wide double crossing.

Beyond Nepopualco the road winds through the mountainous region of N Morelos into the Federal District to (33km) *Milpa Alta* and (45km) *Xochimilco*, see Rte 17.

We continue SW through spectacular scenery to (16km) **Tlayacapan** (c 5000 inhab.; 1705m; P), another congenial checkerboard town amid a rocky landscape, still retaining its 16C barrio chapels altered by time. The *Pal. Municipal* occupies a 16C nucleus and contains contemporary murals. Of greater interest is the convent of *San Juan Bautista*, another massive Augustinian foundation (c 1555–65), its ATRIO, entered by a gateway with pointed arches, occupying the site of a prehispanic religious centre. One simple barrel-vaulted posa survives. The CHURCH is supported by immense buttresses: one on the N wall, serving as a staircase to the roof, and two on the S. The W doorway, between diagonal corner buttresses, is the lowest part of a tall panel, pedimented above the choir window, terminating in an espadaña with five open bays. Traces of the original painting which covered it may still be seen. The N and S wall windows, at different levels, illuminate the vault and the lower parts of the nave. In the sacristy is a notable group of murals, damaged after the removal of later plaster covering, depicting the Crucifixion, Our Lady, angels, and saints.

The five-arched portería, N of the church, was added, c 1569–72, in front of an already existing triple-arched portico open chapel, probably to bring it into line with the new church. Murals (originally in black and white, later filled in in grisaille) have been uncovered: St Catherine of Siena; Presentation of Our Lord in the Temple; Visitation; Dream of St Joseph. The CLOISTER, prow-buttressed, has lower-storey moulded arches resting on half-columns and an upper-storey sloping parapet. Decorative murals line the walks. The refectory is also painted with murals. In a niche on the stairs is an early 16C painting, probably Flemish, of the Virgin and Child with St Augustine.

23km **Oaxtepec** (c 1500 inhab.; 1385m; H,P), a salubrious place amid lush greenery on the S spurs of the Sierra de Totolapan, where Dominicans built their first convent (c 1541–53), *Sto Domingo*, outside Mexico City.

Hot springs here made a suitable location for Moctezuma I Ilhuicamina (1440–68) to construct a sumptuous summer palace and botanical–zoological gardens. With the help of Nezahual-cóyotl, his Texcocan ally, he collected every plant, bird, and animal he could find in Mesoamerica for his garden. Some of the Aztec ruins and a few rock carvings and graffiti of the 15C remain.

The convent was established 6m above the level of the prehispanic town, with its atrio to the N because the ground to the W was too steep and full of springs. There are traces of a processional way inside the outline of the atrio walls.

Buttresses are pierced to accommodate a wall walk halfway up below the parapet of the CHURCH, whose simple façade has an unfinished appearance, probably because of restrictions on elaborate building. In contrast, the interior, though repaired, shows remarkable finish: fine rib vaulting in the long nave and shallow arcades relieving the thickness of N and S walls. The triumphal arch has a Gothic look; the chancel rib vault has pronounced convex-concave curves. Two churrigueresque retables of moderate quality add a touch of colour to the nave. The paintings of SS Hyacinth and Rose are by Juan Sánchez Salmerón.

A decayed masonry block at the NW corner of the façade may be the base of an open chapel facing N; the N doorway is further W than is usual. The two storeys of the CLOISTER, supported by prow buttresses, and roofed by half-barrel vaults, are separated by an apron moulding, and the upper-storey arches spring from classicizing imposts. The lower cloister vaulting is painted in Mudéjar coffering and with frescoes of friars and saints, naive but moving, in the niches formed by the buttresses. At the corners, scenes from the Passion. Among the murals, the Miracle of the Loaves and Fishes may be seen in the refectory.

Oaxtepec's reputation in the 16–17C owed much to the *Hospital de la Sta Cruz*, the ruins of which may also still be seen, founded by Bernardino Alvarez in 1569 and depending on the alms collected by the Brothers of St Hippolytus (see Rte 9). It became the most famous provincial hospital in Spanish America, attracting patients from as far as Guatemala and Peru. The illustrious Spanish physician Francisco Hernández (c 1517–87) worked here during his stay in New Spain (1571–77), as did Gregorio López, who here wrote his 'Tesoro de la Medicina'. By the 18C its decline was complete.

To the S of the convent is the *Centro Vacacional Oaxtepec*, a vacation centre (H, R, swimming pools, thermal baths, gardens, etc.) run by IMSS. On Sun. and public holidays it is open to the general public.

Beyond Oaxtepec the road crosses the Mexico–Cuautla highway (Méx. 115D) to reach (28km) *Cocoyoc*, where an old hacienda has been transformed into a luxury hotel (favoured for conferences). *Yautepec* is 9km E, see Rte 81. 35km *Cuautla*, see below.

92km turning l. into the SW slopes of Popocatépetl, and two important convents.

5km **YECAPIXTLA** (c 6000 inhab.; 1603m; R), on the r. bank of the Río Yecapixtla, where amid the lush greenery rises the convent of **San Juan Bautista**, one of the grandiose Augustinian foundations of the region.

In 1521 Cortés's forces met fierce resistance here, vividly described in his third 'carta de relación'. The river, he wrote, was red with blood for more than an hour and the thirsty troops could not drink. Jorge de Avila, future Augustinian provincial, lived here c 1535–40 and founded the convent, which was mainly finished by 1550.

The L-shaped ATRIO, its wall dense with ornamental merlons, has a complement of four simple posas—that at the SE a recent reconstruction—each with two openings and steps, no doubt to make it easier for processions to file in and out. Indenting the skyline of the CHURCH EXTERIOR along the parapet and surmounting the buttresses, the pointed merlons and garitas create an impression of a medieval fortress. Two diagonal buttresses frame the beautiful façade. The doorway is pure plateresque, strongly European in inspiration, its carving delicate and of the finest quality: arch and jambs studded with vegetal and floral motifs; seraphs in the spandrels; below the pediment, escutcheons representing the stigmata of St Francis (r.) and the Augustinian symbol, the pierced heart (l.); in the frieze, two cherubs riding tritons and a globe covered by a cross; in the bases of the four slender columns, two portraits in relief (one, a friar, perhaps Fray Jorge; the other, a layman, perhaps the architect) and two urns. The pediment envelops a squat crucifix, with a lovely Gothic rose window, rich with tracery, above it. The N portal, though weathered, is even more striking, with its classic round arch, across which runs a line of war trophy relief; human portraits in the spandrels; and urn finials of the elegant baluster columns. Satyrs in low relief decorate the jambs.

INTERIOR. Above the chancel, beyond the pointed triumphal arch, is unusual Gothic rib vaulting. The pulpit is an outstanding piece of flamboyant Gothic, possibly an import from Spain or Portugal, though its ogee arches and foliated finials resemble those of the door into the cloister. Reliefs of four shameless sea monsters decorate the font.

Above the portería the simple elevated open chapel, level with the upper floor of the convent, has been walled up. The CLOISTER, originally of one storey, but with upper parts later added on W and S, is simple in style and could date from c 1540.

15km **Ocuituco** (c 4000 inhab.; 1955m), among peach orchards, where the Augustinians built their first convent, *Santiago Apóstol*, outside Mexico City.

They undertook very ambitious building operations in 1534–36, thoughtless of the welfare of their Indian labourers. In 1536 the Crown intervened, deprived the Order of its rights here, and assigned the convent to Abp Zumárraga, who himself finished the church in 1541. It came into Augustinian hands again in 1554. From the gate, entered by a split stairway, the atrio, uniquely laid out, rises in a three-tier arrangement to the convent block. The church, devastated by fire in the mid-19C, bears few original traces. The lower walk vaults and corner arches of the solid-looking cloister, with narrow bays and square buttresses, are adorned with painted coffering. In the patio, an original hexagonal fountain. The 16C fountain in Pl. Principal is a more elaborate hexagonal example, its two basins decorated with angel and floral relief.

The road climbs to (21km) *Tetela del Volcán*, see below.

96km *Tetelcingo*. At 98km and 99km the roads from *Tepoztlán* and *Yautepec* (see Rte 81) join Méx. 115 on the r.

101km **CUAUTLA** (c 110,000 inhab.; 1291m; H,R,P), in the Valle de Cuautla, is the second city of Morelos, known for its sugar cane, an abundance of fruit and flowers, and its warm climate.

It was the scene of a famous siege during the war of Independence. On 9 Feb. 1812, Morelos, victorious in the region S of Mexico City and planning to march on Puebla, decided to make a stand here, against a large royalist force under the command of Calleja, who reduced the besieged to all the horrors of hunger and famine, and obliged Morelos to break out with what men he could on the night of 3 May. Despite the calamity, Morelos was able to gather fresh forces at Tehuacán and his fame and military reputation increased. Zapata's forces occupied the town in 1911, marking the beginning of his revolutionary movement, and laid siege to it again in 1912. His bullet-ridden body was brought to Cuautla and exhibited after his assassination in Apr. 1919.

On the E side of Pl. Principal is the parish church, formerly the church of the Dominican convent, *Santiago Apóstol*, founded in the 17C. The adjoining cloister served as a refuge for the insurgents in 1812. On the SW side of the plaza, at No. 1 Cjón del Castigo, is the *Casa de Morelos* (Tues.–Sun., 10–5), where Morelos lodged during the siege and including mementoes of it. On the W side of the Alameda, reached by C. de los Bravos, running N from Pl. Principal, is *San Diego* (17C), Hermenegildo Galeana's headquarters and hospital during the siege. The church is empty; the convent is now the railway station.

Méx. 138 goes NW from Cuautla to (18km) *Yautepec*, see Rte 81.

FROM CUAUTLA TO CUERNAVACA VIA CHINAMECA AND ZACATEPEC,
87km. State road 115.

An interesting and scenic route by minor roads through a region of fertile, well-watered valleys descending from the S and SW slopes of Ajusco and Popocatépetl towards the tierra caliente.

7km (r.) *Anencuilco*, birthplace of Emiliano Zapata (1879–1919), caudillo del Sur; the house where he was born is now a national monument. The church of *San Miguel Arcángel* is in fact a large 16–17C open chapel, with a small convent attached, once dependent on the Dominicans from Cuautla. 8km *Ayala* (thermal springs to the S), where on 28 Nov. 1911 Zapata issued his Plan de Ayala, a blistering attack on Pres. Madero, and calling for a redistribution of a third part of the great haciendas among the landless peasants. 13km road r. (W) to (19km) *Tlaltizapán*, see below. 29km *San Rafael Zaragoza*. 2km SE is *Chinameca* where, facing Pl. Principal, is the porfirian hacienda where Zapata was assassinated on 10 Apr. 1919.

Col. Jesús Guajardo, a government officer, had lured him here on the pretence that Guajardo and his men wished to desert to the agrarians. Zapata and his retinue were gunned down when they arrived for the meeting. The bullet holes may still be seen in the entrance porch.
    At *San Pablo Panteón* on the Río Cuautla, 7km SW of San Rafael, David Grove has excavated some 200 ancient burials (c 900–500 BC). Across the river the *La Juana* area was also an ancient cemetery (c 1100–900 BC). La Juana burials included hollow Olmec 'baby-face' figurines and other ceramics identical to those from Olmec San Lorenzo, while the artefacts from San Pablo showed almost no Olmec characteristics.
    Chimalacatlán (local guide advisable) is 20km further SW on the same road. Situated on the *Cerro del Venado* (Stag Hill), the remains comprise a tomb and corbel vault of large basalt stones, and three basalt platforms, two of a single tier and a third of two tiers. Excavations revealed four cultural phases dating from the 1C to the 16C AD, and much evidence of influence from Monte Albán and Teotihuacán during the Classic Period.

From San Rafael Zaragoza the road crosses the valley of the Río Chinameca to (45km) **Tlaltizapán** (P), on the W slopes of the Sierra de Tlaltizapán and on the r. bank of the Río Yautepec. The former Dominican church and convent of *San Miguel Arcángel*, founded in 1591, was built in the 17C. In the atrio is a mausoleum dedicated to Emiliano Zapata. The headquarters of his Revolución del Sur is now a museum (10–2, 4–6; fee), containing mementoes, arms, and photographs. Attached is a reference library specializing in his movement.
    The road N from Tlaltizapán runs along the valley of the Río Yautepec to (25km) *Yautepec*, see below. We continue SW to (53km) **Tlaquiltenango** (c 13,000 inhab.; H), once a rich cochineal-producing town, where the convent of *San Francisco* dates probably from 1540.

It is one of the earliest mendicant establishments in Mexico. When it was ceded by the Franciscans to the Dominicans in 1570, such was the grief of the inhabitants that the whole town put on mourning. By 1586, however, the Franciscans had returned, through, it is said, the intercession of Martín Cortés, 2nd marqués del Valle de Oaxaca.

The large L-shaped atrio, in which three posas have struggled to survive, is mainly S of the church, whose barrel vault was later reinforced by exterior buttresses against the thick (2.5m) nave walls. The sturdy chancel arch rests on rounded jambs. The S side doorway, added after 1552 and of ashlar against a rubble wall, charmingly combines a reticent plateresque with touches of purism—a tall alfíz pierced by a pointed pediment. The plain W doorway, likewise of ashlar, its arch voussoirs emphasized against an alfíz, permits itself decorative touches in the arch imposts and jamb bases. An open chapel, set above the portería, was later walled in, a view of its interior impeded by a porch built in front of the portería. The two-storey cloister (wide bays, three a side, between buttresses) has a pleasing primitive look; in the walks are mural fragments; a mural above the cloister entrance shows the first Dominican friars to arrive in New Spain.

56km *Zacatepec*, with a large sugar refinery and with thermal springs in the vicinity. 15km N is *Chiconcuac*, 5km E of the Cuernavaca–Iguala road, see Rte 82.

Méx. 160 leaves Cuautla to the SE, through the southernmost slopes of the Sierra Nevada. 121km *Amayuca* (P), a little town near crossroads.

FROM AMAYUCA TO CHIAUTLA, 61km. Beyond the town a minor road goes S to (3km) turning l. for (3km SE) *Chalcatzingo*.

The site (2km SE) and valley of **CHALCATZINGO** ('place of the little circles') were influenced by various Mesoamerican cultures from the Preclassic to c AD 1200. The most important phase in its development, however, was as an Olmec 'gateway community' trading centre to the Basin of Mexico.

Relief carvings were discovered in 1932 and the site was visited by Eulalia Guzmán in 1934. Excavations were done by Román Piña Chan (1952), moulds of some of the reliefs taken (1964), the site and region restudied by Carmen Cook (1967), and further excavations done by Carlos Gay (INAH) and David C. Grove (University of Illinois) between 1972 and 1974.

From c 1500 BC the site was a small farming community with few permanent structures, but long-distance trading contacts were already evident in the importation of obsidian from Otumba (E Valle de Teotihuacán), and from sources in Veracruz and Oaxaca. By 1150 BC the pottery from the site resembled that from graves at Tlatilco (Basin of Mexico). By 1000 BC the site was more than 20ha and showed definite signs of contacts with the Olmecs of the Gulf Coast.

The adjacent hillsides were terraced, dams built for water control, and a large central plaza and mound (70m x 40m x 4m high) constructed. Pottery continued to resemble that from the Basin of Mexico, but Olmec designs were also used. The first of the bas-relief rock carvings in Olmec styles were executed, and the first trade items from W Mexico appeared. After 1000 BC obsidian was obtained from sources in Hidalgo and W Mexico.

Perhaps the most flourishing phase was 700–500 BC. Three terraces with stone-faced platforms, an 'élite' residence with a rich offering beneath the floor, and a stone altar of 18 blocks were constructed. Other structures found in excavations included workshops for obsidian, hematite, and serpentine. The site was clearly a religious centre and its location made it a 'gateway' community controlling the long-distance trade between three points: S into Guerrero for exotic minerals, N into the Basin of Mexico, and SE to and from the Olmec heartlands on the Gulf Coast. The site's position at the foot of two imposing cerros indicates that defence was important, and the presence of an 'élite' residence may imply direct Olmec control. Its position was paralleled by the site of Las Bocas on the opposite side of the valley.

The Valle de Amatzinac was a source of kaolin, cotton, lime, and hematite; obsidian and salt came from the Basin of Mexico, more obsidian from Hidalgo and W Mexico, and jadeite, hematite, and other minerals from Guerrero. The sophistication of the site's trading networks in this phase implies a large supporting population and the workshops indicate that the stones traded in were refined and worked at the site. Most of the bas-relief carvings found scattered on the hill slopes above the site date to this phase also, and are the only such Olmec rock reliefs known in the S Central Highlands. Rock-shelter paintings in red and reliefs include human figures, scrolls, volutes, clouds, rain, and 'flame-eyebrows', all in pure Olmec styles. The stylized jaguar-monster-mouth in one carving is thought to represent an Olmec jaguar stone altar, as is the 18-block stone altar and the associated stele. The relief of *El Volador* (Flyer) with a torch in his hand is in Olmec *La Venta* style.

By 500 BC the trade networks had collapsed abruptly for uncertain reasons, but the site continued to be occupied in a less important capacity. Later remains include a Classic Period ball court and a Postclassic Tlahuica sanctuary. There was strong Classic Period Teotihuacano influence in the Amatziner Valley.

The ruins visible today are scattered at the base and up the slopes of the two hills, Cerro Chalcatzingo, and Cerro Delgado. A guide is recommended and caution should be taken in climbing to the relief carvings of Grupos IA and II. The monuments and carvings are divided into four groups:

Grupo IV, seen first on entering the archaeological zone, includes the Olmec 18-block, circular stone altar and its associated broken stelae, a partly un-covered platform or pyramid base, and traces of hillside terracing.

Grupo III is in the valley to the W. Here, widely scattered, are two pyramid bases forming two sides of the PLAZA CENTRAL, several other small mounds, another Olmec altar, a partly excavated ball court, and a Late Postclassic stele, all arranged on a series of terraces. NW of the ballcourt is *Monumento 21*, a stele with the earliest known carving of a female in Mesoamerica.

Grupo IB is c 50m uphill on *Cerro de la Cantera*, the N hill. Here the Postclassic Tlahuica sanctuary comprises two platform structures with staircases. Scattered a few m up the hillside to the E are five Olmec rock bas-reliefs, incl. the *Procesión de Guerreros*, a puma, jaguars attacking humans, and Cipactli, the Mesoamerican mythical earth-monster. These Olmec military reliefs are some of the most violent examples of Olmec art known.

Still farther up the slope, to the W, *Grupo IA* includes 11 bas-reliefs of more military, agricultural, fertility, and mythical scenes, in particular *El Rey* (2.5m high), a seated figure in a stylized jaguar-monster-mouth motif.

Continuing uphill to the W, *Grupo II* has five more reliefs, incl. most notably the La Venta style *El Volador* with a torch in his r. hand.

In shallow caves in the saddle between Cerro Chalcatzingo and Cerro Delgado, and in caves higher up on Cerro Delgado, there are numerous Late Classic Period stick figures and other rock paintings in red.

At (5km) **Jonacatepec** (c 7000 inhab.; 1165m), birthplace of the liberal hero Leandro Valle (1833–61), is the former Augustinian convent of *San Agustín* (c 1566–71). The church is an 18C rebuilding. The three arches of the combined portería and open chapel have been walled up and pierced with window openings. Strikingly quasi-Romanesque in aspect, the cloister, its walls of cut stone and reinforced by prow buttresses, has a sloping upper parapet. Between the arcades the broad smooth band was once covered in murals.

In 1975 José Angulo excavated the site of *Las Pilas*, discovered when excavations were being made for the swimming pool and recreation area. He uncovered several sets of stairs, retaining walls, and the bases of several platforms built using a talud-tablero style similar to that of Monte Albán. The site was probably inhabited by a group contemporary with the inhabitants of Chalcatzingo, to the SE.

16km **TEPALCINGO** (to the r.; c 7000 inhab.; 1220m) stands picturesquely at the foot of a chain of hills running from Atotonilco to the N as far as Ixtlilco to the S and amid sulphur springs. A hot climate and fertile soil were ideal for the sugar-cane haciendas established in the region after the Conquest. The town owes its fame to **Jesús Nazareno**, a much-loved pilgrimage church whose façade is a magnificent, idiosyncratic tour-de-force of provincial carving (1759–82), Gothic, Romanesque, even plateresque, touches superimposed on a baroque mix to conjure up something almost oriental.

The iconography embraces the fall and salvation of man; the history and doctrine of the Church; the Passion; and divine mercy.

The façade resembles a folding screen, its centre panel wider than the two side panels, and consists of two storeys and a gable. The four engaged columns of the lower storey are entirely wayward in conception, but the outer pair smack of the baluster. All break to allow niches holding statues of the Evangelists and all are covered with vegetal and human relief (symbol of suffering humanity), devilish and frog masks, representing the powers of darkness. The spaces between hold quaint niches with statues of SS Peter and Paul (below), Christ ministered to by an angel, and one more saint. Passion symbols—ladders, nails, pelicans, sponges stuck on reeds, etc.—are squeezed in whenever possible. In the doorway arch imposts are a sleeping Adam and a languorous Eve; on extreme l. wall, Christ and Judas; cherub heads crowd the archivolt whose key is a type of shield, on which is stamped the face of Our Lord, supported by hovering angels. Along the frieze above line up the twelve apostles, with Christ holding the Host in the centre.

The upper storey rests upon a capricious arcade, of columns and pilasters, its centre a small temple for an image of the suffering Christ. In the slanting sections, two anachronistic double-headed eagles. Flanking the choir window, two fantastic supports appear like intertwined serpents, each ending in elaborate capitals. In the oblique niches on either side, Christ crowned with thorns and bound to the pillar to be scourged, his tormentors in attendance. In the gable, above a complex cornice, a Calvary, Our Lady and St John standing on huge pedestals; St Mary Magdalen at the foot of the Cross.

The interior contains murals in the form of altarpieces (late 18C) by Juan de Sáenz. The huge paintings of the Descent and Resurrection in the chancel are also by him.
20km W of Tepalcingo, along a minor road, is *Chinameca*, see above.

Our road continues SE to (31km) *Axochiapan*. 7km S, along State road 7, in the State of Puebla, is **Tzicatlán**, where the façade of the church of *San Lucas* is another exuberant manifestation of local mid-18C baroque, but still full of homely touches—like the drapes over window and niches.

Perhaps the most charming of this style is the coloured façade of the church of *La Purísima Concepción de María* at **Jolalpan** (c 8000 inhab.; 820m), 34km SW of Axochiapan and reached by Puebla State road 7. Here the supports of the lower two storeys and the all-pervading relief are the fruit of the most playful and singular imagination. Two swelling engaged outside columns are covered in petatillo mesh; above the cornice they are continued by intertwined serpentine tassels ending in capitals like horns of plenty. The inner lowest-storey pillars are made up of exotic twirling vegetation, with broad faces appearing below the bizarre capitals. Pairs of perilously hovering plump birds draw aside the curtains above the niches (statues of SS Peter and Paul), while jars of flowers in relief are slotted into the spaces on top. In the spandrels, the angels flutter with unexpected grace. Flanking the choir window are two opulent balusters, their capitals—on which sit angels, nonchalantly posed, one plucking a lute, the other bowing a viol—upheld by caryatids. More musical angels, similarly casual, appear beneath the central pediment above the outer tassel supports.
    In the middle of the topmost storey, a huge semicircular pediment, is the niche holding the statue of Our Lady, its frame relief fashioned like tongues of fire. Sainted friars hold back the drapes on either side. From it radiate seven sections, full of fascinating relief: her symbols of sun and moon; four archangels; and the Crucifixion, the cross upheld by angels, above which presides God the Father.

Beyond Axochiapan the road, State road 23, crosses into the State of Puebla (after a turning l. for [33km] *Izúcar de Matamoros*—see Rte 70), to (39km) **Tlancualpican** where the façade of the church of *Sta María* is the fourth example of the area's special kind of mid-18C popular baroque, spontaneous and fresh, this time the columns more recognizably solomonic, the relief a little less dense. Above the arch and in the r. spandrel, Christ dragged by a soldier to Calvary, a poignant touch. Coloured woodwork in the vault is a feature of the interior.
    47km *Huehuetlán el Chico*. 61km **Chiautla** (c 17,000 inhab.; 1025m; H,R,P), on the S slopes of the Sierra Nevada and on the r. bank of the Río Chiautla, is known for its dairy products and honey. The church of the former Augustinian convent of *San Agustín*, founded in the 1550s, was revamped in the early 19C. The cloister, restored in 1991, survives.

From Amayuca a road runs NE to a turning for (2km E) **Jantetelco** (3000 inhab.; 1160m), where the Augustinian convent of *San Pedro* was founded in 1565. The buttressed cloister survives, the second storey unfinished, though with good apron moulding. The present church dates from 1713. Part of the convent, known as the Dormitorio, was adapted as the house of Mariano Matamoros, parish priest here in 1807–11. It is now a museum, with historical paintings, documents, and mementoes of the hero.
    From the turning to Jantetelco the road runs further N to (7km) *Temoac*, where the church of El Señor de la Columna dates from 1821. 9km **Zacualpan de Amilpas** (c 3000 inhab.; 1205m), on the SW slopes of Popocatépetl. Here the Augustinian convent of *La Concepción*, founded in 1535, was built probably in the 1550s, and later rebuilt. The atrio, entered through double-arched baroque gateways, contains two surprising 18C posas (NW and SW corners), a rare revival of a by now obsolescent feature. An addition (late 18C–early 19C?) to the church, the Cap. del Rosario, was decorated by a local sculptor, Higinio López, and contains two late 18C altarpieces and two paintings, the Good Shepherd and St John Nepomuk, by Juan de Sáenz. A beautiful 16C survival is the carved stone font in the baptistery. The arch

of the open chapel, containing murals, is lower than the space behind it. The lower storey of the buttressed cloister has doorways rather than arches; the upper storey, window openings. Its cut stonework is beautifully finished. Among the murals, those in the lower cloister walk showing Augustinian saints were spoiled by 19C restoration.

At (13km) *Tlacotepec* the road forks, both branches (rough roads) climbing into the foothills of Popocatépetl. The l. fork is for (27km) **Tetela del Volcán** (c 7000 inhab.; R), where the restored Dominican convent of *San Juan Bautista* dates from the 1570s. In the sacristy is a beautiful wooden ceiling. The two-storey cloister has original murals.

At *Tescal Pintado*, a cave c 7km SE, are geometric, anthropomorphic, and zoomorphic figures of uncertain date. (A guide and suitable transport should be sought in the town.)

The road running SW and then W from Tetela is for (6km) *Ocuituco*, see above. The r. fork is for (26km) **Hueyapan**, a remote village, where survives the church, much altered, of the Dominican convent of *Sto Domingo* (c 1575–80).

Beyond Amayuca, Méx. 160 runs SE, through the valley of the Río Tenango, into the State of Puebla. 163km *Izúcar de Matamoros*, see Rte 70.

From Izúcar, State road 892 runs SW via (15km) **Chietla** (c 27,000 inhab.; 1163m) and (18km) *Atencingo* (P), with a famous sugar mill, occupying an old hacienda, to (33km) the Axochiapan–Tlancualpican road, see above.

Beyond Izúcar we continue SE on Méx. 190, crossing valleys of the S slopes of the Sierra Nevada, hot dry country in the Mixteca Baja. 210km *Tehuitzingo* (P). 250km **Acatlán** (c 23,000 inhab.; 1213m; H,R,P), in the valley of the Río Acatlán and a sugar-producing region, a town famous for its pottery. 288km (l.) *Chila*, where the Dominican convent of Asunción was founded in 1555; the church, with a new church alongside, is in ruins; the single-storey cloister, partly restored, lies to its N. Beyond Chila we cross the State border into Oaxaca. 312km **Huajuapan de León** (c 23,000 inhab.; 1600m; H,R,P), key commercial and distribution centre for the agricultural produce of the Mixteca Alta.

It was the scene of one of the most renowned actions of the war of Independence, when the insurgent Valerio Trujano was besieged for 111 days in Apr.–July 1812 by royalist troops until Morelos's forces came to his rescue and won the day.

In Pl. de Armas is the attractive *Pal. Municipal* (17C) and the church of *San Juan Bautista*, three-aisled and in deep red stone, once part of a Dominican convent founded in 1578. Its façade was rebuilt in 1953; the priest's residence on the N side was perhaps adapted from the original cloister.

From Huajuapan de León to (120km) *Tehuacán*, see Rte 73.

FROM HUAJUAPAN DE LEON TO PINOTEPA NACIONAL, 301km. The mountain road, of variable and at times of uneasy quality, climbs, W and then S, through the Mixteca Baja to the Mixteca de la Costa across the Sierra Madre del Sur. A sizeable proportion of Mixtec Indians of the typical pueblos of the sierra speak no Castilian. 41km *Tonalá* (1350m), with the large ruined church and convent of Sto Domingo (1555); an open chapel adjoins the N tower. 50km *San Agustín Atenango* (1675m), with a noticeable 19C church. 68km (r.) *Ixpantepec Nieves* (2340m), with an 18C Pal. Municipal and 18C church containing three churrigueresque altarpieces. 98km (r.) *San Sebastián Tecomaxtlahuaca*, a parish set up by the Dominicans in 1582 and famous for its orange trees. The church, in a walled atrio, was partly rebuilt (incl. the façade) in the 18C. 103km **Santiago Juxtlahuaca** (18,000 inhab.; 1650m; simple accommodation, R, P), where the Dominican church was incorporated, as the E transept, in its 18C successor. At 143km we join Méx. 125 from (59km NE) *Tlaxiaco* (see below), and then cross the Sierra Madre del Sur to (301km) *Pinotepa Nacional*, see Rte 82.

From Huajuapan de León, Méx. 190 continues SE through the Mixteca Alta to (354km) **Tamazulapan del Progreso** (c 4000 inhab.; H,R,P) in wooded country on the N of the Sierra de Tamazulapan. The church of *La Natividad*, in an atrio planted with jacarandas, served a Dominican parish set up in 1558; its façade was restored in the 18C.

It contains a beautiful baroque altarpiece into which have been fitted four late 16C paintings (Annunciation, Circumcision, Adoration of the Shepherds, Adoration of the Kings—the first and last repainted), possibly those contracted for by the local Indians with Andrés de la Concha in 1587; although the viceroy intervened, suspecting the townsfolk of extravagance, and may have stopped the work.

The Pal. Municipal dates from 1902. Just N of Tamazulapan is the as yet little-explored site of *Yatachío*. The otherwise unidentified ruins include terraces and several ruined structures, probably of a small Mixtec town. 364km *Tejupan*, where the atrio of the former Dominican convent of Santiago, built c 1572, probably occupies a pre-Conquest ceremonial site. S of the church, whose façade, resurfaced with cement and painted to resemble stone in 1951, includes a coffered arch, are the remains of a handsome two-arched portería, leading to the ruined cloister.

22km NE, along an improved road, is **COIXTLAHUACA** (c 2000 inhab.), set at the far end of a narrow valley in a wooded region of the Mixteca Alta watered by streams which empty into the Rio Papaloapan.

Coixtlahuaca was a Mixtec principality and market, important for the production of cochineal. When its 15C ruler, Atonaltzin, refused to trade with the Aztecs, it was conquered and garrisoned, like its neighbours Tilantongo, Tututepec, Tlaxiaco, and Yanhuitlán, and remained an important market city, visited regularly by caravans from Tlatelolco. It continued to prosper after the Conquest in the 16C, mainly owing to the introduction of a silk industry by the Dominicans. Mismanagement, import of silk from China and the Philippines, and plague ruined local industry, however. In 1679 the Spanish government ordered all mulberry trees destroyed and Coixtlahuaca rapidly declined to a sad village on a bad road, only accessible in the dry season.

Excavations by Alfonso Ortega in the 1940s, and by Ignacio Bernal in the 1960s uncovered foundations for platform structures grouped around patios, and tombs, incl. Mixtec and Aztec pottery. Little remained of the town's 10–11C architecture except some later Zapotec mosaic-work on excavated walls. Tomb 6 has been reconstructed in the Museo Nacional de Antropología.

The convent of **San Juan Bautista**, founded in 1544, finished, entirely in ashlar, probably in 1576, and probably to the design of Fray Francisco Marín, is set in an atrio raised above the village, most likely on rubble formed from the demolition of pre-Conquest shrines.

EXTERIOR. Immediately arresting is the main W façade, underway in the 1560s, fully Renaissance in conception, but too original to be held within plateresque bounds. It is in four harmonious stages, the outer panels of the first three marked by many niches; the lowest and highest by medallions—all offering contrasts of light and shade. Four slender engaged pilasters, divided into coffers punctuated by rosettes, provide the supports for the lowest storey; four even more slender engaged pilasters provide those for the upper two storeys. Above the beautifully moulded coffered archivolt, the pediment of the first storey includes the arms of Philip II; the second an exquisite rose window, like a giant flower whose outer petals show curving moulding dotted with rosettes and inner parts coffers and rosettes. In the centre of the third storey are reliefs of the Holy Trinity and St Barbara; in the side panels, four medallion busts. A recurring dentil motif may be seen in the pediment and entablature, and in the N doorway, analogous but more tequitqui in style, dominated by another rose window, flanked by symbols of the Passion in relief, a Náhuatl speech-glyph issuing from a head on each side. In the central tympanum are three figures in low relief. The pilasters which flank the door and continue through the two upper storeys emphasize verticality.

INTERIOR. The sumptuous rib vaulting of the nave, in four sections, has been shown up by being painted at a later period. Beyond the triumphal arch the vaulting of the apse culminates in a perfect star-shape. In the sections next to the choir and the apse, the tiercerons converge on a ring which surrounds a central boss. The bosses contain geometric relief and figures, of pronounced oriental aspect, that above the choir showing the Crucifixion amid crags, a cypress, and a globe. To the r. of the entrance, the doorway to the baptistery is a basket arch resting on solomonic columns and covered in polychrome relief, the whole perhaps finished off in popular style in the 17C. The side chapels are recesses between internal buttresses.

The high altarpiece, repainted in white and in four storeys, is a mid-18C remake of the 16C original; 18 columns—six with doric and six with ionic captials, and six baluster with Corinthian capitals—coexisting with estípites. Eleven of the paintings, the finest of the late Renaissance in Mexico, are by Andrés de la Concha. In the predella, three out of four paintings of three apostles each remain. Lowest storey: Annunciation, with a beautiful Virgin, delicate, full of grace and diffidence; Adoration of the Shepherds, full of tenderness, the shepherd on the r. especially so. 1st storey: Circumcision, with superb figure painting; Adoration of the Kings, with another lovely Virgin. 2nd storey: Resurrection, Crucifixion, Ascension, with marvellously delineated figures and colouring—notable light violet and dark green shades. In the pediment, God the Father. The paintings in the third storey (St Joachim, St Anne, and, in the centre, two holy kings) are 17C works. The statues in the outer niches of the lower three storeys, representing preachers and doctors of the Church, are of the late 16C, as is that of St John the Baptist, in the centre of the lowest storey.

Also of interest in the church are the early 18C altarpieces dedicated to Our Lady of Guadalupe and Our Lady of Atocha; and an early 17C example, with four fluted columns and baroque touches in the entablatures, in the little chapel by the sacristy.

On the N side of the church are the ruins of a once splendid OPEN CHAPEL, with a square nave and trapezoidal apse. Diagonal buttresses support the back and front corners, and between them a segmental arch spans the entrance. Its archivolt is divided into three sections by mouldings and decorated with superb tequitqui relief: the intrados with flowers; the other two sections with dragon heads and pelicans. The front buttresses were originally planned to incorporate arches springing from the capitals of free-standing columns, emphasizing the lightness of the whole; but the arches were soon filled in, probably to strengthen the building against earthquakes. Most of the vault has disappeared, but what remains shows a fine Gothic intricacy. The horizontal band defining the corbel capitals is composed of dentil motifs. In the r. wall is the arched entrance to a raised rib-vaulted chamber, possibly a sacristy or a musicians' gallery.

The upper storey of the CLOISTER, S of the church, is now in ruins; the lower storey arcade is marked by moulded semicircular arches resting on plain half-columns. The doorway which gives on to the staircase from the choir is deliciously characterful: an ogee arch framed by a thick alfíz which encloses vigorous flower relief.

W of Coixtlahuaca, *Inquitería* was a 15–16C Aztec hilltop ceremonial site (excavated by Ignacio Bernal in the 1970s), comprising two adjoining courts formed by unrestored ruins of platforms and pyramid mounds. In the hillside there are remains of earlier tombs: walled rectangular chambers, vertical shafts, and caverns reached by steps cut into the rock.

376km *Yucura* (R), at an important crossroads.

9km E is *San Pedro Yucunama*, with an 18C church and a museum in the Pal. Municipal containing a small anthropological collection of local ceramics, an ethnographic display, and some local historical pieces.

FROM YUCURA TO PINOTEPA NACIONAL, 269km. Méx. 125 runs S. 13km **TEPOSCOLULA** (c 3500 inhab.; 1670m), pleasant and quiet, set in a deep green valley of the Mixteca Alta.

The Dominicans founded their convent here c 1538, built it during the 1550s and 1560s, and established a silk-raising centre which by the 1550s had achieved extraordinary prosperity, exporting worms to other towns. Salt-mining and cochineal production boosted this success. But by the later 16C decline, aggravated by plague, had set in. Cochineal was still being produced in the 18C.

San Pedro y San Pablo, Teposcolula

Facing away from the W side of Pl. Principal are the church and convent of **San Pedro y San Pablo** (Mon.–Sat., 10–6; fee; Sun. and holidays free), standing in a wide atrio.

EXTERIOR. In the façade, a 17C rebuilding, simple half-columns flank niches enclosing huge saints in high relief, vigorous but primitive, perhaps from the original 16C church, standing on delightfully telling carved supports. The modernized INTERIOR contains two small baroque and two churrigueresque side altarpieces. One of the latter, with particularly fine rococo ornament, has a striking polychrome Descent from the Cross in its central upper niche.

On the N side of the church is the OPEN CHAPEL (c 1549–50; wherever possible restored in 1969), still beautiful in its semi-ruined state, designed with originality, lightness, and grace, all parts so disposed to emphasize the view of the altar at the centre of the E side: the atrio filled with the Indian congregation; the chapel proper reserved for priests, choir, and local notables. Its two naves, once covered with wooden roofs, are set at right-angles to the main church, and spread laterally from a hexagonal central space, on the E side of which was the altar. Five arches, the central one semicircular, run alongside the W nave fronting the atrio. At either end of the E nave lower arches support an upper storey, once reserved perhaps for the choir or other clergy. At the S end is the doorway giving on to the staircase communicating with the church choir. The central space is surrounded by an arcade, covered by rib vaulting, which suffered from years of neglect, and supported on the W by flying buttresses with panelled surfaces, and on the E by wall buttresses. In the vault, decorative detail is late Gothic; on arches and columns, entirely Renaissance, but liberally interpreted. Bases and capitals, obeying no classical order, are bound by thick ring mouldings. In the archivolts run layers of coffering enclosing diamond points; dentils; and pearls of Castile. Between the capital rings are bands of palmettes and egg-shaped relief. Columns show fluting, and counter-fluting—up to halfway in the thicker types of the hexagon, up to two-thirds in the slenderer W arcade, and all the way in the lower interior arcade.

To the r. (S) of the church is the double-arched PORTERIA (freed during restoration), the sculpting of its arches, capitals, and columns among the earliest examples of tequitqui in Oaxaca. It gives access (r.) to the CAP. DE STA GERTRUDIS, notable for its low arches, thick rib vaulting, and a pair of huge, squat twisted columns. The small altarpiece, with four good inner paintings of saints and much excellent detail, dates from the late 16C. The single-storey CLOISTER is reinforced by thick buttresses.

At (22km) *Santiago Yolomécatl* the 18C church of Santiago Apóstol, with a churrigueresque façade and high altar, succeeds the church of a 16C Dominican foundation; remains of the convent and rudimentary posa chapels survive. 31km (l.) *San Martín Huamelulpan*, where the 18C church stands on a prehispanic base. Remains of an earlier open chapel show tequitqui relief in the ogee arch. The nearby hill has remains of a Mixtec site, occupied in the Preclassic and Classic Periods. Here there are groups of terraces, two of which are joined. In one are blocked-out walls and a stairway, and some stone blocks with numeral signs carved in high relief. A second group forms two plazas surrounded by platforms with stone talud-tablero construction covered in stucco. Two stelae with number signs and an Olmec carving from the site have been erected in the Pal. Municipal on the town plaza.

At 39km a rudimentary road (l.) goes E to (22km) **Achiutla**, spectacularly placed on a height. Here the Dominican convent of *San Miguel*, huge though rustic, was built c 1560–80 on top of an ancient pyramid.

A Dominican friar, Fray Hernández, pulverized its large emerald idol. Whenever the 17C Dominican historian Fray Francisco de Burgoa remembered Achiutla, he would offer a prayer of thanks for the loveliness of the church and for the beauty of its setting. Achiutla was the sacred city of the Mixteca, the site of the legendary birth of their ancestors from two trees. The Mixtec federation comprised several main civic centres, each with a tributary territory.

Three posas with thatched roofs still stand in the atrio. The nave of the church (62m long), which contains six baroque and churrigueresque altarpieces, ends in a notable triumphal arch. On its S side is the two-storey convent, ruined, but, on its upper floor, boasting a laundry with ovens for heating water, basins, a kitchen in the wing extending W, and lavatories.

52km **Tlaxiaco** (c 15,000 inhab.; 1998m; H,R,P), in heavily wooded country, was a Postclassic Mixtec principality, important as a market town on the major trade routes (cf. *Tlatelolco*). It was made an Aztec tributary in the mid-15C. The former Dominican convent of *Sta María de la Asunción* (1550–60) is its main monument. Academically Renaissance in inspiration, the church's W doorway, somewhat lost in the immensity of the surface of the façade, has a triple-faceted, coffered basket arch, the coffers continuing into the jambs. Flanking columns end in candelabra finials either side of the triangular pediment. A simple rose window surmounts it. The interior has elegant rib vaulting. On the S the convent is now a school.

Deep in the mountains of the Mixteca Alta, c 30km NW of Tlaxiaco and reached by a track, is *San Juan Mixtepec*, with a three-aisled church in dark red stone, founded by the Dominicans in 1561. Its walled atrio is intact, as is its wooden beam ceiling. Another expedition into the wild and remote Mixteca Alta may be made by rough road to (c 50km S) *Chalcatongo* and thence by track SE and E to (c 90km) *San Pedro Teozacoalco*, site of the capital of a large Mixtec kingdom (cf. *Mixtecas*).

Beyond Tlaxiaco the road winds tortuously through the Sierra Madre del Sur via (93km; l.) *San Andrés Chicahuaxtla*, inhabited by Trique Indians who guard their prehispanic religious rites, to join at 111km the road from Huajuapan de León, see above. 269km *Pinotepa Nacional*, see Rte 82.

Beyond Yucura we continue SE on Méx. 190 to (389km) **YANHUITLAN** (c 8000 inhab.), a sleepy, straggling town set in a spacious valley. Here the former Dominican convent of **Sto Domingo**, lording it above the main road, is a monu-

Convent of Sto Domingo, Yanhuitlán

ment of the greatest importance, its church, in stone of pinkish ochre, the 'behemoth of earthquake-country monastic churches'.

Yanhuitlán was a Postclassic Mixtec principality founded by people from Chachoapan/ Yucuñudahui, and an important market centre with several tributary towns. In the 11C some of the Mixteca from Yanhuitlán moved to the site of Zaachila. Like the contemporary principalities of Coixtlahuaca, Tilantongo, and Tlaxiaco it was conquered by the Aztecs in the 15C.

The first church, begun c 1541 by the encomendero Francisco de las Casas, was, so the story goes, not considered worthy of so important a town. His son Gonzalo, determined to build a better, demolished it. The new structure was built (from c 1543–50) on a slope which necessitated a platform c 107 x 152m and 6m high, formed by the rubble from the old church and several levelled pre-Conquest pyramids. During c 1550–70, 6000 Indians were drafted to labour on church and convent, working in shifts of 400-600. The church was probably designed by the same architect as that at Coixtlahuaca, Fray Francisco Marín, with the builder Fray Antonio de la Serna.

Impending complete collapse was arrested by restoration works directed by José Gorbea Trueba, a specialist in the renewal of historical monuments, during the late 1930s and 1950s. Further restoration is in progress. The Dominicans remained in possession until c 1889. The church is often kept closed. Local enquiry should be made after the sacristan or parish priest, who holds the keys.

The church stands S of the large atrio. EXTERIOR. Two lateral towers project beyond the three-storey façade, started c 1575 and completed a few years later, although the style seems a transition between Mannerism and oaxaqueño baroque, kept within strict bounds. In the lowest and first storeys two pairs of columns end in Tuscan and Corinthian capitals respectively; in the second, pilasters in ionic capitals. Flanking the central relief of Our Lady protecting Dominican saints, accompanied by seraph heads, are two colonnettes with Tuscan capitals. Subdued geometric and vegetal relief is in keeping with the rest. The gable and bell tower are 17C additions, as are two perforated buttresses, one supporting the round apse, the other the NW corner, to compensate for cracks in the fabric.

Strange and involved, the N doorway, a mixture of plateresque and Mannerist, is framed by tall, slender, and complex baluster columns, continued by three-tier finials above the cornice, and echoed by the fluted columns with Corinthian capitals either side of the doorway, topped by bulbous finials above its cornice. Three layers of diamond-point coffering form the rim of the basket arch. Between the finials above, a semicircular fancy, like a carefully creased drape, with a rosette border, gives the illusion of a dome. On either side, two circular medallions of Dominican emblems. Above the upper cornice, a rose window on a Gothic base. Also Gothic-inspired are the traceries of the nave windows, unique in Mexico, set above a moulding which encompasses the building.

INTERIOR. Entered under the wide basket arch of the sotocoro, the high, spacious nave presents a majestic, deeply impressive aspect. Choir and nave are covered by magnificent rib vaulting, with tiercerons and liernes, springing from imposts at the level of the exterior moulding. The ceiling of the sotocoro is a stunning exhibition of coffering, Spanish in inspiration, consisting of hexagons and rhomboids, each hexagon a miniature dome, with a pine-cone boss in the middle and rimmed by a cord. Also noteworthy is the choir balcony, composed of original 16C wooden balusters. Lining the walls are 11 altarpieces (early 17C–late 18C) ranging from Renaissance to churrigueresque, a commentary on changing modes. The doorway from church to cloister, still showing original painting, offers a tentative mixture of styles from the 16C; the rinceaux next to the columns are probably 18C. Drawing all eyes at the E end are the triumphal arch and the high altarpiece, beneath the ribbing of the apse which forms more lovely coffering. Emphatic and extravagant, the arch is larded with polychrome strapwork relief enveloping, high up, niches for statues of angels and SS Peter and Paul. At the bases, twin shrines with blind arches. The high altarpiece, slender and soaring, is one of the pièces de résistance of Mexican art, designed like a folding screen.

C 1567–68 the painter Andrés de la Concha was brought from Seville by Gonzalo de las Casas to do the original altarpiece. The present work, of the late 17C, incorporating Concha's 16 original paintings, was modified in 1718–20. It is in four storeys and seven vertical sections divided by solomonic columns; the centre section broad and ending in an elaborate top-piece; the two centre lateral sections, placed obliquely to it as the screen folds, ending in smaller top-pieces, in fact ornate frames for paintings. The four narrow sections contain niches for statues of saints, probably originals, the work of a local sculptor using estofado, but later overpainted. In the lowest storey are four apostles; in the upper three are four preachers, four doctors of the Church, and four founders of Orders.

The paintings, though faded and maltreated with time, show fine, if sober, colouring. In the predella: SS Mary Magdalen (l.) and Jerome (r.). Lowest storey: Annunciation (l.); Adoration of the Shepherds (r.), with excellent figure painting. 1st storey: Adoration of the Kings (l.); Circumcision (r.). 2nd storey: Ascension (l.); Resurrection (centre); Descent of the Holy Ghost on the Apostles (r.). 3rd storey: Our Lady of the Rosary, surrounded by the mysteries of the Rosary, with donors below (twin of the painting at Tláhuac; see Rte 66); Immaculate Conception (centre); Christ descending into Hell (r.), a magnificent work, strongly italianate, full of vigour and urgency. In the top-piece: Descent from the Cross, archaizing and compelling. In the finial above: St Dominic. At the tops of the oblique sections: SS Catherine of Alexandria and Catherine of Siena.

To the l. of the triumphal arch is the original stone polychrome pulpit. Off the r. side of the triumphal arch opens the Sacristy, on its S wall a moving relief (probably 17C) in polychrome marble, of the Descent from the Cross, the figures just larger than lifesize. Its arched frame is a lovely work; the jambs incorporate two sets of baluster columns.

To the r. of the church façade is the PORTERIA (probably also an open chapel), with a basket arch. Through it we gain access to the CONVENT (10–6; fee). In the long room to its r. is a collection of polychrome statues from 17–18C retables. Around the central patio, shaded by an old cypress, is the two-storey cloister, strongly buttressed, five arches a side, the long openings of the lower storey, resting on Tuscan half-columns, helping to create an impression of height.

Rib vaulting with hanging keystones, and springing charmingly from delightful corbels joined by a dentil cornice, covers the lower walk, on the N side of which two confessionals let into the church wall may be seen. At the SE corner begins the grand staircase to the upper storey; a 16C fresco of St Christopher in the stairwell shows the saint's cloak in parallel folds, a feature of byzantine painting. Immediately to the l. at the top is the friars' communal privy, with finely wrought seats—a feature which excited the admiration of the Peruvian Jesuit Bernabé Cobo in 1630.

397km *San Mateo Yocucuí*, with a church in popular baroque style (1662).

7km SW is **TILTEPEC**, possessor of the large and intriguing church of **Sta María**, seemingly built on top of a prehispanic pyramid, which very likely dates back to the late 16C when it was a *visita* of Yanhuitlán. An almost overwhelming display of Mixtec tequitqui sculpture includes a unique blend of the symbolisms of pre-Conquest tradition and Christianity—in the latter case odd, and not fully mastered. Patching-up, resetting, and repair, doubtless after earthquakes, are evident in many parts of the fabric.

EXTERIOR. Its wide, square façade, set back slightly from two solid tower bases, is divided into two storeys and five vertical sections, and accommodates ten side niches. The archivolt, bevel, and intrados of the supporting jambs of the doorway arch are divided into coffers containing vertical or diagonal bands, or floral motifs. In the block above the keystone appears an owl. Attached to the bevel of each jamb are holy-water stoups; above them, crosses with the emblem INRI, a crown of thorns, and three nails. The columns on either side, highly idiosyncratic, incorporate dot-like motifs in their flutings which run up into feathery tops surmounted by ionic capitals. The four niches, lower on r., are intricately framed and covered by shell canopies. The spaces above them, the spandrels, and the frieze are filled with a wealth of floral relief; that above the r. niches differing markedly from that above those on the l. Main feature of the middle storey is a wide niche with a trilobe arch, the extrados tight with attempts at triglyphs, metopes, and dentils (recurring motifs throughout), the intrados coffered. Supporting pilasters, side columns, and spandrels are crowded with relief, incl. angel heads in the latter. Bearing in upon the octagonal bull's-eye window in the centre of the upper storey is a mass of quaint relief, its area defined by strange twisted columns without capitals. Of greatest interest are the rearing animals on either side: on the l. with jaguar-like ears, mane, and long tail; and above it a rectangular block in which prance what seem like three deer; on the r., more uncanny, with stumpy upper legs, weird head, pointed ears, crinkly mane, and long feathers protruding from its back, and above it another rectangular block with a central eight-petalled flower. High in the S wall (r.) the nave window shows a primitive delicacy, its arch, layer on differing layer, framed by multiple balusters; its alfíz topped by a shell. The S doorway is an extraordinary work (despite obvious rebuilding), tapering upward, yet bulging with repeated motifs as though the craftsmen could not bear to stop. Above the plain arch, whose keystone shows a floral pattern as background for a flute-player, the niche, resting on a pronounced cornice, is framed by columns marked by zigzag relief ending in disproportionately heavy capitals; flanking them are coffers, floral patterns, and pine cones with rosettes on either side. Above the finely done shell canopy appear two full-length figures joined by spine-like vegetation, over which appear tiny heads, to a central crown.

Between niche and triangular frame has been inserted a rectangular slab bearing the date 1689 (to commemorate significant repairs ?); the frame, surmounted by a shell canopy in an alfíz, envelops two rosettes, symbols of the Passion and the risen Christ. On either side are two more rosettes, the sun, and the moon. In the N wall is another singular nave window, flanked by zigzag columns and swelling balusters, their bases laden with petal relief. The N doorway, likewise reset, and aglow with rosettes, resembles the S, except that the niche rests on thick coffered pilasters; between niche and triangular frame an inserted stone shows a chalice and cherub head. Beneath the lower dentilled cornice another slab shows the royal arms in low relief. The arch keystone imitates that of the S portal. In the voussoirs is carved (from keystone to l.; from keystone to r.) VE 20 VITNAIVE defeb vero de 1687 Ab° (uitna jueve

20 de febrero de 1687 AD; uitna in Mixtec meaning today)—Today Thursday 20 February 1687 (another repair date ?).

The INTERIOR is flooded with light from the S door. In the sotocoro are two areas enclosed by wooden balusters, the little hanging pieces between the full balusters a feature of oaxaqueño woodcraft; to the r., images of five saints stand over the baptismal font. The wide choir basket arch and spandrels are covered in relief. The organ dates from the 18C. Four late 17C baroque altarpieces line the nave. The barrel vault of the chancel is much lower than that of the nave. An original polygonal apse was covered by a straight buttressed wall continuing S to form the E side of a later complex, incl. sacristy, a S chapel, and a priest's house, the latter added in 1844. The N chapel was added in 1859.

From (399km) *San Andrés Sinaxtla* a poor road runs S to (25km) **Tilantongo**, where the Dominicans took over the parish of Santiago in 1572. Inscriptions of it survive, although the present church is a modern building.

Tilantongo was an important Mixtec principality, and the birthplace of the legendary 11C king, Eight-Deer-Tiger-Claw (cf. *Mixteca*, Rte 75). His conquests of many smaller centres, and eventual death by sacrifice, are recorded in the Mixtec codices, especially in Codex Nuttall.

The principality was attacked by the Aztecs under Moctezuma I Ilhuicamina in 1455 during the reign of king Dzahuindanda, who defeated the Aztecs twice. With allies and tributaries, allegedly 200,000 warriors and 100,000 tememes (porters), the Aztecs made a third attempt and this time were successful, despite the aid given to the Mixtecs by their own allies from Tlaxcala and Huexotzingo. Dzahuindanda was executed and the town was pillaged in true Aztec vengeance.

At the height of its power, the rulers of Tilantongo were able to appoint rulers in many of their subject towns where there was no legitimate heir, thus strengthening their rule. Despite the Aztec incursion, the city remained a viable commercial centre for Pacific coastal trade, and at the time of the Spanish Conquest was mounting a second attack on Miahuatlán, to the S, to gain more control of this commerce.

C 365m above Tilantongo is **Monte Negro**, a Middle Preclassic Period site on the mountain of the same name. Like Dainzú it was contemporary with *Monte Albán I*, but was abandoned sometime shortly after 300 BC.

Its occupants are a mystery, neither Mixtec nor Zapotec; and although contemporary, its artefacts are not identical to those of *Monte Albán I*, and there were no slab reliefs, hieroglyphic or numerical inscriptions. More typical was a type of tall urn with an Olmec-like face on one side.

The ridge top of Monte Negro was artificially levelled as at Monte Albán and Dainzú, and an alignment of public buildings and plazas built along a principal street running E–W. At the E end, on the N side, is a small patio formed by four rooms with two column stubs each at their fronts, and stairs on either side of the S room. W of it is a second small patio, and another building with a two-columned façade. Continuing W, there is a third patio, identical to the first, but smaller. Next is a much larger plaza, formed by platforms with steps to buildings on its four sides. The E-side structure is a larger temple, incl. a porticoed façade with two columns in front and four central columns.

Along the S side, against the main street, is a small patio, and at the W end of the street several more platforms, the one at the extreme end incl. a rectangular hall with four corner columns and a central patio. There is a tomb on its S side.

C 35m NE of the E end of the principal street there are more terraces and four aligned temple buildings. Each comprises a platform with steps and colonnaded chambers. The largest is on the S end of the line, with a single, large room. The next, to the N, is smaller, with a semidivided chamber with two column stubs at the front and a bench along the rear wall. The next is a platform with ten column stubs, presumably for several rooms. At the N end of the line, offset to the E, is a small patio with colonnaded buildings on three sides.

At 405km a road goes N to (6km) *San Juan Yucuita*, 1km S of which is **Chachoapan** or *Yucuñudahui*; mostly unrestored ruins.

Excavations by Alfonso Caso (1938) uncovered a Mixtec site with a *Juego de Pelota*, a *Templo* thought to have been dedicated to Tláloc, and a mound known locally as *Mogote Grande*, found already looted.

On the adjoining extension of *Cerro Negro* (also known as *Yucuneo*), two mounds had the remains of a small patio formed by four structures, incl. another *Templo*, and a *Tumba*. The tomb comprised five descending steps to a cruciform, stone-lined antechamber, a stone-lined square chamber, and a final chamber with the burial itself. The burial chamber comprised a stone-lined room with a wooden roof of 17 tree trunks. The entrance was blocked by a stone painted with the effigy of Tláloc and the stone walls have Zapotec glyphs. Associated finds indicate a date in the second half of the 3C AD.

Other dating evidence shows a long site history: there was Teotihuacán pottery as well as local ware; and a second tomb has a Mixtec calendar on the walls, indicating occupation in the 11–12C. Yucuñudahui probably dominated the valley during the Classic and Early Postclassic Periods, but for reasons unknown the hill site was abandoned in the 14C or 15C and moved down the valley to Yanhuitlán.

407km (l.) *Nochixtlán*, in the Valle de Nochixtlán. Here the church of Asunción was built by the Dominicans from 1578; its façade was rebuilt in the 18C; the new tower with bells was added in 1957.

Nochixtlán has pre-Spanish origins, but the only visible traces of these are ruins of terracing on the hillsides of Pueblo Viejo and Tinducarrada barrios. In the Postclassic it was probably tributary to Tilantongo or Yanhuitlán (cf. *Mixtecas*, Rte 75).

476km *San Pablo Huitzo*, in the Valle de Etla, watered by the Río Atoyac, where we rejoin Méx. 131, 204km S of Tehuacán, see Rte 73. 491km (r.) **Nazareno Etla**, chief place of the municipio de Etla (c 17 sq km), whose villages in large part bear its name.

The first small Dominican convent here, built during the 1530s, collapsed in 1575 and the present one, *San Pedro*, moved to a higher and firmer site, dates from the 1570s.

Traces of one posa chapel survive, along with part of the atrio wall. The church (completed before 1586 and radically restored in 1940–41) is on a grand scale and marked by a deeply recessed façade and deep interior arcading to reduce the nave span and provide internal buttressing. Instead of a vault, the nave keeps its original wooden ceiling (c 1595). The convent is entered through a four-arched portería with elegant columns. The upper storey of the buttressed cloister (mural fragments) dates from 1636. Remains of the 16C aqueduct may still be seen.

493km turning r. to (4km) **San José Mogote**.

Excavations at sites in the Valle de Etla by Kent Flannery and his students have provided important information on the early growth of village life in the Valle de Oaxaca. *San José Mogote*, an ancient site mostly built over by a modern village, dates from c 1500 BC. Here the ancient villagers had a cluster of huts and a drainage system for agriculture. Huts varied in shape and size, and contained differentially grouped tools typical for 'men's' and for 'women's' work. Between c 1500 and 900 BC the households increased from c 30 to c 240, and there were plastered and painted community buildings as well, oriented 8 degrees W of N. The exploitation of local sources of magnetite and ilmenite had begun, and small iron-ore mirrors were made, to be worn around the neck (as we know from figurines); one house seems to have specialized in the manufacture of these. White-rimmed black-ware pottery, with excised designs, Olmec motifs, rocker stamping, and figurine types C and D similar to figurines in the Basin of Mexico, all show evidence of outside contacts and contemporaneity to Olmec San Lorenzo Tenochtitlán.

By 600 BC San José Mogote was the largest centre in the valley, and boasted a stone-faced platform, supporting a plastered and red-painted community building (as with the earlier public buildings, oriented 8 degrees W of N). Later, contemporary with *Monte Albán I* and *III*, it produced the earliest known evidence in Mesoamerica for the use of a 260-day calendrical cycle. A carved stone slab, set into the threshold of a public building, depicts a figure sprawled as if a captive; between his legs are carved the glyphs for 'one earthquake'. This is the earliest known of the hundreds of such 'captive' reliefs—the most famous at Monte Albán. Although it gives no absolute date in itself, associated artefacts provide evidence for the use of dating and calendrics as early as c 600 BC (cf. *Monte Albán, Tres Zapotes*, and *Chiapa de Corzo*).

A contemporary site, *Tierras Largas* (to the S), grew from c 10 wattle and daub huts to c 80 between c 1300 and 350 BC, as did several other hamlets in the valley before Monte Albán began to dominate the tripartite Oaxaca Valley system. Similar dwellings and artefacts were found at *San Pablo Huitzo* (see above).

In the modern village of San José there are still some terraced platforms, wall remains, and plaster floors to be seen, plus a stele of a 'danzante' figure similar to those at Monte Albán. In a small museum (key kept by the owner of the hut opposite, available during daylight hours on request) there are reconstructed models of the prehistoric huts and some of the artefacts from the excavations, incl. a complete red brazier in the form of a head.

Méx. 190 continues SE through the NW part of the Valle de Oaxaca to (507km) *Oaxaca*.

75 Oaxaca

OAXACA (200,000 inhab.; 1545m), capital of the State of Oaxaca, lies towards the NW of the ample and fertile Valle de Oaxaca and to the E of the Río Atoyac. Its warm, sunny climate; its fame as a gathering place for the Indian peoples of the region who have maintained their ancient customs; its nearness to important prehispanic sites; and the beauty of its historic centre, touched lightly by time, have made it a magnet for visitors. The cathedral and churches, built of green-tinted local stone, called cantera verde ('very solid, yet so soft', wrote Bernabé Cobo in 1630, 'that one can fashion it with a knife'), and displaying sturdy oaxaqueño baroque, combine with thick-walled old houses, with wrought-iron balconies and grilles, to give Oaxaca a wonderfully distinctive stamp, as well as to withstand the earthquakes which have periodically ravaged it.

Airport. 8km S. Frequent flights to *Acapulco, Mexico City*, and *Tapachula*; and to *Puerto Escondido*.

Bus stations. 1st Class. 1036 Calz. Niños Héroes de Chapultepec. Services to *Mexico City* (10 hrs); to *Puebla* (8 hrs); to *Veracruz* (10 hrs); to *Salina Cruz* (5 hrs); to *Tehuantepec* (4½ hrs); to *Villahermosa* (12 hrs); to *San Cristóbal de las Casas* (12 hrs); to *Tapachula* (14 hrs); to *Tuxtla Gutiérrez* (9 hrs); to *Puerto Angel* (7½ hrs); to *Puerto Escondido* (8 hrs); etc.

2nd Class. By the market on the W edge of the city, reached along C. Trujano and then across the Periférico. Frequent services to localities nearer Oaxaca (eg *Cuilapan*); and to *Yanhuitlán* (3½ hrs) and *Teposcolula* (4½ hrs); etc.

Railway station. Av. Madero (continuation W of Av. Independencia). Trains to *Puebla* (12 hrs) and to *Mexico City* (18 hrs).

Hotels throughout the city.

Post Office. Corner of Av. Independencia and C. 20 de Noviembre.

Tourist Office. Pal. Municipal (corner of Av. Independencia and C. García Vigil).

US Consulate. 201 C. Macedonio Alcalá. **Canadian Consulate.** 817 Av. Hidalgo.

Fiestas. Guelaguetza (or Lunes del Cerro; last two Mon. in July) on Cerro del Fortín (tickets at the Tourist Office). 31 Aug.: Blessing of Animals at church of La Merced. 18 Dec.: Our Lady of Solitude. 24 Dec.: Christmas Eve.

In 1522 Spanish settlers from Segura de la Frontera (Tepeaca; see Rte 73) moved to Huaxyácac, a pre-Conquest Aztec garrison town in the valley, but were soon expelled by Cortés. In 1525 a villa, to be called Antequera, was refounded on the site, again to be uprooted in 1526. In 1529 it was settled again, and laid out according to the plans of Alonso García Bravo. Cortés by 1534 had regained control of a part of the region, to be included in the marquesado del Valle de Guaxaca, called Cuatro Villas (Cuilapan, Etla, Guaxaca, Tlapacoya), with its headquarters at Guaxaca (also called Villa del Marquesado), a little to the W of Antequera, and later to be incorporated in it. During the 16C cochineal production and cotton cultivation were to become important industries. In 1626, when c 2000 inhabitants of Spanish origin lived there, Thomas Gage passed through: 'a fair and beautiful City to behold...of so temperate an air'. Later in the 17C the Jesuit Francisco de Florencia gave Oaxaca third place in New Spain after Mexico and Puebla, paying tribute to its 'fruits, meats, fish, sweets of all kinds, and the rest, not only for sustenance, but also to bring delight'. In

1777 the French botanist Thierry de Ménonville described how he smuggled out cochineal insects and the cactus on which they thrived to Sto Domingo where the French wanted to produce the dye themselves. During the war of Independence, Morelos held Oaxaca from Nov. 1812 to Jan. 1813. During the war of the Reform it suffered seven military occupations and four sieges. In Feb. 1865 the imperialists under Marshal Bazaine captured the city from Porfirio Díaz, who recaptured it in Oct. 1866. A formidable yet beneficent later influence on the city was to be Eulogio Gregorio Gillow y Zavalza (1841-1922; bp 1887–91; abp from 1891; comp. Rte 7), an aristocratic Lancastrian-Mexican, who founded free schools, orphanages, and old people's homes; restored various of the city's churches; and was forced to flee when the Revolutionary struggle began.

From 1914 city and State were scene of military action between supporters and opponents of Carranza, ending in the latter's victory. Significant earthquakes are recorded in 1603, 1660, 1787, 1794–95, 1801, 1854, and 1931, the latter two wreaking terrible damage. D.H. Lawrence took up residence in Oaxaca in Nov. 1924: 'a very quiet little town…the Hotel Francia is very pleasant—such good amusing food—4 pesos a day for everything'. He moved to 43 Av. Pino Suárez. He completed 'The Plumed Serpent' in Oaxaca and caught malaria. Then it became: 'I hate the place—a let down'. The city has strong associations with various famous Mexicans: the painter Miguel Cabrera (1695–1768; b. at Tlalixtac, 8km E); Benito Juárez, Benemérito de las Américas (1806–72; b. at Guelatao, see Rte 84) and his wife Margarita Maza (1826–71); Porfirio Díaz (1830–1915); José Vasconcelos (1881–1959), a pioneering secretary for education; and the artist Rufino Tamayo (1899–1991).

The State of **Oaxaca** (93,364 sq km; 3 million inhab.), thanks to its mountain chains, is one of the most rugged states in Mexico. Inland from the coast runs the Sierra Madre del Sur, its E part known as Sierra de Miahuatlán. Approx. down the middle of the State runs the Sierra Madre de Oaxaca, joining the Pico de Orizaba with the Sierra Madre del Sur, its most substantial mass known as the Sierra de Juárez, NE of Oaxaca. A lesser range, the Sierra Atravesada, crosses E to W, joining the Sierra de Chiapas with the Sierra Madre del Sur and forming the spine of the Isthmus of Tehuantepec, mostly low, hot, and arid, the narrowest stretch of Mexican territory, between the Gulf of Mexico and the Pacific.

The largest part of the region known as the *Mixteca* is in the State of Oaxaca: the Mixteca Baja, centring round Huajuapan de León in the NW and extending into S and SW Puebla and into NE Guerrero; the Mixteca Alta, incl. Teposcolula, Tlaxiaco, Yanhuitlán, and Nochixtlán; and the Mixteca de la Costa, between the Mixteca Alta and the Pacific coast. It is the home of the Mixtecs, one of the most important of the indigenous peoples who make up c 40 per cent of the State's population. Towards the Gulf coast the State falls within the Papaloapan and Coatzacoalcos river systems; towards the Pacific, within those of the Ríos Mixteco and others, all deriving from the Río Balsas. Agriculture and mining are mainstays of the economy of what is essentially one of Mexico's poorest States.

The Mixteca. Mixteca origins are uncertain, but they appear to have migrated from the N, from the Pánuco region, simultaneously with the Zapoteca. According to some sources they claimed descent from the seven caves of Chicomoztoc (see Rte 49), led by one Mixtécatl ('Cloud Person'), and in others from the sacred trees at Achiutla (see below). In central and S Oaxaca they formed a loose federation of main civic centres, beginning perhaps by AD 800, each with a tributary territory of smaller towns. The federation was well established by AD 1000.

The legendary 'sacred city' of the Mixteca, where their ancestors were supposed to have issued from two trees, was Achiutla, now only a village. According to the Codex Colombino-Becker, the legendary Eight-Deer-Tiger-Claw, a second-dynasty ruler, founded an 'empire' as the founder-ruler of the city of Tututepec, near the Oaxaca coast. Later, c 1030–63, he co-ruled with his half-brother in the city of Tilantongo as well. The codex also records his five marriages, and his murder of his half-brother in a power-struggle. The Codex Nuttall depicts Eight-Deer in typical Toltec dress while the dress of his courtiers is just as clearly Mixtec, facts used by some scholars to argue that he actually went to Tula to have his power recognized, and to receive a turquoise nose-plug as a symbol of his rank and standing. Eight-Deer's rule came to an end when he offered himself up for sacrifice. More recent studies in the 1980s re-examine these interpretations of the Mixtec codices, even questioning the assumption of their 'Mixtec-ness'.

The Mixtec 'empire' seems more accurately to have been a federation of equals, with the largest centres at Coixtlahuaca, Teozacoalco (identified in the Codex Nuttall with a genealogy of its rulers through to the third ruler and his children, of the third dynasty), Tilantongo, Tlaxiaco, Tututepec, and Yanhuitlán, each jealously guarding its position. Each consolidated its power by conquering and displacing Zapotec centres such as Monte Albán, Mitla, Yagul, and Zaachila. Their influence through trade spread N to Cholula and formed artistic alliance in the Mixteca–Puebla styles in ceramics and mural painting.

Little is known of the plans or architecture of these Mixtec centres, as all are covered by modern towns. Excavations have provided examples of later Zapotec mosaic-work, and at Nochixtlán, a Mixtec tributary village (probably to either Yanhuitlán or Tilantongo), there are some terraces on thg hillside. No ball courts have been found at these centres, but one was excavated at Cerro Yucuñudahui (near modern Chachoapan), from which the later site of Yanhuitlán was founded, proving that the Mixteca knew the game; and one portrayal of Eight-Deer in Codex Nuttall shows him standing in a ball court in Tututepec.

The Mixteca were variously allied with Huexotzingo and Tlaxcala, against the Aztecs, and were also almost constantly in conflict with their Zapotec neighbours to the S. In the 15C all their principal cities were captured by the Aztecs (under Moctezuma I Ilhuicamina, Axayácatl, or Ahuízotl), and occupied by garrisons; but not before inflicting some severe thrashings to Aztec armies, notably at Tilantongo and, in a temporary alliance with the Zapoteca, at Guiengola (see Rte 85).

The first major Spanish expeditions in the area were those of Francisco de Orozco and Pedro de Alvarado in 1521–22. Cortés, interested in possible gold finds, annexed the central Valle de Oaxaca, part of which, as the most significant element of the marquesado del Valle de Oaxaca, remained in possession of his heirs. (By the mid-19C its once vast territories had been whittled away almost to nothing.) By 1524 the pacification of the region was largely complete, and the Dominicans moved in to effect the religious conquest. Governmental complexity was introduced by subdivision into smaller political entities, dominated by alcaldes mayores (deputy governors) and Spanish peninsular merchants. The intendancy of Antequera came into being with the reforms of 1786, becoming one of the States of the republic in 1824. The years 1847–49, 1849–52, and 1856–57 saw the governorships of Benito Juárez, revered as the greatest of all Mexicans, who in 1856 applied the Ley Lerdo, which enabled the sale of church property in the State (814 urban properties and 36 haciendas), realizing 1.3 million pesos. The influence and fame of that other great oaxaqueño, Porfirio Díaz, were confirmed during the war of the Reform, the French intervention, and the struggle against the empire; in 1866 he achieved a series of military successes in the State, culminating in his seizure of Oaxaca in Oct. From his hacienda of La Noria in Nov. 1871 he launched his unsuccessful rebellion against Juárez, and the latter's death in 1872 assured Díaz's triumph, an interlude in which was his governorship in 1881–83. Improvements in the economic infrastructure during the porfiriato could not disguise the all too familiar misery of Indian labour, exemplified by terrible conditions in the Valle Nacional area. During the Revolution zapatista sympathizers fought it out with supporters of Carranza. Recovery, not helped by earthquakes, political repression, and post-second world war student unrest, has been only gradual.

The city centre is PL. DE LA CONSTITUCION, familiarly known as the ZOCALO, closely shaded by Indian laurels and other trees and flowers, a porfirian bandstand in its centre (concerts on Sat. and Sun. evenings), the cafés of its portales favourite places to sit and watch a slower, southern pace of life. On the S side is the **Pal. de Gobierno**, on the site of the old casas consistoriales (1570–), ruined in the earthquake of 1801 and demolished by 1832. The present building, by Francisco de Heredia, set up in 1834–37, was remodelled in the late 1930s and early 1940s. The huge interior staircase mural, detailing the history of Oaxaca, is by A. García Bustos.

On the N side, and facing the adjoining ALAMEDA DE LEON, is the cathedral of **Sta María de la Asunción**, built in broad oaxaqueño baroque and in that soft greenish-brown stone so favoured in the city.

The first cathedral, a primitive affair founded in 1535 and finished c 1544–55, was a likely victim of earthquake damage. The present was built in 1702–03, thanks mainly to Bp Angel Maldonado (1702–28) and to the advice of Pedro de Arrieta. It has since been repaired after further earthquakes. The interior was despoiled from the mid-19C and could not escape the attentions of Abp Gillow.

EXTERIOR. The façade resembles an altarpiece, its horizontality emphasized by the overhanging cornices dividing the three storeys and reaching into the bases of the towers. Five vertical sections, the three central projecting, contain elaborately framed bas-reliefs above the doors and skilfully carved statues of saints between fluted Corinthian columns. A lovely kind of filigree carving winds round doorways, and marks column bases, spaces beneath pedestals, and layered relief frames. The central relief of the Assumption is a profoundly moving work of art: Our Lady, her cloak, carefully arranged, held up by

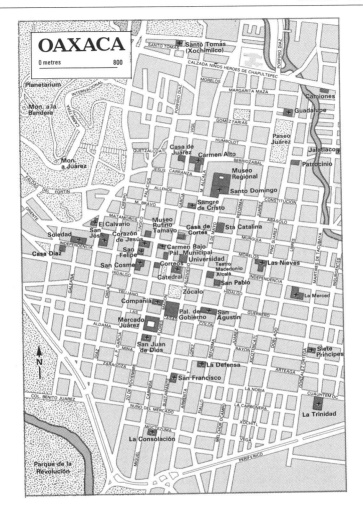

dramatically posed little angels, serenely ascends upon a cloud of cherubs; a solicitous Holy Trinity holds a crown above her head; below, the Apostles manifest surprise, joy, awe, and ecstasy. The relief above, sadly damaged, honours the Blessed Sacrament between parted curtains. The pediment, bearing a central relief of the Holy Ghost, is a modern replacement of the original, torn down in the mid-19C to make way for a clock-tower.

INTERIOR. The high altar, representing the Assumption, and ordered from an Italian sculptor, Tadolini, is typical of Abp Gillow's taste. Among the paintings are a St Christopher (1726) and Archangels in Glory by Marcial de Santaella (l. and r. of main door); among the paintings in the sacristy, a Martyrdom of St Bartholomew (1787) by José Palacios and Assumption and Triumph of the Church attr. Juan de Villalobos.

Facing the cathedral on the W side of the Alameda is the *Hotel Monte Albán*, an elegant 18C mansion.

Opposite the N side of the cathedral, in Av. Independencia between Cs García Vigil and Macedonio Alcalá, are the *Pal. Federal* (State treasury; 1895–1904), the former archiepiscopal palace, and, on the site of the old diocesan seminary, the former *Instituto de Ciencias y Artes* (1899), with a handsome portal, founded in 1827. It is now the headquarters of the *Universidad Benito Juárez*, established in 1955. Diagonally opposite, at the corner of Av. Independencia and C. Valdivieso, another 18C mansion.

Going W on Av. Independencia past the *Correos* (l.) we come to the Oratorian church of **San Felipe Neri**, its façade showing wayward, plateresque-inspired, vigour within the framework of oaxaqueño baroque.

The Oratory was founded here in 1733 and the church consecrated in 1773, although the towers were not finished until 1803. The interior decoration dates from various periods in the 19C. In 1860, during the upheavals of the Reform, the church suffered profanation, which caused Bp Gillow to reconsecrate the high altar in 1888. Benito Juárez and Margarita Maza were married in the church on 31 July 1843.

EXTERIOR. The three-storey façade, in typical greenish stone, is remarkable for its paired baluster supports, elaborately worked in contrasting sections, and diminishing in size with each storey. The great central relief shows St Philip Neri, beneath the top-storey octagonal opening which surrounds a multifoil window frame. The side door is equally interesting for its concentration of geometrical shapes within two storeys.

INTERIOR. The high altarpiece, beautiful, bold, wide, and curving with the apse, is divided into two storeys, the lower occupying two-thirds of the whole, which serves to emphasize its grandeur and allow the development of two pairs of ornamental niche pilasters spanning the height of the lower storey, their topmost parts incredibly sustaining the jagged cornice. In the wide spaces between them, saints in high relief, pushing out of their curving frames, are placed above full-length statues of saints standing beneath baldachins, with luxuriously carved drapery. Framing the central recesses are *estípites*, facing inwards in the middle and upper sections.

The two nave altarpieces are done with a spacious delicacy which enables the rococo ornament to set off the paintings, by Agustín de Santaella. The two in the transepts, oval and churrigueresque, are each flanked by paintings, by José de Páez, in elaborate frames which suggest the rococo.

Opposite, at the corner of Av. Independencia and C. J. P. García, is the church of *San Cosme* (1752), remodelled neo-gothically in the 19C. Further on, Av. Independencia runs alongside (r.) the broad PL. DE LA SOLEDAD, on two levels above it. On the r. is the church and former convent of **San José** (1728–44), built for Capuchinesses from Guatemala. The convent was restored in 1948–50 as the *Escuela Oaxaqueña de Bellas Artes*.

On the W side of the plaza, facing its own atrio, is the church of **La Soledad**, its façade, facing E, one of the abiding masterworks of Mexican baroque, quite distinct from any other work of its period.

Endowed by the archdeacon Pedro de Otálora y Carbajal, it was begun in 1682 and consecrated on 6 Sept. 1690 by Bp Isidro Sariñana. The interior redecoration ordered by Abp Gillow was finished in 1909. The adjoining convent (1690–97), at a higher level than the church, was assigned to Augustinian nuns from Sta Mónica in Puebla who occupied it from 1697 until 1867. The façade, which does not blend with the rest of the church, was built, buttress-like, to be earthquake-proof, and to reinforce the nave.

EXTERIOR. The façade is shaped like a languidly folding altarpiece. Of particular interest is the gradual enriching of the column supports. In the lowest storey the lowest thirds plain, the shafts fluted with Tuscan capitals; in the first, the lowest thirds encompassed by a relief pattern, the shafts fluted, the capitals ionic (emphatically so, resembling scrolls); in the second, the shafts solomonic, the spirals composed of vegetal relief, the capitals Corinthian. By contrast, the gable shows classicizing pilasters. Also of interest are the niche arches—polygonal, ogee, shell. In the niches are expressive statues of saints, among them St Rose of Lima (lowest storey; r.) holding the anchor, symbol of her city, and the infant Christ in a bunch of flowers. The extreme l. second-storey relief shows St Nicholas protecting a child. Across the choir window Our Lady and St Gabriel in high relief enact the Annunciation. The broad central relief, placed to attract all eyes, is of Our Lady of Solitude kneeling before the Cross and a skull representing death, with, behind her, the city of Jerusalem; its purity and stillness set off by the ornateness of its eared frame, made up of layer upon layer of moulding crammed with rich relief. By contrast, the Assumption in the gable is flowingly baroque. On its r., in high relief, is a portrait of Pedro de Otálora.

The S doorway is more Mannerist in style, with pilaster supports and broken pediment more pronounced than on the main façade. The INTERIOR bears all the signs of Abp Gillow's heavy taste. On the high altar is the statue of Our Lady of Solitude, of Guatemalan or Spanish origin, whose miraculous arrival in the city in the late 17C, it is said, spurred on the building of her church. Her crown of gold and precious stones was placed on her head by the abp on 18 Jan. 1909.

In part of the convent is a small museum (entered behind church on l.; Mon.–Sat., 10–2; Sun., 12–2) containing a collection of ex-votos. The handsome building (another part of the convent) on the r. of the church is now State government offices.

To the N of La Soledad in C. Unión is the chapel of *El Calvario* (1729). On the S, in Av. Independencia, between Cs Victoria and Galeana, is the house where Porfirio Díaz was born on 15 Sept. 1830, now functioning as a kindergarten. Opposite, C. División del Norte leads up round the W side of the Cerro del Fortín to *El Marquesado*, at the corner with C. F. Márquez, a charming little neoclassical church (c 1800).

Off the NW corner of the Zócalo is the church of **La Compañía**, its high façade an intriguing mixture of styles which reflects various 17–18C building campaigns after earthquakes.

The Society of Jesus arrived in Oaxaca in 1576 to found their college and church. Earthquakes in 1603–08 and 1727 all but destroyed their first two buildings. The present church, begun after 1727, was left unfinished at the expulsion in 1767. The earthquakes of 1787 and 1800 did further damage—in the latter year causing the cupola to crash. In 1790 church and college were assigned to Conceptionist nuns, who had to abandon the place after the earthquake of 1800; they returned, after its restoration, in 1829–30. With the Reform their convent was broken up; the church became a barracks, a Protestant chapel (which caused a riot), and a meeting-place for a masonic lodge. It was reopened for Catholic worship in 1879, and given new towers.

The church stands on a platform, which emphasizes the height of the façade, its lower storey, as its plateresque motifs indicate, probably salvaged from early 17C rebuilding. Here the canted side panels are marked off by slender baluster columns. Above them, the receding wings of the upper storey are finished off by stepped moulding. The triangular pediment is supported by estípites—the churrigueresque upholding the classical, an astonishing clash.

One block S of La Compañía is the renowned MERCADO BENITO JUAREZ, where local handicrafts and a variety of traditional local dishes are sold. Its annexe, MERCADO 20 DE NOVIEMBRE, is in the next block S on C. Aldama.

It occupies the site of the convent and hospital of the Brothers of St John of God, consecrated in 1702 and largely destroyed by fire in 1864.

The church of **San Juan de Dios** was first rebuilt (late 17C) by the juaninos. The primitive church of c 1532 on the site had served as the first cathedral of Antequera. It was completely restored in 1887–90, but the wooden ceiling kept. The interior murals (part of the restoration), by Urbano Olivera, show scenes from the religious history of Oaxaca, incl. the disturbances caused by the apostasy of the Indians of Cajonos (NE of Oaxaca) in 1700.

From the SE corner of the Zócalo, C. Guerrero leads to the well-buttressed church of **San Agustín** (1699–1722), once belonging to the Augustinian convent, founded in 1586.

EXTERIOR. The finely balanced façade in outline recalls rather Mannerism than baroque. At its centre is a magnificent relief, most beautifully framed, of St Augustine upholding the Church and protecting his friars under his cope, raised by fluttering angels. At his feet are the heads of heretics.

It closely resembles the façade relief of San Agustín in Mexico City (see Rte 7), but here the sculpting is more expressive and fresh.

The column bases, friezes, and other surfaces are covered by a combination of strapwork and floral relief. Of the excellently sculpted statues in the niches, that of St John the Evangelist (lowest storey; r.) carrying the chalice and host is especially good. Part of the convent, rebuilt in the early 18C but abandoned after 1860 and converted into a nursery in 1893, remains, hidden by the houses to the r. of the church.

INTERIOR. Three of the original baroque altarpieces remain. The high altarpiece is an ambitious work in five storeys.

C. Armenta y López runs S. At the crossing with C. Arteaga (l.) is the church of *La Defensa* (1792–95), with a churrigueresque altarpiece, and a little further down in C. Dr Pardo (r.) is the church of **San Francisco**.

It was the church of the convent of discalced Franciscans (dieguinos), founded in 1592, and called San Ildefonso. The present church was built in 1633–36, but badly damaged by earthquakes in 1660 and 1696. A rebuilding took place in the mid-18C; the towers fell down in the earthquake of 1787. The adjoining chapel of *La Tercera Orden*, on the W side, dates from 1733–35. The church was allowed to fall into ruin after the earthquake of 1931 and was stripped of its churrigueresque altarpieces, but has now been restored; the convent has been rebuilt as government offices. The patio has been transformed into a delightful garden.

The main portal, unique in Oaxaca, is churrigueresque, of a rare and elegant reticence, unusually framed in a giant niche. The lower-storey estípites, slender and finely carved, flank statues of SS Francis and Diego of Alcalá. Those of the upper storey end in elaborate finials on either side of a niche framed by miniature estípites, the merest echo of those below, upholding a sort of canopy of stepped moulding.

The church further S along C. Bustamante, at the corner with C. Moctezuma, is *La Consolación* (1706–95; its building thwarted by earthquakes), rebuilt in the early 19C. Its cupola replaces one which collapsed in 1872.

From the NE corner of the Zócalo we take C. Hidalgo E. Within No. 911, and elsewhere in the block (and in the next block to the E), are preserved parts of *San Pablo*, the first Dominican convent founded after the friars' arrival in the city in 1529, abandoned in 1604 because of earthquake destruction, rebuilt by 1728, and demolished after 1862 to open up C. Fiallo. Just to the N, at the corner of Av. Independencia, is the **Teatro Macedonio Alcalá**, in the afrancesado style so dear to the porfiriato.

It was built in 1903–09, as the Teatro-Casino Luis Mier y Terán, to the design of Rodolfo Franco and inaugurated in the latter year with a performance of 'Aida'. Restoration took place in 1936.

INTERIOR. From the lobby rises a small marble staircase; in the ceiling is a medallion fresco, allegories of Music, Poetry, and the Triumph of Art. The auditorium seats 1300. Its ceiling fresco depicts the Nine Muses. The nine medallions in the moulding encircling the ceiling show Shakespeare, Calderón, Ruiz de Alarcón, Molière, Racine, Victor Hugo, Verdi, and Wagner. Above the stage is a relief bust of Luis Mier y Terán (governor in the 1880s). The front curtain shows the Parthenon, Mount Parnassus, and the Chariot of Apollo surrounded by the Muses.

From the theatre we continue E on Av. Independencia. To the l., in C. Pino Suárez, is the church of **Nuestra Señora de las Nieves** (1579–81), once belonging to an early seminary, San Juan. It was rebuilt by order of Bp Miguel Anselmo Alvarez de Abreu in 1766, but preserves more than a trace of sober Renaissance style—and five 17–18C altarpieces.

Further E, at the corner of Av. Independencia and C. Libres, and facing an attractive, shaded plaza, is **La Merced**, the former church of the Mercedarians, dating from the late 17C, rebuilt in the early 18C after earthquake damage in 1696.

Its nave is notable for its four sections of octagonal domical vaulting. A cloister of the former convent, begun in 1646, remains on the N side of the church.

From behind the church C. González Ortega leads S to the church of **Los Siete Príncipes** (the seven archangels), attached to the former convent of *Sta María de los Angeles*.

The church was built in 1744–48, in one of the poorest barrios of the city, and intended for a convent of discalced Capuchinesses, descendants of Zapotec caciques. This was not finished until 1782 when the six founding sisters, from Corpus Christi in Mexico City, arrived, their expenses paid by Bp José Gregorio de Ortigosa.
   The unusual late baroque doorway juts out from the front of the church, upholding the choir with a barrel vault. The convent (N side of the church), a solid mass of a building, entered through a doorway whose jambs and lintel are studded with diamond patterns, houses the *Casa Cultural de Oaxaca* (craft workshops, periodicals library, art exhibitions) and the *Biblioteca Genaro Vázquez*, containing an invaluable collection of books and historical documents of the history of Oaxaca.

From the N side of the cathedral we may take C. García Vigil to its crossing with Av. Morelos. On the l. is the church of *Carmen Bajo*, begun in 1544, rebuilt in 1872 after a fire. Almost opposite, at 503 Av. Morelos, a vigorously characteristic one-storey house (1802), is the **Museo Arqueológico Rufino Tamayo** (Wed.–Mon., 10–2 and 4–6; fee).

The displays are not arranged in strict chronological sequences. Rather the pieces, all exquisite, are arranged to illustrate themes, and are beautifully displayed in lighted cases, clearly labelled, dated, and provenanced where known, with striking, coloured backdrops. The rooms have been numbered in the account below and named after their colour-codes, with directions for proceeding around each room. Two panels in Rooms 1 and 2, in Spanish, English, and French, explain the dedication of the museum to the people of Mexico, and the collection of the pieces in order to save them from the lamentable illicit trade in prehistoric artefacts.

ROOM 1 (pink backdrops). Middle Preclassic (artefacts). Proceed anticlockwise around the room. Olmec figurines from several regions, demonstrating the spread of Olmec trade. These can be compared to the contemporary figurines from early burials in the Huasteca region, to hollow and solid figurines, mostly of women and dogs from Western Mexico (Nayarit, Michoacán, Colima), and figurines from Oaxaca and Morelos. Other cases include anthropomorphic and zoomorphic vessels, tripod vessels, and polychrome pottery from Oaxaca, Morelos, Jalisco, Chupícuaro in Guanajuato, Nayarit, Michoacán, Colima, and Veracruz; and two ground and polished axe-heads of greenstone from S Veracruz. In the centre, stone jaguar head from Oaxaca (AD 200–750).
   R. 2 (blue backdrops; r. from R.1). Anticlockwise. Aztec period jaguar sculpture in volcanic stone, from Guerrero. The rest of the room has Late Preclassic and Late Classic Period materials. The first group (in cases following the Aztec jaguar) includes a carved stone human figure from Guerrero and several cases of red, glossy, hollow figurines from W Mexico, incl. humans engaged in daily activities, house models, a ball court model, and various anthropomorphic and zoomorphic vessels. Toltec figure in volcanic stone, depicting a human wearing a coyote mask. Late Classic pieces include stone figures, jewellery, and ground axe-heads from Guerrero.
   R. 3 (violet backdrops; r. from R. 2). On the r. are stone sculptures, incl.: Toltec figure of a seated man wearing a rabbit mask, standard-bearer (which would have stood in front of a temple doorway), Chicomecóatl (god of nourishment), and Maya stone plaque depicting a leader seated atop two captives. Anticlockwise around the room are cases, first concentrating on the Late Postclassic Period, then on the Classic. The former group includes more red, hollow figurines from W Mexico (dogs, snakes, ducks, and humans), and anthropo-

morphic and zoomorphic vessels, some painted. These continued the long tradition of hollow figurines in Western Mexican culture and can be compared to the earlier dated examples for subtle changes in style. Stone slab (7C AD), carved on one side in Teotihuacano style with a figure of Tláloc, god of rain, and on the reverse with Aztec figures in the 14–15C. For the Classic group, cases contain collections of materials illustrating artistic media, incl. specimens of painted wall plaster comparing styles from Teotihuacán, Oaxaca, and Puebla; clay figurines, and pottery styles from Veracruz and (on the other side of the room) the Huasteca region; and *Monte Albán I, II,* and *III* style green, clay funerary urns, jars, and boxes depicting various deities.

R. 4 (green backdrops) concentrates mostly on the Gulf Coast and on the Maya. Anticlockwise. Yugos, hachas (both associated with the ball game), and various other ground stone artefacts, plus clay figurines of dancing women, children, woman-and-child groups, 'smiling face' figures, and figurines illustrating cranial deformation, all mostly from the central Veracruz Totonac region, and of the Classic Period. Specimens of the Classic Maya Period, and pieces from the Early Postclassic Maya-Toltec phase. Carved stone plaques and stelae, many with hieroglyphic inscriptions; superb examples of Maya polychrome vessels depicting ritual scenes of priests (incl. some with elements inspired by Teotihuacano styles); sculptured stucco heads from architectural embellishments, and carved stone decorations; and a few Toltec stone sculptures (a snake and a head) from central Mexico, for comparison. In the central area, several large sculptures: large, Late Classic, almost naked male figure (with a wide belt and a knot on his chest) from Veracruz; Huastec figure, possibly the goddess of fertility; another Late Classic figure from Veracruz; and a Classic Maya stele depicting a priest in ceremonial regalia.

R. 5 (orange backdrops) concentrates on the Postclassic Period; but first there is a case of Late Teotihuacano funerary urns from Xico. Numerous cases containing Toltec, Aztec and other Postclassic artefacts from the Gulf region and S Mexico, for comparison. Three large painted clay figurines of Xipe Totec and stone sculpture of Xochiquetzal ('richly plumed flower', first wife of Tláloc), all from different regions. Painted jars from Puebla, illustrating the Mixteca–Puebla style, various tripod, polychrome vessels, and some jewellery; two Toltec figures, one of Tonantzin ('little mother'; Earth goddess) and one of Xipe Totec, and a carved stone architectural embellishment. More cases with pottery follow, incl. a late Teotihuacano urn from Xico depicting Tláloc, and polychrome vessels, pipes, and incense burners from Cholula and other sites in central Mexico, and some Maya–Toltec vessels for comparison. Case containing two carved statues of Ehecatl, two of Xochipilli ('flower prince'), a serpent, a grinding stone, and the Toltec Earth goddess. Case with Mixtec monkey-effigy vessel from Puebla, Maya–Toltec stone box in the shape of a jaguar, from Chiapas, Teotihuacano alabaster mask, and Toltec Plumbate Ware vessels.

The final cases contain a collection of incense burners for comparison—from Colima, the Basin of Mexico, and Yucatán; polychrome vessels from Cempoala and polychrome Xochipilli figures from Puebla; carved stone figures of various Toltec and Aztec gods; and miniature tripod vessels from Tzintzuntzan and a 16C bark plan.

In the centre, Aztec carved stone skulls as in a tzompantli (skull rack), Toltec incense burner depicting the god of death, and Aztec stone ritual vase carved with skulls and crossed bones on its exterior wall.

Going E along Av. Morelos we turn l. along C. Macedonio Alcalá, a pedestrian precinct from here northwards. On the opposite side is the so-called **Casa de Cortés**, in fact an early 18C house with a beautiful portal. The balcony window is framed by canopy-like moulding studded with relief and flanked by solomonic columns. Above the cornice, a statue of an angel in a niche and coats-of-arms on either side, marked off by more solomonic columns.

The house is now the **Museo de Oaxaca**, where photographs, models, etc., illustrate the history of the city.

The next turning l. on Av. Morelos, C. 5 de Mayo, passes (r.) the former convent of **Sta Catalina de Sena**, the earliest for nuns in the city.

It was founded in 1576–77, with the backing of the 2nd bp of Oaxaca, Bernardo de Alburquerque, for Dominican nuns. From it was founded the convent of Sta Catalina in Mexico City. The nuns were expelled in 1862 and the buildings later housed the ayuntamiento, a prison, and two schools. From the 1920s the nave of the church served as a cinema. From 1972 church and convent, now thoroughly secularized, were imaginatively restored as the **Hotel Presidente**.

The former nuns' cells have been reconditioned as rooms and the refectory is now the dining room, with jugs and bottles in which olives, olive oil, and wine were once sold. The church and altarpiece date from the early 18C.

Opposite, at the corner of C. 5 de Mayo and Av. Murguía, is the former *Colegio de Niñas*, founded in 1700 to give a basic education in domestic subjects to poor girls; closed in 1860.

Further up we may cross into C. Macedonio Alcalá (l.), through a small plaza. On the l. is the church of *Sangre de Cristo*, begun in 1791. Further, on the r., opens out the atrio of the former convent of **Sto Domingo**, most remarkable and, in its special way, magnificent of the monuments of Oaxaca.

The Dominicans founded their second convent (comp. above) in Oaxaca in 1570 and began building in 1575. Despite earthquake damage in 1603–04, consecration took place in 1608, while reconstruction was proceeding to the original plan.

The cloister, finished c 1619, was rebuilt in 1661 after another earthquake in 1660; the nave was completed in 1657 and the interior stucco work in 1662–65; the façade dates from c 1675; the towers, also badly damaged in 1660, were rebuilt in 1661. The Cap. del Rosario was built in 1724–31, paid for by the father provincial, Dionisio Levanto. The convent served as a strongpoint at various times in the 19C: in 1828, when occupied by Santa-Anna and his troops, in rebellion against the election of Gómez Pedraza to the presidency; in 1836 during the Mixtec rebellion; and in 1859 when conservative forces held it during the war of the Reform. In 1833 the remains of Vicente Guerrero were reburied here after being exhumed from Cuilapan (see below). In 1859 the convent was suppressed, the community having dwindled to three elderly friars, and in 1862 became a barracks, with the church turned into stables. In 1869 Governor Félix Díaz ordered the destruction of the altarpieces. The church was returned to the bishopric in 1898, when Abp Gillow began a judicious restoration programme. He reconsecrated it in Nov. 1902. The Dominicans took charge again in 1938. Further restoration took place in 1976.

EXTERIOR. The church façade is Mannerist, its narrowness and verticality emphasized by the double rows of niches in the two lower storeys, flanked by high fluted columns, and by the sturdiness and strength of the towers topped by lanterns and domes covered in glazed tile, and pierced by twin-arched windows lower down. Above the doorway, a relief of SS Hippolytus and Dominic holding a church, symbol of the Dominican province of Oaxaca. The top two storeys are a noble composition: the broken pediment encloses the shield of the Order. Above perch reliefs of Faith, Hope, and Charity.

Even after extensive restoration (which may have detracted from its pristine beauty) the effect of the gorgeously decorated INTERIOR is overwhelming. The low barrel vault of nave and transepts, the choir vault, the cupola, and the side walls above the side chapel arches are covered in gilded and polychrome stucco relief on a white background. The ceiling of the SOTOCORO, immediately beyond the entrance, is occupied by the family tree of St Dominic's earthly family, the Guzmanes, a wonderfully spontaneous work.

Described in the mid-17C by the provincial, Francisco de Burgoa, as 'a thing sufficiently entertaining', the tree consists of intricate branches from which spring dignified half-figures, interspersed with leaves and bunches of grapes. Empty spaces, intentionally left so by the 17C craftsmen, were filled in during Abp Gillow's restoration, and the pinnacle group of Our Lady, the infant Christ, and angels was added at the same time. At the springing of the two sotocoro vaults are statues of eight Dominican cardinals, surrounded by strapwork and spiral, flower, and pottery motifs.

The CHOIR dome divides into 16 segments along which lines of polychrome half-figures in medallions rise to the apex. The figures in the lower medallions are Dominican saints, those in the upper, angels: a representation of St Dominic's spiritual family on the way to heaven—the Holy Ghost at the summit. In the pendentives are four figures, Dominican martyrs, with their heads in their hands. On the l. (N) side, above the cornice, is a relief of Our Lady protecting members of the Dominican Order; above, a half-figure of St Catherine of Siena. Opposite on the r. (S) side, the corresponding relief shows Our Lady and angels comforting St Dominic after one of his severe penances. On either side stand SS Rose and Agnes of Montepulciano.

The side chapels on either side of the NAVE are separated by thick walls. The statues in the niches between the pilasters are modern replacements. On each side are eight New Testament scenes in high relief, framed in pairs. Above the cornice four frescoes on each side show Old Testament scenes. At the curve of the vault two sets of eight ovals (six canvases and two frescoes) show scenes from the lives of Our Lord and Our Lady. The centre of the vault is lined by paintings of the Immaculate Conception, the Annunciation, and the Assumption; prophets and evangelists; and three Dominican saints (brought to light in 1976).

The CUPOLA is magnificently adorned with strapwork and other geometric relief, and polychrome angel heads and saintly half-figures. In the pendentives, four Dominican popes: Innocent V, Benedict XI, Benedict XIII, Pius V. Above the transept arches, on either side of the windows are reliefs of SS Francis and Dominic (l.) and SS Thomas Aquinas and Raymond of Peñafort (r.). In the spandrels, SS Catherine of Siena and Catherine dei Ricci and Rose and Agnes.

The HIGH ALTARPIECE is a remaking, deserving nothing but praise, of the original of 1681. It is in full baroque style and was done in 1956–59 under the direction of Fr Esteban Arroyo. The statues (except two) and anon. paintings are of the 17C and 18C.

From the r. aisle we reach the **Cap. del Rosario**, another staggeringly colourful creation, containing much that is charming and sweet, more ingenuous than in the main church. The cupola rests on an octagonal drum. In its centre, a relief of Our Lady protecting the Dominican Order; in the lower part of the dome, figures of the apostles; in the pendentives, the four evangelists. In the nave vault is an image of Our Lady in the centre of an elaborate pattern of branches, fruit motifs, musical angels, and medallions containing the glorious mysteries of the rosary. On the side walls, the joyful and sorrowful mysteries around a Madonna and Child and a Pietà. On either side of the choir, SS Thomas Aquinas and Bonaventure, and, at the springing of the nave vault, four fathers of the Church—SS Ambrose, Gregory the Great, Jerome, and Augustine. Flanking the interior door, Judith and St Mary Magdalen. On the E wall beneath the arch, a relief of the Crucifixion against a golden background, with SS Francis and Antony of Padua on either side of the Cross.

The high altarpiece is a felicitous reconstruction, combining baroque and churrigueresque, inaugurated in 1964. The paintings—Our Lady giving the rosary to SS Dominic and Catherine, flanked by medallions of SS Anne and Joachim (above) and four archangels (below)—are original (anon. early 18C) works. In the centre, a venerated image of Our Lady of the Rosary, ordered from a Roman sculptor c 1725.

The former CONVENT is entered through the portería on the r. (N) of the church. The cloister makes a powerful impression; both sets of arcades are firmly buttressed, the arches and interior vaults resting on clustered piers. In the lower walk is preserved the original early 17C rib vaulting and remains of murals. The building now houses the **Museo Regional de Oaxaca** (Tues.–Fri., 10–6; Sat.–Sun., 10–5).

GROUND FLOOR. Proceed straight ahead from the entrance along the cloister, where there are several stone sculptures: a carved tomb slab, architectural decorations, and a stele depicting two opposing men. Next, l. along the cloister: a stele fragment depicting the head of a person speaking, a Maya jaguar sculpture, and a tomb wall- or cap-stone found near Macuixochitl with the glyphs 'eight turquoise' and *five ollin* ('movement').

ROOM A (r. at end of cloister). r., viceregal and 19C artefacts and documents; l., four cases with prehistoric flutes and ocarinas, many decorated with serpents or in the shape of a figurine, figurines of flute players, and various other musical instruments, incl. more flutes, ocarinas, silbatos, and conch-shell horns.

ROOM B has been set up as the 16–17C kitchen of the convent, with all the necessary implements, incl. huge frying pans. ROOM C holds exhibits illustrating the effects (especially on aspects of Indian life) of the Conquest on Oaxaca (incl. Late Postclassic ceramics at the time of the Conquest and Spanish ceramic introductions); the Dominican missions; and the encomienda system. The wars of Independence and the Reform and the effects of the Reform laws are also illustrated.

A small room at the foot of the stairs leading to the Upper Floor has seven stone sculptures: carved slab depicting human figures, tomb cap-stone with glyphs, stele depicting a youth and the glyph 'seven turquoise', stele depicting an old man and the glyph 'nine owl', cap-stone depicting an old man wearing the attributes of the Maize god, and two more slabs carved with a warrior and a human face.

We ascend to the Upper Floor by a magnificent stairway, its walls and vault retaining some of its original decoration and relief work. On the first landing there are several anthropomorphic stone sculptures, incl. a head, and large receptacle, and a glyph stone.

UPPER FLOOR, comprising six rooms: one of Ethnography (First Room), one on Tumba 7 at Monte Albán, four on Oaxaca archaeology (Second to Fifth Rooms).

The rooms are unnumbered, and are therefore referred to by name, as an ordinal, and/or by the different coloured backgrounds to the displays.

Top of stairs: floor plan (but ignore the numbers and follow the colour-coding used below); altar-stone with glyphs for 'five rabbit', 'eight flower', and 'seven turquoise'; and stele from Sta María Papalo. FIRST ROOM: Ethnographic gallery. Life-sized figures in traditional costumes, cases and displays of agricultural implements, fishing implements, textiles, basketry, food preparation, leather work, ceramics, Indian music and musical instruments, and traditional medicine and religious practices. Maps of population change and distribution in Oaxaca for each region (1—Mazatecos, Chinantecos, Cuicatecos, Ixcatecos, Nahuas. 2—Mixes. 3—Zapotecas, Chatinos, Chontales, Huaves, Zoques. 4—Mixtecas).

Begin the archaeological rooms by going back through the ethnographic displays, turning l. onto the balcony, and l. into the TUMBA 7—MONTE ALBAN ROOM. At the entrance, a curved panel with photographs of the excavation. Proceed, basically anticlockwise, to view cases containing the precious finds, perhaps the largest collection of precious objects from one tomb in Mesoamerica: turquoise, greenstone, bone, shell, and pearl jewellery; copper and gold metalwork; alabaster vases and other stone vessels; gold necklaces, pectorals, bracelets, beads; carved jaguar and eagle; skull decorated with turquoise; and three large ceramic burial urns depicting Cocijo (god of rain) and an old man. On the cloister balcony (l.) are several stone sculptures, incl.: serpent heads, stelae depicting warriors, and an altar stone with various glyphs.

SECOND ROOM (white backgrounds; numbers here and in the subsequent rooms refer to numbers on the floor plans). 1. Map of archaeological sites in Oaxaca. 2. Large, complex chart showing the regional and chronological subdivisions used in Oaxaca. 3. Four cases: a—early technology (stone, bone, and various fibres); b—early agriculture; c—ancient diet (grinding stones, cut bone); d—figurine types and chronology, with a colour code.

THIRD ROOM (yellow, then light blue and dark blue backgrounds). Cases 4–7 contain early stone tools from village farming sites, and illustrate the development of ceramic traditions in several chronological sub-phases

(1400–1150, 1150–900, 900–750, and 750–600 BC). 8. Large panel explaining the so-called Observatorio at Monte Albán (see Rte 76). 9. A large-scale model subdivides the room, showing the early civic and ceremonial centre at Monte Negro in the Mixteca Alta; and a case of painted pottery and tripod vessels from this and similar nascent urban centres of the central valleys (600–100 BC). 10. Wall panel showing artist's reconstruction of the plan of Monte Albán, *Phase IIIb*. 11. Two cases containing a variety of decorated vessels, jewellery, figurines, and a skull from early urban centres of the central valleys (100 BC–AD 250). 12. Wall-photograph showing aerial view of Monte Albán. 13. Classic Period pottery and figurines from Zapotec coastal, isthmus (Tehuantepec), and sierra sites (AD 250–750). 14. Pottery with painted, applied, and incised decoration, and stone projectile points from sites in the Mixteca Alta (AD 250–700).

FOURTH ROOM (dark and light blue backgrounds). 15. Ceramic, seated effigy figurine. 16–18. Incised and painted pottery, jewellery and other artefacts from urban sites, contrasting the various regions (coast, isthmus, sierra) as in the earlier displays (AD 250–700). 19. Ñuiñe pottery, and other artefacts from the Mixteca Alta. 20–21. Zoomorphic and anthropomorphic figurines and vessels from Classic Period urban sites. 22. Superb painted bowl with a pelican (or Zopilote bird), from the Saltillo (Juchitán) excavations of 1972. 23. Urn depicting the Zapotec Rain god, Cocijo. 24. Figurine of *Monte Albán IIIb–IV*, deity with bun or topknot headdressing. 25. Seated figurine of *Monte Albán II*, Cuilapan, with the glyphs 'thirteen water' on his headdress and 'thirteen flint' on his chest. 26. Various stone figurines and jewellery.

FIFTH ROOM (green backgrounds). 27. Panel and photographs explaining the architecture at Mitla. 28. Characteristic Late Classic greyware pottery and figurines from Tumba 6 at Lambityeco. 29. Tripod vessels and other pottery, and carved bone, from central valley sites, *Monte Albán IV* (c AD 700). 30. Carved stele depicting a religious ceremony in three panels. 31. Postclassic Period tripod vessels, painted pottery, figurines, and jewellery from central valley sites (AD 900–1521). 32. Polychrome vessels with 'eagle motifs' from a tomb excavated at Etla in 1967. 33. Polychrome jar from Tumba 3b at Coixtlahuaca. 34. Polychrome tripod vessels and other pottery, whitestone projectile point, and axe-head from the Mixteca Alta (AD 700–1521). 35. Polychrome ceramics and figurines from the Teotitlán region. 36. Three polychrome vessels depicting humans from an unknown tomb. 37. Greyware, polychrome vessels, tripod vessels, figurines and jewellery from La Cañada (AD 900–1521). 38. Double case, containing polychrome, handled jars, tripod vessels, greyware, moulded metal axe-heads, jewellery, and other artefacts from the Isthmus of Tehuantepec (AD 700–1521).

In some of the friars' cells may be seen sacred vessels and vestments used by them, and objects which throw light on the history of the convent and Dominican province.

Opposite the convent C. Jesús Carranza goes W across C. García Vigil. Here is **Carmen Alto**, former church of the Carmelites, begun in 1679 with money provided by Manuel Fernández Fiallo (d. 1708), benefactor of the city. The pleasing façade shows a relief of Our Lady of Mount Carmel.

With the expulsion of the friars during the Reform, church and convent served as prison and barracks. In 1871 a gunpowder store exploded and ruined the cupola, since restored. Opposite, at 609 C. García Vigil, is the **Casa de Juárez** (Tues.–Sun., 10–1, 4–7) where Benito Juárez lived in 1818–28.

It belonged to Antonio Salanueva (1770–1835), a member of the Third Order of St Francis, who adopted Juárez when the latter came to Oaxaca from San Pablo Guelatao and made himself responsible for the boy's education. Built around a cool little patio, the rooms contain a rocking chair and table used by Juárez when governor of Oaxaca, state documents, books, portraits, and other furniture. One room has been kitted up as a book bindery, a trade Salanueva taught his pupil. In C. Cosijopi, further up C. García Vigil on the l., is the house where Rufino Tamayo was born in 1899.

To the NE of Sto Domingo is the park called PASEO JUAREZ. At its SE corner is the disused church of *Patrocinio* (1755; rebuilt in the late 19C). On its N side is the church of *Guadalupe* (1686; rebuilt 1870–87). Joined to its E end and built at a right-angle to it (facing S) is the church of *Belén* (1807), former headquarters of the Bethlemite Order, who arrived in Oaxaca in 1685, taking over a house built at the expense of Bp Bartolomé de Benavente y Benavides (1639–52). Here they had their hospital (on the N side of Guadalupe), closed in 1821, converted first into the Hospital Civil in 1862–64, then into a leper hospital and asylum for the destitute in 1867; and bought by Bp Gillow for a seminary in 1888. It is now a school.

Along C. Quetzalcóatl (between Cs Jesús Carranza and Cosijopi) we may reach the CERRO DEL FORTIN, the hill on the NW side of the city. Here are an Observatory and Planetarium (evening visits at 6.30 and 8.30) and the open-air Auditorium where the festival known as Guelaguetza is celebrated on the third and final Mon. of July. Traditional pagan celebrations dating from prehispanic times were gradually infused after the Conquest with Catholic ceremonies. Today the festival offers the visitor an opportunity to see Mixtec, Zapotec, Mazatec, and Mixe Indians perform traditional dances and admire their elaborate and colourful costumes, especially of the women.

Cuilapan and Zaachila

We leave Oaxaca along Av. 20 de Noviembre, as for Monte Albán, and fork l. just after crossing the Río Atoyac. The road runs SW to (9km) **SANTIAGO CUILAPAN**, where, to the r., stands the most remarkable of the Dominican foundations in New Spain, the former convent of **Santiago Matamoros**.

Cuilapan, where the sculpture, *Scribe of Cuilapan*, was found (c 150–1 BC; now in Museo Regional, Oaxaca) was a Mixtec-Zapotec capital. It was also an important market for Aztec pochteca merchants from Tlatelolco in the 15–16C. It became part of the marquesado del Valle de Oaxaca and c 1550 the Dominicans moved the town half a league to its present site at the top of a hill, which was duly levelled. Profits from its silk, fruit, and cochineal wealth enabled the friars to start on an ambitiously planned convent, to minister to c 30,000 Indians. The open chapel, possibly planned by Fray Domingo de Aguiñaga (something of a polymath and friend of Ignatius Loyola), was probably finished by the Portuguese lay brother Antonio Barbosa in 1550–55; the lower floor was completed c 1550–60, the upper c 1560–70, with a S wing added c 1570–75, or perhaps after 1604. The friars' church dates from 1555–70, with the apse finished during 1570–78. The final stages may have been supervised by Fray Agustín de Salazar, who arrived c 1578 and made the Indian builders work 'like angels…as though of their own freewill'.

Since the early 19C the convent has served as school, barracks, and jail. The open chapel lost its roof during the Revolution, and further damage was done during the earthquake of 1931. Behind the convent is a memorial to Vicente Guerrero (2nd president: Apr.–Dec. 1829). Having been ejected from office and having raised rebellion in the south, he was captured with the connivance of the government of Pres. Bustamante, brought to Oaxaca, condemned to death, and shot here on 14 Feb. 1831.

By far the most interesting and important part of the complex is the three-aisled CHAPEL which projects at right-angles to the main church on its N side, but bears no stylistic resemblance to it. Its function may have changed during building. It may well have begun as an open chapel and was probably used as a second church after the abandonment of the other. A wooden-beam ceiling originally covered it and rain spouts may still be seen in the E wall.

Its N façade consists of a main doorway and two side openings surmounted by bull's-eye windows, flanked by round turrets. The detail combines classicism and plateresque, the centre showing engaged columns and a panel in the architrave containing a relief of the Dominican heraldic emblem supported by two dogs (another symbol used by the Order), between two reclining saints. The side doorways are not without a hint of Romanesque. The whole strongly resembles a design by the Italian architectural theorist Sebastiano Serlio (1475–1554). It is out of keeping with the basilica-like interior, where two heavy Romanesque-type arcades (that on the r.—W—now largely disappeared) dividing the nave and side aisles again offer a contrast to the slight outer walls, pierced by low arches and windows. The dark square chapel at the S end, with a rib vault, to the l. of, and in style similar to, the main church, was the sanctuary. The pulpit, with its scallop hood and steps cut into the wall, is strangely set halfway down the E aisle. Note the attractive pair of hooded holy-water stoups at either side of the entrance.

The remains of two more towers (companions of those flanking the N façade) may be seen near the junction of the W wall and the convent church, and in the stairwell to the upper part of the belfry. The nine arched openings in the W wall and eight in the E provided both easy access and ventilation, when the chapel was roofed, in a hot climate.

Both side aisles end in walls aligned with the chancel arch. In that ending the W aisle (c 2.5m from the ground) is set a stone plaque covered with prehispanic hieroglyphs and bearing the date 1555. Behind the walled-up arch, the sanctuary (now converted into a side chapel of the main church) preserves a low five-star vault. On its W side was probably the choir, on its E the sacristy, in which is a fresco of the two Marys and St James the Greater, sword in chest and axe-blade in head (symbols of his martyrdom), in a landscape showing the chapel.

The main convent CHURCH lies across the chapel at its S end. As a result of disputes between the Order and Cortés' heirs, work on it was stopped during the late 1570s, and it was left unroofed. The façade, facing W, is a provincial essay in classicism, satisfying with its clean-cut cantera verde and in the balance of the archivolt resting on jambs of oblique tableros, with a characteristic use of dentil motifs in the pediment. The N doorway shows a different kind of classicism, its inner frame of fluted pilasters and frieze repeating the outer, of fluted engaged columns and frieze.

Inside the W door remain the huge corbel supports for the vault under the choir: those of the upper storey, with elegant beginnings of ribs, more refined and later in construction (1560s). The apse has a coffered barrel-vault c 3m thick. The S nave wall, alongside the N wall of the convent, conceals two confessionals. Its thickness continues into the upper storey, where the sill of the choir doorway lies c 2.5m from the floor level of the adjoining room.

S of the façade, and at right-angles to it, is a nine-arched portería-open chapel. The largest arch gives access to the CONVENT (10–6; fee, except Sun.). Attached to smooth half-columns with Tuscan-like capitals, the prismatic lower-storey buttresses of the beautifully constructed cloister give way to semi-cylindrical ones in the upper, which has a lighter appearance, though its bays are squatter. The lower walk is covered by transverse and diagonal rib-vaulting, springing from corbels joined by an entablature marked by arch-like spaces between dentils; the upper is covered by a cross-beam ceiling. Off the latter are the friars' cells, containing attractive window seats. Murals survive here and on the stairway.

In 1569 the convent was large enough to accommodate novices from San Pablo in Oaxaca (see above), as attested by the number of cells, the eight latrines on the upper floor, and the large kitchen and pantry on the ground floor (W extension of S wing). The ample extension to the S was possibly used for a house of studies (for the Mixtec language) after the convent became a priory in 1604.

The road continues S to (14km) **ZAACHILA**, located in an important position at the head of the Valle de Zaachila (or Ocotlán). Zaachila became the Zapotec capital from c AD 1000, after the decline of Monte Albán.

To the Zapotecs it was known as *Tzapotecapan* ('seat of government'), and to the Aztecs as Teozapotlán. Its population also apparently included Mixtecs who moved there from Yanhuitlán.

According to the 16C manuscript 'Lienzo de Guevea' the Zapotec king married a Mixtec woman in 1280, perhaps bringing a measure of peace between the two peoples. Much later King Cocijoeza of Zaachila (1482–1529) married a daughter of the Aztec king, Ahuitzotl. Their son, Cocijopij, was the last Zapotec king, and died in 1563.

Although long known about, excavation has been hampered because the present-day town covers part of the site and because local belief greatly fears the rousing of the evil spirits of the dead. Roberto Gallegos conducted excavations in 1962 and 1965 under Mexican army guard. More excavations, with similar precautions, were done by Jorge Acosta in 1972.

The major part of Zaachila is on a partly natural, partly man-made hillside. It comprises mainly plaza groups with tombs, and one set of mounds may have been a *Juego de Pelota*.

Montículo B is the largest structure, and from it, on clear days, Monte Albán can be seen 15km to the NE. Montículo B comprises several terraces with at least four courtyards formed by structures. *Montículo A*, slightly lower than *B*, is c 10.5m high and has two tombs at the top: a sunken plaza is formed by stone and adobe rooms, with *Tumbas 1* and *2* beneath the floor of the N building.

Tumba 1 comprises an antechamber and a larger main chamber. In the antechamber the excavators found nine skeletons crumpled against the walls as if fallen where they were killed, presumably as sacrificial victims, and to serve the person of the main burial in his afterlife. Accompanying them were 80 pieces of brilliant polychrome Mixtec pottery, with a lacquer-like surface finish. (Several of the best of these pieces can be seen in the Museo Regional, Oaxaca, and in the Museo Nacional de Antropología.) Other offerings included turquoise mosaic discs and masks, and gold rings.

The walls of the tomb are decorated with modelled stucco figures: humans with calendrical signs identifying them (connected by lines as in a cartoon)—incl. 'five flower' and 'nine flower'; and with a figure of Mictlantecuhtli (god of the Underworld) in front of each.

Tumba 2 also contained a lavish burial, this time with 12 skeletons in the antechamber, interred nater than the principal burial, whose bones were carefully placed in niches. In this tomb only Mixtec greyware vessels were found, but there was also some goldwork and carved bones.

Two other, less sumptuous, tombs were excavated in a small mound beneath the ruins of the church. These were later in date (*Monte Albán Phase* V; c 12–13C), and also contained 124 pieces of fine pottery. Several other burials were also found, one with a beaten gold and turquoise disc, as thin as tissue paper and decorated with seated figures in the style of the Mixtec codices. Two Zapotec urns are embedded in the clock tower of the modern town and several carved monoliths are in the plaza.

Identifying the occupants of these burials has led to some intriguing arguments. The pottery and the Mixtec style of the figures on the walls and on the gold and turquoise disc indicate Mixtec royal or noble burials, perhaps from Yanhuitlán. On the other hand, the historical sources identify Zaachila as a Zapotec capital, although there is also the evidence of intermarriage between the two peoples. Alfonso Caso has used an elaborate genealogical argument to claim that the principal burial in Tumba 1 was Eight-Deer-Fire-Serpent, a ruler born c 1400. Unfortunately a mistake made in a date in one of the codices, used as an important point in his argument, has since weakened it.

Another site, known as *Los Cerritos*, of unrestored mounds, is c 1km S of the town.

Up a slope from the main plaza is the atrio of the former Dominican convent of *Sta María*, founded in 1572. The church, rebuilt in the 18C, preserves a sober Renaissance façade and S doorway; the single-storey convent building is partly ruined, partly in use as a priest's house.

FROM OAXACA TO PUERTO ANGEL. Méx. 175, 249km. The road runs S through the Valle de Oaxaca. 12km *Coyotepec*, known for its pottery (barro negro). At 14km Méx. 131 diverges r. to cross the Sierra de Miahuatlán to (263km) *Puerto Escondido*, see below.

The first 95 or so km are reasonably surfaced. Beyond Sola de Vega its quality deteriorates to gravel as it begins a tortuous climb and descent through the Sierra. It is best attempted in the dry winter months.

29km **Zimatlán** (P), where the parish church of *San Lorenzo*, a Dominican foundation of 1585, keeps a two-tier Renaissance façade; it was rebuilt in 1762 and after an earthquake in 1931. From (43km) *Valdeflores* a road leads r. to (2km) *Sta Cruz Mixtepec*, where the Dominican convent was founded in 1556. The church façade includes an arch decorated with medallion reliefs and set in an alfíz. The two-storey cloister is partly ruined. 53km *Sta María Ayoquezco*, near an archaeological site. 66km. At *San Sebastián de los Fustes* (11km NE), with a ruined 18C church, are subterranean caverns with calcareous formations of great beauty. 95km *San Miguel Sola de Vega*, centre of a mica-producing district. The road winds through the sierra, keeping to the l. just before (179km) *San Juan Lachao*. From (218km) *San Gabriel Mixtepec* a road runs W to (12km) *Santos Reyes Nopala*, a small Mixtec–Zapotec ceremonial centre. Only unrestored platform mounds remain at the site, but some of the finds and stelae are on display in the Pal. Municipal in Puerto Escondido. 263km **Puerto Escondido** (H,R,P), a rapidly growing, still delightful, resort, on a well-sheltered bay, with beaches of fine sand, the heat tempered by cool breezes. High rollers make it popular with surfers; swimmers should beware of strong currents.

32km **Ocotlán de Morelos** (10,000 inhab.; P), in the Valle de Ocotlán, the S part of the Valle de Oaxaca. The convent of *Sto Domingo* was set up in 1555, but later abandoned. The church was rebuilt and given its façade laden with vegetal relief in the 18C. Only four worn finials outside the W door remain from the old construction. The two-storey convent is now a jail. 60km *Ejutla*, known for its specially forged steel implements, made since the mid-18C by the Aragón family, who still jealously guard the tradition. The church of *La Natividad* is successor to a Dominican foundation of the 1560s. 95km **Miahuatlán** (c 16,000 inhab.; 1607m; H,P), an important commercial centre (coffee, castor oil, timber). On a raised platform the ruined church remains from the Dominican convent of *San Andrés* (1562–68). The present parish church combines a neoclassical façade with a churrigueresque high altar. The road crosses the Sierra de Miahuatlán, meeting (at 238km) the coast road (Méx. 200) to (71km W) *Puerto Escondido*, see above. 249km **Puerto Angel** (H,R), a still unspoiled resort, discreetly grown from a fishing village, within reach of Pacific beaches.

10km W the beach at *Cipolite* (simple facilities) is a stretch of fine sand several km long, but with rough seas.

From Puerto Angel Méx. 200 runs along the coast to *Salina Cruz* (175km E). *Sta Cruz Huatulco*, 35km along it, is a new resort being ambitiously developed and based on a series of bays (Bahías de Huatulco) and beaches of fine sand.

76 Monte Albán

Monte Albán ('Green Hill') is the largest, and for a long period the most important, site in the Valle de Oaxaca. It sits on a levelled hilltop, at c 2000m above sea level, 600m above the valley floor. The ancient city was vast, and reached its zenith in the second half of the Classic Period. However, the remains to be visited today represent, as at Teotihuacán, only the central ceremonial zone and a few of the best preserved tombs on adjacent hillocks.

The ancient city was primarily a Zapotec centre, and later both Zapotec and Mixtec. Its history comprises five major phases (the dates of each phase vary from one source to another; in this account, alternative dates are listed in parentheses):

Monte Albán I: c 700–350 BC (or 1000–300 BC; 400–200 BC; 500–200 BC). The Monte Albán phases are applied to the entire Oaxaca Valley system. Population growth in the valley, innovations in agricultural technology, and the resultant development of socio-economic divisions within society, led to the ability at several sites to support élite individuals with special duties and special residences: eg, San José Mogote (Rte 74), Dainzú (Rte 77), Monte Negro (Rte 74), and Mitla (Rte 77). One interpretation is that the increased rivalry between these centres, particularly in economic spheres, caused an 'agreement' to be struck for the establishment of a civic-religious 'capital' on the hilltop at the axial point of the three branch valleys of the Oaxaca system: Etla (N and W), Tlacolula (S and E), and Zaachila (S). Others argue that Monte Albán established its dominance more gradually, as the principal Zapotec foundation able to exert closer control over trade from its strategic ridge-top position.

By c 400 BC Monte Albán was the most powerful civic and religious centre in the valley. It had close contacts with the Olmec centres of the Gulf Coast, in particular with La Venta, and with the Basin of Mexico and Valle de Morelos, especially with Tlatilco. Very little remains of *Monte Albán I* structures, although many earlier foundations no doubt lie beneath the present buildings. The earliest monument known is thg Monumento de los Danzantes, on whose carved stone slabs are some of the earliest examples of writing in the region, and of the Mesoamerican Calendar Round (see Introduction: Mesoamerican Calendrics). (The earliest known Mesoamerican writing and calendrical reference, however, was excavated at San José Mogote in the Valle de Etla, see Rte 77.) At Monte Albán, using the dot and bar numerical system, found first at Tres Zapotes and Chiapa de Corzo, the 260-day and 365-day cycles are referred to, beginning the longest continuous and most complete history of writing in Mesoamerica, from c 600 BC. Two other *Monte Albán I* monuments are beneath the Plataforma Norte, and some stone 'box' tombs in the Pl. Central.

Monte Albán I ceramics include an abundance of yellow and brown wares in a wide variety of forms, and the grey wares that later became the hallmark of the Oaxaqueño potters throughout the Late Preclassic and Classic Periods.

Monte Albán II: c 350 BC–AD 100 (or 300–100 BC; 200 BC–AD 200; 200 BC–AD 100). In this phase Monte Albán was the political capital of the region. Its rulers were able to command greater manpower resources than any other city. They began many new building enterprises and presumably lived at the hilltop centre itself, although no palace-like structures are known to date this early. The population of the surrounding city has been estimated at 10–20,000. The Pl. Central was levelled to form the basis of an extensive ceremonial zone, filling in hollows and utilizing natural outcrops to form terraces. One outcrop, too difficult to remove, was used to form the core of the central group of monuments, which helps to explain its peculiar alignment. Constructions included ball courts, now buried beneath later terraces, Montículo J, and several subterranean tombs. These burials were more elaborate than in the earlier phase, and included steps into antechambers and wall frescoes. In some cases élite individuals were entombed, while in others, retainers, presumably sacrificed, accompanied them (eg, Tumbas 7 and 104). In some cases, stones from the Danzantes complex were re-used in the new buildings, and several dated stelae were erected.

Political and economic ties were developed with cities in Chiapas and Yucatán in addition to the earlier trade links with the Gulf Coast and the Basin of Mexico. *Monte Albán II* ceramics continued earlier tradition; tetrapod vessels anf a tradition of anthropomorphic and zoomorphic figurines and vessels were added.

Transitional Monte Albán II–IIIa: c AD 100–300 and *Monte Albán III:* c 300–900. In the *Transitional Phase* and *Phase III* proper, Monte Albán grew to its largest size and achieved its greatest power. Massive building operations were undertaken to make the Pl. Central symmetrical in general appearance: the E side was built up as a continuous terrace supporting small temples and courts; the N and S platforms were completed; Montículo M and Sistema IV, virtually identical, were built; and the central group comprising Edificios G, H, and I was joined to form a continuous symmetrical system. The present dullish ochre or buff colour of these monuments was originally plastered over and brightly painted. The suburbs reached their greatest extent, covering c 2000 terraces on the surrounding hills and ridges, and included numerous dams and irrigation systems. The population reached c 30–50,000, living in an area of c 6 sq km. There were at least three distinct residential groups around the plaza itself, presumably for the rulers and priests, and an enclosure wall of c 3km on the N and NW sides.

The expansion of Zapotec power was represented on covered stelae and facing stones on the new constructions, showing, in more than 300 sculptures, sacrificial scenes and scenes of captives standing on glyphs clearly representing conquered towns. There are 40 such carvings on the walls of Montículo J alone; and a carving on Plataforma Sur shows a warrior symbolically thrusting his lance through the name-glyph of one town.

Long-distance and closer political and economic relations were maintained with other powers, N and S. Teotihuacán, now the most powerful city in central Oexico, exerted its influence but did not threaten the power of Monte Albán in the Southern Highlands. Monte Albán remained politically and economically independent, but exchanged commercial delegations with Teotihuacán and perhaps with Xochicalco and other cities in central Mexico. (Although there is definite evidence of an Oaxaqueño quarter at Teotihuacán, no reciprocal evidence is known at Monte Albán; and no indisputable Teotihuacano imports have been found on the 2000 terraces surrounding the city.)

Craft specialization developed apace, and there was much experimentation. The medical profession was important and trepanation is known to have been performed on at least ten skulls, incl. some of the best-known examples in Mesoamerica. Death rituals were performed in the tombs, incl. the appearance, in the *Transitional Phase*, of greyware incensarios (urns), depicting in intricate hand-moulded detail a pantheon of 39 gods, incl. Cocijo (god of rain), Xipe Totec (god of springtime and planting), and many others.

Monte Albán IIIa: c AD 300–600 (or AD 200–700; 200–450; 350–600). Economic ties with Teotihuacán and with Classic Maya cities of the Petén reached their florescence. The 'scapulary' tablero, possibly inspired by and developed from the classic Teotihuacano style talud-tablero, became the distinctive architectural form, featuring the use of stone slabs, often carved, to revain terraces and platform walls, with a wide cornice at the top. The Ball Court on the E side of the Pl. Central was built, as were several smaller plazas and temples dedicated to Cocijo, and to a fire god and a bat god (in Edificios G, H, and I). Some 153 elaborately decorated tombs were built into the hillsides. Several new ceramic forms were developed: spouted jars, tripod vessels, polished greywares with engraved and incised decorations, and Thin Orange Ware.

Monte Albán IIIb: AD 600–900 (or AD 450–700; 700–1000). The major building activities reached culmination, incl. the continuous terrace of steps and courts along the E side of the precinct and El Palacio. The Pl. Central was finished and made to look as symmetrical as possible while retaining the earlier, no doubt highly venerated, buildings; and several monumental columns were erected. At the same time, Monte Albán becaoe semi-isolated as the power of Classic Maya cities and Teotihuacán began to wane. Towards the end of the phase Monte Albán's hold over the Oaxaca Valley system began to loosen.

Monte Albán IV: c AD 900–1150 (or *IV–V*: c AD 700–the Spanish Conquest). Political power shifted from Monte Albán to several contemporary cities in the valleys—eg, Mitla. Mixtec peoples began to intermingle on the site with Zapotec. Although not abandoned, the site was used principally as a necropolis, and probably reverted to a residential site mainly for priests keeping the temples and performing death rites. Some of the tombs of earlier phases were re-used (eg, Tumba 7). There was a certain amount of aesthetic and technological malaise, and some Toltec influences.

Monte Albán V: c AD 1150–the Spanish Conquest. Not recognized as a separate phase by all scholars. The Pl. Central was used increasingly as a special Mixtec ceremonial precinct, while valley sites such as Mitla and Yagul served as administrative and civic centres. Rivalry was rife between Zapotec and Mixtec factions, with a few, uneasy, truces, and in the 15C the cities fell one by one to Aztec conquerors.

As the principal builders of Monte Albán, and still the dominant ethnic group in Oaxaca today, the Zapoteca entered the valley sometime before AD 100. They maintained long-distance contacts for political and economic reasons, but remained fiercely independent. In common with the Mixteca they claimed the zapote tree (Náhuatl, *tzapoteca*) as their place of origin, but their own name for themselves was Ban-Zoa ('Cloud People'), also used by the Mixteca. They ruled the Valle de Oaxaca from Monte Albán for c 13–1400 years until *Phase IIIa*, when the ruling house of Zaachila abandoned the site for Teozapotlán. As a theocratic state, their priests exercised considerable power, and worshipped the supreme god Pitac (The Great One) alongside a host of lesser deities. Human sacrifice, although depicted in their sculptures, seems to have featured less prominently than in neighbouring cultures, although a special Zapotec contribution was thg ceremony of Xipe Totec, in which the sacrificial victim was flayed and his or her skin donned by a priest. Elaborate burial rituals were a special forte. They used the Calendar Round from an early date, incl. a special 260-day cycle of four 65-day divisions, each in turn subdivided into five groups of 13 days. 'Astronomer' priests from Monte Albán probably attended the gathering thought to have been held at Xochicalco in the mid-7C. In the Postclassic, Zapotec skill at painting picture chronicles on deerskins was developed into a fine art, justly admired by their neighbours and by the conquering Spaniards.

From c AD 1000 they were under increasing pressure from migrating Toltec-Chichimec groups moving into Oaxaca, causing them eventually to abandon Monte Albán in favour of Yagul, Lambityeco, and Teozapotlán. Throughout this period they intermingled with the Mixteca and, according to legend, their king married a Mixteca in c 1280. Despite this, there was continuous rivalry between the two groups, broken by an alliance of convenience when the Aztecs invaded under Axayácatl (1468–81), whom they defeated and drove back. When Ahuitzotl (1486–1502), attempting a second invasion, was defeated at Guiengola, he tried subterfuge, offering his daughter in marriage to Cocijoeza in the hope that she would act as a spy. The uneasy alliance against the Aztecs continued until the Spaniards arrived and overran the valley with Mixtec help. The last Zapotec king, Cocijopij, son of Cocijoeza and his Aztec wife, died in 1563.

The Archaeological Site

Daily 8–6; fee. City and tourist buses go up the 10km, paved but winding road to the site.

The present archaeological zone includes only the central ceremonial core but traces of the ancient terracing of the surrounding hillsides can be seen from the principal platform (c 200m x 300m).

The ruins of Monte Albán were known throughout the viceroyalty. The first major excavations were undertaken by Alfonso Caso in 1931–32, incl. the discovery of Tumba 7. With José Acosta he excavated more of the site in 1935. Others to excavate and study the site included Ignacio Bernal, Michael D. Coe, Kent Flannery, Marcus Winter, Richard Blanton, John Paddock, and Frank Aveni. The entire tri-valley system has been systematically surveyed by Richard Blanton, Steven Kowalewski, Gary Feinman, and Jill Appel. In addition to the birth and death of Monte Albán itself, their survey examined the settlement patterns in Oaxaca from its earliest villages through to the Spanish Conquest. Their analyses have contributed significantly to understanding the development of early agriculture, village life, urbanization, and empire-building in ancient Mesoamerica; and to reaching conclusions about the foundation of Monte Albán and its domination of the valley, and to estimating its ancient size, utilization of the surrounding hillsides, and population.

From the car-park, a footpath leads straight (c 75m) to the ticket kiosk at the NE corner of the Pl. Central. We proceed along the E, S, and W sides of the

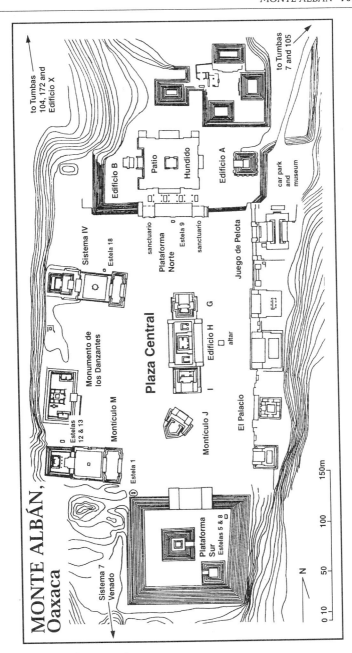

MONTE ALBÁN, Oaxaca

plaza, then explore the N platform and monuments farther N, and then the more outlying tombs.

The **Juego de Pelota** sits embedded in the N end of the continuous terracing along the E side of the plaza, and dates to *Phase IIIa*. It has the usual I-shaped playing field, in this case with vertical end-walls, sloping sides, and narrow, raised viewing platforms. Earlier ball courts have all been covered by later monuments. Three broad staircases lead from the plaza to the terrace block.

In the NE and SW corners of the walls of the playing field are niches, possibly for idols or goal markers. In the excavation of the court, a flat stone disc, possibly used to bounce the ball to start play, was found in the centre of the field, and there were four small shrines on the platform above. Only their fowndations remain, but they had been built and altered several times, incl. two carved monoliths, one with the date 'eight turquoise', in the last construction on the E side.

Aligned one after another S of the Juego de Pelota are seven staircases leading up to platforms and pyramids. Some were the residential compounds of priests, and the two central, higher pyramids supported *Phase IIIb* temples. The first (N) of these pyramids contains a unique interior stairway on its S side; adjoining it is a tunnel (not open to the public), only partly visible, which leads beneath the plaza to its W side.

El Palacio. The last platform on the E-side terrace, reached by the eighth staircase along the terrace, supports the only surviving remains of a palace complex. It comprised a series of rooms around a patio, beneath which was a cruciform tomb. The final pyramid along this terrace is unrestored.

Plataforma Sur. At the S end of the plaza is a vast pyramid-platform, with a wide central staircase (36.5m) flanked by ramps. It is square, c 136.5m each side at the base. At the top are two smaller mound ruins, one in the centre and one to the SE; *Estelas 5* and *8* are in the NE corner. S of this, c 550m away, is *Sistema 7 Venado*, a small rectangular plaza surrounded by mounds, where a stone lintel was found, carved with the date 'seven deer'. From the top of the pyramid can be seen one of the best views of the PL. CENTRAL and its layout. At the NW foot of the platform is *Estela 1*, in situ, carved with two columns of hieroglyphs: on the r.-hand is a figure and writing, incl. dot and bar numerals in the vigesimal system; on the l.-hand is a line of writing and above it symbolic representations of a mountain and a jaguar. (Near this stele, *Estelas, 2, 3,* and *4*, with similar carvings, were also excavated.)

Montículo J. Also known as *Observatorio*, this structure is directly in front (N) of Plataforma Sur, isolated, and unique in its orientation and shape. It comprises three recessed tiers with a staircase on the NE face. At the rear, against the cut-off faces of these tiers, is a low, pointed platform, supporting a similarly shaped structure. On the top tier of the platform is a single-chambered temple, traversed by a corridor oriented 17 deg. W of N.

Montículo J was constructed in *Phase II*, and its builders used over 40 slabs taken from the Monumento de los Danzantes (see below). These were carved with warriors and sacrificial victims, and, at the pointed SW side of the structure, a scene of leaders above glyphs, presumably naming towns that had been captured. These latter may not have been erected until *Phase III*. Montículo J resembles a similar building at the site of Caballito Blanco (see Rte 77), and because of its odd shape and orientation was early thought to have been used to observe heavenly progressions. This theory was tested in 1971 by Frank Aveni and R. M. Linsley, who discovered a 'possible zenith tube' that could have been used to observe the heliacal rising of the bright star, Capella, during the passage of the solar zenith, but no other solar or lunar coincidences, thus leaving the use of the building as inconclusive.

In the SW corner of the plaza sits **Montículo M**, a near twin to Sistema IV, in the NW corner. It comprises a rectangular platform with steps up its E face and down its W face, into a walled enclosure. The E face of the upper level is decorated with stone panels in moulded frames. In the centre of the enclosure there is a small, square oratorio, and on the W side are steps leading to a four-tiered pyramid supporting temple ruins. On the N side of Montículo M lie *Estelas 12* and *13*, both covered with hieroglyphs, and dating to *Phase I*.

The **Monumento de los Danzantes** is the only extant construction from *Phase I*. It comprises two tiers, with sloping walls, on a low platform c 28m x 55m, and 8.5m high. It supports two rectangular temples at the NE and SE corners, and a central W-side square building, around a small patio.

The present structure is in fact a *Phase IIIb* restoration of the original *Phase I* structure. In the original, the sloping face was decorated with flat slabs carved with human figures (now standing in front of the platform) in action attitudes—hence the misnomer 'dancers'. These are thought to be ball players by some, torture victims by others; their features resemble the Olmec art at La Venta. They are nude and many have been sexually mutilated. The date glyphs on them are thought to be 6C BC, and they therefore continued the tradition, begun at San José Mogote, of depicting captives with calendrical glyphs.

At the SE corner of the monument several of these slabs had been buried, and can be seen in situ at the entrance to the excavation tunnel.

Edificios G, H, and I. N of Los Danzantes is an unexcavated mound with traces of dwellings. In the centre of the plaza, facing it, is a tripartite central complex built in *Phase IIIa*. It comprises a symmetrical group of three structures c 90m N–S: Edificio H is a massive rectangular-planned block supporting a two-chambered temple, reached by broad staircases on its E and W sides, although the temple itself faces E. Two smaller, square structures stand to the N and S of the temple, at slightly lower levels.

Edificios G and I are to the N and S of H, respectively, and comprise lower, stepped platforms, each supporting a two-chambered temple. Each temple is reached by a massive staircase at the N and S ends of the complex.

E of Edificio H, between it and the S-side terrace, a small altar was found by the excavators, containing a jadeite bat-mask, now in the Museo Nacional de Antropología. The three vemples of this complex are thought to have been dedicated to the rain god, Cocijo, and to a fire god and a bat god.

N of the Monumento de los Danzantes, in the NW corner of the plaza, **Sistema IV** is a near twin to Montículo M, incl. an altar in the centre of its walled enclosure. Near its N side is *Estela 18*, with very worn hieroglyphs, possibly erected in *Phase II*. A little farther N is a low platform with traces of what were probably dwellings and several small tombs.

Plataforma Norte. The N end of the great plaza is formed by a massive terraced platform, c 7.5m high, with a 36.5m-wide central staircase flanked by two narrower flights of steps. Two small sanctuaries flank the central staircase: that on the E side has a foorjamb carved with a figure wearing a feathered head-dress and holding a staff, itself carved with a human head; facing it is *Estela 9*, carved on all four sides—the glyphs 'eight flower' on the S, two figures and glyphs for '9.K.I.J' and '3.E' on the E, a male figure and two columns of glyphs on the W, and two men and glyphs on the N.

The central staircase leads to the top of the platform where 12 column bases in two equal rows are anl that remain of the open portico. On the opposite side of the rows of columns another set of steps descends into the *Patio Hundido* (Hidden or Sunken Patio), with steps on its N, E, and W sides as well. It is c 45.5m sq. In the centre is a small square altar, which once supported *Estela 10* (now in the Museo Nacional de Antropología).

E and W of the Patio Hundido, at platform level, there are small staircases leading to *Edificios A* and *B*, respectively. These are only partially restored, but B has a small temple room which in its last building phase appears to have been Mixtec (ie, *Phase IV*).

On the SE corner of the platform is a jumble of excavated walls, incl. several phases of construction. One of these can be seen in a modern tunnel, showing a serpent modelled on a clay panel.

N and E of the Patio Hundido steps lead to another, less well preserved patio, formed by four mounds. Those which have been excavated proved to support small temples, interesting for the fact that they dated each from a different phase. They included columns, traces of murals and sculptures. *Estela 11* was also found here (now in the Museo Nacional de Antropología), the only columnar stele at Monte Albán.

Tumba 104 lies N of the Plataforma Norte complex, and is signposted from the plaza. On the way to it various unexcavated mounds are passed, incl. *Edificio X*, a *Phase II* structure with a staircase leading up to a chamber with adobe walls and remains of stone and adobe columns. Tumba 104 has a corniced lintel and a niche containing a clay urn representing Cocijo. The door is a large slab covered with glyphs, leading into the antechamber. The burial chamber is rectangular, flat-roofed, and covered with murals fepicting gods, animals, and numerous glyphs. On one wall, above the niche, is the head of a god in red, with a headdress and the glyph sign 'nine turquoise' next to him.

On the S wall is a figure with a necklace, earplugs, and a headdress, carrying a copal incense bag—possibly representing Xipe Totec. There is also a large yellow bird, standing on a box, with a (?)maize grain in its beak. Another group of figures shows a box, a serpent, and several glyphs with the number 'five'.

The N mural includes another figure in elaborate headgear of feathers and serpents, and carrying a bag—possibly representing Quetzalcóatl—and two glyphs (the number 'five' and an unidentified animal, and 'five bird'). Below Tumba 104, *Tumba 172* has been left in situ.

Tumba 7 is reached by returning to the car park, from which it is signposted. It was built in *Phase IIIb*, and lies beneath a patio, under a chamber with column roof-supports. The antechamber is reached by steps under a sloping roof, which contained *Phase IIIb* urns anf other vessels. Later, in *Phase V*, the tomb was reopened for a Mixtec burial of an élite individual and his nine companions, presumably sacrificed. The funerary offerings included more than 500 artefacts (now in the Museo Regional in Oaxaca) of gold, silver, jadeite, onyx, crystal, and bone.

Tumba 105 lies E of the road leading up to the site, on 'plumage hill'. On the way are the ruins of a second *Juego de Pelota*. Tumba 105 has a wide stone entrance similar to the jambs and lintels found in the Mitla tombs. Like Tumba 7, it is in a patio surrounded by rooms, and has steps leading down to the antechamber.

The burial chamber itself is covered with murals. On the N wall is the head of an old man wearing a 'turban', a jadeite mask around his neck, and a glyph for 'twelve tiger'; facing him is a woman (almost defaced) and the glyph 'one deer'; to either side are two scenes depicting priests or leaders appearing to walk in a procession out of the tomb. Other figures walk towards a central glyph, at the back of the tomb, flanked by god and goddess figures. Above the mural there is a band, symbolic of the 'jaws of heaven' and 'stellar eyes'. In total there are nine male and nine female figures, possibly representing the nine Zapotec gods of death and their wives.

On the S wall there is also painted an old god and the glyph 'one monkey', clasping a (?)copal incense bag and casting grains, and behind him his consort and the glyph 'four tiger', in female dress and a tiger-skin headdress. Behind her follow an old man and the glyph 'four serpent', a rain god, and a female and the glyph 'twelve monkey' (or snake). The W wall retains only faint traces of a oaize god.

On the E wall a figure is discernible, but its identity cannot be made out because of several overpaintings.

There is a small **Museum** with displays in the building at the car park. It contains a large chart showing the chronology of Monte Albán, photographs of the excavation of the site and the restoration work in progress, and three cases. *Case I* contains *Phase I* materials (c 600–150 BC in the case, or 700–350 BC in the chronology used here), incl. plain burnished vessels and two heads of figurines. *Case II* contains *Phase II* and *II/IIIa* materials (c 150 BC–AD 250, or 350 BC–AD 100), incl. plainware jars and bowls, a large tripod bowl, and one figurine head. *Case III* contains *Phase IIIa* and *b* materials (AD 250–700, or AD 300–900), incl. three figurines, a tall, claw-footed vase, some plainware jars, and a cylindrical bowl with lid and inscribed decoration.

77 Oaxaca to Tamazulapan Mixe via Dainzú, Lambityeco, Yagul, and Mitla

Méx. 190, 91km.—18km road S for (2km) Tlacochahuaya de Morelos.—20km turning r. for **Dainzú**.—27km **Lambityeco**.—35km turning for (2km N) **Yagul**.—46km **Mitla**.—91km Tamazulapan Mixe.

We leave Oaxaca to the E on Méx. 190. At 5km (l.) Méx. 175 runs NE to (57km) *Guelatao*, see Rte 84. 10km *Sta María del Tule*. In the atrio of the parish church is a time-honoured giant ahuehuete tree (a kind of cypress), c 2000 years old (40m high, 42m round its base, the greatest girth of any tree in the world). At 18km a minor road (r.) runs S to (2km) **Tlacochahuaya de Morelos**, a small Zapotec town. Here the former Dominican convent of *San Jerónimo* dates from the 1580s, its atrio wall, punctuated by widely spaced merlons, entered through a baroque gateway. Three posas (restored and whitewashed), still in use—especially on Good Friday, when barrio confraternities congregate outside each chapel before processing round the atrio singing hymns of consolation to Our Lady—are integrated into the wall. The CHURCH, rebuilt in the 17–18C, has a spare, four-tier late 17C façade; in the central niche, St Jerome listens to God's voice through an ear trumpet. Redecoration of the interior by local muralists continued until well into the 18C: walls, arches, vaults, and pendentives covered in vividly coloured suns, moons, stars, and Dominican rose motifs. Crowning the arch at the end of the nave is a Holy Trinity, with merry cherubs for company. In the choir is a delightfully painted organ, its decoration spanning baroque and rococo; in a side panel a medallion painting shows an angel playing a viol. The main altarpiece and the two attached to each side of the triumphal arch are of the late 17C. Despite appearances the slim carved pulpit dates from c 1750. In contrast, the small CONVENT (only 25m sq) keeps its 16C sobriety.

The town *picota* (pillory) has survived from the early 17C. It was once used to display the heads of executed criminals and to expose lesser offenders to public ignominy.

C 12km SW is **Teitipac**, where another, large, Dominican convent, *San Sebastián*, founded in the 1560s, was abandoned by the end of the 16C. The convent buildings are now partly ruined, but murals survive in the portería. The façade of the simple church has been covered with cement facing; the towers are new (N, 1950; S, 1956); and the posas, with brick domical vaults, have been restored.

20km turning r. for **DAINZU** (9–6; fee), in the Tlacolula branch of the Valle de Oaxaca, one of the many Preclassic sites later incorporated under Monte Albán (Phase III) rule. Its earlier phases correspond to *Monte Albán I–II* (c 600–100 BC).

Discovered and excavated by Ignacio Bernal in the late 1960s and 1970s, Dainzú was built against a bluff, presumably for defence, and the structures were built directly on bedrock. The site is sometimes referred to as *Macuilxóchitl* after the nearby village, although there is also a separate site of that name (see below).

Dainzú comprises a stepped pyramid-like structure (built against the side of the hill), ball court, and habitation ruins. The pyramid-platform (*Montículo A*) is three tiers with rounded corners and a central stairway, added after the initial construction. Set into the walls of the base tier and S stairway are rows of bas-relief sculptures; 50 have been found, 27 of them in situ. They show considerable Olmec influence: most represent ball players in active poses wearing wide pants, knee guards, visored helmets, gauntlets, and holding balls in their r. hands. Some also wear stone (or wood and leather?) yugos (yokes) around their waists; four figures appear to be priests, perhaps dressed as the gods of the ball game, two as humanized jaguars and two holding torches; four other slabs are carved with hieroglyphics in the same style as the occasional hieroglyph on the other slabs.

The significance of these ball player figures is threefold: both figures and hieroglyphics resemble the Danzantes and hieroglyphics at Monte Albán; they may represent the final Olmec or Olmec-derived influence in the Valle de Oaxaca; and they are some of the earliest representations of the ball game, especially as a ritual. If they depict the early rules of play, holding the balls in their hands, then they differ from the Classic and Postclassic Period games, where the use of hands was prohibited. (Other Preclassic ball players, as figurines, are known from Cuicuilco, San Lorenzo Tenochtitlán, Tlapacoya, Tlatilco, and Xochipak.)

W of the pyramid-platform is Grupo B: habitation buildings—dwellings and walls grouped around courtyards, with interconnecting stairways. There is also a tomb comprising three stone blocks with bas-relief carving representing a jaguar on the fronts (c 300 BC). Farther W and lower down is a *Juego de Pelota*, possibly contemporary with the pyramid-platform. At the top of the hill (access difficult) are several large petroglyphs, mostly of heads, perhaps also related to the city below, but of uncertain date.

21km turning l. for (5km NE) **Teotitlán del Valle**, a predominantly Zapotec town in the foothills of the Sierra de Juárez, famed for its sarapes, tablecloths, and rugs. Designs are inspired by present-day painters.

It was also a prehistoric Zapotec centre, called *Xaquija* (Zapotec: 'at the foot of the mountain'), or *Maquixóchitl*, after the nearby village.

27km (r.) **LAMBITYECO** ('numerous mounds'; 8–6; fee), a Zapotec site, active when Monte Albán was being abandoned by the Zapotecs—*Monte Albán IIIb–IV*, c AD 600–1000—who moved S into the Isthmus of Tehuantepec and to the Pacific Coast. There are over 200 large and small mounds, extending all the way to Tlacolula.

Excavations by John Paddock (1968) show that it was a small village when Monte Albán was founded, but was particularly prosperous between c AD 700 and 775, possibly from salt mining as this commodity became increasingly difficult to obtain from the Isthmus of Tehuantepec. In addition to Zapotec architecture, Maya influences included the use of spiked incense burners, Balancán Fine Orange and Plumbate wares, the use of stepped-fret motifs, and stucco decoration; innovations included paired male and female figurines in tombs, on platforms, and on façades. One spectacular find in one of the tombs was a group of 50 wheeled, animal figurines, the largest single find of such. Paddock concluded that the inhabitants may have moved to Yagul after abandoning Lambityeco, both of which were closely linked to Mitla.

The mounds at Lambityeco show typical Zapotec planning, with large buildings forming sunken plazas, often with a sub-plaza tomb. Restored structures at the site comprise a main *Pirámide*, beneath which was found a house and *Tumba 5*, on the N; and a second house and *Tumba 2*, on the S.

In Tumba 5 an antechamber has stucco heads of a man, with the calendrical glyph for 'one movement', and a woman, with 'ten reed' (l. and r., respectively). On a wall in the house, closing off the tomb, there were originally four painted friezes, two of which remain, depicting two couples, l. to r.: a man ('four face' or 'three movement'); a woman ('ten monkey'); a woman ('three turquoise'); and a man ('eight owl'). After the destruction of the house, the tomb and ruin were used as the base of a platform on which three chambers were built to form a small patio.

To the S, a similar house was built, which underwent five later alterations. It covered Tumba 2, before which stood sculptures of the Zapotec Rain god, Cocijo. These originally adorned the façade of a room on the W of a patio, and belong to the house structure preceding the addition of the tomb.

33km (r.) **Tlacolula** (c 20,000 inhab.; 1650m; P), in the Valle de Tlacolula, a principal Zapotec town, famous for its mezcal. The former Dominican convent of *La Asunción* dates from the 17C. In its atrio are four domed posas. Opening off the church (1647) is the chapel of Sto Cristo, a prototype of oaxaqueño baroque, the exuberant stucco ornament and reliefs of the Passion, martyrdoms, saints, and archangels vying with the doorway grille, choir screen, and pulpit, exquisite examples of wrought-iron work.

At 35km a turning l. leads to (2km N) **YAGUL** (8–6; fee).

The Valle de Tlacolula has yielded evidence of occupation from c 3000 BC, but the site itself was not occupied until c 400 BC, and continued to be occupied right up to the Spanish arrival. The Spanish administration moved the entire population to the town of Tlacolula in the late 16C.

In Zapotec, Yagul means simply 'old town', and the present structures, heavily restored, date mostly to the 7–9C AD. Although little is known of the site's history, excavations have revealed information concerning the everyday lives of the inhabitants. Unlike some of the other sites in the Valle de Tlacolula, Yagul appears to have been more a civic fortress town than a religious retreat (cf. *Mitla*).

Yagul is perched on terracing on the hillside and comprises several plazas, a 'palace' with patios, platforms, tombs (c 30 of them), a ball court, and a look-out fort high up on a promontory above and just N of the palace. This last was built late in the site's history, when Mixtec pressure on Mitla and other sites in the valley became particularly severe in the Postclassic. As a compact hilltop town, Yagul can be compared to Guiengola and Tepexi el Viejo (Rte 73) and contrasted with the huge sprawling site of Xochicalco (Rte 80).

From the car-park, the first group of structures forms PATIO 3, to the NW. Proceed between this and a pyramid mound, heading W, down the main street of the town. The **Juego de Pelota**, reconstructed in the pale green volcanic stone characteristic of the valley, is the first structure encountered. It is compact and completely enclosed, like the ball court at Monte Albán, but nonetheless larger than that court, and lacks niches and ring markers, as do the ball courts depicted in Mixtec codices. There are sets of steps at each corner against the high platforms forming the sides and ends of the I-plan playing field. A serpent head sculpture found at the top of the S wall can now be seen in the Museo Regional in Oaxaca.

SE of the Juego de Pelota the sunken PATIO DE LA RANA (Patio 4) is surrounded by four temple-pyramid mounds. Near the centre of the patio are the foundations of an *Oratorio*, with the entrance to a triple *Tumba* next to it. It is T-shaped and decorated with two human heads, thus relating it both to the tradition of patio-tombs at Mitla and to the duality theme of similar couples above tombs at Lambityeco. At the base of the E-side pyramid is a rounded boulder, carved with a smiling frog-like countenance, whence the name of the plaza. Other tombs were excavated at the base of the W-side pyramid.

NW along the ball court's N wall, the main street leads to another sunken patio (PATIO 1) at the SW corner of the site. This is the best preserved and measures c 35m by 30m, with buildings on the N, E, and W sides: the W building is a long narrow chamber with two pillars at the entrance, reached up a flight of steps; on the E side there are three large, walled divisions on a separate platform, which can be reached by steps from the patio or from the main street; *Tumbas 1* and 2 were excavated at the foot of the patio-side steps; the N side of the plaza is formed by a huge platform supporting a single large room, reached by a flight of steps up to a triple entryway divided by two large square pillars. Because of its size and apparent lack of internal divisions the excavators have dubbed this room *Sala del Consejo* (Council Chamber).

S of the patio, at a lower level, are the walls of another complex of rooms, where *Tumbas 11* and *12* were found.

Returning to the main street, note the remains of the stone slab mosaics along the walls of the smaller street or alley running E–W behind the Sala del Consejo (ie, between it and the next set of terraces). Along with the decorations on the tomb walls, these can be compared to the mosaics at Mitla.

The terraces up the hillside to the N of the main street support a **Palacio** of six complexes of rooms around patios. On the S side there is a wide, open platform with a shallow, rectangular, pillared room on its E end, facing the main street (S). The remainder of the maze of rooms all face into one of six small, sunken patios lettered *A–F* (from W–E, N–S). Most of the rooms are rectangular and shallow, with triple entryways between pillars. Between the sets of *Patios A–D* and *C–F* there are smaller rooms, let off one another and forming an intricate maze of inner chambers. Some rooms were deliberately sealed off during the different minor phases of occupation; and a 'throne' (or 'throne platform') was built in the E end of the S room of *Patio C*. Traces of the pinkish stucco

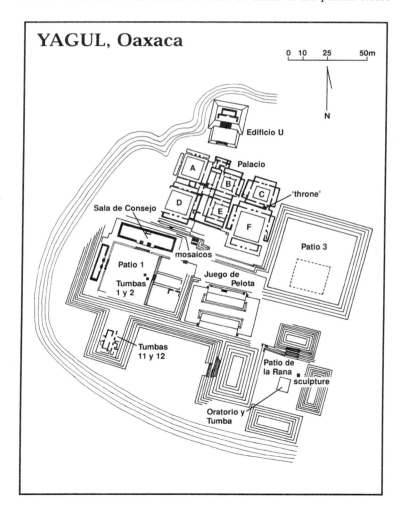

plastering can be seen on the walls and floors of most rooms, and a few still have volcanic-stone grinding tools in them. Tombs were found in Patios A and D, but not in any of the others.

N of the Palacio, on a high outcrop overlooking the site and the valley, are the foundation walls of a look-out fort (*Edificio U*). It is a steep climb, but worth it for the view, especially that obtained from the projecting point across a 'bridge' of stone.

N of the road, between Yagul and Mitla, *Caballito Blanco* was the site of another Mixtec ceremonial centre. It comprises a small group of unrestored ruins, incl. an odd-shaped structure, similar to, but smaller than, the Observatorio (Montículo J) at Monte Albán.

At 42km the road forks, Méx. 190 continuing S to (225km) *Salina Cruz*, see Rte 85. We continue l. to (46km) **MITLA**, distinct from the modern town. The archaeological remains (9–5; fee) comprise a Mixtec–Zapotec town with a blend of the two styles and an important Zapotec ceremonial centre and necropolis right up to the time of the Spanish arrival. There have also been finds of stone tools of much earlier date, showing occupation in the general region from c 5000 BC.

Mitla itself began as a village site c 1000 BC, long before the Zapoteca migrated into the area; and there are Late Preclassic (c 500 BC–AD 1) Mixtec foundations in the town contemporary with *Monte Albán I–II*. The Zapotec town was founded as Mixtec pressure forced them to withdraw from Monte Albán, and the site eventually became a centre for the worship of a 'Lord and Mistress of the Underworld'. The cult continued to operate into the 16C and involved a trained priesthood in ritual sacrifices of dogs, birds, and sometimes humans; ritual blood-letting, fasting, feasting, intoxication; and even cannibalism.

In 1679 Francisco de Burgoa recorded Mitla as a traditional necropolis for the burial of Zapotec priests; indeed the name Mitla is a corruption of Mictlán ('place of the dead'), and the city was apparently ruled as a theocracy. Although not a defensive site, such as partly contemporary Yagul, there are some incompletely explored mounds on *Cerro Guirui* W of the town, overlooking the river, which include walls, ditches, and a cruciform tomb.

Mitla covers c 1–2 sq km, with a hinterland of c 20 sq km, incl. dry terracing on the surrounding hills. It was destroyed by the Aztecs under Ahuitzotl in 1494, along with other towns in the Valle de Tlacolula, incl. Caballito Blanco, Cuilapan, Lambityeco, Loma Larga, Macuilxóchitl, Matatlán, and Yagul.

The site was first described by Fray Martín de Valencia in 1533, then by Diego García de Palacio in 1576, and by Francisco de Burgoa in 1679. Humboldt did not actually visit Mitla, but published (1810) a plan made in 1802 by Luís Martín and Pedro de Laguna. Later 19C visitors included Guillermo Dupaix, A.F. Bandelier, Désiré Charnay, Edouard Seler, William Holmes and Marshall Saville. The first excavations were done by Leopoldo Batres, then by Alfonso Caso and Daniel F. Rubín de la Borbolla in 1934–35, and by Ignacio Bernal and John Paddock in the 1960s. Polychrome tripod vessels, rock crystal and alabaster vessels, and jewellery from these excavations can be seen in the Museo Regional in Oaxaca.

There are five architectural groups, incl. 11 courts, dating to *Monte Albán III, IV*, and *V* (c AD 300–900). In general, two of the groups—Grupo del Sur and Grupo de Adobe—seem to be earlier by virtue of their simpler, more classic, single-plaza plans, surrounded by platforms. The other three—Grupo de Arroyo, Grupo de las Columnas, and Grupo de Curato—are later, palace groups, each comprising a more complex plan of two larger sunken courts, with the platform on the N sides of the N courts in each case leading on to smaller patios surrounded by chambers—altogether a more secretive, private plan. It is also notable that Grupo del Sur and Grupo de Adobe, with their largest platforms on the E sides, have E–W axes, while the other three groups have N–S axes. Minor chronological differences may also be implied by the single alignment of Grupo de Curato and the plans of Grupo de las Columnas and Grupo de Arroyo, each with one court adjoining the others at one corner (the NE) only. Similarly, Grupo de las Columnas is not enclosed, the platforms being unjoined at the corners, while the other two later groups have linked corners. Finally, Grupo de las Columnas also has the unique feature of vertical profiles, cut to lean outwards at the ends of the long horizontal blocks of its construction.

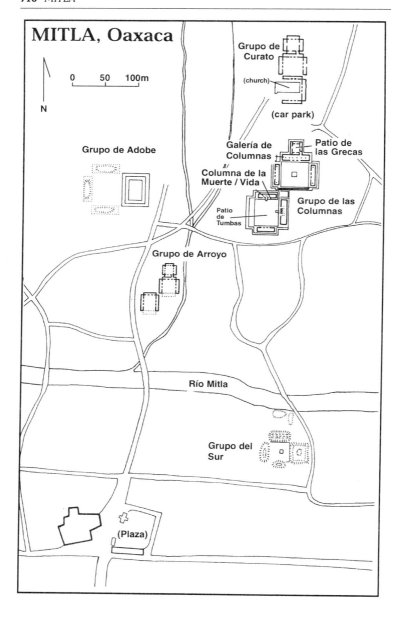

MITLA, Oaxaca

0   50   100m

N

Grupo de Curato

(church)

(car park)

Grupo de Adobe

Galería de Columnas

Patio de las Grecas

Columna de la Muerte / Vida

Grupo de las Columnas

Patio de Tumbas

Grupo de Arroyo

Río Mitla

Grupo del Sur

(Plaza)

The walls of these structures are of mud and loose stone, covered with stone slabs. They comprise a talud at the base, with three panels topped by a cornice, thus constituting a special adaptation of the basic talud-tablero pattern. The vertical panels are decorated in two ways: by mosaics of small stone slabs, or by large relief-carved slabs. Some 150 panels survive in the five groups, decorated with eight different basic patterns and many variations, involving running, interlacing, and stepped fretwork. Huge, poured-slab roofs slope gently to drain rainwater away from the courts.

There is a car park near the central Grupo de las Columnas, S of the church and of Grupo de Curato. These two are the best preserved of the groups.

Grupo de Curato, the most N group, comprises a single alignment (N–S) of two larger courts and a smaller N court, once surrounded by chambers.

Grupo de las Columnas comprises two large sunken courts, formed by platforms and walls unjoined at their corners. The NE court (36.5m x 45.5m) has chambers on the E and W sides; and, up a staircase and through one of three doorways, a large hall or gallery on the N side. This leads in turn, via a dark, narrow corridor, into a small patio (c 3m sq) surrounded by adjoining rooms—known as the *Patio de las Grecas* after the 'Greek key' fretwork on its interior walls.

The SW court, known as *Patio de Tumbas*, is c 35m x 40m. Beneath the N and E platforms, with access through doors in the courtyard, are two cruciform tombs. The tomb beneath the E platform is decorated inside with negative and positive cruciform mosaics. The roof of the N tomb has cracked and has had to be supported by a large central column, known as *Columna de la Muerte* or, more optimistically, *Columna de la Vida*.

Local legend holds that one's lifespan is indicated by one's armspan around the column, although a variety of methods are used to determine this; should one feel the column move, death is said to be imminent.

Grupo de Arroyo is to the SW of the above groups, and has the same, offset plan as Grupo de las Columnas. There are two large courts and a smaller patio to the N of the NE court. The whole is slightly smaller than Grupo de las Columnas and much less well-preserved.

Grupo del Sur and **Grupo de Adobe** are to the SE, across the river, and to the NW, respectively, of Grupo de Arroyo. Each is a single plaza formed by four mounds, the largest in each case being on the E side. Neither is well-preserved.

The church of *San Pablo*, founded in the 1550s as a secular parish church before being taken over by the Dominicans, is substantially of later date. It stands in an atrio with four posa chapels (one rebuilt in 1945, a rare loyalty to an old tradition). The apse rests on three doorways of the S quadrangle.

The **Museo de Mitla de Arte Zapoteca** (daily, 9–5; donation) is in the Posada la Sopresa in the town centre. It comprises four open-plan display rooms.

ROOM 1 (Sala de Urnas; l. of entrance) contains seven cases with Zapotec anthropomorphic and zoomorphic urns, vases, and other vessels of the *Monte Albán II, IIIA*, and *IIIB* periods. Several Zapotec gods figure prominently, eg Cocijo (god of rain), the Old Man god, the bat god, and the jaguar god.

R. 2 has displays of artefacts from *Monte Albán V*, incl. vessels and numerous small animal and bird figurines. One case contains moulds and archaeological fakes. In the courtyard there are several Zapotec anthropomorphic (some with genealogical records) and zoomorphic stone reliefs, and the façade of a temple.

R. 3 displays concentrate on the theme of the containment of creativity in *Monte Albán IV* and V through formalism in periods *II, IIIA*, and *IIIB*. Case 1 shows the evolution of Cocijo, god of rain and lightning, depicted on bottles and urns. A second case has pieces related by their symbolism. Case 3 contains pieces from *Monte Albán I*, from the founding of the ceremonial centre.

R. 4, a long room on one side of the courtyard, has six cases displaying artefacts from various aspects of daily life, from *pre-urban* Monte Albán and from *Monte Albán periods I–IV*: ceramics, stone knives, stone mirrors, jewellery, masks and headgear, and zoomorphic pieces.

At the Hacienda of *Xaaga*, c 3km SE of Mitla, a cruciform tomb, decorated with fretwork, was discovered beneath the floor of the house. On an adjacent hill, *Cerro Guirui*, another cruciform tomb, and traces of ditches and defensive walls, have been found. S of Mitla, in the mountains of the Mixteca Alta, the site of *Diquiyu* was one of several defensive outposts on the approaches to Miahuatlán.

From Mitla the mountain road climbs through the rugged area of the Sierra Madre del Sur inhabited by the Mixe Indians. Typical villages are *San Lorenzo Albarradas* (c 4km S at 58km); *San Juan del Río* (c 14km SW at 70km), both near as yet not fully explored archaeological sites; and (91km) *Tamazulapan Mixe*, with the baroque church of Espíritu Santo, which preserves its old wooden beam ceiling. At 113km the road forks. The l. branch winds N to (c 133km) *Sta María Totontepec* and (154km) *Santiago Choapan*, and then continues NE to join Méx. 147 (Tuxtepec to Palomares; see Rte 84) at 209km. The r. branch goes to (145km) *Zacatepec*, in the foothills of *Cempoaltépetl*, from where it is possible to reach the greater of its two peaks (3390m), the highest point in the State of Oaxaca.

78 Mexico City to Cuernavaca

Méx. 95, 76km.

Most conveniently by the toll road (Méx. 95D; 85km), reached along Av. Insurgentes Sur past the Ciudad Universitaria, across the Anillo Periférico, and beginning SW of Tlalpan. An alternative, and more leisurely, route is the old (free) road (Méx. 95), which runs alongside the toll road for much of the way, and is described below. (Maximilian used to make the journey in a specially built coach drawn by 12 white mules harnessed in turquoise leather.)

21km *San Andrés Totoltepec*. 24km turning r. for (6km W) *San Miguel Ajusco*, see Rte 15. At 28km a road (l.) goes S to (2km) *Topilejo*, see Rte 15. The road goes through the Sierra de Ajusco and crosses from the Federal District into the State of Morelos. 54km turning r. for (3km SW) *Huitzilac*, scene of the assassination in 1927 of Francisco Serrano, candidate for the presidency against the wishes of Calles and Obregón. Crosses along the road commemorate the event. At 60km the free road curves SW, away from the toll road. At 68km we turn l. to enter the N suburbs of Cuernavaca.

76km **CUERNAVACA** (c 300,000 inhab.; 1542m), capital of the State of Morelos, is a surprisingly large and spreading city, famous for its wonderful climate, which has long made it the favourite retreat from the rigours of Mexico City. It occupies the N part of the Valle de Cuernavaca, whose climate is affected by its altitude, ranging from 1800m in the N to 1300m in the S. Flowers bloom everywhere, the poinsettia having become a civic symbol, and the gardens of its suburban private houses, protected behind high walls, contain masses of bougainvillea, jacaranda, and other subtropical plants. A large expatriate community has always been attracted here and the demands of modern tourism have made their mark, not only in the many hotels and restaurants (some enjoying an exceptional reputation), but also in the traffic, crowds of day trippers, and souvenir sellers.

Bus stations. Corner of Cs Abasolo and Netzahualcóyotl. Frequent services to *Mexico City* (1½ hrs). 504 Av. Morelos, N of Jardín Borda. Services to *Mexico City*; to *Acapulco* (c 6 hrs); to *Tasco* (2 hrs); etc. C. Francisco Leyva (behind Pal. de Cortés) and 10 C. Galeana, similar destinations. Av. López Mateos, by the market. Services to *Tepoztlán* (1 hr) and to *Cuautla* (1 hr).

Hotels throughout the town.

Post Office. Pl. de la Constitución.

Tourist Office. 802 Av. Morelos Sur.

Fiestas. Carnival (week before Lent). 2 Feb.: Candlemas. 2 May: Flower festival. 15 May (at Acapantzingo): St Isidore. 8 Sept. (at Tlaltenango): Birth of Our Lady.

The Valle de Morelos was peopled by the Tlahuica, one of the legendary 12C Aztec tribes of the seven caves of Chicomoztoc. However, in N Cuernavaca (and now destroyed beneath it) the site of *Gualupita* yielded evidence of much earlier and continuous occupation, incl. a long ceramic sequence from the mid-Preclassic through to the Postclassic. The earliest levels were contemporary with Tlatilco in the Basin of Mexico and the pottery showed Olmec influence.

Tlahuica is also applied to Morelos pottery, contemporary with Aztec III and Tenayuca Black-on-Orange Ware. The most typical decoration is a lacquer finish.

The principal Tlahuica palace and ceremonial precinct, *Cuauhnáhuac* ('on the edge of the forest'), stood beneath the present Pal. de Cortés, and a second ceremonial precinct stood at *Teopanzolco* (see below) on the outskirts of the present city. At one time, the Tlahuica were forced to provide a tribute of sacrificial victims to Xochicalco (see *Tepozteco*), then were subjugated by the Mexica Aztecs under Itzcóatl (1426–40) and made tributary to Tenochtitlán. His son, Moctezuma I Ilhuicamina (1440–68), was the issue of marriage to the Tlahuica princess of Cuauhnáhuac. The valley was a favourite leisure spot of the Aztec kings and Moctezuma I built a new pyramid over the earlier one at Teopanzolco, and several botanical gardens, in particular at Oaxtepec (Huastepec), SE of Cuernavaca. During the siege of Tenochtitlán, Cortés forced an entry into Cuernavaca and burned Cuauhnáhuac, later razing it for his own palace.

In 1521 Cortés decided to include the region in his marquesado del Valle. Cuernavaca was in viceregal times a stopping point for travellers, and waggons bearing goods from the Orient, from Acapulco to Mexico City and Veracruz. In Feb. 1812 the taking of Cuernavaca was one of Morelos's triumphs; three years later he was brought back as prisoner. In Oct. 1855, after the Plan of Ayutla, Gen. Juan Alvarez was proclaimed interim president here. 'A broad valley blessed by Heaven', it became a much-loved residence of Maximilian and Carlota. In June 1911 the future Pres. Madero met Zapata here, but was unable finally to win him over. The latter's inveterate opposition to him was to be a tragic feature of the Revolution. Since the 1950s the zone has seen industrial development (Ciudad Industrial del Valle de Cuernavaca—CIVAC—E of the city).

The State of **Morelos** (c 1.2 million inhab.; 4941 sq km) lies on the S slopes of the Mexican high plateau, its surface roughly broken by mountain ranges forming many valleys, landscapes of singular beauty, and is drained by the Río Amacuzac, a N tributary of the Balsas. There is wide climatic variation, from the cold and humid higher elevations of the Sierra de Ajusco in the N; the mild and temperate lower spurs; and the subtropical lower valleys. Agriculture flourishes, especially sugar-cane cultivation—it has been termed 'Mexico's sugar bowl'; light and heavy industry has lately made its mark in the Valle de Cuernavaca and at Cuautla; mining has possibilities, but is as yet underdeveloped.

The present State territory formed part of Cortés's marquesado del Valle. Certain rights survived to his heirs after Independence. During the war of Independence, José María Morelos achieved success here, and even greater fame in final defeat at Cuautla. The State of Morelos was created in 1869. Under the porfiriato it is estimated that State lands had fallen to 32 owners, many of them absentees. Harsh conditions on the sugar plantations provoked the uprising of Emiliano Zapata and the zapatistas dominated Morelos. In his campaign of 1916 to exterminate Zapata, Gen. Pablo González laid waste the countryside, looting haciendas and wrecking the sugar industry. Zapata struck back with even worse savagery. The aftermath was predictable desolation. Under Pres. Cárdenas hacienda lands were broken up and redistributed. Present-day economic and social pressures have underlined the need for further reform.

We enter the city from the N along Blvd Emiliano Zapata, passing, on a roundabout at the junction with Av. de los Fundadores del Estado (W from Méx. 97D), a monument to Zapata. Further S on the l. is the chapel of *San José Tlaltenango*, on the site of what was reputed the earliest chapel on the American mainland. Its neighbour is the sanctuary of *La Virgen de los Milagros* (1738).

Opposite, C. San Jerónimo leads to the chapel of *San Jerónimo*, a 16C Franciscan foundation.

Blvd Emiliano Zapata is continued S by Av. José María Morelos, the main N–S artery of the centre, crowded on to a narrow plateau, with ravines falling away on either side. On the l., near the corner with C. Linares, stands **El Calvario**, a square oratory (c 1538–40; restored 1948), resembling a posa chapel, once housing a crucifix before which travellers might pray before leaving the city.

The cross has long been replaced by a statue of Our Lady of Guadalupe. The late Gothic detail is finely worked, especially the capitals and arch mouldings. Cartouche, corner firepots, and central crowning feature are all later than 16C.

Further down Av. Morelos on the r. is the church of *Nuestra Señora de Guadalupe* (1784). Next door is the entrance to the JARDINES BORDA (daily, 9–6; fee).

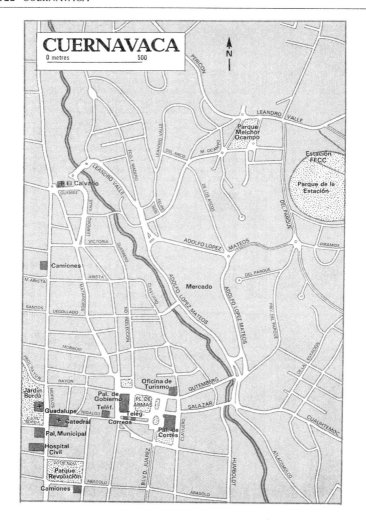

They were laid out and inaugurated in 1783 by Manuel de la Borda, and designed by José Manuel Arrieta, as botanical gardens. The Borda family mansion later became a residence of Maximilian and Carlota.

On the S side of the gardens the *Pal. Municipal* (late 19C) contains murals by Salvador Tarazona and Roberto Cueva del Río, commissioned in the 1930s, some illustrating the imperial pair's life in Cuernavaca.

Opposite, at the corner of Av. Morelos and C. Hidalgo, is the former convent of **La Anunciación de Nuestra Señora**, its atrio wall, topped by merlons, pierced by gateways on its W and N sides.

The fifth Franciscan foundation in New Spain was begun probably in 1525 and completed by the 1550s, although the convent block was remodelled c 1560. It served as retirement home for aged and infirm friars and also housed missionaries before they left for the Philippines. In the 1920s it was a refuge for seminarians during the Calles persecution. The church, since 1891 cathedral of the Cuernavaca diocese, was altered during the 17–19C, and its interior was transformed in 1957 by Matías Goeritz and Gabriel Chávez. The sites of 16C posas are occupied by chapels of later periods.

The longer arm of the L-shaped atrio runs along the church's N side. Its plain stone cross rests on a pre-Conquest base (with a merlon at each corner), showing a skull and crossbones—a hollow square block used by the Aztecs as a container for sacrificial blood and hearts.

In the SW corner of the atrio is the 17C *Cap. de Dolores*; opposite, the *Cap. del Carmen* (late 19C). On the NE side stands the **Cap. de la Tercera Orden** (mainly 18C), its S doorway a puerta abocinada; that on the E more profusely ornamented, the central relief showing St Francis receiving the stigmata. It contains a delightful main altarpiece (1735), by a local craftsman, with unusual estípites alternating with columns and laden with sweetly expressive imagery.

EXTERIOR. The massive walls of the main church, reinforced by flying buttresses on the N, end in lance-like merlons lining the parapet, along which runs a chemin-de-ronde. Remarkable for its diverse elements, an indigenous interpretation of the Renaissance, is the slender N doorway (dated 1552), with its combination of alfíz, outlined by evanescent colonnettes, and steep pediment enclosing a little shrine, containing a mound of bones, guarded by angels and Our Lady's monogram. Resting on its point is a relief of Calvary complete with skull and crossbones.

The second storey of the tower dates from 1713, as does the cupola (finial rebuilt 1882). Modernization of the INTERIOR rediscovered early 17C murals which line the walls and illustrate the martyrdom of St Philip of Jesus and his companions (see Rte 7). On the l., the mass crucifixion preceded by the martyrs being conducted in boats by their Japanese guards to execution.

Remaining from the 16C are the rib vaulting of the sotocoro, under the ample choir balcony; the sunken baptismal font, shaped as a shell and bordered by the Franciscan cord; the confessionals embedded in the wall; and the holy-water stoup.

At a right-angle with the church's W doorway and facing N is the OPEN CHAPEL/PORTERIA (c 1535–40), of outstanding interest.

Its tall façade consists of three generous arches, with excellent moulding, resting on discreetly decorated imposts. Through them is seen another, similar, triple arcade (again, note the pearls of Castile dotted round the imposts): in the centre, the raised chancel, with a rib vault; at either side, two smaller compartments entered through arched doorways, possibly for a choir and musicians. The imposing nave between the two arcades is spanned by a lofty barrel vault, shored up without by two diagonal flying buttresses. Diagonal pier buttresses at the corners of the building provide further support. The façade is topped by a crenellated parapet, beneath which is a band of stuccoed masonry. Above the central arch, dramatically placed, a small pulpit.

On the l. (E) side is the handsome, square entrance to the cloister, the slanting voussoirs of its lintel clearly seen; above, classically framed, a black and white fresco of St Francis and companions presenting their Rule for approval to Pope

Innocent III. The CLOISTER is exceptionally impressive, the arches of the lower storey resting on Tuscan columns, and their archivolts displaying the same fine moulding as those of the open chapel—in contrast to the confining basket arches of the upper storey. Bands of grey and white decorative painting run along the walls of both storeys. On the wall of the lower-storey E walk a fresco in black, white, and ochre shows the spiritual lineage of St Francis. Above the lintel of the doorway giving access to the church, another fresco shows St Francis receiving the stigmata; going through the door, we may find, on the r. of the chancel, a Crucifixion done in grisaille.

A walk E along C. Hidalgo ends in PL. DE ARMAS. On its E side is the **Pal. de Cortés**, oldest extant non-religious building in New Spain.

After his return in 1530, Cortés settled on his encomienda lands around Cuernavaca. He brought with him a vast retinue. His palace was begun in 1533 and here he kept great state, until 1540 when he returned to Spain for good. His widow (Juana Ramírez de Arellano y Zúñiga) continued to live here, most of the time in bed. Their son Martín added to the palace in the later 16C. In 1747 it was repaired by Ildefonso de Iniesta Bejarano y Durán. Repairs since the 1940s have restored much former grandeur. The structure shows innovative characteristics, for Cortés, ruler of vast territories, had to have a palace different from the rest. He had also probably been influenced by that built for Diego Colón (son of Columbus) in Sto Domingo.

It resembles a medieval fortress, the parapet lined with merlons. The NW corner tower is a 19C addition. At the front is a loggia (rare even in contemporary domestic European architecture), two storeys of four round arches each, two extra arches above and below having been covered by later building. There is no central courtyard. At the back is a grander loggia, two storeys of eight arches each. Gothic capitals and the continuous alfíz covering the lower arcade underline the remarkable character of the whole, as do the decorative motifs (based on Castilian pearls) which stud the upper-storey archivolts at both front and rear. (There was also a triple-arched loggia on the S side.)

From the rear upper arcade there is a view across the Valle de Morelos to Popocatépetl—another unusual feature, for scenery was not an early 16C Spanish interest.

In the forecourt are exposed ruins of the former Tlahuica palace, incl. wall foundations and drains. At the entrance to the museum, on the r., is an in situ Tlahuica III adult burial beneath glass casing.

Since 1974 the palace has housed the **Museo Regional de Cuauhnáhuac** (Tues.–Sun., 9.30–7; fee).

The museum comprises two floors with 25 rooms. Each has a theme name related to the objects displayed. Some displays are actually small exhibits on landings, corridors, or balconies rather than in rooms.

GROUND FLOOR. ROOM 1 *Poblamiento de América* (Peopling of the Americas). Maps and charts illustrate the Late Pleistocene Period migrations into the New World from Siberia and the earliest Archaic sites in N and S America. *Mesoamerica* (R.2). In the centre is a huge map of the cultural areas of Mesoamerica; on the walls accompanying charts show the comparative chronologies and cultural divisions of Mexico. Further charts and illustrations show the vegetation of Morelos. A special panel discusses Early Man in the New World, accompanied by two cases with obsidian projectile points, grinding stones for gathered plant foods, and other artefacts, and some mammoth bones. *Preclásico* (R.3; r.). Map of site in the Valle de Morelos. Displays along the walls are reproductions of stone carvings, cases with Preclassic Period ceramics and figurines (especially from sites such as Nexpa, Chalcatzingo, and Cacahua-milpa), and a reconstruction of the Preclassic burial at Tamoanchan.

Clásico (R.4; l.). Concentrates on the Classic Period. Site map of Morelos and photographs of excavations. Panels and illustrations discuss the influence of Teotihuacán in the valley. Cases and freestanding displays include Teotihua-cano pottery, carved stone sculptures, incl. circular ball court marker and stone statue of Tlahuizcalpantecuhtli, god of Venus as both evening and morning star, and of Tláloc, central Mexican god of rain.

Xochicalco (R.5; l.). Devoted to the Classic and Early Postclassic fortress site of Xochicalco. An explanation panel discusses the site and its growth in power and size, especially after the economic and (?)political dominance of Teotihuacán began to decline in the Late Classic. Photographs show the principal structures of the site, incl.: the hall or court, the Pirámide de las Serpientes Emplumadas, and a general aerial view. One case contains stone sculptures from the site, and there are also freestanding sculptures from the altar of Xochiquetzal (goddess of the 'richly-plumed flower'), according to legend the first wife of Tláloc until she was abducted by Tezcatlipoca.

Escritura Pictográfica (R.6; l.). Concentrates on the Postclassic Period, in particular through native chronicles. It begins with a site map for the period. Photographs show various painted, pictographic chronicles, a rich source of myth and legend and of ethnography. Cases contain Postclassic pottery and figurines from the Tetecala excavations and stone slabs with glyphs. Freestanding sculptures include a chacmool (although the head and lower body are missing) and a statue of Tláloc. *El Fuego Nuevo* (passage between sixth and seventh rooms). The New Fire ceremony commemorated the end of a 52-year Mesoamerican calendrical cycle; here a stone sculpture depicts the theme of the ceremony. To the l., in the central courtyard of the capilla there are some exposed remains of *Tlahuica II* and *III* phase structures, corresponding to those at the entrance to the museum.

Las Migraciones (R.7). An explanation panel discusses the 'Tira de la Peregrinación', a post-Conquest codex describing the wanderings of the Aztec tribes. A large photomural shows the Aztec temple at Tepozteco, and there are more Tlahuica remains exposed and a stone sculpture. *The Tlahuica* (R.8; l.). The Tlahuica Aztecs were one of the seven Aztec tribes, in legend migrating S from the land of Aztlán and the seven caves of Chicomoztoc, traditionally somewhere in NW Mexico. A wall map shows the locations of Tlahuica sites, and there are two cases with Tlahuica painted pottery, tripod vessels, figurines, jewellery, and metalwork, and some freestanding stone sculptures.

Influencia Mexica (R.9; straight ahead). The Mexica, more generally referred to as the Aztecs, were the tribe who dominated the Basin of Mexico and then invaded the surrounding valleys. A wall display explains the Aztec tribute system and two cases contain highly decorated pottery, tripod vessels, and a stone head representing influences from the Basin Aztecs, plus Aztec stone sculptures at either end of the room.

Along the colonnaded patio there are several stone sculptures, modern, but in imitation of prehispanic styles; and implements for maize processing. *Los Textiles*. A room at the far end of the colonnaded walk contains examples of prehispanic and post-Conquest textiles, a loom and spinning wheel, and other paraphernalia for textile production. In one corner, some of the earlier foundations of the Palacio have been exposed. *Pal. de Cortés* (l.). This room contains displays illustrating the architectural history of the Pal. de Cortés. At the foot of the staircase there are some more exposed *Tlahuica III* foundations.

The UPPER FLOOR rooms illustrate the history of Morelos since the Conquest. In RR. 1–2 (16C) are wall panels of animals and plants introduced from Europe; glass and metal artefacts; armour; clock machinery; gold objects; wooden ploughs; etc. R.3 (Cortés as Marqués del Valle de Oaxaca) contains wooden and metal chests (one ivory inlaid); documentation and artefacts relating to Cortés. R.4 (16–17C) contains majolica, pottery, tools, etc. R.5 concentrates on imports from the East and the Manila galleon trade. R.6 illustrates the conversion of the Indians to Christianity and Indian influences in religious art. In R.7 a wall map pinpoints the site of the Franciscan, Augustinian, and Dominican convents in Morelos. Works of art from them are also shown, incl. a carved stone font and gold chalices and thuribles. R.8 commemorates José María Morelos and includes his death mask. R.9 (Morelos in the 18–19C) illustrates the importance of the sugar haciendas, the war of Independence, and daily life. R.10 shows later 19C developments and includes portraits of late 19C governors (Carlos Pacheco, Jesús H. Preciado, Manuel Alarcón). In a small side room a photographic display shows Cuernavaca street scenes in the late 19C and early 20C. R.11 includes exhibits on the Revolution, the parts played by Madero and Zapata, and changes in the State's cultural, economic, and social life.

The walls of the upper rear loggia are painted with a series of murals (1930–31) by Diego Rivera, commissioned by US ambassador Dwight W. Morrow as a gift to Cuernavaca and the State of Morelos. Their theme is the conquest and history of Mexico and Morelos. The opulence and colour of the landscape through the arcade are reflected in that which forms the background to the paintings, notable also for the colour and drama of the figures who take part in the scenes—even though time and exposure to the elements have bleached some of the details.

The main themes begin on the N wall. *N Wall and N part of W Wall.* Clash of Aztec and Spanish troops, incl. eagle and tiger knights. *W Wall.* Scene of betrayal, where an Indian guide in a wolfskin directs the Spanish troops, using a massive bent bough as a bridge, over the secret crossing of an otherwise impassable ravine, dense with jungle foliage. Taking of Cuernavaca. Possessing the lands of Cuernavaca by Cortés and the conquistadores—in the background, they and the Tlaxcaltecans loot, kill, and shackle. Building of the Palace of Cortés. Indians toiling on the sugar plantations. *S part of W Wall and S Wall.* The New Religion (Motolinía teaching on r.). Inquisition scene. *S Wall.* Condition of the Indians—Zapata symbolizes revolt.

The grisaille panels (from N wall) show Arrival of Cortés in Mexico; Cortés receiving the emissaries of Moctezuma II Xocoyotzin (1502–20); Cortés winning the support of the Tlaxcaltecans; Siege of Tenochtitlán; Torture of Cuauhtémoc (1520–25); Death of Cuauhtémoc; Destruction of Indian Culture; Indians slaving in the silver mines; Bartolomé de las Casas protecting the Indians; Vasco de Quiroga teaching the Indians new crafts; Assassination of Roquetilla, an Indian leader. On the central piers appear Morelos (with Rivera's features) and Zapata with his white stallion, an enemy cut down by his machete at his feet.

In Jardín Juárez, on the S side of the palace, the bandstand was designed by Alexandre-Gustave Eiffel at the behest of late 19C Austrian residents. From the NW corner of Pl. de Armas we gain the ALAMEDA, with the *Pal. de Gobierno* (finished in 1967) on its W side.

Other points of interest include the small estate (finca) called *El Olvido* (daily, 9–5; fee), with the chalet built by Maximilian for Carlota in 1865–66. It now houses a *Museo de Medicina Tradicional*, illustrating folk medicine. The grounds include a herbarium of tropical plants. It is at 200 C. Matamoros in the district of *Acapacingo* (then a separate village), c 2km SE of the centre, reached from Jardín Juárez along C. Francisco Leyva running S; l. along C. Cuauhtemotzin; r. along Av. Humboldt; and l. again along C. Abasolo until C. Matamoros is reached on the r.

N of the centre, at 1001 Av. Leandro Valle, is the *Casino de la Selva*. The dining room murals were done in the late 1960s by David Alfaro Siqueiros and younger artists.

Siqueiros's studio (*Talleres Siqueiros*; Tues.–Sun., 10–2; 4–6) is at 7 C. Venus (corner with C. Luna) in Colonia Jardines de Cuernavaca. It contains a fascinating photographic collection illustrating his life and work, and the murals of steel geometric forms he was experimenting with before his death in 1974. The adjoining Pl. Siqueiros, dedicated to his memory, was inaugurated in 1977.

C 2.5km NE from the Pal. de Cortés at the end of C. Río Balsas is the ceremonial centre at **Teopanzolco** ('abandoned temple'; Tues.–Sun., 9–6; fee) built on the ancient lava flow of *El Texcal.*

The pyramid ruins were discovered during the Revolution when the main pyramid mound was used as a cannon emplacement. It was excavated in 1921 by Manuel Gamio and José Reygadas Vértiz, in 1922 by Eduardo Noguera, and in 1957, incl. reconstruction work, by Román Piña Chan.

The principal feature is the central pyramid (15C) with its double staircase, mounting the W side, covering an earlier (13–14C) Tlahuica pyramid, also with a double staircase. The Aztec staircase is c 30m wide and the base of the pyramid is c 32m x 50m. Around the base are traces of subsidiary ruins in the SW corner, a small rectangular catchment and adjacent wall at the SE corner, and the first low step of the pyramid retaining wall at the NW corner.

At the top of the staircase, a trench, built in the reconstruction work, has left the earlier staircase exposed; it was in fact better preserved than the Aztec staircase, and the ramps on each side and down the centre end in vertical faces as do those at the contemporary pyramid at Tenayuca. A few traces of painted plaster also remain.

Walls of the double temple on top remain up to c 3m high. The N temple is a single rectangular chamber, with a stone bench along the rear wall, and the stumps of four rectangular roof columns in the corners. The S temple is semi-divided into front and rear chambers, with a stone bench in the latter. On the SW corner of the S temple is the best-preserved example (others are broken off) of a small protruding animal snout in volcanic stone.

From the top of the pyramid the remaining parts of the ceremonial precinct can be viewed before visiting them individually: N are ruins of a small platform with three sets of steps up the W side; NW is a large circular platform, slightly instepped around its rim, with steps up its E side. This is a 16C Aztec construction. Along the W side of the precinct are five low rectangular platforms (the S one has a hollow centre), and a smaller circular platform, all with steps on their E sides. Behind these is a low, rectangular platform with two sets of steps up the E side. Immediately in front of the double staircase of the pyramid is a small rectangular ruin, probably an altar.

Just off the SW corner is a long, low rectangular platform with steps up the N side, and with small wings at the N side corners, plus a rectangular extension off the S side. There are traces of walls on top and a covered drain on the S side. Farther SW are more traces of low, unexcavated mounds. To the S and SE are traces of more unexcavated mounds, probably single platforms or a long, low one.

E of the pyramid is a rather more substantial, but not well preserved, ruin, the *Templo de Tezcatlipoca* (an Aztec creator god), built by the Mexica Aztecs. It has a double staircase (mostly ruined) up the S side, and comprises three tiers with projecting wings on the N and S sides of the front.

S of the main pyramid and E of the long, low platform, is an unidentified circular structure and the ruins of a modern (probably 19C) building with an arched doorway and traces of brick room divisions.

C 7km NW of the centre, at *Sta María Ahuacatitlán*, is the former Benedictine monastery of Sta María de la Resurrección, founded in the 1950s, closed by order of Pope Paul VI in 1967 after a dispute with the Belgian prior, Dom Grégoire Lemercier, over the use of psychoanalysis. The deconsecrated monastery, now known as the Emaus community, was re-established as a centre for psychoanalysis. It is also known for its crafts and chocolate.

79 Cuernavaca to Chalma and Malinalco

85km.—75km Chalma.—85km **Malinalco**.

We leave Cuernavaca to the N. At (22km) *Tres Marías* we turn l. for (25km) *Huitzilac*, see Rte 78. The road runs tortuously along the SW slopes of the Sierra de Ajusco. From 35km we see on the l. the **Lagunas de Zempoala** (2900m), seven lakes formed in volcanic craters. They and their surrounding alpine landscape are now part of a national park. At (50km) *Sta Marta* we meet the road from Chalma to (48km NW) *Toluca*. We turn l. and continue S, gradually descending to (75km) **Chalma** (H,R,P), a shabby town, not recommended despite, or because of, the fact that it is among the most famous pilgrimage centres in Mexico.

Every Sun. pilgrims (sometimes in their thousands) descend on the sanctuary of the *Señor de Chalma*, the church built in 1683, but much altered (and not for the best) since, to house a miraculous statue of Christ. The adjoining convent, recently rebuilt, was for the Augustinian friars who had charge of the sanctuary. Spectacular rituals take place, especially on the first Fri. in Lent and on the feast of the Ascension.

85km **MALINALCO** (c 6000 inhab.; 1500m; P), most beautifully set in a remote and fertile valley. On Pl. Principal is the former Augustinian convent of **El**

Divino Salvador, founded in 1543; by 1571 the church had been built, and the convent was under construction.

The charming atrio, its wall typically lined with thick merlons, is evocatively tree-planted. The church façade (c 1565), doorway and choir window integrated in one design, shows Mannerist influence. Chief feature of the interior is the barrel vault and apse, painted to resemble coffering. Entrance to the cloister is through a five-arched portería-open chapel. The walls of the well-preserved cloister, with its high lower-storey arcade, are covered in frescoes showing floral and vegetal motifs, and Augustinian emblems.

On the cliffs of the Cerro de los Idolos, NW of the town, and 225m above the valley, sits the Aztec sanctuary of **Malinalco** (10–6; fee).

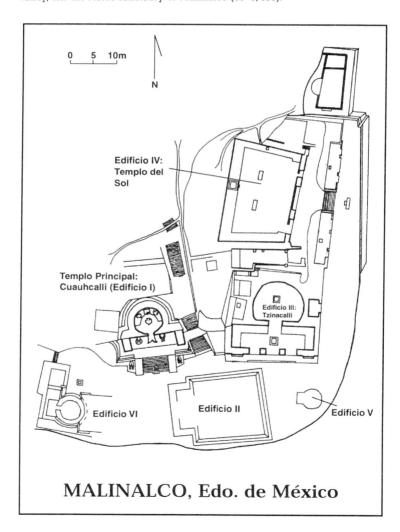

0   5   10m

N

Edificio IV:
Templo del
Sol

Templo Principal:
Cuauhcalli (Edificio I)

Edificio III:
Tzinacalli

Edificio VI

Edificio II

Edificio V

MALINALCO, Edo. de México

The site was discovered by José García Payón in 1936; excavated and restored in 1956–57. Malinalco means 'a turn (or bend) in the road', or, according to one source, is based on *malinalli*, 'a twisted reed'.

According to Aztec chronicles, Axayácatl began his conquests in the Valle de Morelos c 1474 and in his campaign against Cuauhnáhuac several Matlazinca sites were also captured, incl. Ocuila, Chalma, and Malinalco. A certain Citlacoaci was made governor and Malinalco was added to the tribute lists in 1476. The principal Aztec shrine at the site on the cliffs, however, was not begun until the reign of Ahuitzotl (1486–1502), in the year before his death (*nine calli*—'nine house' 1501). Stonemasons (*tetlepanques*) were brought from Tenochtitlán for the task, and it was to be a sanctuary for the military orders of the Eagle Knights and Jaguar Knights, organizations sworn to fight the evil represented by the serpent-mouth doorway to the main temple. Although Ahuitzotl died before its completion, work was continued by his successor, Moctezuma II Xocoyotzin (1502–20), at least until the year *ten acatl*—'ten reed' 1515, and the site was thus unfinished when the Spaniard Andrés de Tapia captured the town in 1521, during the siege of Tenochtitlán. A carved wooden *tlalpanhuéhuetl* drum, allegedly from the site is now in the Museo Nacional de Antropología: carvings on it include eagles, dancing ocelots or jaguars, and solar signs.

The path to the site is signposted from the plaza (c 1km; 424 steps). Much of the site is actually carved out of the cliff face rather than constructed, while other structures have been reconstructed by INAH. There are six principal buildings on a large reversed-L-shaped terrace.

Edificio VI is the first to be encountered, on the r. as we enter the gates to the site. It is circular, 4m in diameter, carved from the cliff stone on a retained terrace. An entryway faces W, with the foundations of rectangular chambers on the W side. *Edificio II*, E of it across a small court, is a small, rectangular, two-tiered platform, c.22m bx 15m, with projecting W-side steps.

On the N side of this court, against and hewn entirely out of the cliffside, is the magnificent **Templo Principal** (*Edificio I*). It was originally covered with coloured stucco, and has been identified as the *Cuauhcalli* (House of the Eagle), according to one interpretation, dedicated to the Sun god. The carved jaguar and eagles inside represent the warrior knights who worshipped here, and were sworn to fight the enemies of the empire and evil in general.

The temple is approached by a wide staircase (c 5.5m), with ramps on either side, leading up to a narrow porch across its face. In the centre of the staircase, on the third step, is the damaged figure of a seated man, a standard holder, carved in the round from the solid rock. On the sloping walls of the platform, to either side of the stairs, are two more carved figures, seated jaguars, perhaps meant to guard the sanctuary; they were originally painted yellow with black spots.

On either side of the porch at the top there is a buttress wall and two pillars to support the portico and temple roof, presumably of thatch, as it has now been reconstructed. To each side of the doorway behind the pillars are two relief carvings: a coiled serpent (r.) with arrowhead scales and the damaged remains of an Eagle Knight seated on top; and a war drum (tlalpanhuéhuetl; l.) with remains of another seated figure, possibly a Jaguar Knight. The door frame is carved as a serpent's jaws, with vicious fangs and forked tongue thrust forward for a threshold.

The temple chamber itself is hollowed out of the cliff face, and forms a circular room 5.8m in diameter, with a raised bench around the rear half. On the floor in the centre is the figure of an eagle, carved in the round, facing the doorway. Directly behind it, on the same axis, is a circular stone *cuauhxicalli* (eagle box; 30cm in diameter), presumably meant to hold the hearts of sacrificial victims. Continuing the line of the axis, on the bench behind these, a jaguar (or jaguar skin) is carved, also facing the door, with its tail on the wall behind it; and on the bench to either side of it is an eagle with spread tail feathers, facing into the centre of the temple. Above the bench are six square slots, possibly niches for shelf supports.

Returning to the court in front of the temple, steps on its E side lead to a platform on the cliff face, above the temple and overlooking Edificio III (described below). More steps lead farther up the cliff, and traces of a drainage system cut into the rock can be seen around the temple and platform.

Passing between the Templo Principal and Edificio II, to the corner of the main terrace, we come to *Edificio V*, partially reconstructed. It is keyhole shaped in plan and was perhaps a small outdoor altar platform.

The front of the Cuauhcalli, Malinalco

Opposite it is **Edificio III**, a large, semicircular temple (c 11m in diameter), with a wide rectangular portico (or chambered entryway; c 19m by 5m). The whole is carved out of the rock of the cliffside.

This building has been interpreted as the *Tzinacalli* (House of Death Rites), in which warrior knights killed in combat, or sacrificed by enemies, were given death and deification rites. In Aztec religion, warriors who died in this manner were believed to be transformed into stars.

There are three entrances between the wing walls and two square pillars of the rectangular antechamber. Inside, a continuous bench lines the side and rear walls to either side of the doorway leading into the semicircular temple. In front of this doorway is a square, stone-lined altar box set into the floor. The restorers of the site found remnants of murals on the walls of the temple, depicting warriors carrying shields and spears, advancing across a stylized ground of feathers (representing the eagle) and jaguar fur, together representing the 'night sky' of Aztec mythology. Within the semicircular chamber there are three flat stones for offerings, arranged around another stone-lined altar box, just off-centre in the floor. The tops of the walls of the temple are the levelled cliff face, into which several smaller rectangular chambers have been carved at a higher level; these are some of the unfinished rooms of the sanctuary.

Continuing around the angle of the reversed-L terrace, to the N, there is the wide façade of **Edificio IV**, actually a complex of rooms carved into the cliff face. This has been interpreted as the *Templo del Sol*, in which the tonal-pohualli ceremonies were celebrated, every 260 days on the day *four ollin*—'four movement' (the Netonatiuhzahualiztli ceremony; see Introduction: Calendrics; and Mesoamerican Religion). A wide terrace frontage is reached by a central staircase between two narrow, rectangular porticoes, each open-fronted with two rectangular pillars, and containing stone-lined altar boxes against their centre, rear walls.

Originally, this temple was entered through a single doorway opposite the stairs; but these were later blocked up and two doorways built at the N and S ends of the façade. Inside there are two rectangular hollows in the floor, presumably for timber roof supports, and a continuous stone bench around the side and rear walls. In the centre of the rear bench is another stone-lined, rectangular altar box, thus opposite the original entrance.

Farther N along the cliff beyond the main terrace, there are more rectangular rooms carved into the cliff face, and the beginnings of another semicircular chamber, all unfinished before the sanctuary was abandoned.

80 Cuernavaca to Xochicalco and Toluca

Méx. 95 and Méx. 55, 189km.—23km junction with Méx. 55.—32km (4km N) **Xochicalco**.—73km Grutas de Cacahuamilpa.—105km Ixtapan de la Sal.—139km Tenancingo.—163km Tenango de Arista.—189km **Toluca**.

We leave Cuernavaca to the S, through the S part of the Valle de Cuernavaca. 8km *Temixco*, where the grounds of the former hacienda have been adapted for entertainment and sports facilities. 11km *Acatlipa*, with a 17C church (restored) and open chapel. At 14km a turning l. leads to (1km) **Xochítepec**, where the former Franciscan convent of *San Juan Evangelista*, founded from Cuernavaca in the 16C, stands in an atrio, its merlon-lined walls pierced by a gateway whose arch holds attractive stylized floral relief. 2km N the former hacienda of *Real del Puente* has been adapted as a recreation centre. At 23km we leave Méx. 95, turning r. on to the Mazatepec road and towards the Sierra de Miacatlán.

32km turning r. for (4km N) **XOCHICALCO** ('place of the house of the flowers'), one of the most fascinating hilltop fortress cities and ceremonial centres in the Highland Plateau. Although little is known of its history, it provides us with tantalizing glimpses of internationalism in the Mesoamerican world and of a site strong enough to resist total subjugation by ever-growing Teotihuacán in the later Classic and Early Postclassic Periods.

Occupation began in the Middle Preclassic as two small hamlets W of the present ceremonial centre. The population continued to grow through the Late Preclassic and Early Classic. A principal phase of monumental construction began in the 4–5C AD, during which the economic power of Teotihuacán overshadowed central Mesoamerica. In the 7–10C it was at its most prosperous and undertook its most ambitious building phase, and was finally abandoned early in the 10C, possibly because of changing trade patterns caused by the migrations of the Early Postclassic after the demise of Teotihuacán, which left it politically and commercially isolated. Only a thin scattering of Aztec pottery on the surface attests to any later use of the site, although its ruins must have been visible to these Postclassic visitors.

Some ancient chronicles refer to the site as *Tamoanchán*, the legendary seat of the 'serpent-bird'. Tamoanchán was the terrestrial paradise of Toltec and Aztec mythology. Of Huastec origin, the word can be traced back to Maya root words: *ta* = of, *moan* = a mythical bird of the 13th Heaven, and *chán*, or *can* = snake or sky; thus the land of the bird-snake or feathered-serpent. In the saga, Quetzalcóatl, the Feathered-Serpent, brought bones from the Underworld to Tamoanchán, which he ground into a powder and mixed with the auto-sacrificial blood of the gods to create man.

Along with Cholula, Cacaxtla, El Tajín, and a few other sites in central Mexico, Xochicalco was an independent city, perhaps hampered by Teotihuacán's economic power, but biding its time. It was able to obtain obsidian from sources outside Teotihuacán's control and maintained trading and diplomatic contacts in its own right. Chief among these, judging from the pottery and architectural styles at the site, were Maya Palenque, Zapotec Monte Albán, and Gulf Coast El Tajín. Xochicalco apparently had its own territory and tributaries also: in legend it exacted an annual sacrificial victim from Tepozteco—an old man who was fed to the 'dragon'; alongside Cholula it exercised a certain amount of control over Teotihuacán's access to Monte Albán via the S trade routes; and to feed its citizens it must have controlled a considerable hinterland of rural towns.

A more detailed history of the building phases at Xochicalco can be drawn from the results of excavation. The Gran Plaza was first created by artificially levelling the hillside in the

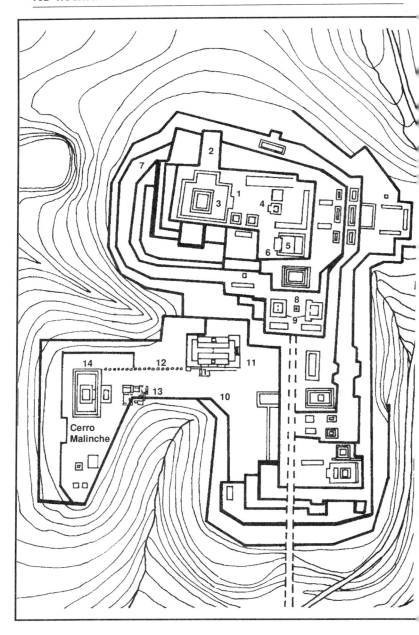

XOCHICALCO, Morelos

Cerro de la Bodega

1 Gran Plaza
2 Observatorio
3 Estructura E
4 Pyrámide de las Serpientes Emplumadas
5 Templo de las Estelas
6 Cámera de las Ofrendas
7 Subterráneos
8 Plaza Inferior and Adoratorio de Estela de los Glifos
9 Estructuras C and D
10 Gran Calzada
11 Juego de Pelota
12 altares
13 Edificio B
14 Edificio A

car park

N

0   50   100m

(old and new approach roads)

3C AD, and the first public monuments of the ceremonial centre were begun. The principal building phase, to which most of the visible restored monuments belong, dates from c AD 600 to 900. Within this period the site grew to cover some 4 sq km with a population of c 20,000, and included pyramids and temples, a ball court, subterranean structures, terraces on the surrounding hillsides, and several massive causeways joining the spurs of the main hilltop. The ceremonial cave itself covered c 63ha. Associated ceramics, and the reliefs on these monuments, show wide-ranging commercial links and use of styles: from Teotihuacán it borrowed the classic talud-tablero technique, but here the talud was emphasized and used to provide a tall, wide surface for carved reliefs; the tablero was short, but flared at the top to form a cornice, as at El Tajín; and stelae and other carvings included figure styles and calendrics from several regions (see below).

In the 7C there are indications that Xochicalco hosted a gathering of 'astronomers' and priests, from Maya, Zapotec, Mixtec, and central Mexican cities. They seem to have met to standardize their calendars and commemorated the event in carvings on the Pirámide de las Serpientes Emplumadas, where several artistic styles are combined.

In the 9C the Xochicalcans reacted to the troubled times by building defensive walls and ditches. Northern tribes were on the move and the region suffered several incursions of the 'Historic' Olmecs from the Mixteca Alta of Oaxaca. In the early 10C, stelae that had been erected in and around the Templo de las Estelas were deliberately broken and painted red as a symbol of destruction and the abandonment of the core of the site. Partial reoccupation took place in the late Postclassic, by Tlahuica peoples, and grew to c 92.5ha in the 13–14C. A ceremonial centre was built on Cerro Temascal, W of the earlier central plaza, but was abandoned again by c 1500. An Aztec garrison was established at Xochicalco just before the Spanish Conquest.

Xochicalco was visited in the 16C by Bernardino de Sahagún and mentioned in the prologue of his first work. The Jesuit José Antonio Alzate conducted some primitive excavations in 1777, uncovering the Pirámide de las Serpientes Emplumadas, and published a paper entitled 'Descripción de las antigüedades de Xochicalco' in 1791. The Jesuit Pedro Márquez also visited the site, and his report was used by Humboldt to describe and publish illustrations of the site in 1810. Other 19C visitors included Guillaume Dupaix, Carlos Nebel ('Viaje pintoresco y arqueológico sobre la República Mexicana', 1829), Manuel Orozco y Berra, and Hubert H. Bancroft (1880s). In 1877 Antonio Peñafiel made the first major study of its monuments since Alzate's. Excavations were undertaken by Leopoldo Batres (1908–10) on the Pirámide de las Serpientes Emplumadas; and studies of the sculpture done by Edouard Seler. Government sponsored excavations were carried out by Eduardo Noguera between 1934 and 1950; and by César Sáenz for INAH from 1961 to 1967. The site and its region were explored by Jaime Litvak King between 1965 and 1972, and by Kenneth Hirth between 1977 and 1984. Excavations on the outer wall were done in the early 1980s by Norberto González and Silvia Garza.

Xochicalco sits at c 1500m above sea level and c 130m above the surrounding plain. The entire ancient city covered c 250ha at its greatest extent. The archaeological zone comprises the hilltop ceremonial core of the city, where a huge levelled causeway, stretching nearly 1200m N–S and 730m E–W, connects the spur of *Cerro Malinche*, on the SW of the Gran Plaza, to the main ridge. The visitor approaches the site up some modern concrete steps from the car-park, opposite the visitors' centre, where tickets are issued.

The GRAN PLAZA is c 350m by 200m, and includes scores of restored and unrestored monuments and terraces, plus numerous unexcavated mounds down the slopes to E, W, and N. It is an artificially levelled platform, the first construction on the site. To the N and NW are walls and uncovered mounds, and a dramatic view into a deep gorge where the ridge drops away abruptly. In the NW corner, just off the plaza, is a ruin known as the *Observatorio*, not, as with similarly named monuments at other sites, for astronomical observations, but as a look-out across the N plains.

Moving S, down the plaza, there are terrace walls up the slope of the hill to the W, to *Estructura E*; and on the E side, the principal restored platforms and buildings. First, on the E side, is an unrestored pyramid mound with ruins showing several stages of construction. Next, two small, square bases of structures in the centre of the plaza.

The **Pirámide de las Serpientes Emplumadas** (Quetzalcóatl; or *Monumento Descubierto*) is a temple platform, built with the talud-tablero technique, but with a tall talud and a relatively short tablero. Both are carved, the former with what has been interpreted as a commemorative scene, and the latter forms a 'flying cornice' reminiscent of the style at El Tajín. An upper wall, also carved, forms a square, open-air building, reached by a staircase on the W side of the platform. One interpretation of this monument is that it was erected to commemorate the gathering of 'astronomer-priests' from all over Mesoamerica. They were there to synchronize watches, so to speak, presumably on the occasion of the approach of a significant calendrical cycle—perhaps AD 650 (see Introduction: Calendrics).

The talud carvings comprise eight plumed serpents, two on each side, which undulate up and down to form frames for alternating hieroglyphs and various seated figures. Glyphs represent the symbol for Fire, and the number nine. The figures sit cross-legged and wear animal masks and flouncing plumes. On either side of the staircase the serpents frame hieroglyphs for three day-signs, held up by hands, possibly representing the calendrical synchronization following astronomical observations. In their dress, arrangement, and facial features these figures are Maya-like rather than central Mesoamerican, and resemble especially the reliefs of Altar Q at Copán in Honduras. On the tableros there are more reliefs, less well preserved, showing more seated figures, also separated by intertwined serpents. On their headgear there are various glyphs, incl. a year-sign. On the 'flying cornice' smaller reliefs depict coils, thought to be plumes, spiral shells, or serpents.

The 'square' temple supported by this platform measures 10.4m by 10.5m, and has relief carvings on the outside walls. These are not well preserved, but can be seen to depict more figures—warriors with darts and shields. The entrance is divided by two pillars, and on the walls to either side there is a carved coyote and more fire symbols. These and the other reliefs were originally painted in bright colours—white, black, blue, red, and yellow—in characteristically Mesoamerican fashion.

Estructura A (*Templo de las Estelas*). C 30m S of the Pyramid another restored platform is ascended by a wide staircase up two tiers, to a platform supporting a third tier and a temple building on its E side. At the top of the steps are pillars which originally supported a portico. Fragments of three stelae were found on the platform itself, and the remaining parts were discovered in a box cut beneath the plastered temple floor. (These are now in the Museo Nacional de Antropología.) Each stele is c 1.8m high and carved on all four sides, constituting a set depicting Tláloc (in this case the Sun god) and his consort, the Moon goddess, and goddess of fertility. The trio are similar in style to reliefs from the coastal Lowlands, especially resembling examples at El Tajín and Palenque. They were erected c AD 600, stood for some 300 years, and were deliberately smashed and buried when the site was abandoned.

The *Cámara de las Ofrendas* (Offertory Chamber) is a small room located against the SW corner of Estructura A. In it the excavators found offerings incl. a stone yugo, used in the ball game ritual, a serpentine figure, a jadeite head, obsidian arrowheads, Nahua and Zapotec hieroglyphic inscriptions on stone, and a human skeleton.

Subterráneos (Underground Chambers). Across the plaza, at the slope on the W side, *Estructura E* sits on the top of the terraces; on the NW slope, beyond the crest, there is a tall terrace retaining wall, and the entrance to some underground passages inside the hill. A large hall is cut into the rock, and, on the far side, three sets of steps with narrow landings. At the top of these is a gallery and the blocked-off steps to another chamber. To the l. of the entrance hall a corridor leads from the base of the stairs, widening as it goes, to another set of steps up to a chamber c 18m by 12m by 3.3m high, with three rectangular pillars. These were originally stucco-covered, and traces of paint can still be seen here and there on the walls and floor. A funnel-shaped hole in one corner provides ventilation and, according to some sources, was an observation site for the equinoxes, when the sun's rays allegedly come straight into the room. There are other passages and chambers that have not yet been cleared.

S of the Templo de las Estelas and the Subterráneos a massive terrace wall separates the Gran Plaza from its lower counterpart, PLAZA INFERIOR, which continues S and, at a still lower level, branches W to join the spur of Cerro Malinche. A huge pyramid backs onto the N side of this plaza, directly S of the Templo de las Estelas. Partially restored steps down its S side lead to the lower plaza and face a small oratory known as *Adoratorio de la Estela de los Glifos*. This is formed by two concentric square walls, with steps, supporting a large stele (2.8m high and 6 tonnes) carved with number glyphs.

The E and W sides of the plaza, flanking the oratory, are formed by *Estructuras C* and *D*, two similar platforms, each supporting an open-fronted temple, with pillars dividing the doorway. Estructura D, on the W, backs onto a retaining wall above the causeway and the Juego de Pelota.

Beyond the Plaza Inferior, to the S, terraces break the E, W, and S slopes of the ridge, and support numerous mounds and traces of other structures, the excavation of some of which revealed them to be densely packed residential units. These did not form apartment-like compounds, as at Teotihuacán or Tula, but were clusters of individual houses on platforms.

Forming a right angle to the above, the GRAN CALZADA, over 100m long and 9m wide at the W end, links the spur of Cerro Malinche to the main ridge. The entire lower plaza covers some 4500 sq m, and from it two other roads lead c 3km out into the countryside with no obvious destinations.

The first, and most conspicuous, structure is the **Juego de Pelota**. This sits along the N side of the Calzada and comprises a massive stone structure of platform walls c 40m long, and lower walls forming an I-shaped playing field c 75m long, between wide, gently sloping platforms. On the main walls the goal rings have been set in place. We see here yet more evidence of international contacts, as this court closely resembles courts on Maya sites, especially the ball court at Cobá in Yucatán.

S of the Juego de Pelota, along the N side of the Calzada, is a long row of square columns. Beyond these, also on the N side of the Calzada, a row of curious circular structures, each c 1.8m in diameter, are thought to be small altars. Opposite these, on the S side of the Calzada, stands *Edificio B*, a large complex of rooms and interconnecting corridors, possibly quarters for the priests who would have served at the altars. To the W of it stands *Edificio A*, a large, ruined pyramid-platform which presumably once supported a temple.

The especially keen can seek two final monuments after returning to the site entrance. First, another causeway leads NE from the site, linking the *Cerro de la Bodega*, which has the ruins of a multichambered structure, probably residential. And second, c 330m N of the plaza, there is a massive rock formation with a small smoothed area inscribed with symbols, possibly recording the event of the New Fire ceremony, celebrated at the end of a 52-year cycle (cf. *Cerro de la Estrella*). On the upper l. is the glyph for the number one, and on the lower l. are two glyphs—'one rabbit' and 'two serpent'—presumably dating the event—and a fire symbol.

The main road passes (l.) the *Lago el Rodeo*, an artificial lake (good fishing; licence necessary), 1500m in diameter. 38km *Miacatlán*, on the E slopes of the Sierra de Miacatlán. 43km *Mazatepec*, where the 18C church of San Lucas incorporates a 16C Franciscan visita chapel.

4km E is **Cuahtetelco** (Náhuatl *Coatetelco*—'serpent mountain'), a small Tlahuica Postclassic ceremonial site (9–6; fee), partly restored just S of the town. It comprises a central plaza surrounded by preserved and unexplored mounds. On the S side is the *Templo Mayor* with a N-side staircase flanked by massive ramps, and with decorated taluds. The N side of the plaza is formed by a large *Juego de Pelota*, flanked by small temples E and W, also with decorated taluds. The other sides of the plaza have relatively unpreserved mounds.

A small *Museum* includes prehistoric and historical displays. Tlahuica and Aztec ceramics; figurines, one from the Preclassic Period, and others from the Teotihuacán Classic (c AD 300–450) and Aztec Postclassic; large stone with small pits—a patolli board, an ancient game similar to pachisi; stone sculptures (incl. Xipe Totec, god of springtime and planting); temalacatl stone carved with symbols of the sun, water, and the annual cycles. Dioramas, artefacts, and photographs depict the Spanish Conquest and later periods.

In the town centre the 18C church of San Juan Bautista is built on the remains of a 16C Franciscan visita chapel.

To the NW is the *Laguna de Coatetelco* (1500m wide, 65m deep) whose waters drain into the Río Tembembe.

48km *Tetecala*. 53km *Coatlán del Río*, in rugged, mineral-rich country, with a 16C Franciscan visita church. At 66km a turning l. leads to (16km SE) the Cuernavaca–Iguala road, see Rte 82. At 71km we cross from Morelos into Guerrero. At 73km we arrive near the entrance to the **Grutas de Cacahuamilpa**, a vast network of underground caves, perhaps the most monumental in Mexico. They are set beneath the Cerro de la Corona, part of the limestone Sierra de Cacahuamilpa, in the S slopes of the volcanic divide.

There are 15 accessible 'halls' (salones) in which stalagtites, stalagmites, and fantastic rock formations, in dazzling colours, have been fashioned by the attrition worked by an underground stream (its run-off carrying calcium carbonate), source of the Río San Jerónimo. Their first systematic exploration, in 1835, was on the initiative of Jean-Baptiste baron de Gros, secretary of the French legation. In 1841, wrote Fanny Calderón de la Barca, 'Some day, no doubt, this cave will become a show-place...as yet, one of its charms consists of its being unhackneyed'.

The prophecy has been fulfilled. In 1970 a visitors' centre, with souvenir shops, and car park were inaugurated. Hundreds of visitors descend daily. Guided tours (10–5; fee) start when a full complement has assembled. The caves are lit by electricity.

A road runs S to join, at 9km, the Cuernavaca–Tasco road, see Rte 82.

We continue N, on Méx. 55, past the village of *Cacahuamilpa* and then through rugged scenery towards the S slopes of the Nevado de Toluca. To the l., the course of the Río Chontalcuatlán, through the deep barranca de Malinaltenango. At 91km we cross into the State of México. 94km turning l. for (2km S) the *Grutas de la Estrella* (guided tours 9–3; fee), more spectacular underground caves, only part of which have been illuminated for visitors. 101km *Tonatico* (1670m), a pretty place with thermal springs and an elaborate 19C parish church. 105km **Ixtapan de la Sal** (c 10,000 inhab.; 1900m; H,R,P), a resort with mineral rich thermal springs, on the S slopes of the Nevado de Toluca. The church of the *Señor del Perdón* retains traces of its 16C foundation. Hence the road winds up to (127km) *Villa Guerrero* (P), famous for its orchards and gardens, the scent of the flowers an irresistible feature. Méx. 55 winds N and then E to (139km) **Tenancingo** (50,000 inhab.; 2022m; H,R,P), a Late Postclassic Matlazinca town, which in the early 16C allied itself with Teotenango against other Matlazinca factions (see below). It has marble quarries and unexploited mineral and opal deposits.

9km SE, on the plateau of Nixcongo, is the former Carmelite convent of *Sto Desierto del Carmen*, founded in the late 18C by friars from the Desierto de los Leones (see Rte 35A) and dedicated in 1801. Stations of the Cross line the way to the convent, surrounded by a stout wall. The surrounding region is a national park.

Méx. 55 climbs N, through cool dry country, cut by barrancas draining S towards the Río Balsas, the Nevado de Toluca on the l. At 151km a road winds NE and then S to (35km) *Chalma* and (45km) *Malinalco*, see Rte 79.

163km **Tenango de Arista** (*Tenango del Valle*; c 15,000 inhab.; 2637m; P), in an intensively cultivated region. On a hill W of the town, and signposted from the town centre, are the Museo del Estado and the site of the ancient city of **TEOTENANGO** ('within divine walls'; 9–6; fee), with its hilltop ceremonial centre and surrounding suburbs, once covering as much as 21 sq km at its greatest extent. It had been neglected by archaeologists until its excavation began in 1971, and restoration work in 1974, by INAH under the direction of Román Piña Chan. Now numerous plazas, courts, platforms, terraces, pyramid-temples, and a ball court have been cleaned and restored. Between these public buildings, streets, markets, and apartment-like complexes of private residences were excavated, whose construction materials revealed socio-economic differentiation among the populace.

The Valle de Toluca was settled by Matlazinca-speaking peoples in the 7C AD. Many other groups either visited or temporarily settled here, incl. Teochichimecas, Otomí, and Nonoalco. Between c AD 750 and 1162, Teotenango became an imposing civic centre, one of many that rose to prominence as Teotihuacán waned in its economic dominance of central Mexico, but nonetheless was heavily influenced by Teotihuacano styles. It is uncertain if Teotenango was captured or dominated by Tula, but Toltec influence was also considerable in the later life of the site.

According to Toltec legend (in the Codex Xólotl), the Toltec prince Nopaltzin, son of the famous Chichimec leader Xólotl, married a girl from the Valle de Toluca, and thereafter the inhabitants were called by the name Matlazinca.

In the mid-12C, perhaps coincident with the fall of Tula, the valley was invaded and taken over by Chichimecs, who established a military rule by a warrior caste, backed up by a priestly caste. Their territory stretched W to the powerful Tarascan principalities, and E to the rim of the Basin of Mexico. There were other Matlazinca settlements N and NW, at Calixtlahuaca, Tecaxic, and Xiquipilco, but Teotenango was the principal Matlazinca civic and ceremonial centre for these and for Malinalco, to the S. Also according to Toltec legend (in the 16C native Ixtlilxóchitl), after the fall of Tula legitimate Toltec heirs were still sent to the valley in order to protect and preserve the line. There was, however, much rivalry between the Matlazinca princes, and wars, capture of prisoners, and mass sacrifices were very endemic.

In the 13C the centre of Teotenango was abandoned and new precincts were established to the S. A strong defensive wall was built, extending around the N end of the hilltop, but the sheer drop on the other three sides rendered other defensive barriers unnecessary. Nevertheless, in the 14C the Matlazinca were forced to accept Chalca rule from the Valle de Anahuac; and in 1415 they were made subject to the powerful Alcoloa of Texcoco. In c 1417 they were temporarily freed when Texcocan power in the Basin of Mexico was seriously challenged by the Tepaneca of Azcapotzalco.

Matlazinca internal rivalry had not abated under foreign rule, and three principal factions emerged. Chimaltecuhtli and the Toluca Matlazinca supported an alliance with the up-and-coming Mexica Aztecs of the Basin, particularly after the Mexica–Alcoloa defeat of Azcapotzalco in 1428; the Hueyebeches Chalchiuhquiauh of Teotenango and the Tezozomoctli of Tenancingo preferred neutrality and independence of any Matlazinca coalition; and the Pirinda Matlazinca ('those in-between') of Tzinacantepec, Tecaxic, and Xiquipilco allied themselves to the Tarascans to the W.

The Matlazinca were famous as slingers, in both war and the hunt, and the first of these three factions served as mercenaries in the Aztec conquest of the Mixteca region and of the Valle de Oaxaca. The Pirinda supported the Tarascans in defence against attacks by the other factions, and especially by the Aztecs in their expansion W towards the Pacific. Together they inflicted a bloody defeat on the armies of Moctezuma I Ilhuicamina in 1464 at Xiquipilco. The Aztecs invaded the Valle de Toluca a second time in 1474 under Axayácatl, and this time were more successful, taking many thousands of sacrificial prisoners and imposing a heavy tribute. The newly conquered domains were presented as a 'fief' to the young heir-potential (later Moctezuma II Xocoyotzin). By 1476 the Aztecs had taken Calixtlahuaca and Tecaxic, Coatepec Harinas, Malacatepec, and Malinalco. Chimaltecuhtli of Toluca, in view of his city's support of the Mexica, was allowed a certain measure of independence, but the tribute exacted from the other Matlazinca princes was so oppressive that they rebelled and had to be severely put down by Tizoc (1481–86), who established garrisons at Calixtlahuaca and Teotenango. Many more captives were taken to Tenochtitlán for sacrifice, incl. prince Tlilcuetzpalin, at the festival of *Tlacaxipehualiztli* (the third Aztec 20-day month). At this feast, in honour of Xipe Totec, the bravest of the captives were made to fight in 'gladiatorial' contests (called tlahuahuanaliztli), in which they were anchored by the ankle to a heavy stone and given a club set with feathers, to fight a freely mobile Aztec champion who wielded a club set with obsidian blades.

At Cortés' arrival the Matlazinca were cautiously interested until they sensed which way the wind blew. Thus, during the siege of Tenochtitlán, when Cortés' lieutenant, Sandoval, led an expeditionary force into the Valle de Toluca and proposed an alliance against the Aztecs, the Matlazinca accepted. Their slingers and bearers took part in the capture of Tenochtitlán, providing manpower and supplies.

The **Museo del Estado** comprises a single floor divided into three areas around a central patio, each area divided by display units. The sequence of displays moves chronologically through Mesoamerican prehistory, and is especially well illustrated by central Mexican sites in the State of México. Proceed counter-clockwise; numbers refer to the floor plan. FIRST AREA. 1. Wall panels, texts, and photographs discuss the entry of early man into the New World, incl.

mammoth kill display, photographs of early skull finds, castes of mammoth bones, and obsidian tools. 2. Panel of figurine photographs and case of Preclassic pottery and figurines from the early village farming sites of Tlatilco, Tlapacoya, Tepalcate, and Chimalhuacán. 3. Case of Preclassic and early Teotihuacano pottery. 4. Panel of photographs and text discussing the Tlapacoya burials. 5. Teotihuacano stone Tláloc sculpture. 6. Two cases of Classic Teotihuacano pottery, figurines, and mica objects. 7. Panel of photographs and text discussing the rise of Teotihuacán. 8. Two cases of Later Teotihuacano ceramics, and conch shell artefacts. 9. Panel-copy of a wall fresco from one of the apartments at Teotihuacán. 10. Several panels showing an artist's reconstructions of the Tenayuca pyramid (Early to Late Postclassic). 11. Stone serpent head sculpture from the Templo Mayor of Tenochtitlán. 12. Postclassic stone sculpture of a woman, possibly a sacrificial victim. 13. Case of Late Classic–Early Postclassic pottery from the Basin of Mexico. 14. Case of artefacts, incl. early metal pieces of Early Postclassic date (here called the 'Military Period'). 15. Stone sculpture of Quetzalcóatl, here portrayed as the 'star' of Venus. 16. Case illustrating stone technology: obsidian projectile points, ground and polished axe-heads, grinding tools, spindle whorls, and loom weights. 17. Case of Early Postclassic pottery from Teotenango, Calixtlahuaca, Malinalco, Tenancingo, and Calimaya; plus pieces of Coyotlatelco and Mazapa wares, representing Toltec influences in the Valle de Toluca. 18. Case of painted pottery, especially jugs and tripod vessels, from Teotenango. 19. Panel of photographs and text discussing the site of Teotenango: pottery, figurine styles, burials, and site structures. 20. Reconstruction of the Teotenango burials and photographs of excavations.

SECOND AREA (at far end of building). 21. Excavation and restoration of Teotenango photographs explaining the site's development and its discovery and excavation. Pottery, clay, and stone figurines (incl. stone face with inlaid shell eyes and teeth), and other artefacts from the site, especially from burials.

THIRD AREA (devoted especially to Teotenango and the Matlazinca). 22. Map of sites in the State of México. 23. Photo-murals of Teotenango. 24. Stone sculpture from the site with the glyph 'One Flower' or 'Cane'. 25. Panel of text and photographs discussing the agricultural economy of Teotenango. 26. Case illustrating Matlazinca technology: obsidian points, ground and polished tools, grinding tools, spindle whorls and loom weights, bone awls and needles. 27. Stelae from Teotenango, incl. glyphs for *Two Atl* ('two water'), *Seven Mázatl* ('seven deer'), *Seven Cóatl* ('seven serpent'), and *Seven Atl* ('seven water'); panel explaining the Aztec system of day and month signs. 28. Two cases of Late Postclassic Matlazinca polychrome pottery (1162–1476). 29. Two cases of late Teotihuacano, Coyotlatelco, and Teotenango pottery, emphasizing the multiple traditions and their sources at Teotenango. 30. Stone sculpture from the site, possibly Quetzalcóatl. 31. Stone sculptures from the site, incl. triangular section with a jaguar on one side and a *Cozcacuauhtli* (the 'vulture', and 16th day of the Aztec month) on the other; and a man wearing a snake helmet. 32. Polychrome pottery illustrating Teotenango's commercial contacts. 33. Case of Postclassic jewellery. 34. Photographs of the stone sculptures at Calixtlahuaca. 35. Famous stone statue from Calixtlahuaca of Ehecatl-Quetzalcóatl in his birdbeak mask. 36. Late Teotenango pottery. 37. Mexica Aztec pottery from the Basin of Mexico to compare with No. 36. 38–39. Panhuehuetl of Teotenango and Malinanco. 40. Panel and photomurals of Malinalco. 41. Stone sculpture representing *Técpatl* ('flint'), the 18th Náhuatl day and one of the four 'Year-Bearers' (along with *Acatl*—reed, *Calli*—house, and *Tochtli*—rabbit); each of these yearbearers began 13 of the 52 years in the Aztec 'century', or 52-year cycle. 42–43. Postclassic stone sculptures. 44. Case of Late Postclassic jewellery. 45. Case illustrating human sacrifice. 46. Two cases containing wooden drums with zoomorphic figures. 47. Carved stone drum-column section. 48. Case of pottery illustrating Matlazinca trade with the Mixteca, Cholulteca, and Tlaxcalteca. 49. Case of Late Aztec Black-on-Orange Ware. 50. Two double cases containing a good representation of the Postclassic Mexican pantheon in stone sculptures.

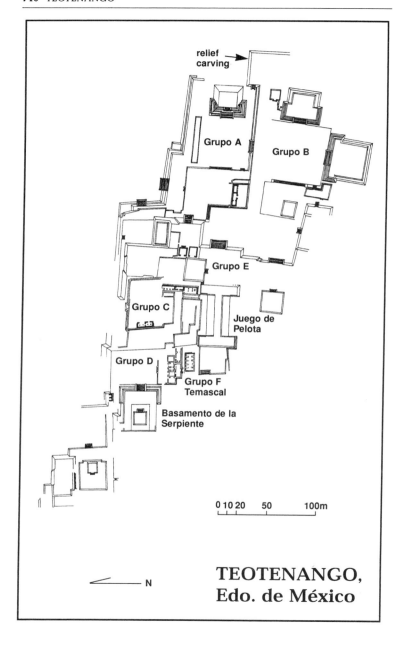

relief carving

Grupo A

Grupo B

Grupo E

Grupo C

Juego de Pelota

Grupo D

Grupo F
Temascal

Basamento de la
Serpiente

0 10 20   50   100m

N

TEOTENANGO,
Edo. de México

51. Panel discussing Aztec conquest of Matlazinca, and later Spanish conquest. 52. Stone sculptures of Quetzalcóatl. 53. Curious carved stone pole with pyramid-like symbols. 54. Relación for Teotenango (1582).

The Archaeological Zone. The main restoration work has been done on the Sistema Norte, but from the tops of its pyramids the terraces and building foundations of other 'systems' can be seen lining the hillsides to the S and W. The hilltop has a strong wall around its N end, but cliffs on the other sides provided natural protection.

The architectural style in general reflects the physical and chronological proximity of Teotihuacán, in the use of talud-tablero walls, court layouts, and in the composition of the plazas, and public and private buildings. The ball court shows the same layout and similar features to those at Tula and Xochicalco. Like those sites, Teotenango used Coyotlatelco and Mazapa ceramics, both featuring red-on-cream vessels and figurines with thin, slab-like bodies and long, pointed noses.

Sistema Norte. This comprises six grupos with public plazas and the monuments surrounding them. In general each ensemble includes stepped platform bases which would have supported temples (of which no trace survives), with monumental staircases, terraces with altars, oratorios, administrative buildings, and streets of residences around the outsides of the huge plazas. The public monuments were built of stone in several tiers, with Classic talud-tablero facings. Private residences were built of adobe bricks. Collective burials of sacrificial victims were often placed at the foot of the pyramid-platforms, especially in front of the stairways. Associated pottery indicates that the earliest such public monuments were built c AD 750–900; the restored monuments here, however, are of the later phases, in the Early Postclassic (c AD 900–mid-12C), but before the Chichimec migration–invasion into the valley.

Grupo A is the first ensemble at the end of the short but steep path, culminating in imposing, wide steps up to the first platform. Just before reaching the first plaza group, however, on the l., against the terrace wall, is a relief carving of a monster (?jaguar) devouring the Náhuatl sun symbol. It is believed to commemorate the eclipse of the sun of 1477 (a date glyph corresponding to that date appears on the carving—*Eleven Calli*—'eleven house'). The ensemble comprises an enormous sunken plaza, enclosed by pyramids with wide staircases, and long, connecting platforms, all faced in cut stone.

Grupo B is S of Grupo A, and at a slightly higher level (it can be seen 'behind' Grupo A from its platforms). It comprises similar structures—a long, high platform, altar, and a monumental pyramid of several tiers rising above its plaza. There is also a smaller patio covered with a stucco floor.

Grupo C is to the W, and appears as a series of horizontal lines of terraces and platforms, with the oblique lines of staircases climbing from terrace to terrace. It includes pyramids for temples and courts at different levels.

Grupo D is W of Grupo C, beyond the Juego de Pelota of Grupo E (below). It comprises a large platform along the main 'street', with groups of interconnecting rooms around patios. A plaza is bordered by the *Basamento de la Serpiente* (Serpent Platform), and a smaller annex; and, on the S side, by another huge platform, bordering another huge plaza believed to have been a market.

Grupo E lies between and S of Grupos C and D, and consists of a *Juego de Pelota* and some earlier structures near it. The ball court is nearly 43m long and 10m wide, conforms to the plans of the ball courts at Tula and Xochicalco, and was probably built during the same period, between c AD 900 and 1150. The playing field is between two sloping walls, with 'stands' on the N wall, and covered with stucco made of a mixture of lime and powdered pumice. The stone goal-ring now in place is a replacement of the broken one found in the excavations. W and E of the court are the foundations of earlier rooms and *Grupo F*—a *Temascal*.

Predating the ball court, the Temascal was a complex of living quarters around a sweat or steam bath.

Such baths are a long tradition in central Mexico, believed to have medicinal and ritually purifying powers. The ill, the wounded, the pregnant or recently delivered, and those about to participate in ceremonies used the sweat baths in preparation or in cure.

Around the N edge of the site remains of the old city wall can be seen, incl. early sections to the W and S. This was not all built at once, but is thought to have been in response to the Chichimec incursions of the mid-12C.

173km turning l. for (5km W) **Calimaya** (c 7000 inhab.; 2475m) where c 1557 the Franciscans founded the convent of *San Pedro y San Pablo* in a small Matlazinca town which had a temple dedicated to their god, Colotzin. The convent is now in ruins, but the four-bay portería-open chapel, with one raised arch facing the chancel, is a handsome survivor. Adjoining it is the baptistery, with an ornate oratory niche (1560s), its arch crowded with embroidery-like floral motifs; guilloches line the jambs.

From Calimaya we may gain (14km) *Toluca* via (6km) *Sta María Natívitas*, with an 18C church and, to one side, an imitative four-arched portería, an earlier survival.

175km turning r. for (2km) *Chapultepec*, see Rte 35B. 177km *Mexicalzingo* and (189km) *Toluca*, see Rte 40B.

81 Cuernavaca to Tepoztlán and Yautepec

33km. 19km **Tepoztlán**. 33km Yautepec.

We leave Cuernavaca to the N along Blvd Emiliano Zapata, turning r. along Av. de los Fundadores del Estado and keeping r. for the Tepoztlán road which passes under Méx. 95D, the toll road for Mexico City. 6km *Ocotepec*, a colourful little town. 15km *Sta Catarina*. The road passes under Méx. 115D, the toll road which branches off Méx. 95D and runs to Cuautla, for (19km) **TEPOZTLÁN** (c 12,000 inhab.; H,R,P), set in a valley into which descend the slopes of the Cerro de Tepozteco, part of a craggy mountain range whose peaks add enchantment to the landscape.

The earliest evidence for occupation at Tepoztlán is dated c 1000 BC, and the site has been occupied ever since. The town became a Tlahuica settlement in the 12C AD when this branch of the Aztec tribes migrated into the Valle de Morelos from N of the Basin of Mexico and established several towns and cities in the valley. In the 15C it was captured by the Aztecs under Itzcóatl (1426–40) or his son Moctezuma I Ilhuicamina (1440–68), and made to pay tribute. Thereafter it became a centre of pilgrimage for the worship of Tepoztécatl (see below).

Anthropological interest in Tepoztlán has continued into modern times, and the town was the focus of studies by Robert Redford in the 1920s and by Oscar Lewis in the 1950s, restudying the town and re-evaluating Redford's conclusions. Their widely differing conclusions concerning the workings of Tepoztlán society caused a minor controversy within the field of anthropological theory and practice.

From the main plaza we descend through an archway in the W wall of the atrio of the former Dominican convent of **La Natividad de Nuestra Señora**, for its austere grandeur one of the finest of Mexico's historical monuments.

The Dominicans set up here c 1556. One of their number, Fray Domingo de la Anunciación, is said to have broken the local idol, Ometochtli, in pieces and sent them to Oaxtepec (see Rte 74) as rubble for the church's foundation.

Immediately to the l., a little tower is crowned by five merlons, the large central one topped by a globe and cross. Of the four elegant POSAS which once graced the precinct only the second, in the NW corner, remains intact, with semi-circular arches, wider at the front, resting on engaged columns whose astragals enclose an ornamental layer with ionic volutes above. In the corner pilasters are deep niches. From the E crowning cornice rises a triangular pediment. The first, NE, posa is joined to the portería.

The massive CHURCH (finished c 1588), supported by highly visible buttresses which add a dimension of extraordinary strength, still preserves at its E end a crowning of merlons, strikingly grouped at the corners and on top of the buttresses where they surmount garitas. The W façade is recessed between two buttresses; their unsatisfactory bell towers are modern additions after an earthquake in 1839. Tall and arresting, the doorway panel is an indigenous interpretation of Renaissance classicism, full of plateresque touches. At the sides, the inner pair of slender fluted colonnettes with ionic capitals rest on low engaged fluted pilasters; the outer pair are upheld by unobtrusive cherubs; both pairs support a cornice below a frieze of medallion reliefs, three held at the sides by hovering angels. Decorative relief crowds the narrow space between the colonnettes, enlivens the semicircular archivolt with seraphim, and invades the spandrels (sun, moon, stars, and dogs). Above the frieze, the pediment is framed by layers of elaborate moulding and encloses figures in flat relief, primitive yet delightful: Our Lady, standing on a half-moon and holding the infant Christ; St Dominic with his dog holding a torch; and St Catherine of Siena offering her heart. On either side stand vases of carnations. Large angels above, out of proportion with the figures below, hold a panel which once contained an inscription.

19C modernization has done nothing to improve the aisleless interior, which has windows only in the S wall; the chancel is covered by a ribbed groin vault. Ruins of an open chapel stand to the r. of the church; its wide chancel arch survives.

The CONVENT buildings were completed by 1580. The cloister, with its widely separated bays, is solid and severe, but the merlons and corner garitas, in turn topped by conical merlons, which line its top parapet are a picturesque addition which blends with the surrounding landscape.

In C. González, on the E side of the convent, a small archaeological *Museum* (10–1, 3–5; fee; poor labelling, dim lighting) displays a collection made by Carlos Pellicer.

In the entrance room are Tlatilco, Chupícuaro, and Olmec pottery and figurines, stone axe-heads, and zoomorphic figurines incl. a fish, duck, and turtle. To the r., and thence counterclockwise through the other rooms, are copies of some of the Teotihuacán murals and cases of Teotihuacano artefacts, incl. a stone eagle; copies of the paintings at Bonampak and cases of Classic Maya artefacts, incl. some figurines from Jaina; artefacts from Veracruz and copies of paintings at Tizatlán; Aztec artefacts; figurines and pottery from Colima and Nayarit, and a central display case with large hollow figurines from Jalisco.

On a volcanic cliff above Tepoztlán (1–1½ hr—600m—climb), **Tepozteco** was first a Tlahuica and later an Aztec sacred shrine. From c 2100m above sea level it looks down on the entire valley.

The summit was artificially levelled to provide a platform for the shrine, originally built by the Tlahuica c AD 1250. After the Aztec conquest of the valley, a rebuilding was begun by Ahuitzotl (1486–1502) but was not finished until near the end of his reign; there is a carved commemoration slab at the site with his glyph and the date 'ten rabbit'. It was probably at this time that it was dedicated to Ometochtli ('two rabbits'), a principal god associated with the fermentation and drinking of pulque.

The temple is also associated with Tepoztécatl, a Moon god, and also associated with drunkenness; he is often depicted with a crescent-moon nose, and with half his face painted red and the other half black. He was believed to help bring the earth out of its winter hibernation and to help with the rebirth of nature; for this reason he was celebrated in an autumn festival (traditionally on 8 Sept.), to lay the seeds for his work. In legend, Tepoztécatl was also a Tlahuica hero, noted for delivering them from the onus of providing the city of Xochicalco with a yearly sacrificial victim—an old man to be eaten by a dragon. In the tale, Tepoztécatl disguised himself as an old woodcutter, and as that year's sacrificial choice, gave the dragon some of his own back, ending the dreadful tribute.

The present stabilized remains at the site (daylight hours; fee) are of the Aztec temple. The main monument sits on a terrace 10m high and is reached by two staircases on E and W. On the terrace sits a three-tiered pyramid (it appears as a four-tiered pyramid from the E, or rear), c 10m high, with a staircase up its W

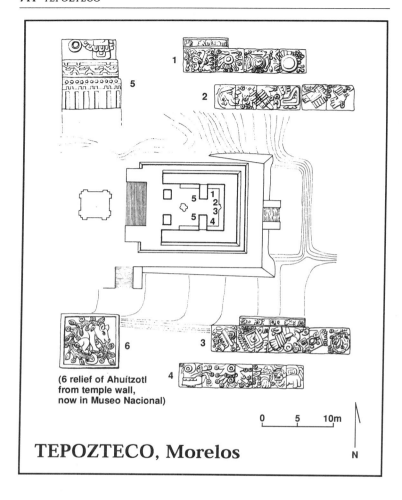

(6 relief of Ahuítzotl
from temple wall,
now in Museo Nacional)

0   5   10m

TEPOZTECO, Morelos

N

face. A small forecourt has the remains of a smaller rectangular structure. The temple on top of the pyramid has two chambers, a portico formed by the square pillars and wall ends across the front, and a doorway into a rear sanctuary. Here a plinth against the rear wall provides a support for the statues of idols. Stone benches along the rear and side walls are carved in bas-reliefs depicting cosmic signs, incl. the 'four suns' that were believed to have preceded the present sun, signs for the cardinal points, and the 20 day-signs of the Aztec month (on a cornice along the vertical face of the benches); plus a crown, shields, and spears symbolizing royal conquest. On the two columns of the doorway there are more reliefs, incl. vertical grooves, fret patterns, and other geometric motifs.

At the foot of the ridge there are traces of a small ball court; evidence of other terracing can be seen down the hillside. S of the pyramid are traces of various walls and floors of annex buildings.

From Tepoztlán we continue E to (22km) *Huilotepec* and then S, across Méx. 115D, to (33km) **Yautepec** (c 15,000 inhab.; 1282m; H,P), in the valley of the Río Yautepec, a rich agricultural region, once a fief of Cortés and with unexcavated remains of the former Postclassic Tlahuica town. The former Dominican convent of *La Asunción* dates probably from the 1560s and was built to the designs of Fray Lorenzo de la Asunción. The church's imposing bulk overshadows the simple open chapel, with a domical vault, to its l. The irregularly shaped buttresses of the upper cloister rest in the projections of the heavy piers which support the barrel vault of the lower storey walk, where original murals may be seen.—Yautepec is the birthplace of Virginia Fábregas (c 1872–1950), Mexico's greatest actress.

The road going S from Yautepec follows the valley to (25km) *Tlaltizapan*, see Rte 74. At (4km) along it) *Atlihuayán* on the Río Yautepec workers making a road cut found a large, hollow Olmec clay figurine, depicting a seated man wearing the skin of a caimán (crocodile), now in the Museo Nacional de Antropología. Subsequent excavations at nearby Iglesia Vieja uncovered grave goods similar to those from the sites of Tlatilco and Chalcatzingo.

We follow Méx. 138 SW, crossing the Sierra de Tetillas, towards Cuernavaca. 50km turning l. for (2km S) **Jiutepec** (3000 inhab.; 1350m), where the former Franciscan convent of *Santiago el Mayor*, founded in the early 1580s, was severely damaged by an earthquake in 1585. The present church is of later date. 55km *Atlacomulco*, an E suburb of Cuernavaca. 58km *Cuernavaca*, see Rte 78.

82   Cuernavaca to Acapulco via Tasco

Méx. 95, 380km.—87km **Tasco**.—123km Iguala.—240km **Chilpancingo**.—380km **Acapulco**.

Cuernavaca to (23km) turning r. for *Xochicalco* and *Toluca*, see Rte 80. 24km turning l. for (11km S) the **Lago de Tequesquitengo** (18 sq km), a favourite resort for water sports, surrounded by modern villas, built for the comfortably off who flock here from Mexico City in winter. A road circling the lake leads to (5km E) **Tequesquitengo** (H,R), chief place of the lake region. 2km N of the lake is the former hacienda of *Vista Hermosa* (reputedly founded by Cortés in 1529), its headquarters building, once a sugar refinery, now converted into a luxury hotel. The arches of an old aqueduct invade the swimming pool.

At 42km a road r. runs NW to join (16km) the Cuernavaca–Toluca road. 49km *Huajintlán*, where the restored parish church dates in part from the 16C. We cross into the State of Guerrero just before (62km) turning r. for (9km N) *Grutas de Cacahuamilpa*, see Rte 80. 66km turning r. for (1km N) *Gruta de Acuitlapan*, more underground caves, discovered in 1934, in the N foothills of the Cerro Techoloapan. 67km *Acuitlapan* has two churches: San Francisco (17C) and San Miguel (16C) with a quaintly plateresque doorway. The road winds spectacularly to (87km) *Tasco*.

TASCO (*Taxco*; c 47,000 inhab.; 1666m), tucked into the folds of the SE slopes of the Cerro del Atachi 'in which more sky than earth appears', is one of the most enchanting spots in Mexico, its irregular layout accentuated by the craggy, uneven terrain, in which the little square houses with their tile roofs seem to tumble down the mountainside. The height called Huisteco shelters it from the N wind and ensures a mild, dry climate.

Bus stations. 126 Av. Kennedy, to the S. Services to *Mexico City* (3 hrs) and to *Acapulco* (5 hrs) via *Iguala*, *Chilpancingo*, and *Zihuatanejo*. 104 Av. Kennedy, to the E. Services to *Acapulco* and to *Mexico City*; to *Toluca* (4 hrs); to *Iguala* (1 hr); to *Cuernavaca* (2½ hrs).

Hotels throughout the town.

Post Office. 6 C. Juárez.

Tourist Office. 1 Av. Kennedy (in Centro de Convenciones).

Fiestas. 17 Jan.: St Prisca (Blessing of Animals). Palm Sunday and Holy Week (famous representation of the Passion). 29 Sept.: St Michael. 1 Dec.: Silver festival. 16–24 Dec.: Posadas (Nativity plays).

Tasco, known as *Tlaxco* ('Ball Court') before the Spanish Conquest, was a Tlahuica city in the W of their territory (cf. *Cuernavaca*). The site of the Postclassic town was c 11km S at *Taxco Viejo*, near silver and tin mines exploited by the Tlahuica, and later much more heavily by the Spaniards. Tlaxco was attacked by the Aztec king Ixcóatl (1426–40), annexed to the empire by Moctezuma I Ilhuicamina (1440–68), and forced to pay a heavy annual tribute.

In his fourth 'carta de relación' (1524) Cortés attests to finds of tin and iron. Spaniards were soon improving mining techniques and silver veins must quickly have been struck: the king's shaft, on a slope of the Cerro de Bermejo (to the E), could be traversed its length of 90m on horseback, and this length was increased to 650m through the efforts of José Vicente de Anza at the end of the 18C. Tasco may have been claimed by Cortés, but by 1534 it seems to have been set aside, as a mining centre, for the crown. Because of population depletion during 16C epidemics, Indian miners were imported from other parts. In 1716 the Aragonese José de la Borda (1699–1778; comp. Rtes 7 and 46) crossed over to New Spain and joined at Tasco his brother Francisco, already working the mine of Tehuilotepec (c 8km E). Here, singleminded and hard-working, he laid the basis of one of history's legendary mining fortunes. It is said that in 50 years he amassed 40 million pesos. In Dec. 1811 Tasco fell to the forces of José María Morelos who was actively assisted by the local magistrate, José Joaquín Fernández de Lizardi. In 1863 Porfirio Díaz took the town after tremendous resistance and his troops went on the rampage in revenge. In the 1920s it began to wake from the isolation into which it had fallen, as an artistic and tourist centre, and in 1929 William Spratling (1900–67), a native of New York state and professor of architecture at Tulane University, settled here to devote much of the rest of his life to the revival of silver crafts. Although born in Mexico City, the great playwright Juan Ruiz de Alarcón (?1580–1639) came from a prominent tasqueño family.

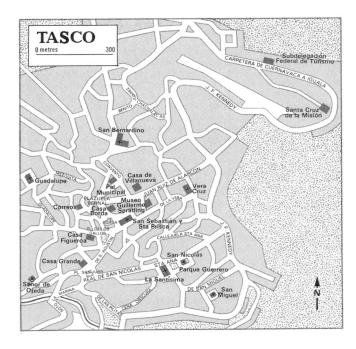

The town centre is the little PL. BORDA, planted with Indian laurels, incongruously full of traffic by day, exquisite by night.

On the E side rises **San Sebastián y Sta Prisca** (always known as *Sta Prisca*), one of the most visible churches in Mexico, dominating the townscape from every viewpoint. It is built of porous, igneous stone, painted a faded rose, on which sun and sky work marvellous effects.

In 1751 José de la Borda was licensed to build and undertook 'with his own wealth to bring the church to a perfect conclusion'. While work was in progress, Borda underwent a financial crisis and was forced to sell treasures intended for Sta Prisca to the cathedral in Mexico City. But he discovered fresh ore in time to embellish his church. The architect was (most likely) Cayetano de Sigüenza, or possibly Diego Durán Berruecos (or a partnership of both). Work finished in 1758 and the consecration, by Manuel Antonio Rojo del Río, abp of Manila, took place in 1759. José's son Manuel was parish priest here in 1759–77.

EXTERIOR. The atrio railings date from 1906–07. The unmistakable towers, slender and light despite their complex ornamentation, and high octagonal cupola, covered with multicoloured azulejo patterns, combine with the façade to give a strongly soaring impression. The façade, audaciously designed, is the earliest manifestation of neostyle baroque, which here takes elements from other, previous and contemporary, styles and shows them in a new guise. In the lower storey stand two pairs of classicizing columns, of the type known as tritóstilo; between them, recessed, highly novel, pilasters on giant bases on which rest statues of SS Peter and Paul. The pilasters continue into the first storey, emphasizing the overall verticality, and end with bases for statues of SS Prisca and Sebastian. On each lower column capital rests not a cornice but part of an intricate entablature crowned by a series of curved pediments, on which in turn rest decorative bases for another cornice substitute above resembling broken pediments, where perch angels holding flowers and palms. Still further up appear more bases, for the sinuous solomonic columns of the first storey.

Above the columns, supported by cherubs, appear two shields: on l., the eagle and Golden Fleece covered by the Spanish crown; on r., the arms of Manuel Rubio y Salinas, abp of Mexico (1749–65).

The central relief is of the Baptism of Christ, homely and ingenuous, but very effective, the work of local craftsmen. Its lovely frame shows all manner of baroque and rococo ornament: volutes, spirals, shells, foliage, cherubs. Going up from the tall doorway, through the hints of an alfíz framing the papal arms, the central relief, and choir window, and continuing beyond the encompassing semicircular moulding of pearl and egg-shaped motifs to clock and finial, the centre panel provides the main statement of the ascending quality of the whole.

The clock, with a single hand, is by Isaac Rogers of London (1753); the finial, carved into a blind balustrade, shows the Immaculate Conception flanked by SS John and Matthew. A simple contrast, yet ornate in itself and well seen, the S doorway shows tritóstilo columns, with composite capitals and an underfringe of pears, against pairs of pilasters, the high bases adorned with lambrequin and foliage relief. Pediments borne up by the capitals form bases for statues of SS Joseph and Christopher. The central relief, of the Coronation of Our Lady, in an eared frame, is enclosed by little almohadilla pilasters. On either side are the beautiful little doorways to the Baptistery (l.) and the Archive Room (r.), loaded with baroque and rococo relief against an almohadilla background, from which stand out the medallions in the jambs and between the lintel and curving cornice.

On all four sides of the lower storeys of the towers are balconies, their bases composed of fantastic mask relief, flanked by pairs of tritóstilo engaged columns. At each corner is a quasi-estípite, its centre a relief medallion. Fantastic heads also show on the balcony bases of the richer and freer upper storeys; beneath them peep cherub heads. The belfry jambs are intricately carved: the engaged columns, on high intricate bases decorated with pearl, Greek fret, foliate, and other motifs, are swathed in undulating ribbon relief. At each corner stands an apostle—eight, complementing the four on the façade.

18C Mexican brilliance, reflecting contemporary religious zeal, has been miraculously preserved in the INTERIOR. Pilasters, arches, and vault bands, in the lightest of rose stone, conspire with the nine altarpieces of nave, sanctuary, and transepts, and shafts of light through cupola and clerestory windows, to give bewitching chiaroscuro effects and tints which change with the hours of the day. The stone itself is fashioned with extraordinary definition: the recurring tablero motif on arch and pilaster, the jutting cornices, curving volutes and scrolls, Corinthian capitals, plentiful foliated relief, and jagged, wavy moulding (enclosing above the arches a winding band of egg-shaped relief) set up a vigorous architectural rhythm, in harmony with the splendour of the matching altarpieces, which become richer as we proceed E.

The latter were designed c 1755 by Isidoro Vicente de Balbás (with one Juan Caballero among his craftsmen) and mark the smoothest of transitions from the Mexican churrigueresque to anastyle baroque. Despite their exuberant fruit, vine, foliate, and other relief, and the skilled use of layers of moulding and pronounced scrolls, volutes, and undulating cornices, and springing imagery, to create a semblance of depth, they stand remarkably flat against the walls and do not invade nave or transept. Their upward movement echoes the thematic pattern of the exterior.

The first pair, facing one another across the sotocoro as we enter—and the smallest and most markedly anastyle of all—are devoted to St Isidore the Farm-worker (l.) and St Lucy (r.). In the former SS George (name spelt English-style in the inscription) and Vitalis stand on pedestals forward of ornamental niches either side of the central shrine; in the medallion above, St Antony Abbot; the finial is a statue of St Roch. In the latter St Lucy is accompanied by SS Catherine and Barbara; St Agnes in the medallion; St Ursula as finial. In both pieces angels and cherubs perilously perch clutching palms, or peep out from the gilded relief.

The second pair along the nave are dedicated to St John Nepomuk and Our Lady of the Pillar (patron of Aragón, Borda's home province). They are gorgeously fringed by floral, foliate, and shell motifs. Their ornamental niche pilasters, merely token supports, include lavish statue bases. In the centres of the cornices, exquisitely framed medallion paintings.

St John Nepomuk is flanked by SS Vincent de Paul and Felix, and, flanking them lower down, SS Peter Arbues and Lawrence. Above are SS Peter Canisius and Francis Xavier. The finial is St Francis Borgia. Our Lady of the Pillar is accompanied by the seven archangels, free in movement, heroic in aspect.

Next come the altarpieces of St Joseph and Our Lady of Sorrows, with elaborately moulded frames using recurring, and much varied, chain, ears-of-corn, and apple motifs, decorated with prominent shells in clusters of four which skirt a high circular vegetal and fruit relief; their central parts divided by the richest of cornices, laden with ornamentation, under which cherubs hold up the shrine curtains. St Joseph is flanked by SS Anne and Joachim and, lower down, by St Anne's parents. The finial is St John the Baptist, with SS Zachary and Elizabeth on either side. Accompanying Our Lady of Sorrows are SS John and Mary Magdalen, Mary Salome and Mary Cleophas. Above, a Crucifixion.

Facing each other, sumptuous and soaring, across the transept are the altarpieces of Our Lady of Guadalupe (l.) and Our Lady of the Rosary (r.)—both shown in central volute flourishes—in which faint estípites, slender and most elaborately finished at their apexes, appear in both storeys; but their support element is dimmed by the wealth of ornament, incl. bishops sprouting from medallions, and cherub heads.

The oval paintings (school of Cabrera) illustrate, in the former, the miracle of Guadalupe. Above Our Lady of Guadalupe, a beautifully framed oval (Our Lady appearing to Juan Diego) pushes up the cornice and is crowned by a shell. The statues are of bishops, culminating in a finial holding St Isidore of Seville. In the altarpiece of Our Lady of the Rosary, the ovals show paintings of scenes from her life; the statues and busts are also of bishops, solicitous cherubs again holding mitres and palms; in the finial is St Nicholas.

Its theme, the triumph of the Church, emphasized by statues of popes and evangelists and busts of more popes, apostles, and doctors, the HIGH ALTAR achieves an incredible exuberance, a dazzling, yet carefully planned, disorder and agitation, bursting out around four detached estípites, huge and complex, in the lower storey, and four more, close together, in the upper. The cornice separating them undulates to form three bases, the central one for the statue of St Peter and the seats of two popes. Among the most imaginative in New Spain, and as assertive as the estípites, the interestípites develop above the little doors at their bases amid a play of geometric mouldings, which with the lavish application of cherubs, seraph heads, garlands, and fruit and foliate relief, are arranged to create an illusion of depth. Their centres are two ornamental niche pilasters for the statues of SS Prisca and Sebastian, the latter the most dynamic sculpture in the church. The middle section, though mutilated by the removal of the tabernacle (by the parish priest Lorenzo Rodríguez c 1890), is still superb.

Its lovely central shrine (1782), enclosing a statue of the Immaculate Conception (glorious even through its glass cover), is sustained by five floating cherubs. Above the shrine perch more cherubs, the upper two holding the Sacred Heart enmeshed in thorns, with St Michael in their midst. Four more cherubs hold aside the baldachin of St Peter. The image of God the Father breaks through the topmost pediment.

Above the S doorway and the entrance to the side chapel opposite are two elegantly framed large half-oval canvases, Martyrdom of St Sebastian and Martyrdom of St Prisca, by Cabrera. The organ has beautiful casing and decoration, and a central medallion of St Cecilia. The pulpit and two ambos on either side of the high altar all show good relief.

On the N side of the nave is the CAP. DEL PADRE JESUS, containing three altarpieces. Opposite the entrance, that dedicated to the Holy Souls is marked off by two fine estípites, the most regular in the church, and paintings by Cabrera: in the upper storey, three ovals—Christ and Our Lady redeeming souls in purgatory (l. and r.), Our Lady of Mount Carmel (centre); lower storey, Salvation of Souls in Purgatory, with Holy Trinity and saints.

The two matching altarpieces, dedicated to Christ (W) and Our Lady (E), incorporate two complex and original niche pilasters, without capitals, on either side of a charmingly framed central painting (Christ carrying the Cross by Cabrera; Immaculate Conception, probably a 17C work). Both impress with their tight geometric patterns and volutes, and lovely brocade-like fringes above the main paintings, adorned with active little angels. In the pilasters are polychrome bas-reliefs (Scourging and Crowning with Thorns; Annunciation and Nativity), a novelty for the period. In the upper storeys, paintings of the Crucifixion and the Holy Trinity, by Cabrera, both in rococo frames, are flanked by statues of Nicodemus and Joseph of Arimathea, and Simeon and Anna the prophetess.

Behind the high altar, reached through a door on the r., is the SACRISTY, a handsome room, with excellent furniture, lined with 14 grandly framed canvases of Scenes from the Life of Our Lady by Cabrera. To the l. of the high altar the room now used as sacristy contains a Presentation of Our Lady and Annunciation, also by Cabrera.

The SALA CAPITULAR, reached through the antesacristy and in an annexe at the SE corner of the church, contains portraits of personages connected with the church, incl. one of Manuel de la Borda (by Cabrera), which gives a good idea of character.

On the N side of the plaza is the *Casa Borda* (1759), said to have been built at the order of José himself—for the parish priest. At the corner of the plaza with the steep C. Agustín Tolsá is the *Casa del Balcón*, with its Spanish-style balcony composed of wooden baluster columns. The rear of the Casa Borda faces Plazuela Bernal, from where C. Pineda leads E to the **Casa Villanueva** (No. 8), a mid-18C house, where Humboldt stayed in Apr. 1803.

From Plazuela Bernal along C. Tolsá we may reach PL. DE LAS CARNICERIAS, in which is the old *Ayuntamiento*, another typical 18C building, buttressed, with a high loggia. Behind it, along C. del Convento, we may climb to PL. DEL CONVENTO, former atrio of the convent of **San Bernardino**, founded by discalced Franciscans in 1592, badly damaged by fire in 1805, and rebuilt by 1824. The cloister was largely destroyed in 1909 to make way for a school. A little further N is the *Cap. de Chavarrieta* (rebuilt 1923), facing a small two-level plaza.

From the SE corner of Pl. Borda, Cjón del Arco runs along the S side of Sta Prisca. In the second turning l. (C. Porfirio Delgado) is the **Museo Spratling** (Tues.–Sun., 10–5; fee), containing the collections formed by William Spratling and arranged by INAH.

The galleries are arranged on two floors, and contain hundreds of pieces representing principally central and W Mexico: Jalisco, Colima, Nayarit, Michoacán, Sinaloa, Guerrero, and Guanajuato; but also have pieces from the Huasteca and other regions of Mexico. There is an important collection of Preclassic pieces from El Opeño and Chupícuaro; and a Post-classic collection from Tzintzuntzan, Ihuatzio, and Pátzcuaro. GROUND FLOOR 1. Stone sculpture, copy of the famous Huastec Youth (original in the Museo Nacional de Antropología—Postclassic). 2. Bas-relief of the Sun god (Postclassic). 3. Stone sculpture of Huehue-téotl, the Old Fire god (Classic Teotihuacano). Also known as Xiuhtecuhtli, he is believed to be of Olmec origin and occupied first place among the nine Lords of Night, or Underworld, and thirteen Lords of Day; his head is shaped into a bowl for holding the fire. 4. Case of fine Huastec jewellery of conch shell and bone. 5. Aztec jaguar head sculpture (15–16C).

UPPER FLOOR. 6. Zoomorphic Zapotec clay funerary urn (Classic Period). 7. Postclassic Huastec stone sculpture of an old man leaning on a cane; probably representing the god of merchants. 8. Case of ceramics and figurines from central Mexico (Teotihuacán), illustrating the typology and development of figurine sculpture from the 2C BC to 7C AD. 9. Zapotec funerary urns from Monte Albán. 10. Display of delicate gold and silver Mixtec pieces. 11. Maya pieces, incl. a calendar and stelae, and carved lintels and stone panels (c AD 300–900). 12. Cases with Preclassic Olmec artefacts (c 1200–300 BC): pottery, incl. a petal-trimmed bowl, polychrome tripod vessels, vases, plates, zoomorphic figurines and masks; stone hachas and palmas used in the ball game; and an explanation panel on the occupation and cultural development of the Gulf Coast.

In the BASEMENT a collection of photographs, documents, manuscripts, and metalwork illustrates the history of Tasco. There are also modern examples of tasqueño silverwork, a craft revived by Spratling.

Cjón del Arco is continued by C. de la Veracruz, which ends in PL. DE LA VERACRUZ, bordered by typical old houses, with wonderful effects at twilight. Here is the *Cap. de la Sta Veracruz*, begun in 1817, finished probably in 1913.

Directly W of Pl. Borda, and higher up, is PL. DE LOS GALLOS, once a cockfighting centre. Beyond, at the beginning of C. de Guadalupe, is the *Casa Figueroa* (l.; adm. by appointment), a two-storey house, containing antique Mexican and European furniture, and objets d'art. From here we may climb up to the barrio of Acayotla and PL. DE GUADALUPE, which affords one of the finest views of the town and fronts the *Cap. de Guadalupe*, in its present form finished in 1877. Also from Pl. de los Gallos we may reach, SW along C. de Ojedo and through Pl. del Progreso, PL. DEL SEÑOR DE OJEDA, on the Cerro del Atachi, with another good view (especially in the morning). The *Cap. del Señor de Ojeda* was rebuilt in the early 19C.

From the SW corner of Pl. Borda runs C. San Agustín (formerly C. Real de los Mercaderes), the most interesting, and only straight, street in Tasco. It ends at PLAZUELA DE SAN JUAN, with, on its N side, the **Casa Grande**, once seat of the alcalde mayor and of the mining court. Morelos lodged here in 1811. On its E side the picturesque Cjón del Nogal winds up to C. de Ojeda (see above). From Plazuela de San Juan, C. Real de San Nicolás goes E to PARQUE GUERRERO, faced by two chapels: on the W side, *La Santísima Trinidad* (1713) and, on the E, *San Nicolás* (rebuilt 1899). To the SE may be seen *San Miguel*, an attractive 18C barrio chapel.

A turning W off Méx. 95 SE of the town centre runs through the W slopes of the Sierra de Tasco past (15km) *Cacalotenango*, a 110m waterfall, to (43km) **Ixcateopan**, where the parish church of *La Asunción*, founded c 1570, has been much altered. The town became subject of heated controversy in 1949 after excavations at the church by Prof. Eulalia Guzmán, who claimed to have found the remains of Cuauhtémoc. The claims were taken up with enthusiasm by press and public; but rejected by two official commissions. The bones rest under the high altar.

Next to the church are some ruins of the Postclassic town, incl. the walls of dwellings, a circular platform, and a stairway. A small *Museum* in two rooms in the town's Cultural Centre (10.30–1, 4–7) has displays of Aztec and some earlier artefacts, reproductions of codices and other Late Postclassic/Conquest Period paintings, and 16C artefacts.

From Tasco, Méx. 95 goes S. 123km **Iguala** (c 90,000 inhab.; 731m; H,R,P), in a valley watered by the Río Cocula.

In 1820 Viceroy Apodaca ordered Iturbide to seek out and defeat Vicente Guerrero, diehard insurgent leader holding out in the mountain fastnesses. After the abrazo of Acatempan (see Rte 31) Iturbide had prevailed on the reluctant Guerrero enough for them both to announce the Plan of Iguala (24 Feb. 1821), acceptable to all shades of creole opinion, and his bid for Independence with himself as leader.

The central PARQUE DE LA BANDERA is shaded by 32 magnificent tamarinds, planted in 1832.

W of Iguala, Méx. 140 runs to (184km) *Ciudad Altamirano*, see Rte 31.

Méx. 95 leaves Iguala to the S and follows the valley of the Río Tepecoacuilco to (176km) **Mezcala**, on the Río Balsas. From the bridge over the river begins, every Nov., the Río Balsas international motorboat marathon, c 700km to the river mouth at Lázaro Cárdenas; then along the coast to Zihuatanejo. Beyond Mezcala the road runs through the cañón de Zopilote.

Mezcala and its environs S of the Río Balsas are known for finds of stone figurines with severely geometrical features dated c 500 BC–AD 400, but resembling Olmec and Teotihuacano styles. The Mezcala style is rendered in straight cuts and planes to represent humans, masks, miniature temples, and animals. Inexplicably, there are more examples of 'Teotihuacano' masks from Guerrero and Puebla than from Teotihuacán itself; and it seems that, because the stone was so easily available in Guerrero, the region became a production centre for serpentine, jadeite, andesite, white nephrite, quartz, turquoise, chalcedony, amethyst, garnet, alabaster, soapstone, and diorite figurines.
   A related style, carved on greenstone, of similar date and origin, is called Chontal; the site of Sultepec (see Rte 40), in the State of México, has yielded the northernmost example, dated c 300–100 BC.
   Ceramic figurines, also with Olmec features, from sites around Xochipala (some dated as early as 1800 BC) have turned up among numerous private collections in the area. Nevertheless, these are known only from surface finds and looted graves, and thus cannot be dated accurately. Paul Schmidt, of UNAM, has recorded as many as 90 sites in this region, but has found no graves, despite local reports of shaft-tombs 2–3m deep. The figurines from his collections include styles dated elsewhere from c 1800 BC to c 800 BC, the earliest showing the sex of the figurine and several other Olmec features. A middle phase style, dated c 1400–1200 BC, included both solid figurines and white-slipped hollow 'baby face' types; and a late phase after c 1200 BC shows a general degeneration of anatomical detail. Among the figurines are some of the earliest representations of ball players, with knee pads and 'yokes', and many dancer figurines with raised hands and naturalistic poses. A late hollow type, painted yellow or red, and as tall as 66cm in one example, also depicts dancers and ball players with flexed-leg stances. Because of their disassociated contexts, the dating of these figurines remains 'floating' in stylistic comparison (cf. *Cuicuilco, Dainzú, San Lorenzo Tenochtitlán, Tlapacoya*, and *Tlatilco*). The pottery from Schmidt's collections, however, includes characteristc mid-Preclassic to Early Classic wares such as white-slipped bowls, composite silhouetted incised bowls, and red-on-white and black-on-white granular wares.
   At 236km the road to the coast between Zihuatanejo and Acapulco branches off NW (r.). At (75km) *Corral de Bravo* a road begins an undulating course N, and then NE, to join (62km) Méx. 95, 17km S of *Mezcala* (see above). We continue SW towards the coast. At 104km a r. turn goes to (c 15km N) *Yextla*, where there are Preclassic (?15C) rock inscriptions and paintings. The road to the coast, through the Sierra Madre del Sur, reaches (263km) Méx. 200 5km NE of *San Jerónimo* (see Rte 30).

240km **CHILPANCINGO** (c 97,000 inhab.; 1360m; H,R,P), in the Valle de Chilpancingo of the Sierra Madre del Sur and on the l. bank of the Río Petaquillas, is an agricultural centre, capital of the State of Guerrero, and seat of a university.

Bus stations. 1st Class. 53 Av. Juárez. Frequent services to *Mexico City* (6 hrs); to *Iguala* (2 hrs); to *Tasco* (3 hrs); to *Cuernavaca* (4½ hrs); to *Acapulco* (2 hrs); etc.
   2nd class. Av. Roberto Masera, on N edge of the town. Services to nearby localities, and to *Mexico City* and *Acapulco*.

Hotels throughout the town.

Post Office. Corner of C. Hidalgo and Av. 5 de Mayo, E of Jardín Bravo.

Information. In Pal. Municipal.

Chilpancingo has two claims to fame. First, as the home town of the four insurgent Bravo brothers—Leonardo (1764–1812), Máximo (d. 1835?), Miguel (d. 1815), and Víctor (d. 1844)—and of Leonardo's son, Nicolás (1786–1854), insurgent and president (1842–43; 1846). Second, as the seat of the Congress of Chilpancingo, whose first session (13 Sept.–6 Nov. 1813) was held here, the first Mexican political assembly. It was summoned by José María Morelos who enunciated here the proposals which would be embodied in the constitution of Apatzingán (see Rte 29): a republic, universal suffrage, abolition of privilege, and the breaking-up of great estates. The congress members were pushed from place to place by Calleja's relentless pressure and Morelos loyally accompanied them, despite their relieving him of his command as responsible for later disasters.

The territory of the State of **Guerrero** (c 2.9 million inhab.; 64,281 sq km) is broken by the Sierra Madre del Sur and its spurs which cover its entire surface, except for the Pacific coastal plain. This plain (tierra caliente), with its famous beaches, bays, and lagoons, enjoys a hot tropical climate, in contrast to the coolness of the mountains (tierra templada), but changes have been caused by too precipitate deforestation. In the W and especially in the E are vast, unexplored areas, probably the wildest and most forbidding terrain in Mexico. To the NE of Acapulco the coast is known as Costa Grande; the stretch further E towards the Isthmus of Tehuantepec is known as Costa Chica. The course of the Río Balsas winds W to E across the State, keeping to the N slopes of the Sierra Madre, receiving the waters of various other rivers, eventually to form the border with Michoacán, crossing the Sierra as it does.

Apart from tourism, centred in Acapulco, Zihuatanejo-Ixtapa, and other smaller coastal resorts, agriculture and mining produce maize, bananas, coffee, and rice; and barytes, lead, zinc, and silver.

From 1521 the Spaniards were attracted to the coast in search of harbours and to the Sierra for its mines, already exploited in prehispanic times. Once pacification was in progress, Indians were brought by force from the mountains to help populate Spanish settlements. The vital artery was the road over the mountains from Acapulco to Mexico City, a mere pathway until 1592 when Viceroy Luis de Velasco ordered its improvement. In 1697 the journey took the Italian traveller Francesco Gemelli Carreri 12 days.

Some of the most significant events of the war of Independence took place in it: in 1813, Morelos's campaign in the S, incl. his capture of Acapulco, his calling of the congress at Chilpancingo, and his expounding of his plans for an independent Mexico. After his capture the struggle was continued by Vicente Guerrero, until the signing of the Plan of Iguala and Guerrero's reconciliation (for the time being) with Iturbide at Acatempan in 1821. Another native, Juan Alvarez, achieved great authority throughout the territory, opposing the hacendados, championing oppressed labour, proving himself a redoubtable liberal foe of Iturbide, Bustamante, and Santa-Anna, and promoting statehood, finally achieved in 1849. By his Plan of Ayutla in 1854 he finally put paid to Santa-Anna and in 1855 occupied the presidency. Liberal traditions remained strong during the Reform and the second empire. Political unrest continued to accompany economic and social reform, culminating in parallel, but unrelated, popular anti-government movements, led by Genaro Vázquez and Lucio Cabañas, during the 1960s and 1970s. Their deaths in 1971 and 1974 (the latter in a confrontation with federal troops) enabled the constitutional powers to reassert their authority.

The town's main buildings face the wide JARDIN NICOLAS BRAVO. On the N side (C. Juan N. Alvarez) is the 18C parish church of *La Asunción*, rebuilt after an earthquake in 1902, where the congress first assembled before removing to the building, now a school, known as *Primer Congreso de Anáhuac*. Further E along C. Alvarez is the *Pal. Municipal* (1903–06), its interior walls decorated with murals of the life of Cuauhtémoc; the war of Independence and the Congress; the Reform; and the Revolution and after, by Luis Arenal, Roberto Cuevas del Río, and Gilberto Aceves Navarro.

On the other side of the jardín is the *Pal. de Gobierno*, rebuilt and inaugurated in 1883 after an earthquake in 1882.

A road goes E of Chilpancingo into the Sierra Madre, one of the remotest and least known regions of Mexico. 16km **Tixtla** (c 13,000 inhab.; 1450m; H,P), birthplace of Vicente Guerrero (1783–1831) and Ignacio Manuel Altamirano (1834–93), poet, novelist, and politician. The church of *San Martín* dates from the 18C. 54km **Chilapa** (15,000 inhab.; 1300m; H,R,P) is a well-known centre for rebozos and basket-making, and its Sun. market is one of the most colourful in the republic. The former Augustinian convent of *La Asunción*, an early foundation, was rebuilt c 1582, and has been much altered since.

Oxtotitlán (2km E of *Acatlán*; c 12km N of Chilapa) is the second of two caves with polychrome paintings attributed to the Olmecs, or at least Olmec-inspired. It lies c 40km N of **Juxtlahuaca** cave, and was discovered in 1968. Michael Coe attributes the paintings to Olmec merchants passing through Guerrero in search of minerals, and considers them to be contemporary with La Venta, slightly later than the paintings at Juxtlahuaca, but both groups as c 900–700 BC.

The first painting is located at the mouth of the cave. One part is almost totally obliterated, but on the upper part of an outcrop is a figure sitting on a jaguar-monster head (cf. *Chalcatzingo* for a similar juxtaposition of a jaguar-monster and cave, in carving; Rte 74). Inside the cave (actually two rock-shelters) various groups of paintings to the N are mainly in black; to the S, others, mainly in red, include jaguars, 'baby-face' figures, and the earliest known 'speech scroll'.

Deep in the hills N of Oxtotitlán, c 18km N of Chilapa at the confluence of the Ríos Balsas and Amacuzac, lies *Teopantecuantitlán*. Here Guadalupe Martínez Donjuán has been excavating for INAH since 1983, and has uncovered an Olmec site dating between c 1400 BC and 600 BC. There is a walled, sunken plaza with four monolithic carved jaguar heads, each weighing c five tons (re-erected). Their faces show characteristic Olmec ovoid eyes and down-turned mouths.

Beyond Chilapa the road continues deep into the Sierra Madre to (146km) turning l. (a rough road) for (39km N) **Olinalá** (c 15,000 inhab.; 1415m; H), famous for its lacquerware, of the rayado type, unique in Mexico. 180km **Tlapa** (10,000 inhab.; 1000m; H,P), centre of the Tlapaneca Indians in the verges of the Mixteca Alta, where the Augustinian convent was set up c 1576 and later abandoned. The market is a magnet for the peoples of the Sierra.

Beyond Chilpancingo Méx. 95 runs SE to (251km) turning l. for (37km E) **Colotlipa**, in the national park of *Juxtlahuaca*. With a guide it is possible to visit the first discovered of two caves with some of the earliest known New World paintings, attributed to the Olmecs, or at least Olmec-inspired.

Juxtlahuaca lies c 7km into the mountains N of Colotlipa, and the **Oxtotitlán** cave is accessible from Chilapa (see above). The paintings, discovered in 1966 by Carlos Gay and Gilbert Griffin, are dated c 900–700 BC, and thus contemporary with Olmec San Lorenzo Tenochtitlán. There are two polychrome paintings (red, black, green, and yellow) located more than 1km inside the cave. The larger is of two figures: one stands, dressed in a huipil (tunic), jaguar-skin gauntlets and leggings, and a feather (quetzal bird?) headdress, and holds a rope-like or trident-shaped instrument towards a much smaller, seated or crouching, bearded man. The second painting depicts a red serpent with St Andrew's cross motifs in the eyes, facing a feline (jaguar?) creature. The paintings may have been done by Olmecs prospecting for rare minerals; their isolated location suggests religious significance, perhaps a shrine.

Méx. 95 undulates through the Sierra Madre via (296km) *Cajeles* and begins its descent to the coast with a magnificent view of the Bahía de Acapulco. At (375km) *Las Cruces* Méx. 200 goes E to (248km) *Pinotepa Nacional*.

The road passes through exuberantly tropical vegetation within reach of the *Costa Chica* and its lagoons. Flooding during the rains can make the going difficult. From (90km) *Cruz Grande* a road runs N to (35km) *Ayutla* where in 1854 Juan Alvarez, Ignacio Comonfort, and other liberals worked out the Plan of Ayutla to bring down Santa-Anna. 97km road S for the *Laguna de Chautengo* (fishing and boating). 131km *Marquelia*, a fishing village on the Bahía Dulce (extensive beaches; few services). From here Méx. 200 goes inland (NE) to (170km) turning l. for (15km) *Ometepec*, a town of Amuzgo Indians, from which two more of their centres, *Sta María* and *Tlacochistlahuaca* (20 and 50km NE), may be reached. The women of the latter are renowned for their expertise in weaving colourful and elegant huipiles. Ometepec's excavated site yielded artefacts of the *Monte Albán III* phase (c AD 300–600).

From the turn to Ometepec, Méx. 200 turns S for (198km) *Cuajinicuilapa*, whose people descend from African slaves. 35km SW on the coast is *Puerto Maldonado*, a remote fishing (varieties of tropical fish) and beach resort (few services). Beyond Cuajinicuilapa the road crosses into the State of Oaxaca to (221km; 2km r.) *El Ciruelo*, near the archaeological zone of *Cola de Palma*, with several unrestored platforms c 3m high and from 59m to 79m long. Anthropomorphic statues of quartz, and one of basalt, were also found.

248km **Pinotepa Nacional** (c 22,000 inhab.; simple H,R,P), chief place of the Mixteca de la Costa, and centre for Amuzgo, Chatino, and Mixtec Indians, among others, and coastal types of African descent.

From Pinotepa, Méx. 200 goes through the foothills of the Sierra de Miahuatlán SE to (144km) *Puerto Escondido*, see Rte 75. From it at 64km we may join a road running N to (9km) *Tututepec*, an early Mixtec capital, founded by the legendary leader Eight-Deer-Tiger-Claw, who later returned to his birthplace, Tilantongo, where he co-ruled the principality with his half-brother. His life is recorded in the Mixtec codices, especially in Codex Nuttall, which depicts him in a temple and in a ball court in Tututepec, identified by its name glyph. Tututepec was important in the trade across the Isthmus of Tehuantepec, between central Mexico and Central America, especially in cotton, cacao, gold dust, and copper. It was conquered by the Aztecs in the 15C.

Other excavated Mixtec sites in the region include *San Francisco de Arriba* (c 8km E); *Cerro Grande* (c 30km W); and *Piedra Parada* (c 15km N of Jamiltepec).

S of Méx. 200 are the *Lagunas de Chacahua*, a paradise for flora, fauna, birds, and tropical fish. 106km *Cacalotepec* has an unspoiled beach. 124km *Manialtepec*, by a laguna, another bird and wildlife sanctuary.

380km *Acapulco*, see Rte 30.

83 Veracruz to Villahermosa

Méx. 180, 485km.—28km (for [35km S] Cerro de las Mesas).—70km Alvarado.—145km Santiago Tuxtla and (30km W) Tres Zapotes.—171km Catemaco.—253km Acayucan.—263km (for [21km S] **San Lorenzo**).—314km Coatzacoalcos.—360km (for [4km N] La Venta).—435km Cárdenas and (40km N) Comalcalco.—485km **Villahermosa**.

We leave Veracruz to the SE. 10km *Boca del Río*, see Rte 71A. At (19km) *Paso del Toro* Méx. 150 branches inland SW to (106km) *Córdoba*, see Rte 71A. We continue SE on Méx. 180, skirting the S shore of the Laguna Mandinga. 28km turning r. (S) for (30km) *Ignacio de la Llave*, c 5km W of which is **Cerro de las Mesas**.

Little remains at Cerro de las Mesas (excavated by M. Stirling and P. Druckerin 1941–42 for the Bureau of American Ethnology and the National Geographic Society) except two large mounds and a few stelae fragments. The larger mound is 60 sq m at the base and 18m high.

Cerro de las Mesas, founded c 600 BC, was a ceremonial and trading centre. Its early pottery was similar to pottery from Izapa, in the Pacific highlands near the Mexico–Guatemala frontier. In one trench the excavators found a cache of 782 jade objects—the largest single group of jades in Mesoamerica—incl. figurines, earspools, beads, and other jewellery of jade, calcite, and serpentine. At least four of the jade objects are in Olmec style, and one jade sculpture is the largest known in Mesoamerica—a crying dwarf 30cm high. One early mound burial contained a carved turtle shell depicting the 'long-lipped god' of Izapan derivation.

In the Classic Period, Cerro de las Mesas expanded and showed strong influences from Teotihuacán. With four plazas, earthen mounds, and stone monuments it was the most important Central Gulf Coast centre until Teotihuacán influence waned from c AD 550. Large clay sculptures became a local tradition, but depicted Teotihuacano gods, especially Tláloc, god of rain, and Huehuetéotl, an ancient god of fire. Much of the pottery was also local, but there was also much Teotihuacano imported ware. At least 15 stelae were erected, depicting stiffly standing or striding figures in early Maya style, with Long Count dates ranging between AD 408 (Stela 6) and 533 (Stela 8) (see Introduction: Counting). In the Early Postclassic Period, Cerro de las Mesas' role in Gulf Coast trade was replaced by El Tajín.

Beyond (47km) *Salinas* the road traverses a spit of land between the Gulf and the Lagunas Camaronero and Alvarado. 70km **Alvarado** (22,000 inhab.; H,R,P), an important fishing port. (The fishermen have a reputation for colourful language.) Beyond Alvarado we cross the mouth of the Río Papaloapan by the Paso Nacional toll bridge (600m). At 85km Méx. 175 branches r. (S) for (338km) *Oaxaca*, see Rte 84. Méx. 180 continues SE away from the coast through a sugar-cane region. 106km *Lerdo de Tejada*. Between the main road and the coast rises the *Sierra de los Tuxtlas*, a volcanic range, always luxuriously green, which reminded Guillermo Prieto of Switzerland. From (122km) *El Trópico* a poor road goes N to some quiet beaches (*Salinas; Punta Roca Partida; Montepío*), apt to be crowded only at Easter, normally a haunt of fishermen using hand nets. 145km **Santiago Tuxtla** (c 16,000 inhab.; 280m; H,R,P), beautifully set on the S slopes of the volcano *San Martín* (1764m) in the valley of the Río Tuxtla. On Pl. Principal is the Cobata Olmec colossal head, the largest yet discovered (11ft; 3.35m). The *Museo Tuxteco* (Tues.–Sat., 9–1, 4–7; Sun., 9–3; fee), at the corner of Cs Ayuntamiento and Zaragoza, has displays from several local sites. Outside are some Olmec stone sculptures from Tres Zapotes.

ROOM 1. Explanatory panels and artefacts illustrating the archaeology and ethnography of the area, incl.: ground stone axe-heads, Totonac carved stone palmas and yugos for the ball game, an Olmec colossal head from Tres Zapotes and other stone sculptures, and objects for ritual healing. R.2. Olmec and Totonac ceramics, clay and stone figurines, and 'smiling face' figures (cf. *Remojadas* and *Nopiloa*). R.3. Olmec and Totonac obsidian tools and other artefacts of daily use; clay sculptures of Cihuateteo—the spirits of women who have died in childbirth, who in Postclassic mythology were believed to lead the souls of fallen warriors to the land of the dead; more 'smiling face' figures, animal figurines. Implements used for witchcraft, a known local practice, though not put on for the outsider, are also displayed.

C 30km W of Santiago Tuxtla is **Tres Zapotes**, reached along the main road S to *Isla* and then by a turn l. at *Tres Caminos* (a dirt road impassable during the rains of May–Dec.). It is the third and latest of the great, well-known Olmec ceremonial centres of the Preclassic Period (cf. *Olmecs*, below). It was primarily occupied between c 800 and 200 BC, contemporary with and eventually succeeding La Venta. The site was excavated by Matthew Stirling in 1938, and by Philip Drucker in 1943, and it was here that the first of the colossal stone heads, with which the Olmecs are so readily identified, was found.

Located in the Arroyo Hueyapan, Tres Zapotes is poorly known except for its stone heads and stelae, and no adequate map of it has ever been made. The earliest phase of occupation included Ocós style ceramics, with oxidized, white-rimmed vessels, cord-marking, shell impressions, and iridescent painted slips, as in the earliest phases at La Venta. There were c 50 mounds here, over an area of c 3 sq km, arranged to form plazas on a N–S axis, two colossal basalt heads, and numerous stelae, both carved and uncarved. One platform mound was faced with cut stone, but the slabs were set in place without mortar. *Stela A* was carved with a characteristic Olmec stylized jaguar mask; *Stela D* with three figures, striding, standing, and kneeling, framed in the mouth of an animal mask; and *Stela C*, carved with another jaguar mask, has the second oldest known hieroglyphic date in the New World—31 BC (see also *Chiapa de Corzo*). (Originally only part of Stela C was found, and many of his colleagues doubted Stirling's confident interpretation of the date from the incomplete inscription; but 33 years later, archaeologists discovered the remaining portion and were able to confirm his extrapolation.) Other finds included Olmec jadeite figurines, some carved with hieroglyphics; five different styles of solid, hand-moulded clay figurines; grooved and everted-rim vessels similar to vessels from Izapa; and a basalt box carved with warriors and a decapitation scene. In its final phase of occupation in the Early Classic it began to show influences from Teotihuacán.

Today there is little to see at the site except grass-covered mounds; the colossal heads, along with the stelae and other finds, have been removed to museums. In the town itself a small *Museum* (Mon.–Sat., 9–1, 4–7; Sun., 9–3; fee) displays monuments from the site. There are four small, open wings with artefacts, incl. the colossal head (*Monumento A*), *Stelae A* and *D*, the upper portion of *Stela C*, and other small stone monuments. (The other Tres Zapotes colossal head, more accurately from *Cerro Nestepe*, is in Santiago Tuxtla.)

At *La Mojarra*, on the Río Acula c 48km NW of Tres Zapotes, between it and Cerro de las Mesas, a basalt stele was found in the river in 1986 by Fernando Winfield Capitaine (now in the Museo de Antropología, Jalapa). It is 2.2m high and weighs c four tons. Its carved face depicts the richly dressed figure of a ruler. Above and beside the figure are 21 columns of 465 hieroglyphs, comprising the earliest deciphered writing of the New World. The text includes the Long Count dates of AD 21 May 143 and 13 July 156, and names the warrior-king Harvest Mountain Lord.

159km **San Andrés Tuxtla** (c 80,000 inhab.; 361m; H,R,P), with narrow winding streets and charming early 19C houses, their patios filled with tropical flowers. The region produces the best-quality tobacco in Mexico and the town has no rival as a cigar-manufacturing centre. The parish church also dates from the early 19C.

Visits are permitted at the Sta Clara cigar factory whose visitors may order supplies marked with their initials.

From *Sihuapan*, on Méx. 180 beyond the town, a dirt road runs S to (8km) the *Salto de Eyipantla* (toll at the bridge of Comoapan), a spectacular waterfall.

167km **Matacapan** is a little-explored Classic Period site, contemporary with Teotihuacán at its height, and with Cerro de las Mesas.

There are 60–70 mounds in several groups around plazas. From surface collections and the excavation of one mound have come local ceramics and a wealth of Teotihuacano and Maya ceramics and other artefacts. The mound platform was constructed with typical Teotihuacano style talud-tablero walls, with a slightly E of N axis. The influence from Teotihuacán is so strong that the site is thought by some sources to have been a colony of that city, located to take best advantage of the trade between central Mesoamerica, Cerro de las Mesas, and El Tajín on the Gulf Coast; and with the Maya, particularly with Kaminaljuyú in the Guatemala Highlands, where a Teotihuacano quarter was established in the city.

To the S and E, around Lago de Catemaco, two other sites may also have been Teotihuacano colonies—*Matacanela* and *Piedra Labrada* (on the coast); excavations at both have recovered stone boxes, basins, and stelae in Teotihuacano style.

171km turning l. for (1km NE) **Catemaco** (c 25,000 inhab.; 335m; H,R,P), set on the W shore of the *Laguna de Catemaco* and popular with holidaymakers from the Veracruz area.

The town has a reputation for its witches, or sorcerers (brujos or hechiceros), who claim infallible remedies for certain illnesses, especially lovesickness. Their services are available to visitors.

Slow launches ply to the small islands, ideal bird sanctuaries, which dot the lake, one of which, *Isla de los Changas*, is home to a colony of Thai monkeys, supervised by the university of Veracruz. On another island are the ruins of the city of *Agaltepe*, occupied between c AD 900 and 1000 by 'Historic Olmecs' or, according to some sources, by roving Toltecs en route to Yucatán. The site was described by Franz Boas and Oscar La Farge in 1925 and partially excavated by J. Valenzuela in 1945, but its courts, plazas, and walls are now covered by mounds and much of the stone used in local house-building by the present-day inhabitants.

From Catemaco a poor road runs away from the W shore of the lake and through the sierra to (13km) *Sontecomapan*, on the S shore of a lagoon, in part surrounded by mangrove swamp, amid splendid scenery (Parque Natural Laguna de Catemaco) as the sierra sweeps down to the sea. Beyond *La Palma*, NW of Sontecomapan, we may reach *Jicacal* and *Playa Escondida*, two semi-deserted beaches of fine white sand.

Beyond the Catemaco turning, Méx. 180 runs along the W shore of the lake and then S through a hilly wooded region. It descends to a great plain devoted to sugar-cane cultivation. 212km *Juan Díaz Covarrubias*, a sugar-processing centre. 253km **Acayucan** (30,000 inhab.; 158m; H,R,P), at the junction with Méx. 185, the highway across the isthmus of Tehuantepec, see Rte 85. At 263km a turning r. on a gravel road via (8km) *Texistepec* to (21km) **SAN LORENZO TENOCHTITLAN**, the collective name for three Olmec sites: San Lorenzo itself, Tenochtitlán (not to be confused with the Aztec capital; or Río Chiquito), and Potrero Nuevo. Of the three, San Lorenzo was the oldest and largest, occupied from c 1500 to 800 BC and eventually succeeded in importance in the Olmec world by La Venta. Excavators (incl. Matthew Stirling, its discoverer, in the 1940s, and Michael Coe and Richard Diehl in the 1960s) and scholars have worked out the following phasing for the site's history.

Ojochí Phase (c 1500–1350 BC). No monumental building, but ceramics show traits of the Ocós style, relating the site to the Soconusco region. *Bajío Phase* (c 1350–1250 BC). The first monumental buildings were erected, especially a 50m-high plateau, made by artificially modifying a natural salt dome. The first mounds or platforms were erected on this, but no 'typical' Olmec artefacts were yet produced. *Chicharras Phase* (c 1250–1150 BC). This was the beginning of the truly Olmec site. Olmec figurines of jadeite and serpentine, as well as of clay, were produced in abundance, incl. the first 'baby-face' examples (the earliest 'baby-face' pieces have been found at San Lorenzo Tenochtitlán, and at another lowland site at Tenexpan). There were also the earliest known figurines of ball players, showing that the game had been invented. White-black, differentially-fired pottery was also made, and fine paste 'kaolin' wares, incl. rocker stamping and the application of hematite slips. *San Lorenzo Phase* (c 1150–900 BC). The site reached its greatest size, population, and production. The population of the ceremonial core itself has been estimated at c 1000. Most of its nearly 200 earthern and clay house-mounds were built on the plateau over an area of c 53ha, and arranged around plazas set in lines, with N–S axes (8 degrees W of N). C 60 stone monuments were also erected, and a special drainage system, the first such in the New World, was built of imported basalt, comprising a network of drains between artificial ponds. The drains were covered with basalt slab lids and were up to 200m long, in all employing some 30 tonnes of stone. A population of c 2500 has been estimated for all three sites, and is thought to represent an élite group supported by and commanding the labour services of a much larger hinterland population. At least ten (the tenth was discovered in May 1993 by Ann Cyphers Guillén) colossal basalt and andesite heads, weighing up to 40 tonnes each, were carved and erected; and artefacts from outside regions to the N, W, and S attest to a well-established trade network. *Nacaste Phase* (c 900–700 BC). Disruptive influences, perhaps even occupation of the site by foreigners, caused the smashing or otherwise defacing and burying of the basalt and andesite heads and other monuments. New pottery and figurine types were prominent as well, and the centre of Olmec cultural power had evidently begun to shift to the site of La Venta from about the beginning of this phase. *Palangana Phase* (c 700–400 BC). The Olmec-ness of the site was all but gone. Pottery types, however, still show close relations with the newer Olmec centres at La Venta, Tres Zapotes, and Laguna de los Cerros (see below). The first known ball court in Mesoamerica was built, comprising an earth and clay basin-shaped court, although the game had obviously already been played for generations. Many of the figurines from this phase depict ball players in the gear they were to wear throughout the succeeding centuries, incl. pads and curious yugos worn around the waist. It is thought that Olmec yugos were of wood and leather, as no stone ones have yet been found. By now the centre of Olmec power had truly shifted to the other sites, and San Lorenzo Tenochtitlán was eventually abandoned. *Reoccupation Phase*. Much later, in the Postclassic Period, San Lorenzo was reoccupied, but it never regained its ancient glory.

Río Chiquito and *Potrero Nuevo*, respectively to the NE and E of San Lorenzo Tenochtitlán, were occupied contemporaneously. These were smaller, dependent sites comprising mounds around plazas, and where carved stone heads and other monuments were also erected (now in Museo de Antropología, Jalapa). Their pottery shows close relationship to that at San Lorenzo Tenochtitlán.

Several other excavated sites in S Veracruz show Olmec occupation contemporary with the rise and decline of the major centres. For example, *La Cañada* in the SW Tuxtla mountains, and *Las Limas* (where a seated greenstone figurine was found, with a 'were-jaguar' baby held in its arms and covered with incised glyphs; now in Museo de Antropología, Jalapa).

Today little remains to be seen at San Lorenzo Tenochtitlán. On the large, grass-covered plateau there are traces of the former house-mounds. Most of the finds are in the Museo Nacional de Antropoligía (incl. colossal stone heads nos 2 and 6), and in the Museo de Antropología, Jalapa (incl. colossal heads nos 1, 3, 4, 5, 7, 8, and 9; no 10 was discovered at the site in 1993).

C 20km NW of Acayucan the huge archaeological zone of **Laguna de los Cerros** was discovered in 1978. Excavations and survey by F.J. Bove show that the site was contemporary with San Lorenzo Tenochtitlán and that it was a fourth large Olmec ceremonial centre. It includes a major mound oriented 8° W of N, together with c 95 other earth and clay structures grouped around plazas. Excavations uncovered carved stone drains, carved stone heads, Olmec torso sculptures, and other carved stones, incl. a single huge rectangular stone block (possibly an altar stone), and numerous small figurines (in Museo de Antropología, Jalapa).

274km *Jáltipan*, one of the principal sulphur-producing centres, see below. 289km **Minatitlán** (c 250,000 inhab.; H,R,P), a petrochemicals centre on the l. bank of the Río Coatzacoalcos.

Its huge oil refinery, the first in Mexico, was planted in 1908, one of the first achievements of Weetman Pearson's Compañía Mexicana del Petróleo El Aguila (see Rte 61). It is joined by oil pipeline across the isthmus to Salina Cruz and is hub of an important network of other oil and natural gas pipelines. The yields from the area's vast sulphur deposits are distributed from here.

Just SE of Minatitlán, at the village of *El Manatí*, Olmec artefacts were discovered in 1987 by villagers near an ancient spring. Excavated by Ponciano Ortíz and Carmen Rodríguez, they incl. polished stone axe-heads, rubber balls, human bones, and red and black painted wooden busts, dated c 1000 BC. Apparently the spring was a place of worship and offering.

From Minatitlán Méx. 180 goes NE through an industrial region, and carrying much heavy traffic, to (314km) **Coatzacoalcos** (237,000 inhab.; H,R,P), a hot and ever-growing port, at the mouth of the Río Coatzacoalcos. It is a centre of the oil and sulphur industries; both sulphur and petroleum products, along with other local produce, are shipped, and the oil rigs are serviced, from here.

It was first developed c 1900, at the N end of the railway across the isthmus (see Rte 85), by S. Pearson and Co. A channel was cut through the bar of the river and long stone breakwaters built out from the river mouth, forming a bottleneck. Through it gushed the river torrent, leaving the channel permanently dredged. Wharves and warehouses were built on the shore of the river where once had been a fishing village, nearly opposite the site of the early Spanish settlement of Espíritu Santo, founded in 1552 by Gonzalo de Sandoval, but abandoned as unhealthy by the late 1580s. From the 1940s the region's rich sulphur deposits, known about since the oil exploration of the early 1900s, have been developed. Early pioneers were the brothers Ashton, Lawrence, and William Brady from Louisiana, who had notable luck at *San Cristóbal* (c 56km S). The US companies Pan American and Gulf Sulphur began operations in the 1950s. In 1967 the Mexican government and private interests acquired a majority shareholding in Pan American. Today the sulphur industry is largely in Mexican ownership.

Coatzacoalcos was a major Aztec trading post on the Gulf Coast. Like Xicalango, Cimatán, and Potonchán, it was a kind of 'free-trade zone' and the Aztecs no doubt kept a garrison in the port. In legend Coatzacoalcos was also the departure point for Topiltzin-Quetzalcóatl, the exiled ruler of Tula, on his way to Yucatán (see *Tula* and *Chichén Itzá*).

We leave Coatzacoalcos across a toll bridge (835m long), spanning the river, and continue past *Pajaritos*, a huge petrochemical complex, and then through a damp, hilly, forested area sometimes cleared for banana and sugar cultivation. Beyond (349km; l.) the turning for *Agua Dulce* we cross the Río Tonalá into the State of Tabasco.

23km S *Arroyo Pesquero* (also called *Las Choapas*), a Preclassic Period Olmec site, was a source of life-sized jade masks, magnetite mirrors, and hundreds of serpentine and jade axe-heads.

At 360km a road (l.) runs N to (4km) **La Venta**, the second major Olmec ceremonial centre. In time it overlapped with and succeeded San Lorenzo Tenochtitlán, was overlapped and succeeded by Tres Zapotes, and was partly contemporary with Laguna de los Cerros. The actual site, *Campo de La Venta* (on the grounds of an oilfield) comprises the grass-covered mounds of the ceremonial centre. Three of the four colossal stone heads, along with various altars and other monumental stones, have been removed and re-erected in their correct relationships at the Parque Museo de la Venta. The fourth colossal head is in the Museo Regional, Villahermosa.

Campo de La Venta was occupied c 1000–400 BC. From c 900 BC it succeeded San Lorenzo Tenochtitlán as the most important Olmec centre, along with Laguna de los Cerros. Excavations and studies have been done by Tulane University (1925), Miguel Covarrubias (1942), Matthew Stirling (1948), Philip Drucker, Robert Heizer, and Robert Squier for the University of California (1955), and John Graham and Michael Coe (1960s). Since 1984, new excavations have been conducted by Rebecca González for INAH. Her work has revealed that La Venta, and presumably the other Olmec 'ceremonial' centres, were thriving communities of prosperous farmers, fishers, traders, and artisans as well as places of worship and élites. Evidence of charred cobs shows that corn-planting at La Venta is as old as 2250 BC.

The earliest inhabitants settled on what was originally an island (c 5 sq km) among marshes on the Río Tonalá. There was abundant food, incl. tapirs, armadillos, peccaries, howler monkeys, jaguars, various reptiles, and fishes. On this site they began to erect an immense fluted cone of earth and clay, with ten alternating ridges and ten valleys, according to one interpreter meant to resemble a volcano. It eventually reached a height of c 33m and covered an area of c 100 sq m. There was no ramp, staircase, or other obvious means of ascent, and it is not certain whether there was ever a structure at the summit, or if the 'pyramid' was actually meant to be climbed. N of this, on a N–S axis (precisely 8° W of N) a large flat plaza was laid out, bound on the E and W by long narrow, rectangular mounds. Within the plaza two smaller rectangular mounds were erected centrally, in alignment with the N and S ends. At the far end of the plaza, two square mounds were erected to hold mosaic floors of green serpentine stone, each of between 450 and 500 pieces, depicting stylized jaguar masks. A third mosaic was laid down in front of the fluted cone. All three mosaics were deliberately buried after construction, presumably as a ritual act, one being covered first with 20 jadeite and serpentine axe-heads, put down in the form of a cross with a hematite mirror at the intersection of the arms. One mosaic was actually at the top of a pit c 7m deep and 15.5m by 18.5m.

Colossal head from La Venta

In a later phase, a second plaza area was laid out to the N of the main plaza, again bound E and W by low rectangular mounds, with a low square mound within the plaza, and a square, stepped pyramid at the N end. The second plaza was also 'fenced' with 2m-long basalt columns, set into adobe brick bases. In the stepped pyramid were buried a tomb and a sarcophagus, with two youths, wrapped individually, and covered with vermilion paint. There were figurine offerings, beads, a jadeite sting-ray spine, and other jadeite objects. Altogether, at least four colossal stone heads, along with numerous stelae and altars, were also erected around and among the mounds of the plazas. Other rectangular mounds and square platforms forming open plazas, but not so formally organized as the original two, were also built to the S.

A supporting population of perhaps 18,000 was needed to erect these monuments and mounds. In the excavations objects of finely polished jadeite, magnetite and ilmenite concave mirrors, and ceramics with rocker stamping, cord marking, shell impressions, and iridescent painted slips were found in abundance. Perhaps the most spectacular find was the famous ceremonial group found in situ (now in the Museo Nacional de Antropología): 6 axe-heads of c 15cm each, erected in a crescent around 16 jadeite, serpentine, and granite figurines, of similar size. The celts are thought to represent a basalt-fenced plaza and the figurines were so arranged as to include onlookers, participants, and principal worshippers.

After abandonment La Venta was succeeded by Tres Zapotes. As at San Lorenzo, abandonment was accompanied by the deliberate defacement and burial of the monuments and altars.

At c 397km Méx. 180 begins to pass the region of the PLAN DE LA CHONTALPA (c 1000 sq km), where marshland has been reclaimed for agriculture and scattered peoples settled on ejidos. 435km **Cárdenas** (c 6500 inhab.; 25m; H,R,P), chief place of the Chontalpa region and headquarters of the Comisión del Río Grijalva, set up in 1951 to promote regional economic development in the Grijalva basin—50,000 sq km in Tabasco, Chiapas, and Oaxaca.

Cimatán, c 2km SE of Cárdenas, was a Postclassic Maya centre for trade across the Isthmus of Tehuantepec (cf. *Tlatelolco*). As were Coatzacoalcos, Potonchán, and Xicalango it was controlled by the Aztecs when the Spaniards arrived.

From Cárdenas a road goes S, never far from the Río Grijalva and through typically lush rain forest, via (21km) *Huimanguillo* to (118km) **Presa Nezahualcóyotl** (*Presa del Mal Paso*) in the State of Chiapas, the second largest dam in Mexico, built in 1960–64 to harness the abundant waters of the Mezcalapa–Grijalva river systems. Flooding took place in 1966. Its capacity is some 13,000 million cubic m, its area c 300 sq km, and it now irrigates 350,000 hectares of rich soil, once regularly devastated by floods.

Méx. 187 runs N of Cárdenas to (40km) **Comalcalco** ('in the earthenware griddle house'; 13,000 inhab.; H,R,P), the westernmost Classic Maya site, in the heartland of the Chontal (or Puuc Maya) region.

Explored by Désiré Charnay in 1880, but otherwise unknown until the first excavations by Franz Blom and Oliver La Farge in 1925; further excavated by Gordon Ekholm in 1956 and 1960; and by Román Piña Chan in the 1970s.

Comalcalco is on the fringe of influence of any Classic Maya regional capital, such as Palenque to the SE, and this may explain the absence of dated inscriptions and Maya polychrome pottery, although the architecture and sculpture resemble that at Palenque. It may have been 'capital' of the Chontalpa frontier region, exchanging cultural features with its Gulf Coast and Mexican neighbours; in Maya legend it was the city of the Maya prince Tabscoob (whence Tabasco). Comalcalco is also rare for the use of kiln-fired bricks (found elsewhere in Mesoamerica only at Santa Rita Corozal [Belize], Zacualpa [Guatemala], Tizatlán, and Tula). The bricks are 19cm x 25cm x 24cm and are cemented with a burnt and crushed oyster-shell-and-lime mortar, often covering an adobe wall and themselves covered over with stucco.

Comalcalco has two groups of structures S and NW of the car park. The NW group is earlier. Two long mounds form the N and S sides of a plaza. On the W side is a pyramid with central stairway leading to *Templo I*, with some stucco figures at the l. base of the steps. *Templo II* is on a smaller platform just NE.

The S group is a much larger platform complex. At the first level, on its NE corner, are *Templos VI* and *VII*, each with central staircases and brick temples atop stepped platforms. *Templo VI* has a superb stucco mask at the base of the steps, and *Templo VII* has stucco decorations of seated people, serpent heads, and other motifs on both its N and S faces. *Templo VIII* is a ruined mound.

The highest, *Acrópolis*, level includes the *Palacio*, of two long brick-built corridors with rooms, *Templos IV* and *V* (both being restored), and a restored *Tumba*. Inside the tomb the three walls each have three bas-relief figures, possibly the Nine Lords of the Underworld. They were painted red when excavated but no trace now remains. The tomb also contained many squared and drilled clam shells and presumably once housed a sarcophagus.

59km **Paraíso** (7000 inhab.; H,R,P) on the Río Seco, with a small Maya site and within reach of the finest beaches on the Tabasco coast. The road NE runs to (7km) *Puerto Ceiba* and (11km) *El Bellote*, where Maya burials were excavated and whence a barge crosses the mouth of the Laguna de Coapa to *Playa Bruja* and (19km) *Chiltepec*, at the mouth of the Río de González.

The road N of Paraíso goes to (6km) *El Limón*. Another road (NW) to (6km) *El Paraíso* beach, amid palm groves, and the adjoining *Playa Azul*, best of the beaches. From the turning to El Paraíso beach a road runs W, skirting the seashore and passing various attractive resorts: (3km; l.) the *Laguna de las Flores*, (6km) *La Unión*, (11km) *Nuevo Paraíso*, and (18km) *Tupilco*, a fishing village on the Laguna de Cocal. At *Ahualulco*, SW along the coast, was another Maya site.

From Cárdenas, Méx. 180 begins to cross swampy land, profusely watered by the Río Grijalva, where bananas grow in abundance. At 446km we reach the Samaria oilfield.

485km **VILLAHERMOSA** (c 460,000 inhab.), capital of the State of Tabasco and seat of a university, in the centre of the plain of Tabasco and surrounded by rivers, is a city which has grown with explosive force on the crest of the oil boom; hot, crowded, with forbidding outskirts, and showing all the signs of its dependence on that industry. The city and State authorities, however, intent on attracting visitors other than business people and oil workers, have done much to improve the centre and have embarked on new civic and cultural precincts. A stay in Villahermosa is mandatory for all serious students of the Olmec and Maya civilizations, for the city boasts two excellent archaeological museums.

Airport. 15km SE. Daily flights to *Cancún, Mérida, Mexico City, Oaxaca*, and *Tuxtla Gutiérrez*.

Bus stations. 1st Class. 297 C. Mina (corner with Av. Lino Merino) in NE part of the city. Services to *Mexico City* (14 hrs); to *Campeche* (7 hrs); to *Mérida* (10 hrs); to *Puebla* (10 hrs); to *Veracruz* (8 hrs); to *Tenosique* (4 hrs); to *San Andrés Tuxtla* (6 hrs); to *Puerto Ceiba* (3 hrs); to *Paraíso* (2½ hrs); to *Palenque* (2½ hrs); etc.

2nd Class. Blvd Grijalva, N of 1st Class station. Services to nearby towns and to *Mexico City*; to *San Cristóbal de las Casas*; etc.

Hotels throughout the city.

Post Office. Corner of Cs Sáenz and Lerdo de Tejada.

Tourist Office. 1504 Paseo Tabasco.

The city had its beginnings in the villa of Sta María de la Victoria, on the coast at the river mouth, established in 1525 on the site of the Chontal ceremonial centre of Potonchén. By 1602, harassed by pirates (especially by an attack in 1597), most of the inhabitants had moved upriver to San Juan Bautista Villahermosa. In 1660 Villahermosa was raided by English pirates and most of the inhabitants moved S to Tacotalpa. By the mid-18C, San Juan Bautista had regained importance as a Spanish-mulatto community. It was officially designated Villahermosa in 1916. Transformation from an isolated, uncomfortable, unhealthy, and backward town (population c 12,000 in 1920) to present raucous modernity has been marked since the 1950s.

The tropical State of **Tabasco** (1.6 million inhab.; 25,267 sq km) mainly comprises the fluvial plain formed by three great rivers and their many distributaries: the Río Mezcalapa in the W; the Río Grijalva in the centre; and the Río Usumacinta in the E. The Mezcalapa (navigable for c 280km) joins the Grijalva (navigable for c 100km) c 4km NE of Villahermosa and then runs N to join the Usumacinta c 16km from the wide estuary beyond Frontera. The Usumacinta, originating in Guatemala, is c 800km long and is navigable for c 500km. Tabasco

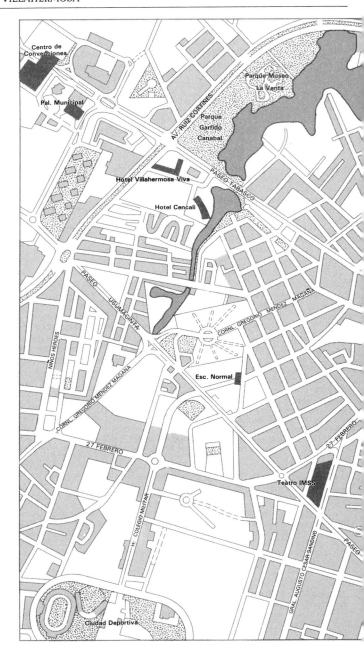

VILLAHERMOSA

0 metres   500

AV. RUIZ CORTINES

JOSÉ PAGES LLERGO

Central Camionera

Hotel Maya Tabasco

Central ADO

Hospital Pemex

Parque Cuauhtémoc

CORNL. GREGORIO MÉNDEZ MAGAÑA

Parque La Paz

PASEO FRANCISCO JAVIER MINA

FRANCISCO-MADERO

JOSE-MARIA-PINO-SUAREZ

Quinta Grijalva

Parque Manuel Mestre

GRAL. IGNACIO ZARAGOZA

Parque Juárez

IGUALA

Correos y Telégrafos

LERDO

JUAREZ

Catedral

Parque Morelos

27 FEBRERO

Casa de la Cultura

REFORMA

Teléfonos

Hotel Miraflores

Parque Hidalgo

PASEO TABASCO

Parque Guerrero

Pal. de Gobierno

MADRAZO

Tribunal Superior de Justicia

Pal. Legislativo

ALLENDE

PL. DE ARMAS

CARLOS A.

La Conchita

ARISTA

PASEO MALECON

GAVIOTAS

Monumento a la Bandera

MARIANO

LAS

PASEO

DE

LA

SIERRA

CENTENARIO INSTITUTO JUAREZ

Museo Histórico

MALECON

Fac. de Derecho

Jardín del Arte

LAS

Ciudad Deportiva Las Gaviotas

Casa del Arte

Teatro Esperanza Iris

CICOM

N

ESPERANZA IRIS

Museo Arqueológico

MALECON

LAS

GAVIOTAS

USUMACINTA

is by far the wettest State in the republic, largely covered by lagoons, watercourses, and swamps, and immense rain forests. During the winter rains (averaging 1500–2000mm near the coast; 4500mm inland) flooding is regular, though the recent building of huge dams in Chiapas aims to control its effects. The S tip of territory touches the N slopes of the N Chiapas highland. Intense exploitation of oil and natural gas has revolutionized the State economy. Fine woods and dyewoods, although not exploited on a regular basis, are the chief wealth of the forests, while fertile soils yield quantities of cacao (highest production in Mexico), copra, sugar cane, bananas, coffee, rice, and tropical fruits.

Juan de Grijalva's expedition of 1518 came inland by the river later named after him. In 1519, Cortés defeated an Indian force at Centla, not far from the river mouth. In 1524–25 he forced his way through the swamps of Tabasco with an army of 3000 Spaniards and Mexicans on his expedition to the coast of Honduras. Francisco de Montejo the elder conquered most of the region in 1529–30. He secured a crown appointment as governor of Tabasco, Yucatán, and the Caribbean coast as far as Honduras. Montejo rule lasted until 1549, after which the audiencia of Guatemala claimed jurisdiction over Tabasco and Yucatán. In 1561 news of a royal decree that both territories should be subject to Mexico City reached Tabasco; and in 1583 the first royal appointment as governor and chief magistrate arrived there. Difficulties of communication and pirate activity along the coast helped ensure Tabasco's isolation and de facto independence from Yucatán. The Spaniards could not penetrate beyond the edge of the jungle and their position was made even more perilous in the later 16C and 17C by English pirates and dyewood traders who established a base on the shores of Laguna de Términos to the E and dominated the Tabasco coast from the 1650s until their expulsion in 1717. In 1824 Tabasco achieved Statehood, yet in 1841–46 maintained independence from central government, and in 1864–67 remained outside the reach of the empire. During 1885–1910 it vegetated under Abraham Bandala, who established complete ascendancy as military chief, cacique, and governor. There followed years of unrest and political violence, unleashed by the Revolution. During 1922–34 the State was under the control of Tomás Garrido Canabal, who pioneered an idiosyncratic form of socialism and carried religious persecution to extremes. In face of fresh unrest, the federal government was forced to intervene in 1935. Since the 1950s oil wealth has brought rescue from isolation, modernization, and the building of an economic infrastructure.

The old city centre, hugging the l. bank of the Río Grijalva, has undergone considerable improvement: its narrow streets repaved, closed to motor traffic, and turned into a pedestrian precinct. On the N side of PL. DE ARMAS is the *Pal. de Gobierno*, handsomely eclectic in style, dating from the 1870s. From its N side Av. 27 de Febrero goes W to the cathedral of *El Señor de Tabasco*, founded in 1614, but much altered since then. Going E from the plaza along Av. 27 de Febrero we come, at the corner with C. Juárez, to the so-called *Casa de los Azulejos*, another fine late 19C building. It contains the *Museo de Historia*, illustrating the city's modern history.

S of the centre (c 1km), between Av. Melchor Ocampo and the Río Grijalva, is **CICOM** (*Centro de Investigación de las Culturas Olmecas y Maya*), a modern cultural complex, incl. museums, a theatre (the *Teatro Esperanza Iris* seats 1200), research centre, garden of art, crafts and book shops, etc., developed since 1980. Its principal attraction is the **Museo Regional Carlos Pellicer** (9–8; fee).

The GROUND FLOOR contains a large display area for 'monumental' artefacts. At the entrance, pride of place is given to the colossal basalt head of a wryly smiling youth, wearing a helmet or close-fitting cap (?leather) and large round earrings (dated Late Preclassic, no. 2 from La Venta; 4 tonnes). The other displays include similar, and many smaller, sculptures. Highlights include: seated figure from La Venta with a grinning feline face, looking up with his head tilted back and his arms curved before him over one crossed leg; numerous carved stone slabs covered with hieroglyphic inscriptions and richly dressed figures from Classic Maya sites—Tortuguero, Macuspana, Balancán, and others; and the Classic Period stele from Balancán depicting a richly dressed, quetzal-feather beplumed figure grasping the hair of an opponent with his l. hand, while his r. hand is raised ready to strike.

The MEZZANINE displays are devoted to no fixed period, but have some of the most exquisite pieces, arranged in cases and pedestals around a central platform with more items. Included are: figurines from Jaina; intricately carved ceremonial axe-heads from La Venta, with characteristic 'baby-face' pouting lips; large figures of sculpted clay Maya priests, wearing an abundance of jewellery and magnificent feather headdresses; more austere, wide-shouldered, and bubble-headed Olmec figurines from La Venta; flamboyant Maya urns with busy decorations surrounding seated figures; Maya polychrome vessels; fragments of stucco glyphs from Palenque; and intricate, relief-decorated vessels for ceremonial use (eg, tall reddish-orange vase with a flared base; and fat, deep pot in the shape of a snail shell).

The chronological displays begin on the SECOND FLOOR. There are semi-divided display units around the centre of the building, beginning to the r. of the lift. The first area contains panels, maps, and chronological charts introducing the archaeology of the New World: migratory routes across the Bering Strait and the possibility of Pacific routes; the Mesoamerican culture area and its divisions; and the culture and development of the first hunter-gatherer groups. The other rooms concentrate on different cultures and time-periods. *Preclassic culture* of the Central Plateau (especially Tlatilco). *Classic Teotihuacán:* pottery, figurines, body-painting stamps, and clay, stone, and alabaster masks. *Zapotec Oaxaca:* Grey Ware ceramics from *Monte Albán Phases I* and *II*, figurines, and elaborate urns (eg, huge seated Cocijo—Rain god—with top-heavy headdress, mask, and pectoral). *Totonac Central Gulf Coast:* mostly a collection from Tenexpan, acquired with funds raised by the State of Tabasco and from don Adolfo Ruiz Cortines. Highlights include caras sonrientes (smiling faces) figurines; diorama showing 12C Totonac thatched hut with figurines eating, drinking, and swinging; female torso with bare breasts and an elaborate shell and (?)bone necklace; hollow clay figure of a seated, mutilated figure; and stone palma, used in the ball game ritual, carved with a bat-winged deity and, on the back, warrior figure holding severed head. *W Mexico:* Ceramics and large hollow, glossy red clay figurines from the shaft-tombs and sites of Sinaloa, Nayarit, Colima, Jalisco, Michoacán, Guanajuato, and Guerrero. *Tarascan* and *Mexica Aztec* Postclassic materials.

The FIRST FLOOR, comprising ten semi-divided rooms, concentrates on the S Gulf Coast and the rise of Olmec culture; and on the Classic and Postclassic Maya. Proceeding r. from the lift, a seated basalt Olmec figure 'smiles', slit-eyed. Information panels and a map show principal Olmec sites and areas of influence; cases contain polished ceremonial axe-heads, Olmec ceramics, and small sculpted heads. Further displays include manos and matates for grinding maize; jade and other stone jewellery. A map of Tabasco shows its regions and the important archaeological sites. The Maya displays begin with information panels, maps, and chronological charts, showing the Highland and Lowland Maya regions and the principal sites. An accompanying figure is in a contorted position, and made of a cement-like material with shell eyes. Cases contain a collection of clay figurine-whistles from Jaina, Campeche, and Jonuta. Ceramics incl. Classic Maya polychromes; elaborate clay urns built up with applied decorations; delicately sculpted faces showing cranial deformation; terracotta urn depicting the 'Long-nosed god', Bolan Dz'acab (God K), wearing elaborate waist band, stiff breastplate, arm-guards, bulky necklace, and fancy hat. Among the leaves around him animals can be seen gripped in human arms. Display of some of the fired bricks from Temple 1 at the site of Comalcalco, one of the two or three sites in Mexico with fired bricks. One depicts a crocodile on its surface, its skin made by applying overlaid bits of clay; another depicts a dead dancer wearing a loincloth; and others depict dancers and other, richly dressed, figures.

On the NW side of the city, in Blvd Adolfo Ruiz Cortines, NE of the junction of Paseo Tabasco and Blvd Grijalva, is the **Parque Museo de La Venta** (8–5; fee), beautifully set on the shores of the *Laguna de las Ilusiones.*

Paths lead to 27 Olmec monuments moved from La Venta and re-erected. The park was designed by Carlos Pellicer; the pieces were transported and erected by Pemex and the Ministry of Hydraulic Resources.

The Olmecs were responsible for the first great ceremonial centres in the S Gulf Coast region, and for the beginnings of many classic Mesoamerican culture-traits. Caution must be taken, however, not to cast them in the role of a 'mother civilization' for all Mesoamerica. Although their developments were prescient, they were paralleled chronologically with developments in both the Central and Southern Highlands. In the Middle Preclassic Period, into the Early Classic (c 1500 BC–AD 300), they established several chronologically overlapping, but successively important, centres: San Lorenzo Tenochtitlán in Veracruz (c 1500–800 BC); La Venta in Tabasco and Laguna de los Cerros in Veracruz (c 1000–400 BC); Tres Zapotes and the smaller sites of Potrero Nuevo and Río Chiquito, and El Trapiche near Cempoala, all in Veracruz.

The name Olmec, in Náhuatl, means 'rubber people' or 'land of rubber', and several arguments have been put forward to explain their origins. Some argue that the Olmecs were intrusive to the S Gulf region, having migrated from the Guerrero highlands; others claim they migrated from the Oaxaca highlands; and still others argue that they were an indigenous development in the Tuxtla mountains, and that their earliest traces lie yet to be discovered beneath the deep layers of volcanic deposits there. The argument is by no means settled.

More conclusively, the Olmecs were the first to spread a unifying influence over a large area of Mesoamerica, in the central and S Gulf region, with visible influence in the Basin of Mexico, to the W into Oaxaca, Guerrero, and Chiapas, and as far S as El Salvador. Just how politically unified their influence was is open to question. Their influence does, however, dramatically demonstrate the development of Mesoamerican long-distance trade, in both artefacts and ideas. Olmec style figurines and ceramics, and artistic influences on indigenous artefacts, are found at contemporary sites and as artistic inspiration in later cultures, incl. the Maya, Mixtec, Zapotec, and even Aztec. They may have been the first to spread a writing and calendrical system, even if the initial development of these systems was actually outside the S Gulf region. The second oldest known dated stele is 31 BC at Tres Zapotes. Many of the deities in Maya and central Mexican pantheons were originally Olmec. They were the first to use the classic Mesoamerican plaza-plan on a large scale, grouping pyramids and platform-mounds around open plazas orientated on a N–S axis; and were the first to build a ball court.

Their artistic style was distinctive. Notable are their colossal stone heads, possibly portraits of their rulers, carved on huge basalt blocks, brought from quarry sites over 100km away. These are, however, restricted to the central Gulf Coast sites, with the single exception of Abaj Takalik in the Guatemalan Highlands, possibly indicating an Olmec antecedent in that region. Smaller sculptures were done in jadeite and serpentine, and highly polished. Characteristic features were the combination of human and feline traits, the plump, 'babyface' image, with turned-down, pouting lips, snarling mouths, toothless gums, and general obesity, all done in naturalistc curves rather than as geometric abstractions. Long-distance trade is evident in the distribution of figurines, and in the rock paintings and carvings attributed to Olmec traders (or at least to Olmec influence) found at Oxtotitlán, Juxtlahuaca, and Teopantecuantitlán in Guerrero, and at Chalcatzingo, Las Bocas, and Gualupita in Morelos. Tlatilco, in the Basin of Mexico, may also have witnessed Olmec presence, and sculptures at Monte Albán, Dainzú, and numerous Maya sites show Olmec influence. Olmec figurines have been found as far afield as El Opeño in Michoacán, and in El Salvador.

I. First monument (l.), 'altar' stone of 30 tonnes, carved with the figure of a monkey on the top. II. Farther along (r.), stone sculpture depicting a monkey gazing at the sky. III. (r.) Small stone basalt sculpture representing a jaguar. IV. Opposite (l.), stone fish sculpture of serpentine. The path then goes l., l. again, then r. to V. Second 'altar' stone, with bas-relief carvings of a figure seated in a niche with a jaguar head above and serpent motifs flanking. The path then leads r., to VI. Reconstructed 'jade' mosaic of a jaguar mask, highly stylized, composed of 498 slabs of blue-green serpentine. VII. (r.) Stele (20 tonnes) carved with a ruler-figure, in elaborate headdress and holding a sceptre; warriors stand on either side. The path then turns l. We continue straight on, passing the T-junction, to the end of a short diversion to VIII. Colossal head of basalt (20 tonnes). He wears a helmet and earplugs, and possibly represents an actual portrait of a ruler. (This head and two others—nos 1, 3 and 4 from La Venta—are originals; a fourth is a *copy* of head no. 2.)

Back to the main path, we turn r. onto it, and on the l. (just before the path veers r.) is (IX) another carved stele, depicting a bearded figure embracing a monster. Farther along (r.) is (X) another carved 'altar' stone (badly preserved) with a figure cradling a child, in a niche. A little farther along are (XI–XIII) a stele of serpentine carved with hieroglyphic signs and numerals, and opposite it an 'altar', partly destroyed, with various figures, in particular a seated, cross-legged figure next to a standing one, and on the l. side two gesticulating figures. Beside XII is an unfinished stone sculpture. The path then turns l. Farther along (r.) is (XIV) another stele carved with a (?)goddess figure, probably the oldest from La Venta. Still farther, after the path turns l. again, are (XV–XVI) serpentine 'throne' (with some inscriptions still visible) and the stone figure of an offering-bearer. XVII. Next (l.), another stele, depicting a bearded man. His features are unlike the general characteristics of other La Venta sculptures, and he may, if the supposition is true that the sculptures represent portraits, depict a stranger from outside. We continue straight on to XVIII. A circular stone monument with a bas-relief of a man walking and holding a small flag-like object in his l. hand. A 'footprint' behind him signifies a journey, and three glyphs are carved in front of him, possibly identifying him.

We return to the main path and continue l. to XIX (r.) A second reconstructed, very stylized, 'jade' jaguar mask mosaic. XX. Next (l.) is a structure of stone rods, possibly imitating a cage or perhaps the basalt fence around the N plaza of the site where Matthew Stirling excavated the cache of buried jadeite figures. XXI. A few m r. is another colossal basalt head, the largest from the site. XXII–XXIII. A branching path leads l. to a third colossal head, a *copy* of one in the Museo Carlos Pellicer, and a second carved head representing an old man.

Back to the main path, we turn l., and after the path veers l., on the l. is (XXIV) a stone 'altar', the smallest, and possibly oldest, from the site. The path then turns l., and farther on (l.) is (XXV) another unfinished colossal basalt head, with inscriptions similar to those on the other heads. Next on the l. (after the path has veered l., then turned l., then r.) is (XXVI) a heavily carved stone monument. In high relief in a niche is a female figure (a goddess?) holding a child, with bas-reliefs on the sides, of male and female figures holding children with jaguar masks. The mutilations of the piece were done in antiquity when the site was abandoned and the sculpture was buried. Just before circling back onto the entrance path (l.; XXVII) is a stone 'altar' carved in bas-relief with owls' heads and a bearded figure. Other figures stand to the l. and r., and one is between the owls' heads. The flanking figures appear to point at a glyph which is partly destroyed. A claw, two human legs, and parts of other figures can also be seen.

Paseo Tabasco joins the old city centre with **Tabasco Dos Mil** (Tabasco 2000), beyond the junction with Blvd Grijalva. It is a vast modern city within the city, incl. a new Pal. Municipal, convention centres, planetarium, fountains, and parks.

On the NE side of the city Av. Universidad passes (l.) the buildings of the *Universidad Benito Juárez*, refounded in 1958. Farther on a l. turn at the Morelos monument runs N to cross the Río Carrizal. From (25km) *Nacajuca*, we may reach various Chontal Indian villages, some with picturesque churches. 32km *Jalpa de Méndez* (8000 inhab.; 42m; H,R,P), another Chontal centre, famous for its beautifully worked jícaras (gourds). From (34km) *Amatitán* a road goes SW to (c 16km) *Cunduacán*, with its quaint painted buildings and famous for the music accompanied by Maya drummers. From Amatitán the road runs N to (43km) *Cupilco*, where the church of Guadalupe has a startlingly coloured façade, incorporating lively stucco scenes of the Guadalupe story. 52km *Comalcalco*, see above.

FROM VILLAHERMOSA TO TUXTLA GUTIERREZ, Méx. 195 and Méx. 190, 288km. The road runs S across the plain to (53km) **Teapa** (11,000 inhab.; 74m; H,R,P), a hot but pleasant town with a fine, large central plaza. Its old church, of which the façade remains, was dynamited during the time of governor Garrido Canabal. 5km NE are the *Grutas de Coconá* (guided visits, with son et lumière sometimes included, Tues.–Sun., 10–5), several km deep, artificially lit. 33km SE is *Tapijulapa*, another picturesque town where the Ríos Amatán and Oxolotán meet to flow into the Río Tacotalpa. C 16km S of Tapijulapa is *Oxolotán*, where the ruins of a 17C Dominican convent are being reclaimed by jungle.

From Teapa, Méx. 195 runs W into the State of Chiapas and to (76km) *Pichucalco* on the Río Blanquillo.

Hence Méx. 195 begins a spectacular, tortuous climb through the N slopes of the N Chiapas highland amid pine forests to (88km) *Ixtacomitán*, where the church has some 16C remains; thence to (136km) *Tapilula* and (144km) *Rayón de Mexcalapa*, with ruined 17C churches, dating from Dominican activity in Tecpatán (see Rte 86), and good highland views.

C 15km SW of Rayón, and difficult of access, is *Tapalapa*, with remains of the 16C Dominican church of San Agustín, in massive style, with a traceried rose window.

167km *Pueblo Nuevo Solistahuacán*, with another 16C (?) church ruin. From (197km) *Puerto Café* a poor road runs NE to (33km) *Simojovel de Allende*, known for its amber. From Puerto Café, Méx. 195 bears sharply W to (207km) *Bochil* and then S to (229km) *Soyaló*, with a ruined 17C church, and (244km) *Ixtapa*. On the W side of the plaza, marked by a venerable ceiba tree, the little parish church retains its rudimentary late 16C appearance, though rebuilt in the 18C. From (254km) the turning l. to (51km E) *San Cristóbal de las Casas* we continue SW to (288km) *Tuxtla Gutiérrez*, see Rte 86.

84 Veracruz to Oaxaca

Méx. 180, Méx. 175, Méx. 190, 431km.—85km junction with Méx. 175.—97km Tlacotalpan.—142km Cosamaloapan.—206km Tuxtepec.—365km Ixtlán de Juárez.—431km **Oaxaca**.

From Veracruz to 85km, see Rte 83. From here Méx. 175 turns S through the marshy region traversed by the Río Papaloapan and its tributaries. 97km **Tlacotalpan** (c 12,000 inhab.; 14m; H,R,P), a charming little town, famed for the beauty of its women. Its narrow streets are lined with pastel-shaded one-storey houses fronted by portals; their patios are filled with flowers. The central PL. CIVICA, full of palm trees and exotic flowers, is bordered by the amply arcaded *Pal. Municipal* and two ornate churches, all built in the 19C.

Of considerable interest is the local museum, *Museo Salvador Ferrando*.

The painter Salvador Ferrando (1830–1908), b. in Tlacotalpan, lived in Italy in 1848–70, where he studied at the Accademia di San Luca in Rome and in 1856 married an English wife, Henrietta Lewes. He returned to Mexico in 1871 and set up as a fashionable painter in Mexico City. He settled in his native town in 1884.

ROOM 1 consists mainly of portraits of local notables painted after 1884. Especially good are those showing ladies dressed in jarocho costume. R2. 19C local furniture. R3. More furniture, and ceramics. R4. Exhibitions of local crafts. A further area is devoted to Olmec, Totonac, and Aztec sculptures and ceramics, and some local ethnic musical instruments and costumes.

The road runs through the basin of the Río Papaloapan, a lush tropical landscape, which includes coconut, sugar-cane, and banana plantations, to (142km) **Cosamaloapan** (c 32,000 inhab.; 65m; H,R,P), a centre of the sugar industry and for fruit distribution. A hurricane in Sept. 1944, which mercilessly battered the Papaloapan basin, brought torrential rain which caused the river to overflow and covered the town to a depth of 3m.

191km *Ciudad Alemán*, planned in 1947 as a model city (a project never brought to fruition, partly because of the intense heat) by the Comisión del Papaloapan (see below).

Hence Méx. 145 runs NW via (43km) *Tierra Blanca* to (79km) *La Tinaja* on the Córdoba–Veracruz road, see Rte 71A. From *La Granja*, 28km along this road from Ciudad Alemán, a road turns off into the State of Oaxaca for (23km SW) *Temascal*, with a hydroelectric plant on the E shore of **Presa Miguel Alemán**, built during 1947–55 by the Comisión del Papaloapan—created in 1947 to organize land reclamation, flood control, and irrigation in those regions of Oaxaca, Veracruz, and Puebla affected by the floods of 1944, and occupied in the main by Mazateca Indians. The dam (880 sq km), full of islands, has a capacity of 8000 million cubic m.

At **Nopiloa**, c 18km NE of Tierra Blanca, excavations have uncovered a small ceremonial site of c AD 500–900, which seems to have been dominant in the S Gulf Coast while El Tajín dominated the N. It was a small town, with little civic architecture, but famous for a style of 'smiling face' figurines distinct from those of Remojadas. These were primarily whistles and rattles with Maya-like faces, similar to the figurines from Jaina and Jonuta.

Excavations at the nearby mound of *El Zapotal* revealed a clay shrine with a macabre death-god model of unbaked clay, representing Mictlantecuhtli (Lord of the Underworld). Burials were also found, guarded by groups of 'smiling face' figurines brandishing knives— perhaps demanding an altered interpretation of the figures' grimaces. One burial comprised a deep pit into which were stacked 80 skulls, to a height of c 3m. It is uncertain whether these represent burials following normal deaths, or the burial of sacrificed victims. Late Teotihuacano pottery was associated, thus dating the burials to the 6–9C AD.

Beyond Ciudad Alemán, at 185km, the road forks. 7km to the l., beyond a toll bridge, Méx. 145, well engineered and surfaced, runs across a richly fertile plain, in parts intensively cultivated, to (125km) *Sayula*, 9km S of Acayucan on Méx. 185 across the isthmus, see Rte 83.

We keep to the r. on Méx. 172 and enter the State of Oaxaca to (206km) **Tuxtepec** where on 1 Jan. 1876 the supporters of Porfirio Díaz published the Plan of Tuxtepec against the continued rule of Pres. Lerdo de Tejada.

Tuxtepec was the site of Postclassic Period *Tochtepec* ('bunny hill'), and was at the end of the first league of an established trade route used by the Aztec pochteca merchants concerned with long-distance trade from Tlatelolco–Tenochtitlán. At Tochtepec the caravan would split, some heading E for the canoe trade of the Yucatán coast, while others headed S for the Tehuantepec and Soconusco trade of the Pacific Coast. An annual tribute was paid to the Aztecs, incl. quotas of rubber, quetzal and parrot feathers, cacao, gold, and crystal jewellery.

From here a minor road goes SW to (36km) *San Lucas Ojitlán*, a Chinanteco town. At 51km a turning r. leads to (10km N) *San Pedro Ixcatlán*, on the S shore of Presa Miguel Alemán (boat hire, fishing).

Beyond Tuxtepec, Méx. 175 crosses a toll bridge. At 215km Méx. 147 (l.) runs SE to (174km) *Palomares* on Méx. 185, see Rte 85. Méx. 175 reaches the foothills of the Sierra de Juárez following the valley of the Río Valle Nacional. 254km *Valle Nacional*, centre of an area made notorious by the US writer John Kenneth Turner whose book 'Barbarous Mexico', published in 1910, exposed the dreadful conditions endured by the tobacco workers under the porfiriato.

The site of *Monte Flor* here was a minor Mixtec town in the Late Postclassic. More generally, this region of N central Oaxaca, known prehistorically as *Chinautla*, showed early Olmec influences, then Maya influence, and finally Mixtec dominance in the 14–15C.

The road climbs through the sierra. Beyond (324km) *Machín* it descends into thickly forested country. 365km **Ixtlán de Juárez** (c 5000 inhab.; 1700m; P), centre of a region producing beans, chickpeas, sweet potatoes, fruits, and coffee and with gold, silver, zinc, and lead deposits. The rosy stone façade of the parish church of *Sto Tomás* (mid-18C) is a lovely, though belated, example of oaxaqueño baroque, incorporating both baluster and solomonic columns. In the centre of the middle storey, an exaggeratedly deep eared frame contains, in high relief, the Incredulity of St Thomas, a superb work, dated 1757, though showing characteristics of an earlier period. Note the human head and filigree-style relief in the panels of the wooden door. The interior has preserved its treasures untouched: 11 superb baroque altarpieces and other furniture in finest woods. In the baptistery, the font at which Benito Juárez was baptized in March 1806.

8km SE, at **Calpulalpan de Méndez** (1300 inhab.; 1980m; R), among conifers in the Sierra de Melacate, the 18C church of *San Mateo* (restored) preserves a wealth of contemporary altarpieces: the four-storey high altarpiece like a folding screen, baroque, with solomonic columns; side altarpieces with singular churrigueresque elements and alive with rocaille relief and angel caryatids, some jauntily posed, interspersed among the estípites—all beneath an original beamed ceiling.

370km **Guelatao de Juárez** (c 700 inhab.; 1885m; P), birthplace on 21 March 1806 of Benito Juárez, son of the Zapotec Indians Marcelino Juárez and Brígida García. It is now more a place of pilgrimage than a lived-in village. The small

Museo Benito Juárez (Tues.–Sun., 8–1, 3–5; fee) is mostly a photographic record of his life. The *Pal. Municipal* also serves as a shrine.

Méx. 175 continues its winding course. At 392km a road r. winds to (5km NW) *Ixtepeji*, with its lovely church of Sta Catarina (late 16C–17C). At 404km we go through the pass of *La Cumbre* (2591m), the entry into the valley of Oaxaca. 431km *Oaxaca*, see Rte 75.

85 Oaxaca to Tehuantepec

Méx. 190, 267km.—126km turning for (8km E) Nejapa.—201km Magdalena Tequisistlán.—221km Jalapa del Marqués.—236km (for [8km N] Guiengola.—249km **Sto Domingo Tehuantepec**.—267km Salina Cruz.

Oaxaca to (42km) turning l. for *Mitla* and *Tamazulapan Mixe*, see Rte 77. We keep r. on Méx. 190, through the Valle de Tlacolula. 49km *Santiago Matatlán*, with a 17C church. It was a Postclassic Zapotec town, the ancient remains of which presumably lie beneath the modern town. At 12 C. Independencia a Zapotec carved anthropomorphic seated figure can be seen.

59km turning r. for (6km W) *San Dionisio Ocotepec*, with another interesting 17C church and (c 21km SW) *San Baltasar Chichicapan*, a small Zapotec town, where the Dominicans established a convent in the 1550s, later abandoned. The present church is a 17C rebuilding. 80km *San Pedro Totolapan*, where the church perhaps dates from the late 16C, as does that at *Sta María Zoquitlán*, 20km SW. Méx. 190 continues E through the N extensions of the Sierra de Miahuatlán to (126km) turning l. for (8km E) **Nejapa** (c 6000 inhab.; 1000m), on the Río Grande de Tehuantepec, founded c 1533, resettled in 1560, as a Spanish villa and garrison to protect the Oaxaca–Tehuantepec high road from the fierce Mixe and Chontal Indians. Once a famed producer of cochineal, indigo, and sugar, the town was struck hard by plague in 1736 and never recovered its prosperity.

The small Dominican convent of *Sto Domingo* was built during the 1560s. The church roof beams, attacked by wood-boring insects, becoming hollow, and invaded by colonies of bats ('con indecible indecencia'), were replaced by vaults c 1650. Heavy arcades along the walls, especially on the S side, were probably once open to give ventilation in the oppressive climate. Above the doorway, the preaching balcony is also later than 16C. The cloister, N of the church, described by Thomas Gage in 1626 as 'very rich', is now in ruins.

171km turning r. for (18km W) **San Bartolo Yautepec**, where the 17C church of *San Bartolo Apóstol* shows profuse relief on its façade and possesses interesting churrigueresque altarpieces. A tree of life in high relief spreads out in the sotocoro vault.

We descend into the hot valley of the Río Tequisistlán to (201km) turning r. for (1km) **Magdalena Tequisistlán**, amid palm trees, where the Dominicans set up a small mission beside the river, probably in the 1560s, and built the bigger church, which stands today (though altered), later in the 16C.

The Dominican friar Francisco de Burgoa (1605–81), whose native place it was, proudly described it as 'like Hebron in its deliciousness'. The settlement produced chocolate, vanilla, coconuts, and bananas, and was home to many parrots. The church's N and S walls allowed for cross-ventilation.

At (21km SW) *Asunción Tlacolulita* prehispanic rock carvings survive on the outskirts of the village.

221km **Jalapa del Marqués** (c 6000 inhab.; 100m; R,P), on the S side of *Presa Benito Juárez* (942 million cubic m), formed by the waters of the Ríos Tequisistlán and Tehuantepec in the 1960s. The small Dominican convent of *Sta María*

(*Asunción*; c 1558) was partly engulfed when the dam was flooded. Trips may be made in hired boats to visit the remains.

A square barrel-vaulted open chapel stands to the N of the church. The convent building was laid out in the form of an H, to maximize ventilation.

At 236km (l.), a track climbs to (8km) **Guiengola** ('great rock'), perhaps the best known example of a Zapotec hilltop fortress.

Nevertheless, it has been little explored since its original description by Edouard Seler in 1896. It was remapped in 1974 by D. A. Peterson and T. D. MacDougall, but no extensive restoration work was done.

Guiengola is of Postclassic date, from c AD 1000 to the Spanish Conquest. It was primarily a fortress refuge, but also served as a religious centre, and according to one source may even have superseded Zaachila as the Zapotec capital, because of Aztec and Mixtec pressures in the last few years before the Spaniards arrived. It is famous as the site of the defeat of the Aztecs under king Ahuitzotl (1486–1502). His predecessor, Axayácatl (1468–81) had originally attempted the conquest of the Mixtecs and Zapotecs, capturing Tehuantepec in 1469. Ahuitzotl made a second attempt c 1497 and reputedly besieged Guiengola, probably repeatedly, over four years of campaigning. Unable to defeat them, the Aztecs attempted to plant, as a spy, the princess 'Cotton Flake' among the Zapotecs, through an arranged marriage to their king, Cocijoeza ('Rain god worshipper'). But the scheme failed (Cotton Flake apparently fell in love with her new husband) and the Aztecs retreated from the region. The temporary alliance between the Zapotecs and Mixtecs also broke off as soon as the immediate danger was over, and the Zapotecs were quick to offer the Spaniards an alliance against the Mixtecs and Aztecs in 1520.

Guiengola is located atop a ridge, taking every advantage of the natural defences, and ringing the entire site with c 40km of double, massive defensive walls, 1.5m thick and 3m high. The only easy access is up a narrow path and stairway. The location also took advantage of two large natural wells and several potholes for water collection on the hill, within the walls. It was never occupied by a large population—the excavations recovered little domestic refuse and no Zapotec polychrome ceramics—and seems to have been principally a princely refuge in times of danger.

At the top there are two principal groups of ruins. Two pyramids, an I-shaped ball court, rooms, and a corner look-out tower form one plaza of 150m in length. A complex of buildings and rooms with patios was apparently a princely residence (of Cocijoeza?) and included another look-out tower, with a view down the Río Tehuantepec valley, where other cliff-forts guarded the approach to Guiengola. Two more towers are located on natural promontories of the ridge.

One of the pyramids has a vertically-faced platform superimposed by a pyramid of three sloping tiers, showing that parts of the site underwent reconstruction during its years of occupation. In general the architecture shows a characteristic Zapotec layout of buildings around patios, similar to the layouts at Mitla, Yagul, or Tepexi el Viejo. Stone slabs set in mortar, carved in 'false' mosaics, and covered with stucco painted red (traces of which still remain), show Zapotec decorations similar to these sites. The narrow terraces along the ridge were apparently a combination of adapting to the natural terrain, defence, and to facilitate the building of other structures.

Méx. 190 skirts the extreme E end of the Sierra de Miahuatlán to (249km) **STO DOMINGO TEHUANTEPEC** (c 45,000 inhab.; H,R,P), an intensely hot and humid town straddling the Río Tehuantepec, and an important commercial, road, and rail centre at the S end of the isthmus. Its matriarchal traditions have made it the focus of much (sometimes a little resented) interest.

The town is of Zapotec origin and was captured by the Aztec king Axayácatl in 1469, thus establishing an Aztec 'tradition' of honouring one's succession to the throne by a feat of arms and by taking many prisoners for public sacrifices in Tenochtitlán. Further Aztec expansion into the area, however, met with stiff resistance and a resort to subterfuge after their ignominious defeat by the Zapotec king Cocijoeza c 1497 at Guiengola. Tehuantepec remained an important Aztec port and market town for merchants travelling from Tlatelolco via Izúcar de Matamoros and Tuxtepec. Cocijopii, Cocijoeza's successor, offered the Spaniards alliance against the Aztecs and Mixtecs. By 1530 Teguantepec (as it was known) and its surrounding province were confirmed as part of Cortés's marquesado. It became a villa on the highway to Guatemala and a major Pacific port with shipyards. In 1626, wrote Thomas Gage, 'There dwell in it some very rich merchants, who trade with Mexico, Peru, and the Philippines, sending their small vessels out from port to port, and these come home richly laden with the commodities of all the southern or eastern parts'. Despite epidemics, Tehuantepec preserved its famous charm, which attracted Diego Rivera and the Russian film-maker Sergei Eisenstein in the 1920s. The coming of the Pan American highway, however, and the development of the oil industry have taken their toll of the old way of life. The local women (tehuanes; more short and generously built than tall, as is often thought) have long had a reputation for their business acumen and for dominating both the social, economic, and political life of the town, and their men. Their rich costume, garnished by heavy necklaces of gold coins, is flaunted at fiesta time, especially in late June.

On JARDIN PRINCIPAL is a bronze statue of Juana Romero who is reputed to have become rich and influential through her long liaison (from the 1860s) with Porfirio Díaz. Facing the plaza is the *Pal. Municipal* (19C), a not unhandsome provincial striving after classicism. At the corner of Av. Guerrero and C. Guadalupe Victoria is the former Dominican convent of **Sto Domingo** (1544–55), the earliest surviving in the State of Oaxaca. Its church was elevated to cathedral status in 1892; notwithstanding earthquake damage in 1897 and 1902, and much rebuilding, it still preserves parts of the original structure.

Despite population decline the convent was raised to priory status in the 1590s, a testimonial of its importance. This building had been generously subsidised by Cocijopii, nephew of Moctezuma and friend of Fray Bernardo de Alburquerque, 2nd bp of Oaxaca. Cocijopii unfortunately apostasized, was tried by the audiencia in Mexico City in 1562–64, and was sentenced to lose all his properties. He died on his way back to Tehuantepec, it is said from apoplectic rage.

The rebuilt brick church has three bays with pointed Gothic ribs and an unusual sanctuary vault: an octagonal dome carried on arched squinches—a throwback to medieval Spain. Through the S doorway we gain access to the open chapel, converted into a three-aisled church by thin metal posts and a metal roof. The groin vault behind its wide central arch, flanked by two lower arched openings, is supported by two solid buttresses (scarcely recognizable today) placed diagonally to the arch columns. The large all-brick convent, N of the church, has been restored as the *Casa de Cultura* after use as jail and home for families of inmates. Its refectory still has its three-star red brick vaulting. On its W side is the bishop's residence.

267km **Salina Cruz** (c 45,000 inhab.; H,R,P), the southernmost isthmus town, terminus of the oil pipeline from Minatitlán, is a steamy, raucous place, without attractions for the discerning visitor.

Its artificial harbour was created in 1901–05, in a dangerous open bay exposed to high winds, as the S terminal of the railway across the isthmus (see below). Further improvements (breakwaters, inner harbour, dry dock, etc.) have recently been made.

4km SE is *La Ventosa* (beach; now open to pollution), on the windy bay of the same name. Méx. 200, the coast road, now links Salina Cruz with *Puerto Angel*, 175km W. This section of the Oaxaca coastline undergoes resort development (see Rte 75).

Reached by a road running NE and across the mouth of the Río Tehuantepec is (31km E) *San Mateo del Mar*, a village of Huave Indians on the peninsula on the S side of the Laguna Superior.

Salina Cruz is also the S terminus of the railway across the **Istmo de Tehuantepec** from Coatzacoalcos. The isthmus, the shortest distance between the Atlantic (Gulf of Mexico) and the Pacific (Gulf of Tehuantepec) on the American continent, except for the Isthmus of Panama, is 215km wide as the crow flies at its narrowest point.

It was an avenue for long-distance trade throughout Mesoamerican prehistory, between the Maya and Central America on the one hand, and central and S Mesoamerica on the other. The coastal region from Tehuantepec down into Guatemala, known as Soconusco (Xoconusco), is occupied by Mixes, Zoques, Huaves, and, to the W up the coast, Chontals. The Zapotecs invaded the region in the Preclassic Period and established several fortified hilltop sites and valley civic and ceremonial centres in S Oaxaca, and were in almost perpetual conflict with their Mixtec neighbours to the N. The two were allied briefly in the late 15C against Aztec invaders, who wished to secure a S port on the Pacific Coast, to tap the rich coastal trade with Central America.

From the 1850s US surveyors and engineers initiated several railway projects, which fell victim to Mexican political turmoil, lack of funds, and civil war. In 1899 Weetman Pearson and his company, S. Pearson and Co., were called in. Construction went ahead in almost unbearable conditions; Indian labourers and European engineers killed by the diseases, especially yellow fever, rife in the region. The 304km of line, capped at each end by the new ports of Coatzacoalcos and Salina Cruz, were inaugurated in Jan. 1907. Pearson and the Mexican government ran the railway as a joint enterprise until 1908, when the latter took control. The opening of the Panama Canal in 1914, however, had already put it into eclipse. Its modernization is now at planning stage. Méx. 185, the trans-isthmus highway, was completed in the 1950s.

FROM SALINA CRUZ TO COATZACOALCOS, 296km. 16km *Sto Domingo Tehuantepec*, see above. From here Méx. 190 crosses the river, traversing an intensively irrigated region NE to (43km) **Juchitán** (c 38,000 inhab.; 39m; H,R,P), once booming with the oil industry, but known for its fiestas, its market, and traditional costumes and music—that of the dance called 'La zandunga' is particularly appealing. A small archaeological collection in the Casa de Cultura includes artefacts from the vicinity, representing several periods and cultures: burial urns and other ceramics, face-shaped stone axe-heads, and a few stelae. 10km SE is *Playa Vicente* on the *Laguna Superior* (30km long and 20km wide), one of the two large saltwater lagoons detached from the Gulf of Tehuantepec by a narrow peninsula (see above). It is separated by a thin stretch of water known as *Mar Tileme*, between two slight sandy peninsulas, from another lagoon, *Laguna Inferior* (30km long and 10km wide), on its E side. Both lagoons are open to the sea through the Boca de San Francisco. The villages on the lagoon shores are home to Huave Indians.

A site called *Laguna Zope* (c 1km W of Juchitán) was excavated by R. N. Zeitlin in the 1970s. It was a prominent site in the Preclassic Period for trade throughout the Oaxaca–Chiapas coastal region from c 1500 to 200 BC, especially in obsidian and shells. By 800 BC it had no rival on the Oaxaca coast and had grown to c 90ha in size. Between 400 and 200 BC contacts became more widespread, extending to the Maya cities in Chiapas and Guatemala. Shortly thereafter, however, unknown factors caused a breakdown of links and the site was eclipsed by inland centres in Puebla.

From Juchitán a road goes NW via (5km) *El Espinal* and (10km) *Asunción Ixtaltepec*, predominantly Zapotec towns on the l. bank of the Río Juchitán, the latter with a charming central plaza, to (17km) **Ciudad Ixtepec** (c 15,000 inhab.; H,R,P), where the market exhibits a variety of local textiles.

From Juchitán, Méx. 190 goes NE to (57km) *La Ventosa*, where the road forks. Méx. 190 continues E to (249km) *Tuxtla Gutiérrez*, see Rte 86. We keep l. along Méx. 185, the trans-isthmus highway, which climbs for its first few km to its maximum elevation of 210m. 87km turning l. for (1km) *Sta María Petapa*, a small Zapotec town. The church contains baroque altarpieces. 102km (l.) **Matías Romero** (c 25,000 inhab.; 201m; H,R,P), a characteristic old railway town with a mixed indigenous population, incl. Zapotecs and Mixes. 119km, just beyond *Piedra Blanca*, turning l. for (13km SW) *San Juan Guichicovi*, a sizeable town in which Mixe Indians predominate. 134km *Palomares*, see Rte 84. Méx. 185 now continues a fast run into the State of Veracruz and to (235km) *Acayucan*. Hence to (296km) *Coatzacoalcos*, see Rte 83.

86 Sto Domingo Tehuantepec to Tuxtla Gutiérrez and San Cristóbal de las Casas

Méx. 190, 375km.—132km San Pedro Tapanatepec (for [289km SE.—by Méx. 200] **Tapachula**).—255km Ocozocoautla.—290km **Tuxtla Gutiérrez** (for [98km N] **Tecpatán**).—305km **Chiapa de Corzo**.—311km turning for (96km SE) Venustiano Carranza and **Copanaguastla**.—375km **San Cristóbal de las Casas**.

Sto Domingo Tehuantepec to (41km) *La Ventosa*, see Rte 85. The road continues across the plain between the Lagunas Superior and Inferior and the western-most heights of the Sierra Madre de Chiapas. At 56km a road runs S to (11km)

Unión Hidalgo, a Zapotec town 4km NW of *Playa Unión* on the N shore of the Laguna Superior. 78km *Niltepec*. 92km road S to (28km) the E shore of the Laguna Inferior. From (101km) *Ostuta* we may gain the sea at (42km S) *Playa Aguachil* (surfing). 132km **San Pedro Tapanatepec**, where the road divides.

Of his experience here in 1626 Thomas Gage wrote: 'the town is one of the sweetest and pleasantest of any we had seen from Oaxaca hither, and it seems God hath replenished it with all sorts of comforts which travellers may need to ascend [Macuilapa, the dangerous pass on the way to Chiapa]. Its top was indeed a head without hair, a top without a tree or branch to shelter a fearful traveller…the height and narrowness of it stupefieth'.

FROM SAN PEDRO TAPANATEPEC TO TAPACHULA, 289km. Méx. 200 runs at first to just N of (9km) *Chahuites*, from where it is possible to reach (9km further S) the N shore of the *Mar Muerto*, a shallow saltwater lagoon approx. 70km long and 12km at its widest point (fishing, water-skiing). From Chahuites, Méx. 200 continues SE into the State of Chiapas and through the hot, humid coastal plain between the surf-pounded beaches with many estuaries behind and the Sierra Madre de Chiapas; the territory of the old Spanish province of Soconusco. 26km road S to *La Gloria* on the Mar Muerto. 45km **Arriaga** (c 25,000 inhab.; 56m; H,R,P), an important communications and commercial centre, from which we may gain Méx. 190 (47km N on Méx. 195) to *Tuxtla Gutiérrez*.

68km **Tonalá** (c 50,000 inhab.; 40m; H,R,P), third most populous town in Chiapas, with a very hot climate (average temperature 26 degrees C). The parish church of *San Francisco*, begun c 1800 and continued probably throughout the first half of the 19C, is curiously four-square in style. Above the triangular pediment is a balustrade topped by a series of curved merlons. A *Museum* at 77 Av. Hidalgo has an archaeological section from the site of Tonalá. It includes Preclassic and Classic Period ceramics, stone knives and spear tips, ground stone axe-heads, manos and matates for grinding, burial urns, and some anthropomorphic figurines. In Parque de Esperanza stands a stone Tláloc statue from nearby *Horcones*, depicting symbols for rain, wind, and the four cardinal directions.

The site of Tonalá is 13km NE. It was explored by Philip Drucker in 1947, and mapped by Edwin N. Ferdon in 1953. Here they found evidence of Olmec influence, chiefly consisting of a stele with a dot and bar numeral; and of the Middle Classic Maya and Teotihuacano trade, part of the traffic across the Isthmus of Tehuantepec and down the Pacific Coast to Izapa and Cotzumalhuapa, in Guatemala.

Although occupied from at least the Middle Preclassic period, most of the existing structures on the site, in five scattered groups, are of Postclassic date: several stone-faced platforms, 1–3.5m high, with wide ramps or central staircases, some with and others lacking side ramps; two stone altars, one carved with a jaguar head and the other with an alligator head; and paved ramps connecting the 'acropolis' with other groups of platform ruins down the slope.

E of Tonalá, at *Tzutzuculi*, excavations by A. J. McDonald in 1977 recovered carvings of a 'were-jaguar' (on a block measuring 0.75m by 0.65m) and a serpent head flanking the stairway of a pyramid dated 410 BC. The entire site comprises some 25 earthen mounds covering an area of c 35ha. Both carvings are of Olmec style.

12 km W *Paredón* is a peaceful spot at the E end of the Mar Muerto. 21km S is **Puerto Arista** (H,R), at the E end of a narrow lagoon, a popular resort and fishing village amid unspoiled coastline, noted for its fine white sand. An archaeological zone along the ridge beside the lagoon has platform mounds and low pyramids. Sculptures from the site show similarities to pieces in the Late Preclassic and Early Classic Olmec and Monte Albán styles, but otherwise are of independent development. In the Late Postclassic the site became a staging post for Aztec pochteca (merchants specializing in luxury goods and given a military escort), and possibly had an Aztec garrison. From Puerto Arista goods were traded along a network stretching across the Isthmus of Tehuantepec and into Soconusco and the Pacific coastal plain of S Chiapas (cf. *Tonalá*).

A poor road runs SE along the coast past *Cabeza de Toro* at the W tip of the meandering *Laguna de la Joya*, to (18km) *Boca del Cielo*, at the lagoon's E end, a much more secluded fishing village, shielded from the sea (dangerous currents) by a sandbar.

Méx. 200, going through the plain between the Sierra Madre and the Pacific, is mostly straight and smooth. 143km **Pijijiapan** (c 8000 inhab.; 39m; H,R,P) is a famous cheese-making centre. 187km *Mapastepec*, S of which are the un-preserved ruins of the small Late Preclassic-Protoclassic Period village site of *Barrancón*. From (217km) **Escuintla** (H,P), a similar Protoclassic village site, a road runs S via (5km) *Acapetagua* towards the lagoons (lush vegetation, man-grove swamps, herons, parakeets) along the coast.

Chantuto, on the coastal estuary c 25km SW of Escuintla, is a Preclassic site of five shell middens, occupied between c 3000 and 2000 BC. The site yielded mano and matate grinding tools, and obsidian tools (traded in from the Highlands to the E and SE), but no pottery. Similar finds came from the site of *Tlacuachero*, c 12km SE.

From (248km) *Huixtla* a road goes NE through the Sierra de Chiapas via (52km) *Motozintla* (1310m; P) to (126km) *Ciudad Cuauhtémoc* (see Rte 88) on the Guatemalan frontier. 265km (1km l.) *Huehuetán* was founded as one of the two Spanish towns of post-Conquest Chiapas (comp. Rte 87). Its church, San Pedro, dates probably from the 16C. At 277km a r. turn for (c 13km W) *Aquiles Serdán*, a site yielding similar finds to those at Chantuto, and (12km SW) *Mazatán*, where Olmec sculptures and rock carvings have been found demonstrating the S extent of Olmec trade. (Olmec trade items have been found as far S as El Salvador and Honduras.)

On the coastal estuary, W of Mazatán, the midden site of *Altamira* (excavated in the 1970s) yielded materials as old as c 2000 BC: obsidian chippings and coarse pottery known as Barra Ware—specializing in bowls, flat-based jars, squash and gourd forms, and tecomates (collar-less spherical vessels with very restricted openings; a very early form). Decoration is incised, punched, and red-slipped, occasionally white-slipped. Barra Ware resembles ceramics from Ecuador, Panama, and N coastal Colombia, and from Ometepe island in Nicaragua, but no direct contact is proven. Similar materials have come from the related site of *La Victoria*, just across the Guatemalan frontier at *Ocós* (cf. *Chantuto* and *Matanchén*).

289km **TAPACHULA** (140,000 inhab.; 137m; H,R,P: airport), second, and fast-growing, town of Chiapas, is pleasant and well laid-out, with a tropical climate. It stands on a plain amid thick jungle vegetation, dominated on the N by the volcano *Tacaná* (4057m).

Tapachula, in the territory of the province of Soconusco, then part of Guatemala, was settled by Spaniards c 1590–1600. In 1794 it became chief place of the district of Soconusco within the intendancy of Chiapa, and that year received the inhabitants of Escuintla (see above), devastated by a hurricane. It suffered terrible damage from earthquake and eruption of the volcano Sta María (near Quetzaltenango in Guatemala) in 1902.

PL. PRINCIPAL is shaded by palms and planted also with topiary trees and flower beds. The neoclassical cathedral of *San Agustín* was built during the 19C. The *Museo Arqueológico del Soconusco* (Tues.–Sun., 9–6), also on the W side of the plaza, contains local finds. In Parque Chapultepec a zoo is home to regional fauna.

27km SW at *Puerto Madero* is the local beach resort.

From Tapachula, Méx. 200 continues E. At 299km a turning r. leads S to (28km) *Ciudad Hidalgo* near the Guatemalan frontier. We continue NE, at 300km meeting the ruins of **IZAPA**, an important site and art style distributed widely in S Mesoamerica. Although the site has the largest collection of Izapan art, it was not necessarily the centre or 'capital' of an Izapan culture, or political unit.

Izapan art is found at numerous sites: Chiapa de Corzo, Chinkultic, Toniná, Tres Zapotes, and Cerro de las Mesas in Chiapas and Veracruz; at Kaminaljuyú in the Guatemala Highlands, and at El Baúl on the coast. There are Izapan style pyramids at Tikal and Uaxactún in the Petén region of Guatemala, and a jaguar altar at Quelepa in El Salvador is also argued to show Izapan influence. The style peaked in the 2C BC, although the earliest stele (from Chiapa de Corzo) is dated 36 BC, and there are regional variations.

According to one interpretation the Izapan style provides a 'link' between the Preclassic Olmec style and the Classic Period Maya, elements of both being represented in Izapan examples. It seems more sensible, however, to view the three styles as overlapping in time and therefore in distribution, borrowing and lending from and to each other. Elements of the style include, in common with Olmec style, jaguar masks on stelae, heads inside jaguar jaws, the St Andrew's cross, a U-shaped motif, the 'long-lipped' god, and skies depicted as scroll-like elements; elements peculiar to Izapan sites include carved trophy heads, descending sky gods, scroll-eyed 'dragon' masks, brandished weapons, and certain glyphs; and elements in common with Maya carving include the portrayal of historical scenes, the double-headed monster, certain other glyph signs, the use of Long Count dates, and the structure and layout of the sites.

Excavations here have been done by M. Stirling (1941, 1943, and 1945), P. Drucker (1948), M. Coe (1957), R. Piña Chan (1960), and S. M. Eckholm (1969), the last incl. restoration work in dark brown stone. The earliest known structure (Montículo 30A) yielded a radiocarbon date of c 627 BC, but pottery from the site indicates occupation from as early as c 1500 BC. Glyph dates at Izapa itself are rare. Izapa's early importance apparently lay in cacao trade, as depicted on some of the stelae.

Izapa lies on either side of the road and includes the town of Tuxtla Chico N of the road. It has over 100 mounds, incl. c 80 temple pyramids. There are several groupings of mounds, platforms, low cylindrical altars, and stelae, forming plazas. There are 244 known stelae, over 50 of them carved and many re-erected in their original positions before altars. *Montículo 30A* was a rectangular, stepped pyramid faced with uncut stone, c 9m high originally, and on which post-holes found by the excavators revealed the existence of a temple structure.

Groups of mounds N of the road have been partially restored and include a platform with a stairway, pyramids, a ball court, altars, and stelae. S of the road, c 1km down a paved road, are more mounds, altars, and stelae. Carvings on the stelae are done in distinctive soft, curved lines depicting narrative scenes of violent action, incl. animals, gods, and humans: water is released and collected by a storm god; jaguars and humans participate in ritual acts; bird gods fly through scroll-like skies; gods ride in canoes on water in which crocodiles and fish swim; gods descend from the heavens; humans watch incense burn in some ritual; and warriors pit their strength and skill against each other. Of particular note are *Stele 5*, which depicts several humans in a ceremony around the 'tree of life'; *Stele 21*, in which two ball players in elaborate headdresses have fought and one holds the loser's head, the body at his feet; and *Stelae 5, 7, and 12*, which have the double-headed monster on them.

307km (r.) *Puente Talismán*, the frontier crossing to Guatemala over the Río Suchiate. The road continues N to (24km) *Unión Juárez* in the foothills of the volcano Tacaná.

From San Pedro Tapanatepec, Méx. 190 crosses the W extremity of the Sierra Madre de Chiapas before emerging into the W end of the great valley known as Depresión Central de Chiapas, beyond the border between Oaxaca and Chiapas. 190km turning r. (Méx. 195) for (47km S) *Arriaga*, see above. 209km (l.) *Cintalapa de Figueroa*. 219km (r.) *Jiquipilas*.

Tracks into the E Chiapas depression, off Méx. 190, lead to several sites: guides are recommended, although there is little to see at most of them. *Campanario* and *Varajonal* are c 13 and 20km N of Jiquipilas; the latter, a Late Classic Maya site dated c AD 550–950, has a large ball court and the only corbel vault known in the region. *Mirador* c 9km S of Jiquipilas, has produced Olmec finds; it was probably a trading station in the distribution of Olmec influence S to the Pacific Coast.

239km turning l. for (3km) *El Aguacero*, a cascade formed by the Río La Venta and a popular excursion spot (few facilities). 255km **Ocozocoautla** (22,000 inhab.; 864m; H,R,P), where the church of *San Juan*, with its elaborate espadaña, is a 19C rebuilding of a 17C original.

Ocozocoautla, as *Javepagouay*, was a 15–16C Zoque principality. Today Zoque is a Macro-Maya language spoken in E Chiapas and Oaxaca. According to Maya chronicles and legend, the Zoque were related to the Maya but were conquered by the Chiapaneca, a Manguespeaking people who migrated from the Cholula area of Puebla, being forced out by the 'Historic Olmec', in the Early Postclassic Period, and established their capital at Chiapa de Corzo in the mid-14C. In the 15C there were four Zoque principalities—Ocozocoautla, Quechula, Mezcalapa, and Zimatán. The Aztecs under Tizoc had conquered the region by 1484, and exacted an annual tribute of cotton, cacao, jaguar skins, feathers, and birds. When the Spaniards arrived, the Zoque were quick to ally themselves against their old Chiapaneca enemies. The Zoque now number perhaps 15,000, scattered between E Chiapas, S Tabasco, and W Oaxaca.

Sites within reach of Ocozocoautla include *Piedra Parada* (c 8km NW), *El Ocote* (c 20km NW), and *Sta Marta Cave* (c 11km N). El Ocote is a ceremonial centre with platforms of huge squared stone blocks, contemporary with the tenth phase at Chiapa de Corzo (c AD 550–900). At Sta Marta Cave a preceramic habitation site was found, dated c 6770–5360 BC, and culturally related to similar cave sites in Oaxaca (Cueva Blanca and Guilá Naquitz), the Valle de Tehuacán (El Riego and Ajuereado), and Tamaulipas (El Infiernillo). Here subsistence relied on hunting and gathering until the domestication of maize in levels dating to c 1500 BC. Artefacts included stone hammers, choppers, knives, grinders, scrapers, gouges and awls, and projectile points, plus charred plant remains.

From Ocozocoautla a minor road runs N to (c 50km) the S ramifications of *Presa Nezahualcóyotl*, see Rte 83. The flora and fauna and forests of the area are protected under the auspices of the State Institute for Natural Resources. 284km turning l. for (92km) *Tecpatán*, see below.

290km **TUXTLA GUTIERREZ** (c 200,000 inhab.; 526m), capital of the State of Chiapas, is a modern city in the Valle de Tuxtla, through which flows the Río Mezcalapa. It is the commercial centre for SE Mexico and draws much of its wealth not only from coffee and tobacco plantations, but also from other agricultural produce, clothing, plastics, and traditional amber. On the E outskirts is perhaps the most interesting zoo in the republic.

Airport. C 35km W. Daily flights to *Mexico City, Tapachula,* and *Villahermosa*; thrice weekly to *Oaxaca*.

Bus stations. 1st Class. 211 C. 2 Norte Poniente. Services to *Mexico City* (19 hrs); to *Tapachula* (7 hrs); to *San Cristóbal de las Casas* (2 hrs); to *Oaxaca* (10 hrs); to *Comitán* (3½ hrs); to *Villahermosa* (7 hrs); etc.

2nd Class. C. 3 Sur Oriente (just W of C. 7 Oriente Sur) and 330 C. 8 Oriente Sur. Services to *Comitán*; to *Mérida* (16 hrs); to *Palenque*; to *San Cristóbal de las Casas*; to *Tapachula*; to *Villahermosa*; etc.

Hotels throughout the city.

Post Office. NE side of Pl. Principal.

Tourist Office. Edificio Plaza de las Instituciones, off Blvd Dr Belisario Domínguez.

Tuxtla, in Zoque Indian country, remained a largely indigenous settlement in the years after the Conquest. Here in 1693 the locals stoned to death the alcalde mayor of Chiapa, Manuel Maesterra y Atocha, and burned alive two village officials. From 1769 Tuxtla became seat of one of the two alcaldes mayores who ruled Chiapa. By the late 18C, the population of c 4280 included a few families of Spanish descent and some mulattoes. Villa status, as San Marcos Tuxtla, was granted in 1813. In 1822, wrote the insurgent general Manuel Mier y Terán, 'the 5000 inhabitants include a considerable number of cultivated persons, in general very obliging...It abounds in foodstuffs, especially beef'. During the 19C State government headquarters changed between Tuxtla and San Cristóbal, the former finally confirmed as capital in 1892. The city was renamed Tuxtla de Gutiérrez in 1848, after Joaquín Miguel Gutiérrez Canales (1796–1838), killed here fighting the forces of a rival governor installed in San Cristóbal.

The Sierra Madre de Chiapas, which runs SE through the State of **Chiapas** (2.5 million inhab.; 73,887 sq km), and whose heights rise to c 4000m, divides the tropical coastal plain (24 to 40km wide), agriculturally rich, yet sparsely populated, from the central valley (Depresión Central de Chiapas), beyond which rise the Chiapas highlands (Meseta Central; maximum elevation c 2500m). The central valley is drained (from SE to NW) by the Río Mezcalapa (called locally Río Grande de Chiapas; and frequently called Grijalva, although, strictly speaking, only on the coastal plain of Tabasco does it join the Río Grijalva river system), whose waters have been harnessed in two mighty dams: La Angostura and Nezahualcóyotl. The frontier with Guatemala in the E is formed by the Río Usumacinta. Climate changes dramatically, from the heat and humidity of the coastal plain; the relative heat and dryness of the central valley; to the often intense cold of the highlands. Plentiful rain falls in March–Nov. on the mountain slopes and coastal plain.

Chiapas is the republic's foremost coffee and banana producer. Timber comes from the forests of the Sierra Madre and Chiapas highlands, and mahogany and dyewoods are exported. (The Lacandón rainforest in the E of the State, home of the isolated and peaceful Lacandón Indians, has been depleted at an alarming and irresponsible rate, prey to multinational companies—a tragedy urgently calling for remedy.) Oilfields in the NW tip, just SW of Villahermosa, have been exploited since the 1970s.

The present-day State of Chiapas comprises two historic provinces, inland Chiapa and coastal Soconusco, divided by the Sierra Madre. By the early 1540s Spanish control of Chiapa, except the Lacandón country in the E, was virtually complete. At first Chiapa was briefly subject to the government of New Spain in Mexico City, but from 1530 (save for the period 1540–44 when it was ruled by Francisco de Montejo the elder) until 1790 it was administered from Guatemala. From c 1560 Soconusco had a series of governors appointed by the crown, who, thanks to the remoteness of the territory, ruled something resembling a personal fiefdom until 1790, when Soconusco was attached to the new intendancy of Chiapa, subordinate to Guatemala. Even as late as the 19C and early 20C this remoteness and isolation were underlined by the absence of decent roads. A journey to Mexico City presented almost insuperable difficulties; it was easier to get to Guatemala, even though the roads were appalling. In 1712 the Tzeltal Indians of the highlands rose in revolt, which was savagely put down the following year. In 1821 Chiapas adhered to newly independent Mexico, but declared its complete independence in 1823 after the fall of Iturbide. In 1824 a plebiscite decided in favour of reincorporation with Mexico. Soconusco, encouraged from Guatemala, pursued an independent line, until 1842 when it finally decided to adhere to Mexico over Guatemalan protests. Exploitation of Indian groups and the confiscation of their lands by caciques have been a sad feature of life in Chiapas, as has the problem of Central American refugees. The insurrection of the Zapatista Army of National Liberation in Jan. 1994 focused attention on poverty and illiteracy among Indian groups and on human rights abuses.

The city centre, developed and improved from the late 1970s, focuses on two large plazas, PL. PRINCIPAL and PL. J.M. GUTIERREZ (or *Pl. San Marcos*), separated by Av. 1 Norte Oriente. On the S side of Pl. J.M. Gutiérrez is the cathedral of *San Marcos*.

Although it dates its foundation from the 17C, it was remodelled in the earlier 20C; its façade, influenced by the neoclassical, with two-storey applied columns, may possibly have been a project of Carlos Z. Flores. Its carrillon is a favourite diversion.

In the NE part of the city, at the intersection of C. 11 Oriente Norte and Av. 5 Norte Oriente, is PARQUE MADERO (Tues.–Sun., 10–6), containing a recreational and cultural complex built in the early 1980s. The *Teatro Emilio Tobasa*, on Av. 5 Norte Oriente, faces the park. To the r. of the public swimming pool is the *Jardín Botánico*. A broad avenue on the r. of the theatre entrance (Calz. de los Hombres Ilustres), lined with busts of heroes of the Revolution, leads to the **Museo Regional de Chiapas** (Tues.–Sun., 9–4; fee; Sat., Sun., holidays, free), founded in 1931; its present building (1982) designed by Pedro Ramírez Vázquez.

GROUND FLOOR. The FIRST ROOM contains principally stone sculptures from the State of Chiapas, incl. Preclassic Olmec and Classic Maya pieces. Explanatory panels and chronological information relate the regional sites to Mesoamerica in general. Zoomorphic and anthropomorphic altarstones, and several fragments of Maya architectural decorations.

Of especial note are the Danzante de Izapa, an Olmec sculpture of a man dancing in a jaguar mask and squared headpiece with a long train down his back, and bells attached to his ankles; and a figure of a cross-legged, seated man carved on a plinth fragment, decorated with curvilinear designs assumed to represent rain—an important example of Jotaná art, a local style in S Chiapas, from c AD 900 to the Spanish Conquest, which was influenced by styles in Central America. SECOND ROOM. Ceramics and figurines, incl. examples from Jaina. Seals for body-painting; clay cylinder depicting in appliqué the Maya Sun god wearing a jaguar mask, resting on a smaller head, representing 'Earth'—dated c AD 300–900; painted Maya fabrics; Totonac carved stone yugos and palmas used in the ball game ritual.

On the UPPER FLOOR is a collection of chiapaneco historical art. A panel from a 16C altarpiece, of local make, its gilding scraped away, shows a relief of the Crucifixion. Another, of the 18C, shows estípites. Among the paintings, Our Lady of Perpetual Succour by the 18C master from San Cristóbal, Eusebio de Aguilar, and a 17C anon. St Simon Stock, an excellent work; Anselmo Rodas (early 19C; from San Cristóbal), Sor María Leonor del Arcángel San Miguel; and an anon. likeness of the dead body of Joaquín Miguel Gutiérrez, which was abandoned naked in the plaza after his assassination.

Beyond the museum an *Orquideario* displays a notable collection of orchids.

Also on the E side of the city, reached along C. 12 Oriente Sur, is the **Parque Zoológico Miguel Alvarez del Toro** (Tues.–Sun., 9–5.30), most imaginatively laid out (c 25 ha), where c 200 species of the beasts and birds native to Chiapas live, as far as possible, in re-creations of their natural habitats.

FROM TUXTLA GUTIERREZ TO TECPATAN. A road pushed ahead in the 1970s, a long drive through and near remote mountain villages, in accidented terrain peopled by Zoques and other indigenous groups. 98km. The road winds NW from Tuxtla through the NW end of the central valley, and ascends gradually NE into the W Chiapas highlands. 48km *Chicoasén*. From here the direction is NW to (77km) **Copainalá** (c 4000 inhab.; 482m; simple accommodation, P), a Zoque Indian town, where the large ruined church of *San Miguel* was built by the Dominicans in the late 16C or very early 17C. Attached to its NW corner is a massive three-storey tower, access to which is by a spiral staircase enveloped by a slim minaret-like structure. The W doorway, framed by two heavy buttresses topped by huge pyramidal finials, is imposingly classical, with (a Gothic touch) a rose window in the gable above; pear-shaped merlons sit upon the outer pilasters. 98km **TECPATAN** (c 5000 inhab.; 338m; R), in a desolate landscape near the E shore of Presa Nezahualcóyotl. Here the former Dominican convent of **Sto Domingo** retains a sturdy grandeur and still dominates the town, despite its sad state of decay.

It was built perhaps from the last quarter of the 16C and continued in the 17C; c 1617 nine friars and one lay brother ministered to 23 towns, incl. Tecpatán, in the province of the Zoques. By the end of the 18C, thanks to the assigning of most of the vast parish among secular priests, only three towns remained to the Dominicans. By 1900 the buildings had sunk into ruin, which since the 1970s the locals have made praiseworthy, but often damaging, efforts to repair.

EXTERIOR. Church and convent are raised from the street on the W side and bounded by the wall which encloses the atrio. The main W façade is in an arresting mixture of styles combined with Mudéjar proportions: the central vertical panel, framed by two shallow pilasters, encloses a deep Romanesque doorway, with a Gothic blind arcade above, its three niches divided by baluster (plateresque) colonnettes; the choir window, with its stepped archivolts, is another Romanesque reminder; above it is a square version of a medieval rose and this in turn is surmounted by a classical low pediment. The strange espadaña, jagged against the sky, may well be a later addition, replacing an original knocked down by an earthquake. The adjoining massive SW tower, unique in the Americas, has Mudéjar antecedents, especially in the Spanish province of Seville.

Two turreted buttresses, one octagonal, one circular, project from the SW and SE corners, while a round spiral staircase tower, with narrow slits for windows, stands out from the W front. The elaborate S doorway panel shows a variety of medieval, plateresque, and Mannerist motifs. Remains of a coat-of-arms show in the attic above the entablature. Above, on a line with the clerestory, parts of a relief honouring the Order of Preachers have survived.

The single-nave INTERIOR, unmarked by pilasters or columns, is still spanned by four (out of an original five) transverse arches springing from a classical entablature running just below clerestory level. Merest traces of the painted pattern which once covered the walls survive. The space of the sotocoro is marked by two semicircular arches which spring from the floor. The chancel, narrower than the nave, is in the form of a huge niche with a scallop vault, once framed by an alfíz. Reached through a doorway in the sotocoro, the tower belfry has preserved its ribbing and some of its painted decoration.

Although ravaged by neglect since c 1767, when the Dominicans were deprived of their extensive parish, the CONVENT may still be admired for its monumental size. The two-storey cloister arcades and the vaults are supported by enormous piers; the vault ribs do not cross on the crown, but join a concave lozenge shape placed in it.

A favourite excursion from Tuxtla Gutiérrez is to (23km N) the narrowest point of the **Cañón del Sumidero**, a precipitous gorge, up to 800m deep, through which rushed the foaming waters of the Río Mezcalapa. Exploration of this enormous tectonic fault began in 1915 and the first crossing of its hitherto unconquered rapids and waterfalls was achieved by a group of eight from Tuxtla in 1960. Completion of Presa de Chicoasén, to the N, has converted the gorge bottom into a calm waterway. **Presa de Chicoasén**, the third dam undertaken in the State to harness the waters of the river, was completed in 1980. Its curtain wall is 260m high, its area c 50sq km, its capacity c 21.6 million cubic m, and its generation capacity 2.4 MW.

Beyond Tuxtla, Méx. 190 skirts the S entry to the Cañón del Sumidero. At 300km a road r. runs SE to (79km) *Venustiano Carranza*, see below. We keep l. for (305km) **CHIAPA DE CORZO** (c 30,000 inhab.; 415m; H,R,P), a town of great interest and historical importance on the Río Mezcalapa.

It is one of the most important sites in SW Mexico by virtue of its long cultural sequence. There are over 100 mounds, some of which were excavated by teams from Tulane University (1940s) and the New World Archaeological Foundation (1950s). There is evidence of occupation as early as 4500 BC, but a continuous sequence begins c 1500 BC. In a palace structure, *Montículo 5*, stratified ceramics provide a complex sequence of 12 phases alongside architectural changes.

In *Phase I* (1400–1000 BC) unslipped, bichrome pottery was used, and some ceramics resembled Ocós Ware from further S, indicating possible influences in style, via Ocós, from Ecuador. In *Phases II* and *III* (1000–750 and 750–500 BC) platforms were built to support simple structures, and pottery showed more variation, incl. three-pronged censers, pottery from Olmec La Venta, blackware whistling vessels, and figurines. *Phase IV* (550–200 BC) pottery shows influence from Monte Albán and a small ceremonial centre with pyramids was constructed.

In *Phase V* (200 BC–AD 1) figurines were no longer made or used, and polished red and black wares were prominent. An important personage was buried in *Tumba I*, accompanied by a long, obsidian-bladed lance, jade jewellery, and three carved human femurs, one with a swimming crocodile and another with a jaguar-masked figure, in Izapa style. A stele from the phase, also in Izapa style, has the earliest known Maya Long Count date, 36 BC, lending credence to the theory that the calendrical systems of Mesoamerica were invented outside the Maya area (see Introduction: Calendrics).

During *Phases VI, VII*, and *VIII* (AD 1–100, 100–200 and 200–350) the first cut-stone architecture appeared, incl. a stone-faced pyramid complex in *Phase VIII*, and fine pottery was imported from Guatemala, El Salvador, and the Gulf Coast. In *Phase IX* (AD 350–550) construction at the site ceased and the palace in *Montículo 5* was destroyed. The phase is associated with the arrival of the Chiapaneca or Zoque peoples in the region and the waning of Maya influence, for the site had been an important centre of trade between the Teotihuacán and Highland zones on the one hand, and the Gulf Coast and the Maya Petén on the other.

In *Phases X, XI*, and *XII* (AD 550–900, 900–1250 and 1250–1524) strong Guatemalan influences continued alongside population increases. Tohil Plumbate pottery was prominent in *Phase IX*, and according to one source the site became the Chiapaneca capital in the mid-14C. At the Conquest the city was called Nenduime.

The Spanish city on the ancient site was founded in 1528 by Diego de Mazariegos. It was planned as a combined Indian and Spanish town, with the Indians confined to their own area, but the Spaniards very soon removed to Villa Real (see Rte 87). It then became known as Chiapa de Indios. By the early 17C is was already termed a pueblo de ladinos—a sign of mestization and the adoption by Indians of a Spanish way of life. 'That one and famous and most populous town of Chiapa of the Indians', recorded Thomas Gage, 'seated upon a river as broad as is the Thames at London'. In 1888 its name was changed in honour of Governor Angel Albino Corzo (1816–75). In 1975 Chiapa suffered a severe earthquake (5.5 points on the Richter scale); the damage to historical buildings has largely been made good.

The town centre is the ample PL. ANGEL ALBINO CORZO. On the S side the portales obey an 18C style; those on the E side are in the neoclassical mode introduced into Chiapas in the early 20C. Its principal feature is the magnificent monumental **Fountain**, made of brick, uniquely devised.

It was designed by the Dominican Fray Rodrigo de León and finished in 1562, to give the town a ready water-supply and to serve as meeting-place. In 1594 a visitor, Juan de Pineda, remarked: '...a fountain very well made, all of brick, and more than a hundred souls can stand inside it without getting wet though it rain'. The style integrates traditional Spanish and Renaissance Italian (the dome); Gothic (the flying buttresses); and Mudéjar (the wealth of patterned brickwork).

Its plan is octagonal. Eight massive piers support the dome, a hemisphere on the exterior, polygonal and rib-vaulted in the interior. Eight semicircular flying buttresses connected with eight freestanding outer buttresses bear the dome's lateral thrust. Under the dome, the octagonal basin. On its NE side a spiral stair is encased in a circular turret. A rare beauty is conveyed by the specially cut bricks: with diamond-shaped bosses for surfaces above the arches; flat and square for the archivolts; flat and polygonal for the applied pilasters of the inner ring of piers supporting the dome, for the dome ribs, and for the upper parts of the outer buttresses; complexly polygonal for the parapets above each bay; and more, specially cut, for the merlons and pinnacles.

No. 35 on the plaza is the **Museo de la Laca** (Tues.–Sat., 9–7; Sun., 9–1, 4–7) containing a choice display of lacquerwork, mainly locally made. Chiapa de Corzo has been, since prehispanic times, one of the three principal centres of this popular art in Mexico. Its production, however, is inferior to that of Olinalá in Guerrero and Uruapan and Pátzcuaro in Michoacán.

S of the plaza, towards the Río Mezcalapa, is the church of **Sto Domingo**, part of an ancient foundation, but much altered by time.

The Dominicans, led by Fray Bartolomé de las Casas, arrived in Chiapa de Indios in 1545 and their convent (replacing an earlier, temporary structure) was built c 1576–88 under Fray Pedro de Barrientos. Additions were probably made after floods in 1652 and further repairs in 1770, when a new roof was put on. The convent fell into ruin during the 19C; what remains gradually fell away. During the 19C and early 20C the church likewise declined. C 1946 the roof was remade, but the original tie-beams left untouched. Repairs were undertaken in the 1960s: W façade transformed, N parapet wall remade with coffered panels, and exterior stucco gone over. The square bell tower at the NE end is an 18C addition, but the bell itself is of 1576.

EXTERIOR. The façade, designed as a huge retable wider than the nave and aisles behind it, is as much the result of a modern imagination (incl. the circular window—though here a reversion to the original, later altered; the dentil course in the cornice of the blind colonnade above; the turret [NW corner] at the top of the spiral staircase; the truncated pediment and the merlons on either side; and column bases on both sides of the doorway) as original work. It nevertheless still shows an amalgam of styles from late Gothic to Mannerist, imposed on a Mudéjar framework. Of the two side doorways on the N side, that in the third bay from the front is probably 16C work; that in the seventh bay by the N transept is elegantly Mannerist, with baroque hints, and dates probably from the late 17C. To the five lower windows improbable ornate canopies were added (late 17C?). The 12 upper windows are divided by mullions, perhaps later additions.

The INTERIOR, with its partly original timber ceiling, presents an unaffectedly harmonious and dignified aspect. The nave is separated from the two side aisles by two-storey arcades, the arches of the lower arcade resting on nine pairs of sturdy piers. The upper arcade faces the clerestory in the outer walls, from which buttresses project into the side aisles to form shallow niches for side-altars. The low vaults of presbytery and transepts, of a type known as pendentive domes, are crossed by unusual decorative ribbing, of Isabeline Gothic inspiration. Three chapels W of the transepts (one on the N, two on the S) are 19C additions. The cupola over the crossing was added after 1770. Above the upper arcade runs an entablature (with doric and Tuscan elements), which could date from the late 17C until the 19C. Over the transverse crossing arch it incorporates the date 1554 (a mistake for 1545—see above), on either side of an oval blazon containing Dominican symbols.

Overlooking the town and the Río Mezcalapa is the ruined church of *San Sebastián*, built probably from the early 17C to the early 18C, and abandoned in 1776; its despoliation dates from the 1860s. A handsome retable façade and nave arcades survive. **El Calvario**, also above the town, another of the churches once administered by the Dominicans, has been completely rebuilt. It preserves, however, various works of art once belonging to Sto Domingo, incl. a beautiful polychrome relief of the Descent from the Cross, once part of an altarpiece.

It is fashioned from hard local wood and dates probably from the late 16C, but is late medieval, even Flemish, in inspiration, showing expert use of estofado. A land and city scape forms a backdrop for the closely grouped figures. The faces of the dead Christ and His sorrowing mother are done with profound sympathy; St Mary Magdalen kneels to kiss His hand. Of the mourners behind, St John stands in the centre, his head obliquely inclined.

Part of the ancient site has been reconstructed at the SE edge of the town, between the continuations of Cs 21 de Octubre and Hidalgo, over 1km from the main plaza. A detailed display of the site shows plans and descriptions of the phases and pottery. One small pyramid has been rebuilt and traces of other buildings show mud construction faced with river cobbles, sometimes covered with stucco, platforms, and two-tiered pyramids. Some completely different structures are on the roadside itself.

Two blocks from the main plaza is an embarkation point for trips (2½ hrs) along the river through the Cañón del Sumidero.

Beyond Chiapa de Corzo, Méx. 190 runs NE to (311km) a road junction.

The turning r. descends into the valley of the Río Mezcalapa. 36km *Acala*, where the church of San Pablo, built in the 19C in an earlier style (façade rebuilt in 1904), stands next to remains of its late 17C predecessor. At 75km the road joins that from Tuxtla, see above. To the S lies **Presa de la Angostura**, the largest dam in Mexico (6360 sq km), built during 1968–74 and filling the major part of the central valley of Chiapas SE almost to the Guatemalan frontier. 96km **Venustiano Carranza** (c 20,000 inhab.; 804m; H,R,P), the former *San Bartolomé de los Llanos*. The *Pal. Municipal*, in 2 Av. Sur, dates from the 18C. In 2 Av. Poniente, the principal church, *San Bartolomé*, the façade covered in coloured stucco mixed with fine gravel, is of comparatively recent date; the cupola was raised in 1890. Next to the primitive little church of *San Sebastián*, on 4 Av. Poniente, is the ruin of its 17C predecessor.

At 112km, just beyond *Pujiltic*, a road winds N into the Chiapas highlands via (4km) **Soyatitán**, where remains (façade, N transept, and apse) of the church of *La Asunción*, built by the Dominicans early in the 17C, attest a once handsome construction, to (36km) *Amatenango del Valle*, see Rte 88.

C 10km S of Pujiltic, and on the land of a plantation called *La Candelaria*, is the site of **COPANAGUASTLA**, now known as a despoblado (uninhabited), but with some simple thatched dwellings.

At the Conquest this was a thriving Chiapaneco Indian community, among those which soon submitted to the Spaniards. In 1545 four Dominican friars arrived to start evangelizing, and their first, temporary, establishment was considered the most important in Chiapas. The convent was officially founded in 1556. The original church was struck by lightning in 1564. Rebuilding took place from 1567, probably to the design of Fray Francisco de la Cruz (d. 1567–68), and may still have been in progress until a few years before the place was finally abandoned in 1629. It is related that the Indians did not take entirely kindly to Christianity: they hid an idol behind Our Lady's altar and the women refused to marry and were apt to drown newborn infants before baptism. In 1617 plague almost wiped out the population. Yet in 1626 Thomas Gage, a guest of the friars, was impressed by what he called 'the head town' of the great valley of Copanabastla, with a population of 800 Indians. In 1629 the survivors were moved to Socoltenango. In 1645 eight or nine Indians lingered on here.

The remains of the once splendid convent of **San Vicente** have been sadly, and alarmingly, despoiled, and put to quite inappropriate uses. Earthquakes have also taken their toll. Traces of the CONVENT can be discerned amid the ruins well back on the N side of the church. Enough of the CHURCH remains vastly to impress. The W façade, set between two diagonal buttresses, is well within a Mannerist framework, but with homely plateresque decorative touches: medallions in the doorway arch and jambs; winged cherub heads in the frieze above; Dominican shields in the corners beneath the upper cornice. On either side of the unusual semicircular pediment, which rests on the more elaborate lower cornice, are two fascinatingly composed finials: from their pedestals jut human heads with huge ears between animal (lamb?) heads; in the finial shaft, long round-bottomed vases; at the top, bowls holding fruit. Three buttresses line the N and S exterior walls; the four windows recall the Romanesque. One transverse nave arch has survived to span the now roofless interior; the springings of the other three, from brackets resting on ornate corbels, may still be seen. From much smaller brackets alongside them spring the arches of the blind clerestories. Remains of the transepts, entered by low semicircular arches, also survive. Among their entrances are three corbels, one once supporting the arch across the transept, two once serving as imposts for rib vaulting.

Méx. 190 begins its spectacular climb towards San Cristóbal. At 324km we reach the road (l.; Méx. 195) to (254km) *Villahermosa*, see Rte 83. 375km *San Cristóbal de las Casas*, see Rte 87.

87 San Cristóbal de las Casas

SAN CRISTOBAL DE LAS CASAS (c 70,000 inhab.; 2100m) lies in the Valle de Jovel, surrounded by forest-covered hills. Partly because of its remoteness and isolation over centuries it has retained a quiet and pleasant provincial atmosphere. Its narrow streets; one-storey old houses, whitewashed or painted in pastel shades, with red-tiled roofs and flower-filled patios; its scattering of historic churches; and the colourful presence of Tzotzil-speaking Indian groups from the surrounding area add to its delightful and picturesque qualities.

Bus stations. Along Carr. Panamericana in S outskirts. Services to *Chiapa de Corzo* (1½ hrs); to *Tuxtla Gutiérrez* (2 hrs); to *Comitán* (1½ hrs); to *Tonalá* (5½ hrs); to *Tapachula* (8–9 hrs); to *Tehuantepec* (7 hrs); to *Oaxaca* (12 hrs); to *Mexico City* (21 hrs); to *Puebla* (18 hrs); to *Ciudad Cuauhtémoc* (3 hrs).
   The stations in C. Allende, just off Carr. Panamericana, and N of the town along Av. Gen. M. Utrilla are best for more local destinations.

Hotels throughout the city.

Post Office. Corner of C. Cuauhtémoc and Av. Crescencio Rosas.

Tourist Office. Pal. Municipal.

Fiestas 25 July: St Christopher. 12 Dec: Our Lady of Guadalupe.

It was founded in 1527 or 1528 by Diego de Mazariegos as Villa Real, exclusively for Spanish settlers, a name soon changed to Villaviciosa, and then to Villa de San Cristóbal de los Llanos. By 1536 the name had been changed again, to Ciudad Real, which was to stick until well into the 19C. In 1545–47 Bartolomé de las Casas, first bp of Chiapas, whose fiery denunciation of Spanish ill-treatment of the Indians earned him and the Dominicans the hostility of the Spaniards, had his residence here. By the early 17C there may have been c 400 Spanish households (c 1600 souls ?) resident in the city, with five attached barrios (El Cerrillo, Cuxtitali, San Antonio, San Diego, and Mexicanos) for various Indian groups. Thomas Gage, who arrived in 1626, was slighting of it: 'one of the meanest cities in all America'. The gentlemen, he wrote, had 'fantastic pride' and 'discourse as shallow-brained as a low brook'. The women 'have learned from the Devil many enticing lessons and baits to draw poor souls to sin and damnation; and if they cannot have their wills, they will surely work revenge either by chocolate or conserves, or some fair present, which will surely carry death along with it'. Yet when he left, he accepted from the governor's wife chocolate, a huge box of conserves, and 'in a handkerchief a dozen pieces of eight'. In 1712 during the revolt of Tzendal Indians, only 1300 men could be mustered to defend Ciudad Real, incl. 500 from Guatemala and

Indians from the barrios. In 1785 occurred the worst of the floods which periodically struck the city, the resulting silt and debris helping to aggravate the decay into which it fell during the 19C. In 1848 its name was officially changed to San Cristóbal Las Casas (in 1943 adjusted to 'de las Casas'). It lost its status as State capital to Tuxtla Gutiérrez for the third and final time during the 19C in 1892. In June 1869, during the Tzotzil uprising, the city was besieged by a force of 13,000 Tzotziles, demanding the release of the ringleaders, who had staged their own crucifixion on Good Friday 1868, held prisoner here. The attack was eventually beaten off, thanks to the intervention of Governor Cleofas Domínguez, but not without damage to the Indian barrios.

Until the Pan American highway (Méx. 190) reached San Cristóbal in 1950, the city remained exceptionally difficult of access. From the Conquest until the 20C it was easier to get to France or Spain than to Mexico City.

The barrio churches of San Cristóbal—Mexicanos, San Antonio, Sta Lucía, Guadalupe—not separately discussed below are mainly 19C and 20C buildings replacing poor originals. *San Cristóbal*, on its hill to the SW, replaces an old hermitage chapel. *San Diego*, on the E side of the Carr. Panamericana on the S edge of the city, retains 18C features.

On the W side of the central PL. 31 DE MARZO is the creamy ochre *Pal. Municipal* (c 1900–30), by Carlos Z. Flores, a successful exercise in the latter-day neoclassical he introduced into Chiapas. On the NW side is the cathedral of **San Cristóbal**, its W front facing Av. 20 de Noviembre.

It was in its predecessor, built in the 1530s, relates Gage, that the ladies of the city were unable to get through Mass 'unless they drink a cup of hot chocolate, and eat a bit of sweetmeats to strengthen their stomachs'. A new, incomplete cathedral was inaugurated in 1696, but rebuilt during 1714–33; further work was carried out in 1769–88; still more at the turn of the century, finished by 1807. Repairs to earthquake damage in 1901 were done in 1920–22 under Carlos Z. Flores, who remodelled the interior, and made exterior changes, especially on the S side.

EXTERIOR. The W façade, typically wide and reached by a lonja, consists of two storeys and three vertical bays divided off by pairs of columns, Tuscan in the lower storey; naively ionic in the upper. Only the inner columns of the upper storey are touched by the floral plaster pattern which covers the façade. Ingenuously carved saints' images stand in the niches between the columns and in the lower arches. The crowning gable, with its curvilinear entablature, is heavily ornate.

INTERIOR. The Corinthian columns (fluted c 1940, after his death) are part of Flores's updating work, as is the new painted artesonado ceiling. The gilded 18C altarpieces at the ends of the aisles, both baroque with solomonic columns, are dedicated to the Passion (l.) and St Joseph (r.). The large painting in the centre of the lowest storey of the former (Our Lady of Sorrows comforted by angels) is by Juan Correa. Later in date, the high altarpiece incorporates paintings by Eusebio de Aguilar, a local artist, and both solomonic columns and estípites. Further back in the aisles, aligning with the high altar steps, are two more altarpieces, that in the S (r.) aisle incl. in its base a portrait of King Edward III of England (in 17C style; a confusion with Edward the Confessor ?), with the insignia of the Order of the Garter in the top r. corner. The pulpit is another notable 18C work.

Adjoining the cathedral, on the NE side of the plaza, is the church of *San Nicolás* (c 1618), its plain façade topped by a large espadaña. It was probably destined for an Indian congregation under Dominican supervision.

N of the cathedral, C. 20 de Septiembre leads to the church and former convent of **Sto Domingo**.

In spite of hostility from local Spaniards the Dominicans, who had arrived in Ciudad Real in March 1545, managed to build their first simple quarters in 1551; the convent was enlarged and rebuilt in the late 16C. The present church dates from the late 17C. The paintings and older works of art in the church, of varying quality, are all by anon. late 17C and 18C artists.

EXTERIOR. The W façade, most sumptuous in the city, with three horizontal storeys and three vertical bays, is a combination of Guatemalan hugeness and Mexican exuberance, emphasized by the perverse spiralling of the columns. Pairs of solomonic columns flank the lateral bays in all three storeys, the inside ones of each pair projecting forward. In the lowest storey the columns are cylindrical in their lowest thirds but covered in dense floral relief; in the upper two-thirds the twisting bands, moving upwards in opposite directions on each pair, are covered in a different type of floral relief. In the middle storey the columns are divided into three equal sections: the centre one has convex bands, the upper and lower, deep narrow furrows twisting in opposite directions to the centre band. The upper-storey columns are similar to those of the lowest, but the spirals wind in the opposite direction. In the side bays and above the choir window saintly statues stand in elaborately framed niches. Stucco floral, vegetal, and other quaint relief invades all surfaces, its design varying from panel to panel. Note the siren figure in the jamb below the outer arch; two more rest lazily at each end of the top cornice. On either side of the central window, medallions display angels attending the Host in a monstrance; in the centre of the upper storey are two Habsburg eagles; in the centre of the gable is a Dominican emblem. Two buttress towers end in squat octagonal belfries, which yet have room for little solomonic columns enclosing niches and alfices covering arches.

The S doorway, a strange composition, and set amid the rough masonry of the exterior wall and strong buttresses, is flanked by broad corrugated pilasters, set forward of which are solomonic columns, on unusually high pedestals, which uphold a pulvinated lintel. At the W end of the S wall are two differing arches, part of a structure (purpose unknown) which once abutted the church.

Nave, presbytery, and N transept of the cruciform INTERIOR are covered by barrel-vaulting, which has suffered from 19C overpainting; the centre of the crossing by a low cupola; and the first section of the S transept (twice as long as the N) by a smaller cupola. Walls and pilasters are lined with gilded wood panelling covered in low relief. In the large niches of the nave six gilded baroque altarpieces (that at mid-r. broken into by the S door), each subtly different in design, continue the dazzling effect.

The altarpieces and intervening pilasters followed a natural progression—paintings of apostles on each altarpiece accompanying the dedicatee; founders of religious orders and archangels on the pilasters—to a culmination in the original high altar (torn out in the 19C to make way for the present), where were placed statues of Christ (at the head of the apostles), St Dominic (for this church, the most important founder), and St Michael (chief of the archangels). *1st altar r.*. In the central niche, statue of the young St Antony of Padua. On either side, paintings of SS Vincent Ferrer and Hyacinth. In the lower part, two archangels. (The date 1795 on the angel on the r. does not correspond to the retable's date.) On the first pilaster, St Bruno, founder of the Carthusians, and the first archangel. *Above the side doorway*. St Dominic is visited by the Holy Family. On the second pilaster, St Augustine and the second archangel. *2nd altar r.*. In the centre, St Thomas Aquinas, his lectern a nude woman representing lust, but yielding to the saintly doctor's chastity. On the r., St Thomas helped by angels to resist the attentions of a prostitute. St Paul here warrants a painting larger than the other apostles. On the third pilaster, St Joseph. On the chancel arch pillars, paintings of SS Dominic and Francis. *1st altar l.*. In the central niche, a young St Joseph holding the infant Christ, a superb Guatemalan work. Paintings of Christ appearing to St Catherine of Siena and St Rose carrying the Cross. On first pilaster, St Francis of Paola, founder of the Minims (the 'least brethren'). *2nd altar l.*, dedicated to St Vincent Ferrer. On second pilaster, St Raymond of Peñafort, founder of the Mercedarians. *3rd altar l.*, with a large painting of St Peter, matching that of St Paul opposite.

The pulpit is a late baroque masterpiece, carved in flamboyant relief. Its balustrade, divided into two panels by relief supports which resemble columns about to dissolve, almost overpowers the pulpit section. The latter, resting on a lavish pedestal, resembles a chalice; the canopy, the lid.

The S transept contains three more baroque altarpieces: at the S end, with wonderfully varied solomonic columns; on the E wall, with white effectively mixed with gold, the columns framing six elegant paintings of the Passion; on the W wall, with columns laden with fruit and vegetal motifs and a moving Trinity in the centre. The painting of SS Catherine and Dominic visited by Our Lady is a fine late 17C work.

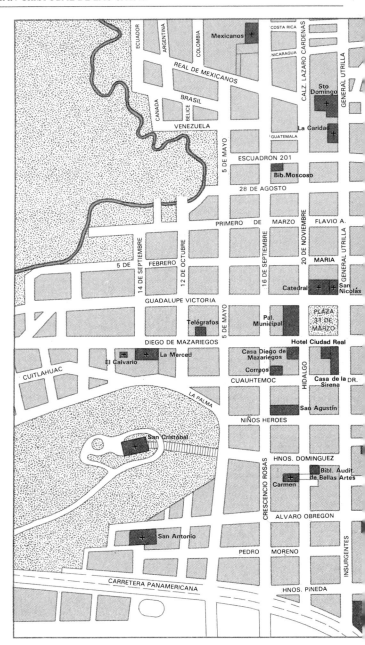

SAN CRISTOBAL
DE LAS CASAS

0 metres   400

The former convent is on the N side of the church. (The balcony in the N transept, with its simple wooden balusters, enabled the friars to watch services or to visit the church for private prayer without having to go into the choir or descend to the nave.) The S corridors of the cloister are built right up against the church wall. It was repaired, after years of neglect, in the early 20C to serve as the prison. After 1969 it was restored and now houses an indigenous co-operative for the sale of embroidery and woven items (expensive) from the surrounding area.

The next turning r. beyond Sto Domingo leads to the MARKET, crowded and colourful, where Indians sell fruit, vegetables, and handicrafts.

Hence we may return to the centre along C. Belisario Domínguez, passing (l.) the barrio church of *Cerrillo* (in its present state 19C and much altered), on the site of a chapel, built in the 16C for manumitted slaves. To the r. at the end of C. Comitán is the church of **La Caridad**, its façade facing a small plaza on the W.

The first church on the site belonged to the Order of St John of God (juaninos), established in Ciudad Real in 1636, who also ran a small hospital. A new church and hospital were built in 1712–14 and repaired in the 1780s. By 1813 the hospital had been closed down. Its L-shaped premises, on the NW side of the church, function today as a dispensary. The church was extensively restored in 1983–84.

EXTERIOR. The strange masonry façade, resembling a large retable, spreads wider than and bears no relation to the church behind, roofed with wood and tiles, and walled in adobe. Its two main horizontal sections are divided into five vertical bays, and the bases of the two towers, the outer bays, form an integral part of the composition. The columns of the lower storey lack bases and capitals, and the archivolt of the doorway niche projects beyond the surface of the façade, continuing alongside the jambs. The upper-storey supports, resembling pairs of consoles one above the other, are unique in Central America. They are repeated on either side of the gable, in the form of an espadaña and higher than the towers, supported on either side and decorated above by volutes, a baroque reminder. Merlons on towers and gable are a typical baroque feature.

The INTERIOR contains a sumptuous baroque high altarpiece, thick with solomonic columns framing central panel niches and outer panel paintings. In the N wing, resembling a separate church, is a churrigueresque altarpiece.

S of La Caridad we may turn r. along C. Escuadrón 201 to C. 16 de Septiembre. The house at the SW corner (29 C. 16 de Septiembre) contains the private library of Prof. Prudencio Moscoso (adm. daily, 4–7, by appointment), a famous collection on the history and customs of Chiapas.

At the SW angle of Pl. 31 de Marzo and at the corner of Cs Diego de Mazariegos and Hidalgo, the low two-storey house popularly known as *Casa de Diego de Mazariegos* is in fact a late 18C building, now partly a school, which may during 1678–1772 have been the local seminary. Following C. Diego de Mazariegos W we come, beyond C. Matamoros, to a small park facing the church of **La Merced**.

The Mercedarians established their first house in America at Ciudad Real in 1537, but never seem to have prospered here. In the later 19C their premises had been rebuilt and converted into a barracks, and then became ruinous. In the 1960s the building next to the church, where the convent had once been, was redesignated as a prison. The present church, its interior design by Carlos Z. Flores, dates from the earlier 20C. Behind the sacristy (not directly accessible from the street) is the simple little chapel of *El Calvario* (probably 18C).

From the SW corner of Pl. 31 de Marzo, C. Hidalgo leads S, past (r.) the neoclassically styled *Escuela de Derecho* (Faculty of Laws) of the University of Chiapas. At the corner with C. Niños Héroes is the former church called **San Agustín**, now used as a lecture hall.

This was, in all probability, the former church of the Jesuits (*La Compañia*), renamed after their expulsion in 1767, and built c 1675–80. Its EXTERIOR, though recently restored, still bears signs of the dilapidation into which it was allowed to fall. Above the choir window on the W façade, which has lost its upper parts, are three pear-like motifs in low relief, worn away, and therefore made more mysterious, by time. In the third bay of the buttressed S wall is a three-storeyed S door, an anachronistic blending of Renaissance and late Gothic. Above the semi-hexagonal arch of the interesting E doorway is the seal of the Society of Jesus, done in plaster—the letters IHS, surmounted by a cross and three nails beneath.

A little further S on C. Hidalgo (r., facing a plaza) is the church of **El Carmen**, once the church of the only convent of nuns in Ciudad Real.

It was founded, as *La Encarnación*, for Conceptionist nuns at the end of the 16C, and was always a poor foundation. The first four nuns arrived from Guatemala in 1609–10. By 1618 the church (an enlargement of the 16C church of San Sebastián which they had been given) was finished, but the convent, which took longer to build, was damaged by earthquake in 1744, unsatisfactorily rebuilt in 1753–66 (the community complained of the cold), and rebuilt again after 1784. The nuns were expelled in 1863; the last survivor died in 1897. Nothing of the convent now remains.

EXTERIOR. The walls of nave and transept (making an L-shape) are partly of adobe and partly of rubble stone and brick covered in stucco. On either side of the nave doorway (c 1753–60) on the N are strange, crude bulbous pilasters which end in top-storey capitals projecting through the ends of the empty frieze to finish in pot-like finials covered with acanthus leaves, from which sprout pestle-like knobs. In the arch spandrels are reliefs of two lions; above the arch, an eagle relief. The transept doorway (1764), facing W, is a poor attempt at grandeur, using slender solomonic columns in the lower storey and at the sides of the niche. In the upper storey the columns are convexly fluted—the outer column left poorly repaired at a later date.

INTERIOR. The nave is covered by a plain wooden ceiling; that in the transept, painted red and gold, is much richer, with lovely tie beams. The wooden interior walls are decorated with gilded arabesques. On the high altar is a statue of St Sebastian, dramatically suffering against a tree trunk, a Guatemalan work (c 1730). In the transept are two good 18C altarpieces, and paintings of the Passion (1762) by Andrés Mazariegos, a chiapaneco artist, ending with a Crucifixion (in the sacristy).

Attached to the E end of the church is the **Torre del Carmen**, unique in the Americas, which spans and narrows the street, and encroaches on the sidewalks.

It was built in response to a petition of 8 Feb. 1677, to serve as bell-tower (replacing a belfry destroyed by a tornado) and to include a passageway to connect a cloister on the S side of the church with another on the E side of the street, on the site of which (or possibly a conversion of which) is now the cultural centre. It may also have served as a choir.

Grand and imposing, in comparison with the humble convent and church, the three-storey base is surmounted by a small, square domed belfry, its vault a four-sided polygon. Most of the first three storeys are sheltered and recessed on both sides under an arch, like a huge niche, topped by a vast alfíz bounded by a column on each side. On the N side, various neoclassical details have been added (perhaps by Carlos Z. Flores); but the S side keeps its original simplicity. Its Mudéjar lineage is obvious, both as a freestanding tower and in the detail: from the plaster reliefs resembling the eight-pointed star in the spandrels of the niche arches to the octagonal wooden vault in the street-level passageway, pinned at its crown by a multi-tiered rosette in an eight-pointed star.

Facing the plaza on the E is San Cristóbal's main cultural complex, incl. a library, the *Instituto de las Bellas Artes*, a concert hall, and the *Casa de Cultura*.

We may return to the centre by going E along C. Hermanos Domínguez and turning l. along Av. Insurgentes. Immediately on the r., facing an atrio, is **San Francisco**, formerly the church of the Franciscan convent.

The first Franciscans arrived in 1577 and their convent, a poor affair never housing more than five friars, took a long time to complete because of their poverty and the fact that they could not compete with the Dominicans. Nothing of the convent has survived.

The church EXTERIOR, part of an 18C rebuilding, is rudimentary, but has an unusual touch in the neo-Romanesque choir window.

The high altarpiece, encasing 12 paintings of Our Lord, Our Lady, and saints, has squarish estípites as supports. The four nave altarpieces follow the same, spare, churrigueresque style and incorporate excellent statues of Our Lady of the Assumption (16C ?; good estofado) and SS Joseph, John Nepomuk, and Salvator of Horta. The pulpit (also 18C) invites comparison with those of the cathedral and Sto Domingo. The altarpiece in the transept is full-bloodedly baroque. Nave and transept walls are hung with acceptable 18C paintings (Annunciation and Holy Family). On the l. of the entrance is the original carved 16C font.

Av. Insurgentes leads back to Pl. 31 de Marzo. At the SE corner of the plaza, on the l., is the **Casa de la Sirena**, now converted into two hotels.

Original ownership of the house has been ascribed to Luis de Mazariegos, son of Diego, or to one Andrés de la Tobilla. It may date from c 1570, but could have been built later. The interior has been much altered to serve various uses, but the large patios, off which rooms open, follow the original pattern.

The doorway facing Av. Insurgentes is a rare example of civil plateresque. It is set against a section of the wall treated with stucco to resemble rusticated masonry. Slim columns stand on top of one another on either side of the door-way, the shafts of the lower pair marked by wide grooves. The upper pair, free of the wall behind, consist of plain shafts resting on coffered cubes encasing rosette motifs. On their capitals crouch lions with their tails curling inwards towards the window. Above the lintel is a blank shield surmounted by a helmet which interrupts a frieze of rosettes overshadowed by a heavy cornice. Above it, a small window, its lintel scalloped to resemble the draping of a curtain. On either side of the window are relief panels marked off by baluster colonnettes which frame reliefs of figures like sea-horses. Remains of the stucco relief (two sirens clinging to a vine) which adorned all the windows may be seen on the upper storey. Attached to the NE corner of the building is the moon-faced stone siren which gives the house its name.

In the NE section of the city, on the edge of the barrio of Cuxtitali, is **Na-Bolom** (House of the Jaguar; corner of Av. Vicente Guerrero and C. Chiapa de Corzo), which includes a library, museum, and research centre of the greatest interest.

The house, built in 1891, was bought in 1950 by the Dane Franz Blom (1893–1963), naturalized Mexican citizen shortly before his death. He and his Swiss wife, Gertrude Duby, have devoted their lives to the study of the Maya and to the welfare of the Lacandón Indians, a dwindling group who live in the rain forest along the Guatemalan frontier, and the protection of their homeland, threatened by deforestation (see Rte 86).

In 1923 Blom was the first director of excavations at *Uaxactún*, a large Maya ceremonial centre and city in Guatemala. He was one of the first to realize and opine on the wealth of material which has become known as the Olmec civilization, and also one of the first to recognize the archaeological importance of Chiapas.

The house includes guest rooms, but only for those with a genuine interest in the work pioneered by Franz and Gertrude Blom. It is essential to enquire about availability well in advance.

Guided tours take place in the afternoons (Tues.–Sun., 4–5.30; fee). The library (Tues.–Sat., 8–1; Mon., 2.30–6) contains a valuable collection of books and journals on the ethnology, anthropology, and history of Chiapas and the Maya, and on Mexico and Guatemala in general. The rest of the main house, with its plant- and flower-filled patios, contains pottery, handicrafts, etc. from the surrounding region. One room is dedicated to archaeological finds from *Moxviquil* (across the valley to the N of San Cristóbal, excavated in the early 1950s), *Hun Chabin, San Bartolomé de los Llanos*, the Valle de Comitán, *San Gregorio*, etc., all in Chiapas. Another illustrates the way of life of the Lacandón Indians. The former chapel contains religious art of the 18–19C.

Further E, reached along Calz. Franz Blom, in C. de los Arcos, is the little church of *Cuxtitali*, dating from 1650, but much altered. Above the central window of the façade, covered in coats of whitewash, may be made out crude reliefs of Crucifixion symbols, and, on either side of them, female angels. In the adjoining bays are representations of the sun and moon.

C 2km W, on the road to Tuxtla Gutiérrez, is the village of *San Felipe Ecatepec*, whose church, the nave walled in adobe, dates from the mid-16C. The façade was completed in the late 17C.

C 7km above San Cristóbal along a rough road (best reached on foot or in a four-wheel drive vehicle) and on private land is the little chapel called **Quinta del Aserradero**, built probably c 1769–74 on an estate used as a retreat by the bps of Chiapas. Two broad little towers stand forward of the façade, forming a porch, across which runs a wooden gallery. The doorway has a trefoil arch. The towers are decorated in incised and modelled stucco: to resemble rusticated stone blocks in the bases; plaque decoration above the moulding; coffers enclosing rosettes in the shafts; balusters in the attics; while the belfries are full of floral motifs, rosettes, and scallop shells.

The probable use of a gallery as an outdoor pulpit or open chapel, the trefoil arch, and the use of rustication betray Peruvian influences, possibly because Manuel de Vargas y Rivera, the bishop who built it, was a native of Lima.

Within a reasonable radius of San Cristóbal are several predominantly Tzotzil-speaking towns keeping their old customs, and colourful traditional dress, and engagingly mixing Catholic and pagan rites.

It has to be said that the coming in recent years of crowds of gawping foreigners attempting to take photographs and (most insensitively) wearing articles of local clothing bought in the markets, or inadequate dress of their own, has made the locals hostile and suspicious. Taking photographs is either prohibited or strongly discouraged. Visitors are warned. Most of the Indian inhabitants live in small settlements in the wider municipio; the town serves as a religious centre.

A rough road winds NW to (7km) **San Juan Chamula** (2300m), once site of a small Classic-Postclassic Maya centre, where the parish church probably dates from the 17C, although the upper part of the façade was altered in 1954. The W doorway, in the form of two niches within an outer niche, has coffered reliefs in archivolts and jambs (reminiscent of 16C examples in central Mexico) and the balcony above could have served as an open chapel. A small ruined church in the outskirts may date from the early 17C. **Zinacantán** (4km SW; 2150m) is another typical place. It was an important Tzotzil Maya trading centre in the Postclassic Period, exporting salt, amber, quetzal feathers, animal pelts, and other raw materials to central Mesoamerica. Despite repeated attempts, the Aztecs were unable to control the principality, but eventually established an enclave of traders in it. The Chiapaneca, neighbours, to the S and W, were also constant trade rivals, often to the extent of open warfare. One Spanish conquistador described the town as full of 'sensible people and many of them traders'.

Today the town and its milperos (farmers) are important to the archaeologist in several ways. Their farming techniques are similar to prehistoric Maya methods of slash-and-burn agriculture. Tracks of land are cleared by cutting and firing the stubble, then planted using a digging stick to punch holes in the soil, into which seeds are dropped by hand, from a net bag or armadillo shell container, and covered using the foot. Beans, squash, and maize are the principal crops. The Zinacantecos continue the Maya practice of 'cargo' systems. These are social sets of ranked civil and religious offices held by adult males; but today only the religious cargoes survive. The cargo-holder must go through four levels in rank, each for one year, during which time he must leave his home and live in the community's ceremonial centre. There, he must pay his own maintenance, plus the costs for hospitality and for necessary ceremonial equipment. His rewards are great community prestige and attention, and personal fulfilment. The religious cargoes of Zinacantán and the neighbouring town of Chamula serve communities of 8000 and 40,000 people, respectively. The Zinacantán 'Earth Owner', the modern equivalent of Maya Chac, the Rain god, must be placated by special ceremonies during planting. He is depicted riding a deer, a tradition thought to have originated when the Maya saw Spaniards on horseback. (When Cortés abandoned his horse at Tayasal, it was deified as Tizimin Chac, god of thunder and lightning.)

The road runs NW to (21km) turning r. for (30km E) **Chenalhó** (1850m; H,R), remote but friendlier. 29km **San Andrés Larraínzar** (1275m; H).

25km NW of San Cristóbal is **Tenejapa** (1970m; H,R), reached by a difficult and winding mountain road, with a co-operative turning out local woven goods.

88 San Cristóbal de las Casas to Ciudad Cuauhtémoc

Méx. 190, 170km.—32km Teopisca.—88km **Comitán**.—104km turning l. for (30km E) Chinkultic and (34km E) the Lagunas de Montebello.—106km La Trinitaria.—136km San Antonio and (c 8km E) **Coneta**.—170km Ciudad Cuauhtémoc.

Beyond San Cristóbal, Méx. 190 continues SE. At 10km the road l. (NE) runs to (195km) *Palenque* and (336km) *Villahermosa*, see Rte 89. At (32km) **Teopisca** (c 8000 inhab.; H,P), now a mestizo town, the large church of *San Agustín*, dating probably from the early 17C, is prefaced by a handsome marble façade. Its nave artesonado ceiling, hexagonally coffered above the chancel, is a reconstruction of 1949. The chancel altarpiece (c 1713), donated by Sebastián Olivera Ponce to the Jesuit church in San Cristóbal, was removed here in 1881.

Thomas Gage passed through Teopisca in 1626: 'a great and fair town of Indians...the church is great and strong, and the music belonging to it sweet and harmonious'.

35km *Amatenango del Valle*, where the church is probably an 18C rebuilding, after earthquake damage in 1714. Its W façade fourth storey espadaña and towers were rebuilt c the 1940s. At (c 8km S; a few km r.) *Cerro Chavín*, a Late Classic Period site, was built high on a hilltop, protected by cliffs. Its isolation and military appearance reflect the troubled times of c AD 900 when the focus of Classic Maya civilization was shifting N into Yucatán. At *Aguacatenango*, a little further S (l.), the church (c 1635–40), with relief figures and symbols in the upper part of its façade almost obliterated by coats of lime wash, has avoided modernization. From 63km it is possible to reach the small classic Maya site of *Yerba Buena*, a few km E of the road.

From here Méx. 190 goes SE through beautiful scenery to (88km) **COMITÁN** (c 80,000 inhab.; 1530m; H,R,P), in a broad valley, with a year-round spring-like climate, sloping streets of one-storey houses, and an abundance of wild orchids.

In the 17C Comitán was a largely Indian (Coxoh- and Cavil-speaking) town, under Dominican care. Another Indian tongue, Tojolabal, has become virtually extinct. In 1840 John L. Stephens found it a commercial centre with a trade in contraband from Guatemala and Belize, a traffic which (from Guatemala) continues today. It is the birthplace of Belisario Domínguez (1863–1913), physician and senator, murdered after his fearless denunciations of the Huerta regime (see Rte 8).

On the E side of the ample PL. PRINCIPAL is the handsome church of **Sto Domingo** whose considerable length (72m) and narrowness are masked by a wide façade.

It is all that remains of the last Dominican establishment in Chiapa, raised to convent status in 1596 and centre of a vast parish. The church was probably started after that date; the convent buildings no longer exist. By 1786, with Dominican influence declining, the church was described as ruined. In 1626 Thomas Gage stayed 'a whole month' as guest of the French prior, Tomás Rocolano; c 1840 John L. Stephens recorded that a number of friars were still in residence.

The simple façade and square tower on its N side present a pleasing ensemble and show different stylistic traits: an alfíz covers the architrave-less arch; above it, a rose window and a gable with broken and curving raking cornices (a baroque touch), on which stand merlons. The tower, composed of a series of cubical layers, complete with parapet and pyramidal finials on which rest globes, is within the Mudéjar tradition.

High above the plaza and reached by a broad flight of steps is the church of *San Caralampio* (19C); in the wide façade of *El Calvario*, also raised above street level, is a 19C celebration of 18C Guatemalan baroque. In the *Casa de Cultura*, on the E side of Pl. Principal, is a local archaeological museum (daily, 9–6), containing Classic Period sculpture and other artefacts, chief among them stele 18 and stucco fragments from the ball court at Chinkultic. In Belisario Domínguez's house (29 Av. Central Sur; Tues.–Sat., 10–6.30; Sun., 9–12.30; fee) have been reproduced his surgery and dispensary, while documents relating to his life are exhibited in other rooms. In the municipal park stands a dressed stele from *La Trinitaria* (to the S).

Just N of Comitán the small, Late Classic Period site of *Hun-Chabin*, excavated in 1926–27 and 1940, has some sculptured monuments and mounds forming a plaza. A few burials were excavated in nearby caves.

102km (c 2km r.) *Tenam (Tenam-Puente)*, a small archaeological zone investigated by Franz Blom (1929), Sylvanus Morley (1937–38), and Tatiana Proskouriakoff (1950).

Stelae from the site give it a Late Classic date, c AD 900. These other stelae found in the valley, and the fine-cut masonry style, indicate Lowland Maya influence, perhaps along with population migrations into the area; some sources even speak of invasion. It has been suggested that there was also Toltec, or Maya–Toltec influence, from Toltecs moving S and establishing themselves at Chichén Itzá (see Introduction: Early Postclassic Period).

Of the two pyramids here, the larger has six tiers; scarce remains of other buildings are on a terraced hillside.

104km turning l.

We go along a reasonable paved road for (27km) another turning l. for (3km N) **Chinkultic** ('Little Sanctuary'; 8–5; fee), a Classic-Late Classic Maya site tucked away amongst tropical vegetation, two lakes, and limestone outcrops.

It was visited in 1895 by Edouard Seler, then surveyed, mapped, and partly excavated by various archaeologists in the 1920s, 1950s, and 1960s, discovering some 200 mounds and several stelae.

The site was probably a porters' stop along the N–S trade route.

The principal structure is 1km from the car park, but c 90m before the entrance gate a barbed-wire enclosure on the l. leads to *Grupo C*, a *Juego de Pelota*, and some unexcavated mounds c 180m off the path. These sit on an artificial terrace, built to divert the river, and the I-shape plan of the ball court is easy to distinguish amongst the mounds. There is a stele on one of the mounds, two more on a path to the l., beyond the ball court's playing field, and a more elaborate, but broken, one under a small shelter at the ball court itself. Altogether, ten stelae have been found on the site, some of which are now in the Museo Nacional de Antropología, together with the beautifully carved stone marker disc from the ball court. *Stela 18* is in the museum in Comitán, and other stelae are in the local museum in Akumal.

The path continues, crossing a bridge over the river between Lagunas Tepancuapan and Chanujabab, to the base of the acropolis of the sanctuary. Here a wide terraced plaza embanks the river, with several unexcavated mounds and a stepped pyramid 8m high.

It is a ten-minute, c 60m climb, to *Estructuras 1* and *2* at the acropolis. The larger pyramid, *Estructura 1*, has been restored, showing at least two phases of construction. The first phase was a Classic Period pyramid and staircase. At the top of the first tier is a niche and a circular, corbel-vaulted receptacle, possibly for offerings or used as a tomb. In the second, Late Classic phase, a larger pyramid, c 8m high, and staircase were built over the first. In front of this second pyramid, *Altar A* was built on a small platform, first used as an altar and later as a tomb.

Estructura 2, unrestored, is a smaller pyramid on the edge of the cenote.

Beyond the turning for Chinkultic the side road continues E to (34km) a turning l. for the entrance, a few km S of the road, to the **Parque Nacional Lagunas de Montebello**, part of a spectacular area of forest and lakes (between 60 and a hundred) which straddles the frontier with Guatemala.

A combination of sunlight, depth, composition of the water, and minerals at the lake bottom gives distinctive hues to the waters of the best-known group of lakes (*Lagunas de Colores*). At c 5km N of the turning is the village of *San Rafael*, where guides can be hired for a serious exploration of the area and its lesser-known attractions (recommended if visitors are not to lose their way). A further 16km E along the side road is the *Laguna de Tziscao* (simple accommodation at the village at its E end), largest of the lakes nearest the road; the waters are crystalline.

From Tziscao a track (usable only in dry weather and in high suspension vehicles, and dangerous for the inexperienced) has run along the frontier to the SE corner of the State (and the republic), called *Zona Marqués de Comillas*, and then NW to Bonampak, Yaxchilán, and Palenque. There are plans to convert it into a paved road. To the E is the Río Usumacinta, originating in Guatemala, forming the frontier for part of its course, running through E Tabasco, and emptying into the Gulf of Mexico.

From the Lagunas de Montebello turning Méx. 190 continues S through some of the loveliest scenery in Mexico. 106km (l.) **La Trinitaria** (c 3000 inhab.; 1530m), with steep streets and agreeable small plazas; its historical name, *La Santísima Trinidad de Zapaluta*. The church of *San Caralampio* (16–17C; restored early 18C) has a crudely attractive retable façade; in its fourth storey a delightful relief of a winged young man in 17C costume, incl. high boots, possibly a representation of St Michael. From (123km) *Tzitul* (r.) may be reached (with difficulty) the ranch called *Coral de Piedra*, near the site of *Coapa*, founded in the late 16C, maintained as a stopping place (unhealthy and swampy) on the old Camino Real, and abandoned in the 1690s. Its ruined church (c 1615–80) is a ghostly survival; on a low mound off its SE corner are what remains of a smaller building with plateresque detail on its W doorway jambs, probably a late 16C chapel.

A few km NW, on the Río San Gregorio, is the site of *Escuintenango*, another 16C town, extinct by the early 19C. The SE tower is a sad memory of its church of Santiago.

136km *San Antonio*. From here it is possible to reach (c 8km E) the site of **CONETA**, lying in a valley, watered by a stream during the summer rains, otherwise arid, now a cattle-ranch.

It was a largely Indian town, founded in the mid-16C, abandoned, after depopulation caused by epidemics, in the mid-18C. In the late 16C the Dominicans had set up a visita, dependent on their convent at Comitán.

To the S and W of the town site stand the church and convent of **San José** (1671–81), the most fascinating historical ruin of the area.

Stephens came upon it in its desolation in 1839, and was impressed by its great size and 'rich and perfect' façade. He and his companions, Frederick Catherwood and Mr Rawlings, inscribed their names in the central belfry.

Its W façade, an uninhibited flight of fancy by an anon. designer-builder using plateresque, baroque, and highly individual stylistic details within a Mudéjar scheme, is divided into five horizontal sections. The lowest storey is a four-arch blind arcade resting on a generous die. In the arches, and in the lower archivolt of the handsome three-layered doorway, are circular and oblong reliefs—poor versions of the rosette and coffer. Traces of red and blue painted decoration (outlines in black) on the inner arches and jambs may still be seen. The second and (narrow) third storeys are full of delightfully idiosyncratic elements. Six strange supports (truncated pyramidal base enclosing a circle with rays [sun symbol ?] holding up a long pilaster interrupted by a bulging ring-like band and a square with a curving underside enclosing another circle with rays) divide the former into five bays—double width over the doorway. In the centre is a rose window; above it a niche within a rectangular frame, flanked by two roundels and covered by an isolated capital, giving the accidental effect of a pre-Conquest mask. On either side of the window is a little niche, framed by broad pilasters, in which two pairs of spiral mouldings shoot up and down from roundels in high relief; above each niche is a freestanding pot. The pattern is reflected in each bay, the pots giving emphasis to the chiaroscuro possibilities of the façade. Seven more most singular pilasters divide the third storey into five similar bays, the chubbier central five pilasters incorporating circular and square motifs in their shafts and surmounted by the sturdiest imitation of capitals. Four niches are composed of a central niche proper and two tiny side bays, formed by pairs of the slenderest baluster colonnettes, with deep circles above. The fourth and fifth storeys, flanked by small domed belfries, are an elaborate gable, within the tradition of Guatemalan baroque, but using slender colonnettes for the three fourth-storey niches and echoes of baluster columns for the fifth-storey bays. Scallop motifs form the niche canopies; two still hold parts of their original statues. Four more freestanding pots are placed two on either side of the central niche and one each on the outside pair of the four stepped, chunky pilasters which divide the storey into three bays. The buttressed nave walls (pierced by four windows), in undressed stone, chancel and polygonal apse, and chancel arch still stand. Remains of two timber brackets which supported the floor beams of the (wooden, destroyed) choir, at the W end, may still be seen.

At 147km a road leads l. (E) to (1km) *Joaquín Miguel Gutiérrez*, an agricultural colony on the l. bank of a river formed by tributaries of the San Gregorio, in turn a tributary of the Mezcalapa. It occupies the site of historic *Aquespala*, founded by the Dominicans c 1548–50, extinct by the early 19C.

What remains is the broad façade of the church of *San Nicolás* (c mid-17C) and bits of the nave and chancel walls.

Méx. 190 skirts the W slopes of the *Cuchumantes*, the mountain range which bestrides the frontier. 167km turning r. (W) for (18km) *Frontera Comalapa*, a little to the S of which, on a ranch, are the ruins of *Cuxu*, the historic Comalapa, another 16C Indian town which faded away as the 18C progressed.

The side road ends at (42km) *Chicomuselo*, a similar settlement, moribund by the mid-19C. Its new church is on the site of the 17C Dominican visita church. For the adventurous, a few km SW are the ruins of the sister town of *Yayaguita*, on the land of a ranch called *Finca Veracruz* or *Pueblo Viejo*, founded in the early 17C.

Méx. 190 ends in Mexico at (170km) *Ciudad Cuauhtémoc*, an inappropriately named locality from where the frontier is negotiated.

89 Villahermosa to Palenque

Méx. 186 and Méx. 199, 146km. Continuation to (118km) Ocosingo (for [14km E] **Toniná**).

Méx. 186 runs E then SE across the plain, an uninspiring landscape with pastureland and some forest. At (32km) a road (l.) runs E to (27km) *Ciudad Pemex*, a new town and oil-drilling centre with a water treatment plant and ancillary installations, and across the Río Tepetitlán to (86km) *Jonuta*, see Rte 91B. 47km turning l. for (6km NE) **Macuspana** (c 10,000 inhab.; 68m; H,R,P), in traditional Chol Indian country, now an active oil-producing area.

Tortuguero, c 10km SE, was the site of a small Maya ceremonial centre, probably within the political sphere of Palenque to the SE. Little remains of its monuments, but a stele dated AD 645 has been found here, together with texts that refer to noblewomen in Palenque, suggesting that small subsidiary towns were bound to the capital by marriage alliances. E of Macuspana, the road parallels the route of Cortés' expedition into Guatemala and Honduras in 1524–25. N of and well off the road (guide necessary), ruins of two Postclassic sites are thought to be those identified by Cortés as *Chilapa* (c 22km E of Macuspana) and *Tepetitán* (c 30km E).

At 64km a road goes S to (4km) *Agua Blanca*, a spa with waterfalls formed by the Río Tulijá and a mirador giving a view of the Tabasco land and riverscape. We then cross the Río Tulijá and enter the State of Chiapas. At 115km, just S of the *Laguna de Catazajá* (fishing, sailing), formed during July–Dec. from the waters of the Río Usumacinta, we turn r. (S; Méx. 199) for (141km) **Palenque** (*Sto Domingo Palenque*; 60,000 inhab.; 60m; H,R,P), a town which offers good headquarters for visitors to the archaeological site, 8km SW.

PALENQUE is perhaps the most celebrated of the great Maya sites, known especially for its rich royal burial, stucco sculptures, and many unique or rare architectural features or omissions. Innovations and high-quality craftsmanship in stucco, jewellery, ceramics, and mosaics set Palenque apart, perhaps along with the site of Yaxchilán, as an artistic centre, for its own special style in the Maya world.

Its name is a Spanish translation of the Palencano-Chol Maya dialect word *otulum*—'fortified houses', or 'palisades'; Palencano-Chol is of NW Tabascan origin, and is still spoken at Palenque and in the Lacandón Forest. More common in ancient times, however, was its name Nachan, meaning 'town of snakes', in the Tzeltal dialect. Its history has been pieced together mostly from the archaeological record, incl. abundant inscriptions and dates from Palenque itself and from other contemporary Maya sites.

Palenque-Nachan was occupied in the Preclassic Period but remained an insignificant, rustic town until the 6C AD. For the relatively short timespan of c 150 years it flourished as a regional capital, during which most of the surviving monuments were built, before it was replaced by another Maya city. Three roughly defined phases can be distinguished in its development: in the Early Classic, when there were no inscriptions and no vaulted buildings; in the Middle Classic, when most of the construction of its civic buildings took place, and it flourished as one of four Maya regional capitals (Tikal in Guatemala, Copán in Honduras, Palenque and Calakmul); and in the early Late Classic, when the city was harassed from the NW, probably by Totonacs from the Gulf Coast (who left their characteristic yugos for the ball game and carvings of flattened heads), and when terraced lines of defences were built and many doorways blocked up as if for siege conditions. The last known inscription is on a pot (AD 799), shortly after which Palenque lost its political control, possibly to Motul, as Maya power shifted to N Yucatán. Interestingly, Piedras Negras (Guatemala), La Mar, El Cayo, and Bonampak (all to the SE) erected their last dated monuments within only a decade after this, while Yaxchilán held out only until AD 840. At its height Palenque included an area of c 24 to 32 sq km, a vast hinterland around a central, monumental core. Its political sphere was fairly well defined, stretching N to Jonuta, NW to Comalcalco (which shares many of Palenque's architectural features), W to Tortuguero (almost certainly a dependent city), E and S to the borders of Piedras Negras and Yaxchilán (to an as yet unidentified site called Pomona in the sources), and to the S to Toniná.

Palenque-Nachan had its own glyph sign, and during the height of its power inscriptions attest to its long-distance trading power; to its political diplomacy, referring to Yaxchilán and Copán (whose glyph signs are also known); and to its dependencies and other noble houses. References to the trio of deities—Chac (god of rain), the Sun god, and his consort (goddess of the moon and of fertility)—attest to connections with central Mexico, to Xochicalco in the Valle de Morelos.

The inscriptions reveal information on Palenque's rulers, incl. the woman rulers Kan-Ik (AD 583–604) and Zac-Kuk (612–627), and the latter's son, Lord Pacal (Shield), whose long reign lasted from 615 to 683. Lord Pacal was succeeded by his sons Chan-Bahlum (640–702) and Hok (702–25). Lord Pacal was born in AD 603, and was only 12½ years old when he ascended the throne under his mother's regency. He claimed a mythological ancestry, and was looked upon as semi-divine. In a power struggle preceding his reign, his uncle was beheaded (duly recorded in a stucco relief sculpture), and it was this uncle's clubfoot that was considered a divine attribute. Similarly, Pacal's mother had an enlarged skull from acromegaly (a disease that causes a growth hormone to produce a tumor in the pituitary gland), also no doubt considered divine. Pacal flaunted his own clubfoot as proof of his divine descent, and the clubfoot was eventually symbolized in Maya art as a serpent and symbol of rulership at Palenque. After AD 912, God K, as he became known (see Introduction: Maya Religion) was depicted with both a serpent foot and an enlarged forehead.

Lord Pacal may have married his mother in order to maintain the divine tradition of marrying within rank; and also his sister, Ahpo-Hel. Thus there seems ample explanation, if this practice had been going on for some time, for the genetic deformities harboured in Palenque's ruling house. During his long reign his and his mother's energies are thought to be responsible for the rise of Palenque as a Maya regional capital, and for most of the civic building programme, incl. several unique structures (see below). At his death he was fittingly given a sumptuous royal burial in the Templo de las Inscripciones, in a plaza he had himself designed.

Sculptures in stucco on the temples of the Cross Group depict the transfer of power to Chan-Bahlum. Bahlum's special deformity was to have six toes on each foot and six fingers on his left hand—polydactyly. Although Pacal had planned his own tomb, it was Bahlum who completed it. He is depicted as a baby on several other monuments, recognizable by his six-toed feet, and his adult portrait head appears in stucco in Templo XIV.

Lord Hok, Pacal's second son, succeeded his brother when he was 38, and ruled for 23 years. It was he who was responsible, as his lasting mark on Palenque, for the remodelling of the Palacio, extending it to massive proportions by adding numerous galleries of rooms and inner patios.

In contrast to these powerful rulers little is known of some of Hok's successors: Chaac, Chac-Zutz, and Kuk, one of whom was responsible for the four-storeyed tower in the Palacio. Lord Kuk is the last we know by name, and as he reigned for c 20 years (to c 784), it is clear that Palenque did not survive as a great power for long after his death.

Architecture. The obsession of the royal house was with maintaining its myth of divinity. This is clear in its sculptures; and it has been suggested that the city was deliberately chosen as a necropolis, associated with the Dying Sun of the W, and with the Underworld in general. Architecturally, it includes many features that set it apart from other Maya cities, despite its close political and economic relations with them. It is laid out on the low foothills overlooking the coastal plain of the Río Usumacinta, blending architectural planning into the local terrain, and taking careful account of the relationships between buildings, as at Uxmal and Tulum. Yet despite this harmony of placement there is no apparent master plan and no great central plaza or acropolis, as in almost all other Maya cities. Many typical Maya traits are either missing or rare. There are no paired stele-and-altar groups (in fact, there are only two known stelae), no sacbeob, and no great caches of imported obsidians, flints, or other stones. Other features are unique or rare, such as the vaulted water channel in the Palacio, the four-storeyed tower, the crypts and their curious 'psychoducts', the style of its centrally positioned roof-combs, and its distinctive ceramics. The ball court, not a rare feature in itself, seems small and plain for a site with such a large palace and powerful ruling house. Palenque's ceramic assemblage included a relatively small percentage of Classic Maya Tepeu polychromes in comparison to other Maya cities; and fine-paste wares, more typical of the Gulf Coast and central Mexico, feature more prominently. There is also a patolli board (on which a pachisi-like game was played), resembling those at Tula, Teotihuacán, and Cuahtetelco.

Thus, Palenque represents a strong regional style of its own, while incorporating the classic Maya elements of roof-combs, palace complexes, stucco moulding, and craftsmanship of high quality. Characteristic features include the use of stepped-platforms to support temples and corbel-arched double galleries of chambers, mansard-like sloping roofs, roof-combs over the central walls of the galleries, and superb stucco portraits and hieroglyphic inscriptions and dates. The temples show a relative dating sequence from simple two-chambered ones to more elaborate, multi-chambered ones. In them, the central dividing wall, rather than a rear wall, supports the roof-comb and is not built as a solid mass, but is broken by many doors, which themselves tend to be wider than at other Maya sites. This practice gives the structures a lighter, more airy feel and appearance.

Stucco portraits are characteristically realistic, a legacy of Chan-Bahlum, especially, and show the deformed heads, limbs, almond eyes, thin lips, long noses, elaborate headdresses, and abundant jewellery of the ruling class. In the crypt structures there are so-called 'psychoducts', tubes from the tombs, through the masonry, to within a few cm of the temple floors above them, thought to provide lasting communication channels between the outer world and the dead.

Palenque was noted and described by several 18C travellers, incl. Ramón de Ordóñez y Aguiar in 1773 (whose report was published in 1784), José Antonio Calderón in 1784, Antonio Bernanconi, and José Antonio del Río in 1787, who was commissioned by and wrote a report (published in London in 1822) for Charles III of Spain. Guillaume Dupaix, commissioned by Charles IV, and the Mexican artist Luciano Castañeda explored and illustrated the site in 1805 (but their book was not published until 1834 in Paris), followed by Jean-Frédéric Maximilien de Waldeck (1766–1875), who explored the ruins in 1834–36, but did not publish his book until 1864. John L. Stephens and Frederick Catherwood visited in 1840, publishing their book of descriptions and illustrations promptly in 1841. In the 1860s Désiré Charnay (the first excavator of Tula) visited the site, followed by Teobart Maler, Alfred Maudslay (who visited it repeatedly between 1889 and 1902), William Holmes, and Leopoldo Batres. At the turn of the 20C came Edouard Seler, then Sylvanus G. Morley, and finally Franz Boas, who conducted the first systematic excavations (although Del Río had actually cleared some of the ruins in 1787).

The importance of the site was officially recognized by the Mexican government in 1940 and INAH began restoration work under the direction of Miguel Angel Fernández the same year. The restoration was continued by Alberto Ruz in 1945–52, who discovered the Templo de las Inscripciones in 1949. Later excavations were conducted by César Sáenz in 1954, and by Ignacio Marquina in 1957.

The Archaeological Zone. Palenque can be visited by special excursion planes from Villahermosa, Mérida, or San Cristóbal de las Casas; tourist buses from the same cities; or by private car. Daily 8–6; fee.

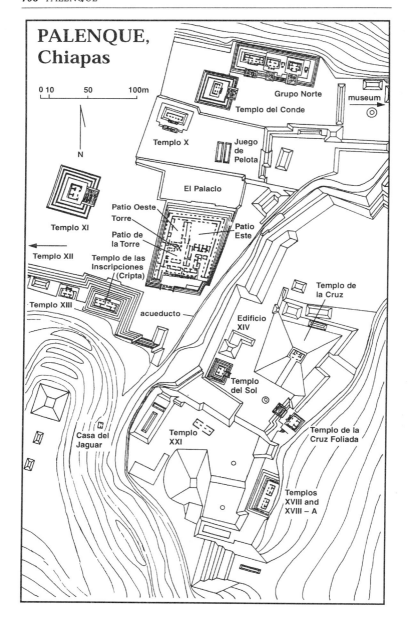

PALENQUE, Chiapas

0 10   50   100m

N

Templo XI

Templo XII

Templo de las Inscripciones (Cripta)

Templo XIII

Patio Oeste
Torre
Patio de la Torre

El Palacio

Patio Este

Templo X

Juego de Pelota

Grupo Norte

Templo del Conde

museum

acueducto

Edificio XIV

Templo de la Cruz

Templo del Sol

Casa del Jaguar

Templo XXI

Templo de la Cruz Foliada

Templos XVIII and XVIII – A

Of the 24–32 sq km of the ancient city only a core zone of c 500m by 275m has been cleared and restored. Other groups of ruins lie under vegetation all around this centre (eg, *Grupo 4*, just before the entrance to the main zone), and a guided excursion to several local waterfalls and natural wells can be made, incl. Misoljá, Motiepá, Laguna Catazajá, and Río Chacamax. The entrance and car park are on the W side of the site; and the first structures to be encountered are on the r. (S) of the footpath.

Templos XII and **XIII** are two small temple ruins of the simpler, earlier type at Palenque. The first has inscribed dates of AD 731 and 764, and a carved stucco relief on one of the pillars of its gallery. In the second, excavators discovered a tomb in a crypt beneath the floor—one of many at Palenque.

The **Templo de las Inscripciones** is the first well-preserved and restored monument encountered. It comprises a pyramid, partly incorporating a hillock, the temple, and the royal burial crypt beneath the temple.

The original pyramid (23m high) was of eight tiers, which were later covered by three blocks. Presently there are eight tiers, a narrow staircase (of the first and second pyramids just described) up the N side, and nine steps of a later, widened staircase (at the foot of the narrower staircase). As the pyramid was built, the crypt and vaulted stairway, turning at the landing, were built simultaneously. The temple was then constructed on top, with close-fitting paving stones over the crypt, one of which had a double row of holes with stoppers and provided the only clue to the existence of the crypt 23m below. When Alberto Ruz lifted this stone in 1949 the stairway was completely filled with rubble, which took four years to excavate scientifically, to reveal the crypt's secrets.

The temple itself is of two parallel galleries entered from the N, up nine steps with side ramps of carved panels and through a portico with four pillars, each carved with life-sized stucco figures holding the child-God K. Originally the mansard-shaped roof supported a painted comb of stucco figures. Inside, the walls of the porticoed gallery and the inner gallery are alike covered with three panels of 620 glyphs, hence the monument's name, recording the successive *katuns* (20-year Maya calendrical divisions). These also report details of the lives of some of Palenque's rulers, incl. Lord Pacal.

The inner gallery contains the entrance to the *Cripta*, two flights of steps covered by ten sections of corbel-arches and stone spanning-rods in the upper vaults. The two 'light galleries' which now provide ventilation are in fact the built-in 'psychoducts' running from the sarcophagus to the temple above. A corridor runs from the foot of the stairway and was originally blocked off by lime-plastered stone slabs.

Against these stood a chest of offerings: jade beads, a pearl, earplugs, pottery vessels, a shell holding red pigment. At the end of this hallway stood a small stone tomb containing the bones of five or six sacrificed children, presumably to accompany their lord into the next life. Lastly, a triangular stone set into the wall of the corridor masked the entrance to the crypt.

When the crypt was finally opened in 1952, the tomb of Lord Pacal, as described in the inscriptions on the outside, was discovered. The burial chamber measures 9.1m by 3.9m, with a 7m high corbel-vaulted ceiling reinforced with stone beams. The walls are lined with stucco reliefs depicting nine priests bearing symbols of the Sun and of Chac, the Rain god. Pottery vessels and two sculptured portrait heads littered the floor.

The sarcophagus containing Lord Pacal's body is a single block c 3m by 2m and 1m high. It rests on six stone piers, the corner ones carved, and is covered by a monolithic lid, in turn covered by a 5-tonne, 4m-long carved stone lid showing Lord Pacal with his clubfoot and wearing an elaborate headdress as God K. He falls into the gaping mouth of the Underworld, together with the symbol of the Dying Sun. There are 14 dates inscribed on the lid, recording Lord Pacal's birth, death, and significant life-events, and pictures of his ancestors.

The skeleton inside bore the pigment (cinnabar) of the red shroud in which it was wrapped, and was bedecked with a piece of jade in his mouth and in each hand, five jade rings on each finger, bracelets, a diadem, a necklace, and earplugs. Over his face was laid a jade-mosaic mask with shell- and obsidian-inlaid eyes. (A reconstruction of the crypt and sarcophagus can also be seen in the Museo Nacional de Antropología.) The rich symbolism of this burial clearly indicates the believed divinity of Palenque's ruling house.

Before descending the pyramid a good view of the rest of the zone can be had from the temple portico.

El Palacio is opposite the Templo de las Inscripciones, to the NE, and comprises a complex of chambered galleries and inner patios. Although not built all at one time, there is a basic division of N and S groups. It is thought that the wider, less-cluttered N section housed the members of the ruling family, while the cramped, smaller-roomed S half housed guards and household servants. The sophistication of Maya civilization is manifest in the vaulted lavatories, in a small inner court near the central tower, built over a channelled stream from the Río Otulum, which runs through the site.

The Palacio complex, c 70m by 55m, stands on a large trapezoidal platform, c 10m high, and measuring c 100m by 79m. The original staircase mounted the W side, and was later covered by a wide (63m) staircase of three flights of nine steps each.

Dominating the central part of the complex, just off-centre in the PATIO DE LA TORRE, stands the unique four-storeyed **Torre**. Its base is a solid mass, 7m by 7.4m, and c 4m high, reinforced at the corners by pilasters, and decorated with carved stone slabs. Above are three corbelled storeys with tall, wide openings on all sides. Each corner and the central core is made up of huge stone blocks, and the centre supports two straight flights of steps to the upper galleries. On the wall of one landing there is a Venus painting, indicating an astronomical function for the structure.

On the day of the winter solstice, when the sun is at its lowest and weakest, observers from the palace would in fact see its last rays through a notch in the ridge behind the Templo de las Inscripciones, spotlighting scenes on the Templo de la Cruz. The rays would further follow the oblique line along the stairs of Lord Pacal's tomb, symbolically sinking, or dying, into his temple.

The rooms of the Palacio are labelled Edificios A through K. Edificios G–K are mostly unrestored.

Edificios C and *D* are found on the E and W sides of PATIO OESTE, and form the NW corner of the complex. Each is two parallel galleries of rooms entered through porticoed façades on the W sides. In *D* there are five doorways with bas-reliefs on the dividing walls, each showing two figures. Traces of more sculptures can be seen on the roof, which also supported a light roof-comb. A treble opening between the two galleries leads to a staircase to the roof. At *C*, across the patio, there are hieroglyphic inscriptions on the walls of the platform and, on the walls separating the doorways, stucco reliefs of a cross-legged, seated figure in an elaborate headdress. More reliefs are inside, and the stairs on the E side have reliefs and dates relating Lord Pacal's birth, accession, and a possible reference to the site of Yaxchilán. There are hieroglyphs in cartouches, the pillars have bas-reliefs painted red, blue, green, and black, and the roof has reliefs of figures and grotesque masks. Between the S end of Edificio C and the Torre is the vaulted lavatory referred to above.

PATIO ESTE and *Edificio A* (on the E side of the patio) form the NE corner of the complex. There are bas-reliefs on the terrace retaining walls and ramps, and on the E façade of Edificio A. This comprises two parallel galleries with a high corbel arch, and a treble doorway. Doorways on both the patio and E sides originally had wooden lintels. The walls separating these doorways have stucco reliefs, each a portrait of a ruler, a sort of aristocratic portrait gallery, bearing a sceptre of authority, each sceptre itself carved with the Long-nosed god. The end walls are carved with hieroglyphs.

Across the N side of the Palacio platform there are three superimposed retaining walls, recessed one behind the other, and decorated with yet more carvings, of masks of the Long-nosed god and of stylized serpents. The *Escalera Norte* (North Stairs) is in the centre and has reliefs of figures on its side ramps. A parallel gallery that stood in front of these steps (ie, on the S side) was later covered when new buildings and a platform were erected around the Patio Este.

Edificio B forms the S side of Patio Este. It is a gallery similar to those previously described, divided into five rooms.

Edificios E and *F* are galleried structures to the S of Patio Este, and form the SE corner of the complex. Edificio E, entered by steps from Patio Este, borders the E side of Patio de la Torre. It is vaulted with stone slabs and divided into four rooms. At the end of the W gallery a staircase leads to the Subterráneos (see below). The E gallery has stucco reliefs, in particular an oval-framed relief of Lord Pacal, sitting on a two-headed jaguar, and of Lady Zac-Kuk, standing on his r., addressing him and offering a headdress. Above a door to the E of this is a relief of an owl mask with spread wings. Edificio F is also of two subdivided galleries.

The S side of the platform is formed by *Edificios G, H,* and *I,* all much-ruined. To the S of these are the *Subterráneos,* underground passages, which may be the earliest structures of the complex. They communicated with the rest of the palace by three stairways. There are sculptured masks along their S façade, beneath a shelter by an older staircase to the platform.

We proceed across the *Acueducto* of the Río Otulum, to visit the scattered temples on the SE of the zone. **Edificio XIV** comprises a restored three-roomed temple on a two-tiered platform. Traces of stucco sculpture can be seen on the stair ramps, and to each side of the central chamber there are stucco figures facing the entrance, and Chac masks emerging from a (?)maize plant at the base. Inside is a large bas-relief carved panel, depicting an offering scene of a woman kneeling and holding out a statue of the Long-nosed god on a cushion, to the figure of a noble. On each side is a column with hieroglyphs and the date inscription for AD 636.

Templo del Sol. This four-tiered pyramid stands just to the S. It comprises several rooms, facing onto an open area towards the Templos de la Cruz y de la Cruz Foliada (described below). In four sections on the façade are stucco reliefs of figures and hieroglyphic inscriptions, and some traces of decorations on the roof, incl. a stone comb. Inside, a carved stone is set into the rear wall. It depicts a central shield-sun symbol supported on two long batons held on an altar, in turn supported by two seated figures, the l. one of which is our old friend Lord Pacal. On either side are hieroglyphs and figures of priests presenting offerings, and a date inscription for AD 642.

Templo de la Cruz and **Templo de la Cruz Foliada** (Leafy Cross). Across the plaza-like area in front of the Templo del Sol stand two temples named for their principal stone carvings. Both stand on terracing around the plaza. The Templo de la Cruz, to the N, is a three-chambered, porticoed structure, now fallen in, to leave only three corbel arches of the roof. A roof-comb contains a staircase from which there is a view a little higher up than that from the Templo de las Inscripciones. In the central chamber once stood a carved stone with a large cross, to either side of which stood Lord Pacal (who else?) and his son, Chan-Bahlum. The two side panels have been returned from having been used(!) in the church of Sto Domingo de Palenque, and depict Maya God L in a jaguar skin, smoking a pipe or cigar (r.), and Chan-Bahlum in an elaborate headdress (l.).

The Templo de la Cruz Foliada faces NW and is also much ruined, leaving only traces of its outer façade and roof-comb. The room plan is similar to the Templo de la Cruz, and contains three carved stones. The flanking stones are almost completely defaced, but the central one shows a central cross of leaves (?maize leaves) with incorporated heads. To either side are Lord Pacal and Chan-Bahlum. The cross appears to issue from a godhead and is surmounted by a serpent-bird figure; the accompanying hieroglyphic inscription includes the date signs for AD 692.

The Templos del Sol, de la Cruz, and de la Cruz Foliada are thought to have been built by Chan-Bahlum, and correspond to the plaza and Templo de las Inscripciones built by his father. Chan-Bahlum's burial may in fact lie beneath one of these temples awaiting discovery.

To the S of the three temples are several ruins, incl. **Templo XXI**, the usual parallel galleried structure, in which a tomb was found (but which had been previously robbed); and to the SE a single structure containing **Templos XVIII** and **XVIII-A**, each of which contained a tomb. In XVIII-A there was a youth (c 20 years old) and a woman, presumably sacrificed to accompany him. From the crypt to just beneath the temple floor was a 'psychoduct'.

To the SW, c 200m, is the **Casa del Jaguar**, a small temple on the hillside. It comprises a porch and chamber, in which Frédéric de Waldeck discovered a relief and made a drawing of it. The published drawing depicts a seated (?)priest on a throne partly in the shape of a jaguar, but only fragments of the original now remain. Stairs lead down to a crypt, corbel-vaulted and presumably once containing a sarcophagus.

There are several more monuments, and a museum, to the N of the Palacio. **Juego de Pelota**. This is the first structure to be encountered in this area. It comprises two parallel platforms of recessed steps and with low benches against each side along the playing field. No stone ring-goals were found. To the NW of the Ball Court is *Templo X*, a single room on a platform facing S. Only its foundations now remain. To the N of these two is the **Templo del Conde**, facing E onto a plaza area, so-called because Frédéric de Waldeck lived in it while he explored the site. It stands on a pyramid with steps up its E side, between ramps. The temple has a tripartite plan, is corbel-arched, and has a roof-comb. Beneath the portico were found three graves with their furniture, but few bones; and traces of stucco decoration can still be seen on the pillars.

Along the N side of the plaza area are long terraces up the hill slope. On them stand the five buildings of **Grupo Norte**, built at different times. From W to E they include: a ruined temple with five entrances; a three-bayed temple with some hieroglyphic inscriptions still visible; a well-preserved temple of a single room; another well-preserved temple of two galleries, each of three rooms; and a temple of which only the foundations remain. All of these had traces of stucco reliefs and roof-combs when excavated.

The **Museum** contains various artefacts from the site, incl. many of the carved reliefs found in the excavations and mentioned above. At the entrance is a stele from the Templo de la Cruz, showing a human figure above a hieroglyphic sign. To either side of the entrance are an archaeological map of Maya sites, and a plan of Palenque.

Inside are: 1. Fossil fish (ichthyolite) of the Tertiary Era found on the site. 2. Stele with hieroglyphic inscriptions, found at the base of the Torre. 3. Display case containing ground and polished stone axe-heads and yugos used in the ball game; these are of Totonac manufacture and are thought to represent the incursion of these peoples on Palenque in the 9–10C. 4. Carved slab, depicting two figures, possibly a priest and a god wearing a mask. On the floor are several stone manos and matates for grinding maize, and a pottery brazier; then several fragments of carved stucco. 5. Stone panel from Templo XXI, depicting a kneeling figure; then two panels from Templo XVIII covered with hieroglyphic inscriptions, incl. dates in the second half of the 7C. 6. Figurines depicting nobles, priestly figures, and deities; clay cylinder with the mask of the Sun god, one of Palenque's characteristic symbols; and a collection of Late Classic pottery. 7. Large carved relief depicting a central figure (?a god), flanked by a priest below whom is a Sun god mask, and a priestess below whom is a deer; below these are two, more humble, figures. 8. Cases with 7–8C ceramics, a painted cylinder from the Templo de la Cruz Foliada, and clay figurine heads. 9. Three carved reliefs depicting: hieroglyphic inscriptions (from the Templo de la Cruz Foliada); figure kneeling and holding a roll of paper or parchment in his r. hand and a (?)stylus or brush in his l. (from the base of the Torre); and kneeling figure holding his hand to his mouth. 10. At the far end of the museum are two clay cylinders depicting various masks of humans, the Sun god, and the Long-nosed god. 11. Towards the entrance, stucco masks; carved architectural fragment from the Templo de la Cruz Foliada; statue whose head is missing—the only known round sculpture from the site; and carved stucco architectural decorations. 12. Artefacts of jade, obsidian, and shell. 13. Carved stucco pieces, in particular a relief from the Palacio depicting a Sun god figure (a masked priest impersonating him) and a Chac figure (masked priestess), incl. the glyph date AD 720.

FROM PALENQUE TO SAN CRISTOBAL DE LAS CASAS, Méx. 199, 210km. A reasonable, mostly paved, winding road through the Chiapas highlands, but it can be dangerous during and after summer rains. Thorough enquiry before starting recommended. 10km road l. (SE) for (approx. 130km) *Lacanjá*, in what remains of the *Selva Lacandona* (suitable only for four-wheel drive vehicles; see Rte 90). 29km turning r. for (1km) *Misol-Ha*, a waterfall formed by a brook playing over a calcareous rock shelf. Waters clear for swimming. 68km turning r. for (4km) *Agua Azul*, numerous waterfalls made by the Río Tulijá (best in the dry season). They form rapids and whirlpools, with calmer stretches for bathing. From (98km) *Temó* a poor road (dry season only) runs NW to (8km) *Bachajón*, (20km) *Chilón*, (33km) *Yajalón*, and (62km) *Tila*, Tzeltal Indian pueblos. 118km **Ocosingo** (c 20,000 inhab.; 900m; H,R,P), a compact, mainly mestizo town and convenient stopping-place. On the E side of Pl. Principal the church of *San Jacinto* (rebuilt) dates from the 18C.

14km E is **TONINA**, principal city of a considerable political and economic state in E Chiapas, much of its trade and contact being with the rulers of Palenque, to the N.

Toniná was excavated in 1925 by a team from Tulane University, and in 1972 by Pierre Becquelin and Claude F. Baudez of the French archaeological mission.

Although occupied in the Preclassic Period, its major phase of building took place in the Late Classic, during the 7–9C AD. It was abandoned once at the end of the 9C, reoccupied briefly c AD 1000, and abandoned again c 1250. In the second phase of occupation, construction was limited to housing complexes, presumably utilizing the existing monumental public architecture.

Many of the smaller centres around it are known, incl. *Sto Ton* (just NE) and *Quexil* (to the E; and where the oldest stele is dated AD 692). In the 7–9C Toniná became known for its regional stele-carving style, incl. sculpture in the round, normally rare in this area of Mesoamerica. Its oldest stele is dated AD 495.

The site sits at the foot of, and on the artificially levelled top of, a mountain spur at the head of the Valle de Ocosingo. The S side of the slope has seven terraces, providing platforms for the public monuments, especially on the upper terraces. The E slope is also terraced, and includes a palace with chambers around a small rectangular courtyard. The base of the slope has been levelled to form a vast plaza, with a few structures around its edges; and to the E, W, and SE there are groups of housing ruins.

The PLAZA contains a temple building and two *Juego de Pelota* ruins, a smaller one at the foot of the first terrace, and a larger one on the E edge of the plaza. The larger court is typically I-shaped, c 72m long, and has a playing field defined by sloping walls forming benches against the main walls. Two circular stone goals were found by the excavators in the centre and N end of the field; and beneath each goal, a pit filled with obsidian blades and pieces of jadeite. The central goal is carved with a figure clutching a rod of authority and several glyphs around its edges. Other carved stones excavated in the playing field included three stelae fragments, a carving of a kneeling figure, and a monster head in the round, all in the regional Toniná style.

The ends of the ball court are formed by freestanding structures: on the S this is a small platform with a staircase leading from the playing field up to four chambers and eight pillars which presumably supported the roof. Also at this end, there are several annex buildings with drains and a stucco-lined basin, interpreted as a temascal (sweat bath; in this case perhaps the 'locker-room').

On the first terrace there are several mound ruins and a stele. In the SW corner, excavations recovered a housing complex, incl. three rooms around a patio, in one of which was a tomb containing Late Classic Period pottery. Traces of ordinary life included food containers, stone storage bins, manos and matates. On the second terrace there are only a few pyramid-shaped mounds. The third terrace also has several mounds, and on the E side, the *Templo del Dintel de Madera* (Wooden Lintel). This is a double-galleried structure with corbel arches, inside which the excavators found a lintel of sapodilla wood, resembling lintels found at Tikal in Guatemala. Fragmentary pieces found in the excavations showed that the temple originally sported a roof-comb over its central wall between the galleries. There is nothing of note on the fourth terrace. On the fifth terrace the excavations of 1972 uncovered a subterranean tomb with benches along the walls and a stone sarcophagus. There are also numerous fragments of bas-reliefs, depicting scenes of war, prisoners under triumphant warriors, and glyphs referring to the scenes depicted.

The sixth and seventh terraces support the principal temples of the site. *Templo I* stands on a stepped pyramid 30m sq at the base and 19m high. The temple itself is badly dilapidated, but originally had two corbel-arched rooms; a stele found in the rear chamber was carved in bas-relief depicting a richly dressed figure holding a spear. The pyramid went through at least two phases of construction, resulting in five tiers on the W and S, and a single tier against the terrace wall on the E and N. There are four stairways, and stylized jaguar heads are sculpted in stucco on the E and N faces. On the sixth terrace were found a stucco-decorated base and a Late Classic statue in the round, unfortunately missing its head. In a pit covered by a single stone slab, in front of the statue, the bones of several children were found, plus grave offerings of jadeite figurines and fishbones (believed to be used in auto-sacrifice). Next to the pit was a tomb containing four adult burials. Another building, known as *Casa A*, contained only the base for a statue, with carved stucco motifs.

From Ocosingo the road winds SW to (173km) **Huistán** (2000m), a 'vacant town', headquarters of the Huistecos, of the Tzotzil group, 10,000 or so who live in the surrounding municipio. The church of *San Miguel*, with a wide handsome façade between corner buttresses (repaired in the early 1970s), dates from the first half of the 17C. At 195km we join Méx. 190 for (210km) *San Cristóbal de las Casas*, see Rte 87.

90 Bonampak and Yaxchilán

The best way to reach these sites in the Lacandón rainforest (*Selva Lacandona*) of E Chiapas is by air. Flights (avioneta—light plane) leave from Palenque (round trip of c 6 hrs), Comitán, San Cristóbal de las Casas, and Tenosique. Services may sometimes be withdrawn, so thorough investigation at local tourist offices is essential. It is also possible to travel from Palenque to Bonampak (153km) by rented four-wheel drive vehicle, or occasional bus or truck adapted to carry passengers. During the rainy season (July–Nov.) the difficult road is rendered even more uncomfortable, if not impossible.

The Selva Lacandona has suffered severely through the insatiable demands of timber companies for valuable mahogany and the lack of a firm conservation policy on the part of the State government. A recent, encouraging, development, however, has been the designation by the Mexican government of the *Montes Azules* Biosphere Reserve (comp. Rte 95) to protect the remaining rainforest. It is the home of the peaceable Lacandón Indians, now approaching extinction in their homeland, a process hastened by their selling, under some pressure, timber rights and exposure to exotic influences. Those who wish to visit their villages of Lacanjá and Najá, on the way to Bonampak, are urged to seek advice from the Na-Bolom centre in San Cristóbal de las Casas and, if counselled against, to abide by that advice. On no account should such a visit be treated as a routine tourist trip.

In the Lacanjá river valley, **BONAMPAK** was a major regional centre, closely associated with Yaxchilán, c 25km NE, to which it probably made tribute payments.

Bonampak was discovered in 1946 by photographer Giles Healey and explorer Charles Frey; Sylvanus Morley named it *Bonampak* ('painted walls'), after its Templo de las Pinturas. The site's murals and architecture have subsequently been studied by Karl Ruppert, Eric Thompson, and Tatiana Proskouriakoff for INAH and the Carnegie Institute in 1955, and by George F. Andrews in 1975.

Bonampak was occupied in the Late Classic Period, from c AD 450 to c 800, when its last dated monument was erected.

Murals in the Templo de las Pinturas provide archaeologists with a major source of information on Maya customs, trade, dress, and warfare; the scenes depicted are believed to be partly historical, recording the investiture of a new ruler. Amongst the items offered to the princely figure in the ceremonial procession are necklaces of jade or greenstone, the nearest sources for which were 300km NW in the Olmec Gulf Coast region, and over 200km SE in the E mountains of Guatemala.

Although most of the site is covered by thick vegetation, the central rectangular plaza (c 275m x 320m) has been cleared and restored. Around it, on terraces and platforms, are seven temples and other buildings, built of block masonry with corbelled roofs and carved lintels. In the centre of the plaza stands *Stele 1* (5m x 3m; c AD 780), broken up on discovery. Its lower fragment is carved with hieroglyphic inscriptions, a Maya profile, and an elaborate mask; another large fragment depicts a warrior.

On the S side of the plaza a wide, partly restored staircase leads up to the first terrace. On the landing between flights are (l.) *Stele 2* (AD 790), depicting two

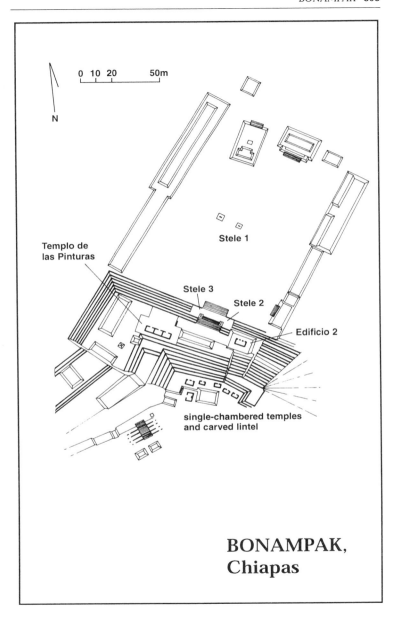

0 10 20 50m

N

Templo de
las Pinturas

Stele 1

Stele 3

Stele 2

Edificio 2

single-chambered temples
and carved lintel

**BONAMPAK,
Chiapas**

richly dressed female figures flanking a male figure; and (r.) *Stele 3* (AD 785) depicting a richly dressed figure standing over a kneeling, bound captive. At the top of the first terrace are the Templo de las Pinturas, and *Edificio 2* (l.), a single-chambered temple. Further staircases lead up more terraces and platforms to more single-chambered temples, one with a carved lintel dated c AD 600.

The **Templo de las Pinturas** comprises three rooms with separate doorways, each with a carved lintel-stone (c AD 800) depicting a warrior and captive, and a niche above it. Inside, the walls and ceiling are covered with murals thought to relate an historical event. Their date is disputed: mid-6C AD, or shortly before the abandonment of the site. Nevertheless it is certain that the paintings were executed in c 48hrs on the wet lime plaster, first as preparatory drawings in red, and then in more detail in black outlines and several colours, incl. red, white, blue, yellow, brown, and black.

The first room has four registers of scenes covering the walls and ceiling. These depict continuous rows of figures—dancers, musicians, and merchants bearing trade-goods—presenting an heir apparent to a group of nobles. In the second room, less rigidly divided registers vividly depict a battle in the forest, then the judgement and punishment of prisoners, incl. figures bleeding and pleading for mercy, and a decapitation. The third room depicts the victory celebrations, showing nobles being entertained by dancers, acrobats, and musicians.

As an incapsulation of ancient Maya ethnography, the paintings show innovative techniques in their representations of violent action and use of depth-of-field, and may have provided a model for murals at Mul-Chic and other sites in the Yucatán. The colours of the originals are now badly faded, but accurate reproductions can be studied at the Carlos Pellicer Museum in Villahermosa or in a full-scale replica of the entire temple in the Museo Nacional de Antropología.

A 10min. flight across the Río Usumacinta lands at **Lacandón Caribal**, or *Lacanjá*, the former site of another ancient Maya centre and a principal village of the Lacandones, descendants of the ancient Maya. Only a few hundred Lacandones remain in the 9000 sq km Lacandón forest, bounded by the Río Lacuntún (S), Usumacinta (E), and Jatate (W), and by the Tenosique region on the N. Their primitive way of life has been the study of anthropologists, incl. Alfred Tozzer, who lived with them in 1901 and 1903, Franz Blom, Gertrude Duby, and Jacques and Georgette Soustelle.

Lacandón social structure seems deceptively simple. They live in two- or three-family groups, in rectangular huts with gabled palm roofs, only rarely subdivided, and with little furniture other than hammocks. Clan lineage is passed down through the father. Clan chiefs often dominate and monopolize the women, causing frequent quarrels, splits, and moves among groups.

Their religion may provide clues to ancient Maya practices, but it is impossible to judge the amount of changes since the Spanish Conquest. Gods are in small temple-huts and sacred caves, in which special pottery vessels, censers, boards on which to burn copal incense, painted gourds, feather brooms, and other paraphernalia are kept. Special beehives are tended in hollow logs near these temples.

They honour some 30 gods, but not all are worshipped by every clan or in each caribal. The ancient site of Yaxchilán still plays a part, particularly as a place of pilgrimage to gods still believed to live there. As with ancient Maya practice, many ceremonies are governed by the seasonal cycles and lunar phases. Burials are often in a stone tumulus.

The Lacandones make use of nearly every tree, plant, and shrub in their environment for food, medicine, art, or religion. Their economy is based on primitive agriculture supplemented by hunting, gathering, and collecting. Their slash-and-burn, milpas-fields require large territories in which to move around, clearing or re-clearing ground as needed. Crops include several fruits, maize, chillies, beans, tomatoes, manioc, sweet potatoes, chayotes, sugar cane, gourds, cotton, and tobacco. Deer, peccaries, armadillos, monkeys, agoutis, iguanas, wild turkeys, curassows, partridges, quail, and fishes are hunted with bows and arrows, traps, nets, and hooks and lines; and snails and wild honey are collected by hand.

Pottery and censers are made by men, while gourd painting, spinning, weaving, and dyeing is done by women, using tools and methods which have changed little since late prehistoric times.

Deep in the Lacandón Forest—requiring a guide and a four-wheel drive vehicle to visit—are two more Maya ceremonial sites, as yet little-explored: c 40km WSW of Lacanjá is *Agua*

Escondida, a small ceremonial centre on two terraces, approached by stairs leading to a multi-tiered pyramid and a three-chambered temple on the upper terrace. To the E, W, and behind these are other platforms and ruins.

C 40km W of Agua Escondida is *Sta Elena Poco Uinic*. Here there is a four-tiered platform with a central staircase, supporting one large and several smaller pyramid-platforms. Along the N side of the plaza several more small pyramids are connected by a low, narrow platform; and within the plaza there are other small pyramid-platforms and some unrestored mounds.

YAXCHILAN was one of the most powerful Late Classic Maya cities in the Southern Lowlands. With Palenque and possibly Calakmul it is one of the few Mexican Maya cities to be identified by its own name-glyph. Despite its being known for a long time, its isolation and relative inaccessibility have resulted in little actual excavation, and most of its history has been reconstructed from its inscriptions.

Its name means 'place of the green stones'. Originally, however, it was called *Menché*, Maya for 'green tree', and at one time had been dubbed *Lorillard*, in honour of the patron of Désiré Charnay's expedition to the site in the 1880s. It was later studied in expeditions led by Teobart Maler for Harvard University at the turn of the century (he gave it the name Yaxchilán), by Sylvanus Morley and John Bolles in 1940, by Tatiana Proskouriakoff in 1960–64, by R. García Moll, and by a US team during the 1970s.

Yaxchilán lies across a heavily forested hillside contained in a loop of the Río Usumacinta, along the Guatemalan frontier. As a powerful city, it had contacts and trade relations throughout the Maya world. It rose to prominence, alongside the city of *Piedras Negras* (c 45km NW across the frontier), as the earlier city of *Altar de Sacrificios* and its tributary, *El Pabellón* (both c 50km SE on either side of the frontier), waned in the 6–7C AD. Bonampak was one of Yaxchilán's principal tributaries, while other sites could be controlled through Piedras Negras, incl.: *El Porvenir* (across the frontier to the NW), *La Mar*, and *El Cayo* (both in Chiapas, SW and S of Piedras Negras, respectively). El Cayo is closely linked artistically to both Piedras Negras and Yaxchilán.

When the civilization of the Classic Period Maya cities crumbled, all these centres ceased building simultaneously: within a decade of the last recorded Long Count date at Palenque (AD 799), Piedras Negras, La Mar, El Cayo, and Bonampak had erected their last dated monuments. Only Yaxchilán held out for a few more decades, erecting its last dated stele in AD 840.

We know something of the history of Yaxchilán from its more than 125 inscriptions and carved scenes on stelae and stone lintels. *Stele 27*, for example, dated AD 514, shows a ruler scattering (?)seeds, a commemoration of the end of a *katun* (a Maya 20-year, or 7300-day, cycle). In the 8C it had a 'Jaguar Dynasty'. Lord Shield-Jaguar was born in AD 647, but not at Yaxchilán—he was brought in from outside. On *Dintel 25* he is shown, with his identifying glyph, as a warrior wearing a Tláloc mask and a year-sign headdress. This combination is a 7–8C practice, possibly spread from Teotihuacán, which had considerable influence at several sites in the Maya Highlands and Southern Lowlands. The significance of the practice is not completely understood, but it was probably a symbol of rulership, or of family connections. Shield-Jaguar ascended the throne of Yaxchilán c AD 701, and four temples dated between AD 692 and 726 are apparently connected with his reign. His successor, Bird-Jaguar, took the throne in AD 752. Bird-Jaguar was not related to Shield-Jaguar, but was also brought in from outside. A commemorative polychrome vessel (the Maya equivalent of a family snapshot) from Altar de Sacrificios, shows Shield-Jaguar attending the funeral of a prominent woman at that city in 754, along with the rulers of Tikal and (?)Alta Verapaz (both in Guatemala). Thus it is possible that all these rulers were related by marriages.

Other inscriptions and scenes on stelae and lintels depict the rulers and nobles of Tikal and Piedras Negras, each identifiable by their city's name-glyphs. Scenes of ceremonial life, and of war and conquest, hint at the troubled times ahead in the 9C, and make Yaxchilán, along with Palenque in the N, an artistic centre for the Classic Maya world. The general style of date inscriptions reflects influences from Campeche, another indication of the site's long-distance connections.

Many of the buildings at Yaxchilán are overgrown with thick vegetation, but there are four main groups, numbered Sectores I–IV, on narrow terraces reached by flights of steps: **Sector I** is along either side of a large plaza, in lines paralleling the river. Scattered structures of residences and public buildings include *Estructura 14*, a large *Juego de Pelota* found with its goals in place. *Estructura 19*, nicknamed 'the labyrinth' for its complex of rooms, has an altar

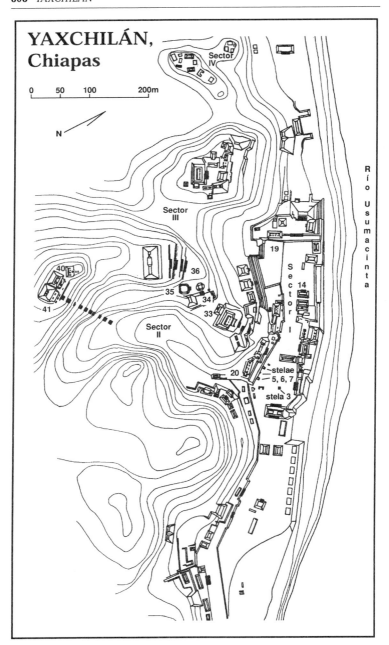

YAXCHILÁN, Chiapas

0   50   100   200m

N

Sector IV

Sector III

Sector II

Sector I

36

35   34

33

40

41

20

19

14

stelae 5, 6, 7

stela 3

Río Usumacinta

of the mid-8C in front of it. *Estructura 20*, in the centre of the plaza, has three stelae (5, 6 and 7) in front of it. Most of the rest of the structures are platforms or temple-pyramids, or chambers with entrances divided by pillars, supporting carved lintels and mansard-shaped roofs. Many have friezes on their upper façades, and open-work roof-combs composed of stone or stucco figures.

Sector II is at a right angle to Sector I, S of it and higher up the hillside. It includes the *Templo de Quetzalcóatl* (Estructura 34), and *Estructuras 35* and *36*, which have staircases carved with hieroglyphics. *Estructura 41* has a stele at the foot of its staircase dating to the early 8C.

Sector III and **Sector IV** are to the W and isolated from the above two. They are grouped along the natural contours of the slope, and the latter has produced evidence that it is the older, 6C, core of the city.

THE YUCATAN

91 Villahermosa to Campeche

A. Via Ciudad del Carmen

Méx. 180, 383km.—171km Ciudad del Carmen.—317km Champotón.—383km **Campeche**.

The coast road, Méx. 180, involves taking three ferries (moderate fees). High winds blowing across the Gulf can cause delays lasting several hours. Erratically kept timetables and ferry breakdowns may also cause delays. Blue sea and sky, white sand, and palms make this route extremely attractive.

Méx. 180 leaves Villahermosa to the N through the fertile plain criss-crossed by streams and lakes formed by tributaries of the Ríos Mezcalapa and Grijalva. 75km *San Román*, at the mouth of the Río Grijalva (which has also received the waters of the Río Usumacinta), just upstream from the site of *Sta María de la Victoria*, see Rte 83. We cross the river by ferry (1km) to **Frontera** (c 16,000 inhab.; H,R,P), a not unattractive fishing port from where the tropical products of Tabasco are shipped.

NW of Frontera, near Punta Frontera, the Putún (or Chontal) Maya are thought to have located **Potonchén**, their chief port for trade to the Ríos Grijalva and Usumacinta region from Yucatán. W of Frontera, at the site of *Centla*, Cortés fought his first major battle in the New World, against the Chontal Maya, after having driven them from Potonchén.

Potonchén was a port also used by the Aztecs, at the end of long-established trade routes from Tlatelolco via Tuxtepec in Oaxaca. The general region, the *Chontalpa*, was known as *Nonoalco* to them, and is associated in legend with Tlapallán ('land of the sunrise'), whence Quetzalcóatl migrated from Tula. The Chontalpa Plain, where the Ríos Grijalva, Usumacinta, and Candelaria converge, was settled by Nonoalca, a Nahuat-Pipil people, after the demise of Teotihuacán. According to the Maya 'Popul Vuh' chronicles, some continued S, to settle in Guatemala (and were ancestral to the Quiché Maya kingdom of the Postclassic Period), while others became part of the Toltec state at Tula. At the fall of Tula in the 12C AD the Nonoalca formed part of the settlement at Chalco in the S Basin of Mexico. Nonoalco (in Náhuatl, 'land of the dumb') was so-called by the Aztecs because its people spoke a difficult language. The Nonoalca were also known for their skill in jade-carving and metal-working.

Also on the Chontalpa plain, a small ceremonial centre, *Sigero* S of Frontera, was excavated by William Sanders in the 1960s: a plaza with a main temple platform on the N side, a residential building on the W side, and a small ball court on the E; other housemounds are scattered over the surrounding countryside.

We reach the coast at (101km) the mouth of the Río San Pedro y San Pablo and cross by ferry (5 minutes) into the State of Campeche. The road runs inland to skirt the *Laguna de Pom*, the *Laguna de Atasta*, the *Laguna de Corte*, and the *Laguna de San Carlos*, interconnecting and flowing into the Laguna de Términos.

The site of *Atasta* (no important standing monuments) is known chiefly from excavated burials. Pottery from the site dates between AD 1300 and 1500, and a standing figure from one burial has Toltec features.

167km *El Zacatal*, from where a ferry crosses the mouth of the Laguna de Términos to (171km) **Ciudad del Carmen** (c 50,000 inhab.; H,R,P), a hot and humid town and fishing port on the W tip of Isla del Carmen, the long sandy island which closes in the huge salt-lake at the SW edge of the Yucatán peninsula. Shipbuilding and timber exploitation are other activities.

On the mainland opposite Ciudad del Carmen, Postclassic Period Maya **Xicalango** (or *Xicalanco*) is thought to have been located near Cerillos on the W shore of the Laguna de Términos, at the swampy delta of the Río Grijalva. It was an important international trading centre, convenient for the canoe traffic up and down the coast, and the principal port city of the Chontal Maya province of *Acalán*. It is also mentioned in the 'Popol Vuh' as one of the stopping places for the Quiché Maya tribes migrating, in the Postclassic, from Mexico into the Guatemalan Highlands.

The trading port seems to have been a 'free trade zone' where Náhuatl was spoken, and where the Aztecs maintained a garrison to keep order and a commercial outpost. Aztec pochteca merchants came here on one of their established routes from Tlatelolco via Tuxtepec to trade central Mesoamerican products for those of the Yucatán. The port was also possibly connected by a paved sacbé to Champotón, up the coast in Campeche, perhaps in order to pick up inland trade. From Xicalango trade items such as gold, copper, cotton, salt, slaves, cacao, and feathers moved between Aztec central Mexico and Mayaland, around the coasts of Yucatán and down into Honduras, and even to S America via other ports such as Chetumal; or overland across the Isthmus of Tehuantepec to the Pacific Coast. According to Diego de Landa, the Cocom Maya rulers of Mayapán even imported Mexican mercenaries from the altiplano to help them control their subject towns.

Into the **Laguna de Términos** (c 70km E to W by 40km N to S) flow, from W to E, the Ríos Palizada, Chumpán, Candelaria, and Mamantel. In 1518 Juan de Grijalva arrived at its E entrance and explored the surrounding area, inhabited by Chontal Indians. Spanish control over the area was established by 1536. From the 1550s the lagoon became occasional headquarters of English, French, and Dutch pirates. C 1658 English logwood-cutters were setting up camps on the shore, taking wood (palo de Campeche) from forests in the hinterland and maintaining their hold, despite sporadic Spanish harassment, thanks to reinforcements from Jamaica. With the arrival of Juan de Vértiz y Hontañón as governor and captain-general of Yucatán in 1715 plans were laid finally to expel the English, who were driven from the island in Dec. 1716 and at last defeated in July 1717. Descendants of the foreign interlopers, with their English, French, and Dutch names and light colouring, may still be seen today.

Isla del Carmen is 39km long and 7.5km at its widest. Shrimps, oysters, turtles, and a variety of fish (especially tarpon) abound. The coastal oil boom has unfortunately left its mark; yet away from the town there are stretches of deserted white-sand beach.

The island was part of the Chontal Maya commercial province of Acalán and Xicalango, a site on the mainland at *Cerrillos* on Laguna de Términos. At the E end of the island are two sites with Postclassic Maya ruins, undoubtedly also satellites of Xicalango.

The main plaza, shaded and flower-filled, is surrounded by pastel-coloured buildings. The two main churches date from the 18C. A small museum contains artefacts from Atasta, incl. a standing figure with Toltec features.

From Ciudad del Carmen, Méx. 180 goes across the island to (208km) *Puerto Real*, since 1983 joined to the mainland at *Isla Aguada* by the *Puente de la Unidad* (3.25km), the longest bridge in Mexico.

At *Pozas de Ventana*, c 4km NW, are several small plazas formed by platforms on the low hills, and at *Los Guarixes* on the E tip of the island some isolated mounds have proved to be stucco-covered pyramids with sand cores.

252km road r. for *Sabancuy*, a pretty fishing village on a long inlet of the Laguna de Términos, with an 18C church. Beyond, the road parallels the mangrove-lined coast, the historic *Costa de Sotavento*, a beautiful drive, to (317km) **Champotón** (c 11,000 inhab.; H,R,P), a fishing port where the Río Champotón flows into the Gulf.

Champotón (or *Champutún*) was occupied by the Itzá Maya from the 8C AD. According to Maya chronicles it was also within the homelands of the Putún, or Chontal Maya, seafaring merchants closely bound up in Itzá history. The location of ancient Chontal *Chakanputún* is uncertain, but one interpretation of the chronicles puts it on the W coast of Campeche, as one of three Putún/Itzá capitals, the other two being Chichén Itzá in Yucatán and Potonchén in the Chontalpa (Chontal Maya) region of E Tabasco–SW Campeche (the Nonoalco region of the Aztecs). According to Maya chronicles, some Itzá migrated S from Yucatán in the 10C, some to the city of Chakanputún. (In another interpretation, the site of Chakanputún is thought to have been *Seibal* in Guatemala.)

Champotón remained a political and economic province, fiercely maintaining its independence after the break-up of the League of Mayapán in AD 1441. In 1517 it stoutly resisted the Spaniards under Francisco Hernández de Córdoba, who had sailed around the Yucatán

Peninsula from E to W (see Rte 97). Fierce fighting broke out before the expedition was able to continue N and W around Yucatán, touching at Canpech, another principality, and then attempting to land at Champotón, where they were attacked and only retained their ships with difficulty. Córdoba himself received 33 wounds and 'sadly' returned with his expedition to Cuba, where he died within two weeks.

The Spaniards' tales of gold and silver whetted appetites of others for more expeditions. In 1530 Francisco de Montejo and Alfonso Dávila linked forces at Champotón, using it as a base in attempting to penetrate Yucatán. Fray Jacobo de Testera visited the town in 1534 and a mission was established in 1537, the sixth town of Salamanca being founded there in the same year. In 1541 El Mozo, son of Francisco de Montejo, landed at the town to begin yet another, the third, campaign to conquer Yucatán. In the 17C the English dominance of the coast (in 1644 the pirate James Jackson and his men attacked Champotón, robbed churches, and made off with two friars) caused the settlement to be moved at times inland; after their expulsion in 1717, movement back to the coast began.

Where Calle 34 meets the seafront are the remains of the 18C fort of *San Antonio*. The simple parish church of *Las Mercedes*, fronting the plaza between Cs 26 and 28, dates from the 17C.

At *Pustunich*, c 35km SE of Champotón, there is an unpreserved Postclassic Maya site near the railway line—to visit it, a guide is recommended.

84km S of Champotón (Méx. 261) is *Escarcega*, see Rte 91B.

Méx. 180 continues N along the coast. From (331km) *Haltunchén* a road runs inland (E) to (58km) *Edzná*, see Rte 93B. 350km *Seybaplaya*, a small fishing port with (S of the town) a narrow long beach and clear water. 383km *Campeche*, see Rte 91B.

B.   Via Francisco Escarcega

Méx. 186, Méx. 261, and Méx. 180, 451km.—136km turning r. for (75km SE) Tenosique.—301km Francisco Escarcega.—451km **Campeche**.

From Villahermosa to (115km) turning S to *Palenque*, see Rte 89. Méx. 186 continues NE through the hot, flat region of lakes and swamps dominated by the Río Usumacinta. 116km (l.) *Catazajá*, see Rte 89. 136km turning r.

This road (Méx. 203) runs to (8km) **Emiliano Zapata** (c 6000 inhab.; 32m; H) in Tabasco, on the l. bank of the Río Usumacinta, known for its charros (displays of horsemanship), a reserve for tropical flora and fauna, and a large nursery for the cultivation of tropical plants. There are several Maya sites in the surrounding jungle, only to be visited with a guide: Tecolpan (NW), *Balancán, Pobileuc* (E), *Arenitas, Chinikiha* (SW), and *Miraflores* (N of Palenque). In the Postclassic this region was the Maya province of Acalán, whose capital (possibly at Río Candelaria) was *Itzamkanae*. 31km *El Tulipán*. From here it is possible to reach by a minor road (29km N across the Usumacinta) **Balancán** (c 4000 inhab.; 218m; H,P), in a marshy region inhabited by Chontal Indians, rapidly being transformed to productive agriculture. Tamarind, mango, and banana trees add to its tropical exuberance. It was a Classic Maya site, where several stelae and ball game paraphernalia were found. Olmec occupation or influence is suggested by finds of Preclassic votive axes. Balancán Z Fine Orange pottery is characterized by flaring-sided bowls with ring-stands and cylindrical vases with an orange, white, or occasionally black slip. A small museum at the municipal library displays yugos (used in the ball game ritual), a Maya stele, ceramics, obsidian blades, face-shaped stone axe-heads, and some 'smiling face' figurines.

Across the border in Chiapas at 52km a road runs S via *Chancalá* to join (27km) the Palenque–Lacanjá road, see Rte 89. We turn l. (E), crossing the Usumacinta and again in Tabasco, for (75km) **Tenosique** (12,000 inhab.; 65m; H,R,P; small airport for local flights; amid thick forest, a departure point for expeditions by plane into the Lacandón rainforest and to Palenque, Yaxchilán, Bonampak, and San Cristóbal de las Casas. An archaeological museum shows local finds. Tenosique is the birthplace of José María Pino Suárez (b. 1869), Madero's vice president, murdered in Feb. 1913.

Méx. 186 crosses the Usumacinta before (158km) a turning l. which runs NW into Campeche to (49km) *San Joaquín*, 4km S of which, in Tabasco, is **Jonuta**, on the r. bank of the Usumacinta, a small Classic Period Maya centre for coastal canoe trade, on the N limits of Palenque's sphere of control.

It was also the source of 'Z'-type—Balancán Z—Fine Orange pottery, distinctive figurines, and Fine Orange paste. The figurines are stylistically similar to those of Palenque and Jaina, and include detailed facial features and dynamic movement. There are groups as well as individual figures, often with whistle insertions on their backs.

19km N of San Joaquín is *Palizada*, in swampy, low country, joined by the Río Palizada to the Laguna de Términos (c 60km NE). The region abounds in mahogany, cedar, and palo de Campeche; mangoes and sugar-cane.

From the turning Méx. 186 begins its long run NE through the coastal hinterland of Campeche, agriculturally rich, and known for its timber, but sparsely populated. 274km turning l. for (57km) the coast W of *Sabancuy*, see Rte 91A. 301km **Francisco Escarcega** (c 10,000 inhab.; H,R,P), something of a frontier town between the Yucatán peninsula and the rest of Mexico, and a convenient, if unattractive, stopping place. From here Méx. 186 continues E into Quintana Roo and (273km) *Chetumal*, see Rte 92.

From Escarcega, Méx. 261 runs N to (385km) *Champotón* and (410km) *Seybaplaya*, see Rte 91A.

451km **CAMPECHE** (c 190,000 inhab.), capital of the State of Campeche, and deep-water port, is a bright and cheerful city, despite its exposed, and often dangerous and violent, past, manifested by the fortifications which still in part surround the picturesque old centre and by outlying forts. The climate is hot and humid, with summer and early autumn rains.

Airport. 10km E. Daily flights to *Mexico City*.

Bus station. Av. Gobernadores, beyond Baluarte de San Pedro. Services to *Mérida* (3 hrs); to *Villahermosa* (8 hrs); to *Mexico City* (18 hrs); to *Puebla* (16 hrs); to *San Andrés Tuxtla* (12 hrs); to *Edzná* (1½ hrs); to *Bolonchén* (2 hrs); to *Kabah* (3 hrs); to *Sta Elena* (3 hrs); to *Uxmal* (3 hrs); to *Iturbide* (for *Dzibilnocac*) (3 hrs); etc.

Hotels throughout the city.

Post Office. Pal. Federal.

Tourist Office. Pl. Moch-Couoh.

Fiesta. 16 Dec.: pre-Christmas celebrations.

Campeche was the principal Postclassic city of Maya Cunpech, or Ah-Kin-Pech, province. It was visited in 1517 by the Francisco Hernández Córdoba expedition on its way along the Yucatán coast to Champotón, where it was forced to turn back. According to an early Spanish account, the town contained an idol depicting a figure with a snake (Maya can) on its head, with a tick (Maya Pech) on its head. In 1518 the natives gave Juan de Grijalva's men a hostile reception. The villa of San Francisco de Campeche was founded in 1541; by 1580 it numbered 80 Spanish families among its inhabitants. By the end of the 18C the population of city and suburbs was c 17,000, incl. 8000 of Spanish descent. Its shipyards, using local timber of highest quality, attained fame from 1580 until the mid-19C throughout the Spanish-speaking world.

As principal port and trading centre of Yucatán it became, from 1561, a magnet for English (who called it Campeachy), Dutch, and French pirates. In the 1670s the Dutchman Laurent Graaf became the scourge of the coast and in 1685 led a particularly vicious sacking which cost many lives and ended with women and children taken by force to sea in rickety boats, cast adrift, and cannonaded by the pirate crews from their ships. By 1704 Campeche was on its way to becoming the first completely fortified city of New Spain: a defensive wall 2.5m thick, and 8m high, and 2536m long, with eight bastions (not completely finished until well into the 18C) and three gates—in addition to six fortresses along the coast. The barrios settled by Indians remained without. In the early 19C Campeche attained economic prosperity as the principal point for exports of chicle and palo de Campeche (palo de tinte; logwood, or dyewood), from which is extracted the red dye then much in demand in Europe and the USA. The city then contained 'a group of cosmopolitan citizens whose polylingual households and attention to refinement, culture and business gave Campeche an air of briskness which travellers thought equal to the best in Europe and perhaps unmatched in Mexico'. By the

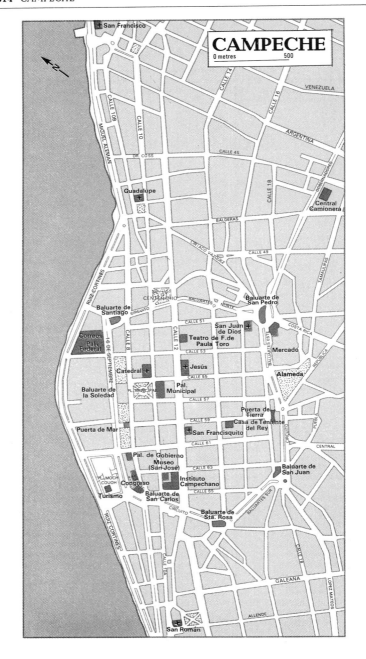

CAMPECHE

0 metres   500

San Francisco

CALLE 14
CALLE 16
VENEZUELA
CALLE 108
MIGUEL ALEMAN
CALLE 10
DR. COSS
CALLE 45
ARGENTINA
GOBERNADORES
CALLE 18
Guadalupe
Central
Camionera
BALDERAS
CIRIACO VAZQUEZ
CALLE 49
RUIZ CORTINES
NIÑO
CENTENARIO
BALUARTES
NORTE
Baluarte de
San Pedro
Baluarte de
Santiago
CIRCUITO
CALLE 51
San Juan
de Dios
COSTA RICA
Correos
Pal.
Federal
16 DE SEPTIEMBRE
CALLE 8
CALLE 12
Teatro de F. de
Paula Toro
BALUARTES ESTE
Mercado
TAMAULIPAS
CALLE 53
Catedral
Jesús
CALLE 55
Alameda
REPÚBLICA
Baluarte de
la Soledad
PL. PRINCIPAL
Pal.
Municipal
CALLE 57
Puerta de Mar
CALLE 59
Puerta de
Tierra
Casa de Teniente
del Rey
PUEBLA
San Francisquito
CALLE 61
CENTRAL
Pal. de Gobierno
Museo
(San José)
CALLE 63
Baluarte de
San Juan
PL. MOCH
COUOH
Congreso
Instituto
Campechano
Turismo
Baluarte de
San Carlos
CALLE 65
BALUARTES SUR
Baluarte de
Sta. Rosa
CIRCUITO
RUIZ CORTINES
CALLE 10
CALLE 18
GALEANA
LÓPEZ MATEOS
ALLENDE
San Román

mid-century the collapse of shipyards and merchant marine, and diminishing logwood exports, brought it into decline. Among famous natives of Campeche are Pedro Sáinz de Baranda y Borreiro (1787–1845), thrice wounded at Trafalgar in 1805 and in 1834–35 an able and uncorrupt governor of Yucatán; José María Gutiérrez Estrada (1800–67), Santa-Anna's foreign minister in 1834–35, and staunch monarchist, Mexican ambassador to Italy in 1861, president of the commission which offered Maximilian the imperial crown, indefatigable adviser to the emperor by letter from his home, the Palazzo Marescotti in Rome; Justo Sierra Méndez (1848–1912), Porfirio Díaz's minister of education, founder of the National University; and the architect Emilio Dondé Preciat (1849–1905).

Demolition of stretches of the wall (600m remain), two of the bastions (San Francisco and San José), and one of the gates began in the late 19C, to make way for tramlines and modern buildings. The old city was declared a national monument in 1936 and further development is governed by strict planning regulations. A quaint spectacle is the horse-drawn carts of water-sellers (aguadores) bearing huge barrels of drinking water which still ply the streets.

The State of **Campeche** (c 510,000 inhab.; 50,813 sq km) occupies the SW part of the Yucatán peninsula. The limestone plain is broken in the N by low hills, the Sierra, not above 300m. The lowest region, inland from the coast, is called La Costa; the S and central regions La Milpa. E and S of the capital excessive rainfall has produced vast forest tracts that became tropical rainforest. Its main products—hardwoods (mahogany, cedar) and chicle—come from the forests, though chemical dyes have cut back the old dyewood trade. Commercial fishing and oil in the SW are other, increasingly significant, economic factors.

Most of the territory was included in the Spanish province of Yucatán; the SW corner formed the separate government of Laguna de Términos, the area surrounding the lake, where Spanish control was established by Francisco de Montejo el Mozo c 1536, and which later was to become a haven for English pirates and logwood-cutters. In 1847 it revolted against the federal government in Mexico City and in 1857–58 separated from the State of Yucatán, an act recognized by the federal government in 1862 and confirmed in 1917. In 1920 agents of Carrillo Puerto in Yucatán, backed by 1500 regular and irregular yucateco troops, invaded Campeche to organize ligas de resistencia and establish the socialist party of the south-east as the only party in the peninsula. In 1923 the rebellion of Adolfo de la Huerta achieved quick success in Campeche. The revolt spread to Yucatán's federal garrison and the troops marched on Mérida, forced Carrillo Puerto's flight, and in Jan. 1924 brought about his death.

On the E side of PL. PRINCIPAL is the cathedral of **La Inmaculada Concepción**, comfortably large in its proportions, the trilobed choir window in its façade a tentative baroque touch. The bulbous spires of the towers are exotic finishes.

It was begun in the mid-17C, but work stopped in 1656. Consecration took place in 1705. The N tower dates from 1758–60; the S from 1849–50; the cupola, upheld by flying buttresses, from c 1760.

The S side of the plaza is occupied by a restored two-storey 17C building complete with portales, once the *Pal. Municipal* (still containing municipal offices). On the NW corner is the house where Justo Sierra Méndez was born. On the N side the *Baluarte de la Soledad* contains an archaeological museum (Museo de las Estelas; Tues.–Sat., 8–8; Sun., 8–1; fee) with carved stone stelae, columns and figures, from Edzná, Itzimté, Chunhuhub, and Xcalumkin and Xcoloc. Other carved stone monuments can be seen near the fountain, outside the courtyard, and beneath the fort arches. Inside there is an arms collection.

Going W along Calle 8 we pass the *Puerta de Mar* (destroyed in 1893, faithfully rebuilt in 1955), one of the surviving city gates, the *Pal. de Gobierno*, and the *Congreso* (State legislative assembly), two controversial buildings which went up in 1965–66. Beyond the Congreso is the *Baluarte de San Carlos* (Mon.–Fri., 9–1, 5–8; Sat., 9–1), with another small museum where scale models tell the history of Campeche.

From here we may walk S along C. 65 to the junction with C. 10. At the NE corner of the block, to the l., is the former church of **San José** (1809), by a Catalan architect, Santiago Casteills; its façade (shades of neostyle baroque) is attractively faced with azulejos. It has been reconditioned as the *Museo de Campeche* (Tues.–Sat., 9–1; Sun., 10–1), a modest affair. The rest of the block is occupied by the **Instituto Campechano**, founded in 1859 as a college of secondary and higher education in the former Jesuit college of *San José*, which had been founded in 1714 and after 1767 had been assigned to the Franciscans. It is now the *Escuela Preparatoria*.

No. 230 in C. 10, the *Hotel Señorial*, is a 17C mansion with a splendidly ornamented façade, with wrought-iron balcony railings and window grilles.

To the W, C. 10A leads beyond Circuito Baluartes Sur to the church of *San Román*, founded in the 1560s, but much altered since then, for the barrio of Mexican Indians. It contains a black Christ crucified on a cross of silver, probably contemporary with the foundation.

From the Baluarte de San Carlos we may follow Circuito Baluartes Sur to the *Baluarte de Sta Rosa*, now a library with books illustrating the history of Campeche (Mon.–Fri., 8.30–2, 4–7). Next, where Circuito Baluartes Sur meets Circuito Baluartes Este, follows the *Baluarte de San Juan*. We go along Circuito Baluartes Este past the *Puerta de Tierra* (1726), beyond which, at the end of C. 57, are the remains of the *Baluarte de San Francisco*. On the S side of the Circuito is the ALAMEDA, inaugurated in 1830; at its S end is the *Puente de las Mercedes*, named in honour of Mercedes López de Santa-Anna (see below). At the SE corner of Cs. 16 and 51, the church of *San Juan de Dios* (c 1635). Circuito Baluartes Norte ends at the *Baluarte de Santiago*, rebuilt in 1857, now enclosing a botanical garden.

C. 12, which runs E–W through the centre of the old city from PL. IV CENTENARIO, passes (l.) the *Teatro de Francisco de Paula Toro* (1832–34), by a French architect, Teodoro Journot.

It was named in honour of the Colombian-born Francisco de Paula Toro (1799–1840), military commander in Yucatán, governor (1835–37), and husband of Mercedes López de Santa-Anna, sister of the dictator.

Between Cs 53 and 55 is the church of *Sto Nombre de Jesús* (17C), built for the mulatto population. Between Cs 59 and 61 is *San Francisquito* and its adjoining convent, now Casa de Cultura, built in the 1650s for the Franciscans. Going l. (E) along C. 59 we reach (No. 26) the **Casa del Teniente del Rey**, built in the 17C (restored) as a residence for the agent of the governor of Yucatán, known as sargento mayor until 1744, when he was redesignated teniente del rey.

It now houses the **Museo Regional de Campeche** (Tues.–Sat., 9–8; Sun., 9–1). On the LOWER FLOOR are prehispanic objects illustrating Maya social life, religion, and funerary customs: Late Classic steles from Calakmul (AD 600–900) and Edzná (one, Stele 9, dated 28 June AD 810); Late Classic anthropomorphic figures from Chunhuhub; column from Xcochac; Early Classic (AD 400–600) treasure from the Tomb of Calakmul, incl. fine jade pieces.

On the UPPER FLOOR are exhibits from the post-Conquest history of Campeche. Bronze culverin (1552), found in a wreck in the Gulf (1890). Arms and armour. 17C ebony rudder in the form of a greyhound coiled by a serpent, merging into a branch adorned with acanthus, discovered in a tributary of the Río Usumacinta. Other objects illustrate piracy and fortifications; religious art; the political history of Campeche; and the economy, incl. trade in palo de tinte with Europe and the sugar industry.

From the E side of Pl. IV Centenario we may follow C. 10 beyond the city. At the intersection of Cs 10B and 47 is *Guadalupe*, a simple, rubble masonry 17C barrio church. After 1km further along C. 10B we come to the church of **San Francisco**, simple but historically significant.

It is part of the Franciscan convent founded in 1546 at a place then called *Campechuelo*, to minister to an Indian congregation. The site is presumed to be where the first Mass in continental America was offered, on 22 March 1517, by Fray Alonso González, chaplain to Hernández de Córdoba.

In 1562 Martín Cortés, 2nd marqués del Valle de Oaxaca, legitimate son of Hernán, put in at Campeche on his way back to Mexico from Europe. His wife, Ana Ramírez de Arellano, gave birth in the convent to their son Jerónimo. By the 17C church and convent were in ruins and what remains is the result of restoration and rebuilding. Chief interest is the two-arched portería-open chapel (one arch closed up), framed by a Franciscan cord and alfíz, which leads into the restored remains of the convent. In the 17C it was the only part of the foundation available for Mass. On its outside corner a column commemorates the Mass of 1517.

C 1km further along the coast road, Av. Gustavo Díaz Ordaz, we may reach the *Fuerte de San Matías*, part of the 17C defensive works. Reached along C. 7, inland from San Francisco, is the *Fuerte de San José el Alto*, not completed until the late 18C.

C 4km SW of the centre, reached by coast road, Av. Justo Sierra and Av. Resurgimiento, is the *Fuerte de San Luis*, and, above it, along Carr. Escénica, the **Fuerte de San Miguel** (3858 sq m), most imposing of the outlying forts, still in good preservation. It houses a *Museo de Arqueología* (Tues.–Sat., 8–12, 3–8; Sun., 9–1), mainly notable for its collection of prehispanic pottery from various parts of Mexico: incl. from the Mixteca, Oaxaca, and the Gulf coast.

92 Francisco Escarcega to Chetumal

Méx. 186, 273km.—90km for (c 68km S) Calakmul.—148km Chicanná (for [20km SW] Hormiguero).—149km **Becán**.—154km Xpuhil.—155km for (16km SE) **Río Bec**.—216km for (9km S) Kohunlich.—273km **Chetumal**.

This road, only completed in the 1970s, runs through the forested and almost deserted S region of Campeche. Buses are infrequent and services almost non-existent. It passes through the Río Bec region, in prehispanic times densely populated. The ancient Maya cities have been engulfed by the forest. To visit the remaining sites (which have resident custodians; daylight hours; fee) a knowledgeable companion is recommended. Mosquitoes are ubiquitous.

At 52km we reach the N shore of *Laguna Noh*. Just beyond it a dirt road (r.) leads to the village of *Silvituk*, the cerro SW of which has overgrown ruins of a small Postclassic Maya site. From (c 90km) *Conhuas* (r.) a gravel road (deteriorating) runs S past (c 32km) the site of *El Ramonal* (l.) to (c 64km) the turn (r.) for (4km W) *Calakmul*.

Calakmul, discovered by C. L. Lundell in 1931 and studied by Sylvanus Morley in 1932, consists of two centres. The larger, W, one is a courtyard and chambers surrounded by platforms and pyramid-towered complexes of buildings generally in the Río Bec style. In the 1970s William Folan and Mexican colleagues mapped some 6500 structures and determined that the ancient city covered c 30 sq km.

Calakmul has produced 108 stelae (some in the Museo Regional at Campeche), the largest number of stelae known from a Maya site. Most have inscriptions of Middle Classic (7C–8C AD) date, but the earliest date is AD 514. The inscriptions also describe several important nobles, their marriages and alliances, and one of the earliest mentions of Motul, a late Maya centre in N Yucatán. Two royal tombs were found, one containing a jadeite portrait mask.
Inscriptions on Stela A at Copán (Honduras) indicate that Calakmul was the centre of an independent political sphere, with a certain deference paid to Tikal, in the Guatemalan Petén. City glyphs have been identified for Tikal, Copán, Palenque, and possibly Calakmul, as the four Maya regional capitals of the 8C AD. Calakmul was surrounded by smaller, dependent sites, constituting a lattice-like, geometrical, politico-economically ranked settlement pattern, comprising *Oxpemul* (to the N), *Muñeca* (NE), *Altamira, Balakbal, Naachtún* (Guatemala), *El Mirador* (Guatemala), *Uxul*, and *Sasilha*, each of these second-rank towns surrounded by its own cluster of villages.

Estructura III dated by associated inscriptions to the 7C AD, is a mixture of pure Río Bec style and the Petén style of N Guatemala. It comprises at least 12 intercommunicating rooms (20.5m x 16m overall), a central tower, and two smaller flanking towers supporting false temples, each with an elaborate roof-comb. Similar buildings are to be found at Río Bec itself, Becán, and Xpuhil, but Calakmul lacks the ornate decoration of these sites.

148km dirt road r. for (c 1km S) **Chicanná** ('serpent-mouth house').

Chicanná was discovered in 1966 by J. Eaton, who excavated the site in the 1960s and early 1970s. It was occupied from the Late Preclassic, but the first construction activities date from c AD 400. The structures now standing are Late Classic, most dating to c AD 550–750, but *Estructuras II* and XX are later, c 750–830. Occupation continued to c 1100 but with little further permanent construction.

There are four monument groups (*A, B, C, D*) scattered in the jungle. The first, *A*, is the GRAN PLAZOLETA, with *Estructuras I* and *II* on its E and W sides.

Estructura I, ruinous, is a Río Bec-style one-storey structure reached from low steps up to its platform. There are ten rooms, with a façade of monster-mask profiles in four panels. Each end of the building comprises typical Río Bec-style false pyramid towers and staircases, with remains of false temples on top.

Estructura II, a one-storey structure of eight rooms on a low, stepped platform, has been partly restored. The façade comprises three doorways with Chenes-style mosaic decoration. The central doorway depicts a monster-mouth, with teeth above the lintel, interpreted as Itzamná, the Maya sky monster and creator deity. To each side there are mosaic monster-masks and stylized serpents, and above the flanking doorways there are stylized pitched roofs. What remains of the central roof-comb has traces of red paint. The three front-rooms have a raised bench around the walls.

Grupo B is c 75m SE of the Gran Plazoleta. Here *Estructura VI* is a two-room building with relief sculptures on the façade and a roof-comb whose perforations are partly lined with seashells.

Grupo C is c 65m SW of the Gran Plazoleta. *Estructura X* is a three-room ruin with some façade mosaics, facing a wide terrace. *Estructura XI* has 11 or 12 rooms, but no mosaic sculptures. Its interior vaulting is of an earlier style and some lintels are still in place. A ruin excavated beneath it is the earliest known construction on the site.

Grupo D is c 275m NW of the Gran Plazoleta. *Estructura XX*, the latest remaining construction, comprises a well-preserved building on two levels. The lower rooms have mostly collapsed, but the upper rooms have serpent-mask motifs and the rounded corners have vertical stacks of the 'Long nosed' deity.

C 20km SW of Chicanná is **Hormiguero**, a small site in the heart of the Río Bec region. The principal attraction is *Estructura II*, a classic Río Bec-style structure with central temple supporting a pitched and crested roof, and side towers with rounded corners and curvilinear Chac (god of rain) masks above the doorposts. The central doorway also has an elaborate Chac mask, and traces of pink stucco geometric decorations can be seen elsewhere on the building. Several chultunes (artificial underground water-storage chambers) have also been found on the site.

149km (l.) **BECAN**, an early village site and later Maya city of some importance.

Becán was discovered in 1934 by Karl Ruppert of the Carnegie Institute and it has since been studied or excavated by several scholars and institutional teams into the mid-1970s.

There is ceramic evidence for the occupation of Becán as early as 2000–1000 BC, but more substantial evidence of a village site dates from c 300 BC. A large platform 14m high, together with smaller platforms and buildings in stone, with stucco facings and thatched roofs, were built in the Late Preclassic after c 50 BC.

Becán is also an early example of a long tradition of Maya fortification (see Introduction: Mesoamerican Architecture). Between AD 100 and 250 a defensive ditch was dug to surround the ceremonial city and two stone-lined reservoirs, and many new or reconstructed public buildings were completed. The ditch has a circumference of 1.9km and varies in width between 3m and 24m, and in depth between 2m and 4m. Parapets on the interior, vertical lip, and possibly a log palisade, presented an 11m obstacle to attackers. It was crossed by seven natural limestone causeways at points left undug, and these show evidence of having been cut and later repaired, presumably before and after an attack on the city. A contemporary population increase in the region, the site's position in the centre of the cross-peninsular trade network, and the unique combination of its isolation in a marshy area and its fortifications, made Becán one of the more powerful Classic Period Maya civic centres.

There is evidence that the city was attacked in c AD 450, possibly by the rival Maya city of Tikal (Guatemala). At the same time, the pottery from the site includes a few Teotihuacano features and obsidian was being traded in from Teotihuacán-controlled mines. In one structure the excavators found a cache of Teotihuacano figurines, comprising one large, hollow figure with ten smaller solid figurines of gods and warriors inside it. Up to c AD 650 many more terraces were built on the surrounding hillsides, indicating a prosperous economy.

In the 7C Río Bec style architecture made its appearance, incl. the extensive use of uncut masonry, rounded corners, and elaborately decorated stucco facings. The Acropolis

(Estructura I) was built, incl. tall end towers topped by small, false, ornamental temples. In the terminal Classic new trade connections began with Highland Guatemala, incl. especially the importation of Tohil Plumbate Ware. By c AD 830, however, the construction and renovation of public buildings had ceased, and the decline of the city is indicated by evidence of squatter occupation in many of the former public buildings.

The present visible remains of Becán are of the Río Bec and Chenes styles. The main plaza is formed by Estructuras I (S), II (W), III (E), and IV (N) in the S part of the ditch enclosure.

Estructura I (7C–8C AD) is a four-tiered rectangular building of classic Río Bec style. There are two pyramidal towers at either end of the platform, overlooking two double ranges of chambers opening onto the plaza.

Estructura II is a pyramid-platform reached by a steep stairway leading to a temple at the top. There are relief sculptures on its S façade and it too is surrounded by multi-chambered buildings of Río Bec style. Estructura II is ruinous and only the mound of *Estructura III* remains.

W of the plaza there is another palace-like structure with stucco-decorated walls and a stone wall carved with elaborate geometrical designs. Much of the rest of the site is covered in jungle growth, but mounds can be seen to form several more plazas. A trail leads from here to PL. CENTRAL, bounded by Estructuras VIII (E), IX (N), and X (W). *Estructura VIII* once had a monumental staircase up its W side. A small entrance on its S side, which one must crawl through, leads to several interconnected rooms. *Estructura IX* is ruinous but still stands c 30m high. *Estructura X* has the lower remains of its stairway and some fine relief sculpture with traces of red paint on its façade.

Immediately W of Estructura X is a small I-shaped *Juego de Pelota* and PL. OESTE. It is mostly ruinous but *Estructura XIII* (W side) forms another group of rooms.

154km **Xpuhil**, which along with Chicanná and Río Bec itself, has one of the finest known examples of the Río Bec style.

The site was mainly occupied between c AD 400 and 900, but the presence of Chicanel monochrome ceramics indicates earlier habitation as well. In settlement pattern studies of the entire region around Río Bec, Becán, and Xpuhil, the Classic Period population has been estimated at an average of c 500 people a sq km.

The site has been studied by K. Ruppert and J. H. Denison (1943), I. Marquina (1951), and A. M. Tozzer (1957), but there are so many mounds in the immediate vicinity that the site has barely yet been touched by archaeology.

There are various dilapidated ruins, but the chief attraction is the ruinous and overgrown, but otherwise excellently preserved, Río Bec style temple. On a low platform with a central staircase, the structure comprises a classic Río Bec triad of a central gallery of three rooms with a tower at the rear, and two flanking pyramid-towers. Each of the three pyramid-towers has a steep, non-functional staircase leading up to a false temple. The temples have remains of roof-combs and doorways in the form of grotesque Chenes style monster-mouths; and there are remains of three more monster-masks on each false stairway. The best-preserved mask, on the central tower, can be seen at closer quarters by walking around to the rear of the structure.

The central building has three doorways with short flights of steps from the platform level, plus doorways at either end of the structure. Over each of the central doorways there are more masks, with stylized snarling lips and evenly spaced teeth hanging down just over the lintels.

From (155km) the village of *Xpuhil* (P) a track runs to (16km SE) **RIO BEC** in Quintana Roo. The term *Río Bec* refers to a specific site, to a general region, and to an architectural style of the Late Classic Period.

The region covers c 100 sq km. It was explored in general by K. Ruppert and J. H. Denison in 1943, but has since been the source of several general surveys, excavations, and analyses. Covering the areas of SE Campeche and SW Quintana Roo, it is rich in Maya sites and produced the distinctive Río Bec architectural style, derived from the earlier Petén style of N

Guatemala. In both space and time it overlapped and was eventually succeeded by the Chenes and Puuc styles. Río Bec architecture featured a tripartite form, comprising a lavishly decorated central building flanked by high, solid tower-like buildings with steep stairways inclining at 20 degrees, leading to false temples. Doorways into these buildings formed horrific, gaping serpent-monster mouths. Aerial reconnaissance and surveys of the region have revealed a sophisticated network of canals, raised fields, and small Maya 'farmsteads', forming the agricultural base necessary to support the ancient population and its ceremonial centres, a population much exceeding that of today. Río Bec itself was a powerful ceremonial centre during the Classic Period, alongside Xpuhil and Becán.

At Río Bec the principal monument is a tripartite structure on a platform. The central building is flanked by tower-like pyramids of six tiers each, with rounded corners and steeply angled staircases and ramps leading to false temples. The entrances to these are stylized Chac, Rain god, masks.

Only the central pyramidal building is functional. It has a wooden-linteled doorway in the form of a huge, grotesque Chac mask, leading into a double gallery. It has a crested and moulded roof, and all three towers have lattice-work and geometric-pattern decorations on their exterior walls.

Other classic Río Bec sites easily accessible on or near main roads include *Xpuhil, Chicanná*, and *Cilvituk*. Many more, like Río Bec, lie in deep jungle, incl. *Calakmul, Hormiguero*, and *Kohunlich* and smaller sites such as *Balakbal* (with a stele dated AD 406 and an unusual building approached by a staircase at front and rear), *Channá, Culucbalom, El Palmar* (with some of the latest dated monuments of the collapse of the Classic Maya), *La Muñeca* (with stelae dated between AD 692 and 909), *Oxpemul* (with stelae dated AD 830 and 879), *Pared de los Reyes, Pasión del Cristo, Payán, Pechal, Peor es Nada, Reforma, Sasilha, Uaacbal*, and *Uxul* in Mexico; plus *El Mirador, La Muralla*, and *Naachtún* (stele dated AD 504) just across the frontier in Guatemala.

A guide and four-wheel drive vehicle are advisable to visit the jungle sites; enquire at the tourist office in Chetumal.

An unsurfaced road (c 17km) leads N from Xpuhil via Zoh Laguna to the remains of a small Maya ceremonial centre known as *Puerto Rico*: a plaza surrounded by platforms and several pyramid ruins. Notable is a large cylindrical tower, probably Late Classic, which survives in good condition, but, mystifyingly, has no ground level entrance, only five narrow, corbel-vaulted openings at c 2m from the ground; it stands on a circular platform 1.5m high and 8.5m in diameter.

Beyond Xpuhil the road crosses into Quintana Roo. From (216km) *Francisco Villa* a road runs S to (9km) **Kohunlich**, a site (8–6; fee) covering c 2 sq km, with over 100 mounds, most of them still unexcavated.

Work by V. Segovia and INAH has cleared and preserved many of the monuments in an area of tropical forest. A general view of the zone can be obtained from the top of the Pirámide de los Mascarones.

From the car park the roadway leads to a restored pyramid on the E side of a large ceremonial plaza. To the l., beyond it, is a small court with buildings and a pyramid with stairway. Built in the Late Classic (c AD 800), it is thought to have been a school or college for Maya nobles. Other buildings around the large plaza are not so well preserved: opposite (W) is a platform with building ruins; on the S, possibly a palace; and on the N, a pyramid and temple. E of the plaza the path leads under shade trees to (c 275m from the car-park) a second, sunken plaza, dominated by the *Pirámide de los Mascarones*.

This is a three-tiered structure on a platform with rounded corners, c 15m high, incl. the restored temple on the top, reached by a staircase 8.5m wide. Flanking the staircase are six large stucco masks; there are in fact two more masks covered by a later, Late Classic, facing of carefully dressed, closely set stones, diminishing in size towards the top. The masks are of Early Classic date and resemble one drawn by Frederick Catherwood at Izamal in 1843; they show possible Olmec influence in the 'baby faces' of thick lips and 'feline' downturned mouths. Other notable features include amber balls in their nostrils, earplugs, symbols on the eyeballs and eye-shaped symbols beside the heads, furrowed eyebrows and high cheekbones, and protruding tongues and mustachios. The highest masks have Maya features similar to masks at Tikal in Guatemala, and may be later in date than the lower masks. The temple on the top has a restored roof and includes a T-shaped Maya tomb and corbel-arched chamber. A structure on the second tier, facing the staircase, was a tomb or altar; and broad buttress-like structures rest on the projecting sills of the first three tiers. From the pyramid, a path leads SW to a restored *Juego de Pelota* with sloping walls forming the playing field.

218km poor road (l.) for (c 20km N) *Dzibanché*, a little-explored Late Classic site, whence came a jade plaque incised with the latest known Long Count date—corresponding to AD 909.

From (249km) *Ucum* a road goes S, alongside the Río Hondo, to (86km) *La Unión*, on the frontier with Belize. 250km turning r. for *Juan Sarabia*, on the Belizean frontier. From 252km, Méx. 307 departs for (358km N) *Puerto Juárez*, see Rte 97.

273km CHETUMAL (c 130,000 inhab.; 5m), the modern capital of the State of Quintana Roo, on the frontier with Belize. It is also a free port and naval station, but has little interest for the traveller.

Airport. 2km NW (Av. Revolución). Flights to *Mexico City, Tuxtla Gutiérrez, Cozumel, Mérida* and *Cancún*.

Bus station. 2km N, at junction of Avs Insurgentes and Belice. Services to *Mexico City* via Villahermosa (22 hrs); to *Francisco Escarcega* (5 hrs); to *Mérida* (9 hrs); to *Cancún* (6–7 hrs); to *Belize* (5 hrs); etc.

Hotels throughout the town.

Post Office. 2A Av. Plutarco Elías Calles.

Tourist Office. Pal. de Gobierno.

Guatemalan Consulate. 342 Av. Obregón (for visas essential for travellers to Guatemala).

Chetumal, once called *Chactumal*, was a Maya city-state in the 15–16C, and a powerful commercial centre. It controlled trade along the E coast of Yucatán, around to Xicalango on the Gulf Coast, and was at the E end of overland, inland trade routes. Cacao, gold, copper, and feathers moved N through Chetumal, while salt and other northern products moved S to Central American cities. Companion centres included Santa Rita (Belize) at the S end of Bahía de Chetumal, Tulum, Tancah, and Xelha. Ichpaatún, Oxtancah, and Nohuchmul were commercial satellites of Chetumal, which also maintained commercial outposts on the Sula Plain (Honduras).

The first Spanish contact occurred in 1511 when a caraval, bound for Santo Domingo from Darien, was wrecked on the shores off Jamaica. Twelve survivors drifted to the E coast of Yucatán and were captured by Maya of Chetumal. Four were immediately sacrificed and eaten in a cannibalistic ritual. Years later the Spaniards found two still surviving—Gerónimo de Aguilar and Gonzalo Guerrero. De Aguilar rejoined his countrymen, brought useful knowledge of the Maya and their language, and helped in their conquest. Guerrero, however, preferred to stay with his Maya wife and family. As a commander in Chetumal's army he fought the Spaniards over Maya commercial interests and was killed in Honduras in 1536, commanding a fleet of war canoes. His body was found, long-haired, tattooed, and pierced with nose, ear, and lip jewellery after the Maya fashions of the day. In 1531 Alonso de Avila with 50 Spaniards founded Villa Real de Chetumal, which hardly thrived. Its recent history began as a settlement called Payo Obispo in 1898, with a naval squadron formed to prevent contraband in the valuable timber (mahogany, cedar, roseapple, and species of gumtree from which chicle is derived) of the hinterland and in arms and ammunition for the Maya rebels (see Rte 94). Hurricanes wreaked terrible damage in 1916, 1942, and 1954. The town reverted to its old name in 1936.

The State of **Quintana Roo** (c 460,000 inhab.; 50,212 sq km) occupies the E part of the Yucatán peninsula. Its level, porous limestone plain has been largely covered by rainforest, now seriously gnawed away by relentless slash and burn; its Caribbean coasts are renowned for their stretches of fine white sand. Part of the longest barrier reef system in the Americas extends along the E coast. The climate is hot and humid. On the mainland 1400mm of rain falls annually; on the island of Cozumel, 1570mm. The forestry industry yields valuable mahogany and cedar, and chicle. Copra is produced on the coast opposite Cozumel. Sponge- and turtle-fishing also have their importance. The development of Cancún has underlined the State's tourist potential. Much damage was done along the coast by the hurricane of 1988.

Spanish control in part of the region was largely assured after the ferocious campaign in 1544–45 of Melchor and Alonso Pacheco; but interior jungle regions remained unconquered. English and other lumbermen (Baymen) operating from Belize and buccaneer representatives of Spain's European rivals preyed along the coasts from the mid-17C. (The appearance of the English and others was recorded as early as c 1570.) After the 1720s the Spaniards managed to contain the Baymen in Belize, although efforts to expel them from there were unsuccessful. In the 19C the region became a dumping ground for political prisoners. After the fiercest period of the war of the Castes, when the cult of the Speaking Cross at Chan Sta Cruz began its hold on the Cruzob (see Rte 100), the Maya who refused to become plantation workers retreated into the eastern fastnesses of the peninsula, even declaring an independent Maya state. Attempts by the Yucatán State government to root them out were made at great cost. By 1902, the Mexican army, using modern artillery, ended Maya resistance. In the same year the new federal territory of Quintana Roo was carved out of the State of Yucatán, much to the anger of the yucateco élite, for it represented an economic loss, a political defeat at the hands of the national government, and their humiliation at the hands of the E Maya. Maya unrest, however, continued. After a chequered existence, the territory became a State of the federation in Oct. 1974.

The road N of Chetumal leads to (8km) *Calderitas*, the local beach resort. 7km N of Calderitas is **Ichpaatún** (unrestored), plundered in 1960 for its stone to pave the streets of Chetumal.

It was a Middle–Late Postclassic Chontal Maya site (explored by William T. Sanders in 1960). Like similar sites farther N along the coast (eg, Tulum, Xelha, or Tancah) it was involved in the sea-trade of coastal Yucatán. There are several platforms around plazas and the architecture reflects the so-called 'decadent' period of Maya culture after the fall of Chichén Itzá. One stele dates between AD 330 and 593 and appears to be a relict brought from elsewhere. Another stele shows a woman with a staff of authority and prisoners, features usually reserved for male rulers; it may reflect an increased importance for women in the late N Maya area (cf. *Cobá* and *Tancah*). There are also remains of a circuit wall.

Calderitas is less well known, but also shows architectural features of Postclassic 'decadent' Maya style; c 1km N of Ichpaatún, *Oxtancah*, and c 6km N, *Nohuchmul*, are two other coastal ruins opposite Isla Tamalcab.

93   Campeche to Mérida

A.   Via Hecelchakán and Calkiní

Méx. 180, 198km.—68km (for 32km W) Jaina.—77km Hecelchakán.—84km Pocboc.—101km Calkiní.—135km for (5km S) Oxkintok.—180km Umán.—198km **Mérida**.

We leave Campeche to the E (Av. Gobernadores), at first through a hilly region before the road straightens one to rolling countryside. At 30km, just before *Chencoyí*, we turn l. on Méx. 180. 59km *Tenabo*. 68km *Pomuch*, known for its sweet spongy bread. Both here and at Tenabo some of the houses were built from stone salvaged from the prehispanic site at *Xcochac*, c 12km E.

C 32km W of Pomuch (gravel road) is the coast opposite the tiny island of **Jaina**, c 2km offshore (accessible only by authorization from INAH), one of the few known Late Classic Maya necropolises. It included a Maya village, the oldest stele of which is dated AD 652, and was the final resting place chosen by many Maya élite. Some of the graves have been excavated, by H. Moedano (1946), R. Piña Chan (1948), and INAH (1964). The most common burial position was flexed, with a figurine placed in the arms, a cloak spread over the body, a jade bead placed in the mouth, and a tripod vessel placed over the head. The grave was then sprinkled with cinnabar paint and other offerings put in. Children were more often placed inside an urn, covered with a tripod vessel or large potsherd. Skulls were often frontally deformed and the teeth often mutilated.

The graves are especially important for their figurines, many of which are in the Museo Regional in Campeche and in several local museums and collections (eg, in Hecelchakán), as well as in the Museo Nacional de Antropología. They are both hand-made (in particular, whistles) and mould-made (rattles), and are among the few Mesoamerican polychrome figurines. They provide a wealth of information on Maya dress and ceremonial wear, incl. skirts, turban-like headdresses, mantles, flowing robes, animal skins, and masks. Some ball-player figurines appear to wear cacao pod pendants. There were three developmental stages: in the first, postures are symmetrical, and there are disc ear-plugs, bulbous heads, and protruding eyes; in the second (5–6C AD), the details of faces, depicting age, sex, status, and of costume are extremely detailed, accurate, and distinct, as if individuals were being portrayed; in the third, possibly from Jonuta, closed-in contours look almost mould-made, but the detail of faces and action continued. Not until the Late Classic do coarser features belie mould-made items.

77km **Hecelchakán** (c 5000 inhab.; 50m; R,P), where the chief attraction is the *Museo Arqueológico del Camino Real de Hecelchakán-Campeche* (Tues.–Sat., 9–6; Sun., 9–1; fee). In it may be seen an important collection of stone sculptures and pottery from Jaina, a model of a Maya village and ceremonial centre, Maya ethnographic materials, and, in the patio, stone stelae, carved columns, lintels, and door-jambs from sites in the vicinity. The buttressed church of *San Francisco*, with attractive sturdy towers, preserves parts of the original Franciscan foundation of c 1579, but is largely of late 17C–early 18C date.

Inspection of four local sites requires a guide and hired jeep (enquire at museum). Excavations at *Kocha* (12km W) uncovered carved stelae depicting Maya priests, and columned buildings. C 20km E of Hecelchakán are clustered *Holactún* (or *Xcalumkin*), *Cumpich*, and *Almuchil*. The first was a Maya centre founded in the 8C AD, of several plazas surrounded by terraces with Puuc style buildings. A principal court, surrounded by four small buildings, typifies the style of the site and of the region. There are plain, vertical façades with decorated and moulded upper friezes, and door-jambs in a style similar to those used at Chichén Itzá—eg, several drums sculpted in single-figure motifs of the earliest Maya tradition. At Cumpich there are burial mounds and a cenote. At Almuchil several single-storey Puuc style buildings stand on terraces and are decorated with friezes of half-columns grouped in sixes and linked by geometric motifs.

At (84km) **Pocboc** is the open chapel of *Los Santos Reyes*, set up in the late 16C as part of a visita of Hecelchakán, now forming the chancel of a ruined church, grafted on to it in 1765, if that is to what the date on a sotocoro column refers.

At (101km) **Calkiní** (c 10,000 inhab.; 52m; H,R,P) the former Franciscan convent of *San Luis Obispo* (c 1555–61) was built on a prehispanic platform. Its single-arch open chapel, now a ruin, over the triple-arch portería, also once used as three chapels, was the largest elevated open chapel in existence. So grand was it that no church was needed.

The Indians would congregate to hear Mass under a ramada (a thatched structure held up by poles, to protect them from the sun) erected before it.

The present church is a 17C building. In contrast, so tiny was the original cloister (two arches a side), that a bigger was built nearby. Over the refectory is one of the largest barrel vaults in Mexico (probably 17C). 109km *Bécal* is famous for its manufacture of Panama hats, known locally as jipijapa. Beyond Bécal we cross into the State of Yucatán. 118km *Halachó*, where the doorway of the 17C church of Santiago is recessed under a scallop-like canopy. 135km *Maxcanú*, with an 18C church.

C 5km S of Maxcanú is the Classic Maya centre of **Oxkintok**. Excavated by Edwin M. Shook in 1940 and re-examined by George Andrews in the 1970s, its scattered ruins remain dilapidated and unrestored.

Over c 1 sq km there are several platform mounds and corbel-vaulted rooms. Between c AD 200 and 475 there was intense construction here, and in a later building phase the architectural style was changed. In the first phase there was block masonry with carved stucco decoration, but no roof-combs or flying façades. A stele (or lintel stone?) erected in AD 475 is the earliest known inscribed date in N Yucatán. Thereafter stele-erecting and glyph-carving spread throughout the region. The second building phase included structures with roof-combs, 'flying' façades, and panelled walls depicting figures in a style different from the previous Early Classic Maya ones. There may therefore have been a change in ethnic composition, with immigrants coming from the Petén (from the Usumacinta valley on the Chiapas–Guatemala border) in the late 5C AD. Ceramics included a controlled-trickle decorated ware found at sites N of Becán, incl. Acancéh and Dzibilchaltún.

At 138km Méx. 184 branches r. for (33km E) *Muna*, see Rte 93B. Excavations at (158km; 2km l.) *Chocholá*, a Maya site, yielded large carved vases, mostly cylindrical in shape. They include paint applied after firing and are Late Classic in date (c AD 600–900). 180km **Umán**, where the enormous church of *San Francisco de Asís* (1766; unfinished) dwarfs the little 16C Franciscan chapel on its N side. The church's doorway is an extraordinary neo-Gothic conception, with four layers of pointed arches. 198km *Mérida*, see Rte 95.

B.   Via Kabah and Uxmal

Méx. 180 and Méx. 261, 254km.—44km Cayal for (18km S) **Edzná** and Méx. 261.—85km Hopelchén for (4km S) Dzibalchén (for [14km SW] Hochob and [20km NE] Dzibilnocac).—116km Xtacumbilxunaan.—146km turning E for Slayil, Xlapak, and Labná.—150km **Kabah**.—160km Sta Elena (for [2km SW] Mul Chic.—175km **Uxmal**.—254km **Mérida**.

Campeche to (32km) *Chencoyí*, see Rte 93A. We continue on Méx. 261. From (44km) *Cayal*, Méx. 261 runs S to (18km) **EDZNA** ('house of echoes') a Late Classic Maya centre with earlier traces of occupation in its 2 sq km zone. Its rulers may have been related to the Sky Dynasty of Tikal in Guatemala.

It has been excavated and studied by E. Polarios in 1936, A. Ruz in 1943–45, I. Marquina in 1951, and G. Andrews in 1975. Stelae from the site, several of which are in the museums of Campeche, date between AD 672 and 810, but occupation is known in the area from c 800 BC and a Late Preclassic pyramid mound and settlement are known from excavations to the W of the Classic Period structures.

The general architectural style at Edzná is a late manifestation of Puuc, but it also has elements of a certain nonconformist style in the chambers. Sculptures from the site provide information on the nature of Classic Maya dress and ornament.

Much of the zone is covered in thick vegetation. The main cleared area is the large central plaza, 159m by 100m, the E side of which is formed by a platform running nearly the whole length. It supports the main *Pirámide*, of five levels with a temple at the top of a central staircase. The base level is solid and 61 m sq, but levels two and three have double vaulted galleries of chambers in them, and levels four and five have single galleries of rooms. The level five chambers also have columnar supports at the façades. The temple is rectangular and faced with masks, and serpent and jaguar heads, in stucco. It has an elegant roof-comb, 6m in height, making the entire pyramid and temple 30m high. The temple is divided into a front and rear chamber, the latter subdivided into a central room and side wings. Traces of earlier constructions have been found throughout, but especially in levels one and two. The older structures were executed in carefully cut stone blocks and the more recent in stone veneer with a lime cement facing over a rubble core. The S side is formed by a platform and restored building that may have been priests' quarters; and other restored structures incl. the *Templo de las Estelas*, the *Temple of the Old Woman*, and two rounded buildings.

To the NW is a *Juego de Pelota* of two block walls with stone benches along the bases; the playing field is c 39.5m long and 9m wide.

Beyond Cayal, Méx. 261 winds through the Sierra of N Campeche to (85km) **Hopelchén** (6000 inhab.; R,P), where the church of *San Antonio* dates in part from its 16C Franciscan foundation.

C 3km NE is *Tohcok*, a Postclassic Maya site where paintings were discovered on some of the door-jambs. C 7km NE of Hopelchén are the little explored ruins of *Nohcuchich*, another small Maya centre.

From Hopelchén State road 269 runs S. 7km (W side of road) *Dzehkabtún*, a small Maya centre, where several low platforms and building ruins are in a plaza group. The architectural style is Puuc. 20km *Komchén*. 35km (r.) **El Tabasqueño** is a small, less well-known Maya site on a hill. Mound ruins here include a pyramid resembling that at Becán. The doorway to one building has carved serpent motifs (cf. *Hochob* and *Dzibilnocac*). The site's Chenes style differs from the more general Río Bec style more in the grouping of buildings than in the decorative motifs carved on them. Near Dzibalchén there are more Chenes style Maya ruins on the outskirts of San Pedro.

41km **Dzibalchén** is midway between two important Maya sites. The rough road SW from Dzibalchén goes to (10km) *Chencoh*, whence a track leads to (c 4km SE) **Hochob**.

Although a large Maya Chenes style site, little work (apart from restoration) has been done here since excavations by a Tulane University team in 1940 and by Ignacio Marquina in 1950. Here again, the Chenes architecture differs from the more general Río Bec less in decorative style than in the groupings and plans of the buildings.

There are three courts formed by small buildings and platforms. The principal court, c 79m x 39.5m, includes a pyramid 6m in height on one side, and to the N of it a three-building group, variously interpreted as a temple or palace. The central, vaulted building lacks Río Bec style towers, but supports the remains of a perforated roof comb formed by two rows of human figures. It is flanked by two smaller buildings at a lower level. All three have façades of cut stone veneer slabs, intricately decorated with highly stylized serpent motifs and serpent-mask doorways in sculpted stucco.

The road running NE from Dzibalchén runs to (20km) *Iturbide*. **Dzibilnocac** ('painted vault'), lies just E of Iturbide.

One of the larger Chenes style Maya sites, it was first studied by Edouard Seler in 1916. Further visits followed; and excavations were done by Brigham Young University 1968–70. It produced a long ceramic sequence dating from the Middle Preclassic to the Early Classic (c 500 BC to AD 1000); most of the material from the site is in the Museo Regional in Mérida.

Its pottery illustrates the cultural and chronological overlap between Maya regions: the Classic Period pottery includes Chicanel 'waxy'-slipped vessels and several features of the Río Bec ceramic tradition, although the majority of the pottery is within the Puuc tradition (cf. *Sta Rosa Xtampak*). Similarly, its Chenes architecture differs from the Río Bec style mainly in the groupings of the building complexes, while decorative motifs are similar.

There are several pyramid ruins and stone walls, but the main structure comprises a double, vaulted structure (c 68.5m x 24m) with three towers in the Río Bec–Chenes style. The central and W towers are ruins. The E tower, however, stands to a considerable height and has carvings all round in the form of an imitation temple. There are stylized, false serpent-mouth doorways on the E and W façades, and real doorways (now collapsed) on the N and S to two small rooms. There is more sculpture on the W side below the temple tower, and projecting serpent masks on three of the tower's corners.

Another small Maya centre, *Huntichmul*, lies c 18km EES of Dzibilnocac, covered by jungle growth (to see it a local guide is strongly recommended).

At **Sta Rosa Xtampak**, c 22km NW of Iturbide, there is a Maya site whose excavation yielded a long ceramic sequence dating from the Middle Preclassic to the Postclassic, and illustrates the spatial overlap of Maya traditions. Both Río Bec and Puuc ceramic styles are represented. Today the ruins of a multi-chambered palace of the Classic (8C) Maya town include two panels of Classic Chenes style architectural embellishment over several rectilinear blocks. Two stelae from the site have date glyphs for c AD 511 and AD 750 (although one authority states AD 771), possibly predating the Chenes buildings (cf. *Dzibilnocac*).

From Hopelchén, Méx. 261 continues N. At 116km a turning l. leads to the caves of **Xtacumbilxunaan** (7–4.30; fee), a series of underground cenotes, the deepest and most dangerous in the peninsula, used by the ancient Maya for religious ceremonies and visited by John L. Stephens in 1841. A guided tour, facilitated by specially built steps, highlights the most fantastic of the stalagtite and stalagmite formations. 119km *Bolonchén de Rejón*, the former Bolonchenticul, where nine prehispanic wells are seen on the plaza. The church of Asunción, high up, is a Franciscan foundation of c 1633.

At c 125km a r. turn leads to **Xkichmook** (or Xkichmul, or Kichmool), with several ruins. *Edificio 1* is a palace facing S, with a central stairway to a two-roomed temple. Rooms extend on each side of the stairway, with Chac masks at the corners of a two-storey section. Another extension of rooms (S) faces a plaza, and also has masks and other decorations on the walls. Two well-preserved rooms SE of Edificio 1 face W onto the plaza, and have circular 'medallions' on their upper façades. A trail leads E from Edificio 1 to two other ruins, one with triangular decorations and the other with mask panels.

At c 127km, **Itzimté** is on the l. Possibly the most southerly Puuc style site, its buildings have friezes less elaborate than those at Uxmal. There are two main groups of ruins on raised platforms. The larger group includes a building (*Estructura 1*) 13m high, with several large rooms—the one beneath the N stairway, for example, is 10.5m long. A path from this structure leads E to another, much more dilapidated, structure (*Estructura 63*), c 22m high, terraced against the hillside. A ruined stairway leads up to ten chambers in the upper floor. To the NW, nearer the road, another group of buildings included several broken stelae (now in the Museo de las Estelas in Campeche) with dates in the Late Classic Period.

We cross into the State of Yucatán. 146km turning l. for *Sayil, Xlapak*, and *Labná*, see Rte 94.

150km **KABAH** (6–6; fee), unlike many other Maya sites, and on the evidence of its pottery, seems to have been occupied and built in the relatively short space of c 250 years.

Its architecture and planning are Late Classic Puuc–Chenes style (c AD 650–900). Its ceramics are of the Cehpech Complex, featuring polychrome pottery, incl. fine paste wares showing central Mexican influences. Warriors with atlatls, carved on some of the door-jambs, also show central Mexican connections. Kabah was a small Maya ceremonial centre, probably a political dependent of its larger neighbour, Uxmal, and like that site, active in the salt trade. A 16km sacbé led NW to Uxmal, and another led SE, to Labná, another Uxmal dependency. The site was discovered by Alberto Ruz in 1948 and studied by Ignacio Marquina in 1950.

Kabah is located on both sides of the highway and can be viewed in general from the car park and ticket office. The most celebrated buildings are on the E side of the road, and show the Puuc–Chenes style at its most extravagant and experimental. The main attraction is the **Pal. de los Mascarones** (or *Codz Po'op*; 'rolled-up mat'). In approaching it, there is an unrestored pyramid on the r., and then a small platform, probably for an altar, in front of it. To the r. of the altar is a white concave circle marking the top of a chultún (water storage chamber).

The Codz Po'op is a palace of two parallel galleries of five corbel-arched chambers (each) at different levels. The interior step between the galleries is in the form of a monster snout or horn, in appearance not unlike a rolled-up reed mat. Other steps on the N end of the platform terrace are similar in form. The façade is a unique example of Puuc architecture, with both lower and upper sections decorated. Sitting on a stepped terrace-platform, with central staircase and a course of stylized masks of inlaid stonework, the Codz Po'op has three stacked rows of Chac masks above and below the central moulding, itself decorated with geometric motifs. Many of the masks are damaged or missing altogether, but there were 250–300 originally, of inlaid limestone, with long, hooked noses, and in various shades of ruddy brown, owing to oxide deposits in the stone. The entire façade is c 46m long, with five portals and a perforated roof-comb c 3m high.

Explored by John L. Stephens and Frederick Catherwood, later studies of Kabah were made by Teobart Maler, Edward Thompson, Sylvanus Morley, Alberto Ruz Chuillier, George Brainerd, and Robert Smith.

On the terrace in front of (W) the Codz Po'op are a small chultun and platform with glyphs.

Behind the Codz Po'op, c 50m NE, are two other palace-like structures. The first is *Tercera Casa* (Third House), a five-chambered, corbel-arched building, unrestored. Beyond it is a sanctuary building called the **Teocalli con Edificio Encima** (Temple with Superimposed Structure).

Its lower storey of chambers is entered through three central doorways, two side portals with central, round column supports, or two doorways at the ends of the façade. Above the medial cornice moulding, the façade is decorated with colonnettes in groups of three. The cornice is of three courses with the central course made up of vertical stones. On the top is part of a two-tiered, perforated roof-comb.

From these structures a path leads c 250m ENE to the *Templo de las Columnas*. This has five doorways in a frontage of c 35m, decorated with ranks of columns along the upper façade.

On the other side of the road there are several more palace-like structures. The *Gran Teocalli* (Great Temple) is a conical hill sanctuary c 25m high. Near it is the unrestored mound called *Edificio de la Bruja* (Witch's House). And c 600m W of the road is the mostly unrestored *Cuadrángulo del Oeste*, the E wing of which has a frieze of stylized masks, and colonnettes.

N of the Cuadrángulo del Oeste are two more temples, *Templo de las Grecas* (Meanders—greek key patterns) and *Templo de los Dinteles*. The former is named for the decoration on its façade and the latter still has its lintels of carved sapodilla wood, and traces of the painted red hand symbol of Itzamná inside (cf. *Izamal*). Between the Gran Teocalli and the above group is the isolated *Arco de Kabah*, spanning c 2.5m and thought to be the beginning of sacbeob to Labná and Uxmal.

From (160km) **Sta Elena**, its church (1779) with a chemin-de-ronde in its thick walls, a dirt track opposite the cemetery leads c 2km SW to the Classic Period Maya site of **Mul Chic**, which comprises a small ceremonial centre of several mounds around a plaza. One of these, *Estructura A*, sits on a platform with other building ruins, and has been excavated and restored. It consists of a single chamber supporting a roof-comb which in profile resembles a Maya hut. This was later filled with masonry rubble, and a five-tiered pyramid built over it, itself supporting a roof-comb with applied stucco figures of a man and a deer, originally painted red, blue, and yellow, and with a staircase c 6m wide.

The original building contained a mural, discovered when the rubble fill was cleared in 1961. Now faded, it depicts a scene similar to that at Bonampak; the dress and ornament on the figures resemble those on carvings at Edzná, Uxmal, Chichén Itzá, and Dzibilchaltún. Its general style is 7C AD and it depicts a procession of priests wearing the symbol of Itzamná (cf. *Izamal*) and Chac Mool. They preside over a battle scene and the massacre of the prisoners, one of which has been hanged, bleeding, from a tree. Trophy skulls hang from the warriors' waist belts, and name glyphs are suspended in cartouches above their heads.

A road leads NE from Sta Elena to (15km) *Ticul*, see Rte 101. Méx. 261 continues to (175km; c 1km l.) *Uxmal*.

UXMAL was one of the largest and most powerful of the N Yucatán cities in the Late Classic and Postclassic Periods. It lies in a heavily wooded valley bounded on the N and S by low hills. As a large centre, it must have been supported by a proportionately vast hinterland; several other Maya cities— Kabah, Sayil, and Labná to the SE—were linked to it by sacbeob and are known to have been its subjects.

The civic core of Uxmal is characterized by wide, uncrowded plazas, covering c 100ha, perhaps inspired by the open Yucatán terrain around it. It characterizes the architectural style known as Puuc, but also demonstrates the contemporaneity of Maya architectural styles: eg, the Pirámide del Adivino comprises a Puuc style structure replaced by a Chenes one; while in the Pal. del Gobernador a Chenes building was replaced by a Puuc one.

> Daily, 6–6; fee. Light and Sound shows, also daily, in Spanish at 7 and in English at 9; separate fee.

History. The Maya Books of 'Chilam Balam' relate something of Uxmal's history, and accounts were gathered by Fray Alonso de Ponce, Fray Diego López de Cogolludo, and others; but for the site's earliest history there is only archaeological evidence. The historical sources relate events spanning the 11–15C; the general style of the architecture, and the stelae associated with the buildings, date mainly within the 8–10C; and radiocarbon measurements of a wooden lintel in Templo I of the Pirámide del Adivino have yielded a date of c AD 569. Thus the site was occupied in the mid-6C, and flourished in the Late Classic and Postclassic Periods.

Sometime in the 11C AD the Xíu Maya, led by Ah Zuitok Tutul Xíu, followed the example of the Itzá Maya and Kukulkán in migrating into N Yucatán. They settled at Uxmal, which according to the 'Chilam Balam' was 'founded' by them. Both families became powerful ruling houses controlling large territories and enriching themselves by trade and marriage alliances. Tensions eventually led to the formation of the 'League of Mayapán' towards the end of the 12C, an alliance of the three Maya houses of Cocom (Mayapán), Itzá (Chichén Itzá), and Xíu Cocom (Uxmal; although some scholars question the primacy of Uxmal, and favour Izamal as the third member of the alliance). In the 13C diplomacy failed to maintain the alliance and Chichén Itzá was destroyed by the armies of Mayapán and Izamal, while Uxmal managed to remain neutral. Nevertheless Xíu princes were virtually held hostage by the ruler of Mayapán until 1441, when Prince Ah Xupán Xíu led a coalition of N Yucatán cities against Mayapán, which was sacked and all but abandoned. By the eve of the Spanish arrival there were about 15 independent N Yucatán principalities. About the same time, the Xíu abandoned Uxmal for reasons not fully understood, and moved to Maní, where they established one of the largest of these principalities.

Architecture. Architecturally Uxmal is the leading example of the Puuc style, and has some of the best-proportioned Maya buildings known. Puuc, in Maya 'land of low hills', was a style derived from and incorporating many elements from the Río Bec and Chenes styles of the Petén region. It featured rubble core walls faced with stone slabs, both freestanding and engaged columns, and façades that were plain up to a medial moulding, then covered with elaborate mosaic friezes. It introduced the use of wide, open plazas, dotted with freestanding palace-administrative buildings and temples with a proportion and simplicity of design balanced by elaborate mosaic embellishments. Column-flanked rectangular doorways relieved alternating rows of whole and half-length, engaged columns and mosaic friezes of lattice-work, stepped-frets, repetitious serpent bodies, and masks.

The buildings at Uxmal are masterfully crafted in soft pink and yellow stone. Although few traces now remain of it, a circuit wall once bore witness to the regional rivalries of the Late Postclassic. Many of the earlier buildings resemble the styles at Hochob, Dzibilchaltún, and Río Bec. Most of the later buildings are purely Maya, but many also include features of central Mexican influence. There are non-Maya inscriptions on some of the stelae, Teotihuacano style Tláloc masks on the temple of the Pirámide del Adivino and the N building of the Cuadrángulo de los Monjas, and a patolli board. Fine paste ware pottery is found as well as local Yucatán wares, and there may have been a barrio for central Mexican merchants within the city. As with all Maya sites, water was of primary importance, and Uxmal was no exception—rainwater was collected in a system of plaster-lined chultunes.

Excavations. Uxmal was visited and described by John L. Stephens and Frederick Catherwood in 1841. The first excavations, however, did not take place until 1929, directed by Franz Blom, who returned in 1936, and in 1938. Restoration work was begun in 1943 under the direction of José A. Erosa for the Mexican Ministry of Education, and has been continued under the auspices of INAH. A special study of the Uxmal sculptures was undertaken by M. Foncerrada de Molina in 1964–65.

The carefully restored **Pirámide del Adivino** (of the Magician, or Prophet) is the first structure encountered after entering the archaeological zone. With its elliptical ground plan and steep, smooth facing, it is unusual in the Maya world. A local legend holds that it was built in one night by a dwarf, hatched from an egg! Unfortunately, it took much longer, incl. five major construction phases between the 6C and 10C. It is oriented not quite N–S, with steep steps up the E and W sides, and comprises three diminishing tiers supporting a temple on top, plus evidence of earlier temples.

Its dilapidated state before restoration has made the exact dimensions difficult to determine, but it appears originally to have been c 85m long and c 31.5m high, to the top of the platform. As late as 1656 the inner temple was used to lay offerings of copal and coca incense in front of idols.

Over its long period of constructions and additions the pyramid incorporated a surprising mixture of architectural styles, incl. Chenes and Puuc Maya as well as Teotihuacano and Toltec.

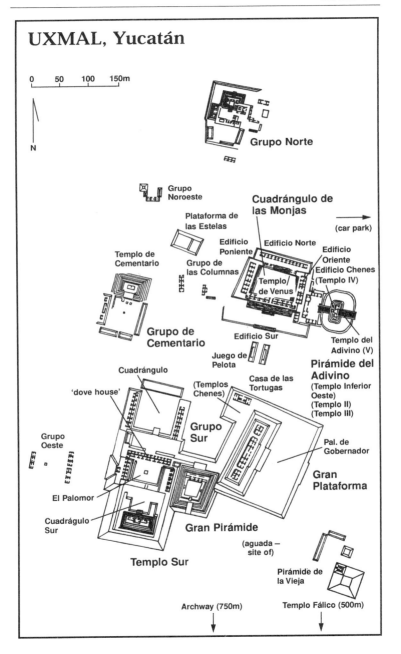

UXMAL, Yucatán

0   50   100   150m

N

Grupo Norte

Grupo Noroeste

Plataforma de las Estelas

Cuadrángulo de las Monjas

(car park)

Edificio Poniente

Edificio Norte

Edificio Oriente

Edificio Chenes (Templo IV)

Templo de Cementario

Grupo de las Columnas

Templo de Venus

Grupo de Cementario

Edificio Sur

Templo del Adivino (V)

Juego de Pelota

Pirámide del Adivino
(Templo Inferior Oeste)
(Templo II)
(Templo III)

Cuadrángulo

'dove house'

(Templos Chenes)

Casa de las Tortugas

Grupo Sur

Grupo Oeste

El Palomor

Pal. de Gobernador

Cuadrágulo Sur

Gran Pirámide

Gran Plataforma

Templo Sur

(aguada — site of)

Pirámide de la Vieja

Archway (750m)

Templo Fálico (500m)

Construction of the first temple began in the 6C AD, when the *Templo Inferior Oeste (Templo I)* was erected on a low platform. It is now completely covered by the pyramid, but can be entered by a tunnel to the r. of the staircase on the W side. It includes a Puuc façade with an upper frieze, over and around both sides of the doorway, comprising engaged colonnettes, checkered mosaic-work, and a set of stacked Chac, Rain god masks. Its wooden door lintel has been submitted to radiocarbon measurements and yielded a date of c AD 569. At the base of the pyramid the excavators also found three masks of Tláloc, the central Mexican Rain god, in Teotihuacano style, with elaborate headdresses bearing year glyphs.

The E face of the pyramid is ascended by a single flight of 90 steep steps, without side ramps, leading directly to the uppermost temple. Originally, however, this side must have had steps only to *Templo II*, on the first tier of the pyramid, now reached by a modern doorway built in the restoration work. This temple was covered in its turn by *Templo III*, and the second and third tiers of the pyramid.

The W face of the pyramid is also ascended by steps, at c a 60° angle, but here they are broken by a narrow landing on the first tier. Stylized masks flank the steps, against the face of the pyramid. Reconstructed steps from the landing lead to the entrance to the *Edificio Chenes (Templo IV)*, backing the second and third tiers. This temple was built in the mid-10C, replacing, and now obscuring, Templos II and III. A projecting Chac mask sits in the middle of these steps in front of the entrance, which forms a stylized, gaping monster-mouth, its teeth hanging down over the lintel. The corners of the projecting façade and the upper frieze comprise smaller masks with protruding, upturned noses. The side walls of the temple also have masks, and lattice-work panels on the frieze. Inside, the temple comprises corbel-arched chambers.

Staircases flanking the Chenes façade lead to the summit of the pyramid, and to the *Templo del Adivino (Templo V)*. In general this is a Puuc style temple, measuring 22m by 3.9m, but it also shows Toltec influence. It is decorated with two panels of flat, interlacing mouldings on each side of the door, and two upper, horizontal mouldings. It originally had five Chac masks above the first moulding, but their pedestals are all that now survives. Inside there are three chambers, the central one entered from the W and the other two from the E.

It is possible to walk around the entire structure on the narrow ledge of the second tier, to view the layout of the rest of the site before returning to the plaza.

Named for the impression it gives of a nuns' convent cloisters, the **Cuadrángulo de las Monjas** is directly W of the Pirámide del Adivino. It comprises a large courtyard (interior = 64m by 45m; exterior = 78m by 65m) formed by four galleried buildings. The courtyard is entered from either the SW corner or through a monumental archway in the building forming the S side. Altogether there are 88 rooms, many of which have their original door lintels of sapodilla wood.

The *Edificio Norte* is clearly the most important, and is characteristically Puuc in design. It stands on a platform, c 100m by 20m, and 6.7m high, and covers an earlier building. The wide central staircase has a stele in the middle, now mostly defaced, and is flanked by two pillared porticoes, four pillars on the l. and two on the r. The building itself comprises parallel galleries of rooms and is two storeys high. The better-preserved l.-hand portico is known as the *Templo de Venus*, and has five emblems attributed to Chac above the medial moulding, Chac masks at the corners, and a frieze of lattice design.

The main building has 11 doorways facing the courtyard and doorways at each end, giving access to 26 rooms. Above the moulding are decorative stone mosaics depicting Maya thatched huts, double-headed serpents (especially at the corners), people, birds, monkeys, interlacing panels of stepped-frets, and checkerboard patterns, plus colonnettes along the walls, and reconstructed

Chac masks forming a crenellated roof-line. Some of the Rain god masks are of Teotihuacano style Tlálocs, with elaborate headdresses bearing year glyphs.

Two radiocarbon measurements were taken from the sapodilla wood lintels, and yielded dates of AD 893 and 653, in both cases plus or minus 100 years. The former date would make the Edificio Norte older than the other structures of the quadrangle.

The *Edificio Sur* was the second to be constructed, and is lower than the others. From the Edificio Norte it is in fact possible to see over the roof, beyond it, to the buildings of Grupo Sur. It has two sets of parallel, corbel-arched galleries on either side of its central archway, and reached by low steps (now very ruinous) running the entire length of the building. Each room is entered by a doorway facing either the courtyard or the open plaza to the S. The axis of the central arch leads directly to the Juego de Pelota, S of the quadrangle. Both the N and S façades are covered with panels of ornamental colonnettes, lattice-work, mosaics depicting Maya huts with palm-leaf roofs, and stylized masks.

The *Edificio Oriente* was the third to be constructed, and, like the others, stands on a low platform. Its parallel galleries form several groups of rooms with a more complex partitioning than in the other buildings. It has a central door-way and two smaller portals to either side. Above the central door there is a stack of Chac masks. The upper frieze consists of moulded interlacing, broken by six frames enclosing two-headed serpents, each surmounted by an 'owl' mask, and stylized masks at the corners of the building.

The *Edificio Poniente* was the last to be built. On a platform with a wide staircase, it comprises the usual double gallery of rooms, with doorways open-ing onto the courtyard. Above the central doorway sits the moulded figure of a turtle, with a human head. Above him there is a large headdress similar to two others found on stelae at Uxmal. Each of the other six doors also has a symbolic figure above it, incl. Maya huts and masks, sets of colonnettes and masks, and small, seated figures. Between two 'flying cornices', friezes filling the rest of the wall include more lattice-work, mosaics, geometric figures, and an undulating serpent with heads at the NE and SE corners of the façade.

The exact use of such a complex 'palace' is uncertain. One romantic fancy has it that it was the residence of virgins in charge of a sacred fire, but archaeologists generally regard such views as the product of overheated imaginations rather than empirical evidence. Considering Uxmal's importance as a prominent seat, if not the capital, of Xíu power, it seems more likely that the quadrangle was a combination of princely residences and administrative offices.

Immediately S of the Cuadrángulo is the **Juego de Pelota**, some 60m away on a low terrace. It has a vertical-walled playing field, c 33m long by 9m wide. Each wall is 6m high and 7m wide on the top, and supports a three-chambered building; the central rooms of these are transverse to the ball court axis, and held tenoned goal rings, one of which was found by the excavators to have glyphs for the date AD 649.

The *Gran Plataforma*, *Gran Pirámide*, and *Grupo Sur* form a collection of structures on a contiguous series of platforms and courtyards. The **Casa de las Tortugas** is directly S of the ball court, on the N corner of the Gran Plataforma. It comprises a multi-chambered structure facing N, and measures 28m by 10m by 6m. Its façade is made up of three parts: a plain base, surmounted by colonnettes, and a frieze of realistically moulded turtles in procession around the top of the building. Inside there are three pairs of corbel-arched rooms, each pair entered by doorways in the N, E, and W façades.

The **Pal. del Gobernador** stands along most of the W side of the *Gran Plata-forma* (180m by 150m by 12m high). The palace itself sits on its own two-tiered base, 121m by 27m by 8m high, and is approached by a wide, central staircase on the E side. The present building was perhaps the latest construction on the site (c AD 987), and is a masterpiece of Puuc design. It covered an earlier structure of Chenes style, some traces of which can be seen at the foot of the terrace on the W side. It comprises a central complex of ten rooms in two interconnecting galleries, and two separate structures at each end, each divided into five rooms. All the rooms open onto the E façade, and the vaulted passages between the three buildings are the tallest known Maya corbel arches. In alterations after the initial construction, these passages were filled in with more room divisions.

The upper façade is a huge frieze of mosaics broken only by the two arches. It includes a central, seated figure with an elaborate headdress, two-headed serpents, masks, lattice-work, and various other designs by now familiar. On the W side, the earlier Chenes building is represented by moulded stucco designs, and a characteristic monster-mouth doorway.

In 1951–52 a small *Adoratorio* was excavated in the middle of the Gran Plataforma by C. Sáenz and A. Ruz. The jade necklace found by them is now in the Museo Regional in Mérida.

The SW corner of the Gran Plataforma is occupied by the **Gran Pirámide** reconstructed in 1972–73. It is 30m high, ascended by a wide staircase on the N side and a narrower one on the S, and supports a typical three-chambered temple. The central doorway to the temple is a grisly monster-mouth, 1.97m high and 3.2m wide. The N façade is decorated with carved guacamayos (macaws), fire symbols (perhaps representing the sun), and Chac masks. The Chac mask on the r.-hand corner has a human head, or perhaps a god's head, protruding from its gaping jaws. Inside the temple the excavators found a tomb with various offerings, now in the museum in Mérida. The view of the site from the top is equal to that from the Pirámide del Adivino.

Along the W side of the Gran Pirámide, and to the S and N, are three contiguous quadrangles, similar in plan to the Cuadrángulo de las Monjas. Running N to S they are: the *Cuadrángulo*—with ruins of rooms on the E, W, and S sides, doorways opening into the courtyard, and a small altar mound off-centre; *El Palomar*—the middle quadrangle, also surrounded by multi-chambered galleries opening onto the courtyard; and the *Cuadrángulo Sur*.

The N building of El Palomar is known for its stone roof-comb, perforated by rectangular openings resembling the niches of a pigeon or dove house. Roof-combs are not a normal feature of the Puuc style; this example, and the one on the *Templo del Cementario* (see below) are collectively unique in W Yucatán. The building itself has two parallel galleries of rooms, divided into two sets by a corbel-arched passage leading onto the plaza and to the Cuadrángulo.

A corresponding arch dividing the S building of the quadrangle leads into the Cuadrángulo Sur, whose surrounding buildings are much ruined. In the centre S of of this last quadrangle stands a raised platform supporting the *Templo Sur*, of four rooms, with yet another row of galleries behind it, to the S, forming the S side of the complex.

To the W of El Palomar are traces of more rooms, *Grupo Oeste*, perhaps once forming another quadrangle. To S and N of these monuments are other, more isolated groups of ruins.

The *Pirámide de la Vieja* stands isolated to the SE of the Gran Plataforma. It consists of a grass-covered mound supporting a small temple, perhaps one of the oldest at Uxmal. Its name comes from a mutilated statue, 1.3m high, of an old woman found near the base. Local legend claims that she was the adoptive mother of the dwarf who built the Pirámide del Adivino.

SW of the Gran Plataforma, c 500m along a path from the Pirámide de la Vieja, is a ruin known as the *Templo Fálico*, because its rain spouts, one of which survives above the cornice, are rather remarkably shaped. Just E of the Gran Plataforma there is also a small collection of phallus stones.

Farther S, c 750m from the Pal. del Gobernador, stands an Archway. It is 5.5m high and 3.5m wide at the base, and stood at the end of the sacbé (causeway) leading through the jungle to a similar freestanding archway at the site of Labná.

SE of the Grupo Sur there was a large *Aguada* (reservoir), one of Uxmal's main chultunes for collecting rainwater. The sides were plastered with several stucco layers to make it watertight.

Returning now to the main plaza N of the Gran Plataforma, there are several monuments on this end of the site.

The *Grupo del Cementario* stands on the W side of the plaza. Another quadrangle of buildings, it is mostly ruinous except for the partly restored *Templo del Cementario* on a stepped pyramid on its N side. It supports another roof-comb, not a regular Puuc feature. Between the Cementario and the Cuadrángulo de las Monjas are some scattered, unrestored ruins known as the *Grupo de las Columnas*.

Beyond these, to the N, are the small, dilapidated ruins of the *Grupo Noroeste*, forming a small, three-sided court of rooms and mounds, and unexcavated terraces, and the much larger **Grupo Norte**. These ruins form yet another huge quadrangle, on a low platform. Although unrestored, and very dilapidated, they can be seen to form several groups of short, multi-chambered galleries, temples, and a pyramid mound. The long mounds form galleried buildings on the S, E, and W sides, surrounding a courtyard in front of a pyramid and temple on the N side.

From the site entrance, taking a last, distant view across the plaza at the façades of these imposing monuments, especially at the Pal. del Gobernador, in the light of a setting sun one cannot but be awed by the simplicity of building lines balanced by the now softened riot of intricate decoration.

Méx. 261 continues N across the low so-called Puuc range (also known as the Sierrita) to (191km) *Muna*, where the façade of the church of Asunción, founded by the Franciscans in the late 16C, incorporates two elaborate three-tier espadañas.

From Muna, Méx. 184 leads NW past (23km) *Calcetohc*, with underground caves, to join (33km) Méx. 261 a little NE of *Maxcanú*, see Rte 93A; and SE to (22km) *Ticul*, see Rte 101.

We go N to (209km) turning r. for (3km) *Abalá*, with a 17C church (good wooden pulpit). At (236km) *Umán* we join Méx. 180 for (254km) *Mérida*, see Rte 95.

94 Sayil, Xlapak, and Labná

These three sites may be reached by the road which turns off Méx. 261. Best negotiated by jeep from Uxmal, Sta Elena, or Kabah, where local enquiry about hire is recommended. The sites are open 8–5; fee.

5km **SAYIL** is another important, although less well-known, Late Classic Maya civic and ceremonial centre, dating from c AD 850. Along with Labná and Kabah it formed the principal cluster of dependent towns around Uxmal.

It was linked to Labná by a sacbé, and possibly also to Kabah. The site was excavated by Edwin M. Shook in 1940 and its magnificent palace studied by Tatania Proskouriakoff in 1950; the entire site was surveyed by George Andrews in the 1970s.

Pottery from the site is of the Classic Maya polychrome tradition, but has distinctive regional features and is known as Sayil 'regional polychrome'; it includes a good proportion of fine paste wares reflecting trade with central Mesoamerica.

Sayil has nearly 100 mounds and buildings, mostly covered in thick vegetation; restoration work by INAH continues. The **Palacio** represents one of the finest Puuc style decorated and planned Maya buildings known. It has an impressive 85m façade of three recessed storeys, the two lower of which are backed onto a central block supporting the third, single galleried, floor. It is approached by a central staircase facing S, at the end of the sacbé.

It is claimed that the complete palace had nearly 100 rooms. Of the present remains, the ground floor sits on a supporting platform and consists of two galleries of corbel-vaulted chambers only 2.5m wide. The first floor is also of two galleries, and is best viewed from the W of the staircase. Its façade is a good example of Puuc decoration, consisting of fields of decorations above and below medial and upper cornice divisions: below the medial cornice are alternating groups of short colonnettes and round columns with square capitals supporting the stone lintels of a portico of six entrances; between the cornices are rows of short colonnettes between stylized Chac masks, and serpent motifs, and, over each portico entrance, a stylized 'descending god' (feet in the air; cf. the Ball Court panels at *El Tajín*) between the jaws of two serpents.

On the second floor is a single gallery of seven narrow rooms each with its own doorway. Its façade is plain except for two projecting, horizontal mouldings, along the top one of which are some unusual square niches above the doorways, except for the central one.

NW of the Palacio, the saucer-like top of a chultún can be seen.

A path to the r., off the sacbé, almost opposite the Palacio staircase, leads through a very dilapidated *Juego de Pelota* to an outbuilding. The impressions of decorative colonnettes can be seen above the medial cornice, with spool-shaped bands on them, another variation of Classic Puuc themes.

On the same path, c 400m from the Palacio, is *El Mirador*, an unrestored temple of two galleries of chambers on a supporting platform. It is entered through a single corbel-vaulted doorway, and the central wall separating the two galleries supports a perforated roof-comb, most of whose decoration is now gone.

On returning, c 27m along the path, a second path to the r. leads c 450m to an anthropomorphic stele with a pronounced phallus. There are several other stelae scattered about the zone.

At 11km lie the dilapidated ruins of **Xlapak** ('old walls'), mostly in the Puuc style. The main structure, the *Palacio* (restored in the mid-1960s), is 20m wide with two construction phases. The older, W part has three chambers with sets of stacked Chac, Rain god, masks above recessed columns in each corner, and above the central doorway; around the entire building are characteristic Puuc engaged colonnettes between the lower and medial cornices. The E wing, backing onto this building, was added later. It presents a façade of seven doorways with five sets of stacked Chac masks between sets of stepped-frets, and a V-shaped decoration formed from engaged columns, resembling the decoration on the monumental archway at Labná.

Like Kabah and Sayil, (15km) **LABNA** was a small ceremonial centre and dependency of Uxmal, and active in the salt trade of the Classic Period. There are some 60 chultunes (underground cisterns) in the zone.

Two main groups of buildings, N and S, are linked by a sacbé; sacbeob also link Labná to Kabah, and possibly to Sayil. The architecture at Labná is Puuc, and very similar to that at Kabah and Sayil, especially in its use of colonnettes on façades.

The S group of structures comprises the Templo Oriente, El Mirador (a pyramid), and the Arco Labná, separating two plazas and the beginning of the sacbé to Kabah. The **Templo Oriente** was an eight-chambered L-shaped structure. It has rectangular doorways of two parallel stone courses dividing rows of short colonnettes, with longer colonnettes between the doorways. Five chambers face W into a plaza and a N wing of three chambers faces S. Across the main plaza to the S is another series of smaller plazas on the NE side of which is **El Mirador**.

Built on two reconstructed platforms, El Mirador is a tiered pyramid, 15m high, which originally had a staircase up its S side (unrestored). On this side there is a rising roof-comb c 10m high. John L. Stephens and Frederick Catherwood, who visited the site in 1842, recorded that traces of painted stucco still remained, depicting a seated figure and a row of death heads. Today, the only surviving stucco decoration is on the SW corner of the temple, above the medial moulding, showing the lower part of a figure.

Separating the plaza W of the Templo Oriente and another plaza NW of it is the **Arco Labná**, a tall corbel arch. The wall running N from it and the buildings W of it are thought to be later additions.

The E side of the arch has a frieze of geometric designs forming a wide V between rectangles, the whole between the medial and upper cornice moulding. The cornice itself has a double stone course with stepped fretwork, and the top of the corbel has a raised horizontal band of stones. The W side stands above a step into the lower plaza, and has trapezoidal doorways and recessed colonnettes flanking it. The medial moulding is a serpent motif between parallel stone courses. Above this are carvings of Maya huts, with steeply pitched thatch roofs, flanked by lattice-work interrupting the moulding.

The chambers on each side of the arch support high roof-combs, each with vertical, rectangular slits. The wall N of the arch is also highly decorated with reliefs, recently restored.

The sacbé from the N side of the central plaza connects the above group with the **Palacio**, a building of stone blocks, levelled with plaster and paved with smoothed stucco. The causeway leads to the SW corner of the easternmost of three plazas, each with galleries of chambers along their N sides. Together these form the largest known multi-chambered palace in the Puuc region, built c AD 800, although at least three building phases are recognized.

The entire façade is 134m long, on a terrace of 168m length. The top, third, storey is 107m long and c 20m high. The main (E) façade looks S, and is on an E–W axis, although the W wing strikes a right-angle to the N, to join with the central façade, the W end of which has a right-angled wing dividing the central and W plazas. All of the façades are highly decorated, but each with slightly differing styles. The E group of six chambers has a frieze of colonnettes and rectangular-framed masks between serpent motifs. At the SW corner of this façade is a gaping serpent's mouth from which emerges the head of a god or priest. Similar decorations of geometric designs, Chac masks, and serpents adorn the central façade, of five chambers with two chambers in the linking right-angled wing between the central and E galleries. Near the steps leading down to the central plaza is the top of a chultún. The wing dividing the central and W galleries had five chambers, while the W gallery had three. These last have a frieze of lattice-work, etc., as above; and one of the Chac masks in the façade has a date of c AD 862. There are traces of further remains N of El Palacio, and more unrestored ruins c 100m to the E, with traces of sacbeob linking them to both El Palacio and El Mirador.

From Labná we may continue NE to (30km) *Yaaxhom*, (34km) *Loltún*, and (42km) *Oxkutzcab*, see Rte 101.

95 Mérida

MERIDA (c 600,000 inhab.; 9m), capital of the State of Yucatán, chief city of the peninsula, and seat of a university, stands at the centre of a dense road network. At the height of its 19C prosperity it was known as 'ciudad blanca', because of its citizens' spotless turn-out and preference for white clothing, and because of its general cleanliness. Its geographical and historical remoteness is reflected in sober ecclesiastical architecture of various epochs, uninfluenced by developments elsewhere in Mexico. Its hot and humid climate promotes a luxuriance of tropical flowers and trees; and the gentle, humorous, and courteous meridanos contribute to a calm and pleasant atmosphere. Mérida offers an ideal base for visitors on the way to explore the Maya archaeological sites.

Laid out on a grid plan, the long straight streets are odd-numbered from E to W (from 1 in the N to over 100 in the S), even-numbered from N to S (from 2 in the E to over 100 in the W). This system, introduced in 1894–95 by Governor Carlos Peón, and gradually adopted after that, displaced designation of the streets by animal and other symbols, two of which remain at corners (Cs 42 and 65, 46 and 65). The churches of Mérida lost some of their interest after the iconoclasm of 1915 (see below); a prominent feature of their exteriors is the espadaña, incorporated into the W façade. Some of the old mansions, in the style of both Castile and Andalucía, keep their 17C stone portals and coats-of-arms in relief.

Airport. 12km SW. Daily flights to *Cancún, Chetumal, Cozumel, Mexico City*, and *Villahermosa*; four times weekly to *Veracruz*; daily flights also to *Miami*; twice weekly to *Houston*.

Bus stations. C. 69 (between Cs 68 and 70). Services to *Mexico City* (24 hrs); to *Campeche* (3 hrs); to *Valladolid* (2½ hrs); to *Cancún* (6 hrs); to *Chichén Itzá* (2 hrs); to *Tulum* (7 hrs); to

Oxkutzcab (2 hrs); to *Ticul* (2 hrs); to *Uxmal* (2 hrs); to *Kabah* (2 hrs); to *Playa del Carmen* (8 hrs); to *Veracruz* (18 hrs); to *Villahermosa* (10 hrs); etc.

524 C. 62 (between Cs 65 and 67). Services to *Dzibilchaltún* (45 minutes) and to *Progreso* (1 hr); and to *Tixcocob, Motul, Izamal, Valladolid,* etc.

Corner of Cs 50 and 67. Services to *Celestún* (2 hrs).

Railway station. C. 55 (between Cs 46 and 48). Trains to *Mexico City* (42 hrs), to *Palenque* (12 hrs), and to *Valladolid* (3 hrs).

Hotels throughout the city.

Post Office. In Pal. Federal (C. 65).

Tourist Office. In Teatro Peón Contreras.

US Consulate. 453 Paseo Montejo. **British Consulate.** Corner of Cs 53 and 58.

Fiesta. Carnival, the week before Lent.

Mérida was founded on 6 Jan. 1542 by Francisco Montejo the younger, on the site of the deserted Maya ceremonial centre of Ichcansihó, later called Tihó. Tihó was within the Chakan principality of the Tutul Xíu Maya lineage, former rulers of Uxmal, who had moved to Maní after the defeat of Mayapán c 1441. Ah Kukum Tutul Xíu, Maní's ruler when the Spaniards arrived in Yucatán, offered his alliance to them at Tihó on 23 Jan. 1542, where he was baptized two months later, as Francisco de Montejo Xíu. Its monuments, more or less intact, were levelled to afford material for the building of the new city. Mérida was seat of government of the Spanish province of Yucatán and from 1786 of the intendancy of Yucatán (or Mérida). Its status as capital remained unaffected during the 19C when the State government periodically refused to recognize the central government in Mexico City. In 1848, at the outset of the war of the Castes (see below), the Maya rebels swept the retreating yucateco whites to the very outskirts of the city and laid siege to it, an attack which the citizens, at a moment of the greatest danger, managed to withstand. (Governor Miguel Barbachano, having written out a proclamation for the city's evacuation, could find no paper on which to print it.) In Nov. 1865 empress Carlota paid an official visit and was overwhelmed by the warmth of her reception, the people shouting for her and Maximilian, but little for Mexico. In 1867 federal troops arrived to snuff out imperialist resistance in 'the final resting place…of Maximilian's fading empire'. With the henequen boom beginning in the 1880s Mérida became a modern and sophisticated city, boasting 'urban services and amenities…that the national capital was hard pressed to match'. A new planter élite flaunted its wealth, importing the latest fashions and consumer goods from Paris and London, and priding itself on its ability to speak foreign languages. On 19 March 1915 the army of Carranza's appointee as governor, Gen. Salvador Alvarado, entered Mérida to begin an enlightened and pragmatic revolutionary regime, though he condoned the wholesale iconoclasm in cathedral and churches. In Dec. 1923, during the uprising of Adolfo de la Huerta, rebellious federal troops overran Mérida and forced Governor Felipe Carrillo Puerto to flee. He was captured later in the month, brought back to the city, and executed, with three of his brothers, on 3 Jan. 1924.

The peninsula of Yucatán comprises the Mexican States of Yucatán, Campeche, and Quintana Roo; and the N regions of the republic of Guatemala and of Belize. It is composed of a bed of coraline and porous limestone rock which forms a low tableland, rising gradually towards the S. Poor, thin soil (State of Yucatán) has militated against most types of agricultural production, except for the tough henequen plant, a cactus from whose fibrous spines agricultural twines and ropes are made, and whose production boom (1880–1915), mainly to satisfy the increasing demands of US cordage factories, made the State of Yucatán the richest in Mexico. The SW and SE regions (Campeche and Quintana Roo) are well-forested. The climate ranges from hot in the N, with varying humidity and with limited rainfall, to more consistently tropical in the S and SE, with more plentiful rains (May–June, Oct.–Nov.).

A regional plan, agreed in 1989 by Mexico, Guatemala, Belize, Honduras, and El Salvador, would halt the indiscriminate felling of rainforest, protect endangered species, promote eco-tourism, minimize road building, and preserve Maya sites. The designation of two Biosphere Reserves in the peninsula—*Calakmul* (Campeche; spanning nearly 4.5 million hectares on either side of the Escarcega–Chetumal road) and *Sian Ka'an* (Quintana Roo; between the Chetumal–Tulum road and the coast), proposed for UNESCO's Man and the Biosphere programme—has followed.

Within living memory, the only means of reaching the Yucatán peninsula from central Mexico was by boat (an uncomfortable voyage) from Veracruz. Proper road and rail links were completed only in the 1960s. Even today the most reasonable approach for travellers whose time is limited is by air.

The State of **Yucatán** (1,260,000 inhab.; 38,402 sq km) occupies the N part of the peninsula and has been called 'one of the harshest regions in the world'. The soil cover, except for a narrow strip in the extreme S, is rarely above 2.5cm thick and water is scarce. Efforts to enrich the former have failed because the porous limestone bed will not retain commercial fertilizers; more recently rock has been dynamited to increase topsoil. There are no rivers. The main, and traditional, source of water has been the natural wells (cenotes; around which the prehispanic Maya built their settlements), formed when the surface limestone rock gives way and collapses into subterranean caves. In the later 19C and early 20C over 10,000 windmills (incl. 3500 in Mérida alone) raised water into galvanized iron storage tanks. In the NW, henequen production is still an economic factor, and production was actually increased in the 1950s; but since the 1960s it has steadily lost ground to synthetic fibres from elsewhere, and the federal-State concern which runs the industry has incurred huge losses. Stockraising (especially pigs; the yucatecos love pork and bacon) has some possibilities, and yucateco honey even more. The coast is low, sandy, and semi-barren. The Puuc range, called also the Sierrita, running NW to SE from approx. Halachó to S of Tzucacab into Quintana Roo, has an average altitude of 100m.

Spanish ships touched the coasts of Yucatán in 1511, 1513, and 1517, the latter expedition meeting defeat in a battle at Champotón. In May 1518 the governor of Cuba sent an expedition under Juan de Grijalva, accompanied by Francisco de Montejo, Alonso de Avila, and Pedro de Alvarado, which reconnoitred the peninsula coast before continuing up the coasts of Tabasco and Veracruz (comp. Rte 102). In Nov. followed Hernán Cortés, with Grijalva's three companions, who followed the same route before continuing N to Veracruz. Montejo led two further, unsuccessful, expeditions to conquer Yucatán in 1527–28 and 1531–34, assisted by his son, Francisco (el Mozo), and nephew, also Francisco. Not until 1540–47 was Spanish control to be assured. In 1549, Francisco de Montejo, the elder, a semi-independent governor, was removed from power, and, after a period of rule by the audiencia of Guatemala, Yucatán became subject to the government in Mexico City, although governors were sent straight from Spain. In 1617 the governor was designated captain-general, his deputies capitanes a guerra. Yucatán, since 1786 one of the intendancies (more in theory than in practice) of New Spain, took no part in the war of Independence, but by 1821 a secessionist movement calling for an independent Yucatán republic emphasized the territory's remoteness and separateness, looking more to the wider world than to the rest of Mexico. Although declared a State of the Mexican republic in 1824 (incl. Campeche until 1857–58 and Quintana Roo until 1902), Yucatán twice seceded, in 1839–43 and 1846–48; in 1847–49, when it considered itself neutral during the US-Mexican war, desperate moves were even afoot to offer sovereignty to Spain or Britain, or above all to the USA in return for help in putting down the Maya rebellion (see below); and in 1864–67 the empire was fervently upheld.

The **War of the Castes**. Until the early 19C the Maya peasantry had been left undisturbed in the cultivation of their own cornfields (milpa). The cattle and maize haciendas of creole landowners had put only mild burdens on them. These haciendas were rapidly replaced by sugar plantations (especially in the S and SE of the present State) which both encroached upon milpa land and demanded intensive Maya labour. In 1841 time-honoured Maya water rights were removed when cenotes began to be commercially exploited by creoles. In 1847 the eastern Maya rose in rebellion and there began the war of the Castes, in its first phase (until 1853), the most savage and terrible Indian uprising in Latin American history, which cost Yucatán nearly half its territory and at least one-third, and probably nearer a half, of its population (300,000 killed). It took the creoles six years, with financial and military assistance from the Mexican government and with the help of 10,000 loyal Maya (known as hidalgos), to reconquer a region as far E as Valladolid and as far S as the Sierrita. Beyond these points the Indians long remained independent and unreachable. The sugar plantations were devastated and henequen replaced sugar as the peninsula's most important cash crop; but this time with federal army detachments and police and State militia helping the hacendados to enforce an even harsher labour regime.

Henequen riches bred a powerful oligarchy of wealth and political power, headed by the family of Olegario Molina (governor 1902–06), known as capitán y amo (lord and master), with strong US business connections. Yucatán remained untouched by the struggles and violence of the Revolution—until 1915 when, after a further attempt at secession, Gen. Salvador Alvarado led an orderly invasion to bring it to heel, and to attempt to unite conservative planters and radicals in a programme, on the whole moderate ('a bourgeois revolution') except for violent attacks upon the Church. After Alvarado's departure in 1918, his erstwhile propaganda chief, Felipe Carrillo Puerto, from 1917 president of the socialist party of the south-east and organizer of the ligas de resistencia as local party instruments, dominated State politics. Endowed by contemporaries and historians with saintlike qualities, in reality a pragmatic and ruthless cacique and regional leader who did not disdain to use

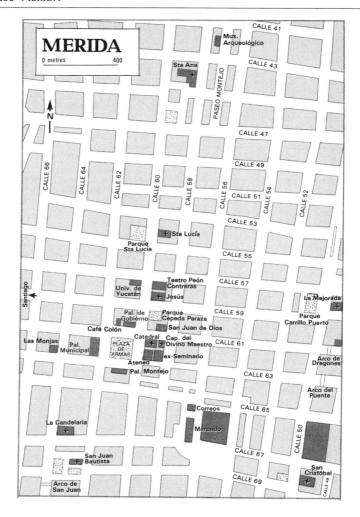

violence to maintain himself in power, Carrillo's views on revolution were far more radical, earning him the hatred of Pres. Carranza who in 1919 drove him into exile in New Orleans. His governorship (1922–23) introduced a sweeping programme of agrarian reform. His judicial assassination at the hands of federal troops in rebellion against Obregón, and in league with henequen-planter interests, brought his reforms to a halt.

In Aug. 1937 Pres. Cárdenas personally supported 'the largest single episode of agrarian reform ever carried out in Mexico', which gave the majority of hacienda lands over to the campesinos. This, however well-intentioned, in its hurry ignored the region's special conditions and traditions; broke up productive units; and hastened the henequen industry's decline. Today Yucatán is one of the republic's most deprived areas, increasingly dependent on federal aid and on receipts from tourism.

The central PL. DE ARMAS (*Pl. Mayor; Pl. Grande*), shaded by dark Indian laurels, almond trees, and tamarinds, is furnished with confidentes, semicircular stone seats in twos, each part facing in opposite directions, ideal for close conversation.

On the E side stands the austere cathedral of **San Ildefonso**, the oldest on the American mainland.

It was begun c 1563 and work continued under the architect Pedro de Aulestia. In 1586 Juan Miguel de Agüero arrived from Havana to take over the work, for a fee of 200 gold pesos, 500 bushels of corn, and 400 hens. He finished it in 1598. The choir, once Spanish-style in the centre of the nave, was removed c 1800, put back in 1830, and finally removed in 1905. The present choir, above the W entrance, upheld by columns and half-columns, with Corinthian capitals, is out of keeping with the rest of the interior. In 1915 a revolutionary mob got to work on the interior, destroying priceless altarpieces and statues. Two side chapels on the S side were then demolished to make way for the narrow street (called Pasaje de la Revolución) between the cathedral and the former archbishop's palace.

EXTERIOR. The unusual façade consists of a high central panel, which does not correspond to the height of the nave, and two towers joined to the centre by high walls. Two small doorways open in these walls and a wide arch frames the centre. Inexplicably out of proportion to their heavy bases, the top two storeys of the towers are later additions; that on the l. went up in 1713. The fine main doorway is inspired by Renaissance classicism. In the niches, endearingly simple images of SS Peter and Paul. The dome, oldest true dome in Mexico, boasts an inscription: 'The architect of this was J.M. de Agüero, the yr 1598'.

Beneath the arch once appeared the arms of Castile and León, substituted after 1822 by the coat-of-arms of the first Mexican empire.

The INTERIOR is the most dignified in Mexico, a dignity paradoxically increased after the iconoclasts had finished their outrages. The thick Tuscan columns which divide nave and two side aisles, all at the same height, and the domical vaults, their interiors in the nave strikingly coffered, recall the spirit of the Romanesque.

To the l. of the high altar is a replica of the venerated Cristo de las Ampollas (Christ of the Blisters) made in Ichmul, blackened and blistered in a fire there, brought to the cathedral in 1645, and destroyed in 1915. Its replacement was made in Querétaro by order of Abp Martín Tritschler y Córdoba (1900–42). Among recent replacements are the huge Cristo de la Unidad in the chancel (1965; the figure of Christ done in birchwood; the cross of mahogany) by the Spanish sculptor Ramón Lapayese del Río. The stations of the Cross, done in brass, bronze, and aluminium, are also by him.

Also on the E side of the plaza is the former **Arzobispado**, dating from 1580, but confiscated and drastically revamped by Manuel Amabilis Domínguez at the orders of the revolutionary government in 1915–18 (at a cost of 2 million pesos 'in paper money') for a new learned society and school of fine arts, the *Ateneo Peninsular*, which didn't last long. Today it houses federal government offices. On the N side of the plaza is the **Pal. de Gobierno** (1883–92), erected, to the designs of Waldemaro G. Cantón, on the site of the palace of the captains-general of Yucatán, but incorporating an exterior arcade of 1783.

Murals in the patio walks and over the staircase, full of Maya symbolism, depicting the Spanish conquest and aspects of Maya culture that have triumphed over years of repression, are by the meridano painter Fernando Castro Pacheco and were completed in the early 1970s after 25 years work. On the first floor is the *Salón de Historia* (Mon.–Sat., 9–8; Sun., 9–5), with more murals by him, incl. a dominant Diego de Landa (comp. Rte 101).

Next door is the *Café Colón*, famous since 1907 for special meridano ices and sorbets made from tropical fruits. On the W is the **Pal. Municipal**.

It occupies the site of the temple called Bakluumchaán, one of the Maya monuments plundered to supply material for the buildings of the new city. It was in large part levelled in 1625 to make room for a new Casa de Gobierno, which was in its turn demolished, with what remained of Bakluumchaán, in 1734. The new ayuntamiento was rebuilt in 1856 and 1859, and reinaugurated, with an inappropriate façade by Carlos Manuel Castillo, in 1928. A gracious portal of the 17C building survives.

No. 505 in Calle 62, which crosses the W side of the plaza, is the *Casa Cárdenas*, with a fine 17C portal, built originally for the conquistador family of Bracamonte, afterwards passing to the Maldonado family.

On the S side of the plaza is the celebrated **Pal. de Montejo**, its doorway façade one of the few remaining examples of civil plateresque (here of a sturdily individual stamp) in Mexico.

It was probably ordered by Francisco de Montejo the elder, adelantado (governor) of Yucatán, built by an Indian mason using Maya labour from Maní, and finished in 1549. Montejo was removed from power that year and returned to Spain, where he died in 1553. His son, Francisco (el Mozo), lived in it till his death in 1565. After the death of his grandson, Juan de Montejo Maldonado, without heirs in 1643, it passed to the Salazar y Montejo family and then to the Solís family, descendants of el Mozo's youngest daughter, Francisca de Montejo y del Castillo; then to members of Yucatán's wealthiest élite, all Montejo descendants: the Ancona y Solís family, who sold it after Independence; then Simón Peón y Cano, whose descendants owned it until 1980, when it was acquired by Banamex. The interior underwent various modifications in the 19C. The windows to the r. of the doorway, complete with caryatids sustaining broken pediments, were altered by Manuel Arrigonaga Gutiérrez in 1890, to conform with then prevailing eclecticism. The heads (all ages) which are such a feature of the decoration may commemorate members of the Montejo family.

The lower storey, more European in style, is flanked by columns, half-fluted, standing forward of pairs of pilasters, all resting on tablero bases. The jambs, lintel panels, and frieze above are full of mythical, bird, animal, and other relief. Above the jambs are two heads, probably Francisco the elder and his wife, Beatriz Alvarez de Herrera; the medallions on each jamb hold what may be the heads of Charles V and his wife, Isabel of Portugal. More heads may be seen in the column and pilaster capitals. In the centre, a crouching bearded man (the master mason ?) supports on his shoulders a keystone placed in the middle of the cornice. Above him is the corbel, composed of child heads, of the curving balcony. For the richly detailed upper storey, less refined in technique, local fancies were allowed free rein. In its two great pilasters stand two warriors in armour, carrying halberds and swords, their feet on the heads of grimacing conquered Indians. On either side of the bases stand wild men in sheepskins and carrying clubs. More child heads appear in the jambs and lintel of the balcony door frame—an interesting composition which includes two stone beams to support the lintel. Above is the Montejo coat-of-arms; the lambrequin of the helmet branches out to form elaborate climbing-plant relief, the stems ending in bell-like fruit. In the frieze three more heads may represent Francisco the elder; his wife; and his daughter, Catalina de Montejo. The crowning pediment holds the inscription, rampant lions on either side, a bearded bust (Francisco the elder ?) on top.

No. 508 C. 63, on its r. (W) is the birthplace of José Peón Contreras (see below). No. 502, on the corner with C. 60, is the *Casa Galera*, preserving good late 16C portals in the later structure, where Carlota stayed in 1865.

She stood on the balcony to acknowledge the plaudits of the crowds in the plaza and was kept awake by their continued enthusiasm.

W of the plaza, at the corner of Cs 63 and 64, is the church known as **Las Monjas** (1633), once part of the Conceptionist convent of *Nuestra Señora de la Consolación*, built in 1589–96.

Drastic restoration in 1983 preserved the Gothic ribbing above the chancel; the nuns' coros alto and bajo also survive, the latter closed in by wide grilles of iron and wood and divided into nave and side aisles by two arcades—a Mudéjar touch. Parts of the convent escaped destruction in 1867, incl. the archaic-looking loggia-mirador on a squat base (1645–48), above the presbytery of the church.

C. 64 runs S to (l.) the church of *La Candelaria*, consecrated in 1609. The tops of its walls are lined with merlons set in an openwork toy battlement. Its baroque altarpiece avoided destruction in 1915. Beyond, to the S, we reach Pl. de San Juan, on whose E side is the church of **San Juan Bautista** (1669), the six engaged columns of its façade resembling a series of unfolding scrolls. The shell motif above doorway and choir window is repeated above the twin side portals. Entrance to the sacristy is gained through a portico whose arches show a remarkable Mudéjar flourish.

From 1808 the sacristy was meeting-place for the sanjuanistas, at first a religious discussion group headed by the priest Vicente María Velázquez, which soon took on political and social reform, and the promotion of yucateco culture, especially after the proclamation of the Constitution of Cadiz in 1812. After the reaction of 1814 in Spain, three members suffered incarceration in San Juan de Ulúa—José Matías Quintana (father of Andrés Quintana Roo), Lorenzo de Zavala, and José Francisco Bates; while Velázquez and another priest, Manuel Jiménez Solís, were imprisoned elsewhere.

Just to the S in C. 64 is the *Arco de San Juan*, one of the three (out of seven) surviving arches erected in the 1690s by Manuel Jorge de Zezera to mark the boundary of the city proper and the barrios beyond.

Beyond the arch, after a short walk we may fork r. into C. 66 (the old road to Campeche) to reach, at the corner with C. 77, the little church of **Sta Isabel** (called *La Ermita* or *Nuestra Señora del Buen Viaje*), built c 1710–20, modified in 1748. Its unusually curved espadaña completes its attraction. Its former cemetery, entered through a stone portal (1636) once belonging to the *Casa Puerto* (a town centre mansion), is now a small open air museum showing Maya and historical fragments.
  Further W, at the corner of Cs 72 and 75, is the church of *San Sebastián*, built for a Maya barrio. In its present state it dates from the late 18C (restored in 1941), though strangely keeping features which remind one of a medieval castle: rubble masonry, stout square tower encompassed by a parapet, and miniature merlons.

From Pl. de Armas C. 61 leads E along the N side of the cathedral. On the l. was once the hospital of *San Juan de Dios*, founded, as Nuestra Señora del Rosario, in 1562, most of it demolished in the 19C. Its chapel survives (now the interesting *Museo de la Ciudad*, Tues.–Sat., 10–8; Sun., 9–2), with a remarkable neo-Romanesque S doorway. Between the delicate mouldings of its archivolt and jambs, interrupted by tiny imposts, runs a string of bead motifs; a pattern repeated in the window resting on the arch crown.

The Brothers of St John of God (juaninos) took over the hospital in 1630. In the 18C it achieved great fame. In 1821 the juaninos were expelled and in 1860–61 the patients were transferred to La Mejorada (see below).

Opposite is the house for priests serving the cathedral, now containing the archives of the archdiocese, and the *Cap. del Divino Maestro*, built for the local confraternity of Jesus the Nazarene in the early 17C, reinaugurated in 1836. To the r. in C. 58 is the entrance to the former seminary (*Seminario Tridentino de Nuestra Señora del Rosario y de San Ildefonso*), opened in 1751 and forming the E quarters of the episcopal palace. In 1915 it became Pal. de Justicia. In the niches of the doorway, still influenced by a late 16C style, are rudimentary, but winning, statues of Our Lady and St Ildefonsus.
  Continuing along C. 61 and turning l. along C. 59 we come to Parque Carrillo Puerto, facing which is the church of **La Mejorada**, imposing in its very simplicity. The façade, recently restored and tentatively Mannerist in inspiration, is bounded by two espadañas. Beautifully understated, the doorway makes play with tableros of various geometric shapes in lintel, jambs, and sunken pilasters supporting the pediment. In the latter, a niche holds a statue of St Francis. The choir window repeats the doorway in miniature. In the third, and crowning, pediment is a relief of the stigmatization of St Francis.

It was built c 1610–40 for the Franciscans, as *Nuestra Señora del Transito*. Its accompanying convent (441 C. 59) was built in 1688–94. The Franciscans were expelled in 1821. In 1859–60 Justo Sierra O'Reilly found a refuge here while he wrote the 'Código Civil', the first systematic setting-out of the republic's common law. During 1861–1906 it served as hospital and from 1916 as army married quarters, which hastened decay. Its later conversion to house the State archives helped to rescue it from ruin.

Going S along C. 50 we pass (l.) two of the three surviving city-limit arches (see above): the *Arco de Dragones*, in C. 61, and the *Arco del Puente*, in C. 63. Further S, between Cs. 67 and 69, is **San Cristóbal** (1756–95), perhaps the most striking, certainly the most atypical, church in Mérida. Flanked by slender three-storey towers, the central panel of its façade is recessed beneath a huge scallop topped by a finial and parapet, while the rim of the outer arch and spaces above the doorway and choir window, as well as their supporting pilasters, are covered in relief—unusually ornate touches. Other notable features are the merlons marking the parapet and cupola, and the chemin-de-ronde which invests the church at window level.

The defensive details are a reminder that the church used to be within the fortress of San Benito (see below) next to the convent of San Francisco.

From San Cristóbal we may make our way W along C. 60 to meet the area of the *Mercado Municipal*, bounded by Cs 54 and 58, and 69 and 65. This historic site, where once had been the highest of the five pyramids of Tihó, was formerly occupied by the convent of *La Asunción de María* (San Francisco), earliest (1546) and most important of the Franciscan foundations in Yucatán, and a renowned centre of missionary and intellectual activity. In 1667 the governor and captain-general, Rodrigo Flores de Aldana, on orders from the crown, surrounded its vast precinct with a fortress. This probably to check the friars' strictures against abuses in the administration and harsh treatment of the Indians. The convent was closed in 1821, the friars were expelled, and their priceless collections of works of art and archaeological antiquities were destroyed and dispersed. Clearance of its ruins began in 1843, but the process did not finish until the end of the century. The fortress, called *San Benito*, was demolished in 1843, to give place to another strong building, also called San Benito, used as barracks and then prison, until demolition in 1895. On its N side, along the line of C. 65, between Cs 54 and 56, used to run an avenue, *Alameda de las Bonitas*, laid out in 1789–90 by order of Lucas Gálvez y Montes de Oca, a popular governor and captain-general. A commemorative stone, embedded in No. 477 of C. 65, marks the place. In C. 65, on the N side of the permanent market building, are the *Correos* and *Telégrafos*, occupying premises put up in 1908 as the *Pal. Federal*. Nos 533–561 in C. 56A, on the W side of the Correos, were the portal of the old grain market (*Mercado de Granos*).

From the Correos we may make our way back to Pl. de Armas along Cs 65 and 60.

From the NE corner of Pl. de Armas C. 60 runs N. At the corner with C. 59 (r.) is a small park, PARQUE CEPEDA PERAZA, with a grandiose monument (1896) to Gen. Manuel Cepeda Peraza (1828–69), who brought imperial rule in Yucatán to an end in June 1867 (see below) and held the governorship in 1867–69.

Opposite is the church of **Jesús** (known also as *Tercera Orden*), its baroque cupola changing colour from grey to ochre during the day, once part of the Jesuit *Colegio de San Francisco Javier*, which occupied the block between Cs 60 and 58 and 57 and 59.

The college was founded in 1618 and mostly demolished in the early 19C when a street was driven through on the N side of the church. Part of the old building on C. 59 is now a small museum of local painting and sculpture (Tues.–Sat., 8–8; Sun., 8–2). The new *Pal. Legislativo*, behind the church in C. 59, is an intruder on a venerable site.

At No. 490 in C. 58, behind the church, died Justo Sierra O'Reilly (1814–61), jurist, journalist, novelist, and statesman, a key figure in yucateco and republican politics during the war of the Castes and the Reform. A walk along C. 59 to the corner with C. 72 brings us to the church of *Santiago* (1637; restored 1893). Its grand espadaña has been likened to an Andalusian ornamental comb. Its roof is supported by original wooden beams.

On the N side of Jesús is the suitably imposing **Teatro Peón Contreras** (1900–08), built to a design by Enrico Deserti, modified by Nicolás Allegretti and Alfonso Cardone.

It occupies the NW part of the former Jesuit site, whose demolition made way in 1807 for the *Teatro de San Carlos*, which caught fire in 1808 while the audience was gripped by a melodrama called 'La huérfana de Bruselas'. The present edifice is named in honour of the meridano poet and dramatist José Peón Contreras (1843–1907).

Opposite in C. 60 is the headquarters of the **Universidad de Yucatán**, occupying part of the old buildings of the *Colegio de San Pedro*, another Jesuit foundation, opened in 1711.

After the Jesuit expulsion in 1767 it became successively a seminary, the customs, and seat of the Academy of Science and Literature. In 1864–67 it was restored as the *Comisariato Imperial*, seat of imperial rule in the peninsula. In it the government headed by Felipe Navarrete and José Salazar Ilarregui presided over three years of peace and economic progress, brought to an end on 15 June 1867 when Mérida capitulated to the republicans after a siege of 56 days. After 1867 the Instituto Literario was installed here, converted in 1922 into the university. By 1942 a third floor and a new façade had been imposed.

Further along C. 60 we come to the charming PARQUE DE STA LUCIA, peaceful, shaded, and favoured by local musicians. The arcades on the N and W sides were built in the early 19C by order of Governor Benito Pérez de Valdelomar (1800–11). The church of *Sta Lucía*, on the E side, dating from 1575, was restored in the early 1970s by Enrique Manero. A continuation along C. 60 brings us to PL. DE STA ANA, laid out in 1880, and the church of **Sta Ana** (1729–33), with idiosyncratic prismatic twin towers.

Buried in the atrio is the church's benefactor, Antonio de Figueroa y Silva Lasso de la Vega y Niño Ladrón de la Vega (d. 1733), governor and captain-general. His tombstone, in the base of the r. tower, refers to his extermination of the English (comp. Rte 91A): 'HAVIENDO HECHO EL EXTERMINIO DE YNGLESES'.

From C. 47, between Cs 58 and 56, begins PASEO DE MONTEJO, a wide and handsome boulevard laid out in the late 19C to reflect the pride of Mérida's rich cosmopolitan élite, whose inner core of some 20 or 30 family groups came to be known as the Casta Divina.

The paseo was decided upon in 1888 by a group of notables headed by Governor Guillermo Palomino and including members of the Peón, Quintero, Casares, and Cantón families. Inauguration took place in 1902 and the first building phase was finished in 1906. Various additions were made up to 1925. Along it those whose wealth was based on the henequen boom raised their town houses, some of which survive, in ostentatiously eclectic fin-de-siècle style. A yucateco visiting France is said to have exclaimed: '¡Si París tuviera un paseo Montejo, sería un Mérida chiquito!'

On the l., beyond C. 43, is the **Pal. Cantón**, the grandest residence of all, built in 1909–11 for Gen. Francisco Cantón Rosado (1833–1917), governor of Yucatán in 1898–1902, by Pio Piacentini and Enrico Deserti. It now houses the **Museo Regional del Estado de Yucatán** (Tues.–Sat., 8–8; Sun., 8–2; fee).

In the Entrance Hall are reproductions of six lithographs done in 1843 by Frederick Catherwood, the English artist and companion of John Lloyd Stephens in exploring the Maya ruins of Yucatán and Central America: 1. Interior view of the corbel-arched room, the *Codz Po'op*, at Kabah. 2. W façade of an annex to the *Las Monjas* complex at Chichén Itzá. 3. Corner detail of a frieze at Labná. 4. Large stucco mask sculpture at Izamal. 5. Stone arch at Labná. 6. Interior view of one of the Bolonchén (Campeche) caves.

The GROUND FLOOR has archaeological displays in seven rooms, each organized around a special theme to illustrate the evolution of Yucatán, both physically and culturally.

In addition, there are two special exhibitions: one on jade (jadeite) artefacts recovered from the Sacred Cenote at Chichén Itzá; and one on stone sculptures, illustrating the artistic development in stone carving and the wider implications of contact and trade in obtaining the stone from various sources in Yucatán.

Medio Ambiente y Prehistoria (Ecology and Prehistory). Displays here illustrate the geological evolution of Yucatán, and the changing ecology from the Pleistocene Period to the present; the early fauna and their hunters, and regional variations in these; the importance of water sources and their manipulation by man in the rise of early agriculture, with examples shown at various

Palacio Cantón, Mérida

sites; the soils and vegetation of Yucatán. Archaeological materials include charts and maps showing the migration of man into Mesoamerica and into Yucatán, and artefacts from the Grutas de Loltún, illustrating Late Pleistocene and Archaic lifeways.

Evolución Social. This room is an extensive series of displays showing the chronological development of pre-Maya, Classic, and Postclassic Maya civilization in Yucatán, incl. abundant references to outside contacts. There is a chronological chart of Mesoamerica and Yucatán, and a site map. The displays are basically chronological, but also concentrate on specific themes, incl.: physical anthropology; linguistics (regions and development); Maya costume, and cranial deformation and dental mutilation; Maya calendrics and codices; economy and social organization.

Archaeological materials include maps, information panels, and a wealth of crania, ceramics, figurines, and other artefacts illustrating these themes. Numerous dioramas provide contexts for these materials.

Ciudades y Estados. The theme here is the evolution of cities and state systems among the Maya, concentrating on the Classic and Postclassic Periods. With models, diagrams, charts and plans, photomurals, and stelae, the great Maya centres are discussed, incl. the layout of Maya cities, the various architectural elements, and their populations. Sub-themes include the definition of the city, the organization of different elements of civic society and the agricultural populations of the hinterland, and inter-city relationships—trade, warfare, political alliances. These themes are further expanded in the succeeding rooms.

Cosmovisión. This room concentrates on Maya religion. Sub-themes include: the Maya concept of the world; class distinctions and religious practices; various gods and goddesses of the Maya pantheon; the calendrical cycles and festivals; the importance of dance and music in Maya religion; the role of water and the sacred cenotes; human sacrifice, and Maya burial practices. These are illustrated through charts, plans, photographs and models, and cases of arte-facts incl. figurines, stelae, ceramics, urns, etc.

Relaciones Inter-regionales. Throughout prehistory Yucatán has been a major network of routes for local, regional, and long-distance trade and contact. This room concentrates on the Classic and Postclassic Periods, but emphasizes the early development of trade from the Preclassic onwards. Sub-themes include: defence and fortification in the Maya world; warfare, illustrated with examples of Maya weapons and armour; commerce, incl. the wealth of products in both short- and long-distance trade; agricultural products of the N peninsula and its provincial divisions, with products traded from one province to another (cotton, honey, feathers, gold, slaves, stone, etc.); the use of cacao, shells, feathers, bells, and mantas (cotton shawls or wraps) as exchange media ('money'); the role of the merchant and deities connected with trade; the various inland foot-routes and coastal canoe trade routes; and the Maya sacbeob.

Trabajo y Producción. This room amplifies information seen in the first room, showing regional topography and geography in Yucatán. Detailed information panels and diagrams show various regions, soils, minerals, and products. Sub-themes include: the evolution of agriculture in the New World; the control of water; early textiles, illustrated by sculptures, figurines, and murals; the role of tobacco in medicinal and religious practices; agricultural practices and the supplemental roles of hunting, fishing, and shellfish collecting, with numerous references to sites and to Spanish and Maya chronicles; the social and sexual divisions of labour; and the development of technology.

Arquitectura y obras públicas. This room naturally concentrates on the Classic Maya architectural styles, illustrated with charts, photographs, plans, and models. Sub- themes include: construction techniques; Maya dwellings; the constructional elements of Maya walls and of the corbel ('false') arch; artistic styles and themes; a general discussion of Mesoamerican architecture by way of illustrating the major Maya architectural styles at various sites; the role of public buildings, the influence of cosmological beliefs in their construction and orientation, and their decoration (stucco and stone carving, murals); the use of sacbeob (causeways) within cities and between cities.

The UPPER FLOOR holds displays on the ethnographic subdivisions of Yucatán.

A progress up the paseo brings us to monuments in honour of two famous yucatecos: at the crossing with C. 37 that to Felipe Carrillo Puerto (1926) by Leopoldo Tomassi López, with a moving inscription: 'A la memoria de mis inolvidables hijos Felipe, Edesio, Benjamín y Wilfrido Carrillo Puerto asesinados el 3 de enero de 1924. Su madre—Adela Puerto de C.'; and, at the crossing with C. 33 (Av. Colón), that to Justo Sierra O'Reilly (1906; statue by Jesús Contreras). To the l., Av. Colón leads to *Parque de las Américas*, with an open-air theatre and other facilities.

Paseo de Montejo ends at the *Monumento a la Patria* (1945–56), an iconographic synthesis in stone of the history of Mexico by the Colombian sculptor Rómulo Rozo.

96 Mérida to Dzibilchaltún and Progreso

Méx. 261, 33km.—13km turning for (5km SE) **Dzibilchaltún**.—33km Progreso.

The road runs N (Paseo de Montejo) from Mérida through monotonous henequen fields to (13km) turning r. for (5km SE) **DZIBILCHALTÚN** (6–5; fee), one of the oldest and most continuously occupied sites in the New World. The civic and ceremonial centre of Dzibilchaltún went through several phases of expansion and decline, but was never totally abandoned.

Dzibilchaltún ('writing on flat stones') was excavated by E. Wyllis Andrews with National Geographic Society backing in 1956–61. In 1963–64 a survey team mapped 31 sq km of the site's 46 sq km core, identifying 8526 structures and estimating a total of c 20,000. The site comprises several ceremonial plazas scattered over a wide area, connected by sacbeob in much the same way as at Cobá. Like Chichén Itzá it is centred on a cenote. A principal sacbé runs E–W for c 2.5km and is 20m wide. A zone of habitation of some 80 sq km, with an estimated population in the tens of thousands (up to 2000 per sq km), was reached at its greatest phase in the Late Classic Period. The more densely populated inner core is estimated at 16 sq km.

From c 1500 BC the earliest habitation comprised a small village, one of the earliest in N Yucatán. Increasing domination of the trade routes of N Yucatán, and a combination of population increase and agricultural success, made Dzibilchaltún a major centre by c 800 BC. There was much public building and the production of a distinctive ash-tempered pottery. Decline set in during the 1C BC, but a stagnant community survived into the Classic Period. By the 5C AD a combination of success in trade and agriculture, population increase, and competition between centres had again led to a burst of public building and civic growth in the Late Classic. During this phase the great platforms around the cenote and the Grupo de las Muñecas were constructed, and the site became known for its distinctive fine-paste pottery. Decline set in again, however, as the site was eclipsed, along with many others, by the rise of Maya–Toltec Chichén Itzá. Yet Dzibilchaltún survived as a small settlement until it could reassert itself after the defeat of Chichén Itzá by Mayapán in the Late Postclassic, but its former glory was never regained.

The architecture at Dzibilchaltún included everything from mud-walled structures to stone masonry buildings supported on vast stone-faced platforms. There are many superimposed structures, and many later buildings were constructed with materials from earlier ones. For example, the Templo de las Siete Muñecas has an earlier, inner sanctuary, and Estructura 450, with its adjacent plaza, is the third of three superimposed temples. Public buildings included plazas, temples, and a large temescal (sweat bath).

Over its long occupation, Dzibilchaltún shows evidence of various influences: much of the architecture is in the Puuc style, the Maya (or corbel) arch was prominently used, and many of its sculptures illustrate Maya dress and ornament; on the other hand, the presence of a tzompantli (skull rack), unusual inscriptions, fine-paste pottery, the style of some of the sculptures, and the presence of a patolli board (on which a pachisi-like game was played) indicates contact with central Mexico, possibly even a central Mexican merchant enclave in the city.

The chief reason for the city's prosperity in all its phases, but especially in the Late Classic, seems to have been its dominance of the salt trade of N Yucatán. Jade from Guatemala was also an important item of trade. From the cenote, divers have recovered some 30,000 artefacts, incl. many jade pieces.

The ruins (some restored) are scattered about a large area. Next to the entrance and site-keeper's house is a small museum containing photographs of the principal cleared ruins, some pottery from the different phases of occupation, sections of architectural sculptures, and examples of finds recovered from the cenote: idols, jade figurines, masks, flutes, rings, and bone awls with hieroglyphic inscriptions.

Around the *Cenote de Xlacah* are two large plazas, formed by platforms, terraces, building ruins, and several pyramid mounds up to 8m high. The cenote, remarkable for its clear waters, is 41m deep.

To the E, c 450m along a sacbé, is the *Grupo de las Muñecas* (Dolls). Here a large platform c 246m x 91m supports various buildings. The largest is the

Templo de las Siete Muñecas, constructed c AD 483, judging from associated date inscriptions. The present temple covers an earlier sanctuary, and is reached by four stairways corresponding to the cardinal points, leading to four doorways, similar to the pyramid and temple Structure VII-sub at Uaxactún (Guatemala). The temple has the rare Maya feature of functional windows. Over each doorway and at each corner there is a carved stone mask. Inside, a corbelled ceiling gives height to the building. Seven crude terracotta figurines, 'dolls' to the excavators, were found inside. These in fact depicted deformed people, incl. hunchbacks, dwarfs, and victims of dropsy. Also on the platform are three other smaller rectangular temples, aligned along a N–S axis, each with two parallel galleries inside. To the W of this platform, on the same axis, is a separate small oratorio on its own platform, with four radiating stairways.

Estructura 450 is a three-tiered platform ruin, with a central staircase and traces of an adjacent plaza contained within a low wall.

Méx. 261 continues N to (33km) **Progreso** (c 30,000 inhab.; H,R,P), historically both a port for the export of henequen and favourite seaside resort (gently shelving beach) of the meridanos. The sea front is partly lined with the fin-de-siècle mansions of henequen-planters; the contemporary pier (2km long) is the relic of the days when ocean liners docked here. 5km W is *Yukalpetén*, since the late 1960s the peninsula's main fishing port.

Two points on the NW coast of the peninsula may also be reached from Mérida, by the Hunucmá road (Méx. 25; continuation of C. 59A), through some of the driest country in the peninsula. At (28km) **Hunucmá** (R,P) the ruined Franciscan convent of *San Francisco* was founded in 1581. The church, with an elaborate espadaña, was added in the 17C, its barrel vault spanned by multifoil arches. The apse was the 16C open chapel. In its 17C altarpiece the top storey conch is sustained by tritóstilo columns.

From Hunucmá we may continue NW to (52km) **Sisal**, developed from 1811 as a port for Mérida, now a fishing village, a pallid shadow of its 19C heyday when it was Yucatán's main henequen-exporting port, and when its name became synonymous with the fibre. Some of its public buildings, now in ruins, incl. the customs house (*Aduana*), barracks, and fortress, date from the 17C; other buildings, in faded stucco, date from the 18C and 19C. The lighthouse, on a 17C fort base, was rebuilt in 1906.

From Hunucmá the road SW (Méx. 281) runs to (37km) *Tetiz*, with a church, San Bernardino, dating from the 17C, (42km) *Kinchil*, where a 16C Franciscan open chapel again serves as apse to a 17C church, and (91km) **Celestún** (c 2000 inhab.; H,R,P), a fishing village on a narrow spit of land separating the Laguna de Esperanza from the Gulf. The coast and hinterland (*Parque Natural Ría Celestún*) is famous for its bird life (especially flamingoes) and designated for protection as a biosphere reserve. The afternoons are made uncomfortable by the strong sea breeze.

97 Mérida to Chichén Itzá, Valladolid, and Puerto Juárez

Méx. 180, 325km.—46km Tahmek for (7km S) Hocabá.—121km Chichén Itzá.—124km Grutas de Balamcanchén.—159km **Valladolid**.—189km Chemax.—320km Cancún.—325km Puerto Juárez.

We leave Mérida to the E along C. 65, into henequen country. From (21km) *Ticapo*, a road runs S to (10km) *Acancéh*, see Rte 101. 46km *Tahmek*, with a 17C church (San Lorenzo).

A road goes S to (7km) *Hocabá*, where the apse of the church of *San Francisco*, raised in a large atrio above the town, was the open chapel of a Franciscan convent founded in the 1570s, and secularized in 1603. It contains a churrigueresque altarpiece. From Hocabá it is possible to continue S and then W to (21km) **Homún**, where the former Franciscan convent of *San*

Buenaventura, still intact, was founded in 1561 and secularized c 1680. 16km NW of Homún is *Acancéh*, see Rte 101.

From (50km) *Hoctún*, where the church of San Miguel dates from 1621, the road NE leads to (21km) *Tekantó*, see Rte 99B. Méx. 180 continues S to (54km) *Xocchel*; the espadaña of the 17C church of San Juan stands out.

From here a road runs SE via (13km) *Huhí* to (36km) **Sotuta** (R,P), site of a Postclassic Maya town, where the Franciscans built the convent of *San Pedro y San Pablo* in the 1560s, only to lose it to the seculars in 1582. The present church, with an attractively curved espadaña, was added in the 17C to the original open chapel and contains a churrigueresque altarpiece; the convent is now in ruins. 12km E of Sotuta is *Tabí*, with the 17C church of La Transfiguración, to which is attached a portería with ogee arches and a chapel of Our Lady (camarín) containing a baroque altarpiece.

From (70km) *Kantunil*, with ancient foundations and linked to Izamal (Rte 99B) by a sacbé, a road runs N to (17km) *Izamal* (see Rte 99B). From (82km) *Holca* a road runs S to (21km) *Sotuta* (see above) via (10km) *Tibolón*, a Maya town where the only surviving Cocom prince of Mayapán, after that site's destruction in c AD 1450, established a small principality (see *Mayapán*).

Nachi Cocom, his descendant, took revenge on the Maní Xíus, the ruling house of Maní, in 1536 when Napot Xíu asked permission to pass through Cocom territory on a pilgrimage to Chichén Itzá's Sacred Cenote. At an honorary fiesta Xíu and his entire entourage were murdered. Such Maya rivalries aided the third Spanish attempt to penetrate and conquer Yucatán, led by Francisco Montejo the Younger.

95km *Libre Unión*.

18km S is **Yaxcabá**, an interesting town with some surviving 17C houses. In a walled atrio the ruined Franciscan convent of *San Francisco*, founded c 1582, dates substantially from the 17C. The church, its singular façade incorporating two espadañas and a central tower, contains a baroque altarpiece and is adjoined by a five-arched open chapel.

Ikil, 8km N of Yaxcabá, was also a Maya site, a Postclassic town and source of one of the books of 'Chilam Balam'. A steep-sided pyramid-temple (Estructura I) is of three tiers, with staircases on all four sides. The temple, c 25m high, is a subsided core of huge stone blocks, with vaulted corridor and two chambers. In the W chamber are five glyph blocks and part of a sixth; in the E chamber there are two (each originally contained ten). A niche in the E chamber has a tenoned stone ring to the l. of it, and, it is assumed, originally also had one to the r.

Yaxuná, c 15km E, was the site of an early Maya settlement by the 7C BC. The site promises to have had a long history, but there has been little excavation as yet, although George Brainard conducted some work at the site in 1958.

There is an early pyramid of the Chicanel style, c 400–200 BC, which introduced many of the Classic Maya traditions: temple-pyramids, plazas, terracing, and early corbel-arching. Other structures are of the early Puuc style, dated c AD 400, when the site prospered from trade and began a new building phase. Perhaps the most interesting feature, however, is its *sacbé*, which connects the site, via six other more minor sites, to Cobá (Rte 102), far to the E. It has been variously measured as 96km, 99km, 100km, and over 100km long.

118km *Piste*, with services for visitors to Chichén Itzá, is joined by road with (17km N) *Dzitás*, see Rte 99B. 121km *Chichén Itzá*, see Rte 98.

124km **Grutas de Balancanchén** (entrance on the hour for guided tours; fee).

The Maya–Toltec cave sanctuaries were discovered by INAH archaeologists in 1959 and studied by E. Wyllis Andrews in 1961. Near the entrance there are traces of a small plaza with stone buildings. A subterranean passage leads c 800m to three raised areas converted into shrines dedicated to Maya Chac Mool—Toltec Tláloc, the Rain god—where offerings were made in several shallow pools. Niches (up to 1m high) for statues were carved into the cave walls and decorative traits indicate contact with the Early Postclassic Toltecs of central Mexico. Radiocarbon dating shows that offerings were made between c AD 850 and the 12C.

The ceremonial objects have been left in situ: one chamber has incense burners depicting Chac Mool–Tláloc and Toltec warriors; another has stone braziers, dishes, manos and matates, and pottery vessels.

At (136km) *Káua*, once the site of a Franciscan visita, the 16C open chapel is incorporated, as its apse, into the now ruined 17C church. Méx. 180 continues via (148km) *Kunkunul* and (156km) *Ebtún*.

159km **VALLADOLID** (c 80,000 inhab.), with a tropical climate, is the second city of the State of Yucatán, for its charm and interest still partly living up to the nickname 'Sultana de Oriente', although, as a centre of creole pride, it suffered severely during the war of the Castes.

Bus station. Near corner of Cs 39 and 46. 1st Class. Services to *Mérida* (2 hrs); to *Cancún* (2 hrs); to *Playa del Carmen* (3 hrs); to *Tizimín* (1 hr). 2nd Class. Services to *Mérida* (3 hrs); to *Cancún* (3 hrs); to *Playa del Carmen* (4 hrs); to *Felipe Carrillo Puerto* (2½ hrs); to *Tizimín* (1 hr); to *Chichén Itzá* (½ hr); to *Izamal* (c 1½ hrs); etc.

Hotels throughout the town.

Post Office. 198A C. 43.

Tourist information. At the hotels on Pl. Principal: eg, Hotel Mesón del Marqués, 293 C. 39 (town plans available).

It was founded in 1544, in face of Maya opposition, at a Maya ceremonial centre called Sací, and became famous as a cloth-making centre, and for its indigo and other vegetable dyes. In 1833–45 the Aurora Yucateca, the first completely mechanized textile factory to use steam power, set up by Pedro Sáinz de Baranda (see Rte 91B) and a Scottish resident, John L. MacGregor, functioned here. The war of the Castes brought devastation and a massacre: in Jan. 1847 Maya troops raised to reinforce secession (see Rte 95), indulged in murder and rape; in March 1848 whites and mestizos, fleeing N, were set upon by the rebellious Maya and slaughtered without mercy. A group of Maya notables in May 1910 signed the Plan of Valladolid, denouncing social and economic conditions in the peninsula, and resorted to arms. Although stifled by the authorities, this revolt has been considered 'the first spark of the Mexican Revolution'.

On the S side of Pl. Principal is the parish church of **San Gervasio** (c 1720–30), with a well-proportioned façade, classically based, its doorway arch, jambs, entablatures, and pilasters enlivened by relief. In the interior two baroque altarpieces are survivors from 19C destruction. On the E side of the plaza, the doubly arcaded *Pal. Municipal* has kept its 16C outline, as has the house, also with an arcade, on the E side of the church.

In the S suburb of *Sisal*, facing C. 41A, are the convent and church of **San Bernardino**, a Franciscan foundation of 1552–60.

A 16C Maya chronicle describes the arrival of the Franciscans: '1552 was the year when the schoolmasters came, and they sang here in Sisal. They came from the west, and they taught us how to sing Mass and vespers, and with organ and flute and plainsong, none of which did we know before'.

The church, built with stones from the Maya temple, has a yucateco severity of style, and is crenellated by pointed merlons. The aisleless interior is relieved by a churrigueresque altarpiece, its estípites strangely composed. From the S flank of the church, at its W end, juts an unusually positioned open chapel, with a high barrel vault, now walled in and used as a baptistery. In front of the church and convent runs an arcade with two small chapels at either end. The convent, raised on rocks which covered an enormous cenote, is partly in ruins, but the two-storey cloister, well-buttressed, with three arches a side, survives. The 17C horse-drawn well, facing C. 49, which irrigated the kitchen garden, has been restored.

Of the city's barrio churches, that of *San Juan de Dios*, in C. 40 S of Pl. Principal, founded by the Brothers of St John of God in 1644, is the most interesting and has a baroque altarpiece. The others are *Sta Ana* (Cs 34 and 41); *Sta Lucía* (C. 27, between Cs 40 and 42); and *La Candelaria* (corner of Cs 35 and 44), facing a plaza on the E side of which are the restored premises of the *Aurora Yucateca*.

In C. 36, between Cs 37 and 39, is the cenote called *Zaci*, one or the two of the original settlement, now a recreation spot despite its uninviting murkiness.

From Valladolid, Méx. 295 runs S to (147km) *Felipe Carrillo Puerto* (see Rte 100) and N to (51km) *Tizimín*, see Rte 99A.

The road running ENE goes to remains of two Franciscan convents: (13km) *Uayma* (Sto Domingo; c 1640) and (21km) *Tinum* (Purísima Concepción; 1581).

From Valladolid, Méx. 180 continues E to (189km) **Chemax**, in a wooded region, where the façade of the church of *San Antonio* (mid-18C), achieving elegance in simplicity, displays estípites, so lacking in ornament as to resemble baluster columns. Its two slender towers are notable for the curious ornamentation of the cornices. We cross into the State of Quintana Roo. 232km *Nuevo X-Can* is linked by a tarmac road to (45km S) *Cobá*, see Rte 102. At 238km a road runs N through marshy land via (29km) *Kantunilkin* to (73km) *Chiquilá* (no services), the uninviting embarkation point (last ferry generally in mid-afternoon) for *Isla Holbox*, an island wilderness off the NE tip of Quintana Roo, from which other islands off *Cabo Catoche* may be reached by fishing boat. 276km *Leona Vicario*.

Several virtually unexplored Maya sites in this corner of Yucatán can only be reached with a guide and four-wheel drive vehicle. Most are simply mounds in the jungle growth, but two relatively close ones are c 1.5km SE of the modern town, comprising three platforms with some building ruins; and *El Dos* (c 8km S), with a cenote and some mounds with building ruins covered in vegetation.

320km *Cancún*, see Rte 102.

325km **Puerto Juárez** (poor H and R; P) is the embarkation point for boats to Isla Mujeres. A car ferry leaves from *Punta Sam*, 4km N along the coast.

Ferries (c 5 a day) take c 45 min. to an hour.
C 3km S of Punta Sam is a small ceremonial centre, *El Meco*. The unpreserved ruins include structures in the Toltec–Chichén style—eg, serpents on the side-ramps of the staircases of a four-tiered pyramid, supporting a porticoed temple on the top.
C 40km N (reached by the road N from Ciudad Cancún and inland from the coast) near *Cabo Catoche*, is where the Spaniards saw a Maya town from their ship, in the province of *Ecab*. Here they officially recorded the discovery of Yucatán, engaged in a light skirmish with the Maya, and named the town 'Gran Cairo' after the pyramids of Egypt, of which it reminded them.

Isla Mujeres (c 13,000 inhab.; H,R), c 7km long and under 2km wide at its widest, is something of an unspoilt Caribbean island paradise, with white-sand beaches (more sheltered on W side; exposed to winds on the E), clear lagoons, and coral reefs. The small township, where ferries dock, is at the NW tip. Buses and taxis exist; but hired mopeds and bicycles are preferred.

The island received its name from the Spanish explorer Hernández de Córdoba, who landed here in 1517, and discovered a shrine with statues of the Itzá Maya goddess Ix Chel. He took several gold objects before sailing around Yucatán to Champotón on the W coast of the peninsula, where he was fatally wounded. Ix Chel was the Itzá goddess of the Moon, consort of the Sun, and patroness of procreation, childbirth, medicine, divination, and weaving—the Maya counterpart of Aztec Coatlícue. Another famous shrine dedicated to her was on Cozumel (Rte 102).
The island was occupied by the Maya from c AD 500.
On the N end is the shrine to Ix Chel, with corbel arches; and several other mounds, one thought to have been an astronomical observatory. On the S end are the mounds of a small ceremonial centre and, c 500m N of these, a lighthouse built on the foundations of a Maya lighthouse or other structure. At the SW end is *El Garrafón* (8–5; fee), a tropical fish reserve on a coral reef. The road running SE from the town leads to Playa Lancheros, inland from which are the ruins of a hacienda built in the 19C by the slave-trader Fermín de Mundaca.
From Isla Mujeres trips may be made to *Isla Contoy*, c 24km N up the coast, a sanctuary for exotic birds.

98 Chichén Itzá

The ancient Maya city of **CHICHEN ITZA** and its region have been explored or studied by dozens of scholars over more than a hundred years, from John L. Stephens and Frederick Catherwood in 1841–42 to the recent studies of the murals by Arthur G. Miller.

The name has been variously translated as: 'at the rim of the well of the Itzás', 'on the edge of the Itzá's well', or 'at the mouth of the well of the Itzá'—clearly indicating the importance of water. There is some evidence that the site was called *Uucil Abnal* ('Seven Bushy Place') in its earlier phase, before the arrival of Toltec-Itzá settlers.

The ruins have been cleared and preserved by INAH.

> 6–6; fee; interior of Templo de los Guerreros 10–11 and 2–3; interior of El Castillo 10–11 and 3–4.

After the visit and description by Stephens and Catherwood in 1841–42 Chichén Itzá was first excavated by Augustus le Plongeon in 1875, planned by Alfred P. Maudslay in 1889, photographed by the German engineer Teobart Maler, and visited by W. H. Holmes as a member of the Field Columbian Expedition to Yucatán in 1895. At the turn of the century Edward H. Thompson bought *Hacienda Chichén Itzá* and set up a centre for research. In 1904–07 he dredged the Sacred Cenote and gave the objects found to the Peabody Museum at Harvard University. Beginning in 1923–24, Sylvanus G. Morley made his career exploring the site for 17 years for the Carnegie Institute, in co-operation with José Reygadas Vértiz of INAH. The objects originally removed by Thompson were returned to the Mexican people in 1959; the Sacred Cenote was systematically explored in 1960–61 by divers from INAH, the National Geographic Society of America, and Mexican INCEDAME.

There were three main phases of occupation, beginning in the 7C AD, but there is also evidence that scattered farmers lived near the wells from c AD 400 and in the general area from the 7C BC.

Phase A (7–10C AD—Classic Maya occupation; traditional Maya dates—AD 692–968. **Phase B** (late 10C AD)—a transitional phase, incl. partial abandonment. **Phase C** (10–12C AD)—Postclassic Toltec-Maya occupation; traditional Maya dates—AD 987–1187.

Water was vital to the location of the city, for agriculture to support a large civic population in N Yucatán is impossible without an assured supply. In the natural chalk of the region there were c two dozen cenotes in the vicinity of the site, and numerous chultunes were dug to catch rainwater. Two large cenotes (one called *Xtoloc*) were used by the city as a water supply and for special cult purposes.

Chichén Itzá's location in the middle of the N Yucatán plain gave it control over trade between the Lowland Maya, the central Mexican Highlands and Central American cultures. Salt, cotton cloth, honey, and slaves were all traded and among the objects recovered from the Sacred Cenote was goldwork from W Mexico, Honduras, Panama, and E Central America. In *Phase C* Toltec ceramics were imported in quantity and its central position was undoubtedly influential in the Toltec decision to conquer the city.

According to the Maya 'Popul Vuh', the site was settled c AD 455 by the Itzá. About 150 years later, however, it was abandoned, or partly abandoned, for uncertain reasons and a large part of the population migrated to the coastal site of Chakanputún (Champotón). Despite traditional dates for *Phase A*, archaeological evidence shows that the site was in fact continuously occupied.

During *Phase A*—as *Uucil Abnal*—the city served as an important ceremonial centre and numerous monuments were constructed: the Akab D'Zib, 'Casa Colorada', 'Casa del Venado', 'Las Monjas', and its annex, the 'Iglesia', and steps down to the waters of Cenote Xtoloc. At this time the city also included *Chichén Viejo* with its 'Phallic Temple', and widely scattered architectural groups connected by sacbeob, of which nine are known. These are in Puuc style, featuring large courts formed by freestanding palace structures decorated by limestone veneers with friezes of fretwork and latticework in repetitious patterns; the 'Anexo' [de Las Monjas] is in the Chenes style.

In *Phase B*, the inner 'Castillo' (or Templo de Kukulkán), a colonnade E of it, and an earlier Templo de Chacmool (beneath the present Templo de los Guerreros pyramid) were built. The phase ended with the infiltration of highland Mexican influences, presumably initially through trade, particularly with Tula. The traditional date for the construction of the Gran Plaza monuments and the arrival of a new group of migrants is AD 987. About 30 years before this, events in Tula resulted in the defeat of Kukulkán by Tezcatlipoca in a power struggle

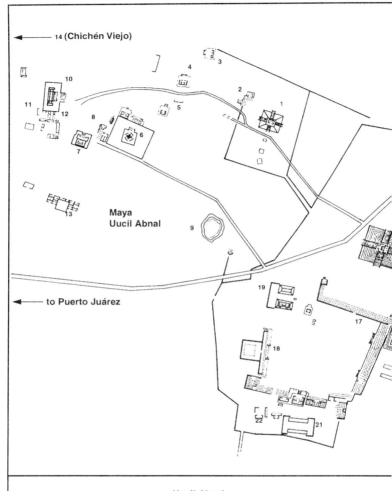

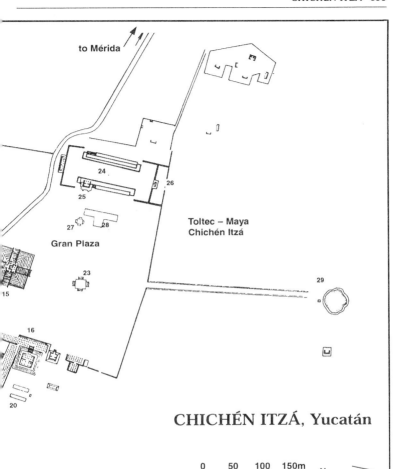

to Mérida

Toltec – Maya
Chichén Itzá

Gran Plaza

CHICHÉN ITZÁ, Yucatán

0   50   100   150m   N ⟶

Chichén Itzá

15 El Castillo and Templo de Kukulkán
16 Templo de los Guerreros
17 Grupo de Mil Columnas y
    Columnata Norte
18 El Mercado
19, 20, 21 juegos de pelota
22 Temascalli

23 Tumba del Chacmool
    or Adoratorio de Venus
24 Juego de Pelota
25 Templo de los Tigres
26 Templo Norte
27 Casa de las Aguilas
28 Tzompantli
29 Cenote de los Sacrificos

between various factions. The Itzá, a Chontal Maya group in the coastal Tabasco region, and presumably the descendants of those who had previously abandoned Uucil Abnal, were led by Kukulkán and his Toltec followers to conquer and resettle the site, renaming it Chichén Itzá.

In this interpretation these events are more or less simultaneous with the departure of the legendary Ce Acatl (of Toltec–Aztec sources) from Tula, who had also been defeated by Tezcatlipoca. Kukulkán (Maya for Quetzalcóatl) is in fact more a generic term meaning leader than a personal name. Whether Ce Acatl and Kukulkán are the same or different leaders is disputed, as are the various dates involved. Some scholars believe that the influence between the two cities went in the opposite direction. (For fuller discussion of dates and nature of Toltec Chichén Itzá, see Introduction: Early Postclassic.)

The settlement of Chichén Itzá by the Toltec–Maya group began *Phase C.* During this phase the Gran Plaza was constructed, N of the earlier city centre, incl. 'El Castillo' (Templo de Kukulkán), Templo de los Guerreros, main Juego de Pelota, and Templo de los Tigres, Caracol (observatory), Tzompantli, Plataforma de los Tigres y las Aguilas, Adoratorio de Venus, El Mercado, and El Osario. According to one source, an irregular polygonal wall (now destroyed) was built around the entire centre, with entrances at the cardinal points. Toltec Tohil Plumbate (although the actual source of manufacture was in highland Guatemala) and Silho Fine Orange pottery were introduced and used extensively.

The city was one of three Putún-Itzá regional capitals (Chichén Itzá, Potponchán, and Chakanputún) ruling N Yucatán. Numerous military and marriage alliances were made between ruling houses, and Toltec Chichén Itzá soon dominated the entire peninsula. Other Late Classic–Early Postclassic Period centres were eclipsed and public building at them ceased. Some were abandoned. As well as controlling coastal trade through Cozumel, Chichén Itzá maintained garrison ports on the NW coast; other, nearby, dependent towns included Ikal to the WSW and Tzebtún to the N. With Mayapán and Izamal (or, according to some sources, Uxmal) it formed the League of Mayapán in the 11C.

Dates for the demise of Chichén Itzá vary widely—AD 1185, 1187, 1194, 1204, c 1250, c 1441–61—but whatever the date, the defeat was at the hands of its rival, Mayapán. According to Maya legend, Hunec Ceel, ruler of Mayapán, conquered Chichén Itzá in revenge for wrongs done to his ally, the ruler of Izamal. Hunec Ceel, in one version, was a mercenary leader imported into Mayapán. He was said to have been thrown into the Sacred Cenote at Chichén Itzá but survived the sacrificial ordeal by spending the night there and emerging the next morning a hero, announcing the rain god's prophecy for a good harvest. Having gained the rulership of Mayapán he persuaded the Itzá ruler, Chac Xib Chac, through sorcery, to abduct the bride of Izamal's ruler at her wedding feast. In feigned indignation he then attacked and conquered Chichén Itzá, presumably his purpose in the first place. The Itzá fled S and eventually settled at Lake Petén (Guatemala), known as Tayasal when the Spaniards arrived. It is of interest, and perhaps not unconnected, to note that both the N and S Toltec centres fell within a few years of each other.

The Toltec-Itzá were apparently not well thought of by their Maya successors in Yucatán. According to the books of Chilam Balam (one of which was found at Káua, c 18km SE, and another at Ikil to the SW), and other Maya sources, the Itzá were regarded as intruders and said to speak Maya brokenly. Their religious practices were regarded as heathen and they were accused of perversity, promiscuity, and phallic worship. In the chronicles they were known as 'the fatherless ones, the motherless ones', perhaps more loosely translated as, 'the freaks'.

The monuments at Chichén Itzá fall into two main groups: those to the S of the road, which bisects the site at an angle, are of Maya *Uucil Abnal;* and those to the N of the road are of the Toltec–Maya city. The entire zone of the ancient city is c 3km x 2km. The principal monuments in each group are the following:

Maya Phases A–B: Akab D'Zib ('Obscure Writing'), Edificio de las Monjas ('Nunnery'), Anexo Este ('Nunnery Annex'), Iglesia, Temazcalli (Sweat Bath), Templo de los Tableros (Temple of Panels), El Caracol (Observatory), Chichán-Chob (or Casa Colorada; Red House), Casa del Venado (Deer House), Casa de los Metates (House of the Grinding Stones), Tumba del Gran Sacerdote (Tomb of the High Priest, or Ossuary), Cenote Xtoloc, and Chichén Viejo.

Toltec–Maya Phase C: El Castillo and Pirámide de Kukulkán, Juego de Pelota, Templo de los Tigres, Templo Norte, Casa de las Aguilas (Eagle House), Tzompantli (Skull Rack), Tumba del Chacmool, or Adoratorio de Venus (Temple of Venus), Templo de los Guerreros (Warriors), Grupo de Mil Columnas y Columnata Norte, El Mercado, Temazcalli (Sweat Bath) and other small ball courts, and Cenote de los Sacrificios (Sacrificial Well or Sacred Cenote).

The archaeological zone is small but uncrowded, the buildings being widely spaced and forming small plaza groupings. The architecture of *Phases A* and *B* is of the Puuc and Chenes styles of the Classic Maya. Stonework at Tula which is contemporary with *Phase C* is said to be of poor quality within the general Mesoamerican tradition, but the use of Maya masons, with their own long stoneworking tradition, produced superior work at Chichén Itzá. *Phase C* is thus a synthesis of former Classic Maya style and Toltec themes.

Sculptures, murals, and symbols all feature martial scenes and scenes of ritual violence. There are some 900 known figures on walls and columns, many of them possibly portraits as each figure has distinct features. Bas-reliefs show warriors and scenes of conquest, priests, skulls, sacrifices, interrogation and torture of prisoners, and phallic worship. Murals depict battle scenes of Toltec conquest, raids on seacoast towns, street fighting, and battles on lakes and along the shore. Sky gods overlook the battles. Maya and Toltec warriors are distinguishable by their gear: the Maya wear feathered headdresses, carry flexible shields and feathered back frames; the Toltecs wear cylinder-shaped helmets with feathers and sometimes earflaps, loincloths, and sandals, and carry round shields. Other scenes depict daily life, with aristocratic figures in all their finery.

To Maya architecture and stone masonry the Toltecs introduced the use of columns; roofed colonnaded spaces; serpentine designs and carved, plastered, and painted benches lining walls; the use of single, huge rooms or of two rooms, one behind the other; sculptured atlantes and banner-bearing figures; and numerous Toltec subjects in bas-relief (serpents of central Mexican style, chacmools, heart-devouring eagles, and jaguars). The combination of roof-supports and the Maya corbel arch allowed vast spaces to be enclosed and roofed, with Maya Chac (Rain god) masks and carvings of the Toltec war glyph side by side.

To the S of the main road is Classic Maya *Uucil Abnal.*

The **Tumba del Gran Sacerdote** is the first monument along the path S of the main road. The pyramid supported a temple reached by narrow staircases up each side; the surrounding gallery of the temple has pillars carved with the feathered serpent and Maya figures. This outer pyramid was built in the late 10C, *Phase B*, over an earlier structure, which had itself been built over an underground cave. The cave is reached down a shaft of steps, capped with large stones, in the temple. At different levels of the shaft were six burials with funerary offerings; and in the cave itself was a burial whose funerary offerings indicated a high-born person, possibly a priest.

Casa de los Metates. Next, to the W of the path, is a small building fronted with columns and containing hollowed, volcanic slabs for grinding corn.

SW of the Tumba del Gran Sacerdote the **Casa del Venado** is a three-room, corbel-vaulted structure so named for the mural of a deer on one of its interior walls (now badly faded). Built in the 7C AD, it was in use right up to the Spanish Conquest.

Chichán-Chob. S of the Casa del Venado, this structure, sometimes also referred to as 'Little Holes', comprises a platform measuring 20m x 17m x 5m high, and a building with rounded corners and roof combs. The front decorations are three Chac masks. Three doorways lead to an inner corridor with a frieze of hieroglyphs, and three rooms off.

At the foot of the platform, excavators found a phallic figure of a crouching man and two anthropomorphic censers. A post excavated in a structure on the opposite side of the courtyard (to the S) may relate Chichán-Chob to the ceremony of the voladores (see Introduction: Mesoamerican Religion). E of the Chichán-Chob are the ruins of a small ball court notable for the carved benches along its sides.

Farther S is the curious round structure called the **Caracol** (Observatorio), after its interior spiral staircase. It comprises a two-tiered platform and circular tower. The first platform is a rectangle with rounded corners of 66.5m x 51.5m. The stairway up the NW side is 14m wide, with an annex on the S side of it. The second platform is a quadrilateral enlargement of an earlier, Classic Period, circular terrace 16.7m in diameter, itself an enlargement of a 10.6m circular terrace. Steps up the W side are at a different axis to the steps of the first platform, and lead, between intertwining serpent side-ramps, to the tower itself. Part way up this stairway a carved stele was discovered in a niche.

The tower is 16.7m in diameter and 2.25m high, and has four doorways corresponding to the cardinal directions. Within are short lengths of wall directly in front of the doorways, thus forming a circular corridor within a circle. Above the doorways are cornices, above which are stylized Chac masks and upper moulding of eight rings with a band running through them. The centre of the tower is the spiral staircase leading up to a rectangular room, with seven narrow, rectangular windows. These were apparently for siting the equinoxes and solstices, leading to the conclusion that the building was a sort of observatory. In 1923, Sylvanus Morley discovered another stele concealed between two divisions of the upper staircase.

To the NW and at the SW corner of the Caracol platform are two small single-room temples with colonnaded porticoes.
Templo de los Tableros. S of the Caracol is a temple ruin with carved relief panels and two rows of six columns each along the bases of three walls. Remains of a later structure, which covered this panelled temple, can be seen in a staircase and fragments of a second temple.
Between these temple ruins and the Caracol are remains of an elaborate **Temazcalli**, a sweat bath, from which a sacbé runs behind the Caracol to the *Cenote Xtoloc.*

Edificio de las Monjas, Anexo Este, La Iglesia. SW of, and facing, the Caracol is a group of structures consisting of a large rectangular pyramid, an adjacent building on the E, and a small square building, among others, also to the E.

The pyramid is 10m high and has a two-part staircase, leading to a temple with two galleries. The Spaniards named this building the 'Nunnery' for the resemblance of the temple and its annex to a convent in Spain. This more elaborate temple and the second part of the staircase succeeded an earlier, single-galleried temple, which was discovered in 1875 when Le Plongeon, using dynamite, attempted to explore the interior of the pyramid.

Against the E side of the pyramid, the Anexo comprises a Chenes style building of ten rooms with façades of carved Chac masks, stylized serpents, geometric mouldings, and, in the doorway, a cross-legged figure seated on a throne and surrounded by plumes and the symbols for maize and water.

The small square Iglesia (so-called by the Spaniards because of its proximity to the 'Nunnery', and thus completing the image of a convent) is a Puuc style building, one of the oldest in Chichén Itzá. It is decorated with Chac masks and fret patterns in relief, and, in panels either side of a doorway, with four Bacabs (bearers of the heavens): a crab, an armadillo, a snail, and a tortoise.

Akab D'Zib ('Obscure Writing'). C 30m E of the 'Nunnery' complex, to a separate clearing, is a complex of rectangular rooms to the N, S, and E of a rectangular platform. The rooms have corbel-arched ceilings and hieroglyphics were found on the lintel stone of one of the rooms in the S group. The underside of this lintel stone has a carved person, seated on a throne. Impressions of hands can be seen in the second room on the r. side of the S group. An earlier building comprised only the centre portion with three doors and two rooms, the wings to the N and S being added in the late 9C. Together with La Iglesia, the Akab D'Zib is one of the oldest structures at Chichén Itzá.

Chichén Viejo. Just W of the 'Nunnery' a path leads S into the jungle to (c 1km; guide recommended) further ruins of Chichén Itzá. (Another path to this area begins S of the Hacienda Chichén Itzá Hotel.) Despite the name, these structures are both Maya and Toltec, and are contemporaneous with the more well-known parts of Chichén Itzá. The ruins include

Templo de Kukulkán and El Castillo, Chichén Itzá

a so-called *Phallic Temple*, where phallus worship was supposedly practised, and just W of it *Telecotes*; the *Templo de las Inscripciones*, whose lintel bears the Maya date AD 619; and two structures known as the *Templo de Quatro Dinteles* and the *Templo de Tres Dinteles*—the first an unrestored ruin except for its four carved lintels, and the latter a beautifully restored, Puuc style building with Chac masks, lattice designs, colonnettes, and hieroglyphs on the lintels. A side trail near the Templo de Tres Dinteles leads to two more cleared ruins, one of which is called the *Castillo de Chichén Viejo*.

To the N of the main road are the principal buildings of the later, Toltec–Maya Chichén Itzá, the whole of which forms the Gran Plaza.

El Castillo and **Templo de Kukulkán**. Dominating the GRAN PLAZA is the nine-tiered, 24m-high Pirámide de Kukulkán, with narrow stairways up each of its four sides, possibly modelled after the earlier Tumba del Gran Sacerdote pyramid (see above). Ramps flank each stairway, with a large serpent head at the base of each. (The serpents at the N stairway are said to represent Kukulkán deified as Quetzalcóatl.) Thus the nine tiers are divided into 18 sections corresponding to the 18 months of the Maya year; the 90 steps in each staircase make the 360 days of the 18 months of 20 days each, leaving, as the Maya did, the five no-month days at the end of the year.

More or less in line with the N stairway, a sacbé leads to the Cenote de los Sacrificios. A second sacbé leads S to the Tumba del Gran Sacerdote.

At the top of the pyramid a multi-chambered temple is entered on the N side through a portico of two serpent columns that would have supported the roof. The heads of the serpents form the bases of the columns, the bodies the shafts, and the rattle tails the capitals. The roof in the main room was supported by two central pillars with a gallery and three doorways around the sides. The door jambs and pillars are all carved and were at one time painted.

Excavations beneath this pyramid have uncovered a smaller, earlier pyramid of Late Classic Maya date. Like its successor it had nine steps, but a staircase mounted only the N side. It was square, 32.75m each side, and 16.5m high. At the top was a two- chambered temple with galleries decorated with jaguar, serpent, flower, shield, and other reliefs. In the front chamber sits a carved stone chacmool for offerings. In the rear chamber was a carved stone jaguar with a flat back for a seat (a 'throne'), or for offerings. At one time painted bright red, it has 73 inset green jade discs, jade eyes, and shell fangs.

To the E of El Castillo lies a second, smaller plaza formed by the **Templo de los Guerreros**, El Mercado (see below), three small ball courts, and colonnades around the sides.

The first is a square pyramid c 39.5m on each side, the present four-tiered pyramid being the last of three superimposed constructions. Its shape and features invite comparison with the main temple at Tula. It has a W side portico of 60 columns, each c 2.6m high, in four rows. Panels on the tiers are decorated with carvings of humans, and animals devouring human hearts.

A stairway up the W side leads to the temple, with an anthropomorphic standard-bearer on each side of the doorway. Before the temple reclines a chacmool for offerings. The temple is entered through the two serpent pillars into the forward chamber, where pillars support the Maya vault. At the rear wall of the inner chamber a large altar table is supported by ten small atlante figures, and pillars also support the vault. The pillars in both chambers are carved with the 'earth-monster', priests or warriors, and Bacabs, in that order from bottom to top. On the door jambs are earth gods in human masks with serpent tongues and more Bacabs. The cornice on the S wall has a restored façade of Puuc style masks between Mexican (ie, central Highland) style reliefs of serpent heads devouring human heads, and bird motifs.

The earlier construction covered by the Templo de los Guerreros was the **Templo de Chacmool**, so-called because a chacmool with a frog-shaped helmet was found in it, among carved and painted columns, when the mound was excavated. Badly-faded paintings discovered on the walls of the temple depicted scenes of seated priests with offerings, a row of kings, or nobles, on thrones with jaguar heads, and the mask of a large-nosed god (similar to the palace at Palenque).

Grupo de Mil Columnas y Columnata Norte. Forming the E side of the Gran Plaza these structures together form another, inward-looking plaza, a new concept in Maya architecture introduced by the Toltecs. However, the various sets of colonnades are of different dates: the Grupo de Mil Columnas is the earliest, antedating the Templo de Chacmool and the Templo de los Guerreros and originally extended farther to the N; the Columnata Norte postdates the Grupo de Mil Columnas and the Templo de los Guerreros. The columns are mostly round, but the S row of the Columnata Norte is of square piers. These colonnades supported Maya vaulting resting on a timber framework.

In the NE corner of the enclosure a separate group of columns has four sculptured pillars and a terrace wall decorated with a procession of warriors and serpents. Along the E side of the enclosure were more buildings and another colonnade, as yet little excavated.

The S side is formed by **El Mercado**, comprising a colonnade and a separate square enclosure, paved and cloister-like. Along the back and side walls of this 'cloister' runs a bench with a procession of warriors and rows of plumed serpents.

The SW corner of the large enclosure is formed by a small *Juego de Pelota*. Two other ball courts lie just outside the enclosure on the E side, together with ruins of another *Temazcalli*, and on the N side, behind the Columnata Norte.

Tumba del Chacmool, or, **Adoratorio de Venus**. Returning to El Castillo the Tumba del Chacmool lies a few m to the N. It is a small, square platform with a stairway up each side, decorated with reliefs of a plumed monster with claws spread, plumed serpents, the symbol for the planet Venus, and other astronomical symbols. (Le Plongeon discovered a chacmool sculpture here, hence its name.)

Juego de Pelota and **Templo de los Tigres** (Jaguars). NW of El Castillo lies a functionally integrated group of monuments, forming the W and NW sides of the Gran Plaza. This Ball Court is the largest known example in Mesoamerica—

its playing field 146m long and 37m wide. The great vertical walls of the terraces forming the sides are 8m high and the stone goal ring is still in place.

Along the bottom of each wall runs a bench with sloping sides carved in bas-relief depicting ball players in ritual dress, in two facing rows with the death symbol between them. The leading figure of the r.-hand row has been decapitated, his blood flowing symbolically in the shapes of serpents, leaves, and flowers. The leading figure of the l.-hand row holds the head and the obsidian knife used in the sacrifice. Above the rows of figures a serpent writhes, with heads at either end of the bench.

A temple sits at either end of the playing field. The S temple is a simple platform with two side stairways and portico facing the field. The N temple is also a terraced platform with a two-pillared porch. On the side of the steps are carvings of a tree whose roots anchor it to Monster-Earth on top of a figure reclining as a chacmool. On the door jambs at the entrance to the temple are carved the Chac and other masks. The corbel-vaulted temple chamber is also carved in relief, although these carvings are badly worn.

On the S end of the E side of the Juego de Pelota terrace stands the larger **Templo de los Tigres**, facing E into the Gran Plaza. The front of the temple, at the top of a steep staircase, has a portico of two serpent columns. There are plumed-serpents on either side at the top of the steps, and along the façade of the portico are friezes, incl. one of walking tigers and shields, giving the temple its name. In the main temple room are jambs with reliefs, once painted; and, inside, a mural of a battle, discovered in a badly-faded state, but copied in the early 20C before deterioration rendered it unintelligible. One group of warriors (Toltecs?), brandishing javelins, spear-throwers, and round shields, attacks a Maya town, while gods look down on them from the sky.

One interpretation, by the art historian Arthur G. Miller, is that the scene depicts a symbolic battle between the armies of two commanders, whom Miller calls 'Captain Serpent' and 'Captain Sun Disk'. An older interpretation suggests that the battle may be the Toltec conquest of Chichén Itzá, but Miller suggests that the battle depicts a scene near Seibal in Guatemala, and the archaeologist Richard Diehl suggests that it is the Itzá conquest of Yucatán.

Below the platform of the temple is a smaller temple, also with a portico of carved columns and with worn reliefs on the roof and walls, some of them of figures fighting with serpents.

Casa de las Aguilas and **Tzompantli**. Just E of the Juego de Pelota are two more platforms. The first is a small square platform with stairs up each side, decorated with carved serpents. On the walls of its temple are reliefs of eagles and jaguars devouring human hearts.

The second, long, rectangular, platform, with a central projecting staircase on its E side, is a Skull Wall or Rack. Along the base of the central projection are carved warriors carrying severed heads, and eagles; and on the bases of the wing walls are carved several rows of human skulls. The wing platforms were the places of sacrifice to the fire god and the skulls of the sacrificial victims would have been displayed on pole-racks set before the platforms.

Cenote de los Sacrificios. On the N side of the Gran Plaza the course of the *sacbé* which begins at El Castillo leads to (300m) the Sacrificial Well. It is c 60.5m across and more than 20m to the water's surface. A small temple stands on the edge of the well, at the end of the sacbé, and it is presumably from here that the offerings and sacrifices were made.

In 1904–07 Edward Thompson dredged up numerous sacrificial offerings, incl. repoussé gold discs, other gold and silver artefacts, copper bells, jade jewellery, rock crystals, amber, carved bone and shell, deformed skulls, and mutilated teeth. Professional divers explored the well again in 1960–61, recovering many more artefacts, incl. fragments of cloth.

Of the human bones recovered, up to 15 adults of both sexes, and up to 21 children between the ages of one and 12, are represented, thus debunking any embroidered myth, dredged up by some overactive imagination, of the exclusive sacrifice of beautiful young virgins.

The dating of the objects recovered, although imprecise, indicates that the well was used for offerings, and possibly for sacrifice as well, as early as the 7C AD. It continued to be a sacred place even after Chichén Itzá was virtually abandoned. Bp Landa records its use in the 16C, and Maya histories record the murder of Napot Xíu, prince of Maní, in 1536 while on his way to Chichén Itzá to make sacrifices for the help of the gods against the invading Spaniards (cf. *Tibolón*).

99 Mérida to Valladolid

A. Via Motul and Tizimín

Méx. 281, Méx. 176, and Méx. 295, 221km.—18km Conkal.—44km **Motul.**—68km Cansahcab and Méx. 176.—169km Tizimín and Méx. 295.—221km **Valladolid**.

The road goes NE to (13km) *Cholul*, where the church of La Asunción, with two typical espadañas, is a 16C foundation. 4km E, at *Sitpach*, the tall espadaña of the 17C church of San Juan is graced by merlon finials. At (18km) **Conkal** the former Franciscan convent of *San Francisco*, now ruined, was founded in 1549. The thickness of the wall of its church, finished in 1675, allows for deep side chapels below a chemin-de-ronde. Murals survive on the triumphal arch and the simple altarpiece, of painted wood, is contemporary with the church. The 18C church of San Bernabé at *Ixil*, 11km NE, contains a baroque altarpiece. 27km *Mocochá*, with the ruined convent of La Asunción, begun in 1609, and its accompanying church with two three-storey espadañas and baroque altarpiece. The open chapel is walled up. From (32km) *Baca*, with a 19C church, roads lead S to (15km) *Tixkokob* (see Rte 99B) and (14km NE) *Dzemul*, see below.

44km **MOTUL** (c 15,000 inhab.; H,R,P), surrounded by the foremost henequen-producing region in Yucatán, is known also for its oranges, bananas, and market gardens. It is the birthplace of Felipe Carrillo Puerto (1882–1924), his parents' house now a museum and library.

Motul was a Maya city, seat of the Pech family at the Spanish Conquest. It has also given its name to a Late Classic ceramic phase (c AD 680–800). The 'Motul Dictionary', composed here in c 1590 by Fray Antonio de Ciudad Real, is the finest Maya-Spanish dictionary extant (now in the John Carter Brown Library in Providence, Rhode Island).

The former Franciscan convent of **San Juan Bautista** dates from 1567; its barrel-vaulted church, begun at the end of the 16C, was finished in 1651.

The Mannerist portal, with paired columns upholding doric capitals and a broken pediment, is surrounded by the plain mass of the façade, which ends in a gable lined with merlon finials and finished off by a modest flourish of volutes. Behind rises a notable cupola. At the N end of the long, five-arched portería is a modest posa chapel, a rare survivor of Revolutionary destruction in Yucatán. On the S side of the church is a walled-up open chapel, its central wide-arched chancel once flanked by a small baptistery (l.) and choir (r.). The 12-sided 18C pulpit displays first-rate carving and estofado; the six wider panels contain reliefs of saints, the six narrower, caryatids. Behind the portería is the two-storey cloister.

The road N to the sea at (27km) *Telchac Puerto* passes (12km) *Telchac*, where the 16C church of San Francisco contains a churrigueresque altarpiece, but ambitiously combining paintings and sculptured figures. 4km W of Telchac is **Dzemul**, with a remarkable 18C church, *Sta Ana*, whose thick walls enclose a double chemin-de-ronde, approached by a spiral staircase, manifested by two lines of windows. Its doorway and choir window show attractive vegetal and geometric relief. The largest altarpiece is a churrigueresque work in three storeys, showing its natural cedarwood. 10km E of Telchac, at *Sinanché*, the 18C church of San Buenaventura contains another churrigueresque retable.

From (59km) *Suma*, where the church dates from 1789, the road SE goes to (25km) *Izamal*, see Rte 99B. We continue N to (68km) *Cansahcab*, where the convent of San Francisco was founded in 1609.

12km N on Méx. 281 is **Dzidzantún** (c 7000 inhab.; R,P), with an unpreserved pyramid, where the Franciscans established the convent of *Sta Clara* in 1567. The church, once reputed the finest in Yucatán, with one of the largest naves in Mexico, is in disrepair.

At *Dzilám González*, 12km NE, John L. Stephens and Frederick Catherwood reported in 1842 seeing what was reputedly the largest pyramid in Yucatán. Unfortunately, it has since been destroyed.

85km *Temax*, with the convent of San Miguel (1591). The church was added c 1617 to the original open chapel.

The road S leads to (27km) *Izamal*, see Rte 99B.

We continue E to (101km) *Buctzotz*, where the 16C church contains a statue of Our Lady (1573), of Guatemalan make. The stretch of road to (151km) *Sucilá* is through henequen and cattle-ranching country.

15km S of Sucilá is *Espitá*, where the church of San José (mid-17C) achieves a certain elegance, its towers decorated with flower finials; its façade with relief bands of stars and lions. 31km SW is *Dzitás*, see Rtes 97 and 99B.

169km **Tizimín** (c 20,000 inhab.; H,R,P), in a region famous for mahogany and cedar. The Franciscans founded the convent of *Los Tres Reyes* here in 1563, originally the convent block and an open chapel, which forms the apse of the present church (mainly 17C). The altarpiece is a local baroque work; the wooden pulpit, also 17C, shows reliefs of the four evangelists.

The road N (Méx. 295) leads to the coast at (52km) **Río Lagartos** (H,R,P), a fishing port on the lagoon of the same name amid dense tropical forest, and within reach of a haunt of flamingoes (part of the significant flamingo colony of the N Yucatán coast) at *Las Coloradas*, 16km E. 12km W of Río Lagartos is *San Felipe*, a smaller fishing village, within reach of mangrove swamps, sandbars, and unspoilt beaches at the W end of the lagoon. The coast and its hinterland—*Parque Natural San Felipe* (W of San Felipe) and *Parque Natural Ría Lagartos* (E of San Felipe)—are designated a biosphere reserve.

E of Tizimín a road runs to (24km) *Buenaventura*, 12km SE of which are the unrestored ruins of the Postclassic Maya site of *Culuba*, just W of the road.

From Tizimín we go S to (183km) *Calotmul*, where the 18C church of La Concepción contains a churrigueresque altarpiece. 221km *Valladolid*, see Rte 97.

B. Via Aké and Izamal

Méx. 80, 160km.—21km Tixkokob for (18km SE) Aké.—69km **Izamal**.— 160km **Valladolid**.

The road runs directly E from Mérida to (16km) *Tixpehual*.

Cuca, c 4km SE, was another Maya centre with defensive walls. Like Chacchob (Rte 101) it was occupied only briefly in the early Postclassic, its defences reflecting those unsettled times. The defences comprise two concentric masonry walls enclosing Puuc style architecture, with sacbeob connecting the walls to the inner settlement. The outer wall is 2255m long, enclosing 0.33 sq km; the inner is 838m long, enclosing 0.046 sq km.

21km *Tixkokob*, where the small Franciscan convent of San Bernardino was founded in 1581. In the 17C the church was added to the open chapel, now the apse. We diverge SE to (18km) **Aké** (accessible but widely scattered over 2 sq km; guides can be applied for at the Museo Regional in Mérida), where a small settlement was established by the 7C BC, one of the few known Preclassic–Classic sites in N Yucatán.

Stephens and Catherwood visited the site in 1842, followed by many others, until in 1966 Lawrence Roys and Edwin Shook surveyed the entire site and identified ten major structures from the 25 conspicuous and over 100 smaller mounds; 7 cenotes, one of which is over 100m in diameter; a possible chultún; and 8 sacbeob. The earliest evidence of occupation comprised traces of mud and loose stone thatched huts.

The importance and long occupation of Aké is indicated by the sizes of its ceremonial plaza and palace, the careful dressing of the cubed pillar-stones and other large stones (1–2m x 1m x 30cm) used in construction, the vaulting in *Estructura 11*, and the large, still uncut stele in the main plaza. Connections with contemporary sites are indicated by the slab-like construction and 'wavy-wall' comparable to Early Classic buildings at Uaxactún (Guatemala) and at Acancéh; vault construction and a triple doorway similar to Early Classic Cobá's; round-cornered substructures as at Kohunlich; and the sacbeob connecting the site to Izamal, Cobá, and possibly to Dzibilchaltún.

In the town itself there is a *stepped pyramid* base just N of the church. A dirt road off Aké town plaza is signposted to the main ruins. A large pyramid-platform is on the r. and the *Palacio* on the l. The latter is built on a terrace and approached up a 40m-wide staircase of steep steps. At the top are 48 pillars, partly reconstructed, which may have supported a roof of mahogany or cedar wood. Large mounds visible from the steps indicate the extent of the plaza of the main centre, and the scale of the site. There is also a surviving section of defensive(?) wall 560m long.

From Tixkokob, Méx. 80 continues E to (37km) *Cacalchén*, with the church and ruined convent of San Pedro y San Pablo, founded in 1609. From (42km) *Bokobá*, where the late 16C church of La Asunción contains a baroque altarpiece, a road goes NW to (16km) *Motul*, see Rte 99A. 50km *Tekantó*, where the convent of San Agustín, founded in 1576, is well preserved; the nave vault of the church (1688) is spanned by multifoil arches upheld by sturdy columns.

5km NE of Tekantó is *Teyá*, 8km SE of Suma on the road to Izamal, see Rte 99A; here the church of San Bernabé, rebuilt from the 18C, with a handsome espadaña, belonged to a Franciscan foundation of 1612.

From Tekantó we proceed S to (58km) *Citilcúm* and then E to (69km) **IZAMAL** (c 40,000 inhab.; simple H,R,P), a quiet, quaint town which may be toured in old-fashioned (somewhat rickety) horse-drawn carriages. Many of its buildings display a distinctive yellow-ochre tint.

Izamal ('Place of the Itzá') was a Classic and Postclassic Maya site described by Bp Diego de Landa in the 16C. It was visited, described, and drawn by John L. Stephens and Frederick Catherwood in 1843, and by Désiré Charnay in 1887; Ignacio Marquina conducted excavations in 1951.

It was important as a centre of trade, particularly in salt, and together with Chichén Itzá and Mayapán comprised the 'League of Mayapán', formed by the Itzá ruling houses to eliminate rivals in N Yucatán. (However, Uxmal is sometimes cited in place of Izamal as the third member of the league.) The league was broken when Mayapán conquered Chichén Itzá, an act in which Izamal played no small part, smarting as it was from the long-standing annual tradition of the sacrifice of some of its youths to Chichén Itzá's serpent god, and the abduction of the ruler's bride by Chac Xib Chac of Chichén Itzá. Izamal was linked with Cobá and Aké, and Kantunil by sacbeob.

According to Maya mythology (in the 'Chilam Balam'), the ruler Votan sent his son, Itzamná, into the region to bring it civilization. At his death a pyramid and temple were built over his grave and he was worshipped as Itzamatul, the 'spirit', or 'the dew', the 'substance from heaven'; or alternatively as Kabul, 'celestial or creative hand'. A red handprint was one of his Maya symbols. Bp Landa recorded 11 or 12 sanctuaries when the Spaniards arrived, with statues of gods, palaces, and temples, but only five survive today as ruined mounds. The principal pyramid was destroyed when the convent was built; foundations of priests' quarters were found opposite.

The *pyramid*, directly N of the convent, was begun c AD 100–200 and was finally 200m long and 20m high with 20 stone steps 30m wide. It was dedicated to Itzamná (Itzamatul) and the Sun god Kinich-katmó (or Kiniah-kaknic, or Kinich Ahau), and had colossal stucco heads around its substructure (now destroyed, although Catherwood drew one of them in 1843); similar stucco masks can be seen at Kohunlich.

Above PL. PRINCIPAL on the E side is the atrio of the Franciscan convent of **San Antonio de Padua**, the finest and most complete in Yucatán, and on the grandest scale.

It was founded in 1549; built in 1553–61 at the instance of Fray Diego de Landa to the design, possibly, of Fray Juan de Mérida, on the platform of the Maya religious centre called Papol Chac (which means 'built of stones of astounding size'). Even after part of the platform had been pulled down along with its temples, an area 158 by 131m was still left, almost rivalling the piazza of St Peter's in Rome. In 1564 the bp of Yucatán, Francisco del Toral, wrote: 'It is a fine thing to behold and a scandal to permit, for without doubt St Francis condemns it in his rule'. Until the new foundation was ready, the friars used an existing Maya temple. In 1558 Fray Diego brought from Guatemala two polychrome images of Our Lady, one for Izamal, the other for San Francisco at Mérida, both the work of Fray Juan de Aguirre. The Izamal statue, credited with miraculous powers, was burnt in 1829, and the identical statue from Mérida, salvaged after the destruction of the convent there, was brought to Izamal. In 1881 it was restored by the sculptor Gumersindo Sandoval. Today both church and convent are again occupied by the Franciscans. In 1943 part of the platform collapsed into one of the side plazas, killing 43 people during a bullfight.

The ATRIO (c 7500 sq m) is entered either up a ramp from the E side of Pl. Principal or up double stairways from the two side plazas to the N and S. The colonnade (c 1618) around the atrio was built to provide shade along the processional walk connecting the four posa chapels, of simple design, now incorporated in the arcade. To the S of the church, fronted by a 19C espadaña, is the open chapel, now *Cap. de la Tercera Orden*, its diaphragm arches carrying a wooden roof. Other 19C additions, the espadaña and horseshoe-shaped window, have altered the church façade, still of the simplest; while the merlons studding the parapet and flying buttresses upholding the apse add to an atmosphere of medieval austerity. The imposing single-nave INTERIOR (c 55m from W door to presbytery [E] wall) is covered by barrel-vaulting, with rib-vaulting above the presbytery. Behind the latter is the Camarín de la Virgen, where the venerated statue of Our Lady of Izamal is kept. On the N side of the church is the convent, still partly ruined, built around two cloisters.

From Izamal it is possible to continue to Valladolid via *Suma* (25km NW; see Rte 99A) or *Kantunil* (17km S; see Rte 97).

A direct, but less satisfactory, road continues E via (75km) *Sitilpech*, (98km) *Tunkás*, and (123km) *Dzitás*, see Rtes 97 and 99A. From here it deteriorates to (139km) *Tinum* and (160km) *Valladolid*, see Rte 97.

100 Chetumal to Felipe Carrillo Puerto

Méx. 186 and Méx. 307, 153km.—19km junction with Méx. 307.—38km Bacalar.—153km Felipe Carrillo Puerto.

We leave Chetumal to the W on Méx. 186, the road to *Francisco Escarcega*, see Rte 92. At 19km we turn r. (N) on Méx. 307. 38km **Bacalar** (R,P), on a hill at the SW end of the narrow *Laguna de Bacalar* (c 50km long by 2km wide).

It was the Classic and Postclassic coastal port-city of *Bakhalal*. According to the 'Chronicles of Maní' the region was colonized by the Itzá from the Petén in katun 6 Ahau (AD 435–55). By c 900 the Putún Maya were penetrating the E Yucatán and the region was known as Ziyancán Bakhalal. From the 10C onwards the port was controlled by the Putún-Acalán Maya state of E Tabasco.

Villa de Salamanca de Bacalar was founded in 1544, but its remote and unhealthy situation ensured that it could not thrive. By the mid-17C English lumbermen (Baymen), with negro and Miskito Indian allies, from their bases in Belize, and from c 1660 reinforced from Jamaica, had begun to raid the area. In 1652 Bacalar was abandoned by the Spaniards, reoccupied by them in 1727 as part of their effort to dislodge the Baymen once and for all, and nearly abandoned again in 1751 when the Baymen made another attempt on it. C 1765 a hundred Spaniards were thought to live in the town, incl. a garrison of 62. By the 1840s, reachable only after a 6–8 day journey by pack trail from the main towns of the peninsula, Bacalar, with a population of 5000, became important as a forwarding centre for English goods from Belize. In 1848–49, during the war of the Castes, it fell to the Maya rebels, who coveted the contents of its warehouses, before being recaptured by yucateco regulars aided by US volunteers. In 1858 Cruzob forces surprised it and butchered part of the garrison of 300 soldiers and 250 women and children despite efforts of the authorities in Belize to save them. It was retaken by Mexican troops in 1901, in the final push against Maya resistance.

The town's narrow little streets which climb up the hill still retain 18C and early 19C houses, witnesses to the ravages of war. The *Fuerte de San Felipe*, built in 1729 in the form of a four-pointed star and with a moat 4m deep, houses the *Museo Regional* (Mon.–Fri., 10–2, 4–7; Sat. and Sun., 10–6; fee), containing archaeological finds.

The road continues N, away from the lake, through lush pastureland and banana plantations. At 75km Méx. 293 branches NW, crossing a region of forest, bogs, and lakes, to join Méx. 184 near (99km) *Polyuc*, 164km SE of *Muna*, see Rte 93B. 88km *Los Limones*, where a three-tiered Maya pyramid ruin lies near the road by a small wooden church. More than a dozen other unrestored, unexcavated mounds are known in the vicinity. C 7km W (l.) of Los Limones is *Chacchoben*, c 12km N of which stands a large but poorly preserved pyramid, part of the Maya ceremonial centre of *Nohbek*.

To the E (r.) of the road (between it and the coast) begins the area designated as the *Sian Ka'an* biosphere reserve, stretching beyond Felipe Carrillo Puerto to just S of Tulum.

C 70km on a direct line E from Laguna Ocom (15km S of Felipe Carrillo Puerto) through the reserve, on Punta Sta Rosa between Bahía de la Ascensión and Bahía del Espíritu Santo, are two Maya sites, shrines along the trade route following the E coast of Yucatán (guides recommended). **Tupak**, on the W, has building ruins with roof-combs and stylized serpent-mouth doorways reminiscent of the Chenes style. At **Chacmool**, to the E, there are Postclassic ruins, incl. a chacmool sculpture in the Maya–Toltec style. N of Bahía de la Ascensión, a long island along the coast has ruins of numerous Maya buildings, all shrines or stop-overs in the coastal trade: *Chamax, Chenocomac, Recodo San Juan, San Francisco,* and *San Miguel de Ruz* (local guides recommended).

153km **Felipe Carrillo Puerto** (c 17,000 inhab.; H,R,P), the modern name (since 1935) of **Chan Sta Cruz**, shrine capital of the Maya during the war of the Castes.

Here in late 1850 began the cult of the speaking cross, brainchild of the mestizo rebel commander José María Barrera, which was for many years to inspire and sustain the Maya of the region between Tulum and Bacalar, who came to be known as Cruzob, in their struggle against the yucateco whites (called ladinos). A wooden cross, sometimes captured and resubstituted (three, clothed in female dress and described as 'daughters of the cross', were installed in the town after the loss of the original to ladino troops in 1851), spoke in a 'hollow quavering Maya voice of God', at first through the aid of a ventriloquist and then, after his death, through other artful devices. The cult itself involved a synthesis of Indian and hispanic religious and political traditions, headed by a tatich (priest or padrón de la cruz), a tata polín (interpreter of the cross), and a secretary; the centre of its ritual, a copy of the Mass. From Chan Sta Cruz marauding guerrilla bands sallied forth against W and NW Yucatán. In 1858 a new church, called Balam Na (House of God), complete with buttresses, was built as a home for the cross. On 4–5 May 1901 the troops of Gen. Ignacio Bravo occupied Chan Sta Cruz and effectively brought to an end the cross's reign, though the tradition was to be tenaciously guarded by two surviving Cruzob groups.

56km NE, on the N shore of Bahía de la Ascensión, is the little resort of *Vigía Chico*, joined to Sta Cruz de Bravo by a railway built from 1904 by convict labour to get forest products to the coast. *Las Milpas*, near the railway line c 5km SW, has two small temples with corbelled roofs, near a cenote.

From Felipe Carrillo Puerto, Méx. 295 runs NW through the forest of Quintana Roo into Yucatán and (147km) *Valladolid*, see Rte 97. From (80km) *Tihosuco* a poor road, but suitable for motor vehicles, goes SW to (c 45km) *Ichmul*, see Rte 101.

From Felipe Carrillo Puerto to *Puerto Juárez*, see Rte 102; to *Mérida*, see Rte 101.

101 Chetumal to Mérida

Méx. 186, Méx. 307, Méx. 184, and Méx. 261, 452km.—153km Felipe Carrillo Puerto and Méx. 184.—285km Peto for (40km E) Ichmul.—331km Tekax (for [8km SW] Chacmultún).—349km Oxkutzcab.—366km Ticul.—388km Muna and Méx. 261.—452km **Mérida**. (Or, from Oxkutzcab, by State road 18.—360km **Maní**.—372km Teabo.—385km Mama.—408km **Mayapán**.—456km **Mérida**.)

From Chetumal to (153km) *Felipe Carrillo Puerto*, see Rte 100. We continue W along Méx. 184 through the jungle of Quintana Roo. 193km turning l. (S) via (4km) *Dzula* for (16km) *Laguna Kana*.

Near the N shore of Laguna Kana is an unexcavated Maya centre buried in undergrowth. Several low platforms support temple buildings around a plaza, of Classic and Postclassic dates. One building is said to be an 'observatory' structure.

Beyond (211km) *Polyuc* turning l. (Méx. 293) for (174km) *Chetumal* via Bacalar, see Rte 100. It passes (20km) a turning r. for *El Ramonal*, an unexcavated Maya Late Classic–Postclassic site. Although covered in thick vegetation, building ruins can still be explored on the low platforms. Beyond (234km) *José María Morelos* the road runs alongside (r.) *Lagunas Esmeralda* and *Chichnánkanab*, long and salty, with no outlet. 243km turning l. for (c 22km SW) *Candelaria*, from where we may reach (c 5km N) *Telantunich*, a Postclassic Maya site noted for phallic reliefs found there. From (254km) *Dziuché* a minor road runs NE to (30km) turning l. for (5km) *Sacalaca*, with a ruined 16C church, remains of the Franciscan visita of La Asunción, and (35km) *Sabán*, where the façade of the now roofless church of Sta Cruz, of 16C foundation, but updated in the 18C and given estípite supports, displays a bas-relief of St Peter and the crowing cock.

Beyond (264km) *Sta Rosa* we reach the border with the State of Yucatán. Here Méx. 184 begins its run through the forested country of Yucatán, diverging N to (285km) **Peto** (H,R,P), a centre for the production of chicle, birthplace of José María Barrera (d. 1852), and much fought over in 1848. The façade of the church of *La Asunción* (1765–85) is notable for a striking doorway panel decorated with stucco vegetal relief and tableros, enclosed within an arch upheld by exceptionally elongated pilasters. This arch echoes the transverse arches which span the interior barrel vault. Above the high cornice the wooden balconies of the windows of the chemin-de-ronde add to the monumental impression.

A worthwhile excursion from Peto may be made by a minor road going E to (c 40km) **Ichmul**, which still bears the signs of its devastation during one of the fiercest actions of the war of the Castes.

Early in Dec. 1847 ladino troops, having advanced from Peto and defeated Maya forces on the way, fortified Ichmul. But Indian bands established in the surrounding forest were ready for them and began an assault, which the Ichmul garrison only just managed to fend off. On 19 Dec. the siege was renewed and the Maya bore mercilessly down until on Christmas morning the defenders, demoralized by the sight of the severed heads of three among them who had been taken prisoner being tossed back into their lines, made a break for it to the S. Women, children, and wounded, followed by the rearguard, managed to get back to Peto.

In the town may be seen houses of immemorial type, built of wood and palm. Bounding a large rectangular plaza are what remains of the less perishable stone buildings. Towards the SW corner is the small, single-storey *Ayuntamiento* (17C ?), with an arcade. On the E side are remains of the huge cloisterless convent of *San Bernardino*, founded in 1576 and secularized in 1602, and, in the NE corner, what appears to be the shell of another church, its two naves forming an L.

The inscriptions on the lintel of the door to the tower staircase and among the reliefs of the S lateral doorway of the unfinished church give the dates 29 May 1765 and 30 May 1768. Above the main doorway, an imitation of Renaissance classicism, appears the date 1802. It was left incomplete after the disasters of 1847. The open chapel next door, quite unlike other examples, was probably a 17C rebuilding by the secular clergy. Its rectangular façade holds a central and two smaller side doorways, giving a generous sight of the interior. Most remarkable is the pediment, in the form of two half-moons studded with stars, their inner curves supporting a base for the central cross, beneath which is an enchanting medallion relief celebrating the Blessed Sacrament. The huge tightly buttressed barrel vault allows room for two lines of parapets, pierced by stars, the upper parapet sinuously curved—features repeated in the rear profile. At the W end of the nave are the long wooden brackets which supported the choir. The buttresses leave room for the side chapels on the N side and three shallower openings on the S; the first on the S, at the W end, is the baptistery, still containing the massive stone font, beautifully carved. Filling the E end is a large painted classicizing altarpiece.

288km turning r. for (21km NW) *Tixmeuac*, where the church dates from 1796. La Asunción (17C) at *Tixcuytún*, c 4km S, boasts one of the most elaborate espadañas, studded with rosettes, in Yucatán.

C 8km NW of Tixmeuac is *Chuchub*, whence we may reach (c 8km NW) **Chacchob**, an early village settlement by the 7C BC (investigated by H. Pollock and G. Stromsvik in 1953, and by David Webster in the 1970s). The site is most noted for its Postclassic surrounding stone wall, oval in plan, c 4–5m wide, up to 3m high, and 1410m long. The town had early Puuc style architecture and a main axis of c 500m, but no other obvious planning, and was occupied only briefly in the Postclassic (cf. *Cuca*).

300km *Tzucacab*, known for sugar-cane, beyond which the road meets the Sierrita. 322km *Ticum*. At (331km) **Tekax** (c 11,000 inhab.; H,R,P), the church of San Juan Bautista was built in 1699, grafted on to an open chapel, part of a Franciscan foundation of 1576.

Signposted from Tekax and c 8km SW is **Chacmultún** ('red stone mounds'; daylight hours; fee) comprising three groups of Late Classic ruins with Puuc architecture. The first group, CERRO CHACMULTÚN (just W of the site road), has three ruined buildings. *Edificio C*, the lowest, has numerous vaulted rooms with carved mouldings, and the second room of a wing facing S has traces of a polychrome mural depicting a ritual procession. Above, to the NE and NW, are *Edificios A* and *B*, each with a ruinous central stairway. *Edificio A* has columned doorways and bands of colonnettes and carved mouldings on its upper façade. The upper W façade has a large hut-like niche. Carved, tenoned fragments of sculpture lie all around the structure. *Edificio B* has two vaulted rooms flanking the stairway and a mass of rubble which may have been an upper storey.

About 200m S is CERRO CABALPAK, comprising five ranges of rooms on four terraces. The lowest group, *Edificio E*, is the best preserved, with a central staircase, S-projecting wings, and 12 rooms. The upper façade has bands of colonnettes and carved mouldings. On the E side of the terrace just above is the mouth of a chultún. A path up the W side leads to the other terraces, with similar but more ruinous ranges of rooms. Some have uncollapsed vaults and lintels, and one upper room has curious foot-shaped carved stones projecting from the vault.

From the lowest range a path leads c 550m E to the third group, *Xetpol*, at the top of a low hill (c 35m). The best preserved structure, *Edificio D*, has a simple, moulded façade and five doorways flanked by short, projecting wings. There is a bench or altar in the most northern room, and the central room has traces of a mural flanking a doorway in its rear wall. Above and behind Edificio D stands another range of rooms, whose terrace provides a good view of the whole site. Just S of it is another, smaller ruin of simple design.

349km **Oxkutzcab** (c 10,000 inhab.; R,P) is in an orange-growing area. The church of *San Francisco* (1693–99), modest and rustic, with two side espadañas, was built on to the original open chapel (c 1581). It contains a notable baroque gilded wooden altarpiece in three storeys, the solomonic columns dividing off delightful reliefs (scenes from the life of Our Lady) and niches, with shell canopies, for statues of saints.

C 8km S, amid the jungle forest of the Sierrita, are the underground caves of **Loltún** (guided tours Tues.–Sun., 9.30, 11.30, 1.30, 3.30; fee), long a place of special veneration among, and source of water for, the Maya and arguably the most spectacular in the republic, full of fantastic stalagtite and stalagmite formations, and plays of light and shade.
    Loltún has the only known Preclassic Period rock sculpture (other than a few portable pieces) in the Maya Lowlands of N Yucatán. Near the cave mouth, it depicts a richly-dressed man facing l. He wears a fancy, helmet-like headdress, a pectoral, a waist garment, and a breech-clout, with a dangling object in front; he holds a curved stick in his r. hand, and a staff—possibly set with obsidian stones—in his l. There is no associated Long Count date, but a partly-damaged hieroglyphic inscription above him opens with a calendrical sign, probably referring to a ritual almanac position. Stylistically the sculpture resembles carvings at Izapa and other early Maya art in the S Lowlands and Highlands.
    Maya carvings, inscriptions, and murals may also be seen.
    A visit demands stamina, for the walk through the caves (c 1.5km) is on slippery and often craggy ground. Among the most impressive caverns are the so-called *Mazorca de Maíz* (corncob); the *Catedral*, beneath a huge vault, once scene of Maya feasts; the *Galerías de los haltunes*, where five cisterns overflow all year round with crystalline water; and the *Cuarto de las columnas musicales*, where deep or high-pitched sounds are made when the column formations are struck with the open hand.
    The serviceable road going S from Oxkutzcab, beyond Loltún, leads to *Cooperativa*, near the departure of the road W to *Labná, Xlapak, Sayil*, and *Kabah* (see Rte 94).

From Oxkutzcab, Méx. 184 continues NW through beautiful country, enlivened by tropical flowers and vegetation, occupied by haciendas. At (352km) **Yotholín** the church of *San Buenaventura* (1762–66) boasts one of the most extraordinary espadañas in Yucatán, covering its entire width. A 16C open chapel, with its own simple espadaña, now serves as sacristy at the far end of the church. 360km *Pustunich*, where the church dates from 1789. At (366km) **Ticul** (c 5000 inhab.; 25m; H,R,P), known for its huipiles, amid banana, orange, and lemon trees, the 17C church of *San Antonio* formed part of a Franciscan foundation of 1591. From here roads run E to (15km) *Maní* and NE to (21km) *Mama*, see below. At *Sacalum*, 13km NW, the church of San Antonio dates from 1788.
    At (388km) *Muna* we join Méx. 261, the Campeche–Mérida road, see Rte 93B. From here to (452km) *Mérida*, see Rtes 93A and 93B.

An alternative route N from Oxkutzcab, by minor roads, is of great interest, though inevitably slower.
    360km **MANI** (c 3500 inhab.), in a maize-growing area, is home to one of the most important and best preserved monuments in Yucatán, the church and convent of **San Miguel Arcángel**.

Maní was seat of the Tutul Xíu Maya noble family. They moved to Maní in the mid-15C from Uxmal and played an important part in the downfall of Mayapán c 1441. They retained the older Maya system of the hanach uinic ('true man'), ruling the capital and several dependent towns. The Xíu bided their time in neutrality when the Spaniards arrived in Yucatán, until they realized the Spaniards would prevail and joined them.
    The region was inhabited much earlier. The Maní cenote has produced narrow-mouth, pointed-base jars with pattern burnishing dated to c 1500 BC, and a small village of mud and loose-stone, thatched huts was established by the 7C BC.
    Maní was also one of the sources of the books of 'Chilam Balam' (Prophet Jaguar), Postclassic Maya historical and mythological chronicles written in Maya, in Latin letters, in the 16C. Another source was *Chumayel*, a site 15km NE. Altogether, there are 18 extant books, from Chumayel, Maní, Káua, Ikil; and the Pérez Codex.
    The Franciscan provincial, Diego de Landa, in the mid-16C described the Chic Kaban ceremony at Maní, beginning on the day sixteen Xul (16th day of the sixth month), and lasting five days. The ceremony honoured Kukulkán, legendary bringer of civilization (see below

and Rte 98), and included a grand procession, ritual food offerings, dancing, and mumming for the collection of gifts to the priests.

The convent was built in seven months during 1548–49, it is said by 6000 Indians under Fray Juan de Mérida. Acting in place of the bp-elect, Francisco del Toral, who had not yet arrived in Yucatán, Diego de Landa, on 12 July 1562 here celebrated an infamous auto de fe. A group of local Maya were flogged and tortured for idolatry; and over 5000 clay 'idols', 40 stone statues, nearly 200 ceremonial vessels, and 27 codices were destroyed. For this he was recalled to Spain for trial, but eventually exonerated. He used his time there to write his own history of Yucatán, 'Relación de las cosas de Yucatán'. 'If ninety-nine hundredths of our present knowledge [of the Maya and their previous history and civilization] is at base derived from what he told us', wrote William E. Gates in 1937, 'it is an equally safe statement that at that Auto de fe…, he burned ninety-nine times as much knowledge of Maya history and sciences as he has given us in his book'. In 1573 he returned to Yucatán as bp. He died at Mérida in 1579. John Lloyd Stephens stayed at the convent in 1841. He described it, despite its then sorry state, as 'among the grandest of these early structures…proud monuments of the zeal and labour of the Franciscan friars'. Restoration, put in hand in 1978, has freed the open chapel of accretions which had walled it up.

Convent and church face a generous square atrio, once planted with orange trees. On the l. of the church is the portería leading to the cloister, its third arch cut into by the new building (see below). Next to the portería is the imposing raised OPEN CHAPEL, with a vault span of c 8m, as high as the upper storey of the convent block, into which it is incorporated. In the 16C, as the focal point of Indian worship, it was the most important part of the foundation. Another restoration is the posa chapel in the corner of the atrio alongside the convent. The large single-nave CHURCH is a later rebuilding (c 1630). In the choirloft are two small Maya carvings of a horse and a tortoise. Among the altarpieces, fashioned in wood, painted red and gilded, a pair in the nave are the finest in Yucatán, provincial work, but beautifully proportioned; they are also unique, without antecedents, even though they hint a late Renaissance style, and date probably from the 1640s.

Their central sections are divided by enchanting female caryatids wearing Corinthian crowns, carrying flowers in their aprons, and standing on bearded male heads. Surfaces are covered with a profusion of flat relief, incl. seraph heads. That on the r., dedicated to St Antony of Padua, shows scenes from his life in the reliefs between the caryatids, and in the predella—note the casual way he leans from the pulpit (upper l.); in the lunette Our Lady, helped by two angels, clothes him in a chasuble. Its companion, commemorating the Passion, has as its central figure a famous statue of Our Lady of Sorrows, her face wonderfully expressive. In the predella, scenes from the Passion and angels holding its symbols; in the lunette, angels hold the Cross, the spear, and the sponge. Another retable, divided by baluster columns and with a lunette relief of St Joseph holding the infant Christ, is possibly of similar date. The high altarpiece, in three storeys divided by Corinthian columns, dates from the 18C.

From Maní the road runs E to (372km) **Teabo** (c 4000 inhab.) where the church of *San Pedro y San Pablo* dates from 1664–96; the ruined open chapel from 1617. A lateral altarpiece, with elongated caryatid supports, is companion to those at Maní.

Now N via (375km) *Chumayel* to (385km) **Mama** (c 3000 inhab.) where the convent of *La Asunción* was founded in the early years of the 17C. The present church (1735), with a chemin-de-ronde in its thick walls and deep side chapels, and fronted by a three-storey espadaña and good stone carving in the façade, was added to the original open chapel. Among the remains of the convent is a water-wheel, covered by a dome. 392km *Tekit*.

408km (1km l.) **MAYAPAN**, whose history comprises two phases, the Toltec–Mayapán settlement period (c AD 1000–1200), when the city was overshadowed by Chichén Itzá, and had an Itzá Maya family lineage, the Cocom, as its ruling house; and the League of Mayapán (c 1200–1441), when Mayapán attacked and overthrew Chichén Itzá.

Mayapán was closely tied to Chichén Itzá. According to legend, Kukulkán (or Quetzalcóatl), the Toltec leader ousted in political rivalries at Tula, founded both cities in AD 987. Nevertheless, Kukulkán was probably a generic name or title rather than a single person (cf. *Tula*

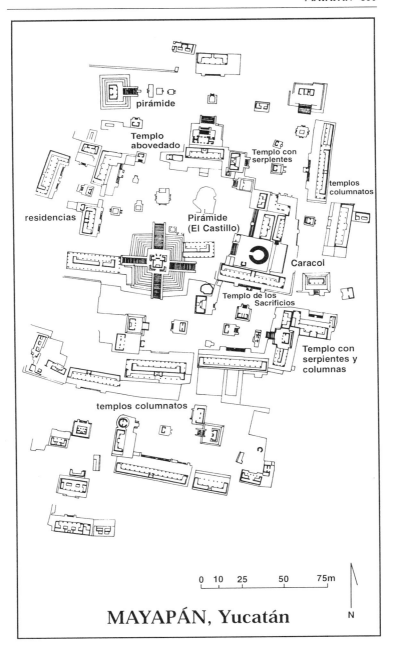

pirámide

Templo
abovedado

Templo con
serpientes

templos
columnatos

residencias

Pirámide
(El Castillo)

Caracol

Templo de los
Sacrificios

Templo con
serpientes y
columnas

templos columnatos

0 10 25   50   75m

MAYAPÁN, Yucatán

N

and *Chichén Itzá*). Despite subordination to Chichén Itzá, Mayapán took its share of the trade in cotton, salt, honey, wax, and slaves to central Mexico and the Gulf Coast, and into the Guatemalan Petén and Highlands as far as Honduras. Trade rivalry led to an uneasy alliance of Mayapán, Chichén Itzá, and Izamal (or possibly Uxmal)—all Itzá ruling houses. Mayapán attacked Chichén Itzá on the excuse that the latter had abducted the bride of the ruler of Izamal. Hunac Ceel, ruler of Mayapán, was an imported mercenary who, having survived the ordeal of being thrown into the Sacred Cenote at Chichén Itzá, emerged to prophesy a good harvest. Chaffing under Itzá domination, at the wedding celebration of the ruler of Izamal he used sorcery to cause Chac Xib Chac, ruler of Chichén Itzá, to be consumed with passion and to abduct the bride-to-be. This, the burden of contributing youths for sacrifice, and trade rivalry, provided adequate excuse for Mayapán and Izamal to sack Chichén Itzá and drive out its inhabitants. Mayapán's dominance lasted only until 1441, when the Tutul Xíu rulers of Uxmal (in fact another branch of the Itzá lineage) revolted, simultaneously sacking Mayapán and moving to Maní. The entire Cocom noble family was massacred in the process, except for one son, who was away on a trading expedition in Honduras (probably to Copán). His descendants, in turn, took revenge on the Xíus of Maní in the 16C (see *Tibolón*, Rte 97).

Mayapán was explored extensively by Edwin M. Shook in 1952–55, and by a team from the Carnegie Institute of Washington, DC, incl. Harry E. D. Pollock, Ralph Roys, Tatiana Proskouriakoff, and Andrew L. Smith, in 1962.

What remains at Mayapán represents the second phase when the city dominated trade in Yucatán. Just as Chichén Itzá was an undefended, religious centre, Mayapán seems to have been prepared as a military centre. Conversant with its violent history the core of the city was surrounded by a wall c 9km in extent, 2.5m thick and c 2m high, enclosing c 4.2 sq km, with a population between 12,000 and 17,500, presumably requiring a large hinterland for support and supply. Different sources list 2000, 2500, 3500, 3600, or 4140 structures inside the walls, planning density decreasing from the centre. (Part of this confusion may be in failing to state whether the number of platforms, or the actual number of structures on platforms, is meant.)

The ceremonial centre of the city (8–6; fee) is small, possibly because the structural groups of private dwellings included numerous small, private shrines and oratories. A typical house group comprised 2–6 structures around a patio on a common platform. The ceremonial centre of c 120 buildings is arranged in functional groups comprising a colonnaded building, shrine, oratory, and assorted buildings, also on a common platform.

The architecture at Mayapán is generally considered degenerate. After the conquest of the Itzá the Cocom attempted to revive the old Maya ways, using corbel arches and carved stucco, and erecting stelae, at least 25 of which have been found on the site. Their artisans, however, were simply not up to the task and their products lack the precise skill of their predecessors. The Templo de Kukulkán and the Caracol are poor copies of those at Chichén Itzá. Similarly, Maya slate pottery, a 1000-year old tradition, went out of fashion, there was no ball court, and no tzompantli (at least none have been found so far). In attempting to centralize their power, the Cocom had to import mercenaries from Xicalango, an old Maya trading port and site of an Aztec colony on the Gulf Coast; and adopted the practice of holding as hostage the nobles of potential rival cities. It seems the only Mayapán innovations were the introduction of large coarse, buff ware ceramics, garishly painted, and the production of large clay anthropomorphic incense burners, depicting deities such as Itzamná (a sky and creator god) and Ek Chuah (god of merchants).

Most of the site is covered in thick vegetation. Near the entrance to the central plaza is a small structure called the *Jaguar House*. The three principal monuments, all in a poor state of preservation, are: the *Pirámide* and *Templo de Kukulkán* (or *El Castillo*); a circular temple known as the *Caracol*; and the *Templo de los Sacrificios*, a colonnaded hall resembling the Templo de los Guerreros at Chichén Itzá, but on a much-impoverished scale. A burial cave was also found, containing two princely burials and 41 other skeletons.

422km **Tecoh** (c 6000 inhab.), the capital or principal city of Chakan Maya province at the time of the Spanish Conquest. The 18C church of *La Candelaria* contains three altarpieces, two modestly churrigueresque, one modestly baroque. The adjoining convent remains from the Franciscan foundation of *La Asunción* (c 1609). At (430km) **Acancéh** (c 5000 inhab.) the church now called *Guadalupe* dates mainly from the 18C. Modern Acancéh, whose Maya name means 'deer lament', is built on the remains of a small prehispanic ceremonial centre.

The ruins were first examined by Edouard Seler in 1905, but extensive excavations were not undertaken until 1941. Of particular importance was the identification of a Classic Period, local pottery style, with 'controlled-trickle' decoration, found at Acancéh, Oxkintok, and Dzibilchaltún, and at sites in Quintana Roo.

Acancéh dates, as a minor ceremonial centre, from the Late Preclassic (c 200 BC). In the Classic it was rebuilt and became a more important Maya civic centre, lasting, in a declining state, until the 15C AD. The central pyramid platform, forming an acropolis, was enlarged in the 9C or 10C AD, and a palace-like structure, *Pal. de los Estucos*, also built. The latter included talud-tablero construction and was covered in painted stucco relief figures in Teotihuacano style, incl. anthropomorphic bats, birds of prey, squirrels, and a feathered serpent. A few remains of the stuccos can be seen on one side at the top of the pyramid, whose stairs and side ramps are still in good condition. The four levels of the pyramid's construction can also be distinguished. The palace's corbel vaulting illustrates the necessarily confined interior space allowed by the technique—in this case only 2m.

A road SE leads via (12km) *Cuzamá*, where the church of La Trinidad (18C) has a stepped espadaña decorated with merlon finials, to (16km) *Homún*, see Rte 97.
  C 6km W of Acanceh, the henequen hacienda of *Timucuy* is a reminder of the industry's 19C apogee.

The road goes gradually NW to (456km) *Mérida*, see Rte 95.

102 Chetumal to Puerto Juárez

Méx. 186 and Méx. 307, 380km.—153km Felipe Carrillo Puerto.—248km (for [42km NW] **Cobá**).—252km **Tulum**.—258km Tancah.—268km Xelha.—275km Akumal.—311km Playa del Carmen (for **Cozumel**).—375km **Cancún**.—380km Puerto Juárez.

From Chetumal to (153km) *Felipe Carrillo Puerto*, see Rte 100. From here Méx. 307 goes NE through hot, forested country on the W edge of the Sian Ka'am Biosphere Reserve to (227km) turning r. to the *Laguna de Chunyaxché*. 232km **Muyil**, a Maya town probably within the political sphere of Tulum, was along the trade route between Cozumel and Chetumal.

It was explored by H. Spinden and G. Mason in 1926. There are four areas of ruins, all Late Classic. The first, just off the highway, comprises mounds and architectural ruins around a plaza. A footpath leads to a second plaza with a temple–pyramid ruin, with its lower staircase intact. A footpath from here continues several hundred m to a multi-chambered temple on a platform. Its rooms have corbel vaults and stucco-covered walls. Other mounds surround it. The fourth area is 1km E of the second plaza, near Laguna de Chunyaxché. Here there is only one small structure—completely collapsed; other mounds are scattered in the jungle, where survey by Michel Peissel in the 1960s identified 108 structures.

248km (beyond the present-day town of *Tulum*) turning l. for (42km) *Cobá* and (c 72km) *Chemax*, see Rte 97.

COBA reached the height of its expansion in the 7C, as the most powerful city in E Yucatán. The entire zone extends c 25 sq km and has 6500 structures, 4000 of which are 'within' the city and have been functionally identified. There are four widely separated groups of structures at Cobá.

The earlier, full name of this large Maya city may have been Cobá-Kinchil ('ruffled waters'—'screeching grouse'). John L. Stephens described Cobá in 1843, but did not visit the site. Later visits were by Teobart Maler at the end of the century, then by Thomas Gann in 1926. Early studies were made by Sylvanus Morley, Eric Thompson, Alfred Kidder, Jean Charlot, and Harry E.D. Pollock (1926–30); then by Norberto González Crespo and George Stuart in the 1960s–70s.

The layout illustrates the dispersed nature of most Maya cities, with central ceremonial groups and public plazas loosely surrounded by residential structures over a wide area. At its height Cobá is estimated to have had c 50,000 inhab., and its importance is indicated by 16 sacbeob radiating from the city centre and numerous (26 have been identified so far) shorter, internal sacbeob between plaza groups. The largest external sacbeob (variously measured at 96, 99, 100, or 'more than 100' km) leads, with seven changes of direction to six smaller sites, to Yaxuná, SW of Chichén Itzá; the second longest, c 20km, leads to Ixil, while a third leads to Izamal. Most of the causeways are c 9m wide and made of compacted stone and limestone rubble, between 0.5m and 2.25m deep according to the terrain. One unusual find at the site was a stone road-roller, 4m long and weighing 5 tons.

So far 32 Classic Period stelae have been found on the site, 23 of them carved, incl. 313 hieroglyphs with dates ranging between AD 610 and 780. Cobá was one of the first Maya centres to decline, its commercial viability, of which a principal item was Guatemalan jade, being undermined by sea transport along the coasts in the Late Classic-Post Classic. Building activity continued, however, especially at the Nohoch Mul group (2km NE of the city centre) after c AD 1200, and the site was probably occupied in some capacity right up to the Spanish arrival.

The architecture is generally related to the S Maya Puuc style, with block masonry, but lacking the roof combs and 'flying' façades of that style. Decoration is usually carved stucco. Preserved structures resemble those at Tulum, and Tikal (Guatemala). Many of the stelae inscriptions refer to S Maya cities; and an unusual number of them memorialize powerful women, often depicted with symbols normally reserved for male rulers—ceremonial bars of authority and prisoners at their feet. One example refers to a noblewoman from Tikal married to the ruler of Cobá. (Similar portraits of important women are known at Tancah and Ichpaatún.)

The four groups of Cobá comprise: *Cobá* proper (Grupo B), *Conjunto las Pinturas, Nohoch Mul* (Grupo C), and *Macanxoc* (Grupo A).

Cobá. Grupo B is opposite the site entrance. This is a large plaza (c 500m x 300m) of platforms and terraces on the isthmus between Lagos Macanxoc and Cobá, two of which are well preserved. *Estructura I* ('Castillo') is a nine-tiered pyramid, 39m x 51m at the base and 24m high. A stairway ascends its W side up to the seventh tier. On top there are temple ruins, inside which a badly eroded stele was found. Near the foot of the stairway *Estructura A*, a small adjoining shrine (3.6 m sq) on its own platform, is reached by a short, broad stairway. *Stela 11* (1.37m high) was found inside, with six columns of seven glyphs each, unfortunately too defaced to be decipherable.

A short, marked path from the plaza leads to a ruined *ball court* a little N of Estructura A, interesting for the fact that excavations produced early evidence for Maya use of ring goal markers.

Along the main path (the sacbé to Nohoch Mul) a short path leads E to **Conjunto las Pinturas**, a five-tiered Postclassic pyramid with a colonnade on the N side. A W-side stairway leads to a single-chambered temple with a W-side doorway divided by a column, and single doorways N and S (the pyramid of Nohoch Mul can be seen from the N doorway). The lintel and three courses above the W doorway bear traces of paintings whose style and Mexican year sign confirm a Postclassic date. A small room at the foot of the stairway contains a carved, eroded stele.

From the NW corner of the pyramid a narrow path leads back to the sacbé. A short path leading E, before reaching Nohoch Mul, ends at three stelae, two under thatch shelters. The protected stelae are carved with figures (one holding a cross) and glyph blocks.

Nohoch Mul. (c 1.5km NE of Grupo B). Grupo C is another, smaller plaza group. Its massive N-side pyramid has several names: *Noho-Chinul, Castillo* or *Pirámide Mayor*. Built in the Late Classic Period, it closely resembles that of Grupo B: 55m x 60m at its base, rising in seven tiers to a height of 36.5m. The stairway of 112 steps up its S side is 11m wide, and splits into two sections at the top. Its Puuc style temple, last of a series, was built c AD 1200, and resembles contemporary Postclassic temples at Tulum. Above its single, corbel-vaulted doorway there were originally three recessed panels (and presumably three on the opposite side). The two surviving niches are carved with figures of the diving god.

Across the plaza, at the foot of the two-roomed, partially restored *Estructura* X is *Stela 20* (beneath a protective covering), carved with the date AD 780. It depicts a Maya lord wearing a jaguar skin, necklaces, armbands, sandles and a ceremonial bar of authority on the chest. His feet rest on a band of glyphs carved on the backs of two smaller figures on all-fours, and to either side are bound, kneeling captives.

Macanxoc. Grupo A, less accessible, is c 2km SE of Cobá (Grupo B). It comprises several pyramid-platforms and terraces, and at least five stelae.

The more adventurous may wish to explore several less accessible groups to the S and E, but it is advisable to use a local guide. S of Grupo B, a sacbé leads to (c 3km) the *Dzib Mul*, a group with two sets of structures around plazas at two different levels. The E set is entered through four doorways, leading to a staircase and a second patio, on which stand three buildings decorated with Maya calendrical glyphs and 14 corbel arches covered with stucco and traces of paintings.

Other less well-known groups include *Chikin Cobá*, on the W shore of Lago Cobá; *Kitamná*, *Nuc Mul*, and *Kucicá*, at the ends of Sacbeob to the S of Grupo B (the last c 5.5km away); *Grupo San Pedro*, to the N; and the *Muluc-baob*, c 4km E of Lago Macanxoc.

252km turning r. for (1km E) **TULUM** (7–5; fee), the main E coast Maya trading port between Cozumel and the Bahía de Chetumal. Through it passed the honey, salt, slaves, feathers, cotton, and precious stones and shells of the Post-classic maritime trade between Yucatán, Central America, and central Mexico.

To the N and S, there are some 500 or more masonry structures along a 60km strip, attesting the importance of this trade, several groups of them forming sizeable subsidiary port towns, probably under Tulum's jurisdiction (eg, Tancah, Xelhá, and Xcaret to the N; Muyil, Chamax, and Tupak to the S).

Tulum, Maya for 'wall' or 'fortification', is a later name, for the site is almost certainly the coastal city of Maya *Zamá* ('dawn city') seen by the Juan de Grijalva expedition of 1518, and described thus by the expedition's chaplain, Juan Díaz: 'we saw from afar a town or village so large that the city of Seville could not appear greater or better; and in it was seen a very great tower'. Here also were enslaved the shipwrecked survivors Gerónimo de Aguilar and Gonzalo Guerrero, the former of whom Cortés found in Cozumel in 1519.

The oldest inscribed stele at Tulum is dated AD 564, and a small group of them date between AD 564 and 593, indicating a foundation date in the initial years of the Classic Period. (There is also a stele with the Long Count date AD 761, but this was imported from the site of Tancah, to the N.) The present architecture, however, dates to the Postclassic, to the 12–13C AD, when Tulum was at its most prosperous. The city was occupied until 1544, when the Spaniards completed their conquest of NE Yucatán.

Tulum appears to be one of the few clear examples of deliberate Maya town-planning. There was undoubtedly some 'urban sprawl' of a perishable nature, beyond the walls, but within them there was a conscious effort to anticipate and control the layout of its 56 structures and streets. There are walls on three sides—N, S, and W—with two sets of corresponding gates in the N and S walls, and one gate in the W wall. Between the N and S walls the buildings are aligned along three parallel streets, two running from gate to gate, and one in between; the E-most is interrupted by the Recinto Interior (see below). In general the architecture is characteristically Postclassic Maya, but many elements reflect the influence of the Early Postclassic Toltec architecture, seen most prominently at Chichén Itzá, and at the contemporary site of Mayapán. Murals in several structures are Maya in content and use of hieroglyphic inscriptions, but reflect the Mixteca–Puebla style of central Mexico in their execution (interestingly, reversing the situation seen in the murals of Cacaxtla). Tulum also differs from most other large Maya sites in its lack of pyramids. Here, the temples are on platforms, and even Tulum's Castillo (the 'tower' remarked on by Juan Díaz) was not planned as a pyramid, but reached its final height only after several building phases. The architecture also reflects the sloppiness of the so-called 'decadent' period, with leaning walls and the defects of poor workmanship carefully covered by plaster.

Tulum was 'discovered' by Juan José Gálvez c 1840, and described by John L. Stephens in 1843. The site was in a good state of preservation when Sylvanus G. Morley and George P. Howe began excavations in 1913. Under the auspices of the Carnegie Institute of Washington these continued from 1916 to 1922. Plans and drawings were made by Samuel K. Lothrop in

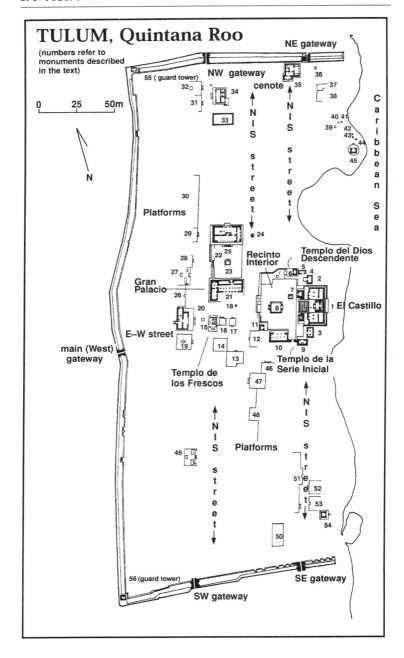

TULUM, Quintana Roo
(numbers refer to monuments described in the text)

1924. Other excavations and studies have been done by Miguel Angel Fernández (1938 and early 1940s), Ignacio Marquina (1951), William T. Sanders (1955 and 1960), and Arthur G. Miller (1971–75).

The entrance to ancient Tulum, as it is today, was through a main gate in its W wall. The E side of the site overlooks the sea, and is protected by the 12m cliffs of the sea front. The monuments are all numbered, and refer to the accompanying site plan.

Tulum was protected on its three landward sides by stout walls, most of which survive. There are c 800m of walls, enclosing an area c 382m by c 164m, of 3–5m in height and 6m in thickness.

The rampart is constructed of stone with a parapet and circuit walk, reached by stairways at irregular intervals around the city. There are five corbel-arched gateways, the NE–SE and NW–SW sets in alignments at the ends of the main city streets. The NE gateway has two small 'guardrooms' set into the wall, and there are several single-chambered temples or other 'guardhouses' at irregular intervals along the top of the wall (eg, the N wall has a well-preserved one with a stepped-fret patterned decorative frieze; and there are 'guard towers' at the NW and SW corners of the long wall—*Estructuras 55* and *56*). Curiously, both the N and S walls end abruptly before actually reaching the cliff edge, and it is thought that the defences were completed by a palisade of wood.

Estructura 20, a temple or palace (or both), is the first to be encountered inside the W gate. It comprises a small platform (1.25m high) supporting a parallel-galleried temple building with a tripartite entrance separated by pillars. Stairs mount the platform from the W and E sides, to a terrace in front of the entrance.

Estructura 19 is just to the SW of Estructura 20. It consists of a platform mounted from the E side, and contained a cruciform tomb in the centre. In the tomb were found a single burial and its funerary offerings, incl. traces of food offerings.

Estructuras 26–28 are all further platforms along the street running N of Estructura 20.

The **Templo de los Frescos** (*Estructura 16*) is the central platform of a ceremonial plaza, and the result of three building phases. The first was a vaulted shrine with decorated walls. In front of it, on the W side, there is a small altar block, *Estructura 15*, and a stele dated c AD 1263 (it is mostly defaced, but has the Short Count date of *katun Two Ahau* ('two sun god'), possibly the date the shrine was dedicated.

The enlargement of the second building phase comprised a portico of columns along the W, N, and S sides, encasing and enlarging the building. In the third phase (c AD 1450) the projecting wing on the N side was filled in with rubble and a second storey added above the room with the frescoes. It was reached by a flight of steps (now destroyed) built on the S side of the building.

The main, W façade of the building has a frieze with three niches: in the central one is a stucco sculpture of the Descending god, and in the other two are seated figures with elaborate Maya headdresses; between the niches are reliefs of another human figure, and a stylized, intertwining serpent. On the upper friezes of the side wings are stucco masks, originally painted red, orange, and black, of the god Itzamná, the deified Classic Maya leader and legendary founder of Izamal (Rte 99B). The second-storey temple also has a niche containing a 'Descending god', above the doorway.

Inside the lower temple, supports, added when the upper storey was built, include a pillar in the doorway and thick slabs added to the walls on each side. A platform spans the width of the rear wall, which forms the primary support for the weight of the upper storey.

The surviving paintings on the E wall, done in turquoise on black, depict scenes of gods performing various ceremonies: there are offerings of maize, flowers, and fruits, a marine scene, and various symbols of death and rebirth, incl. representations of the Upper, Middle, and Lower Worlds of the Maya cosmos. Deities include Itzamná, Chac (god of rain), and Ix Chel (goddess of the Moon, childbirth, medicine, and crafts, and consort of the Sun). To the r. of the main panels are remains of a mural of Chac seated on a four-legged creature.

One interpretation holds that this mural was inspired by the sight of Spaniards on horse-back—the flash and noise of Spanish firearms being associated with the lightning and thunder of Chac. (We know, in fact, that Cortés abandoned his horse at Tayasal, in Guate-mala, and that it was deified by the Maya as Tizimin Chac, god of lightning and thunder; cf. *Zinacantan*.)

Estructuras 17 and 18 are small platforms to the E of the Templo de los Frescos. *Estructuras 13* and *14* are larger platforms to its S. On *13* are two small vaulted tombs in the centre.

Estructuras 46, 47, and 48 are more platforms to the S. Also in this S area are numerous other structures, platforms numbered 49–54: on *Estructura 49* there are some ruins on the SW corner; *Estructuras 50–53* are platforms along the street from the SE gate; and *Estructura 54* is a small, single-chambered temple with a flat roof.

N of the Templo de los Frescos, the **Gran Palacio** (*Estructura 21*) comprises a platform mounted by two flights of steps, and an L-plan, porticoed palace. Its main façade faces S and the columns of the portico supported the masonry blocks for a flat roof. The main entrance is 10.6m wide with four columns, leading to a room 18m by 5.3m, and to a second, larger room in the W wing. This building is thought to have been both a palace and public building, possibly housing the administrative bureaucracy regulating trade. In it the excavators found traces of red and blue paint on the inner walls.

Continuing to walk E from the Gran Palacio, the **Recinto Interior** is entered through its W gate. This is an enclosed compound with *Estructuras 1–12* forming its N, E, and S sides, and an enclosure wall on the W. *Estructura 8*, a low platform (8.2m sq, 2.7m high) with stairs on its E and W sides, stands roughly in the centre. The complex known as **El Castillo** (*Estructura 1*) takes up most of the E side of the compound.

The tallest building in Tulum, the Castillo was not originally intended as a pyramid. It was the result of three building phases: the first was a twin-galleried structure with a W-side colonnaded porch, sitting on a platform 3m high, and reached by a broad (9m) staircase flanked by ramps. The base of this original temple can still be seen behind the small *oratorios* on either side of the staircase at the top. In the second phase, the central section of the galleries was filled in and a new temple was built on the top, comprising two rooms reached by the original staircase, extended to this new height (8m). A buttress wall was also added to the rear (E side) of the original temple to counter the thrust of the upper walls. A narrow, crypt-like corridor was left between the dividing wall of the original galleries and a new wall built to retain the rubble infill. It is on this original wall that the excavators found traces of a polychrome mural, showing that the original temple was painted. In the third building phase, *oratorios* were added to each side of the staircase at the top, the N one covered with a flat roof on wooden beams and the S one vaulted.

The Upper Temple comprises two galleries, the front one a portico divided by two serpent columns; as at Chichén Itzá and Tula, the serpent heads form the bases, the body the column, and the tail the capital. The façade is plain up to the moulding, and then has three niches containing stucco sculptures: a Descending god in the centre, and traces of a standing figure in the N one. This example of the Descending god has bee-like features—an insect abdomen and antennae—and is thought to represent Ah Muzencabab, the 'dying bee', as depicted in the Madrid Codex. Honey was an important item in the coastal trade. On the terrace in front of the temple stands a small stone possibly used for sacrifices. Inside the temple, benches run along the walls of both the porch and the inner room.

Many of these features show the influence of Toltec architecture at Tulum: sloping buttress walls, niches, sacrificial stone, and serpent columns. Thus the main surviving structure was probably built in the 12C or 13C.

The view from the terrace of the Castillo is a vantage point from which to study the full plan of the site, showing the streets running between the N and S gateways—at 17° E of N—and the various structures aligned along them.

Estructuras 2 and *3* are small, single-chambered structures on either side (N and S) of the Castillo. *Estructura 7* is a small temple just N of the main staircase, with four trapezoidal doorways and a tiny altar, 46cm sq and 30cm high.

Templo de la Serie Inicial (see Introduction: Calendrics; *Estructura 9*) is another temple building, in the SE corner of the Recinto Interior. Here Stephens found fragments of Stele 1 in 1848, carved with glyphs for the date AD 564. It is thought that this stele once stood in front of the temple, on its low platform.

Immediately W of the temple is the S entrance to the compound, and S of this, *Estructura 10* forms the SW corner—a single-chambered building with a tri-partite entry divided by columns and an inner row of column roof supports. *Estructura 11* is another small room in the SW corner, against the W wall of the compound.

The N side of the compound is formed by *Estructuras 4–6*. The first and last of these are small, single-chambered structures. The **Templo del Dios Descend-ente** (*Estructura 5*) stands on a low platform (8.2m by 6m), formed when an earlier building was demolished, with a short, off-centre flight of steps on the W side. The building seems to be leaning because the upper parts of its walls jut out at an angle. Above the doorway a niche frames a stucco figure in high relief, depicting another Descending god, similar in form and meaning to the example on the Castillo's temple façade. In its hand, however, this figure grasps the glyph *Kan*, representing the Maize god. The excavators found traces of paint on the façade, now worn away, but on the interior walls, most of a polychrome mural survives, depicting the Sun, Venus, stars, snakes, and a sacrifice.

Estructuras 22–25 form a group to the N of the Gran Palacio: *22* (which has vaulted tombs at either end), *23*, and *24* are all small platforms around *25*, which is another 'palace' structure. It has two parallel galleries entered from the S through the usual colonnaded porch. The inner, or N, gallery contains a polychrome, stucco relief of the Descending god, this time with serpents issuing from his 'tail', and cords twisted around the tail, and hanging on each side of his body.

Moving now to the N half of the site, *Estructuras 31–34* form a group near the NW gate. *31–33* are platforms on either side of the street from the NW gateway, while *34* is a multichambered 'palace', with a tripartite entrance leading to an inner *oratorio*.

Estructura 55 is the NW corner tower, and measures 3.6m sq; with a small altar inside.

Near the NE gateway, *Estructuras 35–38* form another group comprising platforms and a multi-roomed 'palace'. The palace, *35*, covers a cenote, reached by stairs inside the structure. SE of *Estructura 35*, towards the arch of the bay, there are several more structures, mostly the ruins of small temples—*Estructuras 39–45*. *Estructura 45* is a circular platform, the only one at Tulum, supporting a rectangular temple, on the N promontory overlooking the sweep of the bay.

Two small temples are to be found c 100m N of the circuit walls, which the excavators have concluded predate the planned city.

The road continues along the coast to (258km; r.) **Tancah**, where excavations revealed a ceramic sequence of almost continuous occupation from the Late Preclassic to the Late Postclassic Period (from c AD 250 to the Spanish Conquest).

The site was described by Samuel K. Lothrop in 1924, and some investigations were done by Ignacio Marquina in 1951, and by William T. Saunders in 1960. It was an important subsidiary port, probably within the economic, and perhaps political, sphere of Tulum, and participated in the importation of obsidian, granite, jade, pyrite, and slate vessels from the Puuc region, a sort of rock emporium. An important reason for its location must have been the abundance of Strombus gigas shells, which it exported, and which were an important item in Maya ritual practices.

The ruins here, unrestored, date chiefly between AD 300 and 500. They comprise a ceremonial core (just E of the road) and outlying hamlets of house clusters. In the centre there is a principal pyramidal platform, and several other ruins and bases of columns. One palace-like structure (c 40m W of the road) has numerous rooms, the walls of which were discovered to have murals in a style resembling the Codex Tro-Cortesianus; representations of the Maize god were included. (They were discovered by Arthur G. Miller but have been looted.)

Another notable monument is a stele that depicts a woman of importance, portrayed with motifs normally only seen with men—bars of authority and prisoners at her feet.

268km (1km r.) **Xelhá**, in a beautiful setting, a combination of clear semi-freshwater lagoons, full of tropical fish and underwater caves, and the low coastal forest and exotic plants, all now designated a nature reserve. The visual effects as the lagoon waters flow into the sea are fascinating. It is a favourite spot for snorkellers.

Xelhá, like Tancah, was a port town within the economic sphere of Tulum. Here, two ruins are located at the lagoon and just off the highway. From the restaurant car-park the path along the far side of the lagoon passes a miniature temple, less than 1m high. The other ruin lies W of the highway (S of the Xelhá lagoon road) and has traces of red paintings, possibly copies of murals at Tulum.

275km **Akumal** (luxury H), a select resort and water-sport (especially scuba-diving) paradise with a seemingly limitless palm-fringed beach of white sand, is headquarters of the Club de Exploradores y Deportes Acuáticos de México (CEDAM), among whose pursuits are explorations for pirate wrecks and archaeological investigation both underwater and along the coast. In the *Museo Marino y Arqueológico* (partly underwater; casual hours) are exhibited finds from the Cuban galleon 'Nuestra Señora de los Milagros', wrecked on 22 Feb. 1714; arms and trophies from the war of the Castes; and prehispanic stelae and ceramics. C 100m W of Méx. 307 is a small Maya temple ruin.

At 287km (r.) turning to the *Laguna de Chakalal.*

A rough road leads c 400 m to a gate. Another 175m on foot leads to the Late Postclassic single-room temple of *Chakalal* (or Caleta). It has a vaulted roof and a string moulding. Inside traces of murals depict a snake, a jaguar, and handprints.

304km turning r. for (2km) **Xcaret**, whose attractions are reached along two paths. One leads to two cenotes, surrounded by jungle vegetation, whose clear waters take on different shades of turquoise depending on the time of day; the other ends at a cove where the waters (extraordinary shades of blue) form a natural swimming pool.

Xcaret or *Polé*, one of many small ruins along the coast between Cozumel and Chetumal, was, according to the Maya 'Chilam Balam', the mainland landfall of the Itzá Maya when they began their migration–invasion of Yucatán, eventually settling at Chichén Itzá. Xcaret was especially important in the Postclassic as a departure point for pilgrims from Yucatán paying homage to the shrine of Ix Chel, the Moon goddess, on Cozumel, and as a port controlled by Mayapán in the lucrative trade along the E coast of the peninsula. It is thought that the Cobá–Yaxuná sacbé continued on to Xcaret as a major route for transporting goods to and from the port.

Like so many sites along the coast, there is some evidence of Late Preclassic or Early Classic foundations, but the principal surviving ruins are all Postclassic, at Xcaret from c AD 1300. There is a pyramid mound with a temple and doorway on top, a corbel-vaulted shrine, and an unusual two-chambered building with a round doorway, as well as traces of the town's circuit wall.

311km **Playa del Carmen** (H,R,P), a small fishing port now growing as a beach resort.

There are two corbel-arched temple ruins. One has stone columns supporting the wooden lintel of a tripartite doorway; the second is more dilapidated. Both have stucco with simple mouldings.

Playa del Carmen is connected by passenger ferry (thrice daily, at 6am, 12, and 6pm; journey time 1 hour) and frequent air shuttle services (journey time c 7 minutes) with the island of Cozumel.

COZUMEL is separated from the mainland by a 20km wide stretch of the Caribbean through which runs a strong current. It is 47km from N to S and c 15km wide. Its soil is fertile, producing fruit, henequen, and maize, and the dense green forest yields some ebony. The interior plain is broken by a few hillocks. Although the island's fame as a resort has been overshadowed by that of Cancún, it boasts marvellous beaches of white sand: more frequented in the NW and SW, more remote and idyllic on the E.

Cozumel, a corruption of Maya cutzamel ('land of swallows'), was especially important in the Postclassic Period. According to the 'Chilam Balam' of the Chumayel (recorded after the Spanish Conquest), the island was the Itzá point of departure, via mainland Xcaret, in Classic times in their migration-invasion of N Yucatán, and eventual settlement at Chichén Itzá in the 9C or early 10C AD. Under Chichén Itzá, and later Mayapán, the island served as a staging port and commercial centre for maritime trade around, up, and down the E coast of Yucatán (trading cotton cloth, salt, honey, wax, and slaves for cacao, metals, and feathers).

The island was also the location of a shrine to Ix Chel, Moon goddess, consort of the Sun, and patroness of weaving, divination, medicine, and childbirth (see Rte 97). Pilgrims visiting the shrine asked questions of Ix Chel's image, behind which a concealed priest would answer. A Maya sacbé beginning at the nearest mainland point connected Cozumel with Xicalango, Champotón, and other cities in Tabasco and Campeche.

The reconnoitring fleet (four ships and c 200 men) of Juan de Grijalva arrived at Cozumel in May 1518. Early in 1519 Cortés's expedition landed. (Cortés here established contact with Gerónimo de Aguilar, who thereafter followed Cortés as interpreter.) In 1527 Francisco de Montejo the elder disembarked at Cozumel, a first step in his unsuccessful attempt to conquer E Yucatán. By the mid-17C Baymen (see Rte 92) had established camps here. During the second world war the US airforce used the island as a base; the airfield, whose construction obliterated a significant prehispanic archaeological site, has been converted into the present-day airport. Cozumel's heyday as a holiday resort was in the 1950s and 1960s. If it has declined since then, its attractions for divers and snorkellers remain strong.

Ferries from Playa del Carmen and Puerto Morelos put in at the jetty of **San Miguel de Cozumel** (c 14,000 inhab.), the island's only significant town, one block NW of Pl. Principal. An unexciting place, its central part caters for tourists, the shops selling the comparatively rare black coral found on the island reefs.

Airport. 2km N of the town, reached along Blvd Aeropuerto Internacional. Flights to *Mérida* and to *Mexico City*, and to destinations in the USA.

Air shuttle. Every 2 hrs to *Playa del Carmen*.

Ferries to *Playa del Carmen* (changeable timetables).

Car ferry to *Puerto Morelos* at midday.

Hotels. Throughout the town. More desirable, and more expensive, are the W coast hotels near the beaches N and S of the town.

Post Office. Off Av. Rafael Melgar, near junction with Calle 7 Sur.

Tourist Office. SE side of Pl. Principal.

Moped and bicycle rental. Recommended as a good way to explore the island. Shops in Cs Adolfo Rosado Salas, 2 Norte, 10 Norte, 1 Sur, 10 Sur, etc.

The road S leads to (9km) the small freshwater *Laguna Chencanab*, known for its variety of coloured fish and turtles. We pass *Playa de Sta María*, with its palm trees. 15km *Playa San Francisco*, a favoured beach and fishing resort. 5km E at *Cedral*, amid thick jungle undergrowth and trees, are Maya remains and a building used as a jail until the 19C. Offshore beyond Playa San Francisco is *Arrecife Palancar* (reached by boat), a submarine national park, reaching down to c 80m, with tropical fish and plentiful black coral.

Between Playas San Francisco and Palancar the road swings SE across the island to the E coast and then S to the S tip at *Punta Celarain*, where the lighthouse gives good views. The road along the E coast goes by vast stretches of unspoiled beach (exposed to the elements). From *Punta Morena*, halfway along the coast, Carr. Transversal crosses the island to San Miguel de Cozumel. It is possible to continue N by a track from Punta Morena to the N tip at

Punta Molas. The N jungle envelops various prehispanic sites; off the beaches are dangerous currents, rocky little islands, and coral reefs, extremely perilous to snorkellers.

In San Miguel a small *museum* in the Pal. Municipal (Mon.–Sat., 9–1) displays pottery, figurines, and other artefacts from the island's sites, and from an excavated sunken Spanish galleon offshore.

A visit to the museum to consult its map locating the island's sites is recommended before visiting them; and information on local guides can also be asked for.

There are six principal ruins: c 3km S of Punta Molas, at *Aguada Grande*, are platforms surrounded by rectangular and circular building ruins; between Punta Molas and its lighthouse, at *Janan*; at *El Real*, c 6km S of Punta Molas, are vaulted Maya buildings and an altar; at *Miramar*, 3km N of San Miguel, behind the hotels along *Playa del Pilar*, are remains of an idol, carved columns, and a platform topped by buildings with geometric designs on their walls; at **San Gervacio**, c 10km N of Punta Morena, are mounds surrounding a plaza, and, S of these, a structure with columns and a lintel; c 300m E of these are a Maya 'observatory' and buildings on a two-tiered platform, incl. an arch and columns with capitals.

More recent archaeological surveys have identified more than 30 sites or house ruins, mostly near Aguada Grande, incl. walls possibly indicating land divisions and property ownership.

From (343km; r.) *Puerto Morelos* car ferries leave for Cozumel daily at 6am.

375km **CANCUN** (250,000 inhab.; 5m), idyllically located near the NE tip of the Yucatán peninsula on the Mexican Caribbean, has sprung to international fame as a beach and pleasure resort. With its vast stretch of powdery white sand beaches lapped by a sea whose colour changes from emerald green to sapphire blue; its coral reefs and palm groves; its luxurious hotels and restaurants, discos, expensive shops; and its facilities for all kinds of water sports, it is designed mainly for jet-set holidaymakers from abroad and as a conference and convention centre. Sun-worshippers and sybarites will find all they need here.

Airport. C 15km S. Flights to *Mexico City, Mérida, Monterrey, Villahermosa*, and to many destinations in the USA.

Hydrofoil. From behind the Convention Centre. Morning services to *Cozumel*, if weather permits.

Bus station. In Av. Uxmal (W of Av. Tulum). Frequent services to *Mérida* (5 hrs), *Chichén Itzá* (3½ hrs), and to *Valladolid* (2 hrs); to *Playa del Carmen* (1 hr), *Xelha, Tulum*, and *Chetumal*; daily service to *Oxkutzcab*. Buses also leave from Av. Tulum to *Puerto Juárez* and along the Zona Hotelera.

Hotels. Throughout the resort area—very expensive. Advance booking essential. More reasonable rates in Ciudad Cancún.

Post Office. In C. Sunyaxchén, leading W, five blocks W of the main N–S artery, Av. Tulum.

Tourist Office. 26 Av. Tulum.

Cancún, until recently a remote fishing haunt, but considered to possess the whitest sands in the world, was chosen in the late 1960s for development as a tourist centre. Building began in late 1970, helped by a multi-million dollar credit from the Inter-American Development Bank and funds from the federal and State governments and private sources, on plans drawn up by Enrique and Agustín Landa. Ciudad Cancún, on the mainland, is the commercial and residential centre (*Zona Comercial*). It is joined to the N part of the island of Cancún (in fact a narrow sandspit, c 400m wide on average, jutting E, then running c 11km to its S point where it is linked again to the mainland by a road going W), the resort area (*Zona Hotelera*). The lagoon between mainland and sandspit is known as Laguna de Nichapté in the N; Laguna de Bojórquez towards the S. The N point of the sandspit is Punta Cancún; the S point is Punta Nizuc. Cancún suffered particularly severely during the hurricane which struck the Caribbean coast in 1988. Nevertheless, it continues to expand: 140 or so hotels built or under construction in 1990.

From Av. Tulum, Blvd Kukulcán goes E as a causeway (c 8km) joining the mainland and Isla de Cancún (*Zona Hotelera*). It continues the length of the island. Its total distance is c 22km. On the S side of the causeway are the grounds of the *Club de Golf*, in which is a group of Maya ruins, called *Pok-Tapok*. Beyond, at the bend where the island curves S, is the *Centro de Convenciones*, its auditorium seating 2000. Next door is the **Museo de Antropología e Historia** (Tues.–Sat., 8–8; Sun., 9–3; fee).

There are several stone sculptures in the courtyard and collections in one large room. A chart explains the chronology of Quintana Roo, showing the principal sites for each period. 1. Late Preclassic olla from Koxolnah and two vases from Dolores and Alegría. 2. Late Postclassic finds from Kohunlich: five censers, for burning copal incense, and a vase with four female figures on the rim. 3. Stele from Cancún, depicting two unidentified gods, or men dressed as gods, possibly influenced by central Mexican styles. 4. Case of skulls illustrating Maya skull-deformation. 5. Case of jadeite and obsidian jewellery from Tulum, plus other items of jadeite, obsidian, rock crystal, shell, coral, and human bones. 6. Fragment of a polychrome, stucco serpent head from El Meco. 7. Stone manos and matates for grinding maize. 8. Cases containing Late Postclassic incense burners (up to c 45cm high), various domestic ceramics, and some polished jadeite axe-heads from Cozumel. 9. Clay masks illustrating Maya physical 'types'. 10. Maya burnished, polychrome vessels, incl. Classic (c AD 300–600) and Late Postclassic (c AD 1250–1500) Period vessels from Playa del Carmen. 11. Carved stone slabs from a staircase at Resbalón, incl. hieroglyphics, symbols for Venus and the Moon, plus glyphs for a 6C date. 12. Maya painted codex, in five panels. 13. Stone fragment with inscriptions from Tzibanche. 4. Anthropomorphic clay incense burners and various finds from Cozumel. 15. Postclassic stone head from Cancún. 16. Case of funerary items from Cancún, incl. jadeite, shell, and coral jewellery, and ground stone axe-heads. 17. Reconstructions of three of the Cancún burials in circular pits with skeletons in foetal positions and various offerings. 18. Artefacts illustrating the earliest Spanish occupation, incl. finds from the convent at Ecab (glass bowls, gold beads, mother-of-pearl buttons, and pottery).

Beyond the 17km marker, towards the S of the island, are two archaeological sites: *San Miguelito*, on the l. of the boulevard, and *El Rey*, on the r. The sites were occupied in the Preclassic Period by fishermen—who left a shell midden—abandoned, then reoccupied in the Postclassic, when the present structures were built. Burials were also excavated, and some of the finds from them, plus some reconstructions, can be seen in the museum. A small Maya building on a rock outcrop on the beach stands behind the Hotel Camino Real (N shore of the island, 1km W of Punta Cancún).

From Ciudad Cancún, Méx. 307 continues N to join, at 377km, Méx. 180, the Valladolid–Puerto Juárez road. 380km *Puerto Juárez*, see Rte 97.

BAJA CALIFORNIA

The peninsula of **Baja California** (143,791 sq km) is approx. 1220km long and from 40 to 240km wide. Off its coasts appear numerous islands. It is mostly arid and hot, formed by a partly submerged line of volcanoes, manifested from NW to SE by a mountain backbone of grey granite, known in the N as the Sierra de Juárez, continuing as the Sierra San Pedro Mártir, and thereafter under various names. On the E side of the peninsula it descends precipitously into the Gulf of California (Sea of Cortés), whose waters can take on a blood red hue at sunset. On the W side the descent is much more gradual, to broad plains on the Pacific coast. In the central, widest, part a subsidiary series of small volcanic ranges extends SE to NW, forming a great spur, limited on S and W by the Bahía de Sebastián Vizcaíno. Lava flows, broken rock formations, and numerous volcanic cones are ubiquitous. W of La Paz the sierra is interrupted by an isthmus; E of La Paz it continues almost to Cabo San Lucas. Tropical rain falls in late summer in these southernmost mountains and in winter along the Pacific coast N of El Rosario. Otherwise rain is scarce and can, for several years on end, be non-existent. The only rivers worthy of the name are in the NW (Tijuana, Rosario, and Todos Santos). In the extreme NE, where the peninsula borders the State of Sonora, the Río Colorado, plundered for irrigation, runs S towards its delta. To the E its waters irrigate the Valle de Mexicali, closed on the E by the isolated Sierra de Cucapahs. Between the latter and the Sierra de Juárez is the Laguna de Macuata (or Laguna Salada), a vast desert, once invaded by the sea. In the desert aridity are stretches of giant cacti and other exotic plants. Recently established co-operatives have boosted the importance of the fishing industry, among the foremost in the republic. (Some 800 species of fish and 2000 species of invertebrates are estimated to frequent the Gulf, as well as a variety of whales.) The Gulf accounts for about 40 per cent of Mexico's fish production. Overfishing and illegal fishing by foreign fleets threaten seabed habitats and the Gulf's ecosystem. (On its islands are plants and animals found nowhere else in the world.) In the fertile Mexicali area are produced cotton, wheat, alfalfa, maize, linseed, and a variety of fruits. Baja California wines are respectable. In the S, mining, a traditional industry, is still pursued: gypsum on Isla de San Marcos; copper and manganese at Sta Rosalía; and salt extraction in Guerrero Negro and on Isla del Carmen.

'Generally speaking', wrote Clavijero in the 18C, 'California is disagreeable and horrid in aspect; its land broken and arid; exceedingly stony and sandy; lacking in water; covered in thorny plants where it is capable of producing vegetation, and with huge piles of rocks and sand where it is not…If two or three showers fall in a year, the Californians count themselves fortunate'.

Baja California was occupied by man by c 9000 BC at sites such as Laguna Chapala, where traces of pre-projectile point occupation have been found. In the following millennium hunter-gatherer groups related to the Desert Tradition of the Great Basin (USA) and N Mexico, settled in the peninsula and adapted to the seacoast environment. They made numerous shell middens along the small bays, and occupied rock shelters in the hundreds of small arroyos radiating from the rocky spine of the peninsula.

In the Late Prehistoric Period, from c the 5C AD, several cultural groups have been distinguished within the peninsula: in the far N, sites were related to the Desert Tradition and to S Californian coastal cultures; in the extreme NE, an agricultural economy similar to that of the Hohokam culture of the US Southwest was practised; in the middle two-thirds the Comondú culture flourished, famous for its petroglyphs and cave paintings, occupying caves, inland camp sites, and coastal shell middens. Comondú peoples fished with nets, hooks, and lines, and hunted with bows and arrows often tipped with delicately-flaked obsidian points. Plant foods were collected and processed on stationary milling stones with manos (grinders); coiled basketry was common; and pipes were smoked for ritual purposes. Pottery is known only from the historic mission period in the 18C, probably introduced from the US Southwest. In the S third of the peninsula the Las Palmas culture included both shell midden sites, and the occupation of caves and rock shelters (eg, Cerro Cuevoso Cave, Piedra Gorda, and Punta Pescadero). Bows and arrows were used, and the spear- or dart-thrower, tipped with long, slender tanged points, but fishhooks and nets were absent. Manos and millstones were common, but coiled basketry was rare—most Las Palmas baskets were made from sewn strips of bark. Stone scrapers and crudely made stone axes were also used in food gathering and processing. Numerous carved oyster shells have been found, and curious bipointed sticks set with a shark's tooth possibly used in ritual blood-letting.

Baja California, with an estimated Indian population of c 48,000, was first touched in 1533 by the mutinous crew of the 'Concepción', exploring the W coast of New Spain. Having killed their commander, Diego Becerra de Mendoza, they put in at Bahía de la Paz, where most were killed by Indians. In 1535 Cortés himself led an expedition, but his attempts to establish a colony failed. Further expeditions, in 1539–40 and 1542–43, led by Francisco de Ulloa and

Juan Rodríguez Cabrillo, explored the coasts. From the 1550s pearl fisheries began to be exploited, Sebastián Vizcaíno leading a pearling voyage on the Gulf coast in 1596. In 1602–03 he re-explored the Pacific coast. Not until the Jesuits arrived at Loreto in 1697 did permanent settlement from the mainland begin. During 1697–1767 Baja California, in name a military government under the viceroy, was in fact ruled by the Jesuits. In 1769–1804 Alta California (the then vaguely defined area N of approx. the 32nd parallel, now mostly in the USA) was added to the jurisdiction. From 1804 both Californias had separate governments. In 1824 they became the territory 'de las Californias' within the new Mexican federation. But US designs on them soon became apparent. The Treaty of Guadalupe Hidalgo in 1848 assigned Alta California to the USA. In 1888 the peninsula was divided into two districts, N and S, at the 28th parallel. Both were elevated to territories in 1931. In 1952 the N territory, as Baja California, was decreed a State of the federation; the same rank was granted to Baja California Sur in 1974.

Events on the mainland largely passed the peninsula by. The governorship of Abelardo Rodríguez (1923–30) in the N district saw the start of economic advance, a process continued under Pres. Cárdenas (1934–40). The peninsular highway (Méx. 1) from Tijuana to La Paz was inaugurated in 1973. It has eased the passage of visitors from the USA, whose influence has had its effect on local language and customs. The population of Baja California stands today at approx. 2.2 million (80 per cent in Tijuana, Mexicali, and Ensenada); that of Baja California Sur at approx. 325,000.

103 Tijuana to San Ignacio

Méx. 1, 855km.—108km **Ensenada**.—154km Sto Tomás.—242km turning E for (c 80km) Parque Nacional San Pedro Mártir.—275km Lázaro Cárdenas.—292km turning NW for San Quintín.—356km Rosario de Arriba.—478km Cataviñá.—581km Parador Punta Prieta for (68km E) Bahía de los Angeles.—719km turning S for (27km S) Parque Natural de la Ballena Gris.—855km **San Ignacio**.

TIJUANA (over 1.8 million inhab.; 29m), the fourth largest city in Mexico, is a rapidly growing urban sprawl, unattractive in appearance, lying W of the Río Tijuana. Since the mid-1960s it has developed as a business and industrial centre; but it caters particularly for visitors from the USA who come to shop for duty-free jewellery, scent, and liquor, and for Mexican handicrafts. It is also awash with seedy souvenirs cobbled together for the undiscriminating.

Airport. 6km E. Daily flights to *Aguascalientes, Ciudad Obregón, Guadalajara, Hermosillo, La Paz, Los Mochis, Mazatlán, Mexico City, Puerto Vallarta, Zacatecas*; 4 times weekly to *Guaymas*; thrice weekly to *Loreto* and *Torreón*; daily to *Los Angeles*.

Bus station. 5km SE. Services to *Mexico City* (48 hrs); to *Mexicali* (4 hrs); to *La Paz* (22 hrs); to *Mazatlán* (28 hrs); to *Hermosillo* (11 hrs); to *Guadalajara* (36 hrs); to *Los Mochis* (24 hrs); etc.

Hotels throughout the city, cheaper in centre.

Post Office. Corner of Av. Negrete and Calle 11.

Tourist Office. In the Cámara de Comercio de Tijuana, corner of Avs Revolución and Comercio.

US Consulate. 96 Av. Tapachula (off Blvd Agua Caliente, SE of centre).

Bullfights. On Sun., May–Sept., at the Pl. Monumental, 9km W of the city and the Ensenada highway, on the coast; and at the Toreo del Centro, c 3km SE on Blvd Agua Caliente.

In 1829 one Santiago Argüello obtained from José María Echendía six small plots suitable for raising cattle on the ranch called Rancho de Tía Juana. In 1860 a small community formed by the Argüello and Bandini families was in being. The settlement was swept away in 1891 when the Río Tía Juana burst its banks. Refounded on a safer site and given its new contracted name, by 1900 it boasted 242 inhab. and became a target for US filibustering expeditions. During prohibition, Tijuana's bars and brothels became irresistible to repressed US citizens and the second world war boosted its phenomenal growth, not all of it wholesome. Today it attracts thousands of poorer Mexicans desperate to enter (mostly illegally) the USA.

The city's architectural style is indiscriminate and confused. Its main central thoroughfare is the raucous Av. Revolución, known for the tireless efforts of its shopkeepers to attract custom. Towards its N end it is crossed by Av. Benito Juárez, which leads W to the cathedral of *Nuestra Señora de Guadalupe* (1956). From further S on Av. Revolución, Av. Díaz Mirón leads to PARQUE TENIENTE MIGUEL GUERRERO, one of the pleasanter and sometimes quieter spots. Further W is the *Casa de Cultura Fonapas*, a 1930s building reconditioned in 1977. At the corner of Av. Revolución and Calle 7 is the *Frontón Palacios*, in neo-Mudéjar style, which attracts the best jai-alai players in Mexico (every evening, except Thurs., at 8). The **Centro Cultural y Turístico** (fee), on Paseo de los Héroes (corner with C. Mina), SE of the centre, designed by Pedro Ramírez Vázquez and Manuel Rosen, and opened in 1981, offers films on Mexican history and culture, and performances by visiting theatre companies and musical groups. Its *Museo Antropológico e Histórico* (Mon.–Fri., 11–7, Sat.–Sun., 11–8) gives, with the aid of reproductions, a worthy introduction to the country's customs, archaeological sites, and historical monuments.

From Tijuana the quickest route to Ensenada is by toll road Méx. 1D, which runs W to the coast at (9km) *Playas de Tijuana*, the seaside resort, often crowded, but a change after the noise of the city. It is a centre for unorthodox cancer treatment clinics using a drug derived from apricots; it is not approved in the USA—which does not stop US citizens coming S in hope of a cure. The toll road continues alongside and crossing the free road, amid spectacular cliffs overlooking the sea, to (112km) *Ensenada*.

The free road (Méx. 1) runs S to (26km) *Rosarito*, a pleasant enough place with a good wide beach. There is another beach at (34km; 5km W) *Popotla*, at the N point of Bahía Descanso. The road skirts the bay and passes (49km) *El Descanso*, with a new chapel built on the site of a Dominican mission (1814). 65km *La Misión*, named for the Dominican mission of San Miguel (1787), now in ruins. From (98km) *El Sauzal*, with a fish cannery, Méx. 3 goes NE through the Valle de Guadalupe to (117km) *Tecate*, see Rte 106. 108km **ENSENADA** (c 250,000 inhab.; 13m), biggest fishing port in the republic, with canneries and chilling plants; centre of a wine-producing area; and resort on the beautiful Bahía de Todos los Santos, attracts many visitors from the USA. The natives have a reputation for openness and hospitality.

Bus station. Corner of Av. Miramar and C. 11. Services to *Tijuana* (c 1½ hrs); to *La Paz* (c 22 hrs); etc.

Hotels throughout the town.

Post Office. 1347 Av. Juárez.

Tourist Office. 1350 Av. López Mateos.

The bay was used for shelter from the 17C both by the Manila galleons and by pirates lying in wait for them. Ensenada's growth began in 1870 when gold was discovered at Real de Castillo, c 40km E. After gold fever had petered out early in the 20C, the town became an export centre for the products of the Valle de Mexicali. Today it enjoys a reputation second to none for deep-sea fishing.

From the elegant S suburb of *Lomas de Chapultepec* we may gain a superb view of the bay. The largest wine cellar in Mexico, *Bodegas de Sto Tomás*, is at 666 Av. Miramar (guided tours generally Mon.–Sat., 11 and 3).

SE of the centre, at the corner of Blvd Lázaro Cárdenas and Av. Riviera, is the former *Casino Riviera del Pacífico*, built in the 1920s and in its heyday a famous gambling house, once managed by the boxer Jack Dempsey. It is now a cultural centre.

The best beaches begin c 8km to the S. At the tip of the narrow, rocky, and picturesque peninsula which closes the bay, reached by Méx. 1 S until (15km) *Sánchez Taboada* where we turn r. along the peninsula, is (37km) *La Bufadora*, a natural geyser formed by a combination of waves, wind, and tide, and performing with tremendous din at high tide. The two rocky islands in the bay (*Islas de Todos Santos*), the larger c 2km wide, are bird sanctuaries in spring and summer; fishermen also gather here to collect sea urchins, much favoured in local cooking.

From Ensenada, Méx. 3 climbs E via (24km) turning r. for (8km S) *Agua Caliente*, frequented for its hot springs, to (39km; 2km l.) *Ojos Negros* (P), 7km S of *Real de Castillo* (see above), now abandoned. From Ojos Negros it continues SE across the peninsula, an uneasy journey through a barren landscape. Beyond (61km) *San Salvador* and (76km) *Piñón Grande*, at 92km a road goes l. (also SE, but above Méx. 3) via *Agua Blanca* to (8km) *Sta Catarina*, where may be seen ruins of the Dominican mission of Sta Catalina Mártir, founded in 1797, destroyed by the Indians in 1840. Méx. 3 continues to (121km) *Valle Trinidad* (Colonia Lázaro Cárdenas; P), before the Sierra San Pedro Mártir. It then goes NE to join Méx. 5 at (196km) *El Chinero*, see Rte 106.

The road running directly E from Ojos Negros ascends into the *Parque Nacional Constitución de 1857* (c 2000m), in the Sierra de Juárez, where a landscape of conifers replaces the cactus and scrub of the lower altitudes. At 77km (from Ensenada) it passes *Asseradero*, a small lumbering community, 7km NE of which is *Laguna Hanson*, its basin dry except after rains, surrounded by trees, small cultivated patches, and rocks eroded by the wind. The road veers away to the W of the sierra, reaching its end at (169km) *La Rumorosa* on the Tijuana–Mexicali road, see Rte 106.

Beyond Ensenada, Méx. 1 continues S along the coast to (124km) *Maneadero* (r.), where tourist cards are checked, and then goes SE inland. At 151km a road (r.) leads W to a particularly rugged stretch of the coast at *Puerto Sto Tomás*, with a beach suitable for surfing. 154km **Sto Tomás** (107m; H,R,P), named after the Dominican mission of *Sto Tomás de Aquino* (1791; refounded upstream in 1794), now a few outbuilding ruins. The friars planted the vineyards which produce high-quality wine. C 2km W of (192km) **San Vicente** (91m; P), founded in 1780 as mission and garrison, are the ruins of the Dominican mission of *San Vicente Ferrer*. 20km S is the beach of San Isidro, good for surfing. From (230km) *Colonet* (P), centre for a cattle-raising area, two roads run to the coast: to *San Antonio del Mar* (12km W) and *Punta Colonet* (20km SW; good views of Bahía Colonet).

At 242km a dirt road diverges l. (E) for (10km) *San Telmo de Arriba* (last P if proceeding E), with meagre ruins of a Dominican chapel (1800).

At 26km along this road is a junction. The r. branch crosses rolling hills, passing (at 18km from the junction) *Rancho Valladares* and (29km) turning r. for (3km) the *Valladares* mines, and arriving at (39km) *Arroyo San Antonio*, whence a trail leads E to (26km) the ruins of the Dominican mission of *San Pedro Mártir*, founded in 1794, abandoned by c 1806. The l. branch (at 26km) goes to (28km) a road junction. From here we may continue straight ahead via (48km) *Buena Vista* to (75km) *Mike's Sky Ranch*, a country hotel (with airstrip) favoured by US guns. From the road junction at 28km (see above) we may turn r. for (50km) the road leading to the Observatory. At 2km r. is *Rancho Meling*, another hotel, also with an airstrip. From the turning r. at 50km we continue roughly E, climbing steadily into the alpine landscape of the **Parque Nacional San Pedro Mártir** (2700m average), known for its variety of flora and fauna, dramatic granite formations, ponderosa pines, and rolling valleys, and excellent hiking and camping. There is heavy winter snowfall. 75km (r.) *Oak Pasture* camping area (permit needed). 93km *Vallecitos*, from where we can go S by trail to *La Encantada* (meadows and springs). At 97km we reach the gate of the *Observatorio Astronómico* of UNAM (2km walk from gate; 3000m) which possesses the largest telescope (Telmex; one of three) in the hispanic world. In surrounding houses, especially built to withstand the rigours of the climate (15 degrees C below zero in winter), live the staff. (Those wishing to visit are advised to enquire at its offices in Ensenada.) To the E is the N face of the *Peñón del Diablo* (Peña Encantada; 3078m), highest peak in the peninsula.

Méx. 1 descends to (260km) *Camalú* (P). 272km road E to (8km) the ruins of the Dominican mission of *Sto Domingo*, second of their foundations (1775; later moved upstream) in N Baja California. *Rancho Hamilton* (5km E) is favoured by regular (never casual) guests who are game aficionados. 275km **Lázaro Cárdenas** (the former *Colonia Guerrero*; M,R,P), an agricultural centre.

At 292km a poor road diverges NW for **San Quintín** (c 15,000 inhab.; H,M), an unattractive development at the N end of a sheltered lagoon (resembling a U, thanks to the peninsula which juts into it) at the N end of Bahía San Quintín, and centre of an irrigated area—drip irrigation is used to preserve underground water supplies—of market gardens producing vegetables, sugar cane, and cereals. The bay is noted for beautiful beaches and fishing, with multitudes of shrimps and clams. *Isla San Martín*, off the coast, is known for its seal colonies.

In 1888 a US (later English) farming colony, sponsored by the Mexican Land and Colonization Company, was established on the shores of the bay. Withdrawal of company support and drought drove out most of the colonists, although a few lingered on into the 20C. Reminders of the venture are the old cemetery (4km S of the pier on the shore of the bay) and the *Old Mill*, now a motel, c 6km W of Méx. 1 on the bay, where agricultural machinery is preserved.

Beyond the turning for San Quintín, Méx. 1 skirts Bahía San Quintín, with a series of sand and pebble beaches, good centres for fishing and surfing.

356km *Rosario de Arriba* (R,P), with the ruins of the first Dominican mission in Baja California, Nuestra Señora del Rosario Viñadaco (1774), moved a league downstream (W) in 1802 (Rosario de Abajo, also in ruins). Beyond Rosario the road turns inland along the N bank of the Arroyo del Rosario and eventually into an outlandish boulder-strewn desert, with yucca trees, organ-pipe cacti, and other exotic plants—most weird of all, the cirios, with thin, stark trunks (up to 18m) and exiguous tufted tips, which give yellow flowers. At (417km) *San Fernando* is what remains of the mission of San Fernando de Velicatá (1769), the only Franciscan foundation in the peninsula. 439km *San Agustín* (580m; P), whence a track goes NE to *El Mármol*, site of an onyx mine abandoned in 1958. 478km **Cataviñá** (H,R,P), where guides are available to show prehispanic rock paintings. 480km road l. to *Rancho Sta Inés*, whence we may reach (hard going) along a track (c 22km E) the ruins of the last of the Jesuit Californian missions, Sta María de los Angeles, founded to the SE, at Calañujuet, in Oct. 1766, moved here in May 1767.

Méx. 1 continues SE, rising to 800m before descending to skirt (531km) *Laguna Chapala*, a dry lake bed for most of the year and a vast muddy pool after rain. At (559km) *El Crucero* a road N.

It goes to (25km) *Calamajué* and the ruins of *Sta María de los Angeles Calañujuet* (see above). Hence the road continues to (39km) a junction, near *King Richard* (La Josefina), an abandoned gold mine, discovered and worked in the early 1900s by Richard Doggett, from England. By turning r. we may reach the Gulf coast at (55km) *Puerto Calamajué*. The turning l. brings us to Bahía San Luis Gonzaga via (10km) *Las Arrastras* (396km from Mexicali and 194km from San Felipe). At 25km from Las Arrastras is a road r. for (11km) *Puerto San Francisquito* on the coast and *Rancho Punta Final*. The road l. at 25km from Las Arrastras goes to the N headland of Bahía San Luis Gonzaga and to (16km) *San Luis Gonzaga* (H,R,P), a remote resort (good fishing).

At (581km) *Parador Punta Prieta* a road diverges l. (E).

It leads to (68km) **Bahía de los Angeles** (H,R,P), a fishing village, sport fishing centre, and rapidly growing seaside resort beautifully set on a large bay protected by small islands and ringed by mountains.

It is separated by the Canal de las Ballenas from *Isla Angel de la Guarda* (c 600sq km), noted for its fauna, incl. seagulls, iguanas, lizards, venemous snakes, and other reptiles. On its E coast are a few fishing villages whose main activity is oyster catching. The W coast is uninhabited, thanks largely to scorpions and snakes. It is the largest of the chain of islands which goes SE, of which *Isla Raza*, a haunt of migratory birds and now a nature reserve, is the most rewarding.

A research station from UNAM works here each spring to study the tern and Heermann's gull breeding grounds, and has been to the fore in the campaign for proper management of the Gulf's ecosystem.

23km W of Bahía de los Angeles a turning l. from the main road begins a rough ride (4-wheel drive essential) S to (36km) **San Francisco de Borja** (488m), a Jesuit mission started up around the water hole of *Adac*, discovered c 1758, and a doctrinal centre from 1762. By 1767 half the population (c 3000) had fallen prey to European diseases; by 1810–12 the mission was abandoned, although at Independence a handful only of families survived, subsisting on game and wild plants. The remains have been restored by INAH and include the façade of the church, finished by the Dominicans in 1801, walls and adobe constructions, and part of an irrigation system.

From here, this road, only a little improved, runs W and SW, past (45km) *San Ignacito*, a ranch with remains of a Dominican irrigation ditch, to join Méx. 1 at (41km) *Rosarito*, see below.

594km (r.) *Punta Prieta*, whence an alternative road branches off for Bahía de los Angeles. At 604km a road runs SW to the coast at (24km) *Sta Rosalillita*, with good beaches, on Bahía Sta Rosalía. From (632km) *Rosarito* (P) it is possible to reach (35km NE) *San Francisco de Borja*, see above. 642km road r. for (5km) *Playa Altamira*, another unspoiled beach. At 709km we reach the 28th parallel.

It is marked by a 40m-high steel and concrete monument, which commemorates the opening of the highway in 1973. Here watches should be put forward one hour to mark the change from Pacific Standard to Mountain Standard time.

710km turning r. for (5km) **Guerrero Negro** (c 5000 inhab.; H,R,P), a town amid a network of coastal lagoons inland from the huge Bahía Sebastián Vizcaíno.

Its prosperity depends on the exploitation of its vast salt ponds, on which the desert sun accelerates evaporation of sea water and leaves pure white, compact crystals.
　　Estimated production is 20,000 tonnes a day. Deposits of oil and natural gas have been discovered beneath the desert SE of the town. Its local airport connects with the island of *Cedros* (c 275 sq km), once an arrival point of the Manila galleon after the Pacific crossing. From its deep water port freighters transport the salt to the USA, Canada, and Japan. At its SE corner is a famous fish cannery.

At 719km the road r. (not easy and covered in sand) runs S to (27km) the **Parque Natural de la Ballena Gris**, which includes the *Laguna Ojo de Liebre* (also known as *Scammon's Lagoon*). Every year between 10,000 and 20,000 grey whales swim from the Bering Straits to frolic, mate, and spawn along this coast during Dec.–March.

The lagoon bears the name of Charles Melville Scammon, a US whaler who discovered it accidentally in 1856 and paved the way for slaughter over the years until the whales were almost extinct—c 100 survivors at the end of the 19C. Although no longer in danger of extinction, their ecological equilibrium is always delicate. Thanks to protests by conservation groups and action by the Mexican and US governments, the whale is now a protected species. Its average weight is c 20 tonnes and length 15.25m. Its attraction for this region is attributed to the salt content of the waters and their unusual shallowness. All sea and air traffic is forbidden during the breeding season in and over the lagoons and bays of this part of the coast. Visitors must content themselves with looking (binoculars useful) from designated observation points. The former deep-water port of the salt-exporting company (c 11km W of Guerrero Negro; see above) is also a haven; whales swim up to the docks during the day.

Méx. 1 traverses the desolate Desierto de Vizcaíno. At 737km a road (badly paved) branches l. for (42km NE) *El Arco* (290m; P), now almost a ghost town, but scene of gold prospecting from the 1920s, put paid to by scarcity of the metal and labour unrest. Copper prospecting is now in train.

Around El Arco, in the Sierra San Borja numerous caves contain paintings. C 50km NW of El Arco, the *Arroyo Campomonte* has several humans depicted in reds of different shades; and the Sierra de San Juan, SE of Sta Gertrudis, has others.
　　From El Arco a track runs E to (37km) **Sta Gertrudis** (549m), with a partly restored mission. It was founded by the Jesuits at the oasis of La Piedad Calcadañ in July 1752 and its jurisdiction extended far across the peninsula. By 1755 c 400 families lived within a day's journey of the mission; cattle had been brought in; and a mission garden produced maize, wheat, and cotton. In 1750–70 a series of epidemics struck and by 1800 only c 200 Indians were left in the jurisdiction. After 1767 the mission was assigned to the Dominicans, but was abandoned at Independence.

783km turning r. for (5km) *Ejido Vizcaíno*, one of several government-backed farming projects, made possible by the exploitation, through the drilling of deep wells, of water deposits trapped thousands of years ago.
　　At 836km a reasonably surfaced road branches r. (SW) across the desert.

It should be attempted only by the adventurous with 4-wheel drive vehicles, well-equipped with food, drinking water, motor-fuel, spares, and medicine, and above all attracted by desolation, and not deterred by heat, dust storms, and coastal fogs. It runs past the strange and rugged Sierra Sta Clara (r.; W) towards the coast via (100km) *Punta Abreojos*, a small fishing settlement, with a few facilities, and then along the coast via (118km) *La Bocana* to skirt Bahía San Hipólito, with lovely beaches, before reaching (152km) *San Hipólito*. Next comes Bahía de la Asunción and, at its NW point (204km; l.), *Punta Asunción*, also with facilities (M,P). Hence we continue NW and N through the Sierra Placeres to (263km) the ranch of *San*

José de Castro. From here the road continues W to (337km) **Bahía Tortugas** (c 3000 inhab.; simple accommodation; P), to which drinking water has to be imported. C 20km N is *Punta Falsa*, the westernmost point of the Vizcaíno peninsula, off which is the small *Isla Natividad*. 42km N of San José de Castro and reached by dirt road is *Playa Malarrimo*, on the S of Bahía Sebastián Vizcaíno, a magnet for beachcombers hunting remains of wrecks.

855km **SAN IGNACIO** (c 3000 inhab.; 152m; H,R,P), a welcome oasis after the rigours of the desert, watered by an underground stream and rejoicing in date palms, figs, citrus fruits, and vines.

From 1716 the Palermitan Jesuit Francesco Maria Piccolo began missionary activity by the oasis of Cadacaamañ, where a formal mission was founded by Fr Juan Bautista Luyando in 1724 and dedicated in 1728. It became headquarters of a jurisdiction stretching from the Gulf coast W to Isla Cedros—perhaps c 6500 souls, a number drastically reduced by epidemics in 1750–70.

Raised up on the E side of the shady Pl. Principal is the imposing mission church of **San Ignacio**, begun through the efforts of a Croat Jesuit, Fernando Consag, perhaps helped by a local blind builder, Andrés Comanji, and finished by the Dominican Juan Crisóstomo Gómez c 1786. It is built of slabs of volcanic rock c 1.22m thick. The façade, faced with mortar and diluted baroque in style, is crossed by two tiers of pilasters divided by cornice and simple diamond pattern frieze, and punctuated by four rose windows, four slender niches for saints, and coats-of-arms. The four finials on the parapet add a touch of grandeur; the squat tower recalls Dominican structures in SW Mexico.

The imaginative high altarpiece leans towards anastyle baroque (late 18C); the simpler side altarpieces, dedicated to the Life of Our Lady and the Passion, are in the same style and incorporate inferior paintings.

A number of mysterious cave paintings are found within reasonable reach of San Ignacio. Expeditions are organized by guides in San Ignacio and other population centres, and their services are indispensable to the uninitiated. Great technical difficulties prevail and the area where most paintings have been discovered, between latitudes 28 degrees 50' and 26 degrees 15' N, has never been properly mapped. Appearing on the walls and ceilings of shallow caves, and on high ledges, the amazing variety of forms depicted—men (often gigantic figures more than 4m tall), deer, serpents, dolphins, tortoises, etc.—in red, white, black, and shades of ochre attest to a lively artistic sense.

Many of these rock paintings have been known since the missionary period and they were first written about by Clavijero, in his 'Storia della California' (Venice, 1789). The region was later explored by a Dutchman, Ten Kate, in 1874 and in 1883, and by the Frenchman Léon Dignet during 1889–1905, when many more paintings were discovered. A second Frenchman, Georges Enguerrand, explored in 1911–13.

Whether these cave paintings are 5000 years old, or only 200, is unknown. It is a reasonable assumption, however, that they were executed by the Comondú; but as pottery was absent from their cultural baggage until the historic period, and excavations of their sites do not yield any precisely datable artefacts, either internally or by cross-cultural comparison, their date must remain speculative. That they are not of the most recent period is suggested by Indian reports to the earliest Jesuit missionaries that the paintings were made by 'giants from the north' (perhaps suggested to them by the tallness of some of the figures). Some relative dating of the paintings is obvious by the superimposition of figures in many of the caves, and certain stylistic trends or groupings suggest various phases and developments. That the paintings had magico-religious significance is an assumption which seems plausible on a general cross-cultural basis, but which is difficult to prove conclusively. That they represent unique style, or styles, is beyond doubt.

104 San Ignacio to La Paz

Méx. 1, 619km.—70km Sta Rosalía.—131km Mulegé.—266km (3km E)
Loreto, and turning for (33km SW) **San Javier**.—384km Villa Insurgentes.—
410km Ciudad Constitución.—619km **La Paz**.

From San Ignacio, Méx. 1 continues E. From (13km) *Las Palmas* a rough road
winds NW into the Sierra de San Francisco to (c 32km) *Sta Marta*, 5km E of
which are interesting cave paintings (*Cuesta del Palmarito*; guide necessary).
34km *Rancho el Mezquital*, S of the volcano called *Tres Virgenes* (three cones;
2180m), now quiescent.

We reach the coast after an abrupt descent at (70km) **Sta Rosalía** (c 15,000
inhab.; H,R,P; thrice weekly car ferry to *Guaymas*—see Rte 21), a fishing port
still adhering to its copper-mining past.

It grew in the 1870s, thanks to the activities of the French-owned (with Rothschild connections)
El Boleo copper concern, which stayed in business until 1953. Today smaller-scale operations
(copper and manganese) are being continued by Mexican interests.

French architectural influence is especially noticeable in the barrio to the N of
the centre. The prefabricated cast-iron parish church, designed by Gustave
Eiffel for the Paris Exposition Internationale of 1889, as suitable for the African
missions, was bought by the El Boleo directors; packed into innumerable cases;
and shipped by mistake around Cape Horn and up the Pacific coast of America
(instead of to Veracruz). The old smelter, connected to the mines by a narrow-
gauge railway, may still be visited.

From Sta Rosalía, Méx. 1 runs S inland from the coast, past (86km) *San Lucas*,
a fishing village with pleasant beaches facing a sheltered little bay, and (95km)
San Bruno, from where some good beaches on the Chivato peninsula to the E
may be reached—(c 12km) *San Marcos* and (c 33km) *Punta Chivato*. To the N
of San Marcos lies *Isla San Marcos*, with gypsum mines producing c 1.5 million
tonnes a year.

At 101km a road, becoming rougher and suitable only for the hardiest
vehicles, branches off to the r. into the sierra via (18km) *San José Magdalena*,
pleasant and unusually fertile, (44km) *Las Cruces*, and (51km) *San Sebastián*,
both within reach of cave paintings, to (58km) **Guadalupe** (885m), with ruins of
the ample mission of *Nuestra Señora de Guadalupe Guasinapí*, founded in
inhospitable territory by the Jesuit Everardo Helen, a native of Cologne, in
1720; abandoned by 1795.

111km turning r. for (26km SW) the cave of *San Borjita* and some of the best
cave paintings in the peninsula, hunting or battle scenes with human figures of
varying sizes. 131km **Mulegé** (c 3000 inhab.; 8m; H,R,P), an expanding town
with a tropical climate and happily watered by the Río Sta Rosalía (or
Mulegé)—as evidenced by palm, fig, orange, banana, and olive groves—inland
from the Gulf of California.

On the W of the town, reached by pathway S of Pl. Principal, is the former mission of *Sta
Rosalía*, founded in 1705 by the Jesuit Juan de Basaldúa (1675–1718). The church, begun in
1766, was restored in 1973. On a hill to the E is the State prison, devoid of obvious
security—prisoners (if there are any) work in the town during the day and return at night.
An uneven road goes SW from Mulegé to (30km) the ranch of *La Trinidad*, within reach (on
foot or on muleback) of some more spectacular cave paintings (local enquiry essential).

SE of Mulegé the road begins its skirting of the scenic *Bahía Concepción*, 40km
long and 5km wide, sheltered from the Gulf of California by the broad
Peninsula de la Concepción, enveloping little volcanic islands, and rejoicing in
beaches and coves of extraordinary beauty, becoming increasingly popular for
skin-diving, boating, and fishing. 154km *Santispac*, within reach of good
beaches to N and S. 162km *El Coyote*, near cave paintings in the Loma del

Burro, 1km N. From here boats ply across the neck of the bay to the peninsula. 173km *Isla Requesón*, joined at low tide to the mainland by a sandbank. After (8km) *Los Muertitos* the road begins to curve round the S end of the bay before continuing S to (204km) *Rosarito*, a cattle ranch, and (211km) turning r. (W).

From here we may descend W through the N slopes of the Sierra de la Giganta and then SW, beyond (59km) a road SE to *San José de Comondú* (see below), to (67km) *San Isidro* and (71km) *La Purísima* (183m), two small pueblos (P) of c 2500 inhab. between them, in the Valle de la Purísima, intensively irrigated (thanks originally to the Jesuits) for growing of cereals, date palms, fruits, and the vine, and for market gardens, surrounded by stark peaks and desert. A few remains exist of the mission of La Purísima Concepción, founded in 1717, moved to Cadegomo (the old name for La Purísima) in 1730. Only a handful of inhabitants survived by 1820.

From La Purísima the road runs gradually S towards the Pacific coast and (112km) *Poza Grande*, and then straight to (180km) *Villa Insurgentes*, see below.

From the turning at 211km another road, more awkward, runs S through the foothills of the Sierra de la Giganta to (62km) **San José de Comondú** (c 500 inhab.; 466m; R,P), in a well-watered canyon, hemmed in by volcanic rock formations, where fruit and vegetables are cultivated. Here in 1737 was moved the Jesuit mission founded in 1708 c 12 leagues NE. After 1767 it was taken over by the Franciscans and afterwards by the Dominicans. It was abandoned in 1827. What remains is part of the once ample mission buildings (c 1750), reconditioned as a chapel. A drastic restoration was carried out by INAH in 1973. *San Miguel de Comondú*, a settlement of 1714, is c 3km SW across the Río Comondú. The road SW is spectacular and links after 29km with the road from Purísima to *Villa Insurgentes*.

Méx. 1 continues S through the E slopes of the Sierra de la Giganta. At 235km a turning r. leads to (3km W) the remains of *San Juan Bautista Londó*, a visita of Loreto founded in 1699, abandoned by 1745. 247km turning l. for (9km) **Buena Vista**.

5km N are the remains of *San Bruno*, an early fortified settlement (1683–85) which served as base for expeditions inland, established by the governor of Sinaloa, Isidro Atondo y Antillón and the Jesuit Eusebio Francisco Kino.

266km turning l. for (3km) **Loreto** (5000 inhab.; H,R,P; daily flights from airport to *Guadalajara*, *Tijuana*, and *Los Angeles*), now enjoying something of a renaissance as a resort (mainly for fishing and deep-sea diving).

Nuestra Señora de Loreto Conchó was the first permanent European settlement in California, with a garrison to protect and supply the missions. During 1697–1829 it was chief place of Baja California (and Las Californias), the first governor, Gaspar de Portolá, arriving here in 1767. In 1829 it was virtually flattened by a hurricane and the capital was moved to La Paz.

In C. Salvatierra is the former mission of *Nuestra Señora de Loreto*, the first permanent Indian mission, founded by Juan María de Salvatierra in Oct. 1697, and headquarters of the Jesuit Californian missionary effort. The sturdy church was finished and blessed in 1752 and restored in 1973 when the original wooden beams and brackets were repositioned. The tower is a modern (post-1910) addition. Despite hurricane and neglect, original paintings and a fine statue of St Joseph survive in nave and side chapel.

The adjoining (on W side) *Museo de las Misiones de California* (Tues.–Sun., 9–2) contains other works of art once belonging to the mission and illustrates life there.

A steep road bearing r. off Méx. 1 just S of the turning to Loreto leads through one of the finest landscapes in Baja California, climbing SW through the Sierra de la Giganta via (16km) *Las Parras* amid olive and orange groves. At 18km there is a fine view on clear days of the Gulf of California. At c 26km a dirt road goes E to (41km) *San José de Comondú*, see above. We descend S to (33km) **SAN JAVIER** (310m), hemmed in by dark cliffs, and site of the second Jesuit mission in the peninsula.

It was founded as *San Francisco Javier Viggé Biaundó*, by Francesco Maria Piccolo in 1699 and moved to its present site, hitherto a visita called San Pablo Huimiuma, c 1719. One of the more prosperous missions, in 1772 it numbered 74 families and 14 widows, in all 279 souls. From 1773 the Dominicans tended it, but by 1810–12 it was left without a priest; in 1820 only 50 Indians survived throughout its jurisdiction.

The church of **San Francisco Javier**, the most ambitious in the peninsula, built in 1744–58 and restored in 1973, stands in a raised atrio reached by a penitential way on various levels.

EXTERIOR. Its sturdy mass is held in by buttresses and decorated with parapet finials, each different in form. The vertical panel of the façade, dwarfed by the stocky tower, is reminiscent of Franciscan 16C convent churches. Swelling pilasters with Corinthian capitals mark the lowest storey. Jambs, pedestals, and frieze show vegetal relief; the arch face and spandrels geometric motifs. In the keystone, seemingly pinned by a hanging boss, the date of completion; above it, on a sun-like background, the emblem of the Society of Jesus. The middle-storey columns are solomonic, suitably swathed in boltels, cords, and vegetal abstractions. The generous upper storey is covered by a basket arch. Main features of the side portals are the ogee arches enclosed in a type of alfíz formed by little half-pilasters and cornice; the square upper windows with their double frames composed of a strong likeness to the Franciscan cord; and the cross and side supports, full of quaint relief.

The keys of the INTERIOR vault arches (especially good in the choir) hold anagrams of Our Lady and saints, and at the springing of the vaults are piquant conical corbels, with layers of plentiful relief, an idea repeated in the pendentives below the cupola. Of singular interest for its flat, originally designed estípites and variety of frames which hold paintings of the Holy Trinity and saints and statue of St Francis Xavier, the high altarpiece was brought from Mexico 'not yet assembled, but already gilded, packed into two and thirty chests, thus crossing land and sea'. A work of unusual charm, the altarpiece in the r. transept combines chunky estípites and slender solomonic columns; in the centre of the lowest storey, a winning statue of St Ignatius.

From San Javier the road descends to the Pacific plain to join (c 104km) the La Purísima–Villa Insurgentes road, 27km N of *Villa Insurgentes*.

From the Loreto turning Méx. 1 continues S to (277km) *Nopoló*, being developed as a coastal resort. It faces *Isla del Carmen*, distant an average 15km from the shore, 33km long and with a maximum width of 13km. A mountain chain, reaching 480m, lines its central region. Along its shores are extensive salt deposits. 287km *Juncalito* and (290km) *Puerto Escondido*, fishing settlements. 300km turning l. for *Ligüí*, with a rocky beach (5km E) and remains of the Jesuit mission of *San Juan Bautista* (1705). Méx. 1 swings SW across the Sierra de la Giganta towards the Pacific coast plain at (384km) **Villa Insurgentes** (c 9000 inhab.; H,R,P), an agricultural centre from which *Puerto Adolfo López Mateos* (Puerto Matancitas; 43km W), facing the sandspit-lined Pacific coast, may be reached. 410km **Ciudad Constitución** (c 30,000 inhab.; H,R,P; daily flights from airport to *Guadalajara, Los Mochis*, and *Tijuana*), a recent and sudden urban growth, known to local wags as 'ciudad instantanea', which has flourished thanks to the exploitation of water from deep wells and consequent growing of cotton, cereals, and tropical fruits.

From here State road 22 runs W through the irrigated *Praderas de la Magdalena* and then a typical desert zone abounding in cacti and other plants to the mangrove swamp around (57km) *Puerto San Carlos*, export point for the cotton and other produce of the region. In stands to the N of Bahía de Magdalena, the exceptionally secure stretch of water between the mainland and the strangely shaped Isla Sta Magdalena (220 sq km) to the W and Isla Sta Margarita (130 sq km) to the S. The islands are separated by the Boca de la Entrada, entry to the bay. Both have manganese deposits. On the E coast of Isla Sta Margarita is one of Mexico's principal naval bases.

At 429km a serviceable road l. runs E.

It becomes a dirt road after c 20km, running SE to (38km) *San Luis Gonzaga*, with the restored Jesuit doctrinal centre of San Luis Gonzaga Chiriyaqui, founded in 1743, abandoned to become a cattle ranch in 1768. We may continue SE to (64km) a fork l. to (21km) *La Presa San Pedro*, 3km above which are the remains (difficult going) of *Nuestra Señora de los Dolores del Sur de Chillá* (or *La Pasión*), another mission, founded in 1741.

Past (463km) *Sta Rita*, from where a road runs to the coast at (23km) *Puerto Chale*, amid mangroves and with good fishing, Méx. 1 begins to cross the ankle of the peninsula, a dull ride, before arriving at (619km) *La Paz*.

105 La Paz and Southernmost Baja California Sur

LA PAZ (c 160,000 inhab.), capital of Baja California Sur, free port, fishing centre, and increasingly popular resort, stands at the S curve of the wide Bahía de la Paz. It is favoured for its mild winter climate and is especially famous for its fabulous sunsets.

Dec.–Jan. rains can on occasion be violent; in 1976 an exceptional downpour caused havoc. Oppressive summer heat is alleviated by fresh winds at nightfall.

Airport. 13km S. Daily flights to *Cabo San Lucas, Culiacán, Guaymas, Los Mochis, Mazatlán, Mexico City, Tijuana*; six times weekly to *Guadalajara*; thrice weekly to *Ciudad Obregón* and *Hermosillo*; daily to *Los Angeles*.

Ferries, from Pichilingue, 19km N. Daily to *Mazatlán* (16 hrs); four times weekly to *Topolobampo*. Tickets at ferry terminal or at the La Paz office at the corner of Cs Madero and Victoria. Booking for cars at La Paz office only. Cars require their permits stamped at the Registry, at the corner of Cs Belisario Domínguez and Navarro. Ferries always well booked; passengers advised to make reservations well in advance and to be at the office in La Paz by 8am.

Bus stations. Corner of Malecón and C. 5 de Mayo for bus to ferry terminal. Av. Valentín Gómez Farías (corner with C. 5 de Febrero) for services to *Tijuana* (23 hrs); to *Loreto* (5 hrs); to *Sta Rosalía* (8 hrs); to *Guerrero Negro* (11hrs); to *San Quintín* (16 hrs); to *Ensenada* (21 hrs). Other services to *San José del Cabo, Cabo San Lucas*, and *Todos Santos*.

Hotels throughout the city; cheaper in centre.

Post Office. Corner of Av. Revolución and C. Constitución.

Tourist Office. On Malecón (Paseo Obregón) at the junction with C. 16 de Septiembre.

Immigration Office. Corner of Cs Mutualismo and Muelle. Passengers to the mainland are advised to clear their trip here.

The bay was first reached late in 1533 by the mutineers from Diego Becerra's ship 'Concepción'. In Apr. 1683 Governor Isidro Atondo y Antillón, accompanied by the Jesuits Eusebio Kino and Matías Goñi, with two shiploads of settlers arrived at La Paz. Hostile Indians frightened off the colony after 3½ months. In 1720 the Jesuits Juan de Ugarte and Jaime Bravo returned to found the mission of Nuestra Señora del Pilar, which had a short life, interrupted by an Indian revolt in 1734–36, before abandonment in 1749. The site was repopulated in 1811 and in 1830 became capital of Baja California. In 1847 it was captured by US troops and in 1853 occupied by the US adventurer William Walker and his filibusters.

On the E side of Pl. Principal is the cathedral of *Nuestra Señora de la Paz* (1861), in conservative style, probably on the site of the Jesuit mission. To the N, at the corner of Cs 5 de Mayo and Altamirano, is the **Museo del Estado** (Tues.–Sat., 9–1, 4–7) which concentrates on the anthropological past of Baja California Sur.

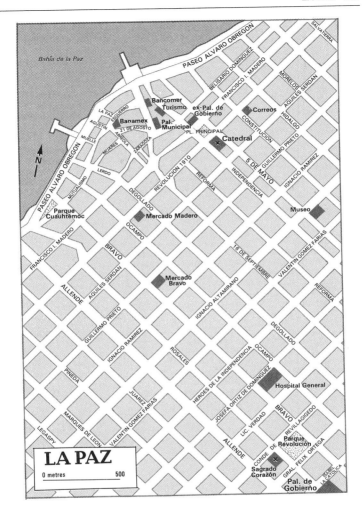

LA PAZ

0 metres   500

S of the cathedral, at the corner of Av. Revolución and C. Degollado, is the *Mercado Madero*, good for local crafts. The area between Av. Revolución and the seafront is the old city nucleus (and commercial centre), with characteristic tree-shaded streets containing some typical old houses, especially C. 16 de Septiembre.

Along the road to (19km N) *Pichilingue*, the ferry terminal, a series of well-sheltered beaches may be gained. Just beyond the ferry landing is Pichilingue beach itself. A dirt road running NE away from Pichilingue leads (c 7km) to the tranquil beach of *Puerto Balandra*, on the Arranca Caballos; beyond that is *Tecolote* and, on the E side of the headland, *El Coyote*, the most remote beach of them all. Lying off Punta Arranca Caballos is the volcanic *Isla Espíritu*

Santo (c 22km long and 8km at its widest), once a haunt of pearl-fishers, an industry for which La Paz was famous in the 19C and early 20C—now gradually reviving.

At c 5km along Méx. 1 S of La Paz a minor road (in reasonable condition) runs SE across the Sierra de la Laguna to (48km) *San Juan de los Planes*, an agricultural and stock-raising centre (thanks to exploitation of aquifers), and then to the coast at (66km) *Ensenada de los Muertos*, at the N end of Bahía de los Muertos and S of *Punta Arena*, a headland enclosing Bahía de la Ventana to the W. The sea here is shark-infested and rich in other fish. To the N is the barren, mountainous, cactus-covered *Isla Cerralvo* (130 sq km; highest peak 770m), whose W coast and the facing E mainland coast were another pearling centre until 1940.

FROM LA PAZ TO CABO SAN LUCAS, 217km. Méx. 1 continues S to (28km) *San Pedro*, where it forks l. to cross the Sierra de la Laguna. 54km *El Triunfo* (564m) was until the mid-1920s a considerable silver-mining centre when abandonment turned it into something of a ghost town. There has been a recent revival of mining activity. From (62km) *San Antonio*, founded in 1756 as a real de minas, and with a contemporary church, a rough road runs N through the sierra to (c 22km) the La Paz–Ensenada de los Muertos road c 3km W of Los Planes, see above. We reach the coast just N of (107km) *Los Barriles*, on Bahía de las Palmas, connected by a coast road to (c 40km N) *Ensenada de los Muertos* via (8km) *Punta Pescadero*, an attractive coastline (H; sailing, diving, fishing). 112km **Buena Vista** (H,R), centre of a tentative resort area.

Beyond Buena Vista at 120km a road l. leads to (4km E) the coast, from where a dirt road (not recommended except for 4-wheel drive vehicles) winds round it for c 92km to *San José del Cabo*, passing small, secluded beaches and budding resorts.

The zone between Punta Pescadero (see above) and *Punta Colorado*, c 5km along this coastal way, is renowned for sportfishing and frequented by US enthusiasts.

Méx. 1 winds SW to (113km) turning r. for (2km W) *Santiago* (457m), site of the Jesuit mission of Santiago de los Coras, removed here from the E coast in 1724, sacked and burned (along with the body of the murdered Fr Lorenzo Carranco) in 1734, and reoccupied by the Spaniards in 1736. The church is a rebuilding of 1948. At 134km we cross the Tropic of Cancer (latitude 23 degrees 27' N).

184km **San José del Cabo** (12,000 inhab.; 23m; H,R,P; daily flights from airport—11km N—to *Guadalajara, Manzanillo, Mazatlán, Mexico City, Puerto Vallarta,* and *Tijuana;* and to *Denver (Col.)* and *Los Angeles;* four times weekly to *San Francisco*), centre of an expensive development, mainly of luxury hotels, residential lots, recreational areas, etc., which threatens to overwhelm the small fishing port.

This grew out of the Jesuit mission of San José del Cabo (also known as Estero de las Palmas), founded in 1730 (its headquarters shifting to various sites), destroyed by rebellious Pericú Indians in 1734, and re-established in 1737, when the Indians were crowded into settlements at gunpoint. Floods in 1799 and an attack by the Chilean fleet commanded by Thomas Cochrane in 1822 aggravated chronic decay. The site was abandoned in 1840. The present church dates from the 1940s.

The area between San José del Cabo and (217km) **Cabo San Lucas**, known as *Los Cabos*, for the chain of capes around the southernmost part of the peninsula, is a spectacularly beautiful coastline, full of little coves enclosing beaches. It is also a fast-growing and expensive tourist area, promoted by the Mexican government and served by the airport N of San José.

Cabo San Lucas (3000 inhab.; H,R,P) is set in a small cove where the peninsula ends in a series of capriciously shaped cliffs and rock formations, and where the warm waters of the Gulf coast meet the cold currents of the Pacific. The small fishing port is being overstamped by the building of luxury hotels. In 1769 José de Gálvez ordered that a non-Indian town be built here; in 1770 there were only two huts.

From Cabo San Lucas a road W (State highway 19) completes the run of the southernmost part of the peninsula and then continues up the Pacific coast past remote beaches to (88km) **Todos Santos** (c 3000 inhab.; H,R,P), a tranquil fishing port, with a pleasant climate and profusion of flowers, fruit trees (especially mangoes), and sugar cane, near the recently rebuilt mission of *Sta Rosa de las Palmas* (also known as Nuestra Señora del Pilar and Todos Santos), set up here in 1734, soon abandoned, but re-established c 1741. 6km SW *Punta Lobos* is being developed as the first modern resort on this coast. The road continues N to (144km) *San Pedro* and thence to (172km) *La Paz*, see above.

106 Tijuana to Hermosillo

Méx. 2, 881km.—52km Tecate.—182km **Mexicali**.—255km San Luis Río
Colorado.—396km Los Vidrios.—456km Sonoita.—605km Caborca.—
637km Altar.—710km Sta Ana.—881km **Hermosillo**.

We leave Tijuana E on Méx. 2, following Blvd Agua Caliente, past the bullring
(r.) and, at 5km, the *Hipódromo Agua Caliente* (horse and greyhound racing).
8km *La Mesa*, a fast-growing conurbation. The road goes SE to (17km) *Presa
Abelardo L. Rodríguez* (finished in 1937; fishing and boating), which harnesses
the waters of the Río de las Palmas to irrigate the Valle de Tijuana, and then
climbs gently to (52km) **Tecate** (c 10,000 inhab.; 565m; H,R,P), with one of
Mexico's most famous breweries and extensive vineyards. To the N is the US
frontier.

Méx. 3 runs S of Tecate to (117km) *Ensenada* (see Rte 103), passing from 76km the fertile *Valle
de Guadalupe*, another significant wine-producing region. In the early 1900s Russian immigrants (of the Malakan religious sect) settled here. A handful of their descendants remain (the
sect has suffered at the hands of land-hungry Mexican agitators), along with Russian-style
wooden houses of the period.

From Tecate, Méx. 2 runs through a valley before approaching the W slopes of
the Sierra de Juárez. At (115km) *La Rumorosa* (1332m; P) summer temperatures
are cool, in contrast to the intense heat of the desert beyond the mountains to
the E; in the winter the road can be dangerously covered by ice. The view of
the desert expanse of the Laguna Salada (can be swampy after rain) to the SE
is breathtaking. The road begins a dizzying descent amid a grotesque rocky
landscape towards the N end of the *Laguna Salada*, c 48km N to S and below
sea level. The area called *Macahuí* (c 30 by 10km), reached at c 147km, on the
N end of the Laguna and on both sides of the highway, between the heights of
Centinela and Colorado, is being studied by INAH. Trace lines and strange
designs, reminiscent of those at Nazca in Peru, have been detected, well seen
from the air.

182km **MEXICALI** (c 690,000 inhab.; 1m), modern, and prosperous, capital of
Baja California, is divided by the frontier from Calexico in California, both cities
set in the Valle Imperial. It is the distribution centre for the agricultural produce
of the intensively irrigated area to the S and its various industries, incl.
industrias maquiladoras (the processing of raw materials from the USA for
re-export), have attracted labour from central Mexico and the Bajío. The climate
is rigorously (sometimes dangerously) hot, with some respite in Dec. and Jan.

Airport. 6km SW. Daily flights to *Hermosillo* and *Mexico City*.

Bus station. c 3km S of centre, near junction of Avs López Mateos and Independencia.
Services to *Tijuana* (3 hrs); to *San Felipe* (3 hrs); to *Hermosillo* (10 hrs); to *Mexico City* (c 45
hrs); etc.

Railway station. Reached (l.) off Av. López Mateos near bus station on way into centre. Trains
twice daily to *Guadalajara* (c 19 hrs), not recommended.

Hotels throughout the city.

Post Office. Av. Madero, facing C. Altamirano.

Tourist Office. C. Azuela.

Formerly a small settlement called Arroyo del Alamo, it and its US counterpart received their
present names in 1902. In 1910 it numbered 462 inhab.; in 1960, 172,000. The fertility of its
valley (c 345,000 hectares), described by the explorer Juan Bautista de Anza in 1775 as
miraculous, increased from the 1930s thanks to the harnessing of the Río Colorado and the
building of Presa Morelos. Despite the treaty of 1944 which guarantees Mexico water supplies
from the river, salinity in soil and river, evaporation in intense heat, and insufficient water
continue to cause problems. Advanced techniques are being investigated to maximize water

supplies and to maintain the valley's abundance. Among principal crops are cotton, alfalfa, wheat, and barley. The city is crowded at weekends with trippers from the USA.

The city's commercial focus has shifted somewhat with the building of the *Centro Cívico y Comercial* along Av. López Mateos, S of the older centre, along Avs Madero and Reforma, which run parallel with the frontier. On the E side of the town, at the corner of Av. Reforma and Calle L, is the *Museo Regional de la Universidad Autónoma de Baja California* (Tues.–Sat., 9–6; Sun., 10–4), which illustrates the geography, ecology, and cultural history of Baja California. The Sala Geológica shows the formation of the peninsula and its geographic features; other rooms illustrate the palaeontology and zoology of Baja, then the early archaeological cultures, chiefly with bone and stone tools. The final room has displays explaining and illustrating the later missionary period and the ethnography and linguistic divisions of Baja during this and recent times.

The Mexicali brewery is just SW of the centre, between Cs D and E and Avs Mariano Arista and Zaragoza.

At 5km from Mexicali, Méx. 5 branches SE off Méx. 2 to run through the W part of the Valle de Mexicali, with the Sierra de Cucapahs to the W. To the E (l.) are the marshy lands where the Río Colorado (now harnessed for irrigation) discharged into the Gulf of California. 25km *Cerro Prieto* where a geothermal plant (adm. by permit—obtainable in Mexicali—only) generates 200,000kW hours of electricity for Tijuana and Mexicali by means of steam from deep water circulating through fractures in hot volcanic rocks. It stands near the *Laguna Vulcano*, a lurid and enigmatic series of mud volcanoes. 116km *La Ventana* (R,P). 152km *El Chinero*, so-called in tragic commemoration of Chinese labourers who, discharged in 1912 during an economic slump from the factories of the frontier zone, met their deaths here through hunger and thirst after wandering across the desert in an effort to reach the coast and make the crossing to Sonora. A road r. is for (72km) *Valle Trinidad*, (154km) *Ojos Negros*, and (193km) *Ensenada*, see Rte 103. 202km **San Felipe** (c 15,000 inhab.; H,R,P), an attractive port which has enjoyed too rapid growth thanks to the exceptional abundance of fish and crowds of (sometimes noisy) visitors from the USA. During late winter and early spring occasionally at high tide the sea sweeps into the centre.

From San Felipe it is possible to follow the coast along a less satisfactory road to (284km) *Puertecitos*, a fishing and sailing resort much favoured by US visitors, and then by dirt road to (357km) *San Luis Gonzaga*, see Rte 103.

Beyond Mexicali, Méx. 2 continues SE and E through the N part of the Valle de Mexicali. We cross the Río Colorado and into the State of Sonora just before (255km) **San Luis Río Colorado** (c 160,000 inhab.; 30m; H,R,P; clocks go forward one hour for standard mountain time), a prosperous frontier town 42km SW of Yuma in Arizona.

From San Luis a trip may be made S to the estuary of the Río Colorado, covered by remains of tidal flooding, at the northernmost point of the Gulf of California. The two islands, *Isla Montague* and *Isla Gore*, at the river mouth are regularly inundated at high tide. The road keeps to the E side of the delta on its way to (114km) *El Golfo de Sta Clara*, a beach resort with good fishing and sailing.

Beyond San Luis Río Colorado the road, once (as a track) known as the Camino del Diablo, runs through the **Desierto del Altar**, a truly formidable wilderness.

The vegetation which begins to appear after c 80km includes the saguaro, a giant cactus reaching c 20m in height; organ-pipe cactus; ocotillos, prickly pears, varieties of agave, and pitahayas. In the early evening the sunset suffuses the desert with deep red, purple, and orange rays.

Beyond (396km) **Los Vidrios** (R,P) a reasonable road leaves S, skirting the **Parque Nacional del Pinacate**.

This huge volcanic zone (c 2500sq km) contains more than 600 craters. Its highest elevation is the dark red *Cerro del Pinacate* (1200m). In addition to areas of desolation, where NASA organized training for US astronauts in the nearest the earth has to offer to lunar conditions, the uplands hold a variety of arachnids and wildlife.

Méx. 2 continues along the frontier to (456km) **Sonoita** (c 5000 inhab.; H,R,P), opposite Lukeville in Arizona.

From Sonoita, Méx. 8 runs SW across the desert and skirts the S part of the Parque Nacional del Pinacate to (100km) **Puerto Peñasco** (c 13,000 inhab.; 61m; H,R,P), on a promontory facing the Gulf of California, which separates Bahía de Adair to the N and Bahía de San Jorge.
   The laying of the railway from Mexicali to Benjamín Hill in 1937–47 and the construction of the road from Sonoita cost many lives, both engineers and labourers—a grim epic.
   Today Puerto Peñasco is a fish farming and sportfishing centre, especially popular with visitors from the USA and Canada. Seri Indians also congregate here to sell their crafts. The universities of Sonora and Arizona collaborate here on a shrimp-breeding programme which has resulted in giant specimens.

Méx. 2 continues S and SE via (541km) *San Luisito* to (605km) **Caborca** (32,000 inhab.; 305m; H,R,P), on the Río de la Asunción, principal town of NW Sonora. It is mainly an agricultural centre and, with its Pima and Pápago inhabitants, preserves something of its indigenous character.

Its foundation dates from the establishment of the Jesuit doctrinal centre in 1695, the last in the NW Pimería Alta, which also served as a point of departure for expeditions across the desert to California. Its resident priest, the Sicilian Francesco Saverio Saeta, was murdered during a Pima rebellion the same year and in 1751, during a revolt of Pimas and Seris, the mission was ravaged and the Jesuit Tomás Antonio Tello killed. On 6 Apr. 1857, 58 US filibusters, commanded by Henry Alexander Crabb, who had invaded Caborca, were defeated and shot (except for the youngest, who was spared)—an event celebrated yearly.

The church of *La Purísima Concepción de Nuestra Señora*, wide and spacious, was finished by the Franciscans in 1809, converted into a fort by the defenders of 1857, flooded in 1927, and restored in 1957 and in the early 1980s. It keeps elements of earlier times, like the cross between baluster columns and estípites for the façade supports, the stucco ornamentation of the altarpieces, and the polychrome motifs of the interior, spoiled by applications of white.

   From (637km) *Altar* a road runs NE, following the course of the Río Altar towards the frontier at (120km) *Sasabe*. At 40km it passes a road r. to (2km SE) **Tubutama**, a peaceful little place, where the Jesuit mission of *San Pedro y San Pablo* was founded in 1691.

It suffered during the rebellions of 1695 and 1751. In the latter year the Pimas besieged the missionaries, the Bohemian Johann Nentvig and the Bavarian Jacob Sedelmayr, in their house and reduced the church to ashes. The present church is a Franciscan building of 1783. It was last restored in 1975.

The church's façade and concave portal (puerta abocinada) are set in the S wall and show a delightful and anachronistic use by indigenous craftsmen of plateresque and baroque themes: baluster columns and exuberant vegetal, floral, shell, angel, and geometric relief. A feature of the interior surfaces is the repetition of octagonal star motifs, favoured by contemporary masons. The side altars, in sculptured stucco, are dedicated to the Passion and Resurrection. The gilded wooden high altarpiece is one of the very few surviving examples in Sonora. In the house adjoining the church is a Museum containing sculpture, paintings, and the 18C works of art once belonging to the mission.
   Beyond Altar, Méx. 2 goes E to (710km) *Sta Ana*. From here to (881km) *Hermosillo*, see Rte 21.

Blue Guides

The Blue Guides series began in 1915 when Muirhead Guide-Books Limited published 'Blue Guide London and its Environs'. Findlay and James Muirhead already had extensive experience of guidebook publishing: before the First World War they had been the editors of the English editions of the German Baedekers, and by 1915 they had acquired the copyright of most of the famous 'Red' Handbooks from John Murray.

An agreement made with the French publishing house Hachette et Cie in 1917 led to the translation of Muirhead's London guide, which became the first 'Guide Bleu'—Hachette had previously published the blue-covered 'Guides Joannes'. Subsequently, Hachette's 'Guide Blue Paris et ses Environs' was adapted and published in London by Muirhead. The collaboration between the two publishing houses continued until 1933.

In 1933 Ernest Benn Limited took over the Blue Guides, appointing Russell Muirhead, Findlay Muirhead's son, editor in 1934. The Muirhead's connection with the Blue Guides ended in 1963 when Stuart Rossiter, who had been working on the Guides since 1954, became house editor, revising and compiling several of the books himself.

The Blue Guides are now published by A & C Black, who acquired Ernest Benn in 1984, so continuing the tradition of guidebook publishing which began in 1826 with 'Black's Economical Tourist of Scotland'. The Blue Guide series continues to grow: there are now more than 60 titles in print with revised editions appearing regularly and many new Blue Guides in preparation.

'Blue Guides' is a registered trade mark.

INDEX

Alphabetical list of archaeologists and the sites they have worked on:

Acosta, Jorge	Monte Albán, Tenayuca, Teotihuacán, Tula (Tollán), Tzintzuntzan
Adams, Richard E.W.	Becan
Almaraz, Ramón	Teotihuacán
Alzate, José Antonio	Xochicalco
Andrews IV & V, E. Wyllys	Acancéh, Becan, Chicanná, Dzibilchaltún
Andrews, George F.	Bonampak, Edzna, Oxkintok, Sayil
Angel Fernández, Miguel	Palenque, Tulum
Angulo, José	Las Pilas
Appel, Jill	Monte Albán
Armillas, Pedro	Teotihuacán, Tula (Tollán)
Aveni, Frank	Monte Albán
Batres, Leopoldo	Mitla, Palenque, Templo Mayor in Tenochtitlán, Teotihuacán, Xochicalco
Baudez, Claude F.	Toniná
Becquelin, Pierre	Toniná
Benfer, Robert A.	Tula (Tollán)
Bernal, Ignacio	Coixtlahuaca, Dainzú, Mitla, Monte Albán, Teotihuacán, Yagul
Blanton, Richard	Monte Albán
Blom, Franz	Chinkultic, Comalcalco, Tenam, Uaxactún (Guatemala), Uxmal
Boas, Franz	Palenque
Bolles, John	Yaxchilán
Borhegyi, Stephan F. de	Chinkultic
Bove, F.J.	Laguna de los Cerros
Breton, Adela	Acancéh
Brush, Ellen and Charles	Barnard Site
Caso, Alfonso	Cerro Negro, Chachoapan (Yucuñudahui), El Potrero de la Isla, Ihuatzio, Mitla, Monte Albán, Tenayuca, Tizatlán, Tzintzuntzan
Castañeda, Luciano	Palenque
Catherwood, Frederick	Aké, Chichén Itzá, Dzibilnocac, Itzamal, Kabah, Labná, Mayapán, Palenque, Sayil, Tulum, Uxmal
Chadwick, Robert	Yagul
Charlot, Jean	Cobá
Charlton, Thomas	Teotihuacán Valley
Charnay, Désiré	Chichén Itzá, Itzamal, Palenque, Teotihuacán, Tula (Tollán), Yaxchilán
Coe, Michael D.	Izapa, La Venta, Monte Albán, San Lorenzo Tenochtitlán
Contreras, Eduardo	Tlatelolco
Cook, Carmen	Chalcatzingo
Covarrubias, Michael	La Venta, Tlatilco
Cuevas, Emilio	Templo Mayor in Tenochtitlán
Cummings, Byron	Cuicuilco
Cyphers Guillén, Ann	San Lorenzo Tenochtitlán
Denison, J.H.	Río Bec, Xpuhil
Díaz, P.	Templo Mayor in Tenochtitlán
Diehl, Richard A.	San Lorenzo Tenochtitlán, Tula (Tollán)
DiPeso, Charles	Casas Grandes
Drucker, Philip	Cerro de las Mesas, Izapa, La Venta, Tonalá
Dupaix, Guillaume	Palenque

Eaton, Jack	Becan, Chicanná
Eckholm, Gordon	Comalcalco, Guasave
Eckholm, Susanna M.	Izapa
Erosa, José A.	Uxmal
Estrada Balmori, Elma	Templo Mayor in Tenochtitlán
Feinman, Gary	Monte Albán
Ferdon, Edwin N.	Tonalá
Flannery, Kent V.	Monte Albán, San José Mogote, Oaxaca Valley
Folan, William	Calakmul
Foncerrada de Molina, M.	Uxmal
Frey, Charles	Bonampak
Gallegos, Roberto	Zaachila
Gamio, Manuel	Chalchihuites, Copilco, Cuicuilco, Templo Mayor in Tenochtitlán, Teopanzolco, Teotihuacán
García Cantú, Gastón	Templo Mayor in Tenochtitlán
García Cubas, Antonio	Tula (Tollán)
García Moll, Roberto	Yaxchilán
García Payón, José	Calixtlahuaca, Castillo de Teayo, Cempoala, El Tajín, Malinalco
Garza Tarazona, Silvia	Xochicalco
Gay, Carlos	Chalcatzingo, Juxtlahuaca, Oxtotitlán
González, Rabecca	La Venta
González Crespo, Norberto	Cobá, Xochicalco
González Rul, Francisco	Tlatelolco
Gorenstein, Shirley	Tepexi el Viejo
Graham, John A.	La Venta
Griffen, Gilbert	Juxtlahuaca, Oxtotitlán
Grove, David C.	Chalcatzingo
Healey, Giles	Bonampak
Heizer, Robert F.	Cuicuilco, La Venta
Hirth, Kenneth G.	Xochicalco
Howe, George P.	Tulum
Jiménez Moreno, Wigberto	Tula (Tollán)
Kelly, J. Charles	Chalchihuites
Kidder, Alfred	Cobá
Kovar, Anton	Teotihuacán
Kowalewski, Steven	Monte Albán
La Farge, Oliver	Chinkultic, Comalcalco
Le Plongeon, Augustus	Chichén Itzá, Uxmal
Linné, S.	Teotihuacán
Litvak King, Jaime	Xochicalco
Lizar di Ramos, César	Huapalcalco
Lombardo, V.	Playa del Oro
López, Diana	Cacaxtla
Lothrop, Samuel K.	Tancah, Tulum
Lundell, C.L.	Calakmul
MacDougal, T.D.	Guiengola
MacNeish, Richard S.	Coxcatlán, El Riego, Tehuacán Valley
Maler, Teobart	Chacmultún, Chichén Itzá, Cobá, Dzibilnocac, Hochob, Kabah, Palenque, Sayil, Xlapak, Yaxchilán
Marcías, Angelina	Sta. Cecilia Acatitlán
Margain, Carlos	Teotihuacán
Márquez, Pedro	Xochicalco
Marquina, Ignacio	Cholula, Edzna, Hochob, Itzamal, Kabah, La Quemada, Palenque, Tancah, Tenayuca, Teotihuacán, Tulum, Xpuhil

Martínez Donjuán, Guadalupe	Teopantecuantitlán
Mason, G.	Muyil
Matos Moctezuma, Eduardo	Templo Mayor in Tenochtitlán, Tula (Tollán)
Maudslay, Alfred P.	Chichén Itzá, Copán (Honduras), Palenque, Quirigua (Guatemala), Tikal (Guatemala), Yaxchilán
Maximilien de Waldeck, Jean-Frédéric	Palenque, Uxmal
McDonald, A.J.	Tzutzuculi
Medellín Zeñil, Alfonso	Castillo de Teayo
Miller, Arthur G.	Chichén Itzá, Tancah, Teotihuacán, Tulum
Millon, René	Teotihuacán
Moedano, Hugo	Cuicuilco, Templo Mayor in Tenochtitlán
Molina, Daniel	Cacaxtla
Morley, Sylvanus G.	Bonampak, Calakmul, Chichén Itzá, Cobá, Kabah, Labná, Mayapán, Palenque, Sayil, Tenam, Tulum, Uxmal, Yaxchilán
Mountjoy, J.B.	Amapa
Mountjoy, R.	Teuchitlán (Ahualulco)
Müller Jacob, Florencia	Huapalcalco
Niederberger, Christine	Tlapacoya, Zohapilco
Noguera, Eduardo	Chalchihuites, Cuicuilco, El Opeño, La Quemada, Tenayuca, Teopanzolco, Teotihuacán, Xochicalco
Olivos, José Arturo	El Opeño
Orellano Tapia, Rafael	Chinkultic, El Tamuín, Teotihuacán
Ortega, Alfonso	Coixtlahuaca
Ortíz, Ponciano	El Manati
Paddock, John	Lambityeco, Mitla, Monte Albán, Yagul
Paradis, L.I.	Tlapacoya, Tlatilco
Pareyón, Eduardo	Sta. Cecilia Acatitlán
Parsons, Jeffrey	Teotihuacán
Paz, Rivera	Ihuatzio
Peñafiel, Antonio	Xochicalco
Pendergast, David M.	Amapa, Playa del Oro
Peterson, D.A.	Guiengola
Piña Chan, Beatriz Barba de	Tlapacoya
Piña Chan, Román	Chalcatzingo, Comalcalco, Izapa, Teopanzolco, Teotenango, Tlatilco
Polarios, E.	Edzna
Pollock, H.E.D.	Chacchob, Cobá, Hochob, Mayapán
Proskouriakoff, Tatiana	Bonampak, Mayapán, Sayil, Tenam, Yaxchilán
Reygadas Vértiz, José	Chichén Itzá, Cholula, Tenayuca, Teopanzolco, Teotihuacán
Rodríguez, Carmen	El Manati
Rosado Ojedo, V.	El Chanal
Roys, Ralph L.	Aké, Mayapán
Rubín de la Barbolla, Daniel	Mitla, Tzintzuntzan
Ruíz, Diego	El Tajín
Ruppert, Karl	Becan, Bonampak, Dzibilnocac, Mayapán, Río Bec, Xpuhil
Ruz, Alberto	Edzna, Kabah, Palenque, Uxmal
Sáenz, César A.	Palenque, Tlatelolco, Uxmal, Xochicalco
Sanders, WilliamT.	Ichpaatún, Sigero, Tancah, Teotihuacán, Tulum
Schmidt, Paul	Xochipala region
Sears, Thomas	El Chanal
Segovia, Víctor	Kohunlich, Tlatelolco

Séjourné de Orfila, Laurette	Teotihuacán
Seler, Edouard	Acancéh, Chinkultic, Dzibilnocac, Guiengola, Hochob, Palenque, Uxmal, Xochicalco
Shook, Edwin M.	Aké, Chinkultic, Mayapán, Oxkintok, Sayil
Sigüenza y Góngora, Carlos	Teotihuacán
Sissons, Edward	Coxcatlán el Viejo, Tehuacán Valley
Smith, Andrew L.	Mayapán
Spinden, H.	Muyil
Squier, Robert	La Venta
Stephens, John L.	Aké, Chichén Itzá, Dzibilnocac, Itzamal, Kabah, Labná, Mayapán, Palenque, Sayil, Tulum, Uxmal
Stirling, Matthew	Cerro de las Mesas, Izapa, La Venta, San Lorenzo Tenochtitlán, Tres Zapotes
Stromsvik, G.	Chacchob
Stuart, George	Cobá
Thompson, Edward H.	Chacmultún, Chichén Itzá, Kabah, Labná, Uxmal
Thompson, Eric S.	Bonampak, Chichén Itzá, Cobá, Mayapán
Tolstoy, Paul	Tlapacoya, Tlatilco
Tozzer, Alfred M.	Xpuhil
Vaillant, George	El Arbolillo, Ixtapaluca, Loma Torremate
Waldeck *see* Maximilien de Waldeck	
Webster, David	Chacchob
Weigand, Philip C.	Chalchihuites, Teuchitlán (Ahualulco)
Wicke, Charles	Yagul
Winter, Marcus	Monte Albán
Wise, M.V.	Playa del Oro
Zeitlin, R.N.	Laguna Zope

Key page to Atlas section

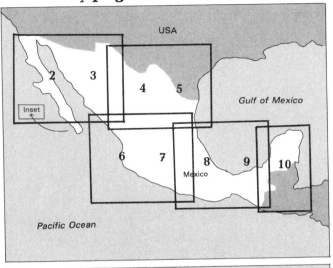

USA

2 3 4 5

Gulf of Mexico

Inset

6 7 8 9 10

Mexico

Pacific Ocean

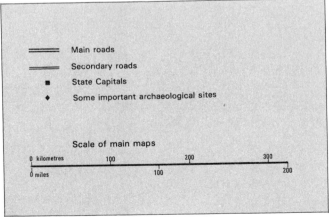

=== Main roads

— Secondary roads

■ State Capitals

◆ Some important archaeological sites

Scale of main maps

0 kilometres   100   200   300

0 miles   100   200

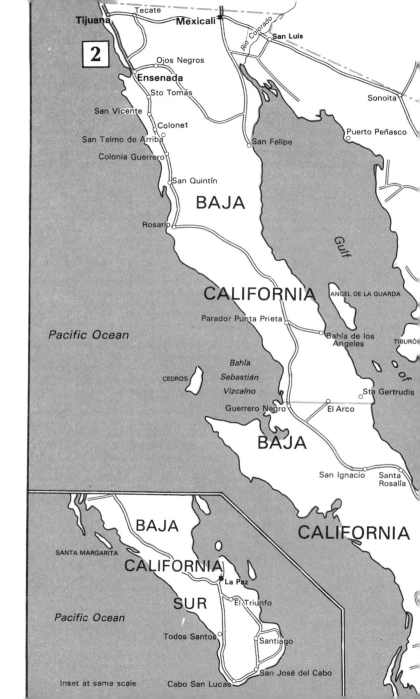

2

Tecate

Tijuana

Mexicali

Rio Colorado

San Luis

Ojos Negros

Ensenada

Sto Tomás

Sonoita

San Vicente

Colonet

Puerto Peñasco

San Telmo de Arriba

San Felipe

Colonia Guerrero

San Quintín

BAJA

Rosario

CALIFORNIA

Gulf

ANGEL DE LA GUARDA

Parador Punta Prieta

Pacific Ocean

Bahía de los Angeles

TIBURÓN

Bahía Sebastián Vizcaíno

CEDROS

of

Sta Gertrudis

Guerrero Negro

El Arco

BAJA

San Ignacio

Santa Rosalía

BAJA

CALIFORNIA

CALIFORNIA

SANTA MARGARITA

La Paz

SUR

El Triunfo

Pacific Ocean

Todos Santos

Santiago

San José del Cabo

Inset at same scale

Cabo San Lucas

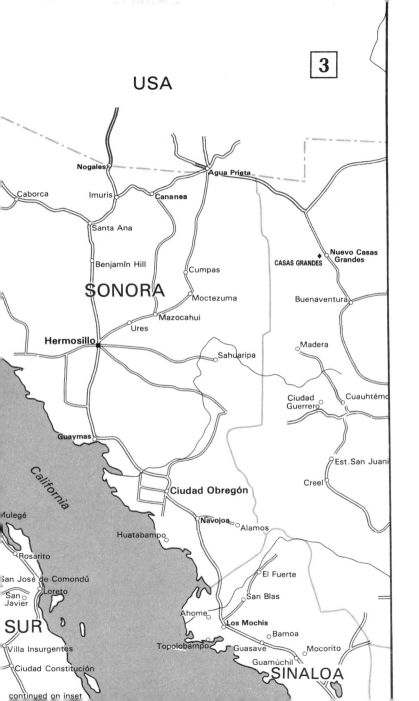

USA

Nogales

Agua Prieta

Caborca

Imuris

Cananea

Santa Ana

Nuevo Casas
Grandes

CASAS GRANDES

Benjamín Hill

Cumpas

SONORA

Moctezuma

Buenaventura

Mazocahui

Ures

Hermosillo

Sahuaripa

Madera

Guaymas

Ciudad
Guerrero

Cuauhtémoc

Est.San Juani

Creel

California

Ciudad Obregón

Mulegé

Navojoa

Alamos

Huatabampo

Rosarito

San José de Comondú

El Fuerte

San
Javier

Loreto

San Blas

SUR

Ahome

Los Mochis

Bamoa

Villa Insurgentes

Topolobampo

Guasave

Mocorito

Ciudad Constitución

Guamúchil

SINALOA

continued on inset

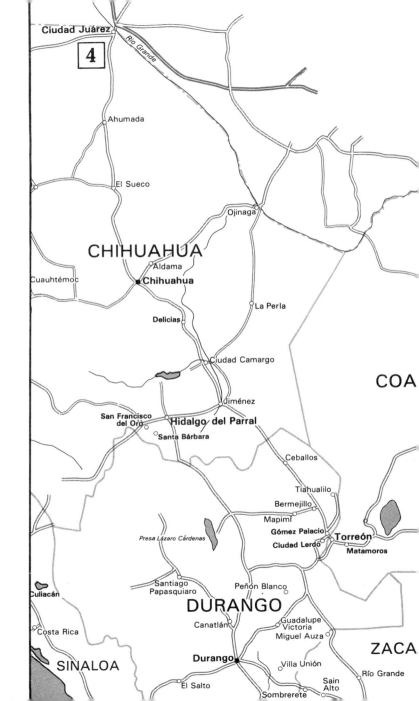

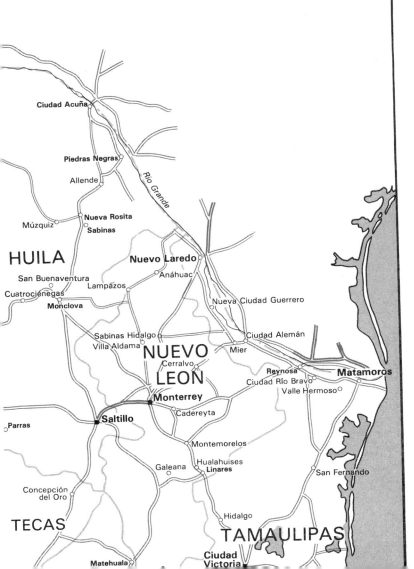

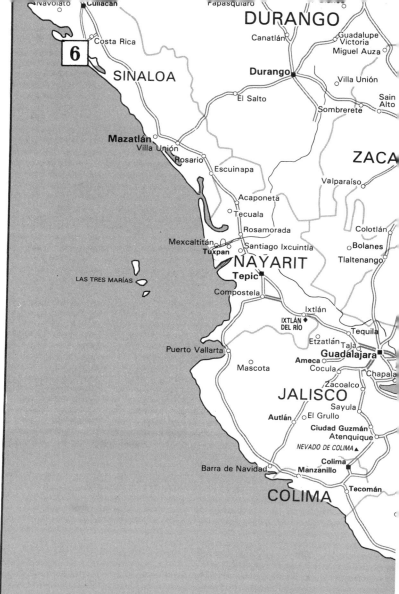

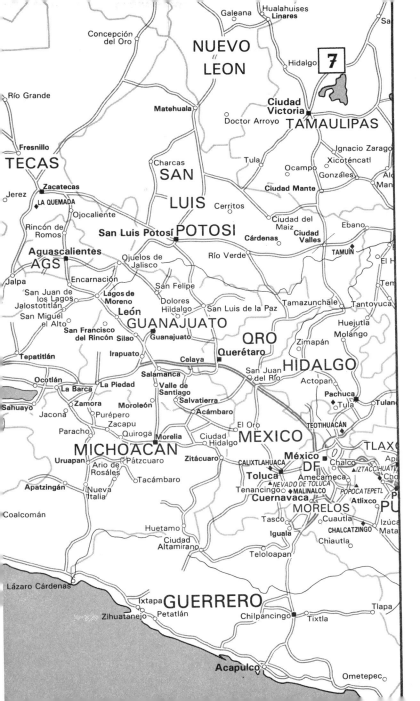

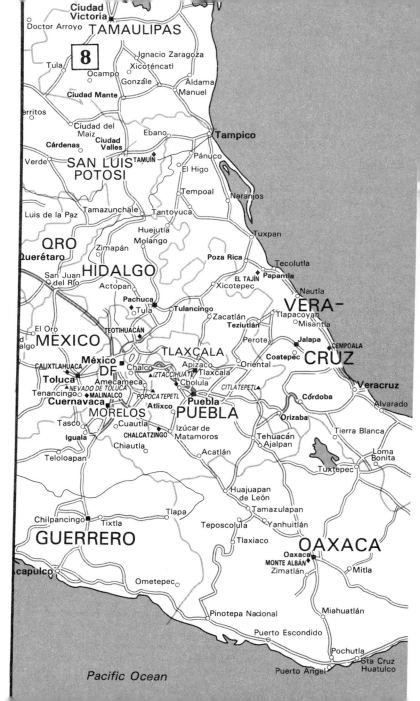

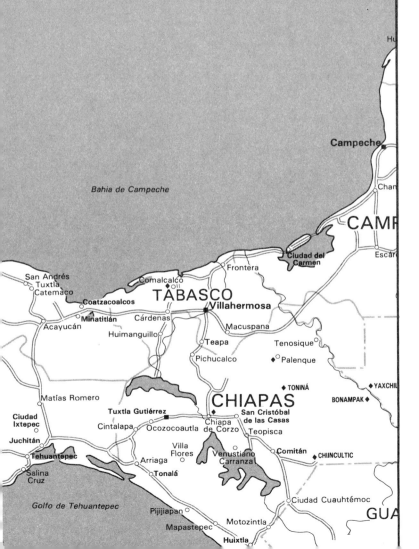

9

Gulf of Mexico

Bahia de Campeche

Campeche

Chan

CAMP

Escár

Ciudad del Carmen

Frontera

San Andrés
Tuxtla
Catemaco

Comalcalco

TABASCO

Villahermosa

Coatzacoalcos

Minatitlán

Cárdenas

Acayucán

Macuspana

Huimanguillo

Teapa

Tenosique

Pichucalco

Palenque

Matías Romero

TONINÁ

YAXCHIL

CHIAPAS

BONAMPAK

Ciudad
Ixtepec

Tuxtla Gutiérrez

San Cristóbal
de las Casas

Juchitán

Cintalapa

Ocozocoautla

Chiapa
de Corzo

Teopisca

Tehuantepec

Villa
Flores

Venustiano
Carranza

Comitán

CHIINCULTIC

Salina
Cruz

Arriaga

Tonalá

Golfo de Tehuantepec

Ciudad Cuauhtémoc

Pijijiapan

GUA

Mapastepec

Motozintla

Huixtla